Sociology

SOCIETY IN HISTORY: TIME LINES

A time line is a visual device that helps us understand historical change. The upper time line represents 5 billion years of the history of the planet Earth. This time line is divided into three sections, each of which is drawn to a different scale of time. The first section, **The Earth's Origins**, begins with the planet's origins 5 billion years before the present (B.P.) and indicates that another full billion years passed before the earliest forms of life appeared. The second section, **Our Human Origins**, shows that plants and animals continued to evolve for billions more years until, approximately 12 million years ago, our earliest human ancestors came onto the scene. In the third section of this time line, **Earliest Civilisation**, we see that what we term civilisation is relatively recent, indeed, with the first permanent settlements occurring in the Middle East a scant 12,000 years

Age of dinosaurs *All humans are hunters and gatherers*

Earth takes form
Earliest life forms
Oldest existing fossils
Earliest mammals
Evolutionary divide, eventually yielding humans and apes
Earliest primates
Bones in Ethiopia attest to 'Stone Age' human ancestors who used tools and fire.

The Earth's Origins

Our Human Origins

| 5 billion B.P. | 4 billion B.P. | 3 billion B.P. | 2 billion B.P. | 1 billion B.P. | 500 million B.P. | 400 million B.P. | 300 million B.P. | 200 million B.P. | 100 million B.P. | 1 million B.P. |

World population 1 billion

Death rates fall in Europe and United States

Colonisation of Latin America/India

Opening of US Western frontier

European colonisation of Africa

US is small, agrarian society

■ Red Cross first established

● First 10-storey skyscraper (Chicago)

■ First postage stamp

■ Emancipation of Russian serfs

▲ Rousseau's Social Contract

Great age of orchestral music

Women's suffrage movement begins

French Revolution begins

● First passenger steam train, England

▲ Comte coins the term 'sociolgy'

▲ Charles Darwin's *Origin of Species*

■ Franco-Prussian War

▲ Karl Marx dies

■ European Enlightment

▲ Malthus dies

| Rev. War | THE MODERN ERA | US Civil War |
| 1775 | 1800 | 1825 | 1850 | 1875 |

▲ Adam Smith dies

● Steam locomotive invented

● Photography invented

● Telegraph invented

● Telephone invented

● Light bulb invented

● Rubber condoms invented

● Pasteur evolves germ theory of disease

● Coca Cola invented

Industrial Revolution transforms Europe

Industrialisation underway

Adam Smith applauds capitalism

Comte coins term 'sociology'

Marx challenges capitalist class conflict

Malthus warns of perilous population increase

ago. But the written record of our species' existence extends back only half this long, to the time humans invented writing and first farmed with animal-driven ploughs some 5,000 years B.P.

Sociology came into being in the wake of the many changes to society wrought by the Industrial Revolution over the last few centuries–just the blink of an eye in evolutionary perspective. The lower time line provides a close-up look at the events and trends that have defined **The Modern Era**, most of which are discussed in this text.

Innovations in technology are charted in the panel below the line and provide a useful backdrop for viewing the milestones of social progress highlighted in the panel above the line. Major contributions to the development of sociological thought are traced along the very bottom of this time line.

Events are coded according to the broad themes as follows:
● Technology
■ National/global events and trends
▲ Sociology as a discipline

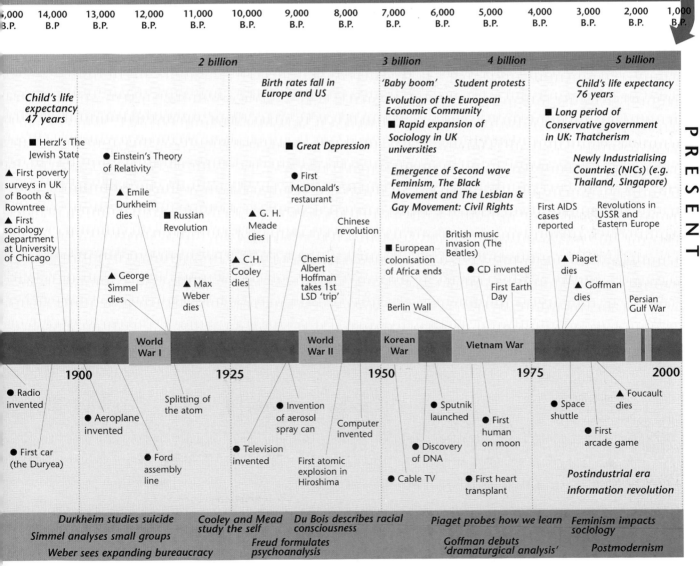

Sociology
A Global Introduction

John J. Macionis
Ken Plummer

PRENTICE HALL EUROPE

NEW YORK ● LONDON ● TORONTO ● SYDNEY ● TOKYO ● SINGAPORE

MADRID ● MEXICO CITY ● MUNICH ● PARIS

Original sixth edition entitled Sociology published by Prentice Hall Inc.
A Simon & Schuster Company
Upper Saddle River
New Jersey, USA
Copyright © 1997 by Prentice Hall Inc.

This edition published by Prentice Hall Europe © 1998
Authorised for sale only in Europe, the Middle East and Africa

Text design by Claire Brodmann

Typeset in 9/12.5pt Stone Serif
by Meridian Colour Repro Ltd, Pangbourne-on-Thames, Berkshire

Printed and bound in Great Britain by Bath Press

Library of Congress Cataloguing-in-Publication Data

Available from the publisher

British Library Cataloguing in Publication Data

A catalogue record for this book is available from
the British Library

ISBN 0–13–664533–X

1 2 3 4 5   02 01 00 99 98

Microsoft® Powerpoint® is a registered trademark of Microsoft Corporation

Contents

Boxes

● Different Voices

● Global Sociology

About the authors

John J. Macionis is Professor of Sociology at Kenyon College in Gambier, Ohio, having graduated from Cornell University and the University of Pennsylvania. At Kenyon, he has chaired the Anthropology–Sociology Department, directed the multidisciplinary programme in Humane Studies and presided over the College's Faculty. He has also been active in academic programmes in many other countries.

His publications are wide-ranging, focusing on community life in the US, interpersonal intimacy in families, effective teaching, humour and the importance of global education. He is co-editor of *Seeing Ourselves: Classic, Contemporary and Cross-Cultural Readings in Sociology*, co-author of *Cities and Urban Life* and author of the concise introductory text, *Society: The Basics*.

Professor Macionis considers himself 'first and foremost...a teacher' who wishes to share his expertise and experience with students both in person and through his textbooks.

Ken Plummer is Professor of Sociology at the University of Essex, and has been actively involved in teaching introductory sociology for the past thirty years. He has been a Senior Lecturer at Middlesex University, and a visiting Professor at the University of California (Santa Barbara) and the University of New York (Stony Brook) – as well as giving lectures in many countries around the world.

Apart from an interest in introductory teaching, his major research interests lie in the fields of sexuality, stigma, methodology and symbolic interactionist theory. He is the author of *Sexual Stigma* (1975), *Documents of Life* (1983) and *Telling Sexual Stories* (1995), as well as the editor of *The Making of the Modern Homosexual* (1981), *Symbolic Interactionism* (1991, 2 vols), *Modern Homosexualities* (1992) and *The Chicago School* (1997, 4 vols). He is also currently the editor of a new journal, *Sexualities*.

Believing sociology has a lot to contribute to the modern world, he thinks it should become more accessible and hopes this textbook will help towards this.

Preface

● Welcome to a new sociology textbook

Why another sociology text?

The book aims to achieve four main goals. These are:

● First, *Sociology: A Global Introduction* aims to provide an introduction to all the main areas of study, the key concepts, the historical debates and basic approaches to the discipline. It assumes you know nothing about sociology; and thus is not an advanced text. It sets its goals as opening up the field of enquiry for the very first time. If you wish to go further, there are suggestions at the end of each chapter for doing this.

● Second, the book provides a global and local introduction. Most textbooks focus upon one country. This textbook has as a prime concern the UK, Europe and North America. But it also takes its orbit to be the world – increasingly it is impossible to understand one country in isolation from others. A recurrent theme through this book is that the modern world is becoming progressively globalised.

● Third, the book provides analyses of a number of newer topics that are not always included in introductory sociology textbooks. We have selected some issues that are becoming increasingly critical as we enter the twenty-first century. These include: the growing number of the elderly (Chapter 14); the rising (global) power of the mass media (Chapter 21); the significance of many countries outside the west who are facing poverty (Chapter 11); and environmental hazards (Chapter 19).

● Finally, the book hopes to present all of this in a distinctly fresh and 'user friendly' way. There is a lot of material to digest, even in a book as introductory as this. And so a number of tools have been provided to help study. These are outlined below.

Some features of the text and how to use it

Sociology: A Global Introduction aims to provide not only a highly readable text, it also provides a number of special features that will help you to study. We hope that this is a 'user friendly' book pitched at a very introductory level for those who have never studied sociology before. Amongst the tools in the book that you should note and work with are:

1. The boxes. These are aimed at focusing you on specific issues. We believe, and hope you do to, that they provide handy tools for thinking and analysing. They come in six forms each identified by an icon.

 Focus on Europe boxes highlight issues in the European Union.

 Different Voices boxes focus on multicultural issues and amplify the voices of people who are outside the mainstream of sociological analysis – such as women, gays and ethnic groups.

 Profile boxes highlight Western sociologists who have shaped or are shaping the discipline of sociology, and provide a capsule guide to some of their ideas.

 Sociological Spotlight boxes focus on issues that are of importance within sociology.

 Controversy and Debate boxes conclude each chapter by presenting different points of view on an issue of contemporary importance.

 Global Sociology boxes focus on issues over a range of different cultures

2. Global and national maps. These are aimed at helping you locate many of the issues discussed in the text through graphic illustration. They come in two forms:

Windows on the World global maps are sociological maps offering a comparative look at a range of sociological issues such as favoured languages and religions, permitted marriage forms, the degree of political freedom, the extent of the world's rain forests, and a host of other issues. Windows on the World use a new, non-Eurocentric projection, devised by cartographer Arno Peters, that accurately portrays the relative size of all the continents.

National maps focus on social diversity within a country or a group of countries.

3. The Time Line. Have you ever wished there was a way to locate at a glance important historical periods and key events? This three-part timeline found at the front of the book locates every era and important development mentioned in the text, and tracks the emergence of crucial trends.

4. Key Concepts, identified by boldfaced type, are followed by a precise, italicised definition. A listing of key concepts with their definitions appears at the end of each chapter, and a complete Glossary is found at the end of the book.

5. Each chapter also contains a numbered **Summary** and some **Critical-Thinking Questions.**

6. Each chapter ends with a list of **Resources for Going Further**. These provide an introductory reading list, identify classic texts of enduring value, note some more advanced readings for essay and project work, and suggest some other sources which will help you in research.

7. Web sites. Included in the Resources for Going Further are a number of relevant web site page addresses. Chapter 1 provides an appendix to introduce them.

In addition the book provides:

Images: photography art.

Vignettes that begin each chapter. These openings hopefully will spark the interest of the reader as they introduce important themes.

Recognition of differences. Readers will encounter the diversity of societies. Although there is an emphasis on Europe and the USA in the book – the dominant Western cultures – there is also a concern with global issues and people from other cultures. There is also an inclusive focus on women and men. Beyond devoting a full chapter to the important concepts of sex and gender, *Sociology* mainstreams gender into every chapter, showing how the topic at hand affects women and men differently, and explaining how gender operates as a basic dimension of social organisation.

Theoretically clear and balanced presentation. The discipline's major theoretical approaches are introduced in Chapter 1 and systematically reappear in later chapters. The text highlights not only the conflict, functional and action paradigms, but incorporates social-exchange analysis, ethnomethodology, cultural theory, sociobiology and developments in the newer postmodern theories where dfferent voices can be heard.

Students are also provided with an easy-to-understand introduction to important social theorists before they encounter their work in later chapters. The ideas of Max Weber, Karl Marx, Emile Durkheim appear in distinct sections.

Emphasis on critical thinking. Critical-thinking skills include the ability to challenge common assumptions by formulating questions, identifying and weighing appropriate evidence, and reaching reasoned conclusions. This text not only teaches but encourages students to discover on their own recent sociological research.

A short note on currency

As currencies vary across all cultures and rates of exchange are constantly in a state of flux the application of any particular unit of currency was a problem. However, the currencies used in our data sources were the pound sterling and the US dollar; for this reason these are the currencies adopted in this book.

Organisation of this text

Part I introduces the foundations of sociology. Underlying the discipline is the sociological perspective, the focus of Chapter 1, which explains how this invigorating point of view brings the world to life in a new and instructive way. Chapter 2 spotlights sociological investigation, or the doing of sociology, and explains how to use the logic of science to study human society. It also provides a guide to planning research.

Part II targets the foundations of social life. Chapter 3 links culture to the concept of society, presenting three time-honoured models of social organisation developed by Emile Durkheim, Karl Marx and Max Weber. Chapter 4 focuses on the central concept of culture, emphasising the cultural diversity that makes up our society and our world. Chapter 5 spotlights socialisation, explaining how we gain our humanity as we learn to participate in society. Chapter 6 provides a micro-level look at the patterns of social interaction that make up our everyday lives. Chapter 7 offers coverage of groups and organisations, two additional and vital elements of social structure. Chapter 8 completes the unit by investigating how the operation of society generates both deviance and conformity.

Part III offers a wide discussion of social inequality, beginning with three chapters devoted to social stratification. Chapter 9 introduces major concepts and presents theoretical explanations of social inequality. This chapter is rich with illustrations of how stratification has changed historically, and how it varies around the world today. Chapter 10 surveys social inequality in a number of Western countries, but mainly the UK, exploring our perceptions of inequality and assessing how well they square with research findings. Chapter 11 extends the analysis with a look at global stratification, revealing the extent of differences in wealth and power between rich and poor societies. Race and ethnicity, additional important dimensions of social inequality both in Europe and the rest of the world, are detailed in Chapter 12. The focus of Chapter 13, gender and sexuality, explains how societies transform the distinction of biological sex into systems of gender stratification, and looks at the ways sexuality is produced. Ageing and the elderly, a topic of increasing concern to greying societies, is addressed in Chapter 14.

Part IV includes a full chapter on each social institution. Chapter 15 leads off investigating the economy, consumption and work, because most sociologists recognise the economy as having the greatest impact on all other institutions. This chapter highlights the processes of industrialisation and postindustrialisation, explains the emergence of a global economy, and suggests what such transformations mean. Chapter 16 investigates the roots of social power and looks at the modern development of social movements. In addition, this chapter includes discussion of the threat of war, and the search for peace. Chapter 17, families, examines the many changes taking place around our personal ways of living together in the modern world,

looking at some of the diversity of family life. Chapter 18, religion, addresses the human search for ultimate meaning, surveys world religions, and explains how religious beliefs are linked to other dimensions of social life. Chapter 19, education, traces the expansion of schooling in industrial societies. Here again, educational patterns in the United Kingdom are brought to life through contrasts with those of many other societies. Chapter 20, health and medicine, shows how health is a social issue just as much as it is a matter of biological processes, and compares UK patterns to those found in other countries. It also looks at a growing area of interest: the sociology of the body. Chapter 21, mass media, looks at forms of communications in societies, focusing especially on the rise of the modern global media.

Part V examines important dimensions of global social change. Chapter 22 focuses on the powerful impact of population growth and urbanisation in Europe and throughout the world. Chapter 23 presents issues of contemporary concern by highlighting the interplay of society and the natural environment. Chapter 24 concludes the text with an overview of social change that highlights traditional, modern and postmodern societies. This chapter rounds out the text by explaining how and why world societies change, and by critically analysing the benefits and liabilities of traditional, modern and postmodern ways of life.

A note on authorship: John J. Macionis wrote the first full text. Ken Plummer has added a chapter, introduced new sections and significantly modified others. Since sociology is a changing and conflictual discipline, neither author necessarily agrees with everything the other has written. But there is strong agreement that sociology is a lively and challenging discipline that should be presented in a lively and challenging way. We hope this book succeeds in this.

Lecturer support

Sociology: A Global Introduction is supported by a range of supplementary teaching materials designed to help lecturers integrate the text into their teaching and assessment. These are available to all lecturers using the textbook on their courses.

The *Instructor's Resource Manual* provides additional examples, questions and extracts keyed to each chapter of the text itself. Each chapter is divided into several sections: a recap of content, detailed chapter objectives, additional discussion questions, a summary of relevant tables and figures on the accompanying Microsoft® Powerpoint® electronic transparencies (see below), short 'pop quizzes', essay questions and additional examples and discussion materials, complete with questions.

The *Instructor's Resource CD-Rom* comprises two items: **A Microsoft® Powerpoint®** set of electronic transparencies which, again by chapter, provide overhead slides for chapter aims and objectives, figures and tables from the text and the 'pop quizzes' from the *Instructor's Resource Manual*. These can be used electronically, or can be printed out for photocopying on to hard-copy transparencies.

The Test Item File provides a series of multiple choice, true–false, short answer and essay questions keyed to the text. The file contains about 100 questions per chapter. Available in Windows format, the Prentice Hall Custom Test is designed to allow for customisation by the lecturer, for example, to provide instructions for students and add/delete questions as required.

Acknowledgements

Ken Plummer wishes to acknowledge the assistance of two excellent research officers: Kimberly Drae Fisher and Travis Kong. All at Prentice Hall should be thanked. In particular, Christina Wipf-Perry for promoting the idea and Ruth Pratten, development editor at Prentice Hall, who provided much support, enthusiasm and back up for what in the end was an extremely pressured production schedule. Anne Rix was a cheerful and dedicated project manager. In addition, Nigel South, Lydia Morris and Colin Samson at the University of Essex gave helpful advice on certain chapters as did the reviewers Derek Williams, Dr van de Braak, Chris Jackman, Raguvald Kalleberg, Dr van Heeriskhuizen and Sue Mew. Finally, my partner, Everard Longland, had to endure a long hot summer with me being locked away at a word processor; as usual his unreserved support and practical help were invaluable.

John Macionis thanks the efforts of dozens of women and men that have resulted in *Sociology*, in particular members of the editorial, production and sales teams at Prentice Hall. It goes without saying that every colleague knows more about some topics covered in this book than the author does. For that reason, he is grateful to the hundreds of faculties and students who have written to offer comments and suggestions. More formally, he is grateful to the people who reviewed some or all of this manuscript.

Photo credits

Grateful acknowledgement is made to the following sources for permission to reproduce material in this book previously published elsewhere. Every effort has been made to trace the correct copyright holders, but if any have been inadvertently overlooked the publisher will be pleased to make the necessary arrangement at the first opportunity. Luc Delahaye/Magnum Photo Inc.; Brown Brothers; New York Public Library Picture Collection; Steve McCurry/Magnum Photo, Inc.; Argas/Gamma-Liaison, Inc.; G. Humer/Gamma-Liaison, Inc.; Mark Peters/SIPA Press; Hinterleiner/Gamma-Liaison, Inc.; Robert Frerck/ Woodfin Camp & Associates; UPI/Bettmann; Elizabeth Crews; Courtesy of the University of Chicago Archives; Danny Lyon/Magnum Photo, Inc.; John L. Focht; Paul Liebhardt; Guide Dogs for the Blind Association; Stephen Shames/Matrix International; Jon Levy/ Gamma-Liaison, Inc.; Benetton; Mirror Syndication International; Ken Marshall/Collection of Joseph M. Ryan; Sebastiao Salgado/Magnum Photo, Inc.; Paula Bronstein/Impact Visuals Photo & Graphics, Inc.; Network Photographers – Carlos Friere Photoflight; Robert Wallis/SABA Press Photos, Inc.; Tim Carlson/Stock Boston; Peter Turnley/Black Star; Miguel Luis Fairbanks; Patrick Aventurier/Gamma-Liaison, Inc.; Tom Stodart/Katz/SABA Press Photos, Inc.; Paul Liebhardt; Commission for Racial Equality; Bettman; Stock Market; Explorer/Y. Layma/Photo Researchers, Inc.; Spencer Rowell; Eve Arnold/Magnum Photo, Inc.; Stephen Castagneto/Gamma-Liaison, Inc.; Antonio Olmos; Mayer/Gamma-Liaison, Inc; David Ball/Picture Cube, Inc.; Peter Northall/Black Star; Baldeu/Sygma; Bo Zaunders/Stock Market; R. Rai/Magnum Photo, Inc.; Hans Hoefer/Woodfin Camp & Associates; Charles Gupton/Stock Boston; Literacy Volunteers of America, Inc; Eric Pasquier/Sygma; Gelehrte Dtld./Bildarchiv Preussischer Kulturbesitz; Popperfoto.

part one

The Foundations
of Sociology

chapter one

Source: Popperfoto

The Sociological Perspective

The Global Village: A Sociological Snapshot of our World

The earth is home to some 5.7 billion people who reside in the cities and countryside of nearly 200 nations. To grasp the social 'shape' of the world, imagine for a moment the planet's population reduced to a single settlement of 1,000 people. A visit to this 'global village' would reveal that more than half (575) of the inhabitants are Asians, including 200 citizens of the People's Republic of China. Next, in terms of numbers, we would find 130 Africans, 125 Europeans, and about 100 Latin Americans. North Americans – including people from the United States, Canada, and Mexico – would account for a mere 65 village residents.

A study of the settlement's ways of life would yield some startling conclusions. The village is a rich place, with a seemingly endless array of goods and services for sale. Yet most of the inhabitants can do no more than dream longingly of such treasures, because half of the village's total income is earned by just 150 individuals.

Food is the greatest source of concern for the majority of the population. Every year, workers produce more than enough food to feed everyone; even so, half the village's people – including most of the children – are poorly nourished and many go hungry. The worst-off 200 residents, who lack food, safe drinking water, and secure shelter, do not have the strength to work and are vulnerable to life-threatening diseases. Villagers boast of their community's many schools, including colleges and universities. About 75 inhabitants have completed a degree and a few even have doctorates, but half of the village's people can neither read nor write.

We in much of the European Union (EU) stand among the most prosperous people of the global village. The sociological perspective reminds us that many of the achievements we attribute to our personal abilities are also products of the privileged position we occupy in the worldwide social system.[1]

[1.] Global village scenario adapted from United Nations data.

Our life chances and our very experiences of social life will differ dramatically according to what kind of society we are born into. Human lives do not unfold according to sheer chance; nor do people live isolated lives relying solely on what philosophers call 'free will' in choosing every thought and action. On the contrary, while individuals make many important decisions every day, we do so within a larger arena called 'society' – a family, a university, a nation, an entire world. The essential wisdom of sociology is that the social world guides and constrains our actions and life choices just as the seasons influence our choices of activities and clothing. It sets the framework in which we make decisions about our lives. And, because sociologists know a great deal about how society works, they can analyse and predict with both insight and accuracy how we all behave.

● The sociological perspective

Formally, the discipline of **sociology** is the *systematic, sceptical study of human society*. At the heart of sociology is a distinctive point of view.

Seeing the general in the particular

Peter Berger (1963) characterised the sociological perspective as *seeing the general in the particular*. He meant that sociologists identify general patterns of social life in the behaviour of particular individuals. While acknowledging that each individual is unique, in other words, sociologists recognise that society acts differently on various *categories* of people (say, children compared to adults, women versus men, the rich as opposed to the poor). We begin to think sociologically as we start to realise how the general categories into which we happen to fall shape our particular life experiences.

Each chapter of this text illustrates the general impact of society on the actions, thoughts, and feelings of particular people. For instance, the differences that distinguish children from the adults reflect not just biological maturity: by attaching meaning to age, society creates what we experience as distinct stages of life. Following these age-scripts, we expect children to be 'dependent' and adults to behave 'responsibly'. And, further along the life course, our society defines old age as a time of diminishing standing and withdrawal from earlier routines (see Chapter 14).

How do we know that society (and not simply biology) is at work here? Looking back in time or around the world today, we see that societies define the stages of life quite differently. Later chapters note that the Native-American Hopi confer on children a surprising degree of independence, while in Abkhasia (part of the Russian Federation) elderly people enjoy the lion's share of social position and esteem.

A sociological look around us reveals the power of class position as well. Chapters 9 and 10 provide ample evidence that how we live – and, sometimes, whether we live at all – has a great deal to do with our ranking in the societal hierarchy.

Seeing the world sociologically also makes us aware of the importance of gender. As Chapter 13 ('Gender and Sexuality') points out, every society attaches meanings (though often different meanings) to being one gender or the other, according women and men different kinds of work and family responsibilities. Individuals experience the workings of society as they encounter advantages and opportunities characteristic of each sex. Figure 1.1 suggests the many factors that shape our lives.

Seeing the strange in the familiar

Especially at the beginning, using the sociological perspective amounts to *seeing the strange in the familiar*. As Peter Berger (1963: 34) says in his *Invitation to Sociology*, 'the first wisdom of sociology is this: things are not what they seem'. For instance, observing sociologically requires giving up the familiar idea that human behaviour is simply a matter of what people *decide* to do and accepting instead the initially strange notion that society guides our thoughts and deeds.

Learning to 'see' how society affects us may take a bit of practice. Asked why you 'chose' to enrol at your

We can easily grasp the power of society over the individual by imagining how different our world would be had we been born in place of any of these children from, respectively, South Africa, Sri Lanka, the People's Republic of China, Brazil and Africa. (Source: Popperfoto)

particular college or university, you might offer any of the following personal reasons:

I wanted to stay close to home.

This college has the best women's rugby team!

A law degree from this university ensures a good job.

My girlfriend goes to university here.

I wasn't accepted by the university I really wanted to attend.

Such responses are certainly grounded in reality for the people expressing them. But do they tell the whole story? The sociological perspective provides additional insights that may not be readily apparent.

Thinking sociologically about going on to further or higher education, we might first realise that, for most people throughout most of the world, university is all but out of reach. Moreover, had we lived a cen-

tury or two ago, the 'choice' to go to university was only an option for the smallest elite. But even in the here and now, a look around the classroom suggests that social forces still have much to do with whether or not one pursues higher education. Typically, college students are relatively young – generally between 18 and 24 years of age. Why? Because in our society going to university is associated with this period of life. But it needn't be – as the recent growth of 'mature students' starts to testify. Likewise, higher education is costly, so college students tend to come from families with above-average incomes. As Chapter 19 ('Education') explains, young people lucky enough to belong to families from the service (middle) classes are some ten times more likely to go to university than are those from manual working class families. There are also significant variations by ethnicity and gender.

Figure 1.1 ● Society as a prison
An essential wisdom of sociology is that society guides our actions and life choices. In this diagram, human beings are located at the centre of numerous social forces: you may like to think about the forces that have shaped your own life – and how your life would be very different if you were born into other languages, institutions or societies.

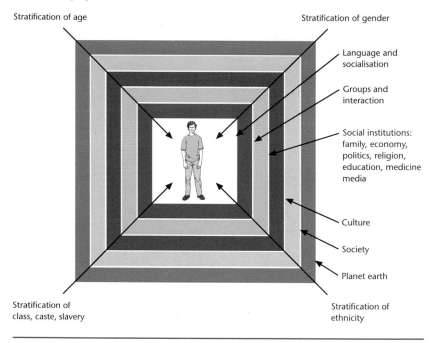

Stratification of age

Stratification of gender

Language and socialisation

Groups and interaction

Social institutions: family, economy, politics, religion, education, medicine media

Culture

Society

Planet earth

Stratification of class, caste, slavery

Stratification of ethnicity

research. If he could show that an intensely individual act like suicide was socially shaped, then he would have made a strong case for sociology. And he did! He was able to demonstrate that social forces figure in the apparently isolated act of self-destruction.

Durkheim began by examining suicide records in and around his native France. The statistics clearly showed that some *categories of people* were more likely than others to choose to take their own lives. Specifically, Durkheim found that men, Protestants, wealthy people, and the unmarried each had significantly higher suicide rates compared to women, Roman Catholics and Jews, the poor, and married people. Durkheim deduced that these differences corresponded to people's degree of *social integration*. Low suicide rates characterised categories of people with strong social ties; high suicide rates were found among those who were more socially isolated and individualistic.

So, at the broadest level, sociology sets out to show the patterns and processes by which society shapes what we do.

Individuality in social context

The sociological perspective often challenges common sense by revealing that human behaviour is not as individualistic as we may think. For most of us, daily living carries a heavy load of personal responsibility, so that we pat ourselves on the back when we enjoy success and kick ourselves when things go wrong. Proud of our individuality, even in painful times, we resist the idea that we act in socially patterned ways.

Perhaps the most compelling demonstration of how social forces affect human behaviour is the study of suicide. Why? Because nothing seems a more personal 'choice' than the decision to take one's own life. This is why Emile Durkheim (1858–1917), a pioneer of sociology writing a century ago who will reappear in many chapters of this book, chose suicide as a topic of

In the male-dominated societies studied by Durkheim, men certainly had more autonomy than women. Whatever freedom's advantages for men, concluded Durkheim, autonomy means lower social integration, which contributes to a higher male suicide rate. Likewise, individualistic Protestants were more prone to suicide than Catholics and Jews, whose rituals foster stronger social ties. The wealthy clearly have much more freedom of action than the poor but, once again, at the cost of a higher suicide rate. Finally, single people, with weaker social ties than married people, are also at greater risk of suicide.

A century later, Durkheim's analysis is still discussed. Figure 1.2 shows suicide rates for European countries. In every country, men are more likely to commit suicide than women. This is also true when you compare age for age. There are lower rates in southern Europe. In general, the Protestant north has higher rates. Whilst there are some exceptions, overall, suicide rates reveal general social patterns in the most personal actions of particular individuals.

(a) The World

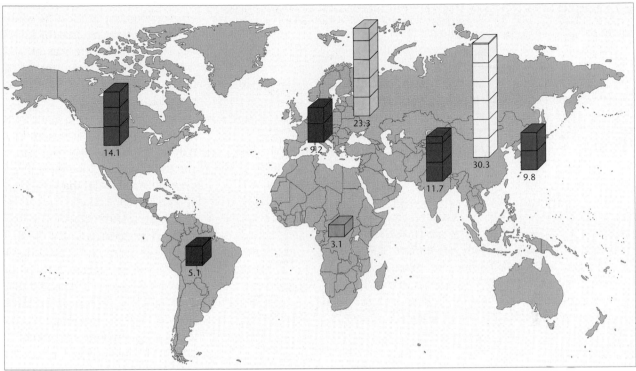

(b) Europe

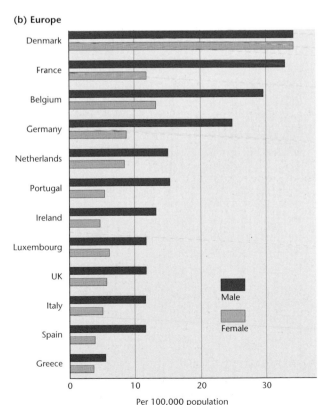

Per 100,000 population

Source: *Sociology Review*, Vol. 5, 1996, p. 34 ('Suicide is Killing Us')

Figure 1.2 ● Suicide figures

Suicide is usually seen as the most intensely personal act. Yet sociologists have long been interested in it, precisely because it shows definite social patterns. Consider what patterns are revealed. Why do you think there are these variations?

But these patterns are not constant around the world. Statistics emerging from China on suicide suggest a very different pattern to the mainly western one described by Durkheim. China, with 22 per cent of the world's people, accounts for some 40 per cent of suicides worldwide: a staggeringly higher rate. But whereas male suicides in the industrial, West outnumber female suicides by roughly three or four to one, in China women's suicides outnumber men's. Likewise, whereas in the West suicide is linked to city life, in China it is three times higher in the countryside (*New Scientist*, 22 March 1997: 34–7). Sociologists, then, look at these statistics to detect broad social patterns that then need explaining.

● Globalisation and the importance of global perspective

In recent years, as even the furthest reaches of the earth have become more easily accessible through advances in technology, many academic disciplines have incorporated a **global perspective**, *the study of the larger world and each society's place in it.* How does a global perspective enhance sociology?

Global awareness is a logical extension of the sociological perspective. Sociology's basic insight is that where we are placed in a society profoundly affects individual experiences. The position of a society in the larger world system affects everyone. The opening story provided a brief sketch of our global village, indicating that people the world over are far from equal in their quality of life.

Map 1.1 provides a visual guide to the relative economic development of the world's countries. The world's **high-income countries** are *industrialised nations in which most people enjoy material abundance.*[2] High-income countries include the United States and Canada, most of Western Europe, and Israel, Japan and Australia. Taken together, these forty societies generate most of the world's goods and services and control most of the planet's wealth. On average, individuals in these countries live well, not because they are particularly bright or exceptionally hard-working, but because they had the good fortune to be born in an affluent region of the world.

A second category of societies comprises the world's **middle-income countries**, which are *nations characterised by limited industrialisation and moderate personal income.* Individuals living in any of the roughly ninety nations at this level of economic development – which include the countries of Eastern Europe and most of Latin America – are more likely to live in rural areas than in cities, to walk or ride bicycles, scooters, or animals rather than to drive automobiles, and to receive only a few years of schooling. Most middle-income countries also have marked social inequality, so that while a few people are extremely rich (Hollywood superstars or sheiks of oil-producing nations in the Middle East, for example), many more lack safe housing and adequate nutrition.

Finally, about half of the world's people live in the sixty **low-income countries**, which are *nations with little industrialisation in which severe poverty is the rule.* As Map 1.1 shows, most of the poorest societies in the world are in Africa and Asia. Here again, a small number of people in each of these nations are rich; but the majority barely get by with poor housing, unsafe water, too little food, little or no sanitation and, perhaps most

seriously of all, little chance to improve their lives.

But the map is constantly changing, and one of the most significant recent developments is the emergence of **newly industrialising countries** (often called NICs), *lower-income countries that are fast becoming high-income ones.* A cluster of (mainly) South East Asian countries are making rapid economic progress. These countries include Hong Kong, Singapore, South Korea, Thailand and Taiwan. Some commentators have suggested that this new 'Asian Way' has been adopting different industrialisation patterns to those traditionally found in the West; and that they are indeed likely to become the trailblazers for the twenty-first century (see in popular vein, Naisbitt, 1997).

Many sociology texts have traditionally focused on one country – like England or the United States. But this is no longer feasible. Thus, Chapter 11 ('Global Stratification') explores the causes and consequences of global wealth and poverty in detail. And every chapter of this text highlights life in the world beyond our own borders. Why? Here are three reasons that global thinking figures prominently in the sociological perspective.

1. *Societies the world over are increasingly interconnected.* A feature of the world over the past 300 years or so has been the ways in which countries have become more and more internationally connected. Initially through 'the great explorers', then through colonialism, slavery and mass migrations; nowadays through tourism and the electronic world. In recent times, the world has become linked as never before. Jet aircraft whisk people across continents in hours, while new electronic devices transmit pictures, sounds and written documents around the globe in seconds.

One consequence of this new technology, as later chapters explain, is that people all over the world now share many tastes in music, clothing and food. With their economic strength, high-income nations cast a global shadow, influencing members of other societies who eagerly gobble up American hamburgers, dance to British 'pop music', and, more and more, speak the English language.

Commerce across national borders has also propelled a global economy. Large corporations manufacture and market goods worldwide, just as global

[2.] The text uses this terminology as opposed to the traditional, but outdated, terms 'First World', 'Second World' and 'Third World'. Chapter 11 ('Global Stratification') delves into the reasons for this shift.

financial markets linked by satellite communications now operate around the clock. Today, no stock trader in London dares to ignore what happens in the financial markets in Tokyo and Hong Kong, just as no fisherman in Scotland can afford to ignore the European common fishing policy! But as the West projects its way of life onto much of the world, the larger world also reacts back. All of this is linked to the process of **globalisation**, *the increasing interconnectedness of societies*. This process will be discussed further in many parts of this book.

2. *A global perspective enables us to see that many human problems we face in Europe are far more serious elsewhere*. Poverty is certainly a serious problem in Europe, and especially Eastern Europe. But, as Chapter 11 ('Global Stratification') explains, poverty is both more widespread and more severe throughout Latin America, Africa and Asia. Similarly, the social standing of women is especially low in poor countries of the world. And, although racism may be very pronounced in the UK, it has even harsher forms throughout many parts of the world. Ethnic cleansings in Bosnia, Islamophobia, and hostility to German 'guest workers' are three examples that will be considered later (Chapter 12). Then, too, many of the toughest problems we grapple with at home are global in scope. Environmental pollution is one example: As Chapter 23 ('Environment and the Risk Society')

demonstrates, the world is a single ecosystem in which the action (or inaction) of one nation has implications for all others.

3. *Thinking globally is an excellent way to learn more about ourselves*. We cannot walk the streets of a distant city without becoming keenly aware of what it means to live in western Europe at the end of the twentieth century. Making global comparisons also leads to unexpected lessons. For instance, Chapter 11 ('Global Stratification') transports us to a squatter settlement in Madras, India. There we are surprised to find people thriving in the love and support of family members, despite a desperate lack of basic material comforts. Such discoveries prompt us to think about why poverty in Europe so often involves isolation and anger, and whether material things – so crucial to our definition of a 'rich' life – are the best way to gauge human well-being.

In sum, in an increasingly interconnected world, we can understand ourselves only to the extent that we comprehend others.

● The sociological perspective in everyday life

Encountering people who differ from ourselves – whether around the world or in our own home towns – inevitably reminds us of the power of social forces

One important reason to gain a global understanding is that, living in a high-income society, we scarcely can appreciate the suffering that goes on in much of the world. The life of this Rwandan boy has been shredded by civil war. But even in more peaceful nations of Africa, children have less than a fifty–fifty chance to grow to adulthood.

Source: Magnum Photos, Inc. – Luc Delahaye

Map 1.1 ● Economic development and global perspective

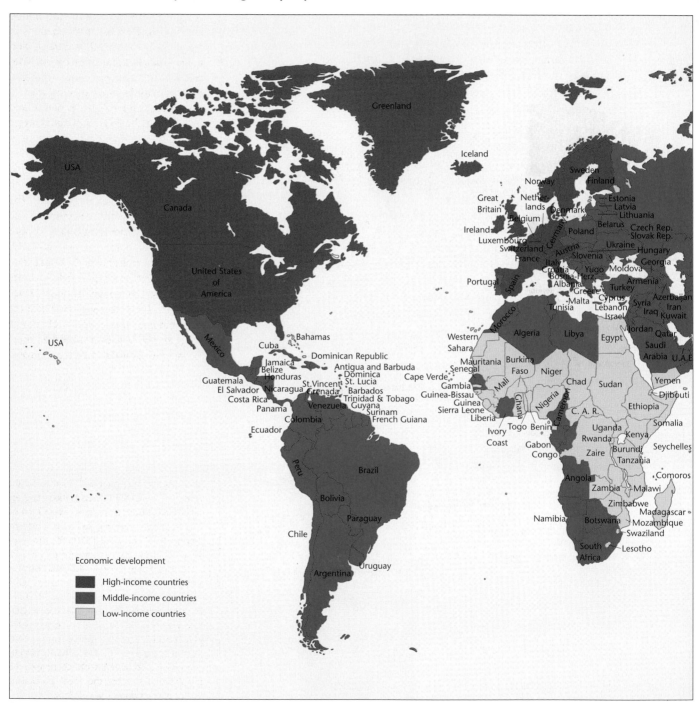

Economic development

■ High-income countries

■ Middle-income countries

□ Low-income countries

Source: prepared by the author using data from the World Bank (1995). Map projection from *Peter's Atlas of the World* (1990)

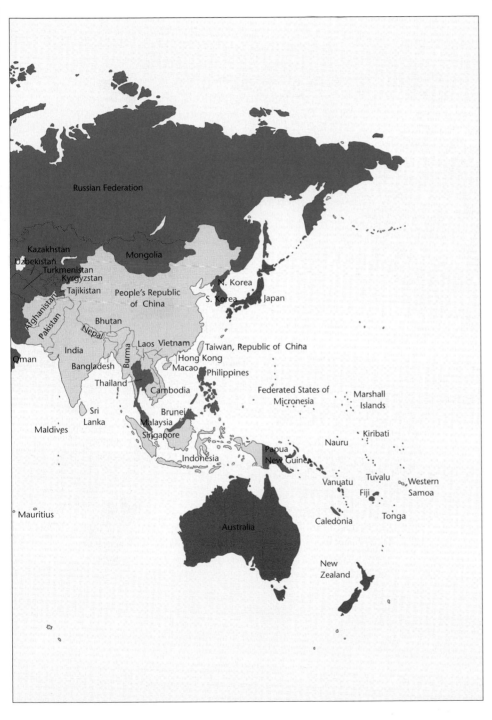

In high-income countries – the United States, Canada, most of the nations of Western Europe, Israel, Australia, and Japan – industrial technology provides people, on average, with material plenty. Middle-income countries – found throughout Latin America and including the nations of Eastern Europe – have limited industrial capacity and offer their people a standard of living that, while about average for the world as a whole, is far below that familiar to most people in Western Europe. The populations of these nations also encompass a significant share of poor people who barely scrape by with meagre housing and diet. In the low-income countries of the world, poverty is severe and extensive. Although small numbers of elites live very well in these poor nations, the majority of people struggle to survive on a small fraction of the income common in Western Europe.

Note: Data for this map are provided by the World Bank and the United Nations and are calculated through dollars. High-income countries have per capita gross domestic product (GDP) of at least $10,000. Many are far richer than this, however; the figure for the United States exceeds $25,000. Middle-income countries have a per capita GDP ranging from $2,500 to $10,000. Low-income countries have a per capita GDP below $2,500. Figures used here reflect the new United Nations 'purchasing power parities' system. Rather than directly converting income figures to US dollars, this calculation estimates the local purchasing power of each domestic currency.

to shape our lives. But two other kinds of situations stimulate a sociological outlook, even before we take a first course in sociology.

Sociology and social marginality

Sociological thinking is especially common among social 'outsiders'. Social marginality is something we all experience from time to time. For some categories of people, however, being an outsider is part of daily living. The more acute people's social marginality, the more likely they are to be keenly aware of their surroundings and to embrace the sociological perspective.

No Turkish guest worker in Germany or Pakistani in England lives for long without learning how much race affects personal experience. But, because white people are the dominant majority in these countries, they think about race only occasionally and often take the attitude that race affects only people of colour rather than themselves as well.

Much the same is true of women, gays and lesbians, people with disabilities, the homeless and the very old. All those relegated to the outskirts of social life typically become aware of social patterns others take for granted. Turning the argument around, for any of us to develop a sociological perspective we must step back a bit from our familiar routines to look on our lives with a new awareness and curiosity. Sociology leads to a questioning of all that is taken for granted. Seeing the world through the eyes of others 'on the margins' can help us see the way the world works more clearly. And it raises challenging questions about how margins and boundaries come about.

Sociology and social crisis

Periods of massive social change or social crisis throw everyone a little off balance, and this, too, stimulates sociological vision. C. Wright Mills (1959), a noted US sociologist, illustrated this principle by recalling the Great Depression of the 1930s. As the unemployment rate in the United States soared to 25 per cent (as it did elsewhere – the depression was 'global'), people out of work could not help but see general social forces at work in their particular lives. Rather than personalising their plight by claiming 'Something is wrong with me. I can't find a job', they took a more sociological approach, observing: 'The economy has collapsed. There are no jobs to be found!'

Conversely, sociological thinking often fosters social change. The more we learn about the operation of 'the system', the more we may wish to change it in some way. As women and men have confronted the power of gender, for example, many have actively tried to reduce the traditional differences that distinguish men and women.

In short, an introduction to sociology is an invitation to learn a new way of looking at familiar patterns of social life. At this point, we might well consider whether this invitation is worth accepting. In other words, what are the benefits of learning to use the sociological perspective?

Benefits of the sociological perspective

As we learn to use the sociological perspective, we can readily apply it to our daily lives. Doing so provides four general benefits.

1. *The sociological perspective becomes a way of thinking, a 'form of consciousness' that challenges familiar understandings of ourselves and of others, so that we can critically assess the truth of commonly held assumptions.* Thinking sociologically, in other words, we may realise that ideas we have taken for granted are not always true. As we have already seen, a good example of a widespread but misleading 'truth' is that Europe is populated with 'autonomous individuals' who are personally responsible for their lives. Thinking this way, we are sometimes too quick to praise particularly successful people as superior to others whose more modest achievements mark them as personally deficient. A sociological approach becomes a way of thinking with an ingrained habit of asking awkward questions. It prompts us to ask whether these beliefs are actually true and, to the extent that they are not, why they are so widely held. Sociology challenges the 'taken for granted'.

2. *The sociological perspective enables us to assess both the opportunities and the constraints that characterise our lives.* Sociological thinking leads us to see that, for better or worse, our society operates in a particular way. It helps us to see the pattern and order that is found in all societies. Moreover, in the game of life, we may decide how to play our cards, but it is society that deals us the hand. The more we understand

the game, then, the more effective players we will be. Sociology helps us to understand what we are likely and unlikely to accomplish for ourselves and how we can pursue our goals most effectively.

3. *The sociological perspective empowers us to be active participants in our society.* Without an awareness of how society operates, we are likely to accept the status quo. We might just think that this is how all societies are, or how all people behave 'naturally'. But the greater our understanding of the operation of society, the more we can take an active part in shaping social life. For some, this may mean embracing society as it is; others, however, may attempt nothing less than changing the entire world in some way. The discipline of sociology advocates no one particular political orientation, and sociologists themselves weigh in at many points across the political spectrum. But it does have a built in 'critical' tendency. And evaluating any aspect of social life – whatever one's eventual goal – depends on the ability to identify social forces and to assess their consequences.

Some thirty years ago, C. Wright Mills claimed that developing what he called the 'sociological imagination' would help people to become more active citizens. This major sociological thinker is highlighted in the Profile box. Other notable sociologists are featured in Profile boxes throughout this book.

4. *The sociological perspective helps us to recognise human differences and human suffering and to confront the challenges of living in a diverse world.* Sociological thinking highlights both the world's remarkable social variety and its sufferings real and potential. 'The British', for example, represent only a small proportion of the world's population, and, as the remaining chapters of this book explain, many human beings live in dramatically different societies. People everywhere tend to define their own way of life as proper and 'natural', and dismiss the lifestyles of those who differ. But the sociological perspective encourages us to think critically about the relative strengths and weaknesses of all ways of life – including our own. It also encourages us to see the many forms of suffering that occur – poverty, marital breakdown, illness, war and so on – and to see how such problems often arise because of the ways in which societies are organised.

Problems with the sociological perspective

Whilst approaching the world sociologically brings many benefits, it also harbours some distinctive problems. Three can be mentioned.

1. *Sociology is part of a changing world.* One of the difficult things about studying sociology is that we are studying a moving object: society can change just as quickly as we study it! A 'finding' from one day may soon be proved wrong when situations and circumstances change. And, since it is a feature of the modern world that societies are changing extraordinarily rapidly, we can expect our knowledge about them to change rapidly too. For instance, many of the statistics you read in this book will be out of date by the time you read them.

2. *Sociologists are part of what they study.* 'I have seen society, and it is me.' As we are all part of society, we are all part of what we study. This cannot be otherwise, but it makes the tasks of a sociologist very difficult. Many other 'sciences' study objects that are separate from the human species: but sociologists do not. Since we are part of the very world we study, we may find it hard to distance ourselves from this world. A sociologist born in Europe may have all kinds of European assumptions which do not hold in Thailand or Brazil. With the best intentions in the world, much sociology remains *ethnocentric* – blinded to a particular cultural view.

3. *Sociological knowledge becomes part of society.* The research and study that sociologists do – the books they write, the arguments they make – eventually become part of a society's knowledge about itself. Sociologist create ideas that can shape the ways in which societies work. Findings on crime – for example, that crimes rates are soaring – can be reported in the media, and people then become more conscious of crime. As a result, even more crime is reported. Sociology has an impact on society.

● The origins of sociology

Major historical events rarely just happen. They are typically products of powerful social forces that are always complex and only partly predictable. So it was with the emergence of sociology itself. Having described the discipline's distinctive perspective and surveyed some of its benefits, we can now consider how and why sociology emerged in the first place.

C. Wright Mills: the sociological imagination

Charles Wright Mills (1916–62) managed to cause a stir with almost everything he did. Even arriving for a class at New York's Columbia University – clad in a sweatshirt, jeans and boots, astride his motorcycle – he usually turned some heads. During the conservative 1950s, Mills not only dressed a bit out of the mainstream; he also produced a number of books that challenged most of the beliefs the majority of us take for granted. He was an American Marxist – and, in the process, he acquired both adherents and adversaries.

As Mills saw it, sociology is not some dry enterprise detached from life. Rather, he held up sociology as an escape from the 'traps' of our lives because it can show us that society – not our own foibles or failings – is responsible for many of our problems. In this way, Mills maintained, sociology transforms *personal problems* into *public and political issues*.

In the following excerpts, Mills describes both the power of society to shape our individual lives, and the importance of connecting our lives (biographies) to history and society:

When a society becomes industrialized, a peasant becomes a worker; a feudal lord is liquidated or becomes a businessman. When classes rise or fall, a man is employed or unemployed; when the rate of investment goes up or down, a man takes new heart or goes broke. When wars happen, an insurance salesman becomes a rocket launcher; a store clerk, a radar man; a wife lives alone; a child grows up without a father. Neither the life of an individual nor the history of a society can be understood without understanding both.

Yet men do not usually define the troubles they endure in terms of historical change. . . . The well-being they enjoy, they do not usually impute to the big ups and downs of the society in which they live. Seldom aware of the intricate connection between the patterns of their own lives and the course of world history, ordinary men do not usually know what this connection means for the kind of men they are becoming and for the kinds of history-making in which they might take part. They do not possess the quality of mind essential to grasp the interplay of men and society, of biography and history, of self and world. . . .

What they need . . . is a quality of mind that will help them to [see] . . . what is going on in the world and . . . what may be happening within themselves. It is this quality . . . that . . . may be called the sociological imagination.

Always keep your eyes open to the image of man – the generic notion of his human nature – which by your work you are assuming and implying; and also to the image of history – your notion of how history is being made. In a word, continually work out and revise your views of the problems of history, the problems of biography, and the problems of a social structure in which biography and history intersect. Keep your eyes open to the varieties of individuality, and to the modes of epochal change. Use what you see and what you imagine as the clues to your study of the human variety . . . know that many personal troubles cannot be solved merely as troubles, but must be understood in terms of public issues – and in terms of the problems of history making. Know that the human meaning of public issues must be revealed by relating them to personal troubles and to the problems of individual life. Know that the problems of social science, when adequately formulated, must include both troubles and issues, both biography and history, and the range of their intricate relations. Within that range the life of the individual and the making of societies occur; and within that range the sociological imagination has its chance to make a difference in the quality of human life in our time (Mills, 1967).

Source: Brown Brothers

This triple focus, on *biography*, *history* and *structure* is sociology's heritage. For a general introduction to Mills work, see John Eldridge (1983).

(Notice that in this excerpt, Mills uses male pronouns to apply to all people. It is interesting – even ironic – that an outspoken critic of society like Mills reflected the conventional writing practices of his time as far as gender was concerned. But he was writing in the 1950s before gender became a key issue for sociology.) ●

Auguste Comte: weathering a storm of change

What sort of person would invent sociology? Certainly someone living in times of momentous change. Comte (1798–1857) grew up in the wake of the French Revolution, which brought a sweeping transformation to his country. And if that wasn't sufficient, another revolution was under way: factories were sprouting up across continental Europe, recasting the lives of the entire population. Just as people enduring a storm cannot help but think of the weather, so those living during Comte's turbulent era became keenly aware of the state of society.

Drawn from his small home town by the bustle of Paris, Comte was soon deeply involved in the exciting events

Source: PH College Archives

of his time. More than anything else, he wanted to understand the human drama that was unfolding all around him. Once equipped with knowledge about how society operates, Comte believed, people would be able to build for themselves a better future. He divided his new discipline into two parts: how society is held together (which he called social statics), and how society changes (social dynamics). From the Greek and Latin words meaning 'the study of society', Comte came to describe his work as sociology. ●

Although human beings have mused about society since the beginning of our history, sociology is of relatively recent origin. It is among the youngest academic disciplines – far newer than history, physics or economics, for example. Only in 1838 did the French social thinker Auguste Comte, introduced in the box, coin the term *sociology* to describe a new way of looking at the world.

Science and sociology

The nature of society was a major topic of inquiry for virtually all the brilliant thinkers of the ancient world, including the Chinese philosopher K'ung Fu-tzu, also known as Confucius (551–479 BCE), and the Greek philosophers Plato (*c.* 427–347 BCE) and Aristotle (384–322 BCE).[3]

Similarly, the medieval thinker St Thomas Aquinas (*c.* 1225–1274), the fourteenth century Muslim Ibn Khaldun, and the French philosopher Montesquieu (1689–1755) all examined the state of human society. There were many such social thinkers. Yet, as Emile Durkheim noted almost a century ago, none of these approached society from a truly sociological point of view.

Looking back in history . . . we find that no philosophers ever viewed matters [with a sociological perspective] until quite recently. . . . It seemed to them sufficient to ascertain what the human will should strive for and what it should avoid in established societies. . . . Their aim was not to offer us as valid a description of nature as possible, but to present us with the idea of a perfect society, a model to be imitated. (1972: 57; orig. 1918)

What sets sociology apart from earlier social thought? Prior to the birth of sociology, philosophers and theologians mostly focused on imagining the ideal society. None attempted to analyse society as it really was. Pioneers of the discipline such as Auguste Comte and

---

[3] Throughout this text, the abbreviation BCE designates 'before the common era'. We use this terminology in place of the traditional BC. ('before Christ') in recognition of religious plurality. Similarly, in place of the traditional AD (*anno Domini*, or 'in the year of our Lord'), we employ the abbreviation CE ('common era'). See also the 'Time Lines' on the inside cover.

Emile Durkheim reversed these priorities. Although they were certainly concerned with how human society could be improved, their major goal was to understand how society actually operates.

The key to achieving this objective, according to Comte, was developing a scientific approach to society. Looking back in time, Comte sorted human efforts to comprehend the world into three distinct stages (1975; orig. 1851–54). The earliest era, extending through to the medieval period in Europe, he termed the *theological stage*. At this point, thoughts about the world were guided by religion, so people regarded society as an expression of God's will – at least insofar as humans were capable of fulfilling a divine plan.

With the Renaissance, the theological approach to society gradually gave way to what Comte called the *metaphysical stage*. During this period, people came to understand society as a natural, rather than a supernatural, phenomenon. Human nature figured heavily in metaphysical visions of society: Thomas Hobbes (1588–1679), for example, posited that society reflected not the perfection of God as much as the failings of a rather selfish human nature.

What Comte heralded as the final, *scientific stage* in the long quest to understand society was propelled by scientists such as Copernicus (1473–1543), Galileo[4] (1564–1642) and Isaac Newton (1642–1727). Comte's contribution came in applying this scientific approach – first used to study the physical world – to the study of society.

Comte was thus a proponent of **positivism**, defined as *a means to understand the world based on science*. As a positivist, Comte believed that society conforms to invariable laws, much as the physical world operates according to gravity and other laws of nature. Even today, most sociologists agree that science plays a crucial role in sociology. But, as Chapter 2 ('Sociological Investigation') explains, we now realise both that human behaviour is often far more complex than natural phenomena and that science is itself more sophisticated than we thought before. Thus human beings are creatures with considerable imagination and spontaneity, so that our behaviour can never be fully explained by any rigid 'laws of society'. Likewise, the universe may be much more 'chaotic' and 'emergent' than we previously thought, making observations and laws much more difficult.

Change, transformation and sociology

The prominent English sociologist Anthony Giddens has argued that sociology was born out of the 'massive social transformation' of the past two centuries. Two great revolutions – the French Revolution of 1789, and the more general 'industrial revolution' traced to England in the eighteenth century, 'have all but totally dissolved the forms of social organisation in which humankind has lived for thousands of years of its previous history' (Giddens, 1986: 4). Striking transformations in eighteenth and nineteenth century Europe, then, drove the development of sociology. As the social ground trembled under their feet, people understandably focused their attention on society.

First came scientific discoveries and technological advances that produced a factory-based industrial economy. Second, factories drew millions of people from the countryside, causing an explosive growth of cities. Third, people in these burgeoning industrial cities soon entertained new ideas about democracy and political rights. We shall briefly describe each of these three changes – though they all reappear for more detailed analysis during this book.

A new industrial economy

During the European Middle Ages, most people tilled fields near their homes or engaged in small-scale *manufacturing* (a word derived from Latin words meaning 'to make by hand'). But, by the end of the eighteenth century, inventors had applied new sources of energy – first water power and then steam power – to the operation of large machines, which gave birth to factories. Now, instead of labouring at home, workers became part of a large and anonymous industrial workforce, toiling for strangers who owned the factories. This drastic change in the system of production weakened families and eroded traditions that had guided members of small communities for centuries.

---

4. Illustrating Comte's stages, the ancient Greeks and Romans viewed the planets as gods; Renaissance metaphysical thinkers saw them as astral influences (giving rise to astrology); by the time of Galileo, scientists understood planets as natural objects behaving in orderly ways.

In the United States, Jane Addams (1860–1935) was a social worker known for her public activism on behalf of poor immigrants to that country. In 1889, Addams founded Hull House, a Chicago settlement house, in a poor, inner-city neighbourhood. There, she engaged with intellectuals and immigrants alike in discussions of the pressing problems of her day. Her contribution to the welfare of others earned Addams a Nobel Peace Prize in 1931. Recently, it has been suggested she is the true founder of the Chicago School (see Chapter 23 and Deegan (1988)).

Source: Brown Brothers

The growth of cities

Factories sprouting across much of Europe became magnets attracting people in need of work. This 'pull' of work in the new industrialised labour force was accentuated by an additional 'push' as landowners fenced off more and more ground, turning farms into grazing land for sheep – the source of wool for the thriving textile mills. This so-called 'enclosure movement' forced countless tenant farmers from the countryside toward cities in search of work in the new factories.

Many villages were soon abandoned; at the same time, however, factory towns swelled rapidly into large cities. Such urban growth dramatically changed people's lives. Cities churned with strangers, in numbers that overwhelmed available housing. Widespread social problems – including poverty, disease, pollution, crime and homelessness – were the order of the day. Such social crises further stimulated development of the sociological perspective.

Political change

During the Middle Ages, as Comte noted, most people thought of society as the expression of God's will. Royalty claimed to rule by 'divine right', and each person up and down the social hierarchy had some other part in the holy plan. With economic development and the rapid growth of cities, changes in political thought were inevitable. Starting in the seventeenth century, every kind of tradition came under spirited attack. In the writings of Thomas Hobbes, John Locke (1632–1704) and Adam Smith (1723–1790), we see a distinct shift in focus from people's moral obligations to remain loyal to their rulers to the idea that society is the product of individual self-interest. The key phrases in the new political climate, therefore, were *individual liberty* and *individual rights*. Echoing the thoughts of Locke, the American Declaration of Independence asserts that each individual has 'certain unalienable rights', including 'life, liberty, and the pursuit of happiness'.

The political revolution in France that began soon afterwards, in 1789, constituted an even more dramatic break with political and social traditions. As the French social analyst Alexis de Tocqueville (1805–1859) surveyed his society after the French Revolution, he exaggerated only slightly when he asserted that the changes we have described amounted to 'nothing short of the regeneration of the whole human race' (1955: 13; orig. 1856). In this context, it is easy to see why Auguste Comte and other pioneers of sociology soon developed their new discipline. Sociology flowered in precisely those societies – France, Germany and England – where change was greatest.

Sociologists reacted differently to the new social order then, just as they respond differently to society today. Some, including Auguste Comte, feared that people would be uprooted from long-established local communities and overpowered by change. So, in a conservative approach, Comte sought to shore up the family and traditional morality.

Taking a different view of these massive changes, Karl Marx (1818–1883) worried little about the loss of tradition. But he could not condone the way industrial technology concentrated its great wealth in the hands of a small elite, while so many others faced hunger and misery. We examine his ideas at length in Chapter 3 ('Society').

Clearly, Comte and Marx advanced radically different prescriptions for the problems of modernity. Yet they had in common the conviction that society rests on much more than individual choice. The sociological perspective animates the work of each, revealing that people's individual lives are framed by the broader society in which they live. This lesson, of course, remains as true today as it was a century ago. In subsequent chapters of this book, we delve into the major issues that concern sociologists. These pivotal social forces include culture, social class, race, ethnicity, gender, the economy and the family. They all involve ways in which individuals are guided, united and divided in the larger arena of society.

● Sociological theory

The task of weaving isolated observations into understanding brings us to another dimension of sociology: theory. A **theory** is *a statement of how and why specific facts are related*. In a sense, we all theorise or generalise all the time. But sociology aims to do this more systematically (see Craib, 1992; Lee and Newby, 1983). Recall that Emile Durkheim observed that certain categories of people (men, Protestants, the wealthy and the unmarried) have higher suicide rates than others (women, Catholics and Jews, the poor and the married). He explained these observations by creating a theory: a high risk of suicide stems from a low level of social integration.

Of course, as Durkheim pondered the issue of suicide, he considered any number of possible theories. But merely linking facts together is no guarantee that a theory is correct. To evaluate a theory, as the next

chapter explains, sociologists use logical thinking and research methods to gather evidence. Facts allow sociologists to confirm some theories while rejecting or modifying others. As a scientist, Durkheim was not content merely to identify a plausible cause of suicide; he set about collecting data to see precisely which categories of people committed suicide with the highest frequency. Poring over his data, Durkheim settled on a theory that best squared with all available evidence.

In attempting to develop theories about human society, sociologists face a wide range of choices. What issues should we study? How should we link facts together to form theories? In making sense of society, sociologists are guided by one or more theoretical 'road maps' or paradigms (Kuhn, 1970). For them, a **theoretical paradigm** is *a basic image of society that guides thinking and research*.

We noted earlier that two of sociology's founders – Auguste Comte and Karl Marx – made sense of the emerging modern society in strikingly different ways. Such differences persist today as some sociologists highlight how societies stay the same, while others focus on patterns of change. Similarly, some sociological theorists focus on what joins people together, while others investigate how society divides people according to gender, race, ethnicity or social class. Some sociologists seek to understand the operation of society as it is, while others actively promote what they view as desirable social change.

In short, sociologists often disagree about what the most interesting questions are; even when they agree on the questions, they may still differ over the answers. Nonetheless, the discipline of sociology is far from chaotic. Over the past hundred years, sociologists have developed three major theoretical paradigms that allow them to analyse effectively virtually any dimension of society. We will introduce these next – and they will reappear at various points in the book. But, like any growing discipline, these are constantly being refined and developed, whilst at the same time newer ones are appearing alongside them. After briefly outlining the mainstream stances, we will turn to some emerging perspectives.

● Mainstream paradigms in sociology

Broadly, three paradigms have dominated sociological thinking: functionalism, conflict, and action theory.

The functionalist paradigm

Functionalism is *a framework for building theory that envisions society as a complex system whose parts work together to promote solidarity and stability*. This paradigm begins by recognising that our lives are guided by **social structure**, meaning *relatively stable patterns of social behaviour*. Social structure is what gives shape to the family, directs people to exchange greetings on the street, or steers events in a university classroom. Second, this paradigm leads us to understand social structure in terms of its **social functions**, or *consequences for the operation of society*. All social structure – from family life to a simple handshake – contributes to the operation of society, at least in its present form.

Functionalism owes much to the ideas of Auguste Comte who, as we have already explained, sought to promote social integration during a time of tumultuous change. A second architect of this theoretical approach, the influential English sociologist Herbert Spencer (1820–1903), is introduced in the box below.

PROFILE

Herbert Spencer: the survival of the fittest

The most memorable idea of the English philosopher Herbert Spencer (1820–1903) was his assertion that the passing of time witnesses 'the survival of the fittest'. Many people associate this immortal phrase with the theory of species evolution developed by the natural scientist Charles Darwin (1809–1882). The expression was actually Spencer's, however, and he used it to refer to society, not to living creatures. In it, we find not only an example of early structural-functional analysis, but a controversial theory that reflects the popular view in Spencer's day that society mirrored biology.

Spencer's ideas, which came to be known as social Darwinism, rested on the assertion that, if left to compete among themselves, the most intelligent, ambitious, and productive people will inevitably win out. Spencer endorsed a world of fierce competition, thinking that as the 'fittest' survived, society would undergo steady improvements.

Society rewards its best members, Spencer continued, by allowing a free-market economy to function without government interference. Welfare, or other programmes aimed at redistributing money to benefit the poor, Spencer maintained, do just the opposite: They drag society down by elevating its weakest and least worthy members. For such opinions, nineteenth-century industrialists loudly applauded Spencer, and the rich saw in Spencer's analysis a scientific justification for big business to remain free of government regulation or social conscience. Indeed, John D.

Source: PH College Archives

Rockefeller, who built a vast financial empire that included most of the US oil industry, often recited Spencer's 'social gospel' to young children in Sunday school, casting the growth of giant corporations as merely the naturally ordained 'survival of the fittest'.

But others objected to the idea that society amounted to little more than a jungle where self-interest reigned supreme. Gradually, social Darwinism fell out of favour among social scientists, though it still surfaces today as an influential element of conservative political thought. From a sociological point of view, Spencer's thinking is flawed because we now realise that ability only partly accounts for personal success, and favouring the rich and powerful does not necessarily benefit society as a whole. In addition, the heartlessness of Spencer's ideas strikes many people as cruel, with little room for human compassion.

For a positive appraisal of Spencer's work, see Jonathan Turner, *Herbert Spencer* (1985). ●

Spencer was a student of both the human body and society, and he came to see that the two have much in common. The structural parts of the human body include the skeleton, muscles and various internal organs. These elements are interdependent, with each contributing to the survival of the entire organism. In the same way, reasoned Spencer, various social structures are interdependent, working in concert to preserve society. The structural-functional paradigm, then, organises sociological observations by identifying various structures of society and investigating the function of each one.

In France, several decades after Comte's death, Emile Durkheim continued the development of sociology. Durkheim did not share the social Darwinist thinking of his English colleague Spencer; rather, his work is primarily concerned with the issue of *social solidarity*, how societies 'hang together'. Because of the extent of Durkheim's influence on sociology, his work is detailed in Chapter 3 ('Society').

As sociology developed in the United States, many of the ideas of Herbert Spencer and Emile Durkheim were carried forward by Talcott Parsons (1902–79). The major US proponent of the functional paradigm, Parsons treated society as a system, identifying the basic tasks all societies must perform to survive and the ways they accomplish these tasks.

Contemporary US sociologist Robert K. Merton has expanded our understanding of the concept of social function in novel ways. Merton (1968) explains, first, that the consequences of any social pattern are likely to differ for various members of a society. For example, conventional families may provide crucial support for the development of children, but they also confer privileges on men while limiting the opportunities of women.

Second, Merton notes, people rarely perceive all the functions of a particular social structure. He described as **manifest functions** the *recognised and intended consequences of any social pattern*. By contrast, **latent functions** are *consequences that are largely unrecognised and unintended*. To illustrate, the obvious functions of higher education include providing people with the information and skills they need to perform jobs effectively. But perhaps just as important, although rarely acknowledged, is a university's function as a chance to meet potential partners. Another function may be to keep millions of young people out of a labour market where, presumably, many of them would not find jobs. And a third less obvious function may well be to reinforce a system of prestige and inequality – by excluding those who do not go to universities from all sorts of work.

Merton makes a third point: not *all* the effects of any social structure turn out to be useful. Thus we designate as **social dysfunctions** *any social pattern's undesirable consequences for the operation of society*. And, to make matters still more complex, people may well disagree about what is useful or harmful. So some might argue that higher education promotes left-wing thinking that threatens traditional values. Others might dismiss such charges as trivial or simply wrong; higher education is dysfunctional for conferring further privileges on the wealthy (who disproportionately attend university) while poorer families find a university course out of their financial reach.

Critical evaluation
The most salient characteristic of the functional paradigm is its vision of society as a whole being comprehensible, orderly and stable. Sociologists typically couple this approach with scientific methods of research aimed at learning 'what makes society tick'.

Until the 1960s, the functional paradigm dominated sociology. In recent decades, however, its influence has waned. How can we assume that society has a 'natural' order, critics ask, when social patterns vary from place to place and change over time? Further, by emphasising social integration, functionalism tends to gloss over inequality based on social class, race, ethnicity and gender – divisions that may generate considerable tension and conflict. This focus on stability at the expense of conflict and change can give the functional paradigm a conservative character.

The conflict paradigm

The **conflict paradigm** is *a framework for building theory that envisions society as an arena of inequality that generates conflict and change*. This approach complements the functional paradigm by highlighting not solidarity but division based on inequality. Guided by this paradigm, sociologists investigate how factors such as social class, race, ethnicity, sex and age are

Figure 1.3 ● A map of traditional sociological theory
The sociological map shows some key western sociologists – when they were born and where. When presented like this it is easy to detect a very strong male bias.

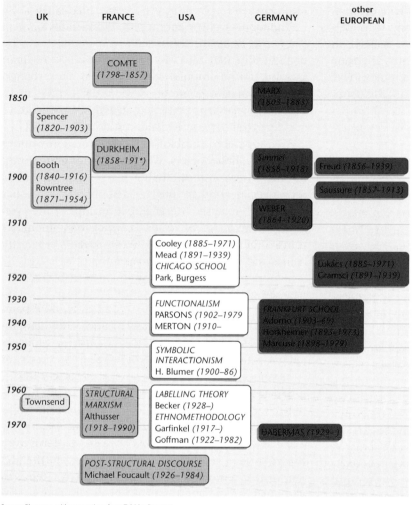

Source: Plummer, with suggestions from Tabitha Freeman

linked to unequal distribution of money, power, education and social prestige. A conflict analysis points out that, rather than promoting the operation of society as a whole, social structure typically benefits some people while depriving others.

Working within the conflict paradigm, sociologists spotlight ongoing conflict between dominant and disadvantaged categories of people – the rich in relation to the poor, white people as opposed to black, men versus women. Typically, those on top strive to protect their privileges; the disadvantaged counter by attempting to gain more resources for themselves.

To illustrate, a conflict analysis of our educational system might highlight how schooling perpetuates inequality by helping to reproduce the class structure in every new generation. The process may start in primary schools and continue as secondary schools stream students. From a functional point of view, this may benefit all of society because, ideally, students receive the training appropriate to their academic abilities. But conflict analysis counters that streaming often has less to do with talent than with a student's social background, as well-to-do students are placed in higher streams and poor students end up in the lower ones.

In this way, privileged families gain favoured treatment for their children from schools. And, with the best schooling behind them, these young people leave university to pursue occupations that confer both prestige and high income. By contrast, the children of poor families are less prepared for college. So, like their parents before them, these young people typically move right from secondary school into low-paying jobs. In both cases, the social standing of one generation is passed on to another, with schools justifying the practice not in terms of privilege but of individual merit (Bowles and Gintis, 1976; and see Chapter 19).

Social conflict extends well beyond schools. Later chapters of this book highlight efforts by working people, women, racial and ethnic and gay and lesbian minorities to improve their lives. In each of these cases, the conflict paradigm helps us to see how inequality and the conflict it generates are rooted in the organisation of society itself.

Finally, many sociologists who embrace the conflict paradigm attempt not just to understand society but to reduce social inequality. This was the goal of Karl Marx, the social thinker whose ideas underlie the conflict paradigm. Marx did not seek merely to understand how society works. In a well-known declaration (inscribed on his monument in London's Highgate Cemetery), Marx asserted: 'The philosophers have only interpreted the world, in various ways; the point, however, is to change it.'

Critical evaluation

The conflict paradigm has developed rapidly in recent decades. Yet, like other approaches, it has come in for its share of criticism. Because this paradigm highlights inequality and division, it glosses over how shared values or interdependence generate unity among members of a society. In addition, say critics, to the extent that the conflict approach explicitly pursues political goals, it relinquishes any claim to scientific objectivity. As Chapter 2 ('Sociological Investigation') explains in detail, conflict theorists are uneasy with the notion that science can be 'objective'. They contend, on the contrary, that the conflict paradigm as well as *all* theoretical approaches have political consequences, albeit different ones.

One additional criticism, which applies equally to both the functional and conflict paradigms: they envision society in very broad terms. 'Society' becomes a thing in itself, describing our lives as a composite of 'family', 'social class', and so on. A third theoretical paradigm depicts society less in terms of abstract generalisations and more in terms of people's everyday, situational experiences.

The action paradigm

Both the functional and conflict paradigms share a **macro-level orientation**, meaning *a focus on broad social structures that characterise society as a whole*. Macro-level sociology takes in the big picture, rather like observing a city from high above in a helicopter, noting how highways carry traffic from place to place and the striking contrasts between rich and poor neighbourhoods. Action theory, by contrast, starts with the ways in which people (or actors) orientate themselves to each other and how they do so on the basis of meanings. This provides a **micro-level orientation**, meaning *a focus on social interaction in specific situations*. The distinction between macro and micro is an important one in sociology and it appears in a number of guises. The box introduces some of these ideas further.

The founder of the **action paradigm** – *a micro theory that focuses on how actors assemble social meanings* – is the highly influential Max Weber (1864–1920), a German sociologist who emphasised the need to understand a setting from the point of view of the people in it. Weber's approach is presented at length in Chapter 3 ('Society'), but here a few ideas can be introduced.

His approach emphasises how human meanings and action shape society. Weber understood the power of technology, and he shared many of Marx's ideas about social conflict. But he departed from Marx's materialist analysis, arguing that societies differ primarily in terms of the ways in which their members think about the world. For Weber, ideas – especially beliefs and values – have transforming power. Thus he saw modern society as the product, not just of new technology and capitalism, but of a new way of thinking. This emphasis on ideas contrasts with Marx's focus on material production, leading scholars to describe Weber's work as 'a debate with the ghost of Karl Marx' (Cuff and Payne, 1979: 73–4).

In all his work, Weber contrasted social patterns in different times and places. To sharpen comparisons, he relied on the **ideal type**, *an abstract statement of the essential, though often exaggerated, characteristics of any social phenomenon*. He explored religion by contrasting the ideal 'Protestant' with the ideal 'Jew', 'Hindu' and 'Buddhist', knowing that these models precisely described no actual individuals. These 'ideal types' can then be contrasted with actual, empirical forms found in reality. Note that Weber's use of the word *ideal* does not mean that something is 'good' or 'the best'; we could analyse 'criminals' as well as 'priests' as ideal types.

Closely allied to Weber is the American tradition of symbolic interactionism. The perspective emerges in the work of the philosopher George Herbert Mead (1863–1931), who looked at how we assemble our sense of self over time based on social experience. His ideas are explored in Chapter 5 ('Socialisation'). The theory is also connected to the Chicago school of sociology (explored more in Chapter 23), which examined city life in this way. The theory leads to careful observing of how people interact. The **symbolic-interaction paradigm**, then, is *a theoretical framework* *that envisions society as the product of the everyday inter-actions of people doing things together.*

How does 'society' result from the ongoing experiences of tens of millions of people? One answer, detailed in Chapter 6 ('Social Interaction in Everyday Life'), is that society arises as a shared reality that its members construct as they interact with one another. Through the human process of finding meaning in our

CONTROVERSY AND DEBATE

Which comes first? Chickens or eggs? Action or structure?
A classic problem for sociologists

Which comes first: the chicken or the egg? This classic conundrum has a parallel question which has persisted throughout sociology's history. It can be put like this: which comes first – society or the individual? And like the chicken and egg problem, there is no simple solution. Indeed, what has to be recognised is that one does not come first – eggs can't simply come before chickens, any more than chickens can simply come before eggs. Both are needed. And it is the interaction of the two that has to be seen. You can't, in short, have one without the other. And the same is true for individuals and societies. What sociologists do is look at both individuals and societies, and at their best they look at them together through dialectical thinking which requires looking at two seeming opposites (like individual and society) and how a new form emerges though them.

Making it happen: Individuals and action

One phase of sociological analysis is indeed to look at human beings. Not as a psychologist would – in terms of individual attributes like drives or personalities. Rather, the task is to look at the ways in which human beings are orientated towards action, to being world makers, creators of history and social life. Human beings make history, and

sociology should look at the ways this happens. We are world makers.

For instance, if you want to understand how our current education system works, one task is to look at the ways in which people make it what it is. This means examining the ways in which legislators passed Acts that provided the framework for schools, teaching, curriculum and exams. These did not just happen: they were made, and sociologists need to look at how they were made. Likewise, a pupil arrives in a class and, along with other students and teachers, sets about making the class happen. Sociologists like to get into the classrooms and observe this 'action' – to see just how human beings make the social world work.

Pattern and prison: social structures as maps

Yet people are also born into worlds that are not of their own making. Indeed, as the sociologist Peter Berger says, 'society is the walls of our imprisonment'. We are born into families, communities and nations over which we have little immediate control; our lives are heavily shaped by the class, gender and ethnicity we are born into; indeed, even the very language we think with and talk with helps set a pattern to our life. And we had no initial choice over which language we plan to speak: it is given to us from early childhood. (It would be very odd, if you were

born in England, if you were made to speak Zqahila.) Thus, one moment of sociological analysis is to look at these broadest patterns of social organisation that shape our lives. Recurrent and habitual patterns of social life may be seen as structures. Think for a moment of the ways in which your own life is 'imprisoned'.

Putting 'Action' and 'Structure' together

So: a *structural* approach tends to map out society as a whole, whilst an *action* approach tends to examine the ways in which individuals and small groups come to make their social worlds.

Of course, ideally both will be done. This is a task for more advanced social theory: Giddens, for example, has introduced the idea of *structuration* to focus on looking at both individuals and structures at the same time. As you read this book, keep this puzzle in mind. And take the discussion further:

● **Continue the debate:**

1. Do you see yourself as 'determined' by social structure? Look at Figure 1.1 again.

2. How far do you think you can change the world? Are you a world maker?

3. Look at attempts that have been made to resolve the problem between individual and society (see Craib, 1992). ●

surroundings, we define our identities, rights, and obligations toward others.

Of course, this process of definition varies a great deal from person to person. On a city street, for example, one person may define a homeless woman as 'a no-hoper looking for a handout' and ignore her. Another, however, might define her as a 'fellow human being in need' and offer assistance. In the same way, one pedestrian may feel a sense of security passing by a police officer walking the beat, while another may be seized by nervous anxiety. Sociologists guided by the symbolic-interaction approach, therefore, view society as a mosaic of subjective meanings and variable responses.

On this foundation, others have devised their own micro-level approaches to understanding social life. Chapter 6 ('Social Interaction in Everyday Life') presents the work of Erving Goffman (1922–82), whose *dramaturgical analysis* emphasises how we resemble actors on a stage as we play out our various roles before others. Other contemporary sociologists, including George Homans and Peter Blau, have developed *social-exchange analysis*. In their view, social interaction amounts to a negotiation in which individuals are guided by what they stand to gain and lose from others. In the ritual of courtship, for example, people typically seek mates who offer at least as much – in terms of physical attractiveness, intelligence and social background – as they provide in return.

Critical evaluation

The action paradigm helps to correct a bias inherent in all macro-level approaches to understanding society. Without denying the usefulness of abstract social structures such as 'the family' and 'social class', we must bear in mind that society basically amounts to *people interacting*. Put another way, this micro-level approach helps convey more of how individuals actually experience society and how they do things together (cf. Becker, 1986).

The trouble is that by focusing on day-to-day interactions, these theorists can obscure larger social structures. Highlighting what is unique in each social scene risks overlooking the widespread effects of our culture, as well as factors such as class, gender and race.

Table 1.1 summarises the important characteristics of the functional, conflict and action paradigms. As we have explained, each paradigm is especially helpful in answering particular kinds of questions. By and large, however, the fullest understanding of society comes

from linking the sociological perspective to all three. The three theoretical paradigms certainly offer different insights, but none is more correct than the others. Applied to any issue, each paradigm generates its own interpretations so that, to fully appreciate the power of the sociological perspective, you should become familiar with all three. Together, they stimulate key debates and controversies, many of which are presented in the chapters that follow.

● Emerging perspectives in sociological theory: other voices

Although functionalism, conflict theory and action sociology are still the dominant positions within sociology and are the major theories you will encounter in this book, there have been many others which have emerged over the past two decades. It is the sign of a lively subject, that as society changes so too do some of the approaches being adopted within it.

Some of them are really just further developments of the above theories. They may, for example, focus on different aspects of 'action' such as language and conversation (conversational analysis) ; or the idea that people are rational actors (rational choices theory). Or they may focus on different aspects of structure, focusing on the way the state works, for example (as in Althusserian Marxism). At this stage in your introductory studies, you perhaps need not be concerned with these.

Other developments, however, are seen by some to go deeper than this. A number of critics of sociology suggest the discipline has now entered a stage of 'crisis' in which many of its older ideas and paradigms are seen as being too narrowly conceived. Broadly, the newer approaches highlight different *perspectives*, *standpoints* or *voices*: they are much more conscious that all of sociology has to come from a perspective, a position or a point of view. We can never grasp the full truth of society, a completely full picture of it, so we should be more open about the partial perspectives we adopt. Sociology will always be selective. Max Weber himself recognised this long ago when he said: 'There is no absolutely "objective" scientific analysis of culture or . . . of "social phenomena" independent of special and "one-sided" viewpoints according to which . . . they are selected, analysed and organised' (Weber, 1949: 72).

This recognition of *perspectives*, *points of view*s, or *standpoints* from which analysis proceeds has become more and more important for modern sociology. And

Table 1.1 ● The three major theoretical paradigms: a summary

Theoretical paradigm	Orientation	Image of society	Core questions
Functional	Macro-level	A system of interrelated parts that is relatively stable based on widespread consensus as to what is morally desirable; each part has functional consequences for the operation of society as a whole	How is society integrated? What are the major parts of society? How are these parts interrelated? What are the consequences of each one for the operation of society?
Conflict	Macro-level	A system characterised by social inequality; each part of society benefits some categories of people more than others; conflict-based social inequality promotes social change	How is society divided? What are the major patterns of social inequality? How do some categories of people attempt to protect their privileges? How do other categories of people challenge the status quo?
Symbolic-interaction	Micro-level	An ongoing process of social interaction in specific settings based on symbolic communications; individual perceptions of reality are variable and changing	How is society experienced? How do human beings interact to create, sustain, and change social patterns? How do individuals attempt to shape the reality perceived by others? How does individual behaviour change from one situation to another?

this means that it helps to be explicit and open about the perspective we take. At its most critical, many of the new perspectives suggest that the major perspective of the past has been that of white, Western (predominantly Anglo-American) heterosexual men. Whether the sociologist was a functionalist, conflict or action theorist, they all shared common assumptions derived from their male and Western position. In contrast, the newer perspectives generally see a range of other voices that have been missed out of sociology in the past. Taken together they provide a lot more 'angles' from which to approach society.

Although some of them are very critical of the dominant, earlier approaches, at present it may be most helpful to see them as complementing and not replacing these earlier 'paradigms'. They do, however, disagree with these early theories whenever they suggest they are telling the whole story of society: only partial stories are possible in this newer view. They speak of the 'death of the metanarrative' as a way of rejecting any idea that there is one, and only one, Big Story of Sociology.

What, then, are these new voices? They include women, racial and ethnic minorities, colonised peoples throughout the world, gays and lesbians, the elderly, disabled people and various other marginalised or overlooked groups. You may well belong to one of these many groups, and should read this book with this in mind. Taken together a number of criticisms of classical sociology can be briefly summarised as:

1. Sociology has mainly looked at research by men for men and about men – and for men, read white and heterosexual and relatively affluent. As such it has had a persistently limited, even biased approach.

2. That areas of significance to other groups – racism for ethnic groups; reproduction, mothering and patriarchy for women; homophobia for gays; colonisation for other cultural groups – have often been overlooked.

3. That these areas of significance, when they have been included, have often been presented in a distorted fashion: often sociology has been sexist, racist and homophobic.

Beatrice Webb (née Potter) (1853–1943) leading social historian and reformer and founder with her husband, Sidney Webb, of the Fabian Society.

Source: courtesy of Halton Getty

Feminist sociology

Whilst there are many voices missing in sociology, the most apparent absence until recently has been that of women's voices: sociology has been by men, about men and largely for men. All this is changing with the development of both feminist sociology and feminist methodology. Broadly, these place gender at the centre of their analysis, and see a more political role for sociologists in trying to reduce or eliminate women's subordination and oppression in societies. Although you will find a chapter in this book that looks at gender specifically (Chapter 13 'Gender and Sexuality'), you will also find that gender as an issue will be considered in nearly every chapter. Bringing a feminist gender perspective to any analysis helps to widen and deepen understanding (cf. Abbott and Wallace, 1997).

And other voices

Following from all this, there are many new developments in sociology and you will encounter these throughout this book. For instance, Chapter 4 ('Culture') introduces ideas around multiculturalism and postcolonialism; Chapter 8 introduces ideas around 'discourse theory'; Chapter 12 debates antiracist theory; Chapter 13 will extend feminist theory and introduce Queer theory; whilst Chapter 24 will present some ideas around postmodern social theory. As in any introduction, we cannot take these newer ideas very far. But at least you will sense that sociology is a continuously growing and changing discipline of study that is always bringing new challenges to its students.

SUMMARY

1. The sociological perspective reveals 'the general in the particular' or the power of society to shape our lives.

2. Because people in Europe tend to think in terms of individual choice, recognising the impact of society on our lives initially seems like 'seeing the strange in the familiar'.

3. Emile Durkheim's research demonstrating that suicide rates are significantly higher among some categories of people than among others shows that society affects even the most personal of our actions.

4. Global awareness enhances the sociological perspective because, first, societies of the world are becoming more and more interconnected; second,

many social problems are most serious beyond the borders of European countries; and, third, recognising how others live helps us better understand ourselves. Globalisation is an emerging widespread process by which social relations acquire relatively distanceless and borderless qualities.

5. Socially marginal people are more likely than others to perceive the effects of society. For everyone, periods of social crisis foster sociological thinking.

6. There are four general benefits to using the sociological perspective. First, it challenges our familiar understandings of the world, helping us separate fact from fiction; second, it helps us appreciate the opportunities and constraints that frame our lives; third, it encourages more active participation in society; fourth, it increases our awareness of social diversity in the UK and in the world as a whole.

7. There are three problems in studying sociology. First, societies change very rapidly; second, we are part of the societies we study; and third, sociology itself becomes a part of society.

8. Auguste Comte gave sociology its name in 1838. Whereas previous social thought had focused on what society ought to be, Comte's new discipline of sociology used scientific methods to understand society as it is.

9. Sociology emerged as a reaction to the rapid transformation of Europe during the eighteenth and nineteenth centuries. Three dimensions of change – the rise of an industrial economy, the explosive growth of cities, and the emergence of new political ideas – each focused people's attention on the operation of society.

10. Building theory involves linking insights to gain understanding. Various theoretical paradigms guide sociologists as they construct theories.

11. The functional paradigm is a framework for exploring how social structures promote the stability and integration of society. This approach minimises the importance of social inequality, conflict and change.

12. The conflict paradigm highlights social inequality, conflict and change. At the same time, this approach downplays the extent of society's integration and stability.

13. In contrast to these broad, macro-level approaches, the action paradigm is a micro-level theoretical framework that focuses on face-to-face interaction in specific settings.

14. Because each paradigm spotlights different dimensions of any social issue, the richest sociological understanding is derived from applying all three.

15. Newer developments in sociological theory have highlighted how all sociology must work from perspectives or different voices. Classically, sociology has heard only the voices of white, Western, heterosexual men: other voices are now being heard. Feminist sociology is a prime example.

16. Sociological thinking involves the action–structure debate.

KEY CONCEPTS

action theory a micro theory that focuses on how actors assemble social meanings

conflict paradigm a framework for building theory that envisions society as an arena of inequality that generates conflict and change

functional paradigm a framework for building theory that envisions society as a complex system whose parts work together to promote solidarity and stability

global perspective the study of the larger world and our society's place in it

globalisation the increasing interconnectedness of societies

high-income countries industrial nations in which most people enjoy material abundance

ideal types an abstract statement of the essential, though often exaggerated, characteristic of any social phenomenon

latent functions consequences of any social pattern that are unrecognised and unintended

low-income countries nations with little industrialisation in which severe poverty is the rule

macro-level orientation a focus on broad social structures that characterise society as a whole

manifest functions the recognised and intended consequences of any social pattern

micro-level orientation a focus on patterns of social interaction in specific situations

middle-income countries nations characterised by limited industrialisation and moderate personal income

newly industrialising countries (NICs) lower-income countries that are fast becoming higher-income ones

positivism a means to understand the world based on science

social dysfunction the undesirable consequences of any social pattern for the operation of society

social function the consequences of any social pattern for the operation of society

social structure relatively stable patterns of social behaviour

sociology the systematic study of human society

stereotype an exaggerated description applied to every person in some category

symbolic-interaction a theoretical framework that envisions society as the product of the everyday interactions of people doing things together

theoretical paradigm a basic image of society that guides sociological thinking and research

theory a statement of how and why specific facts are related

CRITICAL-THINKING QUESTIONS

1. In what ways does using the sociological perspective make us seem less in control of our lives? In what ways does it give us greater power over our surroundings?

2. Consider this statement: Sociology would not have arisen if human behaviour were biologically programmed (like that of, say, ants); nor could sociology exist if our behaviour were utterly chaotic. Sociology thrives because human social life falls in a middle ground – as thinking people, we create social patterns, but they are variable and changeable.

3. Give a sociological explanation of why sociology developed where and when it did. Examine whether it had 'biases', and if so what they were.

4. Guided by the discipline's three major theoretical paradigms, what kinds of questions might a sociologist ask about (a) television, (b) war, (c) sport, (d) colleges and universities, and (e) men and women?

5. Your flatmates tell you that studying sociology is a waste of time. Consider what some of the popular objections to it are, and then mount your defence!

6. Start keeping a 'sociological glossary' of key new words you find in sociology. Try and make sure you can say (a) what the word means, (b) what debates and research it is applied in, and (c) whether you find it helpful or not: does it enable you to see society more sharply or does it confuse and hinder?

7. Take the map of sociological theories presented on page 21 and start filling it out in more detail.

8. What is the action-structure debate? How might you resolve it?

GOING FURTHER

Sociology has been an area of study for nearly 200 years, though it is only in the past forty years that it has become really popular amongst students. The research and writing in sociology is now enormous and this book is only meant as an opening guide. Every topic discussed in the book could (and should) be taken further – much further! We hope that there will be many areas you would like to follow up, so at the end of each chapter you will find a guide to ways you can pursue your thinking and study further. These sources will also be of great help in writing essays, doing research or engaging in discussions.

Introductory reading

Two short, readable guides to sociology by UK sociologists are: Anthony Giddens, *Sociology: A Brief but Critical Introduction* (London: Macmillan, 2nd edn, 1986). Zygmunt Bauman, *Thinking Sociologically,* (Oxford: Blackwell, 1990).

An introductory text which provides a feminist perspective is Pamela Abbott's and Claire Wallace's *An Introduction to Sociology: Feminist Perspectives* (London: Routledge, 2nd edn, 1997). This is a very valuable book with a clear focus on women. What it also manages to display so clearly in its own bias towards women is just how 'biased' most mainstream (or 'malestream') sociology is.

In addition, there is a 'cartoon style' introduction by Richard Osborne and Borin Van Loon, *Sociology for Beginners* (Cambridge: Icon Books, 1996). Although it is full of cartoons, its messages are pretty serious.

Jon Gubbay, Chris Middleton and Chet Ballard, *The Student's Companion to Sociology* (Oxford: Blackwell, 1997) is a useful reference source for sociology students.

A guide to key quotations in sociology may be found in: Kenneth Thompson, *Key Quotations in Sociology* (London: Routledge, 1996).

Finally, there is a glossary of key concepts at the end of this book. But sometimes you will wish to explore the meanings of concepts more fully. For this, you will need a dictionary of sociology. There are many available. Amongst them are *The Penguin Dictionary of Sociology* (Harmonsworth, Middlesex: Penguin, 2nd edn, 1988), and *The Concise Oxford Dictionary of Sociology* (Oxford: Oxford University Press, 1994).

Classic sources

C. Wright Mills, *The Sociological Imagination* (New York: Oxford University Press, 1959).

> This classic elaborates on the benefits of learning to think sociologically and links this perspective to the possibilities for social activism.

Peter Berger, *An Invitation to Sociology* (Garden City, NY: Anchor Books, 1963).

> Berger's readable classic account of the sociological perspective highlights its value for enhancing human freedom.

Introductory texts on sociological theory

There are many textbooks on sociological theory that greatly amplify the above. Here is a selection:

E. Cuff, Wes Sharrock and D. Francis, *Perspectives in Sociology* (London: Unwin Hyman/ Routledge, 3rd edn, 1990).

David Lee and Howard Newby, *The Problem of Sociology* (London: Hutchinson/Routledge, 1983).

> Two good general introductions to the world of sociological theories.

Ian Craib, *Classical Social Theory* (Oxford: Oxford University Press, 1997), and Ian Craib, *Modern Social Theory* (London: Harvester Wheatsheaf, 2nd edn, 1992).

> Highly readable introductions both to the classics – Marx, Durkheim, Weber, Freud and Simmel – and to the more contemporary debates, especially around 'action' and 'structure'.

Charles Lemert (ed.), *Social Theory: The Multicultural and Classic Readings* (Oxford: Westview, 1993).

> A major compendium of articles that debates the full range of sociological theories – classical and newer. It is a very large volume! But for anyone very interested in the full range of sociological theory from the original authors it is an invaluable starting point.

George Ritzer, *Sociological Theory* (New York: McGraw-Hill, 3rd edn, 1992).

> A classic overview theory text book.

Martin Albrow, *The Global Age* (Oxford: Policy Press, 1996).

> A wide ranging introduction to the idea of 'the global' in modern sociology.

Other sources

Journals and magazines

Much useful reading is contained in magazines or journals, which come out at regular intervals: in fact, academics are very dependent on these for the latest findings. Two very readable popular magazines for sociology students – even worth subscribing to – are:

Sociology Review
> from Philip Allan Publishers Ltd., Market Place, Deddington, Oxfordshire, OX15 0SE

Published four times a year. Full of short up-to-date articles on key issues in sociology and well illustrated. A strong focus on the UK. This is a must for the budding sociologist.

New Internationalist
from : PO Box 79, Hertford, SG14 1AQ
Published monthly. This takes a clear political stance, and it is packed full of valuable information on the 'global state' of the world.

Video
Sociology II
A useful video which introduces Sociology – and includes interviews with students who have just graduated. Available from Sociology Department, University of Glasgow, G12 8RT.

Sociological associations
The British Sociological Association
Unit 39, Mountjoy Research Centre, Stockton Road, Durham, DH1 3UR
e mail: britsoc@dial.pipex.com
http://dspace.dial.pipex.com/britsoc/

The European Sociological Association
ESA, SISWO, Plantage Muidergracht 4,
TV Amsterdam, The Netherlands
e mail: kruithof@siswo.uva.nl

American Sociological Association
1722 North Street, NW,
Washington, DC 20036, USA
e mail: executive.office@asanet.org

International Sociological Association
Facultad C.C. Politicas y Sociologia,
Universidad Complutense,
28223 Madrid, Spain
e mail: isa@sis.ucm.es

Sociology, Computers and WebSites
Computers and the new information technology are playing an increasingly prominent role in sociology. Currently, probably the most common uses for students are to be found in

● word processing (when you prepare your essays and projects),

● research (when you need statistical techniques such as those discussed in Chapter 2)

● searching various data bases (the most common of which is probably your university library, when you retrieve information on books).

But information technology is also being used more and more by students for a much wider range of activities. For instance, some students are using electronic mail (e mail) to talk both to their lecturers and fellow students. They set up 'discussion lists' where they find students and others with similar interests (such as wanting to find out more about post-modern culture, feminism or Marx), and then chat away on the 'e mail'. All you need for this, basically, is an e mail account – and it is quite likely that your university will provide one of these for you at no cost. An e mail address usually looks like this:

smith@essex.ac.uk

where the smith identifies the communicator, @essex identifies the location, and uk identifies the country.

Sociology on the Web
Even more interesting is the development of the World Wide Web Sites. This is a system that helps you gain systematic access to all the information housed in the vast world wide network of computer networks (known as the Internet). It connects you up to libraries, businesses, research centres, voluntary organisations, etc. all over the world.

The trouble with the internet is that it contains millions of bits of disconnected data: in order to make sense of it and find what you want, you will need a web browser such as 'Netscape Navigator' which enables you to be more systematic in your searches.

Every document on the Internet has a URL – a Uniform Resource Locator – or address. This is what you need to know when you start your search for sociology web sites. But once you are inside a web page, you can usually 'click' on a number of items, and you will find yourself rapidly transported to these items. (Technically, this is called hypertext.) So many 'web searches' involve just jumping from one site to another.

There are now a great many sociological web sites. So where to start? A good number of them have been listed in:

Joan Ferrante and Angela Vaughn's *Let's Go Sociology: Travels on the Internet*, Belmont California, Wadsworth Publishing, 1997

which is also to be found on http://www.thomson.com./wadsworth.html

To unravel what this address means (and this can help you remember web site addresses more easily) note that most addresses start with http (or ftp, or gopher). This stands for hypertext transfer protocol and enables you to navigate the system. Then follows (between // and /) what is called 'the domain name' (in this case thompson – a branch of thompson publishing), followed by a suffix like com. (which means commercial), edu (which indicates educational) gov. (Governmental) or org (organisational). Finally, comes the name of the particular people or groups web page that you are searching.

A word of warning

There is a huge amount of sociological data on the Web, and although it can be very easy to access it, it can also bring problems. Throughout this book, we will from time to time suggest web sites, but we do so with some anxiety because:

● Web sites keep changing. There is no guarantee that a site will not be closed or its name changed. Even whilst preparing this book, we found a number that had 'vanished' and others that had opened for just a few weeks.

● The quality of web sites is very variable: we have checked most of the sites listed in this book and they were 'good' at that time. But they change, and sometimes they can be the home page of one 'crank' who is really only listing his or her own private interests. So use carefully and critically.

● The usage of web sites at key times can be colossal. So a cardinal rule is to be patient!

● And, finally, note that accuracy matters. Do not change addresses from lower cases to capitals, or miss out slashes and points. The web site address must be precise.

Below are listed a number of general web sites.

Sociologists/perspectives:

● http://csf.colorado.edu:80/psn/marx/index.html

Archive of Marx/Engels which contains detailed chronologies, biographies, photos plus their concepts and related ideas. All the major works of them can also be accessed through this website.

● http://www.lang.uiuc.edu/RelSt/Durkheim/Durkheim Home.html

A web site for Durkheim which contains his biography, chronology and writings as well as a glossary of his ideas.

● http://www.socioweb.com

A large resource centre that links to major sociology departments, sociological associations, resources, calendars of events and activities and publications.

● http://www.asanet.org/

Homepage of the American Sociological Association (ASA). Currently updated and contains information about the ASA and links to meetings, conferences, and publications.

● http://dspace.dial.pipex.com/britsoc/

Homepage of the British Sociological Association

Further Reading: See: Rob Kling 'The Culture of Cyberspace: The Internet for Sociologists', in *Contemporary Sociology*, July 1997, Vol. 26, No. 4, pp. 434–44

And for a good guide to the internet, see Angus J. Kennedy *The Internet and World Wide Web: The Rough Guide 2.0*, London: Penguin, 1996

chapter two

Source: Popperfoto

Sociological Investigation

While on a visit to Atlanta during the holiday season at the close of 1984, North American sociologist Lois Benjamin (1991) paid a call on the mother of an old friend from college. Benjamin was anxious to learn what had become of her friend, Sheba, who had shared her own dream of earning a Ph.D., finding a teaching position, and writing books. Benjamin was proud that she had fulfilled her dream. But, as she soon found out, Sheba had fallen disastrously short of her goal.

There had been early signs of trouble, Benjamin recalled, after they had finished college. Enrolling in a graduate programme in Canada, Sheba was increasingly critical of the world around her and became cut off from others. In letters to Benjamin, Sheba attributed her bitterness to racism; as an African-American woman, she claimed she was the target of racial hostility. Before long, her resentment overwhelmed her and she dropped out of graduate school, blaming her white professors for her failure. At this point, she left North America, finally earning a Ph.D. in England and then settling in Nigeria. Since then, Benjamin had not heard a word from her long-time friend.

Entering the house, Benjamin's initial delight at finding that Sheba had returned to Atlanta dissolved into shock when she confronted her comrade. Sheba had suffered a mental breakdown and was barely responsive to anyone.

Many months later, Sheba's emotional collapse still troubled Benjamin. She knew that many factors combine to cause such a personal tragedy. But, having experienced the sting of racism in her own career, Benjamin was convinced that this form of hatred played a major role in Sheba's story. Partly as a tribute to her old friend, Benjamin set out to explore the effects of race in the lives of bright and well-educated blacks in the United States.

Doing so, Benjamin was aware, challenged conventional wisdom that race poses less of a barrier to talented African Americans today than in previous generations (Wilson, 1978). Benjamin knew, too, that some of her colleagues in sociology think of racism as a problem for poor black people far more than for those with prestigious jobs and high incomes. But her own experiences, and those of her friend Sheba, contradicted such thinking.

To test her contention, Benjamin spent the next two years asking 100 successful African Americans around the country how race affected their lives and shaped their work. In the words of these 'talented one hundred' men and women, she found evidence that, even among privileged African Americans, racism remains a heavy burden.

Later in this chapter, we will take a closer look at Lois Benjamin's research.

Sociology involves a way of thinking, which we saw in the last chapter. But it also involves a way of doing: a practice that looks at problems and then digs out the best 'data', 'evidence' or 'facts' that it can. This chapter will look at some of the ways sociologists actually go about studying the world.

This chapter, then, highlights the methods that sociologists use to conduct research. Along the way, we shall see that sociological research involves not just procedures for gathering information but controversies about whether that research should strive to be objective or to offer a bold prescription for change. Certainly, for example, Lois Benjamin did not undertake her exploration of racism simply to document its existence; she sought to bring racism out into the open as a way to eradicate it. We shall tackle questions of values after addressing the basics of sociological investigation.

The issues this chapter raises should help you think about the adequacy of the methods used in the sociological studies you read about. It should also enable you to start thinking about how you could conduct your own research – the chapter ends with some basic guidelines for you to plan your own project.

● The basics of sociological investigation

Sociological investigation begins with two simple requirements. The first was the focus of Chapter 1: *look at the world using the sociological perspective*. Suddenly, from this point of view, all around us we see curious patterns of behaviour that call out for further study.

Lois Benjamin's sociological imagination prompted her to wonder how race affects the lives of talented African Americans. This brings us to the second

requirement for sociological investigation: *be curious and ask questions*. Benjamin wanted to find out how racial identity figured in the lives of people with significant personal achievements. She asked questions. What effect does being part of a racial minority have on self-identity? Do black people and white people understand racial dynamics in the same way? Are racial tensions easing or becoming more pronounced?

These two requirements – seeing the world sociologically and asking questions – are fundamental to sociological investigation. Yet they are only the beginning. They draw us into the social world, stimulating our curiosity. But then we face the challenging task of finding answers to our questions. To understand the kind of insights sociology offers, it helps to divide the research process into three kinds of issues. These are:

● *Theoretical/epistemological questions.* Here we ask about the kind of truth we are trying to produce. Do we, for example, want to produce a strong 'factual' scientific kind of truth with lots of evidence? Or do we wish to provide a wider theoretical understanding of what is going on? As we shall see, there are different versions of sociology and it helps to be clear which kind of sociology is being done.

● *Technical questions.* Here we ask questions about how to use tools and procedures which enable our 'findings' to be as good as they can be. There is the matter of the kinds of research tools to use – interviewing, observing, giving out questionnaires, for example; and then making sure they measure what they should measure adequately.

● *Ethical, political and policy questions.* Here we ask questions about the point of doing the research and consider what consequences it might have: for us, for our research subjects, and even for the wider world.

The discussion in this chapter will be framed by these questions. You can use it as a guide for thinking about your own research projects. But it is only a guide, and suggestions for taking it further will – as usual – be found at the end of the chapter.

● A matter of epistemology

The first question to ask of social research is a *very* hard one. 'What kind of truth am I trying to produce?' This raises questions of **epistemology**, *that branch of philosophy that investigates the nature of knowledge and truth.* Our opening concern is to realise that there are different kinds of 'truth'.

When we say we 'know' something, we can mean any number of things. Some people, for instance, claim to believe in the existence of God. Whilst only a few may say that they have had direct contact with God, they are believers all the same. We call this kind of knowing 'belief' or 'faith'. A second kind of truth rests on a pronouncement by some recognised expert. When worried about your health, you approach a doctor or other expert. You may not always believe them, but they have some claim to be listened to on the basis of their authority. A third type of truth is based on simple agreement among ordinary people. We come to 'know' that, say, stealing is wrong because virtually everyone in our society says it is.

People's 'truths' differ the world over, and we often encounter 'facts' at odds with our own. Imagine being a volunteer with Voluntary Service Overseas (VSO) and arriving in a small, traditional village in Africa. With the job of helping the local people to grow more food, you take to the fields, observing a curious practice: farmers carefully planting seeds and then placing a dead fish directly on top of each one. In response to your question, they reply that the fish is a gift to the god of the harvest. A local elder adds sternly that the harvest was poor one year when no fish were offered as gifts.

From that society's point of view, using fish as gifts to the harvest god makes sense. The people believe in it, their experts endorse it, and everyone seems to agree that the system works. But, with scientific training in agriculture, you have to shake your head and

wonder. The scientific 'truth' in this situation is something entirely different: the decomposing fish fertilise the ground, producing a better crop.

Our VSO worker example does not mean, of course, that people in traditional villages ignore what their senses tell them, or that members of technologically advanced societies reject non-scientific ways of knowing. A medical researcher using science to seek an effective treatment for cancer, for example, may still practise her religion as a matter of faith; she may turn to experts when making financial decisions; and she may derive political opinions from family and friends. In short, we all embrace various kinds of truths at the same time.

But science represents a very distinctive way of knowing, and one that has come to dominate in the modern Western world.

Common sense versus scientific evidence

Scientific evidence sometimes challenges our common sense. Here are five statements that many people assume are 'true', even though each is at least partly contradicted by scientific research.

1. *Poor people are far more likely than rich people to break the law.* Watching a crime show on TV, one might well conclude that police arrest only people from 'bad' neighbourhoods. And, as Chapter 8 ('Deviance and Control') explains, poor people are arrested in disproportionate numbers. But research also reveals that police and prosecutors are more likely to treat apparent wrongdoing by well-to-do people more leniently. Further, some researchers argue that our society drafts laws in such a way as to reduce the risk that affluent people will be criminalised.

2. *We now live in a middle class society in which most people are more or less equal.* Data presented in Chapter 10 ('Class, Poverty and Welfare') show that a very small group of people throughout the world control wealth. If people are equal, then some are much 'more equal' than others.

3. *Differences in the behaviour of females and males reflect 'human nature'.* Much of what we call 'human nature' is created by the society in which we are raised, as Chapter 4 ('Culture') details. Further, as Chapter 13 ('Gender and Sexuality') argues, some

societies define 'feminine' and 'masculine' very differently from the way we do.

4. *People change as they grow old, losing many former interests while becoming focused on their health.* Chapter 14 ('Ageing and the Elderly') reports that ageing actually changes our personalities very little. Problems of health increase in old age but, by and large, elderly people retain their distinctive personalities.

5. *Most people marry because they are in love.* To members of our society, few statements are so self-evident. But as surprising as it may seem, research shows that, in most societies, marriage has little to do with love. Chapter 17 ('Families') explains why.

These examples confirm the old saying that 'It's not what we don't know that gets us into trouble as much as the things we *do* know that just aren't so'. We have all been brought up believing conventional truths, bombarded by expert advice, and pressured to accept the opinions of people around us. Sociology teaches us to evaluate critically what we see, read and hear. Like any way of knowing, sociology has limitations, as we shall see. But sociology gives us the tools to assess many kinds of information.

● The three sociologies: positivist, realist and humanistic sociologies

The trouble is that precisely what is meant even by 'science' is not agreed upon by philosophers of knowledge. Broadly, they take one of three views: positivism, realism and humanism. They correspond roughly (but not wholly) to the functionalist, conflict and action theories introduced in Chapter 1.

The first is positivism. Here, **Science 1** is *a logical system that bases knowledge on direct, systematic observation.* It usually seeks out law-like statements of social life that can be tested. The work of Durkheim on suicide introduced in Chapter 1 would be an instance of this. Standing apart from faith, the wisdom of 'experts', and general agreement, scientific knowledge rests on **empirical evidence** (for Durkheim, recall, these were suicide rates) meaning *information we can verify with our senses.* But even here there is controversy amongst philosophers over the true nature of science, as we shall soon see.

The second is realism. Here, **Science 2** is *a theoretical system of concepts that are evolved to handle a partic-ular problem* (like how the economy, our minds or even the solar system works). Whilst it may also gather empirical evidence, this is not crucial to its research – since it argues that 'empirical evidence' is never straightforward. We can never be sure of 'facts'. What we need, therefore, are strong explanations – built from theoretical tools that will help us do this. The work of Marx is usually seen as a realist theory. For him, the problem was how capitalism works. To explain this, he developed the idea of the **mode of production** – *the way a society is organised to produce goods and services.*

The third position is humanism. **Humanist epistemology** sees that studying the human world is very different from studying the physical, biological or material world. As such, social science must produce a different kind of knowledge, one that seeks to understand meanings. Research in this tradition will look at the empirical world (as in positivism) but will highlight the importance of understanding and interpretation.

Sociological investigations can employ any or all three of these epistemologies. In what follows we will focus mainly on Science 1 (positivism) and humanism.

● The positivist baseline

Positivist sociologists apply science to the study of society in much the same way that natural scientists investigate the physical world. Whether they end up confirming a widely held opinion or revealing that it is completely groundless, sociologists use scientific techniques to gather empirical evidence. The following sections of this chapter introduce the major elements of positivist investigation.

The ideal of objectivity

Assume that ten writers who work for a magazine in Amsterdam are collaborating on a story about that city's best restaurants. With their editor paying, they head out on the town for a week of fine dining. Later, they get together to compare notes. Do you think one restaurant would be everyone's clear favourite? That hardly seems likely.

In scientific terms, each of the ten reporters probably operationalises the concept 'best restaurant' differently. For one, it might be a place that serves Indonesian food at reasonable prices; for another, the choice might turn on a superb view of the canals; for yet another, stunning decor and attentive service might be the deciding factor. Like so many other things in life, the best restaurant turns out to be mostly a matter of individual taste.

Personal values are fine when it comes to restaurants, but they pose a challenge to scientific research. On the one hand, every scientist has personal opinions about the world. On the other, science endorses the goal of **objectivity**, *a state of personal neutrality in conducting research*. Objectivity in research depends on carefully adhering to scientific procedures in order not to bias the results. Scientific objectivity is an ideal rather than a reality, of course, since complete impartiality is virtually impossible for any researcher to achieve. Even the subject a researcher selects to study and the framing of the questions are likely to grow out of personal interest, as the research on race by Lois Benjamin attests. But scientists cultivate detachment and follow specific methods to lessen the chance that conscious or unconscious biases will distort their work. As an additional safeguard, researchers should try to identify and report their personal leanings to help readers evaluate their conclusions in the proper context.

The influential German sociologist Max Weber expected personal beliefs to play a part in a sociologist's selection of research topic. Why, after all, would one person study world hunger, another investigate the effects of racism, and still another examine one-parent families? But Weber (1958; orig. 1918) warned that even though sociologists select topics that are *value-relevant*, they should conduct research that is *value-free* in their pursuit of conclusions. Only by being dispassionate in their work (as we expect any professional to be), can researchers study the world *as it is* rather than telling others how they think *it should be*. In Weber's view, this detachment was a crucial element of science that sets it apart from politics. Politicians, in other words, are committed to a particular outcome; scientists try to maintain an open-minded readiness to accept the results of their investigations, whatever they may be.

By and large, sociologists accept Weber's argument, though most concede that we can never be completely value-free or even aware of all our biases. Moreover, sociologists are not 'average' people: most are white people who are highly educated and more politically liberal than the population as a whole (Wilson, 1979).

Sociologists need to remember that they, too, are affected by their own social backgrounds.

One strategy for limiting distortion caused by personal values is **replication**, *repetition of research by other investigators*. If other researchers repeat a study using the same procedures and obtain the same results, they gain confidence that the original research (as well as their own) was conducted objectively. The need for replication in scientific investigation is probably the reason that the search for knowledge is called *research* in the first place.

In any case, keep in mind that the logic and methodology of science hold out no guarantee that we will grasp objective, absolute truth. What science offers is an approach to knowledge that is *self-correcting* so that, in the long run, researchers stand the best chance to overcome their own biases and achieve greater understanding. Objectivity and truth, then, lie not in any particular research method, but in the scientific process itself.

Some limitations of scientific sociology

The first scientists probed the operation of the natural world. Many sociologists use science to study the social world; however, the scientific study of people has several important limitations.

1. *Human behaviour is too complex to allow sociologists to predict precisely any individual's actions.* Astronomers calculate the movement of planets with remarkable precision, announcing years in advance when a comet will next pass near the earth. But planets and comets are unthinking objects; humans, by contrast, have minds of their own. Because no two people react to any event in exactly the same way, the best that sociologists can do is to show that categories of people typically act in one way or another. This is no failing of sociology; it is simply consistent with the nature of our task: studying creative, spontaneous people.

2. *Because humans respond to their surroundings, the mere presence of a researcher may affect the behaviour being studied.* An astronomer gazing at the moon has no effect whatever on that celestial body. But people usually react to being observed. Some may become anxious, angry or defensive; others may try to 'help' by providing the answers or actions they think researchers expect of them.

3. *Social patterns change constantly; what is true in one time or place may not hold true in another.* The laws of physics apply tomorrow as well as today; they hold true all around the world. But human behaviour is too variable for us to set down immutable sociological laws. In fact, some of the most interesting sociological research focuses on social diversity and social change.

4. *Because sociologists are part of the social world they study, being value-free when conducting social research can be difficult.* Barring a laboratory mishap, chemists are rarely personally affected by what goes on in test tubes. But sociologists live in their 'test tube' – the society they study. Therefore, social scientists face a greater challenge in controlling – or even recognising – personal values that may distort their work.

5. *Human behaviour differs from all other phenomena precisely because human beings are symbolic, subjective creatures.* Human beings – unlike planets or molecules – are always constructing meaning. And what marks us off from other animals is the elaborate symbolic systems we weave for ourselves. Therefore, sociologists cannot simply study societies from outside; they have to take on board ways of 'entering' these worlds of meaning.

A basic lesson of social research is that being observed affects how people behave. Researchers can never be certain precisely how this will occur; while some people resent public attention, others become highly animated when they think they have an audience.

The importance of subjective interpretation

As we have explained, scientists tend to think of 'subjectivity' as 'bias' – a source of error to be avoided as much as possible. But there is also a good side to subjectivity, since creative thinking is vital to sociological investigation in three key ways.

First, science is basically a series of rules that guide research, rather like a recipe for cooking. But just as more than a recipe is required to make a great chef, so scientific procedure does not, by itself, produce a great sociologist. Also needed is an inspired human imagination. After all, insight comes not from science itself but from the lively thinking of creative human beings (Nisbet, 1970). The genius of physicist Albert Einstein or sociologist Max Weber lay not only in their use of the scientific method but also in their curiosity and ingenuity.

Second, science cannot account for the vast and complex range of human motivations and feelings, including greed, love, pride and despair. Science certainly helps us gather facts about how people act, but it can never fully explain the complex meanings people attach to their behaviour (Berger and Kellner, 1981).

Third, we also do well to remember that scientific data never speak for themselves. After sociologists and other scientists 'collect the numbers', they face the ultimate task of *interpretation* – creating meaning from their observations. For this reason, good sociological investigation is as much art as science.

Source: Magnum Photos – Steve McCurry/Gamma-Liaison Inc. – Argas

● The humanities baseline

The recognition of all these limitations leads many sociologists to adopt a somewhat difference stance towards their study. They do not claim to be scientists as above, but instead try to make sociology a more humanistic discipline concerned with understanding. In his study of *Sociology as an Art Form*, Nisbet reflects 'How different things would be . . . if the social sciences at the time of their systematic formation in the nineteenth century had taken the arts in the same degree they took the physical science as models' (Nisbet, 1976: 16).

This corrective sociology may be called 'humanistic' and has at least four central criteria. It must pay tribute to *human subjectivity and creativity*, showing how individuals respond to social constraints and actively assemble social worlds. It must deal with concrete human experiences – talk, feelings, actions – through their *social, and especially economic, organisation* (and not just their inner, psychic or biological structuring). It must show a naturalistic *'intimate familiarity'* with such experiences – abstractions untempered by close involvement are ruled out. And there must be a self-awareness by the sociologist of the ultimate *moral and political role* in moving towards a social structure in which there is less exploitation, oppression and injustice and more creativity, diversity and equality. A list like this is open to detailed extension and revision, but it is hard to imagine a humanistic sociology which is not so minimally committed to these criteria.

Figure 2.1 summarises some of the wide ranging contrasts between the positivistic and humanistic approaches to sociological investigation.

● The technical questions of sociological investigation

Whichever stance is to be adopted, sociological research always involves learning some 'tricks of the trade'. These are very practical matters – tools that are needed to make sure that you are doing the research as best you can.

Figure 2.1 ● A bridgeable divide?

	Towards the humanities	Towards the positivistic sciences
Foci	Unique and idiographic Human centred The inner: subjective meaning, feeling	General and nomothetic Structure centred The outer: objective, 'things', events
Epistemology	Phenomenalist Relativist Perspectivist	Realist Absolutist/Essentialist Logical positivist
Task	Interpret, understand Describe, observe	Causal explanation Measure
Style	'Soft', 'Warm' Imaginative Valid-'real', 'rich'	'Hard', 'Cold' Systematic Reliable, 'replicable'
Theory	Inductive and grounded 'Story telling'	Deductive and abstract 'Operationalism'
Values	Ethically and politically committed Egalitarianism	Ethically and politically neutral 'Expertise and elites'

Source: derived from Plummer (1983)

Concepts, variables, and measurement

A crucial element of science is the **concept**, *a mental construct that represents some part of the world, inevitably in a simplified form*. 'Society' is itself a concept, as are the structural parts of societies, including 'the family' and 'the economy'. Sociologists also use concepts to describe individuals, by noting, for example, their 'sex', 'race', or 'social class'.

A **variable** is *a concept whose value changes from case to case*. The familiar variable 'price', for example, changes from item to item in a supermarket. Similarly, people use the concept 'social class' to evaluate people as 'upper class', 'middle class', 'working class', or 'lower class'.

The use of variables depends on **measurement**, *the process of determining the value of a variable in a specific case*. Some variables are easy to measure, such as adding up income at tax time. But measuring many sociological variables can be far more difficult. For example, how would you measure a person's 'social class'? You might be tempted to look at clothing, listen to patterns of speech, or note a home address. Or, trying to be more precise, you might ask about someone's income, occupation and education.

Researchers know that almost any variable can be measured in more than one way. Having a very high income might qualify a person as 'upper class'. But what if the income is derived from selling cars, an occupation most people think of as middle or even working class? And, would leaving school at 16 make the person 'lower class'? To resolve such a dilemma, sociologists sensibly (if somewhat arbitrarily) combine these three measures – income, occupation and education – into a single composite assessment of social class, called socio-economic status, which is described in Chapters 9 and 10.

Sociologists also face the challenge of describing thousands or even millions of people according to some variable of interest such as income. Reporting an interminable stream of numbers would carry little meaning and tell us nothing about the people as a whole. Thus sociologists use *statistical measures* to describe people efficiently and collectively. The box explains how.

Measurement is always a bit arbitrary because the value of any variable depends, in part, on how one defines it. **Operationalising a variable** means *specifying exactly what one is to measure in assigning a value to a variable.* If we were measuring people's social class, for example, we would have to decide whether we were going to measure income, occupational prestige, education or something else and, if we measure more than one of these, how we will combine the scores. When reporting their results, researchers should specify how they operationalised each variable, so that readers can evaluate the research and fully understand the conclusions.

SOCIOLOGICAL SPOTLIGHT

Three useful (and simple) statistical measures

We all talk about 'averages': the average price of a litre of petrol or the average salary for graduates. Sociologists, too, are interested in averages, and they use three different statistical measures to describe what is typical.

Assume that we wish to describe the salaries paid to seven members of a company: £23,000, £28,500, £27,800, £28,000, £23,000, £52,000 and £23,000.

The simplest statistical measure is the mode, defined as the value that occurs most often in a series of numbers. In this example, the mode is £23,000 because that value occurs three times, while each of the others occurs only once. If all the values were to occur only once, there would be no mode; if two values occurred three times (or twice), there would be two modes. Although the mode is easy to identify, sociologists rarely make use of it because this statistic provides only a crude measure of the 'average'.

A more common statistical measure, the mean, refers to the arithmetic average of a series of numbers, and is calculated by adding all the values together and dividing by the number of cases. The sum of the seven incomes is £205,300; dividing by 7 yields a mean income of £29,329. But notice that the mean is actually higher than the income of six of the seven members. Because the mean is 'pulled' up or down by an especially high or low value (in this case, the £52,000 paid to one member who also serves as a director), it has the drawback of giving a distorted picture of any distribution with extreme scores.

The median is the value that occurs midway in a series of numbers arranged in order of magnitude or, simply, the middle case. Here the median income for the seven people is £27,800, because three incomes are higher and three are lower. (With an even number of cases, the median is halfway between the two middle cases.) Since a median is unaffected by an extreme score, it usually gives a more accurate picture of what is 'average' than the mean does. ●

Reliability and validity of measurement

Useful measurement involves two further considerations. **Reliability** is *the quality of consistent measurement*. For a measure to be reliable, in other words, repeating the process should yield the same result. But consistency is no guarantee of **validity**, which is *the quality of measuring precisely what one intends to measure*. Valid measurement, in other words, means more than getting the *same* result time and again – it means obtaining a *correct* measurement.

To illustrate the difficulty of valid measurement, say you want to investigate how religious people are. A reasonable strategy would be to ask how often they attend religious services. But, in trying to gauge *religiosity* in this way, what you are actually measuring is *attendance at services*, which may or may not amount to the same thing. Generally, religious people do attend services more frequently, but people also participate in religious rituals out of habit or because of a sense of duty to someone else. Moreover, some devout believers shun organised religion altogether. Thus, even when a measurement yields consistent results (making it reliable), it can still miss the real, intended target (and lack validity). In sum, sociological research is no better than the quality of its measurement.

Relationships among variables

Once they achieve valid measurement, investigators can pursue the real payoff, which is determining how variables are related. The scientific ideal is **cause and effect**, *a relationship in which we know that change in one variable causes change in another*. A familiar cause-and-effect relationship occurs when a girl teases her brother until he becomes angry. *The variable that causes the change* (in this case, the teasing) is called the **independent variable**. *The variable that changes* (the behaviour of the brother) is known as the **dependent variable**. The value of one variable, in other words, is dependent on the value of another. Why is linking variables in terms of cause and effect important? Because doing so is the basis of *prediction* – that is, researchers using what they do know to predict what they don't know.

Because science puts a premium on prediction, people may be tempted to think that a cause-and-effect relationship is present any time variables change together. Consider, for instance, that the marriage rate in the United Kingdom falls to its lowest point in January, exactly the same month our national death rate peaks. This hardly means that people die because they fail to marry (or that they don't marry because they die). In fact, it is the dreary weather during January (and perhaps also the post-holiday blues) that causes both a low marriage rate and a high death rate. The converse holds as well: the warmer and sunnier summer months have the highest marriage rate as well as the lowest death rate. Thus, researchers often have to untangle cause-and-effect relationships that are not readily apparent.

To take a second case, sociologists have long recognised that juvenile delinquency is more common among young people who live in crowded housing. Say we operationalise the variable 'juvenile delinquency' as the number of times (if any) a person under the age of 18 has been arrested, and assess 'crowded housing' by looking at the total square footage of living space per person in a home. We would find the variables related; that is, delinquency rates are, indeed, high in densely populated neighbourhoods. But should we conclude that crowding in the home (the independent variable) is what causes delinquency (the dependent variable)?

Not necessarily. **Correlation** is *a relationship by which two (or more) variables change together*. We know that density and delinquency are correlated because they change together, as shown in part (a) of Figure 2.2. This relationship *may* mean that crowding causes misconduct, but often some third factor is at work causing change in both the variables under observation. To see how, think what kind of people live in crowded housing: people with less money, power and choice – the poor. Poor children are also more likely to end up with police records. Thus, crowded housing and juvenile delinquency are found together because *both* are caused by a third factor – poverty – as shown in part (b) of Figure 2.2. In other words, the apparent connection between crowding and delinquency is 'explained away' by a third variable – low income – that causes them both to change. So our original connection turns out to be a **spurious correlation**, *an apparent, though false, association between two (or more) variables caused by some other variable*.

Unmasking a correlation as spurious requires a bit of detective work, assisted by a technique called **control**, *holding constant all relevant variables except one in order to clearly see its effect*. In the example above, we suspect that income level may be behind a spurious connection between housing density and delinquency. To check, we control for income (that is, we hold it constant) by

Figure 2.2 ● **Correlation and cause: an example.**

(a)

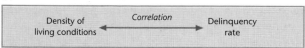

If two variables vary together, they are said to be correlated. In this example, density of living conditions and juvenile delinquency increase and decrease together.

(b)

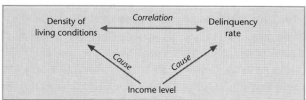

Here we consider the effect of a third variable: income level. Low income level may cause *both* high-density living conditions *and* a high delinquency rate. In other words, as income level decreases, both density of living conditions and the delinquency rate increases.

(c)

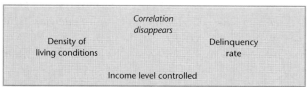

If we control income level — that is, examine only cases with the same income level — do those with higher-density living conditions still have a higher delinquency rate? The answer is *no*. There is no longer a correlation between these two variables.

(d)

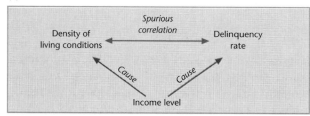

This finding leads us to conclude that income level is a cause of both density of living conditions and the delinquency rate. The original two variables (density of living conditions and delinquency rate) are thus correlated, but neither one causes the other. Their correlation is therefore *spurious*.

using as research subjects only young people of the same income level and looking again for a correlation between density and delinquency. If, by doing this, a correlation between density and delinquency remains (that is, if young people living in more crowded housing show higher rates of delinquency than young people with the same family income in less crowded

housing), we gain confidence that crowding does, in fact, cause delinquency. But if the relationship disappears when we control for income, as shown in part (c) of the figure, we confirm that we have been dealing with a spurious correlation. Research has, in fact, shown that virtually all correlation between crowding and delinquency disappears if income is controlled (Fischer, 1984). So we have now sorted out the relationship among the three variables, as illustrated in part (d) of the figure. Housing density and juvenile delinquency have a spurious correlation; evidence shows that both variables rise or fall according to people's income.

To sum up, correlation means only that two (or more) variables change together. Cause and effect rests on three conditions: (1) a demonstrated correlation, but also (2) that the independent (or causal) variable precedes the dependent variable in time, and (3) that no evidence suggests a third variable is responsible for a spurious correlation between the two.

Natural scientists identify cause-and-effect relationships more easily than social scientists because the laboratories used for study of the physical world allow control of many variables at one time. The sociologist, carrying out research in a workplace or on the streets, faces a considerably more difficult task. Often, sociologists must be satisfied with demonstrating only correlation. In every case, moreover, human behaviour is highly complex, involving dozens of causal variables at any one time.

● The methods of sociological research

A **research method** is *a systematic plan for conducting research*. The remainder of this chapter introduces five commonly used methods of sociological investigation. There are others. None is inherently better or worse than any other. Rather, in the same way that a carpenter selects a particular tool for a specific task, researchers choose a method according to whom they choose to study and what they wish to learn.

Testing a hypothesis: the experiment

The logic of positivist science is most clearly expressed in the **experiment**, *a research method for investigating cause and effect under highly controlled conditions*. Experimental research is *explanatory*, meaning that it asks not just what happens but why. Typically, researchers turn to an experiment to test a specific **hypothesis**, *an unverified statement of a relationship between variables.*

Ideally, we evaluate a hypothesis in three steps. First, the experimenter measures the dependent variable (the 'effect'); second, the investigator exposes the dependent variable to the independent variable (the 'cause' or 'treatment'); and third, the researcher again measures the dependent variable to see if the predicted change took place. If the expected change did occur, the experiment lends support to the hypothesis; if not, the hypothesis is discounted.

But a change in the dependent variable may be due to something other than the assumed cause. To prevent this, researchers must carefully control any and all extraneous factors that might intrude into the experiment and affect what is being measured. Such control is most easily accomplished in a laboratory, an artificial setting specially constructed for research purposes. Another strategy for neutralising outside influences is dividing subjects into an *experimental group* and a *control group*. At the outset, the researcher measures the dependent variable for subjects in both groups but exposes only the experimental group to the independent variable or treatment (the control group typically gets a 'placebo', an apparently comparable treatment known to have no experimental effect). Then the investigator measures the subjects in both groups again. Any factor (such as some news event) occurring during the course of the research that influences people in the experimental group would do the same to the control-group subjects, thus neutralising the factor. In short, the use of a control group 'washes out' many extraneous factors; comparing before and after measurements of the two groups, a researcher is able to assess how much of the observed change is due only to the independent variable.

Yet subjects may alter their behaviour simply in response to a researcher's attention, as one classic experiment revealed. In the late 1930s, the Western Electric Company hired researchers to investigate worker productivity in its Hawthorne factory near Chicago (Roethlisberger and Dickson, 1939). One experiment examined whether increasing the available lighting would raise worker output. To test this idea, researchers measured initial productivity (the dependent variable); then they increased the lighting (the independent variable); finally, they measured productivity a second time. Productivity increased, supporting the hypothesis. But when the research team subsequently *reduced* the lighting, productivity again increased, contradicting the initial hypothesis. In time, the researchers realised that the employees were working harder (even if they could not see as well) simply because people were paying attention to them. From this research, social scientists coined the term **Hawthorne effect** to refer to *a change in a subject's behaviour caused simply by the awareness of being studied.*

Examples of such research will be found in Chapter 7, when studies that use the experimental method to look at group conformity will be discussed (see especially the work of Stanley Milgram).

Asking questions: survey research

A **survey** is *a research method in which subjects respond to a series of items in a questionnaire or an interview.* The most widely used of all research methods, surveys are particularly well suited to studying attitudes that investigators cannot observe directly, including political and religious beliefs or the subjective effects of racism. Although surveys can shed light on cause and effect, most often they yield *descriptive* findings, as researchers seek to paint a picture of subjects' views on some issue.

Population and sample

The researcher begins a survey by designating a **population**, *the people who are the focus of research.* Lois Benjamin, whose research we introduced at the beginning of this chapter, focused on the population of talented African Americans as she explored the effects of racism. As another example, political pollsters try to predict election returns using surveys that treat every adult in the country as the population. And if you wanted a random sample of your university, you would initially need a sampling frame of everybody attending it!

Obviously, however, contacting millions of people – or everybody at your university – would overwhelm even the most well-funded and patient researcher. Fortunately, there is a far easier alternative that produces accurate results: researchers collect data from a **sample**, *a part of a population that represents the whole.* The now familiar national political surveys utilise a sample of some 1,500 people to gauge the political mood of the entire country.

Although the term may be new to you, you use the logic of sampling all the time. If you look around a lecture room and notice five or six students nodding off, you might conclude that the class finds the day's lecture dull. Such a conclusion involves making an inference about *all* the people (the 'population') from observing *some* of the people (the 'sample'). But how do we know if a sample actually represents the entire population?

One way to do this is through *random sampling*, in which researchers draw a sample from the population in such a way that every element in the population has the same chance of ending up in the sample. If this is the case, the mathematical laws of probability dictate that the sample they select will, in the vast majority of cases, represent the population with a minimal amount of error. Seasoned researchers use special computer programs to generate random samples. Novice researchers, however, sometimes make the mistake of assuming that 'randomly' walking up to people on the street produces a sample representative of an entire city. But such a strategy does not give every person an equal chance to be included in the sample. For one thing, any street – whether in a rich neighbourhood or a 'university city' – contains more of some kinds of people than others. For another, any researcher is apt to find some people more approachable than others, again introducing a bias.

Although good sampling is no simple task, it offers a considerable saving in time and expense. We are spared the tedious work of contacting everyone in a population, while obtaining essentially the same results.

Questionnaires and interviews

Selecting subjects is only the first step in carrying out a survey. Also needed is a plan for asking questions and recording answers. Surveys fall into two general categories: questionnaires and interviews.

A **questionnaire** is *a series of written questions a researcher supplies to subjects requesting their responses.* One type of questionnaire provides not only the questions but a series of fixed responses (similar to a multiple-choice examination). This *closed-ended format* makes the task of analysing the results relatively easy, yet narrows the range of responses in a way that might distort the findings. By contrast, a second type of questionnaire, using an *open-ended format*, allows subjects to respond freely, expressing various shades of opinion. The drawback of this approach is that the researcher later has to make sense out of what can be a bewildering array of answers.

How to present questions to subjects forms another part of the research strategy. Most often, researchers employ a *self-administered survey*, in which they mail questionnaires to respondents with a request to complete the form and mail it back. Since no researcher is present when subjects read the questionnaire, it must be both inviting and clearly written. Pre-testing a self-administered questionnaire with a small number of people before sending it to the entire sample can preclude the costly problem of finding out – too late – that its instructions or questions were confusing.

Using the mail (or, more recently, electronic mail) has the advantage of allowing a researcher to contact a large number of people over a wide geographical area at minimal expense. But many people treat such questionnaires as 'junk mail'; typically, no more than half are completed and returned. Researchers often send out follow-up mailings to coax reluctant subjects to fill out the questionnaire.

Finally, keep in mind that many people are not capable of completing a questionnaire on their own. Young children obviously cannot, nor can many hospital patients, as well as a surprising number of adults who simply lack the reading and writing skills needed to wade through a comprehensive questionnaire.

An **interview** is *a series of questions a researcher addresses personally to respondents.* Interviews come in several forms. In a *closed-ended* interview, researchers would read a question or statement and then ask the subject to select a response from several alternatives. Generally, however, interviews are *open-ended* so that subjects can respond in whatever way they choose and researchers can probe with follow-up questions. In the ensuing conversation, however, the researcher must guard against influencing a subject, a problem that can creep in through subtle gestures such as the raising of an eyebrow when a person begins to answer.

Closed-ended and open-ended interviews are both relatively formal. But there is another kind of informal conversational interview, which is more commonly used in the qualitative field research described in the next section. With this mode of interviewing the goal is to encourage the respondent to participate fully and equally in discussion with the interviewer. Certain key themes provide the shape for the discussion but there is no questionnaire as such, and the relationship between interviewer and respondent is much more casual, friendly, and egalitarian. This mode of research is more suitable to gaining 'in-depth' understanding and for researching more sensitive topics. The 'conversations' are usually taped. This can lead to problems of a mass of data that is much less organised and accessible to analysis than the data found with more formal interviewing.

Comparing the interview with the questionnaire, experienced investigators know that a subject is more likely to complete a survey if contacted personally by the researcher. Yet interviews have some disadvantages: tracking people down and personally interrogating them is costly and time consuming, especially if all subjects do not live in the same area. And while telephone interviews clearly allow far greater 'reach', the impersonality of 'cold calls' by telephone may result in a low completion rate.

In both questionnaires and interviews, the wording of questions has a significant effect on answers. When asked if they object to homosexuals serving in the military, for example, most adults say 'yes'. Yet, asked if the government should exempt homosexuals from military service, most say 'no' (NORC, 1991). Moreover, emotionally loaded language can easily sway subjects. For instance, the term 'single mothers', as opposed to 'women who receive social security', injects an emotional element into a survey and encourages respondents to answer more negatively. In still other cases, the wording of questions may hint at what other people think, thereby steering subjects. For example, people are more likely to respond positively to the question 'Do you *agree* that the police force is doing a good job?' than to a similar question 'Do you *think* that the police force is doing a good job?' Similarly, respondents are more likely to endorse a statement to 'not allow' something (say, public speeches against the government) than a statement to 'forbid' the same activity (Rademacher, 1992).

Finally, researchers may inadvertently confuse respondents by asking double questions like 'Do you think that the government should cut spending and raise taxes to reduce the deficit?' The problem here is that a subject could very well agree with one part of the question but reject the other, so that saying *yes* or *no* to the two-part question distorts the person's true opinion.

An illustration: studying the African-American elite

We opened this chapter with a brief account of Lois Benjamin's investigation of the effects of racism on talented African-American men and women. Contrary to some published research, she was convinced that personal achievement did not lift minorities above the ordeal of hostility based on colour. Her own experiences as the only black professor in the history department of the University of Tampa confirmed this view. But was she the exception or the rule? To answer this question, Benjamin set out to discover whether – and how – racism had tainted the achievements of others like herself.

Opting to conduct a survey, Benjamin chose to do interviews rather than distribute a questionnaire because, first, she wanted to enter into a conversation with her subjects, to ask follow-up questions, and to be able to pursue topics that she could not have anticipated in advance. A second reason she favoured interviews over questionnaires is that racism is a sensitive topic. Subjects tend to shy away from painful questions in the absence of a supportive relationship with the investigator.

The choice to conduct interviews carried with it the requirement to limit the number of people in the study. Benjamin settled for 100 men and women. Given the time needed to complete interviews, even this small number kept Benjamin busy for more than two years of scheduling, travelling, and meeting with informants. Another two years was needed to transcribe the tapes of her interviews, to sort out what the hours and hours of heartfelt conversation told her about the issue of race, and to write up her results.

Once a researcher selects a survey technique, the next order of business is selecting a sample. At first, Benjamin considered using all the people listed in *Who's Who in Black America* as her population of talented African Americans; from this list, she could easily have drawn a random sample of people to contact. But she rejected this idea in favour of starting out with people she knew and asking respondents to suggest others to include in the sample. This strategy is called *snowball sampling* because the number of individuals included in the sample grows rapidly over time.

Snowball sampling offers an easy and pleasant way to do research – we begin with familiar people who provide easy introductions to their friends and colleagues. However, snowball sampling rarely produces a sample that is representative of the larger population. In this case, the social networks into which Benjamin entered probably contain many like-minded individuals and it was certainly biased toward people willing to talk openly about race. Benjamin understood these problems, and did try to make her sample as varied as she could in terms of sex, age, and region of the country. Table 2.1 provides a statistical profile of the people who participated in her investigation.

Benjamin based all her interviews on a series of questions, but adopted an open-ended format so her subjects could pursue whatever issues they wished. Like many interviewers, Benjamin conducted her interviews in a wide range of settings. She met subjects in offices (hers or theirs), in hotel rooms and in cars. In each case, Benjamin tape-recorded the conversation – which lasted from two-and-a-half to three hours – so that the task of taking notes would not distract her. After completing all the interviewing, however, she faced the arduous task of transcribing some 300 hours of tape-recorded conversations.

As research ethics demand, Benjamin offered full anonymity to any individual who wanted it. Even so, many of her respondents – including such notables as Vernon E. Jordan, Jr (former president of the National Urban League) and Yvonne Walker-Taylor (first woman president of Wilberforce University) – were accustomed to being in the public eye and permitted Benjamin to use their names.

Table 2.1 ● The talented one hundred: Lois Benjamin's African-American elite

Sex	Age	Childhood racial setting	Childhood region	Highest educational degree	Occupational sector	Income	Political orientation
Male 63%	35 or younger 6%	Mostly black 71%	West 6%	Doctorate 32%	College/ university 35%	More than $50,000 64%	Radical 13%
Female 37%	36 to 54 68%	Mostly white 15%	North/ central 32%	Medical/ law 17%	Private, profit 17%	$35,000 to $50,000 18%	Liberal 38%
	55 or older 26%	Racially mixed 14%	South 38%	Master's 27%	Private, nonprofit 9%	$20,000 to $34,999 12%	Moderate 28%
			Northeast 12%	Bachelor's 13%	Government 22%	Less than $20,000 6%	Conservative 5%
			Other 12%	Less 11%	Self-employed 14%		Depends on issue 14%
					Retired 3%		Unknown 2%
100%	100%	100%	100%	100%	100%	100%	100%

Source: Adapted from Lois Benjamin, *The Black Elite, Facing the Color Line in the Twilight of the Twentieth Century* (Chicago: Nelson-Hall, 1991), p. 276

What surprised Benjamin the most, however, was how eagerly many informants responded to her request for an interview. These normally busy men and women appeared to go out of their way to contribute to this project. Furthermore, once the interviews were under way, many displayed a high degree of emotion. Benjamin reports that, at some point in the conversation, about 40 of her 100 subjects shed tears. For many, apparently, the interviews provided an opportunity to release feelings and share experiences never revealed before. How did Benjamin herself respond to such sentiments? She reports that she laughed, reflected, or cried along with her respondents. In light of this close rapport, we might reasonably wonder whether a more formal and aloof researcher could have completed this research, and whether or not a white investigator could have done so.

As we noted at the beginning of this chapter, other researchers have documented important gains in social standing among African Americans in recent decades. But Benjamin's interviews caution us that race continues to shape the daily lives of talented people of colour. Many reported anxiety that their racial identity would at some point undermine their success. Others feared that a race-based 'glass ceiling' stands between them and the highest positions in society. Summing up her respondents' thoughts and feelings, Benjamin states that, despite the improving social standing of African Americans, black people in the United States continue to feel the sting of racial hostility. Just as important, we see that a position in the nation's professional elite is no shield from racism.

Finding a persistent 'colour line' in US society, Benjamin ends her study by expressing her commitment to change. Following the lead of pioneer African-American sociologist W. E. B. Du Bois (1868–1963) (see Box in Chapter 12), she asserts that research is not merely a source of knowledge but a strategy for assisting those we study (and, perhaps, ourselves).

SOCIOLOGICAL SPOTLIGHT

Table reading: an important skill

A table provides a great deal of information in a small amount of space, so learning to read tables can increase your reading efficiency. When you spot a table, look first at the title to see what information it contains. In Table 2.1, the title tells us that the table provides a profile of the 100 subjects participating in Lois Benjamin's research. Across the top of the table, you will see eight variables that define these men and women. Reading down under each one, note the various categories, each with a percentage; the percentages in each column add up to 100.

Starting at the top left, we see that Benjamin's sample was mostly men (63 per cent versus 37 per cent women). In terms of age, most of the respondents (68 per cent) were in the middle stage of life, and we see, too, that most grew up in a predominantly black community either in the south or in the north-central region of the United States.

These individuals do, indeed, constitute a professional elite. Notice that half have earned either a doctorate (32 per cent) or a medical or law degree (17 per cent). Given their extensive education (and Benjamin's own position as a professor), we should not be surprised that the largest share (35 per cent) work in academic institutions. In terms of income, these are affluent individuals, with most (64 per cent) earning more than $50,000 (£33,300) annually (a salary commanded by only 14 per cent of all workers in the United States).

Finally, we see that these 100 individuals generally claim to be left-of-centre in their political orientations. In part, this reflects their extensive schooling (which encourages progressive thinking) and the tendency of academics to lean towards the liberal side of the political spectrum. ●

In the field: participant observation

The most widely used strategy for humanistic field study is **participant observation**, *a method by which researchers systematically observe people while joining in their routine activities.*

Researchers choose participant observation in order to gain an inside look at social life in settings ranging from night clubs to religious seminaries. Cultural anthropologists commonly employ participant observation (which they call *fieldwork*) to study communities in other societies. They term their descriptions of unfamiliar cultures *ethnographies*; sociologists prefer to describe their accounts of people in particular settings as *case studies*.

At the outset of a field study, social scientists typically have just a vague idea of what they will encounter. Thus, most field research is *exploratory* and *descriptive*. Researchers might have hypotheses in mind, but it's just as likely that they may not yet realise what the important questions will turn out to be.

As its name suggests, participant observation has two facets. On the one hand, gaining an 'insider's' look depends on becoming a participant in the setting – 'hanging out' with others, attempting to act, think and even feel the way they do. Compared to experiments and survey research, then, participant observation has fewer hard-and-fast rules. But it is precisely this flexibility that allows investigators to explore the unfamiliar and to adapt to the unexpected.

Unlike other research methods, participant observation requires a researcher to become immersed in the setting, not for a week or two, but for months or even years. For the duration of the study, however, the researcher must maintain some distance as an 'observer', mentally stepping back to record field notes and, eventually, to make sense of the action. The tension inherent in this method comes through in the name: 'playing the *participant*' gains for the researcher acceptance and access to people's lives; yet 'playing the *observer*' affords the distance and perspective needed for thoughtful analysis. The twin roles of 'insider' participant and 'outsider' observer, then, often come down to a series of careful compromises.

Most sociologists carry out participant observation alone, so they must remain mindful that results depend on the interpretations of a single individual. Participant observation is typically **qualitative research**, meaning *investigation by which a researcher gathers subjective, not numerical, data.* (The informal conversational interviews we encountered earlier are also part of this approach.) Unlike experiments or surveys, participant observation and informal interviews usually involves little **quantitative research**, *investigation by which a researcher collects numerical data.* Some scientists disparage a 'soft' method like participant observation as lacking in scientific rigour. Yet, much qualitative research has become very rigorous in recent years, even to the point of having computer programs like *The Ethnograph* and *NUDIST* to enable a rigorous analysis of 'soft' data. Further, its personal approach – relying so heavily on personal impressions – is also a strength: while a highly visible team of sociologists attempting to administer formal surveys would disrupt many social settings, a sensitive participant-observer can often gain considerable insight into people's natural day-to-day behaviour.

An illustration: Street Corner Society

In the late 1930s, a young graduate student at Harvard University named William Foote Whyte became fascinated by the lively street life of a nearby, rather run-down section of Boston. His curiosity ultimately led Whyte to carry out four years of participant observation in this neighbourhood, which he called 'Cornerville', producing a sociological classic in the process.

At the time, Cornerville was home to first- and second-generation Italian immigrants. Many were poor and lived economically precarious lives, quite unlike the more affluent Bostonians familiar to Whyte. Popular wisdom in Boston held that Cornerville was a place to avoid: a poor, chaotic slum inhabited by racketeers. Unwilling to accept easy stereotypes, Whyte set out to discover for himself exactly what kind of life went on inside this community. His celebrated book, *Street Corner Society* (1981; orig. 1943), describes Cornerville as a highly organised community with a distinctive code of values, complex social patterns, and particular social conflicts.

Beginning his investigation, Whyte considered a range of research methods. Of course, he might have taken a pile of questionnaires to one of Cornerville's community centres and asked local people to fill them out. Or he could have asked members of the community to come to his Harvard office for interviews. But it is easy to see that such formal strategies would have prompted little cooperation from the local people and yielded few insights. Whyte decided, therefore, to ease into Cornerville life and patiently seek out the keys to understanding this rather mysterious place.

Soon enough, Whyte discovered the challenges of just getting started in field research. After all, an upper middle class Anglo-Saxon graduate student from Harvard did not exactly 'fit in' to Cornerville life. And, as Whyte quickly found out, even what he intended as a friendly overture could seem pushy and rude to others. Early on, Whyte dropped in at a local bar, hoping to buy a woman a drink and encourage her to talk about Cornerville. He looked around the room, but could find no woman alone. Presently, he thought he might have an opportunity when a fellow sat down with two women. He gamely remarked 'Pardon me. Would you mind if I joined you?' Instantly, he realised his miscalculation:

There was a moment of silence while the man stared at me. Then he offered to throw me down the stairs. I assured him that this would not be necessary, and demonstrated as much by walking right out of there without any assistance. (1981: 289).

As this incident suggests, gaining entry to a community – that is, becoming a participant – is the crucial (and sometimes hazardous) first step in this type of research. 'Breaking in' typically depends on patience, ingenuity and a little luck. For Whyte, a big break came in the form of a young man named 'Doc', whom he met in a local social service agency. Listening to Whyte's account of his bungled efforts to make friends in Cornerville, Doc sympathetically decided to take Whyte under his wing and introduce him to others in the community. With Doc's help, Whyte soon became a 'regular' in the neighbourhood.

Whyte's friendship with Doc illustrates the importance of a *key informant* in field research. Such people not only introduce a researcher to a community but often continue to be sources of help and information on a host of issues. But using a key informant also has its risks. Because any person has a particular circle of friends, a key informant's guidance is certain to introduce bias into the study. Moreover, in the eyes of others the reputation of the key informant – for better or worse – usually rubs off on the investigator. In sum,

while relying on a key informant at the outset, a participant-observer soon must seek a broader range of contacts.

Now that he had entered the Cornerville world, Whyte began his work in earnest. But he soon realised that the careful field researcher needs to know when to speak up and when to simply listen, look and learn. One evening, he joined a group of Cornerville people engaged in a discussion of neighbourhood gambling. Wanting to get the facts straight, Whyte asked naively 'I suppose the cops were all paid off?' In a heartbeat,

The gambler's jaw dropped. He glared at me. Then he denied vehemently that any policeman had been paid off and immediately switched the conversation to another subject. For the rest of that evening I felt very uncomfortable.

The next day, Doc offered some sound advice:

'Go easy on that "who", "what", "why", "when", "where" stuff, Bill. You ask those questions and people will clam up on you. If people accept you, you can just hang around, and you'll learn the answers in the long run without even having to ask the questions.' (1981: 303)

In the months and years that followed, Whyte became familiar with life in Cornerville, and even married a local woman. In the process, he learned that this neighbourhood was hardly the stereotypical slum. On the contrary, most immigrants were working hard, many had earned considerable success, and some could even could boast of having sent children to college. In short, his book makes fascinating reading about the dreams, deeds and disappointments of one ethnic community, and it contains a richness of detail that only long-term participant observation can provide.

In Whyte's work, we also see that participant observation is a method rife with tensions and contrasts. Its flexibility helps a researcher respond to an unfamiliar setting but makes replication difficult for others. Insight depends on getting close to others, while scientific observation demands detachment. Participant observation calls for little expense, because no elaborate equipment or laboratory is needed, but a comprehensive community study does take time – typically a year or more. Perhaps this long-term commitment explains why participant observation is used less often than other methods described in this chapter. Yet the depth of understanding gained through research of this kind has greatly enriched our knowledge of many types of human communities.

Using available data: secondary and historical analysis

Not all research requires investigators to collect their own data personally. In many cases, sociologists engage in **secondary analysis**, *a research method in which a researcher utilises data collected by others*.

The most widely used statistics in social science are gathered by government agencies. The Office for National Statistics in the UK continuously updates information about the UK population, and offers much of interest to sociologists. Comparable data on Europe is available via *Eurostats*, from the Office for Official Publications of the European Communities in Luxembourg. Global investigations benefit from various publications of the United Nations and the World Bank. And much of the data of previous research is housed in archives such as the Social Science Research Data Archive at the University of Essex, UK. In short, a wide range of data about the whole world is as close as the university library. And most of these data sets, these days, are available on CD-ROM or on the World Wide Web.

Clearly, using available data – whether government statistics or the findings of individuals – saves researchers time and money. Therefore, this approach holds special appeal to sociologists with low budgets. Just as important, the quality of government data is generally better than what even well-funded researchers could hope to obtain on their own.

Still, secondary analysis has inherent problems. For one thing, available data may not exist in precisely the form one might wish; further, there are always questions about the meaning and accuracy of work done by others. For example, in his classic study of suicide, Emile Durkheim realised that he could not be sure that a death classified as an 'accident' was not, in reality, a 'suicide' and vice versa. And he also knew that various agencies use differing procedures and categories in collecting data, making comparisons difficult. In the end, then, using second-hand data is a little like shopping for a used car: Bargains are plentiful, but you have to shop carefully to avoid being stuck with a 'lemon'.

To illustrate, let's assume that reading about Lois Benjamin's account of African-American elites sparks our interest in North America's affluent minorities. How many such people are there? Where do they live? Map 2.1 graphically displays Census Bureau data that address these questions. These statistics are the best available on the topic, and they are readily available at no cost. Yet to use them means accepting the Census Bureau's racial and ethnic categories as well as the accuracy of people's self-reported income on government questionnaires. Further, if you were to use this map for your own purposes, not only would these problems remain, but you would have to accept our definitions of 'affluent' and 'above average'.

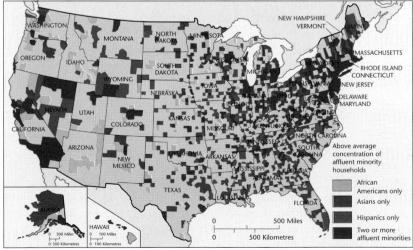

Map 2.1 ● Affluent minorities across the United States.
Based on 1990 census data, this map identifies the counties of the United States that contain an above-average share of affluent minority households – those earning at least $50,000 annually. (For the entire country, 13.2 per cent of African Americans, 16.1 per cent of Hispanics, and 35.0 per cent of Asians fall into this favoured category.) Where in the United States do affluent members of each minority category live? Do members of one category tend to live where members of another category predominate? Can you explain this pattern?

Source: adapted from *American Demographics*, Dec. 1992, pp. 34–35. Reprinted with permission. C. 1992 *American Demographics*, Ithaca, New York. Data from the 1990 decennial census

Table 2.2 ● Four research methods: a summary

Method	Application	Advantages	Limitations
Experiment	For explanatory research that specifies relationships among variables; generates quantitative data	Provides greatest ability to specify cause-and-effect relationships; replication of research is relatively easy	Laboratory settings have artificial quality; unless research environment is carefully controlled, results may be biased
Survey	For gathering information about issues that cannot be directly observed, such as attitudes and values; useful for descriptive and explanatory research; generates quantitative or qualitative data	Sampling allows surveys of large populations using questionnaires; interviews provide in-depth responses	Questionnaires must be carefully prepared and may produce a low return rate; interviews are expensive and time consuming
Participant observation	For exploratory and descriptive study of people in a 'natural' setting; generates qualitative data	Allows study of 'natural' behaviour; usually inexpensive	Time consuming; replication of research is difficult; researcher must balance roles of participant and observer
Secondary analysis	For exploratory, descriptive, or explanatory research whenever suitable data are available	Saves time and expense of data collection; makes historical research possible	Researcher has no control over possible bias in data; data may not be suitable for current research needs

Emerging research tools: from life stories to video

So far, we have described the four most common tools used by sociologists to dig out data and understand the world. They are compared in Table 2.2. But there is a fifth that is becoming increasingly common: we call them 'documents of life' (cf. Plummer, 1983). These are accounts of peoples lives told by themselves – usually in words, but sometimes through other media such as video. The world is crammed full of these personal documents. People keep diaries, send letters, take photos, make their own video diaries, write memos, tell biographies, scrawl graffiti, publish their memoirs, write letters to the papers, leave suicide notes, inscribe memorials on tombstones, shoot films, paint pictures, make music and try to record their personal dreams. All of these expressions of personal life are hurled out into the world by the millions and can be of interest to anyone who cares to seek them out.

They are all in the broadest sense 'documents of life', and are there to be gathered and analysed by sociologists. They come in a number of forms, which include:

Life histories

The life history method was established with the 300-page story of a Polish émigré to Chicago, Wladek Wisniewski, written in three months before the outbreak of World War I. It was one volume of the massive study by W. I. Thomas and F. Znaniecki, *The Polish Peasant in Europe and America*, first published between 1918 and 1920. Wladek describes the early phases of his life in the Polish village of Lubotynborn as the son of a rural blacksmith, his early schooling, his entry to the baker's trade, his migration to Germany to seek work, and his ultimate arrival in Chicago and his plight there. Following the classic work, life histories became an important tool in the work of Chicago and Polish sociologists. The authors have claimed this to be the best form of sociological method.

We are safe in saying that personal life records, as complete as possible, constitute the *perfect* type of sociological material, and that if social science has to use other materials at all it is only because of the practical difficulty of obtaining at the moment a sufficient number of such records to cover the totality of sociological problems, and of the enormous amount of work demanded for an adequate analysis of all the personal material necessary to characterise the life of a social group. (Thomas and Znaniecki, 1958: 1832–3)

Diaries

For Allport (1942: 95), the diary is the document of life *par excellence*, chronicling as it does the immediately contemporaneous flow of public and private events that are significant to the diarist. The word 'contemporary' is crucial here, for each diary entry – unlike life histories – is sedimented into a particular moment in time. In some recent research on sexual behaviour and AIDS, researchers have asked subjects to keep diaries of their sexual activities and they have then analysed them (Coxon, 1997).

'Logs' and 'time budgets'

Sorokin pioneered this method when he asked informants to keep detailed 'time-budget schedules' showing just how they allocated their time during a day (Sorokin and Berger, 1938). The anthropologist Oscar Lewis's particular method focused on a few specific families in Mexico, and the analysis of a 'day' in each of their lives. Of course, his actual familiarity with each family was in no way limited to a day. He 'spent hundreds of hours with them in their homes, ate with them, joined in their fiestas and dances, listened to their troubles, and discussed with them the history of their lives' (Lewis, 1959: 5). But in the end he decided that it would be analytically more valuable, for both humanistic and scientific purposes, to focus upon 'the day' as a unit of study. Thus each family – Martinez, Gomez, Gutierez, Sanchez and Castro – is first presented as a 'cast of characters' and then followed through one arbitrarily chosen but not untypical day of their life. Lewis believed that a study of a day had at least a threefold value: practically, it was small enough to allow for intensive observation; quantitatively, it permitted controlled comparisons across family units; and qualitatively, it encouraged a sensitivity to the subtlety, immediacy and wholeness of life.

Letters

Letters remain a relatively rare document of life in the social sciences. The most thoroughgoing use of letters is still to be found in Thomas and Znaniecki's *Polish Peasant*, where on discovering that there was extensive correspondence between Poles and Polish émigrés to America, an advertisement was placed in a Chicago journal offering to pay between 10 to 20 cents for each letter received. Through this method they were able to gain many hundreds of letters, 764 of which are printed in the first volume of their study, totalling some 800 pages and arranged in fifty family sequences. Each sequence is prefaced with a commentary that introduces the family members and the main concerns.

Photographs

Until recently, sociologists have not taken much interest in what should now be viewed as a major tool for investigation. The lead has primarily come from anthropologists, and in particular the pioneering work of Gregory Bateson and Margaret Mead (1942) who provided a volume devoted entirely to photographic images from the culture of the Balinese, and from journalistic photographers, such as Jacob A. Riis's visual depiction of impoverished styles in New York City's slums (Riis, 1971).

Film and video

If social scientists have only occasionally considered the benefits of photography to their work, most have never countenanced the significance of film. Yet with improvements in film technology, the rise in videotaping and the relative drop in costs, film-making is fast becoming a hobby and interest open to many: the photograph album will probably be replaced by the video selection in many Western homes by the end of the century. Here should be the ethnographer's dream: life as it is lived, accurately recorded as it happens, and constantly available for playback and analysis (see Gottdiener, 1980).

Critique

Life documents can provide very valuable insights into the subjective experiences of people as they live life. They are increasingly becoming part of the repertoire of qualitative research (see above). But they are subject to many of the problems of this style of work. Thus, they are often accused of being overly impressionistic and subjective. They are also accused of technical inadequacy, of not paying proper attention to the issues of representativeness, validity and objectivity (discussed above).

● Ethical, political and policy questions

As Max Weber observed long ago, a fine line separates politics from science. Most sociologists endorse Weber's goal of value-free research. But a growing number of researchers are challenging the notion that politics and science can – or should – be distinct.

Alvin Gouldner (1970a, 1970b) was among the first to claim that the ideal of 'value-free' research paints a 'storybook picture' of sociology. Every element of social life is political, he argues, in that it benefits some people more than others. If so, Gouldner reasoned, the topics sociologists choose to study and the conclusions they reach also have political consequences.

If sociologists have no choice about their work being political, Gouldner continues, they do have a choice about *which* positions are worthy of support. Moreover, as he sees it, sociologists are obligated to endorse political objectives that will improve society. Although this viewpoint is not limited to sociologists of any one political orientation, it prevails among those with left-leaning politics, especially those guided by the ideas of Karl Marx. Recall Marx's (1972: 109; orig. 1845) claim that the point is not simply to understand the world but to change it.

Researchers must always remain respectful of subjects and mindful of their well-being. In part, this means investigators must become familiar – well ahead of time – with the cultural patterns of those they wish to study.

Such thinking, colliding with the value-free approach, has carried many universities into a spirited debate over 'political correctness'. In simple terms, this controversy pits advocates of Weberian value-free teaching and research against proponents of Marx's view that, since all knowledge is political, sociologists should strive to promote positive societal change.

Feminist methodology: gender and research

One political dimension of research involves **gender**, *the significance members of a society attach to being female or male*. Sociologists have come to realise that gender often plays a significant part in their work. Margrit Eichler (1988) identifies five threats to sound research that relate to gender.

1. *Androcentricity*. Androcentricity (*andro* is the Greek word for 'male'; *centricity* means 'being centred on') refers to approaching an issue from a male perspective. Sometimes researchers enter a setting as if only the activities of men are important while ignoring what women do. For years, for example, researchers studying occupations focused on the paid work of men while overlooking the housework and child care traditionally performed by women (Counts, 1925; Hodge, Treiman and Rossi, 1966). Clearly, research that seeks to understand human behaviour cannot ignore half of humanity.

   Eichler notes that the parallel situation of *gynocentricity* – seeing the world from a female perspective – is equally limiting to sociological investigation. However, in our male-dominated society, this narrowness of vision arises less frequently.

2. *Overgeneralising*. This problem occurs when researchers use data drawn from only people of one sex to support conclusions about both sexes. Historically, sociologists have studied men and then made sweeping claims about 'humanity' or 'society'. Gathering information about a community from a handful of public officials (typically, men) and then drawing conclusions about the entire community illustrates the problem of overgeneralising.

   Here, again, the bias can occur in reverse. For example, in an investigation of child-rearing practices, collecting data only from women would allow researchers to draw conclusions about 'motherhood' but not about the more general issue of 'parenthood'.

3. *Gender blindness*. This refers to the failure of a researcher to consider the variable of gender at all. As we note throughout this book, the lives of men and women typically differ in virtually every setting. A study of growing old in Europe that overlooked the fact that most elderly men live with spouses while elderly women generally live alone would be weakened by its gender blindness.

4. *Double standards*. Researchers must be careful not to distort what they study by applying different standards to men and women. For example, a family researcher who labels a couple as 'man and wife' may define the man as the 'head of household' and treat him accordingly, while assuming that the woman simply engages in family 'support work'.

5. *Interference*. In this case, gender distorts a study because a subject reacts to the sex of the researcher in ways that interfere with the research operation. While studying a small community in Sicily, for instance, Maureen Giovannini (1992) found that many men responded to her as a woman rather than as a researcher, compromising her research efforts. Gender dynamics precluded her from certain activities, such as private conversations with men, that were deemed inappropriate for single women. In addition, local residents denied Giovannini access to places considered off-limits to members of her sex.

Of course, there is nothing wrong with focusing research on one sex or the other. But all sociologists, as well as people who read their work, should stay mindful about how gender can affect the process of sociological investigation.

Feminist research

Sociology's pervasive attention to men in the past has prompted some contemporary researchers to make special efforts to investigate the lives of women. Advocates of feminist research embrace two key tenets: (1) that their research should focus on the condition of women in society, and (2) that the research must be grounded in the assumption that women generally experience subordination. Thus feminist research rejects Weber's value-free orientation in favour of being overtly political – doing research in pursuit of gender equality.

Some proponents of feminist research advocate the use of conventional scientific techniques, including all those described in this chapter. Others maintain that feminist research must transform the essence of science, which they see as a masculine form of knowledge. Whereas scientific investigation traditionally has demanded detachment, feminists deliberately foster a sympathetic understanding between investigator and subject. Moreover, conventional scientists take charge

of the research agenda by deciding in advance what issues to raise and how to study them. Feminist researchers, by contrast, favour a less structured approach to gathering information so that participants in research can offer their own ideas on their own terms (Stanley and Wise, 1983; Nielsen, 1990; Stanley, 1990; Reinharz, 1992).

Such alterations in research premises and methods have led more conventional sociologists to charge that feminist research is less science than simple political activism. Feminists respond that research and politics should not – indeed cannot – ever be distinct. Therefore, traditional notions that placed politics and science in separate spheres have now given way to some new thinking that merges these two dimensions.

Research ethics

Like all investigators, sociologists must be mindful that research can be harmful as well as helpful to subjects or communities. For this reason, the British Sociological Association – the major professional association of sociologists in the UK – has established formal guidelines for the conduct of research. (For addresses of sociological associations, see 'Going further' at the end of Chapter 1.)

The prime directive is that sociologists strive to be both technically competent and fair-minded in conducting their research. Sociologists must disclose all their findings, without omitting significant data. Further, they must point out various interpretations of data, and they are ethically bound to make their results available to other sociologists, some of whom may wish to replicate the study.

Whether social scientists need to inform people that they are the objects of study is a matter of continuing debate among sociologists. No one objects to studying public behaviour (say, observing how people interact in a gambling casino or a park) without announcing one's presence. But most sociologists agree that a researcher must not target specific individuals for study without their permission. Taking this debate one step further, should researchers employ deception in their work? Obviously, if researchers tell people exactly what they are looking for, they will not observe natural behaviour. On the other hand, misleading subjects may generate understandable resentment. Sociologists disagree about such ethical quandaries, but there is a trend toward greater sensitivity for the well-being of subjects in research.

Virtually everyone agrees, however, that researchers must strive to protect the safety of people involved in a research project. Sociologists are obligated to terminate research, however promising it may seem, if they become aware of any danger to participants. And if research is likely to cause subjects substantial discomfort or inconvenience, sociologists must ensure in advance that all participants understand and accept any risks.

In addition, sociologists must include in their published results the sources of any and all financial support. They must never accept funding from any organisation that seeks to influence the research process for its own purposes.

Finally, there are also global dimensions to research ethics. Before beginning research in other countries, investigators must become familiar enough with the society to be studied to understand what people *there* are likely to perceive as a violation of privacy or a source of personal danger. In a multicultural society like ours, of course, the same rule applies to studying people whose cultural background differs from one's own.

Technology and research

In recent decades, new information technology has changed our lives considerably, and this applies to the practice of research as well. Personal computers – which came on the scene only about fifteen years ago – now give individual sociologists remarkable technical ability to randomly select samples, perform complex statistical analysis, and prepare written reports efficiently. Today's average office computer is far more powerful than even the massive mainframe devices that filled entire rooms on the campus a generation ago. The development of the Internet (the so-called 'electronic superhighway') is certain to further enhance our research capabilities in the years to come.

First, the Internet now links over 50 million computers in 175 countries of the world, allowing an unprecedented level of communication. Contemporary sociologists are capable of building networks across the country and around the globe that will facilitate collaboration and prompt comparative research. Second, we can readily access a rapidly increasing amount of statistical information on the Internet. A number of these sites are listed at the end of the chap-

ters and you are encouraged to try using them. The problem here is that such sites can come and go quite quickly; some are very good and others are poor. A lot of time can be wasted 'browsing'. But once good sources are found, they can save a lot of time and provide much valuable information.

Such developments – and other as-yet-unimagined forms of technological change – promise to transform sociological investigation as we enter the next century (Morton, 1995).

The interplay of theory and method

There are, of course, some research tasks that remain unaffected by technological change. No matter how we gather data, sociologists must ultimately transform facts into meaning by building theory.

Actually, sociological investigators move back and forth between facts and theory. **Inductive logical thought** is *reasoning that transforms specific observations into general theory*. In this mode, a researcher's thinking runs from the specific to the general something like this: 'I have some interesting data here; what are the data saying about human behaviour?'

A second type of logical thought works 'downwards' in the opposite direction. **Deductive logical thought** is *reasoning that transforms general theory into specific hypotheses suitable for scientific testing*. This time,

Figure 2.3 ● Deductive and inductive logical thought

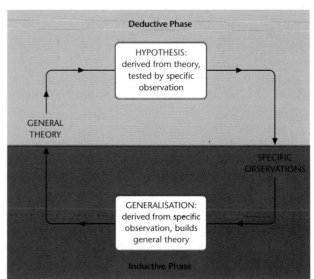

the researcher's thinking goes from the general to the specific: 'I have this hunch about human behaviour; let's put it in a form we can test, collect some data, and see if it is correct.' Working deductively, the researcher first states the theory in the form of a hypothesis and then selects a method by which to test it. To the extent that the data support the hypothesis, we conclude that the theory is correct; data that refute the hypothesis alert the researcher that the theory should be revised or perhaps rejected entirely.

Just as researchers commonly employ several methods over the course of one study, they typically make

CONTROVERSY AND DEBATE

Can people lie with statistics?

Is scientific research always as objective and 'factual' as we think? Not according to the great English politician Benjamin Disraeli, who once noted wryly: 'There are three kinds of lies: lies, damned lies, and statistics!' In a world that bombards us with numbers – often in the form of 'scientific facts' and 'official figures' – it is well worth pausing to consider that 'statistical evidence' is not synonymous with truth. For one thing, as this chapter has explained, every method of data collection is prone to error; for another, because data do not speak for themselves, someone has to interpret them to figure out what they mean. And, sometimes, people (even social scientists) 'dress up' their data almost in the way politicians whip up a campaign speech – with an eye more to winning you over than getting at the truth.

The best way to uncover statistical manipulation is to understand how these tricks are performed. Here are three ways people can lie with statistics.

1. *People choose their data.* Many times, the data we confront are not wrong; they just do not tell the whole story. Let's say someone claims that television is ruining our way of life and, as evidence, offers statistics indicating that we watch more TV today than a generation ago, and that some national measure of educational attainment has fallen during that time. Such data may be correct; however, they are selectively chosen. Another person could just as correctly counter that people spend much more on books today than they did a generation ago, suggesting that there is no cultural crisis at all. In short, plenty of statistics are available for people on all sides of a political debate to use as ammunition to bolster their arguments.

2. *People interpret their data.* Another way people manipulate statistics is to 'package' them inside a ready-made interpretation, as if to say 'Here are the numbers, and this is what they mean.' One recent publication, for example, presented the results of a study of US children living in poverty in 1992 (National Centre for Children in Poverty, cited in

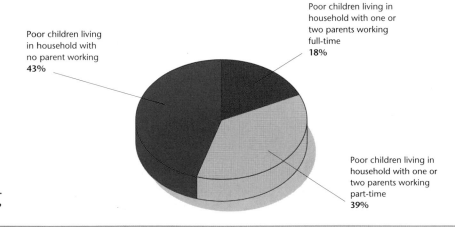

Poor children living in household with one or two parents working full-time
18%

Poor children living in household with no parent working
43%

Poor children living in household with one or two parents working part-time
39%

Figure 2.4 ● Can people lie with statistics?

use of *both* types of logical thought. Figure 2.3 illustrates the two phases of scientific thinking: inductively building theory from observations and deductively making observations to test our theory.

Finally, it is worth noting that statistics, too, play a key part in the process of turning facts into meaning.

Commonly, sociological researchers provide quantitative data as part of their research results. And precisely how they present their numbers affects the conclusions their readers draw. In other words, data presentation always provides the opportunity to 'spin' reality in one way or another.

Figure 2.5 ● Inflation and deflation of trends

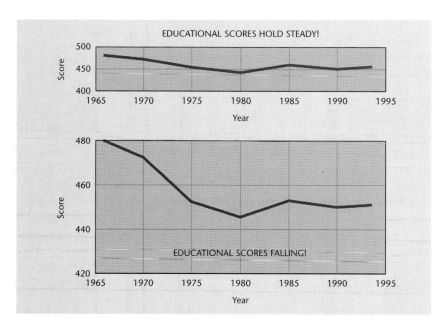

Population Today, 1995). As the pie chart (Figure 2.4) shows, the researchers reported that 43 per cent of these children lived in a household with no working parent, 39 per cent lived in a household with one or two parents employed part-time, and 18 per cent lived in a household with one or two parents working full-time. The researchers labelled this figure 'Majority of children in poverty live with parents who work'. Does this title accurately portray the data or mislead the reader?

3. *People use graphs to 'spin' the 'truth'.* Especially in newspapers and other popular media, we often encounter graphic representations of statistical data. While graphs make comprehending data easy (showing, for example, an upward or downward trend), they also provide the designer with the opportunity to 'spin' data in various ways. Where trends are concerned, one common technique for casting data in a particular light involves compressing or expanding the graph's time frame. A graph of the crime rate over only the last several years, for example, would reveal a downward trend;

shifting the time frame to include the last few decades, however, would show a sharp increase.

A second manipulation technique occurs when the designer chooses a graph's scale specifically to 'inflate' or 'deflate' a trend. An illustration of this is shown in Figure 2.5. Both graphs present identical data for Educational scores between 1967 and 1993. But the left-hand graph stretches the scale to make a downward trend more pronounced; the right-hand graph compresses the scale to minimise any change over

time. So, understanding what statistics really mean depends on being a careful reader!

● **Continue the debate:**

1. Why do you think people are so quick to accept 'statistics' as true?

2. Would Max Weber's 'value-free' approach to research forbid 'dressing up' one's data? What about a Marxist approach?

3. Can you cite a piece of research that you think presented biased data or conclusions? Specify the biases. ●

Often, we conclude that an argument must be true simply because there are statistics to back it up. However, readers must use a cautious eye when encountering statistical data. After all, researchers choose what data to present, they offer interpretations of the statistics, and they may use tables or graphs to encourage others to reach particular conclusions. The final box in this chapter takes a closer look at these important issues.

● Putting it all together: planning a sociological project

Drawing together the elements of sociological investigation presented in this chapter, a typical project in sociology will include each of the following 13 steps. The emphasis here is upon planning the project well.

1. *Get yourself a research problem and define the topic of investigation.* Being curious and looking at the world sociologically can generate ideas for social research anywhere. The issue you choose to study is likely to have some personal significance. But a social problem is not a sociological problem and you need to be clear how you can pose a sociological question.

2. *Start keeping a log and record files.* Keep a log of how you develop your research, how you change your views and problems, and how you make key decisions. This will be useful in helping you reflect; but it may also provide good source material for writing up the methodology chapter in your study – if you are to have one. Keep all your notes well organised, and plan this early.

3. *Find out what others have learned about the topic.* You are probably not the first person to develop an interest in a particular issue. Spend time in the library to see what theories and methods researchers have applied to your topic in the past. In reviewing existing research, note problems that may have come up before. Check on the findings.

4. *Assess the requirements for carrying out the research.* How much time and money will the research require? What special equipment or skills are necessary? Can you do the work yourself? What sources of funding are available to support the research? You should answer all these questions before beginning to design the research project.

5. *Specify the research questions.* Are you seeking to explore an unfamiliar social setting? To describe some category of people? Or to investigate cause and effect among variables? If your study is exploratory, identify general questions that will guide the work. If it is descriptive, specify the population and the variables of interest. If it is explanatory, state the hypothesis to be tested and carefully operationalise each variable. Make a long list of what puzzles you; and then work to narrow it to a firmer focus.

6. *Specify your theoretical orientation, and perhaps your disciplinary links.* You should try to locate your own research within certain traditions. For example, some research might be historical, some anthropological, and some more theoretical. And if it is to be theoretical, what kinds of theories will you use: to return to Chapter 1, would you find a functionalist, conflict or action approach most suitable?

7. *Consider ethical issues.* Not all research raises serious ethical issues, but you should be sensitive to this matter throughout your investigation. Could the research harm anyone? How might you design the study to minimise the chances of injury? Do you plan to promise anonymity to the subjects? If so, how will you ensure that anonymity will be maintained?

8. *Devise a research strategy.* Consider all major research strategies – as well as innovative combinations of approaches. Keep in mind that the appropriate method depends on the kind of questions you are asking as well as the resources available to support your research.

9. *Draw up a written research proposal in which you outline the above stages and say what you will be doing.* This is very valuable in providing a guide and checklist for doing the research.

10. *Gather and record the data.* The way you collect data depends on the research method you choose. Be sure to record accurately all information in a way that will make sense later (it may be some time before you actually write up the results of your work). Remain vigilant for any bias that may creep into the research. Bias may be inevitable, but you should be aware of it.

11. *Interpret the data.* Scrutinise the data in terms of the initial questions and decide what answers they suggest. If your study involves a specific hypothesis, you should be able to confirm, reject or modify the hypothesis based on the data. In writing up your research report, keep in mind that there may be several ways to interpret the results of your study, consistent with different theoretical paradigms, and you should consider them all.

12. *State your conclusions.* As you write your final report, specify conclusions supported by the data. Consider the significance of your work both to sociological theory and to improving research methods. Of what value is your research to people outside of sociology? Finally, evaluate your own work, noting problems that arose and questions left unanswered. Note ways in which your own biases may have coloured your conclusions.

13. *Share your results.* Consider submitting your research paper to a campus newspaper or magazine, or making a presentation to a seminar, a meeting of any people you have been involved in studying, or perhaps a meeting of professional sociologists. The important point is to share what you have learned with others and to let others respond to your work.

SUMMARY

1. Two basic requirements for sociological investigation are (1) viewing the world from a sociological perspective, and (2) being curious and asking questions about society.

2. Sociological research involves asking questions about three issues: (1) epistemology, (2) technical tools, and (3) ethics and politics.

3. Three approaches to epistemology can be found within sociology: positivism, realism and humanism.

4. Measurement is the process of determining the value of a variable in any specific case. Sound measurement is both reliable and valid.

5. A goal of science is discovering how variables are related. Correlation means that two or more variables change value together. Knowledge about cause-and-effect relationships is more powerful, however, because a researcher can use an independent variable to predict change in a dependent variable.

6. Although investigators select topics according to their personal interests, the scientific ideal of objectivity demands that they try to suspend personal values and biases as they conduct research.

7. Human curiosity and imagination must infuse the scientific method; moreover, researchers must always bring their data to life through interpretation.

8. Investigators should avoid examining issues from the point of view of only one sex or basing generalisations about humanity on data collected from only men or women.

9. Rejecting conventional ideas about scientific objectivity, some sociologists argue that research inevitably involves political values; with this in mind, research should be directed toward promoting desirable social change.

10. Because sociological research has the potential to cause discomfort and harm to subjects, sociological investigators are bound by ethical guidelines.

11. Experiments, which are performed under controlled conditions, attempt to specify causal relationships between two (or more) variables.

12. Surveys, which gather people's responses to statements or questions, may employ questionnaires or interviews.

13. Through participant observation, a form of field research, sociologists directly observe a social setting while participating in it for an extended period of time.

14. Secondary analysis, or making use of available data, is often preferable to collecting one's own data; it is also essential in the study of historical questions.

15. Documents of life are records of personal lives recorded by the subjects themselves. They help to gain an understanding of subjective experience, and include life histories, diaries and letters.

16. Feminist methodologies take gender bias very seriously and aim to correct it.

17. Theory and research are linked through two kinds of thinking. Deductive thought transforms general ideas into specific hypotheses suitable for testing. Inductive thought organises specific observations into general ideas.

KEY CONCEPTS

cause and effect a relationship in which change in one variable (the independent variable) causes change in another (the dependent variable)

concept a mental construct that represents some part of the world, inevitably in a simplified form

control holding constant all relevant variables except one in order to observe its effect

correlation a relationship by which two (or more) variables change together

deductive logical thought reasoning that transforms general ideas into specific hypotheses suitable for scientific testing

dependent variable a variable that is changed by another (independent) variable

documents of life research documents produced in the natural world by the subjects themselves, like letters and diaries

empirical evidence information we can verify with our senses

epistemology branch of philosophy that investigates the nature of knowledge and truth

experiment a research method for investigating cause and effect under highly controlled conditions

gender the significance members of a society attach to being female or male

Hawthorne effect a change in a subject's behaviour caused simply by the awareness of being studied

humanism stance that takes the human subjects seriously and is concerned with their meanings

hypothesis an unverified statement of a relationship between variables

independent variable a variable that causes change in another (dependent) variable

inductive logical thought reasoning that transforms specific observations into general theory

interview a series of questions a researcher administers personally to respondents

mean the arithmetic average of a series of numbers

measurement the process of determining the value of a variable in a specific case

median the value that occurs midway in a series of numbers arranged in order of magnitude or, simply, the middle case

mode the value that occurs most often in a series of numbers

objectivity a state of personal neutrality in conducting research

operationalising a variable specifying exactly what one intends to measure in assigning a value to a variable

participant observation a research method in which researchers systematically observe people while joining in their routine activities

population the people who are the focus of research

positivism scientific method that copies the methods of the physical sciences

qualitative research investigation by which a researcher gathers subjective, not numerical, data

quantitative research investigation by which a researcher collects numerical data

questionnaire a series of written questions a researcher supplies to subjects requesting their responses

realism scientific method that theorises a 'problematic' in order to see what is really going on

reliability the quality of consistent measurement

replication repetition of research by others

research method a systematic plan for conducting research

sample a part of a population that researchers select to represent the whole

science a logical system that bases knowledge on direct, systematic observation

secondary analysis a research method in which a researcher utilises data collected by others

spurious correlation an apparent, though false, relationship between two (or more) variables caused by some other variable

survey a research method in which subjects respond to a series of items in a questionnaire or an interview

validity the quality of measuring precisely what one intends to measure

variable a concept whose value changes from case to case

CRITICAL-THINKING QUESTIONS

1. What does it mean to state that there are various kinds of truth? What is the basic rationale for relying on science as a way of knowing?

2. Is sociology a science? Should it be? And if so, what kind?

3. What sorts of measures do scientists adopt as they strive for objectivity? Why do some sociologists consider objectivity an undesirable goal?

4. Identify several ways in which sociological research is similar to – and different from – research in the natural sciences.

5. What considerations lead a sociologist to select one method of research over another?

6. Dissect any one sociological study in order to evaluate its methodology.

7. If there can be a feminist methodology, can there also be an anti-racist methodology, or a gay methodology?

GOING FURTHER

Introductory reading

Judith Bell, *Doing your Research Project: A Guide for First-Time Researchers in Education and Social Science* (Buckingham: Open University Press, 2nd edn, 1993).

A standard guide to understanding research projects.

Julia O'Connell Davidson and Derek Layder, *Methods, Sex and Madness* (London: Routledge, 1994).

Covers the whole field in an introductory, readable way – but with an emphasis on research conducted into sexuality.

Classical sources

C. Wright Mills, *The Sociological Imagination* (Oxford: Oxford University Press, 1959).

Already introduced in Chapter 1, this has a useful appendix on how to do sociology.

Alvin Gouldner, *The Coming Crisis in Western Sociology* (New York: Avon Books, 1970).

In this volume, Alvin Gouldner provided one of the earliest and best efforts to evaluate the place of values and politics in sociological research.

More advanced reading

David Rose and Oriel Sullivan, *Introducing Data Analysis for Social Scientists* (Buckingham: Open University Press, 2nd edn, 1996).

A text designed for an introductory course on quantitative methods, which includes basic statistical measures, an introduction to computing ideas, and a series of examples from the British Class Survey and the British Household Panel Survey. A disk for a Windows version of SPSS is included.

Norman K. Denzin and Yvonna S. Lincoln (ed.), *Handbook of Qualitative Research* (London: Sage, 1994).

This is an expensive 'library book'. But it covers – through 36 articles – a full range of questions about qualitative research, from ethnography and photography to biography and interviewing.

Steiner Kvale, *Interviews: An Introduction to Qualitative Research Interviewing* (London: Sage, 1996).

A tour of all the issues in qualitative interviewing, with a number of useful study boxes on such things as 'types of interviewer questions' and 'seven stages of an interview investigation'.

Robert Burgess, *In the Field* (Allen and Unwin, 1984).

Martin Hammersley and Paul Atkinson, *Ethnography: Principles in Practice* (London: Routledge, 2nd edn, 1995).

Two useful guides to fieldwork in sociology

Ruth Levitas and Will Guy (eds), *Interpreting Official Statistics* (London: Routledge, 1996).

Looks at the statistics around unemployment, health and crime – and shows their critical weaknesses. A valuable critique of official statistics.

Liz Stanley and Sue Wise, *Breaking Out Again: Feminist Ontology and Epistemology* (London: Routledge, 2nd edn, 1993).

One of the founding statements for a feminist methodology, here updated.

Other resources

Research/Web sites

● http://www.stir.ac.uk/socinfo/

Homepage of SocInfo, the CTI (Computer in Teaching Initiative) Centre for sociology, politics and social policy. Links to useful resources such as university departments, SOSIG (Social Science Information Gateway, UK), SCROL (Sociological Research Online UK), ESRC data archive homepage, and other social science gateways.

● http://www.bowleer-saur.co.uk/service/

Access to homepage of European Research and Development Database, which contains a comprehensive guide to organisations and individuals carrying out research across European countries. Registration required.

● http://www.irc.essex.ac.uk

Homepage of ESRC Research Centre on Micro-Social Change (also known as the British Household Panel Study (BHPS)), provides studies relating to individual and household change, including income dynamics, employment change, household structure, living standards, and social values.

Finally, there are now a number of CD rom packages which are designed to facilitate the research process. These function at both advanced and introductory levels. They would only really be available in libraries where they would usually be 'on line'. They are too expensive to buy. See for example:

BIDS – The Bath Information and Data Service
Provides access to databases across a range of fields of enquiry, including the humanities and social sciences

Details on http://www.bids.ac.uk

British Humanities Index Plus
Some 250 international humanities journals and UK quality newspapers are recorded

Details on http://www.bowker-saur.co.uk/service/

IBSS – The International Bibliography of the Social Sciences
A vast guide to reading in the social sciences

Details on http://www.bids.ac.uk

Sociofile
Covering the whole field of sociology, it contains abstracts from some 2,300 journals and a lot more besides.

Details on http://www.accessinn.com/socabs/

Methodologists Toolchest, CD-ROM, Scolari Sage Software, 1997
This enables you to plan your project, prepare your research design, and keep a check on problems.

Details on http://www.sagepub.co.uk

part two

The Foundations of Society

chapter three

Source: Popperfoto

Society

'I thought at first it was a doll's head', said Helmut Simon, a German tourist who, in 1991, made one of the scientific finds of the century. Simon was hiking across a huge glacier in south-west Austria near the Italian border when he stumbled upon a familiar shape protruding from the melting ice. He soon realised that it was not a doll but a human body: the so-called Iceman, who died some 5,300 years ago (before the construction of the Great Pyramids of Egypt), making him the oldest member of our species to be discovered essentially intact.

Experts from around the world soon were buzzing with excitement. At the time of his death, they estimate the Iceman was about thirty years of age, with a height of five feet two inches and weighing about 110 pounds. He was a shepherd, tending his flock high in the Alps in early autumn, scientists speculate, when he was overtaken by a cold storm that forced him to take refuge in a narrow ridge in the mountain. Tired from his ordeal, he lay down and fell asleep, and, as the temperature continued to drop, he painlessly froze to death. Deep snows and a wall of ice soon entombed his body in a massive glacier. There, at a flesh-preserving temperature of –6°C he remained for 53 centuries. Only an unusual melt of the glacier – and the luck of a sharp-eyed hiker – led to the Iceman's discovery.

Source: Gamma-Liaison, Inc. – Hinterleiner

Examining the Iceman's garments, scientists were astonished at how advanced this 'cave man's' society was. The Iceman's hair was neatly trimmed, and his body displayed numerous tattoos that probably symbolised his standing in his home community. He wore a skillfully stitched leather coat over which a woven grass cape provided greater protection from the elements. His shoes, also made of leather, were stuffed with grass for comfort and warmth. He carried with him an axe, a wood-handled knife, and a bow that shot feathered arrows with flint points. A primitive backpack held additional tools and personal items, including natural medicines made from plants (Rademaekers and Schoenthal, 1992).

Imagine you were born some 300 years ago, in the year 1700. Although this is very recent in terms of the billions of years of the existence of Planet Earth, you would still have been living in a remarkably different world. You would probably be living in a very small community and you would not have travelled anywhere except perhaps to a nearby town. You would never have been to a shop, let alone a shopping centre. You would never have encountered the world of railways, cars, telephones, camera, PCs, faxes, mobile phones, planes, videos . . . . And more than this, the idea of voting for your government, going to a university, choosing your religion, or even choosing your identity would all have been rare. Welcome to the modern world!

As we saw in Chapter 1 ('The Sociological Perspectives'), sociology was born out of a concern with this rapidly changing character of the modern, industrial world: with where we have come from and where we are heading. This chapter takes a look back at this historical development of human societies, offers insights about their present state, and points to some future trends. The central concept of **society** refers to *people who interact in a defined space and share culture*. In this sense, both Europe, and specific countries such as Norway or England, may be seen as societies (see the box on pages 68–9).

We shall start by describing the changing character of human society over the last 10,000 years. This is a very difficult task! The remainder of the chapter then analyses the main patterns of different kinds of society, and presents classic visions of society developed by three of sociology's founders, already introduced in earlier chapters. Karl Marx understood human history as a long and complex process of social change. His

concern was with the ways the economy generates *conflicts and inequalities* around the production of material goods in order to live; and how these conflicts provided the motor force for change. Max Weber recognised the importance of productive forces as well, but he sought to demonstrate the power of *human ideas* (especially those found in religions) to animate society. Weber believed that rational thinking underlies modern society and promotes change. Finally, Emile Durkheim investigated patterns of *social solidarity*, noting that the bonds uniting traditional societies are strikingly different from those uniting their modern counterparts. All of them were concerned with the momentous changes taking place in European societies in their times; and with how the future would develop.

All three visions of society try to answer key questions:

● How do societies of the past and present differ from one another?

● How and why does a society change? What forces divide a society? What forces hold it together?

● Are societies getting better or worse?

The theorists profiled in this chapter all probed these questions, but they disagree on the answers. We shall highlight the similarities and differences in their views as we go along.

● Changing patterns of society

The Iceman, introduced at the opening of this chapter, was a member of a very early human society. He had already died before a great empire flourished in Egypt, before the flowering of culture in ancient Greece, and before any society in Europe could boast of a single city.

As people who take for granted rapid transportation and instant global communication, we look on this ancestor from our distant past with keen curiosity. But sociologists who study the past (working with archaeologists and anthropologists) have learned quite a bit about our human heritage. Gerhard Lenski and Jean Lenski have chronicled the great differences among societies that have flourished and declined throughout human history. Just as important, the work of these researchers helps us better understand how we live today. The Lenskis call the focus of their research **sociocultural evolution**, *the process of change that results from a society's gaining new information, particularly technology* (Lenski, Nolan and Lenski, 1995: 75). Rather like a biologist examining how a living species evolves over millennia, a sociologist employing this approach observes how societies change over centuries as they gain greater ability to manipulate their physical environments. Societies with rudimentary technology can support only a small number of people who enjoy few choices about how to live. Technologically complex societies – while not necessarily 'better' in any absolute sense – develop large populations which are more likely to be characterised by diverse, highly specialised lives.

The greater the amount of technological information a society has in its grasp, the faster the rate at which it changes. Technologically simple societies, then, change very slowly; in fact, some of the clothing worn by the Austrian Iceman differs only slightly from garments used by shepherds in the same area early in this century. By contrast, industrial, high-technology societies change so quickly that people witness dramatic transformations in the span of their lifetimes. Again, consider some familiar elements of contemporary culture that would probably puzzle, delight, but most likely alarm people who lived just a few generations ago: fast food, faxes, mobile phones, computer 'cybersex', artificial hearts, laser surgery, test-tube babies, genetic engineering, computer-based virtual reality, fibre optics, smart bombs, the threat of nuclear holocaust, space shuttles, transsexual surgery, and 'tell-all' talk shows transmitted across the world to all countries! It is indeed a strange modern world we have arrived in – even when compared with the world of the recent past.

As a society extends its technological reach, the effects ripple through the cultural system, generating countless repercussions. When our ancestors first harnessed the power of the wind by using a sail, they set the stage for discovering kites, sailing ships, windmills and, eventually, aircraft. Consider, as more recent examples, the many ways modern life has been changed by atomic energy or the computer.

Drawing on the Lenskis' work, we will describe five general types of society distinguished by their technology: hunting and gathering societies, horticultural and pastoral societies, agrarian societies, industrial societies, and postindustrial societies.

Technological determinism: a cautious word

Whilst different kinds of technologies may well create preconditions for different kinds of societies, there are two cautions that need to be given about the account which follows.

First, the technology does not *determine* societies. There is no automatic connection between the kinds of technologies a society has available and the form of that society. It takes people to decide how to use technologies – and they may use them in very different ways, developing different skills and meanings. Under Nazi Germany, for example, the weight of modern technology was used to exterminate millions of people. The technologies of the Incas or the Egyptians were very sophisticated, but also involved systems of domination and slavery. As we will see later, modern information or computer societies need actions from people to use them – and they may be used for good or bad. Technology is neutral: it is people who shape technology.

Second, we must be very wary of saying these five societies *evolve* into each other, as if there is some kind of automatic progress. In fact, in the twentieth century all of these societies may be said to coexist. Many indigenous peoples may have hunting, pastoral or agrarian societies with highly evolved technologies of their own. It is often a 'Eurocentric' view that wants to see them as prior to or more simple than European culture. We will return to some of these problems when we discuss multiculturalism in the next chapter.

Hunting and gathering societies

Hunting and gathering refers to *simple technology for hunting animals and gathering vegetation*. From the emergence of our species until about 12,000 years ago,

What is European society?

Marx, Weber and Durkheim – discussed in this chapter – were not just seeking to understand the nature of industrial societies; they were Europeans largely in search of understanding industrial Europe. But it is hard to know quite what 'Europe' is. Before going on, make a list of ways you might define Europe, and ponder what are its common elements and what are its differences.

In one sense it is hard to see Europe as anything coherent. There are over 40 countries, and even more languages. They are scattered over diverse climates – from Scandinavia to the Mediterranean – and diverse cultures – from 'Spanish' to 'Nordic'. There are diverse histories, rituals, politics, economic systems and religions. Northern Europe has more individualistic values than southern Europe and Ireland (where religious values are stronger). It is hard to see what the Nordic cultures of Denmark, Finland, Sweden and Norway have in common with the cultures of Spain, Italy or Portugal. And within each of these countries there are internal splits

and differing ethnic groups (France has Algerians; Germany has guest workers; and the United Kingdom has Scots, Welsh and Irish alongside people of Asian and Afro-Caribbean descent). Most introductory UK textbooks ignore the diversity of this Europe and focus on the one voice of England (often with a diluted voice from North America). But clearly the English voice is not the French voice or the Norwegian one.

Yet despite this, people speak of a European society. What can be meant by this?

One way is to search for some common elements. A common history, common lands and geography and – perhaps – some broad common, cultural

Map 3.1 ● Greater Europe: the widening domain of the EU
A geography of the European Union – a regional and economic perspective.

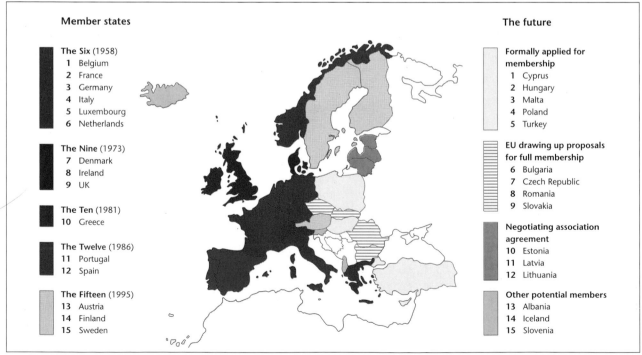

Member states

The Six (1958)
1 Belgium
2 France
3 Germany
4 Italy
5 Luxembourg
6 Netherlands

The Nine (1973)
7 Denmark
8 Ireland
9 UK

The Ten (1981)
10 Greece

The Twelve (1986)
11 Portugal
12 Spain

The Fifteen (1995)
13 Austria
14 Finland
15 Sweden

The future

Formally applied for membership
1 Cyprus
2 Hungary
3 Malta
4 Poland
5 Turkey

EU drawing up proposals for full membership
6 Bulgaria
7 Czech Republic
8 Romania
9 Slovakia

Negotiating association agreement
10 Estonia
11 Latvia
12 Lithuania

Other potential members
13 Albania
14 Iceland
15 Slovenia

Source: Wintle (1996)

Some landmarks in the making of the European Union	
April 1951	Treaty of Paris establishes the European Coal and Steel Community (with France, West Germany, Italy, Belgium, The Netherlands and Luxembourg). Britain does not join
March 1957	Treaties of Rome signed again by the above six, establishes the European Economic Community and The European Atomic Energy Community. Also includes new parliament, new court and eliminates customs duties amongst member states
1 January 1958	Treaties of Rome become law. In effect, this is the start of the European Economic Community (EEC)
1964	Common agricultural policy established with uniform prices to start in 1967
22 January 1972	Britain, Denmark, Ireland and Norway admitted to membership from January 1973. Conservative government in the UK with Prime Minister Edward Heath takes Britain into the EEC, but a referendum in Norway rejects membership
June 1975	Labour government in UK wishes to withdraw and holds a referendum: 67% of voters decide they want to stay in
December 1975	Elected European Parliament planned to start in 1979. No powers to introduce legislation, but powers to advise?
1978	Members agree to ECU (European Currency Unit)
1 January 1981	Greece becomes tenth member
January 1983	Common fishing policy
January 1985	First European passports issued. Jacques Delors is first president of European Commission
January 1986	Spain and Portugal join
February 1986	The Single Act; streamlining, with legalisation now passed by a majority
October 1990	Former East Germany becomes part of the Community
October 1991	European Free Trade Association (EFTA – Austria, Finland, Iceland, Liechtenstein, Norway, Sweden, Switzerland) agrees an extended cooperation project – the European Economic Area (EEA) – within the Community and EFTA creating an integrated trade area
November 1991	Associations with Poland, Hungary and Czechoslovakia (but stopping short of full membership)
1992	The internal market
1992	Maastricht: The Treaty on European Union (seeking monetary union by the millennium)

elements that could be seen as similar. It may indeed be what Benedict Anderson has called an 'imagined community', held together by a common sense of history and culture. In part this may be because most of these cultures have deep values that link to being the first industrialising countries, the first modern democratic cultures and the first Christian cultures. As we will see, these values are pervasive. Taken together, it may be, as Agnes Heller argues, that 'European culture is modernity – cumulative knowledge and progress, technology and wealth – along with nation states and ideas of freedom and equality' (Wintle 1996: 11).

Another way is to approach them as countries themselves seeking to be united. Since World War 1 (itself a curiously unifying factor), there have been persistent attempts to create a European Union. Starting with the Congress of Europe in 1948 at The Hague, the European Union has grown through many stages. In 1951 Jean Monnet called the European Coal and Steel Community 'the first expression of the Europe that is being born'. But this only involved six countries: Belgium, France, Italy, West Germany, Luxembourg and The Netherlands. The chart and the map aim to give some sense of the European Union's growth in the past, and also the projected plans for the future.

To date, Britain has been an 'awkward partner' in Europe. Until the election of a Labour government on 1 May 1997, successive Conservative governments were the embodiment of 'euroscepticism'. Giving priority to UK national sovereignty, and worried about the seeming dominance of Franco-Germany, they suspected that federalism meant centralisation. ●

all humans were hunters and gatherers. Although hunting and gathering societies remained common several centuries ago, only a few persist today, including the Aka and Pygmies of central Africa, the Bushmen of south-western Africa, the Aborigines of Australia, the Kaska Indians of north-west Canada, and the Batek and Semai of Malaysia (Endicott, 1992; Hewlett, 1992).

With scarcely any technology to make food production efficient, most members of these societies must search continually for game and edible plants. Only in lush areas where food is plentiful would hunters and gatherers have any leisure time. Moreover, foraging for food demands a large amount of land, so hunting and gathering societies comprise small bands of a few dozen people living at some distance from one another. These groups are also nomadic, moving on as they deplete vegetation in one area or in pursuit of migratory animals. Although they periodically return to favoured sites, they rarely form permanent settlements.

Hunting and gathering societies are based on kinship. The family obtains and distributes food, protects its members, and teaches necessary skills to children. Most activities are common to everyone and centre on seeking the next meal; some specialisation, however, corresponds to age and sex. The very young and the very old contribute only what they can, while healthy adults secure most of the food. The gathering of vegetation – the more reliable food source – is typically the work of women, while men take on the less certain job of hunting. Although the two sexes have somewhat different responsibilities, then, most hunters and gatherers probably accorded men and women comparable social importance (Leacock, 1978).

Hunting and gathering societies have few formal leaders. Most recognise a *shaman*, or spiritual leader, who enjoys high prestige but receives no greater material rewards than other members of the society and must help procure food like everyone else. Other individuals who are especially skilful at obtaining food may also have high prestige; overall, however, the social organisation of hunters and gatherers is relatively simple and egalitarian.

Hunting and gathering societies rarely use their weapons – the spear, the bow and arrow, and stone knife – to wage war. Nonetheless, they are often ravaged by the forces of nature. Storms and droughts can easily destroy their food supply, and they stand vulnerable to accident and disease. Such risks encourage cooperation and sharing, a strategy that increases everyone's odds of survival. Even so, many die in childhood, and perhaps half perish before the age of 20 (Lenski, Nolan and Lenski, 1995: 104).

During this century, technologically complex societies have slowly closed in on the few remaining hunters and gatherers, reducing their landholdings and depleting game and vegetation. The Lenskis predict that the 1990s may well witness the end of hunting and gathering societies on earth. Yet, whilst many of these 'indigenous' peoples, such as the Innuit in Canada, are finding their cultures increasingly destroyed by the industrial west, there are many signs that such cultures are also fighting back to protect their own ways of life.

Horticultural and pastoral societies

Ten to twelve thousand years ago, a new technology began to change many hunting and gathering societies. **Horticulture** is *technology based on using hand tools to cultivate plants*. The most important tools of horticulturalists are the hoe to work the soil and the digging stick to punch holes in the ground for seeds. Humans first used these tools in fertile regions of the Middle East and, later, in Latin America and Asia. Cultural diffusion spread knowledge of horticulture throughout most of the world by about 6,000 years ago.

Not all societies were quick to abandon hunting and gathering in favour of horticulture. Hunters and gatherers living amid plentiful vegetation and game probably saw little reason to embrace the new technology (Fisher, 1979). The Yanomamö of the Brazilian rainforest (described in Chapter 4, 'Culture'), illustrate the common practice of combining horticulture with more traditional hunting and gathering (Chagnon, 1992).

Then, too, people in particularly arid regions (such as the Middle East) or mountainous areas (such as in the Alps, where the Iceman lived) found horticulture to be of little value. Such people turned to a different strategy for survival, **pastoralism**, which is *technology based on the domestication of animals*. Still others combined horticulture and pastoralism to produce a variety of foods. Today, many horticultural–pastoral societies thrive in South America, Africa and Asia.

The domestication of plants and animals greatly increased food production, enabling societies to support not dozens but hundreds of people. Pastoralists remained nomadic, leading their herds to fresh grazing lands. Horticulturalists, by contrast, formed settlements, moving on only when they depleted the soil. These settlements, joined by trade, comprised multi-centred societies with overall populations often in the thousands.

Domesticating plants and animals generates a *material surplus* – more resources than necessary to sustain day-to-day living. A surplus frees some people from the job of securing food, allowing them to create crafts, engage in trade, cut hair, apply tattoos or serve as priests. In comparison to hunting and gathering societies, then, horticultural and pastoral societies display more specialised and complex social arrangements.

Hunters and gatherers recognise numerous spirits inhabiting the world. Horticulturalists, however, practise ancestor worship and conceive of God as creator. Pastoral societies carry this belief further, viewing God as directly involved in the well-being of the entire world. This view of God ('The Lord is my shepherd . . .', Psalm 23) is widespread among members of our own society because Christianity, Islam and Judaism originated as Middle Eastern, pastoral religions.

Expanding productive technology also intensifies social inequality. As some families produce more food than others, they assume positions of relative power and privilege. Forging alliances with other elite families ensures that social advantages endure over generations, and a formal system of social inequality emerges. Along with social hierarchy, rudimentary government – backed by military force – is formed to shore up the power of elites. However, without the ability to communicate or to travel quickly, a ruler can control only a limited number of people, so empire-building proceeds on a small scale.

The domestication of plants and animals surely made simpler societies more productive. But advancing technology is never entirely beneficial. Compared to hunters and gatherers, horticulturalists and pastoralists display more social inequality and, in many cases, engage in slavery, protracted warfare, and even cannibalism.

Agrarian societies

About 5,000 years ago – at about the time the Iceman roamed the earth – another technological revolution was under way in the Middle East that would eventually transform most of the world. This was the discovery of **agriculture**, *the technology of large-scale farming using ploughs harnessed to animals or more powerful sources of energy*. The social significance of the animal-drawn plough, along with other technological innovations of the period – including irrigation, the wheel, writing, numbers, and the expanding use of metals – clearly suggests the arrival of a new kind of society.

Farmers with animal-drawn ploughs cultivated fields vastly larger than the garden-sized plots worked by horticulturalists. Ploughs have the additional advantage of turning, and thereby aerating, the soil to

Of Egypt's 130 pyramids, the Great Pyramids at Giza are the largest. Each of the three major structures stands more than forty stories high and is composed of 3 million massive stone blocks. Some 4,500 years ago, tens of thousands of people laboured to construct these pyramids so that one man, the pharaoh, might have a god-like monument for his tomb. Clearly social inequality in this agrarian society was striking.

Source: Woodfin Camp & Associates – Robert Frerck

increase fertility. Such technology encouraged agrarian societies to farm the same land for decades, which in turn led to humanity's first permanent settlements. Large food surpluses, transported on animal-powered wagons, allowed agrarian societies to expand to unprecedented land area and population. As an extreme case, the Roman Empire at its height (about 100 CE) boasted a population of 70 million spread over some 2 million square miles (Stavrianos, 1983; Lenski, Nolan and Lenski, 1995).

As always, increasing production meant greater specialisation. Tasks once performed by everyone, such as clearing land and securing food, became distinct occupations. Specialisation made the early barter system obsolete and prompted the invention of money as a common standard of exchange. The appearance of money facilitated trade, sparking the growth of cities as economic centres with populations soaring into the millions.

Agrarian societies exhibit dramatic social inequality. In many cases, peasants or slaves constitute a sig-

nificant share of the population and labour for elites. Freed from manual work, elites can then devote their time to the study of philosophy, art and literature.

Among hunters and gatherers and also among horticulturalists, women are the primary providers of food. The development of agriculture, however, appears to have propelled men into a position of social dominance (Boulding, 1976; Fisher, 1979). The box looks more closely at the declining position of women at this point in the course of sociocultural evolution.

Religion reinforces the power of agricultural elites. Religious doctrine typically propounds the idea that people are morally obligated to perform whatever tasks correspond to their place in the social order. Many of the 'wonders of the ancient world', such as the Great Wall of China and the Great Pyramids of Egypt, were possible because emperors and pharaohs wielded virtually absolute power to mobilise their people to endure a lifetime of labour without pay.

In agrarian societies, then, elites gain unparalleled power. To maintain control of large empires, leaders

DIFFERENT VOICES

Technology and the changing status of women

In technologically simple societies of the past, women produced more food than men did. Hunters and gatherers valued meat highly, but men's hunting was not a dependable source of nourishment. Thus vegetation gathered by women was the primary means of ensuring survival. Similarly, tools and seeds used in horticulture developed under the control of women, who already had primary responsibility for providing and preparing food. For their part, men engaged in trade and tended herds of animals. Only at harvest time did both sexes work together.

About 5,000 years ago, humans discovered how to mould metals. This technology spread by cultural diffusion, primarily along trade networks forged by men. Thus it was men who devised the metal plough and, since they already managed animals, they soon thought to hitch the implement to a cow.

This great innovation propelled the transition from horticulture to agriculture and, for the first time, thrust men into a dominant position in the production of food. Elise Boulding explains how this technological breakthrough undermined the social standing of women:

The shift of the status of the woman farmer may have happened quite rapidly, once there were two male specialisations relating to agriculture: plowing and the care of cattle. This situation left women with all the many subsidiary tasks, including weeding and carrying water to the fields. The new fields were larger, so women had to work just as many hours as they did before, but now they worked at more secondary tasks. This would contribute further to the erosion of the status of women. ●

Sources: Based on Boulding (1976) and Fisher (1979).

require the services of a wide range of administrators. Consequently, along with the growing economy, the political system becomes established as a distinct sphere of life.

Agrarian societies have greater specialisation and more social inequality. And, compared to horticultural and pastoral societies, agrarian societies differ more from one another because advancing technology can increase human control over the natural world.

Industrial societies

Industrialism is *technology that powers sophisticated machinery with advanced sources of energy*. Until the industrial era, the major source of energy was the muscle power of humans and other animals. At the dawning of the *Industrial Revolution*, about 1750, mills and factories relied on flowing water and later steam to power ever-larger and more efficient machinery.

Once this technology was at hand, societies began to change faster, as shown in Figure 3.1. Industrial societies transformed themselves more in a century than they had in thousands of years before. As explained in

Chapter 1 ('The Sociological Perspective'), this stunning change stimulated the birth of sociology itself. During the nineteenth century, railways and steamships revolutionised transportation, and steel-framed skyscrapers recast the urban landscape, dwarfing the cathedrals that symbolised an earlier age.

As the twentieth century opened, the internal combustion engine further reshaped Western societies, and electricity was fast becoming the basis for countless 'modern conveniences'. Electronic communication, including the telephone, radio and television, was mass-producing cultural patterns and gradually making a large world seem smaller and smaller. More recently, transportation technology has given humanity the capacity to fly faster than sound and even to break the bonds of earth. Nuclear power has also changed the world for ever. And, during the last generation, computers have ushered in the *Information Revolution*, dramatically increasing humanity's capacity to process words and numbers.

Work, too, has changed. In agrarian societies, most men and women work in the home and on the land. Industrialisation, however, creates factories near centralised machinery and energy sources. Lost in the process are close working relationships and strong kinship ties, as well as many of the traditional values, beliefs and customs that guide agrarian life.

Industrialism engenders societies of unparalleled prosperity. Although health in the industrial cities of Europe and North America was initially poor, a rising standard of living and advancing health-related technology gradually brought infectious diseases under control. Consequently, life expectancy increased, fuelling rapid population growth. Industrialisation also draws people from the countryside to the cities where the factories are built. So, while roughly one in ten members of agrarian societies lives in cities, three out of four people in industrial societies are urbanites.

Occupational specialisation, which expanded over the long course of sociocultural evolution, has become more pronounced than ever. Industrial people often size up one another in terms of their jobs, rather than according to their kinship ties as agrarian people do. Rapid change and movement from place to place also generate anonymity and cultural diversity, sparking the formation of numerous subcultures and countercultures, as described in Chapter 4 ('Culture').

Figure 3.1 ● The increasing number of technological innovations
This figure illustrates the number of technological innovations in Western Europe after the beginning of the Industrial Revolution in the mid-eighteenth century. Technological innovation occurs at an accelerating rate because each innovation spins off existing cultural elements to produce many further innovations.

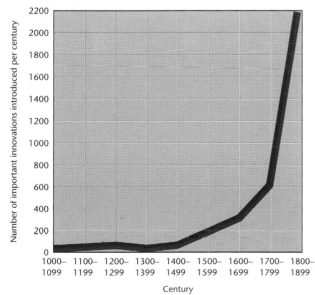

Source: Lenski, Nolan and Lenski (1995)

Industrial technology recasts the family, too, diminishing its traditional significance as the centre of social life. No longer does the family serve as the primary setting for economic production, learning, and religious worship. And, as Chapter 17 ('Families') explains in detail, technological change also underlies the trend away from so-called traditional families to greater numbers of single people, divorced people, single-parent families, lesbian and gay coupling, and stepfamilies.

Early industrialisation concentrated the benefits of advancing technology on a small segment of the population, with the majority living in poverty. In time, however, the material benefits of industrial productivity spread more widely. Poverty remains a serious problem in industrial societies, but compared to the situation a century ago, the standard of living has risen fivefold, and economic, social and political inequality has declined. Some social levelling, detailed in Chapter 9 ('Social Stratification'), occurs because industrial societies demand a literate and skilled labour force. While most people in agrarian societies are illiterate, industrial societies provide state-funded

Table 3.1 ● Sociocultural evolution: a summary

Type of society	Historical period	Productive technology	Population size	Settlement pattern
Hunting and gathering societies	Only type of society until about 12,000 years ago; still common several centuries ago; the few examples remaining today are threatened with extinction	Primitive weapons	25–40 people	Nomadic
Horticultural and pastoral societies	From about 12,000 years ago, with decreasing numbers after about 3000 BCE	Horticultural societies use hand tools for cultivating plants; pastoral societies are based on the domestication of animals	Settlements of several hundred people, interconnected through trading ties to form societies of several thousand people	Horticulturalists form relatively small permanent settlements; pastoralists are nomadic
Agrarian societies	From about 5,000 years ago, with large but decreasing numbers today	Animal-drawn plough	Millions of people	Cities become common, though they generally contain only a small proportion of the population
Industrial societies	From about 1750 to the present	Advanced sources of energy; mechanised production	Millions of people	Cities contain most of the population
Postindustrial societies	Emerging in recent decades	Computers that support an information-based economy	Millions of people	Population remains concentrated in cities

schooling and confer numerous political rights on virtually everyone. Industrialisation, in fact, intensifies demands for political participation, as seen recently in South Korea, Taiwan, the People's Republic of China, the former Soviet Union, and the societies of Eastern Europe.

Postindustrial societies

Many industrial societies now appear to be entering yet another phase of technological development. A generation ago, sociologist Daniel Bell (1973) coined the term **postindustrialism** to refer to *technology that supports an information-based economy*. While production in industrial societies focuses on factories and machinery that generate material goods, postindustrial production focuses on computers and other electronic devices that create, process, store and apply information. At the individual level, members of industrial societies concentrate on learning mechanical skills; people in postindustrial societies, however, work on honing information-based skills for work involving computers, facsimile machines, satellites and other forms of communication technology.

As this shift in key skills indicates, the emergence of postindustrialism dramatically changes a society's occupational structure. Chapter 15 ('The Economy, Consumption and Work') examines this process in detail, explaining that a postindustrial society utilises less and less of its labour force for industrial production. At the same time, the ranks of clerical workers, managers, and other people who process information (in fields ranging from academia and advertising to marketing and public relations) swell rapidly.

The Information Revolution is, of course, most pronounced in industrial, high-income societies, yet the reach of this new technology is so great that it is affecting the entire world. As explained in Chapter 4 ('Culture'), the unprecedented worldwide flow of information originating in rich nations like our own has the predictable effect of tying far-flung societies together and fostering common patterns of global culture. This extends the process of **globalisation**.

Table 3.1 summarises how technology helps shape societies at different stages of sociocultural evolution.

The limits of technology

While technology remedies many human problems by raising productivity, eliminating disease, and sometimes simply by

Social organisation	Examples
Family centred; specialisation limited to age and sex; little social inequality	Pygmies of central Africa Bushmen of south-western Africa Aborigines of Australia Semai of Malaysia Kaska Indians of Canada
Family centred; religious system begins to develop; moderate specialisation; increased social inequality	Middle-Eastern societies about 5000 BCE Various societies today in New Guinea and other Pacific islands Yanomamö today in South America
Family loses significance as distinctive religious, political and economic systems emerge; extensive specialisation; increased social inequality	Egypt during construction of the Great Pyramids Medieval Europe Numerous nonindustrial societies of the world today
Distinct religious, political, economic, educational and family systems; highly specialised; marked social inequality persists, diminishing somewhat over time	Most societies today in Europe and North America, Australia and Japan generate most of the world's industrial production
Similar to industrial societies with information processing and other service work gradually replacing industrial production	Industrial societies noted above are now entering postindustrial stage

relieving boredom, it provides no 'quick fix' for deeply rooted social problems. *Poverty* remains the plight of millions of women and men in Europe (detailed in Chapter 10 'Class, Poverty and Welfare') and of 1 billion people worldwide (see Chapter 11, 'Global Stratification'). Moreover, with the capacity to reshape the world, technology has created new problems that our ancestors hardly could have imagined. Industrial societies provide more personal freedom, often at the cost of the sense of community that characterised agrarian life. Further, although the most powerful societies of today's world infrequently engage in all-out warfare, *international conflict* now poses unimaginable horrors. Should nations ever unleash even a fraction of their present stockpiles of nuclear weapons, human society would almost certainly regress to a technologically primitive state if, indeed, we survived at all.

Another stubborn social problem involves humanity's relation to the *physical environment*. Each stage in sociocultural evolution has introduced more powerful sources of energy and accelerated our appetite for the earth's resources at a rate even faster than population is growing. We now face an issue of vital concern – one that is the focus of Chapter 23 ('Environment and the Risk Society'): Can humanity continue to pursue material prosperity without subjecting the planet to damage and strains from which it will never recover?

In some respects, then, technological advances have improved life and brought the world's people closer together within a 'global village'. Yet in technology's wake are daunting problems of establishing peace, ensuring justice, and sustaining a safe environment – problems that technology alone can never solve.

● Karl Marx: society and conflict

The first of our classic visions of society comes from Karl Marx (1818–83), who is introduced in the box. Few observed the industrial transformation of Europe as keenly as he did. Marx spent most of his adult life in London, then the capital of the vast British Empire. He was awed by the productive power of the new factories; not only were European societies producing more goods than ever before, but a global system of commerce was funnelling resources from around the world through British factories at a dizzying rate.

Marx saw that the concentration of industry's riches were increasingly in the hands of a few. A walk almost anywhere in London revealed dramatic extremes of splendid affluence and wretched squalor. A handful of aristocrats and industrialists lived in fabulous mansions, well staffed by servants, where they enjoyed luxury and privileges barely imaginable by the majority of their fellow Londoners. Most people laboured long hours for low wages, living in slums or even sleeping in the streets, where many eventually succumbed to poor nutrition and infectious disease.

Throughout his life, Marx wrestled with a basic contradiction: in a society so rich, how could so many be so poor? Just as important, Marx asked, how can this situation be changed? He was motivated by compassion for humanity, and sought to help a society already badly divided forge what he hoped would be a new and just social order.

The key to Marx's thinking is the idea of **social conflict**, *struggle between segments of society over valued resources*. Social conflict can, of course, take many forms: individuals may quarrel, some towns have longstanding rivalries, and nations sometimes go to war. For Marx, however, the most significant form of social conflict involved clashes between social classes that arise from the way a society produces material goods.

Society and production

Living in the nineteenth century, Marx observed the early stage of industrial capitalism in Europe. This economic system, Marx noted, transformed a small part of the population into **capitalists**, *people who own factories and other productive enterprises*. A capitalist's goal is profit, which results from selling a product for more than it costs to produce. Capitalism transforms most of the population into industrial workers, whom Marx called the **proletariat**, *people who provide labour necessary to operate factories and other productive enterprises*. Workers sell their labour for the wages they need to live. To Marx, an inevitable conflict between capitalists and workers has its roots in the productive process itself. To maximise profits, capitalists must minimise wages, generally their single greatest expense. Workers, however, want wages to be as high as possible. Since profits and wages come from the same pool of funds, ongoing conflict occurs. Marx argued that this conflict would end

Karl Marx: an agenda for change

Few names evoke as strong a response as Karl Marx. Some consider him a genius and a prophet, while others see only evil in his ideas. Everyone agrees that Marx stands among the social thinkers with the greatest impact on the world's people. Today, more than one-fifth of all humanity live in societies that consider themselves Marxist.

Nor was Marx a stranger to controversy during his lifetime. Born in the German city of Trier, he earned a doctorate in 1841 and began working as a newspaper editor. But his relentless social criticism sparked clashes with government authorities, who managed to drive Marx from Germany to Paris. Soon controversy forced him to flee from France as well, and Marx spent the rest of his life in London.

Along with Max Weber and Emile Durkheim, Marx was a major figure in the development of sociology, as we saw in Chapter 1 ('The Sociological Perspective'). However, sociologists in the United States paid relatively

Source: Brown Brothers

little attention to his ideas until the 1960s. Why? The answer lies in Marx's explicit criticism of industrial-capitalist society. Early sociologists often dismissed his ideas as mere 'politics' rather than serious scholarship. But for Marx, scholarship was politics. While most sociologists heeded Max Weber's call for value-free research by attempting to minimise or conceal their own values (see Chapter 2, 'Sociological Investigation'), Marx placed values at the centre of his thinking. Marx did not merely observe society; he offered a rousing prescription for profound social change. Now that we have come to recognise the extent to which values shape all ideas, Marx's social analysis has finally received the attention it deserves as a pivotal approach to sociology. ●

only when people abandoned the capitalist system.

All societies are composed of **social institutions**, defined as *the major spheres of social life, or society's subsystems, organised to meet basic human needs*. In his analysis of society, Marx contended that one specific institution – the economy – dominates all others when it comes to steering the direction of a society. Drawing on the philosophical doctrine of historical *materialism*, which asserts that how humans produce material goods shapes the rest of society, Marx claimed that all the other major social institutions – the political system, family, religion and education – operated under the influence of a society's economy. Marx argued that the economy is 'the real foundation. . . . The mode of

production in material life determines the general character of the social, political, and spiritual processes of life' (1959: 43; orig. 1859).

Marx therefore viewed the economic system as the base or social *infrastructure* (*infra* is Latin meaning 'below'). Other social institutions, including the family, the political system and religion, which are built on this foundation, form society's *superstructure*. These institutions extend economic principles into other areas of life, as illustrated in Figure 3.2. In practical terms, social institutions reinforce the domination of the capitalists, by legally protecting their wealth, for example, and by transferring property from one generation to the next through the family.

Figure 3.2 ● Karl Marx's model of society
This diagram illustrates Marx's materialist view that the process of economic production underlies and shapes the entire society. Economic production involves both technology (industry, in the case of capitalism) and social relationships (for capitalism, the relationship between the capitalists, who control the process of economic production, and the workers, who are simply a source of labour). Upon this infrastructure, or foundation, are built the major social institutions as well as core cultural values and ideas. Taken together, these additional social elements represent the society's superstructure. Marx maintained that every part of a society operates in concert with the economic system.

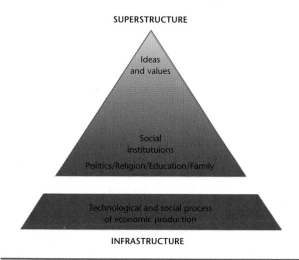

Generally speaking, members of industrial-capitalist societies do not view their legal or family systems as hotbeds of social conflict. On the contrary, individuals come to see their rights to private property as 'natural'. Many people find it easy to think that affluent people have earned their wealth, while those who are poor or out of work lack skills or motivation. Marx rejected this kind of reasoning as rooted in a capitalist preoccupation with the 'bottom line' that treats human well-being as a market commodity. Poverty and unemployment are not inevitable; as Marx saw it, grand wealth clashing with grinding poverty represents merely one set of human possibilities generated by capitalism (Cuff and Payne, 1979).

Marx rejected capitalist common sense, therefore, as **false consciousness**, *explanations of social problems grounded in the shortcomings of individuals rather than the flaws of society*. Marx was saying, in effect, that industrial capitalism itself is responsible for many of the social problems he saw all around him. False consciousness, he maintained, victimises people by obscuring the real cause of their problems.

Conflict in history

Marx studied how societies have changed throughout history, noting that they often evolve gradually, though they sometimes change in rapid, revolutionary fashion. Marx observed that change is partly prompted by technological advance. But he steadfastly held that conflict between economic groups is the major engine of change.

Early hunters and gatherers formed primitive communist societies. The word *communism* refers to a social system in which the production of food and other material goods is a common effort shared more or less equally by all members of society. Because the resources of nature were available to all hunters and gatherers (rather than privately owned), and because everyone performed similar work (rather than dividing work into highly specialised tasks), there was little possibility for social conflict.

Horticulture, Marx noted, introduced significant social inequality. Among horticultural, pastoral, and early agrarian societies – which Marx lumped together as the 'ancient world' – the victors in frequent warfare forced their captives into servitude. A small elite (the 'masters') and their slaves were thus locked in an irreconcilable pattern of social conflict (Zeitlin, 1981).

Agriculture brought still more wealth to members of the elite, fuelling further social conflict. Agrarian serfs, occupying the lowest reaches of European feudalism from about the twelfth to the eighteenth centuries, were only slightly better off than slaves. In Marx's view, the power of both the Church and the State defended feudal inequality by defining the existing social order as God's will. Thus, to Marx, feudalism amounted to little more than 'exploitation, veiled by religious and political illusions' (Marx and Engels, 1972: 337; orig. 1848).

Gradually, new productive forces undermined the feudal order. Commerce grew steadily throughout the Middle Ages as trade networks expanded and the power of guilds increased. Merchants and skilled crafts workers in the cities formed a new social category, the *bourgeoisie* (a French word meaning 'of the town'). Profits earned through expanding trade brought the bourgeoisie increasing wealth. After the mid-eighteenth century, with factories at their command, the bourgeoisie became true capitalists with power that soon rivalled that of the ancient, landed nobility. While the nobility regarded this upstart 'commercial' class with disdain, the latter's increasing wealth gradually shifted the control of European societies to the capitalists.

Industrialisation also fostered the development of the proletariat. English landowners converted fields once tilled by serfs into grazing land for sheep to secure wool for the prospering textile mills. Forced from the land, serfs migrated to cities to work in factories, where they joined the burgeoning industrial proletariat. Marx envisioned these workers one day joining hands across national boundaries to form a unified class, setting the stage for historic confrontation, this time between capitalists and the exploited workers.

Capitalism and class conflict

Much of Marx's analysis centres on destructive aspects of industrial capitalism – especially the ways in which it promotes class conflict and alienation. In examining his views on these topics, we will come to see why he advocated the overthrow of capitalist societies.

'The history of all hitherto existing society is the history of class struggles.' With this declaration, Marx and his collaborator Friedrich Engels began their best-known statement, the *Manifesto of the Communist Party* (1972: 335; orig. 1848). The idea of social class is at the heart of Marx's critique of capitalist society. Industrial capitalism, like earlier types of society, contains two major social classes – the dominant people and the oppressed – reflecting the two basic positions in the productive system. Capitalists and proletarians are the historical descendants of masters and slaves in the ancient world and nobles and serfs in feudal systems. In each case, one class controls the other as productive property. Marx used the term **class conflict** (and sometimes *class struggle*) to refer to *antagonism between entire classes over the distribution of wealth and power in society*.

Class conflict, then, dates back to civilisations long gone. What distinguishes the conflict in capitalist society, Marx pointed out, is how it has come out into the open. Agrarian nobles and serfs, for all their differences, were bound together by long-standing traditions and a host of mutual obligations. Industrial capitalism dissolved those ties so that pride and honour were replaced by 'naked self-interest' and the pursuit of profit in a blatant exercise of oppression. Marx believed that the proletariat, with no personal ties to the oppressors, had little reason to stand for its own subjugation.

But, though industrial capitalism brought class conflict out in the open, Marx realised that fundamental social change would not come easily. First, he claimed, workers must *become aware* of their shared oppression and see capitalism as its true cause. Second, they must *organise and act* to address their problems. This means workers must replace false consciousness with **class consciousness,** *the recognition by workers of their unity as a class in opposition to capitalists and, ultimately, to capitalism itself.* Because the inhumanity of early capitalism was plain for him to see, Marx concluded that industrial workers would inevitably rise up *en masse* to destroy industrial capitalism.

In the twentieth century, Marxism became one of the world's most influential social movements, and shaped the economic and political life of one-fifth of the world's people including China, the Soviet Union and Eastern Europe. But the socialist regimes of Eastern Europe and the former Soviet Union collapsed in the late 1980s. The political transformation of this world region is symbolised by the removal of statues of Vladimir Lenin (1870–1924), architect of Soviet Marxism, in city after city during the last few years.

Source: Gamma-Liaison, Inc.

And what of the workers' adversaries, the capitalists? The capitalists' formidable wealth and power, protected by the institutions of society, might seem invulnerable. But Marx saw a weakness in the capitalist armour. Motivated by a desire for personal gain, capitalists fear the competition of other capitalists. Thus Marx thought that capitalists would be reluctant to band together, even though they too share common interests. Furthermore, he reasoned, capitalists keep employees' wages low in their drive to maximise profits. This strategy, in turn, bolsters the resolve of workers to forge an alliance against them. In the long run, Marx surmised, capitalists would only contribute to their own undoing.

Capitalism and alienation

Marx also condemned capitalism for producing **alienation**, *the experience of isolation resulting from powerlessness*. Dominated by capitalists and dehumanised by their jobs (especially monotonous and repetitive factory work), proletarians find little satisfaction in, and feel individually powerless to improve, their situation. Herein lies another contradiction of capitalist society: as human beings devise technology to gain power over the world, the productive process increasingly assumes power over human beings.

Workers view themselves as merely a commodity, a source of labour, bought by capitalists and discarded when no longer needed. Marx cited four ways in which capitalism alienates workers.

1. *Alienation from the act of working*. Ideally, people work both to meet immediate needs and to develop their long-range personal potential. Capitalism, however, denies workers a say in what they produce or how they produce it. Furthermore, much work is

DIFFERENT VOICES

Alienation and industrial capitalism

These excerpts from the book *Working* by Studs Terkel illustrate how dull, repetitive jobs can generate alienation for men and women.

Phil Stallings is a 27-year-old car worker in a Ford assembly plant in Chicago.

I start the automobile, the first welds. From there it goes to another line, where the floor's put on, the roof, the trunk, the hood, the doors. Then it's put on a frame. There is hundreds of lines. . . .

I stand in one spot, about two- or three-feet area, all night. The only time a person stops is when the line stops. We do about thirty-two jobs per car, per unit. Forty-eight units an hour, eight hours a day. Thirty-two times forty-eight times eight. Figure it out. That's how many times I push that button.

The noise, oh it's tremendous. You open your mouth and you're liable to get a mouthful of sparks. [Shows his arms.] That's a burn, these are burns. You don't compete against the noise. You go to yell and at the same time you're straining to manoeuvre the gun to where you have to weld.

You got some guys that are uptight, and they're not sociable. It's too rough. You pretty much stay to yourself. You get involved with yourself. You dream, you think of things you've done. I drift back continuously to when I was a kid and what me and my brothers did. The things you love most are what you drift back into.

It don't stop. It just goes and goes and goes. I bet there's men who have lived and died out there, never seen the end of the line. And they never will – because it's endless. It's like a serpent. It's just all body, no tail. It can do things to you. . . .

Twenty-four-year-old Sharon Atkins is a college graduate working as a telephone receptionist for a large midwestern business.

I don't have much contact with people. You can't see them. You don't know if they're laughing, if they're being satirical or being kind. So your conversations become very abrupt. I notice that in talking to people. My conversation would be very short and clipped, in short sentences, the way I talk to people all day on the telephone. . . .

You try to fill up your time with trying to think about other things: what you're going to do on the weekend or about your family. You have to use your imagination. If you don't have a very good one and you bore easily, you're in trouble. Just to fill in time, I write real bad poetry or letters to myself and to other people and never mail them. The letters are fantasies, sort of rambling, how I feel, how depressed I am.

. . . I never answer the phone at home. ●

Source: Terkel (1974).

tedious, involving countless repetitions of routine tasks. The modern-day replacement of human labour by machines would hardly have surprised Marx; as far as he was concerned, capitalism had turned human beings into machines long ago.

2. *Alienation from the products of work*. The product of work belongs not to workers but to capitalists, who dispose of it for profit. Thus, Marx reasoned, the more workers invest of themselves into their work, the more they lose.

3. *Alienation from other workers*. Marx saw work itself as the productive affirmation of human community. Industrial capitalism, however, transforms work from a cooperative venture into a competitive one. As the box on page 80 illustrates, factory work often provides little chance for human companionship.

4. *Alienation from human potential*. Industrial capitalism alienates workers from their human potential. Marx argued that a worker 'does not fulfill himself in his work but denies himself, has a feeling of misery rather than well-being, does not freely develop his physical and mental energies, but is physically exhausted and mentally debased. The worker, therefore, feels himself to be at home only during his leisure time, whereas at work he feels homeless' (1964: 124–5; orig. 1844). In short, industrial capitalism distorts an activity that should express the best qualities in human beings into a dull and dehumanising experience.

Marx viewed alienation, in its various forms, as a barrier to social change. But he hoped that industrial workers eventually would overcome their alienation by uniting into a true social class, aware of the cause of their problems and galvanised to transform society.

Revolution

The only way out of the trap of capitalism, contended Marx, was deliberately to refashion society. He envisioned a more humane and egalitarian productive system, one that would enhance rather than undermine social ties. He called this system *socialism*. Marx knew well the obstacles to a socialist revolution; even so, he was disappointed that he never lived to see workers in England overthrow industrial capitalism. Still, convinced of the basic immorality of capitalist society, he was sure that in time the working majority would realise that they held the key to a better future in their own hands. This transformation would certainly be revolutionary, perhaps even violent. What emerged from the workers' revolution, however, would be a cooperative socialist society intended to meet the needs of all.

The discussion of social stratification in Chapter 9 ('Social Stratification') reveals more about changes in industrial-capitalist societies since Marx's time and why the revolution he championed has not taken place. Later chapters also delve into why people in the societies of Eastern Europe recently revolted against established socialist governments. But, in his own time, Marx looked towards the future with hope (1972: 362; orig. 1848): 'The proletarians have nothing to lose but their chains. They have a world to win.'

● Max Weber: the rationalisation of society

With a broad understanding of law, economics, religion and history, Max Weber (1864–1920) produced what many regard as the greatest individual contribution to sociology. He generated ideas that were very wide ranging, Here, we limit ourselves to his vision of how modern society differs from earlier types of social organisation (see the box).

As we saw earlier (Chapter 1, 'The Sociological Perspective') Weber's sociology was an action theory. Weber understood the power of technology but he departed from Marx's materialist analysis. For him, ideas – especially beliefs and values – have transforming power. Thus he saw modern society as the product, not just of new technology and capitalism, but of a new way of thinking. As we have seen, Weber also used **ideal types**, contrasting the ideal 'Protestant' with the ideal 'Jew', 'Hindu' and 'Buddhist'. We have already compared 'hunting and gathering societies' and 'industrial societies' as well as 'capitalism' and 'socialism'.

Tradition and rationality

Rather than categorise societies in terms of technology or productive systems, Max Weber highlighted differences in the ways people view the world. In simple terms, Weber concluded that members of preindustrial societies cling to *tradition*, while people in industrial-capitalist societies endorse *rationality*.

By **tradition**, Weber meant *sentiments and beliefs passed from generation to generation*. Thus traditional societies are guided by the past. Their members evaluate particular actions as right and proper precisely because these actions have been accepted for so long.

Max Weber: expanding the boundaries of sociology

To be called merely a 'sociologist' would probably have offended Max Weber. Not that he disliked the study of society; in fact, he spent most of his life doing just that. But Weber's contribution to understanding humanity is so broad and rich that no single discipline can claim him.

Born to a prosperous German family, Weber completed law school and set off on a legal career. But he soon felt confined by the work of a lawyer. Continuing his studies, he became a college professor. With his curiosity racing across the entire human condition, he compiled an amazing legacy of scholarship.

The influence of Weber's parents stands out in his work. His mother's devout Calvinism probably encouraged Weber's study of world religions and his classic study of Calvinism and its impact

on industrial capitalism, which we take up shortly. From his father, a notable politician, Weber clearly gained insights into the workings of political life and bureaucracy.

Weber flirted with politics, and his wife Marianne was a leading feminist of

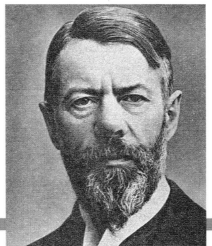

Source: PH College Archives

her time. But Weber found politics to be incompatible with scholarly work. The former, he claimed, demands action and personal conviction, while the latter requires impartiality and patient reflection. Weber tried to resolve this personal dilemma by urging his colleagues to become involved in politics outside the classroom while striving for scientific neutrality in their professional work.

For many reasons, Weber's life was far from happy. He did not get on well with his father, and soon after his father's death Weber began to suffer from psychological problems. Illness sharply limited his ability to work during the remainder of his life. Even so, the exceptional number of major studies he conducted has led many to regard him as the most brilliant sociologist in history. ●

People in modern societies take a different view of the world, argued Weber, embracing **rationality**, *deliberate, matter-of-fact calculation of the most efficient means to accomplish a particular goal*. Sentiment has no place in a rational world-view, which treats tradition simply as one kind of information. Typically, modern people choose to think and act on the basis of present and future consequences, evaluating jobs, schooling and even relationships in terms of what we put into them and what we expect to receive in return.

Weber viewed both the Industrial Revolution and capitalism as evidence of a historical surge of rationality. He used the phrase **rationalisation of society** to denote *the historical change from tradition to rationality*

as the dominant mode of human thought. Modern society, he concluded, has been 'disenchanted', as scientific thinking and technology have swept away sentimental ties to the past.

The willingness to adopt the latest technology, then, is one good indicator of how rationalised a society is. Indicating the global pattern of rationalisation, Map 3.2 shows where in the world facsimile (fax) machines are found. In general, the high-income countries of Europe and North America utilise these devices to the greatest degree while, in low-income nations, they are quite rare.

Drawing on Weber's comparative perspective – and the data found in the map – we deduce that various societies place different values on technological advancement. What one society might herald as a breakthrough, another might deem unimportant, and a third might strongly oppose as a threat to tradition. Inventors in ancient Greece, for instance, devised many surprisingly elaborate mechanical devices to perform household tasks. But since elites were well served by slaves, they viewed such inventions as mere entertainment. In Europe today, many small communities are guided by their traditions to staunchly oppose modern technology.

In Weber's view, then, technological innovation is promoted or hindered by the way people understand their world. He concluded that people in many societies discovered keys to technological change; however, only in the rational cultural climate of Western Europe did people exploit these discoveries to spark the Industrial Revolution (1958; orig. 1904–5).

Rationality, Calvinism and industrial capitalism

Is industrial capitalism a rational economic system? Here again, Weber and Marx came down on opposite sides of the issue. Weber considered industrial capitalism as the essence of rationality, since capitalists pursue profit in eminently rational ways. Marx, however, dismissed capitalism as the antithesis of rationality, claiming that it failed to meet the basic needs of most of the people (Gerth and Mills, 1946: 49).

But, to look more closely at Weber's analysis, how did industrial capitalism emerge in the first place? Weber contended that industrial capitalism was the legacy of Calvinism – a Christian religious movement spawned by the Protestant Reformation. Calvinists, Weber explained, approached life in a highly disciplined and rational way. Moreover, central to the religious doctrine of John Calvin (1509–64) was *predestination*, the idea that an all-knowing and all-powerful God has preordained some people for salvation and others for damnation. With everyone's fate set before birth, Calvinists believed that people could do nothing to alter their destiny. Nor could they even know what their future would be. Thus the lives of Calvinists were framed by hopeful visions of eternal salvation and anxious fears of unending damnation.

For such people, not knowing one's fate was intolerable. Calvinists gradually came to a resolution of sorts. Why shouldn't those chosen for glory in the next world, they reasoned, see signs of divine favour in *this* world? Such a conclusion prompted Calvinists to interpret worldly prosperity as a sign of God's grace. Anxious to acquire this reassurance, Calvinists threw themselves into a quest for success, applying rationality, discipline and hard work to their tasks. This pursuit of riches was not for its own sake, of course, since self-indulgently spending money was clearly sinful. Calvinists also were little moved to share their wealth with the poor, because they saw poverty as a sign of God's rejection. Their ever-present duty was to carry forward what they held to be their personal *calling* from God.

As they reinvested their profits for greater success, Calvinists built the foundation of capitalism. They piously used wealth to generate more wealth, practised personal thrift, and eagerly embraced whatever technological advances would bolster their efforts.

These traits, Weber explained, distinguished Calvinism from other world religions. Catholicism, the traditional religion in most of Europe, gave rise to a passive, 'otherworldly' view of life with hope of greater reward in the life to come. For Catholics, material wealth had none of the spiritual significance that so motivated Calvinists. And so it was, Weber concluded, that industrial capitalism became established primarily in areas of Europe where Calvinism had a strong hold.

Weber's study of Calvinism provides striking evidence of the power of ideas to shape society (versus Marx's contention that ideas merely reflect the process of economic production). But always sceptical of simple explanations, Weber knew that industrial capitalism had many roots. In fact, one purpose of this research was to counter Marx's narrow explanation of modern society in strictly economic terms.

As religious fervour weakened among later generations of Calvinists, Weber concluded, success-seeking personal discipline remained strong. A *religious* or, more precisely, *Protestant* ethic became simply a '*work* ethic'. From this point of view, industrial capitalism emerged as 'disenchanted' religion, with wealth now valued for its own sake. It is revealing that 'accounting', which to early Calvinists meant keeping a daily record of moral deeds, now refers simply to keeping track of money.

Map 3.2 ● High technology in global perspective

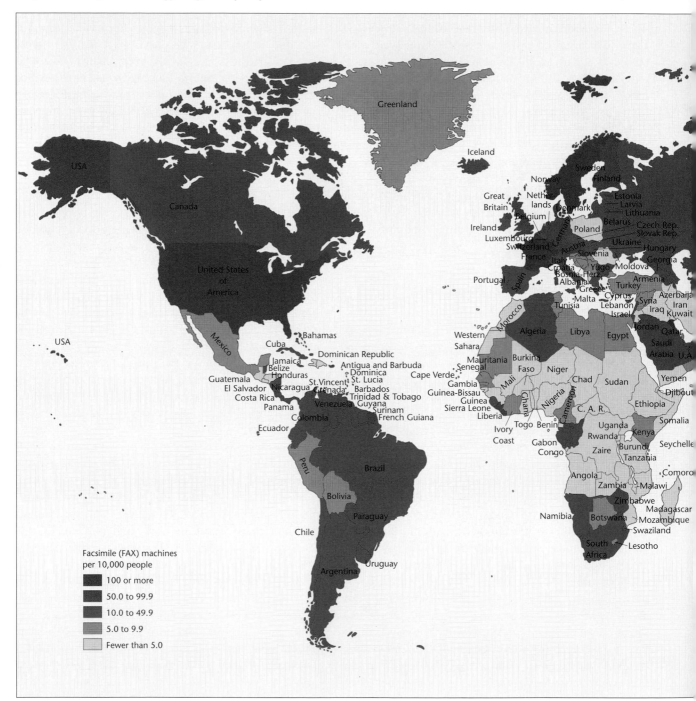

Facsimile (FAX) machines
per 10,000 people

- 100 or more
- 50.0 to 99.9
- 10.0 to 49.9
- 5.0 to 9.9
- Fewer than 5.0

Source: *Peters Atlas of the World* (1990)

Countries with traditional cultures ignore or even resist technological innovation; nations with highly rationalised ways of life eagerly embrace such changes. Facsimile (fax) machines, one common form of high technology, are numerous in high-income countries, where 5 million faxes fly along the 'information super-highway' every hour. In low-income nations, by contrast, fax machines are unknown to most people. Notice that, in Asia, fax machines are widely available only in Japan, South Korea, Taiwan, and the business centres of Hong Kong and Singapore.

Rational social organisation

Weber contended that, by unleashing the Industrial Revolution and sparking the development of capitalism, rationality had defined the character of modern society. Rational social organisation confers the following seven traits on today's social life.

1. *Distinctive social institutions.* Among hunters and gatherers, the family was the centre of virtually all activities. Gradually, however, other social institutions, including religious, political and economic systems, broke away from family life. In modern societies, institutions of education and health care have also appeared. The separation of social institutions – each detailed in a later chapter – is a rational strategy to address human needs more efficiently.

2. *Large-scale organisations.* Modern rationality is exemplified by a proliferation of large-scale organisations. As early as the horticultural era, political officials oversaw religious observances, public works and warfare. In medieval Europe, the Catholic Church grew larger still with thousands of officials. In modern, rational societies, the employees of national governments may number in the millions, and most people work for a large organisation.

3. *Specialised tasks.* Unlike members of traditional societies, individuals in modern societies pursue a wide range of specialised activities. The enormous breadth of occupations can be seen in any city's 'Yellow Pages', which typically runs to more than one thousand pages.

4. *Personal discipline.* Modern society puts a premium on self-directed discipline. For early Calvinists, of course, such an approach to life was rooted in religious belief. Although now distanced from its religious origins, discipline is still encouraged by cultural values such as achievement, success and efficiency.

5. *Awareness of time.* In traditional societies, people measure time according to the rhythm of sun and seasons. Modern people, by contrast, schedule events precisely by the hour and minute. Interestingly, clocks began appearing in European cities some five hundred years ago, just as commerce was starting to expand; soon, people began to think (to borrow Benjamin Franklin's phrase) that 'time is money'.

6. *Technical competence.* Members of traditional societies evaluate one another largely on the basis of *who* they are – how they are joined to others in the web of kinship. Modern rationality, by contrast, prompts us to judge people according to *what* they are – that is, with an eye towards their skills and abilities.

7. *Impersonality.* Finally, in a rational society, technical competence takes priority over close relationships, rendering the world impersonal. Modern social life can be viewed as the interplay of specialists concerned with particular tasks, rather than people broadly concerned with one another. Weber explained that we tend to devalue personal feelings and emotions as 'irrational' because they often are difficult to control.

Rationality and bureaucracy

Although the medieval church grew large, Weber argued that it was never entirely rational because its goal was to preserve tradition. Truly rational organisations, with the principal focus on efficiency, appeared only in the last few centuries. The organisational type that Weber called *bureaucracy* became pronounced along with capitalism as an expression of rationality.

Chapter 7 ('Groups and Organisations') explains that bureaucracy is the model for modern businesses, government agencies, trades unions and universities. For now, note that Weber considered this organisational form to be the clearest expression of a rational world-view because its chief elements – offices, duties and policies – are intended to achieve specific goals as efficiently as possible. By contrast, the inefficiency of traditional organisation is reflected in its hostility to change. In short, Weber asserted that bureaucracy transformed all of society in the same way that industrialisation transformed the economy.

Still, Weber emphasised that rational bureaucracy has a special affinity to capitalism. He wrote:

Today, it is primarily the capitalist market economy which demands that the official business of public administration be discharged precisely, unambiguously, continuously, and with as much speed as possible. Normally, the very large capitalist enterprises are themselves unequalled models of strict bureaucratic organisation. (1978: 974; orig. 1921)

Rationality and alienation

Max Weber joined with Karl Marx in recognising the unparalleled efficiency of industrial capitalism. Weber also shared Marx's conclusion that modern society generates widespread alienation, though for different reasons. For Weber, the primary problem is not the economic inequality that so troubled Marx, but the stifling regulation and dehumanisation that comes with expanding bureaucracy. It leads to an increasing 'disenchantment with the world'.

Bureaucracies, Weber warned, treat people as a series of cases rather than as unique individuals. In addition, working for large organisations demands highly specialised and often tedious routines. In the end, Weber envisioned modern society as a vast and growing system of rules seeking to regulate everything and threatening to crush the human spirit.

An irony found in the work of Marx reappears in Weber's thinking: rather than serve humanity, modern society turns on its creators and enslaves them. In language reminiscent of Marx's description of the human toll of industrial capitalism, Weber portrayed the modern individual as 'only a small cog in a ceaselessly moving mechanism that prescribes to him an endlessly fixed routine of march' (1978: 988; orig. 1921). Thus, knowing well the advantages of modern society, Weber ended his life deeply pessimistic. He feared that the rationalisation of society would end up reducing people to robots.

● Emile Durkheim: society and function

'To love society is to love something beyond us and something in ourselves.' These are the words of Emile Durkheim (1858–1917), another architect of sociology, introduced in the box. This curious phrase (1974: 55; orig. 1924) distills one more influential vision of human society.

PROFILE

Emile Durkheim: unmasking the power of society

Why would being a professor of sociology be controversial? Because there weren't any, at least not in France, until Emile Durkheim became the first one in 1887. Up to that time, the study of human behaviour was left to biologists and psychologists. But Durkheim made the assertion – widely disputed at the time – that one can understand people, not by looking at individuals, but only by examining their society.

Durkheim's investigation of suicide, detailed in Chapter 1 ('The Sociological Perspective'), offers persuasive evidence of society's power to shape human behaviour. In this classic study,

Durkheim showed that people's place within the social system – as women or men, rich or poor, Catholic, Jew or Protestant – affects even this most personal act.

Durkheim's work, like that of Marx and Weber, is discussed in many later chapters. His contributions to the understanding of crime figure prominently in Chapter 8 ('Deviance and Control'). Durkheim also spent much of his life investigating religion, which he held to be a key foundation of social integration (see Chapter 18, 'Religion'). Just as important, Durkheim is also one of the major architects of the structural-functional paradigm, which we refer to in almost every chapter that follows. ●

Source: Corbis-Bettmann

Structure: society beyond ourselves

First and foremost, Emile Durkheim recognised that society exists beyond ourselves. Society is more than the individuals who compose it; society has a life of its own that stretches beyond our personal experiences. It was here long before we were born, it makes claims on us while we are alive, and it will remain long after we are gone. Patterns of human behaviour, Durkheim explained, form established *structures*; they are *social facts* that have an objective reality beyond the lives and perceptions of particular individuals. Cultural norms, values, religious beliefs – all endure as social facts.

And because society looms larger than individual lives, it has the *power* to shape our thoughts and actions, Durkheim noted. So studying individuals alone (as psychologists or biologists do) can never capture the essence of human experience. Society is more than the sum of its parts; it exists as a complex organism rooted in our collective life. A reception class in a primary school, a family sharing a meal, people milling about a country auction – all are examples of the countless situations that have an organisation apart from any particular individual who has ever participated in them.

Once created by people, then, society takes on a momentum of its own, confronting its creators and demanding a measure of obedience. For our part, we experience society's influence as we come to see the order in our lives or as we face temptation and feel the tug of morality.

Function: society in action

Having established that society has structure, Durkheim turned to the concept of *function*. The significance of any social fact, he explained, extends beyond individuals to the operation of society itself.

To illustrate, consider crime. Most people think of lawbreaking as harmful acts that some individuals inflict on others. But, looking beyond individuals, Durkheim saw that crime has a vital function for the ongoing life of society itself. As Chapter 8 ('Deviance and Control') explains, only by recognising and responding to acts as criminal do people construct and defend morality, which gives necessary shape to our collective life. For this reason, Durkheim rejected the common view of crime as 'pathological'. On the contrary, he concluded, crime is quite 'normal' for the most basic of reasons: a society could not exist without it (1964a, orig. 1895; 1964b, orig. 1893).

Personality: society in ourselves

Durkheim contended that society is not only 'beyond ourselves', it is also 'in ourselves'. Each of us, in short, builds a personality by internalising social facts. How we act, think and feel – our essential humanity – is drawn from the society that nurtures us. Moreover, Durkheim explained, society regulates human beings through moral discipline. Durkheim held that human beings are naturally insatiable and in constant danger of being overpowered by our own desires: 'The more one has, the more one wants, since satisfactions received only stimulate instead of filling needs' (1966: 248; orig. 1897). Having given us life, then, society must also instil restraints in us.

Nowhere is the need for societal regulation better illustrated than in Durkheim's study of suicide (1966; orig. 1897), detailed in Chapter 1. Why is it that, over the years, rock stars have been so vulnerable to self-destruction? Durkheim had the answer long before anyone made electric music: it is the *least* regulated categories of people that suffer the *highest* rates of suicide. The greater licence afforded to those who are young, rich and famous exacts a high price in terms of the risk of suicide.

Modernity and anomie

Compared to traditional societies, modern societies impose fewer restrictions on everyone. Durkheim acknowledges the advantages of modern freedom, but he warned of a rise in **anomie**, *a condition in which society provides little moral guidance to individuals*. What so many celebrities describe as 'almost being destroyed by their fame' is one extreme example of the corrosive effects of anomie. Sudden fame tears people away from their families and familiar routines, disrupting society's support and regulation of an individual, sometimes with fatal results. Durkheim instructs us, therefore, that the desires of the individual must be balanced by the claims and guidance of society – a balance that has become precarious in the modern world.

Evolving societies: the division of labour

Like Marx and Weber, Durkheim witnessed at first hand the rapid social transformation of Europe during the nineteenth century. Analysing this change, Durkheim saw a sweeping evolution in the forms of social organisation.

In preindustrial societies, explained Durkheim, strong tradition operates as the social cement that binds people together. In fact, what he termed the *collective conscience* is so strong that the community moves quickly to punish anyone who dares to challenge conventional ways of life. Durkheim called this system **mechanical solidarity**, meaning *social bonds, based on shared morality, that unite members of preindustrial societies*. In practice, then, mechanical solidarity springs from *likeness*. Durkheim described these bonds as 'mechanical' because people feel a more or less automatic sense of belonging together.

Durkheim considered the decline of mechanical solidarity to be a defining trait of modern society. But this does not mean that society dissolves; rather, modernity generates a new type of solidarity that rushes into the void left by discarded traditions. Durkheim called this new social integration **organic solidarity**, defined as *social bonds, based on specialisation, that unite members of industrial societies*. In short, where solidarity was once rooted in likeness, it now flows from *differences* among people whose specialised pursuits make them rely on one another.

For Durkheim, then, the key dimension of change is a society's expanding **division of labour**, or *specialised economic activity*. As Max Weber explained, modern societies specialise in order to promote efficiency. Durkheim fills in the picture by showing us that members of modern societies count on the efforts of tens of thousands of others – most of them complete strangers – to secure the goods and services they need every day.

So modernity rests far less on *moral consensus* (the foundation of traditional societies) and far more on *functional interdependence*. That is, as members of modern societies, we depend more and more on people we trust less and less. Why, then, should we put our faith in people we hardly know and whose beliefs may differ radically from our own? Durkheim's answer: 'Because we can't live without them'. In a world in which morality sometimes seems like so much shifting sand, then, we confront what might be called 'Durkheim's dilemma': the technological power and expansive personal freedom of modern society come only at the cost of receding morality and the ever-present danger of anomie.

Like Marx and Weber, Durkheim had misgivings about the direction society was taking. But, of the three, Durkheim was the most optimistic. Confidence in the future sprang from his hope that we could enjoy greater freedom and privacy while creating for ourselves the social regulation that had once been forced on us by tradition.

● Critical evaluation: three visions of society

This chapter opened with several important queries about human societies. We will conclude by summarising how each of the three key visions of society answers these questions.

How have societies changed?

We started with a view – sociocultural evolution, furthest developed by the North American sociologists Gerhard and Jean Lenski (1995) – in which societies differ primarily in terms of changing technology. Modern society stands out in this regard because of its enormous productive power. Karl Marx also stressed historical differences in productive systems, yet pointed to the persistence of social conflict throughout human history (except perhaps among simple hunters and gatherers). For Marx, modern society is capitalist, and is distinctive because it brings that conflict out in the open.

Max Weber looked at this question from another perspective, tracing evolving modes of thought. Preindustrial societies, he claimed, are guided by tradition, while modern societies espouse a rational worldview. Bureaucracies take on a key role. Finally, for Emile Durkheim, traditional societies are characterised by mechanical solidarity based on moral consensus. In industrial societies, mechanical solidarity gives way to organic solidarity based on productive specialisation.

Why do societies change?

Marx's materialist approach pointed to the struggle between social classes as the 'engine of history', pushing societies toward revolutionary reorganisation. Weber's idealist view argues that modes of thought also contribute to social change. He demonstrated how rational Calvinism bolstered the Industrial Revolution, which in turn reshaped much of modern society. Finally, Durkheim pointed to an expanding division of labour as the key dimension of social change.

What holds societies together?

Marx spotlighted social division, not unity, treating class conflict as the hallmark of human societies throughout history. From his point of view, elites may force an

Is our society getting better or worse? The problem of progress

A major contrast between the USA and Europe is the former's sense of optimism. In Europe, generally, burdened by the sense of a long and troubled history, the fate of human kind is often looked upon with foreboding. Much of its intellectual tradition highlights critique, disenchantment, cynicism, despair and pessimism. Weber, for instance, wrote of the 'disenchantment of the world'. Freud, introduced in Chapter 5, saw civilisation as advancing at the cost of human happiness. And, perhaps most significant, this has been the tragic century that has witnessed two world wars and the Holocaust. In contrast, optimism has been a key trait of US society; as time goes on life gets better.

Robert Nisbet has argued that one of the defining features of modernity has been a belief in progress, often in spite of problems. Indeed, Swedish sociologist Therborn also sees this as the key in distinguishing between premodernity, modernity and postmodernity. Progress is the definer of the modern world. He writes:

> Pre-modernity is looking back over its shoulder, to the past, to the latter's example of wisdom, beauty, glory, and to the experiences of the past. Modernity looks to the future, hopes for it, plans for it, constructs it, builds it. Post-modernity has lost or thrown away any sense of direction. . . . Modernity ends when words like progress, advance, development, emancipation, liberation, growth, accumulation, enlightenment, embetterment, avant-garde, lose their attraction and their function as guides to social action. (Therborn, 1995: 4)

So is there progress or has it come to an end as we move into the twenty-first century? Just what's going on here?

To begin, we can point to some good reasons for society's belief in progress. Since the beginning of this century, for example, the scope of education has expanded to an unprecedented level. Moreover, even taking account of inflation, average income and national products have grown significantly. In addition, back in 1900, it was a rare home that had a telephone and, outside large cities, none had access to electricity. No one had even heard of television, and cars were still on the drawing boards. Today, almost every Western home is served by a telephone, a host of electric appliances, one or more television sets, and a video cassette recorder (VCR); many also are equipped with satellite or cable TV. Most important of all, people born in

---

uneasy peace between the classes, but true social unity would emerge only if production were to become a truly cooperative endeavour. To Weber, members of a society share a distinctive world-view. Just as traditional beliefs joined people together in the past, so modern societies have created rational, large-scale organisations with their own organisational cultures that fuse and guide people's lives. Finally, Durkheim made solidarity the focus of his work, contrasting the morality-based mechanical solidarity of preindustrial societies with modern society's more practical organic solidarity.

Where is society going?

Finally, there is the question of where society may now be headed (see the box). For Marx, capitalism would generate the seeds of its own destruction: revolutionary change should bring about a new communist social order. For Weber, there was a strong pessimistic streak: he saw the world as an Iron Cage, with growing rationality creating an ever-spreading 'disenchantment with the world'. Durkheim held out hope for new forms of association to emerge that would bind people together through their differences and resolve the problem of anomie.

Like a kaleidoscope that shows us different patterns as we turn it, these approaches reveal an array of insights into society. Yet no one approach is, in an absolute sense, right or wrong. Society is exceedingly complex, and we gain the richest understanding from using all of these visions, as we do in the concluding box.

1900 lived an average of just 47 years; children born today can look forward to 30 additional years of life.

But some trends, especially during the last 25 years, have been troubling. It is true that some countries seem to be enjoying higher standards of living etc., but is this at the expense of others? Contrasts of inequality are massive, as Chapters 9 to 11 will show. To give one figure from these chapters: 20% of the world (some 1 billion) lack the nutrition to work regularly, and 800 million are at risk for their lives. Add to this problems of cities, of pollution, of media, of environment, of risk, of crime – and so on. Rising crime rates have undermined people's sense of personal safety even in their own homes. Our relative affluence coupled with our capacity to move farther and faster than ever before seems to have eroded our sense of responsibility for others, unleashing a wave of individualism that often comes across as unbridled selfishness. As a result, not only is pessimism on the rise, many people have been

losing confidence in the direction of society.

So, which is it? Is society getting better or worse?

The theorists whose ideas we have examined in this chapter shed some light on this question. It is easy to equate 'high tech' with 'progress'. But we should make such assumptions cautiously, the Lenskis maintain, because history shows us that, while advancing technology does offer real advantages, it is no guarantee of a 'better' life. Marx, Weber and Durkheim also acknowledged the growing affluence of societies over time; yet each offered a pointed criticism of modern society because of a dangerous tendency toward individualism. For Marx, capitalism is the culprit, elevating money to godlike status and fostering a culture of selfishness. Weber's analysis claims that the modern spirit of rationality wears away traditional ties of kinship and neighbourhood while expanding bureaucracy, which, he warned, both manipulates and isolates

people. In Durkheim's view, functional interdependence joins members of modern societies, who are less and less able to establish a common moral framework within which to judge right and wrong.

In the end, what human societies gain through technological advances may be offset, to some extent, by the loss of human community.

● **Continue the debate:**

1. Draw up a balance sheet of 'progress' in the modern world. Do you think life in the modern world is getting better or worse? Why?

2. Is our society's increasing level of affluence entirely good? What might Marx, Weber and Durkheim say?

3. Do you think people in low-income countries are aware of the 'advances' in Europe or the United States? Would they see them as advances? ●

SUMMARY ....

1. Sociocultural evolution explores the societal consequences of technological advancements.

2. The earliest hunting and gathering societies were composed of a small number of family-centred nomads. Such societies have all but vanished.

3. Horticulture began some 12,000 years ago as people devised hand tools for the cultivation of crops. Pastoral societies domesticate animals and engage in extensive trade.

4. Agriculture, about 5,000 years old, is large-scale cultivation using animal-drawn ploughs. This tech-

nology allows societies to grow into vast empires, more productive, more specialised, and unequal.

5. Industrialisation began 250 years ago in Europe as people harnessed advanced energy sources to power sophisticated machinery.

6. In postindustrial societies, enterprise shifts from the production of material things to the creation and dissemination of information; computers and other information-based technology replace the heavy machinery of the industrial era.

Karl Marx

7. Marx's materialist analysis pointed to historical and contemporary conflict between social classes.

8. Conflict in 'ancient' societies involved masters and slaves; in agrarian societies, it places nobles and serfs in opposition; in industrial-capitalist societies, capitalists confront the proletariat.

9. Industrial capitalism alienates workers: from the act of working, from the products of work, from fellow workers, and from human potential.

10. Once workers had overcome their own false consciousness, Marx believed they would overthrow capitalists and the industrial-capitalist system.

Max Weber

11. Weber's idealist approach reveals that modes of thought have a powerful effect on society.

12. Weber drew a sharp contrast between the tradition of preindustrial societies and the rationality of modern, industrial societies.

13. Weber feared that rationality, embodied in efficiency-conscious bureaucratic organisations, would stifle human creativity.

Emile Durkheim

14. Durkheim explained that society has an objective existence apart from individuals.

15. His approach relates social elements to the larger society through their functions.

16. Traditional societies are fused by mechanical solidarity based on moral consensus; modern societies depend on organic solidarity based on the division of labour or productive specialisation.

KEY CONCEPTS

agriculture the technology of large-scale farming using ploughs harnessed to animals or more powerful sources of energy

alienation the experience of isolation resulting from powerlessness

anomie Durkheim's designation of a condition in which society provides little moral guidance to individuals: the breakdown of norms, or normlessness

capitalists people who own factories and other productive enterprises

class conflict antagonism between entire classes over the distribution of wealth and power in society

class consciousness Marx's term for the recognition by workers of their unity as a social class in opposition to capitalists and to capitalism itself

division of labour specialised economic activity

false consciousness Marx's term for explanations of social problems grounded in the shortcomings of individuals rather than the flaws of society

horticulture technology based on using hand tools to cultivate plants

hunting and gathering simple technology for hunting animals and gathering vegetation

ideal type Weber's term for an abstract statement of the essential characteristics of any social phenomenon

industrialism technology that powers sophisticated machinery with advanced sources of energy

mechanical solidarity Durkheim's designation of social bonds, based on shared morality, that unite members of preindustrial societies

organic solidarity Durkheim's designation of social bonds, based on specialisation, that unite members of industrial societies

pastoralism technology based on the domestication of animals

postindustrialism technology that supports an information-based economy

proletariat people who provide labour necessary to operate factories and other productive enterprises

rationality deliberate, matter-of-fact calculation of the most efficient means to accomplish a particular goal

rationalisation of society Weber's term for the historical change from tradition to rationality as the dominant mode of human thought

social conflict struggle between segments of society over valued resources

social institution a major sphere of social life, or societal subsystem, organised to meet a basic human need

society people who interact in a defined space and share culture

sociocultural evolution the Lenskis' term for the process of change that results from a society's gaining new information, particularly technology

tradition sentiments and beliefs passed from generation to generation

CRITICAL-THINKING QUESTIONS

1. Assess the notion that technological advance amounts to 'progress'.

2. As general approaches to understanding society, contrast Marx's concept of materialism with Weber's idealism.

3. How does Marx's concept of alienation differ from Durkheim's concept of anomie?

4. Contrast the theories of Marx, Durkheim and Weber on the emergence of the modern world. Which do you find most helpful – and why?

5. How do these visions of society explain the changing standing of women? What issues might be raised by a feminist critique of each of these theories?

GOING FURTHER

Introductory reading

For the long historical view of the evolution of society – going back a mere five million years! – a highly readable account is Colin Tudge's *The Day before Yesterday: Five Million Years of Human History* (London: Cape, 1995).

David Frisby and Derek Sayer, *Society* (London: Routledge, 1986).
  A short introduction to the different sociological conceptions of society

Classical sources

Hans Gerth and C. Wright Mills, *From Max Weber: Essays in Sociology* (London: Routledge & Kegan Paul, 1948).

Kenneth Thompson (ed.), *Readings from Emile Durkheim* (London: Routledge, 1985).

R. C. Tucker (ed.), *The Mark–Engels Reader* (New York: W. W. Norton, 2nd edn, 1978).
  These volumes provide classic sets of readings around the work of the founding theorists: Marx, Weber and Durkheim.

For commentaries on their work, which are many, see:

Ian Craib, *Classical Social Theory* (Oxford: Oxford University Press, 1997), and David Lee and Howard Newby, *The Problem of Sociology* (London: Hutchinson/ Routledge, 1984).

More advanced reading

Gerhard Lenski, Patrick Nolan and Jean Lenski, *Human Society: An Introduction to Macrosociology* (New York: McGraw-Hill, 7th edn, 1995).
  A comprehensive account of Gerhard and Jean Lenski's analysis of human societies is found in this textbook. This has been drawn upon quite extensively in this chapter, and it is worth reviewing in more detail. They place a great emphasis upon technological change.

Barry Lopez, *Arctic Dreams* (London: Picador, 1986).
  An account of society in the Arctic which shows the high level of technological sophistication amongst Arctic people.

The work of Krishan Kumar is also a very valuable source for looking at these broad changes. His first study, *Prophecy and Progress: The Sociology of Industrial and Post-Industrial Society* (Harmondsworth: Penguin, 1978), takes further much of the discussion in this chapter. His more recent *From Post-Industrial to Post-Modern Society: New Theories of the Contemporary World* (Oxford: Blackwell, 1995) reviews current debates about the 'information society', 'Fordism' (discussed in Chapter 15 of this book), and postmodernism.

On the 'Progress' debate, you could read Eric Hobsbawm's *Age of Extremes: The Short Twentieth Century, 1914–1991* (London: Michael Joseph, 1994). This is a full account of the history of the world this century, and leaves one at the very least being cautious about any simple view of progress. It could be read in conjunction with his other works on European history: *The Age of Revolution* (1962), *The Age of Capital* (1975) and *The Age of Empire* (1987) (Weidenfeld and Nicolson).

For the background to British society in the twentieth century see Paul Johnson (ed.), *20th Century Britain: Economic, Social and Cultural Change* (London: Longman, 1994), and A. H. Halsey, *Change in British Society* (Oxford: Oxford University Press, 1986).

On Europe

The most important sociological study of Europe to date is by the Swedish sociologist Goran Therborn: *European Modernity and Beyond: The Trajectory of European Societies*, 1945–2000 (London: Sage, 1995).

The background to European societies as the first modern industrial society is to be found in D. Hay, *Europe: The Emergence of an Idea* (Edinburgh: Edinburgh University Press, 2nd edn, 1968; orig. 1957).

Books providing valuable information on European societies include: Joe Bailey (ed.), *Social Europe* (London: Longman, 1992), David Edye and Valerio Lintner (eds.), *Contemporary Europe* (Hemel Hempstead: Prentice-Hall, 1996), and Tony Spybey (ed.), *Britain in Europe: An Introduction to Sociology* (London: Routledge, 1997).

A helpful guide to the European Union is Philippe Barbour (ed.), *The European Union Handbook* (London: Fitzroy Dearborn, 1996). The weekly newspaper, *The European*, can be a good guide to current concerns.

Other sources

The statistics profile of Europe can be found in *Eurostats, Europe in Figures*, 4th edn, 1995 (it is regularly updated), *The Eurostats Yearbook* (annual), and *Demographic Statistics* (annual). Regular bulletins – *Employment Bulletin, Women of Europe*, etc. – are produced through the European Commission's offices in Brussels and Luxembourg.

Web sites

The Marx and Durkheim web sites were introduced in Chapter 1. Web sites connected to Europe include:

● http://ibwww.essex.ac.uk/plus/eur.html

European Union: a homepage with links to European Community information home pages, including links to Europe full text electronic journals, EU-related sites, press releases, the current Presidency homepage, Maastricht Treaty, Treaty of Rome, etc.

● http://europa.eu.int/index-en.html

Europa, the European Union's server to the Parliament, the Council, the Commission, the Court of Justice, the Council of Auditors and other EU bodies. This server offers news, simple answers to key questions, information on policies, information on institutions, and links to Eurostat. Available in all EU languages.

chapter four

Source: Popperfoto

Culture

We were flying into Hong Kong shortly before it was taken back into Chinese rule in 1997. The air stewardess welcomed us to the land, but with a cryptic message. She informed us that Hong Kong was the land where half the people had mobile phones but the other half believed in ghosts! And here, in a nutshell, is the clash of two cultures – a modernising West touching a superstitious East.

Everywhere one turns in Hong Kong the contrast is visible. The bustling, dirty old temples where women cry and wail at the altars of their ancestors; the glittering, elaborate shopping malls – amongst the largest in the world – where consumerist capitalism is at its most spectacular. Spirituality versus materialism. Or the Chinese schoolchildren elaborately dressed in their formal 'Western' school uniforms complete with satchels – clambering over the houseboats in the harbour to their overcrowded houseboat homes. Or the Bank of Hong Kong – a monument to modern architecture, but built with full regard to 'evil spirits' and designed to keep them at bay. Here are rich and vibrant cultures pushing against each other.

Or consider another example: New York real estate broker Barry Lewen, after six months of tough negotiations with a group of Taiwanese investors, is on the verge of signing what any broker would regard as a dream deal – the sale of a $14 million building on New York's Madison Avenue – But the investors soberly informed Lewen of 'one final concern'. Before any sale would go through, they explained, they would have to enlist the services of a master of *feng shui* (pronounced 'fung shway', Chinese words that mean 'wind and water'). After flying to New York from Taiwan, this practitioner of the ancient Chinese art would inspect the building; only if he declared the structure to be acceptable would the sale be completed.

Several days later, a jet carrying the *feng shui* master landed at a New York airport and a car whisked him directly to the Madison Avenue building. A small crowd of anxious onlookers had assembled and they watched intently as he surveyed the setting, took account of the surrounding buildings, and, for thirty tense minutes, walked through the structure noting the shape and length of hallways, the location of doorways and lifts, and the presence of mirrors, fountains and even air conditioners. 'I can tell you there were a lot of sweaty palms', recounts Barry Lewen. In the end, the master turned to the apprehensive audience, smiled, and formally approved the building. A wave of relief broke over the group.

To the West's way of thinking, the merit of a building is a matter of its location, size, and the state of its plumbing and other systems. Such concerns are also of great importance to the Chinese. But, historically, members of south-east Asian societies have also considered how physical space affects human feelings and emotions. From this point of view, a 'life force' or qi (pronounced 'chee') flows through all of nature – including buildings – so that the physical design of a home or office building will either help or hinder this flow. A 'good' building – that is, one that stands in harmony with nature – will enhance the luck, health and prosperity of the people living or working inside (Dunn, 1994).

Understanding how such cultural differences work is a crucial part of sociology, and this chapter sets out to explore them.

The 5.7 billion people on the earth today are members of a single biological species: *Homo sapiens*. Even so, the differences among people the world over can delight, puzzle, disturb and sometimes even overwhelm us. Some differences in lifestyles are simply arbitrary matters of convention – the Chinese, for example, wear white at funerals while people in European countries prefer black. Similarly, Chinese people associate the number four with bad luck, in much the same way that people in England think of the number thirteen. Or, take the practice of kissing: most people in Europe kiss in public, most Chinese kiss only in private; the French kiss publicly twice (once on each cheek), while Belgians kiss three times (starting on either cheek); for their part, most Nigerians don't kiss at all. At weddings, moreover, North American couples kiss, Koreans bow, and a Cambodian groom touches his nose to the bride's cheek! If you have travelled much, you will be very aware of these differences.

Other cultural differences, however, are more profound. The world over, people wear much or little clothing, have many or few children, venerate or shunt aside the elderly, are peaceful or warlike, embrace different religious beliefs, and enjoy different kinds of art and music. In short, although we are all the same creatures biologically, the human beings on this planet have developed strikingly different ideas about what is pleasant and repulsive, polite and rude, beautiful and ugly, right and wrong. This capacity for startling difference is a wonder of our species: the expression of human culture.

● What is culture?

Sociologists define **culture** as *the values, beliefs, behaviour and material objects that constitute a people's way of life*. Culture includes what we think, how we act and what we own. But as our social heritage, culture is also a bridge to the past as well as a guide to the future (Soyinka, 1991). One classic account puts it like this:

Believing, with Max Weber, that man is an animal suspended in webs of significance he himself has spun, I take culture to be those webs, and the analysis of it to be therefore not an experimental science in search of law but an interpretive one in search of meaning . . . (Geertz, 1995: 5)

To begin to understand all that culture entails, it is helpful to distinguish between thoughts and things. What sociologists call **non-material culture** is *the intangible world of ideas created by members of a society* that span a wide range from altruism to zen. **Material culture**, on the other hand, constitutes *the tangible things created by members of a society*; here again, the range is vast, running from armaments to zips.

Not only does culture shape what we do, it also helps form our personalities – what we commonly (yet inaccurately) describe as 'human nature'. For sociologists, there is no such thing as human nature: 'nature' is produced through our varying histories and

Human beings around the globe create diverse ways of life. Such differences begin with outward appearance: Contrast the women and men shown here. Top row: South America, India, Namibia; middle row: Ethiopia, China, Nigeria; bottom row: India, Thailand, India.

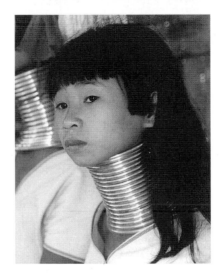

Source: Popperfoto

Culture shock: confronting the Yąnomamö

A small aluminium motorboat chugged steadily along the muddy Orinoco River, deep within South America's vast tropical rainforest. Anthropologist Napoleon Chagnon was nearing the end of a three-day journey to the home territory of the Yąnomamö, one of the most technologically primitive societies on earth.

Some twelve thousand Yąnomamö live in villages scattered along the border of Venezuela and Brazil. Their way of life could hardly be more different from our own. The Yąnomamö wear little clothing and live without electricity, cars or other conveniences most people in Europe take for granted. Their traditional weapons, used for hunting and warfare, are the bow and arrow. The Yąnomamö have had few encounters with the outside world. Thus Chagnon would be as strange to them as they would be to him.

By 2.00 in the afternoon, Chagnon had almost reached his destination. The hot sun made the humid air almost unbearable. The anthropologist's clothes were soaked with perspiration, and his face and hands swelled from the bites of innumerable gnats swarming around him. But he scarcely noticed, because of his anticipation that in just a few moments he would be face to face with people unlike any he had ever known.

Chagnon's heart pounded as the boat slid onto the riverbank near a Yąnomamö village. Sounds of activity came from nearby. Chagnon and his guide climbed from the boat and walked toward the village, stooping as they pushed their way through the dense undergrowth. Chagnon describes what happened next.

I looked up and gasped when I saw a dozen burly, naked, sweaty, hideous men staring at us down the shafts of their drawn arrows! Immense wads of green tobacco were stuck between their lower teeth and lips making them look even more hideous, and strands of dark green slime dripped or hung from their nostrils – strands so long that they clung to their [chests] or drizzled down their chins.

My next discovery was that there were a dozen or so vicious, underfed dogs snapping at my legs, circling me as if I were to be their next meal. I just stood there holding my notebook, helpless and pathetic. Then the stench of the decaying vegetation and filth hit me and I almost got sick. I was horrified. What kind of welcome was this for the person who came here to live with you and learn your way of life, to become friends with you? (1992: 11–12).

Fortunately for Chagnon, the Yąnomamö villagers recognised his guide and lowered their weapons. Reassured that he would survive at least the afternoon, Chagnon was still shaken by his inability to make any sense of the people surrounding him. And this was to be his home for a year and a half! He wondered why he had forsaken physics to study human culture in the first place. ●

Source: Chagnon, 1997.

Culture shock: confronting the Yąnomamö

Source: Gamma-Liaison, Inc. – G Humer

cultures. This is often hard for students to grasp, but it is another example where common sense gets challenged by sociology.

Consider the example of the warlike Yąnomamö of the Brazilian rainforest who look on aggression as natural in their children, just as, halfway around the world, the Semai of Malaysia expect their young to be peaceful and cooperative. The cultures of the UK and China both stress achievement and hard work; but in the UK, people value individualism more than do the

Chinese, who place a stronger emphasis on tradition and group living.

Given the extent of cultural differences in the world and the tendency of all of us to view our own way of life as 'natural' it is no wonder that travellers commonly experience **culture shock**, *personal disorientation that comes from encountering an unfamiliar way of life*. The box presents one researcher's personal experience of cultural shock.

No cultural trait is inherently 'natural' to humanity, even though most people around the world view their own way of life that way. What is natural to our species is the capacity to create culture in our collective lives. Every other form of life – from ants to zebras – behaves in uniform, species-specific ways. To a world traveller, the enormous diversity of human life stands out in contrast to the behavior of cats and other creatures, which is the same everywhere. Most living creatures are guided by *instincts*, biological programming over which animals have no control. A few animals – notably chimpanzees and related primates – have the capacity for limited culture: researchers have observed them using tools and teaching simple skills to their offspring. But the creative power of humans far exceeds that of any other form of life; in short, *only humans rely on culture rather than instinct to ensure the survival of their kind* (Harris, 1987). To understand how this came to be, we must briefly review the history of our species on earth.

Culture, intelligence and the 'dance through time'

In a universe some 15 billion years old, our planet is a much younger 4.5 billion years of age. For a billion years after the earth was formed, no life at all appeared on our planet. Huge geological changes kept changing the earth's surface. Several billion more years went by before dinosaurs ruled the earth and then disappeared. And then, some 65 million years ago, our history took a crucial turn with the appearance of the creatures we call primates.

What sets primates apart is their intelligence, based on the largest brains (relative to body size) of all living creatures. As primates evolved, the human line diverged from that of our closest relatives, the great apes, about 12 million years ago. But our common

lineage shows through in the traits humans share with today's chimpanzees, gorillas and orang-utans: great sociability, affectionate and long-lasting bonds for child rearing and mutual protection, the ability to walk upright (normal in humans, less common among other primates), and hands that manipulate objects with great precision.

Studying fossil records, scientists conclude that, about 2 million years ago, our distant ancestors grasped cultural fundamentals such as the use of fire, tools and weapons, created simple shelters, and fashioned basic clothing. Although these Stone Age achievements may seem modest, they mark the point at which our ancestors embarked on a distinct evolutionary course, making culture the primary strategy for human survival.

To comprehend that human beings are wide-eyed infants in the larger scheme of things, Carl Sagan (1977) came up with the idea of superimposing the 15-billion-year history of our universe on a single calendar year. The life-giving atmosphere of the earth did not develop until the autumn, and the earliest beings who resembled humans did not appear until 31 December – the last day of the year – at 10.30 at night! Yet not until 250,000 years ago, which is mere minutes before the end of Sagan's 'year', did our own species finally emerge. These *Homo sapiens* (derived from Latin meaning 'thinking person') have continued to evolve so that, about 40,000 years ago, humans who looked more or less like we do roamed the earth. With larger brains, these 'modern' *Homo sapiens* produced culture at a rapid pace, as the wide range of tools and cave art from this period suggests.

Still, what we call 'civilisation', based on permanent settlements and specialised occupations, began in the Middle East (in what is today Iraq and Egypt) only about 12,000 years ago (Hamblin, 1973; Wenke, 1980). In terms of Sagan's 'year', this cultural flowering occurred during the final *seconds* before midnight on New Year's Eve. And what of our modern, industrial way of life? Begun only 300 years ago, it amounts to a mere millisecond flash in Sagan's scheme. It is with this millisecond that most of this book is concerned. We are 'latecomers to a global party that has been in progress for at least 3.5 billion years, since life began, and will continue till the death of the planet itself. It is a fabulous party, with billions of participants from all walks of life' (Tudge, 1995: 76).

GLOBAL SOCIOLOGY

Travellers beware! The meaning of gestures in other societies

A young man from Amsterdam is enjoying a summer trip in the African nation of Nigeria. He stands by the side of a country road, trying to 'thumb a ride' to the next town. A dusty cloud on the horizon soon turns into a truck carrying half a dozen local people. They look him over and come to a screeching halt. But they are not about to offer a ride to our hapless visitor; instead, they pile out of the truck, angrily denounce him, rough him up, and leave him sitting dazed and confused on the ground.

What has happened here? Are Nigerians hostile to foreigners? Not at all. But like people everywhere, they don't take kindly to insults. What the young man from Europe meant as a request for a ride, Nigerians see as a crude and offensive gesture.

Since much human communication involves not words but gestures and body language – especially when we encounter people whose language differs from our own – we need to be mindful that the innocent use of even a simple hand movement may provoke an angry response. Here are six bodily gestures that seem innocent enough to members of our society but that may evoke a stern response from people elsewhere.

Images (a) and (b) each would offend members of Islamic societies. Since Muslims typically perform toilet hygiene with the left hand, they recoil at the sight of a person eating with that hand, illustrated in (a). Islam also holds that the sole of a shoe is unclean; therefore, any display of the bottom of the foot, as in (b), conveys insult. Photo (c) displays the common 'A-OK' gesture by which people in North America express approval and pleasure. In France, however, this symbol imparts the snub 'You're worth zero', while Germans take this gesture as a crude word for 'rectum'. Photo (d) shows the simple curling of a finger, meaning 'come here'. Malaysians attach the same meaning to this gesture as we do, but they use it exclusively for calling animals; thus, they take no pleasure in being beckoned in this way. Photo (e) shows the familiar 'thumbs up' gesture widely employed in North America to mean 'Good job!' or 'All right!' In Nigeria (as the hapless hitchhiker learned), and also in Australia, flashing this gesture (especially with a slight upward motion) transmits the insulting message 'Up yours!' Finally, (f) shows a gesture that members of our society read as 'Stop!' or 'No, thanks'. But display this gesture to a motorist or street vendor anywhere in western Africa and you will probably have a fight on your hands. There it means 'You have five fathers' or, more simply, 'You bastard!' ●

Sources: Examples are drawn from Ekman et al., 1984, and Axtell, 1991.

Human culture, then, is very recent and was a long time in the making. As culture became a strategy for survival, our ancestors descended from the trees into the tall grasses of central Africa. There, walking upright, they discovered the advantages of hunting in groups. From this point on, the human brain grew larger allowing for greater human capacity to create a way of life – as opposed to simply acting out biological imperatives. Gradually, culture pushed aside the biological forces we call instincts so that humans gained the mental power *to fashion the natural environment for ourselves*. Ever since, people have made and remade their worlds in countless ways, which explains today's extraordinary cultural diversity.

Culture, nation and society

At this point, we might well pause to clarify several similar terms – 'culture', 'nation' and 'society'. *Culture* refers to a shared way of life. A *nation* is a political entity – that is, a territory within designated borders such as Canada, Argentina, or Zimbabwe (discussed in Chapter 16). *Society*, the topic of the previous chapter, is the organised interaction of people in a

(a)   (b)   (c)

(d)   (e)   (f)

Source: Popperfoto

nation or within some other boundary. We correctly describe each of Sweden, Norway or Belgium, then, as both a nation and as a society. But many societies are *multicultural*, meaning that they encompass various ways of life that blend (and clash) in our everyday lives.

In the world as a whole, how many cultures are there? The number of cultures comprising the human record is a matter of speculation. Experts have documented the existence of 5,000–6,000 human languages, suggesting that at least this many cultures have existed on the earth (Durning, 1993). High-technology communication, rising international migration and the expanding global economy have combined to lessen the cultural diversity of the contemporary world. Even so, at least 1,000 distinct cultures continue to flourish, and hundreds of them thrive in Europe.

The tally of world nations has risen and fallen throughout history as a result of political events. The dissolution of the former Soviet Union and the former Yugoslavia, for example, added 19 nations to the count. In 1995, there were 191 politically independent nations in the world.

● The components of culture

Although the cultures found in all the world's nations differ in many ways, they all are built on five major components: symbols, language, values, norms and material objects. We shall consider each in turn.

Symbols

Human beings not only sense the surrounding world as other creatures do, we build a reality of *meaning*. In doing so, humans transform elements of the world into **symbols**, *anything that carries a particular meaning recognised by people who share culture*. A whistle, a wall of graffiti, a flashing red light, and a fist raised in the air all serve as symbols. We can see the human capacity to create and manipulate symbols reflected in the very different meanings associated with the simple act of winking the eye. In some settings this action conveys interest; in others, understanding; in still others, insult.

We are so dependent on our culture's symbols that we take them for granted. But entering an unfamiliar society also reminds us of the power of symbols; culture shock is nothing more than the inability to 'read' meaning in one's surroundings. We feel lost and isolated, unsure of how to act, and sometimes frightened – a consequence of being outside the symbolic web of culture that joins individuals in meaningful social life.

Culture shock is a two-way process. On the one hand it is something the traveller **experiences** when encountering people whose way of life is unfamiliar. On the other hand, it is also what the traveller **inflicts** on others by acting in ways that may well offend them. For example, because the English consider dogs to be beloved household pets, travellers to northern regions of the People's Republic of China might well be appalled to find people roasting dogs as a winter-time meal. On the other hand, visitors to England from much of South-East Asia can be shocked to find how much alcohol we consume! Indeed, global travel provides almost endless opportunities for misunderstanding. When in an unfamiliar setting, we need to remember that even behaviour that seems innocent and quite normal to us may be anathema to others. The 'Travellers beware!' box takes a closer look at this phenomenon.

Then, too, symbolic meanings vary even within a single society. A fur coat, prized by one person as a luxurious symbol of success, may represent to another the inhumane treatment of animals. Cultural symbols also change over time. Blue jeans were created more than a century ago as sturdy and inexpensive clothing for people engaged in physical labour. In the liberal political climate of the 1960s, this working class aura made jeans popular among affluent students – many of whom wore them simply to look 'different' or perhaps to identify with working people. A decade later, 'designer jeans' emerged as high-priced 'status symbols' that conveyed quite a different message. In recent years, everyday jeans remain as popular as ever; most people choose them simply as comfortable apparel.

In sum, symbols allow people to make sense of their lives, and without them human existence would be meaningless. Manipulating symbols correctly allows us to engage others readily within our own cultural system. In a world of cultural diversity, however, the misuse of symbols may give rise to embarrassment, and loyally supporting one cultural symbol while opposing another can even generate conflict.

The study of *the symbols and signs* is called **semiotics**. Broadly, semiotics suggests that meanings are never inherent in objects but are constructed around them through a series of practices. The American pragmatist Peirce, the French language specialist de Saussure and the French philosopher Roland Barthes have made special studies of the ways in which any sign – a T-shirt, a flag, a pop song, a menu, a word – can be given different meanings. We return to this in Chapter 21 ('Mass Media') where we look at the semiological analysis of the mass media.

Language

Helen Keller (1880–1968) became a national celebrity in the United States because she overcame the daunting disability of being blind and deaf from infancy. The loss of two key senses cut off this young girl from the symbolic world, greatly limiting her social development. Only when her teacher, Anne Mansfield Sullivan, broke through Keller's isolation by teaching her sign language did Helen Keller begin to realise her human potential. This remarkable woman, who later became a renowned educator herself, recalls the moment she grasped the concept of language.

We walked down the path to the well-house, attracted by the smell of honeysuckle with which it was covered. Someone was drawing water, and my teacher placed my hand under the spout. As the cool stream gushed over one hand, she spelled into the other the word *water*, first slowly, then rapidly. I stood still, my whole attention fixed upon the motions of her fingers. Suddenly I felt a misty consciousness as of something forgotten – a thrill of returning thought; and somehow the mystery of language was revealed to me. I knew then that 'w-a-t-e-r' meant the wonderful cool something that was flowing over my hand. That living word awakened my soul; gave it light, hope, joy, set it free! (1903: 21–4)

Language, the key to the world of culture, is *a system of symbols that allows members of a society to communicate with one another*. These symbols take the form of spoken and written words, which are culturally variable and composed of the various alphabets used around the world. Even conventions for writing differ: in general, people in Western societies write from left to right, people in northern Africa and western Asia write from right to left, and people in eastern Asia write from top to bottom.

Map 4.1 shows where in the world one finds the three most widely spoken languages. Chinese is the official language of 20 per cent of humanity (about 1.2 billion people). English is the mother tongue of about 10 per cent (600 million) of the world's people, with Spanish the official language of 6 per cent (350 million). Whilst these are major languages, there are thousands of minor ones – estimates usually vary from 5,000 to 6,000. A quarter of these languages have less than 1,000 speakers; half have fewer than 10,000. Many are dying out. And this has led to a number of language revivals that aim to rekindle interest in languages such as Welsh (Crystal, 1997: 287).

Due to the worldwide influence of Britain over the past 200 years, and more recently of the United States, English is now becoming a global tongue that is a favoured second language in many of the world's nations. It is used as an official or semi-official language in over 60 countries, and is the main language of the World Wide Web, air traffic control, business conferences and pop music. But in many countries there is considerable concern about this. So much so that there is now a European Bureau of Lesser Used Languages which tries to promote and conserve these less-used languages (with a bulletin, *Contact*, published three times a year). And some countries, like France

and Wales, are trying hard to resist the weakening of their language by challenging English words.

The European Union is a Tower of Babel. The European Commission in Brussels employs 400 full time staff to deal with translation problems. There are at present 11 official languages, though this could grow: the theoretically possible number is 30 (Crystal, 1997: 56).

For people everywhere, language is the major means of **cultural reproduction**, *the process by which one generation passes culture to the next*. Just as our bodies contain the genes of our ancestors, so our symbols carry our cultural heritage. Language gives us the power to gain access to centuries of accumulated wisdom.

Throughout human history, people have transmitted culture through speech, a process sociologists call the *oral cultural tradition*. Only as recently as 5,000 years ago did humans invent writing, and even then, just a favored few ever learned to read and write. It was not until this century that nations (generally the industrial high-income countries) have boasted of nearly universal literacy (see Chapter 21 'Mass Media'). Even so, in many industrial countries there are still large number of people who are functionally illiterate – approximately one in five people in the UK have literacy, and numeracy problems – an almost insurmountable barrier to opportunity in a society that increasingly demands symbolic skills. In low-income countries of the world, illiteracy rates range from 30 per cent (People's Republic of China) to as high as 80 per cent (Sierra Leone in Africa).

Language skills not only link us with others and with the past, they also set free the human imagination. Connecting symbols in new ways, we can conceive of an almost limitless range of future possibilities. Language – both spoken and written – distinguishes human beings as the only creatures who are self-conscious, mindful of our limitations and aware of our ultimate mortality. Yet our symbolic power also enables us to dream, to envision a better world, and to work to bring that world into being.

Is language uniquely human?

Creatures great and small direct sounds, smells and gestures toward one another. In most cases, these signals are instinctive. But research shows that some animals have at least a rudimentary ability to use symbols to communicate with one another and with humans.

Map 4.1 ● Language in global perspective

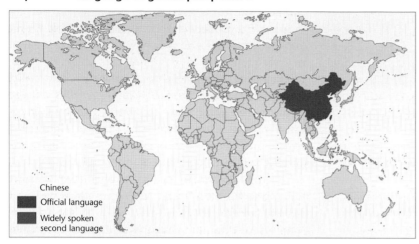

Chinese (including Mandarin, Cantonese, and dozens of other dialects) is the native tongue of one-fifth of the world's people, almost all of whom live in Asia. Although all Chinese people read and write with the same characters, they employ any of several dozen dialects. The 'official' dialect, taught in schools throughout the People's Republic of China and the Republic of Taiwan, is Mandarin (the dialect of Beijing, China's historic capital city). Cantonese (the language of Canton, which differs in sound from Mandarin roughly the way French does from Spanish) is the second most common Chinese dialect.

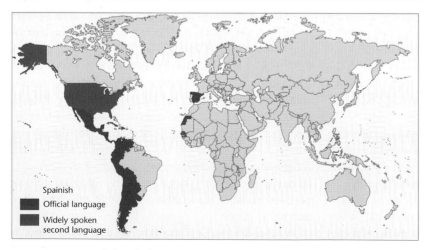

English is the native tongue or official language in several world regions and has become the preferred second language in most of the world.

The largest concentration of Spanish speakers is in Latin America and, of course, in Spain. Spanish is also the preferred second language of the United States.

Source: *Peters Atlas of the World* (1990)

Consider the remarkable achievement of a 12-year-old pygmy chimp named Kanzi. Chimpanzees lack the physical ability to mimic human speech. But researcher E. Sue Savage-Rumbaugh discovered that Kanzi was able to learn language by listening and observing people. Under Savage-Rumbaugh's supervision, Kanzi has amassed a vocabulary of several hundred words, and he has learned to 'speak' by pointing to pictures on a special keyboard. Kanzi has correctly responded to requests like 'Will you get a nappy for your sister?' and 'Put the melon in the potty'. More intriguing, Kanzi's abilities surpass mere rote learning because he can respond to requests he has not heard before. In short, this remarkable animal has the language ability of a $2^1/_2$ year-old human child (Linden, 1993).

Despite such accomplishments, the language skills of chimps, dolphins and a few other animals are limited. And even specially trained animals cannot, on their own, teach language skills to others of their kind. But the demonstrated language skills of Kanzi and others caution us against assuming that humans alone can lay claim to culture.

Does language shape reality?

Do the Chinese, who think using one set of symbols, actually experience the world differently from Swedes who think in Swedish or the English who think in English? The answer is yes, since each language has its own, distinct symbols that serve as the building blocks of reality.

Edward Sapir (1929, 1949) and Benjamin Whorf (1956), two anthropologists who specialised in linguistic studies, noted that each language has words or expressions with no precise counterparts in other tongues. In addition, all languages fuse symbols with distinctive emotions. Thus, as multilingual people can attest, a single idea often 'feels' different if spoken in, say, German rather than in English or Chinese (Falk, 1987).

Formally, then, what we now call the **Sapir–Whorf hypothesis** states that *people perceive the world through the cultural lens of language*. Using different symbolic systems, a Filipino, a Turk and a Brazilian actually experience 'distinct worlds, not merely the same world with different labels attached' (Sapir, 1949: 162). They combine two principles. **Linguistic determinism** suggests that *language shapes the way we think*. Whilst **linguistic relativity** states that *distinctions found in one language are not found in another*. Whorf's classic case studies involved the Hopis, who only had one word for everything that flies – insects, planes, pilots – except birds; and the Inuit, who had many different words for snow.

The capacity to create and manipulate language also gives humans everywhere the power to alter how they experience the world. For example, many African Americans hailed it as a step toward social equality with white people when the word 'Negro' was replaced by the term 'black' and, more recently, by 'African American' or 'person of colour'. Likewise, homosexuals redefined themselves as 'gay' during the 1970s, creating a more forceful, positive self-definition.

In short, a system of language guides how we understand the world but does not limit how we do so. We will return to the importance of language in Chapters 5 ('Socialisation') and Chapter 6 ('Social Interaction in Everyday Life').

Values and beliefs

What accounts for the popularity of film characters like James Bond, Rambo, and Thelma and Louise? Each is ruggedly individualistic, suspicious of 'the system', and relies on personal skill and savvy. In applauding such people, we celebrate a sturdy strain of individualism, traditionally for men but increasingly for women, too.

Sociologists call these judgments **values**, *culturally defined standards by which people assess desirability, goodness and beauty, and which serve as broad guidelines for social living*. From the standpoint of a culture, values are statements about what ought to be.

Values are broad principles that underlie **beliefs**, *specific statements that people hold to be true*. While values are abstract standards of goodness, in other words, beliefs are particular matters that individuals consider to be true or false.

Cultural values and beliefs not only colour how we perceive our surroundings, they also form the core of our personalities. We learn from families, schools and religious organisations to think and act according to approved principles, to pursue worthy goals, and to believe a host of cultural truths while rejecting alternatives as false.

In a continent as large and diverse as Europe, of course, few cultural values and beliefs are shared by everyone. In fact, with a long history of immigration from the rest of the world, Europe may be seen as a cultural mosaic. Even so, there may be some broad shape to European life. First, it is largely the sediment of what might be called 'The Age of the Enlightenment' (Gay, 1969). That is, it holds broadly to the values of rationality, science and progress that came with the *philosophes* – great writers and thinkers, mainly of the eighteenth century. This was a period marked by significant improvements in some lives due to reason, science, medicine. People started to sense they were the makers of their own futures, that they could exert some rational control over their world, that they could bring about change.

Secondly, Europe has been dominated by versions of the Christian religion, and its subsequent secularisation. Much of its heritage cannot be understood without grasping the long struggles between Catholic groups and emerging Protestant ones, and the twentieth century weakening of both. The very calendar year and most of its key holidays – Christmas, Easter – are bound up with Christian values, culture and identity: 'To be a European is to celebrate Christmas and Easter' (Therborn, 1995: 234). (For an interesting history of British Christmas, see Hutton, 1996.)

Thirdly, it has been characterised by the development of nation states, and their citizenship. Finally, it may be seen as a culture that has highlighted individualism and class (cf. Therborn, 1995: 273). European culture, in the broadest of strokes, is clearly different from, say, North American culture or Asian cultures. The box highlights some North American values, many of which may be taken more broadly to exemplify Western capitalist culture. You may like to consider how far these differ from European ones.

Values: inconsistency and conflict

Cultural values can be inconsistent and even outright contradictory (Lynd, 1967; Bellah et al., 1985). Living in Europe, we sometimes find ourselves torn between the 'me first' attitude of an individualistic way of life and the opposing need to belong and contribute to some larger community. Similarly, we affirm our belief in equality of opportunity, only to turn around and promote or degrade others because of their ethnicity, gender or sexual preference. Value inconsistency reflects the cultural diversity of society and the process of cultural change by which new trends supplant older traditions.

Norms

In China, people curious about how much money colleagues are paid readily ask about their salaries. In Europe, people consider such a question rude. Such patterns illustrate the operation of **norms**, *rules and expectations by which a society guides the behaviour of its members*. Some norms are *proscriptive*, mandating what we should not do, as when Chinese parents scold young lovers for holding hands in public. *Prescriptive* norms, on the other hand, spell out what we *should* do, as when some European schools teach practices of 'safe sex'.

Most important norms apply virtually anywhere and at any time. For example, parents expect obedience from children regardless of the setting. Many normative conventions, by contrast, are situation-specific. In Europe, we expect audience applause at the end of a musical performance; we discourage it when a priest or a rabbi finishes a sermon.

Mores and folkways

William Graham Sumner (1959; orig. 1906), an early US sociologist, recognised that some norms are more crucial to our lives than others. Sumner used the term **mores** to refer to *a society's standards of proper moral conduct*. Sumner counted among the mores all norms essential to maintaining a way of life; because of their importance, he contended that people develop an emotional attachment to mores and defend them publicly. In addition, mores apply to everyone, everywhere, all the time. Violation of mores – such as our society's prohibition against sexual relations between adults and children – typically brings a swift and strong reaction from others.

Sumner used the term **folkways** to designate *a society's customs for routine, casual interaction*. Folkways, which have lesser moral significance than mores, include notions about proper dress, appropriate greetings and common courtesy. In short, while mores distinguish between right and wrong, folkways draw a line between right and *rude*. Because they are less important than mores, societies afford individuals a measure of personal discretion in matters involving folkways, and punish infractions leniently. For example, a man who does not wear a tie to a formal dinner party is, at worst, guilty of a breach of etiquette. If, however, the man were to arrive at the dinner party wearing *only* a tie, he would be challenging the social mores and inviting more serious sanctions.

GLOBAL SOCIOLOGY

Core national values: the case of the USA

Sociologist Robin Williams (1970) identified the following ten values as central to the way of life in the United States of America. How do they differ from European values?

1. *Equal opportunity*. People in the United States endorse not equality of *condition* but equality of *opportunity*. This means that society should provide everyone with the opportunity to get ahead; at the same time, though, people's varying talents and efforts should end up making some people more successful than others.

2. *Achievement and success*. The American way of life encourages competition so that each person's rewards should reflect personal merit. Moreover, greater success confers worthiness on a person – the mantle of being a 'winner'.

3. *Material comfort*. Success, in the United States, generally means making money and enjoying what it will buy. People may quip that 'money won't buy happiness', but most diligently pursue wealth all the same.

4. *Activity and work*. US heroes, from Olympic figure skating star Kristi Yamaguchi to film's famed archaeologist Indiana Jones, are 'action figures', people who get the job done. Members of US society prefer *action* to *reflection*; through hard work,

they try to control events rather than passively accept their fates. For this reason, many Americans take a dim view of cultures that appear more easygoing or philosophical.

5. *Practicality and efficiency*. People in the United States value the practical over the theoretical; 'doers' over 'dreamers'. Activity has value to the extent that it earns money. Moreover, Americans praise the ability to solve problems with minimal effort. 'Building a better mousetrap' is a cultural goal, especially when it is done in the most cost-effective way.

6. *Progress*. Americans are an optimistic people who, despite periodic waves of nostalgia, believe that the present is better than the past. This embrace of progress comes through in marketing that equates the 'very latest' with the 'very best'.

7. *Science*. Americans often turn to scientists to solve problems, convinced that the work of scientific experts will improve their lives. They believe that they are rational people, which accounts for the cultural tendency (especially among men) to devalue emotions and intuition as sources of knowledge.

8. *Democracy and free enterprise*. Members of US society recognise numerous individual rights that cannot be overridden by government.

The political system has come to be based on the ideal of free elections in which all adults select their own leaders. In the same way, Americans believe that the US economy responds to the needs and choices of individual consumers.

9. *Freedom*. Their cultural value of freedom means that Americans favour individual initiative over collective conformity. Although they acknowledge that everyone has responsibilities to others, they believe that individuals should be free to pursue personal goals with minimal interference from anyone else.

10. *Racism and group superiority*. Despite prevailing ideas about individualism and freedom, most people in the United States still evaluate individuals according to their sex, race, ethnicity and social class. US society values males above females, whites above people of colour, people with northwestern backgrounds above those whose ancestors came from other lands, and more privileged people above those who are disadvantaged. Although they like to describe themselves as a nation of equals, there is little doubt that some Americans rank as 'more equal than others'. ●

Material culture and technology

In addition to intangible elements such as values and norms, every culture encompasses a wide range of tangible (from Latin meaning 'touchable') human creations that sociologists term *artifacts*. The Chinese eat with chopsticks rather than knives and forks, the Japanese place mats rather than rugs on the floor, and many men and women in India prefer flowing robes to the tighter clothing common in much of Europe. An unfamiliar people's material culture may seem as strange to us as their language, values and norms.

The artefacts common to a society typically reflect cultural values. The fact that poison-tipped arrows are a prized possession of Yanomamö males in the Amazon rainforest, for example, surely reflects the importance that society places on warfare and militaristic skills.

In addition to reflecting values, material culture also reveals a society's **technology**, *knowledge that a society applies to the task of living in a physical environment*. In short, technology ties the world of nature to the world of culture. Among the most technologically simple people on earth, the Yanomamö interfere little with the natural environment. They remain keenly aware of the cycles of rainfall and the movement of animals they hunt for food. By contrast, technologically complex societies have an enormous impact on the natural world, reshaping the environment (for better or ill) according to their own interests and priorities.

Because we accord science such great importance and praise the sophisticated technology it has produced, members of our society tend to judge cultures with simpler technology as less advanced. Some facts would support such an assessment. For example, life expectancy for children born in Europe now exceeds 75 years; the lifespan of the Yanomamö stands at only about 40 years.

However, we must be careful not to make self-serving judgements about cultures that differ from our own. Although many Yanomamö are eager to gain modern technology (such as steel tools and shotguns), they are generally well fed by world standards and most are quite satisfied with their lives (Chagnon, 1992). Remember, too, that while our powerful and complex technology has produced work-reducing devices and seemingly miraculous forms of medical treatment, it has also contributed to unhealthy levels of stress, eroded the quality of the natural environment, and created weapons capable of destroying in a blinding flash everything that humankind has managed to achieve throughout history.

Finally, technology is another cultural element that varies substantially within Europe. Although many of us cannot imagine life without CD players, televisions and microwave ovens, some Europeans cannot afford such items, and others reject them on principle. Generally, northern Europe is wealthier than the sun drenched southern countries.

The ethnicity boom

From the mid 1960s onwards, North America and Western Europe experienced something of an 'ethnicity boom' – a widespread awareness of different ethnicities having their own languages. Thus, of 230 million people over the age of 5 in the United States, the 1990 Census reports that 32 million (14 per cent) typically speak a language other than English at home. Of these people, 54 per cent speak Spanish, 14 per cent use an Asian language, and the remaining 32 per cent employ some other tongue (the Census Bureau lists 25 languages, each of which is favored by more than 100,000 people). In Europe, there are wide variations in language too, often generating conflicts. In Spain, Basque (Euskera) was banned under Franco from the mid-1930s: books written in it were publicly burnt. In the 1960s, policy changed and by March 1980, the first Basque Parliament was elected and Euskera became its official language. In Britain, although English dominates, there are speakers of Punjabi, Bengali, Urdu, Gujarati and Cantonese, not to mention German, Polish, Italian, Greek and Spanish. There is also 'Black English Vernacular' (BEV) linked to the use of a Creole English, used by the first blacks in America. (cf. Crystal, 1997: 36).

● Cultural diversity: many ways of life in one world

When contractors and estate agents in New York take account of the Chinese art of *feng shui*, as noted in the opening to this chapter, we can see a nation of striking cultural diversity. In fact, between 1980 and 1990, the number of people in the United States with Chinese or other Asian ancestry more than doubled. Historical isolation makes Japan the most *monocultural* of all industrial nations; heavy immigration over centuries, by contrast, makes the United States the most *multicultural* of all industrial nations.

Between 1820 (when the US government began keeping track of immigration) and 1990, more than 55 million people travelled to the United States from other countries. A century ago, as shown in Figure 4.1, most immigrants hailed from Europe. By the 1980s, however, a large majority of newcomers were arriving from Latin America and Asia.

Cultural variety has also always characterised Europe, and has not just been a feature of the United States. We return to this in Chapter 12.

High culture and popular culture

Much cultural diversity has roots in social class. In fact, in everyday conversation, we usually reserve the term 'culture' for sophisticated art forms such as classical literature, music, dance and painting. We praise university professors, film directors or dance choreographers as 'cultured', because they presumably appreciate the 'finer things in life'. The term 'culture' itself has the same Latin root as the word 'cultivate', suggesting that the 'cultured' individual has cultivated or refined tastes.

By contrast, we speak less generously of ordinary people, assuming that everyday cultural patterns are somehow less worthy. In more concrete terms, we are tempted to judge the music of Mozart as 'more cultured' than Motown, fine cuisine as better than fish fingers, and polo as more polished than ping pong.

Such judgments imply that many cultural patterns are readily accessible to some but not all members of a society (Hall and Neitz, 1993). Sociologists use the shorthand term **high culture**[1] to refer to *cultural patterns that distinguish a society's elite*; **popular culture**, then, designates *cultural patterns that are widespread among a society's population*.

Common sense may suggest that high culture is superior to popular culture. After all, history chronicles the lives of elites much more than those of ordinary women and men. But sociologists are uneasy with such a sweeping evaluation, and generally use the term 'culture' to refer to *all* elements of a society's way of life, even as they recognize that cultural patterns vary throughout a population (Gans, 1974).

We should resist quick judgements about the merits of high culture as opposed to popular culture for two key reasons. First, neither elites nor ordinary people have uniform tastes and interests; people in both categories differ in numerous ways. Second, do we praise high culture because it is inherently better than popular culture, or simply because its supporters have more money, power and prestige to begin with? For example, there is no difference between a violin and a

---

[1] The term 'high culture' is derived from the more popular term 'highbrow'. Influenced by phrenology, the bogus nineteenth century theory that personality was determined by the shape of the human skull, people a century ago contrasted the praiseworthy tastes of those they termed 'highbrows' with the contemptible appetites of others they derided as 'lowbrows'.

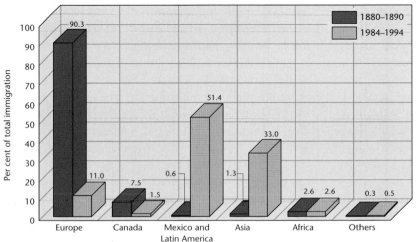

Source: US Immigration and Naturalisation Service (1995)

Figure 4.1 ● **Recorded immigration to the United States, by region of birth, 1880–1890 and 1984–1994**

fiddle; however, we refer to the instrument one way when it is used to produce music typically enjoyed by people of higher social position, and the other way when the musician is playing works appreciated by individuals with lower social standing.

Subcultures and countercultures

The term **subculture** refers to *cultural patterns that set apart some segment of a society's population*. Rastafarians, young gays and lesbians, frequent-flyer executives, jazz musicians, old people's homes, homeless people, campus poets and offshore powerboat racers all display subcultural patterns. It is easy – but often inaccurate – to place people into subcultural categories. Almost everyone participates simultaneously in numerous subcultures, and we often have little commitment to many of them.

In some cases, however, important cultural traits such as ethnicity or religion do set off people from one another – sometimes with tragic results. Consider the former nation of Yugoslavia in south-eastern Europe. The ongoing turmoil there has been fuelled by astounding cultural diversity. This *one* small country (which, before its breakup, was about half the size of England, with a population of 25 million) made use of *two* alphabets, professed *three* religions, spoke *four* languages, was home to *five* major nationalities, was divided into *six* political republics, and absorbed the cultural influences of *seven* surrounding countries. The cultural conflict that plunged this nation into civil war reveals that subcultures are a source not only of pleasing variety but also of tensions and outright violence (see Chapter 16 'Power, the State and Social Movements' and Sekulic et al., 1994).

Cultural diversity involves not just *variety* but also *hierarchy*. Too often, what we view as 'dominant' or 'highbrow' cultural patterns are those favoured by powerful segments of the population, while we relegate the lives of the disadvantaged to the realm of 'subculture'. This dilemma has led some researchers to highlight the experiences of less powerful members of our society in a new approach called multiculturalism (see Box 'Whose culture? Whose voice?' on page 122).

Cultural diversity also includes outright rejection of conventional ideas or behaviour. **Counterculture** refers to *cultural patterns that strongly oppose those widely accepted within a society*. An example of this would be the youth-orientated counterculture of the 1960s that

rejected the cultural mainstream as overly competitive, self-centred and materialistic. Instead, hippies and other counterculturalists favoured a cooperative lifestyle in which 'being' took precedence over 'doing' and the capacity for personal growth – or 'expanded consciousness' – was prized over material possessions like homes and cars. Such differences led some people at that time to 'drop out' of the larger society. Counterculture may involve not only distinctive values, but unconventional behaviour (including dress and forms of greeting) as well as music. Many members of the 1960s counterculture, for instance, drew personal identity from long hair, headbands and blue jeans; from displaying a peace sign rather than offering a handshake; and from drug use and the energy of ever-present rock-and-roll music.

Cultural change

Perhaps the most basic human truth is that 'All things shall pass'. Even the dinosaurs, who thrived on this planet for some 160 million years, exist today only as fossils. Will humanity survive for millions of years to come? No one knows. All we can say with certainty is that, given our reliance on culture, for as long as we survive, the human record will be one of continuous change.

Change in one dimension of a culture usually accompanies other transformations as well. For example, women's rising participation in the labour force has paralleled changing family patterns, including later age at first marriage, a rising divorce rate, and a growing share of children being raised in households without fathers. Such connections illustrate the principle of **cultural integration**, *the close relationship among various elements of a cultural system*.

But all elements of a cultural system do not change at the same speed. William Ogburn (1964) observed that technology moves quickly, generating new elements of material culture (like 'test-tube babies') faster than non-material culture (such as ideas about parenthood) can keep up with them. Ogburn called this inconsistency **cultural lag**, *the fact that cultural elements change at different rates, which may disrupt a cultural system*. In a culture with the technical ability to allow one woman to give birth to a child by using another woman's egg, which has been fertilized in a laboratory with the sperm of a total stranger, how are we to apply the traditional notions of motherhood and fatherhood?

Cultural changes are set in motion in three ways. The first is *invention*, the process of creating new cultural elements. Invention has given us the telephone (1876), powered aircraft (1903) and the aerosol spray can (1941), all of which have had a tremendous impact on our way of life. The process of invention goes on constantly, as indicated by the thousands of applications submitted annually to the European Patent Office.

Discovery, a second cause of cultural change, involves recognising and understanding something not fully understood before – from a distant star, to the foods of another culture, to the athletic prowess of US women. Many discoveries result from scientific research. Yet discovery can also happen quite by accident, as when Marie Curie left a rock on a piece of photographic paper in 1898 and serendipitously discovered radium.

The third cause of cultural change is *diffusion*, the spread of cultural traits from one society to another. The technological ability to send information around the globe in seconds – by means of radio, television, facsimile (fax) and computer – means that the level of cultural diffusion has never been greater than it is today.

Certainly, our own society has contributed many significant cultural elements to the world, ranging from computers to jazz music. But diffusion works the other way as well; for example, much of what we assume is inherently 'British' actually comes from other cultures. Ralph Linton (1937) explained that many commonplace elements of our way of life – most clothing and furniture, clocks, newspapers, money, and often the food we eat – are all derived from other cultures.

Ethnocentrism and cultural relativity

Western travellers are among the world's greatest shoppers. They delight in surveying hand-woven carpets in China or India, inspecting finely crafted metals in Turkey, or collecting beautifully coloured porcelain tiles in Morocco. And, of course, all these items are wonderful bargains. But one major reason for the low cost is unsettling: many products from low- and middle-income countries of the world are produced by children, many as young as 5 or 6, who work long days for extremely low wages.

We think of childhood as a time of innocence and freedom from adult burdens like regular work. In poor countries throughout the world, however, families depend on income earned by children. So what people in one society think of as right and natural, people elsewhere find puzzling and even immoral. Perhaps the Chinese philosopher Confucius had it right when he noted that 'All people are the same; it's only their habits that are different'.

Just about every imaginable social habit is subject to at least some variation around the world, and such differences cause travellers excitement and distress in about equal measure. The tradition in Japan is to name road *junctions* rather than streets, a practice that regularly confuses Europeans, for example, who do the opposite; Egyptians move very close to others in conversation, irritating any foreign visitors who are used to maintaining several feet of 'personal space'; bathrooms lack toilet paper throughout much of Morocco, causing great agitation among Westerners unaccustomed to using one's left hand for bathroom hygiene!

Because a particular culture is the basis for everyone's reality, it is no wonder that people everywhere exhibit **ethnocentrism**, *the practice of judging another culture by the standards of one's own culture*. On one level, some ethnocentrism is inevitable if people are to be emotionally attached to a cultural system. On another level, however, ethnocentrism generates misunderstanding and sometimes conflict.

For example, take the seemingly trivial matter of people in Europe referring to China as the 'Far East'. Such a term, which has little meaning to the Chinese, is an ethnocentric expression for a region that is far east *of Europe*. For their part, the Chinese refer to their country with a word translated as 'Middle Kingdom', suggesting that, like us, they see their society as the centre of the world.

Is there an alternative to ethnocentrism? The logical alternative is to imagine unfamiliar cultural traits from the point of view of *them* rather than *us*. The casual observer of an Amish farmer in Pennsylvania tilling hundreds of hectares with a team of horses rather than a tractor might initially dismiss this practice as hopelessly backward and inefficient. But, from the Amish point of view, hard work is a foundation of religious discipline. The Amish are well aware of tractors; they simply believe that using such machinery would be their undoing.

This alternative approach, called **cultural relativism**, is *the practice of judging a culture by its own standards*. Cultural relativism is a difficult attitude to

DIFFERENT VOICES

Youth cultural styles

The idea of 'culture' and all its linked concepts becomes clearer once we focus on a particular group. Young people are a good example. In many societies, new cultures spring from adolescence (Spates, 1976, 1983; Spates and Perkins, 1982). These have certainly not always been with us: most societies have no conception of a youth culture. Indeed, they only started to appear in very distinctive form in the period after World War 2. Here was a period of relative affluence in the West, the extension of schooling, and the emergence of a pervasive consumer market. Relatively disconnected from the responsibilities of adult family life, young people were a noticeable consumer market. Many new products – from records and films, to sports gear and clothing styles – could be directed at them. From these 'material conditions', youth cultures started to appear with their own 'ways of life', their own 'webs of meaning'. In the United Kingdom, for instance, a string of cultural styles developed: Teddy Boys came first in the 1950s (in the wake of the first rock 'n roll record and film – Bill Haley's *Rock around the Clock*); Mods and Rockers followed in the 1960s and adopted distinctive dress, music styles and values. These were followed by a whole gallery of youth types: skinheads, hippies, punks, rastas, grunge, goths, acid heads, new travellers and others. Some of these dominated for brief periods, but by the mid-1990s the situation was largely one of mixture – what some have called postmodern youth styles.

Sociologists in the cultural studies tradition (see the box later in this chapter) have asked many questions about the nature and development of such cultures. At one level, these sociologists simply describe what's going on – they do participant observation and ethnographies which depict the symbols, languages, values and material cultures in which young people live. Style becomes important and often parodies the consumer culture they are part of: to put it generally, punks, bikers, goths,

crusties, hippies dress down; mods, soul boys, home boys dress up!

At another level, sociologists try to show how these cultures work. Generally, they argue, such cultures 'express and resolve, albeit magically, the contradictions which remain hidden or unresolved in the parent culture' (Cohen, 1980: 82–3). Thus youth cultures may be seen as active ways of dealing with the problems generated by both the wider culture (with all its pushes towards getting jobs, consuming goods, getting on in school, becoming men and women) and the immediate 'adult' culture of the parents. These are stressful times, and young people have to develop and negotiate their own responses. Youth styles may come to be seen as forms of resistance, in which the young work up their own cultures as a way of handling a string of problems.

These days, youth cultural styles are amongst the most global in the world. Partly because of a widely common youth language of pop music, cable and satellite TV, film and the like, much of youth culture depends on borrowing from many sources. Young people play around with the dominant culture, creating a 'bricolage' of diverse bits in their own lives, mixing styles of fashion, music, consumption. The photographs capture some of the dress styles of different male youth. Why do young people wear such clothes, and adopt values and languages to go with them? ●

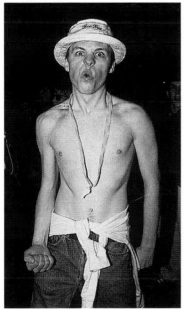

Source: Popperfoto

See Sarah Thornton, *Club Cultures* (Cambridge: Polity, 1995)

Most people in the affluent West take for granted that childhood should be a carefree time of life devoted to learning and play. In low-income societies of the world, however, poor families depend on the income earned by children, some of whom perform long days of heavy physical labour. We may not want to accept all cultural practices as 'natural' just because they exist. But what universal standards can be used to judge social patterns as either right or wrong?

Source: SIPA Press – Mark Peters

adopt because it requires that we not only understand the values and norms of another society but also suspend cultural standards we have known all our lives. But, as people of the world come into increasing contact with one another, so we confront the need to understand other cultures more fully.

The world may need greater cultural understanding, but cultural relativity introduces problems of its own. Virtually any kind of behaviour is practised somewhere in the world; does that mean that every-

thing is equally right? Just because Indian and Moroccan families benefit from having their children work long hours, does that justify such child labour?

Since we all are members of a single species, surely there must be some universal standards of proper conduct. But what are they? And, in trying to develop them, how can we avoid imposing our own standards of fair play on others? There are no simple answers. But here are some general guidelines to keep in mind when dealing with other cultures.

First, while cultural differences fascinate us, they can also be deeply disturbing. Be prepared to experience an emotional reaction when encountering the unfamiliar. Second, resist making a snap judgement so that you can observe unfamiliar cultural surroundings with an open mind. Third, try to imagine the issue from *their* point of view rather than *yours*. Fourth, after careful thought, try to evaluate an unfamiliar custom. After all, there is no virtue in passively accepting every cultural practice. But, in reaching a judgement, bear in mind that – despite your efforts – you can never really experience the world as others do. Fifth, and finally, turn the argument around and think about your own way of life as others might see it. After all, what we gain most from studying others is insight into ourselves.

A global culture?

Today, more than ever before, we can observe many of the same cultural patterns the world over. Walking the streets of Seoul (South Korea), Kuala Lumpur (Malaysia), Madras (India), Cairo (Egypt) and Casablanca (Morocco), we find familiar forms of dress, hear well-known pop music, and see advertising for many of the same products we use at home. Just as important, as illustrated by Map 4.1, English is rapidly emerging as the preferred second language of most of the world. So are we witnessing the birth of a global culture?

The world is still divided into around 200 nation-states and thousands of different cultural systems. Further, as recent violence in the former Soviet Union, the former Yugoslavia, the Middle East, Sri Lanka, and elsewhere attests, many people are intolerant of others whose cultures differ from their own. Yet, looking back through history, we see that societies around the world now have more contact with one another, and enjoy more cooperation, than ever before. These global connections involve the flow of goods, information and people.

FOCUS ON EUROPE

Old cultures and new cultures in Europe

However unified Europe may or may not seem, it is clear that it harbours many different cultures with different ways of life and ways of doing things. Think of the following:

● *Breakfasts*. Whilst in the UK it is cereals or a fry-up, in France they will have croissants and in The Netherlands, cheese and hams.

● *The working day*. Whilst in the UK, to have a 'siesta' would be looked upon as outrageously lazy, in most Mediterranean countries the whole system shuts down after lunch for a couple of hours. Workers in Spain or Italy tend to be very casual and relaxed, even chaotic; in Germany, everything is much more formal.

● *Consuming*. The English tend to form queues, but this is not so in many EU countries. Further, the English tend to accept the prices of goods from street sellers; not so in most of Europe. In UK bars you order drinks at the bar, pay straight away and do not tip; in most of the EU, you are served, pay at the end, and leave a tip.

Yet these cultural differences – many and small – are starting to change. Increasingly, for instance, breakfasts offered at hotels throughout Europe would give a choice of cereals, fry-ups, croissants, cheese and ham, and even Japanese noodles. Cultural differences are both recognised and breaking down.

And the new cultures

Nowhere was this clearer than when Disney came to Paris. Disneylands all over the world have been a favourite topic of cultural studies (see p. 81–2 of Bryman for a listing). Euro Disneyland, covering about 1,500 acres 20 miles east of Paris and housing six themed hotels, opened on 12 April 1992. EuroDisney was derided by French intellectuals as a cultural Chernobyl, and the unions objected to an almost fascist concern with uniformity that is anathema to the French. 'No one on the Disney payroll is allowed to smoke, wear flashy jewellery, chew gum, tint their hair an unnatural shade, possess a visible tattoo, be fat or fail to subdue their sweat glands. Men must wear their hair short, and may not have a beard or a moustache' (Bryson, 1993: 77).

In its opening years it was a significant failure, losing as much as $60 million in one three-month period and raising fears of closure. Many reasons were put forward for this – including the high costs and the poor weather. But at the heart of the complaints was a fear that Disney had come to the wrong place. It was out of culture.

Thus whilst the French value food, here it was all fast food. Whilst the French have a lugubrious and nonchalant manner, here the workers had to be cheery and efficent. The French could not easily play the smiling hosts. There was a cultural resistance and cultural contagion. Slowly, EuroDisney has become more successful: there is a lot of money in it, after all. And traditional cultures look less and less stable in the light of McDisney Worlds... ●

See Alan Bryman, *Disney and His Worlds* (London: Routledge, 1995).

Source: Popperfoto

1. *The global economy: the flow of goods*. The extent of international trade has never been greater. The global economy has introduced many of the same consumer goods (from cars to TV shows to T-shirts) the world over.

2. *Global communications: the flow of information*. A century ago, communication around the world depended on written messages delivered by boat, train, horse and wagon, or, occasionally, by telegraph wire. Today's satellite-based communication system enables people to experience sights and sounds of events taking place thousands of miles away – often as they happen.

3. *Global migration: the flow of people*. Knowledge about the rest of the world motivates people to move where they imagine life will be better. Moreover, today's transportation technology – especially air travel – makes relocating easier than ever before. As a result, most countries now contain significant numbers of people born elsewhere.

These global links have made the cultures of the world more similar, at least in superficial respects. It has also generated a deep contrast in world peoples. Some – usually poor and in low-income cultures – remain heavily restricted to a local world. But others have developed a much more flexible, global character. Ulf Hannerz describes this as a **cosmopolitan character**, who adopts:

a stance towards diversity . . . towards the coexistence of cultures in the individual experience . . . a willingness to engage with the other . . . a stance of openness toward divergent cultural experiences . . . a search for contrasts rather than toward uniformity . . . a state of readiness, a personal ability to make one's way into other cultures, through listening, looking, intuiting and reflecting . . . (Hannerz, 1990: 239)

But there are three important limitations to the global culture thesis. First, the flow of goods, information and people has been uneven throughout the world. Generally speaking, urban areas (centres of commerce, communication and people) have stronger ties to one another, while rural villages remain more isolated. Then, too, the greater economic and military power of North America and Western Europe means that these regions influence the rest of the world more than the other way around.

Second, the global culture thesis assumes that people everywhere are able to afford various new goods and services. As Chapter 11 ('Global Stratification') explains, the grinding poverty in much of the world deprives millions of even the basic necessities of a safe and secure life.

Third, although many cultural traits are now found throughout the world, we should not conclude that people everywhere attach the same meanings to them. Do teenagers in Tokyo understand rap music the way their counterparts in New York or Los Angeles do? Similarly, we mimic fashions from around the world with little knowledge of the lives of people who first came up with them. In short, people everywhere look at the world through their own cultural 'lenses' (Featherstone, ed., 1990; Hall and Neitz, 1993). This process has been identified as **glocalisation**, *the ways in which global phenomenon are responded to differently in local cultures*. Karaoke may have been sent round the world from Japan, but it takes on different meanings, songs and rituals when it is done in Thailand, London or San Francisco.

● Theoretical analysis of culture

Through culture, we make sense of ourselves and the surrounding world. Sociologists and anthropologists, however, have the special task of comprehending culture. They do so by using various theoretical paradigms.

Functional analysis

Recall from Chapter 1 ('The Sociological Perspective') that functional analysis presents society as a relatively stable system of integrated parts designed to meet human needs. From this point of view, then, the significance of various cultural traits lies in how they function to maintain the overall operation of society.

The reason for the stability of a cultural system, as functionalists see it, is that core values anchor its way of life (Parsons, 1964; Williams, 1970). The assertion that ideas (rather than, say, the system of material production) are the basis of human reality aligns functionalism with the philosophical doctrine of *idealism*. Core values give shape to most everyday activities, in the process binding together members of a society. New arrivals, of course, will not necessarily share a society's core orientations. But, according to the functionalist melting-pot scheme, immigrants learn to embrace such values over time.

Thinking functionally is also helpful in making sense of an unfamiliar way of life. Recall, for example, the Amish farmer ploughing hundreds of acres with a team of horses. This practice may violate the more widespread cultural value of efficiency; however, from the Amish point of view, hard work functions to generate discipline, which is crucial to Amish religious life. Long days of teamwork, along with family meals and recreation at home, not only make the Amish self-sufficient, but unify families and local communities.

Of course, Amish practices have dysfunctions as well. Farm living is hard work, and some people find strict religious discipline too confining, ultimately choosing to leave the community. Then, too, different interpretations of religious principles have generated tensions and sometimes lasting divisions within the Amish world (Hostetler, 1980; Kraybill, 1989; Kraybill and Olshan, 1994).

Because cultures are strategies to meet human needs, we would expect that societies the world over would have some elements in common. The term **cultural universals** refers to *traits that are part of every known culture*. Comparing hundreds of cultures, George Murdock (1945) found dozens of traits common to them all. One cultural universal is the family, which functions everywhere to control sexual reproduction and to organise the care and upbringing of children. Funeral rites, too, are found everywhere, because all human communities cope with the reality of death. Jokes are also a cultural universal, acting as a relatively safe means of releasing social tensions.

Critical evaluation
The functional paradigm shows how culture operates as an integrated system for meeting human needs, yet by emphasising cultural stability, this approach downplays the extent to which societies change. Similarly, functionalism's assertion that cultural values are embraced by every member of a society overlooks the range of cultural diversity. Finally, the cultural patterns favoured by powerful people often dominate a society, while other ways of life are pushed to the margins. Thus, cultures typically generate more conflict than functional analysis leads us to believe.

The conflict analysis of culture

Conflict analysis draws attention to links between culture and inequality, and highlights the ways in which any cultural trait benefits some members of society at the expense of others. Conflict theory asks basic questions about why certain values dominate a society in the first place, and examines the ways in which people might come to create their own alternative 'cultures of resistance'. Sociologists using this paradigm, especially those influenced by Marx, argue that values reflect a society's system of economic production. 'It is not the consciousness of men that determines their existence', Marx proclaimed. 'It is their social existence that determines their consciousness' (1977: 4; orig. 1859). Conflict theory, then, is rooted in the philosophical doctrine of *materialism*, the assertion that how people meet their material needs (in Europe, through a capitalist economy) has a powerful effect on other dimensions of their culture. Such a materialist approach contrasts with the idealist leanings of functionalism.

There are a number of more recent analyses that have developed Marx's ideas (such analysts are sometimes called neo-Marxists). One is the tradition of 'critical theory' developed by the Frankfurt School in the 1930s. Theodor Adorno (1903–69), a leading proponent, suggested that the emerging 'mass culture' – of popular music and film, for example – weakened critical consciousness and manipulated the working masses. He studied the workings of the 'culture industry' and the ways in which it standardised culture, made people passive and served to make people uncritical. For Adorno, the 'culture industry perpetually cheats its consumers of what it perpetually promises' (Adorno and Horkheimer, 1972: 120–3).

Another Marxist tradition was spearheaded by the Italian Antonio Gramsci (1891–1937). A militant in the Italian Communist party, he spent ten years imprisoned by Mussolini. During this time he wrote his famous Prison Notebooks which developed the idea of **hegemony**: *the ways in which one class dominates another through consent rather than force*. 'Culture' in its many forms may thus serve as a mechanism for encouraging people to accept the existing social order uncritically; as a means of 'winning consent'. Through culture, coercive power may not be needed to maintain dominance. Watching a regular diet of soaps, daytime TV and sports programmes may be sufficient! This argument has been taken further by an English group of sociologists centred on Stuart Hall. These are described in the box.

From culture to cultural studies

Over the past thirty years, sociology has been challenged by a number of newer disciplines. One of these has been 'cultural studies', which can be dated from three important books written by socialist historians and literary critics. They differ from much of the discussion of this chapter, which focuses upon 'culture' as an anthropological and sociological term. Instead, each of these books switched attention to the study of the values, beliefs, behaviour and material culture of the working class in England. The three books are Richard Hoggart's *Uses of Literacy*, Raymond Williams's *Culture and Society*, and E. P. Thompson's *The Making of the English Working Class*. What each of these books does is show that working class culture is an intelligible, active, even coherent and vibrant culture that has historical roots. These authors highlighted the active nature of the working class – how they made their culture.

Uses of Literacy looks at popular culture and locates the attitudes and response they have to books and entertainment. *The Making of the English Working Class* traces 'the growth of class consciousness, especially through trade unions, friendly societies, educational and religious movements, political organisations and periodicals – working class intellectual traditions, working class community pattern, and a working class structure of feeling' (E. P. Thompson, 1968). What this tradition highlights is the way in which working class groups both create their own cultures and resist other (dominant) ones.

Stuart Hall

This tradition was taken up and pushed further in the work of Stuart Hall, first at the Birmingham Centre for Contemporary Cultural Studies, and later when he became Professor of Sociology at the Open University.

With Stuart Hall, 'cultural sudies' comes into its own. Drawing from Hoggart et al., Hall makes culture a much more political idea. Indeed, as he says, popular culture is 'an arena of consent and resistance. It is partly where hegemony arises, and where it is secured. It is not a sphere where socialism, a socialist culture – already fully formed – might be simply expressed. But it is one of the places where socialism might be instituted. That is why "popular culture" matters' (Hall, in Storey, 1996: 3).

Hall has influenced a whole generation of young scholars studying ethnic, gendered and class based cultures. They have looked at the ways media 'represent' gender; how ethnic groups battle over their identities; and how dominant political forces – such as Thatcherism in the UK – have been resisted through the creation of alternative cultures, rituals and identities. ●

Conflict analysis reveals that cultural systems address human needs unequally and that a key function of cultural elements is to maintain the dominance of some people over others. This inequity, in turn, generates pressure toward change. Yet by stressing the divisiveness of culture, this paradigm understates the ways in which cultural patterns integrate members of society. Thus we should consider both conflict and functional insights to gain a fuller understanding of culture.

Sociobiology

We know culture is a human creation; but does our biological humanity influence the development of culture? A third theoretical paradigm, standing with one leg in biology and one in sociology, attempts to answer this question. **Sociobiology**, then, is *a theoretical paradigm that explores ways in which our biology affects how humans create culture.*

A multidisciplinary theoretical scheme, sociobiology rests on the logic of evolution. In *On the Origin of*

Species, Charles Darwin (1859) asserted that living organisms change over long periods of time as a result of *natural selection*, a matter of four simple principles. First, all living things live to reproduce themselves. Second, the blueprint for reproduction lies in the genes, the basic units of life that carry traits of one generation into the next. Genes vary randomly in each species; in effect, this genetic variation allows a species to 'try out' new life patterns in a particular environment. Third, due to genetic variation, some organisms are more likely than others to survive and to pass on their advantageous genes to their offspring. Fourth and finally, over thousands of generations, specific genetic patterns that promote reproduction survive and become dominant. In this way, as biologists say, a species *adapts* to its environment, and dominant traits emerge as the 'nature' of the organism.

In the case of humans, culture itself emerged as human nature. That is, rather than being biologically 'wired' for specific behaviour, humans developed the intelligence and sociability to devise many ways of life. Such flexibility has allowed our species to flourish all over the planet. Even so, sociobiologists point out, we are all one species – a fact evident in the large number of cultural universals.

Consider, for example, sex researcher Alfred Kinsey's observation: 'Among all people everywhere in the world, the male is more likely than the female to desire sex with a variety of partners' (quoted in Barash, 1981: 49). What insights does sociobiology offer into the so-called 'double standard'?

To begin, we all know that children result from joining a woman's egg with a man's sperm. But the biological significance of a single sperm and a single egg differ dramatically. For healthy men, sperm represent a 'renewable resource' produced by the testes throughout most of the life course. A man releases hundreds of millions of sperm in a single ejaculation – technically, enough to fertilise every woman in North America (Barash, 1981: 47). A newborn female's ovaries, however, contain her entire lifetime allotment of follicles or immature eggs. A woman commonly releases a single mature egg cell from her ovaries each month. So, while a man is biologically capable of fathering thousands of offspring, a woman is able to bear only a relatively small number of children.

Given this biologically based difference, each sex is well served by a distinctive reproductive strategy. From a strictly biological perspective, a man reproduces his genes most efficiently by being promiscuous – that is, readily engaging in sex. This scheme, however, opposes the reproductive interests of a woman, whose relatively few pregnancies demand that she carry the child for nine months, give birth, and care for the infant for some time afterwards. Thus, efficient reproduction on the part of the woman depends on carefully selecting a mate whose qualities (beginning with the likelihood that he will simply stay around) will contribute to their child's survival and successful reproduction (Remoff, 1984).

The 'double standard' certainly involves more than biology, and is tangled up with the historical domination of women by men (Barry, 1983). But sociobiology suggests that this cultural pattern, like many others, has an underlying bio-logic. Simply put, it has developed around the world because women and men everywhere tend toward distinctive reproductive strategies.

Critical evaluation
Sociobiology has generated intriguing theories about the biological roots of some cultural patterns, especially those that are universal. But sociobiology remains controversial for several reasons.

First, some critics fear that sociobiology may revive biological arguments, common a century ago, touting the superiority of one race or sex. But defenders counter that sociobiology rejects the past pseudoscience of racial superiority. On the contrary, they contend, sociobiology actually unites all of humanity by asserting that all people share a single evolutionary history. With regard to sex, sociobiology does rest on the assumption that men and women differ biologically in some ways that culture cannot overcome – if, in fact, any society sought to. But, far from asserting that males are somehow more important than females, sociobiology emphasises how both sexes are vital to human reproduction.

Second, say the critics, sociobiologists have as yet amassed little evidence to support their theories. A generation ago, Edward O. Wilson (1975, 1978), generally credited as the founder of this field, optimistically claimed that sociobiology would reveal the biological roots of human culture. But research to date concludes that biological forces do not determine human behaviour in any rigid sense. Rather, abundant evidence supports the conclusion that human behaviour is *learned*

Whose culture? Whose voice? Eurocentrism, multiculturalism and postcolonialism in sociology

Europe has long been seen as the cradle of the modern world. Indeed, for the Swedish sociologist Goran Therborn, 'There is no doubt that Europe was the pioneer of modernity and the centre of it. Neither the Islamic, the Black African, the Hindu nor the East Asian Confucian world seems to have discovered the future as a new place, attainable but never visited before. . . . Europe became the undisputed centre of modernity in terms of knowledge as well as in terms of power'. It was the 'chief organiser' of this modern world. For Therborn, there are many features of this. Europe's 'modernity' brought new knowledge, new settlements around the world, new technologies and capital investment, as well as the development of all the 'isms' – socialism, communism, anarchism, liberalism, Protestantism, etc.

But 'a sense of Europe' can go back a long way. Some writers suggest that European culture can be defined by four elements that mark it off from the rest of the world:

● The Hellenistic and Roman Empires – rediscovered through the Renaissance – which helped establish a sense of art, politics and philosophy that shapes a characteristic 'humanistic' temper

● Christianity, which for two millennia, and despite oppositions and internal schisms, has pervaded the European idea (and at times the very words 'Europe' and 'Christendom' were synonymous)

● The Enlightenment – the creation of a scientific, sceptical, creative intellectual climate helps to define it – as does the 'Europabild' literature

● Industrialisation: whilst not alone, and these days overtaken by many other countries, it was the first region to foster the industrial world . . . (Hay, 1968; Joll, 1969)

Yet there are serious problems with this commonly held 'Eurocentric' view. Taking a European view of the world often minimises the importance of other cultures: Asian, Latin American, African etc. It also cultivates a view of Europe as an entity with a history of continuity, which on closer inspection is hard to sustain. Greek history, for example, is as much connected to the Middle East and the Orient. Indeed, the eminent historian Arnold Toynbee saw this continuity as a 'thorough going misinterpretation of the history of Mankind' – a dangerous tendency that minimised the contribution of many other cultures. These days, this is recognised as the twin problem of 'multiculturalism' and 'postcolonialism'.

Originally emerging as an education policy in the United States, **multiculturalism** *recognises past and present cultural diversity and promotes the equality of all cultural traditions. This movement represents a sharp turn from the view where cultures are defined through their European links.* **Postcolonialism** *recognises how many cultures have been made through oppressor–subject relationships and seeks to unpack these, showing how cultures are made.*

The European Flag

Source: Popperfoto

For more than two centuries, historians have highlighted people of English and other European ancestry and chronicled events from their point of view. In the process, little attention has been paid to the perspectives and accomplishments of other cultures. Multiculturalists condemn this pattern as **Eurocentrism**, *the dominance of European (particularly English) cultural patterns*. Molefi Kete Asante, a leading advocate of multiculturalism, draws a historical analogy: like the fifteenth century Europeans who could not let go of the idea that the earth was the centre of the universe, many today find it difficult not to view European culture as the centre of the social universe (1988: 7).

Few deny that our culture has wide-ranging roots. But multiculturalism is controversial because it demands that we rethink the norms and values at the core of our society. Not surprisingly, battles are now raging over how to describe culture. To counter pervasive Eurocentrism, some multiculturalists are calling for **Afrocentrism**, *the dominance of African cultural patterns*, which they see as a corrective for centuries of minimising or altogether ignoring the cultural achievements of African societies.

And other cultures are making similar claims. Throughout much of history the world has been colonised by other countries and nations. Many countries have been invaded by others and had their cultures uprooted, transformed, even destroyed. And today, whenever we look at cultures, we tend to see them from the point of our own.

Frantz Fanon analysed the impact of white colonialism on blacks. He aimed through his writings to liberate the consciousness of the oppressed. In the first phase he sees how blacks may become assimilated to dominant white culture; a second phase sees the black writer disturbed; and a third sees the native writers turning themselves into awakeners of the people. But labels like African, Muslim, American, 'Chinese' or, worse, 'Chineseness' are no more than starting points. The object then is to 'deconstruct' them – to take them apart and see what lies behind them.

Although multiculturalism and postcolonialism have found widespread favour in the last several years, they have provoked criticism as well. Opponents think they encourage divisiveness rather than unity by urging individuals to identify with their own category rather than with common elements. Similarly, rather than recognise any common standards of truth, say critics, multiculturalism maintains that we should evaluate ideas according to the race (and sex) of those who present them. Common humanity thus dissolves into an 'African voice', an 'Asian voice', and so on.

Critics say that multiculturalism and postcolonialism may not end up helping minorities, as proponents contend. They argue that multiculturalist initiatives (from African-American studies to all-black college accommodation) seem to demand precisely the kind of racial segregation we do not want. Then, too, an Asiacentric curriculum may well deny children a wide range of crucial knowledge and skills by forcing them to study only certain topics from a single point of view. Whose voices are to be heard?

Is there any common ground in this debate? Virtually everyone agrees that all people in Europe need to gain greater appreciation of the extent of cultural diversity. Eurocentric views distort an appreciation of the emergent global cultures, all with their differing languages, symbols, countercultures, etc. But precisely where the balance is to be struck is a burning issue for a new generation of sociologists.

● **Continue the debate:**

1. Do you think there is a truly distinctive 'European' culture with history and roots? What does it look like, and what is its history? Does it have a coherence, or does it conceal many voices?

2. How does the multiculturalism debate shape our views on school curriculums and language learning? What are the pros and cons of different curriculums and languages?

3. Whose voices are being heard once you adopt a 'postcolonial' voice? ●

Sources: Michael Wintle (ed.), *Culture and Identity in Europe* (Avebury, 1996); Stephen Castles and Mark J. Miller, *The Age of Migration* (London: Macmillan, 1993).

within a cultural system. The contribution of sociobiology, then, lies in its explanation of why some cultural patterns seem 'easier to learn' than others (Barash, 1981).

● Culture and human freedom

Throughout this chapter, we have touched on the extent to which cultural creatures are free. Does culture bind us to each other and to the past? Or does culture enhance our capacity for individual thought and independent choices?

Culture as constraint

Over the long course of human evolution, culture became the human strategy for survival. Truly, we cannot live without culture. But the capacity for culture does have some drawbacks. We may be the only animals who name ourselves; yet, as symbolic beings, we are also the only creatures who experience alienation. Moreover, culture is largely a matter of habit, limiting our choices and driving us to repeat troubling patterns, such as racial prejudice, in each new generation. And, in an electronic age, we may wonder at the extent to which the news media and businesses manipulate people into believing they must see the latest films or wear the latest styles of clothing.

Moreover, while our society's insistence on competitive achievement urges us toward excellence, this same pattern also isolates us from one another. Material comforts improve our lives in many ways, yet our preoccupation with acquiring things distracts us from seeking the security and satisfaction of close relationships or cultivating spiritual strength. Our emphasis on personal freedom affords us privacy and autonomy, yet our culture often denies us the support of a human community in which to share life's problems (Slater, 1976; Bellah et al., 1985).

Culture as freedom

Human beings may seem to be prisoners of culture, just as other animals are prisoners of biology. But careful thought about the ideas presented in this chapter reveals a crucial difference. Biological instinct operates in a ready-made world; culture, by contrast, gives us the responsibility to make and remake a world for ourselves.

Therefore, although culture seems at times to circumscribe our lives, it always embodies the human capacity for hope, creativity and choice. There is no better evidence of this than the fascinating cultural diversity of our own society and the far greater human variety of the larger world. Furthermore, far from being static, culture is ever-changing; it allows our imagination and inventiveness to come to the fore. The more we discover about the operation of our culture, the greater our capacity to use the freedom it offers us.

SUMMARY

1. Culture refers to a way of life shared by members of a society. Several species display a limited capacity for culture, but only human beings rely on culture for survival.

2. As the human brain evolved, the first elements of culture appeared some 2 million years ago; the development of culture reached the point we call 'the birth of civilisation' approximately 12,000 years ago.

3. Humans build culture on symbols by attaching meaning to objects and action. Language is the symbolic system by which one generation transmits culture to the next.

4. Values represent general orientations to the world around us; beliefs are statements that people who share a culture hold to be true.

5. Cultural norms guide human behaviour. Mores consist of norms of great moral significance; folkways guide everyday life and afford greater individual discretion.

6. High culture refers to patterns that distinguish a society's elites; popular culture includes patterns widespread in a society.

7. Subculture refers to distinctive cultural patterns adopted by a segment of a population; counterculture means patterns strongly at odds with a

conventional way of life. Multiculturalism represents educational efforts to enhance awareness and appreciation of cultural diversity.

8. Invention, discovery and diffusion all generate cultural change. When parts of a cultural system change at different rates, this is called cultural lag.

9. Because we learn the standards of one culture, we evaluate other cultures ethnocentrically. An alternative to ethnocentrism, cultural relativism, means judging another culture according to its own standards.

10. The functional paradigm views culture as a relatively stable system built on core values. Cultural traits function to maintain the overall system.

11. The conflict paradigm envisions culture as a dynamic arena of inequality and conflict. Cultural patterns typically benefit some categories of people more than others.

12. Sociobiology investigates the influence of humanity's evolutionary past on present-day cultural patterns.

13. Culture can constrain human needs and ambitions; yet, as cultural creatures, we have the capacity to shape and reshape the world to meet our needs and pursue our dreams.

14. Multiculturalism and postcolonialism help us develop ways of thinking outside of our own cultures.

KEY CONCEPTS

Afrocentrism the dominance of African cultural patterns

beliefs specific statements that people hold to be true

counterculture cultural patterns that strongly oppose those widely accepted within a society

cultural conflict political opposition, often accompanied by social hostility, rooted in different cultural values

cultural integration the close relationship among various elements of a cultural system

cultural lag the fact that cultural elements change at different rates, which may disrupt a cultural system

cultural relativism the practice of judging a culture by its own standards

cultural transmission the process by which one generation passes culture to the next

cultural universals traits that are part of every known culture

culture the beliefs, values, behaviour and material objects that constitute a people's way of life

culture shock personal disorientation that comes from encountering an unfamiliar way of life

ethnocentrism the practice of judging another culture by the standards of one's own culture

Eurocentrism the dominance of European (especially English) cultural patterns

folkways a society's customs for routine, casual interaction

glocalisation the ways in which global phenomenon are responded to differently in local cultures

hegemony the ways in which one class dominates another through consent rather than force.

high culture cultural patterns that distinguish a society's elite

ideal culture (as opposed to real culture) social patterns mandated by cultural values and norms

language a system of symbols that allows members of a society to communicate with one another

material culture the tangible things created by members of a society

mores a society's standards of proper moral conduct

multiculturalism an educational approach recognising past and present cultural diversity in a society and promoting the equality of all cultural traditions

non-material culture the intangible world of ideas created by members of a society

norms rules and expectations by which a society guides the behaviour of its members

popular culture cultural patterns that are widespread among a society's population

postcolonialism recognises how many cultures have been made through oppressor subject relationships and seeks to unpack these, showing how cultures are made

real culture (as opposed to ideal culture) actual social patterns that only approximate to cultural expectations

Sapir–Whorf hypothesis the hypothesis that people perceive the world through the cultural lens of language

social control various means by which members of a society encourage conformity to norms

sociobiology a theoretical paradigm that explores ways in which our biology affects how humans create culture

subculture cultural patterns that set apart some segment of a society's population

symbol anything that carries a particular meaning recognised by people who share culture

technology knowledge that a society applies to the task of living in a physical environment

values culturally defined standards by which people assess desirability, goodness and beauty, and which serve as broad guidelines for social living

CRITICAL-THINKING QUESTIONS

1. What is the cultural significance of a carefully manicured lawn in a highly mobile and largely anonymous society? What does a well-tended (or untended) front garden say about a person?

2. Do you think European cultural values are changing? If so, how and why?

3. Using some of the key concepts developed in this chapter – language, values, material culture etc. – present an analysis of any one cultural group you know (such as a religious culture, a sport culture, a youth culture or a 'deviant' culture). (Hint: also look back to Chapter 2 on ways of doing research.)

4. Look at this text – or any other student text you use – and consider how far it is shaped by Eurocentrism.

5. How far do you think young people in your own country have more in common with youth of other countries than with older people in their own? Discuss in relation to the idea of globalisation introduced in Chapter 1 and glocalisation introduced in this chapter.

GOING FURTHER

Introductory reading

Two short introductions to the field are John Storey's *Cultural Studies and the Study of Popular Culture* (Edinburgh University Press, 1996), and Chris Jenks, *Culture* (London: Routledge, 1993). The former is more limited to 'cultural studies' not culture; the latter is more theoretical.

Classic sources

'Culture' has long been a prime concern of anthropology. A leading general statement here is Clifford Geertz, *The Interpretation of Cultures* (London: Hutchinson, 1975) – a classic book that also introduces the important term 'thick description'.

Napoleon A. Chagnon, *Yanomamö: The Fierce People* (New York: Holt, Rinehart and Winston, 5th edn, 1997).
 Napoleon Chagnon's updated account of the Yanomamö offers fascinating insights into a culture very different from our own. It is also a compelling

tale of carrying out fieldwork in an unfamiliar world. The 1997 edition comes with a CD ROM Yanomamö Interactive: The Ax Fight.

Margaret Mead. *Coming of Age in Samoa: A Psychological Study of Primitive Youth for Western Civilization* (New York: Wm. Morrow, 1961, 1928).
 Margaret Mead, perhaps the best-known student of culture, carried out this study of the Samoan Islands, which demonstrates the variability of cultural systems.

Raymond Williams, *Culture* (London: Fontana, 1981) is generally considered to be one of the prime English introductions.

More advanced reading

Colin Tudge, *The Day before Yesterday: Five Million Years of Human History* (London: Cape, 1995).
 This is a highly readable account of the 'long history' of planet Earth, in which we have appeared

only very recently. It enables human societies to be located in a very broad context of geological change.

William W. Zellner, *Counter Cultures: A Sociological Analysis* (New York: St Martin's Press, 1994).

This recent book investigates a host of groups at the margins of US society, including skinheads, the Ku Klux Klan, Satanists, survivalists, and followers of Scientology and the Unification Church.

Mike Featherstone (ed.), *Global Culture: Nationalism, Globalisation, and Modernity* (London: Sage, 1990).

These two dozen essays explore various ways in which a global culture is emerging.

Joana McIntyre Varawa, *Changes in Latitude: An Uncommon Anthropology* (New York: Harper & Row, 1990).

This fascinating book describes how a woman from Hawaii past mid-life travelled to Fiji on vacation only to find a new home, a new husband, and a host of new challenges.

Craig Storti, *The Art of Crossing Cultures* (Yarmouth, MN: Intercultural Press, 1990).

This brief book explores the excitement as well as the difficulties of cross-cultural experience.

On cultural studies

This new field of study should not be confused with 'culture', which generally has a much broader set of concerns. The histories of cultural studies and analysis of it may be found in: Patrick Bratlinger, *Crusoe's Footprints: Cultural Studies in Britain and America* (New York: Routledge, 1990); G. Turner, *British Cultural Studies*, (London: Unwin Hyman/Routledge, 1990) and B. Agger, *Cultural Studies as Critical Theory* (London: Falmer, 1992).

For fairly classic 'readings' in the field, see Simon Duhring (ed.), *The Cultural Studies Reader* (London: Routledge, 1993), which includes articles by Adorno, Hall, Williams, Bordieu and many others.

The 'state of the field' essays in the early 1990s are to be found in Lawrence Gorssberg, Cary Nelson and Paula Treichler, *Cultural Studies* (London: Routledge, 1992).

To go further with the youth culture debate, see: Ken Gelder and Sarah Thornton (eds.), *The Subcultures Reader* (London: Routledge, 1997), a collection of both classic and recent articles; and Johan Fornas, Ulf Lindeberg and Oue Sernhede, *In Garageland: Rock, Youth and Modernity* (London: Routledge, 1995) – recent research of one youth form.

Web sites

Rumoured to be a creative web site on 'postmodern culture' is gopher://jefferson.village.virginia.
EDV/11/pubs/pmc

● http:/deil.lang.vivc.edu/exchange/

This is the web site of *Exchange* which welcomes submissions from non-native English speakers around the world.

chapter five

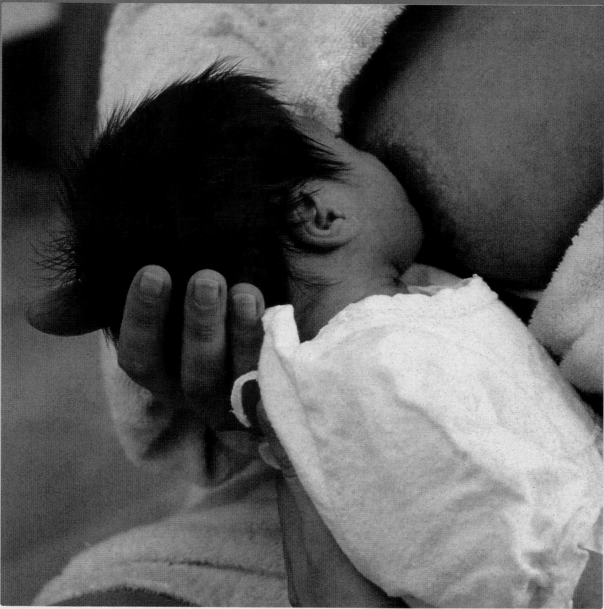

Source: Popperfoto

Socialisation

On a cold winter day in 1938, a social worker walked anxiously to the door of a rural Pennsylvania farmhouse. Investigating a case of possible child abuse, the social worker soon discovered a 5-year-old girl hidden in a second-floor storage room. The child, whose name was Anna, was wedged into an old chair with her arms tied above her head so that she could not move. She was dressed in filthy garments, and her arms and legs – looking like matchsticks – were so frail that she could not use them.

Anna's situation can only be described as tragic. She was born in 1932 to an unmarried and mentally impaired woman of 26 who lived with her father. Enraged by his daughter's 'illegitimate' motherhood, the grandfather did not even want the child in his house. Anna therefore spent her first six months in various institutions. But her mother was unable to pay for such care, so Anna returned to the hostile home of her grandfather.

At this point, her ordeal intensified. To lessen the grandfather's anger, Anna's mother moved the child to the attic room, where she received little attention and just enough milk to keep her alive. There she stayed – day after day, month after month, with essentially no human contact – for five long years.

Upon learning of the discovery of Anna, sociologist Kingsley Davis (1940) travelled immediately to see the child. He found her at a county home, where local authorities had taken her. Davis was appalled by Anna's condition. She was emaciated and feeble. Unable to laugh, smile, speak or even show anger, she was completely unresponsive, as if alone in an empty world.

● The importance of social experience

Here is a deplorable but instructive case of a human being deprived of virtually all social contact. Although physically alive, Anna hardly seemed human. Her plight reveals that, isolated in this way, an individual develops scarcely any capacity for thought, emotion and meaningful behaviour. In short, without social experience, an individual is more an *object* than a *person*.

This chapter explores what Anna was deprived of – the means by which we become fully human. This process is **socialisation**, *the lifelong social experience by which individuals develop their human potential and learn patterns of their culture*. Unlike other living species whose behaviour is biologically set, human beings rely on social experience to learn the nuances of their culture in order to survive.

Social experience is also the foundation of **personality**, *a person's fairly consistent patterns of thinking, feeling and acting*. We build a personality by internalising our social surroundings. As personality develops, we participate in a culture while remaining, in some respects, distinct individuals. But in the absence of social experience, as the case of Anna shows, personality does not emerge at all.

Social experience is vital for society just as it is for individuals. Societies exist beyond the life span of any person, and thus each generation must teach something of its way of life to the next. Broadly speaking, then, socialisation amounts to the ongoing process of cultural transmission.

Human development: nature and nurture

Virtually helpless at birth, the human infant depends on others for care and nourishment as well as learning. Although Anna's short life makes these facts very clear, a century ago most people mistakenly believed that human behaviour was the product of biological imperatives.

Charles Darwin, whose groundbreaking ideas are summarised in Chapter 4 ('Culture'), held that each species evolves over thousands of generations as genetic variations enhance survival and reproduction. Biologically rooted traits that enhance survival emerge as a species' 'nature'. As Darwin's fame grew, people assumed that humans, like other forms of life, had a fixed, instinctive 'nature' as well.

Such notions are still with us. People sometimes claim, for example, that our economic system is a reflection of 'instinctive human competitiveness', that some people are 'born criminals', or that women are more 'naturally' emotional while men are 'inherently' more rational. We often describe familiar personality traits as *human nature* as if people were born with them, just as we are born with five senses. More accurately, however, our human nature leads us to create and learn cultural traits, as we shall see.

People trying to understand cultural diversity also misconstrued Darwin's thinking. Centuries of world exploration and empire building taught Western Europeans that people around the world behaved quite differently from themselves. They attributed such contrasts to biology rather than culture. It was a simple – although terribly damaging – step to conclude that members of technologically simple societies were biologically less evolved and, therefore, less human. Such a self-serving and ethnocentric view helped justify colonial practices, including land seizures and slavery, since it is easier to exploit others if you are convinced that they are not truly human in the same sense that you are.

In the twentieth century, social scientists launched a broad attack on naturalistic explanations of human behaviour. Psychologist John B. Watson (1878–1958) devised a theory called *behaviourism*, which held that specific behaviour patterns are not instinctive but learned. Thus people the world over have the same claim to humanity, Watson insisted; humans differ only in their cultural environment. For Watson, 'human nature' was infinitely malleable:

Give me a dozen healthy infants . . . and my own specified world to bring them up in, and I will guarantee to take any one at random and train him [or her] to become any type of specialist that I might select – doctor, lawyer, artist, merchant, chief, and yes, even beggar-man and thief – regardless of his [or her] talents, penchants, tendencies, abilities, vocations, and race of his [or her] ancestors. (1930: 104)

Anthropologists weighed in on this debate as well, showing how variable the world's cultures are. An outspoken proponent of the 'nurture' view, anthropologist Margaret Mead summed up the evidence: 'The differences between individuals who are members of different cultures, like the differences between individuals within a culture, are almost entirely to be laid to differences in conditioning, especially during early childhood, and this conditioning is culturally determined' (1963: 280; orig. 1935).

Today, social scientists are cautious about describing any type of behaviour as instinctive. Even sociobiology, examined in Chapter 3, holds that human behaviour is primarily guided by the surrounding culture. Of course, this does not mean that biology plays *no* part in human behaviour. Human life, after all, depends on the functioning of the body. We also know that children share many biological traits with their parents, especially physical characteristics such as height, weight, hair and eye colour, and facial features. Intelligence and various personality characteristics (for example, how one reacts to stimulation or frustration) have some genetic component, as does the potential to excel in such activities as art and music. But whether a person develops an inherited potential depends on the opportunities associated with social position (Herrnstein, 1973; Plomin and Foch, 1980; Goldsmith, 1983).

In sum, the evidence shows that nurture is far more important than nature in determining human behaviour. We should not think of nature as opposing nurture, though, since we express our human nature as we build culture. For humans, then, nature and nurture are inseparable.

Social isolation

For obvious ethical reasons, researchers cannot subject human beings to experimental isolation. Consequently, much of what we know about this issue comes from rare cases of abused children like Anna. Researchers have, however, studied the impact of social isolation on animals.

Effects of social isolation on non-human primates

Psychologists Harry Harlow and Margaret Harlow (1962) conducted a classic investigation of the effects of social isolation on non-human primates. They observed the consequences of various conditions of isolation on rhesus monkeys, whose behaviour is in some ways remarkably similar to that of humans.

The Harlows found that complete social isolation for even six months (with adequate nutrition) seriously disturbed the monkeys' development. When these monkeys subsequently returned to their group, they were anxious, passive and fearful.

The Harlows then isolated infant rhesus monkeys, but provided an artificial 'mother' made of wire mesh with a wooden head and the nipple of a feeding tube where the breast would be. These monkeys survived but they, too, subsequently displayed emotional damage.

But when the researchers covered the artificial 'mother' with soft terry cloth, the infant monkeys would cling to it, apparently deriving emotional benefit from the closeness. Subsequently, these monkeys revealed less emotional distress. The Harlows thus concluded that normal emotional development requires affectionate cradling as part of parent–infant interaction.

The Harlows made two other discoveries. First, as long as they were surrounded by other infants, monkeys were not adversely affected by the absence of a mother. This finding suggests that deprivation of social experience, rather than the absence of a specific parent, has devastating effects. Second, the Harlows found that lesser periods of social isolation – up to about three months – caused emotional distress, but only temporarily. The damage of short-term isolation, then, can be overcome; longer-term isolation, however, appears to inflict on monkeys irreversible emotional and behavioural damage.

Effects of social isolation on children

The case of Anna, described earlier, is the best-known instance of the extended social isolation of a human infant. After her discovery, Anna benefited from intense social contact and soon showed improvement. Visiting her in the county home after ten days, Kingsley Davis (1940) noted that she was more alert and even smiled with obvious pleasure. During the next year, Anna made slow but steady progress, showing greater interest in other people and gradually learning to walk. After a year and a half, she could feed herself and play with toys.

Consistent with the observations of the Harlows, however, it was becoming apparent that Anna's five years of social isolation had left her permanently damaged. At the age of 8 her mental and social development was still less than that of a 2-year-old. Not until she was almost 10 did she begin to grasp language. Of course, since Anna's mother was mentally retarded, perhaps Anna was similarly disadvantaged. The riddle was never solved, because Anna died at the age of 10 from a blood disorder, possibly related to her years of abuse (Davis, 1940, 1947).

A second, quite similar case involves another girl, found at about the same time as Anna and under strikingly similar circumstances. After more than six years of virtual isolation, this girl – known as Isabelle – displayed the same lack of human responsiveness as Anna. Unlike Anna, though, Isabelle benefited from a special learning programme directed by psychologists. Within a week, Isabelle was attempting to speak, and a year and a half later, her vocabulary included nearly 2,000 words. The psychologists concluded that intensive effort had propelled Isabelle through six years of normal development in only two years. By the time she was 14, Isabelle was attending sixth-grade classes, apparently on her way to at least an approximately normal life (Davis, 1947).

Like other children subjected to prolonged isolation, Genie never did develop a normal facility with language. Many researchers conclude that, unless a child learns language at an early age, this ability is permanently hindered. But others counter that children may well be mentally retarded by such abuse. Thus, cases such as Genie do not settle 'nature–nurture' debates about human development.

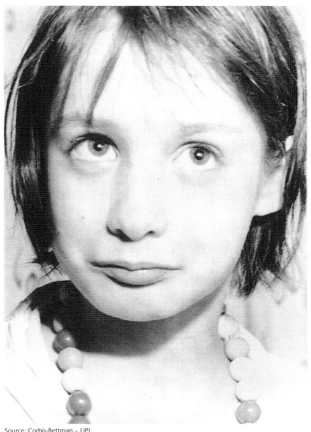

Source: Corbis-Bettman – UPI

A final case of childhood isolation involves a 13-year-old California girl victimised in a host of ways by her parents from the age of 2 (Curtiss, 1977; Pines, 1981; Rymer, 1994). Genie's ordeal included extended periods of being locked alone in a garage. Upon discovery, her condition mirrored that of Anna and Isabelle. Genie was emaciated (weighing only 59 pounds) and had the mental development of a 1-year-old. She received intensive treatment by specialists and thrived physically. Yet even after years of care, her ability to use language remains that of a young child, and she lives today in a home for developmentally disabled adults.

All the evidence points to the crucial role of social experience in personality development. Human beings are resilient creatures, sometimes able to recover from even the crushing experience of abuse and isolation. But there is a point – precisely when is unclear from the limited number of cases – at which social isolation in infancy results in irreparable developmental damage.

● Understanding the socialisation process

Socialisation is a complex, lifelong process. The following sections highlight the work of five men and women who have made lasting contributions to our understanding of human development.

Sigmund Freud: the elements of personality

Sigmund Freud (1856–1939) lived in Vienna at a time when most Europeans considered human behaviour to be biologically fixed. Trained as a physician, Freud gradually turned to the study of personality and eventually developed the celebrated theory of psychoanalysis. Many aspects of this work bear directly on our understanding of socialisation.

Basic human needs
Freud contended that biology plays an important part in social development, though not in terms of the simple instincts that guide other species. Humans, Freud theorised, respond to two general needs or drives. First, humans have a basic need for pleasure and bonding, which Freud called the life instincts, or *eros* (from the Greek god of love). Second, opposing this need, are aggressive drives, which Freud termed the death instincts, or *thanatos* (from the Greek meaning

Sigmund Freud (1856–1939)

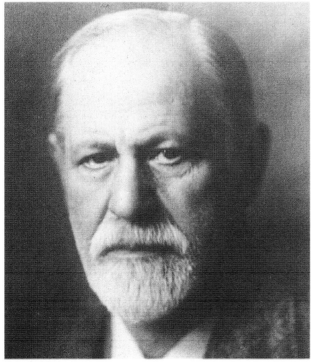

Source: Popperfoto

'death'). Freud postulated that these opposing forces, operating primarily at the level of the unconscious mind, generate deeply rooted inner tensions.

Freud's model of personality

These basic drives need to be controlled and Freud incorporated them and the influence of society into a model of personality with three parts: id, ego and superego. The **id** represents *the human being's basic drives*, which are unconscious and demand immediate satisfaction. Rooted in our biology, the id is present at birth, making a new-born a bundle of needs demanding attention, touching and all kinds of nervous and sexual experiences. But society does not tolerate such a self-centred orientation, so the id's desires inevitably encounter resistance. Because of this cultural opposition, one of the first words a child comprehends is 'no'.

To avoid frustration, the child learns to approach the world realistically. This accomplishment forms the second component of the personality, the **ego** (Latin for 'I'), which is *a person's conscious efforts to balance innate, pleasure-seeking drives with the demands of society.*

The ego arises as we gain awareness of our distinct existence; it reaches fruition as we come to understand that we cannot have everything we want. It is guided by the reality principle.

Finally, the human personality develops the **super-ego** (Latin meaning 'above' or 'beyond' the ego), which is the *operation of culture within the individual.* With the emergence of the superego, we can see *why* we cannot have everything we want. The superego consists of cultural values and norms – internalised in the form of conscience – that define moral limits. The superego begins to emerge as children recognise parental control; it matures as they learn that their own behaviour and that of their parents – in fact, everyone's behaviour – reflects a broader system of cultural demands.

Personality development

The id-centred child first encounters the world as a bewildering array of physical sensations and need satisfactions. With the gradual development of the superego, however, the child's comprehension extends beyond pleasure and pain to include the moral concepts of right and wrong. Initially, in other words, children can feel good only in the physical sense; but, after three or four years, they feel good or bad as they evaluate their own behaviour according to cultural standards.

Conflict between id and superego is ongoing; but, in a well-adjusted person, these opposing forces are managed by the ego. Unresolved conflicts, especially during childhood, typically result in personality disorders later on.

As the source of superego, culture operates to control human drives, a process Freud termed *repression*. Some repression is inevitable, since any society must coerce people to look beyond themselves. Often the competing demands of self and society are resolved through compromise. This process, which Freud called *sublimation*, transforms fundamentally selfish drives into socially acceptable activities. Sexual urges, for example, may lead to marriage, just as aggression gives rise to competitive sports.

Freud and the Oedipal Complex

Central to Freud's thought, and to his theory of socialisation, is his concept of the Oedipus Complex: a metaphor for the emotional and psychic struggles and conflicts a young child experiences with its mother and father. The term is derived from the Greek tragedy when Oedipus marries his mother and murders his father, and looks at the passionate 'little love affairs' that children have with their families in the earliest years of life.

Broadly, Freud suggests that new-born children initially feel a stong closeness and attachment to the mother, and that the father is experienced as something of a threat to this attachment. The child thus starts to harbour hostile feelings towards the father, for which it feels increasingly guilty. This little dilemma can be experienced very profoundly. Freud uses the term 'castration complex' to suggest a powerful threat to the child. And in order to resolve this threat, the child starts to identify with the father instead.

The Oedipus Complex is the key to getting the Id and all its desires under control: the father becomes part of the superego as an authority figure. Freud is outlining a basic predicament in becoming social: how to cope with all our desires and become a socialised adult with a conscience. And he does this through seeing a struggle in emotional identification.

Critical evaluation

Freud's work sparked controversy in his own lifetime, and some of that controversy still smoulders today. The world he knew vigorously repressed human sexuality, so that few of his contemporaries were prepared to concede that sex is a basic human need. More recently, Freud has come under fire for his depictions of humanity in allegedly male terms, thereby devaluing the lives of women (Donovan and Littenberg, 1982). But Freud provided a foundation that influenced virtually everyone who later studied the human personality. Of special importance to sociology is his notion that we internalise social norms and that childhood experiences have a lasting impact on socialisation.

Jean Piaget: cognitive development

Jean Piaget (1896–1980) is also among the foremost psychologists of the century. Much of his work centred on human *cognition* – how people think and understand. Early in his career, Piaget was fascinated by the behaviour of his three children, wondering not only what they knew but *how* they comprehended the world. His observations led him to conclude that children's thinking undergoes dramatic and patterned changes as children mature biologically and gain social experience. Piaget identified four stages of cognitive development.

The sensorimotor stage

In Piaget's scheme, first comes the **sensorimotor stage**, *the level of human development at which individuals experience the world only through sensory contact*. At this stage, roughly the first two years of life, the infant explores the world with the five senses: touching, tasting, smelling, looking and listening.

Children's social skills at this early point are limited to imitating others; infants cannot yet comprehend symbols. So 'knowing' to very young children amounts to direct, sensory experience.

The preoperational stage

The second plateau in Piaget's account of development is the **preoperational stage**, *the level of human development at which individuals first use language and other symbols*. At about age 2, children begin to engage the world mentally; their capacity to *think* moves reality beyond the senses. The ability to use symbols also gives flight to children's imagination; they learn to distinguish between dreams and reality and they can enjoy the element of fantasy in fairy tales (Kohlberg and Gilligan, 1971; Skolnick, 1986). Unlike adults, however, they attach names and meanings only to specific things. A child at this stage – roughly from age 2 to 6 – can describe a favourite toy, for example, but is still unable to describe the qualities of toys in general.

Without abstract concepts, a child also cannot judge size, weight or volume. In one of his best-known experiments, Piaget placed two identical glasses containing equal amounts of water on a table. He asked several children aged 5 and 6 if the amount in each glass was the same. They nodded that it was. The children then watched Piaget take one of the glasses and pour its contents into a taller, narrower glass, raising the level of the water. He asked again if each glass held the same amount. The typical 5- and 6-year-old now insisted that the taller glass held more water. But children of 7 or 8, who are able to think abstractly, could comprehend that the amount of water remained the same.

We have all seen young children place their hands in front of their faces and exclaim, 'You can't see me!' They assume that if they cannot see you, then you are unable to see them. This behaviour reveals that preop-

In a well-known experiment, Jean Piaget demonstrated that children over the age of 7 had entered the concrete operational stage of development because they could recognise that the quantity of liquid remained the same when poured from a wide beaker into a tall one.

Source: Elizabeth Crews Photography

erational children maintain an egocentric view of the world; they cannot yet perceive that any situation may appear different to another person.

The concrete operational stage

Next comes the **concrete operational stage**, *the level of development at which individuals first perceive causal connections in their surroundings*. At this level of development, typically between ages 7 and 11, children begin to grasp how and why things happen, gaining a far greater ability to manipulate their environment.

In addition, girls and boys now can attach more than one symbol to a particular event or object. For instance, if you say to a girl of 5, 'Today is Wednesday', she might respond, 'No, it's my birthday!' indicating the ability to use just one symbol at a time. Within a few years, however, she would be able to respond, 'Yes, this Wednesday is my birthday!'

Also during the concrete operational stage, children transcend earlier egocentrism so that they can now imagine themselves from the point of view of another person. As we shall explain shortly, the ability to 'stand in another's shoes' is the key to participating in complex social activities, such as games.

The formal operational stage

The final level in Piaget's model is the **formal operational stage**, *the level of human development at which indi-*

viduals think abstractly and critically. By about the age of 12, children begin to reason in abstract terms rather than thinking only of concrete situations. If, for example, you were to ask a child of 7 or 8, 'What would you like to be when you grow up?' you might prompt a concrete response such as, 'A teacher'. But a teenager might well respond abstractly, saying 'I would like a job that is exciting'. At this point, young people's surging energy is matched by their creativity and imagination, sometimes evident in a passion for science fiction or poetry.

Also at this stage, children can comprehend metaphors. Hearing the phrase 'A penny for your thoughts' might lead a young child to ask for a coin, but the adolescent will recognise a gentle invitation to intimacy. Then, too, adolescents begin to favour or reject thoughts or actions 'in principle', a trait especially pronounced among teenagers.

Critical evaluation

While Freud envisioned personality as an ongoing battle between opposing forces of biology and society, Piaget viewed the human mind as active and creative. Piaget's contribution to understanding socialisation lies in showing that the capacity to engage the world unfolds predictably as the result of biological maturation and increasing social experience.

Some challenge Piaget's scheme by questioning whether people in every society progress through all four of the stages he identified. For instance, living in a traditional society that changes very slowly is likely to inhibit the capacity for abstract and critical thought. Finally, even in our own society, as many as 30 per cent of 30-year-olds may never reach the formal operational stage at all (Kohlberg and Gilligan, 1971: 1065). Thus people exposed to little creative and imaginative thinking do not generally develop this capacity on their own.

Lawrence Kohlberg: moral development

More recently, Lawrence Kohlberg (1981) used Piaget's theory as a springboard for a study of moral reasoning – the ways in which individuals come to judge situations as right or wrong. Following Piaget's lead, Kohlberg argues that moral development proceeds in stages.

Young children who experience the world in terms of pain and pleasure (Piaget's sensorimotor stage) are at the *preconventional* level of moral development. At this early stage, in other words, 'rightness' amounts to 'what serves my needs' or 'what feels good to me'.

The *conventional* level of moral development, Kohlberg's second stage, begins to appear among teenagers (corresponding to Piaget's last, formal operational stage). At this point, young people shed some of their selfishness and begin to define right and wrong in terms of what pleases parents and what is consistent with broader cultural norms. In reaching moral judgements, individuals at this stage try to assess intention in addition to simply observing what others do.

A final stage of moral development, the *postconventional* level, moves individuals beyond the specific norms of their society to ponder more abstract ethical principles. At this level, people philosophically reflect on the meaning of liberty, freedom or justice. Individuals are now capable of actively criticising their own society and of arguing, for instance, that what is traditional or legal still may not be right.

Critical evaluation

Like the work of Piaget, Kohlberg's model explains that moral development occurs in more or less definable stages. Thus, some of the criticisms of Piaget's ideas also apply to Kohlberg's work. Whether this model

applies to people in all societies, for example, remains unconfirmed. Then, too, many people in advanced industrial societies apparently do not reach the postconventional level of moral reasoning, though exactly why is also, at present, an open question.

Another problem with Kohlberg's research is that his subjects were all boys. Kohlberg commits the research error, described in Chapter 2 ('Sociological Investigation'), of generalising the results of male subjects to all of humanity. This problem prompted his colleague Carol Gilligan to investigate how gender affects moral reasoning.

Carol Gilligan: bringing in gender

Carol Gilligan, who is introduced in the box, was disturbed that Kohlberg's research had overlooked girls. This narrow focus, as she sees it, is typical of much social science, which uses the behaviour of males as the norm for how everyone should act.

Therefore Gilligan (1982, 1990) set out systematically to compare the moral development of females and males. Simply put, her conclusion is that the two sexes make moral judgements in different ways. Males,

Carol Gilligan: socialisation and girls' self-esteem

Carol Gilligan, an educational psychologist at Harvard University, studies the personality development of young girls. Initially, she attempted to correct a research bias by which others had investigated only boys. As her work progressed, Gilligan discovered that boys and girls employ distinctive standards in making moral decisions.

Gilligan's more recent work targets the issue of self-esteem. Her research team interviewed more than 2,000 girls, ranging from 6 to 18 years of age, over a five-year period. Their responses

point up a clear pattern: young girls start out with considerable confidence and self-esteem, only to find these vital resources slipping away as they pass through adolescence.

Why? Gilligan claims that the answer lies in culture. Our way of life, she argues, still defines the ideal woman as calm, controlled and eager to please. Then, too, as girls move from the elementary grades to secondary school, they encounter fewer women teachers and find that most authority figures are men. So by their late teens, women are

struggling to regain much of the personal strength they had a decade before.

Illustrating this trend, Gilligan and her colleagues returned to a girls' school – one site of their research – to present their findings. Most younger girls who had been interviewed were eager to have their names appear in the forthcoming book; the older girls, by contrast, were hesitant: many were fearful that they would be talked about. ●

Sources: Gilligan, 1990, and Winkler, 1990.

she contends, have a *justice perspective*, relying on formal rules and abstract principles to define right and wrong. Girls, on the other hand, have a *care and responsibility perspective*, judging a situation with an eye towards personal relationships and loyalties. Stealing, as boys see it, is wrong because it breaks the law and violates common moral sentiments. Girls, however, are more likely to wonder why someone would steal, looking less severely upon an individual who did so with the intention of helping another person.

Kohlberg treats the abstract male perspective as superior to the person-based female approach. Yet Gilligan, who takes a more subtly shaded view, points out that the impersonal application of rules has long dominated men's lives in the workplace. Concern for attachments, by contrast, has been more relevant to women's lives as wives, mothers and caregivers. But, Gilligan asks, should we set up male standards as the norms by which we evaluate everyone?

Critical evaluation

Gilligan's work both sharpens our understanding of human development and highlights the problems related to gender in conducting and evaluating research. Yet what accounts for the differences she documents between females and males? Is it nature or nurture? Although it is impossible to rule out inherent differences between the sexes, Gilligan believes that these patterns reflect cultural conditioning. Thus, we might predict that, as more women organise their lives around the workplace, the moral reasoning of women and men will show greater similarity.

George Herbert Mead: the social self

Our understanding of socialisation stems in large part from the life work of George Herbert Mead (1863–1931), who is introduced in the box. Mead (1962; orig. 1934) described his approach as *social behaviourism*,

PROFILE

George Herbert Mead: the self is born of society

Few people were surprised that George Herbert Mead became a college professor. He was born to a Massachusetts family with a strong intellectual tradition, and both his parents were academics. His father was both a preacher and a teacher at a number of colleges, and his mother served for a decade as president of Mount Holyoke College.

But Mead also had a hand in shaping his own life, rebelling against the strongly religious atmosphere of his home and community. After completing college, he restlessly travelled throughout the Pacific Northwest, surveying for the railroad and reading voraciously. He gradually settled on the idea of studying philosophy, an acade-

mic endeavour he pursued at Harvard and in Europe.

Mead took a teaching position at the new University of Chicago. But his outlook still veered from the conventional. He rarely published, going

against a long-standing tradition among academics. Mead's reputation and stature grew only after his death, when colleagues and former students collected and published his lecture notes. Mead drew together a wide range of ideas to help launch the new field of social psychology.

Never content with life as it was, Mead was an active social reformer. To him, the course of an entire society was as ongoing and changeable as the life of any individual. This insight follows from his basic contention: society may have the power to shape individuals, but people also have the capacity to mould their society. ●

Sources: based, in part, on Coser, 1977, and Schellenberg, 1978.

Source: University of Chicago Archives

calling to mind the behaviourism of psychologist John B. Watson described earlier. Both recognised the power of the environment to shape human behaviour. But Watson focused on outward behaviour, while Mead highlighted inward *thinking*, which he contended was humanity's defining trait.

The self

Mead's central concept is the **self**, *a dimension of personality composed of an individual's self-awareness and self-image.* Mead's genius lay in seeing that the self is inseparable from society, a connection explained in a series of steps.

First, Mead asserted, *the self emerges from social experience.* The self is not part of the body, and it does not exist at birth. Mead rejected the position that personality is guided by biological drives (as asserted by Freud) or biological maturation (as Piaget claimed). For Mead, the self develops *only* through social experience. In the absence of social interaction, as we see from the cases of isolated children, the body may grow but no self will emerge.

Second, Mead explained, *social experience is the exchange of symbols.* Using words, a wave of the hand or a smile, people create meaning, which is a distinctively human experience. We can use reward and punishment to train a dog, after all; but the dog attaches no meaning to these actions. Human beings, by contrast, make sense of actions by inferring people's underlying intentions. In short, a dog responds to *what you do*; a human responds to *what you have in mind* as you do it.

Return to our friendly dog for a moment. You can train a dog to walk to the porch and return with an umbrella. But the dog grasps no meaning in the act, no intention behind the command. Thus, if the dog cannot find the umbrella, it is incapable of the *human* response: to look for a raincoat instead.

Third, says Mead, *to understand intention, you must imagine the situation from another person's point of view.* Using symbols, we can imaginatively place ourselves in another person's shoes and thus see ourselves as that person does. This capacity allows us to anticipate how others will respond to us even before we act. A simple toss of a ball requires stepping outside ourselves to imagine how another will respond to our throw. Social interaction, then, involves seeing ourselves as others see us – a process that Mead called *taking the role of the other.*

The looking-glass self

In social life, other people represent the mirror or looking glass in which we perceive ourselves. Charles Horton Cooley (1864–1929), one of Mead's colleagues, used the phrase **looking-glass self** to designate *the image people have of themselves based on how they believe others perceive them* (1964; orig. 1902). Whether we think of ourselves as clever or clumsy, worthy or worthless, depends in large measure on what we think others think of us. This insight goes a long way toward explaining Carol Gilligan's finding that young women lose self-confidence as they come of age in a society that discourages women from being too assertive.

The I and the Me

Our capacity to see ourselves through others implies that the self has two components. First, *the self is subject* as we initiate social action. Humans are innately active and spontaneous, Mead claimed, dubbing this subjective element of the self the *I* (the subjective form of the personal pronoun).

Second, *the self is object* because, taking the role of another, we form impressions of ourselves. Mead called this objective element of the self the *Me* (the objective form of the personal pronoun). All social experience begins with someone initiating action (the I-phase of self) and then guiding the action (the me-phase of self) by taking the role of the other. Social experience is thus the interplay of the I and the me: our actions are spontaneous yet guided by how others respond to us.

Mead stressed that thinking itself constitutes a social experience. Our thoughts are partly creative (representing the I), but in thought we also become objects to ourselves (representing the me) as we imagine how others will respond to our ideas.

Development of the self

According to Mead, gaining a self amounts to learning to take the role of the other. Like Freud and Piaget, Mead regarded early childhood as the crucial time for this task, but he did not link the development of the self to biological maturation. Mead maintained that the self emerges over time with increasing social experience.

Infants respond to others only in terms of *imitation*. They mimic behaviour without understanding underlying intentions. Unable to use symbols, Mead concluded, infants have no self.

Children first learn to use language and other symbols in the form of *play*, especially role playing. Initially, they model themselves on key people in their lives – such as parents – whom we call *significant others*. Playing 'mummy and daddy', for example, helps children imagine the world from their parents' point of view.

Gradually, children learn to take the roles of several others at once. This skill is the key to moving from simple play (say, playing catch) involving one other to complex *games* (like baseball) involving many others. Only by the age of 7 or 8 have most children acquired sufficient social experience to engage in team sports that demand taking the role of numerous others simultaneously.

Figure 5.1 shows the logical progression from imitation to play to games. But a final stage in the development of the self remains. A game involves taking the role of others in just one situation. But members of a society also need to see themselves as others in general might. In other words, we recognise that people in any situation in society share cultural norms and values, and we begin to incorporate these general patterns into the self. Mead used the term **generalised other** to refer to *widespread cultural norms and values we use as references in evaluating ourselves.*

Of course, the emergence of the self is not the end of socialisation. Quite the contrary: Mead claimed that socialisation continues as long as we have social experience, so that changing circumstances can reshape who we are. The self may change, for example, with divorce, disability or unexpected wealth. And we retain some control over this process as we respond to events and circumstances and thereby play a part in our own socialisation.

Critical evaluation

The strength of Mead's work lies in exploring the nature of social experience itself. He succeeded in explaining how symbolic interaction is the foundation of both the self and society.

Some critics disparage Mead's view as radically social because it acknowledges no biological element in the emergence of the self. In this position, he stands apart from Freud (who identified general drives within the organism) and Piaget (whose stages of development are tied to biological maturation).

Mead's concepts of the I and the Me are often confused with Freud's concepts of the id and the superego. But Freud rooted the id in the biological organism, while Mead rejected any link between the self and biology (though he never specified the origin of the I). Freud's concept of the superego and Mead's concept of the me both reflect the power of society to shape personality. But for Freud, superego and id are locked in continual combat. Mead, however, held that the I and the me work closely and cooperatively together (Meltzer, 1978).

● Agents of socialisation

Every social experience we have affects us in at least some small way. In modern industrial and postindustrial societies, however, several familiar settings have special significance in the socialisation process.

The family

The family is the most important agent of socialisation because it represents the centre of children's lives. As we have seen, infants are almost totally dependent on others, and the responsibility to meet their needs almost always falls on parents and other family members. At least until the onset of schooling, the family also shoulders the task of teaching children cultural values, attitudes and prejudices about themselves and others.

Figure 5.1 ● Building on social experience
George Herbert Mead described the development of the self as the process of gaining social experience. This is largely a matter of taking the role of the other with increasing sophistication.

Family-based socialisation is not all intentional. Children learn continuously from the kind of environment that adults create. Whether children learn to think of themselves as strong or weak, smart or stupid, loved or simply tolerated, and whether they believe the world to be trustworthy or dangerous largely stem from this early environment.

Parenting styles aside, research points to the importance of parental *attention* in the social development of children. Physical contact, verbal stimulation and responsiveness from parents and others all foster intellectual growth (Belsky, Lerner and Spanier, 1984).

The family also confers on children a social position; that is, parents not only bring children into the physical world, they also place them in society in terms of race, ethnicity, religion and class. In time, all these elements become part of a child's self-concept. Of course, some aspects of social position may change later on, but social standing at birth affects us throughout our lives.

We know children are born both to rich and poor parents. What is less evident – and probably just as important – is that parents at varying class positions provide children with 'cultural capital' in the form of differing aspirations. In many ways, then, parents teach their children to follow in their footsteps. This is discussed further in Chapter 19 (Education).

Schooling

Schooling enlarges children's social world to include people with social backgrounds that differ from their own. As children confront social diversity, they learn the significance society attaches to people's race and sex and often act accordingly: studies document the tendency of children to cluster together in play groups composed of one race and gender (Lever, 1978; Finkelstein and Haskins, 1983).

Formally, schooling teaches children a wide range of knowledge and skills. But schools convey a host of other lessons informally through what sociologists call the *hidden curriculum*. Activities such as spelling tests and sports teach children key cultural values such as competitive achievement and success. Children also receive countless formal and informal messages promoting their society's way of life as morally good.

Moving beyond the personal web of family life, children entering school soon discover that evalua-tions of skills like reading and arithmetic are based on impersonal, standardised tests. Here, the emphasis shifts from *who* they are to *how* they perform. Of course, the confidence or anxiety that children develop at home can have a significant effect on how well they perform in school (Belsky, Lerner, and Spanier, 1984).

School is also most children's first experience with rigid formality. The school day runs on a strict time schedule, subjecting children to impersonal regimentation and fostering punctuality. Not surprisingly, these are the same traits expected by most of the large organisations that will employ them later in life.

Finally, schools socialise children with regard to gender. Raphaela Best (1983) points out that, in primary school, boys engage in more physical activities and spend more time outdoors, while girls tend to be more sedentary, sometimes even helping the teacher with various housekeeping chores. Gender distinctions continue in the higher grades and persist right through college and university: women, for example, encounter pressure to select degrees in the arts or humanities, while men are steered towards the physical sciences.

The peer group

By the time they enter school, children have also discovered the **peer group**, *a social group whose members have interests, social position and age in common*. A young child's peer group generally consists of neighbourhood playmates; later, peer groups are composed of friends from school or elsewhere.

Unlike the family and the school, the peer group allows young people to escape from the direct supervision of adults. With this new-found independence, members of peer groups gain valuable experience in forging social relationships on their own and developing a sense of themselves apart from their families. Peer groups also give young people the opportunity to discuss interests that may not be shared by adults (such as styles of dress and popular music) or are not looked on favourably by parents (such as drugs and sex).

For the young, the appeal of the peer group lies in the ever-present possibility of activity not condoned by adults; for the same reason, parents express concern about who their children's friends are. In a rapidly changing society, peer groups often rival parents in influence, as the attitudes of parents and children diverge along the lines of a 'generation gap'. The primacy of peer groups typically peaks during adolescence, as young people begin to break away from their families and think of themselves as responsible adults. At this stage of life, young people often display anxious conformity to peers because this new identity and sense of belonging eases some of the apprehension brought on by breaking away from the family.

The conflict between parents and peers may be more apparent than real, however, for even during adolescence children remain strongly influenced by their families. Peers may guide short-term concerns such as style of dress and musical taste, but parents retain greater sway over the long-term goals of their children. One study, for example, found that parents had more influence than even best friends on young people's educational aspirations (Davies and Kandel, 1981).

Finally, any local community or school operates as a social mosaic composed of numerous peer groups. As we will see in Chapter 7 ('Groups and Organisations'), members tend to perceive their own peer group in positive terms while discrediting others. Moreover, individuals are also influenced by peer groups they would like to join, a process sociologists call **anticipatory socialisation**, *social learning directed toward gaining a desired position*. In school, for example, young people may mimic the styles and banter of the group they hope to join. Or, at a later point in life, a young lawyer who hopes to become a partner in her law firm may conform to the attitudes and behaviour of the firm's partners to ease her way into this rarefied group.

The mass media

The **mass media** are *impersonal communications directed to a vast audience*. The term 'media' comes from Latin meaning 'middle', suggesting that the media function to connect people. The development of *mass* media occurs as communications technologies (first newspapers and, more recently, radio and television) disseminate information on a mass scale.

The mass media have an enormous influence on our lives. For this reason, they are an important component of the socialisation process. Television, introduced in 1939, has rapidly become the dominant medium throughout the world. Just how 'glued to the television' are we? Figures vary by group, nation, class and gender, but 'average households' may well keep a television on for seven hours or more each day. Years before children learn to read, watching television has become a regular routine and, as they grow up, young girls and boys spend as many hours in front of a television as they do in school. Indeed, television consumes as much of children's time as interacting with parents. (This is discussed further in Chapter 21.)

● Socialisation and the life course

Although childhood is critical to the socialisation process, learning continues throughout our lives. The following overview of the life course reveals that our society organises human experience according to age, resulting in distinctive stages of life: childhood, adolescence, adulthood and, finally, old age.

Childhood

Charles Dickens's classic novel *Oliver Twist* is set in London early in the nineteenth century, when the Industrial Revolution was rapidly transforming English society. Oliver's mother died in childbirth, and, barely surviving himself, he began life as an indigent orphan, 'buffeted through the world, despised by all, and pitied by none' (Dickens, 1886: 36; orig. 1837–39). As was typical for a poor child of his time, Oliver Twist was soon facing the toil and drudgery of a workhouse, labouring long hours to pay for filthy shelter and meagre food.

Today, we think of *childhood* – roughly, the first 12 years of life – as a time of freedom from the burdens of the adult world. But until about a century ago, as *Oliver Twist* testifies, children in Europe and North America shouldered most of the burdens of adults. According to historian Philippe Ariès (1965), once children were able to survive without constant care, medieval Europeans expected them to take their place in the world as working adults. Although 'child labour' is now scorned in Europe, this historical pattern persists in poor societies today, especially in Africa and Asia. Map 5.1 shows that work is commonplace for children in low-income nations of the world.

We can be shocked by the notion of young children working long hours because common sense tells us

WINDOW ON THE WORLD

Map 5.1 ● Child labour in global perspective

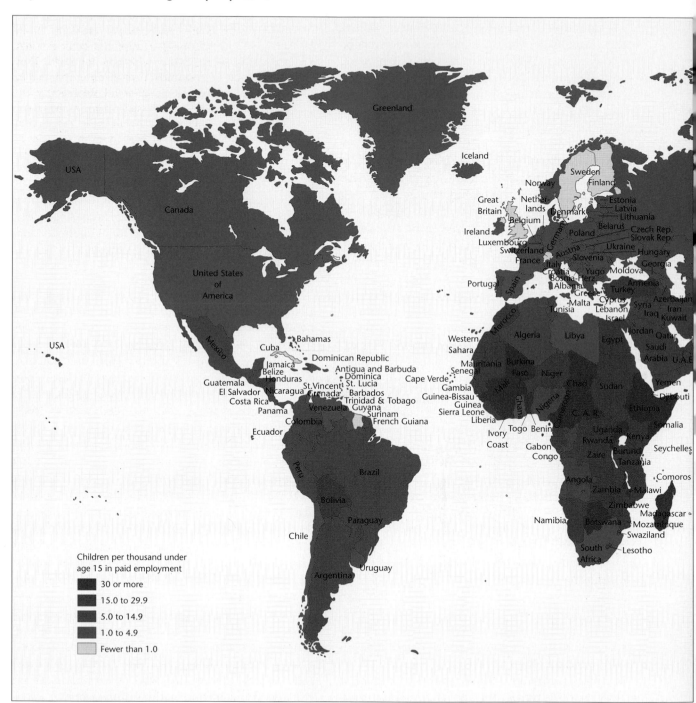

Children per thousand under
age 15 in paid employment

- 30 or more
- 15.0 to 29.9
- 5.0 to 14.9
- 1.0 to 4.9
- Fewer than 1.0

Source: *Peters Atlas of the World* (1990)

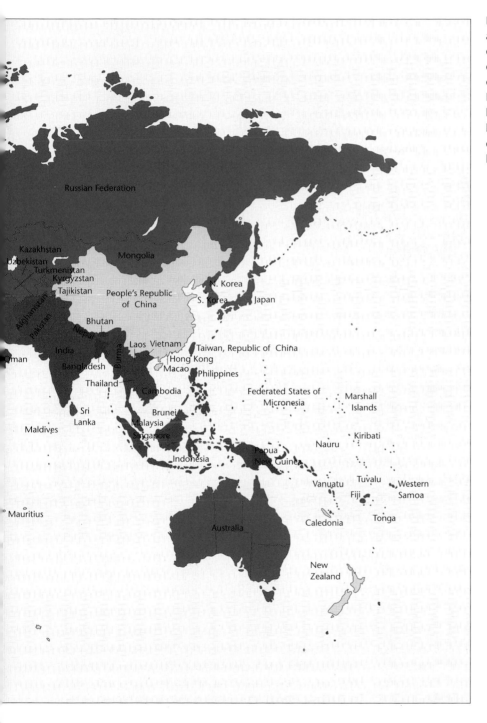

Industrialisation prolongs childhood and discourages children from engaging in work and other activities deemed suitable only for adults. Thus child labour is relatively uncommon in Europe and other industrial societies. In less industrialised nations of the world, however, children serve as a vital economic asset, and they typically begin working as soon as they are able.

that youngsters are very different from adults – physically immature and inexperienced in the ways of the world. But, although this difference is certainly biological, it is also rooted in culture. High-income societies are rich enough that many people – including children – do not need to work. In addition, societies with sophisticated technology extend childhood, so young people have time to learn the many complex skills required for adult activities. Thus, we construct the life course so that 'irresponsible' children are looked after by 'responsible' adults (Benedict, 1938).

Recently, some social scientists have declared that our conception of childhood is changing yet again. In an age of high divorce rates, mothers and fathers in the workforce, and an increasing level of 'adult' programming on television, they point out that children are no longer 'protected' from grown-up concerns as in the past. Rather, we are seeing the development of a 'hurried child' syndrome, meaning that children have to grapple with sex, drugs and violence as well as fend more and more for themselves (Elkind, 1981; Winn, 1983). Critics of this view, however, counter that there is no convincing evidence of any dramatic shift in our society's conception of childhood. Further, they note, the 'hurried child' thesis overlooks the fact that children in the lower class have always assumed adult responsibilities sooner than their middle and upper class counterparts (Lynott and Logue, 1993).

Adolescence

As industrialisation gradually framed childhood as a distinct stage of life, adolescence emerged as a buffer between childhood and adulthood. Corresponding roughly to the teenage years, this is the stage of life when young people establish some independence and learn specialised skills required for adult life.

We generally associate adolescence with emotional and social turmoil; young people experience conflict with their parents and struggle to develop their own, separate identities. Since adolescence commonly occurs at the onset of puberty, we may be tempted to attribute teenage turbulence to physiological changes. However, comparative research indicates that, like childhood, adolescence is a variable product of culture. Studying the Samoan Islanders in the 1920s, Margaret Mead (1961; orig. 1928) found little evidence of stress among teenagers; there, children appeared to

move easily to adult standing. Western societies, however, tend to define childhood and adulthood more in opposing terms, making the transition from one to the other more difficult.

As is true of all stages of life, the experience of adolescence varies according to social background. Most young people from working class families move directly from secondary school into the adult world of work and parenting. Wealthier youth, however, has the resources to attend colleges and universities, which may extend adolescence into the late twenties and even the thirties. For different reasons, of course, poverty also may extend adolescence. Especially in the inner cities, many young minorities cannot attain full adult standing because jobs are not available.

Adulthood

At the age of 35, Eleanor Roosevelt, wife of President Roosevelt and one of the most widely admired women in the United States in her time, wrote in her diary: 'I do not think I have ever felt so strangely as in the past year . . . all my self-confidence is gone and I am on the edge, though I never was better physically I feel sure' (quoted in Sheehy, 1976: 260). Eleanor Roosevelt may have been troubled by the attention her husband was paying to another, younger woman; or, looking into the future, she may have been trying to imagine what challenges or accomplishments might bring further satisfaction to her life.

But as Eleanor Roosevelt struggled with what today we might call a 'mid-life crisis', there was much that she could not foresee. Her husband, Franklin Delano Roosevelt, was shortly to become disabled by poliomyelitis, although his rising political career ultimately would lead to the White House. And Eleanor herself was to become one of the most active and influential of all First Ladies. After her husband's death, she would remain in public life, serving as a delegate to the United Nations.

Eleanor Roosevelt's life illustrates two major characteristics of *adulthood*, which our culture defines as beginning during the twenties. First, adulthood is the period during which most of life's accomplishments typically occur, including pursuing careers and raising families. Second, especially in later adulthood, people reflect upon what they have been able to accomplish, perhaps with great satisfaction or with the sobering realisation that many of the idealistic dreams of their youth will never come true.

Early adulthood

By the onset of adulthood, personalities are largely formed. Even so, a marked shift in an individual's life situation – brought on by unemployment, divorce or serious illness – can significantly change the self (Dannefer, 1984).

Early adulthood – from 20 to about age 40 – is generally a time of working towards many goals set earlier in life. Young adults break free of parents and learn to manage for themselves a host of day-to-day responsibilities. With the birth of children, parents draw on experiences from their own upbringing, although, as children, they may have only vaguely perceived what adult life entailed. In addition, young adults typically try to master patterns of intimate living with another person who may have just as much to learn.

Early adulthood is also a period of juggling conflicting priorities: parents, partner, children, schooling and work (Levinson et al., 1978). Women, especially, confront the difficulty of 'doing it all', since our culture still confers on them primary responsibility for child rearing and household chores, even if they have demanding occupations outside the home (Hochschild, 1989).

Middle adulthood

Young adults usually cope optimistically with such tensions. But in middle adulthood – roughly, from 40 to 60 – people begin to sense that marked improvements in life circumstances are less likely. The distinctive character of middle adulthood takes shape as people assess actual achievements in light of earlier expectations. At mid-life, people also become more aware of the fragility of health, which the young typically take for granted.

Some women who have already spent many years raising a family find middle adulthood especially trying. Children grow up and require less attention, husbands become absorbed in their careers, leaving these women with spaces in their lives that they find difficult to fill. Women who divorce during middle adulthood may experience serious financial problems (Weitzman, 1985). For all these reasons, an increasing number of women mark middle adulthood by undertaking the challenge of returning to colleges or universities and then launching their careers.

Growing older means that both men and women face the reality of physical decline, but our society's traditional socialisation has made this prospect more painful for women. Because good looks are defined as more important for women, wrinkles, weight gain and loss of hair are more traumatic for them. Men, of course, have their own particular difficulties. Some confront limited professional achievement, knowing that their careers are unlikely to change for the better. Others, now realising that the price of career success has been neglect of family or personal health, harbour uncertainties about their self-worth even as they bask in the praise of others (Farrell and Rosenberg, 1981). Women, too, who devote themselves single-mindedly to careers in early adulthood, may experience regrets about what they have given up in pursuit of occupational success.

Eleanor Roosevelt's mid-life crisis may well have involved some of the personal transitions we have described. But her story also illustrates that most people passing mid-life have yet to experience their greatest productivity and personal satisfaction. Socialisation in our youth-orientated culture has convinced many people (especially the young) that life ends at 40. But as life expectancy has increased, such limiting notions have begun to dissolve. Major transformations may become less likely, but the potential for learning and new beginnings still infuses this stage of life with promise.

Old age

Old age comprises the later years of adulthood and the final stage of life itself, beginning about the mid-sixties. Here again, societies attach different meanings to a time of life. Pre-industrial people typically grant elders great influence and prestige. As explained in Chapter 14 ('Ageing and the Elderly'), traditional societies confer on older people control of most of the land and other wealth; moreover, since their societies change slowly, older people amass a lifetime of wisdom, which earns them great respect (Sheehan, 1976; Hareven, 1982).

In industrial societies, however, most younger people work apart from the family, becoming more independent of their elders. Rapid change and our society's youth orientation combine to define what is older as unimportant or even obsolete. To younger people, then, the elderly are dismissed as unaware of new trends and fashions, and their knowledge and experience are often deemed irrelevant.

No doubt, however, this anti-elderly bias will diminish as the proportion of older people steadily increases. The share of our population over 65 has almost tripled since the beginning of this century, so that today more men and women are elderly than in their teens. Moreover, life expectancy is still increasing, so that most men and women in their mid-sixties (the 'young elderly') can look forward to decades more of life. Looking to the next century, the fastest-growing segment of our population will be those over 85, whose numbers will soar sixfold.

At present, this final phase of the life course differs in an important way from earlier stages. Growing up typically means entering new roles and assuming new responsibilities; growing old, by contrast, entails the opposite experience of leaving roles that provided both satisfaction and social identity. Retirement, for example, may indeed fit the common image as a period of restful activity. But it may also mean the loss of valued activity and, for some people, outright boredom. Like any life transition, retirement demands learning new and different patterns while simultaneously *un*learning familiar routines. A nearly equal transition is required of the non-working wife or husband, who must now accommodate a partner spending more time at home.

Dying

Through most of human history, death caused by disease or accident came at any stage of life because of low living standards and primitive medical technology. Today, however, almost 85 per cent of people in Western countries die after the age of 55. Therefore, although most senior citizens can look forward to decades of life, growing old cannot be separated from eventual physical decline and ultimate death.

After observing many dying people, Elisabeth Kübler-Ross (1969) described death as an orderly transition involving five distinct responses. A person's first reaction to the prospect of dying is usually

Figure 5.2 ● The seasons of life
Daniel Levinson's research into human development depicts the life span as a series of critical transitions.

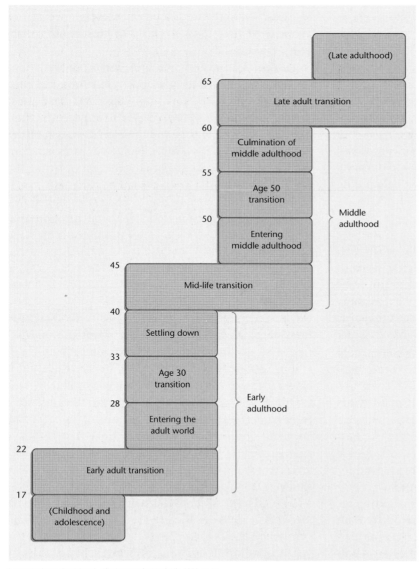

Source: Levinson, Daniel et al., *The Seasons of a Man's Life*, 1978, p. 57

denial, since our culture tends to ignore the reality of death. The second phase is *anger*, by which a person begins to accept the idea of dying but views it as a gross injustice. Third, anger gives way to *negotiation*, the attitude that death may not be inevitable and that one might strike a bargain with God so life can continue. The fourth response, *resignation*, is often accompanied by psychological depression. Finally, adjustment to death is completed in the fifth stage, *acceptance*. At this point, rather than being paralysed by fear and anxiety, the person whose life is ending sets out to make the most of whatever time remains.

As the proportion of women and men in old age increases, we can expect our culture to become more comfortable with the idea of death. In recent years, for example, people have been discussing death openly more than in decades past, and the trend is to see dying as preferable to painful or prolonged suffering in hospitals or at home. Moreover, more married couples now anticipate their own deaths with legal and financial planning. This openness may ease the disorientation that generally accompanies the death of a spouse – a greater problem for women, who usually outlive their husbands.

The life course: an overview

This brief examination of the life course points to two sweeping conclusions. First and more important, although each stage of life is linked to the biological process of ageing, the life course is largely a social construction. For this reason, people in other societies may experience a stage of life quite differently, or not at all. Second, each stage of any society's life course presents characteristic problems and transitions that involve learning something new and unlearning familiar routines.

Note, too, that just because societies organise human experience according to age, this in no way negates the effects of other forces, such as class, race, ethnicity and gender. Thus, the general patterns we have described are all subject to further modification as they apply to various categories of people.

Finally, people's life experiences also vary depending on when, in the history of the society, they were born. A **cohort** is *a category of people with a common characteristic, usually their age.* Age-cohorts are likely to have been influenced by the same economic and cul-

tural trends so that members typically display similar attitudes and values (Riley, Foner and Waring, 1988). The lives of women and men born early in this century, for example, were framed by an economic depression and two world wars – events unknown to their children or grandchildren. For their part, younger people today are entering adulthood during a period of economic uncertainty that has dampened the optimism that characterised the generation that came of age during the 1960s.

● Resocialisation: total institutions

A final type of socialisation involves being confined – often against a person's will – in prisons or mental hospitals. This is the special world of the **total institution**, *a setting in which people are isolated from the rest of society and manipulated by an administrative staff.*

According to Erving Goffman (1961), total institutions have three distinctive characteristics. First, staff members supervise all spheres of daily life, including

The demand by guards that new prisoners publicly disrobe is more than a matter of issuing new clothing; such a degrading ritual is also the first stage in the process by which the staff in a total institution attempts to break down an individual's established social identity.

Source: Magnum Photos, Inc. – Danny Lyon

where residents (often called 'inmates') eat, sleep and work. Second, a rigid system provides inmates with standardised food, sleeping quarters and activities. Third, formal rules and daily schedules dictate when, where and how inmates perform virtually every part of their daily routines.

Total institutions impose such regimentation with the goal of **resocialisation**, *radically altering an inmate's personality through deliberate manipulation of the environment*. The power of a total institution to resocialise is also enhanced by its forcible segregation of inmates from the 'outside' by means of physical barriers such as walls and fences topped with barbed wire and guard towers, barred windows and locked doors. Cut off in this way, the inmate's entire world can be manipulated by the administrative staff to produce lasting change – or at least immediate compliance – in the inmate.

Resocialisation is a two-part process. First, the staff tries to erode the new inmate's autonomy and identity through what Goffman describes as 'abasements, degradations, humiliations, and profanations of self' (1961: 14). For example, inmates must surrender personal possessions, including clothing and grooming articles used to maintain their distinctive appearances. In their place, the staff provides standard-issue items that make everyone look alike. In addition, inmates all

CONTROVERSY AND DEBATE

Are we free within society?

Throughout this chapter we have returned to one key theme: society shapes how we think, feel and act. But, if this is so, in what sense are we free?

Sociologists speak with many voices when addressing this question. One response, with politically liberal overtones, is that individuals are not free of society – in fact, as social creatures, we never could be. But if we are condemned to live in a society with power over us, it is important to do what we can to make our home as just as possible – that is, to lessen class differences and eliminate barriers to opportunity based on sex and race. Another approach, this one with conservative overtones, is that we are free because society can never control the aspirations or break the will of people committed to their dreams, whatever these may be. The history of the United States, for example – right from the revolutionary act that led to its founding – is the story of one individual after another who persisted in pursuit of personal goals, often overcoming great odds in the process.

We find both of these orientations in the work of George Herbert Mead, who made a crucial contribution to our understanding of socialisation. Mead recognised the power of society to make demands on us, sometimes setting itself before us as a barrier. But he also reminded us that human beings are spontaneous and creative, capable of continually acting back – individually or collectively – on society. Thus Mead acknowledged the power of society while still affirming the human capacity to evaluate, criticise and, ultimately, to choose and to change.

In the end, then, we may resemble puppets, but only superficially. A crucial difference – one that allows us to claim a significant measure of freedom – is that we have the power to stop, and peer upward at the 'strings' that animate much of our action, and perhaps even to jerk down on them defiantly (Berger, 1963: 176). If our pull is persistent and powerful enough, we may accomplish more than we might imagine. As Margaret Mead once mused, 'Do not make the mistake of thinking that concerned people cannot change the world; it's the only thing that ever has.'

● **Continue the debate:**

1. Do you think our society affords more freedom to males than to females? Why, or why not?

2. What about modern, industrial countries compared to traditional, agrarian nations? Are some of the world's people more free than others?

3. How does an understanding of sociology enhance personal freedom? ●

receive standard haircuts, so that, once again, what was personalised becomes uniform. The staff also subject new inmates to 'mortifications of self', including searches, medical examinations and fingerprinting, and then assign them a serial number. Once inside the walls, individuals surrender the right to privacy; guards may demand that inmates undress publicly as part of the admission procedure and may routinely monitor their living quarters.

The second part of the resocialisation process includes efforts to systematically build a different self. The staff manipulate inmate behaviour through a system of rewards and punishments. The privilege of keeping a book, watching television or making a telephone call may seem trivial to outsiders, but, in the rigid environment of the total institution, this can form a powerful motivation to conform. Bucking the system, on the other hand, means that privileges will be withdrawn or, in more serious cases, that the

inmate will suffer further isolation or additional punishment. The duration of confinement in a prison or mental hospital also depends on how well an inmate cooperates with official rules and regulations. Goffman emphasises that the staff also seek to win the hearts and minds of inmates, punishing even those who toe the line but have 'an attitude problem'. In principle, total institutions can bring about considerable change in inmates. Yet the resocialisation process is extremely complex, and no two people respond to such programmes in precisely the same way. Moreover, while some inmates are deemed 'rehabilitated' or 'recovered', others display little change at all, and still others only become confused, hostile or bitter. Furthermore, over a long period of time, a rigidly controlled environment may destroy a person's capacity for independent living; such *institutionalised* personalities lose the capacity to deal with the demands of the outside world.

SUMMARY

1. For individuals, socialisation is the process of building our humanity and particular identity through social experience. For society as a whole, socialisation is the means by which one generation transmits culture to the next.

2. A century ago, people thought most human behaviour was guided by biological instinct. Today, the nature–nurture debate has tipped the other way as we understand human behaviour to be primarily a product of a social environment. So-called human nature is actually the capacity to create variable cultural patterns.

3. The permanently damaging effects of social isolation reveal the importance of social experience to human development.

4. Sigmund Freud envisioned the human personality as composed of three parts. The id represents general human drives (the life and death instincts), which Freud claimed were innate. The superego embodies cultural values and norms internalised by individuals. Competition between the needs of the id and the restraints of the superego are mediated by the ego.

5. Jean Piaget believed that human development reflects both biological maturation and increasing social experience. In his view, socialisation proceeds through four major stages of development: sensorimotor, preoperational, concrete operational and formal operational.

6. Lawrence Kohlberg applies Piaget's approach to the issue of moral development. Individuals, he claims, first judge rightness in preconventional terms, according to their individual needs. Next, conventional moral reasoning takes account of the attitudes of parents and the norms of the larger society. Finally, postconventional moral reasoning allows for a philosophical critique of society itself.

7. Beginning with a critique of Kohlberg's reliance on male subjects, Carol Gilligan discovered that gender affects moral reasoning. Females, she asserts, look to the effect of decisions on relationships, while males rely more on abstract standards of rightness.

8. To George Herbert Mead, socialisation is based on the emergence of the self, which he viewed as partly autonomous (the I) and partly guided by

society (the me). Mead contended that, beginning with imitative behaviour, the self develops through play and games and eventually recognises the 'generalised other'.

9. Charles Horton Cooley used the term 'looking-glass self' to underscore that the self is influenced by how we think others respond to us.

10. Commonly the first setting of socialisation, the family has the greatest influence on a child's attitudes and behaviour.

11. School exposes children to greater social diversity and introduces the experience of impersonal evaluation. In addition to formal lessons, schools informally teach a wide range of cultural ideas, including attitudes about competitiveness and achievement.

12. Members of youthful peer groups are subject to adult supervision less than in the family or in school. Peer groups take on great significance among adolescents.

13. The mass media, especially television, have a considerable impact on the socialisation process. The average child now spends as much time watching television as attending school.

14. As with each phase of the life course, the characteristics of childhood are socially constructed. Medieval Europeans scarcely recognised childhood as a stage of life. In high-income societies, people define childhood as very different from adulthood.

15. Adolescence, the transition between childhood and adulthood, is considered a difficult period in our society. This is not the case in all societies, however.

16. During early adulthood, socialisation involves settling into careers and raising families. Later adulthood is marked by considerable reflection about initial goals in the light of actual achievements.

17. In old age, people make many transitions, including retirement. While the elderly typically enjoy high prestige in preindustrial societies, industrial and postindustrial societies are more youth orientated, relegating older people to the sidelines of life.

18. Members of industrial and postindustrial societies typically fend off death until old age. Adjustment to the death of a spouse (an experience more common to women) and acceptance of one's own death are part of socialisation for the elderly.

19. Total institutions such as prisons and mental hospitals strive for resocialisation – radically changing the inmate's personality.

20. Socialisation demonstrates the power of society to shape our thoughts, feelings and actions. Yet, as free humans, we also have the capacity to act back on society and, in so doing, shape our lives and our world.

KEY CONCEPTS

anticipatory socialisation social learning directed towards gaining a desired position

cohort a category of people with a common characteristic, usually their age

concrete operational stage Piaget's term for the level of human development at which individuals first perceive causal connections in their surroundings

ego Freud's designation of a person's conscious efforts to balance innate, pleasure-seeking drives and the demands of society

formal operational stage Piaget's term for the level of human development at which individuals think abstractly and critically

generalised other George Herbert Mead's label for widespread cultural norms and values that we use as references in evaluating ourselves

id Freud's designation of the human being's basic drives

looking-glass self Cooley's term for the image people have of themselves based on how they believe others perceive them

mass media impersonal communications directed toward a vast audience

peer group a social group whose members have interests, social position and age in common

personality a person's fairly consistent patterns of thinking, feeling and acting

preoperational stage Piaget's term for the level of human development at which individuals first use language and other symbols

resocialisation radically altering an inmate's personality through deliberate manipulation of the environment

self George Herbert Mead's term for a dimension of personality composed of an individual's self-awareness and self-image

sensorimotor stage Piaget's designation for the level of human development at which individuals experience the world only through sensory contact

socialisation the lifelong social experience by which individuals develop their human potential and learn patterns of their culture

superego Freud's designation of the operation of culture within the individual in the form of internalised values and norms

total institution a setting in which people are isolated from the rest of society and manipulated by an administrative staff

CRITICAL-THINKING QUESTIONS

1. What do cases of social isolation teach us about the importance of social experience to human development?

2. Describe the two sides of the nature–nurture debate. In what sense are human nature and nurture not opposed to one another?

3. In what ways does a comparison of the theories of Freud, Piaget, Kohlberg, Gilligan and Mead suggest that research findings build on one another? In what ways do they seem incompatible?

4. Proportionately speaking, television features many more physically attractive people than there are in the population as a whole. Develop arguments for and against this practice. How does this practice affect the way we think about others – and ourselves?

5. How much change do you think is possible in adult life?

6. Attempt to draw a map of the stages of your life and, using some of the concepts and theories above, assess which theory you think makes most sense of it.

GOING FURTHER

Introductory reading

Colin Thurnbull, *The Human Cycle* (London: Cape, 1984).

An anthropologist looks at human development

Classic sources

George Herbert Mead, *Mind, Self, and Society from the Standpoint of a Social Behaviourist*, edited by Charles W. Morris (Chicago: University of Chicago Press, 1962; orig. 1934).

Compiled after Mead's death by his students, this paperback presents Mead's analysis of the development of self.

Margaret Mead, *Coming of Age in Samoa* (New York: Dell, 1961; orig. 1928).

While still in her early twenties, Margaret Mead completed what is probably the best-known book in anthropology, in which she argues that the problems of adolescence are socially created rather than rooted in biology.

More advanced reading

Anthony Giddens, *Self Identity and Late Modernity* (Cambridge: Polity, 1991).

Important study that suggests how socialisation processes are changing in the modern world.

Carol Gilligan, *In a Different Voice* (Cambridge, MA: Harvard University Press, 1982).

    A very influential book that critiques 'male models' of development.

Daniel J. Levinson et al., *The Seasons of a Man's Life* (New York: Knopft, 1978).

    Looks at the stages of adult development. Should be read in conjunction with Gail Sheehey's *Passages*.

Grace Craig, *Human Development* (Englewood Cliffs, NJ: Prentice-Hall, 7th edn, 1995).

    This book is a good general reference for understanding socialisation across the life course.

Alba N. Ambert and Marie D. Alvarez (eds.), *Puerto Rican Children on the Mainland: Interdisciplinary Perspectives* (New York: Garland, 1992).

    This collection of essays sketches a statistical portrait of Puerto Ricans on the mainland and investigates distinctive dimensions of socialisation among young people.

M. E. J. Wadsworth, *The Imprint of Time: Childhood, History, and Adult Life* (Oxford: Clarendon Press, 1991).

    Long-term studies of cohorts are difficult and, therefore, rare in social science. This book reports on an ongoing study of more than 5,000 men and women living throughout Britain, all born in 1946 and interviewed periodically since then.

Web sites

● http://www.unicef.org/sowc96/contents.htm

    This is the UNICEF 'State of the Worlds' Children' site, and provides information and statistics on children around the world.

● http://plaza.interport.net/nypsan/freudarc.html

    Web site of Sigmund Freud which contains his biography, writings, photos, libraries and museums.

● http://www.wpi.edu/~isg_501/nsushkin.html

    Worcester Polytechnic Institute page of development theories, including Piaget's stages of intellectual development and his archive.

chapter six

Source: Popperfoto

Social Interaction in Everyday Life

Tony and Margaret are on their way to another couple's home in an unfamiliar part of town. They are now late, because for the last twenty minutes they have travelled in circles looking for Rosabelle Avenue. Tony, gripping the wheel ever tighter, is driving very slowly. Margaret, sitting next to him, looks straight ahead, afraid to utter a word. Both realise the evening is off to a bad start.

Here we have a simple case of two people unable to locate the home of some friends. But Tony and Margaret are lost in more ways than one, since they fail to grasp why they are growing more and more enraged at their situation and at each other.

Consider the predicament from Tony's point of view. Like most men, Tony cannot tolerate getting lost. The longer he drives around, the more incompetent he feels. Margaret is seething, too, but for a different reason. She does not understand why Tony does not pull over and ask someone where Rosabelle Avenue is. If she were driving, she fumes to herself, they already would have arrived and would now be comfortably settled with drink in hand.

Why don't men ask for directions? Men value their independence and so are uncomfortable asking for help (and also reluctant to accept it). To men, asking for assistance is an admission of inadequacy, an acknowledgement that others know something they don't. If it takes Tony a few more minutes to find Rosabelle Avenue on his own – and secure his self-respect in the process – he thinks the bargain is a good one.

If men pursue self-sufficiency and are sensitive to hierarchy, women are more attuned to others and strive for connectedness. Asking for help seems right to Margaret because, from her point of view, sharing information reinforces social bonds. Requesting directions seems as natural to Margaret as continuing to search on his own appears to Tony. But the two people will not resolve their situation as long as neither one grasps the other's point of view. (Cf. Tannen, 1990: 62)

Analysing such examples of everyday life is the focus of this chapter. We begin by presenting many of the building blocks of common experience and then explore the almost magical way in which face-to-face interaction generates reality. Throughout, the discussion highlights the importance of gender to our everyday experiences.

The central concept is **social interaction**, which may be defined as *the process by which people act and react in relation to others*. Social interaction is the key to creating the changing reality we perceive. And in our everyday lives we interact with one another according to particular social guidelines.

● Social structure: a guide to everyday living

Members of every society rely on social structure to make sense out of everyday situations. So what, then, are the building blocks of our daily lives?

Status

One basic element of social structure is **status**, *a recognised social position that an individual occupies*. Notice that the sociological meaning of the term 'status' differs from its everyday meaning of 'prestige'. In common usage, a bank manager has more 'status' than a bank clerk. Sociologically, however, both 'bank manager' and 'bank clerk' are statuses because they represent socially defined positions, even though one does confer more power and prestige than the other.

Every status involves particular duties, rights and expectations. The statuses people occupy thus guide their behaviour in any setting. In the University lecture theatre, for example, lecturers and students have distinctive, well-defined responsibilities. Similarly, family interaction turns on the interplay of mother, father, daughters, sons and others. In all these situations, statuses connect us to others, which is why, in the case of families, we commonly call others 'relations'. In short, a status defines who and what we are *in relation to* others.

Status is also a key component of social identity. Occupational position, for example, is a major part of most people's self-concept throughout life and is quickly offered as part of a social introduction. Even long after retirement, people continue to identify themselves in terms of their life's work.

Status set

Everyone occupies many statuses simultaneously. The term **status set** refers to *all the statuses a person holds at a given time*. A girl may be a *daughter* to her parents, a *sister* to her siblings, a *friend* to members of her social circle, and a *goalie* to others on her hockey team. Just as status sets branch out in many directions, they also change over the life course. A child grows into an adult, a student becomes a lawyer, and people marry to become husbands and wives, sometimes becoming single again as a result of divorce or death. Joining an organisation or finding a job enlarges our status set; withdrawing from activities diminishes it. Individuals gain and lose dozens of statuses over a lifetime.

Ascribed and achieved status

Sociologists classify statuses in terms of how people obtain them. An **ascribed status** is *a social position that someone receives at birth or assumes involuntarily later in life*. Examples of ascribed statuses include being a daughter, a Norwegian, a teenager or a widower. Ascribed statuses are matters about which people have little or no choice.

By contrast, an **achieved status** refers to *a social position that someone assumes voluntarily and that reflects personal ability and effort*. Among achieved statuses are being a sociology student, an Olympic athlete, a spouse, a computer programmer or a thief. In each case, the individual has significant choice in the matter.

In practice, of course, most statuses involve some combination of ascription and achievement. That is, people's ascribed statuses influence the statuses they achieve. Adults who achieve the status of lawyer, for example, are likely to share the ascribed trait of being born into relatively privileged families. And any person of a privileged sex, race, ethnicity or age has far more opportunity to realise desirable achieved statuses than does someone without such advantages. By contrast, many less desirable statuses, such as criminal, drug addict or being unemployed are more easily 'achieved' by people born into poverty.

Master status

Some statuses matter more than others. A **master status** is *a status that has exceptional importance for social identity, often shaping a person's entire life*. For many people, occupation is often a master status, because it conveys a great deal about social background,

We learn from what we see. Thus each one of us selects others as role models, people whose behaviour we wish to emulate. The National Civil Rights Museum in Memphis, Tennessee, contains this sculpture of Rosa Parks, a woman of colour and a seamstress, who boarded a public bus on December 1, 1955, in Montgomery, Alabama. Although she took her place in the section reserved for African Americans, the driver ordered her to give up her seat to a white man. When she courageously refused, police arrested her. The episode led to the Montgomery Bus Boycott, which lasted for a year and finally brought an end to racial segregation on that city's buses.

Source: John L. Focht

education and income. At the extreme, being Prince Charles or Queen Elizabeth is enough by itself to push an individual into the limelight.

In a negative sense, serious disease also operates as a master status. Sometimes even lifelong friends shun cancer patients or people with acquired immune deficiency syndrome (AIDS), simply because of their illness. Most societies of the world also limit the opportunities of women, whatever their abilities, making gender, too, a master status.

Finally, we sometimes dehumanise people with physical disabilities by perceiving them only in terms of their impairments. In the box, two people with physical disabilities describe this problem.

Role

A second major component of social interaction is **role**, *behaviour expected of someone who holds a particular status*. Think of a role as the dynamic expression of a status: individuals *hold* a status and *perform* a role

(Linton, 1937). The obligations and privileges of being a student, for example, require you to fulfil that role by attending lectures and completing assignments and, more generally, devoting much of your time to personal enrichment through academic study.

Both statuses and roles vary by culture. In the UK, the status 'uncle' refers to a sibling of either one's mother or father; in Vietnam, by contrast, specific terms designate uncles on each side of the family, and responsibilities differ accordingly. In every society, too, actual role performance varies according to an individual's unique personality, though some societies permit more personal latitude than others do.

Role set

Because we occupy many statuses simultaneously – a status set – everyday life is a mix of multiple roles. Robert Merton (1968) introduced the term **role set** to identify *a number of roles attached to a single status*.

Figure 6.1 illustrates the status set and corresponding role sets of one individual. Four statuses are presented, each linked to a different role set. First, this woman occupies the status of 'wife', with corresponding roles in relation to her husband ('conjugal roles' such as confidante and sexual partner), with whom

Figure 6.1 ● Status set and role set

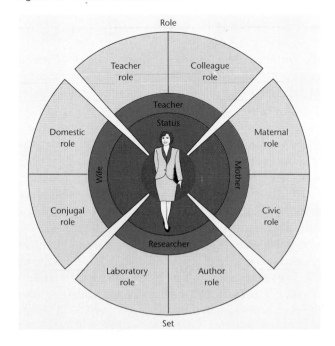

DIFFERENT VOICES

Physical disability as master status

In these research interviews, two women explain how a physical disability can become a master status, defining an individual. The first voice is that of 29-year-old Donna Finch, who holds a master's degree in social work and lives with her husband and son in Muskogee, Oklahoma. She is also blind.

Most people don't expect handicapped people to grow up, they are always supposed to be children. . . . You aren't supposed to date, you aren't supposed to have a job, somehow you're just supposed to disappear. I'm not saying this is true of anyone else, but in my own case I think I was more intellectually mature than most children, and more emotionally immature. I'd say that not until the last four or five years have I felt really whole.

Rose Helman is an elderly woman living near New York City. She suffers from spinal meningitis and is also blind.

Source: Guide Dogs for the Blind Association

You ask me if people are really different today than in the 20s and 30s. Not too much. They are still fearful of the handicapped. I don't know if fearful is the right word, but uncomfortable at least. But I can understand it somewhat; it happened to me. I once asked a man to tell me which staircase to use to get from the subway out to the street. He started giving me directions that were confusing, and I said, 'Do you mind taking me?'

He said, 'Not at all'. He grabbed me on the side with my dog on it, so I asked him to take my other arm. And he said, 'I'm sorry, I have no other arm'. And I said, 'That's all right, I'll hold onto the jacket'. It felt funny hanging onto the sleeve without the arm in it. ●

Source: Orlansky and Heward, 1981.

she would share a 'domestic role' in terms of maintaining the household. Second, she also holds the status of 'mother', with routine responsibilities for her children (the 'maternal role') as well as obligations to their school and other organisations (the 'civic role'). Third, as a professor, she interacts with students (the 'teacher role') as well as with other academics (the 'colleague role').

Fourth, her work as a researcher (the 'laboratory role') generates the data she uses in her publications (the 'author role'). Of course, Figure 6.1 lists only some of this person's status and role sets, since an individual generally occupies several dozen statuses at one time, each linked to a role set. This woman might be, additionally, a daughter caring for ageing parents and a member of the city council.

Role conflict and role strain

Members of industrial societies routinely juggle a host of responsibilities demanded by their various statuses and roles. As most mothers can testify, parenting as well as working outside the home taxes both physical and emotional strength. Sociologists thus recognise **role conflict** as *incompatibility among roles corresponding to two or more statuses.*

We experience role conflict when we find ourselves pulled in various directions while trying to respond to the many statuses we hold. Some politicians, for example, decide not to run for national office because the demands of a campaign would impoverish family life; in other cases, ambitious people defer having children or choose to remain childless in order to stay on the 'fast track' for career success.

Even the roles linked to a single status may make competing demands on us. The concept of **role strain** refers to *incompatibility among roles corresponding to a single status*. A factory supervisor may enjoy being friendly with other workers. At the same time, however, the supervisor's responsibility for everyone's performance requires maintaining some measure of personal distance from each employee. In short, performing the roles attached to even one status may involve something of a balancing act.

One strategy for minimising role conflict is 'compartmentalising' our lives so that we perform roles linked to one status at one time and place, and carry out roles corresponding to another status elsewhere at another time. A familiar example of this scheme is heading home while leaving the job 'at work'.

Role exit

After she herself left the life of a Catholic nun to become a university sociologist, Helen Rose Fuchs Ebaugh (1988) began to study *role exit*, the process by which people disengage from important social roles. Studying a range of 'exes', including ex-nuns, ex-doctors, ex-husbands and ex-alcoholics, Ebaugh identified elements common to the process of 'becoming an ex'.

According to Ebaugh, people initiate the process of role exit by reflecting critically on their existing lives and grappling with doubts about their ability or willingness to persist in a certain role. As they imagine alternative roles, they ultimately reach a point when they decide to pursue a new life.

Even at this point, however, a past role may continue to influence our lives. 'Exes' retain a self-image shaped by an earlier role, which may interfere with the drive to build a new sense of self. An ex-nun, for example, may hesitate to wear stylish clothing and makeup.

'Exes' must also rebuild relationships with people who may have known them in their 'earlier life' and who may not realise just how new and unfamiliar their present role may be. And learning new social skills poses another challenge. For example, Ebaugh reports, nuns who begin dating after decades in the Church are often startled to learn that sexual norms are now vastly different from those they knew as teenagers.

● The social construction of reality

More than fifty years ago, the Italian playwright Luigi Pirandello skillfully applied the sociological perspective to social interaction. In The *Pleasure of Honesty*, Angelo Baldovino – a brilliant man with a chequered past – enters the fashionable home of the Renni family and introduces himself in a most peculiar way:

Inevitably we construct ourselves. Let me explain. I enter this house and immediately I become what I have to become, what I can become: I construct myself. That is, I present myself to you in a form suitable to the relationship I wish to achieve with you. And, of course, you do the same with me. (1962: 157–8)

This curious introduction reveals that, while behaviour is guided by status and role, each human being has considerable ability to shape what happens moment to moment. 'Reality', in other words, is not as fixed as we may think.

The phrase **social construction of reality** was introduced by Peter Berger and Thomas Luckmann (1967) to identify *the process by which people creatively shape reality through social interaction*. This idea stands at the foundation of sociology's symbolic-interaction paradigm, as described in earlier chapters. As Angelo Baldovino's remark suggests, especially in an unfamiliar situation, quite a bit of 'reality' remains unclear in everyone's mind. So as Baldovino 'presents himself' in terms that suit his purposes and, as others do the same, a complex reality emerges, though few people are so 'up front' about their deliberate efforts to foster an impression.

Social interaction, then, amounts to negotiating reality. Most everyday situations involve at least some agreement about what's going on, but participants perceive events differently to the extent that they are motivated by disparate interests and intentions.

Steering reality in this way is sometimes referred to as 'street smarts'. In his biography *Down These Mean Streets*, Piri Thomas recalls moving to a new apartment in New York City's Spanish Harlem, which placed him squarely on the turf of the local street gang. Returning home one evening, young Piri found himself cut off by Waneko, the gang's leader, who was flanked by a dozen of his cohorts.

'Whatta ya say, Mr. Johnny Gringo,' drawled Waneko.

Think man, I told myself, *think your way out of a stomping. Make it good.* 'I hear you 104th street coolies are supposed to have heart,' I said. 'I don't know this for sure. You know there's a lot of streets where a whole 'click' is made out of punks who can't fight one guy unless they all jump him for the stomp.' I hoped this would push Waneko into giving me a fair one. His expression didn't change.

'Maybe we don't look at it that way.'

Crazy, man, I cheer inwardly, *the* cabron *is falling into my setup* . . . . 'I wasn't talking to you,' I said. 'Where I come from, the pres is president 'cause he got heart when it comes to dealing.'

Waneko was starting to look uneasy. He had bit on my worm and felt like a sucker fish. His boys were now light on me. They were no longer so much interested in stomping me as seeing the outcome between Waneko and me. 'Yeah,' was his reply. . . .

I knew I'd won. Sure, I'd have to fight; but one guy, not ten or fifteen. If I lost, I might still get stomped, and if I won I might get stomped. I took care of this with my next sentence. 'I don't know you or your boys,' I said, 'but they look cool to me. They don't feature as punks.'

I had left him out purposely when I said 'they'. Now his boys were in a separate class. I had cut him off. He would have to fight me on his own, to prove his heart to himself, to his boys, and most important, to his turf. He got away from the stoop and asked, 'Fair one, Gringo?' (1967: 56–7)

This situation reveals the drama – sometimes subtle, sometimes savage – by which human beings creatively build reality. There are limits, of course, to what even the most skilful and persuasive personality can achieve. And, of course, not everyone enters a negotiation with equal standing. Should a police officer have come on the scene of the fight that ensued between Piri and Waneko, both young men might well have ended up in jail.

The Thomas theorem

By displaying his wits and boxing with Waneko until they both grew tired, Piri Thomas won acceptance that evening and became one of the group. W. I. Thomas (1966: 301; orig. 1931) succinctly expressed this insight in what has come to be known as the **Thomas theorem**: *situations we define as real become real in their consequences.*

Applied to social interaction, Thomas's insight means that, although reality is initially 'soft', as it is fashioned it can become 'hard' in its effects. In the case of Piri Thomas, having succeeded in defining himself as worthy, this young man *became* worthy in the eyes of his new comrades.

Ethnomethodology

Rather than assume that reality is something 'out there', the symbolic-interaction paradigm posits that reality is created by people in everyday encounters. But how, exactly, do we define reality for ourselves? Answering this question is the objective of *ethnomethodology*.

The term itself has two parts: the Greek *ethno* refers to people and how they understand their surroundings; 'methodology' designates a set of methods or principles. Combining them makes **ethnomethodology**, *the study of the way people make sense of their everyday lives*. Ethnomethodology is largely the creation of Harold Garfinkel (1967), who challenged the then-dominant view of society as a broad, abstract 'system' (recall the approach of Emile Durkheim, described in Chapter 3, 'Society'). Garfinkel wanted to explore how we make sense of countless familiar situations. On the surface, we engage in intentional speech or action; but these efforts rest on deeper assumptions about the world that we usually take for granted.

Think, for a moment, about what we assume in asking someone the simple question, 'How are you?' Do we mean physically? Mentally? Spiritually? Financially? Are we even looking for an answer, or are we 'just being polite'?

Ethnomethodology, then, delves into the sense-making process in any social encounter. Because so much of this process is ingrained, Garfinkel argues that one effective way to expose how we make sense of events is to purposely *break the rules*. Deliberately ignoring conventional rules and observing how people respond, he points out, allows us to tease out how people build a reality. Thus, Garfinkel (1967) directed his students to refuse to 'play the game' in a wide range of situations. Some students living with their parents started acting as if they were boarders rather than children; others entered stores and insisted on bargaining for items; others recruited people into simple games (like tic-tac-toe) only to intentionally flout the rules; still others initiated conversations while slowly moving closer and closer to the other person.

The students first noticed people's reactions. Typically, the 'victims' of these rule violations became

Cultures frame reality in different ways. This man lay on the street of Bombay, India, for several hours and then quietly died. In Britain, such an event would probably have provoked someone to call the rescue squad. In a poor society in which death on the streets is a fact of everyday life, however, many Indians responded not with alarm but with simple decency by stopping to place incense on his body before continuing on their way.

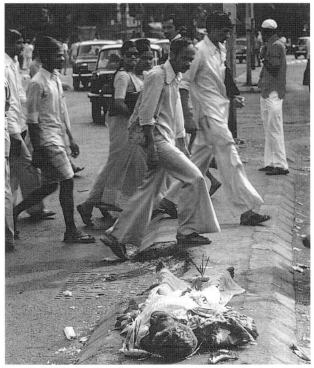

Source: Paul W. Liebhardt

agitated, indicating that even if reality is taken for granted it is very important to us. Then the students tried to identify exactly *why* people were disturbed, leading to insights about the unspoken agreements that underlie family life, shopping, fair play and the like.

Reality building in global perspective

People do not build everyday experience 'out of thin air'. In part, how we act or what we see in our surroundings depends on our interests. Scanning the night sky, for example, lovers discover romance, while scientists perceive the same stars as hydrogen atoms fusing into helium. Social background also directs our perceptions, since we build reality out of elements in the surrounding culture. For this reason, some residents of,

say, London's Hampstead experience the world differently from some of those living in poorer Brixton.

In truth, there are few common elements to the reality construction that goes on across England and Europe. And in global perspective, reality construction is even more variable. People waiting for a bus in London typically queue up in a straight line; people in New York are rarely so orderly. The law forbids women in Saudi Arabia from driving a car, a constraint unheard of in the West. Fear of crime in the big cities of the United States is considerably greater than it is elsewhere – including London, Paris, Rome, Calcutta and Hong Kong – and this sense of public danger shapes the daily realities of tens of millions of US citizens.

From these examples, we conclude that people build reality from the surrounding culture. Chapter 4 ('Culture') explained how people the world over derive different meanings from specific gestures, so that sometimes travellers find themselves building a most unexpected reality! Similarly, what we 'see' in a book or a film also depends on the assumptions we make about the world.

If people the world over inhabit different realities, are some happier than others? Those living in a high-income society have reason to feel fortunate. As Figure 6.2 indicates, global survey data reveal that members of Swedish society claim to be happier than most.

Figure 6.2 ● Happiness: a global survey
Survey question: 'We are interested in the way people are feeling these days. During the past few weeks, did you ever "feel on top of the world", feeling that life is wonderful?'

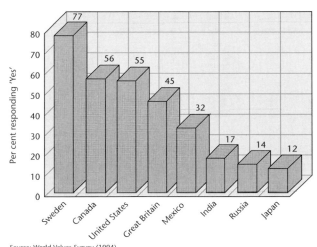

Source: World Values Survey (1994)

Finally, what about the full range of human emotions? Are emotions generically human and, therefore, much the same everywhere? Or is what we feel derived from our culture? Cross-cultural researchers conclude that emotions are rooted in biology – and culture – as the box on pages 164 and 165 explains.

● Dramaturgical analysis: 'the presentation of self'

Erving Goffman (1922–82) is this century's leading microsociologist. He greatly enhanced our understanding of everyday life by noting that people interacting behave much like actors performing on a stage. By imagining ourselves as directors scrutinising what goes on in some situational 'theatre', we engage in what Goffman called **dramaturgical analysis**, *the investigation of social interaction in terms of theatrical performance.* Dramaturgical analysis offers a fresh look at two now-familiar concepts. In theatrical terms, a status mirrors a part in a play, and a role serves as a script, supplying dialogue and action for each of the characters. Moreover, in any setting, a person is both actor and audience. Goffman described each individual's 'performance' as the **presentation of self**, *an individual's effort to create specific impressions in the minds of others.* Presentation of self, or *impression management*, contains several distinctive elements (Goffman, 1959, 1967).

Performances

As we present ourselves in everyday situations, we convey information – consciously and unconsciously – to others. An individual's performance includes dress (costume), any objects carried along (props) and tone of voice and particular gestures (manner). In addition, people craft their performance according to the setting (stage). We may joke loudly in the street, for example, but assume a more reverent manner upon entering a church. In addition, individuals design settings, such as a home or office, to enhance a performance by invoking the desired reactions in others.

Consider, for example, how a doctor's surgery conveys information to an audience of patients. Doctors enjoy prestige and power, a fact immediately grasped by patients upon entering the surgery or health centre. First, the doctor is nowhere to be seen. Instead, in what Goffman describes as the 'front region' of the

setting, the patient encounters a receptionist who functions as a gatekeeper, deciding if and when the patient can meet the doctor. A simple survey of the waiting room, with patients (often impatiently) awaiting their call to the inner sanctum, leaves little doubt that the medical team controls events.

The doctor's private examination room or surgery constitutes the 'back region' of the setting. Here the patient confronts a wide range of props, such as medical books and framed degrees, which together reinforce the impression that the doctor has the specialised knowledge necessary to be in charge. In the surgery the doctor usually remains seated behind a desk – the larger and grander the desk, the greater the statement of power – while the patient is provided with only a chair.

The doctor's appearance and manner convey still more information. The common hospital doctor's costume of white lab coat may have the practical function of keeping clothes from becoming soiled, but its social function is to let others know at a glance the doctor's status. A stethoscope around the neck or a black medical bag in hand has the same purpose. A doctor's highly technical terminology – frequently mystifying – also emphasises the hierarchy in the situation. The use of the title 'Doctor' by patients who, in turn, are frequently addressed only by their first names, also underscores the physician's dominant position. The overall message of a doctor's performance is clear: 'I will help you only if you allow me to take charge'.

Non-verbal communication

Novelist William Sansom describes a fictional Mr Preedy – an English holidaymaker on a beach in Spain:

He took care to avoid catching anyone's eye. First, he had to make it clear to those potential companions of his holiday that they were of no concern to him whatsoever. He stared through them, round them, over them – eyes lost in space. The beach might have been empty. If by chance a ball was thrown his way, he looked surprised; then let a smile of amusement light his face (Kindly Preedy), looked around dazed to see that there were people on the beach, tossed it back with a smile to himself and not a smile *at* the people. . . .

. . . [He] then gathered together his beach-wrap and bag into a neat sand-resistant pile (Methodical and Sensible Preedy), rose slowly to stretch his huge frame (Big-Cat Preedy), and tossed aside his sandals (Carefree Preedy, after all). (1956; quoted in Goffman, 1959: 4–5)

Through his conduct, Mr Preedy offers a great deal of information about himself to anyone caring to observe him. Notice that he does so without uttering a single word. This illustrates the process of **non-verbal communication**, *communication using body movements, gestures and facial expressions rather than speech.*

Virtually any part of the body can be used to generate *body language*; that is, to convey information to others. Facial expressions form the most significant element of non-verbal communication. As noted in the box, smiling and other facial gestures express basic emotions like pleasure, surprise and anger the world over. Further, people project particular shades of meaning with their faces. We distinguish, for example, between the deliberate smile of Kindly Preedy on the beach, a spontaneous smile of joy at seeing a friend, a pained smile of embarrassment and a full, unrestrained smile of self-satisfaction that we often associate with the 'cat who ate the canary'.

Eye contact is another crucial element of non-verbal communication. Generally, we use eye contact to initiate social interaction. Someone across the room 'catches our eye', for example, sparking a conversation. Avoiding the eyes of another, on the other hand, discourages communication. Hands, too, speak for us. Common hand gestures in our culture convey, among other things, an insult, a request for a lift, an invitation for someone to join us or a demand that others stop in their tracks. Gestures also supplement spoken words. Pointing in a menacing way at someone, for example, intensifies a word of warning, just as shrugging the shoulders adds an air of indifference to the phrase 'I don't know', and rapidly waving the arms lends urgency to the single word 'Hurry!'

But, as any actor knows, the 'perfect performance' is an elusive goal. In everyday performances, some element of body language often contradicts our intended meaning. A teenage boy offers an explanation for getting home late, for example, but his mother doubts his words because he avoids looking her in the eye. The movie star on a television talk show claims that her recent flop at the box office is 'no big deal', but the nervous swing of her leg belies her casual denial. In practical terms, carefully observing non-verbal communication (most of which is not easily controlled) provides clues to deception, in much the same way that a lie detector records tell-tale changes in breathing, pulse rate, perspiration and blood pressure.

Yet detecting lies is difficult, because no single bodily gesture directly indicates deceit in the way that, say, a smile indicates pleasure. Even so, because any performance involves so many expressions, few people can confidently lie without allowing some piece of contradictory information to slip through, arousing the suspicions of a careful observer. Therefore, the key to detecting deceit is to scan the whole performance with an eye for inconsistencies and discrepancies.

Paul Ekman (1985) suggests scrutinising four elements of a performance – words, voice, body language and facial expression – for clues to deception.

1. *Words.* Good liars can mentally rehearse their lines and manipulate words with ease. But they may not be able to avoid a simple slip of the tongue – something the performer did not mean to say in quite that way. For example, a young man who is deceiving his parents by claiming that his room mate is a male friend rather than a female lover might inadvertently use the word 'she' rather than 'he' in a conversation. The more complicated the deception, the more likely a performer is to make a revealing mistake.

2. *Voice.* Tone and patterns of speech are hard to control, so a person trying to hide a powerful emotion, for example, cannot easily prevent the voice from trembling or breaking. Similarly, the individual may speak quickly (a clue to anger) or slowly (indicating sadness). Nervous laughter, inappropriate pauses between words, or non-words, such as 'ah' and 'ummm', also hint at discomfort.

3. *Body language.* A 'leak' of body language may tip off an observer to deception as well. Subtle body movements, for example, give the impression of nervousness, as does sudden swallowing or rapid breathing. These are especially good clues to deception because few people can control them. Sometimes, *not* using the body in the expected way to enhance words – as when a person tries to fake excitement – also suggests deception.

4. *Facial expressions.* Because facial expressions, too, are hard to control, they give away many phony performances, as indicated by Figure 6.3. A sad person feigning happiness, for example, generally 'flashes' momentary frowns through a crooked smile. By contrast, raising and drawing together the eyebrows signals genuine fear or worry, since this expression is virtually impossible to make wilfully.

Emotions in global perspective: do we all feel the same?

On a busy London street, a woman reacts angrily to the roller blade skater who zooms past her. Apart from a few choice words, her facial expression broadcasts a strong emotion that Europeans easily recognise. But would an observer from Nigeria, Nicaragua or New Guinea be able to interpret her emotion? In other words, do people the world over share similar feelings, and do they express them in the same way?

Paul Ekman (1980a) and his colleagues studied emotions around the world, even among members of a small society in New Guinea. They concluded that people throughout the world experience six basic emotions: anger, fear, disgust, happiness, surprise and sadness. Moreover, people everywhere recognise these feelings in the same distinctive facial gestures. To Ekman, this commonality means that much of our emotional life is universal – rather than culturally variable – and that the display of emotion is biologically programmed in our facial features, muscles and central nervous system.

But if the reality of emotions is rooted in our biology, Ekman and other researchers note three ways in which emotional life differs significantly in global perspective.

First, what triggers an emotion varies from one society to another. Whether people define a particular situation as an insult (causing anger), a loss (calling forth sadness), or a mystical event (provoking surprise and awe) depends on the cultural surroundings of the individual.

Second, people display emotions according to the norms of their culture. Every society has rules about when, where and to whom an individual may exhibit certain emotions. For example, people in the United States typically express emotions more freely in the home among family members than among colleagues in the workplace. Similarly, we expect children to express emotions to parents, though parents are taught to guard their emotions in front of children.

Third, societies differ in terms of how people cope with emotions. Some societies encourage the expression of feelings, while others belittle emotions and demand that their members suppress them. Societies also display significant gender differences in this regard. In England, most people consider emotional expression as feminine, expected of women but a sign of weakness in men. In other societies, however, this sex typing of emotions is less pronounced or even reversed.

In sum, emotional life in global perspective has both common and variable elements. People around the world experience the same basic feelings. Witnessing our angry Londoner who opened this box, an individual from New Guinea quickly would comprehend her expression. But what sparks a particular emotion, to whom someone expresses it, and whether people encourage or discourage the display of emotions are variable products of social learning. ●

Sources: Ekman, 1980a, 1980b; Lutz and White, 1986, and Lutz, 1988.

In sum, lies are detectable, but training is the key to noticing relevant clues. Another key to spotting deception is knowing the other person well, the reason that parents can usually pick up deceit in their children. Finally, almost anyone can unmask deception when the liar is trying to cover up strong emotions.

Gender and personal performances

Because women are socialised to be less assertive than men, they tend to be especially sensitive to non-verbal communication. In fact, gender is a central element in personal performances. Based on the work of Nancy Henley, Mykol Hamilton and Barrie Thorne (1992), we can extend the present discussion of personal performances to spotlight the importance of gender.

Demeanour
Demeanour – that is, general conduct or deportment – reflects a person's level of social power. Simply put, powerful people enjoy far greater personal discretion

To most people in Europe these expressions convey happiness, anxiety, fear, anger and surprise.

Source: Popperfoto

in how they act; subordinates act more formally and self-consciously. Off-colour remarks, swearing or casually removing shoes and putting feet up on the desk may be acceptable for the boss, but rarely for employees. Similarly, people in positions of dominance can interrupt the performances of others with impunity, while others are expected to display deference by remaining silent (Smith-Lovin and Brody, 1989; Henley, Hamilton and Thorne, 1992; Johnson, 1994).

Since women generally occupy positions of lesser power, demeanour is a gender issue as well. As Chapter 13 ('Gender and Sexuality') explains, about half of all working women in Europe and the United States hold clerical or service jobs that place them under the control of supervisors, who are usually men. Women, then, craft their personal performances more carefully than men and display a greater degree of deference in everyday interaction.

Figure 6.3 ● Which is an 'honest face'

Telling lies is no easy task because most people lack the ability to manipulate all their facial muscles. Looking at the three faces below, the expression of grief in sketch (a) is probably genuine, since few people can deliberately lift the upper eyelids and inner corners of the eyebrows in this way. Likewise, the apprehension displayed in (b) also appears authentic, since intentionally raising the eyebrows and pulling them together is nearly impossible. People who fake emotions usually do a poor job of it, as illustrated by the phoney expression of pleasure shown in (c). Genuine delight, for most people would produce a balanced smile.

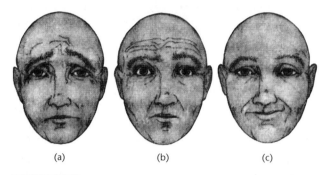

(a)   (b)   (c)

Use of space

How much space does a personal performance require? Here again, power plays a key role, since using more space conveys a non-verbal message of personal importance. According to Henley, Hamilton and Thorne (1992), men typically command more space than women do, whether pacing back and forth before an audience or casually lounging on the beach. Why? Our culture traditionally has measured femininity by how *little* space women occupy (the standard of 'daintiness'), while gauging masculinity by how *much* territory a man controls (the standard of 'turf').

The concept of **personal space** refers to *the surrounding area to which an individual makes some claim to privacy*. In the United Kingdom, for example, people typically position themselves several feet apart when speaking; throughout the Middle East, by contrast, individuals interact within a much closer space.

Throughout the world, gender further modifies these patterns. In daily life, men commonly intrude on the personal space of women. A woman's encroachment into a man's personal space, however, is likely to be construed as a sexual overture. Here again, women have less power in everyday interaction than men do.

Staring, smiling and touching

Eye contact encourages interaction. Typically, women employ eye contact to sustain conversation more than men do. Men have their own distinctive brand of eye contact: staring. By making women the targets of stares, men are both making a claim of social dominance and defining women as sexual objects.

Although frequently signalling pleasure, *smiling* has a host of meanings. In a male-dominated world, women often smile to indicate appeasement or acceptance of submission. For this reason, Henley, Hamilton and Thorne maintain, women smile more than men; in extreme cases, smiling may reach the level of nervous habit.

Finally, *touching* constitutes an intriguing social pattern. Mutual touching conveys feelings of intimacy and caring. Apart from close relationships, however, touching is generally something men do to women (though rarely, in our culture, to other men). A male doctor touches the shoulder of his female nurse as they examine a report, a young man touches the back of his woman friend as he guides her across the street, or a male skiing instructor looks for opportunities to touch his female students. In these examples – as well as many others – touching may evoke little response, so common is it in everyday life. But it amounts to a subtle ritual by which men express their dominant position in an assumed hierarchy that subordinates women.

Idealisation

Complex motives underlie human behaviour. Even so, according to Goffman, we construct performances to *idealise* our intentions. That is, we try to convince others (and perhaps ourselves) that what we do reflects ideal cultural standards rather than more selfish motives.

Idealisation is easily illustrated by returning to the world of doctors and patients. In a hospital, consultants engage in a performance commonly described as 'making the rounds'. Approaching the patient, the doctor often stops at the foot of the bed and silently examines the patient's chart. Afterward, doctor and patient converse briefly. In ideal terms, this routine involves a doctor making a personal visit to inquire about a patient's condition.

In reality, something less exemplary is usually going on. A doctor who sees several dozen patients a day may remember little about most of them. Reading the chart gives the doctor the opportunity to rediscover the patient's identity and medical problems. Openly revealing the actual impersonality of much medical care would undermine the culturally ideal perception of the doctor as deeply concerned about the welfare of others.

Idealisation is woven into the fabric of everyday life in countless ways. Doctors, university lecturers and other professionals typically idealise their motives for entering their chosen careers. They describe their work as 'making a contribution to science', 'helping others', 'answering a calling from God', or perhaps 'serving the community'. Rarely do such people concede the less honourable, though common, motives of seeking the income, power, prestige and leisure these occupations confer.

Taking a broader view, idealisation underlies social civility, since we smile and make polite remarks to people we do not like. Such small hypocrisies ease our way through social interactions. Even when we suspect that others are putting on an act, rarely do we openly challenge their performance, for reasons we shall explain next.

Embarrassment and tact

The eminent professor consistently mispronounces the dean's name; the visiting dignitary rises from the table to speak, unaware of the napkin that still hangs from her neck; the president becomes ill at a state dinner. As carefully as individuals may craft their performances, slip-ups of all kinds frequently occur. The result is *embarrassment*, which, in dramaturgical terms, means the discomfort that follows a spoiled performance. Goffman describes embarrassment simply as 'losing face'.

Embarrassment looms as an ever-present danger because, first, all performances typically contain some measure of deception. Second, most performances involve a complex array of elements, any one of which, in a thoughtless moment, may shatter the intended impression.

Interestingly, an audience usually overlooks flaws in a performance, thereby allowing an actor to avoid embarrassment. If we do point out a mis-step ('Excuse me, but do you know that your fly is open?'), we do it discreetly and only to help someone avoid even greater loss of face. In Hans Christian Andersen's classic fable *The Emperor's New Clothes*, the child who blurts out that the emperor is parading around naked is telling the truth, yet is scolded for being rude.

But members of an audience usually do more than ignore flaws in a performance, Goffman explains; typically, they help the performer recover from them. *Tact*, then, amounts to helping another person 'save face'. After hearing a supposed expert make an embarrassingly inaccurate remark, for example, people may tactfully ignore the comment as if it were never spoken at all. Alternatively, mild laughter may indicate that they wish to dismiss what they have heard as a joke. Or a listener may simply respond, 'I'm sure you didn't mean that', acknowledging the statement but not allowing it to destroy the actor's performance.

Why is tact such a common response? Because embarrassment provokes discomfort not simply for one person but for *everyone*. Just as the entire audience feels uneasy when an actor forgets a line, people who observe awkward behaviour are reminded of how fragile their own performances often are. Socially constructed reality thus functions like a dam holding back a sea of chaotic possibility. Should one person's performance spring a leak, others tactfully assist in making repairs. Everyone, after all, jointly engages in building culture, and no one wants reality to be suddenly swept away.

In sum, Goffman's research shows that, while behaviour is spontaneous in some respects, it is more patterned than we like to think. Almost four hundred years ago, William Shakespeare captured this idea in memorable lines that still ring true:

All the world's a stage,
And all the men and women merely players:
They have their exits and their entrances;
And one man in his time plays many parts. . . .
(*As You Like It*, II)

● Interaction in everyday life: two illustrations

We have now examined many elements of social interaction. The final sections of this chapter illustrate key lessons by focusing on two important, yet quite different, elements of everyday life.

Language: the gender issue

As Chapter 4 ('Culture') explains, language is the thread that ties members of a society together in the symbolic web we call culture. In everyday life, language conveys meaning on more than one level. Besides the obvious message in what people say, a host of additional meanings are embedded in our language. One such message involves gender. Language defines men and women differently in at least three ways, involving control, value and attention (Henley, Hamilton and Thorne, 1992).[1]

Language and control

A young man astride his new motorcycle rolls proudly into the petrol station, and eagerly says to the attendant, 'Isn't she a beauty?' On the surface, the question has little to do with gender. Yet, curiously, a common linguistic pattern confers the female 'she', and never the male 'he', on a man's prized possession.

As we noted at the beginning of this chapter, the language men use often reveals their concern with competence and control. In this case, a man attaches a female pronoun to a motorcycle (car, yacht or other object) because it reflects *ownership*.

A more obvious control function of language relates to people's names. Traditionally, in many parts of the world, a woman takes the family name of the man she marries. While few people consider this an explicit statement of a man's ownership of a woman, many believe that it reflects male dominance. For this reason, an increasing proportion of married women (currently 10 per cent) have retained their own name or merged two family names (Brightman, 1994).

Language and value

Language usually treats as masculine whatever has greater value, force or significance. Although we may not think much about it, this pattern is deeply rooted in the English language. For instance, the positive adjective 'virtuous', meaning 'morally worthy' or 'excellent', is derived from the Latin word *vir* meaning 'man'. By contrast, the derogatory adjective 'hysterical' is derived from the Greek word *hyster*, meaning 'uterus'.

In numerous, more familiar ways, language also confers different value on the two sexes. Traditional masculine terms such as 'king' or 'lord' have retained their positive meaning, while comparable terms, such as 'queen', 'madam' or 'dame' have acquired negative con-

notations in contemporary usage. Language thus both mirrors social attitudes and helps to perpetuate them.

Similarly, use of the suffixes '-ette' and '-ess' to denote femininity generally devalues the words to which they are added. For example, a 'major' has higher standing than a 'majorette', as does a 'host' in relation to a 'hostess'. And, certainly, men's groups with names such as the Los Angeles Rams carry more stature than women's groups with names like the Radio City Music Hall Rockettes.

Language and attention

Language also shapes reality by directing greater attention to masculine endeavours. Consider our use of personal pronouns. In the English language, the plural pronoun 'they' is neutral as it refers to both sexes. But the corresponding singular pronouns 'he' and 'she' specify gender. According to traditional grammatical practice, we use 'he' along with the possessive 'his' and the objective 'him' to refer to all people. Thus, we assume that the bit of wisdom 'He who hesitates is lost' refers to women as well as to men. But this practice also reflects the traditional cultural pattern of ignoring the lives of women. Some research suggests that people continue to respond to allegedly inclusive male pronouns as if only males were involved (MacKay, 1983).

The English language has no gender-neutral, third-person singular personal pronoun. In recent years, however, the plural pronouns 'they' and 'them' increasingly have gained currency as singular pronouns ('A person should do as they please'). This usage remains controversial because it violates conventional grammatical rules. Yet, there is no doubt that English is now evolving to accept such gender-neutral constructions.

Even as the English language changes, gender is likely to remain a source of miscommunication between women and men. In the box, Tony and Margaret – whose misadventures when looking for a friend's home opened this chapter – return to illustrate how the two sexes often seem to be speaking different languages.

Humour: playing with reality

Humour plays a vital part in everyday life. Comedians are among our favourite entertainers, most newspapers carry cartoons, and even professors and members of the clergy include a joke or two in their performances. As with many aspects of social life, however, we largely take humour for granted. While everyone

---

[1.] The following sections draw primarily from Henley, Hamilton and Thorne, 1992. Additional material comes from Thorne, Kramarae and Henley, 1983, and others, as noted.

SOCIOLOGICAL SPOTLIGHT

Gender and language: 'You just don't understand!'

In the story that opened this chapter, a couple face a situation that rings all too true to many people: when they are lost, men grumble to themselves, sometimes blaming their partners, but avoid asking others for directions. For their part, women can't understand why not.

Deborah Tannen's work in the United States has become best selling. She has conducted extensive research on the linguistic differences that separate the sexes and explains why. Men and women are fascinated by it.

Men, she claims, see almost every encounter as potentially competitive; thus, getting lost is bad enough without a man asking for help and thereby letting someone else 'one up' him. By contrast, because women hold a generally subordinate position, they are socialised to ask for help. Sometimes, Tannen points out, women will ask for assistance even when they don't need it.

A similar gender-linked problem common to couples involves what men call 'nagging'. Consider the following exchange (Adler, 1990: 74):

Margaret: What's wrong, honey?
Tony: Nothing . . .
Margaret: Something is bothering you; I can tell.
Tony: I told you nothing is bothering me. Leave me alone.
Margaret: But I can see that something is wrong.
Tony: OK. Just why do you think something is bothering me?
Margaret: Well, for one thing, you're bleeding all over your shirt.
Tony: [now irritated] It doesn't bother me.
Margaret: [losing her temper] WELL, IT SURE IS BOTHERING ME!
Tony: I'll go change my shirt.

The problem couples face in communicating is that what one partner intends by a comment is not always what the other hears in the words. To Margaret, her opening question is an effort at cooperative problem solving. She can see that something is wrong with Tony (who has carelessly cut himself) and she wants to help solve the problem. But Tony interprets her point-

ing out his problem as belittling, and tries to close off the discussion. Margaret, confident that Tony would take a more positive attitude toward her if he just understood that she only wants to be helpful, repeats herself. This reaction sets in motion a vicious cycle in which Tony, thinking Margaret is trying to manipulate him and make him feel incapable of looking after himself, responds by digging in his heels. His response, in turn, makes Margaret all the more sure that there is a problem that requires attention. And round it goes until somebody loses patience.

In the end, Tony gives in only to the extent that he agrees to change his shirt. But notice that he still refuses to discuss the original problem. Misunderstanding his wife's motives, Tony just wants Margaret to leave him alone. For her part, Margaret fails to understand her husband's view of the situation and walks away thinking that he is unnecessarily grouchy and insensitive. ●

Sources: Adler, 1990; Tannen, 1990.

---

laughs at a joke, in other words, few people think about what makes something funny or why humans everywhere like to laugh. Many of the ideas developed in this chapter provide insights into the character of humour, as we shall now see.

The foundation of humour

Humour is a product of reality construction; specifically, it stems from the contrast between two, incongruous realities. Generally, one reality is *conventional*, corresponding to what people expect in a specific situ-

ation. The other reality is *unconventional*, representing a significant violation of cultural patterns. Humour, therefore, arises from contradiction, ambiguity and 'double meanings' generated by two differing definitions of the same situation. Note how this principle works in one of Woody Allen's lines: 'I'm not afraid to die; I just don't want to be there when it happens'.

In this example, the first phrase represents a conventional notion; the second half, however, interjects an unconventional – even absurd – meaning that collides with what we are led to expect.

This same simple pattern holds true for virtually all humour. Yogi Berra's quip, 'If you come to a fork in the road, take it', sounds like useful advice, but ends up offering nothing at all. Or, notice the twin realities in the statement by frustrated parents: 'For their birthday, we're taking the twins to America. Next year, maybe we'll go back to get them'.

Of course, there are countless ways to mix realities and thereby generate humour. In some cases, contrasting realities emerge simply from reordering syllables, as in the case of the (probably fictitious) country song 'I'd rather have a bottle in front of me than a frontal lobotomy'.

Of course, a joke can be built the other way around, so that the comic leads the audience to *expect* an unconventional answer and gets a very ordinary one. When a reporter asked the famous desperado Willie Sutton why he robbed banks, for example, he replied dryly: 'Because that's where the money is'. However a joke is constructed, the greater the opposition or incongruity between the two definitions of reality, the greater the potential for humour.

When telling jokes, the comedian can strengthen this opposition in various ways. One technique, favoured by Groucho Marx and a host of other comics, is to present the first, or conventional, remark in conversation with another actor, then to turn toward the audience (or the camera) when delivering the second, or unconventional, line in a slightly different tone of voice. In one of his films, Groucho swaggers in front of a young woman and brags 'This morning I shot a lion in my pyjamas'. Then, dropping his voice and turning to the camera, he adds, 'What the lion was doing in my pajamas *I'll never know. . .*' This 'shift of channel' underscores the incongruity of the two parts. Following the same logic, many stand-up comedians also 'reset' the audience to conventional expectations by interjecting 'But, seriously, folks. . .' after one joke and before the next one.

To construct the strongest contrast in meaning, comedians pay careful attention to their performances – the precise words they use, as well as the timing of each part of the delivery. A joke is 'well told' if the comic creates the sharpest possible opposition between the realities, just as humour falls flat in a careless performance. Since the key to humour lies in the opposition of realities, it is not surprising that the climax of a joke is called the *punch* line.

The dynamics of humour: 'getting it'

If people fail to understand both the conventional and unconventional realities embedded in a joke, they usually say, with a puzzled expression, 'I don't get it'. To 'get' humour, members of an audience must understand the two realities underlying the joke well enough to perceive their incongruity.

But getting a joke can be more challenging still, because comics may deliberately omit some of the information listeners must grasp. The audience, therefore, must pay attention to the stated elements of the joke, and then fill in the missing pieces on their own. As a simple case, consider the reflection of movie producer Hal Roach upon reaching his one hundredth birthday:

If I had known I would live to be 100, I would have taken better care of myself!

Here, 'getting' the joke depends on realising that Roach must have taken pretty good care of himself because he lived to be 100 in the first place. Or take one of W. C. Fields's lines: 'Some weasel took the cork out of my lunch'. 'Some lunch', we think to ourselves to 'finish' the joke.

Of course, some jokes demand more mental effort than others. A more complex example is the following, written on the wall of a university lavatory:

Dyslexics of the world, untie!

To get this one, you must know, first, that dyslexia is a condition in which people routinely reverse letters; second, one must identify the line as an adaptation of Karl Marx's call to the world's workers to unite; third, one must recognise 'untie' as an anagram of 'unite', as one might imagine a disgruntled dyslexic person would write it.

Why would an audience be required to make this sort of effort in order to understand a joke? Simply because our enjoyment of a joke is heightened by the pleasure of having completed the puzzle necessary to 'get it'. In addition, once we understand a complex joke, we gain favoured status as an 'insider' in the larger audience. These insights explain the frustration that accompanies *not* getting a joke: the fear of mental inadequacy coupled with a sense of being socially excluded from a pleasure shared by others. Not surprisingly, 'outsiders' in such a situation may fake 'getting' the joke; sometimes, too, others may tactfully explain a joke to end another's sense of being left out.

But, as the old saying goes, if a joke has to be explained, it won't be very funny. Besides taking the edge off the language and timing on which the *punch* depends, an explanation completely relieves the audience of any mental involvement, substantially reducing their pleasure.

The topics of humour

People throughout the world smile and laugh, signifying humour as a universal human trait. But, living in diverse cultures, the world's people differ in what they find funny. Musicians frequently perform for receptive audiences around the globe; comedians rarely do this, however, demonstrating that humour does not travel well.

What is humourous to the Japanese may be lost on the Chinese, Iraqis or the English. To some degree, too, the social diversity of our own nation means that even within one country people will find humour in different situations. Greeks, Italians and the Dutch have their own brands of humour, as do those in the north of England and the Welsh, 15- and 40-year-olds, City bankers and construction workers.

But, for everyone, humour deals with topics that lend themselves to double meanings or *controversy*. For example, the first jokes many of us learned as children concerned the cultural taboo, sex. The mere mention of 'unmentionable acts' or even certain parts of the body can dissolve young faces in laughter. Are there jokes that do break through the culture barrier? Yes, but they must touch upon universal human experiences such as, say, turning on a friend.

The controversy inherent in humour often walks a fine line between what is funny and what is considered 'sick'. During the Middle Ages, the word *humours* (derived from the Latin *humidus*, meaning 'moist') referred to a balance of bodily fluids that regulated a person's health. Today's researchers have come up with scientific justification for the notion that 'Laughter is the best medicine': Maintaining a sense of humour is thought to reduce a person's level of unhealthy stress (Robinson, 1983; Haig, 1988). At the extreme, however, people who always take conventional reality lightly go beyond the bounds of a sense of humour and risk being defined as deviant or even mentally ill (a common stereotype depicts insane people laughing uncontrollably, and we have long dubbed mental hospitals 'funny farms').

And then there are certain topics that every social group declares as too sensitive for humorous treatment. Of course, one can joke about such things, but doing so courts criticism for telling a 'sick' joke (and, therefore, *being* sick). People's religious beliefs, tragic accidents or appalling crimes are the stuff of 'sick' jokes.

The functions of humour

If humour is a cultural universal, it must make a significant contribution to social life. Functional analysis points out that humour serves as a social 'safety valve', allowing people to release potentially disruptive sentiments safely. By means of humour, we can acceptably discuss a host of cultural taboos, from sex to prejudice to hostility toward parents.

Having strayed into controversy, an individual may also use humour to defuse the situation. Called to account for a remark an audience takes as offensive, a speaker may simply state, 'I didn't mean anything by what I said; it was just a joke!' Likewise, an audience may use humour as a form of tact, smiling, as if to say, 'We could take offence at what you said, but we'll assume you were only kidding'.

Like theatre and art, humour allows a society to challenge orthodox ideas and to explore alternatives to the status quo. Sometimes, in fact, humour may actually promote social change by loosening the grip of convention.

Humour and conflict

If humour holds the potential to liberate those who laugh, it can also be used to oppress others. Men who tell jokes about feminists, for example, typically are voicing some measure of hostility toward them (Powell and Paton, 1988; Benokraitis and Feagin, 1995). Similarly, jokes at the expense of gays and lesbians can reveal the tensions surrounding sexuality in much of Europe and the United States. Generally speaking, humour is a sign of real conflict in situations where one or both parties choose not to bring the conflict out into the open (Primeggia and Varacalli, 1990).

'Put down' jokes, which make one category of people feel good at the expense of another, are common around the globe. After collecting and analysing jokes from many societies, Christie Davies (1990) concluded that conflict among ethnic groups is one driving force behind humour virtually everywhere. In the typical ethnic joke, the jokester and audience label some

Is new technology changing our reality?

When Thomas Edison successfully tested the first telephone in 1874, observers were amazed by the feat of talking to others who were 'not there'. No doubt, people were just as astounded when the first powered aircraft defied gravity and lifted off the ground (1903) or when images appeared out of nowhere on the first television screen (1928).

Is today's new information technology once again reconstructing reality? Absolutely, and the changes are no less amazing. Consider, first, that computers and other information technology have fundamentally altered modern economies. The production of material things (clothing and cars) that defined the industrial age is quickly being replaced by the creation of ideas and images (computer programs and television shows). This trend is changing not only the nature of work, but the skills needed to find employment – working with one's hands is steadily giving way to working with one's head. Moreover, even our legal conception of property is in flux. A million-pound investment used to mean a factory or a hotel; today, the programming on a single floppy disk can make or break a major company.

Second, new information technology is eroding the importance of place in our lives. The telephone greatly extended our 'reach'; however, with sound tied to wires, a caller knew exactly where the call was going. Today's cellular technology allows a person to key in a number and reach another person who could be, quite literally, anywhere in the country, and beyond – at home, moving in a car or flying eight miles high.

Similarly, the emerging high-technology workplace is now anywhere one can position a computer terminal and fax machine.

Even the centuries-old concepts of national boundaries and citizenship have grown fuzzy, shaken by new technology. Say an employee logs onto a computer terminal in Mexico City and, travelling the 'information superhighway', connects to a UK bank in London where she processes transactions throughout the day. Is this 'electronic immigrant' part of the labour force of Mexico or the United Kingdom?

Third, there is no more basic foundation of our reality than the timeless adage, 'Seeing is believing'. But digital imagery now allows photographers to combine and manipulate pictures to show anything, computer animation enables movie producers to have humans interact with life-like dinosaurs, and the technology of 'virtual reality' means that, connected to computers, we can see, hear and even feel the 'touch' of another person thousands of miles away.

Change is coming to the higher education scene as well. Historically, students have read textbooks, which augment the 'live' performance they observe in lectures. But books are becoming a smaller and smaller part of publishers' offerings, as we witness a proliferation of images on tape, film and computer disks. (Not coincidentally, Prentice-Hall, publisher of this text, is owned by the entertainment giant Viacom.) In the years to come, textbooks themselves will be gradually replaced by CD ROMS or downloaded directly from Web sites on the Internet. And, in a world of interactive computer-based instruction, will students need to travel to classrooms to learn? Indeed, will the lecture or seminar itself eventually become obsolete?

● **Continue the debate:**

1. What dangers do you see in new information technology? Might this technology render life more impersonal or threaten our privacy?

2. What changes has technology brought to your university or college? To the library? To lectures?

3. In the 'electronic decades' to come, what changes would you predict in everyday routines involving recreation, entertainment, paying bills, getting medical check-ups and shopping? ●

disadvantaged category of people as stupid or ridiculous, thereby imputing greater wisdom and skills to people like them. Within the United States, given its long standing Anglo-Saxon traditions, Poles and other ethnic and racial minorities have long been the 'butt' of jokes, as have the Irish in England, Sikhs in India, Turks in Germany, Hausas in Nigeria, Tasmanians in Australia and Kurds in Iraq.

Disadvantaged people, of course, also make fun of the powerful. Women have long joked about men, just as Afro-Carribeans portray white people in humorous ways, and poor people poke fun at the rich. Throughout the world, people target their leaders with humour, and officials in some countries take such jokes seriously enough to repress them vigorously.

In sum, the significance of humour is no laughing matter. Michael Flaherty (1984, 1990) points out that humour amounts to a means of mental escape from a conventional world that is not entirely to our liking. As long as we maintain a sense of humour, then, we assert our freedom and are never prisoners of reality. And, in doing so, we change the world and ourselves just a little.

SUMMARY

1. Social structure provides guidelines for behaviour, rendering everyday life understandable and predictable.

2. A major component of social structure is status. Within an entire status set, a master status has particular significance.

3. Ascribed statuses are essentially involuntary, while achieved statuses are largely earned. In practice, however, many statuses incorporate elements of both ascription and achievement.

4. Role is the dynamic expression of a status. The incompatibility of roles corresponding to two or more statuses generates role conflict; likewise, incompatible roles linked to a single status produce role strain.

5. The phrase 'social construction of reality' conveys the important idea that we all build the social world through our interaction.

6. The Thomas theorem states: 'Situations defined as real become real in their consequences'.

7. Ethnomethodology seeks to reveal the assumptions and understandings people have of their social world.

8. Dramaturgical analysis studies how people construct personal performances. This approach casts everyday life in terms of theatrical performances, noting the settings of interaction, the use of body language and how performers often idealise their intentions.

9. Social power affects performances; our society's underlying subordination of women makes them craft their behaviour differently from men's.

10. Social behaviour carries the ever-present danger of embarrassment. Tact is a common response to a 'loss of face' by others.

11. Language is vital to the process of socially constructing reality. In various ways, language defines females and males differently, generally to the advantage of males.

12. Humour stems from the contrast between conventional and unconventional definitions of a situation. Because comedy is framed by a specific culture, people throughout the world find humour in very different situations.

KEY CONCEPTS

achieved status a social position that someone assumes voluntarily and that reflects personal ability and effort

ascribed status a social position that someone receives at birth or assumes involuntarily later in life

dramaturgical analysis Erving Goffman's term for the investigation of social interaction in terms of theatrical performance

ethnomethodology Harold Garfinkel's term for the study of the way people make sense of their everyday lives

master status a status that has exceptional importance for social identity, often shaping a person's entire life

non-verbal communication communication using body movements, gestures and facial expressions rather than speech

personal space the surrounding area to which an individual makes some claim to privacy

presentation of self an individual's effort to create specific impressions in the minds of others

role behaviour expected of someone who holds a particular status

role conflict incompatibility among the roles corresponding to two or more statuses

role set a number of roles attached to a single status

role strain incompatibility among roles corresponding to a single status

social construction of reality the process by which people creatively shape reality through social interaction

social interaction the process by which people act and react in relation to others

status a recognised social position that an individual occupies

status set all the statuses a person holds at a given time

Thomas theorem W. I. Thomas's assertion that situations we define as real become real in their consequences

CRITICAL-THINKING QUESTIONS

1. List a dozen of your own statuses. Do both ascription and achievement play a part in each?

2. Consider ways in which a physical disability can serve as a master status. How do people commonly characterise, say, a person with the physical disability cerebral palsy with regard to mental ability? With regard to sexuality? What interaction strategies may be employed by those with disabilities to smooth their interactions?

3. George Jean Nathan once quipped, 'I only drink to make other people interesting'. What does this mean in terms of reality construction? Identify the elements of humour within this statement.

4. Paralleling the dramaturgical analysis of a doctor's surgery found in this chapter, develop a similar analysis of a university classroom. How about a lecturer's office?

GOING FURTHER

Introductory reading

John P. Hewitt, *Self and Society* (London: Allyn and Bacon, 5th edn, 1991).

Provides an account of the symbolic interactionist tradition on which much of this chapter is based, and details more fully than the text allows a number of important concepts including self, role and language.

Classical sources

Erving Goffman, *The Presentation of Self in Everyday Life* (Garden City, NY: Anchor Books, 1959).

Erving Goffman's first book is his best-known work.

Peter L. Berger and Thomas Luckmann, *The Social Construction of Reality: A Treatise in the Sociology of Knowledge* (Garden City, NY: Doubleday Anchor Books, 1967).

This book elaborates on the argument that individuals generate meaning through their social interaction.

More advanced reading

Philip Manning, *Erving Goffman and Modern Sociology* (Cambridge, Polity, 1992).

A full review and assessment of Goffman's work

Stanley Cohen and Laurie Taylor, *Escape Attempts: The Theory and Practice of Resistance to Everyday Life* (London: Routledge, 2nd edn, 1995).

Looks at the ways in which people 'get through the day' and 'handle everyday life'. Influenced by Goffman, it is a prime example of microsociology at work.

Adam Phillips, *On Flirtation* (Cambridge, MA: Harvard University Press, 1994).

Flirtation allows us to experiment, and shows that social interaction proceeds in a fluid, unplanned way.

William Rathje and Cullan Murphy, *Rubbish: The Archeology of Garbage* (New York: HarperCollins, 1991).

Researchers at the University of Arizona learned a great deal about people by studying their garbage.

Michele Fine and Adrian Ash, *Women with Disabilities* (Philadelphia: Temple University Press, 1990).

How do people define others with physical disabilities and how do the disabled construct their own identity? This book provides some intriguing insights.

Catherine A. Lutz, *Unnatural Emotions: Everyday Sentiments on a Micronesian Atoll and Their Challenge to Western Theory* (Chicago: University of Chicago Press, 1988).

This report of research on a Pacific island points up how emotions, and the way people think about them, are culturally variable.

Christie Davies, *Ethnic Humour around the World: A Comparative Analysis* (Bloomington: Indiana University Press, 1990).

Relatively little attention has been paid to the sociological analysis of humour. This book applies a global perspective to the issue.

Web sites

● http://sun.soci.niv.edu/~sssi/papers/papers,html

The web site of the Society for the Study of Symbolic Interaction. A good source for developing ideas about symbolic interactionism.

chapter seven

Source: Popperfoto

Groups and Organisations

Sixty years ago, the opening of a new restaurant in Pasadena, California, attracted little attention from the local community and went unnoticed by the world as a whole. Yet this seemingly insignificant small business, owned and operated by Mac and Dick McDonald, would eventually spark a revolution in the restaurant industry and provide an organisational model that would be copied by countless other businesses and even schools and churches.

The basic formula the McDonald brothers put into place – which we now call 'fast food' – was to serve food quickly and inexpensively to large numbers of people. They trained employees to perform highly specialised jobs, so that one person grilled hamburgers, while others 'dressed' them, made French fries, whipped up milkshakes, and presented the food to the customers in assembly-line fashion.

As the years went by, the McDonald brothers prospered, and they moved their single restaurant from Pasadena to San Bernardino. It was there, in 1954, that events took an unexpected turn when Ray Kroc, a travelling blender and mixer merchant, paid a visit to the McDonalds.

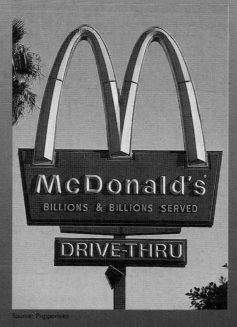

Source: Popperfoto

Kroc was fascinated by the brothers' efficient system, and, almost immediately, he saw the potential for a greatly expanded system of fast-food restaurants. Initially, Kroc launched his plans in partnership with the McDonald brothers. Soon, however, he bought out their interests and set out on his own to become one of the greatest success stories of all time. Today, 15,000 McDonald's restaurants serve people throughout the world.

From a sociological point of view, the success of McDonald's reveals much more than the popularity of hamburgers. As this chapter will explain, the larger importance of this story lies in the extent to which the principles that guide the operation of McDonald's are coming to dominate social life in very many parts of the world. Close intimate groups are everywhere giving way to fast, efficient but distant ones.

We begin by examining *social groups*, the clusters of people with whom we associate in much of our daily lives. As we shall see, the scope of group life has expanded greatly during this century. From a world built on kin and community – usually small, local, face-to-face and intense, the structure of our society now turns on the operation of vast businesses, bureaucracies and formal organisations – usually large, impersonal and fleeting. And even more recently, we can 'log on' to our computer and surf the Net with a vast array of unknown individuals across the world. How this changing and expanding scale of life has come to dominate society, and what it means for us as individuals, are the chapter's key objectives.

● Social groups

Virtually everyone moves through life with a sense of belonging; this is the experience of group life. A **social group** refers to *two or more people who identify and interact with one another*. Human beings continually come together to form couples, families, circles of friends, neighbourhoods, churches, businesses, clubs, communities and numerous large organisations. Whatever the form, groups encompass people with shared experiences, loyalties and interests. In short, while maintaining their individuality, the members of social groups also think of themselves as a special 'we'.

Groups, categories and crowds

People often use the term 'group' imprecisely. We now distinguish the group from the similar concepts of category and crowd.

Category

A *category* refers to people who have some status in common. Women, single fathers, military recruits, home owners and Roman Catholics are all examples of categories. Why are categories not considered groups? Simply because, while the individuals involved are aware that they are not the only ones to hold that particular status, the vast majority are strangers to one another.

Crowd

A *crowd* refers to a temporary cluster of individuals who may or may not interact at all. Students sitting together in a lecture theatre do engage one another and share some common identity with their fellow students; thus, such a crowd might be called a loosely formed group. By contrast, passengers on an underground train or bathers enjoying a summer day at the beach pay little attention to one another and amount to an anonymous aggregate of people. In general, then, crowds are too transitory and too impersonal to qualify as social groups.

The right circumstances, however, could turn a crowd into a group. People riding on an underground train that crashes under the city streets generally become keenly aware of their common plight and begin to help each other. Sometimes such extraordinary experiences become the basis for lasting relationships.

Primary and secondary groups

Acquaintances commonly greet one another with a smile and the simple phrase 'Hi! How are you?' The response is usually a well-scripted 'Fine, thanks. How are you?' This answer, of course, is often more formal than truthful. In most cases, providing a detailed account of how you are *really* doing would prompt the other person to beat a hasty and awkward exit.

Sociologists classify social groups by measuring them against two ideal types based on members' level of genuine personal concern. This variation is the key to distinguishing *primary* from *secondary* groups.

According to Charles Horton Cooley (1864–1929), who is introduced in the box, a **primary group** is *a small social group whose members share personal and enduring relationships*. Bound together by *primary relationships*, individuals in primary groups typically spend a great deal of time together, engage in a wide range of common activities and feel that they know one another well. Although not without periodic conflict, members of primary groups display sincere concern for each other's welfare. The family is every society's most important primary group.

Cooley characterised these personal and tightly integrated groups as *primary* because they are among the first groups we experience in life. In addition, the family and early play groups also hold primary importance in the socialisation process, shaping attitudes, behaviour and social identity.

The strength of primary relationships gives people a comforting sense of security. In the familiar social circles of family or friends, people feel they can 'be themselves' without constantly worrying about the impressions they are making.

Members of primary groups generally provide one another with economic and other forms of assistance as well. But, as important as primary ties are, people generally think of a primary group as an end in itself rather than as a means to other ends. In other words, we prefer to think that kinship or friendship links people who 'belong together', rather than people who expect to benefit from each other. For this reason, we readily call on family members or close friends to help us move into a new apartment, without expecting to pay for their services. And we would do the same for them. A friend who never returns a favour, by contrast, is likely to leave us feeling 'used' and questioning the depth of the friendship.

Moreover, this personal orientation means that members of a primary group view each another as unique and irreplaceable. We typically do not care

who cashes our cheque at the bank or takes our money at the supermarket checkout. Yet in the primary group – especially the family – we are bound to specific others by emotion and loyalty. So even though brothers and sisters do not always get along, they always remain siblings.

In contrast to the primary group, the **secondary group** is *a large and impersonal social group whose members pursue a specific interest or activity*. In most respects, secondary groups have precisely the opposite characteristics of primary groups. *Secondary relationships* usually involve weak emotional ties and little personal knowledge of one another. Secondary groups vary in duration, but they are frequently short term, beginning and ending without particular significance. Students following a university course, for instance, who may not see one another after the term ends, exemplify the secondary group.

Weaker social ties permit secondary groups to include many more people than primary groups do. For example, dozens or even hundreds of people may work together in the same office, yet most of them pay only passing attention to one another. Sometimes the passing of time will transform a group from secondary to primary, as with co-workers who share an office for many years. Generally, however, the boundary separating members of a secondary group from non-members is far less clear than it is for primary groups.

Secondary groups lack strong loyalties and emotions because members look to one another only to achieve limited ends. So while members of primary groups display a *personal orientation*, people in secondary groups reveal a *goal orientation*. Secondary ties are not necessarily always aloof or cold, of course. Social interactions among students, co-workers, and business associates are often quite pleasant, even if they are rather impersonal.

In primary groups, members define each other according to *who* they are – that is, in terms of kinship or unique, personal qualities. Members of secondary groups, by contrast, look to one another for *what* they are or what they can do for each other. In secondary groups, in other words, we are always mindful of what we offer others and what we receive in return. This 'scorekeeping' comes through most clearly in business relationships. Likewise, the people next door typically expect that a neighbourly favour will be reciprocated.

Charles Horton Cooley: the primary group is morally good

Many people fear that life now moves at such a fast pace that individuals are losing touch with one another. This is nothing new: Charles Horton Cooley shared this concern a century ago, growing up in a small town and witnessing rapid change all around him.

Home for Cooley was Ann Arbor, Michigan, where he spent his childhood and later returned to teach at the University of Michigan from 1892 until his death. His major contribution to sociology was exploring the character of the primary group.

Cooley noted a disturbing trend: as the United States was becoming more urban and industrialised, people seemed to become ever more individualistic and competitive, displaying less concern for the traditional family and local neighbourhood. This transformation made Cooley uneasy because he was convinced of the crucial impor-

Source: Library of Congress

tance of small, cooperative groups to social life. Primary groups are morally good, he declared, because they engender in people a sense of secure belonging as well as a spirit of fairness and compassion.

Cooley hoped that calling attention to the importance of primary groups might support traditional values and sustain social cohesion. Certainly, the United States has continued to change since Cooley's lifetime, and not entirely in ways he would have liked. But even though he died some 70 years ago, many of Cooley's social concerns are with us still. ●

Sources: Rieff, 1962, and Coser, 1977.

The goal orientation of secondary groups encourages individuals to craft their behaviour carefully. In these roles, we remain characteristically impersonal and polite. The secondary relationship, therefore, is one in which the question 'How are you?' may be asked without really expecting a truthful answer.

Table 7.1 summarises the characteristics that distinguish primary and secondary groups. Keep in mind that these traits define two types of social groups in ideal terms; actual groups in our lives may well contain elements of both. By placing these concepts as ends of a continuum, however, we devise a useful scheme for describing and analysing group life.

Do some regions of Europe have a more primary orientation than others? A long-standing sociological assertion holds that rural areas and small towns tend toward a greater emphasis on primary relationships while large cities are typically more secondary. While this generalisation holds much truth, some urban neighbourhoods – especially those populated by people of a single ethnic or religious category – are quite tightly knit.

Finally, what about the world as a whole? In general, primary relationships predominate in low-income preindustrial societies throughout Latin America, Africa and Asia in which people's lives revolve around families and local villages. In these countries, especially in rural areas, strangers stand out in the social landscape. By contrast, secondary ties take precedence in high-income industrial societies, in which people assume highly specialised social roles. Most people in England, especially in cities, routinely

Table 7.1 ● Primary groups and secondary groups: a summary

	Primary group ←→	Secondary group
Quality of relationships	Personal orientation	Goal orientation
Duration of relationships	Usually long term	Variable; often short term
Breadth of relationships	Broad; usually involving many activities	Narrow; usually involving few activities
Subjective perception of relationships	As ends in themselves	As means to an end
Typical examples	Families; circles of friends	Co-workers; political organisations

engage in impersonal, secondary contacts with virtual strangers – people about whom we know very little and whom we may never meet again (Wirth, 1938).

Group leadership

How do groups operate? One important dimension of group dynamics is leadership. Groups vary in the extent to which members recognise leaders. Large, secondary groups generally place leaders in a formal chain of command; a small circle of friends may have no leader at all. Parents assume leadership roles in families, though husband and wife may disagree about who is really in charge.

Two leadership roles

Groups typically benefit from two kinds of leadership (Bales, 1953; Bales and Slater, 1955). **Instrumental leadership** refers to *group direction that emphasises the completion of tasks*. Members look to instrumental leaders to 'get things done'. **Expressive leadership**, by contrast, *focuses on collective well-being*. Expressive leaders take less of an interest in the performance goals of a group than in group morale and minimising tension and conflict among members.

Because they concentrate on performance, instrumental leaders usually have formal, secondary relations with other group members. Instrumental leaders give orders and reward or punish people according to their contribution to the group's efforts. Expressive leaders, however, cultivate more personal, primary ties. They offer sympathy to a member having a tough time, work to keep the group united and lighten serious moments with humour. While successful instrumental leaders enjoy more distant respect from members, expressive leaders generally garner more personal *affection*.

In the traditional European family, this differentiation of leadership is linked to gender. Conventional cultural norms bestow instrumental leadership on men so that, as fathers and husbands, they assume primary responsibility for earning income, making decisions and disciplining children. By contrast, expressive leadership is the traditional purview of women. Historically, mothers and wives have encouraged supportive and peaceful relationships among family members. This division of labour partly explains why many children have greater respect for their fathers but closer personal ties with their mothers (Parsons and Bales, 1955; Macionis, 1978).

Of course, increasing equality between men and women has blurred this gender-based distinction between instrumental and expressive leadership. In most group settings, women and men now assume both of these leadership roles.

Three leadership styles

Sociologists also characterise group leadership in terms of three orientations to power. *Authoritarian leadership* stresses instrumental concerns, taking personal charge of decision-making and demanding strict compliance from subordinates. Although this leadership style may win little affection from group members, a fast-acting authoritarian leader often earns praise in a crisis situation. *Democratic leadership* has a more expressive focus, making a point of including everyone in the decision-making process. Although less successful when crises afford little time for discussion, democratic leaders generally draw on the ideas of all members to forge reflective and imaginative responses to the tasks at hand. *Laissez-faire leadership* allows the group to function more or less on its own. This style typically is the least effective in promoting group goals (White and Lippitt, 1953; Ridgeway, 1983).

Group conformity

In most of the Western world, people do not like to think they are 'conformists', that they follow the group. Most people like to think they are unique individuals, that they in some way stand out from the crowd. But think for a minute of the main groups you belong to – at school, university, in sport, at home. Think of your peer group and how you want (or even need) to be accepted by them. Maybe you do stand out as a less conformist person, but many social psychological studies have shown that group conformity is very likely. This section looks at some of the classic studies that suggest this. Social scientists confirm the power of group pressure to shape human behaviour and report that it remains strong in adulthood as well as in adolescence.

Asch's research

Solomon Asch (1952) conducted a classic investigation that revealed the power of group conformity. Asch recruited students for an alleged study of visual perception. Before the actual experiment, however, he revealed to all but one member in each small group that their real purpose was to impose group pressure on the remaining subject. Placing all the students around a table, Asch asked each, in turn, to note the length of a 'standard' line, as shown on Card 1 in Figure 7.1, and match it to one of three lines on Card 2.

Figure 7.1 ● Cards used in Asch's experiment (Asch, 1952) in group conformity

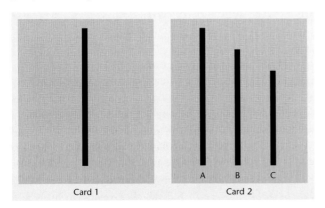

Card 1   Card 2

Anyone with normal vision could easily see that the line marked 'A' on Card 2 was the correct choice. Initially, as planned, everyone made the matches correctly. But then Asch's secret accomplices began answering incorrectly, making the naive subject (seated at the table in order to answer next to last) bewildered and uncomfortable.

What happened? Asch found that one-third of all subjects placed in this situation chose to conform to the others by answering incorrectly. His investigation indicates that many people are willing to compromise their judgements to avoid the discomfort of being different from others, even from people they do not know. Think about yourself for a minute: do you think you would conform like this?

Milgram's research

In an equally famous (even notorious) set of experiments, Stanley Milgram – former student of Solomon Asch – conducted conformity experiments that were even more surprising. In Milgram's initial study (1963, 1965; Miller, 1986), a researcher explained to male recruits that they were about to engage in a study of how punishment affects learning. One by one, he assigned them the role of 'teacher' and placed another individual – an insider to the study – in a connecting room as the 'learner'.

The teacher saw the learner sit down in an ominous contraption resembling an electric chair with an electrode attached to one arm. The researcher then had the teacher read aloud pairs of words. In the next step, the teacher repeated the first word of each pair and asked the learner to recall the corresponding second word.

As mistakes occurred, the researcher instructed the teacher to shock the learner using a 'shock generator', a bogus but forbidding-looking piece of equipment with a shock switch and a dial marked to regulate electric current from 15 volts (labelled 'mild shock') to 300 volts (marked 'intense shock') to 450 volts (marked 'Danger: Severe Shock' and 'XXX').

Beginning at the lowest level, the researcher told the teacher to increase the shock by 15 volts every time the learner made a mistake. The shocks, explained the researcher, would become painful but cause no permanent damage. And so it went. At 75, 90 and 105 volts, the teacher heard audible moans from the learner; at 120 volts, shouts of pain; at 270 volts, screams of agony; and, after 330 volts, deadly silence.

The results show just how readily authority figures can obtain compliance from ordinary people. None of 40 subjects assigned in the role of teacher during the initial research even questioned the procedure before 300 volts had been applied, and 26 of the subjects – almost two-thirds – went all the way to 450 volts.

Milgram (1964) then modified his research to see if Solomon Asch had documented such a high degree of group conformity only because the task of matching lines seemed trivial. What if groups pressured people to administer electrical shocks?

To investigate, he varied the experiment so that a group of three teachers, two of whom were his accomplices, made decisions jointly. Milgram's rule was that each of the three teachers would suggest a shock level when the learner made an error and they would then administer the lowest of the three suggestions. This arrangement gave the naive subject the power to lessen the shock level regardless of the other two teachers' recommendations.

The accomplices called for increasing the shock level with each error, placing group pressure on the third member to do the same. Responding to this group pressure, subjects applied voltages three to four times higher than in control conditions in which subjects acted alone. Thus Milgram's research suggests that people are surprisingly likely to follow the directions not only of 'legitimate authority figures', but also of groups of ordinary individuals.

Reference groups

How do we assess our own attitudes or behaviour? Frequently, we make use of a **reference group**, *a social group that serves as a point of reference in making evaluations or decisions.*

A young man who imagines his family's response to a woman he is dating is using his family as a reference group. Similarly, a banker who assesses her colleagues' reactions to a new loan policy is using her co-workers as a standard of reference. As these examples illustrate, reference groups can be primary or secondary. In each case, the motivation to conform to a group means that the attitudes of others can greatly affect us.

We also use groups that we do *not* belong to for reference. People preparing for job interviews typically notice how those in the company they wish to join dress and act, adjusting their personal performances accordingly. The use of groups by non-members illustrates the process of *anticipatory socialisation*, described in Chapter 5 ('Socialisation'), by which individuals use conformity as a strategy to win acceptance to a particular group.

Stouffer's research

Samuel A. Stouffer (1949) and his associates conducted a classic study of reference group dynamics during the Second World War. In a survey, researchers asked soldiers to evaluate the chances of promotion for a competent soldier in their branch of the service. One might guess that soldiers serving in outfits with a high promotion rate would be optimistic about their future advancement. Yet survey results supported the opposite conclusion: soldiers in branches of the service with low promotion rates were actually more optimistic about their own chances to move ahead.

The key to this paradox lies in sorting out the groups against which the soldiers measured their progress. Those in branches with low promotion rates looked around them and saw people making no more headway than they were. That is, they had not been promoted, but neither had many others, so they did not feel unjustly deprived.

Soldiers in service branches with high promotion rates, however, could easily think of people who had been promoted sooner or more often than they had. With such people in mind, even soldiers who had been promoted themselves were likely to feel short-changed. So these were the soldiers who voiced more negative attitudes in their evaluations.

Stouffer's research demonstrates that we do not make judgements about ourselves in isolation, nor do we compare ourselves with just anyone. Instead, we use specific social groups as standards in developing individual attitudes. Whatever our situation in *absolute* terms, then, we assess our well-being subjectively, *relative* to some specific reference group (Merton, 1968; Mirowsky, 1987).

Ingroups and outgroups

Everyone favours some groups over others, sometimes based on political outlook, social prestige or simply manner of dress. On the university campus, for example, left-leaning student activists may look down on fellow students whom they view as conservative; and arts students may snub computer 'nerds'. People in virtually every social setting develop a comparable cluster of positive and negative evaluations.

Such judgements illustrate another key element of group dynamics: the opposition of ingroups and outgroups. An **ingroup** is *a social group commanding a member's esteem and loyalty*. An ingroup exists in relation to an **outgroup**, *a social group towards which one feels competition or opposition*.

Social life is the interplay of both kinds of groups. A campus rugby team, for example, is both an ingroup to its members and an outgroup for students with no interest in sport. A town's left-wing politicians generally think of themselves as an ingroup in relation to the local right-wing supporters. All ingroups and outgroups work on the principle that 'we' have valued characteristics that 'they' lack.

Tensions among groups often help to sharpen their boundaries and give people a clearer sense of social identity. However, this form of group dynamics also promotes self-serving distortions of reality. Specifically, research shows, members of ingroups construct overly positive views of themselves and hold unfairly negative views of various outgroups (Tajfel, 1982).

Power also guides intergroup relations. With greater power, members of one ingroup may socially injure people they view as an outgroup. For example, white people have historically viewed people of colour in negative terms and subjected them to social, political and economic disadvantages. Internalising these negative attitudes, minorities often struggle to overcome negative self-images. In short, ingroups and outgroups foster loyalty as well as generate tension and conflict.

● Group size

If you are the first person to arrive at a party, you can observe some fascinating group dynamics. Until about six people enter the room, everyone generally shares a single conversation. But as more people arrive, the group divides into two or more smaller clusters. It is apparent that size plays a crucial role in how group members interact.

To understand why, consider the mathematical connection between the number of people in a social group and the number of relationships among them. As Figure 7.2 shows, two people form a single relationship; adding a third person generates three rela-

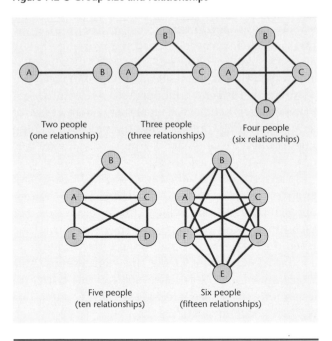

Figure 7.2 ● Group size and relationships

Two people (one relationship)

Three people (three relationships)

Four people (six relationships)

Five people (ten relationships)

Six people (fifteen relationships)

tionships; adding a fourth person yields six. Increasing the number of people one at a time, then, boosts the number of relationships much more rapidly, since every new individual can interact with everyone already there. Thus, five people produce ten relationships and, by the time six people join one conversation, fifteen 'channels' connect them. This leaves too many people unable to speak, which is why the group usually divides at this point.

The dyad

The German sociologist Georg Simmel (1858–1918) explored social dynamics in the smallest social groups. Simmel (1950; orig. 1902) used the term **dyad** to designate *a social group with two members*. Throughout the world, most love affairs, marriages and the closest friendships are dyadic.

What makes the dyad a special relationship? First, explained Simmel, social interaction in a dyad is typically more intense than in larger groups since, in a one-to-one relationship, neither member shares the other's attention with anyone else. Thus dyads have the potential to be the most meaningful social bonds we ever experience.

Second, Simmel explains, like a stool with only two legs, dyads have a characteristic instability. Both members of a dyad must actively sustain the relationship; if either one withdraws, the group collapses. Because of the importance of marriage to society, the marital dyad is supported with legal, economic and often religious ties. By contrast, a large group such as a charity run by volunteers is inherently much more stable, as it can survive the loss of many members.

Marriage in our society is dyadic; ideally, we expect powerful emotional ties to unite husbands and wives. As we shall see in Chapter 17 ('Families'), however, marriage in other societies may involve more than two people. In that case, the household is usually more stable, though many of the marital relationships are weaker.

The triad

Simmel also probed the **triad**, *a social group with three members*. A triad encompasses three relationships, each uniting two of the three people. A triad is more stable than a dyad because, should the relationship between any two members become strained, the third can act as a mediator to restore the group's vitality. This bit of group dynamics helps explain why members of a dyad (say, a married couple) sometimes seek out a third person (a counsellor) to air tensions between them.

Nonetheless, two of the three can form a coalition to press their views on the third, or two may intensify their relationship, leaving the other feeling like a 'third wheel'. For example, two members of a triad who develop a romantic interest in each other will understand the old saying 'Two's company, three's a crowd'.

PROFILE

Georg Simmel: a sociology of forms

When students encounter sociology, they invariably hear of the three giants – Marx, Durkheim, Weber – who have already been introduced several times in this book. They may hear of a fourth 'founding theorist' – Simmel (1858–1918). But rarely will they ever consider him in any detail. Yet his influence has been very profound.

Simmel adopted a distinctive and wide-ranging approach to sociology, studying many things from money and gender to cities and 'strangers'. He viewed society as interaction, and believed the task of the sociologist was to study the interactive webs that people entered into. He was keen to depict the ways in which changing numbers and scales of interactions brought about profoundly different relation-ships. In the text, you see how he contrasted simple dyads with triads and the difference this makes.

But he also looked at how social relations changed as cities emerged and relationships became more and more impersonal. He provided a socio-logical portrait of people's changing consciousness under modernity, and especially cities. He saw there was a down side to this: people kept their distance from each other. But there was also an up side: people became more tolerant and even sophisticated (see Chapter 22 on the city).

Simmel invented a style of sociology known as formal sociology: a sociology which studies the underlying forms of interaction in society. To do this, he distinguished between content and form. Social life is about content in so far as it studies things like marriage, war, education and drug-taking. But for sociology to be systematic it needed more than studies of little areas of social life and their contents: instead it also needed to piece together the underlying social processes that they have in common. Thus, for instance, one common process found in social life is conflict: you can look at marriages, wars, education and drug-taking and you will usually find elements of social interaction involving conflicts. Sociologists needed not just to study contents, then, but also forms.

A brilliant essayist, Simmel left his mark on much contemporary sociology which looks at forms of interaction. ●

For a short guide to Simmel's work, see David Frisby, *Georg Simmel* (London: Tavistock, 1984).

As groups grow beyond three members, they become progressively more stable because the loss of even several members does not threaten the group's existence. At the same time, increases in group size typically reduce the intense personal interaction possible only in the smallest groups. Larger groups are thus based less on personal attachments and more on formal rules and regulations. Such formality helps a large group persist over time, though the group is not immune to change. After all, their numerous members give large groups more contact with the outside world, opening the door to new attitudes and behaviour (Carley, 1991).

Does a social group have an ideal size? The answer depends on the group's purpose. A dyad offers unsurpassed emotional intensity, while a group of several dozen members is more stable, capable of accomplishing larger, more complex tasks, and better able to assimilate new members or ideas. People typically find more *personal pleasure* in smaller groups, while deriving greater *task satisfaction* from accomplishments in larger organisations (Slater, 1958; Ridgeway, 1983; Carley, 1991).

Social diversity

Social diversity affects group dynamics, especially the likelihood that members will interact with someone of another group. Peter Blau (1977, 1982; South and Messner, 1986) points out four ways in which the composition of social groups affects intergroup association.

1. *Large groups turn inwards*. Extending Simmel's analysis of group size, Blau explains that the larger a group, the more likely its members are to maintain relationships exclusively among themselves. The smaller the group, by contrast, the more members will reach beyond their immediate social circle.

   To illustrate, consider the efforts of many universities to include a wider range of students from overseas. Increasing the number of international students may add important dimensions to a campus, but, as their numbers rise, these students eventually are able to maintain their own distinctive social group. Thus intentional efforts to promote social diversity may well have the unintended effect of promoting separatism.

2. *Heterogeneous groups turn outwards*. The more internally heterogeneous a group is, the more likely its members are to interact with members of other

groups. We would expect, for example, that campus groups that recruit members of both sexes and people of various ethnic and geographic backgrounds would promote more intergroup contact than those that choose members of only one social type.

3. *Social parity promotes contact*. An environment in which all groups have roughly equal standing encourages people of all social backgrounds to mingle and form social ties. Thus, whether groups insulate their members or not depends on whether the groups themselves form a social hierarchy.

4. *Physical boundaries foster social boundaries*. Blau contends that physical space affects the chances of contacts among groups. To the extent that a social group is physically segregated from others (by having its own accommodation or dining area, for example), its members are less apt to engage other people.

Networks

Formally, a **network** is *a web of social ties that links people who identify and interact little with one another*. Think of a network as a 'fuzzy' group that brings people into occasional contact without a group's sense of boundaries and belonging. Computer networks, or other high-technology links, now routinely connect people living all over the world. If we consider a group as a 'circle of friends', then, we might describe a network as a 'social web' expanding outwards, often reaching great distances and including large numbers of people.

Some network contacts are regular, as among college friends who years later stay in touch by mail and telephone. More commonly, however, a network includes people we *know of* – or who *know of us* – but with whom we interact infrequently, if at all. As one woman with a widespread reputation as a community organiser explains, 'I get calls at home, someone says, "Are you Roseann Navarro? Somebody told me to call you. I have this problem…"' (quoted in Kaminer, 1984: 94). For this reason, social networks amount to 'clusters of weak ties' (Granovetter, 1973).

Network ties may be weak, but they serve as a significant resource. For example, many people rely on their networks to find jobs. Even the scientific genius Albert Einstein needed a hand in landing his first job. After a year of unsuccessful interviewing, he obtained employment only when the father of one of his fellow students put him in touch with an office manager who hired him (Clark, 1971; cited in Fischer, 1977: 19). This use of networks to one's advantage suggests that, as the saying goes, *who you know* is often just as important as *what you know*.

Networks are based on peoples' colleges and universities, clubs, local communities, political parties and informal cliques. Some networks encompass people with considerably more wealth, power and prestige than others do, which is the essence of describing someone as 'well connected'. And some people have denser networks than others – that is, they are connected to more people – which is also a valuable social resource. Typically, the most extensive social networks are maintained by people who are young, well educated, and living in urban areas (Marsden, 1987; Kadushin, 1995).

Gender, too, shapes networks. Although the networks of men and women are typically the same size, women include more relatives in their networks, while those of men are filled out with more co-workers. Women's networks, therefore, may not carry quite the same clout as the 'old boy' networks do. Even so, research indicates that, as gender inequality lessens, this difference is diminishing over time (Moore, 1991, 1992).

Finally, new information technology has generated a global network of unprecedented size in the form of

SOCIOLOGICAL SPOTLIGHT

The Internet: welcome to cyberspace!

Its origins seem right out of the 1960s Cold War film Dr Strangelove. Three decades ago, US government officials and scientists were trying to imagine how to run the country after an atomic attack, which, they assumed, would instantaneously eliminate telephones and television. The brilliant solution was to devise a communication system with no central headquarters, no one in charge and no main power switch – in short, an electronic web that would link the country in one vast network.

By 1985, the US federal government was installing high-speed data lines around the country and the Internet was about to be born. Today, thousands of government offices, as well as colleges and universities across the world, are joined by the Internet and share in the cost of its operation. Add to this mix millions of other individuals who connect their home computers to this 'information superhighway'

through a telephone-line modem and a commercial 'gateway' such as America OnLine, Prodigy and CompuServe.

No one knows precisely how many people make use of the Internet. But a rough 1995 estimate put the total at 50 million individuals in 175 (of 191) countries around the world, making it the largest network in history. And the numbers are doubling each year.

What is available on the Internet? Far more than anyone could ever list in a single directory. Popular activities include electronic mail (start a cyber-romance with a pen pal, write to your textbook author, or even send a message to the president of the United States: president@whitehouse.gov), participating in discussion groups or receiving newsletters on a wide range of topics, or searching libraries across the campus or around the world for books or other information. Because the Internet has no for-

mal rules for its use, its potential defies the imagination.

Ironically, perhaps, it is precisely this chaotic quality that has many people up in arms. Pundits warn that 'electronic democracy' may undermine established political practices, parents fear that their technologically sophisticated children may discover sex 'on line', and purists bristle at the thought that the Internet may soon be flooded with advertising and other commercial ventures.

In many respects, the 'anything goes' character of the Internet mirrors the real world. Not surprisingly, therefore, more and more users are now employing passwords, fees and other 'gates' to build restricted subnetworks limited to people like themselves. From one vast network, then, is emerging a host of smaller social groups. ●

Sources: Based, in part, on Elmer-DeWitt, 1993, 1994, and Hafner, 1994.

Map 7.1 ● Cyberspace: a global network

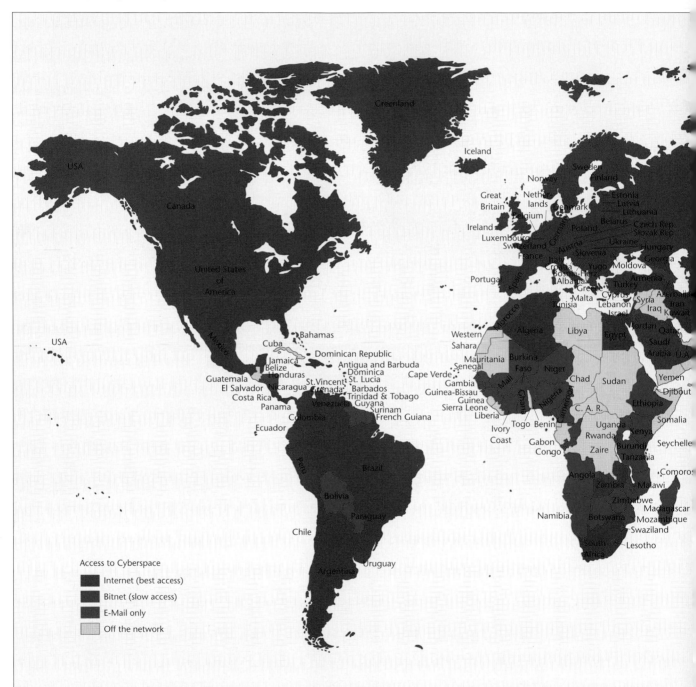

Access to Cyberspace

- Internet (best access)
- Bitnet (slow access)
- E-Mail only
- Off the network

Source: Copyright C. 1993/1995 by The New York Times Co. Reprinted by permission.

While 175 of 191 world nations are connected to the Internet, a majority of the world's people have no access to this valuable resource. For one thing, computers are expensive, well out of reach of ordinary people in low-income countries, especially in Africa. Thus the vast majority of Internet sites are in the United States, Canada, Western Europe and Australia. But another barrier to global communication is language: Born in the US, the Internet's available software demands that users read and write in the Latin alphabet using English. But experts around the world are at work developing keyboards and interface programs that will link people using various languages. Perhaps, in the near future, the Internet may be as multicultural as the world it connects.

the Internet. The box takes a closer look at this twenty-first century form of communication, while Map 7.1 shows its extent.

● Formal organisations

Throughout human history, most people lived in small groups of family members and neighbours; this pattern was still widespread in Europe and the United States a century ago. Today, families and neighbourhoods persist, of course, but our lives revolve far more around **formal organisations**, *large, secondary groups that are organised to achieve their goals efficiently.*

Formal organisations, such as corporations and government agencies, differ significantly from families and neighbourhoods: their greater size renders social relationships less personal and fosters a planned, formal atmosphere. In other words, formal organisations operate to accomplish complex jobs rather than to meet personal needs.

When you think about it, organising a continent like Europe, with some 500 million members, is a remarkable feat. Countless tasks are involved, from collecting taxes and delivering the mail to the production and distribution of consumer goods. To meet most of these tasks, we rely on large, formal organisations. From national governments to private corporations, millions of people are employed in them. Such vast organisations develop lives and cultures of their own, so that as members come and go, the statuses they fill and the roles they perform remain unchanged over the years.

Types of formal organisations

There are a number of classifications of organisations. One by Amitai Etzioni (1975) identifies three types, distinguished by why people participate – utilitarian organisations, normative organisations and coercive organisations.

Utilitarian organisations

Just about everyone who works for income is a member of a *utilitarian organisation*, which provides material rewards for its members. Large business enterprises, for example, generate profits for their owners and income in the form of salaries and wages for their employees. Joining utilitarian organisations is usually a matter of individual choice, though most people must join one or another utilitarian organisation to make a living.

Normative organisations

People join *normative organisations* not for income but to pursue goals they consider morally worthwhile. Sometimes called *voluntary associations*, these include community service groups (such as the Boy Scouts and Girl Guides or the Red Cross), political parties, religious organisations, and numerous other confederations concerned with specific social issues (such as Greenpeace or Liberty). In 1996, about 10 per cent of adults in Britain belonged to an environmental organisation or charity – The National Trust and the Royal Society for the Protection of Birds are the largest; Greenpeace comes a respectable third with 380,000 members (*Social Trends*, 1997: 189).

Coercive organisations

In Etzioni's typology, *coercive organisations* are distinguished by involuntary membership. That is, people are forced to join the organisation as a form of punishment (prisons) or treatment (psychiatric hospitals). Coercive organisations have extraordinary physical features, such as locked doors and barred windows, and are supervised by security personnel (Goffman, 1961). These are settings that segregate people as 'inmates' or 'patients' for a period of time and sometimes radically alter their attitudes and behaviour. Recall from Chapter 5 ('Socialisation') the power of *total institutions* to transform a human being's overall sense of self.

From differing vantage points, any particular organisation may fall into *all* these categories. A psychiatric hospital, for example, serves as a coercive organisation for a patient, a utilitarian organisation for a psychiatrist and a normative organisation for a part-time hospital volunteer.

Origins of bureaucracy

Formal organisations date back thousands of years. Elites who governed early empires relied on government officials to extend their power over millions of people and vast geographical regions. Formal organisation allowed these rulers to collect taxes, undertake military campaigns and construct monumental structures such as the Great Wall of China and the pyramids of Egypt.

The power of these early organisations was limited, however, not because elites lacked grandiose ambition, but by the traditional character of preindustrial societies. Typically, cultural patterns placed greater importance on preserving the past or carrying out 'God's will' than on organisational efficiency. Only in the last few centuries did there emerge what Max Weber called a 'rational world view', as described in Chapter 3 ('Society'). In the wake of the Industrial Revolution, the organisational structure called *bureaucracy* became commonplace in Europe and North America.

Characteristics of bureaucracy

Bureaucracy is *an organisational model rationally designed to perform complex tasks efficiently*. In a bureaucratic business or government agency, officials deliberately enact and revise policy to make the organisation as efficient as possible. To appreciate the power and scope of bureaucratic organisation, consider that any one of 150 million phones in the United States can connect anybody, within seconds, to any other phone – in homes, businesses, automobiles, even in the middle of a baseball field. Such instant communication is beyond the imagination of those who lived in the ancient world.

Of course, the telephone system depends on technological developments such as electricity, fibre optics and computers. But the system could not exist without the organisational capacity to keep track of every telephone call – noting which phone called which other phone, when and for how long – and presenting all this information to tens of millions of telephone users in the form of regular bills.

What specific traits promote organisational efficiency? Max Weber (1978; orig. 1921) identified six key elements of the ideal bureaucratic organisation.

1. *Specialisation.* Through most of human history, everyone pursued the basic goals of securing food and shelter. Bureaucracy, by contrast, assigns to individuals highly specialised duties.

2. *Hierarchy of offices.* Bureaucracies arrange personnel in a vertical hierarchy of offices. Each person is thus supervised by 'higher-ups' in the organisation while, in turn, supervising others in lower positions.

3. *Rules and regulations.* Cultural tradition holds scant sway in bureaucracy. Instead, operations are guided by rationally enacted rules and regulations. These rules control not only the organisation's own func-

tioning but, as much as possible, its larger environment. Ideally, a bureaucracy seeks to operate in a completely predictable fashion.

4. *Technical competence.* A bureaucratic organisation expects officials to have the technical competence to carry out their official duties. Bureaucracies regularly monitor the performance of staff members. Such impersonal evaluation based on performance contrasts sharply with the custom, followed through most of human history, of favouring relatives – whatever their talents – over strangers.

5. *Impersonality.* In bureaucratic organisations, rules take precedence over personal whim. This impersonality encourages uniform treatment for each client as well as other workers. From this detached approach stems the notion of the 'faceless bureaucrat'.

6. *Formal, written communications.* An old adage states that the heart of bureaucracy is not people but paperwork. Rather than casual, verbal communication, bureaucracy relies on formal, written memos and reports. Over time, this correspondence accumulates into vast *files*. These files guide the subsequent operation of an organisation in roughly the same way that social background shapes the life of an individual.

These traits represent a clear contrast to the more personal character of small groups. Bureaucratic organisation promotes efficiency by carefully recruiting personnel and limiting the unpredictable effects of personal tastes and opinions. In smaller, informal groups, members allow one another considerable discretion in their behaviour; they respond to each other personally and regard everyone as more or less equal in rank. Table 7.2 summarises the differences between small social groups and large formal organisations.

The informal side of bureaucracy

Weber's ideal bureaucracy deliberately regulates every activity. In actual organisations, however, human beings have the creativity (or the stubbornness) to resist conforming to bureaucratic blueprints. Sometimes informality helps to meet a legitimate need overlooked by formal regulations. In other situations informality may amount to simply cutting corners in one's job (Scott, 1981).

In principle, power resides in offices, not with the people who occupy them. Nonetheless, the personali-

GLOBAL SOCIOLOGY

Bureaucracy's darkest hour: killing 20 million people in the Holocaust

One of the most significant events of twentieth century history was Hitler's Final Solution: the mass extermination of over 20 million people – 6 million Jews, along with gypsies, gays, 'impure races' and others throughout the Second World War. There have been many other genocides in history (see Chapter 16), but the Holocaust must be seen as unique because it involved the systematic, huge scale extermination of large numbers of people through bureaucratic means in concentration camps such as Auschwitz in a mechanical way. People were 'rounded up'; trains took them to the death camps; there they were stripped, numbered, herded; and led finally to the gas chambers or other execution.

Zygmunt Bauman, in his powerful sociologi-cal study *Modernity and the Holocaust* (1989), shows that 'we live in a type of society that made the Holocaust possible' (p. 88). Indeed, the modern world facilitated the mass exterminations. Drawing from Max Weber's analysis of bureaucracy, and Durkheim's analysis of the division of labour, he suggests that these very characteristic features of modern society made the Holocaust possible. People could exterminate large numbers of others simply because they were distant links in a work chain, following the abstract rules that most jobs now dictate. There was an abrogation of personal responsibility, fostered by bureaucracy that made it all possible then – and indeed possible again now. People become dehumanised, and moral standards become irrelevant to the success of the technical operation.

When society seemed to be at its most advanced, and most civilised, the dark atrocities of mass extermination became a routine, bureaucratic commonplace. The challenge for sociology is to see this extreme horror – even 'evil' – as part of the routine workings of modern societies, and to ponder: can it happen again? ●

See Zygmunt Bauman, *Modernity and the Holocaust* (Cambridge: Polity Press, 1989).

Belsen concentration camp, World War 2. Note the heap of shoes from those who have been killed in the gas chambers.

Source: Popperfoto

ties of officials greatly affect patterns of leadership. For example, studies of corporations document that the qualities and quirks of individuals – including personal charisma and interpersonal skills – have a tremendous impact on organisational outcomes.

Authoritarian, democratic and laissez-faire types of leadership – described earlier in this chapter – also reflect individual personality as much as any organisa-tional plan. Then, too, in the 'real world' of organisations, leaders and their cronies sometimes seek to benefit personally through the abuse of organisational power. And perhaps even more commonly, leaders take credit for the efforts of their subordinates. Many secretaries, for example, have far more authority and responsibility than their official job titles and salaries suggest.

Table 7.2 ● Small groups and formal organisations: a comparison

	Small groups	Formal organisations
Activities	Members typically engage in many of the same activities	Members typically engage in distinct, highly specialised activities
Hierarchy	Often informal or non-existent	Clearly defined, corresponding to offices
Norms	Informal application of general norms	Clearly defined rules and regulations
Criteria for membership	Variable, often based on personal affection or kinship	Technical competence to carry out assigned tasks
Relationships	Variable, typically primary	Typically secondary, with selective primary ties
Communications	Typically casual and face-to-face	Typically formal and in writing
Focus	Person orientated	Task orientated

Communication offers another example of how informality creeps into large organisations. Formally, memos and other written communications disseminate information through the hierarchy. Typically, however, individuals cultivate informal networks or 'grapevines' that spread information much faster, if not always accurately. Grapevines are particularly important to subordinates because high officials often attempt to conceal important information from them.

Throughout the hierarchy, employees modify or ignore rigid bureaucratic structures for a host of reasons. A classic study of the Western Electric factory in Chicago revealed that few employees reported fellow workers who violated rules, as the company required

(Roethlisberger and Dickson, 1939). On the contrary, workers took action against those who *did* blow the whistle on their colleagues, shunning them as 'squealers'. Although the company formally set productivity standards, workers informally created their own definition of a fair day's work, criticising those who exceeded it as 'rate-busters' and those who fell short as 'chisellers'.

Such informal social structures suggest that people act to personalise rigidly defined social situations. This leads us to take a closer look at some of the problems of bureaucracy.

Problems of bureaucracy

Despite our reliance on bureaucracy to manage countless dimensions of everyday life, many members of our society are ambivalent about this organisational form. The following sections review several of the problems associated with bureaucracy, ranging from its tendency to dehumanise and alienate individuals to the threats it poses to personal privacy and political democracy.

Bureaucratic alienation

Max Weber touted bureaucracy as a model of productivity. Nonetheless, Weber was keenly aware of bureaucracy's potential to *dehumanise* those it purports to serve. That is, the same impersonality that fosters efficiency simultaneously denies officials and clients the ability to respond to each other's unique, personal needs. On the contrary, officials must treat each client impersonally as a standard 'case'.

The impersonal bureaucratic environment, then, gives rise to *alienation*. All too often, Weber contended, formal organisations reduce the human being to 'a small cog in a ceaselessly moving mechanism' (1978: 988; orig. 1921). The trend towards more and more formal organisation, therefore, left him deeply pessimistic about the future of humankind. Although formal organisations are designed to benefit humanity, he feared that humanity might well end up serving formal organisations.

Bureaucratic inefficiency and ritualism

Then there is the familiar problem of inefficiency, the failure of a bureaucratic organisation to carry out the work it was created to perform. Perhaps the greatest challenge to a large, formal organisation is responding to special needs or circumstances. Anyone who has ever tried to replace a lost driving licence, return defective merchandise to a discount store or change an address on a magazine subscription knows that bureaucracies sometimes can be maddeningly unresponsive.

The problem of inefficiency is captured in the concept of *red tape* (a phrase derived from the red tape used by eighteenth century English administrators to wrap official parcels and records; Shipley, 1985). Red tape refers to a tedious preoccupation with organisational routines and procedures. Sociologist Robert Merton (1968) points out that red tape amounts to a new twist on the already familiar concept of group conformity. He coined the term **bureaucratic ritualism** to designate *a preoccupation with rules and regulations to the point of thwarting an organisation's goals.*

Ritualism impedes individual and organisational performance as it stifles creativity and imagination. In part, ritualism emerges because organisations, which pay modest, fixed salaries, give officials little or no financial stake in performing efficiently. Then, too, bureaucratic ritualism stands as another expression of the alienation that Weber feared would arise from bureaucratic rigidity (Whyte, 1957; Merton, 1968; Coleman, 1990; Kiser and Schneider, 1994).

Bureaucratic inertia

If bureaucrats sometimes have little motivation to be efficient, they certainly have every reason to protect their jobs. Thus, officials typically strive to perpetuate their organisation even when its purpose has been fulfilled. As Weber put it, 'once fully established, bureaucracy is among the social structures which are hardest to destroy' (1978: 987; orig. 1921).

Bureaucratic inertia refers to *the tendency of bureaucratic organisations to perpetuate themselves.* Formal organisations, in other words, tend to take on a life of their own beyond their formal objectives. Occasionally, a formal organisation that meets its goals will simply disband, as the anti-British Sons of Liberty did after the American Revolution. More commonly, an organisation stays in business by redefining its goals so it can continue to provide a livelihood for its members.

For example, consider the history of the US National Association for Infantile Paralysis, the sponsor of a fundraising campaign known as the March of Dimes' (Sills, 1969). This organisation came into being as part of the drive to find a cure for polio. The goal

was accomplished in the early 1950s when Dr Jonas Salk developed the polio vaccine. Subsequently, however, the March of Dimes did not close down; rather, it redirected its efforts towards other medical problems, such as birth defects, and continues to this day.

Oligarchy

Early in this century, Robert Michels (1876–1936) pointed out the link between bureaucracy and political **oligarchy**, *the rule of the many by the few* (1949; orig. 1911). According to what Michels called 'the iron law of oligarchy', the pyramid-like structure of bureaucracy places a few leaders in charge of vast and powerful government organisations.

Preindustrial societies did not possess the organisational means for even the most power-hungry ruler to control everyone. But the power of elites increased with the steady expansion of formal organisations and the development of technology over the centuries.

Max Weber credited bureaucracy's strict hierarchy of responsibility with increasing organisational efficiency. By applying Weber's thesis to the organisation of government, Michels reveals that this hierarchical structure concentrates power and thus endangers democracy. While the public expects organisational officials to subordinate personal interests to organisational goals, people who occupy powerful positions can – and often do – use their access to information and the media, plus numerous other advantages, to promote their personal interests. Furthermore, bureaucracy also insulates officials from public accountability, whether in the form of a corporate president who is 'unavailable for comment' to the local press or a national president seeking to control information by claiming 'executive privilege'. Oligarchy, then, thrives in the hierarchical structure of bureaucracy and undermines people's control over their elected leaders (Tolson, 1995).

Parkinson's Law and the Peter Principle

Finally, and on a lighter note, we acknowledge two additional insights concerning the limitations of bureaucratic organisations. The concerns of C. Northcote Parkinson and Laurence J. Peter are familiar to anyone who has ever been a part of a formal organisation.

Parkinson (1957) summed up his understanding of bureaucratic inefficiency with the assertion: *Work expands to fill the time available for its completion.* There is enough truth underlying this tongue-in-cheek assertion that it is known today as Parkinson's Law. To illustrate, assume that a bureaucrat working at the Driver and Vehicle Licensing Centre processes 50 driving licence applications in an average day. If one day this worker had only 25 applications to examine, how much time would the task require? The logical answer is half a day. But Parkinson's Law suggests that if a full day is available to complete the work, a full day is how long it will take.

Because organisational employees have little personal involvement in their jobs, few are likely to seek extra work to fill their spare time. Bureaucrats do strive to *appear* busy, however, and their apparent activity often prompts organisations to take on more employees. The added time and expense required to hire, train, supervise and evaluate a larger staff make everyone busier still, setting in motion a vicious cycle that results in *bureaucratic bloat*. Ironically, the larger organisation may accomplish no more real work than it did before.

In the same light-hearted spirit as Parkinson, Laurence J. Peter (Peter and Hull, 1969) devised the Peter Principle: *Bureaucrats rise to their level of incompetence.* The logic here is simple: employees competent at one level of the organisational hierarchy are likely to earn promotion to higher positions. Eventually, however, they will reach a position where they are in over their heads; there, they perform poorly and thus are no longer eligible for promotion.

Reaching their level of incompetence dooms officials to a future of inefficiency. Adding to the problem, after years in the office they have almost certainly learned how to avoid demotion by hiding behind rules and regulations and taking credit for work actually performed by their more competent subordinates.

Gender and race in organisations

Rosabeth Moss Kanter has analysed how ascribed statuses such as gender and race figure in the power structure of bureaucratic hierarchies. To the extent that an organisation has a dominant social composition, the gender- or race-based ingroup enjoys greater social acceptance, respect, credibility and access to informal social networks.

As Figure 7.3 shows, white men in the United States represent about 42 per cent of the US population between the ages of 20 and 64 but hold 63 per cent of management jobs. White women, a category of comparable size, trail with about 26 per cent of managerial positions (US Equal Employment Opportunity Commission, 1996). The members of various minorities lag further behind, even taking account of their smaller populations.

A smaller representation in the workplace, argues Kanter, may leave women, people of colour and those from economically disadvantaged backgrounds feeling like members of socially isolated outgroups. They are often uncomfortably visible, taken less seriously and given fewer chances for promotion. Understandably, minorities themselves often end up thinking that they must work twice as hard as those in dominant categories to maintain their present position, let alone advance to a higher position (Kanter, 1977; Kanter and Stein, 1979).

Kanter (1977) finds that providing a structure of unequal opportunities has important consequences

Figure 7.3 ● US managers by race, sex and ethnicity, 1995

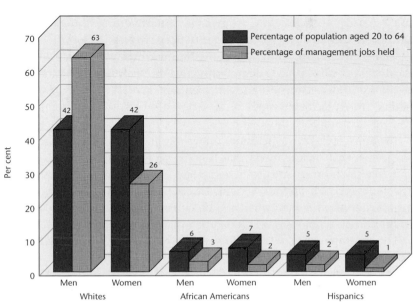

Source: US Equal Employment Opportunity Commission (1996), Census Bureau (1996) and Merton (1968)

for everyone's on-the-job performance. A company with many 'dead-end' jobs, she explains, only encourages workers to become 'zombies' with little aspiration, poor self-concept and little loyalty to the organisation. Widespread opportunity, by contrast, motivates employees, turning them into 'fast-trackers' with higher aspirations, greater self-esteem and stronger commitment to the organisation.

Finally, Kanter claims that in a corporate environment with wide-open opportunity for advancement, leaders value the input of subordinates and seek to bolster their morale and well-being. It is officials with no real power, she maintains, who jealously guard their own privileges and rigidly ride herd over subordinates.

Organisational research in recent years has also spotlighted differences in management styles linked to gender. Deborah Tannen (1994) claims, for example, that women have a greater 'information focus' and more readily ask questions in order to understand an issue. Men, she maintains, share an 'image focus' that makes them hesitate in the same situation, wondering what effect asking questions will have on their reputation. In another study of women executives, Sally Helgesen (1990) notes three additional gender-linked patterns. First, women tend to share information more than men do; that is, they 'stay involved' and place greater value on communication skills.

Second, women are more flexible in their approach to leadership and typically allow subordinates greater autonomy. Third, Helgesen notes, rather than emphasise a narrow specialisation, women are attentive to the interconnectedness of all organisational operations. Because many of today's leading business organisations operate more democratically and seek flexibility in order to contend with complex environments, Helgesen concludes that women bring a 'female advantage' to the workplace.

In sum, one key conclusion drawn from recent research is that organisations that become more open and adaptable bring out the best in their employees. The converse of this trend – in which women are playing a major part – is that, when allowed a more flexible environment, employees best serve the organisation.

Humanising bureaucracy

Humanising bureaucracy means *fostering a more democratic organisational atmosphere that recognises and encourages the contributions of everyone.* Research by Kanter (1977, 1983, 1989; Kanter and Stein, 1980) and others (Peters and Waterman, Jr, 1982) suggests that 'humanising' bureaucracy produces both happier employees and healthier profits. Based on the discussion so far, we can identify three paths to a more humane organisational structure.

1. *Social inclusiveness.* The social composition of the organisation should, ideally, make no one feel 'out of place' because of gender, race or ethnicity. The performance of all employees will improve to the extent that no one is subject to social exclusion.

2. *Sharing of responsibilities.* When organisations ease rigid organisational structures, they spread power and responsibility more widely. Managers cannot benefit from the ideas of employees who have no channels for expressing their opinions. Knowing that superiors are open to suggestions encourages all employees to think creatively, increasing organisational effectiveness.

3. *Expanding opportunities for advancement.* Expanding opportunity reduces the number of employees stuck in routine, dead-end jobs with little motivation to perform well. The organisation should give employees at all levels a chance to share ideas and try new approaches, defining everyone's job as the start of an upward career path.

Kanter's work takes a fresh look at the concept of bureaucracy and its application to business organisations. Rigid formality may have made sense in the past, when organisations hired unschooled workers primarily to perform physical labour. But today's educated workforce can contribute a wealth of ideas to bolster organisational efficiency – if the organisation encourages and rewards innovation.

There is broad support for the idea that loosening up rigid organisations improves performance. Moreover, companies that treat employees as a resource to be developed rather than as a group to be controlled stand out as more profitable. But some critics challenge Kanter's claim that social heterogeneity necessarily yields greater productivity. In controlled comparisons, they maintain, it is homogeneous work groups that typically produce more, while heterogeneous groups are better at generating a diversity of ideas and approaches. Optimal working groups, then, appear to be those that strike a balance: team members bring to the decision-making process a variety of backgrounds and perspectives, yet are similar enough in outlook and goals to effectively coordinate their efforts (Hackman, 1988).

Self-managed work teams

After the Second World War, most formal organisations in Europe were typically conventional bureaucracies, run from the top down according to a stern chain of command. Today, especially as businesses face growing global competition, rigid structures are breaking down. One important element of this trend is the increasing use of the *self-managed work team*. Members of these small groups have the skills necessary to carry out tasks with minimal supervision. By allowing employees to operate within autonomous groups, organisations enhance worker involvement in the job, generate a broader understanding of operations and raise employee morale. A few corporations (such as Procter & Gamble) have had autonomous work units since the 1960s. In recent years, many more are following suit.

Even though it is difficult to compare the performance of organisations with disparate goals and operations, research indicates that self-managed work teams do boost productivity while heading off some of the problems – including alienation – of the traditional bureaucratic model. In the business world, many companies have found that decentralising responsibility in this way also raises product quality and lowers rates of employee absenteeism and turnover (Yeatts, 1991, 1995; Maddox, 1995).

Organisational environment

How any organisation performs depends not only on its internal structure but also on the **organisational environment**, *a range of factors external to an organisation that affects its operation*. Such factors include technology, politics, population patterns and the economy, as well as other organisations.

Technology is especially critical in the modern organisational environment. We have already noted that today's organisations could hardly exist without the communications links provided by telephone systems and facsimile (fax) machines and the ability to duplicate, process and store information afforded by copiers and computers.

Technological changes currently under way are likely to have two somewhat contradictory consequences for organisational structure. On the one hand, the proliferation of personal computers and fax machines affords employees unprecedented access to information; this may produce some levelling in the traditional hierarchy by which top officials kept information and decision-making to themselves. On the other hand, computer technology also enables organisational leaders to monitor the activities of workers more closely than ever before (Markoff, 1991).

A second dimension of the organisational environment is *politics*. Changes in law often have dramatic consequences for the operation of an organisation, as many industries have learned in the face of new environmental standards imposed by government. In global perspective, a radical change like the reorganisation of the Soviet government in 1991 rippled through virtually every organisation in that country.

Third, *population patterns* – such as the size and composition of the surrounding populace – also affect organisations. The average age, typical education and social diversity of a local community shape both the available workforce and the market for an organisation's products or services.

Fourth, the state of the *economy* figures prominently in an organisation's well-being. Businesses expand or contract along with cycles in the overall economy. Even people's ability to get an organisation off the ground depends on the availability of funds, which varies according to economic trends and banking policies (Pennings, 1982). An equally important factor is the rising international competition within the global economy that has propelled the drive towards more flexible and efficient organisations.

Fifth, *other organisations* also form part of the organisational environment. The people who operate a hospital in the UK, for example, must be responsive to doctors' and nurses' associations and unions of other hospital workers, as well as the National Health Service. Similarly, to remain effective, a hospital must be keenly aware of the kinds of equipment and procedures available at other facilities (Fennell, 1980).

In sum, no organisation operates in a social vacuum. But, just as formal organisations are shaped by their environment, organisations themselves have an impact on the surrounding society, as we shall now explain.

The future of postmodern cyber-relations

The intimate face-to-face relationships of the primary group have been breaking down and replaced by the more impersonal and transitory relationships of the secondary group for a long time. Indeed, most of us have come to accept that there is a part of our life where the primary group matters most; but for much of our daily activities – from work to shopping to entertainment – we depend more and more on secondary groups. The world has changed.

But it may well be that this is about to change again! Indeed, many of the themes found in this text suggest that a new set of relationships are starting to happen. Some might even call them 'postmodern cyber-relations'. One way of thinking about these is to look at your relationships with the world of hi-tech gadgetry: what do you use – faxes, videos, multi-media, mobile phones, video games, interactive web sites, and most important of all: your personal computer. Now think about how much time you spend doing these things, away usually from face-to-face contact with people. For many, this will be a lot of time. Indeed, we know many students who seem to spend 24 hours a day on their computer: they cannot be taken away from it! They do their work, their play, their shopping and their relationships all through it!

But think for a minute how this is changing our group involvement.

Sociologist, Sherry Turkle, and social psychologist, Ken Gergen, have both been studying these changes. They see a new way of relating and a new way of life starting to appear. Consider some of the changes:

● Personal face-to-face talking relationships are replaced by distanced writing relationships on the screen: face-to-face contact ceases in this medium.

● Close primary groups and even secondary groups give way to global groups: providing you are connected up to the web, you can talk with anybody in the world. Intimacy can now spread across the globe (and it does, literally, through computer sex lines – or cybersex).

● Straightforward linear thinking – as in most writing – becomes taken over by 'hypertext' where the reader jumps around, splices the text, moves in and out of different 'MUDS' (Multi-user domains). Ways of thinking start to shift.

● Identities are no longer given in face-to-face interaction (e.g. as a man or a woman), but assembled through the machine. In a literal sense, you can make yourself anybody you wish.

This is just an opening listing. You may like to continue it. But the big question becomes: what will happen when we all start to conduct our lives like this, as many argue we will?

There may be many downsides to this. What happens when people cannot afford a computer – and, as we will see in Chapter 11, most of the world not only cannot afford it, but remains illiterate. Might this divide the world into a new form of stratification – the cyberclasses and the non cyberclasses?

There again, what happens when people can afford it? Some researchers are starting to suggest that there has been an increase in shyness and an inability to communicate with others since the computer has arrived. We avoid primary groups and face-to-face relationships, and are only comfortable with machines and text talk.

So there are pluses and minuses to the arrival of this new technology.

● **Continue the debate:**

1. Does the new information technology damage our relationships? Draw up a pros and cons list of the dangers and merits.

2. What is cybersex? How can people have sex with or on a computer? Is this the way ahead for all our sexual problems?

3. Doesn't the new technology lead to a growing inequality? ●

See: Kenneth Gergen *The Saturated Self*, New York, Basic, 1991, and Sherry Turkle *Life on the Screen: Identity in the Age of the Internet*, London: Weidenfeld, 1996

The 'McDonaldisation' of society

Everywhere your authors have travelled, they have not been far away from a McDonalds! And sometimes in the most surprising of places. Whilst visiting Hong Kong, both of us have visited the Portuguese colony of Macau – a little nub jutting from the Chinese coast. Few people here speak English, and life on the streets seems a world apart from the urban rhythms of London, Amsterdam or Los Angeles – where you would certainly expect to find a McDonalds. Strolling the old streets, we turn the corner and stand face to face with (who else?) Ronald McDonald! After eating who-knows-what for so long, forgive our failure to resist the lure of the Big Mac! But the most amazing thing is that the food – the burger, fries and drinks – looks, smells and tastes exactly the same as it does thousands of miles away in the United States!

As noted in the opening to this chapter, McDonald's has enjoyed enormous success.[1] From a single store in the mid-1950s, McDonald's now operates nearly 20,000 restaurants throughout much of the world. There are more than 850 pairs of golden arches in Japan, for example, and the world's largest McDonald's recently opened for business in China's capital city of Beijing.

McDonald's has become a symbol of the modern world. Even more important, the organisational principles that underlie McDonald's are steadily coming to dominate our entire society. Our culture is becoming 'McDonaldised' – an awkward way of saying that we now model many aspects of life on the famous restaurant chain. Parents buy toys at worldwide chain stores like Toys Я Us; face-to-face communication is giving way more and more to voice mail over the telephone, e-mail via computer and junk mail at the door; more vacations take the form of resort and tour packages; television presents news in the form of ten-second sound bites; colleges devise mass courses based on pre-packaged 'modules'; admissions officers size up students they have never met by glancing over their grades; and lecturers assign ghostwritten textbooks and evaluate students with tests mass-produced for them by publishing companies. The list goes on and on.

---

[1] This section draws on George Ritzer's (1993) book of the same name.

McDonaldisation: four principles

What do all these developments have in common? According to George Ritzer, the 'McDonaldisation of society' involves four basic organisational principles.

1. *Efficiency*. Ray Kroc, the marketing genius behind the expansion of McDonald's, set out with the goal of serving a hamburger, French fries and a milkshake to a customer in 50 seconds. Today, one of the company's most popular items is the Egg McMuffin, an entire breakfast in a single sandwich. In the restaurant, customers clear their own trays or, better still, drive away from the pickup window taking the packaging and whatever mess they make with them.

   Efficiency is now a value virtually without critics in our society. Almost everyone believes that anything that can be done quickly is, for that reason alone, good.

2. *Calculability*. The first McDonald's operating manual declared the weight of a regular raw hamburger to be 1.6 ounces, its size to be 3.875 inches across, and its fat content to be 19 per cent. A slice of cheese weighs exactly half an ounce. Fries are cut precisely $^9/_{32}$ of an inch thick.

   Think about how many objects around the home, the workplace or the university campus are designed and mass-produced uniformly according to a calculated plan. Not just our environment but our life experiences – from travelling on motorways to sitting at home watching television – are now more deliberately planned than ever before.

3. *Uniformity and predictability*. An individual can walk into a McDonald's restaurant anywhere and receive the same sandwiches, drinks and desserts prepared in precisely the same way. Predictability, of course, is the result of a highly rational system that specifies every course of action and leaves nothing to chance.

4. *Control through automation*. The most unreliable element in the McDonald's system is human beings. People, after all, have good and bad days, sometimes let their minds wander, or simply decide to try something a different way. To eliminate, as much as possible, the unpredictable human element, McDonald's has automated its equipment to cook food at fixed temperatures for set lengths of time. Even the cash register at a McDonald's is little more than pictures of the items so as to minimise the responsibility of the human being taking the customer's order.

The scope of McDonaldisation is expanding throughout Europe. Automatic banking machines are replacing banks, highly automated bakeries now produce bread with scarcely any human intervention, and chickens and eggs (or is it eggs and chickens?) emerge from automated hatcheries. In supermarkets, laser scanners are phasing out (less reliable) human checkout operators. Most of this country's shopping now occurs in large precincts, in which everything from temperature and humidity to the kinds of stores and products are subject to continuous control and supervision.

Can rationality be irrational?

No one would challenge the popularity or the efficiency of McDonald's and similar organisations. But there is another side to the story.

Max Weber viewed the increasing rationalisation of the world with alarm, fearing that the expanding control of formal organisations would crush the human spirit. As he saw it, rational systems were efficient, but at the terrible cost of dehumanisation. Each of the four principles noted above depends on reining in human creativity, discretion and autonomy. Moreover, as George Ritzer contends, McDonald's food is not particularly good for people nor is the company's extensive use of packaging good for the natural environment. Taking a broader perspective, Ritzer echoes Weber's concern, asserting that 'the ultimate irrationality of McDonaldization is that people could lose control over the system and it would come to control us' (1993: 145).

Formal organisations in Japan

We have described efforts to 'humanise' formal organisations. Interestingly, however, organisations in some countries have long been more personal than those in others. For instance, organisations in Japan, a nation that has had remarkable economic success, thrive within a culture of strong collective identity and solidarity. Unlike much of Europe and the United States, where individualism is a strong tradition, the Japanese maintain traditions of cooperation.

Because of Japan's social cohesiveness, formal organisations in that society approximate to very large primary groups. William Ouchi (1981) highlights five distinctions between formal organisations in Japan and their counterparts in industrial societies of the West. In each case, the Japanese organisation reflects that society's more collective orientation.

1. *Hiring and advancement*. Organisations in Europe hold out promotions and raises in salary as prizes won through individual competition. In Japanese organisations, however, companies hire new graduates together, and all employees of a particular age cohort receive the same salary and responsibilities. Only after several years is anyone likely to be singled out for individual advancement.

2. *Lifetime security*. Employees in much of Europe expect to move from one company to another to advance their careers. Companies are also quick to lay off employees when economic setbacks strike. By contrast, most Japanese firms hire employees for life, fostering strong, mutual loyalties among members. Japanese companies avoid lay-offs by retraining expendable workers for new jobs in the organisation.

3. *Holistic involvement*. European workers tend to see the home and the workplace as distinct spheres. Japanese organisations take a different tack, playing a broad role in their employees' lives by providing home mortgages, sponsoring recreational activities and scheduling social events. Such interaction beyond the workplace strengthens collective identity and offers the respectful Japanese worker an opportunity to voice suggestions and criticisms informally.

4. *Non-specialised training*. Bureaucratic organisation in Europe is based on specialisation; many people spend their entire working life at a single task. From the outset, a Japanese organisation trains employees in all phases of its operation, again with the idea that employees will remain with the organisation for life.

5. *Collective decision-making*. In Europe, important decisions fall to key executives. Although Japanese leaders also take responsibility for their organisation's performance, they involve workers in 'quality circles' that seek employee input in any decision that affects them. A closer working relationship is also encouraged by greater economic equality between management and workers. The salary differential between executives and lower-ranking employees is much less.

These characteristics give the Japanese a strong sense of organisational loyalty. The cultural emphasis on *individual* achievement in our society finds its parallel in Japanese *groupism*. By tying their personal interests to those of their company, workers realise their ambitions through the organisation.

Stuart Clegg (1990, 1992) has taken this argument further, suggesting that Japanese firms approximate to what he calls the postmodern firm. Such organisations are much more flexible and fluid than firms of the past. Strict demarcations are weakened, and they employ the 'Just in Time' system (JIT) of production. Here, goods are produced as required – there is no mass stocking of parts. And this in turn makes the system more adaptable and flexible.

● Groups and organisations in global perspective

As this chapter has explained, formal organisations and their surrounding society interact, with each influencing the other. Yet a global perspective reveals that bureaucracy does not take a consistent organisational form; formal organisations in Europe and the United States for example, differ in significant ways from those in Japan.

Organisations have also changed over time. Several centuries ago, most businesses in Europe and the United States were small family enterprises. But the Industrial Revolution propelled large impersonal organisations to the fore. Within this context, officials in Europe and the United States came to define primary relationships at work (such as *nepotism*, favouritism shown to a family member) as an unethical barrier to organisational efficiency.

The development of formal organisations in Japan followed a different route. Historically, that society was even more socially cohesive, organised according to family-based loyalties. As Japan rapidly industrialised, people there did not discard primary relationships as inefficient, as Westerners did. Rather, the Japanese modelled their large businesses on the family, transferring traditional kinship loyalties to corporations.

From our point of view, then, Japan seems to be simultaneously modern and traditional, promoting organisational efficiency by cultivating personal ties. There are indications that Japanese workers are now becoming more individualistic. Yet the Japanese model still demonstrates that organisational life need not be so dehumanising.

Economically challenged as never before, businesses are taking a closer look at organisational patterns elsewhere, especially in Japan. In fact, many efforts to humanise bureaucracy are clear attempts to mimic the Japanese way of doing things.

Beyond the benefits for most Western business organisations, there is another reason to study the Japanese approach carefully. Our society is less socially cohesive now than the more family-based society Weber knew. A rigidly bureaucratic form of organisation only further atomises the social fabric. Perhaps by following the lead of the Japanese, formal organisations can promote – rather than diminish – a sense of collective identity and responsibility.

As some analysts point out, many US and European organisations are still the envy of the world for their productive efficiency. But the extent of global diversity and change demands that we be cautious about asserting any 'absolute truths' about formal organisations and, just as important, that we remain open to new possibilities for reorganising our future.

SUMMARY

1. Social groups – important building blocks of societies – foster personal development and common identity as well as performing various tasks.

2. Primary groups tend to be small and person orientated; secondary groups are typically large and goal orientated.

3. Instrumental leadership is concerned with realising a group's goals; expressive leadership focuses on members' collective well-being.

4. The process of group conformity is well documented by researchers. Because members often seek consensus, work groups do not necessarily generate a wider range of ideas than do individuals working alone.

5. Individuals use reference groups – both ingroups and outgroups – to form attitudes and make decisions.

6. Georg Simmel characterised the dyad relationship as intense but unstable; a triad, he noted, can easily dissolve into a dyad by excluding one member.

7. Peter Blau explored how the size, internal homogeneity, relative social parity and physical segregation of groups all affect members' behaviour.

8. Social networks are relational webs that link people who typically have little common identity and limited interaction. The Internet is a vast electronic network linking millions of computers worldwide.

9. Formal organisations are large, secondary groups that seek to perform complex tasks efficiently. According to their members' reasons for joining, formal organisations are classified as utilitarian, normative or coercive.

10. Bureaucratic organisation expands in modern societies to perform many complex tasks efficiently. Bureaucracy is based on specialisation, hierarchy, rules and regulations, technical competence, impersonal interaction and formal, written communications.

11. Ideal bureaucracy may promote efficiency, but bureaucracy also generates alienation and inefficiency, tends to perpetuate itself beyond the achievement of its goals and contributes to the contemporary erosion of privacy.

12. Formal organisations often mirror oligarchies. Rosabeth Moss Kanter's research has shown that the concentration of power and opportunity in US corporations can compromise organisational effectiveness.

13. Humanising bureaucracy means recognising people as an organisation's greatest resource. To develop human resources, organisations should spread responsibility and opportunity widely. One way to put this ideal into action is through self-managed work teams.

14. Technology, politics, population patterns, the economy and other organisations combine to form the environment in which a particular organisation must operate.

15. The trend toward 'the McDonaldisation of society' involves increasing automation and impersonality.

16. Reflecting the collective spirit of Japanese culture, formal organisations in Japan are based on more personal ties than are their counterparts in the United States and Europe.

KEY CONCEPTS

bureaucracy an organisational model rationally designed to perform complex tasks efficiently

bureaucratic inertia the tendency of bureaucratic organisations to perpetuate themselves

bureaucratic ritualism a preoccupation with rules and regulations to the point of thwarting an organisation's goals

dyad a social group with two members

expressive leadership group leadership that emphasises collective well-being

formal organisation a large secondary group organised to achieve its goals efficiently

groupthink the tendency of group members to conform by adopting a narrow view of some issue

humanising bureaucracy fostering a more democratic organisational atmosphere that recognises and encourages the contributions of everyone

ingroup a social group commanding a member's esteem and loyalty

instrumental leadership group leadership that emphasises the completion of tasks

network a web of social ties that links people who identify and interact little with one another

oligarchy the rule of the many by the few

organisational environment a range of factors external to an organisation that affects its operation

outgroup a social group toward which one feels competition or opposition

primary group a small social group in which relationships are both personal and enduring

reference group a social group that serves as a point of reference in making evaluations or decisions

secondary group a large and impersonal social group devoted to some specific interest or activity

social group two or more people who identify and interact with one another

triad a social group with three members

CRITICAL-THINKING QUESTIONS ....

1. Identify various primary and secondary groups in your own life. What do you like or dislike about each type of setting?

2. What are some of the positive functions of group conformity (for example, fostering team spirit)? Note several dysfunctions.

3. What does the 'McDonaldisation of society' mean? Cite familiar examples of this trend beyond those discussed in this chapter.

4. How do Japanese organisations differ from those found in Europe? Which organisational type do you prefer? Why?

GOING FURTHER ....

Introductory reading

Stuart R. Clegg, *Modern Organisations: Organisation Studies in the Postmodern World* (London: Sage, 1990).
An important review of earlier studies of organisations which also comes right up to date with the postmodern organisation. There are some intriguing case studies too of the French bread industry, the Italian fashion industry, and 'post-Confucian' Asian enterprises. Pays much attention to the strengths and weaknesses of the Japanese firm.
In a short article, Stuart Clegg ('Modern and Postmodern Organisations', *Sociology Review*, April 1992) provides some of the key ideas.

George Ritzer, *The McDonaldization of Society* (Thousand Oaks, California: Pine Forge Press, 2nd edn, 1996).
A highly readable and lively account of the McDonalds phenomenon and how it provides a blueprint for contemporary organizational life.

Classic sources

George C. Homans, *The Human Group* (New Brunswick, NJ: Transaction, 1992; orig. 1950).
This is an early and enduring sociological investigation of the group, the setting for much of our lives.

A. Paul Hare, Edgar F. Borgatta and Robert F. Bales, *Small Groups: Studies in Social Interaction* (New York: Alfred A. Knopf, rev. edn, 1965).
This collection of classic contributions to the study of small groups contains important essays by Emile Durkheim, Charles Cooley, Georg Simmel, Solomon Asch, and other notable pioneers in the field.

More advanced reading

John P. Walsh, *Supermarkets Transformed: Understanding Organisational and Technological Innovations* (New Brunswick, NJ: Rutgers University Press, 1993).
Industrial-organisational sociology applies many of this chapter's ideas to the real world of business. This study illustrates this process by focusing on a familiar setting.

Sally Helgesen, *The Female Advantage: Women's Ways of Leadership* (New York: Doubleday, 1990).
This intriguing book argues that women typically have a more humanised leadership style that works to the advantage of corporations.

Patricia Caplan, *Class and Gender in India: Women and Their Organisations in a South Indian City* (New York: Tavistock, 1985).
This author analyses women's associations in the context of national politics in India.

Boye De Mente, *Japanese Etiquette and Ethics in Business* (Lincolnwood, IL: NTC Business Books, 5th edn, 1987).
This is one of the best books contrasting formal organisations in the United States with those in Japan.

The Internet age

Two good books that introduce changes in our relationships that are emerging as a consequence of the hi tech world are: Sherry Turkel, *Life on the Screen: Identity in the Age of the Internet* (London: Weidenfeld & Nicolson, 1996); and Kenneth J. Gergen, *The Saturated Self: Dilemmas of Identity in Contemporary Life* (New York: Basic Books, 1991).

chapter eight

Source: Popperfoto

Deviance and Control

Sweden once had an image throughout the world as being something of a permissive society. It had a free and open approach compared with most societies. In matters of sexuality, for example, it was the society of 'free love', tolerance and civility. And it had a much more radical approach to the roles of men, women and children outside of traditional family forms. During the 'swinging sixties' Sweden also had quite a reputation for drug smoking amongst hippies – second only, perhaps, to those in Haight Ashbury, San Francisco. These were the fun loving, beautiful people who smoked pot quite openly. Cannabis may have been officially illegal, but it was accepted everywhere.

All that has changed. Whilst it remains liberal on matters of welfare and sexuality, Sweden today may have one of the most repressive drug policies in the world. The 1970s brought an end to this open and tolerant scene; and largely through the crusading work of the RNS Riksorbundet Narkotikafritt Samhalle (National Union for a Narcotics Free Society), new policies have been adopted that have made the approach to drug use more and more severe.

Sweden now has one of the toughest drug policies and laws in Europe, criminalising drug use as well as possession. Passing a joint is trafficking and carries a compulsory prison sentence. Drugs generally are now invisible. The use of drugs has been driven underground.

There has been so strong an opposition to drug use that it is very hard to find people who will speak out in any kind of liberal way in favour of drug use. The term for people who favour the liberalisation of laws, *drogliberal*, has become a term of abuse! People are regarded with suspicion as 'drug legalisers' and excluded from public debate. And the media has a strong consensus of disapproval.

Lief Lenke, Professor of Criminology at Stockholm University, comments:

At a conference organised by the National Health Institute, I dared raise a couple of questions about drugs. (I asked) If it is credible to assert that cannabis is as dangerous as heroin, and if it is right that Sweden refuses to give clean syringes to addicts when even the WHO recommends it. There was immediately a very unpleasant uproar. People whistled, shouted, and interrupted. I was called a 'legaliser'. I had been invited to speak on European narcotic policy at a meeting of Sweden's social service officers. They telephoned me to say they had heard certain things about me and had chosen another speaker. Now the Social Services Department has informed me that I may no longer sit as Sweden's representative on the Council of Europe Committee for narcotic questions. . . .

When the Director of the National Health Institute, Jakob Lindberg, was asked about the above, he said 'Everyone should know that we are completely, fully and uncompromisingly against drugs. There is great unity on this in Sweden.'

But there is little evidence that the 'war against drugs' in Sweden is working. On the contrary, despite harsh penalties, some 20 per cent of young Swedes in the larger cities use drugs (mainly cannabis), organised crime has grown, and there has been an escalation in many drugs related crimes. Adult crime in Stockholm has risen by some 80 per cent since 1975.

Sources: John Yates, 1996; Arthur Gould, 1996; and *Dagens Nyheter*, Stockholm, 26 October 1995.

The 'drug debate' is just one of the very many issues of crime and deviance facing almost every country in the world today. Crimes of all sorts seem to be on the increase. And many of our concerns – like drug trafficking and control – stretch across the globe. Anxieties and fears about crime are up; our changing penal responses to crime are becoming more and more repressive. Nowadays, most governments make 'crime control' one of their central political arguments in elections. And the message is to 'get tough on crime'. Everywhere in the world it is an issue.

This chapter explores some of many questions dealing with deviance and conformity. Why do societies create cultural norms, including laws, in the first place? Why are some people more likely than others to be accused of violations? How do we control crime, and what impact does this have?

● Defining deviance and control

Deviance involves two elements: labels and norms. Typically, deviance involves *the labelling of the violation of cultural norms*. Norms guide virtually all human activities, so the concept of deviance covers a correspondingly broad spectrum. For instance, there are health norms, sexual norms and religious norms. People who violate such norms are ill, perverts or heretics.

One distinctive category of deviance is **crime**, *the violation of norms a society formally enacts into criminal law*. Even criminal deviance is extensive, ranging from minor traffic violations to serious offences such as murder. A subcategory of crime, **juvenile delinquency**, refers to *the violation of legal standards by the young*.

Some instances of deviance barely raise eyebrows; other cases command a swift and severe response. Members of our society pay little notice to mild nonconformity like left-handedness or boastfulness; we take a dimmer view of reckless driving or dropping out of school, and we dispatch the police in response to a violent crime like rape.

Not all deviance involves action or even choice. For some categories of individuals, just *existing* may be sufficient to provoke condemnation from others. To the young, elderly people sometimes seem hopelessly 'out of it'; to whites who are in the majority, the mere presence of people of colour may cause discomfort. And affluent people of all ages and races may view the poor as disreputable to the extent that they fall short of conventional middle class standards.

Most examples of non-conformity that come readily to mind are negative instances of rule breaking, such as stealing from a supermarket, neglecting a pet or driving while intoxicated. But, given our shortcomings,

Streaker at England versus France rugby international, April, 1974.

Source: Mirror Syndication Intl

we also define especially righteous people – students who speak up too much in class or people who are enthusiastic about paying their taxes – as deviant, even if we accord them a measure of respect (Huls, 1987). What deviant actions or attitudes – whether negative or positive – have in common is some evaluation of *difference* that prompts us to regard another person as an 'outsider' (Becker, 1966).

Social control

Because societies have rules, members target each other with efforts at social control. Much of this process is informal, as when we receive praise or criticism from parents, friends and teachers. Cases of more serious deviance, however, may provoke a response

from the **criminal justice system**, *a societal reaction to alleged violations of law utilising police, courts and prison officials.*

In sum, deviance is much more than a matter of individual choice or personal failing. *How* a society defines deviance, *whom* individuals brand as deviant and *what* people decide to do about non-conformity are all issues of social organisation. Only gradually, however, have people recognised this essential truth, as we shall now explain.

● Theories of crime and control

The biological context

Chapter 5 ('Socialisation') explained that people a century ago understood – or, more correctly, misunderstood – human behaviour as an expression of biological instincts. Understandably, early interest in criminality emphasised biological causes as well. In 1876 Caesare Lombroso (1835–1909), an Italian physician who worked in prisons, declared that criminals have a distinctive physique – low foreheads, prominent jaws and cheekbones, protruding ears, excessive hairiness and unusually long arms that, taken together, made them resemble the apelike ancestors of human beings.

But Lombroso's work was flawed. Had he looked beyond prison walls, he would have realised that the physical features he attributed exclusively to prisoners actually were found throughout the entire population. We now know that no physical attributes, of the kind described by Lombroso, distinguish criminals from noncriminals (Goring, 1972; orig. 1913).

At mid-century, William Sheldon (1949) took a different tack, positing that body structure might predict criminality. He categorised hundreds of young men in terms of body type and, checking for any criminal history, concluded that delinquency occurred most frequently among boys with muscular, athletic builds. Sheldon Glueck and Eleanor Glueck (1950) confirmed Sheldon's conclusion, but cautioned that a powerful build does not necessarily cause or even predict criminality. The Gluecks postulated that parents treat powerfully built males with greater emotional distance so that they, in turn, grow up to display less sensitivity toward others. Moreover, in a self-fulfilling prophecy, people who expect muscular boys to act like bullies may provoke such aggressive behaviour.

Recent genetics research continues to seek possible links between biology and crime. To date, no conclusive evidence connects criminality to any specific genetic flaw. Yet people's overall genetic composition, in combination with social influences, may account for some variation in criminality. In other words, biological factors probably have a real, if modest, effect on whether or not individuals engage in criminal activity (Rowe, 1983; Rowe and Osgood, 1984; Wilson and Herrnstein, 1985; Jencks, 1987).

Critical evaluation

At best, biological theories that trace crime to specific physical traits explain only a small proportion of all crimes. Recent sociobiological research – noting, for example, that violent crime is overwhelmingly committed by males or that adults are more likely to abuse foster children than natural children – is promising, but, at this point, we know too little about the links between genes and human behaviour to draw any firm conclusions (Daly and Wilson, 1988).

Then, too, because a biological approach spotlights individual behaviour, it offers no insight into how some kinds of behaviours come to be defined as deviant in the first place. Therefore, although human biology may affect behaviour, research currently places far greater emphasis on social influences (Gibbons and Krohn, 1986; Liska, 1991).

Personality factors

Like biological theories, psychological explanations of deviance focus on cases of individual abnormality, this time involving personality. Some personality traits are hereditary, but most psychologists believe that temperament is shaped primarily by social experiences. Episodes of deviance, then, are viewed as the product of 'unsuccessful' socialisation.

The work of Walter Reckless and Simon Dinitz (1967) illustrates the psychological approach. These researchers began by asking teachers to categorise 12-year-old boys as either likely or unlikely to engage in juvenile delinquency. Interviews with both categories of boys and their mothers allowed them to assess each boy's self-concept and how well he related to others. Analysing their results, they concluded that the 'good boys' displayed a strong conscience (or superego, in Sigmund Freud's terminology), coped well with frustration, and identified positively with cultural norms and values. The 'bad boys', by contrast, had a weaker conscience, showed little tolerance for frustration, and felt less in tune with conventional culture.

Furthermore, the researchers found that the 'good boys' went on to have fewer contacts with the police than the 'bad boys'. Since all the boys Reckless and Dinitz studied lived in areas where delinquency was widespread, the investigators attributed the tendency to stay out of trouble to a personality that reined in impulses toward deviance. Based on this conclusion, Reckless and Dinitz call their analysis *containment theory*.

Critical evaluation

Psychologists have demonstrated that personality patterns have some connection to delinquency and other types of deviance. Nevertheless, the value of this approach is limited by one key fact: the vast majority of serious crimes are committed by people whose psychological profiles are *normal*.

In sum, both biological and psychological approaches view deviance as an individual attribute without exploring how conceptions of right and wrong initially arise, why people define some rule breakers but not others as deviant, and the role of social power in shaping a society's system of social control. We now turn to these issues by delving into sociological explanations of deviance.

The social foundations of deviance

Although we tend to think of deviance in terms of the free choice or personal failings of individuals, all behaviour – deviance as well as conformity – is shaped by society. There are three social foundations of deviance, identified below.

1. *Deviance varies according to cultural norms*. No thought or action is inherently deviant; it becomes

deviant only in relation to particular norms. The life patterns of rural Icelanders, urban Californians and Welsh mining communities differ in significant ways; for this reason, what people in each area prize or scorn varies as well. Laws, too, differ from place to place. In Amsterdam, for instance, soft drug use is permitted: and there are even shops for their sale. In the rest of Europe, marijuana is outlawed.

In global context, deviance is even more diverse. Albania outlaws any public display of religious faith, such as 'crossing' oneself; Cuba can prosecute its citizens for 'consorting with foreigners'; police can arrest people in Singapore for selling chewing gum; US citizens risk arrest by their own government for travelling to Libya or Iraq.

2. *People become deviant as others define them that way.* Each of us violates cultural norms regularly, occasionally to the extent of breaking the law. For example, most of us have at some time walked around talking to ourselves or have 'borrowed' supplies, such as pens and paper, from the workplace. Whether such activities are sufficient to define us as mentally ill or criminal depends on how others perceive, define and respond to any given situation.

3. *Both rule making and rule breaking involve social power.* The law, Karl Marx asserted, amounts to little more than a strategy by which powerful people protect their interests. For example, the owners of an unprofitable factory have a legal right to close their business, even if doing so throws thousands of people out of work. But if workers commit an act of vandalism that closes the same factory for a single day, the workers are subject to criminal prosecution. Similarly, a homeless person who stands on a street corner denouncing the city government risks arrest for disturbing the peace; a politician during an election campaign does exactly the same thing while receiving extensive police protection. In short, norms and their application are linked to social inequality.

● Why we need deviance: the functional theory of crime

Functionalist theory teaches us a great paradox about crime and deviance: that far from always being disruptive, it may contribute to a social system and underlie the operation of society.

Emile Durkheim: the functions of deviance

In his pioneering study of deviance, Emile Durkheim (1964a, orig. 1895; 1964b, orig. 1893) made the remarkable assertion that there is nothing abnormal about deviance; in fact, it performs four functions essential to society.

1. *Deviance affirms cultural values and norms.* Culture involves moral choices. Unless our lives dissolve into chaos, people prefer some attitudes and behaviours to others. But any conception of virtue rests upon an opposing notion of vice. Just as there can be no good without evil, then, there can be no justice without crime. Deviance, in short, is indispensable to the process of generating and sustaining morality.

2. *Responding to deviance clarifies moral boundaries.* By defining some individuals as deviant, people draw a

No social class stands apart from others as being either criminal or free from criminality. According to various sociologists, however, people with less stake in society and their own future typically exhibit less resistance to some kinds of deviance. Photographer Stephen Shames captured this scene on a Bronx, New York, rooftop in 1983.

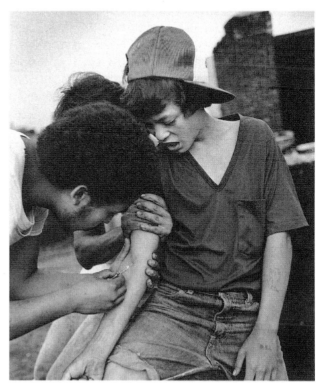

Source: Matrix International – Stephen Shames

social boundary between right and wrong. For example, a university marks the line between academic honesty and cheating by disciplining those who commit plagiarism.

3. *Responding to deviance promotes social unity.* People typically react to serious deviance with collective outrage. In doing so, Durkheim explained, they reaffirm the moral ties that bind them. For example, most US citizens joined together in a chorus of condemnation after a terrorist bombed the federal building in Oklahoma City in 1995.

4. *Deviance encourages social change.* Deviant people, Durkheim claimed, push a society's moral boundaries, suggesting alternatives to the status quo and encouraging change. Moreover, he declared, today's deviance sometimes becomes tomorrow's morality (1964a: 71). In the 1950s, for example, many people denounced rock-and-roll music as a threat to the morals of youth and an affront to traditional musical tastes. Since then, however, rock-and-roll has been swept up in the musical mainstream, becoming a multibillion-dollar industry.

An illustration: the Puritans of Massachusetts Bay

Kai Erikson's (1966) historical investigation of the early Puritans of Massachusetts Bay illustrates Durkheim's analysis. Erikson showed that even the Puritans – a disciplined and highly religious group – created deviance to clarify their moral boundaries. In fact, Durkheim might well have had the Puritans in mind when he wrote:

Imagine a society of saints, a perfect cloister of exemplary individuals. Crimes, properly so called, will there be unknown; but faults which appear [insignificant] to the layman will create there the same scandal that the ordinary offence does in ordinary consciousness . . . For the same reason, the perfect and upright man judges his smallest failings with a severity that the majority reserve for acts more truly in the nature of an offence. (1964a: 68–9).

Deviance, in short, is not a matter of how good or bad individuals are; it is a necessary product of social living.

But the *kind* of deviance a society condemns depends on the moral issues that members of that society seek to clarify. Over time, the Puritans confronted a number of 'crime waves'. In responding to them, the Puritans sharpened their views on crucial moral quandaries. Thus, they answered questions about how much dissent to allow or what their religious goals should be by celebrating some of their members while branding others as deviants. And, perhaps most fascinating of all, Erikson discovered that, even though the offences changed, the Puritans declared a consistent proportion of their number as deviant over time. This stability, concludes Erikson, confirms Durkheim's contention that deviants serve as ethical markers, outlining a society's changing moral boundaries. By constantly defining a small number of people as deviant, in sum, Puritan society ensured that the social functions of deviance were carried out.

Merton's strain theory

While deviance is inevitable in all societies, Robert Merton (1938, 1968) argues that excessive violations arise from particular social arrangements. Specifically, the scope and character of deviance depend on how well a society makes cultural *goals* (such as financial success) accessible by providing the institutionalised *means* (such as schooling and job opportunities) to achieve them.

Writing originally about North American Society in the 1930s, Merton argued that the path to *conformity* was to be found in pursuing conventional goals by approved means. The true 'success story', in other words, is someone who gains wealth and prestige through talent and hard work. But not everyone who desires conventional success has the opportunity to attain it. Children raised in poverty, for example, may see little hope of becoming successful if they 'play by the rules'. As a result, they may seek wealth through one or another kind of crime – say, by dealing cocaine. Merton called this type of deviance *innovation* – the attempt to achieve a culturally approved goal (wealth) by unconventional means (drug sales). Figure 8.1 characterises innovation as accepting the goal of success while rejecting the conventional means of becoming rich.

According to Merton, the 'strain' between a culture's emphasis on wealth and the limited opportunity to get rich gives rise, especially among the poor, to theft, the selling of illegal drugs or other forms of street hustling. In some respects, at least, a 'notorious gangster' like Al Capone was quite conventional – he pursued the fame and fortune at the heart of the 'American dream'. But, like many minorities who find the doors to success closed, this bright and enterprising man blazed his own trail to the top. As one analyst of the criminal world put it:

> The typical criminal of the Capone era was a boy who had . . . seen what was rated as success in the society he had been thrust into – the Cadillac, the big bankroll, the elegant apartment. How could he acquire that kind of recognisable status? He was almost always a boy of outstanding initiative, imagination, and ability; he was the kind of boy who, under different conditions, would have been a captain of industry or a key political figure of his time. But he hadn't the opportunity of going to Yale and becoming a banker or broker; there was no passage for him to a law degree from Harvard. There was, however, a relatively easy way of acquiring these goods that he was incessantly told were available to him as an American citizen, and without which he had begun to feel he could not properly count himself as an American citizen. He could become a gangster. (Allsop, 1961: 236)

The inability to become successful by normative means may also prompt another type of deviance that Merton calls *ritualism* (see Figure 8.1). Ritualists resolve the strain of limited success by abandoning cultural goals in favour of almost compulsive efforts to live 'respectably'. In essence, they embrace the rules to the point where they lose sight of their larger goals. Lower-level bureaucrats, Merton suggests, often succumb to ritualism as a way of maintaining respectability.

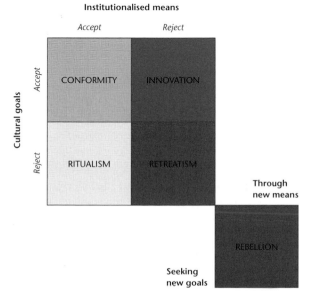

Figure 8.1 ● Merton's strain theory of deviance

A third response to the inability to succeed is *retreatism* – the rejection of both cultural goals and means so that one, in effect, 'drops out'. Retreatists include some alcoholics and drug addicts, and some of the street people found in cities. The deviance of retreatists lies in unconventional living and, perhaps more seriously, in accepting this situation. The fourth response to failure is *rebellion*. Like retreatists, rebels reject both the cultural definition of success and the normative means of achieving it. Rebels, however, go one step further by advocating radical alternatives to the existing social order. Typically, they call for a political or religious transformation of society, and often join a counterculture.

Deviant subcultures

Richard Cloward and Lloyd Ohlin (1966) extended Merton's theory in their investigation of delinquent youth. They maintain that criminal deviance results not simply from limited legitimate opportunity but also from available illegitimate opportunity. In short, deviance or conformity grows out of the *relative opportunity structure* that frames young people's lives.

Consider, once again, the life of Al Capone. An ambitious individual denied legitimate opportunity, he organised a criminal empire to take advantage of the demand for alcohol in the United States during Prohibition (1920–1933). As Capone's life shows, illegal opportunities foster the development of *criminal subcultures* that offer the knowledge, skills and other resources people need to succeed in unconventional ways. Indeed, gangs may specialise in one or another form of criminality according to available opportunities and resources (Sheley et al., 1995).

But some poor and highly transient neighbourhoods may lack almost any form of opportunity – legal or illegal. Here, delinquency often surfaces in the form of *conflict subcultures* where violence is ignited by frustration and a desire for fame or respect. Alternatively, those who fail to achieve success, even by criminal means, may sink into *retreatist subcultures*, dropping out through abuse of alcohol or other drugs.

Albert Cohen (1971) asserts that delinquency is most pronounced among lower class youths because it is they who contend with the least opportunity to achieve success in conventional ways. Sometimes those whom society neglects seek self-respect by building a deviant subculture that 'defines as meritorious the characteristics they *do* possess, the kinds of conduct of which they *are* capable' (1971: 66). Having a notorious street reputation, for example, may win no points with society as a whole, but it may satisfy a youth's gnawing desire to 'be somebody'.

Walter Miller (1970) agrees that deviant subcultures typically develop among lower class youths who contend with the least legitimate opportunity. He spotlights six focal concerns of these deviant subcultures: (1) *trouble*, arising from frequent conflict with teachers and police; (2) *toughness*, the value placed on physical size, strength and athletic skills, especially among males; (3) *smartness* (or 'street smarts'), the ability to out-think or 'con' others, and to avoid being similarly taken advantage of; (4) *excitement*, the search for thrills, risk or danger to escape from a daily routine that is predictable and unsatisfying; (5) a preoccupation with *fate*, derived from the lack of control these youths feel over their own lives; and (6) *autonomy*, a desire for freedom often expressed as resentment toward figures of authority.

Critical evaluation
Durkheim's pioneering work on the functions of deviance remains central to sociological thinking. Even so, recent critics point out that a community does not always come together in reaction to crime; sometimes, in fact, fear of crime drives people to withdraw from public life altogether (Liska and Warner, 1991).

Derived from Durkheim's analysis, Merton's strain theory has also come under criticism for explaining some kinds of deviance (theft, for example) far better than others (such as crimes of passion or mental illness). In addition, not everyone seeks success in conventional terms of wealth, as strain theory implies. As we noted in Chapter 4 ('Culture'), members of our society embrace many different cultural values and are motivated by various notions of personal success.

The general argument of Cloward and Ohlin, Cohen, and Miller – that deviance reflects the opportunity structure of society – has been confirmed by subsequent research (Allan and Steffensmeier, 1989). However, these theories, too, fall short by assuming that everyone shares the same cultural standards for judging right and wrong. Moreover, we must be careful not to define deviance in ways that unfairly focus attention on poor people. If crime is defined to include stock fraud as well as street theft, offenders are more likely to include affluent individuals. Finally, all structural-functional theories imply that everyone who violates conventional cultural standards will be branded as deviant. Becoming deviant, however, is actually a highly complex process, as the next section explains.

● Labelling theory

The central contribution of symbolic-interaction analysis is **labelling theory**, *the assertion that deviance and conformity result, not so much from what people do, but from how others respond to those actions.* Labelling theory stresses the relativity of deviance, meaning that the same behaviour may be defined in any number of ways. Howard S. Becker claims that deviance is, therefore, nothing more than 'behaviour that people so label' (1966: 9).

Consider these situations. A woman takes an article of clothing from a room mate; a married man at a convention in a distant city has sex with a prostitute; a Member of Parliament drives home intoxicated after a party. In each case, 'reality' depends on the response of others. Is the first situation a matter of borrowing or is it theft? The consequences of the second case depend largely on whether news of the man's behaviour follows him back home. In the third situation, is the official an active socialite or a dangerous drunk? The social construction of reality, then, is a highly variable process of detection, definition and response.

Because 'reality' is relative to time and place, one society's conventions may constitute another's deviance. The box describes cockfighting: is this popular sport a meaningful cultural ritual or simply a vicious abuse of animals?

Primary and secondary deviance
Edwin Lemert (1951, 1972) notes that many episodes of norm violation – say, truancy or underage drinking – provoke little reaction from others and have little effect on a person's self-concept. Lemert calls such passing episodes *primary deviance*.

But what happens if other people take notice of someone's deviance and make something of it? If, for example, people begin to describe a young man as a 'boozer' and push him out of their social circle, he may become embittered, drink even more and seek the company of others who condone his behaviour. So the response to initial deviance can set in motion *secondary deviance*, by which an individual engages in repeated norm violations and begins to take on a deviant identity. The development of secondary deviance is one application of the Thomas theorem, which states, 'Situations defined as real become real in their consequences'.

CONTROVERSY AND DEBATE

Cockfighting: cultural ritual or abuse of animals?

One of the great national sports amongst the wealthy in England has been fox hunting. Controversial because of its cruelty to animals, it may be made illegal in the near future. But most countries have some kind of sports in which animals are ritually abused. In Spain it is bullfighting.

Whilst you won't see much of it in Europe, one of the popular sports of the world is cockfighting. Legal in parts of North America (Louisiana, Texas, Arizona), cockfighting is big business in Mexico, and approaches something of a national pastime in the Philippines. There, the local cockpit is as important as strolling the Italian Piazza: every settlement has one, and it attracts a crowd on weekends and fiesta days.

On the surface, cockfights are about gambling. An afternoon or evening event might include ten fights. The process begins as the cock owners display their birds to one another, calling out for bets on which is the stronger bird. Members of the audience weigh in with their own cash as a pair of cocks prepares to fight. Taking the money and confirming the bets is the *cristo*, by which Filipinos mean that

he is expected to be as honest as Christ.

Once the odds of winning have been set and the money is on the table, the actual combat begins. Roosters fight in pairs, each outfitted with a small, sharp blade (each region of the world has its favourite variation as to shape and length) strapped to the rear of the left leg. The cocks need little encouragement to fight, but the owners engage in a bit of strutting of their own, swinging their birds back and forth in front of each other before dropping them on lines drawn in the pit sand. Immediately upon hitting the ground, the hackles rise and the birds fly at one another, merging in a blur of legs and feathers.

Within a few minutes, one bird may collapse from exhaustion; the owner

steps in to revive his cock and the process is repeated. Before long, however, a blade finds its mark. The victor, the bird who will live to fight another day, ends up perching on the vanquished, who will not.

In many parts of the world, cockfighting ranks among the most important male rituals. Many men lavish on their birds the kind of attention they otherwise reserve for their sons. Typically, men raise their roosters for about two years, often at considerable expense, before their fighting careers begin. At that point, cocks take on a crucial cultural function for men. That is, through the ritual of the cockfight, men test their own claims to manhood, establish their own standing in the community pecking order, and pass on to their sons significant lessons about honour, competition and masculinity.

An outside observer, easily repulsed by the brutality of the cockfight, may readily condemn the practice as unethical. But, sensing the deep importance of the ceremony to insiders, one hangs – looking both ways – on the uneasy edge of uncertainty. ●

Source: Based on *The Economist*, 1994, Harris, 1994, and Plummer's research in the Philippines.

Source: Gamma-Liaison, Inc. – Jon Levy

Stigma

The onset of secondary deviance marks the emergence of what Erving Goffman (1963) called a *deviant career*. As individuals develop a strong commitment to deviant behaviour, they typically acquire a **stigma**, *a powerfully negative social label that radically changes a person's self-concept and social identity*.

Stigma operates as a master status (see Chapter 6, 'Social Interaction in Everyday Life'), overpowering other dimensions of social identity so that an individual is diminished and discounted in the minds of others and, consequently, socially isolated. Sometimes an entire community formally stigmatises individuals through what Harold Garfinkel (1956) calls a *degradation ceremony*. A criminal prosecution is one example, operating much like a university graduation except that people stand before the community to be labelled in a negative rather than a positive way.

Retrospective labelling

Once people have stigmatised a person, they may engage in **retrospective labelling**, *the interpretation of someone's past consistent with present deviance* (Scheff, 1984). For example, after discovering that a priest has sexually molested a child, others may rethink his past, perhaps musing, 'He always did want to be around young children'. Retrospective labelling distorts a person's biography in a highly selective and prejudicial way, guided more by the present stigma than by any attempt to be fair. This process often deepens a person's deviant identity.

Labelling and mental illness

Is a woman who believes that Jesus rides the bus to work with her every day seriously deluded or merely expressing her religious faith in a highly graphic way? If a man refuses to bathe, much to the dismay of his family, is he insane or simply unconventional? Is a homeless woman who refuses to allow police to take her to a city shelter on a cold night mentally ill or simply trying to live independently?

Psychiatrist Thomas Szasz – a maverick among mental health professionals – charges that people apply the label of insanity to what is only 'difference'; therefore, he concludes, the notion of mental illness should be abandoned (1961, 1970, 1994, 1995). Illness, Szasz argues, is physical and afflicts only the body; mental illness, then, is a myth. The world is full of people whose 'differences' in thought or action may irritate us, but difference is no grounds on which to define someone as sick. To do so, Szasz claims, simply enforces conformity to the standards of people powerful enough to impose their will on others.

Many of Szasz's colleagues reject the notion that all mental illness is a fiction. But some have hailed his work for pointing out the danger of abusing medical practice in the interest of promoting conformity. Most of us, after all, experience periods of extreme stress or other mental disability from time to time. Such episodes, although upsetting, are usually of passing importance. If, however, others respond with labelling that forms the basis of a social stigma, the long-term result may be further deviance as a self-fulfilling prophecy (Scheff, 1994).

The medicalisation of deviance

Labelling theory, particularly the ideas of Szasz and Goffman, helps to explain an important shift in the way our society understands deviance. Over the last fifty years, the growing influence of psychiatry and medicine has prompted the **medicalisation of deviance**, *the transformation of moral and legal issues into medical matters*.

In essence, medicalisation amounts to swapping one set of labels for another. In moral terms, we evaluate people or their behaviour as 'bad' or 'good'. However, the scientific objectivity of modern medicine passes no moral judgement, utilising instead clinical diagnoses such as 'sick' and 'well'.

To illustrate, until the middle of this century, people generally viewed alcoholics as weak and morally deficient people, easily tempted by the pleasure of drink. Gradually, however, medical specialists redefined alcoholism so that most people now consider alcoholism a disease, rendering individuals 'sick' rather than 'bad'. Similarly, obesity, drug addiction, child abuse, promiscuity and other behaviours that used to be moral matters are today widely defined as illnesses for which people need help rather than punishment.

The significance of labels

Whether we define deviance as a moral or medical issue has three profound consequences. First, it affects *who responds* to deviance. An offence against common morality typically provokes a reaction by ordinary people or the police. Applying medical labels, however, places the situation under the control of clinical specialists, including counsellors, psychiatrists and physicians.

A second difference is *how people respond* to deviance. A moral approach defines the deviant as an 'offender' subject to punishment. Medically, however, 'patients' need treatment (for their own good, of course). Therefore, while punishment is designed to fit the crime, treatment programmes are tailored to the patient and may involve virtually any therapy that a specialist thinks will prevent future deviance (von Hirsh, 1986).

Third, and most important, the two labels differ on the issue of *the personal competence of the deviant person*. Morally speaking, people take responsibility for their behaviour whether right or wrong. If we are sick, however, we lose the capacity to control (or even comprehend) our behaviour. Defined as incompetent, the deviant person becomes vulnerable to intense, often involuntary, treatment. For this reason alone, attempts to define deviance in medical terms should be made only with extreme caution.

Sutherland's differential association theory

Learning any social patterns – whether conventional or deviant – is a process that takes place in groups. According to Edwin Sutherland (1940), any person's tendency toward conformity or deviance depends on the relative frequency of association with others who encourage conventional behaviour or norm violation. This is Sutherland's theory of *differential association*.

Sutherland's theory is illustrated by a study of drug and alcohol use among young adults in the United States (Akers et al., 1979). Analysing responses to a questionnaire completed by junior and senior high school students, researchers discovered a close link between the extent of alcohol and drug use and the degree to which peer groups encouraged such activity. The investigators concluded that young people embrace delinquent patterns as they receive praise and other rewards for defining deviance rather than conformity in positive terms.

Hirschi's control theory

In his *control theory*, Travis Hirschi (1969, 1995) claims that the essence of social control lies in people's anticipation of the consequences of their behaviour. Hirschi assumes that everyone finds at least some

deviance tempting. Imagining condemnation from family or friends is sufficient to deter most people from temptation; concerns about how transgressions will affect their careers will give others pause. By contrast, individuals who have little to lose from deviance are most likely to become rule-breakers.

Hirschi asserts that conformity arises from four types of social controls.

1. *Attachment*. Strong social attachments encourage conformity; weak relationships in the family, peer group and school leave people freer to engage in deviance.

2. *Opportunity*. The more one perceives legitimate opportunity, the greater the advantages of conformity. A young person bound for university, one with good career prospects, has a high stake in conformity. By contrast, someone with little confidence in future success drifts more toward deviance.

3. *Involvement*. Extensive involvement in legitimate activities – such as holding a job, going to school and completing homework, or pursuing hobbies – inhibits deviance. People with few such activities – who simply 'hang out' waiting for something to happen – have time and energy for deviant activity.

4. *Belief*. Strong beliefs in conventional morality and respect for authority figures restrain tendencies toward deviance. By contrast, people with a weak conscience are more vulnerable to temptation.

Hirschi's analysis draws together a number of ideas presented earlier about the causes of deviant behaviour. Note that both relative social privilege and strength of moral character are crucial in generating a stake in conformity to conventional norms (Wiatrowski, Griswold and Roberts, 1981; Sampson and Laub, 1990; Free, 1992).

Critical evaluation
The various symbolic-interaction theories share a focus on deviance as process. Labelling theory links deviance not to *action* but to the *reaction* of others. Thus some people come to be defined as deviant while others who think or behave in the same way are not. The concepts of stigma, secondary deviance and deviant career demonstrate how people can incorporate the label of deviance into a lasting self-concept.

Yet labelling theory has several limitations. First, because this theory takes a highly relative view of deviance, it glosses over how some kinds of behaviour, such as murder, are condemned virtually everywhere (Welfare, 1980). Labelling theory is thus most usefully applied to less serious deviance, such as sexual promiscuity or mental illness.

Second, the consequences of deviant labelling are unclear. Research is inconclusive as to whether deviant labelling produces subsequent deviance or discourages further violations (Sherman and Smith, 1992).

Third, not everyone resists the label of deviance; some people may actually relish being defined as deviant (Vold and Bernard, 1986). For example, individuals may engage in civil disobedience leading to arrest to call attention to social injustice.

Both Sutherland's differential association theory and Hirschi's control theory have had considerable influence in sociology. But they provide little insight into why society's norms and laws define certain kinds of activities as deviant in the first place. This important question is addressed by social-conflict analysis, the focus of the next section.

● Conflict and crime

Conflict theory demonstrates how deviance reflects inequalities and power. This approach holds that the cause of crime may be linked to inequalities – of class, race and gender; and that who or what is labelled as deviant depends on the relative power of categories of people.

Conflict theory links deviance to power in three ways. First, the norms – and especially the laws – of any society generally bolster the interests of the rich and powerful. People who threaten the wealthy, either by seizing their property or by advocating a more egalitarian society, come to be tagged as 'common thieves' or 'political radicals'. As noted in Chapter 3 ('Society'), Karl Marx argued that the law (together with all social institutions) tends to support the interests of the rich. Echoing Marx, Richard Quinney makes the point succinctly: 'Capitalist justice is by the capitalist class, for the capitalist class, and against the working class' (1977: 3).

Second, even if their behaviour is called into question, the powerful have the resources to resist deviant labels. Corporate executives who order the dumping of hazardous wastes are rarely held personally account-able for these acts. And, as the O. J. Simpson trial in United States made clear, even when charged with violent crimes, the rich have the resources to vigorously resist being labelled as criminal. (Although this particular case – and the main reason for so much interest in it – was complicated by race: O. J. Simpson is not just wealthy, but black.)

Third, the widespread belief that norms and laws are natural and good masks their political character. For this reason, we may condemn the unequal application of the law but give little thought to whether the *laws themselves* are inherently fair (Quinney, 1977).

Conflict criminologies

Although there is a long history of conflict theories of crime (from at least Marx onwards), since the 1970s there has been a significant revitalisation of interest. A key book here was Taylor, Walton and Young's *The New Criminology* 1973, which was a substantial critique of all the theories outlined above. Broadly, they argued that most existing theories of crimes had not looked at a wide enough range of questions (to take in the structural explanations of control as well as of crime, for instance); and had often ignored wider material conflicts at the root of much of the criminal process. The authors were all Marxists.

Applying deviant labels: the conflict view

Spitzer (1980), also following the Marxist tradition, argues that deviant labels are applied to people who impede the operation of capitalism. First, because capitalism is based on private ownership of wealth, people who threaten the property of others – especially the poor who steal from the rich – are prime candidates for labelling as deviants. Conversely, the rich who exploit the poor rarely are called into question. Landlords, for example, who charge poor tenants high rents and evict those who cannot pay are not considered a threat to society; they are simply 'doing business'.

Second, because capitalism depends on productive labour, those who cannot or will not work risk deviant labelling. Many members of our society think of people out of work – even if through no fault of their own – as deviant.

Third, capitalism depends on respect for figures of authority, so people who resist authority are labelled as deviant. Examples are children who play truant or talk back to parents and teachers; adults who do not cooperate with employers or police; and anyone who opposes 'the system'.

Fourth, anyone who directly challenges the capitalist status quo is likely to be defined as deviant. Into this category fall anti-war activists, environmentalists and labour organisers.

To turn the argument around, society offers positive labels to whomever enhances the operation of capitalism. Winning athletes, for example, have celebrity status because they express the values of individual achievement and competition vital to capitalism.

Additionally, Spitzer notes, we condemn using drugs of escape (marijuana, psychedelics, heroin and crack) as deviant, while espousing the use of drugs that promote adjustment to the status quo (such as alcohol and caffeine).

The capitalist system also strives to control threatening categories of people. Those who are a 'costly yet relatively harmless burden' on society, says Spitzer, include Robert Merton's retreatists (for example, those addicted to alcohol or other drugs), the elderly and people with mental and/or physical disabilities. All are subject to control by social welfare agencies. But those who challenge the very underpinnings of the capitalist system, including the inner city 'underclass' and revolutionaries – Merton's innovators and rebels – come under the purview of the criminal justice system and, in times of crisis, military forces such as the US National Guard.

Note that both the social welfare and criminal justice systems apply labels that blame individuals and not the system for the control they exert over people's lives. Welfare recipients are deemed unworthy freeloaders; poor people who vent rage at their powerlessness are labelled rioters; anyone who actively challenges the government is branded a radical or a communist; and those who attempt to gain illegally what they cannot otherwise acquire are called common thieves.

The emergence of Left realism

Since the mid 1980s a new debate has appeared within British criminology. One group of criminologists – from a conflict, Marxist background – have introduced the idea of Left realism (Jock Young, Roger Matthews and John Lea, all based at Middlesex University). Seeing crime as a serious problem, especially in inner city areas, that has grown in recent years, they analyse what they call 'the square' of crime – the state, society and the public at large, offenders and victims (Figure

8.2). All need to be looked at for all types of crime. Crucial, though, is the fact the victims of crime are overwhelmingly the working class – for example, unskilled workers are twice as likely to be burgled as other workers. Crime, then, is largely done by the working class on the working class. The causes of crime need to be looked for in deep structural inequalities (see Chapter 10). Crime is produced by relative deprivation – *a perceived disadvantage arising from a specific comparison* – and marginalisation, where people come to live on the edge of society. All this calls for the pursuit of justice at a wide level, with calls being made for fundamental shifts in economic situations, enlightened prison policies, environmental design and accountable police.

Like other analyses of deviance, however, conflict theory has its critics. First, this approach implies that laws and other cultural norms are created directly by and exclusively for the rich and powerful. At the very least, this assumption is an oversimplification, since many segments of our society influence, and benefit from, the political process. Laws also protect workers, consumers and the environment, sometimes in opposition to the interests of the rich.

Second, conflict analysis implies that criminality springs up only to the extent that a society treats its members unequally. However, as Durkheim noted, all societies generate deviance, whatever their economic system.

Figure 8.2 ● **The square of crime**

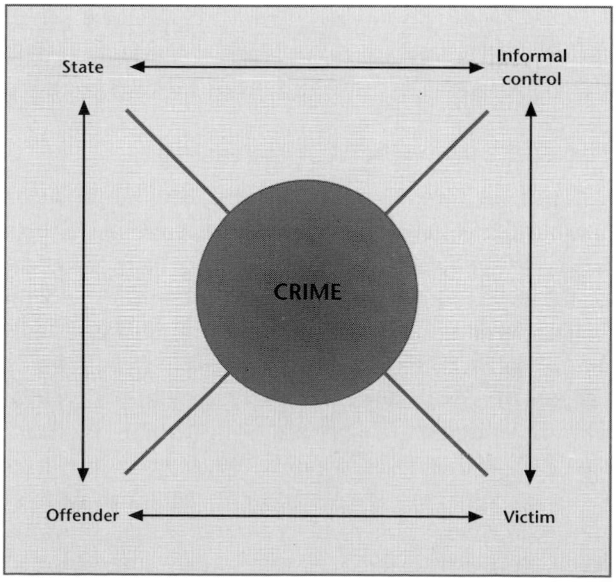

Source: Jock Young

Table 8.1 ● Sociological explanations of deviance: a summary

Theoretical paradigm	Major contributions
Functional analysis	While what is deviant may vary, deviance itself is found in all societies; deviance and the social response it provokes sustain the moral foundation of society; deviance may also guide social change.
Symbolic-interaction analysis	Nothing is inherently deviant but may become defined as such through the response of others; the reactions of others are highly variable; the label of deviance may lead to the emergence of secondary deviance and deviant careers.
Conflict analysis	Laws and other norms reflect the interests of powerful members of society; those who threaten the status quo generally are defined as deviant; social injury caused by powerful people is less likely to be considered criminal than social injury caused by people who have little social power.

We have now presented various sociological explanations for crime and other types of deviance. Table 8.1 summarises the contributions of each approach.

The rise of a feminist criminology

In a notable irony, conflict analysis – despite its focus on social inequality – has long neglected the importance of gender. If, as conflict theory suggests, economic disadvantage is a primary cause of crime, why do women (whose economic position is much worse than that of men) commit far fewer crimes than men do?

Until the 1970s, the study of crime and deviance was very much a male province. And when you think about it, crime does seem to be a male preserve. Statistics repeatedly show that more men than women commit crimes. They are also more likely to come before courts and they are more likely to end up in

prison. Although there are women's prisons, they are greatly outnumbered by men's. Given all this, then, it might seem obvious that in the past criminology should have focused upon the study of men.

But these facts alone should alert us to something very interesting going on. If there is such a skew towards men, could this mean that the whole process of crime is connected to gender? It must be a strong probability. We need, for instance, to explain why it is that men commit more crimes and women fewer. And indeed, once we start to ask these question a whole new field of questions and problems arises.

For instance, in virtually every society in the world there would seem to be more stringent controls on women than men. Historically, our society has restricted the role of women to the home. Even in much of Europe today, many women find limited opportunities in the workplace, in politics and in the military. In many bars of Europe, women remain decidedly unwelcome: these places are men's domains. And more, women on their own in public places may be looked upon with some suspicion. And elsewhere in the world, the normative constraints placed on women are often greater still. In Saudi Arabia, women cannot vote or legally operate motor vehicles; in Iran, women who dare to expose their hair or wear makeup in public can be whipped.

So we now have two questions at least. How is crime gendered? And how is control gendered? Questions likes these have given rise to a whole new branch of criminology, known as feminist criminology.

Carol Smart's book *Women, Crime and Criminology*, published in 1976, is generally considered to be the start of this field of study. In this book, she both documented the ways in which women had been neglected in the study of crime and deviance and showed that, when they had been included, the approach had usually been highly sexist or outright misogynist. For instance, in one notorious case, a criminologist Otto Pollak proposed that women are in fact more criminal than men: it is just they are also more devious and cunning and hence can 'cover up their crimes' better!

Given the importance of gender to the social construction of deviance, we need to pause a moment to see how gender figures in some of the theories we have already discussed. Robert Merton's strain theory, for example, has a masculine cast in that it defines cultural goals in terms of financial success. Traditionally,

DIFFERENT VOICES

Hate crimes in the USA: punishing actions or attitudes?

Types of crimes are not fixed once and for all. Definitions of crime are socially produced and change. More than a decade ago the concept of **hate crime** came into use in North America to designate *a criminal act motivated by a manifest prejudice based on race, religion, sexual orientation or ethnic origin.* A hate crime, then, involves both a violation of criminal law and a bias on the part of the offender towards the victim on the basis of race, religion, ancestry, sexual orientation or physical disability.

Although hate crimes are nothing new, the US federal government has only tracked them since 1990. While still a small share of all crime, their numbers are rising. A survey conducted in eight US cities by the National Gay and Lesbian Task Force (cited in Berrill, 1992: 19–20) found that 20 per cent of lesbians and gay men had been physi-

cally assaulted because of their sexual orientation; more than 90 per cent claimed to have been at least verbally abused for this reason. Research indicates that hate-motivated violence is especially likely to target people who contend with multiple stigmas, such as black gay men.

Three-fifths of US states have now adopted laws enhancing sentences for crimes motivated by bias. Supporters of hate-crime legislation make three arguments in favour of this trend. First, an offender's intentions have always figured in criminal deliberations, so weighing evidence of hatred represents nothing new. Second, crimes motivated by homophobia, sexism, racial or other bias inflame public sentiment more than those carried out for more pedestrian reasons like monetary gain. Third, advocates contend, victims of hate crimes typically suffer

greater injury than victims of crimes with other motives.

Critics counter that most hate crimes involve not hard-core homophobia or racism, but impulsive and situational behaviour, often involving juveniles. Even more important, critics maintain, hate-crime law is a direct threat to free speech. Under such a law, they explain, courts sentence offenders not just for actions but for underlying attitudes. As Harvard law professor Alan Dershowitz cautions, 'As much as I hate bigotry, I fear much more the Court attempting to control the minds of its citizens.' In short, according to the critics, hate-crime statutes open the door to punishing beliefs rather than behaviour. ●

See Gregory M. Herek and Kevin T. Berrill, *Hate Crimes* (Beverly Hills: Sage, 1992).
Sources: Greenhouse, 1993; Jacobs, 1993; and Terry, 1993.

at least, this goal has had more to do with the lives of men, while women have been socialised to view success in terms of relationships, particularly marriage and motherhood (Leonard, 1982). A more woman-focused theory might point up the 'strain' caused by the cultural ideals of equality clashing with the reality of gender-based inequality. It could help us see that different forms of deviance may emerge for women: those that are linked to marriage and motherhood. Indeed, women who do not marry ('spinsters') and who do not have children are often seen as 'problems' (see Hutter and Williams, 1981; Smart, 1984; Richardson, 1993).

Labelling theory, the major approach in symbolic-interaction analysis, offers greater insight into ways in which gender influences how we define deviance. To

the extent that we judge the behaviour of females and males by different standards, the very process of labelling involves sex-linked biases. Further, because society generally places men in positions of power over women, men often escape direct responsibility for actions that victimise women. In the past, at least, men engaging in sexual harassment or other assaults against women have been tagged with only mildly deviant labels, if they have been punished at all.

But feminist criminologists have gone much further than reappraising past theories. They have opened up a whole field of new questions and issues. Amongst the issues have been: the importance of the fear of crime in women's, and especially older women's, lives (see Chapter 14); the gendering of sexual violence, and especially the growth of domestic violence, rape and incest (see Chapter 17); and the gendering of social control. This last topic concerns the ways in which women are handled differently by police, courts and prisons – often through a code of chivalry or through a mechanism by which women are pathologised and rendered as having medical problems. The classic debate here suggested that whilst men became criminals, women went mad! Feminist criminologies have thrown critical thought over such statements (see Busfield, 1997).

One further contribution of feminist criminology has been to raise the issue of men, violence and masculinity. They have suggested that since more men are involved in violent crimes, and more young men are involved in 'yob culture', there may be a link between forms of masculinity and forms of crime.

Race and ethnicity

Race and ethnicity have been correlated both to crime victimisation and to crime rates. In the UK, for instance, ethnic minorities are more likely to be victims of crimes than the white population: some 26 per cent of all black households are likely to be a victim of theft compared to 20 per cent of white households. The figures are 22 per cent for those of Indian origin, and 25 per cent for Pakistani/Bangladeshi origin (Morgan and Newburn, 1997: 27)

Looking at crime rates in the UK, in 1995 people of Afro-Caribbean origin made up around 1.5 per cent of the total population, but 11 per cent of males in prison. For women, the figure was of greater disparity – some 20 per cent of women in prisons are Afro-Caribbean. For other ethnic groups in the UK, the figures are different: thus south Asians account for 2.7 per cent of the population and about 3 per cent of the prison population.

In the USA, the figures are even more striking – and more alarming. Official statistics indicate that 66.9 per cent of arrests for crimes in 1993 involved white people. However, arrests of African Americans were higher than for whites in proportion to their numbers: black people represent 12.5 per cent of the population and 33.2 per cent of arrests for property crimes (versus 64.4 per cent for whites) and 45.7 per cent of arrests for violent crimes (52.6 per cent for whites) (US Federal Bureau of Investigation, 1994).

What accounts for the disproportionate level of arrests among Afro-Caribbeans and African Americans? Several factors stand out. To the degree that prejudice related to colour or class prompts white police to arrest black people more readily and leads citizens more willingly to report 'blacks' to police as suspected offenders, people of colour are overly criminalised (Liska and Tausig, 1979; Unnever, Frazier and Henretta, 1980; Smith and Visher, 1981; Holmes et al., 1993). In the UK, a 'stop and search' policy shows that in 1994–5, 22 per cent of people from ethnic minorities (compared with 5 per cent of the population) were stopped and searched: the figure in London was 37 per cent. This certainly suggests that 'blacks' are more likely to be placed under suspicion (ISTD Factsheet, 1997).

Second, race is closely linked to inequalities (see Chapter 12), and as we have seen above, many of the categories of crime suggest that crime is linked to inequality. Criminality is promoted by the sting of being poor in the midst of affluence as poor people come to perceive society as unjust. Looking only at the US figures, unemployment among African-American adults is double the rate among whites, two-thirds of black children are born to single mothers (in contrast to one in five white children), and almost half of black

The creators of this photograph, part of the United Colours of Benetton advertising campaign, intended to make the statement that people are linked together regardless of colour. But so strong are our notions about crime and ethnicity that many individuals mistakenly interpreted the photograph as a white police officer escorting a black suspect. What can sociology contribute toward a more accurate understanding of the connection between crime and ethnicity?

Source: Benetton USA, Corp.

children grow up in poverty (as opposed to about one in six white children). With these patterns of inequality, no one should be too surprised at proportionately higher crime rates for African Americans (Sampson, 1987). And the broad pattern also holds for the UK.

Third, remember that the official crime index excludes arrests for offences ranging from drunk driving to white-collar violations. Clearly, this omission contributes to the view of the typical criminal as a person of colour. If we broaden our definition of crime to include driving while intoxicated, insider stock trading, embezzlement and cheating on income tax returns, the proportion of white criminals rises dramatically.

Finally, some categories of the population have unusually low rates of arrest. People of south Asian descent, who account for about 3 per cent of the population, figure in only 1 per cent of all arrests. As Chapter 12 ('Race, Ethnicity and Migration') documents, south Asians enjoy higher than average incomes and have established a more successful record of educational achievement, which enhances job opportunities. Moreover, the cultural patterns that characterise Asian communities emphasise family solidarity and discipline, both of which inhibit criminality.

● Crime and crime statistics

Recent years have shown a persistent increase in the growth of crime. Indeed, there was a remarkably low rate of crime in the UK until the 1950s and the 1960s, when it took off most significantly. There was an annual recorded figure of roughly 100,000 recorded offences between 1876 and 1920, growing to half a million by 1950, two and a half million in 1980, and well over 5 million in 1990. But, apart from not taking the significant population increases into account, such figures can be seriously misleading in a number of ways. We will discuss these problems below.

Criminal statistics

Statistics gathered by the Home Office and published annually as *Criminal Statistics in England and Wales* show that crime rates have largely been rising in recent decades, although the total amount of recorded crime has fallen a little since 1990 (*Social Trends*, 1997: 153). The peaking of noticeable offences to the police was 10.5 for every 100 people in 1992. (It was 9.5 per 100 in 1995.)

In the United States, the crime rate is extremely high: during the 1990s, police have tallied some 8 million serious crimes annually. But, as in the UK, there is evidence that crime rates have been levelling off, and even falling, in recent times. As we shall see below, however, there are real problems in knowing exactly what criminal statistics such as the above mean.

Types of crime

From reading the newspapers you could easily believe that sexual and violent crimes were everywhere. In fact, 93 per cent of all recorded crimes in England and Wales are property offences – and often linked to theft of or from cars. Whilst killings attract much attention, they account for around 600 or 700 offences a year, and well over a half of these are 'domestic'. The isolated street murder is therefore relatively rare in the UK. Looking at criminal statistics, the following generalisations may be made:

● Households found in inner cities are most likely to be victims of burglaries (twice as likely as elsewhere)

● Young adults between 14 and 20 account for 4 in 10 offenders

● Most offenders have already been convicted of an offence (7 in 10 males in 1994)

● The peak age for offending for males in 1995 was 18 (almost 9 per cent)

● A small proportion of offenders are responsible for a large proportion of offences

● The number of girls and women found guilty of indictable offences is significantly lower for all indictable offences (see Table 8.2).

Problems of measuring crime

The crime statistics presented above – like all statistics – must be read with extreme caution. One way of understanding the construction of crime statistics is to see them like a flow, through which smaller and smaller numbers of offences get counted. This is presented in Figure 8.3 which shows the process of reporting and recording crimes. We start with a very large pool of actual offences where the numbers are unknown and unknowable. There is then a sharp drop in numbers at each stage. It seems likely that as little as 2 in 100 offences result in a conviction. The *hidden*

Table 8.2 ● Offenders found guilty of, or cautioned for, indictable offences: by gender, type of offence and age, 1995

England and Wales						Percentages
	10–13	14–17	18–20	21–34	35 and over	All aged 10 and over (=100%) (thousands)
Males						
Theft and handling stolen goods	8	24	16	37	15	160.9
Drug offences	—	13	24	53	10	71.9
Burglary	8	30	20	37	5	43.9
Violence against the person	4	21	14	43	17	41.8
Criminal damage	10	24	15	39	12	12.2
Sexual offences	4	14	8	30	45	6.8
Robbery	7	36	19	32	6	5.3
Other indictable offences	1	8	17	58	17	52.4
All indictable offences	5	20	18	43	14	395.2
Females						
Theft and handling stolen goods	12	28	12	32	16	60.1
Drug offences	—	10	19	56	16	7.9
Burglary	12	43	15	24	4	1.9
Violence against the person	8	36	11	34	12	7.7
Criminal damage	8	27	13	35	17	1.2
Sexual offences	6	13	6	50	24	0.1
Robbery	7	55	16	20	2	0.5
Other indictable offences	—	9	15	59	16	5.0
All indictable offences	10	26	13	36	15	84.4

Source: Home Office

amount of crime – that does not get into the statistics – is called the **dark figure**.

Official statistics of 'recorded crimes' only include crimes reported to the police. (But they may not include all the crimes reported – some, for instance, may not be crimes or may be very trivial.) So getting crimes reported is the first key issue in statistic construction and, quite clearly, not all crimes are reported, though this differs with offence. The police learn about almost nearly all killings, but assaults – especially among acquaintances – are far less likely to be reported. The police record an even smaller proportion of property crimes, especially when losses are small. Some victims may not realise that a crime has occurred, or they may assume they have little chance of recovering their property even if they notify the police. And reports of rape, although rising over time, still grossly understate the extent of this crime.

The majority of crimes come to police attention by being reported by the public (about 90 per cent). Their responsiveness is shaped by such issues as:

● tolerance of certain kinds of crimes (such as vandalism)

● seriousness of offence (such as very minor thefts or brawls)

● confidence in the police ('nothing can be done')

● crimes without victims (such as drug offences)

● awareness that it is a crime (for example, some fraud)

There are alternative ways of measuring crime (and by implication, considering the reliability of official crime statistics). One is through a *victimisation survey*, in which a researcher asks a representative sample of

Figure 8.3 ● Attrition within the criminal justice system

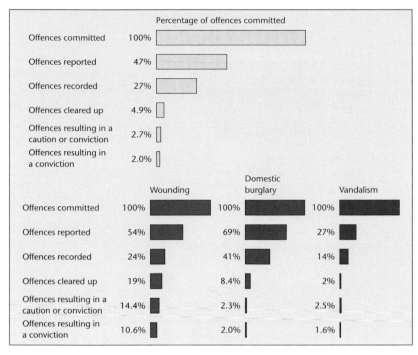

Source: Morgan and Newburn, *The Future of Policing*, Oxford University Press, 1997, p. 36

people about their experience with crime. People do not always respond fully or truthfully to such surveys, experts acknowledge, but the results of these surveys indicate that actual criminality occurs at a rate two or three times higher than what official reports suggest.

In England, since 1982, there has been a regular major victim survey of crime: the *British Crime Surveys*. Here a random sample of about 5,000 adults are asked questions about being victims of crime, whether they reported the crimes or not, and their fear of crime. These studies raise further doubts about the value of crime statistics, as they have persistently shown both much higher rates and significant discrepancies for different kinds of crime. At the same time, these figures also suggest that the overall growth of crime may have been exaggerated, since crime statistics are so dependent on the vagaries of reporting.

A second way of measuring crime is through *self reporting* studies. Here a sample of people are asked about the crimes they have committed and whether these were reported or not. Thus, for example, The Youth Lifestyles Survey (YLS) conducted in the UK in 1992–3 suggested that offending is much more widespread amongst young people. One in four males aged

18–21 admitted to a theft or burglary, and 1 in 8 females aged 14–17 (*Social Trends*, 1997: 159). Those with single-parent or step families were more likely to commit.

● **Crime in global perspective**

Because it is impossible to be accurate about measuring crime in any one society such as the UK, it becomes even harder to compare crimes across cultures. In many low-income countries, the data are significantly flawed anyway. Despite these problems, crime rates do appear to differ significantly throughout the world (Figure 8.4).

Thus, although violent crime is significantly on the increase in many countries of Europe – especially in Germany, France and the UK, the violent crime rate in the United States generally emerges as about five times greater; and the rate of property crime is twice as high. With differences as great as this, it seems reasonable to conclude that crime is higher in the USA than in Europe. But the contrast may be even greater with many nations of Asia, including India and Japan, where rates of violent and property crime seem to be amongst the lowest in the world. In Iran, and many Muslim countries, rates of crime are generally low.

Yet in some of the largest cities of the world, like Manila in the Philippines and São Paulo in Brazil, crime rates appear to be soaring. These are the cities that have rapid population growth and millions of desperately poor people (see Chapter 22). By and large, however, the traditional character of less economically developed societies and their strong family structure allow local communities to control crime informally (Clinard and Abbott, 1973; *Der Spiegel*, 1989).

The globalisation of deviance

As noted in earlier chapters, we are experiencing 'globalisation' on many fronts, including crime and deviance. Some types of crime have always been multinational, including terrorism, espionage and arms

Figure 8.4 ● **Perceptions of crime across the world**

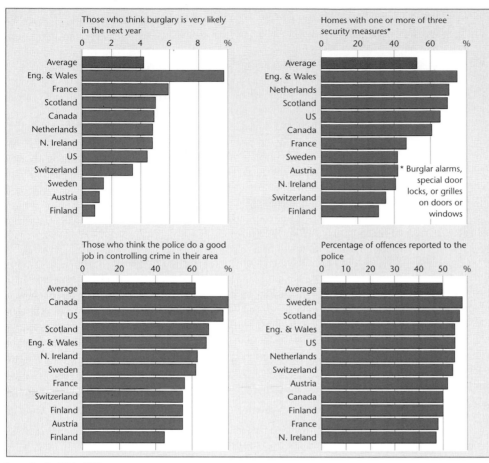

Source: *Guardian*, 27 May 1997

then, understanding crimes such as drug dealing requires analysing social conditions both in the country of consumption and around the world. More and more, the comprehension of crime and deviance requires moving beyond the borders of one country to look at a host of international connections.

● **The social control system**

A **social control system** involves *planned and programmed responses to expected deviance* (Cohen, 1985: 2). At the most visible level, this involves the police, the courts and punishments, from prisons to probation. The criminal justice system is a society's formal response to crime. In some countries, military police keep a tight rein on people's behaviour; in others, officials have more limited powers to respond to specific violations of criminal law. But there are also less visible networks of control: from the monitoring done by social workers and psychiatrists to the closed circuit surveillance in shops and shopping centres, the development of electronic tagging and the rise of private policing. Some of these will be discussed below.

Key features of the modern Western control system – often called 'penality' – emerged at the end of the eighteenth century. Although, for instance, jails existed prior to this time, they were not the large scale places with individual cells and strict rules that exist

dealing (Martin and Romano, 1992). But newer ones are appearing as crimes travel through countries and know no borders.

A case in point is the illegal drug trade. In part, the proliferation of illegal drugs in the United States and Europe stems from 'demand': there is a very profitable market for cocaine and other drugs, as well as many young people willing to risk arrest or even violent death by engaging in the lucrative drug trade. But the 'supply' side of the issue also propels drug trafficking. In the South American nation of Colombia, at least 20 per cent of the people depend on cocaine production for their livelihood. Furthermore, not only is cocaine Colombia's most profitable export, but it outsells all other exports combined (including coffee). Clearly,

Homegrown drugs in The Netherlands: changing drugs policies

Amsterdam is known as 'Europe's drugs capital'. Since 1976 it has operated a policy of 'decriminalisation' for soft drugs, making it a misdemeanour and not a crime. Individuals can own up to 30 grams of marijuana or hashish, which can be purchased in coffee shops (which are not allowed to deal in any kind of hard drug) and grown at home. The aim of this highly liberal and pragmatic policy (to be contrasted with the one described at the start of this chapter) is prevention and harm reduction: reducing the dangers to both community and the individual.

The key distinction in this policy is that between hard and soft drugs. Hard drugs are seen as very harmful and must be prohibited; soft drugs are much less harmful and may even be less harmful than currently permitted 'drugs' like cigarettes (nicotine) and drink (alcohol). They are only a danger for specific groups (like children) and are not likely to lead to escalation. Indeed, there are an estimated 675,000 people in The Netherlands who smoke soft drugs; but only 25,000 are involved with cocaine. By contrast, rates of use are much higher in most of Europe where the 'addict rate' is 2.7 people per thousand. In The Netherlands, it is 1.6 and there are few signs of pot leading to harder drugs.

At various times the Dutch government has argued that it would like soft drugs to be completely legal so that prices would fall and criminal connections would be disconnected. Soft drugs, it is argued, only need the kinds of controls that have been routinely applied to alcohol (such restrictions as age limits, driving restrictions and advertising restrictions).

Most other countries condemn the Dutch policy on drugs, not least because it has an impact upon them. They argue that it weakens international prohibitions; that it encourages drugs tourism (people crossing borders seeking 'better class drugs', which are more accessible and cheaper); that it makes too simple a distinction between hard and soft drugs; and ultimately that it does not drive out organised criminal networks.

The mounting criticisms, and a concern about its international reputation, has recently made The Netherlands start to reconsider its policies. ●

Source: Maris, 1996

now. Instead they were smaller, local and held crowds of people who were undifferentiated by crime and offence. Often they were just 'holding places' on the way to the gallows (cf. Ignatieff, 1978). Likewise, policing was organised on a local basis. Only in 1829 was the Metropolitan Police force established in England.

But, with industrialisation and the emergence of the modern world, all this changed. *Control processes became subject to bureaucratisation, professionalisation and State funding.* Thus, control became organised through bureaucratic, rule bound organisations run by new professions such as prison officers and policemen, and central government started to play a significant role in legislation and in the funding of control. In 1995–6, in England and Wales, £6.6 billion was spent on the police (a third higher than 1986), and £1.7 bil-

lion was spent on prisons. Some 198,000 people were employed by the police (as well as 57,000 civilians, and 21,000 Special Constables), and 40,000 by the prison service (double on 1971). This scale is mirrored in most other industrial countries: everywhere social control today is a large part of public/State spending.

Foucault's classic book *Discipline and Punish: The Birth of the Prison* (1975) depicts this change dramatically. In the striking opening pages – well worth a read! – he compares the earlier forms of brutal and chaotic punishment on the body with the more recent forms of surveillance and imprisonment which are intensely rule governed. As he says, it is the difference between the spectacle of a *public execution* and a *timetable*. The former leads to the following normal event in 1757:

on a scaffold that will be erected (at the Place de Grève), the flesh will be torn from his breasts, arms, thighs and calves with red hot pincer, his right hand . . . burnt with sulphur, and, on those places where the flesh will be torn away, poured molten lead, boiling oil, burning resin, wax and sulphur melted together and then his body drawn and quartered by four horses and his limbs and body consumed by fire, reduced to ashes and thrown to the winds . . . (Foucault, 1977: 3)

while the latter leads, eighty years on, to:

Art. 17. The prisoners' day will begin at six in the morning in winter and at five in the summer . . . they will work for nine hours a day. . . .

Art 18. Rising. At the first drum roll, the prisoners must rise and dress in silence . . . at the second drum-roll, they must be dressed and make their beds. At the third, they must line up and proceed to the chapel for morning prayer . . .

Art 19. The prayers are conducted by the chaplain and followed by a moral or religious reading. This exercise must not last more than half an hour . . . (Foucault, 1977: 6)

The differences in systems of control are clearly illustrated.

Emerging control patterns

The modern control system may be characterised in three ways. First, the old system of public control financed by the state of prisons and policing laid down during the nineteenth century has continued to expand. New prisons are being built and in some countries prison populations have increased dramatically.

Second, a new and largely informal system of control has been grafted on to this. This brings an ever increasing number of people into the control network. Young offenders for instance who were once cautioned may now be placed on a community care order or required to attend some form of therapy group. The British criminologist, Anthony Bottoms has called these first two developments the bifurcation of the system: 'put crudely, this bifurcation is between, on the one hand the so called "really serious offender" for whom very tough measures are typically advocated; and on the other hand, the "ordinary offender" for whom we can afford to take a much more lenient line' (Bottoms, 1983).

Third, the system overall has expanded greatly to include a wide range of surveillance techniques, and many of these are privately sponsored and funded. For some, the modern world can be characterised as a surveillance society: whoever says modernity says surveillance. In non-industrial societies, surveillance operates in an informal manner, often through primary groups (see Chapter 7). But larger organisations require a much more complex monitoring of events. Since the rise of industrial society, more and more energy has been given over to collecting records on the lives of citizens and monitoring their behaviour.

Most noticeable here has been the dramatic increase in closed circuit television (CCTV) in recent years. In shops, on motorways and in all kinds of public places, surveillance can now take place 24 hours a day, 365 days a year. Crime detection is no longer dependent upon the police being called; they can systematically monitor and video record crimes, sending appropriate squads to deal with them.

New digital technologies can also put faces into an electronic file of suspects so that previous shoplifters in stores can be identified as soon as they enter! Developing systems are also going to be able to electronically identify people through the unique iris patterns in their eyes or through their unique voices. This could mean, for example, that passports or credit cards will become things of the past, as features of our body are digitally scanned as a unique identifying personal bar code!

But not all surveillance operates so formally. Another interesting development has been the informal operation of Neighbourhood Watch Schemes. Starting in 1983, there has been an enormous growth in the numbers of people who want to watch over their communities. By 1996, it was estimated there were some 143,000 schemes in the UK (Morgan and Newburn, 1997: 62)

The downside of all this, of course, is a civil liberties concern: we may never quite know who is watching us; or when; or where. George Orwell's nightmare world of 1984 may finally be upon us (Criminal Justice Matters, No. 20, 1995).

In sum, there has been a major expansion in social control and surveillance in modern societies. Boundaries of control are being blurred and many new deviants are being 'created' through this system.

Prisons

Prisons seem to be expanding and growing in nearly all countries. Nils Christie calls this the 'Prison Industrial Complex'. There has been a massive

Michel Foucault: power and surveillance

The French philosopher Michel Foucault 1926–1984 is one of the late twentieth century's most influential thinkers. He has examined a number of major changes that mark out the distinctive ways we think in 'the modern world' when compared with past ones; and he has developed an important theory of power–knowledge–discourse.

Always a radical and critical thinker, he saw dramatic ruptures with the past and suggested that these modern developments are not signs of simple 'enlightened' progress, but rather evidence of extending power and increasing surveillance. For Foucault, power is everywhere and works its way through **discourses** – *bodies of ideas and language often backed up by institutions.* Thus, criminology is a discourse that invents or produces its own set of ideas and languages about the criminal as an object to be studied, backed up by many institutions like the prison and the courts. Power works its way distinctly

through this discourse to help shape the whole society's view of crime. 'Knowledge' in this view may act as a way of keeping people under control.

His work looks at such changes as (1) the appearance of the modern prison along with the rise of criminology; (2) the 'birth of the clinic' as a distinctly modern way of handling health; (3) the development of the psychiatric discourse and modern approaches to madness, through grasping the appearance of a very distinctive modern way of reasoning; and (4) the development of our modern languages around sexu-

Source: Network Photographers – Carlos Friere

ality. Very wide ranging, he even asks questions about the very idea of what it means to be an 'individual' human being in Western societies.

Many of Foucault's ideas challenge common sense. He argues, for instance, the following. That 'sexuality' has not always existed: it is a creation of the modern world. That prisons, far from solving the crime problem, actually extend it.

His most accessible book is *Discipline and Punish* (1977), in which he traced the development of the modern prison system. A brief extract from this is given in the text.

His ideas are controversial and much discussed. Some say he was one of the most brilliant figures of twentieth century thought. Others feel that his difficult writing and complexity has detracted from engagement with what is happening in the world. For an introduction to Foucault's work, see Barry Smart, *Michel Foucault* (London: Routledge, 1985). ●

expansion in numbers going to prison, as well as numbers of prisons (see Figure 8.5).

The United States is frequently cited as the most extreme case. Its prison population doubled between 1985 and 1995, with some 1.6 million inmates, enough to fill a medium-sized city like Philadelphia (Young, 1997: 37). In June 1994, the number sentenced to more than a year was as high as 373 prisoners per 100,000 of the population – double on the previous decade. (Roughly 1 in 37 was under some

form of correctional supervision.) The cost of the US prison service was astronomical – in 1990 something around $20 billion (James et al., 1997: 1–2).

In Europe, the trend may not be quite so developed (Figure 8.5). Indeed, some countries like Sweden, Norway and The Netherlands have long been seen as having the most humane and contained prison systems in the world. But even here, in recent years, there have been significant changes. Prison use is on the increase and the treatment of prisoners is getting worse. For instance in the Netherlands in 1975, there were 2,356 prison cells and the rate of imprisonment was 17 per 100,000. By the end of 1996, there were 12,000 prisoners and a rate of nearly 80 per 100,000. (Stern, 1997: 6). The UK had the second largest prison population in Europe: with nearly 60,000 and a rate of 100 per 100,000 (Matthews, 1977: 15). Portugal had the largest prison population overall.

Imprisonment has become a mega industry and a system in crisis in the late twentieth century. Part of this may be due to new policies such as the 'three strikes' policy (first introduced in Washington in 1992) which produces a mandatory life sentence after three offences. Part of this may also be due to a decisive penal shift in many countries to be 'tough on crime and tough on the causes of crime'. There has been a clear shift from policies of rehabilitation to policies of punishment over the past decade.

Privatising prisons

In the late twentieth century, there has been a turn away from State investment in prisons towards privatisation. Although private arrangements for running prisons can be traced back some time (for instance to early arrangements of labour leasing – the chain gangs), since the early 1990s more and more countries have come to see privatisation as one fruitful way of handling the 'penal crisis'.

Initially, privatisation was applied in the United States to the 'soft end' of the control process – to small facilities for juveniles, low security prisons and women's prisons. The first contracted-out house for juveniles was in 1975 in Pennsylvania. A little later, Corrections Corporation of America (CCA) and Wakenhut started getting contracts for adult prisons.

Those in favour of private prisons argued that they were more economic, more flexible and more efficient – they provided new and better facilities and costs were reduced in both prison building and operations. Critics suggested it was 'punishment for profit'. It was an area where markets and profits could be against the public and individual good.

The system has grown throughout the world. Most extensively it has been taken up in Australia, but most European countries take it seriously too. France has had one of the strongest involvements, with at least 17 private institutions accommodating over 10,000 prisoners. But privatisation is also to be found in Germany, The Netherlands and the UK (see James et al., 1997).

Punishment

In the autumn of 1994, Iraqi television offered viewers in Baghdad special coverage of the punishment meted out to a man convicted of theft. Viewers saw a close-up of a severed human hand, followed by the offender staggering in pain as he clutched the stump of his forearm. Careful observers could also see a black cross that had been branded on his forehead.

Barbaric? Maybe. But this televised punishment was a desperate act by Iraq's leaders to control a rising tide of theft, and it highlights key questions surrounding the act of punishment. Why do governments punish at all? If punishment is necessary, how should it be carried out?

First, the point of punishment. On this score, four justifications for punishment are made.

Retribution

The celebrated justice of the US Supreme Court, Oliver Wendell Holmes, stated: 'The first requirement of a sound body of law is that it should correspond with

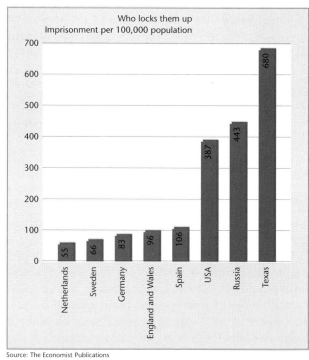

Figure 8.5 ● Imprisonment across the world

Who locks them up
Imprisonment per 100,000 population

- Netherlands 55
- Sweden 66
- Germany 83
- England and Wales 96
- Spain 106
- USA 387
- Russia 443
- Texas 680

Source: The Economist Publications

The prison population in the UK increased by 50 per cent in the 1990s to record breaking figures. It now has the largest prison population in Europe (over 60,000) except for Portugal. So significant was the growth that new prisons had to be found like this first prison boat which the Conservative government brought to Portland Harbour in 1997.

Source: Photoflight

the actual feelings and demands of the community.' Because people react to crime with a passion for revenge, Holmes continued, 'the law has no choice but to satisfy [that] craving' (quoted in Carlson, 1976).

One key reason to punish, then, is to satisfy a society's need for **retribution** or *moral vengeance by which society inflicts suffering on the offender comparable to that caused by the offence*. Retribution rests on a view of society as a moral entity in balance. When criminality upsets this balance, punishment exacted in comparable measure restores the moral order, as suggested by the biblical dictum 'An eye for an eye'.

Retribution stands as the oldest justification for punishment. During the Middle Ages, most people viewed crime as sin – an offence against God as well as society – that warranted a harsh response. Today, critics charge that retribution does little to reform the offender; even so, this principle retains widespread support.

Deterrence

A second justification for punishment, **deterrence**, amounts to *the attempt to discourage criminality through punishment*. Deterrence reflects the eighteenth century Enlightenment notion that, as calculating and rational creatures, humans will forgo deviance if they perceive that the pain of punishment outweighs the pleasure of mischief.

Deterrence emerged as reform directed at the harsh punishments based on retribution. Why cut off a hand for stealing, critics asked, if theft can be discouraged with a prison sentence? As the concept of deterrence gained acceptance, execution and physical mutilation of criminals in most industrial societies were replaced by milder forms of punishment such as incarceration.

Punishment may deter crime in two ways. *Specific deterrence* demonstrates to an individual offender that crime does not pay. Through *general deterrence*, the punishment of one person serves as an example to others.

Rehabilitation

The third justification for punishment is **rehabilitation**, *a programme for reforming the offender to preclude subsequent offences*. Rehabilitation paralleled the development of the social sciences in the nineteenth century. According to sociologists of that time (and also since), crime and other deviance spring from an unfavourable environment marked by poverty or a lack of parental supervision. Logically, then, if offenders learn to be deviant, they can also learn to obey the rules; the key is controlling the environment. *Reformatories* or *houses of correction* served as a controlled setting to help people learn proper behaviour (recall the description of total institutions in Chapter 5, 'Socialisation').

Rehabilitation resembles deterrence in that both motivate the offender toward conformity. But rehabilitation emphasises constructive improvement, while deterrence (like retribution) inflicts suffering on an offender. In addition, while retribution demands that the punishment fit the crime, rehabilitation tailors treatment to the offender. Thus identical crimes would prompt similar acts of retribution but might call for different programmes of rehabilitation.

Societal protection

A final justification for punishment is **societal protection**, *a means by which society renders an offender incapable of further offences temporarily through incarceration or permanently by execution*. Like deterrence, societal protection is a rational approach to punishment and seeks to protect society from crime.

Table 8.3 ● Four justifications of punishment: a summary

Retribution	The oldest justification of punishment that still holds sway today. Punishment is atonement for a moral wrong by an individual; in principle, punishment should be comparable in severity to the deviance itself.
Deterrence	An early modern approach. Deviance is considered social disruption, which society acts to control. People are viewed as rational and self-interested; deterrence works because the pains of punishment outweigh the pleasures of deviance.
Rehabilitation	A modern strategy linked to the development of social sciences. Deviance is viewed as the product of social problems (such as poverty) or personal problems (such as mental illness). Social conditions are improved and offenders subjected to intervention appropriate to their condition.
Societal protection	A modern approach easier to implement than rehabilitation. If society is unable or unwilling to rehabilitate offenders or reform social conditions, people are protected from further deviance by incarceration or execution of the offender.

Table 8.3 summarises these four justifications of punishment.

Critical evaluation

We have identified four justifications for punishment. Assessing the actual consequences of punishment, however, is no simple task.

The value of retribution reminds us of Durkheim's contention that punishing the deviant person bolsters people's moral consciousness. To accomplish this objective, punishment was traditionally a public event. Public executions occurred in England until 1868; the last public execution in the United States took place in Kentucky in 1937. Even today, the mass media ensure public awareness of executions carried out inside prison walls (Kittrie, 1971). Nonetheless, it is difficult to prove scientifically that punishment upholds social morality. Often it advances one conception of justice at the expense of another, as when our government imprisons people who refuse to perform military service.

To some degree, punishment serves as a specific deterrent (Wright, 1994). Yet US and European society also have high rates of **criminal recidivism**, *subsequent offences committed by people previously convicted of crimes*. A 1991 study of US state prison inmates found that 62 per cent had been imprisoned before, and 45 per cent had been sentenced three or more times (US Bureau of Justice Statistics, 1991). Put more simply, once released from jail, half of the former inmates return to prison within several years. Such a high rate of recidivism raises questions about the extent to which punishment actually deters crime. Then, too, only about one-third of all crimes are known to police and, of these, only about one in five results in an arrest. The old adage that 'crime doesn't pay' rings rather hollow when we consider that such a small proportion of offences ever result in punishment.

General deterrence is even more difficult to investigate scientifically, since we have no way of knowing how people might act if they were unaware of punishments meted out to others. In the US debate over capital punishment, which is permitted in 36 states, critics of the practice point to research indicating that the death penalty has limited value as a general deterrent in the United States, which is the only Western industrial society that routinely executes serious offenders (Sellin, 1980; van den Haag and Conrad, 1983; Archer and Gartner, 1987; Lester, 1987; Bailey and Peterson, 1989; Bailey, 1990; Bohm, 1991).

Prisons accomplish short-term societal protection by keeping offenders off the streets, but they do little to reshape attitudes or behaviour in the long term (Carlson, 1976; Wright, 1994). Rehabilitation may be an unrealistic expectation, since, according to Sutherland's theory of differential association, locking someone up among criminals for months or years should simply strengthen criminal attitudes and skills. And because imprisonment severs whatever social ties inmates may have in the outside world, individuals may be prone to further crime upon their release, consistent with Hirschi's control theory.

So what can be done about crime?

People across Europe are fearful – and fed up – with crime. Dogs for protection, special locks and security systems have never been more popular. Fear of crime is on the increase: many adults are afraid to walk alone at night in the vicinity of their own homes. Government spending on crime prevention has risen steadily over the past few decades, but so has the crime rate. What is to be done?

Travis Hirschi, sociologist and author of the well-known 'control theory', recently offered the radical suggestion that we abandon the criminal justice system as we know it in favour of a new approach. Although his proposals will surely be controversial, they are grounded in decades of research about crime and offenders.

Hirschi begins by pointing out two key characteristics that define the population of criminal offenders. The first is age; specifically, crime is a young person's (typically a young man's) game. Crime rates are high in the late teens and early twenties, and they fall quickly thereafter. Second, Hirschi continues, offenders are individuals who take a short-term view of their lives. Most law breakers, claims Hirschi, are individuals 'relatively unable to sustain a course of action toward some distant goal, whether that goal be education, friendship, employment or criminal gain. In fact, the defining characteristic of offenders appears to be low self-control.'

These two facts alone, he reasons, mean the criminal justice system, as it currently operates, is not up to the task. For one thing, punishment from the courts is too uncertain (most crimes, after all, go unpunished), and too far removed in time (arrest, trial and imprisonment of criminals often takes a year or more) to deter the typical offender. Thus, Hirschi explains, popular calls for 'stiffer sentences' actually have little effect in suppressing crime. And even when offenders are sent off to prison, all but the small percentage of habitual offenders are cared for at the taxpayer's expense at a time when they are moving beyond the peak 'crime years' simply because they are growing older. Statistically speaking, then, offenders ageing in prison represent a crime threat already shrinking on its own.

Therefore, rather than trying to incapacitate or rehabilitate adults, society would better protect itself by adopting a whole new approach. Hirschi reasons that we must intervene earlier, directing resources towards young people before they commit crimes. One proposal he advances is to restrict the unsupervised activities of teenagers – those at highest risk of criminal behaviour. Effective crime control, he explains, depends on regulating the access of teenagers not only to guns and drugs, but also to alcohol, cars and perhaps even to each other.

A second initiative takes effect even earlier in the life course. The most effective way to control crime, Hirschi concludes, is for our society to raise children who learn the key trait of self-control. Teaching children to understand the long-term consequences of their behaviour is a task ill-suited to government, Hirschi cautions; it is the responsibility of parents. But government can help by targeting seriously dysfunctional fami-lies for assistance and by any other means that fosters strong – preferably two-parent – families. Simply 'delaying pregnancy among teenage girls', he predicts, 'would probably do more to affect long-term crime rates than all the criminal justice programs combined'. By increasing the number of caregivers relative to children, Hirschi concludes, society would increase the care and educational resources available to our children and, in the process, protect everyone from crime.

Proposals of this kind will surely provoke criticism. If we reduce support for police and prisons, don't we risk a further outbreak of crime? Without locking up today's offenders, how can we satisfy our society's desire for retribution? Shouldn't we attack the broader conditions that breed crime, such as poverty and racial prejudice? And is it fair to curb the civil rights of all teenagers just so that some would be prevented from committing crimes?

● **Continue the debate:**

1. Do you think limiting teenagers' freedom would reduce crime? What civil rights issues are raised by such a plan?

2. Do you think increasing the share of two-parent households would cut the crime rate? Can society realistically shape families in this way?

3. Would economic programmes directed at reducing poverty diminish the crime problem? What specific programmes would you suggest? ●

Source: Based on Gottfredson and Hirschi, 1995.

Finally, inmates returning to the surrounding world contend with the stigma of being ex-prisoners, often an obstacle to successful integration. One study of young offenders in Philadelphia found that boys who were sentenced to long prison terms – and thus likely to acquire a criminal stigma – later committed both more crimes and more serious ones (Wolfgang, Figlio, and Sellin, 1972).

Ultimately, we should never assume that the criminal justice system – the police, courts and prisons – can eliminate crime. The point here, made strongly in the final box as it has been throughout this chapter, is simple: crime and all other deviance are more than simply the acts of 'bad people'; they are inextricably bound up with the operation of society itself.

SUMMARY

1. Deviance refers to normative violations ranging from mild breaches of etiquette to serious violence.

2. Biological investigation, from Caesare Lombroso's nineteenth century observations of convicts to recent research in human genetics, has yet to offer much insight into the causes of crime.

3. Psychological study links deviance to abnormal personality stemming from either biological or environmental causes. Psychological theories help to explain some kinds of deviance.

4. Deviance has societal rather than individual roots because it (1) exists in relation to cultural norms, (2) results from a process of social definition, and (3) is shaped by the distribution of social power.

5. Using the structural-functional paradigm, Durkheim asserted that responding to deviance affirms values and norms, clarifies moral boundaries, promotes social unity and encourages social change.

6. The symbolic-interaction paradigm is the basis of labelling theory, which holds that deviance arises in the reaction of others to a person's behaviour. Acquiring a stigma of deviance can lead to secondary deviance and the onset of a deviant career.

7. Following the approach of Karl Marx, social-conflict theory holds that laws and other norms reflect the interests of powerful members of society. Social-conflict theory also spotlights white-collar crimes, which cause extensive social harm even though the offenders are rarely branded as criminals.

8. Official statistics are not reliable, and reflect a number of social processes. Alternatives to these statistics include victim surveys like the British Crime Survey.

9. Official statistics indicate that arrest rates peak in late adolescence, then drop steadily with advancing age. Three-quarters of those arrested for property crimes are males, as are almost nine out of ten people charged with violent crimes.

10. Afro-Caribbeans are arrested more often than whites in proportion to their respective populations.

11. Feminist criminology has grown as a response to a neglect of gender issues in the study of crime. It has led to many new developments, including the study of masculinity and its link to criminality; and the gendering of social control processes.

12. Social control has seen three major developments: the old system expands; a new one is grafted on; and surveillance increases.

13. Modern societies are surveillance societies.

14. There has been a significantly expansion of prison populations throughout the world, along with the introduction of the privatisation of prisons.

15. Justifications for punishment include retribution, deterrence, rehabilitation and societal protection. Because its consequences are difficult to evaluate scientifically, punishment – like deviance itself – sparks controversy among sociologists and the public as a whole.

KEY CONCEPTS

crime the violation of norms a society formally enacts into criminal law

crimes against the person (violent crimes) crimes that direct violence or the threat of violence against others

crimes against property (property crimes) crimes that involve theft of property belonging to others

criminal justice system a societal reaction to alleged violations of the law utilising police, courts and prison officials

criminal recidivism subsequent offences committed by people previously convicted of crimes

deterrence the attempt to discourage criminality through punishment

deviance the recognised violation of cultural norms

hate crime a criminal act against a person or a person's property by an offender motivated by racial or other bias

juvenile delinquency the violation of legal standards by the young

labelling theory the assertion that deviance and conformity result not so much from what people do, as from how others respond to those actions

medicalisation of deviance the transformation of moral and legal issues into medical matters

plea bargaining a legal negotiation in which the State reduces the charge against a defendant in exchange for a guilty plea

rehabilitation a programme for reforming the offender to preclude subsequent offences

retribution moral vengeance by which society inflicts suffering on an offender comparable to that caused by the offence

retrospective labelling the interpretation of someone's past consistent with present deviance

social control system planned and programmed responses to expected deviance

societal protection a means by which society renders an offender incapable of further offences temporarily through incarceration or permanently by execution

stigma a powerfully negative social label that radically changes a person's self-concept and social identity

victimless crimes violations of law in which there are no readily apparent victims

white-collar crime crimes committed by persons of high social position in the course of their occupations

CRITICAL-THINKING QUESTIONS

1. How does a sociological view of deviance differ from the common-sense notion that bad people do bad things?

2. Identify Durkheim's functions of deviance. From his point of view, could anyone forge a society free from deviance? Why or why not?

3. How does social power affect deviant labelling? How do gender, race and class figure in this process?

4. Examine the ideas of Michel Foucault on crime and prisons. Do you agree with his implicit view that our so-called 'humane treatment' of prisoners is in fact a controlling and corroding use of power.

5. Why do you think crime rates have been rising in much of the world over the last 50 years?

6. Do you agree or disagree with Travis Hirschi's prescription for crime control presented in the chapter's final box? Why?

7. Why do you think crime rates are lower in some countries than others?

8. Trace the emergence of the modern control system. Does it work?

9. Examine the policy of increasing the numbers going to prison. Is this an effective response to crime for the twenty-first century?

GOING FURTHER ·

Introductory reading

David Downes and Paul Rock, *Understanding Deviance* (Oxford: Clarendon Press, 2nd edn, 1988).

> A sophisticated guide to the full range of deviance theories.

Malcolm Davies, Hazel Croall and Jane Tyrer, *Criminal Justice: An Introduction to the Criminal Justice System in England and Wales* (London: Longmans, 1995).

> Readable account of the workings of the UK penal system.

Sandra Walkgate, *Gender and Crime.* (Prentice Hall, 1995).

> A good guide to feminist criminology and gender concerns

Clive Coleman and Jenny Moynihan, *Understanding Crime Data* (Milton Keynes: Open University Press, 1996).

> A clear introductory statement on crime figures and their limits.

Classical sources

Kai Erikson, *Wayward Puritans: A Study in the Sociology of Deviance* (New York: Wiley, 1966).

> This historical account of the Puritans of Massachusetts Bay reinforces Durkheim's functional theory of deviance.

Thomas Szasz, *The Myth of Mental Illness: Foundations of a Theory of Personal Conduct* (New York: Harper & Row, 1970, 1961).

> This influential and controversial treatise condemns the concept of mental illness as a fiction designed to impose conformity on those who are different.

More advanced reading

Mike Maguire, R. Morgan and R. Reiner, et al., *The Oxford Handbook of Criminology* (Oxford: Clarendon Press, 2nd edn, 1988).

> This has become the key text: very comprehensive coverage of the whole field of crime and control by specialist writers. Expensive, but indispensable for the budding criminologist.

Gregory M. Herek and Kevin T. Berrill, *Hate Crimes: Confronting Violence against Lesbians and Gay Men* (Newbury Park, CA: Sage, 1992).

> This collection of essays analyses the legal, psychological and social issues surrounding bias crimes against homosexual men and women.

Ikuyo Sato, *Kamikaze Biker: Parody and Anomie in Affluent Japan* (Chicago: University of Chicago Press, 1991).

> In the tradition of Emile Durkheim, this account of juvenile delinquency in Japan highlights the breakdown of traditional social controls that often accompanies material affluence.

On social control see:

Stanley Cohen, *Visions of Social Control* (Cambridge: Polity Press, 1985).

> This important study details many of the major changes in social control happening at the end of the century including policing, prisons and alternatives to prison. Although now a little old, it remains highly recommended.

David Garland, *Punishment and Modern Society* (Oxford University Press, 1990).

> A comprehensive review of the history of modern 'penality'.

Adrian L. James, A. Keith Bottomley, Alison Liebling and Emma Clare, *Privatising Prisons: Rhetoric and Reality* (London: Sage, 1997).

> Reviews the history and problems of private prisons internationally and provides an evaluation of the UK situation.

Rod Morgan and Tim Newburn, *The Future of Policing* (Oxford: Clarendon Press, 1997).

> Short but comprehensive guide to major issues facing society around policing today. Contains a lot of valuable background information, and a guide to current debates about crime.

Vincento Ruggiero, Mick Ryan and Joe Sim (eds.), *Western European Penal Systems: A Critical Anatomy* (London: Sage, 1995).

Bill Hebenton and Terry Thomas. *Policing Europe* (London: Macmillan, 1995).

> Monitoring law and order in Europe comes under the 'third pillar' of the EU, and was consolidated by

the Maastricht Treaty. It has established a number of European priorities such as drugs, Europol and dealing with terrorism. These two books provide some readings around this field.

Other sources

Organisations that can provide useful briefing sheets and background data include:

The Institute for the Study and Treatment of Delinquency (ISTD)
King's College London, Strand, London WC2R 2LS
This organisation produces a regular and very readable magazine on crime called *Criminal Justice Matters (CJM)*, as well as the *British Journal of Criminology*.

NACRO (the National Association for the Care and Resettlement of Offenders) also provides regular study sheets and bulletins.

Groups concerned especially with prisons include:

Prison Reform International, 169 Clapham Road, London SW9 0PU
Prison Reform Trust, 15 Northburg Street, London EC1V 0AH

For official data on crime, see

British Crime Survey
Home Office *Statistical Bulletins*
Police Statistics, England and Wales
Office for National Statistics, via Home Office:
tel. 0181 760 8340

Web sites

● ftp://www.ojp.vsdoj.gov/bjs/abstract/walesus.htm
provides a profile of inmates in the United States, England and Wales.

part three

Social Inequality

chapter nine

Source: Popperfoto

Social Stratification

On 10 April 1912, the ocean liner *Titanic* slipped away from Southampton docks on its maiden voyage across the North Atlantic to New York. A proud symbol of the new industrial age, the towering ship carried 2,300 passengers, some enjoying more luxury than most travellers today could imagine. By contrast, poor immigrants crowded the lower decks, journeying to what they hoped would be a better life in the USA.

Two days out, the crew received radio warnings of icebergs in the area but paid little notice. Then, near midnight, as the ship steamed swiftly and silently westwards, a lookout was stunned to see a massive shape rising out of the dark ocean directly ahead. Moments later, the *Titanic* collided with a huge iceberg, almost as tall as the ship itself, which split open its starboard side as if the grand vessel were nothing more than a giant tin can.

Sea water surged into the ship's lower levels, and within 25 minutes people were rushing for the lifeboats. By 2.00 am, the bow of the *Titanic* was submerged and the stern reared high above the water. Clinging to the deck, quietly observed by those in the lifeboats, hundreds of helpless passengers solemnly passed their final minutes before the ship disappeared into the frigid Atlantic (Lord, 1976).

The tragic loss of more than 1,600 lives made news around the world. Looking back dispassionately at this terrible accident with a sociological eye, however, we see that some categories of passengers had much better odds of survival than others. In an age of conventional gallantry, women and children boarded the boats first, so that 80 per cent of the casualties were men. Class, too, was at work. Of people holding first-class tickets, more than 60 per cent were saved, primarily because they were on the upper decks, where warnings were sounded first and lifeboats were accessible. Only 36 per cent of the second-class passengers survived, and of the third-class

Source: Ken Marshall

passengers on the lower decks, only 24 per cent escaped drowning. On board the *Titanic*, class turned out to mean much more than the quality of accommodation: it was truly a matter of life or death.

The fate of the *Titanic* dramatically illustrates the consequences of social inequality for the ways people live – and sometimes whether they live at all. This chapter explores the important concept of social stratification. Chapter 10 ('Class, Poverty and Welfare') continues the story by highlighting social inequality in the USA, Europe and, more specifically the UK, and Chapter 11 ('Global Stratification') examines how this fits into a global system of wealth and poverty.

● What is social stratification?

Most societies exist with systems of stratification, through which entire categories of people are elevated above others, providing one segment of the population with a disproportionate amount of money, power and prestige. Sociologists use the concept **social stratification** to refer to *a system by which a society ranks categories of people in a hierarchy*. Social stratification is a matter of four basic principles.

1. *Social stratification is a characteristic of society, not simply a reflection of individual differences.* Members of industrial societies consider social standing as a reflection of personal talent and effort, though we typically exaggerate the extent to which people control their destinies. Did a higher percentage of the first-class passengers survive the sinking of the *Titanic* because they were smarter or better swimmers than the second- and third-class passengers? Hardly. They fared better because of their privileged position on the ship. Similarly, children born into wealthy families are more likely than those born into poverty to enjoy health, achieve academically, succeed in their life's work and live well into old age. Neither rich nor poor people are responsible for creating social stratification, yet this system shapes the lives of them all.

2. *Social stratification persists over generations.* To understand that stratification stems from society rather than individual differences, note how inequality persists over time. In all societies, parents confer their social positions on their children, so that patterns of inequality stay much the same from generation to generation.

   Especially in industrial societies, however, some individuals do experience **social mobility**, *change*

The personal experience of poverty is captured in Sebastiao Salgado's haunting photograph, which stands as a universal portrait of human suffering. The essential sociological insight is that, however strongly individuals feel its effects, our social standing is largely a consequence of the way in which a society (or a world of societies) structures opportunity and reward. To the core of our being, then, we are all the products of social stratification.

Source: Network Photographers – Sebastiao Salgado

in one's position in a social hierarchy. Social mobility may be upwards or downwards. Our society celebrates the achievements of a Madonna or the Beatles, all of whom rose to prominence from modest beginnings. But we also acknowledge that people move downward as a result of business setbacks, unemployment or illness. More often, people move *horizontally* when they exchange one occupation for another that is comparable. For most people, however, social standing remains much the same over a lifetime.

3. *Social stratification is universal but variable.* Social stratification is found everywhere. At the same time, *what* is unequal and *how* unequal it is vary from one society to another. Among the members of technologically simple societies, social differentiation is minimal and based mostly on age and sex. With the development of sophisticated technology for growing food, societies also forge complex and more rigid systems for distributing what people produce. As we shall see, industrialisation has the effect of increasing social mobility and of reducing at least some kinds of social inequality.

4. *Social stratification involves not just inequality but beliefs.* Any system of inequality not only gives some people more resources than others but defines certain arrangements as fair. Just as *what* is unequal differs from society to society, then, so does the explanation of *why* people should be unequal. Virtually everywhere, however, people with the greatest social privileges express the strongest support for their society's system of social stratification, while those with fewer social resources are more likely to seek change.

For a long time, sociologists focused primarily upon one major system of stratification: that which deals with social and economic positions. Broadly, this is how people are ranked in terms of their economic position, their power and their prestige (see Weber below). But more recently, sociologists have recognised that social divisions and stratification systems can be organised through other key social processes such as gender, ethnicity and age. Thus, there are hierarchies which can be introduced as:

● social and economic stratification
● gender stratification
● ethnic stratification
● age stratification

There are others, too, including disabilities, language and dialect, and sexuality, which you will encounter if you read further than this simple introduction.

This section of the book looks at aspects of these systems, gives examples of them and raises some debates around them. This chapter considers some broad features of social-economic stratification. Chapter 10 then looks at how social and economic stratification works in countries like the UK and the United States. The next chapter (11) then examines the wider world, looking at such issues as global poverty. Chapter 12 turns to the ethnic stratification system and discusses matters of race and migration. Chapter 13 introduces the idea of patriarchy and sexism to see how gender acts as a major system of stratification. Finally, Chapter 14 looks at age stratification, focusing especially on both the growth of, and the increasing exclusion of, the elderly. One key problem with these varying systems of stratification is how they all interconnect. We will discuss this as we go along.

● Systems of social and economic stratification: slavery, caste, estate and class

In describing social stratification in particular societies, sociologists often use two opposing standards: 'closed' systems that allow little change in social position, and 'open' systems that permit considerable social mobility (Tumin, 1985).

The slavery system

A **slave system** is a *form of social stratification in which people are owned by others as property.* Chattel slavery turns human beings into things to be bought or sold. Many early civilisations such as Egypt and Persia (now Iran), as well as the ancient Greeks and Romans, relied heavily on slave labour. But it was not just a pervasive feature of 'classical worlds'. Between the fifteenth and nineteenth centuries, there was a massive slave trade into the New World.

The forms that slavery has taken have been highly variable. The legal rights and autonomy of slaves varied. In classical Athens, for example, slaves could often hold positions of great responsibility even though they were owned by their masters. But slaves who worked building pyramids, or excavating mines, or on plantations were much more regulated and treated as less than human. People caught in warfare often became slaves.

The British Empire abolished slavery in 1833, and the American Civil War brought slavery in the United States to an end in 1865. Although slavery no longer

GLOBAL SOCIOLOGY

Race as caste: a report from South Africa

South Africa was home to 45 million people in 1995. Dutch traders and farmers appropriated land around indigenous African people in the mid-seventeenth century. Early in the nineteenth century, a second wave of British colonists pushed the descendants of the Dutch settlers inland. By the beginning of this century, the British had gained control of the entire country, naming it the Union of South Africa.

In subsequent years it became an independent state, and by 1961 all ties with the United Kingdom ended. But freedom was a reality only for the white minority who dominated the society by imposing the policy of apartheid, or racial separation. A common practice for many years, apartheid was enshrined in a 1948 law denying the black majority South African citizenship, ownership of land and any formal voice in the government.

Apartheid rendered blacks a subordinate caste, and offered them only the education needed to perform low-paying jobs deemed inappropriate for whites. So separate were the races that white people earned four times the average black salaries, and even whites of limited means became accustomed to having a black household servant. A final plank in the platform of apartheid was the forcible resettlement of millions of blacks to so-called 'homelands' – very poor and desolate areas.

The prosperous white minority defended apartheid, claiming that blacks threatened their cultural traditions or, more fundamentally, were inferior beings. But resistance to apartheid rose steadily, prompting whites to resort to brutal military repression to maintain their power. Under racially based law, police could arrest and detain any black person for any violation of or opposition to apartheid.

Despite severe repression, violent confrontations became an almost everyday occurrence, sparked primarily by younger blacks impatient for a political voice and economic opportunity. Support for change also swelled outside the country: many corporations severed economic ties with South Africa, and consumers boycotted the sale of South African goods. This foreign divestiture staggered the South African economy and effectively pressured the government into making significant reforms.

In 1984, the government granted all South Africans the right to form trades unions, to enter various occupations once restricted to whites and to own property. Soon afterwards, officials abolished a host of 'petty apartheid' regulations

exists in its classical forms, it does still persist as forced labour, child prostitution and forced marriages (where women are given in marriage without the right to refuse) in many parts of the world today. Indeed, agencies working in this field suggest that numbers may well run into hundreds of millions.

The caste system

A **caste system** amounts to *social stratification based on ascription*. A pure caste system, in other words, is 'closed' so that birth alone determines one's social destiny with no opportunity for social mobility based on individual efforts. Caste systems rank categories of people in a rigid hierarchy.

Two illustrations: India and South Africa

A number of the world's societies – most of them agrarian – approximate to caste systems. One example is India, or at least India's traditional villages in which most people still live. The Indian system of castes (or *varna*, a Sanskrit word that means 'colour') is composed of four major categories: Brahmin, Kshatriya, Vaishya and Shudra. On the local level, however, each is composed of hundreds of subcaste (or *jati*) groups.

Caste also played a key role in South Africa until recently. In this nation's former policy of *apartheid*, the 5 million South Africans of European ancestry enjoyed a commanding share of wealth and power, dominating some 30 million black South Africans. In a middle position were another 3 million mixed-race people,

that segregated the races in public places, including beaches and hospitals.

In 1990, the legalisation of the anti-apartheid African National Congress (ANC) and the release from prison of its leader, Nelson Mandela, raised hopes for more basic change. In 1992, a majority of white voters endorsed, in principle, an end to apartheid. Two years later, all South African adults, regardless of race, voted in a national election that swept Nelson Mandela into office as South Africa's new president.

The great promise of change has not fully filtered through South African society. The legal right to own property means little to millions of black people who are desperately poor; opening hospitals to people of every race is an empty gesture for those who cannot afford to pay for medical care; ending racial barriers to the professions offers scant real opportunity to people without much schooling. The harsh reality is that more than one-third of all black adults cannot find any work at all, and, by the government's own estimate, half of all black

people live in desperate conditions.

The worst off are those called *ukuhleleleka*, which means 'the marginal people' in the Xhosa language. Some 7 million black South Africans fall into this category, living on the edge of society and on the edge of life itself. In Soweto-by-the-Sea, an idyllic-sounding community, thousands of people live crammed into shacks built of packing

---

Nelson Mandela, leader of the African National Congress (ANC), who was imprisoned by the white apartheid government for 27 years, celebrates his election victory as South Africa's first black president.

Source: Impact Visuals Photo & Graphics, Inc. – Paula Branstein

crates, corrugated metal, cardboard and other discarded materials. There is no electricity for lights or refrigeration. Without plumbing, people haul sewage in buckets, and a single tap provides water for more than 1,000 people. Jobs are hard to come by, partly because Ford and General Motors closed their factories in nearby Port Elizabeth and partly because people keep migrating to the town from regions where life is even worse. Those who can find work are lucky to earn £100 a month.

South Africa has ended white minority rule and, most analysts agree, there is no turning back. Yet undoing centuries of racial caste cannot be accomplished by simple legal mandate. Even when deeply rooted notions about racial inequality are finally overcome, this still-divided society will face the daunting challenge of resolving the underlying problem of intense and persistent poverty among most of its people. ●

Sources: Fredrickson, 1981; Price, 1991; Wren, 1991; Contreras, 1992; and various news reports.

known as 'coloureds', and about 1 million Asians. The box details the problems of dismantling South Africa's racial caste system.

In a caste system, birth determines the fundamental shape of people's lives in four crucial respects. First, traditional caste groups are linked to occupation, so that generations of a family perform the same type of work. In rural India, although some occupations (such as farming) are open to all, castes are identified with the work their members do (as priests, barbers, leather workers, street sweepers and so on). In South Africa, whites still hold most of the desirable jobs, with most blacks consigned to manual labour and other low-level service work.

No rigid social hierarchy could persist if people regularly married outside their own categories, as then most children would have uncertain rank. To shore up the hierarchy, then, a second trait of caste systems is mandating that people marry others of the same ranking. Sociologists call this pattern *endogamous* marriage (*endo* stems from Greek, meaning 'within'). Traditionally, Indian parents select their children's marriage partners, often before the children reach their teens. Until 1985, South Africa banned marriage and even sex between the races. Even now, interracial couples are rare since blacks and whites continue to live in separate areas.

Third, caste guides everyday life so that people remain in the company of 'their own kind'. Hindus in India enforce this segregation with the belief that a ritually 'pure' person of a higher caste will be 'polluted' by contact with someone of lower standing. Apartheid in South Africa achieved much the same effect. Fourth, and finally, caste systems rest on powerful cultural beliefs. Indian culture is built on Hindu traditions that mandate accepting one's life work, whatever it may be, as a moral duty. And, although apartheid is no longer a matter of law, South Africans still cling to notions distinguishing 'white jobs' from 'black jobs'.

Caste and agrarian life

Caste systems are typical of agrarian societies, because the lifelong routines of agriculture depend on a rigid sense of duty and discipline. Thus, caste still persists in rural India, half a century after being formally outlawed, even as its grip is easing in the nation's more industrial cities, where most people exercise greater choice about their work and marriage partners (Bahl,

1991). Similarly, the rapid industrialisation of South Africa elevated the importance of personal choice and individual rights, making the abolition of apartheid increasingly likely. Note, however, that the erosion of caste does not signal the end of social stratification. On the contrary, it simply marks a change in its character, as the next sections explain.

The class system

Agrarian life relies on the discipline wrought by caste systems; industrial societies, by contrast, depend on developing specialised talents. Industrialisation thus erodes caste in favour of a **class system**, *social stratification based on individual achievement*. A class system is more 'open' so that people who gain schooling and skills may experience some social mobility in relation to their parents and siblings. Mobility, in turn, blurs class distinctions. Social boundaries also break down as people immigrate from abroad or move from the countryside to the city, lured by greater opportunity for education and better jobs (Lipset and Bendix, 1967; Cutright, 1968; Treiman, 1970). Typically, newcomers take low-paying jobs, thereby pushing others up the social ladder (Tyree, Semyonov and Hodge, 1979).

People in industrial societies come to think that everyone is entitled to 'rights', rather than just those of particular social standing. The principle of equal standing before the law steadily assumes a central place in the political culture of industrial class systems. Class systems are no different from caste systems in one basic respect: people remain unequal. But social stratification now rests less on the accident of birth. Careers become not a matter of moral duty but an issue of individual choice; likewise, class systems allow more individual freedom in the selection of marriage partners.

Status consistency

Status consistency refers to *the degree of consistency of a person's social standing across various dimensions of social inequality*. In a caste system, limited social mobility generates high status consistency so that the typical person has the same relative ranking with regard to wealth, power and prestige. By contrast, the greater mobility of class systems allows for lower status consistency. In industrial nations such as Sweden or Canada, then, a university professor with an advanced degree might enjoy high social prestige while receiving a modest income. Such low status consistency is the key reason that *classes* are less well defined than *castes*.

An example: Japan

Social stratification in Japan also mixes the traditional and the contemporary. Japan is at once the world's oldest, continuously operating monarchy and a modern society in which wealth follows individual achievement.

Feudal Japan

As early as the fifth century CE, Japan was an agrarian society with a rigid caste system composed of nobles and commoners and ruled by an 'imperial family'. Despite the people's belief that the emperor ruled by divine right, limited government organisation forced the emperor to delegate much authority to a network of regional nobles or *shoguns*.

Below the nobility stood the *samurai*, or warrior caste. The word *samurai* means 'to serve', indicating that this second rank of Japanese society comprised soldiers who cultivated elaborate martial skills and pledged their loyalty to the nobility. To set themselves off from the rest of the commoners, the *samurai* dressed and behaved according to a traditional code of honour.

As in Great Britain, the majority of people in Japan at this time in history were commoners who laboured to eke out a bare subsistence. Unlike their European counterparts, however, Japanese commoners were not the lowest in rank. The *burakumin*, or 'outcasts', stood further down in that country's hierarchy, shunned by lord and commoner alike. Much like the lowest caste groups in India, 'outcasts' lived apart from others, engaged in the most distasteful occupations and, like everyone else, had no opportunity to change their standing.

Japan today

Important changes in nineteenth century Japan – industrialisation, the growth of cities, and the opening of Japanese society to outside influences – combined to weaken the traditional caste structure. In 1871, the Japanese legally banned the social category of 'outcast', though even today people look down on women and men who trace their lineage to this rank. After Japan's defeat in the Second World War, the nobility, too, lost legal standing, and, as the years have passed, fewer and fewer Japanese accept the notion that their emperor rules by divine right.

Thus social stratification in contemporary Japan is a far cry from the rigid caste system in force centuries ago. Analysts describe the modern-day Japanese population in terms of social gradations, including 'upper', 'upper-middle', 'lower-middle', and 'lower'. But since classes have no firm boundaries, they disagree about what proportion of the population falls in each.

Today's Japanese class system also reveals this nation's fascinating ability to weave together tradition and modernity. Because many Japanese people revere the past, family background is never far from the surface in assessing someone's social standing. Therefore, despite legal reforms that assure everyone of equal standing before the law and a modern culture that stresses individual achievement, the Japanese continue to perceive each other through the centuries-old lens of caste.

This dynamic mix echoes from the university campus to the corporate boardroom. The most prestigious universities – now gateways to success in the industrial world – admit students with outstanding scores on rigorous entrance examinations. Even so, the highest achievers and business leaders in Japan are products of privilege, with noble or *samurai* background. At the other extreme, 'outcasts' continue to live in isolated communities cut off from opportunities to better themselves (Hiroshi, 1974; Norbeck, 1983).

Finally, traditional ideas about gender still shape Japanese society. Despite legal reforms that confer formal equality on the sexes, women are clearly subordinate to men in most important respects. Japanese parents are more likely to push sons than daughters towards university and the nation thus retains a significant 'gender gap' in education (Brinton, 1988). As a consequence, women predominate in lower-level support positions in the corporate world, only rarely assuming leadership roles. In this sense, too, individual achievement in Japan's modern class system operates in the shadow of centuries of traditional privileges.

The Russian Federation

The Russian Federation, which rivalled the USA as a superpower while it existed as the Soviet Union, was born out of revolution in 1917. The feudal estate system ruled by a hereditary nobility came to an abrupt end as the Russian revolution transferred most farms, factories and other productive property from private ownership to state control.

A classless society?

This transformation was guided by the ideas of Karl Marx, who argued that private ownership of productive property was the basis of social classes (see Chapter 3, 'Society'). As the State gained control of the economy, Soviet officials claimed that they had engineered a remarkable achievement: humanity's first classless society.

Analysts outside the Soviet Union were sceptical about this claim of classlessness (Lane, 1984). The occupations of the people in the former Soviet Union, they pointed out, clustered into a four-level hierarchy. At the top were high government officials, or *apparatchiks*. Next came the Soviet intelligentsia, including lower government officials, university lecturers, scientists, physicians and engineers. Below them stood the manual workers and, in the lowest stratum, the rural peasantry.

Since people in each of these categories enjoyed very different living standards, the former Soviet Union was never classless in the sense of having no social inequality. But one can say, more modestly, that placing factories, farms, colleges and hospitals under State control did rein in economic inequality (although not necessarily differences of power) compared to capitalist societies such as the members of the Europe Union.

The 1917 Russian revolution radically recast the society as prescribed by Karl Marx (and revolutionary Russian leader Vladimir Lenin). Then in the 1980s, the Soviet Union underwent another sweeping transformation. Economic reforms accelerated when Mikhail Gorbachev came on the scene in 1985. His economic programme, popularly known as *perestroika*, meaning 'restructuring', sought to solve a dire problem: while the Soviet system had succeeded in minimising economic inequality, everyone was relatively poor and living standards lagged far behind those of other industrial nations. Simply put, Gorbachev hoped to stimulate economic expansion by reducing inefficient centralised control of the economy.

Gorbachev's reforms soon escalated into one of the most dramatic social movements in history, as popular uprisings toppled one socialist government after another throughout Eastern Europe and, ultimately, brought down the Soviet system itself. In essence, people blamed their economic plight as well as their lack of basic freedoms on a repressive ruling class of Communist party officials.

From the Soviet Union's founding in 1917 until its demise in 1991, the Communist party retained a monopoly of power. Near the end, 18 million party members (6 per cent of the Soviet people) still made all the decisions about Soviet life while enjoying privileges such as vacation homes, chauffeured cars and access to prized consumer goods and elite education for their children (Zaslavsky, 1982; Shipler, 1984; Theen, 1984). The second Russian revolution, then, mirrors the first in that it was nothing less than the overthrow of the ruling class.

The transformation of the Soviet Union into the Russian Federation demonstrates that social inequality involves more than economic resources. Figure 9.1 confirms that Soviet society lacked the income disparity typical of EU states and the United States. But elite

In recent years, the former Soviet Union has moved towards a market economy. Thus economic reforms have made some people quite wealthy, while others have been reduced to selling household goods in order to buy food.

Source: SABA Press Photos, Inc. – Robert Wallis

Figure 9.1 ● Economic inequality in selected countries, 1980–1992
The former Soviet Union did not provide data on economic inequality. The figure is the author's estimate based on UN data for various nations in the Soviet bloc and other sources

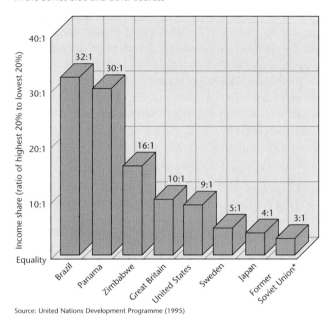

Source: United Nations Development Programme (1995)

standing in the former Soviet Union was based on power rather than wealth. Thus, even though Mikhail Gorbachev and Boris Yeltsin earned far less than a US president, they wielded awesome power.

And what about social mobility in Russia? Evidence indicates that during this century there was more upward social mobility in the Soviet Union than in Great Britain, Japan or the United States. Why? For one thing, Soviet society lacked the concentrated wealth that families elsewhere pass from one generation to the next. Even more important, industrialisation and rapid bureaucratisation during this century pushed a large proportion of the working class and rural peasantry upwards to occupations in industry and government (Dobson, 1977; Lane, 1984; Shipler, 1984). Nevertheless, this pattern has begun to change as dynasties, sometimes linked with organised crime, have formed in Russia in the last few years.

Often, as the Russian experience attests, widespread societal changes affect people's individual social standing in a process sociologists call **structural social mobility**, *a shift in the social position of large numbers of people due more to changes in society itself than to indi-vidual efforts.* Half a century ago, industrialisation in the Soviet Union created a vast number of new factory jobs that drew rural people to cities. Similarly, the growth of bureaucracy propelled countless Soviet citizens from ploughing to paperwork. Now, with new laws sanctioning individual ownership of private property and business, some experts monitoring the changing Russian scene predict further structural social mobility along with greater economic inequality (Róna-Tas, 1994). But, equal or not, everyone hopes to enjoy a higher standard of living.

Ideology: stratification's 'staying power'

Looking around the world at the extent of social inequality, we might wonder how societies persist without distributing their resources more equally. Caste-like systems in Great Britain and Japan lasted for centuries, concentrating land and power in the hands of several hundred families. Even more striking, for 2,000 years most people in India accepted the idea that they should be privileged or poor because of the accident of birth.

One key reason for the remarkable persistence of social hierarchies is that they are built on **ideology**, *cultural beliefs that serve to justify social stratification.* Any beliefs – for example, the claim that the rich are clever while the poor are lazy – are ideological to the extent that they bolster the dominance of wealthy elites and suggest that poor people deserve their plight.

Plato and Marx on ideology

The ancient Greek philosopher Plato (427–347 BCE) defined justice as agreement about who should have what. Every society, Plato explained, teaches its members to view some stratification system as 'fair'. Karl Marx, too, understood this process, though he was far more critical of inequality than Plato was. Marx took capitalist societies to task for channelling wealth and power into the hands of a few, all the while defining the practice as simply 'a law of the marketplace'. Capitalist law, Marx continued, defines the right to own property as a bedrock principle. Then, laws of inheritance, which are tied to kinship, funnel money and privileges from one generation to the next. In short, Marx concluded, ideas as well as resources are controlled by a society's elite, which helps to explain why established hierarchies are so difficult to change.

Both Plato and Marx recognised that ideology is rarely a simple matter of privileged people conspiring together to propound self-serving ideas about social inequality. By contrast, ideology usually takes the form of cultural patterns that evolve over a long period of time. As people learn to embrace their society's conception of fairness, they may question the rightness of their own position but are unlikely to challenge the system itself.

Historical patterns of ideology

The ideas that shore up social stratification change along with a society's economy and technology. Early agrarian societies depended on slaves to perform burdensome manual labour. Aristotle (384–322 BCE) defended the practice of slavery among the ancient Greeks, arguing that some people with little intelligence deserved nothing better than life under the direction of their natural 'betters'.

Agrarian societies in Europe during the Middle Ages also required the daily farm labour of most people to support the small aristocracy. In this context, noble and serf learned to view occupation as rightfully determined by birth and any person's work as a matter of moral responsibility. In short, caste systems always rest on the assertion that social ranking is the product of a 'natural' order.

The rise of industrial capitalism transformed wealth and power into prizes won by those who display the greatest talent and effort. Class systems celebrate individualism and achievement, so that social standing serves as a measure of personal worthiness. Thus poverty, which called for charity under feudalism, became under industrial capitalism a scorned state of personal inadequacy. The box on 'ideology' takes a closer look at the transition from the medieval notion of divinely sanctioned inequality to the modern idea that stratification reflects unequal effort and ability.

Throughout human history, most people have regarded social stratification as unshakeable. Especially as traditions weaken, however, people begin to question cultural 'truths' and unmask their political foundations and consequences. Historic notions of a 'woman's place' today seem far from natural and are losing their power to deprive women of opportunities. For the present, however, the contemporary class system still subjects women to caste-like expectations that they perform traditional tasks out of altruism while men are financially rewarded for their efforts. Most chefs are men who work for income while most household cooks are women who perform this role as a household duty.

Yet, while gender differences persist in Europe and elsewhere, there is little doubt that people are steadily becoming more equal in important respects. The continuing struggle for racial equality in South Africa also exemplifies widespread rejection of apartheid, which for decades shaped economic, political and educational life in that nation. Apartheid has never been widely accepted by blacks, and it has lost its support as a 'natural' system among whites who reject ideological racism (Friedrich, 1987; Contreras, 1992).

● The functions of social stratification

Why are societies stratified at all? One answer, consistent with the functional paradigm, is that social inequality plays a vital part in the operation of society. This influential – and controversial – argument was set forth over 50 years ago by Kingsley Davis and Wilbert Moore (1945).

The Davis–Moore thesis

The **Davis–Moore thesis** is *the assertion that social stratification has beneficial consequences for the operation of a society*. How else, ask Davis and Moore, can we explain the fact that some form of social stratification has been found everywhere? Davis and Moore describe our society as a complex system involving hundreds of occupational positions of varying importance. Certain jobs, say, changing spark plugs in a car, are fairly easy and can be performed by almost anyone. Other jobs, such as transplanting a human organ, are quite difficult and demand the scarce talents of people who have received extensive (and expensive) education. Positions of high day-to-day responsibility that demand special abilities are the most functionally significant.

In general, Davis and Moore explain, the greater the functional importance of a position, the more rewards a society will attach to it. This strategy pays off, since rewarding important work with income, prestige, power and leisure encourages people to do these things. In effect, by distributing resources unequally, a society motivates each person to aspire to the most significant work possible, and to work better, harder and

SOCIOLOGICAL SPOTLIGHT

Ideology: when is inequality unjust?

Inequality is not always injustice; on the contrary, all societies endorse some dimensions of inequality as fair while condemning others as wrong. Justifications for social stratification, then, are culturally variable across history and from place to place.

A millennium ago, a rigid estate system in Europe rested on Church teachings that such arrangements reflected the will of God. More specifically, the Church endorsed as divinely sanctioned a system by which most people laboured as serfs, driving the feudal economy with their muscles. According to the Church, nobility was charged with responsibility for defending the realm and maintaining public order. To question this system meant challenging the Church and, ultimately, defying God. The religious justification that supported the medieval estate system for centuries is expressed in the following stanza from the nineteenth century English hymn 'All Things Bright and Beautiful'.

The rich man in his castle,
The poor man at his gate,
He made them high and lowly
And ordered their estate.

The Industrial Revolution opened the way for newly rich industrialists to topple the feudal nobility. In the process, industrial culture advanced a new ideology. Capitalists mocked the centuries-old notion that social hierarchy should depend on the accident of birth. Under God's law, the new thinking went, the most talented and hard-working individuals should dominate society.

The American John D. Rockefeller (1839–1937), who made a vast fortune in oil, defended the wealth and power of early industrialists as the product of extraordinary effort and initiative. Such a scheme, he contended, was consistent with the laws of nature. The same thinking recast the poor from objects of charity into unworthy people lacking ability and ambition. The ideological shift from birth to individual achievement as the basis of social inequality was well established by the time early nineteenth century German writer Johann Wolfgang von Goethe quipped:

Really to own
What you inherit,
You first must earn it
With your merit.

Clearly, medieval and modern justifications for inequality differ dramatically: what an earlier era viewed as fair, a later one rejected as wrong. Yet both cases illustrate the pivotal role of ideology – cultural beliefs that define a particular kind of hierarchy as fair and natural. ●

longer. The overall effect of a social system of unequal rewards – which is what social stratification amounts to – is a more productive society.

Davis and Moore concede that every society could be egalitarian. But, they caution, rewards could be equal only to the extent that people were willing to let *anyone* perform *any* job. Equality also demands that someone who carries out a job poorly be rewarded on a par with another who performs well. Logic dictates that such a system offers little incentive for people to make their best efforts, and thereby reduces a society's productive efficiency.

The Davis–Moore thesis points out why *some* form of stratification exists everywhere; it does not endorse any *particular* system of inequality. Nor do Davis and Moore specify precisely what reward should be attached to any occupational position. They merely point out that positions a society deems crucial must yield sufficient rewards to draw talent away from less important work.

Meritocracy

The Davis–Moore thesis implies that a productive society is a **meritocracy**, *a system of social stratification based on personal merit*. Such societies hold out rewards to develop the talents and encourage the efforts of everyone. In pursuit of meritocracy, a society promotes equality of opportunity while, at the same time, mandating inequality of rewards. In other words, a pure class system would be a meritocracy, rewarding everyone based on ability and effort. In addition, such a society would have extensive social mobility, blurring social categories as individuals move up or down in the social system depending on their performance.

For their part, caste societies can speak of 'merit' (from Latin, meaning 'worthy of praise') only in terms of persistence in low-skill labour such as farming. Caste systems, in short, offer honour to those who remain dutifully 'in their place'.

Although caste systems waste human potential, they are quite orderly. And herein lies a clue to an important question: why do modern industrial societies resist becoming pure meritocracies by retaining many caste-like qualities? Simply because, left unchecked, meritocracy erodes social structure such as kinship. No one, for example, evaluates family members solely on the basis of performance. Class systems in industrial societies, therefore, retain some caste elements to promote order and social cohesion.

Critical evaluation

By investigating the functions of social stratification, Davis and Moore made a lasting contribution to sociological analysis. Even so, critics point to several flaws in their thesis. Melvin Tumin (1953) wonders if functional importance really explains the high rewards that some people enjoy. Can we even measure functional importance? Surgeons may perform valuable service in saving lives, but a related profession, nursing, is vastly less well paid. Popular footballers and pop singers earn more in a few years than most primary school teachers and childminders earn in their working lives – and the latter are responsible for raising the next generation!

Second, Tumin argues that the Davis–Moore thesis exaggerates social stratification's role in developing individual talent. Our society does reward individual achievement, but we also allow families to transfer wealth and power from generation to generation in caste-like fashion. Additionally, for women, people of colour and others with limited opportunities, stratification still raises barriers to personal accomplishment. In practice, Tumin concludes, social stratification functions to develop some people's abilities to the fullest while barring others from ever reaching their potential.

Third, by contending that social stratification benefits all of society, the Davis–Moore thesis ignores how social inequality promotes conflict and, sometimes, even outright revolution. This assertion leads us to the social-conflict paradigm, which provides a very different explanation for the persistence of social hierarchy.

● Stratification and conflict

Conflict analysis argues that, rather than benefit society as a whole, social stratification provides advantages to some people at the expense of others. This theoretical perspective draws heavily on the ideas of Karl Marx, though additional contributions were made by Max Weber.

Karl Marx: class and conflict

Karl Marx, whose approach to understanding social inequality is detailed in Chapter 3 ('Society'), identified two major social classes corresponding to the two basic relationships to the means of production: individuals either (1) own productive property or (2) labour for others. In medieval Europe, the nobility and the Church owned the productive land; peasants toiled as farmers. Similarly, in industrial class systems, the capitalists (or the bourgeoisie) own and operate factories, which utilise the labour of workers (the proletariat).

Marx noted great disparities in wealth and power arising from the industrial-capitalist productive system, which, he contended, made class conflict inevitable. In time, he believed, oppression and misery would drive the working majority to organise and, ultimately, to overthrow capitalism.

Marx's analysis was grounded in his observations of capitalism in the nineteenth century, when great industrialists dominated the economic scene. In North America, for example, Andrew Carnegie, J. P. Morgan and John Jacob Astor (one of the few very rich passengers to perish on the *Titanic*) lived in fabulous mansions filled with priceless art and staffed by dozens of servants. Their fortunes were staggering: John Jacob Astor accumulated $25 million; Andrew Carnegie reportedly earned more than $20 million a year as this century began (worth close to $100 million in today's terms) – all at a time when the wages paid to the average US worker totalled roughly $500 a year (Baltzell, 1964; Pessen, 1990).

According to Marx, the capitalist elite draws its strength from more than the operation of the economy. He noted that through the family, opportunity

Fat cats: are the rich worth what they earn?

For an hour of work, a residential care worker in Southern England earns about £3.25; a university teaching assistant earns about £4; and a computer programmer earns between £9 and £30. These wages seem insignificant in comparison to the hundreds of thousands to millions earned annually by actors like Rowan Atkinson (Mr Bean), sports stars like Eric Cantona, and music chart toppers like the Spice Girls. The Duchess of York paid off a personal debt in excess of £1 million (a debt greater than the lifetime earnings of many Britons) by writing children's stories and working the talk show and lecture circuits in the United States.

The Davis–Moore thesis states that rewards reflect an occupation's value to society. But are the antics of Mr Bean worth as much to our society as the work of all teachers in several primary schools? In short, do earnings really reflect people's social importance?

Salaries in industrial-capitalist societies like the UK are a product of the market forces of supply and demand. In simple terms, if you can do something better than others, and people value it, you can command greater rewards. According to this view, movie stars, top athletes, skilled professionals and many business executives have rare talents that are much in demand; thus, they may earn many times more than the typical worker in the UK.

But critics claim that the market is really a poor evaluator of occupational importance. First, they claim, the British economy is dominated by a small proportion of people who manipulate the system for their own benefit. Corporate executives – like the directors of the much-berated Camelot, which runs the British lottery, for example – pay themselves multimillion pound salaries and bonuses even in years when their companies flounder. Japanese executives, by contrast, earn far less than their counterparts in this country, yet most Japanese corporations have comfortably outperformed their rivals in the UK.

A second problem with the idea that the market measures people's contributions to society is that many people who make clear and significant contributions receive surprisingly little money for their efforts. Hundreds of thousands of teachers, counsellors and health-care workers contribute daily to the welfare of others for very little salary.

Using social worth to justify income, then, is hazardous. Some defend the market as the most accurate measure of occupational worth; what, they ask, would be better? But others contend that what is lucrative may or may not be socially valuable. From this standpoint, a market system amounts to a closed game in which only a handful of people have the money to play. ●

and wealth are passed down from generation to generation. Moreover, the legal system defends this practice through inheritance law. Similarly, exclusive schools bring children of the elite together, encouraging informal social ties that will benefit them throughout their lives. Overall, from Marx's point of view, capitalist society *reproduces the class structure in each new generation.*

Critical evaluation
Exploring how the capitalist economic system generates conflict between classes, Marx's analysis of social stratification has had enormous influence on sociological thinking in recent decades. Because it is revolutionary – calling for the overthrow of capitalist society – Marxism is also highly controversial.

One of the strongest criticisms of the Marxist approach is that it denies one of the central tenets of the Davis–Moore thesis: that motivating people to perform various social roles requires some system of unequal rewards. Marx separated reward from performance, endorsing an egalitarian system based on the principle of 'from each according to ability; to each according to need' (1972: 388). Critics argue that severing rewards from performance is precisely the flaw that generated the low productivity characteristic of the former Soviet Union and other socialist economies around the world.

Defenders of Marx rebut this line of attack by pointing to considerable evidence supporting Marx's general view of humanity as inherently social rather than unflinchingly selfish (Clark, 1991; Fiske, 1991). They counter that we should not assume that individual rewards (much less monetary compensation alone) are the only way to motivate people to perform their social roles. Table 9.1 on page 254 compares the functional and conflict paradigms.

In addition, although few doubt that capitalist society does perpetuate poverty and privilege, as Marx asserted, the revolutionary developments he considered inevitable have failed to materialise. The next section explores why the socialist revolution Marx predicted and promoted has not occurred, at least in advanced capitalist societies.

Why no Marxist revolution?

Despite Marx's prediction, capitalism is still thriving. Why have workers in the UK and other industrial societies not overthrown capitalism? Some while ago, Ralf Dahrendorf (1959) pointed to four reasons.

1. *The fragmentation of the capitalist class.* First, the century since Marx's death has witnessed the fragmentation of the capitalist class in Europe. A century ago, *single families* typically owned large companies; today, *numerous stockholders* fill that position. The diffusion of ownership has also stimulated the emergence of a managerial class, who may or may not be major stockholders (Wright, 1985; Wright, Levine and Sober, 1992). We will find more evidence of this in the next chapter (see Scott, 1991).

2. *White-collar work and a rising standard of living.* A 'white-collar revolution' has transformed Marx's industrial proletariat. As Chapter 15 ('The Economy, Consumption and Work') details, the majority of workers in Marx's time laboured either on farms or in factories. They had **blue-collar or manual occupations**, *lower-prestige jobs involving mostly manual labour*. By contrast, most workers today hold **white-collar jobs**, *higher-prestige work involving mostly mental activity*. These occupations include positions in sales, management and other service work, frequently in large, bureaucratic organisations.

While many of today's white-collar workers perform repetitive tasks like the industrial workers known to Marx, evidence indicates that most do not think of themselves in those terms. Rather, most white-collar workers now perceive their social positions as higher than those of their blue-collar parents and grandparents. One key reason is that

workers' overall standard of living in Europe rose fourfold over the course of the century, even as the work week decreased. As a result of a rising tide of social mobility, society seems less sharply divided between rich and poor than it did to people during Marx's lifetime (Edwards, 1979; Gagliani, 1981; Wright and Martin, 1987).

3. *More extensive worker organisation.* Employees have organisational strengths they lacked a century ago. Workers have won the right to organise into trades unions that can and do make demands of management backed by threats of 'working to rule' and strikes. Although union membership is declining, research suggests that well-established unions continue to enhance the economic standing of the workers they represent (Rubin, 1986). Further, today's negotiations between labour and management typically are institutionalised and peaceful, a picture quite different from the often-violent confrontations common before the mid-century.

4. *More extensive legal protections.* Since Marx's death, the government has extended laws to protect workers' rights and has given workers greater access to the courts for redressing grievances. Government programmes such as National Insurance, disability protection and social security also provide workers with substantially greater financial resources than the capitalists of the last century were willing to grant them.

Taken together, these four developments mean that, despite persistent stratification, many societies have smoothed out some of capitalism's rough edges. Consequently, social conflict today may be less intense than it was a century ago.

A counterpoint

Many sociologists continue to find value in Marx's analysis, often in modified form (Miliband, 1969; Edwards, 1979; Giddens, 1982; Domhoff, 1983; Stephens, 1986; Boswell and Dixon, 1993; Hout et al., 1993). Conflict theorists respond with their own set of four key points, defending Marx's analysis of capitalism.

1. *Wealth remains highly concentrated.* As Marx contended, wealth remains in the hands of the few. In Europe, about half of all privately controlled corporate stock is owned by just 1 per cent of individuals, who persist as a capitalist class.

2. *White-collar positions offer little to workers.* As defenders of Marx's thinking see it, the white-collar revolution has delivered little in the way of higher income or better working conditions compared to the factory jobs of a century ago. On the contrary, much white-collar work remains monotonous and routine, especially the low-level clerical jobs commonly held by women.

3. *Progress requires struggle.* Labour organisations may have advanced the interests of the workers over the last half century, but regular negotiation between workers and management hardly signals the end of social conflict. In fact, many of the concessions won by workers came about precisely through the class conflict Marx described. Moreover, workers still strive to gain concessions from capitalists and, in the 1990s, they struggle to hold on to the advances already achieved. As an example, half of all workers in the United States and much of Europe have no company-sponsored pension scheme.

4. *The law still favours the rich.* Workers have gained some legal protections over the course of this century. Even so, the law still defends the overall distribution of wealth in Europe. Just as important, 'average' people cannot use the legal system to the same advantage as the rich do.

Richard Branson – wealthy entrepreneur.

Source: Popperfoto

Max Weber: class, status and power

Max Weber, whose approach to social analysis is described in Chapter 3 ('Society'), agreed with Karl Marx that social stratification sparks social conflict, but he differed with Marx in several important respects. Weber considered Marx's model of two social classes simplistic. Instead, he viewed social stratification as a more complex interplay of three distinct dimensions. First is economic inequality – the issue so vital to Marx – which Weber termed *class* position. Weber's use of 'class' refers not to crude categories but to a continuum on which anyone can be ranked from high to low. A second continuum, *status*, measures social prestige. Finally, Weber noted the importance of *power* as a third dimension of social hierarchy.

The socioeconomic status hierarchy

Marx believed that social prestige and power derived from economic position; thus he saw no reason to treat them as distinct dimensions of social inequality. Weber disagreed, recognising that stratification in industrial societies has characteristically low status consistency. An individual, Weber pointed out, might have high standing on one dimension of inequality but a lower position on another. For example, bureaucratic officials might wield considerable power yet have little wealth or social prestige.

So while Marx viewed inequality in terms of two clearly defined classes, Weber saw something more subtle at work in the stratification of industrial societies. Weber's key contribution in this area, then, lies in identifying the multidimensional nature of social rankings. Sociologists often use the term **socioeconomic status** (SES) to refer to *a composite ranking based on various dimensions of social inequality.*

A population that varies widely in class, status and power – Weber's three dimensions of inequality – creates a virtually infinite array of social categories, all of which pursue their own interests. Thus, unlike Marx, who focused on conflict between two overarching classes, Weber considered social conflict as highly variable and complex.

Inequality in history

Weber also made a key historical observation, noting that each of his three dimensions of social inequality stands out at different points in the evolution of human societies. Agrarian societies, he maintained,

Table 9.1 ● Two explanations of social stratification: a summary

Functional paradigm	Conflict paradigm
Social stratification keeps society operating. The linkage of greater rewards to more important social positions benefits society as a whole.	Social stratification is the result of social conflict. Differences in social resources serve the interests of some and harm the interests of others.
Social stratification encourages a matching of talents and abilities to appropriate positions.	Social stratification ensures that much talent and ability within society will not be utilised at all.
Social stratification is both useful and inevitable.	Social stratification is useful to only some people; it is not inevitable.
The values and beliefs that legitimise social inequality are widely shared throughout society.	Values and beliefs tend to be ideological; they reflect the interests of the more powerful members of society.
Because systems of social stratification are useful to society as a whole and are supported by cultural values and beliefs, they are usually stable over time.	Because systems of social stratification reflect the interests of only part of society, they are unlikely to remain stable over time.

Source: Adapted in part from Arthur L. Stinchcombe, 'Some Empirical Consequences of the Davis–Moore Theory of Stratification', *American Sociological Review*, Vol. 28, No. 5 (October 1963): 808

emphasise status or social prestige, typically in the form of honour or symbolic purity. Members of these societies gain such status by conforming to cultural norms corresponding to their rank.

Industrialisation and the development of capitalism level traditional rankings based on birth, but generate striking material differences in the population. Thus, Weber argued, the crucial difference among people in industrial-capitalist societies lies in the economic dimension of class.

In time, industrial societies witness a surging growth of the bureaucratic state. This expansion of government, coupled with the proliferation of other types of formal organisations, brings power to the fore in the stratification system. Power is also central to the organisation of socialist societies, as we see in their extensive government regulation of many aspects of life. The elite members of such societies are mostly high-ranking officials rather than rich people.

This historical analysis underlies a final disagreement between Weber and Marx. Looking to the future, Marx believed that social stratification could be largely eliminated by abolishing private ownership of productive property. Weber doubted that overthrowing capitalism would significantly diminish social stratification in modern societies. While doing so might

lessen economic disparity, Weber reasoned, the significance of power based on organisational position would only increase. In fact, Weber imagined, a socialist revolution might well *increase* social inequality by expanding government and concentrating power in the hands of a political elite. Recent popular uprisings against entrenched bureaucracies in Eastern Europe and the former Soviet Union lend support to Weber's argument.

Critical evaluation

Weber's multidimensional analysis of social stratification retains enormous influence among sociologists, especially in Europe. Some analysts (particularly those influenced by Marx's ideas) argue that while social class boundaries have blurred, striking patterns of social inequality persist in the industrial world.

As we shall see in Chapter 10 ('Class, Poverty and Welfare'), the enormous wealth of the most privileged members of our society contrasts sharply with the grinding poverty of millions who barely meet their day-to-day needs. Moreover, the upward social mobility that historically fuelled optimism in this country all but came to a halt in the 1970s, and, during the 1980s, evidence points to an increase in economic inequality. Against this backdrop of economic polarisation, the 1990s are marked by a renewed emphasis on 'classes' in conflict rather than on the subtle shadings of a 'multidimensional hierarchy'.

● Stratification and technology in global perspective

We can weave together a number of observations made in this chapter by considering the relationship between a society's technology and its type of social stratification. Gerhard Lenski and Jean Lenski's model of sociocultural evolution, detailed in Chapter 3 ('Society'), puts social stratification in historical perspective and also helps us to understand the varying degrees of inequality found around the world today (Lenski, 1966; Lenski, Nolan and Lenski, 1995).

Hunting and gathering societies

Simple technology limits the production of hunting and gathering societies to only what is necessary for day-to-day living. No doubt some individuals are more successful hunters or gatherers than others, but the group's survival depends on all sharing what they have. With little or no surplus, therefore, no categories of people emerge as better off than others. Thus social stratification among hunters and gatherers, based simply on age and sex, is less complex than among societies with more advanced technology.

Horticultural, pastoral and agrarian societies

Technological advances generate surplus production, while intensifying social inequality. In horticultural and pastoral societies, a small elite controls most of the surplus. Agrarian technology based on large-scale farming generates even greater abundance; but marked inequality means various categories of people lead strikingly different lives. The social distance between the elite hereditary nobility and the common serfs who work the land looms as large as at any time in human history. In most cases, lords wield godlike power over the masses.

Industrial societies

Industrialisation reverses the historical trend, prompting some decrease in social inequality. The eclipse of tradition and the need to develop individual talents gradually erode caste rankings in favour of greater individual opportunity. Then, too, the increasing productivity of industrial technology steadily raises the living standards of the historically poor majority. Specialised, technical work also demands the expansion of schooling, sharply reducing illiteracy. A literate population, in turn, tends to press for a greater voice in political decision-making, further diminishing social inequality. As already noted, continuing technological advances transform much blue-collar labour into higher-prestige white-collar work. All these social shifts help to explain why Marxist revolutions occurred in agrarian societies – such as the former Soviet Union (1917), Cuba (1959) and Nicaragua (1979) – in which social inequality is most pronounced, rather than in industrial societies, as Marx predicted more than a century ago.

Initially, the great wealth generated by industrialisation is concentrated in the hands of a few – the pattern so troubling to Marx. In time, however, the share of all property in the hands of the very rich declines

Figure 9.2 ● Social stratification and technological development: the Kuznets curve
The Kuznets curve reveals that greater technological sophistication is generally accompanied by more pronounced social stratification. The trend reversed itself, however, as industrial societies gradually become more egalitarian. Rigid caste-like distinctions are relaxed in favour of greater opportunity and equality under the law. Political rights are more widely extended, and there is even some levelling of economic differences. The Kuznets curve may also be usefully applied to the relative social standing of the two sexes.

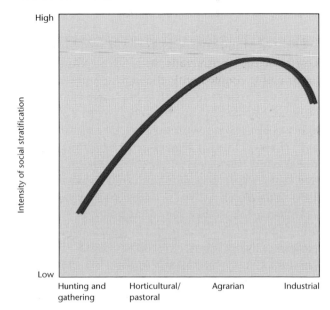

CONTROVERSY AND DEBATE

The bell curve debate: are rich people really smarter?

It is rare that the publication of a new book in the social sciences captures the attention of the public at large. But *The Bell Curve: Intelligence and Class Structure in American Life* by Richard J. Herrnstein and Charles Murray did that and more, igniting a firestorm of controversy over why pronounced social stratification divides US society and, just as important, what to do about it. Although the book speaks specifically about the USA, its general argument has been made for many countries. In Europe, for instance, its main proponent has been the psychologist Hans Eysenck.

The Bell Curve is a long (800 page) book that addresses many critical issues and resists simple summary. But its basic thesis is captured in the following propositions:

1. Something we can describe as 'general intelligence' exists; people with more of it tend to be more successful in their careers than those with less.

2. At least half the variation in human intelligence (Herrnstein and Murray use figures of 60 to 70 per cent) is transmitted genetically from one generation to another; the remaining variability is due to environmental factors.

3. Over the course of this century – and especially since the 'Information revolution' – intelligence has become more necessary to the performance of industrial societies' top occupational positions.

4. Simultaneously, the best US universities have shifted their admissions policies away from favouring children of inherited wealth to admitting young people who perform best on standardised tests.

5. As a result of these changes in the workplace and higher education, US society is now coming to be dominated by a 'cognitive elite', who are, on average, not only better trained

than most people but actually more intelligent.

6. Because more intelligent people are socially segregated on the university campus and in the workplace, it is no surprise that they tend to pair up, marry and have intelligent children, perpetuating the 'cognitive elite'.

7. Near the bottom of the social ladder, a similar process is at work. Increasingly, poor people are individuals with lower intelligence, who live segregated from others, and who tend to pass along their modest abilities to their children.

Resting on the validity of the seven assertions presented above, Herrnstein and Murray then offer, as an eighth point, a basic approach to public policy:

8. To the extent that membership in the affluent elite or the impoverished underclass is rooted in intelligence

somewhat. According to estimates, the proportion of all wealth controlled by the richest 1 per cent of US families peaked at about 36 per cent just before the stock market crash in 1929; during the entrepreneurial 1980s, this economic elite owned one-third of all wealth (Williamson and Lindert, 1980; Beeghley, 1989; *1991 Green Book*).

Finally, industrialisation diminishes the domination of women by men, a pattern that is strongest in agrarian societies. The movement towards social parity for the sexes derives from the industrial economy's need to cultivate individual talent as well as a growing belief in basic human equality.

The Kuznets curve

The trend described above can be distilled into the following statement. *In human history, technological progress first sharply increases but then moderates the intensity of social stratification.* So if greater inequality is functional for agrarian societies, then industrial societies benefit from a more egalitarian climate. This historical shift, recognised by Nobel Prize winning economist Simon Kuznets (1966), is illustrated by the Kuznets curve, shown in Figure 9.2.

Current patterns of social inequality around the world generally square with the Kuznets curve. As shown in Map 9.1, industrial societies have somewhat

and determined mostly by genetic inheritance, programmes to assist underprivileged people will have few practical benefits.

The book has prompted considerable debate. Critics first questioned exactly what is meant by 'intelligence', arguing that anyone's innate abilities can hardly be separated from the effects of socialisation. Of course, rich children perform better on intelligence tests, they explained: these people have had all the advantages! Some critics dismiss the concept of 'intelligence' outright as phony science. Others take a more moderate view, claiming that we should not think of 'intelligence' as the sole cause of achievement, since recent research indicates that mental abilities and life experiences are interactive, each affecting the other.

In addition, while most researchers who study intelligence agree that genetics does play a part in transmitting intelligence, the consensus is that no more than 25 to 40 per cent

is inherited – only about half what Herrnstein and Murray claim. Therefore, critics conclude, The *Bell Curve* wrongly misleads readers into thinking that social elitism is both natural and inevitable. In its assumptions and conclusions, moreover, The *Bell Curve* amounts to little more than a rehash of the social Darwinism popular a century ago, which heralded the success of industrial tycoons as merely 'the survival of the fittest'.

Perhaps, as one commentator noted, the more society seems like a jungle, the more people think of stratification as a matter of blood rather than upbringing. But, despite its flaws and exaggerations, the book's success suggests that *The Bell Curve* raises many issues we cannot easily ignore. Can a democratic system tolerate the 'dangerous knowledge' that elites (including not only rich people but also political leaders) are at least somewhat more intelligent than the rest of us? What of *The Bell Curve*'s description that elites are increasingly insulating themselves from social problems such as

crime, homelessness and poor schools? As such problems have become worse in recent years, how do we counter the easy explanation that poor people are hobbled by their own limited ability? And, most basically, what should be done to ensure that all people have the opportunity to develop their abilities as fully as possible?

● **Continue the debate:**

1. Do you agree that 'general intelligence' exists? Why or why not?

2. In general, do you think that people of higher social position are more intelligent than those of low social position? If you think intelligence differs by social standing, which factor is cause and which is effect?

3. Do you think sociologists should study controversial issues such as differences in human intelligence? Why or why not? ●

Sources: Herrnstein and Murray, 1994; Jacoby and Glauberman, 1995.

---

less income inequality – one important measure of social stratification – than nations that remain predominantly agrarian. Specifically, mature industrial societies, such as those in the European Union, Australia and the United States, exhibit less income inequality than the less industrialised countries of Latin America, Africa and Asia.

Yet income disparity reflects a host of factors beyond technology, especially political and economic priorities. Societies that have had socialist economic systems (including the People's Republic of China, the Russian Federation and the nations of Eastern Europe) display relatively little income inequality. Keep in mind, however, that an egalitarian society like the

People's Republic of China has an average income level that is quite low by world standards; further, on non-economic dimensions such as political power, China's society reveals pronounced inequality.

And what of the future? Although the global pattern described by the Kuznets curve appears to be valid, this analysis does not necessarily mean that industrial societies will gradually become less and less stratified. In the abstract, members of our society endorse the principle of equal opportunity for all; even so, this goal has not been and may never become a reality. The notion of social equality, like all concepts related to social stratification, is controversial, as the final section of this chapter explains.

Map 9.1 ● Income disparity in global perspective

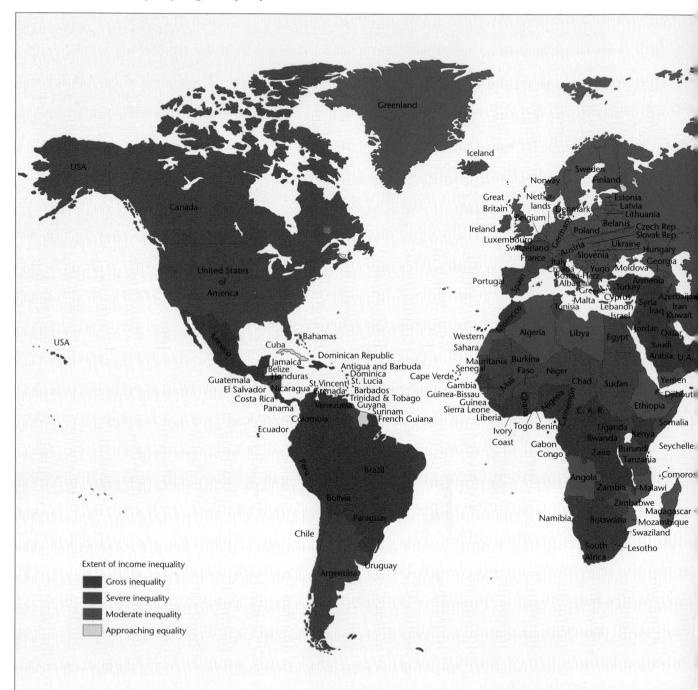

Extent of income inequality

■ Gross inequality
■ Severe inequality
■ Moderate inequality
□ Approaching equality

Source: *Peters Atlas of the World* (1990)

Societies throughout the world differ in the rigidity and intensity of social stratification as well as in overall standard of living. This map highlights income inequality. Generally speaking, countries that have had centralised, socialist economies (including the People's Republic of China, the former Soviet Union and Cuba) display the least income inequality, although their standard of living has been relatively low. Industrial societies with predominantly capitalist economies, including the United States and most of Western Europe, have higher overall living standards, accompanied by severe income disparity. The low-income countries of Latin America and Africa (including Mexico, Brazil and Zaire) exhibit the most pronounced inequality of income.

● Social stratification: facts and values

The year was 2081 and everybody was finally equal. They weren't only equal before God and the law. They were equal every which way. Nobody was smarter than anybody else. Nobody was better looking than anybody else. Nobody was stronger or quicker than anybody else. All this equality was due to the 211th, 212th, and 213th Amendments to the Constitution and the unceasing vigilance of agents of the Handicapper General . . .

With these words, novelist Kurt Vonnegut, Jr (1961) begins the story of 'Harrison Bergeron', an imaginary account of a future United States in which social inequality has been totally abolished. There have been many such 'utopian' novels of a much dreamed of equality. George Orwell's *Animal Farm* and *1984* are other instances. Yet while most people probably find equality appealing in principle, Vonnegut and Orwell warn that it can be a dangerous concept in practice. Vonnegut's story describes a nightmare of social engineering in which every individual talent that makes one person different from another has been systematically neutralised by high-handed government agents.

In order to neutralise differences that make one person 'better' than another, the State mandates that physically attractive people wear masks that render them average looking, that intelligent people don earphones that generate distracting noise and that the legs of the best athletes and dancers be precisely fitted with weights to make their movements just as cumbersome as everyone else's. In short, although we may imagine that social equality would liberate people to make the most of their talents, Vonnegut concludes that an egalitarian society would only succeed in reducing everyone to a lowest common denominator.

This chapter's explanations of social stratification also involve value judgements. The Davis–Moore thesis, which cites universal social stratification, interprets this pattern as evidence that inequality is a necessary element of social organisation. Class differences, then, reflect both variation in human abilities and the importance of occupational roles. From this point of view, the spectre of equality is a threat to a society of diverse people, since such uniformity could exist only as the product of the relentless and stifling efforts of officials like Vonnegut's fictitious 'Handicapper General'.

The conflict theory of Marx interprets universal social inequality in a very different way. Rejecting the notion that inequality is in any sense necessary, Marx condemned social hierarchy as a product of greed. Guided by egalitarian values, he advocated social arrangements that would enable everyone to share all important resources equally. Rather than undermining the quality of life, Marx maintained that equality would enhance human well-being.

Our concluding Controversy and Debate discussion (see the box on pages 256 and 257) addresses the link between intelligence and social class. This issue, also a mix of facts and values, is among the most troublesome in social science, partly because of the difficulty in defining and measuring 'intelligence', but also because the idea that elites are inherently 'better' than others challenges our democratic culture.

The next chapter ('Class, Poverty and Welfare') takes a close look at inequality in our own society. But, here again, even people who agree on the basic facts often interpret them quite differently. This lesson is repeated in Chapter 11 ('Global Stratification'), which examines inequality among the world's nations and offers two opposing explanations for it. At all levels, then, the study of social stratification involves a complex, ongoing debate that yields no single or simple truth.

SUMMARY ....

1. Social stratification refers to categories of people ranked in a hierarchy. There are four major stratification systems: socio-economic, ethnic, gender and age.

2. Stratification is (1) a characteristic of society, not something that merely arises from individual differences; (2) persistent over many generations; (3) universal, yet variable in form; and (4) supported by cultural beliefs.

3. Caste systems, typical of agrarian societies, are based on ascription and permit little or no social mobility. Caste hierarchy, which rests on strong moral beliefs, shapes a person's entire life, including occupation and marriage.

4. Class systems, common to industrial societies, reflect a greater measure of individual achievement. Because the emphasis on achievement opens the way for social mobility, classes are less clearly defined than castes.

5. Historically, socialist societies have claimed to be classless, based on their public ownership of productive property. While such societies may exhibit far less economic inequality than their capitalist counterparts, they are notably stratified with regard to power.

6. Social stratification persists for two reasons – support from various social institutions and the power of ideology to define certain kinds of inequality as both natural and just.

7. The Davis–Moore thesis states that social stratification is universal because it contributes to the operation of society. In class systems, unequal rewards motivate people to aspire to the occupational roles most important to the functioning of society.

8. Critics of the Davis–Moore thesis note that (1) it is difficult to assess objectively the functional importance of any occupational position; (2) stratification prevents many people from developing their abilities; and (3) social stratification often generates social conflict.

9. Karl Marx, a key architect of social-conflict analysis, recognised two major social classes in industrial societies. The capitalists, or bourgeoisie, own the means of production in pursuit of profits; the proletariat, by contrast, offer their labour in exchange for wages.

10. The socialist revolution that Marx predicted has not occurred in industrial societies such as Germany or the United States. Some sociologists see this as evidence that Marx's analysis was flawed; others, however, point out that our society is still marked by pronounced social inequality and substantial class conflict.

11. Max Weber identified three distinct dimensions of social inequality: economic class, social status or prestige, and power. Taken together, these three dimensions form a complex hierarchy of socio-economic standing.

12. Gerhard Lenski and Jean Lenski explained that, historically, technological advances have been associated with more pronounced social stratification. A limited reversal of this trend occurs in advanced industrial societies, as represented by the Kuznets curve.

13. Social stratification is a complex and controversial area of research because it deals not only with facts but with values that suggest how society should be organised.

KEY CONCEPTS

blue-collar or manual occupations lower-prestige work involving mostly manual labour

caste system a system of social stratification based on ascription

class system a system of social stratification based on individual achievement

Davis–Moore thesis the assertion that social stratification is a universal pattern because it has beneficial consequences for the operation of a society

ideology cultural beliefs that serve to justify social stratification

meritocracy a system of social stratification based on personal merit

slavery a form of stratifcation in which people are owned by others as property

social mobility change in people's position in a social hierarchy

social stratification a system by which society ranks categories of people in a hierarchy

socioeconomic status (SES) a composite ranking based on various dimensions of social inequality

status consistency the degree of consistency of a person's social standing across various dimensions of social inequality

structural social mobility a shift in the social position of large numbers of people due more to changes in society itself than to individual efforts

white-collar occupations higher-prestige work involving mostly mental activity

CRITICAL-THINKING QUESTIONS ....

1. How is social stratification evident in your university or college?

2. Why are agrarian societies typically caste systems? Why does industrialisation replace castes with classes?

3. Examine different kinds of slavery systems: for instance the plantation system of the USA and the ones at work in the world today.

4. According to the Davis–Moore thesis, why is a university Vice-chancellor paid more than a lecturer? Do you agree with this analysis?

5. In what respects have the predictions of Karl Marx failed to materialise? In what respects does his analysis ring true?

6. Consider the mix of class, ethnicity, gender and age as systems of stratification. Are they all equally important; and can they be usefully combined?

7. Locate your own position in the stratification system. Compare it with those of friends and family.

GOING FURTHER ....

Introductory reading

Steven Edgell, *Class* (London: Routledge, 1993).
A short overview of the field.

Classical source

C. Wright Mills, *The Power Elite* (New York: Oxford University Press, 1956).
In this treatise, written in the Marxist tradition, Mills argues that US society is dominated by a small, well-integrated group that controls the economy, the government and the military.

More advanced readings

John Scott, *Stratification and Power: Structures of Class, Status and Command* (Oxford: Polity, 1996).
Addresses the current crisis in class theory, and provides a Weberian account of stratification.

Lillian Breslow Rubin, *Worlds of Pain: Life in the Working-Class Family* (New York: Basic Books, 1976).
Based on interviews with 50 working-class families; Rubin skilfully explores the effects of social stratification on everyday life.

Mary J. Jackman, *The Velvet Glove: Paternalism and Conflict in Gender, Class, and Race Relations* (Berkeley and Los Angeles: University of California Press, 1994).

According to this research, relations between elites and subordinates are typically characterised by paternalism, not overt conflict.

Russell Jacoby and Naomi Glauberman (eds.), *The Bell Curve Debate: History, Documents, Opinions* (New York: Times Books, 1995).
Presenting the ideas of dozens of scholars and journalists, this is an excellent collection of commentary and analysis of the *Bell Curve* thesis – the alleged link between intelligence and social class.

Simon Bekker, *Ethnicity in Focus: The South African Case* (Durban: Indicator South Africa, 1993).
This book traces the recent and complex process by which South Africa seeks to shed the racial foundations of its social inequality.

James Curtis and Lorne Tepperman (eds.), *Haves and Have Nots: An International Reader on Social Inequality* (Englewood Cliffs, NJ: Prentice-Hall, 1994).
This collection of essays presents a global survey of social stratification.

Other sources

For more information on modern slavery, contact: Anti-Slavery International, Stableyard, Broomgrove Road, London SW9 9TL.

chapter ten

Source: Popperfoto

Class, Poverty and Welfare

Imagine an hour long parade of people with heights matched to income. What a parade it would be! For more than twenty-five minutes, all the toddlers and 'vertically challenged' would march by. Three-quarters of an hour would pass before we saw people of average height or taller. Suddenly, for the last minute we would be stunned to see people who would be twenty metres or so tall. Then in the final seconds, huge, colossal figures start to emerge, their heads lost in the clouds. Just a few massive people, and yet such vast numbers of small ones. One of the world's richest men, John Paul Getty, could stand as tall as 10 miles (Goodman et al., 1997).

This is an example of the colourful language used in several recent reports on inequality. It makes a point. More prosaically, we can say that most Western societies are characterised by extremes of inequality: huge numbers with low incomes and a few with large incomes. But statistics conceal the experiences. At one end there is the life of luxury – a level of wealth that most of us can only imagine. But at the other extremes are what sociologist Richard Sennett has called 'the hidden injuries of class'. These are the deep scars often thrust upon a life because of no work or demeaning work over which one has little control; because of poor housing or no housing, because money is tight and there are no assets, and, maybe worst of all, a deep sense of being outside of society, at the bottom of the heap.

All contemporary societies have class structures, though not every society treats class as an issue of premium social importance. In the United States, where racial divides are foremost in people's minds, there is only moderate interest in class, and people tend to see themselves as being much less class bound. Any visitor to the UK, in contrast, will soon hear people talk about class. Indeed they may soon see it, with hereditary peers in the House of Lords, gentleman's's clubs and elite educational institutions from public schools to Oxford and Cambridge universities being but a few examples. At the other extreme, street beggars, slums and large numbers of unemployed mark the British lower classes. And never the two shall meet. You can walk in one world and be quite unaware of the other.

Yet, all main political parties in the UK, at least rhetorically, claim to want to create conditions for upward social mobility – a world where we all can 'make it'. Indeed, both of the last two Conservative Prime Ministers, John Major and Margaret Thatcher, came from 'humble' origins: he, the son of a circus acrobat and garden gnome salesman; she, the daughter of a grocer from Grantham.

In this chapter, we will examine the nature of classes, wealth and poverty in industrial capitalist societies, focusing on the UK, the European Union, and the United States. The chapter will ask how we can measure class, and outline some of the key variables in doing this. It will then present a 'portrait' of class life as it is lived in the UK and much of the rest of Europe. Poverty will be highlighted. Then we will consider just how class 'mobile' people are in the United States – the society that prides itself on being the most mobile of all. Finally, we will consider the emergence of 'welfare states' as a means of dealing with some of the problems that inequalities generate.

● Stratification in Europe

Goran Therborn has suggested that social class is one of the key defining features of modern Europe, as Europe was the first major arena of industrialisation. More than anywhere in the world, class is to be found here (1995: 68). Europe as a whole, he contends, first experienced the rise of a manual working class through the industrialisation period, followed much more recently by a decline in this section of the population. Nowadays, 'less than a third of the economically active population is engaged in industrial labour' (1995: 76), marking the shrinking size of the working class population.

Other commentators have suggested that Western Europe could now be characterised as a rugby ball – with a large middle class and smaller working classes and upper classes at the ends. The middle class accounts for around 45–50 per cent of Western European societies – and has grown as traditional manual occupations decline (Eyde and Lintner, 1996: 108).

Despite such changes, Europe remains highly stratified. Not only do the rich have controlling stakes in most businesses, they also benefit from the most schooling, enjoy the best health care, and consume the greatest share of almost all goods and services (Scott, 1991). Such privileges contrast sharply with the emergence of higher levels of unemployment throughout Europe, and the poverty of millions of people who struggle from day to day

The UK's Conservative Party brought 'monetarism' and 'marketisation' to the forefront of its social policy programme.

Source: Popperfoto

simply to buy food and keep a roof over their heads. And yet more and more people think that Europe's countries are all becoming middle class. It is easy to underestimate the extent of stratification in our society for four reasons:

1. *We support equal standing under the law.* Because our legal system accords equal rights to everyone, we tend to think that all people have basically the same social standing.

2. *Our cultures celebrate individual autonomy and achievement.* Our belief that people forge their own destinies through talent and hard work leads us to downplay the significance of birth on social position.

3. *We tend to interact with people like ourselves.* Throughout Europe, primary groups, including family, neighbours and friends, are typically composed of people with similar social standing. While we may speak of 'how the other half lives', generally we have only brief and impersonal encounters with people very different from ourselves.

4. *Europe generally boasts affluent societies.* The overall standard of living in Europe is amongst the highest in the world, though there are sharp variations. Relative to most regions of the world, few Europeans confront the most severe forms of life threatening inequalities. Such affluence lulls us into believing that everyone in our societies is relatively well off, and that we are egalitarian. Yet research over the past few years has suggested that, although a larger middle class may have generally emerged, the gaps between the wealthy and the poor in Europe have been growing; and the number of poor have been increasing (Funken and Cooper, 1995; Joseph Rowntree Foundation, 1995). We will return to this research later in this chapter.

● Dimensions of social inequality

Sociologists have long debated just what social class is, and we have enountered some of these debates in Chapter 9. Some are very theoretical – building on the ideas of Marx and Weber developed in the last chapter. Some adopt the large scale survey approach – attempting to measure 'classes'. Still others provide descriptive case studies. We will look at some of this research as we go along. In what follows, we will show some of the major ways class has been measured, discuss broad features of different classes and consider whether people are generally moving between classes. We will not, however, be concerned with the detailed complexities of the debates. It will be sufficient for our purposes to provide the broadest contours.

Defining and measuring class

As Chapter 9 ('Social Stratification') explained, people living in rigid caste systems can tell at a glance anyone's social ranking. Assessing social position in a more fluid class system, however, poses a number of challenges. In part, these challenges arise from the ways we think about class in our everyday lives. People often speak of a 'ladder' of social class, as if inequality were a matter of a single factor such as money. Social class, as we shall see, has more subtle dimensions.

Karl Marx defined class in terms of those who own the means of production and those who do not (with a residual class in between). Erik Ohlin Wright elaborated on Marx's model by dividing ownership into three categories: those controlling resource allocation; those controlling the means of productuon; and those controlling labour power. Ohlin Wright defines all low-level employees as working class, and suggests that the rest in the middle occupy a contradictory position in which they may identify either with the capitalists or the working classes. Others break down Marx's original distinctions further into six (Warner and Lunt, 1941) or even seven (Coleman and Rainwater, 1978) categories. The separation of management and 'capital', and the failure of radical class consciousness to emerge among working people, have made such class definitions difficult to translate into numbers we can meaningfully measure and compare.

Other scholars endorse Max Weber's contention that, rather than clear-cut classes, people are ranked in a multidimensional status hierarchy. Those elaborating on Weber often examine socioeconomic status (SES), introduced in Chapter 9, a composite measure of social position which includes a person's income, wealth, kind of occupation and 'spending power' in the market. Some sociologists also add a status dimension that takes account of a person's lifestyle, communities, sense of who they are, consciousness and identity. These definitions of class likewise run into problems because of the relatively low level of status consistency in European societies. Especially around the middle of hierarchies, standing on one dimension often contradicts one's position on another. A government official, for example, may have the power to administer a multimillion-pound budget, yet earn a modest personal income. Similarly, members of the clergy typically enjoy ample prestige but only moderate power and low pay. Or consider a lucky professional gambler who may win little respect but who accumulates considerable wealth.

Other researchers, particularly those working for government agencies, define class through the people's work situation (their work tasks and the degree of control they have over their working timetables and methods) and market situation (people's life chances, which depend upon such things as their income and opportunity for promotion). John Scott, for example, breaks down capitalist classes into three types: entrepreneurs, who own and control their own businesses; internal capitalists (top career managers); and finance capitalists, who own and manage big finance companies and big business. To more directly examine the challenges of defining class, we will now look at two scales that have been widely used.

The Registrar General's scale of social class
The Registrar General's scale of social class provides the most straightforward and most widely used classification of social classes. This scale builds on the Weberian notion of life chances, and ranks the prestige, salary and general power associated with different kinds of occupations. Table 10.1 illustrates the categories in this scale.

The Goldthorpe scale
John Goldthorpe, one of the most prominent of British class analysts, has modified the Registrar General's scale. Goldthorpe groups workers into three main categories of work, and further subdivides each group. His scale is as follows: *service class* ((a) professional and managerial workers; (b) supervisors of non-manual workers); *intermediate class* ((a) routine non-manual workers; (b) small proprietors; (c) supervisors of manual workers; (d) lower grade technicians); and *working class* ((a) skilled; (b) semi-skilled; (c) unskilled manual workers). Both of the scales make allowances for three factors that determine the general social power people gain from their occupation: prestige, income and wealth.

Prestige

For more than half a century, sociologists have assessed **prestige**, or the *value people in a society associate with various occupations*. In general, people attach high prestige to occupations such as medicine, law and engineering that also generate high income. But prestige reflects more than just pay, since favoured occupations typically require considerable ability and demand extensive education and training. By contrast, less prestigious work, such as that of a cleaner or porter, not only pays less but usually requires less ability and schooling. Nevertheless, as previously discussed, high prestige and high income do not always go hand in hand. Even so, occupational prestige rankings are much the same in all industrial societies (Ma, 1987; Lin and Xie, 1988). Almost everywhere, more highly ranked work that involves mental activity, free from extensive supervision, confers greater prestige than lower class occupations that require supervised manual labour. In any society, privileged categories of people tend to fill high-prestige occupations.

Income

A second important dimension of inequality involves **income**, *wages or salaries and earnings from investments*. We will look briefly at the situation in Britain (Figure 10.1). In 1996, the avergage gross weekly

Table 10.1 ● Registrar General scale categories		
Class	Name of the class	Examples
I	Professional	Solicitors, accountants
II	Managerial and technical	Managers, teachers, nurses
III N	Skilled non-manual	Estate agents, secretaries, shop workers
III M	Skilled manual	Bricklayers, electricians, drivers
IV	Partly skilled manual	Postal carriers, pub/bar staff
V	Unskilled manual	Cleaners, labourers

earnings in Britain were highest in Greater London at over £450, and lowest in Blaenau Gwent at £255. The gap between high incomes and low incomes grew very rapidly in the UK in the 1980s, growing faster than in any other country in the OECD except New Zealand. It has been more stable since the early 1990s. Even so, in 1995, the Joseph Rowntree Foundation found that the poorest one-fifth of households earned less than £126 per week; two-thirds fell below £254; while only one-fifth earned more than £342 per week. The disturbing feature is that inequalities have grown: between 1979 and 1992, income *grew* by 36 per cent for the population as a whole, yet *fell* by 17 per cent for the poorest 10 per cent of people. Between 1983 and 1993, income for the top 5 per cent of earners rose nearly 50 per cent to £550 per week; for the bottom 5 per cent it hardly changed, and this gap continued to grow through 1997 (Joseph Rowntree Foundation, 1995; *Social Trends*, 1997; Goodman et al., 1997). It has been estimated that by the year 2000 there will be 200,000 millionaires in the UK (in 1997 there were 120,000). This is one in every 480 people. So some people are getting much richer, whilst many others are getting poorer. This signposts a country of increasing inequalities.

In the United States, the richest 20 per cent of families (earning at least $70,000 annually, with a mean of about $115,000) received 46.8 per cent of all income, while the bottom 20 per cent (earning less than $18,000, with a mean of about $10,000) received only about 4.2 per cent. The highest-paid 5 per cent of US families, who earn six-figure incomes (with a mean of $198,336), secured 20.1 per cent of all income, surpassing in earnings the lowest-paid 40 per cent. At the very top of the pyramid, the richest 0.5 per cent earn at least $1 million annually. In short, the bulk of the income earned in the United States is 'earned' by a small proportion of families, while the rest of the population makes do with far less. Similarly to the UK, income disparity in the United States increased during the 1980s as a result of tax policies, more two-earner couples and cuts in social programmes that assist low-income people (Levy, 1987; Reich, 1989; Cutler and Katz, 1992). Since 1990, however, income disparity in the United States has eased downwards, a trend accelerated in 1993 by higher income tax rates on the top-earning 5 per cent.

Whilst both the UK and the United States may have less income inequality than, say, Venezuela, Kenya or Sri Lanka, income inequality in these countries is higher than in other industrial societies. The ratio of high to poor incomes in Britain is 10:1, while this ratio is only 8:1 in France and 6:1 in Germany.

Wealth

Income is one component of a person's **wealth**, *the total value of money and other assets, minus outstanding debts*. Assets contributing to wealth include such items as houses, property, jewels, cars, artworks, boats, shares in a stock market, deposited money and racehorses. As Figure 10.2 shows, an increasing proportion of people have an expanding share of the national wealth. While the richest 1 per cent of Britons controlled 69 per cent of the national wealth in 1911, today they control 20 per cent. Nevertheless, as Figure 10.2 reflects, the richest 1 per cent in Britain hold roughly the same amount of wealth as the poorest 50 per cent! In the United States, once financial liabilities are balanced against assets, the least affluent 40 per cent of households have virtually no wealth at all – with the poorest 20 per cent living in debt. The figure also illustrates that social mobility in industrial class systems has been most pronounced near the middle, where people's social position is most likely to change. This mobility has blurred the lines between social classes, suggesting that the 'capitalist classes' have 'fragmented into millions of tiny pieces' (yet they have still managed to retain power over the classes of people working for subsistence wages or surviving with state benefits).

Even though the wealth base has broadened, the wealthiest people still command considerable resources. Some examples among the richest 25 people in Britain include the former Beatle Paul McCartney, whose personal wealth exceeds £400 million, Richard Branson (the entrepreneur who founded the various Virgin companies – see photo on page 253), with a personal fortune exceeding £895 million, and the Duke of Westminster, wielding wealth of £1,500 million. Such wealth gives the mega-rich considerable influence, from the field of national politics (where the rich can sponsor politicians, fund their own political campaigns, or, in the cases of the European millionaire Sir James Goldsmith (now deceased) and US business tycoon H. Ross Perot, even found their own political parties), to minor business transactions. The super-rich

Figure 10.1 ● Who really earns what

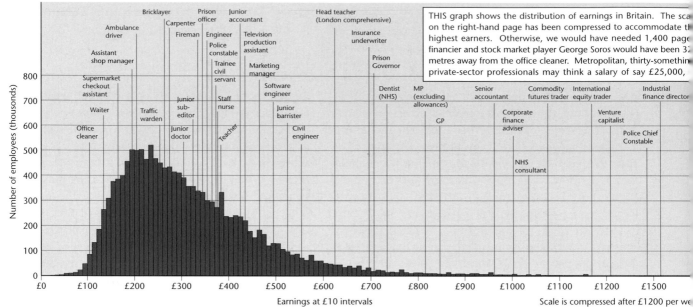

Source: Office for National Statistics; Income Data Source (from *Independent on Sunday* 3 November 96)

---

also tend to reinforce and protect each other's interests. As John Scott notes, the elite 0.1 per cent of industrial populations often share similar backgrounds, swap directorships of high-performing companies, and are dominant shareholders in the leading businesses.

Figure 10.2 ● Income disparities for selected industrial countries

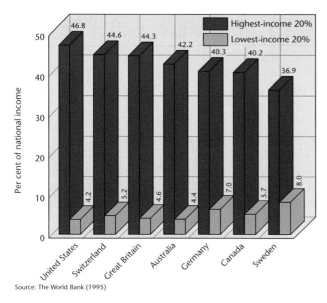

Source: The World Bank (1995)

Problems of defining class

Even when we have identified the key components of social class, we still encounter problems with measuring and identifying class. While some people live solitary lives, managing their wealth or lack of wealth personally, many people live in partnerships or families where ownership of wealth (or responsibility for debt) is spread among members of the household. Until the 1970s, most social science researchers assumed that men headed households and that the fortunes of these men determined the life chances of women, children and other adult male members of the household (Parkin, 1971, Goldthorpe, 1980). Class was thus measured by the prestige, income and wealth of the male 'head of the household'. Though men remain more likely to hold the higher prestige and higher income occupation in dual-career couples (Goldthorpe, 1987), increasing numbers of women now head households, not only as single parents but also as primary earners. Moreover, researchers faced the challenge of defining the class of households formed by unions of people from very different economic positions. We cannot always safely assume that the lower class partner will simply assume the class status of the higher class partner. We will now explore the layers of class in more depth.

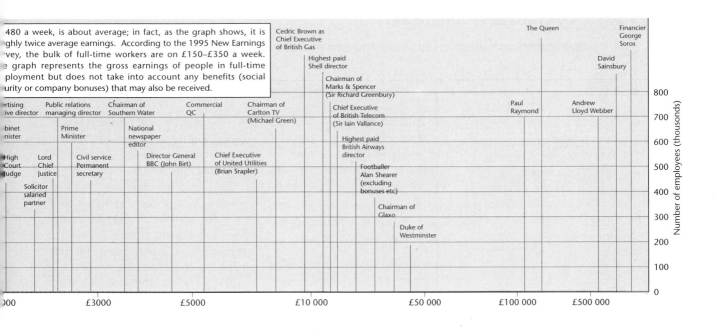

480 a week, is about average; in fact, as the graph shows, it is ...ghly twice average earnings. According to the 1995 New Earnings ...vey, the bulk of full-time workers are on £150–£350 a week. ...e graph represents the gross earnings of people in full-time ...ployment but does not take into account any benefits (social ...urity or company bonuses) that may also be received.

● Layers of social class

Having expressed the necessary reservations, we now proceed to identify four social classes that are probably found across the industrialised world: the upper class, the middle class, the working class and the underclass. Will Hutton suggests that roughly 30 per cent of the British population falls into the underclass; 30 per cent into the marginal working class; and 40 per cent into the privileged middle and upper classes. The box offers more detail on his 30:30:40 proposal. Hutton's view, which appears to fit roughly into the popular view of class in the UK today, however, does not hold up to more substantial review. Runciman (1990) instead has documented that the proportions of people at the different levels of the British class structure are as follows:

Upper class	0.2–0.1%
Lower upper class	less than 10%
Upper middle and service class	15%
Lower middle class	20%
Skilled working class	20%
Unskilled working class	30%
Underclass	5%

We will now examine each of these groups in some detail.

Figure 10.3 ● The shapes of class

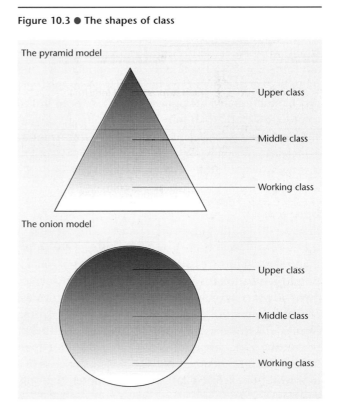

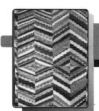

The 30–30–40 society

The English economist Will Hutton has put forward a popular account of the changing shape of Britain's economy and class structure. It is a 'popular account' but one that raises some key issues about the broad structuring of the UK class system. He argues that Britain has become a society split three ways.

● *The privileged*: the top 40 per cent who have stable, long-term employment, and a market (consumption) power that is considerable.

● *The marginalised and insecure*: a middle 30 per cent made up of part-time and casual workers with little job security and few benefits, and many who earn way below average wages.

● *The disadvantaged*: a bottom 30% who are unemployed or married to economically inactive partners.

This description of Britain is compatible with many of the ideas about a 'flexible' labour market and an emerging underclass. Britain now has a highly deregulated society: one group works more and more; others can find no work at all. With the weakening security of work for many, relationships and friendships may be becoming more and more insecure.

But there are problems with this analysis. Each of these groups is itself fractured and split into many others. Most importantly, Hutton ignores the divisions that come about through ethni-city or gender. Do you find this characterisation of the British class structure convincing? ●

Source: Will Hutton, *The State We're In* (London: Cape, 1995).

The upper classes

In industrialised countries, the upper classes make up anything from 5 to 10 per cent of the populations, and include a small cadre of the super-rich (around 0.2 per cent). Traditionally, the upper classes have been linked to old aristocratic traditions and to significant ownership of property (especially land). But this 'old' money is increasingly being joined by 'new' money. We might distinguish two groups: the upper-uppers and the lower-uppers.

Upper-uppers

Membership of the upper-upper class is almost always the result of ascription or birth. In much of Europe, many large landed estates have passed from generation to generation for centuries. The British aristocracy owns 40 per cent of British land. These families possess enormous wealth, primarily inherited rather than earned. For this reason, we sometimes say that members of the upper-upper class have *old money*. Set apart by their wealth, members of the upper-upper class live in a world of exclusive affiliations. Children typically attend private secondary schools with others of similar background, completing their formal education at high-prestige colleges and universities.

Lower-uppers

Most upper-class people actually fall into the *lower-upper class*. From most people's point of view, this group is every bit as privileged as the upper-upper class. The major difference, however, is that lower-uppers are the 'working rich' who depend on earnings rather than inherited wealth as the primary source of their income. They include what we have come to call the 'fat cats', whose incomes often rise to extraordinary heights. The lower-upper class also includes 'the jet set rich' – the very visible and very famous, such as the footballer who accepts a million-pound contract to play in the First Division; the computer whiz who designs a program that sets a standard for the industry; or the musician whose work tops the charts – these are the lucky and talented achievers who reach the level of the lower-upper class. Celebrities like Elton John or Andrew Lloyd Weber are included here. But there are also the entrepreneurial rich, including people like Richard Branson, the Guinness family (the brewers); the Sieff family (Marks and Spencers) and Anita Roddick of the Body Shop. Entrepreneurial capitalists, rentiers, executive and finance capitalists generally make the majority of their money through wise investments of stocks and bonds.

Especially in the eyes of members of 'society', the lower-upper class are merely the 'new rich' who can never savour the status enjoyed by those with rich and famous grandparents. Thus, while the new rich typically live in the biggest homes, they often find themselves excluded from the clubs and associations of old-money families.

The middle classes

The middle classes used to be the 'middle group' between poor and rich, who gained income through trade and manufacturing. Weber predicted its growth and Marx its demise. In fact, however, the middle classes have increasingly made up a larger and larger proportion of most of the class structure of Europe. Middle class occupations have material and cultural advantages over working class employment, generally offering more security, higher pay and higher prestige. The middle class encompasses far more racial and ethnic diversity than the upper class. While many upper class people (especially upper-uppers) know each other personally, such exclusiveness and familiarity do not characterise the middle class. We can identify three general shades of middle class: the upper (or traditional) middle class, the service class and the lower middle class. It is a large and highly fragmented group (cf. Savage, 1995).

The upper middle class

The more powerful end of this category, also dubbed the traditional middle class, earns above-average incomes. Family income may be even greater if both wife and husband work. High income allows upper middle class families to gradually accumulate considerable property, a comfortable house in a fairly expensive area, several cars and investments. A majority of upper middle class children receive university educations, and postgraduate degrees are common. Many go on to high-prestige occupations (as doctors, engineers, lawyers, accountants or business executives). Lacking the power of the upper class to influence national or international events, the upper middle class nonetheless often plays an important role in local political affairs.

The service class

The service class includes people who provide highly valued and well-paid services to employers, including middle-level bureaucrats, management of health, welfare and education services, technically trained secretaries and business consultants. This group also includes many people who work in media, teaching, fashion and therapy professions. Service class people enjoy a lot of autonomy in their work, usually exercise and delegate authority, and tend to have secure careers (cf. Goldthorpe, 1982; Lash and Urry, 1987). David Lockwood (1992) further subdivides this group into: professionals, who rely on cultural capital (knowledge); managers; and petty bourgeois (traders and small property owners). People in this class also tend to own property (though in less fashionable districts), to own vehicles (though less expensive models) and to have relatively high levels of education, though they are more likely to work to pull maximum advantage from state-sponsored education and to have attended second-tier colleges and universities.

The lower middle class

The rest of the middle class falls close to the centre of the class structure. People in the lower middle class typically work in less prestigious white-collar occupations (such as bank clerks, middle managers or sales clerks) or in highly skilled blue-collar jobs (including electrical work and carpentry). Commonly, lower middle class households earn incomes around the national average. Income at this level provides a secure, if modest, standard of living. Lower middle class people generally accumulate some wealth over the course of their working lives, mostly in the form of a house. People in this class generally complete some post-secondary school qualifications, though not necessarily university degrees.

The working classes

Two distinct phases have marked out the working class. Working class life used to be defined in terms of strong identities based in communities associated with a particular field of labour, such as found in traditional mining communities (Dennis, 1956), traditional steel communities (Beynon, 1991), traditional fishing communities, and so forth. But to name these communities is to sense their demise. In the UK the old coalfields around Durham or the steel furnaces blasting out around Middlesborough have gone and the fishing communities around the country are rapidly shrinking. With them went jobs, income, security and communities. After long periods of unemployment and demoralisation, some benefit from new patterns of work that emerge. But these patterns are very different, often involving relocation and work that is much more fragmented. We have moved from work in the mine to work in McDonald's. And with that, working class communities are in steep decline.

But a new working class has also emerged. This is one that will own their own homes, live in suburbs and be more affluent, with cars and video recorders. It is even unlikely that they will see themselves as working class.

The blue-collar occupations of the working class generally yield a household income somewhat below the national average. Working class families thus find themselves vulnerable to financial problems, especially when confronted by unemployment or illness. Besides generating less income, working class jobs typically yield less personal satisfaction. Tasks tend to be routine, requiring discipline but rarely imagination, and workers are usually subject to continual supervision. Such jobs also provide fewer benefits, like private medical insurance and pension schemes. About half of working class families own their homes, usually in lower-cost districts.

The underclass

The **underclass** comprises those people *'under the class structure' who are economically, politically and socially marginalised and excluded.* Typically, these people live between unemployment and the labour market of casual and temporary work. They usually live on state benefits or charitable aid. Encompassing the frail pensioners, the single 'trapped' parents and the long-term unemployed, they are in a sense 'outside' the system of work and even class! In 1987, Dahrendorf estimated that about 5 per cent of the British population fell within the underclass – and that this percentage was growing rapidly.

The idea of an underclass has a long and controversial history. Marx spoke of the *lumpenproletariat* (the social scum of vagrants, misfits, dregs). Booth and Mayhew described the 'dangerous classes' of 'paupers, beggars and outcasts with a repugnance to regular labour'. There is a long history of distinguishing undeserving, disreputable poor from 'respectable' people trapped in a 'cycle of deprivation' (Morris, 1994) – a debate which the box examines in greater detail. All these writings point to a heavily stigmatised group at the bottom, excluded from work, living in dire poverty. The least generous observers suspect the underclass of turning to crime and, as we shall discuss more later, this view often associates racial and underclass issues.

The American Sociologist Charles Murray has recently popularised the use of the term 'underclass'. Looking at the USA, in his book *Losing Ground* (1984) he charted what he saw as the failure of welfare policies, where he argued that more and more people had become dependent on the State. In the late 1980s he brought these ideas to the UK and they became serialised in *The Sunday Times* (26 November 1989). For Murray, this underclass lives in a different world, raises its children differently and has different values. He ponders: 'How is a civilised society to take care of the deserving without encouraging people to become undeserving? How does it do good without engendering vice?'.

In Europe, the problem of the underclass is often linked to problems of migration. Workers who cannot find work in their own countries want to go to others where work may be found. But in this process – as new arrivals, often with different ethnic backgrounds – all they can find is casual work. Algerians in France, Turks in Germany, Moroccans in Spain and Bangladeshis in the UK often confront both formal and informal barriers against their entering the regular labour market. People who have illegally joined family and friends in the European Union face an even more tenuous position, as they cannot even apply for benefits to meet basic needs. The drive for daily survival focuses the attention of underclass people more on the present. Without much prospect of work, people in the underclass live on the margins of society.

Although many people experience the conditions implied by the term 'underclass', the academic use of this term is problematic. 'Underclass' is often used as an abusive 'catch all' phrase that lumps together many different kinds of experiences, and then proceeds to

DIFFERENT VOICES

What a difference a class makes

Why do sociologists spend so much time talking about class? The answer is that there is little doubt that social stratification affects nearly every dimension of our lives. While class alone does not define our sense of place in society, class is one of the most significant influences on our lives. Our class status affects us objectively – that is, in our health, our education, our possessions and our lifestyle – but it also affects us subjectively – the way we see ourselves, our language, our values, our ideas, our 'cultural capital'. Here are a few examples of the impact of class on various aspects of life in the UK:

Infant mortality	working class children may be three times more likely to die in first year of life
Health	working class is three times more likely to have long-term serious illness
Death	measuring differences in the risk of death from birth to age 65, the child of the unskilled manual worker will die around 7 years earlier than a counterpart born to professional parents
Divorce	four times higher among manuals than professionals
Education	in 1984, just 1 per cent going to university came from the unskilled manual class, whilst 70 per cent came from the top two classes
Income	by definition, the lower class gets lower incomes and has much less wealth
Job security	much less job security for working class occupations than middle class professions
Unemployment	In 1993, unemployment rates were 13 per cent for those with previous manual experience and 5.6 per cent for non-manual
Home ownership	90 per cent of professionals were owner occupiers; only 42 per cent of unskilled manuals were ●

Source: *Social Trends*, 1995; Hart, 1985; Reid, 1989

stigmatise them. It is the most recent term – in a long line – for blaming the poor for their poverty. So sociologists have to be very careful how they come to use it.

● Social mobility and the 'American Dream'

As we discussed in Chapter 9 ('Social Stratification'), in industrial societies, people's class status is not rigidly fixed by birth. Earning a university degree, securing a higher-paying job or becoming a member of a two-career household contributes to *upward social mobility*, while dropping out of school, losing a job or starting to live in a female-headed household may signal *downward social mobility*. Sociologists also distinguish

between changes within a single generation and shifts between generations of a family. **Intragenerational social mobility** refers to *a change in social position occurring within a person's lifetime*. Sociologists pay even greater attention to **intergenerational social mobility**, *upward or downward social mobility of children in relation to their parents*, because social mobility across generations reflects structural changes in society that affect virtually everyone.

Some commentators in the United States have claimed that Americans are the most socially mobile people in the world. 'Rags to riches' stories comprise an important part of the American dream. Nevertheless, even though many people in the United States see class as little more than a transitory marker, even in the USA, class plays an important role in stratifying people across the power spectrum in that country. Although many people are mobile, many others are trapped.

Studies of intergenerational mobility in the United States (that, unfortunately, have focused almost exclusively on men) show that almost 40 per cent of the sons of working class men attain white-collar jobs, and almost 30 per cent of sons born into white-collar families end up doing blue-collar work. Horizontal mobility – a change of occupation at one class level – is even more common, so that about 80 per cent of sons show at least some type of social mobility in relation to their fathers (Blau and Duncan, 1967; Featherman and Hauser, 1978). Available research points to four general conclusions about social mobility in the United States.

1. *Social mobility among men has been fairly high.* The widespread notion that the United States has considerable social mobility is basically true. We would expect such mobility in an industrial class system.

2. *The long-term trend in social mobility has been upwards.* Industrialisation, the expansion of the US economy and the growth of white-collar work over the course of this century have greatly boosted average incomes and living standards.

3. *Within a single generation, social mobility is usually incremental, not dramatic.* Only a very few move 'from rags to riches'. While sharp rises or falls in individual fortunes may command public attention, most instances of social mobility involve subtle shadings *within* one class level rather than striking changes *between* classes.

4. *The short-term trend has been stagnation, with some income polarisation.* The rise in living standards that carried through most of this century hit a plateau in the early 1970s. Real income (adjusted for inflation) for the US population as a whole also changed little during the 1980s, rising slowly in the early 1990s (Veum, 1992). Well-to-do families (the highest 20 per cent) saw their average incomes jump from $89,696 in 1980 to $115,608 in 1994, a 29 per cent increase. People in the second 20 per cent also made gains, albeit a more modest 9.5 per cent. While the middle of the population held about even, the lowest-income 20 per cent suffered a 6.4 per cent loss in earnings (US Bureau of the Census, 1996).

In 1993, the national government classified 39.3 million US citizens (15.1 per cent of the population) as poor. While the majority of poor people in the United States are white, non-white people, particularly those of African, Latin American or indigenous descent, are disproportionately represented at the low end of the socioeconomic scale. Indeed, white and Asian incomes have generally risen faster than the incomes of Americans from other ethnic groups. African-American households earned a smaller percentage relative to white household income in 1992 (58 per cent) than in 1970 (61 per cent); and earnings of Hispanics relative to whites slipped from 72 per cent in 1975 to 69 per cent in 1993 (US Bureau of the Census, 1994). Single mothers and their children are also far more likely than most other groups of Americans to live in poverty.

More disturbingly, the poor in the United States – particularly the poor from ethnic minority groups – are very much more likely to be segregated from the rest of US society in run-down inner city areas, with few jobs, poor-quality schools and little prospect of contact with role models who have escaped the poverty trap (Jacob, 1986). This is not to say that poor neighbourhoods lack any sense of community or drive. In a study conducted in the poor section of a northern city, Carol Stack (1975) noted that, far from lacking initiative and responsibility, residents devised ingenious means to survive. Even so, financial institutions have expressed historical reluctance to lend money to people who seek to buy or improve property in poor inner city areas. Poor inner city communities often face disintegration or agonising battles to survive if their areas are targeted for gentrification. The bottom line, then, is that social mobility exists for many, but is a particularly remote option for the poor in the United States, who are more likely to be single mothers and disproportionately non-white.

● Class and gender

As previously mentioned in this chapter, conventional ways of defining class until very recently focused on male heads of households. As in so much early sociology, women were excluded. Much of class theory may therefore be misconceived. Certainly, bringing women into the picture shifts the focus of class questions, such as how child bearing and child rearing fit into the labour structure. Moreover, women as a group earn less than men – even at comparable levels of education and experience. While overt sex discrimination is illegal in the European Union (as well as in most other industrialised countries), women remain more likely to be ghettoised into lower paid occupations like social work, nursing, child care, primary school teaching and secretarial roles (see Chapter 15 for details of the European situation). In the United States as well, the income gap between women and men has narrowed. Women working full time earned 60 per cent as much as men working full time in 1980, and 72 per cent in 1993; however, much of this change was due to a *drop* in men's earnings through the 1980s, while the income of women remained about the same (US Bureau of the Census, 1995).

● The 'Death of Class' debate

The past 30 years have seen so many changes in the socioeconomic environment that it would be surprising if there had not been changes in the nature of class and the way we study it. Leading British sociologists now disagree about both its importance and how it should be studied. John Scott (1994: 19) argues that 'class remains the sociological key to understanding the structure of society'; whilst Ray Pahl (1989) contends that 'class as a concept is ceasing to do any useful work for sociology'. Which is it?

Some sociologists argue that we have become more and more of a classless society and that the concept of class cannot incorporate the scope of the changes that are happening in the modern world. It is not a question of whether inequalities persist – all agree that they do (and many suggest they are widening) – but whether and how these inequalities can be traced back to class.

There has been a general levelling up, with traditional working class communities largely vanishing and new working class lives heavily shaped by home ownership and consumerism. Working class no longer holds the clear social distinctions that it once did. There has been a clear failure of working class based action and a decline of working class identity and trade unionism. Indeed, one Marxist, André Gortz (1982), calls his book *Farewell to the Working Class*. The divides now occur around consumption and lifestyles, which cut across old class lines. Pahl maintains that 'if the cathedral of the nineteenth century was the factory chimney, that of the twentieth century is the shopping mall'. More important, perhaps, are the new divides between those who rely on market and those who rely on State; between those who own their houses and those who rent them; between those who work and those who are unemployed; between 'work-rich' and 'work-poor' households. Klauss Elder suggests that classes now need to be linked to the 'texture' of cultures and the key role of (largely middle class) social movements.

For this group of scholars, class analysis has become so complicated that the nature of what we are studying ceases to be clear! A myriad of variables are important to studying inequality, they argue, and 'class' as a concept can no longer handle this range. 'Class' is being replaced by 'lifestyle', 'differences' and all sorts of other inequalities linked to ethnicity and gender (see Chapters 12 and 13). The failure of class analysis to seriously incorporate these concerns has made it weaker and weaker: an area of academic study restricted to a few ivory tower academics!

But another group of sociologists, like John Scott, still take class as the central feature of societies. The nature of class may be changing, but it is still the central organising feature of industrial countries. Class here is not in dispute, but its changing character may be. These class theorists often point to a number of key changes, which include:

1. the decreasing importance of the manual/non-manual labour distinction as manual work declines;

2. the collapse of a very traditional working class (for example, around mining communities);

3. the growth and diversity of the middle class, including the expansion of the service sector;

4. the identification of an underclass who are largely outside the class system, and, indeed society;

5. the introduction of both gender and ethnicity into various class schemas as a complicating factor.

These sociologists try to incorporate many of the issues raised by those who have suggested the end of class. They conclude that class is still very important. Class, and class analysis, is far from dead. Indeed, this chapter should have clearly shown that although class patterns are changing, they are deep and widespread. 'Classlessness' may have been exaggerated, for there remains a very clear, powerful and strong upper class. People in Europe in particular still strongly identify with class groups; and new divisions and polarisations continue to appear.

● Shifting work patterns in global perspective

Underlying a phenomenon described as the **middle class slide**, *a trend towards declining living standards and economic security at the centre of industrial societies*, is a global economic transformation. Much of the industrial production that offered high-paying jobs to European, Canadian and American workers a generation ago has been transferred to the developing world (Rosen, 1987; Thurow, 1987). Many popular consumer items, including cars, stereos, cameras and computers,

CONTROVERSY AND DEBATE

Blaming the poor: who is to blame?

That the richest regions on earth – Europe and North America – are home to tens of millions of poor people raises serious questions. It is true, as some analysts remind us, that many of the people counted among the officially poor in industrialised countries are better off than the poor in other countries – 40 per cent of poor families in the United States, for instance, own their home and 60 per cent own a car (Jenkins, 1992). But it is also the case, as noted earlier, that malnutrition and outright hunger are quite widespread, along with violence, illness and a host of other problems that accompany economic deprivation. We now examine more closely the arguments underlying each of these two approaches to the problem of poverty. Together, they frame a lively and pressing political debate.

Blaming the poor: cycles of deprivation and cultures of poverty

One side of the issue is based on the following view: *The poor are primarily responsible for their own poverty*. Since the creation of the English Poor Laws, some thinkers in industrial nations have drawn distinctions between the 'deserving' and the 'undeserving' poor. Believing that social standing primarily reflects talent and individual effort, these people contend that industrial societies offer considerable opportunities to anyone able and willing to take advantage of them. The poor, then, are those who cannot or will not work, people with fewer skills, less schooling or simply lower motivation. While some people (historically, widows, orphans and the disabled) command our compassion as 'worthy poor', this line of reasoning leads us to condemn many people as, in one way or another, responsible for their own fate, and hence undeserving.

Some researchers have offered a different view, suggesting that a *culture of poverty* holds down the poor,

---

Figure 10.4 ● Assessing the causes of poverty

Survey question: 'Why are there people in this country who live in need?' Percentages reflect respondents' identification of either 'personal laziness' or 'societal injustice' as the primary cause of poverty. Percentages for each country do not add up to 100 because less frequently identified causes of poverty were omitted from this figure.

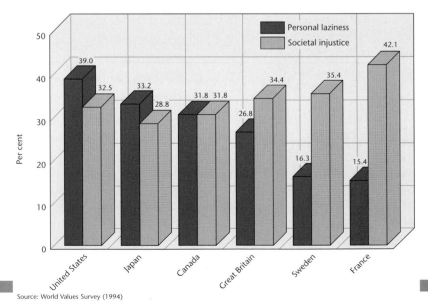

Source: World Values Survey (1994)

are produced in Korea, Singapore and elsewhere.

High-paying jobs in manufacturing, which used to account for a large proportion of the labour force in the earlier part of this century, have now been seriously reduced in number. In their place, the economy now offers jobs in various types of 'service work', which typ-ically pay far less. Indicative of this shift, old steel plants and mines have been closed down – leaving weakened working class communities behind them – whilst fast food chains like McDonald's enjoy a rapid expansion. Traditional working class jobs remain; but the new ones that appear are low paid and much less secure.

fostering resignation to poverty as a matter of fate. Anthropologist Oscar Lewis (1961), who investigated the poor barrios of Latin American cities, is one of the early proponents of this view. Although Lewis doubted that most poor people could do much about their plight, he did not blame them individually for their poverty. Instead, he claimed that the barrio environment socialised children to believe that there is little point in aspiring to a better life. The result is a self-perpetuating cycle of poverty, as one generation transmits its way of life to the next. In the UK, this has been a widely influential model too.

Research in the United States led Charles Murray (1984) to much the same conclusion. Especially in areas of intense poverty such as the inner cities, claims Murray, a lower-class subculture has taken hold, eroding personal ambition and achievement. One element of this subculture, as he sees it, is a present-time orientation that encourages living for the moment. While a future orientation guides most better-off people to study, plan, work hard and save, Murray saw poor people as failing to look beyond the moment. In living for the present, he concluded, the poor perpetuate their own poverty and, therefore, reap what they deserve.

Blaming society: social exclusion and structural divisions

The other side of the issue can be summed up as follows: *Society is primarily responsible for poverty.* This alternative position, argued by William Ryan (1976), holds that social structures – not people themselves – distribute the resources unequally and are, therefore, responsible for poverty. Looking at societies around the world from this point of view, we see that those that distribute wealth very unequally (like the United Kingdom) also have high levels of relative poverty; while societies that strive for more economic equality (such as Sweden and Japan) lack such extremes of social stratification.

Poverty, Ryan insists, is not inevitable. Low income, not personal deficiencies, cause the problem. Ryan interprets any lack of ambition on the part of poor people as a *consequence* rather than a *cause* of their lack of opportunity. He therefore dismisses Lewis's analysis as little more than 'blaming the victims' for their own suffering. In Ryan's view, social policies that empower the poor would give them real economic opportunity and yield more economic equality.

Weighing the evidence

Each of these explanations of poverty has won its share of public support, and each has advocates among policymakers. As Murray sees it, society should pursue equality of opportunity, especially for the young, but otherwise people should take responsibility for themselves, and their success will correspond to their talents and interests.

Ryan takes a more activist approach, asserting that public policy should reduce poverty through more equitable redistribution of income. Programmes like comprehensive child care, for example, could help poor mothers gain job skills; indeed, the living standard of every poor person could be raised by a tax-funded, guaranteed minimum income for every family.

Certainly, both of these views could be put into practice, and many societies periodically lean towards one or the other. Typically, conservative policies are sympathetic toward the first; while left-leaning and liberal strategies are usually more in tune with the second.

● **Continue the debate:**

1. What are the major groups in the communities of poor people? Is it reasonable to divide some of them into 'deserving' and some into 'undeserving' categories?

2. Why do you think poverty in Europe seems to be constantly on the increase?

3. Discuss strategies for reducing poverty. ●

The global reorganisation of work may not be bad news for everyone. This growing global economy is driving the upward social mobility of a highly educated managerial class who specialise in areas such as law, finance, marketing and computer technology. Moreover, the increasing value of global companies has vastly expanded the wealth of the richest members of industrial societies. But surging global competition has also unleashed a trend toward 'downsizing', which has prompted the largest corporations to eliminate about a quarter of all jobs since 1980. To make matters worse, many individuals of moderate income have been left without work as their factory jobs have been 'exported' overseas (Reich, 1989, 1991).

Just as industrialisation spawned prosperity a century ago, today's deindustrialisation has hurt the standard of living and shaken the confidence of many people. Compared to a previous generation, far fewer now expect to improve their social position and a growing number worry about being able to maintain the way of life they knew as children in their parents' homes.

● Poverty

Social stratification simultaneously creates 'haves' and 'have nots'. Poverty is therefore an inevitable product of all systems of social inequality. Sociologists address the concept of poverty in two different ways, however. **Relative poverty** refers to *the deprivation of some people in relation to those who have more*. Relative poverty is universal and unavoidable; even a rich society has some members who live in relative poverty. It depends on the values and standards of living that a particular society sets; those falling below it are 'poor'. In contrast, **absolute poverty** is *a deprivation of resources that is life threatening*. It depends upon a universally agreed minumum for adequate nutrition and living.

As the next chapter ('Global Stratification') explains, the global dimensions of absolute poverty place the lives of perhaps 800 million people – one in seven of the earth's entire population – at risk. Yet even in Europe, the most affluent region of the whole world as defined by its Gross Domestic Product (GDP), people go hungry, become homeless or live in inadequate housing and endure poor health because of the wrenching reality of poverty. This chapter now turns to the problems of studying the problems of the least well-off.

Measuring poverty

Some of the earliest attempts to measure poverty were conducted in Britain in the latter part of the nineteenth century. Aware of the shocking conditions brought about through rapid industrialisation in major cities like Manchester and London, the philanthropist and businessman Charles Booth set about a door to door survey in large areas of London, enumerating the numbers of people occupying each dwelling and measuring poverty in terms of their income. Poverty, for Booth, was taken to be absolute and objective: it was the amount of money people had to live on. If it fell below a certain breadline of nutritional needs it meant that people were poor.

Seebohm Rowntree conducted three surveys between 1899 and 1951 in the city of York (and concluded in the last study that poverty had more or less been eradicated in the UK by 1951). He defined absolute poverty in subsistence terms: 'nothing must be bought but that which is absolutely necessary for the maintenance of physical health and what is bought must be of the plainest and most economical description'. Subsequent researchers developed more sophisticated modes of measurement (see John Scott, 1994, for an excellent review of the work of Booth and Rowntree).

More recently, poverty in the UK has been studied by Peter Townsend, who has conducted research in this area for over four decades. Townsend defines poverty as 'the lack of the resources necessary to permit participation in the activities, customs and diets commonly approved by society' (1979: 81). After a major survey, using a national random sample, Townsend concluded that poverty and deprivation almost certainly begin to occur at a level which is over 50 per cent above the official government definition of poverty for means-tested social assistance rates. Social assistance rates are fixed by governments at minimum levels; Townsend and many subsequent researchers see this as far too low and basic, failing to take into account the relative need for 'participation' in a society.

A little later, Mack and Lansley took Townsend's ideas of relative poverty one step further. For a television series called 'Breadline Britain', they investigated the 'British standard of living' by conducting a public opinion poll – asking people what they regarded necessary for a good standard of living – and then documenting the level of missing necessities experienced by a national quota sample of over 1,000 people (see

Table 10.2 ● Lack of necessities

1983 Necessity	Percentage of households unable to afford
1 Holiday	21
2 Two pairs of shoes	9
3 Meat or fish every other day	8
4 Hobby	7
4 Damp-free house	7
4 Warm coat	7
4 Weekly roast	7
8 Leisure equipment for children	6
8 New clothes	6
8 Washing machines	6
1990	
1 Regular savings	30
2 Holiday	20
3 Decent decoration	15
4 Outing for children	14
5 Insurance	10
6 Out-of-school activities	10
7 Separate bedrooms	7
7 Hobby	7
7 Telephone	7
10 Best outfit	8
10 Entertaining of children's friends	8

Source: Frayman, 1991: 6, reprinted in Scott, 1994

Table 10.2). Defining the poor as those 'excluded from the way of life that most people take for granted' (Mack and Lansley, 1985: 15), they found that the number of poor people, especially children, increased in Britain between 1983 and 1990.

The Mack and Lansley style approach consistently moves the poverty line upwards over time, as expectations of living standards shift (Table 10.2). These days, for instance, students increasingly need computers for their work. You might ask yourself whether a student who is is unable to afford to buy a computer is poor.

Given the complexities of these more sophisticated sociological approaches, it is most common, these days, for poverty to be measured relatively through income. Until 1987, poverty was measured as living below whatever was the government's current supplementary benefit level. (It moves under various names in various countries. Currently, in the UK it is the incomes support level). Nowadays, below average income is the most common measure.

The extent of poverty

Given the complexities of measuring poverty, estimates of it are notoriously variable. Indeed, the UK Conservative governments of 1979–97 more or less tried to ignore poverty by arguing that 'officially poverty does not exist in Britain. The government does not define a poverty line. It argues that an objective definition is impossible, that any attempt to count the poor is doomed because it will depend on the subjective definitions of experts about what it is to be poor' (Frayman, 1991: 2).

It is certainly true that 'poverty figures' can be quite wide ranging. Rowntree in 1950 found only 1.5 per cent of York living in poverty, but he was applying very strict absolute standards. Under the more lenient relative standards of recent times, poverty is found to be anywhere between a tenth and a third of the population. Thus, Townsend found in 1969 that 21.8 per cent of the population were below 140 per cent of the Supplementary Benefit line, and 22.9 per cent below his deprivation standard. More recently, in 1993, the Low Pay Unit estimated a third of the population lived in poverty; the OECD suggested there were 12 million poor in the UK (a quarter of Europe's 50 million living in poverty); and 10 per cent of people claimed income support (5.6 million people) (Skellington, 1996: 105–11).

In the *European Union*, poverty and social exclusion has generally been rising – despite a series of programmes to combat it. In 1975, it was recorded at some 38 million, but by the 1990s it was being registered at some 50 million. It involves roughly 15 per cent of the European population. Usually, it is measured as those with per capita incomes below 50 per cent of the national average.

Poverty does not affect all European countries equally, and three clusters of countries have been identified. These are:

- high levels of poverty: Greece, Ireland, Portugal, Spain and the UK
- average levels of poverty: France, Italy
- lower levels of poverty: Belgium, Denmark, Germany, The Netherlands (see Figure 10.7). (Bernt Schulte, 1995, in Funken and Cooper, 1995: 127).

Figure 10.5 ● **The changing shape of inequality globally**

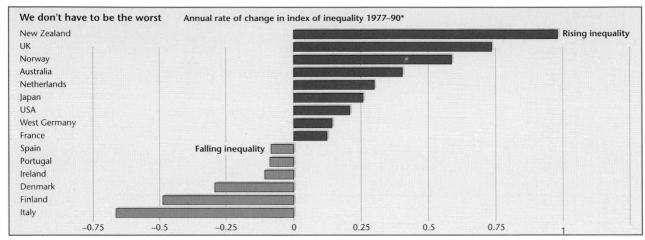

Source: Rowntree Inquiry into Welfare * The precise period varies from country to country, *The Observer*, 13 April 1997

Figure 10.6 ● **Poverty and deprivation in the UK**

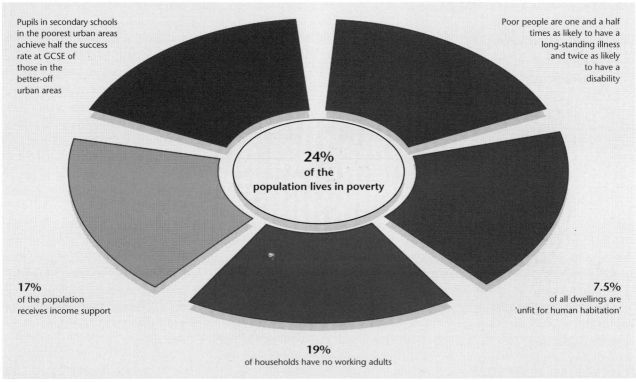

Source: *The Observer*, 13 April 1997

The *United States*, despite being one of the richest nations on earth, has a very high level of relative poverty. In 1993, a total of 39.3 million men, women and children – 15.1 per cent of the US population – were officially living in poverty. Another 12.5 million people – the *marginally poor* – were supported by incomes no greater than 125 per cent of the poverty threshold. For two adults and two children living in an urban area in 1993, the poverty threshold was $14,763. The income of the typical poor family, however, is about $5,960 *below* the poverty threshold. And estimates suggest that 40 per cent of the poor – those we might term *the poorest of the poor* – struggle to get by on no more than half the income specified as the poverty threshold (US Bureau of the Census, 1995).

Figure 10.7 ● Distribution of poverty in Europe using 'national'* and EU† poverty lines, 1985

Notes *The poverty line used is 50 per cent of national average household expenditure adjusted for family size. Luxembourg is not included in the Eurostat figures.

†The poverty line used is 50 per cent of community average household expenditure adjusted for family size

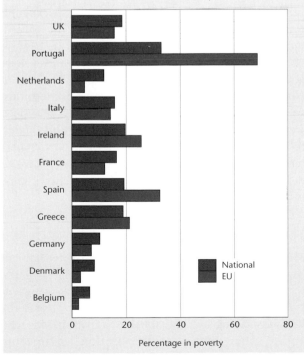

Percentage in poverty

Source: Eurostat, 1990

Who are the poor?

Although no single description covers all poor people, poverty is pronounced among certain categories of the population. In particular, it is likely to hit people who are disadvantaged in other ways: low-wage earners, the unemployed, disabled people. Here we will briefly focus on four groups: children, the elderly, ethnic groups and women are all at high risk of being poor. Where these categories overlap, the problem of poverty is especially serious.

Age

A generation ago, the elderly were at greatest risk of poverty. They still remain at risk, but studies now conclude that a 'new poverty' has emerged amongst the young and children. The numbers of elderly needing assistance fell from 1.8 million in 1974 to 1.4 million in 1991. Today, the burden of poverty falls most heavily on children. Thus, numbers of children under 16 needing assistance in the UK rose from 800,000 in 1974 to 2.3 million in 1991. Ten per cent of children live below the poverty line (Funken and Cooper, 1995: 12).

The same story is true in much of the rest of Europe. And in the USA, it is even more extreme. In 1993, 22.7 per cent of people under the age of 18 (15.7 million children) were officially classified as poor. Tallied another way, four in ten of the US poor are children under the age of 18.

Race and ethnicity

Studies strongly suggest that 'mutiple deprivations' affect ethnic minorities, leading to significantly higher levels of poverty. The Joseph Rowntree Foundation's (1995) study of poverty in the UK was 'particulary concerned . . . at what is happening to the non-white population'. One in three of the non-white population was in the poorest fifth of the population. Most significant here were alarming rates of unemployment (worst of all among people of Pakistani origin) and the difficulties of ethnic women, not least Afro-Caribbean single parent families. Many of these groups were contributing to an emerging underclass (see above).

Ethnicity is important across the world when looking at poverty. In the United States, for example, in absolute numbers, two-thirds of all poor people are white. But in relation to their overall numbers, African Americans are about three times as likely as white

A widespread stereotype links poverty to people of colour in the inner cities of the United States. Although minorities are more likely to be disadvantaged, most of the US poor are white people. Furthermore, although inner cities have the greatest concentration of poverty, rural residents are at higher risk of poverty than their urban counterparts.

Source: Stock Boston – Tim Carlson

people to be poor. In 1993, 33.1 per cent of African Americans (10.9 million people) lived in poverty, compared to about 30.6 per cent of Latinos (8.1 million), 15.3 per cent of Asians and Pacific Islanders (1.1 million), and 9.9 per cent of non-Latino white people (18.9 million).

Gender and family patterns

The term **feminisation of poverty** describes *the trend by which women represent an increasing proportion of the poor*. Peter Townsend (1987) has identified four groups of women that make up the 'female poor':

● single (including divorced) women with children
● elderly women pensioners
● 'carers' who look after children or other dependents
● women with low earnings

The feminisation of poverty is part of a larger change: the rapidly increasing number of households – at all class levels – headed by single women. This trend, coupled with the fact that households headed by women are at high risk of poverty, explains why women (and their children) represent an increasing share of the European poor. Black women appear in all these categories, and for them poverty becomes even more likely (see Glendinning and Millar, 1993).

● Citizenship and the rise of welfare states

An important development of modern, industrial capitalist societies has been the evolution of welfare states. A narrow definition of this would be 'the involvement of the state in social security and social services' (Cochrane and Clarke, 1993: 4). More broadly, some definitions of the welfare state include a commitment to full employment and a whole arena of welfare polices to do with education, health and families. Welfare states are therefore very much bound up with improving the quality of life for a society's citizens and reducing the problems generated through inequalities.

Most modern industrialised nations are welfare states – they increasingly have to deal with public problems and deal with them through public expenditure. In Britain, in 1981, 56.3 per cent of the government's budget was spent on welfare; and in 1993, it was 64.1 per cent. This was despite an anti-welfare government! (Much of the rise, though, was due to costs of increased unemployment etc.). Some industrial societies, such as Sweden, have highly developed welfare states, whilst others, such as the United States, have only minimal ones. Nevertheless, it is a characteristic feature of modern societies that they have to devote large sums to welfare. Figure 10.8 shows some comparative spending on welfare.

The citizenship approach

The growth of State involvement with the 'welfare' of its citizens parallels the growth of industrial societies. In the optimistic version, this is a story of growing 'citizenship rights'. The key thinker in this area is the British sociologist T. S. Marshall (1893–1981), who argued that with industrialisation, citizenship emerged in three ways. These were:

FOCUS ON EUROPE

The Social Charter: social policies in the European Union

In May 1989, the European Community Charter of the Fundamental Social Rights of Workers – commonly known as The Social Charter – was approved. It was subsequently incorporated as the 'Social Chapter' into the Maastricht Treaty in 1991 (see Chapter 3). The Charter's main provisions included the following rights and guarantees of workers who hold citizenship in EU countries:

The rights:

● to work in the EU country of one's choice

● to a fair wage

● to continuing improvements in living and working conditions

● to adequate social protection and social security

● to belong to a trade union (or professional body) and to be represented in collective bargaining

● to satisfactory health care and safe working conditions

The guarantees:

● equal treatment for men and women in the workplace, and 'enabling men and women to rec-oncile their occupational and family obligations'

● consultation between employers and workers

● protection of children and adolescents; with a minimum working age of 15, fair pay and reasonable hours

● minimum decent standard of living for the elderly

● changes to make it easier for the disabled to become part of the workforce

Until 1997, the UK opted out of the Chapter. In practice, the UK did recognise many of the conditions, but the former Conservative government objected to the regulations of maximum hours and minimum wages, as well as to fathers being given a statutory three months' unpaid leave after the birth of a child. The Conservatives argued that these provisions would increase industrial costs to a level that would make the UK less competitive with the USA, Japan and the newly industrialising countries. The Labour government elected in 1997 rejected these arguments, and signed up to the Social Chapter.

Like most such mission statements, these ideal goals are not always followed in practice. Although there is a clear statement that men and women should be treated equally, in practice there remain significant pay and opportunity differentials. Additionally, the charter does not always allow for consistent enforcement. Some issues, including a 48 hour maximum working week and a common retirement age for men and women, are laid down centrally, but other matters, including the power to set the age of retirement, remain at the discretion of national governments.

Through the Social Protection in Europe Directive (1993), all EU countries must provide a basic level of support in unemployment benefits, pensions, cover for work accidents, health cover and maternity benefits. A predictable pattern emerges: a high level of protection in Sweden, as is the case for Luxembourg and The Netherlands. A low level of protection exists in Spain, Portugal, Ireland, Greece and the UK; and middle levels of support in France, Germany, Finland, Denmark, Belgium and Austria. Figure 10.8 shows the level of benefits and social protection provided by some EU member states as compared with Japan and the US. ●

1. *Civil*: the rights necessary for individual freedom – liberty of the person, freedom of speech, thought and faith, the right to own property and to conclude valid contracts, and the right to justice. The key institutions to implement this would be the civil and criminal courts of justice.

2. *Political*: the right to participate in the exercise of political power, as a member of a body invested with political authority or as an elector of such a body. This included such institutions as parliament and local elective bodies, along with the extension of political suffrage.

Figure 10.8 ● Percentage spent by government on welfare

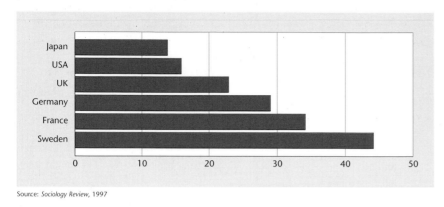

Source: *Sociology Review*, 1997

3. *Social*: the whole range from the right to a modicum of economic welfare and security to the right to share to the full in the social heritage and to live the life of a civilised being according to the standards prevailing in the society. The educational and social welfare institutions are the key here.

For Marshall, each of these sets of rights appears in distinct periods. In the Middle Ages, they were 'wound together' but weak. Civil rights emerged most clearly in the eighteenth century, political rights in the nineteenth and social rights in the twentieth century.[1] Many do not agree with the precise periodisation and remark that Marshall's model was developed through one case study only – that of the UK. When applied to other countries it does not fit so well. Bryan Turner (1990), for example, has suggested that the foundations of citizenships differ for France, Germany and Sweden. Marshall's model does raise a series of key issues about the emerging rights and responsibilities in modern societies.

A Marxist approach

Marxists see the welfare state differently: instead of seeing it as a benign set of institutions that foster security and equality, they argue that it helps contribute to the smooth running of the capitalist order. In order for

capitalism to work, it needs a well trained labour force that is reasonably healthy and secure. The welfare state ensures this. Marxists suggest advanced capitalism needs welfare to 'buy off' working class dissent and maintain social order with a secure workforce (Piven and Cloward, 1972).

The three worlds of welfare capitalism

In 1990, Costa Esping-Andersen published a much discussed study of different kinds of welfare regimes. For him, 'The welfare system is not just a mechanism that intervenes in . . . inequality; it is, in its own right, a system of stratification' (1990: 23). He argued that there were three major kinds of welfare systems, though they are a little like ideal types (see Chapter 1). These three main 'worlds' are:

1. *Social democratic*. This argues for universal rights, equality and a kind of 'universal solidarity' in favour of the welfare state. It is largely anti-market. It takes on many family responsiblities and is a universalist model. Scandinavian countries largely adopt this approach.

2. *Corporatist/'Bismarck'*. Here, welfare is mainly organised through work itself, through business, tradition, Church and existing powers. This approach does not enourage redistribution. Whilst the state may deliver welfare, its aim is the maintenance of traditional families. This is a conservative model, found in Austria, France, Germany and Italy.

3. *Liberal*. This intervenes in the market as little as possible and gives benefits that are subject to strict entitlement rules. It is a basic safety net approach, showing a direct line of inheritance from the old Poor Laws. It leads to market based insurance for the wealthy and means testing for the poor. Private schemes are encouraged. Examples are the USA, Australia and Canada. The UK used to be close to the social democratic model, but under Thatcherism moved closer and closer to the market/liberal model.

---

[1] There is talk, at the end of the twentieth century, of the emergence of a fourth cluster of citizen rights which may become important in the twenty-first century. These are the cluster around 'Intimate citizenship'.

Esping-Andersen derived this classification from his own research into pensions, unemployment insurance and sickness benefits. He examined levels of benefit, protection against risks and strictness of rules that govern access across a number of countries. It was on this basis that he could classify societies thus:

● lowest scores for welfare – liberal: USA and UK

● intermediate scores for welfare – corporatist: France, Germany, Italy, Switzerland

● highest scores for welfare – social democratic: Scandinavia, Belgium, The Netherlands.

More recently, Leibfreid has added a fourth group – the 'Latin Rim countries' – Spain, Greece, Portugal, Southern Italy and part of France which have 'rudimentary welfare states'.

The welfare state in the UK

The UK is quite close to the liberal model but it is, at least historically, a bit of a mixture of all three. Its roots go back to the Poor Law in Elizabethan and Tudor England, where government started to impose an elementary framework on what had previously been the task of churches and charities. But this rudimentary care of the sick broke down with mass industrialisation and the arrival of capitalism. In 1834 the Poor Law Amendment Act set up a national Poor Law Commission to oversee the development of a system with links eventually growing to state education and health care. All this shapes the 'State' links to a society's population, and especially its 'poor' and 'working class'.

Bit by bit, a system that was heavily laissez faire gave way to a system that is more central and state controlled. By the start of the twentieth century, legislation such as the Pensions Act of 1908 and National Insurance Act of 1911 provided cover for sickness and unemployment for some workers, introducing the 'insurance principle' into British social security.

The period 1945–75 may be seen as the years of the 'classic welfare state'. It was spearheaded by the work of William Beveridge in several major reports. Waging war on the 'five great evils' of 'Want, Disease, Ignorance, Squalor and Idleness', his plan for social security was to abolish Want – but only if the others could simultaneously be abolished (Beveridge Report, paragraph 8). This was a time when there was a commitment to a mixed economy, to full employment and to a welfare state that would provide universal rights. At this stage, the welfare state in the UK was closest to the social democratic model described above. In education, health, child care and welfare provisions, the UK seemed to be moving towards this social democratic welfare state. There were 'means tested' systems, but the broad principles stressed universality.

This was also the period when the National Health Service came into existence – a time very different from our own, when most people rented their houses, nobody had televisions but instead listened to the wireless, few had overseas holidays, only a minority had telephones, nobody had computers, and few had cars so most were dependent upon public transport. Social democratic thinkers believed the welfare state would create citizenship for all and would combat inequality. But by the mid-1970s – as unemployment surged forward and huge economic changes were in the offing – it was clear that it had not been especially successful in redistribution. Indeed, a number of commentators saw most of the benefits of the system going to the middle classes (Le Grand, 1982).

A new period was ushered in from the mid-1970s onwards. Most notably, from 1979 there emerged a much more 'anti welfare state' approach. It was, as Prime Minister Margaret Thatcher bluntly put it, a rejection of the Nanny State. Monetarist theory (to be outlined in Chapter 15) was put into practice and at the same time the 'classic' welfare state began to be 'marketised'.

Marketisation is *an economic system based on the principles of the market, including supply, demand, choice and competition.* Thatcherism (discussed in Chapter 16) attempted to bring marketisation into all spheres of life, including much of the welfare state. Thus, as we shall see, both education (Chapter 19) and health (Chapter 20) were to move to the principles of the market. Even prisons, as we saw in Chapter 8, moved towards privatisation.

The new Labour government elected in 1997 may change some of this; but in the first weeks of its office and in its election manifesto it showed that it also favoured market models in many areas of the welfare state. The UK model therefore seems increasingly to be aligning itself with the liberal rather than the social democratic approach. What this means for the reduction of inequalities remains to be seen.

SUMMARY

1. Social inequality involves disparities in a host of variables, including income, wealth and power.

2. Occupation is one way in which class is measured. The Registrar General's classification is the most commonly used such classification in the UK.

3. Income and wealth are other ways in which social class is often measured.

4. Marxists would adopt an approach to measuring class that focuses upon the ownership of the means of production.

5. Ascription has a powerful impact on stratification; ancestry, race and ethnicity, gender and religion are all related to social position.

6. The upper class, which is small (about 5 per cent), includes the richest and most powerful families. Members of the upper-upper class, or the old rich, derive their wealth through inheritance over several generations; those in the lower-upper class, or the new rich, depend on earned income as their primary source of wealth.

7. The middle class includes 40 to 45 per cent of the population. The upper middle class may be distinguished from the rest of the middle class on the basis of higher income, higher-prestige occupations and more schooling.

8. The working class, sometimes called the lower middle class, includes about one-third of our population. With below-average income, working class families have less financial security than those in the middle class. Only one-third of working class children reach college and most eventually work in blue-collar or lower-prestige white-collar jobs.

9. There is a growing 'underclass' – people outside society and the class system.

10. Social class affects nearly all aspects of life, beginning with health and survival in infancy and encompassing a wide range of attitudes and patterns of family living.

11. Social mobility is common in the United States as it is in other industrial societies; typically, however, there are only small changes from one generation to the next.

12. Since the early 1970s, changes in the economy have reduced the standard of living for low- and moderate-income families. One important contemporary trend is a decline in manufacturing industries, paralleling growth in low-paying, service-sector jobs.

13. Oscar Lewis and Charles Murray advanced the *culture of poverty* thesis, which holds that poverty is perpetuated by the social patterns of the poor themselves. Opposing this view, William Ryan argues that poverty is caused by a society's unequal distribution of wealth.

14. An important development of modern capitalist societies has been the development of welfare states alongside the idea of 'citizenship'.

KEY CONCEPTS

absolute poverty a deprivation of resources that is life threatening

feminisation of poverty the trend by which women represent an increasing proportion of the poor

income occupational wages or salaries and earnings from investments

intergenerational social mobility upward or downward social mobility of children in relation to their parents

intragenerational social mobility a change in social position occurring during a person's lifetime

marketisation an economic system based on the principles of the market, including supply, demand, choice and competition.

middle class slide a trend towards declining living standards and economic security at the centre of industrial societies

occupational prestige the value that people in a society associate with various occupations

relative poverty the deprivation of some people in relation to those who have more

underclass a group 'under the class structure' which is economically, politically and socially marginalised and excluded

wealth the total value of money and other assets, minus outstanding debts

CRITICAL-THINKING QUESTIONS ....

1. Assess your own social class. Does your family have consistent standing on various dimensions of social stratification? Why do most people find talking about their own social position awkward?

2. Identify some of the effects of social stratification on health, values, politics and family patterns.

3. Discuss the nature of (a) the middle classes and (b) the underclass. Consider how they have changed over the past 20 years.

4. Is class dead? If so, why?

5. What categories of people are at high risk of poverty in Europe? Does any evidence support the assertion that the poor are responsible for their situation? Does any evidence suggest that society is primarily responsible for poverty?

6. Discuss the origins of 'welfare states'. Are they better driven by collective concerns or market forces?

7. Compare three 'welfare states'. Why is public assistance for the poor more controversial in some countries than in others?

8. Discuss the reasons for the emergence of 'citizenship' in modern welfare states?

GOING FURTHER ....

Introductory reading

Ivan Reid, *Social Class Differences in Britain* (London: Fontana, 3rd edn, 1989).

    A valuable review of links between class and matters like housing, education and health.

John Scott, *Poverty and Wealth* (London: Longman, 1994).

    Packs a great deal of information into a short book.

Classical sources

David Lockwood, John Goldthorpe, Frank Beckhoffer and Jennifer Platt, *The Affluent Worker* series (Cambridge: Cambridge University Press, 1967).

    These three classic volumes of empirical English class analysis look at the 'embourgeoisement' thesis.

Robert S. Lynd and Helen Merrell Lynd, *Middletown in Transition: A Study in Cultural Conflicts* (New York: Harcourt, Brace & World, 1937).

    In their second sociological study of Muncie, Indiana, a team of researchers led by the Lynds examines life in a Middle American town with a keen eye on the effect of social class.

More advanced reading

Alan Cochrane and John Clarke, *Comparing Welfare States: Britain in International Context* (London: Sage, 1993).

    A readable comparison which looks at Hong Kong, Sweden, Ireland, Germany and the UK.

David Lee and Bryan Turner (eds.), *Conflicts about Class: Debating Inequality in Late Industrialism* (London: Longman, 1996).

    A series of articles which debate the current concerns over class analysis.

Martin Bulmer and Anthony M. Rees (eds.), *Citizenship Today: The Contemporary Relevance of T. H. Marshall* (London: UCL Press, 1996).

    A series of essays which review and debate the important and influential work of the British sociologist T. H. Marshall and his theory of citizenship.

Rosemary Crompton, *Class and Stratification* (Cambridge: Polity, 1993).

    Although an introduction, quite a complex review of the field, from someone who is unapologetically sympathetic to class analysis.

Fiona Devine, *Class in Britain and America* (Edinburgh: University of Edinburgh Press, 1996).

A detailed study that compares the two countries' systems of stratification.

Klaus Eder, *The New Politics of Class* (London: Sage, 1993). Anthony Giddens, *Beyond Left and Right* (Cambridge: Polity, 1994).

Both offer new class theories.

Robert Erikson and John H. Goldthorpe, *The Constant Flux: A Study of Class Mobility in Industrial Societies* (Oxford: Clarendon Press, 1992).

This report of a massive research effort explains why rates of social mobility are basically the same in all industrial societies.

C. Esping-Andersen, *The Three Worlds of Welfare Capitalism* (London: Polity Press, 1990).

The now classic study of modern welfare which distinguishes three types (and clearly favours the Scandinavian model).

Michael Hill, *Understanding Social Policy* (Oxford: Blackwell, 5th edn, 1997).

A classic standard text on social policy, regularly revised.

Joanna Mack and S. Lansley, *Poor Britain* (London: Routledge, 2nd edn, 1993).
C. Oppenheim, *Poverty: The Facts* (London: Child Poverty Action Group, 2nd edn, 1993).

Two good general reviews of poverty in the UK.

Lydia Morris, *Dangerous Classes: The Underclass and Social Citizenship* (London: Routledge, 1994).

Provides a guide to the history of the underclass and discusses current controversies, including the work of Charles Murray and problems emerging in Europe.

chapter eleven

Global Stratification

Fed by methane from the decomposing garbage, the fires never go out on Smokey Mountain, Manila's vast garbage dump. The smoke envelops the hills of refuse like a thick fog. But Smokey Mountain is more than a dump; it is home to thousands of people. The residents of Smokey Mountain are the poorest of the poor, and one is hard pressed to imagine a setting more hostile to human life. Amidst the smoke and the squalor, men and women walk deliberately about, doing what they can to survive, picking plastic bags from the garbage and washing them in the river, stacking flat cardboard boxes up the side of a family's plywood shack. And all over Smokey Mountain are children – *children* – kids who must already sense the enormous odds against them. The girls and boys we see are the lucky ones, of course. But what chance do they have, living in families that earn scarcely a few hundred dollars a year? With barely any opportunity for schooling? Year after year, breathing this air?

Although they seem worlds away from the comfortable lives of many people in Europe, the residents of Manila's Smokey Mountain are far from unique. Their counterparts live throughout Latin America, Africa and Asia, and indeed in almost every country of the world. There is, of course, much poverty in Europe too. But, as we shall see, poverty in the poor countries of the world is not only more widespread; it is usually far more severe.

● Global economic development

Chapter 10 ('Class, Poverty and Welfare') detailed the income inequality that marks our own society. In global perspective, however, social stratification is even more pronounced. Figure 11.1 divides the total global income by fifths of the population: the richest 20 per cent of the global population receives fully 70 per cent of all income. At the other end of the social scale, the poorest 20 per cent of the world's people, by contrast, struggle to survive on just 2 per cent of global income.

Because global income is so concentrated, the average member of a rich society (such as most of Europe) lives extremely well by world standards. In fact, the living standard of most people below the poverty threshold far surpasses that of the majority of the earth's people.

The problem of terminology

After the Second World War, analysts generated a familiar scheme to describe the unequal distribution of global income. They labelled the rich, industrialised countries the 'First World', called the somewhat less industrialised, socialist countries the 'Second World',

Figure 11.1 ● **Distribution of world income**

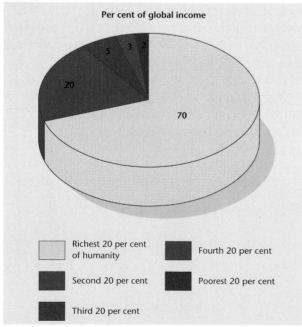

Per cent of global income

5 3 2
20
70

☐ Richest 20 per cent of humanity

■ Fourth 20 per cent

■ Second 20 per cent

■ Poorest 20 per cent

■ Third 20 per cent

Source: Based on Sivard (1988) and The World Bank (1993)

and dubbed the remaining non-industrialised, poor countries the 'Third World'.

Although widely used for decades, this 'three worlds' model has lost validity in recent years. For one thing, it was a product of Cold War politics by which the capitalist West (the First World) faced off against the socialist East (the Second World), while the rest of the world (the Third World) remained more or less on the sidelines. But the sweeping transformation of Eastern Europe and the former Soviet Union means that there no longer exists a distinctive Second World; just as important, the superpower opposition that defined the Cold War has faded in recent years.

A second problem with the model is that it lumped together in the Third World more than a hundred countries at different levels of development. Some relatively better-off nations of the Third World (such as Chile in South America) have ten times the per-person productivity of the poorest countries of the world (including Ethiopia in eastern Africa).

The changes and social differences that mark today's world call for a modestly revised system of classification. Utilising the terms introduced in Chapter 1, *high-income countries* are the richest 40 nations with the most-developed economies and the highest overall standard of living for their people. Next, the world's 90 *middle-income countries* are somewhat poorer nations whose economic development is more or less typical for the world as a whole. Finally, the remaining 60 *low-income countries* are marked by the lowest productivity and the most severe and extensive poverty.

Compared to the older 'three worlds' system, this new form of classification has two main advantages. First, it focuses on the key issue of economic development while ignoring the question of whether societies are capitalist or socialist. Second, this revision provides a more precise picture of the relative economic development of the world's countries because it does not lump together all less-industrialised countries into a single Third World.

Nonetheless, classifying the approximately 200 nations on earth into any three categories (or, even more crudely, to divide them into the rich 'North' and the poor 'South') ignores pronounced differences in their ways of life. The countries at each of the three levels of economic development have rich and varied histories, speak hundreds of languages and encompass diverse peoples, proud of their cultural distinctiveness.

Keep in mind, too, that just as the world's nations form a social hierachy that ranges from very rich to very poor, every country on earth is also internally stratified. This means that the extent of global inequality is actually greater than national comparisons suggest, since the most well-off people in rich countries (like Norway or the United States) live worlds apart from the poorest people in low-income countries (like India). With this striking contrast in mind, we can better appreciate the power of visiting Manila's Smokey Mountain dump-dwellers, described at the beginning of this chapter.

Measuring a country's economic productvity is usually done through the GNP and the GDP. GDP or **gross domestic product** refers to *all the goods and services on record as produced by a country's economy in a given year*. Income earned outside the country by individuals or corporations is excluded from this measure; this is the key difference between GDP and **gross national product** (GNP), which *includes foreign earnings*. For countries that invest heavily abroad (Kuwait, for example), GDP is considerably less than GNP; for countries in which other nations invest heavily (such as Hong Kong), GDP is much higher than GNP. For countries that both invest heavily abroad and have considerable foreign investment at home (like the United States), the two measures are roughly comparable. In what follows we will examine some of the striking differences in productivity of the various world economies.

High-income countries

High-income nations are rich because theirs were the first economies to be transformed by the Industrial Revolution more than two centuries ago, increasing their productive capacity a hundredfold. To grasp how this development enriched our own region of the world, consider that the typical Euopean household may well spend more today just caring for their pets than the average European household did to meet all its needs during the Middle Ages.

A look back at Map 1.1 identifies the 40 high-income countries of the world. They include most of the nations of Western Europe, including the UK, where industrialisation first took hold about 1750. Canada and the United States are also rich nations; in North America, the Industrial Revolution was well under way by 1850. In Asia, one of the world's leading economic powers is Japan; recent economic growth

also places Hong Kong and Singapore in this favoured category. Finally, to the south of Asia in the global region known as Oceania, Australia and New Zealand also rank as industrial, high-income nations.

Taken together, countries with the most-developed economies cover roughly 25 per cent of the earth's land area – including parts of five continents – while lying mostly in the northern hemisphere. In mid-1996, the total population of these nations was 870 million, representing about 15 per cent of the earth's people. By global standards, rich nations are not densely populated; even so, some countries (such as Japan) are crowded while others (like Canada) are sparsely settled. Inside their borders, however, about three-quarters of the people in high-income countries congregate together in or near cities.

High-income countries reveal significant cultural differences – the nations of Europe, for example, recognise more than 30 official languages. But these countries share an industrial capacity that generates, on average, a rich material life for their people. Per capita income in these societies ranges from about US $10,000 annually (in Portugal and Cyprus) to more than US $20,000 annually (in the United States and Switzerland).[1] This prosperity is so great that citizens of high-income countries enjoy more than half the world's total income.

Finally, just as people in a single society perform specialised work, so various regions form a global division of labour. Generally speaking, high-income countries dominate the world's scientific efforts and employ the most complex and productive technology. Production in rich societies is capital-intensive, meaning high investments in factories and related machinery. High-income countries also stand at the forefront of new information technology; the majority of the largest corporations that design and market computers, for instance, are centred on rich societies. With the lion's share of wealth, high-income countries also control the world's financial markets: ups and downs on the financial exchanges of New York, London and Tokyo affect people throughout the world.

[1.] High-income countries have per capita annual income of at least US $10,000. For middle- and low-income countries, the comparable figures are $2,500 to $10,000 and below $2,500. All data reflect the United Nations' concept of 'purchasing power parities', which avoids distortion caused by exchange rates when converting all currencies to US dollars. Instead, the data represent the local purchasing power of each nation's currency.

Middle-income countries

Middle-income countries are those with per capita income ranging between US $2,500 and $10,000, or roughly the median for the world's *nations* (but higher than that of the world's *people* since most people live in low-income countries). These nations have experienced limited industrialisation, primarily centred on cities. But about half their people still live in rural areas and engage in agricultural production. Especially in the countryside, schooling, medical care, adequate housing and even safe water are hard to come by, which represents a standard of living far below what members of high-income societies take for granted.

At the high end of this category, Barbados (Latin America), Greece (Europe) and South Korea (Asia) provide people with about $5,000 in annual income. Ecuador (Latin America), Albania (Europe) and Sri Lanka (Asia) hover at the lower end of this category with roughly $1,750 annually in per capita income. Looking back at Map 1.1 shows that about 90 of the world's nations fall into this classification, and they are a very diverse lot.

One group of middle-income countries includes the former Soviet Union and the nations of Eastern Europe (in the past, also known as the Second World). The former Soviet Union's military strength rivalled that of the United States, giving it 'superpower' status. Its satellite states in Eastern Europe, including Poland, the German Democratic Republic (East Germany), Czechoslovakia, Hungary, Romania and Bulgaria, had predominantly socialist economies until popular revolts between 1989 and 1991 swept aside their governments. Since then, these nations have begun to introduce market systems. This process, detailed in Chapter 15 ('The Economy, Consumption and Work'), has yet to solve serious economic woes; on the contrary, in the short term, at least, nations of the former Eastern Bloc are battling high inflation and some people enjoy fewer consumer goods than ever.

In the second category of middle-income countries are most of the oil-producing nations of the Middle East (or, less ethnocentrically, western Asia). These nations, including Saudi Arabia, Oman and Iran, are very rich, but their wealth is so concentrated that most people receive little benefit and remain poor. The third, and largest, category of middle-income countries can be found in Latin America and northern and western Africa. These nations (which might be termed the better-off countries of the Third World) include Argentina and Brazil in South America as well as Algeria and Botswana in Africa. Although South Africa's white minority lives as well as people in the United States, this country, too, must be considered middle income because its majority black population scrapes by with far less income.

Taken together, middle-income countries span roughly 40 per cent of the earth's land area; and upwards of 2 billion people, or one-third of humanity, call these nations home. Compared to high-income countries, therefore, these nations are densely populated though, again, some countries in this category (such as El Salvador) are far more crowded than others (like Russia).

Low-income countries

Low-income countries of the world, where most people are very poor, are primarily agrarian societies with little industry. These 60 nations, identified in Map 1.1, are found primarily in central and eastern Africa as well as in Asia. Low-income countries (or the poorest nations within the so-called Third World) represent about 35 per cent of the planet's land area but are home to half its people. Combining these facts, the population density for poor countries is generally high, though it is much higher in Asian countries (such as Bangladesh and India) than in more sparsely settled central African nations (like Chad or Zaire).

In poor countries, barely 25 per cent of the people live in cities; most inhabit villages and farm as their families have done for centuries. In fact, half the world's people are peasants, and most of them live in the low-income countries. By and large, peasants are staunchly traditional, following the folkways of their ancestors. Living without industrial technology, peasants are not very productive – one reason many endure severe poverty. Hunger, minimal housing and frequent disease all frame the lives of the world's poorest people.

This broad overview of global economic development gives us a foundation for understanding the problem of global inequality. For people living in affluent nations, the scope of human want in much of the world is difficult to grasp. From time to time, televised scenes of famine in very poor countries such as Ethiopia and Bangladesh give us a shocking glimpse of the absolute poverty that makes every day a life-and-

By and large, rich nations such as the United States wrestle with the problem of relative poverty, meaning that poor people get by with less than we think they should have. In poor countries such as Somalia, absolute poverty means that people lack what they need to survive. Here people gather near the Juba River to bury in a common grave family members who died from starvation.

Source: Black Star – Christopher Morris/*Time*

death struggle. Behind these images lie cultural, historical and economic forces that we shall explore in the remainder of this chapter.

● Global wealth and poverty

To classify a country as 'low income' does not mean that only poor people live there. On the contrary, the rich districts of Manila and Madras testify to the high living standards of some. Indeed, given the low wages paid to most urbanites in these countries, the typical well-to-do household is staffed by several servants and served by a gardener and chauffeur. But for the majority in the world's poor countries, poverty is the rule. Moreover, with incomes of only several hundred pounds a year, the burden of poverty is greater than it is among the poor in high-income societies.

The severity of poverty

Poverty in poor countries is more severe than it is in rich nations. The data in Table 11.1 suggest why. The first column of figures shows the gross domestic product

(GDP) for countries at each level of economic development. Industrial societies have a high economic output primarily because of their industrial technology. A large industrial nation like the United States had a 1993 GDP of about $6.3 trillion; Japan's GDP stood at about $4.2 trillion. Comparing GDP figures shows that the world's richest nations are thousands of times more productive in terms of goods and services than the poorest countries on earth.

The second column of figures in the table indicates per capita GDP in terms of what the United Nations (1995) calls 'purchasing power parities', the value of people's income in terms of what it can buy in a local economy. The resulting figures for rich countries like the United States, Switzerland and Canada are very high – in the range of $20,000. Per capita GDP for middle-income countries, including Brazil, Poland and Iran, are much lower – in the $5,000 range. And in the world's low-income countries, per capita annual income is no more than just a few hundred dollars. In the African nations of Zaire or Ethiopia, for example, a typical person labours all year long in order to earn what the average worker in the United States reaps in just several days.

The table's final column measures quality of life in the various nations. The quality of life index, calculated by the United Nations (1995), is a composite measure based on a country's life expectancy, income and education (rates of adult literacy and average number of years of schooling). Index values are decimals that fall between hypothetical extremes of 1 (highest) and zero (lowest). By this calculation, Canadians enjoy the highest quality of life (0.950), with residents of the United States and Japan close behind (0.937); at the other extreme, people in the African nation of Niger have the world's lowest quality of life (0.207).

A key reason for marked disparities in quality of life is that economic productivity is lowest in precisely the regions of the globe where population growth is

Table 11.1 ● Wealth and well-being in global perspective, 1992

Country	Gross domestic product (US $ billion)	GDP per capita (PPP$)*	Quality of life index
High-income countries			
Canada	494	20,520	0.950
United States	5,920	23,760	0.937
Japan	3,671	20,520	0.937
Sweden	221	18,320	0.929
Australia	295	18,220	0.927
Switzerland	241	22,580	0.925
Germany	1,789	21,120	0.921
United Kingdom	903	17,160	0.916
Middle-income countries			
Eastern Europe			
Hungary	35	6,580	0.856
Poland	84	4,830	0.855
Russian Federation	388	6,140	0.849
Lithuania	5	3,700	0.769
Latin America			
Argentina	229	8,860	0.882
Mexico	329	7,300	0.842
Brazil	360	5,240	0.804
Asia			
South Korea	296	9,250	0.882
Thailand	110	5,950	0.827
Middle East			
Iran	110	5,420	0.770
Saudi Arabia	111	9,880	0.762
Africa			
Botswana	4	5,120	0.763
Algeria	36	4,870	0.732
Low-income countries			
Latin America			
Honduras	3	2,000	0.578
Haiti	—	1,046	0.362
Asia			
China	506	1,950	0.594
India	215	1,230	0.439
Africa			
Zaire	—	523	0.384
Guinea	3	592	0.237
Ethiopia	6	330	0.227

* These data are the United Nations' new 'purchasing power parity' calculations that avoid currency rate distortion by showing the local purchasing power of each domestic currency.
Source: United Nations Development Programme, *Human Development Report* (New York: Oxford University Press, 1995)

highest. Figure 11.2 shows the division of global population and global income for countries at each level of economic development. High-income countries are by far the most advantaged with 55 per cent of global income supporting just 15 per cent of the world's people. Middle-income nations contain about 33 per cent of the global population; these people earn about 37 per cent of the world's income. This leaves more than half the planet's population with a scant 8 per cent of total global income. Factoring together income and population, for every unit of currency received by individuals in the low-income countries, their counterparts in the high-income nations enjoy roughly 28 more!

Relative versus absolute poverty

A distinction made in the last chapter has an important application to global inequality. The members of rich societies typically focus on the *relative poverty* of some of their members, highlighting how those people lack resources that are taken for granted by others. Relative poverty, by definition, cuts across every society, rich or poor.

But especially important in a global context is the concept of *absolute poverty*, a lack of resources that is life threatening. Human beings in absolute poverty commonly lack the nutrition necessary for health and long-term survival. To be sure, some absolute poverty exists in Europe. Inadequate nutrition that leaves children or elderly people vulnerable to illness and even outright starvation is a reality in this nation. But such immediately life-threatening poverty strikes only a small proportion of the population; in low-income countries, by contrast, one-third or more of the people are in desperate need.

Since absolute poverty places people at risk of death, we can see the extent of this problem by examining the median age at death around the world. In other words, by what age have half of all people born in

Figure 11.2 ● Relative share of income and population by level of economic development

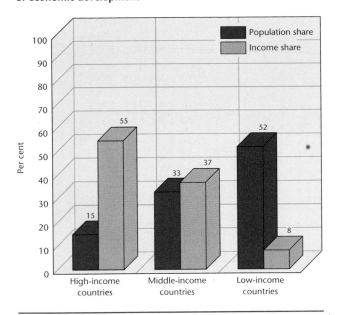

a society died? Map 11.1 shows that death in high-income countries, on average, occurs among the elderly beyond the age of 75. Death occurs somewhat earlier in middle-income nations, reflecting a lower standard of living. But in many low-income countries of Africa and western Asia, the greater extent of absolute poverty is brought home by the fact that half of all deaths occur among children under the age of 10.

The extent of poverty

Poverty in poor countries is more extensive than it is in rich nations. Chapter 10 noted that poverty in Europe may well effect one in five of the population – the figure varies dramatically by country and region. But in low-income countries, however, most people live no better than the poor in our nation and many people are living close to the edge of survival. As the high death rates among children suggest, the extent of absolute poverty is greatest in Africa, where half the population is malnourished. In the world as a whole, at any given time, 20 per cent of the people (about 1 billion) lack the nutrition they need to work regularly. They are in absolute poverty. Of these, at least 800 million are at risk for their lives (Sivard, 1988; Helmuth, 1989; United Nations Development Programme, 1993).

Members of rich societies tend to be overnourished. On average, a member of a high-income society consumes about 3,500 calories daily, an excess that contributes to obesity and related health problems. Yet most people in low-income countries not only do more physical labour, but they consume less than 2,000 calories daily. In short, they do not consume enough food or, just as important, enough of the right kinds of food.

In simple terms, lack of necessary nutrition makes death a way of life in poor societies. In the ten minutes it takes to read through this section of the chapter, about 300 people in the world will die of starvation. This amounts to about 40,000 people a day, or 15 million people each year. Even more than in Europe, the burden of poverty in poor countries falls on children. As we have seen, in the poorest nations of central Africa, half of all children die before they reach age 10.

Two further comparisons reveal the human toll of global poverty. First, at the end of the Second World War, the United States obliterated the Japanese city of Hiroshima with an atomic bomb. The worldwide loss of life from starvation reaches the Hiroshima death toll *every three days*. Second, the annual loss of life stemming from poverty is ten times greater than that resulting from all the world's armed conflicts. Given the magnitude of this problem, easing world hunger is one of the most serious responsibilities facing the world today.

Poverty and children

As the last chapter explained, poverty in the United States and Europe hits children hardest. The same holds true worldwide, and the extent and severity of child poverty are greatest in low-income countries. As we have already explained, death often comes early in poor societies, where families lack adequate food, safe water, secure housing and access to medical care. In many cases, too, children in poor countries leave their families because their chances to survive are better on the streets.

Organisations combating child poverty in the world estimate that poverty forces some 75 million city children in poor countries to beg, steal, sell sex or serve as couriers for drug gangs in order to provide income for their families. Such a life almost always

WINDOW ON THE WORLD

Map 11.1 ● Median age at death in global perspective

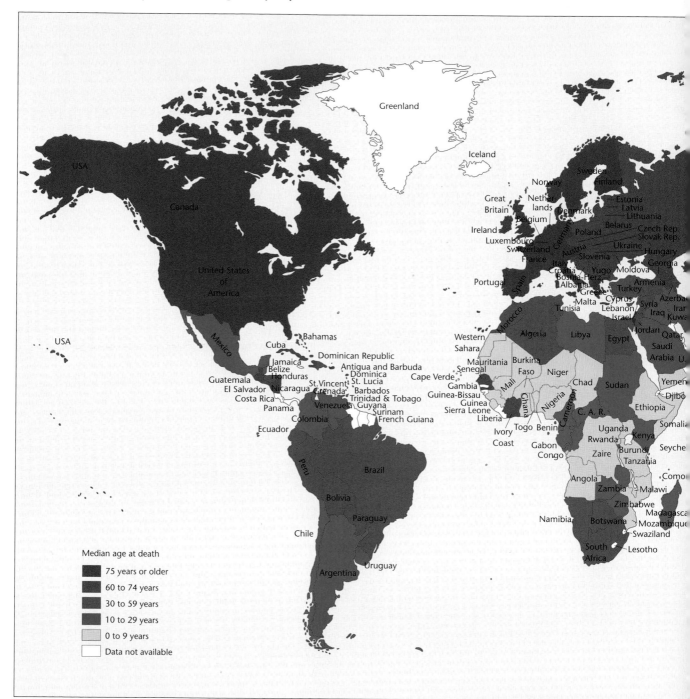

Median age at death

- 75 years or older
- 60 to 74 years
- 30 to 59 years
- 10 to 29 years
- 0 to 9 years
- Data not available

Source: The World Bank (1993); map projection from *Peters Atlas of the World* (1990)

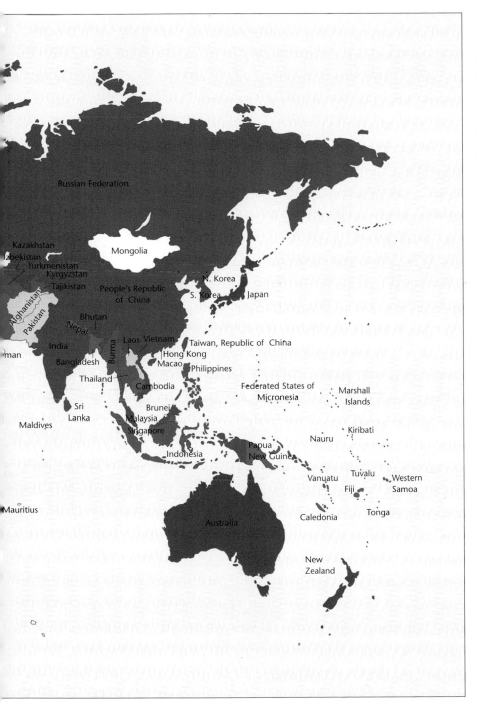

This map identifies the age below which half of all deaths occur in any year. In the high-income countries of the world, it is the elderly who face death – that is, people age 75 or older. In middle-income countries, including most of Latin America, most people die years or even decades earlier. In low-income countries, especially in Africa and parts of Asia, it is children who die, with half of all lives ending before individuals reach 10 years of age.

Will the world starve?

The animals' feet leave their prints on the desert's face.
Hunger is so real, so very real,
that it can make you walk around a barren tree looking for nourishment.
Not once,
Not twice,
Not thrice . . .

These lines, by Indian poet Amit Jayaram, describe the appalling hunger found in Rajasthan, in north-west India. As this chapter has explained, however, hunger casts its menacing shadow not only over regions of Asia, but also over much of Latin America, most of Africa, and even parts of North America. Throughout the world, hundreds of millions of adults do not consume enough food to enable them to work. And, most tragically, some 10 million of the world's children die each year because they do not get enough to eat.

At the closing of the last century, humankind took a major step forward by abolishing slavery almost everywhere on the planet. As we near the end of this century, however, what are the prospects for eradicating the wretched misery of human beings enduring daily hunger?

It is easy to be pessimistic. For one thing, the population of poor countries is currently increasing by 90 million people annually – equivalent to adding another Mexico to the world every year. Poor countries can scarcely feed the people they have now; looking ahead a generation to the future, how will they ever feed double their current populations?

In addition, as detailed in Chapter 22 ('Environment and Society'), hunger forces poor people to exploit the earth's resources by using short-

term strategies for food production that will lead to long-term disaster. For example, to feed the swelling populations of poor tropical countries, farmers are cutting rainforests in order to increase their farmland. But, without the protective canopy of trees, it is only a matter of time before much of this land turns to desert.

Taken together, rising populations and ecological approaches that borrow against the future raise the spectre of hunger and outright starvation escalating well beyond current levels. Regarded pessimistically, the world's future is bleak: unprecedented hunger, human misery and political calamity. But there are also some grounds for optimism. Thanks to the Green Revolution, food production the world over is up sharply over the last 50 years, even outpacing the growth in popula-

means dropping out of school and places children at high risk of illness and violence. Many street girls, with little or no access to medical assistance, become pregnant – a case of children who cannot support themselves having still more children.

Another 25 million of the world's children have deserted their families altogether, sleeping and living on the streets as best they can. Roughly half of all street children are found in Latin America. Brazil, where much of the population has flocked to cities in a desperate search for a better life, has millions of street children – many not yet teenagers – living in makeshift huts, under bridges or in alleyways. Public response to street children is often anger directed at the children themselves. In Rio de Janeiro, police try to keep the numbers of street children in check; when

this unrealistic policy fails, however, death squads may sweep through a neighbourhood, engaging in a bloody ritual of 'urban cleansing'. In Rio, several hundred street children are murdered each year (Larmer, 1992; US House of Representatives, 1992).

Poverty and women

Women in Sikandernagar, one of India's countless rural villages, begin work at 4.00 in the morning, lighting the fires, milking the buffalo, sweeping floors and walking to the well for water. They care for other family members as they rise. By 8.00, when many people in Europe are just beginning their day, these women move on to their 'second shift', working under the hot sun in the fields until 5.00 in the afternoon. Returning

tion. Taking a broader view, the world's economic productivity has risen steadily, so that the average person on the planet has more income now to purchase food and other necessities than ever before.

This growth has increased daily calorie intake as well as life expectancy, access to safe water and adult literacy, while infant mortality is going down. In fact, looking at these social indicators, we can see the gap between rich and poor countries actually narrowing. So what are the prospects for eradicating world hunger – especially in low-income nations? Overall, we see less hunger in both rich and poor countries; that is, a smaller share of the world's people faces starvation now than, say, in 1960. But as global population increases, with 90 per cent of children born in middle- and low-income countries, the number of lives at risk is as great today as ever before. Moreover, even though living standards are rising, there has not been any narrowing of the economic gap between rich and poor countries.

Also bear in mind that aggregate data mask different trends in various world regions. The 'best case' region of the world is eastern Asia, where incomes (controlled for inflation) have tripled over the last generation. It is to Asia that the 'optimists' in the global hunger debate typically turn for evidence that poor countries can and do raise living standards and reduce hunger. The 'worst case' region of the world is sub-Saharan Africa, where living standards have actually fallen over the last decade, and more and more people are pushed to the brink of starvation. It is here that high technology is least evident and birth rates are highest. Pessimists typically look to Africa when they argue that poor countries are losing ground in the struggle to keep their people well nourished.

Television brings home the tragedy of hunger every year or so when news cameras focus on starving people in places like Ethiopia and Somalia. But hunger – and the early death from illness that it brings on – is the plight of millions all year round. The world does have the technical means to feed everyone; the question is do we have the moral determination to do so?

● **Continue the debate:**

1. In your opinion, what are the primary causes of global hunger?

2. Do you place responsibility for solving this problem on poor countries or rich ones? Why?

3. Do you expect the extent of global hunger to increase or decrease? Why? ●

Sources: United Nations Development Programme, 1994, 1995.

home, the women gather wood for their fires, all the time searching for whatever plants they can find to enrich the evening meal. The buffalo, too, are ready for a meal and the women tend to them. It is well past dark before their 18-hour day is over (Jacobson, 1993: 61).

In rich societies, the work women do is typically unrecognised, undervalued and underpaid; women receive less income for their efforts than men do. In low-income countries, this pattern is even more pronounced. Women do most of the work in poor societies, and families depend on women's work to provide income. At the same time, just as tradition keeps many women from school, it also accords them primary responsibility for child rearing and maintaining the household. In poor societies, the United Nations estimates, men own 90 per cent of the land, representing a far greater gender disparity in wealth than is found in industrial nations. Clearly, multilayered systems of tradition and law subordinate women in poor societies. Caught in a spiral of circumstance that promises little hope for change, women are disproportionately the poorest of the poor. More than 500 million of the world's 800 million people living in absolute poverty are women.

Women in poor countries have limited access to birth control (which obviously raises the birth rate), and they typically give birth without the assistance of any trained health personnel. Figure 11.3 draws a stark contrast between high- and low-income countries in this regard. Overall, gender inequality is strongest in low-income societies, especially in Asia where cultural traditions overwhelmingly favour males. As the box explains, this

Life expectancy is closely related to social-class position. Poor people – especially young males – who struggle to get by in cities around the world, have a strikingly high rate of death and injury from illness, accident and violence. Some individuals caught up in poverty engage in perilous behaviour because they have little reason to think the future will be brighter than the present. The boy shown here, from a poor neighbourhood in Rio de Janeiro, died in a 'train surfing' accident shortly after this photograph was taken.

Source: Miguel Luis Faribanks

pattern of denigrating women affects virtually every dimension of life and has produced a stunning lack of females in some regions of the world (Kishor, 1993).

Correlates of global poverty

What accounts for the severe and extensive poverty in low-income countries? The rest of this chapter weaves together explanations from the following facts about poor societies.

1. *Technology*. Almost two-thirds of people in low-income countries farm the land; the productive power of industrial technology is all but absent in these poorest nations. Energy from human muscles or beasts of burden falls far short of the force unleashed by steam, oil, gas or nuclear fuels – the power sources that propel complex machinery. Moreover, poor societies' focus on farming, rather than on specialised production, inhibits development of human skills and abilities.

2. *Population growth*. As Chapter 22 ('Population and Urbanisation') explains in detail, countries with the

least-developed economies have the world's highest birth rates. Despite the death toll from poverty, the populations of poor countries in Africa, for example, double every 25 years. There, more than half the people have yet to enter their child bearing years, so the wave of population growth will roll into the future. Even an expanding economy cannot support vast population surges. During 1993, for example, the population of Kenya swelled by 4 per cent; as a result, even with some economic development, living standards actually fell.

3. *Cultural patterns*. Poor societies are typically very traditional. Kinship groups pass folkways and mores from generation to generation. Adhering to long-established ways of life, people resist innovations – even those that promise a richer material life. The members of poor societies often accept their fate, although it may be bleak, in order to maintain family vitality and cultural heritage. Such attitudes bolster social bonds, but at the cost of discouraging development. The box on page 307 ('A different kind of poverty') explains why traditional people in India respond to their poverty differently than poor people in Europe commonly do.

Figure 11.3 ● **Per cent of births attended by trained health personnel**

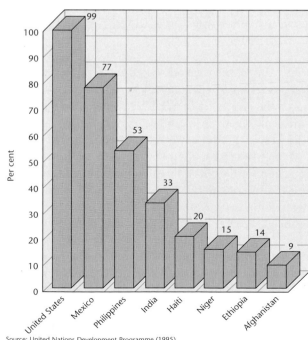

Source: United Nations Development Programme (1995)

Infanticide and sexual slavery: reports from India and Thailand

Rani, a young woman living in a remote Indian village, returned home from the hospital after delivering a baby girl. There was no joy in the family. On the contrary, upon learning of the birth, the men sombrely filed out of the mud house. Rani and her mother-in-law then set about the gruesome task of mashing oleander seeds into several drops of oil to make a poisonous paste, which they forced down the baby's throat. The day came to an end as Rani returned from a nearby field where she had buried the child.

As she walked home, Rani felt not sadness at losing her daughter but bitterness at not bearing a son. Members of her village, like poor people throughout the world (and especially Asia), favour boys while defining girls as an economic liability. Why? Because, in poor societies, most power and wealth falls into the hands of men. Parents recognise that boys are a better investment of their meagre resources, since males who survive to adulthood will provide for the family. Then, too, custom dictates that parents of a girl offer a dowry to the family of her prospective husband. In short, given the existing social structure, families are better off with boys and without girls.

One consequence of this double standard is high rate of sex-selective abortion throughout rural India, China and other Asian nations. Curiously, in India, even villages that lack running water typically have a doctor who performs high-tech amniocentesis or ultrasound to determine the sex of a foetus.

The woman's typical response, upon hearing the results of the test, is either elation at carrying a boy or resolve to terminate the pregnancy quickly so that she may 'try again'. Although there are no precise counts of abortion and female infanticide, analysts point out that, in some rural regions of Asia, men outnumber women by as many as ten to one.

For girls who manage to survive infancy, gender bias presents overwhelming barriers. Generally speaking, parents provide girls with less food, schooling and medical care than they give to boys. In times of drought or other crisis, families may leave girls to die while they channel what little resources they have toward the survival of a son.

A global pattern is that poverty forces women into sexual slavery as prostitutes. These four Vietnamese women working in a brothel in Cambodia will never escape their poverty and may well fall victim to AIDS, which is spreading rapidly across Southeast Asia.

Source: Gamma-Liaison, Inc. – Patrick Aventurier

Another dimension of gender bias is the exploding growth of sexual slavery involving young women, which has spread rapidly across South-east Asia. Bangkok, Thailand, is emerging as the sex-tourism capital of the world; prostitution in that country currently claims as many as 800,000 females, half under the age of 18. In some cases, parents sell female infants to agents who pay others to raise them, then 'harvest their crop' when the girls approach their teenage years and are old enough to work the sex trade. In other cases, girls who see little future in a rural village make their own way to the city, only to fall into the hands of pimps who soon have them working in brothels, soliciting in bars or performing in sex shows. Pimps provide girls with clothes and housing, but at a price that exceeds the girls' salaries. The result is a system of debt bondage that keeps women virtual prisoners of their unscrupulous employers. Those who run away are pursued by agents and forced to return.

The numbers involved are rapidly mounting: Thailand alone now has 1 to 2 million prostitutes (perhaps 8 per cent of the country's female population); about half of these are under the age of 18. The future for these girls and women is bleak. Most suffer from a host of diseases brought on by abuse and neglect, and 40 per cent are now infected with the virus that causes AIDS. ●

Sources: Anderson and Moore, 1993, and Santoli, 1994.

chapter twelve

Source: Commission for Racial Equality

Race, Ethnicity and Migration

Bosnia, a federal state of the former Yugoslavia, is a country marked by multicultural and ethnic differences. Its chronicler, Noel Malcolm, has said: 'There is no such thing as a typical Bosnian face: there are fair haired and dark haired Bosnians, olive skinned and freckled, big boned and wiry limbed. The genes of innumerable people have contributed to this human mosaic' (1996: 1). In its 1,000-year history it has been touched by all the great empires of the European past: Rome, Charlemagne, the Ottomans and the Austro-Hungarians. It has harboured most of the major faiths: Western Christianity, Eastern Christianity, Judaism and Islam. And it has been home to migrants from all over Europe bringing their own languages and culture. It has long been home to Slavs (who arrived 1,000 years ago), and Muslims and Croats whose own states bordered it (Croatia and Serbia).

Yet 1992 marked Bosnia's destruction. A bloody civil war erupted between the Serbs (Orthodox Christians), the Croatians (Catholics) and the Bosnian Muslims. Estimated to have cost the lives of some 500,000, unleashing some three and a half million refugees, it involved the systematic rape of thousands of Muslim women, the destruction of much of the country's infrastructure, the desecration of its great ancient mosques and churches. Whole cities were destroyed, as each group claimed its territories and aimed to 'cleanse' other ethnic groups. The biggest and most hideous ethnic cleansing was of the Bosnian Muslims, attacked by the Serbs.

Although it was a 'local war', it provoked international interventions. But even this could not prevent this large and devastating civil war. It was a modern 'ethnic' war complete with horrendous atrocities. Today, most wars are not between nation states. They are tribal conflicts between different ethnic groupings. Between 1989 and 1992 there were 80 armed conflicts – but only three of them were between countries. The rest were internal wars. Currently, in 1997, there are some 30 civil wars taking place all over the world.

Map 12.1 ● Post-1945 Yugoslavia: republics, autonomous provinces, historic regions and cities

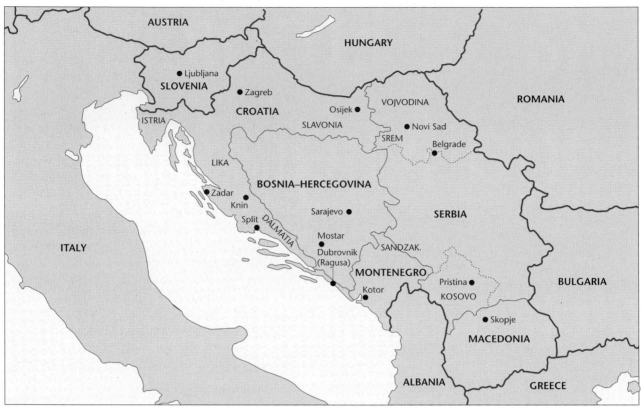

Source: Noel Malcolm 'Bosnia'

It may be, then, that the days of the big wars are over. What we have seen growing at the end of the twentieth century is a proliferation of civil wars and 'tribal conflicts'. In Turkey between the government and Kurdish nationalists. In Sudan between north Muslim Arabs and southern blacks, both Christian and animist – going on since the 1950s. In Sri Lanka between Hindu Tamils and Buddhist Sinhalese. In Rwanda between Hutus and Tutsis. In Israel between Jews and Palestinians. In Iraq between Kurds and Marsh Arabs. The list goes on and on. Conflicts for over 30 years in Angola, for 17 years in Afghanistan, and 13 years in Sri Lanka . . .

Sources: Noel Malcolm, *Bosnia: A Short History* (London: Macmillan, 1994). Migrants and Refugees: a briefing (1996)

Globally, the pattern of inequality and conflict based on colour and culture becomes ever more pronounced. The extermination of Jews and other minorities in the Holocaust marks this century's extreme low point (see Chapter 7). But ethnic strife has continued. With the collapse of the former Soviet empire, Ukrainians, Moldavians, Azerbaijanis and a host of other ethnic peoples in Eastern Europe are struggling to recover their cultural identity after decades of Soviet subjugation. In the Middle East, deep-rooted friction divides Arabs and Jews, while blacks and whites strive to establish a just society in South Africa. In the African nation of Rwanda, the Asian countries of India and Sri Lanka, in the Balkans and elsewhere in the world, racial and ethnic rifts frequently flare into violent confrontation. In the United States, ethnic tensions exist in most large, urban cities – exploding intermittently as with the Los Angeles 'Riots' of 1992. And in Europe, reports suggest a tellingly high number of violent crimes against ethnic minorities. Across the globe, ethnic antagonism is an accelerating and important issue.

Colour and culture: these are two traits that can be a source of great pride. They can also foment hatred and violence, and propel violence and war. This chapter examines the meaning of race and ethnicity, explains how these social constructs have shaped our history and suggests why they continue to play such a central part – for better or worse – in the world today.

● The social significance of race, ethnicity and migration

People throughout Europe and elsewhere in the world frequently use the terms 'race' and 'ethnicity' imprecisely and interchangeably. For this reason, we begin with important definitions.

Race

A **race** is *a category composed of people who share biologically transmitted traits that members of a society deem socially significant.* People may classify each other into races based on physical characteristics such as skin colour, facial features, hair texture and body shape.

Racial diversity appeared among our human ancestors as a result of living in different geographical regions of the world. In regions of intense heat, for example, people developed darker skin (from the natural pigment melanin) that offers protection from the sun; in regions with moderate climates, humans have lighter skin. But such differences are superficial; individuals of all races are members of a single biological species.

People the world over display a bewildering array of racial traits. This variety is the product of migration and intermarriage over the course of human history, so that many genetic characteristics once common to a single place are now evident throughout the world. The most striking racial variation appears in the Middle East (that is, western Asia), that has long served as a 'crossroads' of human migration. Striking racial uniformity, by contrast, characterises more isolated

DIFFERENT VOICES

What's in a word?

Using the 'correct' language in the study of race and ethnicity can be very difficult. Race, as we have seen, is a very muddled concept and can easily lead to racialisation. Ethnicity is a valuable term, but not when it is applied only to groups that differ from us: everybody on the planet is part of complex ethncities. Much of this leads to discussions of migration patterns, hybridities and diasporas – so we understand the paths along which different ethnicities have travelled in the world. Some commentators prefer the language used by different ethnicities themselves: the

word 'black' (in the UK) or 'people of colour' (in the USA). The trouble here is that there is no agreement within these groups: some, often more political, people prefer one word, others may prefer another. For example, 'Asian' black feminist Kum-Kum Bhavnani suggests that 'black' is used in Britain as a political category for racialised groups – all those non-white groups who experience racism. This would include Pakistani, Bangladeshi and Indian groups. The word would become a unifying force for a 'black movement'.

But others do not agree. Tariq

Modood argues that 'black' is not suitable for Asians in the UK because it generates a false sense of essential unity and is itself used inconsistently (it sometimes only means people of African descent). Indeed he argues that most Asians do not use the term, and that what is really needed is a language of Asian pride with its own historical and cultural roots.

When other groups are considered – Chinese, Maltese, Cypriots, Arabs – the debates become even more complexly drawn. ●

Sources: Bhavnani (1993) and Modood (1994)

Map 12.2 ● Black and white Britain

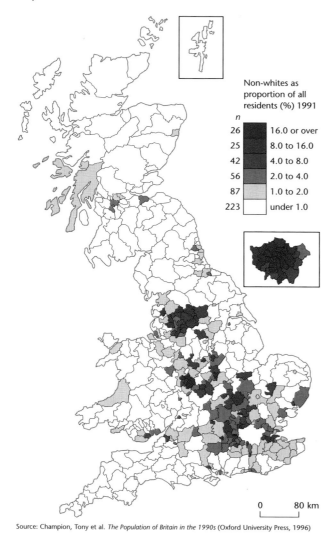

Source: Champion, Tony et al. *The Population of Britain in the 1990s* (Oxford University Press, 1996)

Sociologists consider such categories very misleading, since we now know that no society is composed of biologically pure individuals. In fact, the world traveller notices gradual and subtle racial variations from region to region. The people we might call 'Caucasian' (or 'Indo-Europeans' or, more commonly, 'white people') actually display skin colour that ranges from very light (typical in Scandinavia) to very dark (widespread in southern India). We also find the same variation among so-called 'Negroids' ('Africans' or, more commonly, 'black people') and 'Mongoloids'. In fact, many 'white people' of southern India actually have darker skin than many 'black people', including the blond Negroid aborigines of Australia.

Although we often distinguish 'black' and 'white' people, populations are genetically mixed. Over many generations, the biological traits of Negroid Africans, Caucasian Europeans and Mongoloid Native Americans (whose ancestors were Asian) spread widely throughout the world. Many 'black' people, therefore, have a significant proportion of Caucasian genes and many 'white' people have some Negroid genes. In short, no matter what people may think, race is no black-and-white issue.

Yet, despite this reality of biological mixing, however, people around the world are quick to classify each other racially and rank these categories in systems of social inequality. This *process of ranking people on the basis of their presumed race* is called **racialisation**. As explained later, people may also defend racial hierarchy with assertions that one category is inherently 'better' or more intelligent than another, though no sound scientific research supports such beliefs. But, because so much is at stake, it is no wonder that societies strive to make racial labelling much more clear than facts permit. Earlier in this century, for example, many southern states in the USA legally defined as 'coloured' anyone who had as little as one-thirty-second African ancestry (that is, one African-American great-great-great grandparent). Today, with less of a caste distinction in the United States, the law enables parents to declare the race of a child, if they wish to do so at all.

Ethnicity

Ethnicity is *a shared cultural heritage*. Members of an *ethnic category* have common ancestors, a language or a religion that, together, confer a distinctive social identity. The forebears of Pakistani, Indonesian,

peoples such as the island-dwelling Japanese. But no society lacks genetic mixture, and increasing contact among the world's people will ensure that racial blending will accelerate in the future.

Nineteenth-century biologists responded to the world's racial diversity by developing a three-part scheme of racial classifications. They labelled people with relatively light skin and fine hair as *Caucasian*; they called those with darker skin and coarser, curlier hair *Negroid*; and people with yellow or brown skin and distinctive folds on the eyelids were termed *Mongoloid*.

Table 12.1 ● The major groups of Asians in Britain

Place of origin	Religion	First language	Community known as
(a) **From the Indian subcontinent**			
(i) *India*			
Punjab State	mainly Sikhs some Hindus	Punjabi	Punjabi Sikh Punjabi Hindu
Gujarat State	mainly Hindus some Muslims	Gujarati (some Kitchi)	Gujarati Hindu Gujarati Muslim (Kutchi Muslim)
(ii) *Pakistan*			
Punjab	Muslims	Punjabi (some Urdu)	Punjabi Muslim
Mirpur (Azad Kashmir)	Muslims	Punjabi (Mirpuri dialect)	Mirpuri
NW Frontier Province (very few)	Muslims	Pashto	Pathan
(iii) *Bangladesh*			
Sylhet District	Muslims	Bengali	Bengali Muslim
(b) **From East Africa** most people have come from: Uganda, Kenya, Tanzania some people have come from: Malawi, Zambia the families of most East African Asians originated in these areas of the Indian subcontinent:			
(i) Gujarat State (main group)	Hindus some Muslims	Gujarati (some Kutchi)	EA Gujarati Hindu EA Gujarati Muslim (EA Kutchi Hindu) (EA Kutchi Muslim)
(ii) Punjab State (India)	Sikhs Hindus	Punjabi	EA Punjabi Sikh EA Punjabi Hindu
(iii) Punjab (Pakistan)	Muslims	Punjabi (some Urdu)	EA Punjabi Muslim

Source: adapted from Coombe and Little, 1986: 38

Caribbean, Hong Kong or Chinese Europeans – to name just a few! – may well retain cultural patterns rooted in particular areas of the world. In 1995, there were over a million foreign students in French schools (and three-quarters of a million in Germany) where German, English, Spanish, Italian, Portugese, Arabic, Hebrew, Russian, Japanese, Dutch, Chinese and Turkish were taught. In Britain, there exist around 100 minority languages – about a quarter of them taught in English schools (see Crystal, 1997: 36–7). And in the United States, more than 30 million people speak a language other than English in their homes.

But it goes deeper than just language. Most Europeans and Americans of Spanish, Italian and Polish ancestry are Roman Catholic, while others of Greek, Ukrainian and Russian ancestry are members of the Eastern Orthodox church. There are more than 6 million Jewish Americans (with ancestral ties to various nations) who share a distinctive religious history. Similarly, several million women and men in Europe have a Muslim heritage.

Race and ethnicity, then, are quite different, since one is biological (and now very muddled) and the other is cultural. But the two sometimes go hand in hand. Gujarati Hindus, for example, can have distinctive physical traits and – for those who maintain a traditional way of life – cultural attributes as well. But ethnic distinctiveness should not be viewed as racial. For example, Jews are sometimes described as a race although they are distinctive only in their religious beliefs as well as their history of persecution (Goldsby, 1977).

Finally, ethnicity involves even more variability and mixture than race does, for most people identify with more than one ethnic background, (a person might claim to be, say, German and English). Many Asians in the UK, for example, identify with quite specific ethnicities in Asia, as well as 'being British'. The communities vary from Punjabi Hindus (who speak Punjabi) and Gujarati Muslims (who speak Gujarati) who come from Indian states (Punjab and Gujarat), to those from Pakistan (such as Mirpuri Muslims), Bangladesh (such as Bengali Muslims) and East Africa (such as Uganda or Kenya). Table 12.1 provides a listing of the major groupings.

Moreover, people may intentionally modify their ethnicity over time. Many West Indian immigrants to England have gradually shed their cultural background, becoming less 'West Indian' and absorbing new ethnic traits from others. In a reversal of this pattern, others have highlighted

Table 12.2 ● Racial and ethnic categories in the United States, 1990

Racial or ethnic classification	Approximate US population	Per cent of total population
African descent	**29,986,060**	**12.1%**
Hispanic descent	**22,354,059**	**9.0**
Mexican	13,495,938	5.4
Puerto Rican	2,727,754	1.1
Cuban	1,043,932	0.4
Other Hispanic	5,086,435	2.1
Native-American descent	**1,959,234**	**0.8**
American Indian	1,878,285	0.8
Eskimo	57,152	<
Aleut	23,797	<
Asian or Pacific Islander descent	**7,273,662**	**2.9**
Chinese	1,645,472	0.7
Filipino	1,406,770	0.6
Japanese	847,562	0.3
Asian Indian	815,447	0.3
Korean	798,849	0.3
Vietnamese	614,547	0.2
Hawaiian	211,014	<
Samoan	62,964	<
Guamanian	49,345	<
Other Asian or Pacific Islander	821,692	0.3
European descent	**200,000,000**	**80.0**
German	57,947,000	23.3
Irish	38,736,000	15.6
English	32,652,000	13.1
Italian	14,665,000	5.9
French	10,321,000	4.1
Polish	9,366,000	3.8
Dutch	6,227,000	2.5
Scotch-Irish	5,618,000	2.3
Scottish	5,314,000	2.1
Swedish	4,681,000	1.9
Norwegian	3,869,000	1.6
Russian	2,953,000	1.2
Welsh	2,034,000	0.8
Danish	1,635,000	0.6
Hungarian	1,582,000	0.6

People of Hispanic descent can be of any race. Many people also identify with more than one ethnic category. Thus figures total more than 100 per cent. White people represent 80 per cent of the US population.

< Indicates less than 1/10 of 1 per cent.

Source: US Bureau of the Census (1995)

North America: the land of migration – and the coming majority?

Although Europe may be seen as a continent of migration, the figures of ethnic groups present here are small when compared with those found in the United States, truly the modern land of migration. Table 12.2 shows just how many groups have settled in the United States, and any visit to Ellis Island off New York – the place where most of the migrating people first arrived – would soon confirm the enormity of this migration pattern.

With such a vast pattern of migration, the argument is now made that 'white' groupings are about to become a minority. During the 1980s, Manhattan, the central borough of New York City, gained a minority-majority. This means that people of African, Asian and Latino descent, together with other racial and ethnic minorities, became a majority of the population. The same transformation has taken place in 186 counties across the United States (some

6 per cent of the total – Map 12.3). As early as 2050, according to some projections, minorities will represent a majority of the country.

A look at the US 1990 census data confirms the prospect of a minority-majority. Between 1980 and 1990, the 'majority' white, non-Hispanic population increased by a modest 6 per cent. The number of Asians or Pacific Islanders, however, more than doubled, soaring by 108 per cent. The Hispanic population increased by more than half (53 per cent), and the number of Native Americans, Eskimos or Aleuts jumped by 37 per cent. African Americans increased their numbers by 13 per cent – twice the white rate. This population growth is highly concentrated, however, with more than half the increase taking place in just three states: California, Florida and Texas.

Not everyone accepts the conclusion that the United States will have a

minority-majority in the foreseeable future. Stephan Thernstrom (1990) points out that such a projection rests on two questionable assumptions. First, he explains, the US immigration rate must remain at its current high level despite government projections of a coming downturn. Beyond that, he asks, who can be sure? Second, the high birth rates that characterise many immigrant minorities today must continue. But, Thernstrom points out, as the years pass, immigrants typically begin to behave more or less like everyone else.

But whatever the specific projections, few people doubt that a great change in the racial and ethnic profile of the United States is under way. It seems only a matter of time before white people – largely of European ancestry – will become minorities as a host of others emerge as the majority in the United States. ●

their background through 'Rastafarianism' (see below). Likewise, many people with Native-Irish ancestry have recently taken a renewed interest in their traditional ethnicity, enhancing this dimension of their identity. In short, ethnicity is about varying cultures (see Chapter 4) which are themselves changeable and fluid.

Minorities

A racial or ethnic **minority** is *a category of people, distinguished by physical or cultural traits, who are socially disadvantaged.* Distinct from the dominant 'majority', in other words, minorities are set apart and subordinated. The breadth of the term 'minority' has

expanded in recent years beyond people with particular racial and ethnic traits to include people with physical disabilities; as the next chapter explains, some analysts view all women as minorities as well. Gays and lesbians have also been placed in a minority framework.

White people continue to predominate numerically; about 80 per cent of the US (it is about 95 per cent in the UK) population falls into this broad category. But the absolute numbers and share of population for virtually every minority category grew rapidly during the 1980s. As the 'North America' box above explains, some researchers even project that the historical *minorities*, taken together, will constitute a *majority* of people in the United States sometime during the coming century.

Minorities have two major characteristics. First, they share a *distinctive identity*. Because race is highly visible (and virtually impossible – Michael Jackson apart – for a person to change), minority men and women typically have a keen awareness of their physical distinctiveness. The significance of ethnicity (which people can change) is more variable. Some people (many Reform Jews among them) have downplayed their historic ethnicity, while others (including many Orthodox Jews) have retained their cultural traditions and lived in distinctive ethnic enclaves.

A second characteristic of minorities is *subordination*. As the remainder of this chapter will demonstrate, racialised minorities typically have less income, lower occupational prestige and more limited schooling than their counterparts in the majority. This is true in the UK, but also throughout Europe and the world. With this in mind, we can see that class, race and ethnicity, as well as gender, are not mutually exclusive issues but are overlapping and reinforcing dimensions of social stratification.

Of course, not all members of any minority category are disadvantaged. Some Afro-Caribbeans are quite wealthy, certain Asians are celebrated business leaders. But even the greatest success rarely allows individuals to transcend their minority standing (Benjamin, 1991). That is, race or ethnicity often serves as a *master status* (described in Chapter 6, 'Social Interaction in Everyday Life') that overshadows personal accomplishments.

The term 'minority' suggests that these categories of people constitute a small proportion of a society's population. But this is not always the case. For example, black South Africans are a numerical majority in their society, though they are grossly deprived of economic and political power by whites. In the United States, women represent slightly more than half the population but are still struggling to obtain opportunities and privileges enjoyed by men.

● Prejudice

Prejudice is *a rigid and irrational generalisation about an entire category of people*. A prejudice is an attitude – a prejudgement – that one applies indiscriminately and inflexibly to some category with little regard for the facts. People commonly hold prejudices about individuals of a particular social class, sex, sexual orientation, age, political affiliation, race or ethnicity.

Prejudices can be positive or negative. Our positive prejudices tend to exaggerate the virtues of people like ourselves, while our negative prejudices condemn those who differ from us. Negative prejudice runs along a continuum, ranging from mild aversion to outright hostility. Because attitudes are rooted in culture, everyone has at least some measure of prejudice. Most people recognise that white people commonly hold prejudiced views of minorities. But minorities, too, harbour prejudices, sometimes of whites and often of other minorities.

Map 12.3 ● Where the minority-majority already exists

As recorded by the 1990 census, minorities predominate in 186 counties (out of 3,014 in the United States). That is, the total number of African Americans, Asian Americans, Hispanics and other minorities exceeds 50 per cent of the population. The map also identifies some 40 counties in which minorities together exceed 75 per cent of the population and more than 200 counties in which minority population surpasses the 25 per cent mark. Why do you think most of these counties are in the South and Southwest?

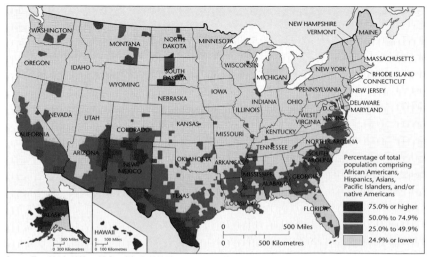

Source: *Time*, 12 July 1993, p. 15 Copyright C. 1993 Time Inc. Reprinted by permission.
Data from the 1990 decennial census.

Stereotypes

Prejudices combine to form a *stereotype* (*stereo* is derived from Greek meaning 'hard' or 'solid'), described in Chapter 1 ('The Sociological Perspective') as *a prejudicial, exaggerated description of some category of people*. Because many stereotypes involve emotions like love and loyalty (generally towards members of ingroups) or hate and fear (towards outgroups), they are exaggerated images that are hard to change even in the face of contradictory evidence. For example, some people have a stereotypical understanding of the poor as lazy and irresponsible spongers who would rather rely on welfare than support themselves (Waxman, 1983; NORC, 1994). As Chapter 10 explained, however, this stereotype distorts reality because most poor people tend to be children, women, working adults or elderly people.

Stereotypes have been devised for virtually every racial and ethnic minority, and such attitudes may become deeply rooted in a society's culture. In the United States, for example, half of white people stereotype African Americans as lacking motivation to improve their own lives (NORC, 1994: 236). Such attitudes assume that social disadvantage is a matter of personal deficiency, which, in most cases, it is not. Moreover, stereotypes of this kind ignore the fact that most poor people in the United States are white and that most African Americans work as hard as anyone else and are *not* poor. In this case the bit of truth in the stereotype is that black people are more likely than white people to be poor (and slightly more likely, if poor, to receive welfare assistance). But by building a rigid attitude out of a few selected facts, stereotypes grossly distort reality.

Racism

A powerful and destructive form of prejudice, **racism** refers to *the belief that one racial category is innately superior or inferior to another*. Racism has pervaded world history. The ancient Greeks, the peoples of India and the Chinese – despite their many notable achievements – were all quick to view 'others' as inferior. Racism has also been widespread in our own history, especially as a justification for the enslavement of people of African descent. Today, overt racism in the UK and United States has subsided to some degree because of a more egalitarian culture that urges us to evaluate people, in Dr Martin Luther King's fine words, 'by the content of their character, not the colour of their skin'.

Yet racism persists and, whether blatant or subtle, it continues to cause injury and humiliation to people of colour (Feagin, 1991).

Racism and social domination

Historically, the assertion that one specific category of people is innately inferior to another has served as a powerful justification for subjecting the targets of these taunts to *social* inferiority. By the end of the last century, European nations and the United States had forged vast empires, often ruthlessly and brutally subjugating foreign peoples with the callous claim that they were somehow less human than the explorers who enslaved them.

In this century, racism was central to the Nazi proclamation that a so-called Aryan super-race of blond-haired, blue-eyed Germans was destined to rule the world. Such racist ideology encouraged the systematic slaughter of anyone deemed inferior, including some 6 million European Jews and millions of Poles, gypsies, homosexuals and people with physical and mental disabilities.

More recently, racial conflict has intensified in Western Europe with the immigration of people from former colonies as well as from Eastern Europe seeking a higher standard of living. In Germany, France, Britain and elsewhere, growing public intolerance of immigrants has fuelled a resurgence of Nazi-style rhetoric and tactics. The United States, too, is experiencing increasing racial tensions in cities and on college campuses. Racism – in thought and deed – remains a serious social problem everywhere as people still contend that some racial and ethnic categories are 'better' than others.

Theories of prejudice

If prejudice does not represent a rational assessment of facts, what are its origins? Social scientists have come up with various answers to this vexing question, citing the importance of frustration, personality, culture and social conflict.

Scapegoat theory of prejudice

Scapegoat theory holds that prejudice springs from frustration. Such attitudes, therefore, are common among people who are themselves disadvantaged (Dollard, 1939). Take the case of a white woman frustrated at the low wages she earns working in a textile factory. Directing hostility at the powerful people who operate the factory carries obvious risks; therefore, she may

W. E. B. Du Bois: race and conflict

One of sociology's pioneers, who has not received the attention he deserves, is William Edward Burghardt Du Bois (1868–1963). Born to a poor Massachusetts family, Du Bois showed extraordinary aptitude as a student. After graduating from high school, he went to college, one of only a handful of the young people in his small town (and the only person of African descent) to do so. After graduating from Fisk University in Nashville, Tennessee, Du Bois realised a childhood ambition and enrolled at Harvard, repeating his junior and senior years and then beginning graduate study. He earned the first doctorate awarded by Harvard to a person of colour.

Du Bois believed sociologists should direct their efforts to contemporary problems, and for him the vexing issue of race was the paramount social concern. Although he was accepted in the intellectual circles of his day, Du Bois believed that US society consigned African Americans as a whole to an existence separate and apart. Unlike white people, who can make their way in the world simply as 'Americans', Du Bois pointed out, African Americans have a 'double consciousness', reflecting their status as Americans who are never able to escape identification based on colour.

Politically speaking, his opposition to racial separation led Du Bois to serve as a founding member of the National Association for the Advancement of Colored People (NAACP). Du Bois maintained that his research, too, should attempt to address pressing racial problems. Later in his life, Du Bois reflected (1940: 51):

I was determined to put science into sociology through a study of the condition of my own group. I was going to study the facts, any and all facts, concerning the American Negro and his plight.

After taking a position at the University of Pennsylvania in Philadelphia, Du Bois set out to conduct the research that produced a sociological classic, *The Philadelphia Negro: A Social Study* (1899). In this systematic investigation of Philadelphia's African-American community at the turn of the century, Du Bois chronicled both the strengths and weaknesses of people wrestling with overwhelming social problems. Running against the intellectual current of the times (especially Spencer's Social Darwinism), Du Bois rejected the widespread notion of black inferiority, attributing the problems of African Americans to white prejudice. But his criticism extended also to successful people of colour, whom he scolded for being so eager to win white acceptance that they abandoned all ties with those still in need. 'The first impulse of the best, the wisest and the richest', he lamented, 'is to segregate themselves from the mass' (1899: 317).

At the time *The Philadelphia Negro* was published, Du Bois was optimistic about overcoming racial divisions. By the end of his life, however, he had grown bitter, believing that little had changed. At the age of 93, Du Bois left the United States for Ghana, where he died two years later. ●

Sources: Based, in part, on Baltzell, 1967, and Du Bois, 1967; orig. 1899.

Source: Brown Brothers

well attribute her low pay to the presence of minority co-workers. Prejudice of this kind may not go far towards improving the woman's situation, but it serves as a relatively safe way to vent anger and it may give her the comforting feeling that at least she is superior to someone.

A **scapegoat**, then, is *a person or category of people, typically with little power, whom people unfairly blame for* *their own troubles*. Because they are often 'safe targets', minorities are easily used as scapegoats. The Nazis blamed the Jewish minority for all of Germany's ills fifty years ago. And today some Europeans attribute troubles at home to the presence of Turkish, Pakistani or other immigrants from abroad.

Authoritarian personality theory

T. W. Adorno (1950) and his colleagues claimed that extreme prejudice was a personality trait of particular individuals. They based this conclusion on research showing that people who displayed strong prejudice towards one minority were usually intolerant of all minorities. Such people exhibit *authoritarian personalities*, rigidly conforming to conventional cultural values, envisioning moral issues as clear-cut matters of right and wrong and advocating strongly ethnocentric views. People with authoritarian personalities also look upon society as naturally competitive and hierarchical, with 'better' people (like themselves) inevitably dominating those who are weaker.

By contrast, Adorno found, people tolerant towards one minority were likely to be accepting of all. They tend to be more flexible in their moral judgements and believe that, ideally, society should be relatively egalitarian. They feel uncomfortable in any situation in which some people exercise excessive and damaging power over others.

According to these researchers, authoritarian personalities tend to develop in people with little education and harsh and demanding parents. Raised by cold and insistent authority figures, they theorised, children may become angry and anxious people who seek out scapegoats whom they come to define as their social inferiors.

Cultural theory of prejudice

A third approach holds that, while extreme prejudice may be characteristic of certain people, some prejudice is common to everyone because such attitudes are embedded in culture. As noted in Chapter 4 ('Culture'), the social superiority of some categories of people is a core value of US culture. Recent multicultural research echoes this idea and calls for educational programmes to help people in the United States move beyond their traditionally Eurocentric attitudes to gain an appreciation of the culture and contributions of those of non-European descent (Asante, 1987, 1988).

For more than forty years, Emory Bogardus (1968) studied the effects of culturally rooted prejudices on interpersonal relationships. He devised the concept of *social distance* to gauge how close or distant people feel in relation to members of various racial and ethnic categories. Interestingly, his research shows that people throughout the United States share similar views in this regard, leading Bogardus to conclude that such attitudes are culturally normative.

Bogardus found that members of US society regarded most positively people of English, Canadian and Scottish background, welcoming close relationships with and even marriage to them. There was somewhat less of a premium on interactions with people of French, German, Swedish and Dutch descent. The most negative prejudices, Bogardus discovered, targeted people of African and Asian descent.

If prejudice is widespread, can we dismiss intolerance as merely a trait of a handful of abnormal people, as Adorno asserted? A more all-encompassing approach recognises some bigotry is within us all as we become well adjusted to a 'culture of prejudice'.

Conflict theory of prejudice

A fourth view, following the conflict approach, claims that powerful people utilise prejudice as a strategy to oppress minorities. To the extent that the public looks down on illegal Latino immigrants in the south-west United States, for example, rich landowners are able to pay these people low wages for hard work. Similarly, elites benefit from prejudice that divides workers along racial and ethnic lines and discourages them from working together to advance their common interests (Geschwender, 1978; Olzak, 1989).

A different conflict argument, advanced by Shelby Steele (1990), holds that minorities themselves spark conflict by cultivating a climate of *race consciousness*, designed to win them greater power and privileges. Race consciousness, Steele explains, amounts to the assertion that minorities are victims and white people their victimisers. Because of this historical disadvantage, minorities claim they are now entitled to special considerations based on their race. While this strategy may yield short-term gains for minorities, Steele cautions that such policies may precipitate a backlash from white people or others who condemn 'special treatment' for anyone on the basis of race or ethnicity.

CONTROVERSY AND DEBATE

Dangerous extremists: Islamic fundamentalists or Islamophobes?

slam is the dominant faith in some 40 states throughout the world, and is seen by many to be the fastest growing religion. (In Chapter 18, we discuss its features in some more detail). In the UK, there has been a growth from 0.1 per cent to 0.6 per cent over the past 25 years. This is small in absolute numbers, but very significant in its expansion. It is estimated that there are now about 1 million Muslims in the UK and 3 million in France. Overall, Muslims account for some 3 per cent of European faith.

Islam has come to symbolise key questions about ethnicity, prejudice and tolerance. This can be seen from the prominence given to the debate over the Salman Rushdie affair and the Iranian fatwah (death threat) imposed upon him (see the opening vignette to

Chapter 18). It is also seen in the Gulf War waged against Iraq in 1992. Some have even claimed that this is a new Holy War between East and West, where the traditional forces of the anti-Western, anti-Rational and anti-Modern Islamic regions are in spiritual and moral combat with the modernising but decadent West. Benjamin Barber, for one, sees this as a clash of civilisations, a conflict between the Jihad (Holy War) and the materialism symbolised by McDonaldisation (see Chapter 7 and Chapter 16). It is a conflict which may also be linked to ethnicity and some see it as the major world conflict in the twenty-first century.

On the one hand, some westerners argue that Islam is a dangerous force in the world. It is seen as a fundamentalist

religion (see Chapter 18) holding strongly to traditionalist views, emphasising religious texts and looking back to its past to affirm its puritan vision. It is seen to hold particular prejudices against many modern concerns of the West: the liberation of women, the 'open and free society', the decline of religion, the acceptance of diversity such as homosexuality and 'sexual freedom'. And it is seen to favour an absolutist religious state where nothing can exist outside of the religion. Indeed, of the forty or so states where Islam is dominant, few can be called democratic. All of this clashes with the modern values of the Western state.

Such claims as above certainly do have some basis in fact. But the critics argue that such statements are extreme: the Islamic faith actually comes in a

---

The efforts of these four women greatly advanced the social standing of African Americans in the United States. Pictures below, from left to right: Sojourner Truth (1797–1883), born a slave, became an influential preacher and outspoken abolitionist who was honoured by President Lincoln at the White House. Harriet Tubman (1820–1913), after escaping from slavery herself, masterminded the flight from bondage of hundreds of African-American men and women via the 'Underground Railroad'. Ida Wells-Barnett (1862–1931), born to slave parents, became a partner in a Memphis newspaper and served as a tireless crusader against the terror of lynching. Marian Anderson (1897–1993), an exceptional singer whose early career was restrained by racial prejudice, broke symbolic 'colour lines' by singing in the White House (1936) and on the steps of the Lincoln Memorial to a crowd of almost 100,000 people (1939).

Source: Corbis Bettmann/Culver Pictures, Inc. Schomburg Centre for Research in Black Culture/Corbis-Bettmann

number of varieties, and many of its supporters do not adopt these extreme positions. Just as Christianity as a number of its own divides, so too do the Muslims. Most are not extreme. Indeed, a key divide lies between Shi'ism and the Shi'ites (who hold more traditional and rigid views) and the Sunnis (who accept more diversity and change). In the UK, for instance, the majority of Muslims must be distinguished from small extreme groups like Al-Muhajiroun which calls for Islamic government in the UK (*Khilafah*).

It is the more extreme views which get reported most often. And it is these ideas which form the basis of a new form of prejudice growing in Europe called '**Islamophobia**' – *a hatred of all things Muslim*. Where once the Jews or blacks or 'Asians' were prime objects of attack in the UK, increasingly Muslims have become the new objects of prejudice and discrimination. Not only is the incidence of violence attacks against

Muslims increasing, but prejudicial views are being widely held. No one, for example, blames the Catholics for IRA bombings in Ireland: the IRA is recognised as a more extreme group. So why blame Muslims for much of what is in fact only an extreme edge? In the UK, Muslims are generally amongst the most economically successful of new migrant groups, and this success may well be one basis for the prejudice.

In 1996, the Runnymede Trust – a major organisation which promotes and researches a multi-cultural society – announced a commission to look into what they considered as the most rapidly growing form of prejudice in the UK. They were concerned to look at such things as anti-Islamic and anti-Muslim attitudes; the relations between Islam and secular outlooks and other world faiths; the treatment of Islam and Muslim concerns in the media; and the contributions of British Muslims to government and society. The Trust has highlighted a

major emerging form of prejudice in Western societies, one that is likely to become more and more recognised.

These divides raise serious issues around prejudice and discrimination. How far can a multi-cultural society which claims to accept religious and ethnic diversity pursue such outright attacks upon different religions? At the same time, how far can a religious strand which rejects tolerance and diversity be allowed to propagate its views? This is a classical dilemma of freedom for those who may advocate unlimited freedom.

Consider some possible scenarios of what might happen in Europe and the West in the future. Will more and more Muslims be co-opted into Western secular individualism? Will more and more Muslims stay with their own faith, whilst accepting multi-cultural values? Or will a strong defence of Islamic fundamentalism lead to growing ethnic conflicts? ●

Source: Benjamin Barber, 1995.

● Discrimination

Closely related to prejudice is the concept of **discrimination**, *any action that involves treating various categories of people unequally*. While prejudice refers to attitudes, discrimination is a matter of behaviour. Like prejudice, discrimination can be either positive (providing special advantages) or negative (placing obstacles in front of particular categories of people). Discrimination also varies in intensity, ranging from subtle to blatant.

Prejudice and discrimination often – but not always – occur together. A personnel manager prejudiced against members of a particular minority may refuse to employ them. Robert Merton (1976) describes such a person as an *active bigot*. Fearing legal action, however, another prejudiced personnel manager may not discriminate, thereby becoming a *timid bigot*. What Merton calls *fair-weather liberals* may be generally tol-

erant of minorities yet discriminate when it is expedient to do so, such as when a superior demands it. Finally, Merton's *all-weather liberal* is free of both prejudice and discrimination.

Not all kinds of discrimination are wrong. Individuals discriminate all the time, preferring the personalities, favouring the looks or admiring the talents of particular people. Discriminating in this basic sense of *making distinctions* is necessary to everyday life and rarely causes problems. But discriminating on the basis of race or ethnicity is another matter.

All societies praise some forms of discrimination, in other words, while condemning others. Universities, for example, systematically favour applicants with greater abilities over those with less aptitude. This kind of discrimination is entirely consistent with our culture-based expectation that the greatest rewards go to people with more ability or those who work harder.

which others should aspire. Many immigrants, too, have been quick to pursue assimilation in the hope that it will free them from the prejudice and discrimination directed against distinctive foreigners and encourage upward social mobility (Newman, 1973). But multiculturalists find fault with the assimilation model because it tends to paint minorities as 'the problem' and define them (rather than the elites) as the ones who need to do all the changing.

Certainly some assimilation has occurred. In the UK, whilst Afro-Caribbean cultures and Asian cultures may be strong, they have also taken on many key features of British society. In the United States, as fast as some urban 'ethnic villages' disappear, new ones emerge, the product of a steady and substantial stream of immigrants. Almost 30 per cent of today's New Yorkers are foreign born – the highest percentage in 50 years. No wonder some analysts argue that race and ethnicity endure as basic building blocks of US society (Glazer and Moynihan, 1970; Alba, 1985).

As a cultural process, assimilation involves changes in ethnicity but not in race. For example, many Americans of Japanese descent have discarded their traditional way of life but still maintain their racial identity. However, racial traits do diminish over generations as the result of **miscegenation**, *biological reproduction by partners of different racial categories*. Miscegenation (typically outside of marriage) has occurred throughout US history despite cultural and even legal prohibitions. Norms against miscegenation are now eroding and, while the share of officially recorded interracial births in the United States is still just 4 per cent, it is rising steadily.

Segregation

Segregation refers to *the physical and social separation of categories of people*. Some minorities, especially religious orders like the Amish of Pennsylvania, have voluntarily segregated themselves. Mostly, however, majorities segregate minorities involuntarily by excluding them. Various degrees of segregation characterise residential districts, schools, occupations, hospitals and even cemeteries. While pluralism fosters distinctiveness without disadvantage, segregation enforces separation to the detriment of a minority.

South Africa's system of apartheid (described in Chapter 9, 'Social Stratification') illustrates racial

segregation that has been both rigid and pervasive. Apartheid was created by the European minority it served, and white South Africans historically have enforced this system through the use of brutal power (Fredrickson, 1981). South Africa is now in the process of dismantling apartheid but, as yet, the basic racial structure of South Africa has changed little and the nation remains essentially two different societies that touch only when blacks provide services for whites.

In the United States, too, racial segregation has a long history. Centuries of slavery gave way to racially separated lodging, schooling and transportation. Decisions such as the 1954 *Brown* case have reduced overt and *de jure* (Latin meaning 'by law') discrimination in the United States. However, *de facto* ('in fact') segregation continues.

In the 1960s, Karl and Alma Taeuber (1965) assessed the residential segregation of black people and white people in more than 200 cities in the United States. On a numerical scale ranging from zero (a mixing of races in all neighbourhoods) to 100 (racial mixing in no neighbourhoods), they calculated an *average* segregation score of 86.2. Subsequent research has shown

---

Only a full century after the abolition of slavery did the US government take action to dismantle the 'Jim Crow' laws that continued to separate people of European and African ancestry. Until the early 1960s, these laws formally segregated hotels, restaurants, parks, buses and even drinking fountains. More than three decades later, de facto racial segregation in housing and schooling remains a reality for millions of people of colour in the United States.

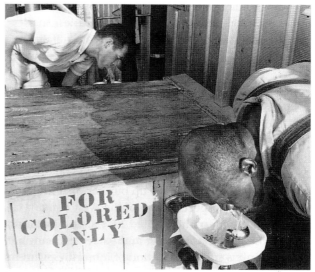

Source: Corbis-Bettmann

that segregation has decreased since then, but only slightly; even African Americans with high incomes continue to find that their colour closes off opportunities for housing (Hwang et al., 1985; Calmore, 1986; Saltman, 1991; Wilson, 1991; Farley and Frey, 1994; NORC, 1994).

We associate segregation with housing but, as Douglas Massey and Nancy Denton (1989) point out, racial separation involves a host of life experiences beyond neighbourhood composition. Many African Americans living in inner cities, these researchers concluded, have little social contact of any kind with the outside world. Such *hypersegregation* affects about one-fifth of all African Americans but only a small fraction of comparably poor whites (Jagarowsky and Bane, 1990).

In short, segregation generally means second-class citizenship for a minority. For this reason, many minority men and women have struggled valiantly against such exclusiveness. Sometimes the action of a single person can make a difference. On 1 December, 1955, Rosa Parks boarded a bus in Montgomery, Alabama and sat in a section designated by law for black people. When a crowd of white passengers boarded the bus, the driver asked Parks and three other African Americans to give up their seats. The three did so, but Rosa Parks refused. The driver left the bus and returned with police, who arrested her for violating the racial segregation laws. A court later convicted Parks and fined her $14. Her stand (or sitting) for justice sparked the African-American community of Montgomery to boycott city buses, ultimately bringing this form of legal segregation to an end (King, 1969).

Genocide

Genocide is *the systematic annihilation of one category of people by another*. A more recent term for this is **ethnic cleansing**, a term used especially in the Bosnia conflict described at the start of this chapter. This racist and ethnocentric brutality violates nearly every recognised moral standard; nonetheless, it has occurred time and again in the human record.

Genocide figured prominently in centuries of contact between Europeans and the original inhabitants of the Americas. From the sixteenth century on, the Spanish, Portuguese, English, French and Dutch forcefully colonised vast empires. These efforts decimated the native populations of North and South America,

allowing Europeans to gain control of the continents' wealth. Some native people fell victim to calculated killing sprees; most succumbed to diseases carried by Europeans and to which native peoples had no natural defences (Cottrell, 1979; Butterworth and Chance, 1981; Matthiessen, 1984; Sale, 1990).

Unimaginable horror befell the Jews of Europe during Adolf Hitler's reign of terror in this century. Ultimately, the Nazis exterminated more than 6 million Jewish men, women and children in what has become known as the Holocaust. (See Chapter 7 'Groups'.) In Cambodia between 1975 and 1980, Pol Pot's communist regime slaughtered anyone thought to represent capitalist cultural influences. Condemned to death were men and women able to speak any Western language and even individuals who wore eyeglasses, viewed as a symbol of capitalist culture. In all, some 2 million people (a quarter of the population) perished in the Cambodian 'killing fields' (Shawcross, 1979).

These four patterns of minority–majority interaction have all been played out in Europe and the United States.

● Migration, ethnicity and race

We live in a world of 100 million immigrants – 19 million of them refugees (Sowell, 1996). Migration patterns – the movements of people in and out of societies – offer crucial clues to the workings of societies. Not only do they help in understanding demographic patterns (discussed in Chapter 21), they focus sharp attention upon the dynamics of different groups in a society. Often these 'migratory' groups become singled out for the processes of racialisation and discrimination described above. And indeed it is hard to find any society where some outsider ethnic groups do not exist.

There have always been migratory movements: sometimes voluntary, sometimes planned, sometimes forced. 'Deportation and evacuations, exile and forcible repatriation, compulsory transfers and panic stricken flight are an essential part of European history' (Stola, in Sowell, 1996: 2). In the past, the distances travelled were often short, but with new modes of travel, vast distances have often been covered. Sometimes there have been enforced geographical dispersals of a people (for example, Jews). These are the **diasporas**. Sometimes peoples have been assimilated

chapter thirteen

Source: Popperfoto

Gender and Sexuality

We tend to think that 'becoming a man' or 'becoming a woman' is a straightforward process of 'natural' development. But sociologists and anthropologists have shown quite otherwise. North American anthroplogist Gilbert Herdt, for instance, has studied a number of New Guinean societies. In one – the Sambia – boys aged 7 to 10 are taken from their mothers to a special place outside of the village. Here they experience powerful homosexual fellatio activities. For a number of years, they daily fellate, for some years as fellator and then later as fellated. Elders teach that semen is absolutely vital; that it should be consumed daily since it is the basis of biological maleness; and that their very masculinity depends on it! At the same time, they must avoid women who are seen to be contaminating. When they are young men, they are returned to society, where they settle down and marry women. With fatherhood, their homosexuality ceases. But then the cycle starts all over again when the men steer their own young sons into this erotic pattern. As Herdt says, 'homoeroticism is the royal road to Sambia manliness'.

This is a ritualised form of homosexuality, and for the Sambia it is absolutely essential that men engage in these fellating activities in order to establish both their masculinity and, ultimately, their heterosexuality. Masculinity, here, is the outcome of a regime of ritualised homosexuality leading into manhood.

Some may find such research a little unsettling! Masculinity is often said to be the very opposite of homosexuality. Life among boys and men in the Sambia is clearly not like life among boys and men in modern Europe! In Europe, there is no ritualised homosexuality among all young boys in order for them to become men. Quite the opposite. If boys are found to be involved in sex with other boys, they are presumed quite often to be passing through a brief homosexual phase, or they are seen as being effeminate and queer. It is certainly not seen as 'manly' (Herdt, 1981).

Cultural meanings about what is considered masculine and feminine, and what is not, vary from one society to another and from one historical period to another. Not only do such meanings vary, but so do the sexual activities in which people engage. In Ancient Greece the notion of masculinity included homosexuality, whereas in our culture the two tend to be seen as mutually exclusive. In Ancient Greece sexual activity between males was required in some social relationships – between a mature aristocratic man and a younger male – for example. Love between two males was held in high esteem at the time of Plato in the city state of Athens. *The Symposium* – one of the main texts written by Plato – consists of a discussion of love in a culture which assumed, without much argument, that homosexual love between men was a higher form of love than that between a husband and wife. Nor was this confined to the Athenians: the soldiers of the army of Sparta practised homosexuality. The assumption was that such relationships led to soldiers fighting better in order to protect their lovers.

In every society, people assume certain jobs, patterns of behaviour, and ways of dressing are 'naturally' feminine while others are just as obviously masculine. But, in global perspective, we see remarkable variety in such social definitions. These men, Wodaabe pastoral nomads who live in the African nation of Niger, are proud to engage in a display of beauty most people in European society would consider feminine.

Source: The Stock Market – Aspect Picture Library

What it means to be masculine or feminine differs across cultures and history. Research suggests that 'our concept of masculinity seems to be a fairly recent historical product, a few hundred years old at most' (Connell, 1995: 68). Indeed, the leading sociologist of masculinity, R. W. Connell, suggests that the way we think about masculinity today was closely linked to the rise of individualism in early modern European society. Prior to this, whilst women were regarded as different from men, they were seen as 'incomplete' men: there was not the clear split into masculinity and femininity we have today.

Many people claim that what it is to be a man or a woman, a heterosexual or a homosexual, reflects basic and innate differences between the sexes. But, as we shall see, the different social experiences of women and men are the creation of society far more than biology. To begin, we shall distinguish between the key concepts of sex and gender. We will then examine how people become gendered, before moving on to an analysis of sexism, patriachy and gender stratification. We will see how the women's movement emerged to challenge gender stratification. Finally, we will look briefly at some recent accounts of sexuality.

● Sex and gender

Several distinctions are commonly made. **Sex** refers to *the biological distinction between females and males*, and is usually taken to have six major components: chromosome makeup, reproductive organs, external genitals, hormonal states, internal genitals and secondary sex characteristics. In general, we can speak of a female as having XX chromosomes, clitoris and vagina, ovaries, oestrogen and breast development; and the male as having XY chromosomes, penis and testicles, gonads, testosterone and a beard. There are, however, enormous variations within the two sexes in genetic and hormonal endowment. For example, an infant may be born with too few or too many X or Y chromosomes, giving it the chromosome makeup of one sex and the genitals of another.

The term **gender**, introduced in Chapter 2 ('Sociological Investigation'), refers to *the social aspects of sexual differences* of female and male. Gender is evident throughout the social world, shaping how we think about ourselves, guiding our interaction with others and influencing our work and family life. But gender involves much more than difference; it also involves hierarchy, because men enjoy a disproportionate share of most social resources.

Thus, whereas sex may be male or female, gender refers to the social meaning of masculinity and femininity. Since this stresses the social aspects, you will note that it is gender that sociologists are interested in: 'sex' would be more appropriate for a course in biology. In any event, 'sex' itself is not always a clearcut matter. A hormone imbalance before birth can produce a **hermaphrodite** (a word derived from Hermaphroditus, the offspring of the mythological Greek gods Hermes and Aphrodite, who embodied both sexes), *a human being with some combination of female and male internal and external genitalia*. Because our culture is uneasy about sexual ambiguity, we often look upon hermaphrodites with confusion and even disgust. By contrast, the Pokot of eastern Africa are indifferent to what they consider a simple biological error and the Navajo regard hermaphrodites with awe, viewing them as the embodiment of the full potential of both the female and the male (Geertz, 1975).

Under the term 'gender' are several key linked concepts. **Gender identity** refers to the psychological state in which someone comes to say 'I am a man' or 'I am a woman'. It is perfectly possible – and not uncommon – to believe that one is a woman whilst having all the biological sex attributes of a male. Currently, such experiences are often designated as either **transsexualism** or **transgenderism**. Hermaphrodites may undergo genital surgery to gain the appearance (and occasionally the function) of a sexually normal female or male. Surgery is also commonly considered by **transsexuals**, *people who feel they are one sex though biologically they are the other*. Tens of thousands of transsexuals across the world have medically altered their genitals to escape the sense of being 'trapped in the wrong body' (Restak, 1979, cited in Offir, 1982: 146). **Gender role** refers to learning and performing the socially accepted characteristics for a given gender. The content of this may differ enormously across cultures and even within a culture. Again, it is possible to hold a gender identity (such as 'I am a man') that crosses with a gender role (for example, 'I wear a dress'). This is the case of what contemporarily is referred to as **transvestism**.

All the above issues of sex and gender need to be distinguished from the sexual and the erotic. Whereas sex and gender involve languages of 'male' and 'female'

Adam Perry with baby. When this photo appeared in 1986, Perry was for a while seen as the embodiment of the caring, sensitive 'new man' – one of the many gender changes seen to be happening at the end of the twentieth century.

Source: Spencer Rowell

and 'masculinity' and 'femininity' respectively, the sexual and the erotic involve a language of desire: of heterosexuality, homosexuality and more. This language is much more concerned with types of sexual activities and partners. Again this has a biological substratum – of orgasms and physiological changes around arousal – but most of what is distinctive about human sexuality comes from the fact that it is hugely symbolic and social. Gender identity – 'I am a man' – often becomes the basis for organising the erotic – 'therefore I am a heterosexual interested in women', but it does not have to. Most male homosexuals have no doubt that they are men; but have a sexual interest in the same sex. In that sense, it is quite mistaken to see male homosexuality as necessarily linked to effeminacy.

● Becoming gendered: the case of gender socialisation

The first question people usually ask about a newborn – 'Is it a boy or a girl?' – looms large because the answer involves not just sex but the likely direction of

SOCIOLOGICAL SPOTLIGHT

It's only natural: the social construction of gender and sexuality

Some of the most popularly held assumptions about gender rest upon conceptions of it as somehow 'natural' and 'biological'. 'Motherhood is natural to women', 'sex is a naturally powerful drive', 'men are naturally more aggressive', 'some men can't help rape – it's their sex drive which is too strong', 'men are naturally promiscuous' – these and hundreds of similar observations (perhaps you could list some more) are pervasive 'common sense' assumptions found in everyday life. Sexual differences are – after all – 'only natural'.

Turning to the scientific literature, it is easy to find a large amount of research to justify this 'only natural' view of the world. From the writings of the early social Darwinians to contemporary sociobiologists, from research on 'hormones' to research on 'sex differences in the brain', from theories of 'aggression' to theories of 'male bonding', many writers who claim the authority of science have been concerned with laying out the biological foundations for gender.

Now, although nobody would wish to deny the role of the biological substratum in human activities – it clearly sets constraints on what is humanly possible – social scientists suggest that some of these biological claims are extravagant and overstated. The main criticisms that social scientists present against 'natural' or 'biological' explanations of patterns of human behaviour are the following.

● *The problem of history, culture, the social and the symbolic.* Whatever the biological substratum of human life, there is much evidence from the humanities and the social sciences that suggests significant variations in human experience across cultures and history – from classic anthropological work which claims to show that men may be 'feminine' and women may be 'masculine' to historical research which suggests how living arrangements such as 'the family' can be organised very differently. The 'biological' always has to be mediated by the symbolic in order for it to be social. Imagine, for

instance, what human sexuality would be like if it was unmediated by meaning – a world of uncoordinated erections and lubrications, of sexuality without rule or fantasy, of fumbling inabilities to interpret acts, orgasms, objects or people as sexual. Biology may provide cues, impulses and constraints, but all of this has to be interpreted through history and culture. Human beings are symbol manipulators who make and inhabit worlds of meaning which can be transmitted and modified from generation to generation. We have 'culture' and a 'history' in ways that other animals do not.

● *The problem of reductionism.* Biological arguments have a tendency to be overly simple, reducing vastly complex human civilisations and historical epochs to a chromosome, a hormone, a gene. It is suggested by some sociobiologists (for example, Goldberg) that all the complexities of long historical processes and variations can be

the child's entire life. In fact, gender is at work even before the birth of a child, since parents generally hope to have a boy rather than a girl. As we noted in Chapter 11 ('Global Stratification'), in China, India and other strongly patriarchal societies, female embryos are at risk because parents may abort them, hoping later to produce a boy, whose social

value is greater (United Nations Development Programme, 1991).

Sociologist Jessie Bernard (1981) asserts that soon after birth family members usher infants into the 'pink world' of girls or the 'blue world' of boys. Parents convey gender messages to children by how they themselves act, and even unconsciously in the way they

squashed into one hormone. Often, such claims are used not only to capture the past and the present, but also the future. Consider a famous observation by one of the world's leading sociobiologists, E. O. Wilson:

In the hunter-gatherer societies, men hunt and women stay at home This strong bias persists in agricultural societies and on that ground alone appears to have a genetic origin. The genetic basis is intense enough to cause a substantial division of labour even in the most free and most egalitarian of future societies. (quoted in Sayers, 1982)

Even without any training in sociobiology, you can probably see some criticisms which might be made. Would it be fair to say it is reductionist and oversimple – that is, does it reduce complex social phenomena to unitary biological ones? Wilson is one of the most sophisticated sociobiologists and there is much of value in his work, but he is still capable of making generalisations that pay no attention to the complex variations of human societies.

● *Problems of science and refutation.* Although there are many biological explanations of most social phenomena, from crime and race relations to the family and gender, in most cases there are strong disagreements among biologists. Claims of truth are made prematurely. There are endless controversies even within biology over the role of hormones, chromosomes and genes. Those interested in reading a biologist's analysis of the evidence on gender might find the book by Anne Fausto-Sterling (*Myths of Gender: Biological Theories about Men and Women* (1985)) to be valuable. She is a biologist, and reviews the evidence on such issues as hormones and aggression, menstruation and female behaviour, intelligence and men, and in all cases she finds little evidence of straightforward biological causation of human behaviour.

● *Problems of ideology.* It is important to ask just why the 'it's natural' type of arguments are so popular when the world is more complex and the explanations it provides are too simple. The answer to this may well lie not in the truth of the biological claims but in the ways in which they can be socially used. They come to serve ideological functions – in providing simple, uncomplicated answers that typically reaffirm the existing social order and the division of gender roles.

● *Problems of the future and change.* However biological sex may be, we are also moral and political animals. Hence biological arguments cannot be produced to legitimate biological male dominance and biological male aggression. The moral dimension is not the same as the biological. As Janet Radcliffe Richards, a 'sceptical feminist', has put it:

And suppose that men are naturally dominant because of the miraculous testosterone of which we hear so much these days. Why should feminists be reluctant to admit or anti-feminists to think that it clinches their case? Even If men are naturally inclined to dominance it does not follow that they ought to run everything. Their being naturally dominant might be an excellent reason for imposing special restrictions to keep their nature under control. We do not think that the men whose nature inclines them to rape ought to be given free rein to go around raping, so why should the naturally dominant be allowed to go around dominating? (Richards, 1982). ●

handle daughters and sons. One researcher (at an English university) presented an infant dressed as either a boy or a girl to a number of women; her subjects handled the 'female' child tenderly, with frequent hugs and caresses, while treating the male child more aggressively, often lifting him up high in the air or bouncing him on the knee (Bonner, 1984). The lesson is clear: the female world revolves around passivity and emotion, while the male world places a premium on independence and action.

There is a huge amount of research and theorising on gender development, but three broad traditions can be briefly distinguished.

1. *Social learning theories.* These suggest that differences in gender behaviour are learnt, in the same way as all behaviours, through a mixture of rewards, reinforcements and punishments. From its earliest day the baby boy is rewarded for behaving in 'boyish' ways and punished for being 'girl-like'. Often, this theory suggests how boys come to model themselves upon or imitate the behaviour of other men and boys, as this will be most highly praised and rewarded. The boy, in effect, thinks 'I want rewards. I am rewarded for doing boy things, therefore I want to be a boy'. It is a very widely held theory, and a very simple one.

2. *Cognitive theories.* These suggest that differences in gender emerge through a categorization process in which boys come to place themselves in a 'masculine' category and proceed to organise their experiences around it. Here the boy in effect says 'I am a boy, therefore I want to do boy things'. Some of these theories suggest that there may be preformed stages at which such identifications can take place, while others suggest that the identities emerge out of social contexts. Kohlberg is a major proponent of this view.

3. *Psychodynamic theories.* These, derived from Freud (introduced in Chapter 5), suggest that differences in gender emerge out of emotional struggles between the infant and its caretakers in the earliest years of life. Most classically, a boy's emotional structure emerges from the conflict between the love of his mother and the fear of his father which, if resolved successfully, will eventually lead the boy to identify strongly with his father and hence with masculinity. Psychodynamic theorists disagree with each other over the nature of this conflict and its timing, but it is basic to this theory that gender is structured 'unconsciously' into a deep emotional form in early childhood.

Each of these theories has many variants, is very widely held and has spawned a massive research and analytic literature. In general, the virtues of one theory are the weaknesses of the others, and each theory has its own emphasis, behaviour, cognition or emotion. It is way beyond the scope of this book to review all this material. But here we will focus on the Freudian tradition.

Nancy Chodorow and mothering

How do little girls grow up to become mothers? Why don't boys? Chodorow starts her analysis by criticising some of the most popular explanations of gender differences – those that stress biology, social learning and role learning. Although such theories may be partially correct, they all fail to deal adequately with the way in which gender differences are organised into the deep psychic structuring of individuals. She prefers to use a Freudian theory (introduced in Chapter 5). For her, masculinity and femininity are rooted in strong emotional structures established very early in life and are very hard to transform. Men in Anglo-Saxon culture tend, on the whole, to become more emotionally restricted yet more independent, and more work and achievement orientated than women, who seem to 'connect better'. Men often lack a 'connectedness' to relate to loved ones, whilst girls tend to develop stronger attachments and reproduce this in mothering. Of course, these are generalisations. (They are not that dissimilar to Talcott Parsons's distinctions between expressive and instrumental roles, discussed below.)

Chodorow argues that in order to understand the development of these strong emotional structures, we have to go back to the intense connections between child and mother in which both baby boy and baby girl are overwhelmingly dependent upon the mother. (Note: this is true of this culture; it is by no means true of all.) From the beginning of life there is a process of forming strong attachments and dependencies with the mother, and an accompanying sense of anxiety and fear when she is absent. There is a massive identification of both boy and girl with the 'mother' – the primary caregiver who suckles, shelters and comforts the baby. The image of the mother is incorporated and internalised by the child.

So far, the description holds for both boys and girls. Bit by bit, the child has to break away from the strong identification with the carer, to test its competence against the outside world. Although both the baby girl and baby boy are primarily attached to the mother, the girl remains attached while the boy breaks away. The little girl does not outgrow her dependency, she does not develop a strong sense of separateness and boundaries, and this leads her ultimately to identify with the needs of others more than boys. In later life this asserts itself as the need for mothering. 'The basic feminine sense of self is connected to the world, the basic masculine sense of self is separate' (Chodorow, 1978: 169).

While the little girl stays in close identification with the mother and ultimately attains a less separate, more connected sense of identity, the little boy is pushed into a sharper, stronger and earlier separation. This rupture may be experienced as an abandonment and generate life-long anxieties around rejection. For many boys, so the story goes, this leads to a turning to the outer world (especially of hitherto relatively insignificant fathers) and the establishment of a separate, autonomous identity – one fearful of connecting in case of abandonment, and often open to rage against the long-lost love object, the mother. In one swoop male autonomy, male inexpressiveness and male hostility towards women is explained!

Critical evaluation
Although this theory is influential, critics have worried that the evidence for it is inadequate: it depends on a few clinical cases for generalisations. Feminist critics have also accused the theory of 'blaming the victim', of ultimately blaming mothers for the reproduction of male power in their sons (see Treblicott, 1984). Other critics also see the theory as presenting a model of development that is too unchangeable. These days, for example, we see many 'modern' 'new' men who are very seriously involved in 'mothering' – or 'parenting' as it is increasingly called.

Chodorow responds by saying that although gender identity is established in early lives, it is only a provisional structure and one that is open to change in later life. Indeed, she advocates fathers being much more involved in raising children, so that it breaks the cycle of motherhood and both boys and girls find nurturance in fathers as well as mothers (Chodorow, 1987).

Gender across the life-cycle

Chodorow's theory needs supplementing by looking at both wider influences on the child (peer group, school, workplace), and transformations over the life-cycle. There is, for instance, a considerable body of research that suggests that childhood worlds are highly segregated by gender and that this segregation works to structure gender identity. Likewise, there is research on the male life-cycle that suggests that as men become

older they often change into more emotionally responsive and less powerfully autonomous people than was evidenced in their youth and childhood.

Gender emerges over the entire life-cycle through a series of ever-changing encounters in which meaning is built up, modified and transformed. Gender is not something fixed at any time, but is a process constantly open to historical changes in the wider world, local changes in situation and biographical shifts over the life-cycle.

Gender and the peer group

As children reach school age, their lives spill outside the family as they forge ties with others of the same age. Peer groups further socialise their members according to normative conceptions of gender. A series of feminist researchers in the UK – Sue Lees, Christine Griffin and Angele McRobbie amongst them – have interviewed girls and discovered the ways in which their 'femininity' is shaped from early years. Likewise, some male sociologists – Paul Willis, Martin Macan Ghaill amongst them – have studied boys. Reading their studies, it is not hard to sense the overwhelming pressures placed on young boys and girls to conform to gender stereotypes, and to sense the sanctions they will experience if they step out of these roles.

Carol Gilligan (1982), whose work is highlighted in Chapter 5 ('Socialisation'), provides a gender-based theory of moral reasoning. Boys, Gilligan contends, reason according to abstract principles. For them, 'rightness' amounts to 'playing by the rules'. Girls, by contrast, consider morality more a matter of their responsibilities to others. Thus, the games we play have serious implications for our later lives.

Gender and schooling

As children near school age, their reading promotes distinctions of gender. A generation ago, children's books typically made males the focus of attention (Weitzman et al., 1972). Males were the main characters, typically mentioned in book titles and shown in illustrations. Stories portrayed boys as engaged in interesting activities, while girls – more like dolls than living beings – were attractive and compliant observers who concentrated on supporting and pleasing the males at the centre of the action.

More recently, a growing awareness among authors, publishers and teachers of the limiting effects of gender stereotypes on young people has led to changes. Today's books for children portray females and males in a more balanced way.

Through primary and secondary school, however, classroom curricula still encourage children to embrace appropriate gender patterns. For example, schools have long offered young women instruction in typing and home-centred skills such as nutrition and sewing. Classes in woodworking and car mechanics, conversely, contain mostly young men. But even out of school, the trend for girls' and boys' magazines serves to further reinforce notions of masculinity and femininity (see McRobbie, 1991).

In college and university, the pattern continues, with men and women tending towards different subjects. Men are disproportionately represented in the natural sciences – including physics, chemistry, biology and mathematics. Women cluster in the humanities, the fine arts (painting, music, dance and drama), education courses and the social sciences (including anthropology and sociology). New areas of study are also likely to be sex linked. Computer science, for example, with its grounding in engineering, logic and abstract mathematics, predominantly enrols men, while courses in gender studies, by contrast, are popular among women.

Gender and work

Andrew Tolson in what was the first major English study of masculinity, *The Limits of Masculinity* (1977), suggested that in addition to early family experiences there are three major sites for boys and men in which gender is formed and structured: the peer group, the school and the workplace. He is particularly keen to emphasise the importance of the workplace in reinforcing male identity. Just as adult female lives often become swamped by thinking about 'their children', so male lives become overwhelmed by 'their work' – seeking success in it, dealing with boredom from it, finding alternatives to it, being humiliated by lack of it. In many ways this concern with work as a key to male identity simply reflects the earlier experiences of childhood – the quest for power, autonomy and the concomitant anxiety about failure and rejection.

Gender and the mass media

Since it first captured the public imagination in the 1950s, television has placed the dominant segment of our population – white males – at centre stage. Racial and ethnic minorities were all but absent from television until the early 1970s; only in the last decade have programmes featured women in prominent roles.

Even when both sexes appear on camera, men generally play the brilliant detectives, fearless explorers and skilled surgeons. Women, by contrast, continue to be cast as the less capable characters, often prized primarily for their sexual attractiveness.

Change has come most slowly to advertising, which sells products by conforming to widely established cultural norms. Advertising thus presents the two sexes, more often than not, in stereotypical ways. Historically, ads have shown women in the home, happily using cleaning products, serving foods, modelling clothing and trying out new appliances. Men, on the other hand, predominate in ads for cars, travel, banking services, industrial companies and alcoholic beverages. The authoritative voiceover – the faceless voice that promotes products on television and radio – is almost always male (Busby, 1975; Courtney and Whipple, 1983).

In a classic study of magazine and newspaper ads, Erving Goffman (1979) found other, more subtle biases. Men, he concluded, are photographed to appear taller than women, implying male superiority. Women were more frequently presented lying down (on sofas and beds) or, like children, seated on the floor. The expressions and gestures of men exude competence and authority, whereas women are more likely to appear in childlike poses. While men focus on the products being advertised, women direct their interest to men, conveying their supportive and submissive role.

The beauty myth

Advertising also actively perpetuates what Naomi Wolf calls 'the beauty myth'. She argues that society teaches women to measure personal importance, accomplishment and satisfaction in terms of physical appearance (Backman and Adams, 1991). Curiously, however, this myth also sets up unattainable standards of beauty for most women (such as the *Playboy* centrefold or the skinny Paris fashion model), making the quest for beauty ultimately self-defeating. It should not be surprising, argues Wolf, that the beauty myth surfaced

PROFILE

Margaret Mead and Samoa

Margaret Mead (1901–1978) was one of the world's leading anthropologists and, although her work has recently been criticised, she produced a number of classic studies in the earlier part of this century.

In one of these studies, Margaret Mead studied three societies of New Guinea (1963; orig. 1935). Trekking high into the mountains, Mead observed the Arapesh, whose men and women were remarkably similar in attitudes and behaviour. Both sexes, she reported, were cooperative and sensitive to others – what our culture would label 'feminine'.

Moving south, Mead then studied the Mundugumor, whose culture of head-hunting and cannibalism stood in striking contrast to the gentle ways of the Arapesh. Here, Mead reported, females and males were again alike, though they were startlingly different from the Arapesh. Both Mundugumor females and males were typically selfish and aggressive, traits defined as more 'masculine' in Europe and the United States.

Source: Popperfoto

Finally, travelling west to survey the Tchambuli, Mead discovered a culture that, like our own, defined females and males differently. Yet the Tchambuli reversed many of our notions about gender: females tended to be dominant and rational, while males were submissive, emotional and nurturing towards children.

Based on her observations, Mead concluded that what one culture defines as masculine another may consider feminine. Further, she noted that societies can exaggerate or minimise the importance of sex. Mead's research, then, makes a strong case that gender is a variable creation of culture. It can be sharply distinguished from sex, which is the biological substratum of gender. ●

in our culture during the 1890s, the 1920s and the 1980s – all times of anxiety and heightened debate about the social standing of women.

The beauty myth society teaches women to prize relationships with men, whom, presumably, they attract with their beauty. The relentless pursuit of beauty not only drives women towards being highly disciplined, but it also forces them to be keenly attuned and responsive to men. Beauty-minded women, in short, strive to please men and avoid challenging male power. More, through this myth men learn to want to possess women who embody beauty. In other words, our concept of beauty both reduces women to objects and motivates men to possess them as if they were dolls rather than human beings.

In short, Wolf asserts, beauty is as much about behaviour as appearance. The myth holds that the key to women's personal happiness lies in beauty (or, for men, in possessing a beautiful woman). In fact, however, beauty amounts to an elaborate system – which this chapter explores – through which society teaches both women and men to embrace specific roles and attitudes that place them in a social hierarchy. The equation runs something like this: by embracing traditional notions of femininity and masculinity, we raise our prospects for personal and professional success. Thus, advertising commands masculine men to drive the 'right' car and feminine women to use beauty aids that will help them look younger and more attractive to men.

Gender and adult socialisation

Reinforced in so many ways by the surrounding culture, gender identity and gender roles come to feel natural long before we reach adulthood. As a result, the attitudes and behaviour of adults commonly follow traditional feminine and masculine patterns (Spender, 1980; Kramarae, 1981).

Chapter 6 ('Social Interaction in Everyday Life') reviewed Deborah Tannen's (1990) account of why women and men see many routine situations so differently. Men hate to ask for directions, Tannen notes, because interpersonal exchanges establish a hierarchy, and asking for help amounts to accepting a subordinate place in that hierarchy. But to women, who draw strength from forging and maintaining connections with others, asking for directions is both practical and sensible. The two sexes, therefore, perceive different meanings in a wide range of everyday experiences.

● Patriarchy, gender stratification and sexism

Gender goes to the heart of social organisation and three terms will help clarify this. First, the concept of **gender stratification** refers to *a society's unequal distribution of wealth, power and privilege between the two sexes.* In Europe, as throughout the world, societies allocate fewer valued resources to women than to men.

Second, **patriarchy** (literally, 'the rule of fathers'), is *a form of social organisation in which men dominate, oppress and exploit women* (cf. Walby, 1990: 20). While some degree of patriarchy may be universal, there is significant variation in the relative power and privilege of females and males around the world. In Saudi Arabia, for example, the power of men over women is as great as anywhere on earth; in Norway, by contrast, the two sexes approach equality in many respects. Sylvia Walby has argued that patriarchy is composed of six overlapping and changing structures, which are discussed both in this chapter and throughout the book. These elements are: paid work (see below and Chapter 15), the household (see below and Chapter 17), the State (see Chapter 22), violence (see below and Chapter 8), sexuality (see below), and culture (see above and Chapter 21) (see Walby, 1990: 20). Walby argues that these elements take on different forms in different cultures and at different times. She argues in

Table 13.1 ● Traditional notions of gender identity	
Feminine traits	**Masculine traits**
Submissive	Dominant
Dependent	Independent
Unintelligent and incapable	Intelligent and competent
Emotional	Rational
Receptive	Assertive
Intuitive	Analytical
Weak	Strong
Timid	Brave
Content	Ambitious
Passive	Active
Cooperative	Competitive
Sensitive	Insensitive
Sex object	Sexually aggressive
Attractive because of physical appearance	Attractive because of achievement

particular that the twentieth century in the West has seen a move from **private patriarchy** (where *men regulate in the home*) to **public patriarchy** (where *the state and the labour market shape women's lives*). The case is strongest for the Scandinavian countries.

Among the most striking consequences of patriarchy in China is the ancient practice of 'foot-binding', by which young girls' feet are tightly wrapped as they grow, with predictable results. Although this practice – now rare – produces what people deem 'dainty' proportions, what effect would you imagine this deformity has on the physical mobility of women?

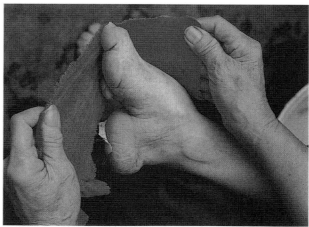

Source: Photo Researchers, Inc. – Explorer/Y Layma

GLOBAL SOCIOLOGY

Patriarchy breaking down: a report from Botswana

As the judge handed down the decision, Unity Dow beamed a smile towards the friends sitting all around her; people in the courtroom joined together in hugs and handshakes. Dow, then a 32-year-old lawyer and citizen of the southern African nation of Botswana, had won the first round in her efforts to overturn the laws by which, she maintains, her country defines women as second-class citizens.

The law that sparked Unity Dow's recent suit against her government specifies the citizenship rights of children. Botswana is traditionally patrilineal, meaning that people trace family membership through males, making children part of their father's – but not their mother's – family line.

Under the law, a child of a Botswanan man and a woman of another nationality is a citizen of Botswana, since in that country legal standing passes through the father. But the child of a Botswanan woman and a

man from another nation has no rights of citizenship. Because she married a man from the United States, Unity Dow's children had no citizen's rights in the country where they were born.

The Dow case attracted broad attention because its significance extends far beyond citizenship to the overall legal standing of women and men. In rendering the decision in Dow's favour, High Court Judge Martin Horwitz declared, 'The time that women were treated as chattels or were there to obey the whims and wishes of males is long past'. In support of his decision, Horwitz pointed to the constitution of Botswana, which guarantees fundamental rights and freedoms to both women and men. Arguing for the government against Dow, Ian Kirby, a deputy attorney general, conceded that the constitution confers equal rights on the two sexes, but he claimed that the law can and should take account of sex where such

patterns are deeply rooted in Botswanan male-dominated culture. To challenge such traditions in the name of Western feminism, he continued, amounts to cultural imperialism by which some people seek to subvert an established way of life by advancing foreign notions that are popular elsewhere.

Women from many African nations attended the Dow court case, sensing that a historic change was at hand. And, indeed, this has proven to be the case. As a result of the Dow ruling, the constitution of Botswana was amended to extend citizenship to children such as her own. Symbolically, this transformation greatly enhances the social standing of that nation's women.

To many people in Europe, the Dow case may seem strange, since the notion that men and women are entitled to equal rights and privileges is widely endorsed throughout the European Union. ●

Thirdly, **sexism**, *the belief that one sex is innately superior to the other*, stands as an important ideological underpinning of patriarchy. Historically, patriarchy has rested upon a belief in the innate superiority of males who, therefore, legitimately dominate females. Sexism has much in common with racism: both are ideologies that support the social domination of one category of people by another. As we shall see presently, *institutionalised sexism* pervades the operation of the economy, with women highly concentrated in jobs that are less challenging and that offer relatively low pay. Similarly, the legal system has his-

torically turned a blind eye towards violence against women, especially violence committed by boyfriends, husbands and fathers (Landers, 1990).

Patriarchy at work

For women, there are two important areas of work: paid employment and work done at home (domestic labour). The relationship between the two is also important.

Paid work: as Chapter 15 shows, the number of women in the workforce has grown substantially this

WINDOW ON THE WORLD

Map 13.1 ● Women's paid employment in global perspective

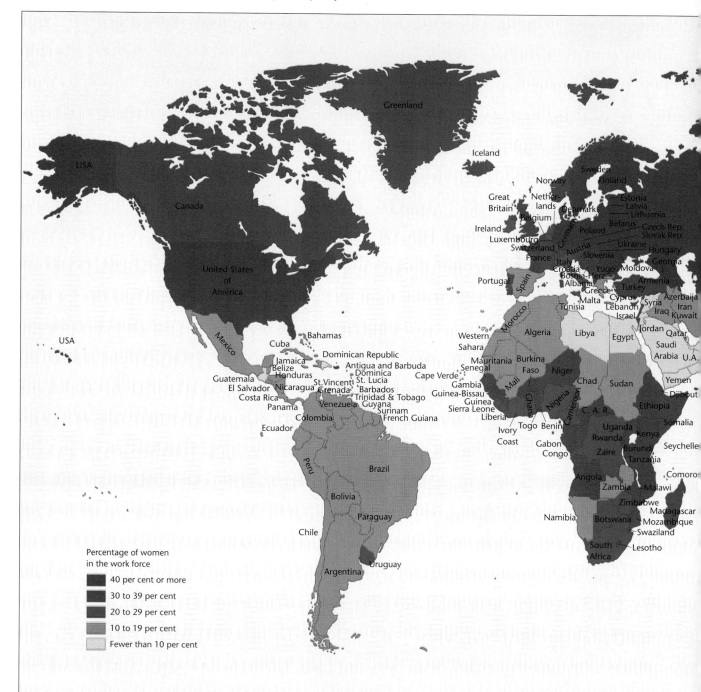

Percentage of women
in the work force

- 40 per cent or more
- 30 to 39 per cent
- 20 to 29 per cent
- 10 to 19 per cent
- Fewer than 10 per cent

Source: *Peters Atlas of the World* (1990)

Throughout the industrialised world, at least one-third of the paid labour force is made up of women. In poor societies, however, women work even harder, but they are less likely to be paid for their efforts. In Latin America, for example, women represent only about 15 per cent of the paid labour force; in Islamic societies of northern Africa and the Middle East, the figure is even lower.

WINDOW ON THE WORLD

Map 13.2 ● Housework in global perspective

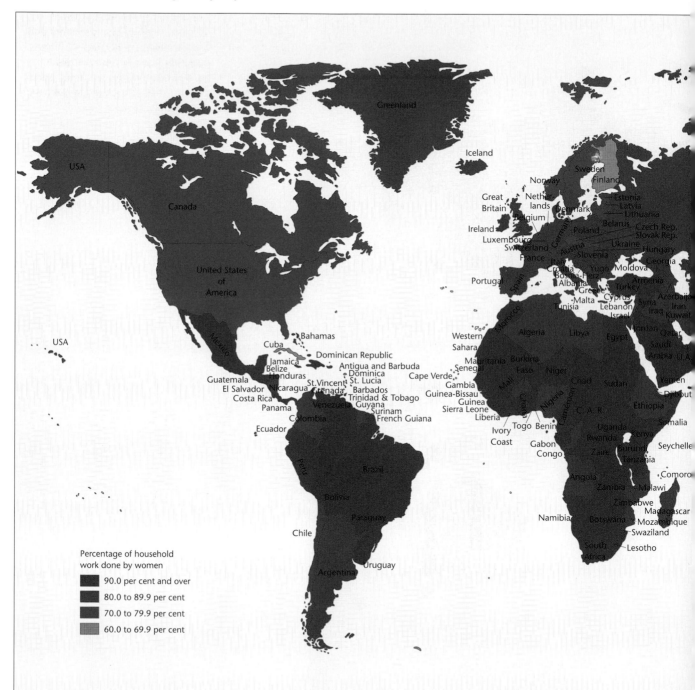

Percentage of household
work done by women

- 90.0 per cent and over
- 80.0 to 89.9 per cent
- 70.0 to 79.9 per cent
- 60.0 to 69.9 per cent

Source: *Peters Atlas of the World* (1990); updated by the author

Throughout the world, a major component of women's routines and identities involves housework. This is especially true in poor societies of Latin America, Africa and Asia, where women are not generally in the paid labour force.

century. Industrial nations consider women working for income to be the rule rather than the exception. The traditional view that working for income is a 'man's role' no longer holds true. Today, 60 per cent of married couples depend on two incomes. As Map 13.1 shows, however, this is not the case in many of the poorer societies of the world.

Household production: a second indicator of the global pattern of patriarchy is the extent to which housework – cleaning, cooking and caring for members of the family (from children to the sick to husbands to the elderly) is the province of women. Map 13.2 shows that, in general, members of industrial societies divide housework more evenly than people in the poor societies of the world do. But in no nation on earth is housework shared equally. And, despite women's rapid entry into the labour force, the amount of housework performed by women has declined only slightly (and the proportion done by men has not changed at all). Although the typical couple shares in disciplining the children and managing finances, men routinely perform home repairs and outdoor work while women see to most daily tasks of shopping, cooking and cleaning. Consuming, on average, 26 hours a week, housework amounts to a 'second shift' that women undertake after returning from the workplace each day. In general, then, housework adds stress to many women's lives; those who have help in maintaining the household suffer less, as do those who choose only the role of full-time homemaker (Schooler et al., 1984; Fuchs, 1986; Hochschild, 1989; Presser, 1993; Keith and Schafer, 1994; Benokraitis and Feagin, 1995).

In sum, men support the idea of women entering the labour force and count on the money women earn. But men nonetheless resist modifying their own behaviour to help their partners establish and maintain careers and manageable home lives. Women with high-prestige, high-income jobs certainly have greater power in the household to limit their own housework roles (by hiring outside help). But, typically, men call special attention to any housework they perform, while taking for granted the contributions of women (Komarovsky, 1973; Cowan, 1992; Robinson and Spitze, 1992; Lennon and Rosenfeld, 1994; Heath and Bourne, 1995).

Looking at these two issues together – paid work and housework – English social policy expert Jane Lewis has suggested there are strong, weak and moder-

ate 'male breadwinner states' (Lewis, 1992). In the strong state, wives are largely dependent upon their husbands (the UK, Germany and The Netherlands are prime examples). In the weak breadwinner state, women are workers, independent of their partners (Norway, Sweden, Denmark are prime examples). In the moderate state, women act as both workers and child carers (France and Belgium are instances of this).

Is patriarchy inevitable?

Technologically simple societies have little control over biological forces. Thus, men's greater physical strength, as well as women's common experience of pregnancy, combine to bolster patriarchy. Technological advances, however, give members of industrial societies a wider range of choices about gender. Industrial machinery has diminished the primacy of muscle power in everyday life, just as contraception has given women control over pregnancy. Today, then, biological differences provide little justification for patriarchy.

Categorical social inequality – whether based on race, ethnicity or sex – also comes under attack in the more egalitarian culture of industrial societies. In many industrial nations, law mandates equal employment opportunities for women and men and equal pay for comparable efforts.

Nonetheless, in all industrial societies, the two sexes continue to hold different jobs and receive unequal pay, as we will explain presently. So does the persistence of patriarchy mean that it is inevitable? Some sociologists contend that biological factors underlie sex-based differences – especially a greater level of aggressiveness on the part of males. If this is so, of course, the eradication of patriarchy would be difficult and perhaps even impossible (Goldberg, 1974, 1987; Rossi, 1985; Popenoe, 1993). However, most sociologists believe that gender is primarily a social construction, subject to change. Simply because no society has yet eliminated patriarchy, then, does not mean that we must remain prisoners of the past.

To understand why patriarchy has persisted throughout human history, we need to see how gender is rooted and reproduced in society, a process that begins with the way we learn to think of ourselves as children and continues through the work we perform as adults.

● Theoretical analysis of gender

Although they come to differing conclusions, the functional and conflict paradigms each point up the importance of gender to social organisation.

Functional analysis

The functional paradigm views society as a complex system of many separate but integrated parts. In this approach, every social structure contributes to the overall operation of society.

As Chapter 3 ('Society') explained, members of hunting and gathering societies had little power over the forces of biology. Lacking effective birth control, women experienced frequent pregnancies, and the responsibilities of child care kept them close to home. Likewise, to take advantage of greater male strength, norms guided men towards the pursuit of game and other tasks away from the home. Over many generations, this sexual division of labour became institutionalised and largely taken for granted (Lengermann and Wallace, 1985).

Industrial technology opens up a vastly greater range of cultural possibilities. Human muscle power no longer serves as a vital source of energy, so the physical strength of men loses much of its earlier significance. At the same time, the ability to control reproduction gives women greater choice in shaping their lives. Modern societies come to see that traditional gender roles waste an enormous amount of human talent; yet change comes slowly, because gender is deeply embedded in social mores.

Talcott Parsons: gender and complementarity

In addition, as Talcott Parsons (1942, 1951, 1954) explained, gender differences help to integrate society – at least in its traditional form. Gender, Parsons noted, forms a *complementary* set of roles that links men and women together into family units that carry out various functions vital to the operation of society. Women take charge of family life, assuming primary responsibility for managing the household and raising children. Men, by contrast, connect the family to the larger world, primarily by participating in the labour force.

Parsons further argued that distinctive socialisation teaches the two sexes their appropriate gender identity and skills needed for adult life. Thus society teaches boys – presumably destined for the labour force – to be

rational, self-assured and competitive. This complex of traits Parsons termed *instrumental*. To prepare girls for child rearing, their socialisation stresses what Parsons called *expressive* qualities, such as emotional responsiveness and sensitivity to others.

Society, explains Parsons, promotes gender-linked behaviour through various schemes of social control. People incorporate cultural definitions about gender into their own identities, so that failing to be appropriately feminine or masculine produces guilt and fear of rejection by members of the opposite sex. In simple terms, women learn to view non-masculine men as sexually unattractive, while men learn to avoid unfeminine women.

Critical evaluation

Functionalism advances a theory of complementarity by which gender integrates society both structurally (in terms of what people do) and morally (in terms of what they believe). Although influential at mid-century, this approach is rarely used today by researchers exploring the impact of gender.

For one thing, this analysis assumes a singular vision of society that is not shared by everyone. Poor women, for example, have always worked outside the home as a matter of economic necessity; today, more and more women at all social levels are entering the labour force for various reasons. A second problem, say the critics, is that Parsons's analysis minimises the personal strains and social costs produced by rigid, traditional gender roles (Giele, 1988). Third and finally, to those whose goals include sexual equality, what Parsons describes as gender complementarity amounts to little more than male domination.

Conflict analysis

From a conflict point of view, gender involves not just differences in behaviour but disparities in power. Conventional ideas about gender have historically benefited men while subjecting women to prejudice, discrimination and sometimes outright violence, in a striking parallel to the treatment of racial and ethnic minorities (Hacker, 1951, 1974; Collins, 1971; Lengermann and Wallace, 1985). Thus, conflict theorists claim, conventional ideas about gender promote not cohesion but tension and conflict, with men seeking to protect their privileges while women challenge the status quo.

As earlier chapters noted, the conflict paradigm draws heavily on the ideas of Karl Marx. Yet Marx was a product of his time insofar as his writings focused almost exclusively on men. His friend and collaborator Friedrich Engels, however, did explore the link between gender and social class (1902; orig. 1884).

Friedrich Engels: gender and class

Looking back through history, Engels noted that in hunting and gathering societies the activities of women and men, though different, had comparable importance. A successful hunt may have brought men great prestige, but the vegetation gathered by women constituted most of a society's food supply (Leacock, 1978). As technological advances led to a productive surplus, however, social equality and communal sharing gave way to private property and, ultimately, a class hierarchy. At this point, men gained pronounced power over women. With surplus wealth to pass on to heirs, upper class men took a keen interest in their children. The desire to control property, then, prompted the creation of monogamous marriage and the family. Ideally, men could be certain of paternity – especially who their sons were – and the law ensured that wealth passed to them. The same logic explains why women were taught to remain virgins until marriage, to remain faithful to their husbands thereafter and to build their lives around bearing and raising children.

According to Engels, capitalism intensifies this male domination. First, capitalism creates more wealth, which confers greater power on men as wage earners as well as owners and heirs of property. Second, an expanding capitalist economy depends on defining people – especially women – as consumers and convincing them that personal fulfilment derives from owning and using products. Third, to allow men to work, society assigns women the task of maintaining the home. The double exploitation of capitalism, as Engels saw it, lies in paying low wages for male labour and no wages for female work (Eisenstein, 1979; Barry, 1983; Jagger, 1983; Vogel, 1983).

Critical evaluation

Conflict analysis highlights how society places the two sexes in unequal positions of wealth, power and privilege. As a result, the conflict approach is decidedly critical of conventional ideas about gender, claiming that society would be better off if we minimised or even eliminated this dimension of social structure.

But conflict analysis, too, has its limitations. One problem, critics suggest, is that this approach casts conventional families – defended by traditionalists as morally positive – as a social evil. Second, from a more practical standpoint, conflict analysis minimises the extent to which women and men live together cooperatively and often quite happily. A third problem with this approach, for some critics, is its assertion that capitalism stands at the root of gender stratification. Agrarian countries, in fact, are typically more patriarchal than industrial-capitalist nations.

And socialist societies, too – including the People's Republic of China – remain strongly patriarchal (Moore, 1992).

● Feminism

Feminism is *the advocacy of social equality for the sexes, in opposition to patriarchy and sexism.* With roots in the English Revolution and the French Revolution – each with their concern over equality – the 'first wave' of the feminist movement was initiated with Mary Wollstonecraft's *A Vindication of the Rights of Women* (1792) and continued with the liberal classic by John Stuart Mill and Harriet Taylor Mill, *The Subjection of Women* (1869). They argued against women's perceived (biologically) inferior status and argued for improved education and equality before the law. Many of the initial campaigns centred on morality and sexuality, and an end to slavery. Perhaps the primary objective of the early women's movement was securing the right to vote, which British women first exercised in the General Election on 14 December 1918 (Banks, 1981; Rowbottom, 1997). But other disadvantages persisted and a 'second wave' of feminism arose in the 1960s and continues today.

Basic feminist ideas

Feminism views the personal experiences of women and men through the lens of gender. How we think of ourselves (gender identity), how we act (gender roles), and our sex's social standing (gender stratification) are all rooted in the operation of our society.

Although people who consider themselves feminists disagree about many things, most would probably support five general principles:

The London suffragettes demonstrate and are arrested, 1910.

Source: Popperfoto

1. *The importance of change*. Feminist thinking is decidedly political; it links ideas to action. Feminism is critical of the status quo, advocating social equality for women and men.

2. *Expanding human choice*. Feminists maintain that cultural conceptions of gender divide the full range of human qualities into two opposing and limited spheres: the female world of emotion and cooperation and the male world of rationality and competition. As an alternative, feminists pursue a 'reintegration of humanity' by which each person develops *all* human traits (French, 1985).

3. *Eliminating gender stratification*. Feminism opposes laws and cultural norms that limit the education, income and job opportunities of women.

4. *Ending sexual violence*. A major objective of today's women's movement is eliminating sexual violence. Feminists argue that patriarchy distorts the relationships between women and men and encourages violence against women in the form of rape, domestic abuse, sexual harassment and pornography (Millet, 1970; Dworkin, 1987; Kelly, 1988).

5. *Promoting sexual autonomy*. Finally, feminism advocates women's control of their sexuality and reproduction. Feminists support the free availability of birth control information. As Figure 13.1 shows use of contraception in a range of countries, with Norway (and other Scandinavian countries) leading in use. In addition, most feminists support a woman's right to choose whether to bear children or to terminate a pregnancy, rather than allowing men – as husbands, doctors and legislators – to regulate sexuality. Many feminists also align with the gay and lesbian movement to overcome homophobia and heterosexism (which will be discussed later) (Vance, 1984; Segal, 1997).

Variations within feminism

One way in which feminism varies is simply by country. Whilst 'North American feminism' has probably become the most organised, public and vocal in the world, it has also bred what might be called a 'superstar feminism' whereby a number of women

Figure 13.1 ● Use of contraception by married women of childbearing age

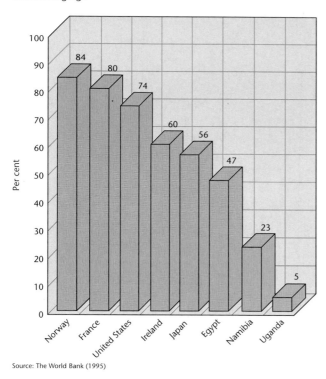

Source: The World Bank (1995)

become very prominent through their writing and media work.

In Europe, feminists are less likely to be so media focused, and each country develops its own 'style' and set of conflicts. Angela Glasner has observed that

Feminism in Europe exhibits a wide variety of forms . . . the political context has . . . been important in determining the specific form, and indeed in prescribing or proscribing feminism altogether. In Italy, Holland, Denmark and Norway, the second wave has been strongly influenced by left wing politics and has been predominantly led by middle class women. In France, the movement has been largely contained within the academic community, and in Germany it has been significantly diluted by conservatism. (Glasner, 1992: 76–7).

We can also say that in Italy, Britain, Holland, Denmark and Norway it has been a more broadly based movement with alliances to the left. In Sweden the initiatives for change came much earlier: as a result, a strong collectivist culture emerged with women as a notable presence. Hence, there was little second wave feminism as such. In the new democracies, by contrast (Spain, Portugal), hindered by both past authoritarian-

ism and by the Roman Catholic background, the women's movement has been slower to develop.

People pursue the goal of sexual equality in different ways, yielding three major divisions within feminism. Although the distinctions among them are far from clear-cut, each describes the problem of patriarchy in somewhat different terms and calls for correspondingly distinctive strategies for social change (Banks, 1981; Barry, 1983; Jagger, 1983; Stacey, 1983; Vogel, 1983).

Liberal feminism

Liberal feminism is grounded in classic liberal thinking that individuals should be free to develop their own talents and pursue their own interests. Liberal feminists accept the basic organisation of our society but seek to expand the rights and opportunities of women. Liberal feminists support equal rights and oppose prejudice and discrimination that block the aspirations of women.

Liberal feminists also endorse reproductive freedom for all women. Some respect aspects of the family as a social institution, calling for widely available maternity leave and child care for women who wish to work. Others are critical of the way in which the family reproduces gender and argue that freedom is not possible for women until families are dramatically changed (Okin, 1989).

With their strong belief in the rights of individuals, liberal feminists do not think that all women need to march in step toward any political goal. Both women and men, working individually, would be able to improve their lives if society simply ended legal and cultural barriers rooted in gender.

Socialist feminism

Socialist feminism evolved from Marxist conflict theory, in part as a response to how little attention Marx paid to gender, in part as a strategy to challenge both patriarchy and capitalism. Engels claimed that patriarchy (like class oppression) has its roots in private property; thus, capitalism intensifies patriarchy by concentrating wealth and power in the hands of a small number of men.

Socialist feminists view the reforms sought by liberal feminism as inadequate. The bourgeois family must be restructured, they argue, to end 'domestic slavery' in favour of some collective means of carrying out housework and child care. The key to this goal, in turn, is a socialist revolution that creates a state-centred economy operating to meet the needs of all. Such a basic transformation of society requires that women and men pursue their personal liberation together, rather than individually, as liberal feminists maintain. (Further discussion of this view can be found in Chapter 17; Barrett, 1980).

Radical feminism

Radical feminism, too, finds the reforms called for by liberal feminism inadequate and superficial. Moreover, radical feminists claim that even a socialist revolution would not end patriarchy. Instead, this variant of feminism holds that gender equality can be realised only by eliminating the cultural notion of gender itself. Fundamentally, say radical feminists, patriarchy rests on the subordination of women through sexuality and reproduction. Men exert power over and through women's bodies. We will consider this view in more detail below, when we discuss sexuality. Radical feminists seek to overthrow 'male sexuality', heterosexual parenting and the family.

There are many disagreements from within, however. Thus, some would support the new reproductive technologies – conception here can take place outside the body, so that there is no necessary link between women's bodies, men and child bearing. With the demise of motherhood, radical feminists reason, the entire family system (including conventional definitions of motherhood, fatherhood and childhood) could be left behind, liberating women, men and children from the tyranny of family, gender and of sex itself (Dworkin, 1987). But others see the new reproductive technologies as based on patriarchy and male science – a way of robbing women's rights over their own wombs. Further, they celebrate women's key role as mothers (see Richardson, 1993).

In general, radical feminists seek a revolutionary overthrow of the patriarchal order. Andrea Dworkin is a leading North American feminist who has suggested the centrality of male power and outlined its seven key dimensions. She writes as follows:

The power of men is first a metaphysical assertion of self – an I am that exists a priori, bedrock, absolute, no embellishment or apology required, indifferent to denial or challenge. Second, power is physical strength used over and against others less strong or without the sanction to use strength as power. Third, power is the capacity to terrorize, to use self and strength to inculcate fear – fear in a whole class of persons of a whole class of persons. The acts of terror run the gamut from rape to battery to sexual abuse of children to war to murder to maiming to torture to enslaving or kidnapping to verbal assault to cultural assault to threats of death to threats of harm backed up by the ability and sanction to deliver. The symbols of terror are commonplace and utterly familiar – the gun, the knife, the bomb, the fist, and so on. Even more significant is the hidden symbol of terror – the penis. Fourth, men have the power of naming, a great and sublime power. This power of naming enables men to define experience, to articulate boundaries and values, to designate to each thing its realm and qualities, to determine what can and cannot be expressed, to control perception itself. Fifth, men have the power of owning. Historically, this power has been absolute, denied to some men by other men in times of slavery and other persecution, but in the main upheld by armed force and law. In many parts of the world, the male right to own women and all that issues from them, children and labour, is still absolute. Sixth, the power of money is a distinctly male power. Money speaks, but it speaks with a male voice. In the hands of women, money stays literal, count it out, it buys what it is worth or less. In the hands of men, money buys women, sex, status, dignity, esteem, recognition, loyalty, all manner of possibility. In the hands of men, money does not only buy – it brings with it qualities, achievements, honour, respect. On every economic level, the meaning of money is significantly different for men than for women. Seventh, men have the power of sex. They assert the opposite, that this power resides in women, whom they view as synonymous with sex. He fetishizes her body as a whole and in its parts. He exiles her from every realm of expression outside the strictly male-defined sexual or male-defined maternal. He forces her to become that thing that causes erection, then holds himself helpless and powerless when he is aroused by her. His fury when she is not that thing, when she is either more or less than that thing, is intense and punishing. (Dworkin, 1981: 1)

● Sexualities

Closely linked to gender, but different, is **sexuality**. Here we are concerned with *aspects of the body and desire that are linked to the erotic*. This is usually seen as such a personal area of life that sociologists have not spent a great deal of time studying it.

Indeed, most of our contemporary understanding of sexuality comes from the work of biologists, medical researchers and sexologists. They tend to look at hormones, brain structures, drives and instincts. From the writings of the earliest social Darwinians to the

Kinsey and the social survey approach to sexuality

Alfred Kinsey (1849–1956), a professor of zoology, is usually credited with the first major surveys of sexual behaviour. In several large, academic but best-selling books – including *The Sexual Behavior of the Human Male* (1948) and *The Sexual Behavior of the Human Female* (1953) – he interviewed some 12,000 volunteers about their sexual behaviour. His study was a 'bombshell' when it was published because it showed that there was much more sexual activity taking place in the USA than people had hitherto thought. Remember that when he wrote, sexuality was much more of a taboo topic than it is today. Not only

were matters like premarital and extra-marital sex much less common, so too were activities like homosexuality. What he also found was that there were significant social influences on sexuality – it was patterned by such factors as class and region.

Many have suggested that the very publication of the Kinsey volume was a social event that changed North America, where the book was first published. His findings were also seen as so extraordinary that people started to discuss them publicly. The world of 'public sex talk' grew as a result of him.

Kinsey produced a great deal of data. But because of his 'volunteer'

samples, his work was heavily criticised. He nevertheless established that it was indeed possible to conduct such research, and that people were willing to talk about their sexual lives. Recently, some major surveys – generated because of concern about AIDS – have produced findings based upon random samples (see Chapter 2). Unlike Kinsey's findings, they have generally discovered that people are much more conservative in their sexuality than many thought.

Source: Kaye Wellings et al., 1994; Edward O. Laumann et al., 1994.

---

contemporary sociobiologists (see Chapter 4) and more recent research on hormones and differences in the brain, most researchers have been concerned with laying out the biological foundations of sexuality. This is also true of much common sense, too. People tend to assume that 'sex is only natural'. But recall from Chapter 1 that sociologists tend to challenge these natural, taken for granted views.

Thus, when sociologists started to study human sexuality, they soon realised that it is profoundly unlike that found in other animals! As the box on pp. 352–3 suggests, sociologists generally find problems with the overstatement of biological factors. Most sociologists who study sexuality – though they do not deny the role of biological components – argue that what is distinctive about human sexuality is that it is symbolic and meaningful. As we saw in Chapter 6, language, symbols and communications are vital to human beings: it is through these that we become distinctively social beings. It should not therefore be surprising to find that this what sociologists highlight.

It may be an interesting exercise to think about all the ways in which human sexuality differs from animal sexuality. Being firmly embedded in language and communication, we become the 'talking' and 'thinking' sex. Animals do not. Further, we often tend to use sex for social ends, not just biological goals like reproduction. Far from it just being biological sex, we come to use it for many reasons: as an expression of love, as a means to establish bonding, as a way of being clear about our manliness or womanliness, or indeed our maturity. It can be used to show our aggression (as in rape) or to fill up our boredom or as a kind of hobby. It can be used as play, as performance, as power and as a form of work (such as sex work like prostitution).

Constructionism and scripting theory

Drawing on this, William Simon and John Gagnon were the founders of what has now become commonly known as the 'social constructionist' approach to sexuality. Both worked at the Kinsey Institute for Sexual

Behavior in the 1960s, collecting and unearthing mounds of empirical data (see box on page 370). And yet in the midst of this, both felt the need to look at what was happening in a more sociological way. To do this, they suggested that the metaphor of *script* was much more useful in understanding sexuality for humans than was biology.

In scripting theory, human sexualities are best seen as drama. In Chapter 6, we saw how Erving Goffman viewed social life as drama. This idea can also be applied to sexuality. An elaborate set of stagecraft rules and performance guides our sexualities and brings them into action. There is no automatic sexual release for humans; instead sexuality must have life breathed into it through drama. Sexual scripts help define who, what, where, when and even why we have sex.

Discourse and sexualities

Closely linked is the 'discourse' approach to sexuality. Following on from the work of Michel Foucault (introduced in Chapter 8), many sociologists see sexuality as an elaborate language structure that organises power relations. They are concerned with seeing the ways in which language shapes the way we see sex.

A language approach to sex might, for instance, look at the ways in which 'chat shows' like *Oprah* let people talk about sex on television, and how this has some influences in the wider society. Or it may look at the ways in which new categories of sexual problems – sex addiction, AIDS, child sex abuse – come to be constructed and how they develop a language of their own. Much of our sexual life is lived through these discourses and sociologists have increasingly turned their attention to them.

Feminist theories of sexuality

A second important impetus for the sociological study of sexuality has come from feminists, though they have far from agreed on their approach. (See the discussion of different positions above.) We will look briefly at two: radical feminist and libertarian socialists.

Radical feminism

In the radical feminist version, sexuality is seen to be one of the key mechanisms through which men have regulated women's lives. The nineteenth century feminists recognised this when they waged war on prosti-

tution, venereal disease, the low age of consent and immorality of all forms. They saw this as generated by men: as Frances Swiney wrote: 'women's redemption from sex slavery can only be achieved through man's redemption from sex-obsession'. The solution to the problem was 'votes for women and chastity for men' (see Sheila Jeffreys, 1987). Through establishing anti-vice organisations, their aim was to stop men's debauchery.

Late twentieth century radical feminists have taken these arguments even further. They characterise the central features of sexuality as being male. Thus sexuality is centred on the penis, is aggressive, takes place devoid of emotional sensitivity and is often extremely fixated and fetishistic. It is men who rape, abuse and harass. It is men who buy and use pornography and pay sex workers. It is men who become serial sex killers and become sex offenders.

Radical feminists argue that it is through men's sexuality exerting control over women's bodies that women are subordinated. Rape is the clear symbol here: it is not about sexual release, so much as it is about male power and violence. It is a mechanism through which 'all men keep all women in a constant state of fear'.

Out of this wing of the women's movement have grown the campaigns over pornography, the battles against child sex abuse and over violence against women in the home, and the development of new arguments about rape and the setting up of rape crisis centres. Two of these will be briefly considered below.

The case of sexual harassment

Sexual harassment refers to *comments, gestures or physical contact of a sexual nature that are deliberate, repeated and unwelcome*. During the 1990s, sexual harassment became an issue of national importance that has already significantly redefined the rules for workplace interaction between the sexes.

Most victims of sexual harassment are women. This is because, first, our culture encourages men to be sexually assertive and to perceive women in sexual terms; social interaction in the workplace, on campus and elsewhere, then, can readily take on sexual overtones. Second, most individuals in positions of power – including business executives, doctors, assembly-line supervisors, university lecturers and military officers – are men who oversee the work of women. Surveys carried out in widely different work settings confirm that

GLOBAL SOCIOLOGY

Sexuality in Japan

Modern Japan seems lodged in two worlds: a classic traditional one where body and sexuality is 'wrapped' (Hendry, 1995) in fine etiquette and rules and where traditional gender roles are firmly maintained. It is not, however, an anti-sex world (as the Anglo-American one largely is). For it is a world where the geisha can provide an ideal of female companionship for men which includes the explictly erotic, and the samuarai can provide an ideal of homoerotic passion. It is a structured world of genteel sex (for men, that is!).

And yet whilst Japan clearly still has a classical culture, it also has long been at the forefront of a modern industrialising zeal. In Nicholas Bornhoff's *Pink Samurai* (1992) a growing preoccupation with sex in all its guises appears.

● *The comic strip book, or Manga, is everywhere in Japan (and now widely exported).* White has estimated that of 1.9 billion comic books produced in 1989, 474 million were explictly sexual (White, 1993: 176). These are read by adults and children alike; and as one commentator remarks, 'Many comics are wild: scenes of violence, unnatural sex, and scatology are common, even in comics for children...' (Schodt, 1986: 16). With titles like 'No Panty Angels', 'Teach Me Love', 'Hunt of the Sex Maniac', (and drawings to match) they leave little to the imagination!

● *Japanese men were taking to virtual reality games around sex. Exciting Memory*, for example, a virtual real-ity game, offered love, friendship and nudity, and had been purchased by 600,000 men in the 16–35 age range. In these virtual worlds men could assemble romantic and erotic little worlds in which they could once again establish their control over women, a control that has become increasingly lost (*Guardian*, 8 April 1996: 9).

● *The existence of 'love hotels'* (*Rabu Hoteru*) is a widepread and common phenomenon in Japan: a mode of having sex outside the home both for the young and the older. Often garish in form and likened to Disneyland in their curious combination of childishness, innocence yet commercialism, in 1984 there were estimated to be 35,000 nationwide

half of women respondents report receiving unwanted sexual attention (Loy and Stewart, 1984; Paul, 1991).

Sexual harassment is sometimes blatant and direct, as when a supervisor solicits sexual favours from a subordinate, coupled with the threat of reprisals if the advances are refused. Behaviour of this kind – which not only undermines the dignity of an individual but prevents her from earning a living – is widely condemned. Courts have declared such *quid pro quo* sexual harassment (the Latin phrase means 'one thing in return for another') to be an illegal violation of civil rights.

However, the problem of unwelcome sexual attention often involves subtle behaviour – sexual teasing, off-colour jokes, pinups displayed in the workplace – none of which any individual may *intend* as harassing to another person. But, using the *effect* standard favoured by many feminists, such actions add up to creating a *hostile environment* (Cohen, 1991; Paul, 1991). Incidents of this kind are far more complex because they involve very different perceptions of the same behaviour. For example, a man may think that showing romantic interest in a co-worker is paying the woman a compliment; she, on the other hand, may deem his behaviour offensive and a hindrance to her job performance.

Women's entry into the workplace does not in itself ensure that everyone is treated equally and with respect. Untangling precisely what constitutes a hostile working environment, however, demands clearer standards of conduct than exist at present. Creating such guidelines – and educating the public about them – is likely to take some time (Cohen, 1991; Majka, 1991). In the end, courts (and, ultimately, the court of

and 4,000 in Tokyo. Bornhoff's account remarks: 'The scope of fantasy is large: tatami matting and plastic cherry trees for a classic Japanese touch, Hawaiian tropical, medieval Western torture chambers, heated swimming pools . . . in one instance the bed is like an island anchored in the middle of the pool, in another the bed suggests a 1950s Cadillac sitting complete . . . in the middle of what looks like an ornate Chinese restuar-ant' . . . (Bornhoff: 1992: 46-7).

● *There is a fascination with an array of 'sexualities'*, often in fantasy only such as *roricon* (The Lolita Complex) or paedophilia, or an interest in younger girls and 'cute' boys too, and 'panties' (see Borhoff, 1992: 119–22).

This last interest has led to reports of speciality shops and even vending machines selling girls' used under-wear (and shoes) – at the height of

this craze in 1993, it has been esti-mated some 6,000–10,000 girls sold their underpants along with a photo of themselves in Tokyo for as much as US $50 (5,000 yen) (*Newsweek*, 23 December 1996: 28).

● *The growth of a teenage girl sex industry* – replete with erotic dancers, sex video catalogues and the phe-nomenon of telephone clubs. Here, men rent out booths showing soft porn and with telephones where girls can ring them up (*Guardian*, 'Teenage kicks', 30 October 1966: 4).

● *The emergence of more and more couples who seem to be abstaining from sex*, and are 'sexless' (*Newsweek*, 23 December 1996: 30).

● *The emergence of a new kind of fam-ily structure* in which men have become increasingly absent, often through work but often through

staying late at bars at night. Women seeking more egalitarian relations are leaving these men in growing numbers. 'Singlehood... has become partially recognised as a possible life style' (Yoshizumi, 1995: 96).

● *The emergence of a brand of comic that treats young gay male love romantically* – dreamlike, kissing in clouds – but that is marketed for teenage heterosexual girls, such as Kizuna by female illustrator Kazuma Kodoka (though they are also mar-keted in the United States for a gay audience, which often finds the romantic attraction between men to be very different from the erotic emphasis in US publications) (*4Front*, 22 January 1997, citing the analysis of New York Design Critic, Abby Denson). ●

Sources: Bornhoff, 1992; White, 1993.

public opinion) will draw the line between what amounts to 'reasonable friendliness' and behaviour that is 'unwarranted harassment'.

Rape and date rape

Another important area of action is that of rape. For a long time, the academic study of rape was mainly the province of male criminologists who saw rape through two main lenses. The first argued that rapists were pathological people and few and far between. The sec-ond suggested that many women said no to sex when they actually wished to participate; further, it was often precipitated by them.

Such arguments have been roundly condemned by feminists over the past thirty years, and through their campaigns they have brought about change. Critical here has been the growth of rape crisis centres,

offering both support to rape victims and campaign materials that have worked to change police and court practice, as well as the law.

Libertarian and socialist perspectives

As the box on the 'politics of pornography' indicates, not all feminists agree on the anlaysis of sexuality and men provided by radical feminists. These feminists – who count liberals and socialists in their number – charge that radical feminism is too extreme, too fixed in its conceptions of what male sexuality is and ulti-mately adopts a position that makes heterosexuality impossible. It is also too sex-negative.

Many feminists are trying to develop an account of sexuality that recognises that, whilst there is often *dan-ger* in (male) sex, there can also be *pleasure* (Vance, 1984).

Feminism and the politics of pornography

Pornography may be taken as a major symbol of our time because it condenses many of our fears and anxieties concerning sexuality and gender. For the past two decades, there has been an ongoing debate from many different positions about the role of pornography in society. One of the most telling debates has come not from the traditional conservatives and sexual radicals, but from within feminism itself. One group of feminists have made strong attacks on pornography and have tried to have it outlawed. Other feminists have been very critical of such actions.

On one side, radical feminists and others argue that pornography should be a major issue because it strikes at the core of gender and sexuality. Indeed, it shows you the very nature of what men desire and what male sexuality is. They argue that pornography is really a *power* issue because it fosters the notion that men should control both sexuality and women.

Catharine MacKinnon (1987) has branded pornography as one foundation of male dominance in the United States because it portrays women in dehumanising fashion as the subservient playthings of men. Worth noting, in this context, is that the term 'pornography' is derived from the Greek word *porne*, meaning a harlot who acts as a man's sexual slave.

A related charge is that pornography promotes violence against women. Certainly, anyone who has viewed more recent 'hard-core' videos finds this assertion plausible. Yet demonstrating a scientific cause-and-effect rela-tionship between what people watch and how they act is difficult. Research does support the contention, however, that pornography gives men licence to think of women as objects rather than as people.

● Pornography – like most of male sexuality – degrades and abuses women. It is violent, voyeuristic, objectificatory, dehumanising and is designed to satisfy the male's concern with masturbation.

● Pornography is about male power. It shows how men seek to control women, both in the porn itself – the male eye takes the women over, the woman is represented as being there for the man – but also in the making of the porn: here women have often been turned into abuse objects and actually become prostitutes and whores for men.

● Pornography is an ideology that promotes sexual violence in society. By encouraging an objectificatory and abusive approach to women, it actually encourages rape and sexual violence. In the famous epigram: 'pornography is the theory, rape is the practice'.

Many feminists do not agree with these arguments (and have set up movements to challenge the above). They argue:

● The pornography issue gives too much weight to sexuality as a source of women's oppression and deflects attention from other more important sources such as their weak position in the labour market, how racism compounds their problems, exploitation at home in the domestic labour market . . .

● The pornography issue encourages censorship, and this works against women's interests. Indeed, in some places where porn has been banned, so have all kinds of women's publications, especially those for lesbians.

● The pornography issue side-steps the issue of women's sexuality and their growing desire for their own erotica. Women make pornography for themselves; it is not all male. And anti-porn feminists make women seem to be passive, asexual victims of male desire. They are not.

● Finally, the representations of pornography do not have one clear meaning. They have different meanings to different groups and, whilst they can be about male power and violence, this is certainly not the only meaning.

Anti-porn feminists argue back that many of the above arguments either misrepresent their position or are themselves weak. What do you think?

● **Continue the debate:**

1. Do you think sexuality is largely defined by men for their own needs? What might a non-male sexuality look like?

2. What kinds of images in pornography would not be sexist, and would not subordinate women?

3. Where do we draw boundaries? Is there never a case for censorship? ●

Of course, acts of rape and coercive degradation remain unacceptable to all feminists; but they argue there should also be explorations about what it is that women desire, how women can have sexual relations with men that are not degrading and how new patterns of sex-positive sexuality can be developed (see Segal, 1994).

● Gay and lesbian relations

Although same-sex erotic experiences exist across cultures and throughout history with varying degrees of acceptability and frequency, it was not until the nineteenth century in Europe and America that homosexuality was invented as an object of scientific investigation. The term itself was introduced by a sympathetic Hungarian doctor, Benkert, in 1869 amidst a flurry of attempts at classifying sexuality. From this time until the 1970s, the dominant mode of thinking about homosexuality was clinical – it was primarily viewed through a medical framework as a pathology, its causes were located in biological degeneracy or family pathology, and treatments ranging from castration to psychoanalysis were advocated. Although such an approach still continues amongst a few, since 1973 the American Psychiatric Association has officially removed homosexuality from its clinical listing of pathologies, seeing it as non-pathological in itself. Ironically, some of the leading clinicians, and notably Freud, had never viewed it as a pathology: in 1935 Freud could write in a famous 'letter to a mother' that 'whilst homosexuality is assuredly no advantage, it is nothing to be classified as an illness; we consider it to be a variation of the sexual development'.

While the nineteenth century saw the ascendancy of the clinical model of homosexuality, it also saw the growth of writing and campaigning that challenged the orthodox heterosexual assumptions. Thus Magnus Hirschfield established the Scientific Humanitarian Committee and the Institute for Sexual Science in Germany in 1897 and campaigned through scientific research for the acceptance of homosexuality up until the 1930s, when the Nazi movement stopped such advocacy and started a policy of extermination instead. Others, such as Edward Carpenter in England and André Gide in France, pursued a more literary defence. It was not, however, until the period after the Second World War that a substantial body of published research suggested the ubiquity and normality

of homosexual experience. Pivotal to this enterprise was the publication of the Kinsey Report in 1948 and 1953, which contained the findings of interviews with well over 12,000 American men and women. Among the men, Kinsey found that 37 per cent had experienced some post-adolescent homosexual orgasm and 4 per cent had a preponderance of such experience; among the women, the figures were around 13 per cent and 3 per cent respectively. When Kinsey added that such responses were to be found among all social groups and in all walks of life, he created a social bombshell. When he concluded that homosexual behaviour was neither unnatural nor neurotic in itself but an 'inherent physiologic capacity', he established an outrageous view that was later to be turned into something of an orthodoxy in the research of others like Hooker in America and Schofield in England (see the box on the 'Kinsey Report').

Throughout this period, however, homosexuality was strongly condemned by law in most European countries and in all American states. It was not until the 1960s, and a decade or so after proposals for change in the British Wolfenden report and the American New Model Code, that the legal situation changed. Despite the progressive growth of organised groups during the 1950s, it was the New York 'Stonewall Riots' of 1969 that are generally taken to symbolise the birth of the modern international 'Gay Movement' (Weeks, 1977). The scientifically imposed term 'homosexual' was shifted to the self-created term 'gay'; medical rhetoric was converted to political language; organisations for gays became widespread in most large cities and millions of gay men and women started to 'come out' and positively identify with the term 'gay'. The 1970s therefore demonstrated a real change in gay experiences.

Heterosexism and homophobia

Heterosexism – like racism and sexism – describes an ideology that categorises and then unjustly dismisses as inferior a whole group of fellow citizens; in the case of heterosexism, the group are people who are not heterosexual. It is institutionalised in our laws, media, religions and language, and in all too many family units. Attempts to enforce heterosexuality are as much a violation of human rights as racism and sexism, and are now increasingly challenged with equal determination.

Homophobia is the fear of and resulting contempt for homosexuals. The term **homophobia** was coined in the early 1970s by an American psychiatrist George Weinberg, who defined it as *the dread of being in close quarters with homosexuals* (Weinberg, 1973). Figure 13.2 is a very simple homophobia scale that Weinberg introduces in his book. You may like to try it. It's fairly obvious which items indicate 'homophobia' so you could rank yourself! In fact, this is a very naive and indeed bad measurement device, but it is beyond our scope to consider the methodological difficulties involved in scaling attitudes. There is a huge critical literature on this. You might, however, like to ponder what you think is wrong with the scale.

A number of researchers have used scales such as Weinberg's and suggested that people intolerant of homosexuals are likely to be:

more authoritarian, more dogmatic, more cognitively rigid, more intolerant of ambiguity, more status conscious, more sexually rigid, more guilty and negative about their sexual impulses, and less accepting of others in general (Morin and Garfinkle, 1978).

Queer theory

As lesbians, gays and bisexuals have 'come out', and become both more visible and more accepted within the mainstream of many Western societies, so their voices have increasingly entered sociology and social science debates. There has been a growth of lesbian and gay studies (Plummer, 1992).

Nevertheless, **Queer theory** argues that most sociological theory still has a bias towards 'heterosexuality' and that non-heterosexual voices need to be heard. Such theorists would argue that all the topics discussed in this book – from stratification and ethnicity, to religion and economy – would be greatly enhanced if the position of 'non-heterosexual voices' were placed at the centre. For example, it suggests that many religions have been organised around 'homophobic' persecutions; that a new form of economy is emerging that is based upon the spending power of young middle-class gay men – the pink economy; and that the experience of being lesbian or gay can differ significantly across different ethnic minority communities (Seidman, 1996).

Homosexuality and AIDS

In the early 1980s, AIDS appeared as a major life-threatening disease (see Chapter 19). Although around the world it is overwhelmingly a disease that affects heterosexuals, in most of the West gay men have been heavily impacted. Especially in the large cities of the Western world that contain relatively large groups of active gay men – New York, Los Angeles, San Francisco in the United States; Berlin, Paris, Amsterdam, London in Europe – it is hard to find a gay man who hasn't been affected by awareness of AIDS. Indeed, whereas in the 1970s the key to understanding gay life was the politicisation flowing from the Gay Liberation Front and from Stonewall, when gay men rioted against a police raid on this gay club in New York, now it has become AIDS that shapes the gay community. As one gay journalist put it so clearly, 'There's a whole new batch of gay men in their mid-twenties and younger who see the health crisis, not Stonewall, as the decisive historical force shaping their gay identity.' Or, as another gay man put it, 'AIDS has infected my dreams'.

AIDS has had a dual impact on the gay community, simultaneously decimating it and, ironically, strengthening it – yet, out of this enormous suffering, gay men have organised themselves into a new culture of resistance; they have fought back through a whole arena of new organizations. The old gay movement hardly survives; what has taken its place is a massive proliferation of self-help groups covering every aspect of the health crisis. It is the text-book case study of self-help. From help lines and 'buddy support' to advocacy and education, from fundraising and community

Yukon 1995. Gays move to remote region of Yukon in search of greater freedom and tolerance.

Source: Popperfoto

Figure 13.2 ● The Standard Homophobia Scale

	Yes	No
Homosexuals should be locked up to protect society	☐	☐
It would be upsetting for me to find out I was alone with a homosexual	☐	☐
Homosexuals should be allowed to hold government positions	☐	☐
I would not want to be a member of an organisation which had any homosexuals in its membership	☐	☐
I find the thought of homosexual acts disgusting	☐	☐
If laws against homosexuality were eliminated, the proportion of homosexuals in the population would probably remain about the same	☐	☐
A homosexual could be a good President of the United States	☐	☐
I would be afraid for a child of mine to have a teacher who was homosexual	☐	☐
If a homosexual sat next to me on the bus I would get nervous	☐	☐

Source: Weinberg (1973)

education to 'safer sex' campaigns and nursing facilities, not one aspect of gay life has remained untouched by AIDS. Indeed, the gay community has provided many blueprints for responses in the heterosexual world (Altman, 1986).

● Social change and sexuality

AIDS and the gay movement are but one instance of major changes taking place in sexuality. The English sociologist Anthony Giddens, in his book *The Transformation of Intimacy* (1992), talks about a number of other recent changes. Most important here is the arrival of 'plastic sexuality' and the 'pure relationship'. By the former he means that modern sexuality has broken away from its long historical connection to reproduction and has opened up into a much wider array of ways of doing sex. This is closely connected, of course, to the widespread availability and acceptability of contraceptive techniques. He also sees this 'plastic sex' as closely linked to the idea of the pure relationship, by which communication is enhanced between men and women and greater equality happens around sexual and emotional experiences.

Giddens recognises that there is also room for danger in contemporary developments. For as women

gain more and more equality, so some men feel more and more threatened. Modern times thus bring a growing potential for both an increasing democratisation of personal relationships and at the same time a growing potential for a gender war between men and women. We return to this thorny issue in Chapter 17, when we consider changes in the family.

● Looking ahead: gender in the twenty-first century

Predictions about the future are, at best, informed speculation. Just as economists disagree about the inflation rate a year from now and political scientists can only guess at the outcome of upcoming elections, sociologists can offer only general observations about the likely future of gender and sexuality.

But certainly, change in the gender and sexuality spheres has been remarkable. Two centuries ago, women in the West occupied a position that was clearly and strikingly subordinate. Husbands controlled property in marriage, laws barred women from most jobs, from holding political office and even from voting. Although women today remain socially disadvantaged, the movement toward equality has surged ahead. Note, further, that two-thirds of people entering the workforce during the 1990s will be women. Truly, today's economy *depends* on the earnings of women (Hewlett, 1990).

Many factors have contributed to this transformation. Most important, industrialisation has both broadened the range of human activity and shifted the nature of work from physically demanding tasks that favoured male strength to jobs that require more human thought and imagination, which places the talents of women and men on an even footing. Additionally, technology has afforded us control over reproduction, so that women's lives today are less constrained by unwanted pregnancies.

Many women and men have also made deliberate efforts in pursuit of social equality. Sexual harassment complaints, for example, are now taken much more seriously in the workplace. And, as more women assume positions of power in the corporate and political worlds, social changes in the twenty-first century may turn out to be even greater than those we have already witnessed.

Likewise, with sexuality. As we have shown, the shifts in sexuality over the past thirty years have been remarkable. Not only have gay men and lesbians been able to 'come out' and gain a considerable degree of positive support, but women's sexuality has been transformed.

Nevertheless, a clear 'backlash' against feminism persists. Traditionalists argue that gender still forms an important foundation of personal identity and family life and that it is deeply woven into the moral fabric of our society. They see feminism as a threat to social stability. But others recognise the variability of genders throughout cultures and history and sense that there are now many ways of being men and many ways of being women. Still others argue even more radically for the need to transcend all gender boundaries. On balance, however, this century has clearly witnessed a great many changes across the boundaries of sexuality and gender, changes that seem likely to continue.

SUMMARY

1. Sex is a biological concept; a human foetus is female or male from the moment of conception. Hermaphrodites represent rare cases of people who combine the biological traits of both sexes. Transsexuals are people who feel they are one sex when biologically they are the other.

2. Heterosexuality is the dominant sexual orientation in virtually every society in the world, though people with a bisexual or exclusively homosexual orientation make up a small percentage of the population everywhere.

3. Gender involves how cultures assign human traits and power to each sex. Gender varies historically and across cultures. Some degree of patriarchy, however, exists in every society.

4. Through the socialisation process, people link gender with personality (gender identity) and actions (gender roles). Three theories dominate socialisation theory: behavioural learning, cognitive learning and pyschodynamic learning. Learning to mother is an important part of this socialisation process. The major agents of socialisation – the family, peer groups, schools and the mass media – reinforce cultural definitions of what is feminine and masculine.

5. Gender stratification entails numerous social disadvantages for women. Although most women are now in the paid labour force, a majority of working women hold low-paying clerical or service jobs. Unpaid housework also remains predominantly a task performed by women.

6. Women earn less than men do. This disparity stems from differences in jobs and family responsibilities as well as discrimination.

7. Women now earn a slight majority of all bachelor's and master's degrees. Men still receive a majority of all doctorates and professional degrees.

8. The number of women in politics has increased sharply in recent decades. Still, the vast majority of people elected are men.

9. Minority women encounter greater social disadvantages than white women.

10. Violence against women is a widespread problem in the UK. Our society is also grappling with the issues of sexual harassment and pornography.

11. Functional analysis holds that preindustrial societies benefit from distinctive roles for males and females reflecting biological differences between the sexes. In industrial societies, marked gender inequality becomes dysfunctional and slowly decreases. Talcott Parsons claimed that complementary gender roles promote the social integration of families and society as a whole.

12. Conflict analysis views gender as a dimension of social inequality and conflict. Friedrich Engels tied gender stratification to the development of private property. He claimed that capitalism devalues women and housework.

13. Feminism endorses the social equality of the sexes and actively opposes patriarchy and sexism. Feminism also strives to eliminate violence against women, and to give women control over their sexuality.

14. There are three variants of feminist thinking. Liberal feminism seeks equal opportunity for both sexes within current social arrangements; socialist feminism advocates abolishing private property as the means to social equality; radical feminism aims to create a gender-free society.

15. There are two central approaches to the sociological study of sexuality: social constructionism, which highlights scripts, languages and symbols; and feminism, which highlights power and gender.

16. Same-sex relations – gay and lesbian relationships – have undergone profound changes in the last hundred years.

17. 'Plastic sex' and 'pure relationships' may be future patterns of sexuality. They both indicate a growing flexibility, openness and potential equality in relationships.

KEY CONCEPTS

feminism the advocacy of social equality for the sexes, in opposition to patriarchy and sexism

gender identity traits that females and males, guided by their culture, incorporate into their personalities

gender roles (sex roles) attitudes and activities that a society links to each sex

gender stratification a society's unequal distribution of wealth, power and privilege between the two sexes

hermaphrodite a human being with some combination of female and male internal and external genitalia

patriarchy a form of social organisation in which males dominate females

primary sex characteristics the genitals, used to reproduce the human species

secondary sex characteristics bodily development, apart from the genitals, that distinguishes biologically mature females and males

sex the biological distinction between females and males

sexism the belief that one sex is innately superior to the other

sexual harassment comments, gestures or physical contact of a sexual nature that are deliberate, repeated and unwelcome

sexuality aspects of the body and desire that are linked to the erotic

transsexuals people who feel they are one sex though biologically they are the other

CRITICAL-THINKING QUESTIONS

1. Describe the main behaviour patterns of a Sambian boy with (a) other boys and (b) women. Do Sambian boys grow up to become adult homosexuals?

2. A recent cover story in a national news magazine characterised bisexuality as 'the wild card of erotic life' and a 'potent threat to monogamy'. Do you agree? Why or why not?

3. Why is gender a dimension of social stratification? How does gender interact with inequality based on race, ethnicity and class?

4. What do feminists mean by asserting that 'the personal is political'? Explain how liberal, socialist and radical feminisms differ from one another.

5. How would you define the following: (a) patriarchy, (b) gender identity, (c) homophobia?

6. What problems do you find with biological explanations for masculinity? Suggest some examples of how male gender roles vary cross-culturally.

7. Distinguish briefly between a psychodynamic, behavioural and cognitive theory of gender socialisation.

8. What do you understand by the 'heterosexism' and the 'homophobia'? Why are they such important issues in understanding homosexuality?

9. What are the most significant changes in gender and sexuality over the past twenty years. Why have they happened?

GOING FURTHER ....

Introductory reading

Sylvia Walby, *Theorizing Patriarchy* (Cambridge: Polity Press, 1990).

> Not strictly an introduction, it nevertheless provides a detailed analysis of the workings of patriarchy, with both theoretical critique and empirical evidence. The figures provided now need a little updating.

Sheila Rowbottom, *A Century of Women: The History of Women in Britain and the United States* (London: Viking, 1997).

> Readable (and illustrated) account of women's role this century. A good guide and introduction.

Jeffrey Weeks, *Sexuality* (London: Routledge, 1986).
Gail Hawkes, *A Sociology of sex and sexuality* (Buckingham: Open University Press, 1996).

> Two short guides to the field of sexuality studies

Classic sources

Margaret Mead, *Sex and Temperament in Three Primitive Societies* (New York: William Morrow, 1963; orig. 1935).

> This comparative study carried out in New Guinea was an early effort to advance the social equality of the sexes.

Jessie Bernard, *The Female World* (New York: The Free Press, 1981).

> This more recent classic explores how females and males live in different, socially constructed worlds.

More advanced reading

R. W. Connell, *Masculinities* (Cambridge: Polity Press, 1995).

> A key text for reviewing and examining the developing field of men's studies, though this is clearly from a strong sociological perspective.

Rosemarie Tong, *Feminist Thought: A Comprehensive Introduction* (London: Unwin Hyman, 1989).

> Broadens the 'three perspectives' of feminism outlined above to include another five. Fairly advanced reading, and certainly not an introduction!

Judith Lorber, *Paradoxes of Gender* (New Haven, CT: Yale University Press, 1994).

> This comprehensive survey of the state of gender research argues for classifying gender as a social institution because it shapes all aspects of human behaviour.

Marnia Lazreg, *The Eloquence of Silence: Algerian Women in Question* (New York: Routledge, 1994).

> This historical survey of the lives of women in a North African nation suggests that women everywhere – despite profound cultural differences – confront many of the same basic problems.

Cynthia Enloe, *Bananas, Beaches, and Bases: Making Feminist Sense of International Politics* (Berkeley: University of California Press, 1990).

> This book pushes the issue of gender into the international arena, arguing that gender (along with

race and class) are important dimensions of the geopolitical system.

Anne Fausto Sterling, *Myths of Gender: Biological Theories about Men and Women* (New York: Basic Books, 1985).

Written by a feminist biologist, this is a valuable review of biological evidence on genders and a broader consideration of their ideological functions.

Lynne Segal, *Straight Sex: The Politics of Pleasure* (London: Virago 1994).

A leading socialist feminist locates the problem of heterosexuality and debates many of the issues around sexuality that have been at the heart of modern feminism for the past 30 years.

Steven Seidman (ed.), *Queer Theory/Sociology* (Oxford: Blackwell, 1996).

Reviews the history of the sociology of homosexuality, before presenting some original articles on 'Queer theory'.

Other sources

There are huge libraries, databases and journals associated with everything discussed in this chapter. For a start, try some web sites:

● http://www.feminist.org/

Women's web world! Homepage of Feminist Majority Online which links to plenty of information concerning women such as news and events, political actions, publications, arts and entertainment. Also links to feminist university network and feminist Internet gateway.

● http://www.igc.apc.org/womensnet/

Womensnet is a unionised Internet service provider that provides information on women's issues.

● http://www.acusd.edu/ethics

This web site links to many other resources on ethical issues such as abortion, sexual orientation, gender and sexism, world hunger, poverty, etc. with suggested journals, articles and books.

● http://www.qrd.org/

Queer resource directory, which links to various issues concerning 'queer' people such as education, health, family, youth, religion, cultures, law and politics by regions.

chapter fourteen

Source: *Observer*, 15 June 1997

Ageing and the Elderly

Nellie Bruton is 104. Her husband died about thirty years ago and she has one son. Her two brothers died young: one from meningitis as a baby, the other killed in the First World War. She remembers Queen Victoria coming to review local troops returning from the Boer War, and also recalls a memorial service in her local church after the Queen's death. For much of her working life she was the village postmistress; her husband was an agricultural worker.

Mrs Bruton has lived in the same Somerset house since she retired in the 1950s. She lives on her own, but is supported by friends, her church and 'meals on wheels'. She walks to church every week and still sings in the church choir – in which she has been a member since 1916! She recalls the time when the village baker came round, when milk was delivered by the bucket, and there was a grocer, butcher and a post office. None now remains. For Mrs Bruton, the secret of her long life has been 'Good plain living – not beefburgers like it is now. And a drop of sherry every morning. I've come to like it.'

Mrs Bruton is one of a rapidly growing group of centenarians. By the year 2030, there may well be 30,000 people living beyond their 100th birthday in Britain. In 1951, there were only 271, but by the 1991 census, this number had risen to 4,400. Projections suggest there are about 8,000 centenarians living today. An unprecedented 'oldie' boom is on the way – with the numbers of the '100-somethings' predicted to grow rapidly (DGAA Homelife, 1997).

● The greying of the Western world

A quiet but powerful revolution is reshaping the Western world: the number of elderly people (aged 65 and over) is dramatically increasing, and with this comes new concerns. The changes in the United States are shown in Figure 14.1. At the start of this century, a typical European city would probably have had one elderly person for every 20 people. By 1996, the ratio had become one in every seven; and by 2020 it is predicted to be one in every five (Walker and Maltby, 1997: 1). The effects of this 'greying' of Europe promise to be profound.

Looking at Britain, a few statistics may bring this change into sharp focus. In 1880 less than 5 per cent of the population was over 65; in 1995, this was 16 per cent – with 7 per cent over 75 (*Social Trends*, 1977: 29). As 'baby boomers' reach their sixties around 2007, the elderly will rise even more steeply – perhaps to 19 per cent in 2035 (Field, 1992). Looking at absolute numbers, the elderly population jumped from 1.52 million in 1901 to 7.27 million in 1981. The population over 75 is projected to be 6.8 million in 2034 (*Social Trends*,

1997: 17; Coleman and Salt, 1992: 230; Champion, 1996: 16).

Similar change is occurring across the rest of Europe. Within the EU, the percentage of people over 60 rose from 16 per cent in 1960 to 20 per cent in 1990, and is predicted to rise to 30 per cent by 2020 (Figure 14.2). But there are differences across countries – with Ireland having the youngest population of EU countries and Sweden having the oldest (followed closely by Germany, France and the UK). Italy has the highest proportion of the elderly in the world – by the year 2000, out of a population of 57 million, nearly 10 million will be over 65 (Drake, 1994: 70; Walker and Maltby, 1997: 11).

Women outnumber men in the elderly population (due to their greater longevity) and the discrepancy increases with advancing age: at ages 70–74 there are roughly four women for every three men; at 80–84 there are two women for every man; and by 95, the ratio becomes three to one (Walker and Maltby, 1997: 11). Figure 14.3 shows 'the feminisation of old age ratio'. Women over pensionable age are the largest group of single person households (around 11 per cent).

The dependency ratio

This greying of society characterises all industrial countries. Typically, rich nations have low birth rates, coupled with increasing longevity. This is sometimes called the 'demographic time bomb' and it highlights the **dependency ratio**: *the numbers of dependent children and retired persons relative to productive age groups* (Coleman and Salt, 1992: 542). This has been hovering around 58 and 53 over the past 25 years. Recently, because of falling fertility and family size it has been declining; it is not a problem yet. But changes predicted for the next century suggest a growth in the dependency ratio – there will be fewer and fewer people of working age, and more and more will be dependants.

This century has witnessed a remarkable increase in life expectancy. Barely half of 20-year-olds living in 1900 could expect to live to 65; women born in 1900 lived, on average, only about 48 years, while men lived 46 years. By contrast, most women born in 1994 can look forward to 79 years of life; and men to just over 74 years (*Social Trends*, 1997: 122). This represents an increase of over 60 per cent since the start of the century.

Underlying this striking gain in life span are medical advances that have virtually eliminated infectious

Figure 14.1 ● **The greying of society**

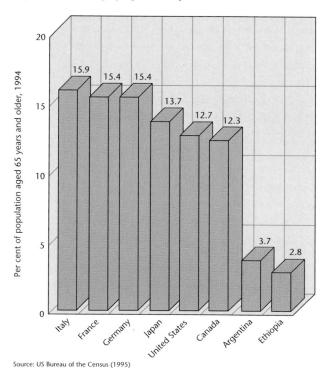

Source: US Bureau of the Census (1995)

Figure 14.2 ● Percentage of the population aged 60 and over in the EU countries, 1993 and 2020 (projected)

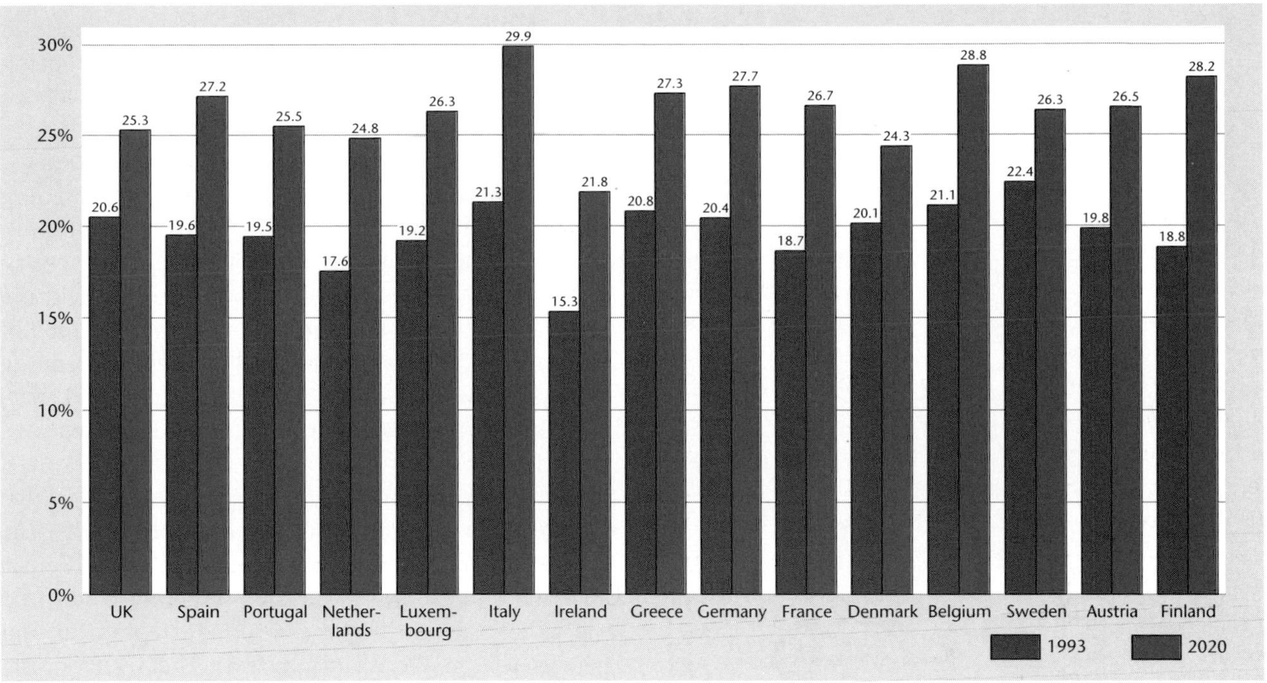

Source: Eurostat (1995), Table B4, pp. 17, 192

diseases such as smallpox, diphtheria and measles, which killed many infants and young people in the past. Just as important, more recent medical strides fend off cancer and heart disease, afflictions common to the elderly. Looking beyond the elderly population, a rising standard of living during this century has promoted the health of people of all ages.

We can only begin to imagine the consequences of this massive increase in the elderly population. As elderly people steadily retire from the labour force, the proportion of non-working adults will generate ever-greater demands for social resources and programmes. And the ratio of elderly people to working-age adults, which analysts call the *old-age dependency ratio*, will almost double in the next 50 years (rising from 20 to 37 elderly people per 100 people aged 18 to 64).

One key area of concern is the health-care system, because the elderly today account for a quarter of all medical expenditures. With the skyrocketing costs of medical care, tens of millions of additional elderly men and women will place an unprecedented demand on health-care systems throughout the world.

In terms of everyday experience, interacting with elderly people will become commonplace in coming decades. In recent history, our society has been marked by a considerable degree of age segregation. The young rarely mingle with the old, so that most people know little about ageing. In the twenty-first century, as the elderly population of Europe increases, this pattern will probably change. But, tomorrow as well as today, how frequently younger people interact with the elderly depends a great deal on where in the country we live. Map 14.1 looks at residential patterns for people aged 65 and older.

Finally, the elderly represent an open category in which all of us, if we are lucky, end up. But the category represents great diversity, representing all cultures, classes, sexes, sexual orientations and ethnic groups. Even so, several broad distinctions between the elderly have become common. One is the distinction between 'the third age' (50–74) – *a period of life often free from parenting and paid work when a more active, independent life is achieved* – and a 'fourth age' – *an age of eventual dependence* (Laslett, 1987; 1994). Another distinction is

Map 14.1 ● Where are the elderly most likely to live in the UK?

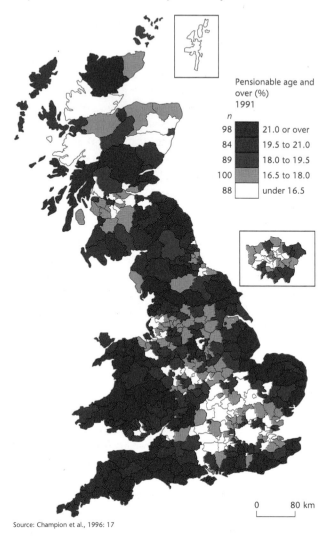

Pensionable age and over (%) 1991

n		
98		21.0 or over
84		19.5 to 21.0
89		18.0 to 19.5
100		16.5 to 18.0
88		under 16.5

0   80 km

Source: Champion et al., 1996: 17

between a very large group – the 'younger elderly' (65–75) – who enjoy good health and financial security, are typically autonomous and are likely to be living as couples. The 'older elderly' (75–85) become increasingly dependent on others because of both health and money problems. Finally, there is a growing group of 'very old'. Both these ways of grouping the elderly suggest a move from periods of increased activity and autonomy to one of growing dependency.

● Growing old: biology and culture

Tracking the greying of Europe is one focus of **gerontology** (derived from the Greek word *geron*, meaning 'an old person'), *the study of ageing and the elderly*. Gerontologists explore the biological processes of ageing, ask if personalities change as we grow older and investigate how cultural assumptions about ageing vary around the world.

Biological changes

Ageing amounts to a series of gradual, ongoing changes. How we think about life's transitions – whether we cheer our maturity or bemoan our physical decline – depends largely on whether our culture labels such changes as positive or negative. In much of Europe and the Western world, a youth-orientated way of life is stressed. Through childhood and adolescence, we gain responsibility and look forward to expanded legal rights.

But Western cultures often take a more negative view of the biological changes that unfold later in life. We commiserate with those entering old age and make jokes about ageing to avoid the harsh conclusion that the elderly are on a slippery slope of physical and mental decline. We assume, in short, that by about age 40, people cease growing *up* and begin growing *down*.

Growing old does bring on certain physical problems. Grey hair, wrinkles, loss of height and weight, and an overall decline in strength and vitality all begin in middle age. After the age of 50, bones become more brittle, so injuries take longer to heal, and the odds of suffering from chronic illnesses (such as arthritis and diabetes) as well as life-threatening conditions (like heart disease and cancer) rise steadily. The sensory abilities – taste, sight, touch, smell and especially hearing – also become less keen with age (Colloway and Dollevoet, 1977; Treas, 1995).

Yet, without denying that health becomes more fragile with advancing age, the vast majority of older people are neither discouraged nor disabled by their physical condition. Evidence from the European Observatory on Ageing suggests that the proportion of people over 65 who are incapacitated is less than 10 per cent (and less than 5 per cent for the population aged 60–69). After 80, however, this increases sharply to 30 per cent (Walker and Maltby, 1997: 92).

Bear in mind, too, that patterns of well-being vary greatly within the elderly population. More health problems beset the 'older elderly', those past the age of 75. Moreover, because women typically live longer than men do, women spend more of their lives suffering from chronic disabilities like arthritis. In addition, the better off are often more likely to live and work in a healthy and safe environment, which pays benefits well into old age. And, of course, richer people can afford much more preventive medical care.

Psychological changes

Just as we tend to overstate the physical problems of ageing, so it is easy to exaggerate the intellectual and psychological changes that accompany growing old. Looking at intelligence over the life course, the conventional wisdom can be summed up in the simple rule: 'What goes up must come down' (Baltes and Schaie, 1974).

In recent years, however, gerontologists have cast a critical eye on this assertion. If we operationalise intelligence to spotlight sensor/motor coordination – such as the ability to arrange objects to match a drawing – we indeed find a steady decline after mid-life. The facility to learn new material and to think quickly appears to subside as well, though not until much later – typically around the age of 70. But the ability to apply familiar ideas holds steady with advancing age, and some studies actually show improvement in verbal and mathematical skills (Baltes and Schaie, 1974; Schaie, 1980).

Most people wonder if they will think differently or have a different outlook when they are older. Gerontologists assure us, for better or worse, that the answer is usually no. Personality changes with advancing age are usually limited to becoming more introspective – that is, more engaged with our own thoughts and emotions – and less materialistic. Generally, therefore, two elderly people who were childhood friends would recognise in each other many of the same personality traits that distinguished them as youngsters (Neugarten, 1971, 1972, 1977; Wolfe, 1994).

Ageing and culture

When do people grow old? How do younger people regard society's oldest members? The variable answers to these questions demonstrate that, while ageing is universal, the significance of growing old is a variable element of culture.

At one level, how well – and, more basically, how long – people live is closely linked to a society's technology and overall standard of living. Throughout most of human history, as the philosopher Thomas Hobbes (1588–1679) put it, people's lives were 'nasty, brutish, and short' (though Hobbes himself persisted to the ripe old age of 91!). In his day, most people married and had children while in their teens, became middle-aged in their twenties and began to succumb to various illnesses in their thirties and forties. It took several more centuries for a rising standard of living and advancing medical technology to curb deadly infectious diseases. Living to, say, age 50 became commonplace only at the beginning of this century. Since then, a surging standard of living coupled with medical advances has added 20 years to people's longevity in industrial nations.

But living into what we call 'old age' is not yet the rule in much of the world. Map 14.2 shows that, in the poorest countries, the average life span is still barely 50 years. Beyond longevity, however, we must examine how societies view their senior members. As Chapter 9 ('Social Stratification') details, all societies display systematic inequality with regard to basic resources. We now turn to how ageing figures in this process.

Age stratification: a global assessment

Like race, ethnicity and gender, age is a basis for socially ranking individuals. **Age stratification**, then, is *the unequal distribution of wealth, power and privileges among people at different stages in the life course* (see also Chapter 5). As is true of other dimensions of social hierarchy, age stratification varies according to a society's level of technological development.

In hunting and gathering societies, as Chapter 3 ('Society') explains, without the technology to produce a surplus of food, hunters and gatherers are nomadic. Their survival depends on physical strength and stamina; thus, as members of these societies become elderly (in this case, reaching about age 30) they become less active, often leading others to consider them an economic burden (Sheehan, 1976).

In pastoral, horticultural and agrarian societies, with control over raising crops and animals, societies gain the capacity to produce a material surplus; consequently, individuals may accumulate considerable wealth over a lifetime. The most privileged members of these societies are typically the elderly, promoting **gerontocracy**, *a form of social organisation in which the elderly have the most wealth, power and prestige*. Old people, particularly men, are honoured (and sometimes

WINDOW ON THE WORLD

Map 14.2 ● Life expectancy in global perspective

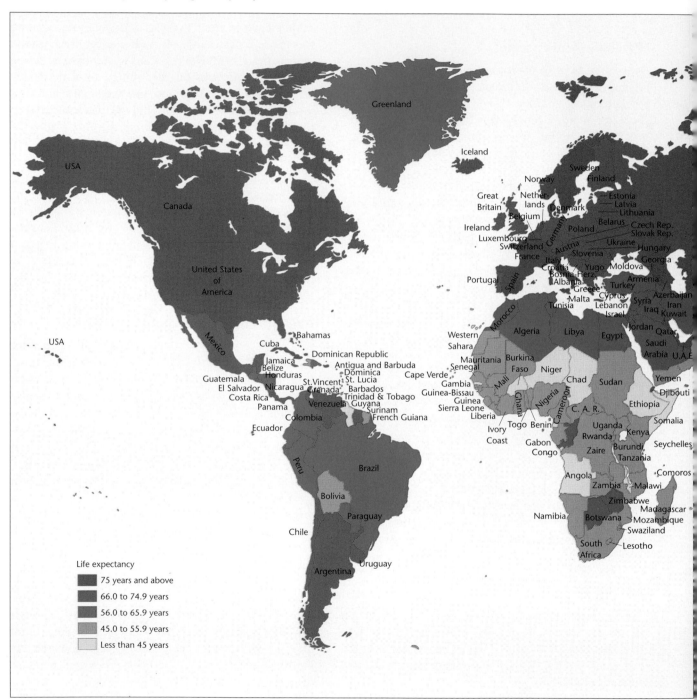

Life expectancy

- 75 years and above
- 66.0 to 74.9 years
- 56.0 to 65.9 years
- 45.0 to 55.9 years
- Less than 45 years

Source: *Peters Atlas of the World* (1990)

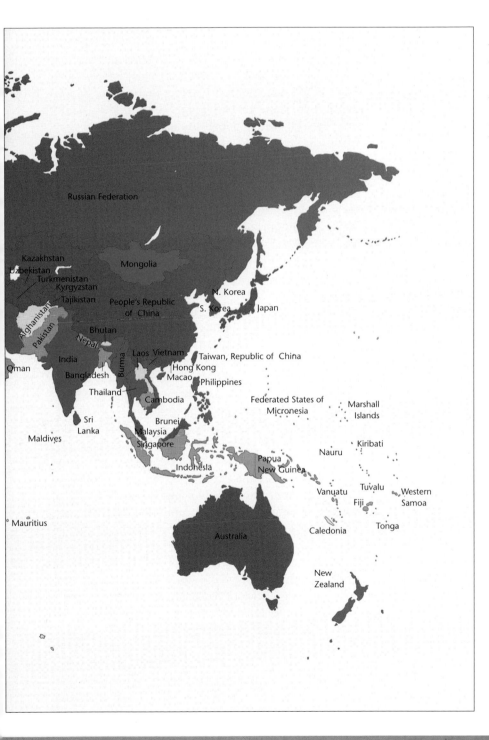

Life expectancy has shot upward over the course of this century in industrial countries including Canada, the United States, the nations of Western Europe, Japan and Australia. A new-born in the United Kingdom can expect to live about 75 years, and our life expectancy would be greater still were it not for the high risk of death among infants born into poverty. Since poverty is the rule in much of the world, lives are correspondingly shorter, especially in parts of Africa where life expectancy may be as low as 40 years.

feared) by their families and, as the box reports, in the case of the Abkhasians they remain active leaders of society until they die. This veneration of the elderly also explains the widespread practice of ancestor worship in agrarian societies.

Industrial societies

Industrialisation pushes living standards upwards and advances medical technology, which, in turn, increases life expectancy. But these same forces simultaneously erode the power and prestige of the elderly. In part, this decline reflects a shift in the prime source of wealth from land (typically controlled by the oldest members of society) to factories and other goods (often owned or managed by younger people). The peak earning years for most workers, for instance, occur around age 50; after that, earnings generally decline.

Urban living also separates the generations physically and encourages children to depend less on their parents and more on their own earning power. Furthermore, because industrial, urban societies change rapidly, the skills, traditions and life experiences that served the old seem less relevant to the young. Finally, the tremendous productivity of industrial nations means that some members of society do not need to work; as a result, most of the very old and the very young remain in non-productive roles (Cohn, 1982).

Over the long term, all these factors are transforming *elders* (a term with positive connotations) into the *elderly* (commanding far less prestige). In mature, industrial societies such as Europe and the United States, economic and political leaders are usually middle-aged people who combine seasoned experience with up-to-date skills. In the late 1990s, the combination of UK Prime Minister Tony Blair and US President Bill Clinton – both youthful in their looks – highlighted the decline of the 'older statesman'. In rapidly changing sectors of the economy – especially high-tech fields – many key executives are much younger and sometimes not long out of college or university. Industrial societies often consign older people to marginal participation in the economy because they lack the knowledge and training demanded by a fast-changing marketplace.

Certainly, some elderly men and women remain at the helm of businesses they own but, more commonly, older people predominate in traditional occupations (such as barbers, tailors and seamstresses) and jobs that involve minimal activity (night security guards, for instance) (Kaufman and Spilerman, 1982).

Japan: an exceptional case

Japan stands out as an exception to the rule. With a large proportion of elderly people (about 14 per cent and rising rapidly), Japan also maintains a traditional culture that elevates the prestige of older people. Most aged people in Japan live with an adult son or daughter and continue to play a significant role in family life. Elderly men in Japan are also more likely than their counterparts in Europe to remain in the labour force and, in many Japanese corporations, the oldest employees enjoy the greatest respect. But even Japan is steadily becoming more like other industrial societies, in which growing old means giving up a large measure of social importance (Harlan, 1968; Cowgill and Holmes, 1972; Treas, 1979; Palmore, 1982; Yates, 1986).

● Transitions and problems of ageing

Chapter 5 ('Socialisation') explained that we confront change at each stage of life. People must unlearn self-concepts and social patterns that no longer apply to their lives, and must simultaneously learn to cope with new circumstances. Of all stages of the life course, however, old age can present some of the greatest personal challenges.

Although physical decline in old age is less serious than most younger people think, this change can cause emotional stress. Older people endure more pain, become resigned to limited activities, adjust to greater dependence on others and see in the death of friends or relatives frequent reminders of their own mortality. Moreover, because our culture places such a premium on youth, ageing may spark frustration, fear and self-doubt (Hamel, 1990). As one retired psychologist recently said of his old age: 'Don't let the current hype about the joys of retirement fool you. They are not the best of times. It's just that the alternative is even worse' (Rubenstein, 1991: 13).

Erik Erikson (1963, 1980) points out that elderly people must resolve a tension that springs from 'integrity versus despair'. No matter how much they still may be learning and achieving, older people recognise that their lives are nearing an end. Thus the elderly spend much time reflecting on their past accomplishments and disappointments. To shore up

Growing (very) old: a report from Abkhasia

Anthropologist Sula Benet was sharing wine and conversation with a man in Tamish, a small village in the Republic of Abkhasia, once part of the Soviet Union. Judging the man to be about 70, she raised her glass and offered a toast to his long life. 'May you live as long as Moses', she exclaimed. The gesture of goodwill fell flat: Moses lived to 120, but Benet's companion was already 119.

An outsider – especially an open-minded anthropologist who studies many of the world's mysteries – should be sceptical of the longevity claims made by some Abkhasians. In one village of 1,200 visited by Benet, for example, 200 people declared their age to be more than 80. But government statistics confirm that, even if some Abkhasians exaggerate their longevity, most outlive the average European.

What accounts for this remarkable life span? The answer certainly is not the advanced medical technology in which people in Europe place so much faith; many Abkhasians have never seen a physician nor entered a hospital. The probable explanation is cultural, includ-

ing diet and physical activity. Abkhasians eat little saturated fat (which is linked to heart disease), use no sugar and drink no coffee or tea; few smoke or chew tobacco. They consume large amounts of healthful fruits and vegetables and drink lots of buttermilk and low-alcohol wine. Additionally, Abkhasians maintain active lives built around regular physical work for people of all ages.

Moreover, Abkhasians live according to a well-defined and consistent set of traditional values, which confers on all a strong feeling of belonging and a clear sense of purpose. Here the elderly remain active and valued members of the community, in marked contrast to

Source: Magnum Photo, Inc. – Eve Arnold

our own practice of pushing old people to the margins of social life. As Benet explains: 'The old, when they do not simply vegetate, out of view and out of mind, keep themselves "busy" with bingo and shuffleboard.' For their part, the Abkhasians do not even have a word for old people and have no notion of retiring. Furthermore, younger people accord their senior members great prestige and respect since, in their minds, advanced age confers the greatest wisdom. Elders are indispensable guardians of culture and preside at important ceremonial occasions where they transmit their knowledge to the young. In Abkhasia, in short, people look to the old, rather than the young, for decisions and guidance in everyday life.

Given their positive approach to growing old, Abkhasians expect to lead long and useful lives. They feel needed because, in their own minds and everyone else's, they are. Far from being a burden, elders stand at the centre of society. ●

Source: Based on Benet, 1971.

their personal integrity, Erikson explains, older women and men must face up to past mistakes as well as savour their successes. Otherwise, this stage of life may turn into a time of despair – a dead end with little positive meaning.

Research indicates that most people cope fairly well with the challenges of growing old. In a classic

study of people in their seventies, Bernice Neugarten (1971) acknowledged that some people develop *disintegrated and disorganised personalities* because they find it nearly impossible to come to terms with old age. Despair is the common thread in these lives, sometimes to the point of making them passive residents of hospitals or nursing homes.

Another segment of Neugarten's subjects, those with *passive-dependent personalities*, were only slightly better off. They have little confidence in their abilities to cope with daily events, sometimes seeking help even if they do not actually need it. Always in danger of social withdrawal, their level of life satisfaction remains relatively low.

A third category of people had *defended personalities*, living independently but fearful of advancing age. Such people try to shield themselves from the reality of old age by valiantly fighting to stay youthful and physically fit. While concerns about health are certainly positive, setting unrealistic standards for oneself can only breed stress and disappointment.

Most of Neugarten's subjects, however, fared far better, displaying what she called *integrated personalities*. As she sees it, the key to successful ageing lies in maintaining one's dignity, self-confidence and optimism while accepting the inevitability of growing old. This seems by far the most common pattern. Given the youth orientation of most European societies, it may be easy to imagine that the elderly are generally unhappy. But research suggests that, while personal adjustments and problems are inevitable, the experience of growing old may also provide positive experiences – many old people do not even see themselves as old. As they say, 'I don't feel old' (Thompson, Ibsen and Auerldstern, 1990). A European survey of the elderly found that only one in five were not satisfied with their lives, whilst two out of three reported they were very busy or leading full lives (Walker and Maltby, 1997: 23, 122).

● Some problems of the elderly

The transition from working life to retirement has been romanticised in European cultures, but retirement poses some problems for many older people. Moreover, elderly people are also more likely than the whole population to experience social isolation, poverty and abuse. Finally, as popular culture enshrines the value of youth, the elderly encounter discrimination and ageism.

Retirement

The pattern of work is changing in industrial societies, and there is a pronounced tendency for people to retire at earlier and earlier ages – sometimes by choice,

sometimes through compulsory redundancies. Although the idea of retirement is familiar to us, it is actually a recent creation, becoming commonplace only in industrial societies during the last century (Atchley, 1982). Advancing technology reduces the need for everyone to work, as well as placing a premium on up-to-date skills. Retirement permits younger workers, who presumably have the most current knowledge and training, to predominate in the labour force. Some of the lowering of retirement ages may be linked to the growth of unemployment – stimulating early retirement polices in many countries (Laczo and Walker, 1985). The establishment of private and public pension schemes provided the economic foundation for retirement. In poor societies that depend on the labour of everyone, and where no pension schemes exist, most people work until they become incapacitated.

Work provides not only earnings; it also figures prominently in our personal identity. Hence, retirement from paid work usually brings a significant reduction in income and sometimes entails a diminished status and even a loss of purpose in life (Chown, 1977).

Class differences are often important in retirement. Working class retirement may often lack 'an active concept of retirement', whereas middle class retirement – with better resources – has led to an expanding consumer market and culture (Fennell, Phillipson and Evers, 1988: 83). For many older people, fresh activities and new interests minimise the personal disruption and loss of prestige brought on by retirement. They join what Peter Laslett has called the third age – a time of active leisure. Volunteer work can be personally rewarding, allowing individuals to apply their career skills to new challenges and opportunities. But for others, and especially older women, this might be little more than a 'bourgeois option, unavailable to those who have low incomes and poor health' (Arber and Ginn, 1995: 8)

Around the world, there is little agreement as to when (or even if) a person should retire from paid work. In the light of such variability, one might wonder if a society should formally designate any specific age for retirement. Vast differences in the interests and capacities of older people make the notion of a fixed retirement age controversial. In the United States, as a result, Congress began phasing out mandatory retirement policies in the 1970s and virtually ended the practice by 1987. It is one of the few countries that have legislated against age discrimination – France, Spain, Canada, New Zealand and Australia being others (Walker and Maltby, 1997: 80).

In Europe, men more than women have faced the transition of retirement. Elderly women who spend their lives as homemakers do not retire *per se*, though the departure of the last child from home serves as a rough parallel. As the proportion of women in the labour force continues to rise, of course, both women and men will experience the changes brought on by retirement.

Social isolation

One of the most apparent concerns of the elderly is being 'old and alone' (Tunstall, 1966): there is a problem of both potential isolation and loneliness. Retirement may cut the old off from friends and workmates; the death of a spouse may leave the old on their own; and illness may bring limited mobility and a reduced chance to meet others. In Europe, '15% of those aged 60–4 live alone. This percentage doubles for those 70–4 and is almost 48% for those aged over 80' (Walker and Maltby, 1997: 13). This is much more likely in the northern states (the UK, The Netherlands, France, Belgium) and less likely in the southern states (Greece, Portugal and Spain). But living alone is not the same as feeling lonely. Indeed, in the European survey, loneliness almost runs in reverse to living alone (Table 14.1). The elderly in Portugal and Greece are more likely to feel lonely, and those living in Germany, the UK and Denmark are least likely (Walker and Maltby, 1997: 26). And whilst many do live alone, most old people seem to keep regular contact with

their children – either by phone or by living near to them. It is what one writer has called 'Intimacy at a distance' (Rosenmayer and Kockeis, 1963).

One of the greatest causes of social isolation is the inevitable death of significant others. Few human experiences affect people as profoundly as the death of a spouse or family member. One study found that almost three-quarters of widows and widowers cited loneliness as their most serious problem (Lund, 1989). Widows and widowers must rebuild their lives in the glaring absence of people with whom, in many instances, they spent most of their adult lives. Some survivors choose not to live at all. One study of elderly men noted a sharp increase in mortality, sometimes by suicide, in the months following the death of their wives (Benjamin and Wallis, 1963).

But there are other problems of isolation. Modern societies have often made going out very difficult for the elderly. There is, for instance, a growing concern about 'crime' amongst the elderly often associated with a 'fear of crime'. This often means they become housebound. In The Netherlands, more than half those aged 65 or over no longer go out after dark; in Denmark, two-fifths of women aged 60 or over are afraid of being exposed to violence in the evening. Large numbers of old people are thus becoming stranded in their own homes.

The problem of social isolation falls most heavily on women, who typically outlive their husbands. Over 40 per cent of older women (especially the 'older elderly') live alone, compared to 16 per cent of older men. As with everything to do with old age, it is strongly structured by gender (Arber and Ginn, 1997).

Poverty and inequalities

For most people in Europe, retirement leads to a significant decline in income. While some of the elderly are quite affluent (a new category – 'woopies', well off older persons, has started to appear!), many lack sufficient savings or pension benefits to be self-supporting. John A. Vincent has argued that

The inequalities in the rest of society are reproduced in old age, and appear to be amplified. After retirement, the inequalities resulting from low pay, unemployment, disability, ill health, sex discrimination and racial discrimination are carried through into old age. The decline in the value of savings and pensions . . . means the worst off are the very old. (1996: 23–4)

Table 14.1 ● Old and lonely: proportion of older people who often feel lonely by country (percentages)

Percentage feeling lonely often	Country
< 5	Denmark
5–9	Germany, The Netherlands, the UK
10–14	Belgium, France, Ireland, Luxemburg, Spain
15–19	Italy
20 or more	Portugal, Greece (36%)

Source: Walker and Maltby, 1997

Figure 14.3 ● (a) Feminisation ratio, 1992 (EUR 12); (b) Feminisation ratio in the 0–19 and 60+ age groups, 1992

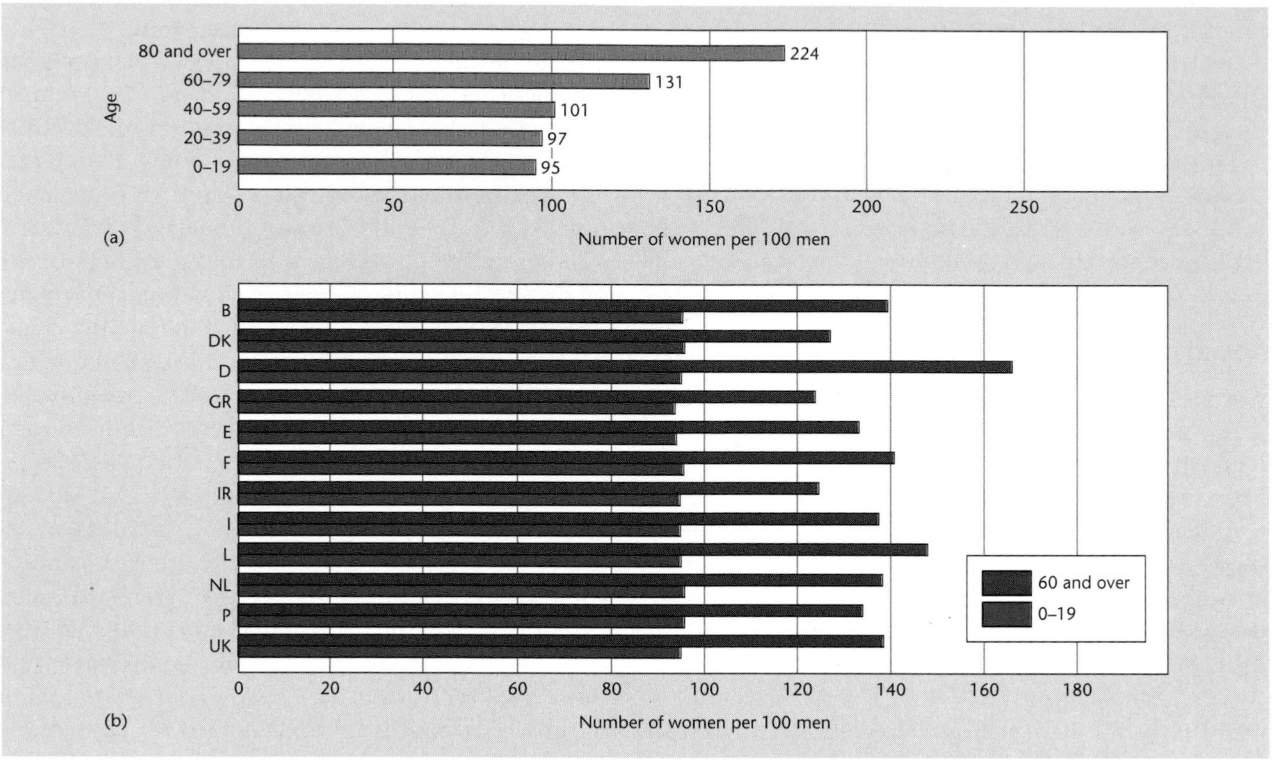

(a)

(b)

Source: *Women and Men in Europe: A Statistical Portrait*, Office for Official Publications of the European Community, Eurostat: (1995), p. 13

He argues that the elderly are the most disadvantaged in society, and yet they are often excluded from mainstream studies of class and inequality. Simple matters like income invariably decrease. There is a systematic curve that shows that income starts low in early life, increases until middle age and then declines through later years. Citing evidence from the General Household Survey, Vincent shows that the income of men over 74 in the UK may drop an average of £80 per week, whilst a woman's may drop nearly £60 (Vincent, 1996: 22). More of their income has to be spent on the 'bare necessities' of life: food, fuel, housing. And the older one gets, the poorer one becomes.

Throughout Europe a major source of income for the elderly is the pension. Generally, this is a two-tier system: public and private (usually an occupational pension). The latter is much more available to men, once again reinforcing the weaker position of women in old age. The value of this often decreases over time,

so the elderly become relatively poorer. Only Denmark, Finland and Sweden have a universal flat rate pension as a right of citizenship with no distinctions based on age or gender built into it (Walker and Maltby, 1997: 45), though at the time of writing, the Swedish system is undergoing radical reform.

Poverty rates also rise significantly as people enter old age, making an increasing gap between the wealthy elderly and the poor elderly. The UK stands out in this polarisation of groups (Walker and Maltby, 1997: 48), and it has been much studied since the pioneering work of Peter Townsend. Looking at Europe generally, the European Observatory on Ageing has concluded that although the living standards of older people have generally been rising in recent years, there are wide differences across countries. In general, there are low poverty rates in Denmark, Germany, Ireland and Luxembourg; medium poverty rates in Belgium, France, Italy and The Netherlands; and the countries with the highest poverty rates are Greece, Portugal, Spain and the UK. This said, however, when compared with the poverty rates found in the United States, all these levels are relatively low. One study ranking poverty levels gives Norway an index of 4.8 (low), the UK an index of UK 8.8 (middling) and the United States as an index of 16.9 (high) (Vincent, 1996: 28).

In Europe, then, although many elderly are faring better than ever before, growing old (especially among women and other minorities) still means a growing risk of poverty, one that is feminised (more women experience it) and polarised (there is a sharp divide between the poor old and the wealthy old). What is distinctive about the deprivation of the elderly, however, is that it is often hidden from view. Because of personal pride and a desire to maintain the dignity of independent living, many elderly people conceal financial problems, even from their own families. It is often difficult for people who have supported their children for years to admit that they can no longer provide for themselves, even though it may be through no fault of their own.

Abuse of the elderly

Problems of family violence became increasingly recognised in Europe during the 1970s and the 1980s. First came 'wife battering', then 'child abuse' (see Chapter 17: 'Families'). Most recently, an increasing number of researchers have noticed the phenomenon of 'granny battering' – or elder abuse. Abuse of older people takes many forms, from passive neglect to active torment, and includes verbal, emotional, financial and physical harm. Research suggests that between 3 and 4 per cent of elderly people (mainly women) suffer serious maltreatment each year and three times as many sustain abuse at some point. Like family violence against children or women, it is difficult to determine how widespread abuse of the elderly is because victims are understandably reluctant to talk about their plight. But as the proportion of elderly people rises, so does the incidence of abuse (Bruno, 1985; Clark, 1986; Glendenning, 1993; Pillemer, 1988; Holmstrom, 1994). Nevertheless, most elderly people suffer from none of these things, and it has been suggested that these figures may be very unreliable (Whittaker, 1997).

What motivates people to abuse the elderly? Often the cause lies in the stress of caring – financially and emotionally – for ageing parents. Today's middle-aged adults represent a 'sandwich generation' who may well spend as much time caring for their ageing parents as for their own children. This caregiving responsibility is especially pronounced among adult women who not only look after parents and children but hold down jobs as well.

Even in Japan – where tradition demands that adult children care for ageing parents at home – more and more people find themselves unable to cope with the caregiving role. Abuse appears to be most common where the stresses are greatest: in families with a very old person suffering from serious health problems. Here, family life may be grossly distorted by demands and tensions that caregivers simply cannot endure, even if their intentions are good (Douglass, 1983; Gelman, 1985; Yates, 1986).

Ageism and discrimination

In earlier chapters, we explained how ideology – including racism and sexism – seeks to justify the social disadvantages of minorities. Sociologists use the parallel term **ageism** to designate *prejudice and discrimination against the elderly*. Like racism and sexism, ageism can be blatant (as when individuals deny elderly women or men a job simply because of their age) or subtle (as when people speak to the elderly with a condescending tone, as if they were children) (Kalish, 1979). Also, like racism and sexism, ageism builds physical traits into stereotypes; in the case of the elderly, people consider greying hair, wrinkled skin and stooped posture as signs of personal incompetence. Negative stereotypes picture the aged as helpless, confused, resistant to change and generally unhappy (Butler, 1975). Even sentimental notions of sweet little old ladies and charmingly eccentric old gentlemen gloss over older people's individuality, their distinct personalities and their long years of experience and accomplishment (Bytheway, 1995).

Ageism, like other expressions of prejudice, may have some foundation in reality. Statistically speaking, old people are more likely than young people to be mentally and physically impaired. But we slip into ageism when we make unwarranted generalisations about an entire category of people, most of whom do not conform to the stereotypes. Recently Betty Friedan, a pioneer of the contemporary feminist movement, asserted that ageism is central to our culture. The box takes a closer look at this issue.

The elderly: a minority?

As a category of people in this country, the elderly do face social disadvantages. But sociologists disagree as to whether the aged form a minority in the same way as, say, Asian Europeans or people with disabilities do. Leonard Breen (1960) was the first to pronounce the elderly a minority, noting that older people have a clear social identity based on their age and, as a category, are subject to prejudice and discrimination. Yet, Gordon Streib (1968) countered, minority status is

usually both permanent and exclusive. That is, a person is an Asian or a woman *for life* and cannot become part of the dominant category of white males. Being elderly, Streib continued, is an *open* status because, first, people are elderly for only part of their lives and, second, everyone who has the good fortune to live long enough eventually grows old.

Streib made a further point. The social disadvantages faced by the elderly are less substantial than those experienced by the minorities described in earlier chapters. For example, old people have never been deprived of the right to own property, to vote or to hold office, as Asian Europeans and women have. Some elderly people, of course, do suffer economic

---

DIFFERENT VOICES

The fountain of ageing

In 1953, the French philosopher Simone de Beauvoir published a best-selling book, *The Second Sex* (orig. 1949 in France) in which she argued that women were defined in and through men as 'the other'. Ten years later, American author Betty Friedan argued in *The Feminine Mystique* that Western societies defined women only in sexual relation to men – as wives, mothers or sex objects. Thirty years later, having long established their feminist voices, both Friedan and de Beauvoir issued another call for change, this time in the way we view the elderly.

Surveying the mass media, Friedan concluded that elderly people are still conspicuous by their absence; only a small percentage of television shows, for example, feature central characters who are over 60. In addition, when members of many Western societies do think about older people, it is in negative terms: the elderly lack jobs, have lost

their vitality and look back to their youth. In short, the 'ageing mystique' is that we define being old as little more than a disease, marked by decline and deterioration, for which there is no cure.

This culture-based ageism is as widespread as it is powerful. Why do we still equate being old with living in an institution? Why do social service agencies foster dependency in older

Betty Friedan

Source: Gamma-Liaison, Inc. – Stephen Castagneto

people rather than encouraging them to live – actively and independently – in society's mainstream?

Responding to this pervasive pessimism, Friedan claims that it is time we started seeking the 'fountain of ageing' by highlighting the potential and possibilities of this stage of life. All over North America and Europe, older people are discovering that they have more to contribute than others give them credit for. Playing in orchestras, assisting small business owners, designing housing for the poor, teaching children to read – there are countless ways in which older people can enhance their own lives by engaging people around them. The bottom line, concludes Friedan, is that people do not stop living when they grow old; they grow old when they stop living. ●

Source: based on Friedan, 1993. See also de Beauvoir, 1971, and Bytheway, 1995: 33–6.

disadvantages, but these do not stem primarily from old age. Instead, most of the aged poor also happen to fall into categories of people likely to be poor at any age. To Streib, the truth is that 'the poor grow old', *not* that 'the old grow poor'.

In light of this reasoning, and the rising economic fortunes of the elderly, it seems reasonable to conclude that old people are not a minority in the same sense as, say, Asian Europeans and women are. Perhaps the best way to describe the elderly is simply as a distinctive segment of our population with characteristic pleasures and challenges. In sum, growing old involves numerous problems and transitions. Some are brought on by physical decline. But others – including social isolation, adjustment to retirement, risk of poverty, abuse by family members and ageism – are social problems. In the next section, we will delve into various theoretical perspectives on how society shapes the lives of the elderly.

● Theoretical analysis of ageing

Each of sociology's major theoretical paradigms sheds light on the process of ageing in Europe. We examine each in turn.

Functional analysis: ageing and disengagement

In the early 1960s, Cumming and Henry (1961) developed one of the first social theories of ageing. Based on the ideas of Talcott Parsons – an architect of the functional paradigm – they argued that ageing threatens society with disruption as physical decline and death take their toll. Society's response, they claim, is to *disengage* the elderly – to gradually transfer statuses and roles from the old to the young so that tasks are performed with minimal interruption.

Disengagement is thus a strategy to promote the orderly functioning of society by removing ageing people from productive roles while they are still able to perform them. Such disengagement has an added benefit in a rapidly changing society, because young workers typically have the most up-to-date skills and training. Formally, then, **disengagement theory** is *the proposition that society enhances its orderly operation by disengaging people from positions of responsibility as they reach old age.*

Disengagement may benefit elderly people as well as society. Ageing individuals with diminishing capac-

Simone de Beauvoir, April 1983, aged 78.

Source: Popperfoto

ities presumably look forward to relinquishing some of the pressures of their jobs in favour of new pursuits of their own choosing (Palmore, 1979b). Society also grants older people greater freedom, so that unusual behaviour on their part is construed as harmless eccentricity rather than dangerous deviance.

Although this is an old theory, it is still widely cited because some see it as explaining why rapidly changing, industrial societies typically define their oldest members as socially marginal. But it is largely rejected, and for four reasons. First, many workers cannot readily disengage from paid work because they do not have sufficient financial security to fall back on. Second, many elderly people – regardless of their financial circumstances – do not wish to disengage from their productive roles. Disengagement, after all, comes at a high price, including loss of social prestige and social isolation. Third, there is no compelling evidence that the benefits of disengagement outweigh its costs to society, which range from the loss of human resources to the increased care of people who might otherwise be able to fend better for themselves. Indeed, as the numbers of elderly people swell, devising ways to help seniors remain independent is a high national priority.

Then, too, any useful system of disengagement would have to take account of the widely differing abilities of the elderly themselves. But fourth, and perhaps most significant, it makes the elderly appear too passive and too much like victims. And many studies show this is not true.

Humanistic analysis: activity and biography

This latter criticism is picked up by the symbolic-interaction paradigm. **Activity theory** is *the proposition that a high level of activity enhances personal satisfaction in old age*. Because all individuals build their social identities from statuses and roles, this theory maintains, disengagement in old age is bound to undermine the satisfaction and meaning many elderly people find in their lives. What seniors need, in short, are productive and recreational activities that imbue their retirement with meaning and joy.

Activity theory proposes that, to the extent that elderly people do disengage, they substitute new roles and responsibilities for the ones they leave behind. The elderly pursue active lives as much as the young do. Indeed, study after study suggests the importance to the elderly of following their interests, remaining engaged with daily activities and relationships, etc. (Havighurst, Neugarten and Tobin, 1968; Neugarten, 1977; Palmore, 1979a; Moen, Dempster-McClain and Williams, 1992).

Activity theory thus shifts the focus of analysis from the needs of society (as stated in disengagement theory) to the needs of the elderly themselves. This second approach also highlights social diversity among elderly people, which is an important consideration in formulating any government policy.

However, from a functionalist point of view, this approach tends to exaggerate the well-being and competence of the elderly. Functionalists might ask if we really want elderly people actively serving in crucial roles, say, as physicians or airline pilots. From another perspective, activity theory falls short by overlooking the fact that many of the problems that beset older people have more to do with how society, not any individual, operates.

The biographical approach

Of growing interest to both gerontologists and sociologists in recent times has been a biographical approach to ageing. This is a humanistic approach that aims to listen to the stories of the lives of the elderly. Three types can be distinguished.

First is the *reminiscence* story. Gerontologists have found that a characteristic of many elderly is their desire to tell, and tell again, some key highlights of their life. These can perform important functions both practically for the researcher – in providing key jumping off points for further questions – but also therapeutically, since the telling of these stories is often an important part of the elderly person's adjustment process.

Second is the *oral history*. Here the life is told in order to throw light on the times of the elderly person. Stories of the Second – or First – World War; stories of the Depression; stories of illegitimate children and the problem this led to. All this and more help provide the oral historian fill out the portraits of the historical past (see Thompson, 1990). Closely allied to this is the gathering of a family history. (These days, many bookshops provide rather elaborate 'family history' albums that facilitate this.)

Third, is the *sociological life history*. Here the life is told through a series of stages and themes which help us understand the workings of a life over the life course. Does the life, for instance, fit into the stages discussed in Chapter 5 of this book? What might be the life's major organising themes – possibly linked to power, intimacy, work, play and love.

Conflict analysis: ageing and inequality

Conflict theories highlight how different age categories compete for scarce social resources, a fact that contributes to age stratification. By and large, middle-aged people in Europe enjoy the greatest social privileges, while the elderly (as well as children) contend with less power and prestige and face a higher risk of poverty. Employers often shunt elderly workers aside in favour of younger men and women as a means of keeping down wages. As a consequence, conflict theorists note, older people become second-class citizens (Atchley, 1982; Phillipson, 1982).

To conflict theorists, age-based hierarchy is inherent in industrial-capitalist society. Capitalist culture has an overriding concern with profit, and hence facilitates the devaluation of those categories of people who are economically unproductive. Viewed as mildly deviant because they are less productive than their younger counterparts, the elderly are destined to be marginal members of a society consumed by material gain. In recent years, a cluster of British sociologists – Townsend, Walker, Phillipson and Vincent – have all highlighted the links between old age, dependency, divisions of labour and structures of inequality. The key to their work is the idea of **structured dependency**: *the process by which some people in society receive an unequal share in the results of social production* (Vincent, 1996: 186). Originally, in the work of Townsend and Walker, this referred to material dependency and focused upon the ways the elderly were structured out of work and into low incomes and poverty, and how this was reflected in welfare, health and care policies generally. More recently, it has become concerned with interpersonal dependence; with the ways the elderly are often infantilised into a form of helplessness, and how they may become segregated not only in institutions but also in the growing practices of keeping the elderly 'off the streets'. New dependencies can exclude the old from an autonomous 'normal' life.

Conflict analysis also draws attention to social diversity in the elderly population. Differences of class, ethnicity and gender splinter older people as they do everyone else. Those in higher social classes have far more economic security, greater access to top-flight medical care and more options for personal satisfaction in old age than others do. Likewise, elderly WASPs typically enjoy a host of advantages denied to older minorities. For ethnic groups, ageing is confounded by 'triple jeopardy': because they are old, usually poor and also black. And throughout this chapter we have seen how women – who represent an increasing majority of the elderly population with advancing age – experience the social and economic disadvantages of both ageism and sexism (Arber and Ginn, 1995).

Critical evaluation
Social-conflict theory adds to our understanding of the ageing process by underscoring age-based inequality and explaining how capitalism devalues elderly people who are less productive. The implication of this analysis is that the aged fare better in non-capitalist societies, a view that has some support in research (Treas, 1979).

One shortcoming of this approach goes right to its core contention: rather than blame *capitalism* for the lower social standing of elderly people, critics hold

A sign of the future? Two centenarians.

Source: *Observer*, 15 June 1997, p. 3; Photo: Antonio Olmos

that *industrialisation* is the true culprit. Thus, they claim, socialism does little to lessen age stratification. Furthermore, the notion that capitalism dooms the elderly to economic distress is challenged by the steady rise in the income of the elderly population in recent decades.

● Death and dying

To every thing there is a season,
And a time for every matter under heaven:
A time to be born and a time to die . . .

These well-known lines from the Book of Ecclesiastes in the Bible convey two basic truths about human existence: the fact of birth and the inevitability of death. Just as life varies in striking ways across history and around the world, so does death. We conclude this chapter with a brief look at the changing character of death – the final stage in the process of growing old.

Historical patterns of death

Throughout most of human history, confronting death was commonplace. No one assumed that a newborn child would live for long, a fact that led parents

CONTROVERSY AND DEBATE

When is the time to die? The 'right to die' debate

Because death struck at any time, often without warning, our ancestors would have found the question 'Can people live too long?' to be absurd. But as increasing numbers of people live longer and longer, new questions arise about the best time and ways to die. One issue is the right of the elderly (and terminally ill) to die when they choose – the euthanasia debate. Another issue concerns the medical prolonging of life. While there is widespread support for using technology to prolong life, the high cost of nursing care for the elderly puts impossible burdens on the health service, prompting people to wonder how much old age we can now afford.

Recent decades, with a surge in the elderly population, have thus generated major new ethical debates. The question of how we die – by natural causes, by self-inducement or by physician assisted death (PAD) – is on the worldwide agenda. And it is an issue that divides philosophers, doctors, ethicists, politicians and religious leaders around the world. In The Netherlands, whilst not 'legalised', PAD is allowed. And for a short while in 1997, in the Northern Territory of Australia, it was legalised (but only for seven months – before it was recriminalised due to public outcry). In the same year in the UK, a 47-year-old woman with motor neurone disease received her doctor's assistance in easing her death, prompting a British Medical Association enquiry. Everywhere these issues are arriving on the agenda of public debate.

In the United States, Derek Humphrey is a founder and executive director of the Hemlock Society. Since 1980, this organisation has offered support and practical assistance to people who wish to die. Humphrey argues that the time has come for people to have straightforward information about how to end their own lives. Hence he published the book *Final Exit* – a 'suicide, how to' manual that gives specific instructions for killing (swallowing sleeping pills, self-starvation, suffocation etc.). It was an immediate and remarkably popular best-seller – especially among the elderly – suggesting that millions of people agree with him. Not surprisingly, when *Final Exit* was published, it sparked controversy. While supporters view the work as a humane effort to assist people who are painfully and terminally ill, critics claim that it encourages suicide by people who are experiencing only temporary depression (Angelo, 1991).

But the appearance of *Final Exit* also raises broader questions that are no less disturbing and controversial. Older people are, on the one hand, fearful of not being able to afford the medical care they may need and, on the other, alarmed at the prospect of losing control of their lives to a medical establishment that often seeks to prolong life at any cost. People of all ages worry

to delay naming children until they had survived for a year or two. For those fortunate enough to survive infancy, illness prompted by poor nutrition, accidents and natural catastrophes such as drought or famine combined to make life uncertain, at best.

In times of great need, death was often deliberate, the result of a strategy to protect the majority by sacrificing a group's least productive members. *Infanticide* is the killing of new-born infants; *geronticide*, by contrast, is the killing of the elderly.

If death was routine, it was also readily accepted. Medieval Christianity assured Europeans, for example, that death fitted into the divine plan for human existence. To illustrate, historian Philippe Ariès describes how Sir Lancelot, one of King Arthur's fearless Knights of the Round Table, prepared for his own death when he believed himself mortally wounded:

> His gestures were fixed by old customs, ritual gestures which must be carried out when one is about to die. He removed his weapons and lay quietly upon the ground. . . . He spread his arms out, his body forming a cross . . . in such a way that his head faced east toward Jerusalem. (1974: 7–8)

As societies gradually gained control over many causes of death, death became less of an everyday occurrence. Fewer children died at birth, and accidents and

whether the health-care system can meet the escalating demands of seniors only by short-changing the young.

Against the spiralling costs of prolonging life, then, we may well have to ask if what is technically possible is necessarily socially desirable. As we enter the next century, warns gerontologist Daniel Callahan, a surging elderly population ready and eager to extend their lives will eventually force us either to 'pull the plug' on old age or to short-change everyone else. Raising this issue highlights the problem of priorities and selectivity in the health service. Callahan makes a bold case for limits. He reasons, first, that to spend more on behalf of the elderly we must spend less on others. With a serious problem of poverty among children, he asks, can we continue to direct more money toward the needs of the oldest members of our society at the expense of those just growing up?

Second, Callahan reminds us, a longer life does not necessarily make for a better life. Costs aside, does stressful heart surgery that may prolong

the life of an 84-year-old person by a year or two truly improve quality of life? Costs considered, would those resources yield more 'quality of life' if used, say, to transplant a kidney into a 10-year-old boy? Third, Callahan urges us to reconsider our notion of death. Today many people rage against death as an enemy to be conquered at all costs. Yet, he suggests, a sensible health-care programme for an ageing society must acknowledge death as a natural end to the life course. If we cannot make peace with death for our own well-being, limited financial resources demand that we do so for the benefit of others.

A compelling counterpoint, of course, is that those people who have worked all their lives to make our society what it is should, in their final years, enjoy society's generosity. Moreover, in light of our tradition of personal independence and responsibility, can we ethically deny an ageing individual medical care that this person is able and willing to pay for? What Is clear from everyone's point of view is that, in

the next century, we will face questions that few would have imagined even 50 years ago. Is optimum longevity good for everyone? Is it even possible for everyone?

● **Continue the debate:**

1. Should governments devise legislation to permit euthanasia? If yes, what safeguards need to be incorporated?

2. Evaluate the suggestion that doctors and hospitals should devise a double standard, offering more complete care to younger people but more limited care to society's oldest members.

3. Do you think we have a cultural avoidance of death that drives us to extend life at all costs?

4. Is the idea of rationing medical care really new? Hasn't our society historically done exactly this by allowing some people to amass more wealth than others? ●

Sources: Callahan, 1987; Humphrey, 1991.

---

disease took a smaller toll among adults. Except in times of war or catastrophe, people came to view dying as quite *extra*ordinary, except among the very old. In 1900, about one-third of all deaths in Europe occurred before the age of 5, another third occurred before the age of 55, and the remaining one-third of men and women died in what was then defined as old age. By 1995, 85 per cent of our population died *after* the age of 55. Thus death and old age have become fused in our culture.

The modern separation of life and death

Now removed from everyday experience, death seems to us unnatural. If social conditions prepared our

ancestors to accept their deaths, modern society, with its youth culture and aggressive medical technology, has fostered a desire for immortality, or eternal youth. In this sense, death has become separated from life.

Death is also *physically* removed from everyday activities. The clearest evidence of this is that many of us have never seen a person die. While our ancestors typically died at home in the presence of family and friends, most deaths today occur in impersonal settings such as hospitals and nursing homes. Even hospitals commonly relegate dying patients to a special part of the building, and hospital morgues are located well out of sight of patients and visitors alike (Sudnow, 1967; Ariès, 1974).

documents the changing fortunes of the elderly in a classic study and shows the importance of reciprocity and intergenerational attachment.

Robert N. Butler, *Why Survive? Being Old in America* (New York: Harper & Row, 1975).

> This Pulitzer Prize winning book coined the term 'ageism' and launched a growing social movement critical of society's approach to ageing.

More advanced reading

Sara Arber and Jay Ginn (eds), *Connecting Gender and Ageing: A Sociological Approach* (Buckingham: Open University Press, 1995).

> Looks at the differential social effects of ageing on women's and men's roles, relationships and identity.

Ken Blakemore and Margaret Boneham, *Age, Race and Ethnicity: A Comparative Approach* (Buckingham: Open University Press, 1993).

> The first definitive study of ageing among black and Asian people in Britain.

Jennie Keith et al., *The Ageing Experience: Diversity and Commonality Across Cultures*, (London: Sage, 1994).

> Compares the experience of the elderly in Ireland, Botswana, the USA and Hong Kong.

Anne Jamieson, Sarah Harper and Christian Victor (eds), *Critical Approaches to Ageing and Later Life* (Buckingham: Open University Press, 1997).

> An up to date series of essays by 'advanced' experts in the field, who engage with all the latest debates.

John A. Vincent, *Inequality and Old Age* (London: UCL Press, 1996).

> Focuses sharply on the elderly as a major, but neglected, pattern of inequality and provides both theory and evidence to support this claim.

Alan Walker and Tony Maltby, *Ageing Europe* (Buckingham: Open University Press, 1997).

> Using research from the EU's 'Observatory on Ageing and Older People' and Eurobarometer surveys of both attitudes to the elderly in Europe and the attitudes of the elderly, this is an up-to-date review of the situation of the elderly across the EU.

World Bank, *Averting the Old Age Crisis: Policies to Protect the Old and Promote Growth* (Oxford: Oxford University Press, 1994).

> World figures and world analysis of the impending problems.

Other sources

Age Concern, The National Council on Ageing, 1268 London Road, London SW16 4ER; phone 0181 679 8000; fax 0181 679 6069.

> This agency works to improve the quality of life for older people in the UK, publishing books and research on the elderly via the Age Concern Institute of Gerontology at King's College London.

The Centre for Policy on Ageing, at 25–31 Ironmonger Row, London EC1V 3QP, has a 'state of the art' database, held on CD ROM; phone 0171 253 1787.

part four

Social Institutions

chapter fifteen

Source: Popperfoto

The Economy, Consumption and Work

Take a few minutes, and think about what you have eaten in the last few days. Do you know where each item was produced? The chances are that many minimally processed products you may have eaten, such as fresh fruit and vegetables, were imported from countries on the other side of the globe. More heavily processed products, from chocolates to frozen meals, probably included ingredients produced and processed by many groups of people from many different countries, some of whom have prospered by selling the product you ate and some of whom themselves are worrying when they may get their next meal. If you were to trace the processes of producing each of the items you consumed in your last meal, Harvey reflects, you would discover:

a relation of dependence upon a whole world of social labour conducted in many different places under very different relations and conditions of production. That dependency expands even further when we consider the materials and goods used in the production of goods we directly consume. Yet we can in practice consume our meal without the slightest knowledge of the intricate geography of production and the myriad social relationships that puts it upon our table. (Harvey, 1990).

For better or worse, the products we use each day have become part of a cycle of international exchange which is reshaping the way people around the world live and work.

This chapter explores the operation and significance of the economy, widely considered to be the most influential of all social institutions. We also will investigate the changing character of work in today's world and note how the economies of the world are now more closely interconnected than ever before.

● The economy: historical overview

The **economy** is *the social institution that organises the production, distribution and consumption of goods and services.* To call the economy an 'institution' implies that it functions in an established manner that is predictable, at least in its general outlines. This is not to say the economy operates to everyone's liking, of course, and sociologists debate the merits of particular economic arrangements as they critically examine the shape and scope of the other social institutions. *Goods* are commodities ranging from necessities (such as food, clothing and shelter) to luxury items (such as cars, swimming pools and yachts). *Services* refer to valued activities that benefit others (including the work of religious leaders, doctors, police officers and telephone operators).

We value goods and services because they ensure survival or because they make life easier, more interesting or more aesthetically pleasing. The things we produce and consume are also important to our self-image and social identity. How goods and services are distributed, then, shapes the lives of everyone in a number of basic ways.

The complex economies that mark modern industrial societies are themselves the product of centuries of technological innovation. The following sections highlight three technological revolutions that reorganised the means of production and, in the process, brought sweeping changes to many other dimensions of social life.

The Agricultural Revolution

As Chapter 3 ('Society') explained, members of the earliest human societies relied on hunting and gathering to live off the land. In these technologically simple societies, there was no distinct economy; rather, production, distribution and consumption of goods were all dimensions of family life.

The development of agriculture about 5,000 years ago brought revolutionary change to these societies. Agriculture emerged as people harnessed animals to ploughs, increasing the productive power of hunting and gathering more than tenfold. The resulting surplus freed some people in society from the demands of food production. Individuals began to adopt specialised economic roles, forging crafts, designing tools, raising animals and constructing dwellings.

With the development of agriculture under way, towns emerged, soon to be linked by networks of traders dealing in food, animals and other goods (Jacobs, 1970). These four factors – agricultural technology, productive specialisation, permanent settlements and trade – were the keys to a revolutionary expansion of the economy.

In the process, the world of work became distinct from family life, though production still occurred close to home. In medieval Europe, for instance, most people farmed nearby fields. Both country and city dwellers often laboured in their homes – a pattern called *cottage industry* – producing goods sold in frequent outdoor 'flea markets' (a term suggesting that not everything was of high quality).

The Industrial Revolution

By the middle of the eighteenth century, a second technological revolution was proceeding apace, first in England and soon afterward elsewhere in Europe and North America. The development of industry was to transform social life even more than agriculture had done thousands of years before. Industrialisation introduced five notable changes to the economies of Western societies.

1. *New forms of energy.* Throughout history, people derived energy from their own muscles or those of animals. Then, in 1765, James Watt pioneered the development of the steam engine. Surpassing muscle power a hundred times over, steam engines soon operated large machinery with unprecedented efficiency.

2. *The centralisation of work in factories.* Steam-powered machinery soon rendered cottage industries obsolete. Factories – centralised and impersonal workplaces separate from the home – proliferated. Work moved from the private sphere to the public sphere – that is, people 'went out to work'.

3. *Manufacturing and mass production.* Before the Industrial Revolution, most work involved cultivating and gathering raw materials, such as crops, wood and wool. The industrial economy shifted

most jobs into manufacturing that turned raw materials into a wide range of saleable products. For example, factories mass-produced timber into furniture and transformed wool into clothing.

4. *Specialisation*. Typically, a single skilled worker in a cottage industry fashioned a product from beginning to end. Factory work, by contrast, demands specialisation so that a labourer repeats a single task over and over again, making only a small contribution to the finished product. Thus as factories raised productivity, they also lowered the skill level of the average worker (Warner and Low, 1947). Deskilling occurred.

5. *Wage labour*. Instead of working for themselves or joining together as households, industrial workers entered factories as wage labourers. They sold their labour to strangers who often cared less for them than for the machines they operated. Supervision became routine and intense. Incomes were usually pitifully low and workers were hence subject to great exploitation.

The impact of the Industrial Revolution gradually rippled outwards from the factories to transform all of society. Whilst working conditions were very poor for many, greater productivity steadily raised the standard of living as countless new products and services filled an expanding marketplace. Especially at the outset, however, the benefits of industrial technology were shared very unequally. Some factory owners made vast fortunes, while the majority of industrial workers hovered perilously close to poverty. Children, too, worked in factories or deep in coal mines for pennies a day. Women factory workers, among the lowest paid, endured special hardships.

The Information Revolution and the postindustrial society

Industrialisation is by nature an ongoing process. In Europe and North America, workers gradually formed trades unions to represent their collective interests in negotiations with factory owners. During this century, governments outlawed child labour, forced wages upwards, improved workplace safety and extended schooling and political rights to a larger segment of the population.

The nature of production itself has also changed. By the middle of this century, most European countries were transforming into **postindustrial economies**, *productive systems based on service work and high technology*.

Automated machinery reduced the role of human labour in production, while bureaucracy simultaneously expanded the ranks of clerical workers and managers. There were few managers a century ago; now they account for up to a third of the labour force (Heilbroner, 1985). More broadly, service industries – such as public relations, health care, education, media, advertising, banking and sales – now employ the bulk of workers. Distinguishing the postindustrial era, then, is a shift from industrial work to service jobs.

Driving this economic change is a third technological transformation: the development of the computer. The *Information Revolution* in Europe, the United States, much of newly industrialising Asia and elsewhere is generating new kinds of information and new forms of communication, and changing the character of work just as factories did two centuries ago. The Information Revolution has unleashed three key changes.

1. *Tangible products to ideas*. The industrial era was defined by the production of goods; in the postindustrial era, work revolves around creating and manipulating symbols. Computer programmers, writers, financial analysts, advertising executives, architects and all sorts of consultants represent the workers of the Information Age.

2. *Mechanical skills to literacy skills*. Just as the Industrial Revolution offered opportunities to those who learned a mechanical trade, the Information Revolution demands that workers have literacy skills – the ability to speak, write and use computer technology. People who can communicate effectively enjoy new opportunities; those who cannot face declining prospects.

3. *Decentralisation of work away from factories*. Just as industrial technology (steam power driving massive machines) drew workers together into factories, computer technology now permits many people to work almost anywhere. Indeed, laptop computers and facsimile (fax) machines linked to telephone lines now make the home, a car or even a plane a 'virtual office'. New information technology, in short, is reversing the industrial trend and bringing about a return of home-based 'cottage industries'. The virtual workplace and 'telecommuting' is becoming a reality for many.

The need for face-to-face communication as well as the availability of supplies and information still keep most workers in the office. On the other hand, today's more educated and creative labour force no longer requires – and often resists – the close supervision that marked yesterday's factories.

Post-Fordism and disorganised capitalism

Capitalism is clearly changing its form, and this has been characterised as a shift in the flexibility of production: from Fordism to post-Fordism. At the turn of the twentieth century, the American car manufacturer Henry Ford developed the assembly line to produce cheap cars that could be purchased by the masses. **Fordism**, named after Ford's innovation, is *an economic system based on mass assembly line production, mass consumption and standardised commodities*. It depends upon dedicated machinery and tools producing identical components; centralised unskilled labour used intensively on specific tasks; and low cost production of vast quantities of goods. Workers do repetitive work over long periods: they are paid reasonably well and this increases their consumer spending. Fordism is technically limited and not very flexible.

Whilst Fordist production techniques have continued through much of the twentieth century, newer more flexible ones have emerged alongside them (especially in Japan and South-East Asia). This newer process has involved the following:

● shifts in production: more flexible systems of production
● more flexible time: part-time, temporary and self-employed workers
● decentralisation of labour into smaller, less hierarchical units
● 'just-in time' rapid production
● movement from standardised goods to goods including options
● gradual replacement of 'mass marketing and advertising' by 'niche marketing', targeted at specific groups
● globalisation, with a new international division of labour

Called **post-Fordism**, this is *a new economic system emerging mainly in the 1970s based on flexibility (rather than standardisation), specialisation and tailor-made goods*. We have already seen some of this at work in organisational forms in Chapter 7 (where they were identified as 'postmodern'). These modes are not just to be found in work practices, but in consumption in the home as well.

Sectors of the economy

The three revolutions just described reflect a shifting balance among the three sectors of a society's economy. The **primary sector** is *the part of the economy that generates raw materials directly from the natural environment*. The primary sector, which includes agriculture, animal husbandry, fishing, forestry and mining, predominates in preindustrial societies. Figure 15.1 indicates that 63 per cent of the economic output of low-income countries is produced by the primary sector. The importance of the primary sector declines with economic development. Thus, this sector represents 32 per cent of economic activity among middle-income nations and around 4 per cent of production among high-income areas like Europe. Indeed, in 1992, agriculture accounted for only 2.1 per cent of the European Union's Gross Domestic Product (GDP). In Greece it is as high as 10 per cent but in the UK it is as low as 1 per cent (Eurostat, 1995: 250). Everywhere it is in decline.

The **secondary sector** is *the part of the economy that transforms raw materials into manufactured goods*. This sector grows quickly as societies industrialise, just as

Figure 15.1 ● **The size of economic sectors by income level of country**

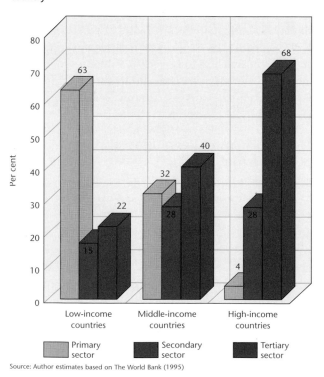

Source: Author estimates based on The World Bank (1995)

manufacturing surged in Europe during the first half of this century. Secondary-sector production includes the refining of petroleum and the use of metals to manufacture tools and automobiles. Employment levels in manufacturing in the EU fell from 27 million in 1980 to 21 million in 1993 (Eurostat, 1995: 288). Work in Eastern Europe remains more industrial and class based than in Western Europe today.

The **tertiary sector** is *the part of the economy that generates services rather than goods.* Accounting for just 22 per cent of economic output in low-income countries, the tertiary sector grows with industrialisation, and dominates the economies of high-income nations as they enter the postindustrial era. This marks the most significant change in modern economies. In 1970, manufacturing accounted for over 40 per cent of EU GDP; by 1992, the service sector was in the lead accounting for around 60 per cent of employment and GDP. In the United States, 70 per cent of the labour force are involved in some form of service work (cf. Eurostat, 1995: 319).

The global economy

As technology draws people around the world closer together, another important economic transformation is taking place. Recent decades have witnessed the emergence of a **global economy**, *economic activity spanning many nations of the world with little regard for national borders.* The development of a global economy has four main consequences. First, we are seeing a global division of labour by which each region of the world specialises in particular kinds of economic activity. As Map 15.1 shows, agriculture occupies

more than 70 per cent of the workforce in low-income countries. Map 15.2 indicates that industrial production

Map 15.1 ● Agricultural employment in global perspective
The primary sector of the economy predominates in societies that are least developed. Thus, in the poor countries of Africa and Asia, half, or even three-quarters, of all workers are farmers. This picture is altogether different among the world's most economically developed countries – including the United States, Canada, Great Britain, and Australia – which have less than 10 per cent of their work force in agriculture

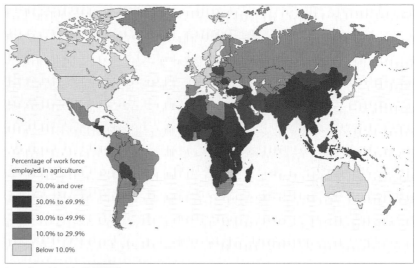

Source: *Peters Atlas of the World* (1990)

Map 15.2 ● Industrial employment in global perspective
The world's poor societies, by and large, have yet to industrialise. For this reason, in the countries of Latin America, Africa and Asia, a small proportion of the labour force engages in industrial work. The nations of Eastern Europe, along with the Russian Federation, have far more of their workers in industry. In the world's richest societies, we see a reversal of this trend, with more and more workers moving from industrial jobs to service work.

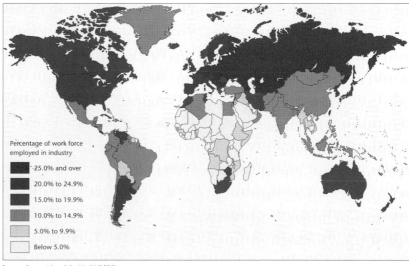

Source: *Peters Atlas of the World* (1990)

is concentrated in the middle- and high-income nations of the world. The economies of the richest nations, including Europe, now specialise in service-sector activity.

Second, an increasing number of products pass through the economies of more than one nation. Consider, for instance, that workers in Taiwan may manufacture shoes, which a Hong Kong distributor sends to Italy, where they receive the stamp of an Italian designer; another distributor in Rome forwards the shoes to New York, where they are sold in a department store owned by a firm with its headquarters in Tokyo. As Figure 15.2 shows, it takes many countries to produce a car.

Figure 15.2 ● Global manufacturing: the component network for the European model of Ford Escort

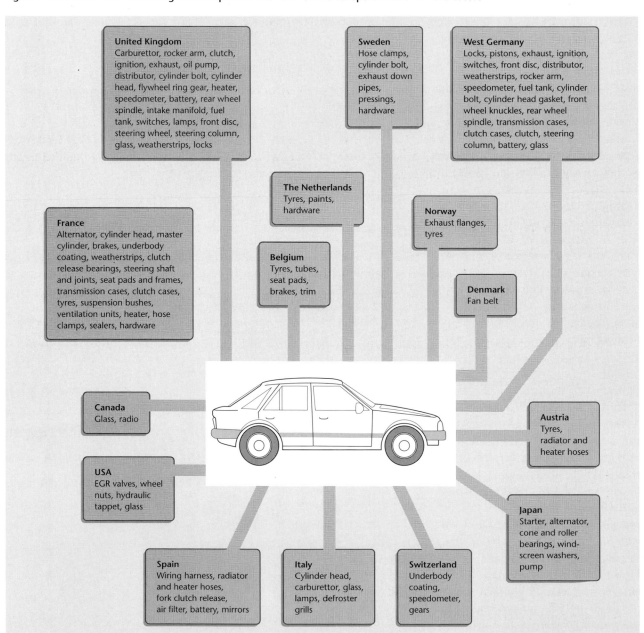

Source: Peter Dicken, *Global Shift*, New York: Harper and Row (1986), p. 304

A third consequence of the global economy is that national governments no longer control the economic activity that takes place within their borders. In fact, governments cannot even regulate the value of their national currencies, since money is now traded around the clock in the financial centres of Tokyo, London and New York. Global markets are one consequence of satellite communications that forge information links among the world's major cities. Indeed this gives rise to **global cities** (see Chapter 22).

The fourth consequence of the global economy is that a small number of businesses, operating internationally, now control a vast share of the world's economic activity. One estimate concludes that the 600 largest multinational companies account for fully half of the earth's entire total economic output (Kidron and Segal, 1991). The world is still divided into approximately 200 politically distinct nations. But, in light of the proliferation of international economic activity, 'nationhood' has lost much of its former significance.

● **Comparative economic systems**

Economies of the world can be analysed in terms of two abstract models – capitalism and socialism. No society has an economy that is either purely capitalist or purely socialist; these models represent two ends of a spectrum along which all actual economies can be located. Indeed, many countries move along this continuum in one direction or the other.

Most European countries have degrees of 'mixed economies'. They are neither pure capitalism nor pure planning, but a mixture of both which differs in each country. Sweden and the other Scandinavian countries are generally seen as an extreme version of the social market approach – highly interventionist, corporatist and planned. But they are on the process of being pulled towards the German model, which is more inclined towards a social market. The system in the UK was mixed until the advent of Thatcherism in 1979. But since then it has moved more and more towards a privatised market system, a system that the New Labour government of 1997 seems unlikely to change. In short, in Europe 'there has been considerable convergence around the German social market model' (Edye and Lintner, 1996: 183).

Capitalism

Capitalism refers to *an economic system in which natural resources and the means of producing goods and services are privately owned*. Ideally, a capitalist economy has three distinctive features.

Figure 15.3 ● GDPs for the United States, Japan and EU countries

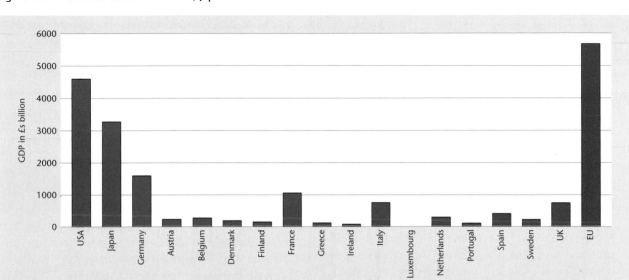

Source: Evans-Pritchard (1997), p. 7

Thatcherism, privatisation and markets: does 'the market' serve the public interest?

When Margaret Thatcher came to power in the UK in 1979, she started to revolutionise the way in which both the economy and the government were to be run. So influential was she that a whole ideology – **Thatcherism** – was named after her. Broadly, this is *a system of political beliefs based on free markets and economic individualism*. What she achieved was to radically shift the grounds of debate to a focus on the importance of market mechanisms. Before 1979, for example, very few people discussed health or education provision through market models. But it is a sign of her deep influence that the new Labour government of 1997 has actually continued to stress the importance of markets in many areas of life.

The debate is not a new one however. Thatcher just 'modernised' it for the UK. Historically, most European societies have had a mix of market and government intervention – hence, mixed economies. From 1946 to 1979, the British government regularly intervened in the economy, both through the welfare state and the through its extensive programme of nationalisation. The Scandinavian countries also had a pronounced 'welfare' and interventionist background. By contrast, US society has relied on 'the market' for most economic decisions: the market sets prices, as potential buyers and sellers bid for goods and services upwards or downwards in a changing balance of supply and demand.

With the rise of Thatcherism, the UK followed the US model – though even more intensely. It privatised all the nationalised industries (including telephones, water, gas, electricity and rail), and embarked on a programme to introduce internal markets into the welfare state (especially in health care and schools).

Defenders praise the market for encouraging choice, diversity and flexibility: in so doing, the market coordinates the efforts of countless people, each of whom – to return to Adam Smith's crucial insight – is motivated only by self-interest. It is also praised for discouraging some social bad habits such as racial prejudice. Industrialist J. P. Morgan once commented that, while he would sail only with a gentleman, he would do business with anyone – explicit acknowledgement that market transactions focus on value, not the social traits of traders. Economists Milton and Rose Friedman note that a more-or-less freely operating market system has provided many members of capitalist societies with an unprecedented economic standard of living.

But others celebrate the role of government in the operation of European economies. At one level, government steps in to accomplish some tasks that no one would do for profit. Even Adam Smith looked to government to defend the country against external enemies. Government also has a key role in constructing and maintaining public projects such as roads, utilities and schools. And in some countries the involvement of government goes much further – the Scandinavian countries probably take intervention further than in most other democratic, capitalist systems.

Free-marketeers such as the Friedmans counter that virtually any

1. *Private ownership of property*. A capitalist economy supports the right of individuals to own almost anything. The more capitalist an economy is, the more private ownership there is of wealth-producing property such as factories, real estate and natural resources. The downside of this can be a mass accumulation of profits by relatively few people, which can generate polarisation and cleavages between groups – the 'haves' and the 'have nots'. A potential for conflict is generated.

2. *Pursuit of personal profit*. A capitalist society encourages the accumulation of private property and defines a profit-minded orientation as natural and simply a matter of 'doing business'. Further,

task government undertakes, it performs inefficiently. They claim that the products we enjoy – such as computers, household appliances and the myriad offerings of supermarkets and shopping centres – are primarily products of the market. By contrast, the least-satisfying goods and services available today – and the Friedmans place schools, public transport and health services among these – are those operated by governments. Thus, while some government presence in the economy is necessary, supporters of free markets maintain that an economy that operates with minimal state regulation serves the public interest well.

Conservative government and privatisation

Other analysts, however, all but dismiss the market as a negative force. For one thing, critics point out, the market has little incentive to produce goods and services that generate little profit, which include just about everything consumed by poor people. Government-directed public housing, for example, stands as a vital resource that no profit-seeking developer would offer independently. Second, critics look to government to curb what they see as the market system's self-destructive tendencies. The formation of economic monopolies, for example, can threaten the public interest. Government can perform a host of regulatory functions, intervening in the market to control inflation, to enhance the well-being of workers (by imposing workplace safety standards) and to benefit consumers (through product quality controls). Indeed, the power of global corporations is so great, conclude the critics, that even government cannot effectively defend the public interest. And as we shall see in Chapter 22, with increasing environmental degradation being heaped upon the planet, often through self-interested corporations, surely there is a need for international governments to provide some regulation?

Third, critics support government's role in curbing what they see as another market flaw: magnifying social stratification. As we have seen, capitalist economies characteristically concentrate income and wealth; a government system of taxation (typically applying higher rates to the rich) counters this tendency in the name of social justice. For a number of reasons, then, the market operating alone does not serve the public interest.

Does the market's 'invisible hand' feed us well or pick our pockets? Although many – perhaps most – people in Europe view the market as good, they also support some government role in economic life to benefit the public. Indeed, government assists not only citizens but business itself by providing investment capital, constructing roads and other infrastructure and shielding companies from foreign competition. Yet the precise balance struck between market forces and government decision-making continues to underlie much of the political debate in Europe and around the world.

Continue the debate:

1. Why do defenders of the free market assert that 'the government that governs best is the government that governs least'?

2. Does a market system meet the needs of European countries? Does it serve some better than others?

3. What is your impression of the successes and failures of Thatcherism? Compare it with socialist economic systems? ●

Sources: Friedman, 1980; Erber, 1990; Hall and Jacques, 1989.

claimed Scottish economist Adam Smith (1723–90), the individual pursuit of self-interest helps an entire society prosper (1937: 508; orig. 1776). Others argue that it leads to the exploitation of the mass by the few, and generates a class system.

3. *Free competition, consumer sovereignty and markets.* A purely capitalist economy would operate with no government interference, sometimes called a *laissez-faire* approach. Adam Smith contended that a freely competitive economy regulates itself by the 'invisible hand' of the laws of supply and demand.

Smith maintained that the market system is dominated by consumers who select goods and services that offer the greatest value. Producers compete with one another by providing the highest-quality goods and services at the lowest possible price. Thus, while entrepreneurs are motivated by personal gain, everyone benefits from more efficient production and ever-increasing value. In Smith's time-honoured phrase, from narrow self-interest comes the 'greatest good for the greatest number of people'. Government control of an economy would inevitably upset the complex market system, reducing producer motivation, diminishing the quantity and quality of goods produced and short-changing consumers.

Pure, ideal capitalism is non-existent. The United States is the leading capitalist society – private markets are more extensive than in Europe. Yet even there the guiding hand of government does plays a role in economic affairs. Through taxation and various regulatory agencies, the government influences what companies produce, the quality and costs of merchandise, the products businesses import and export, and the consumption and conservation of natural resources. The federal government also owns and operates a host of businesses, including the US Postal Service, the Amtrak railway system and the Nuclear Regulatory Commission (which conducts atomic research and produces nuclear materials). The entire US military is also government operated. Federal officials may step in to prevent the collapse of businesses, as in the recent 'bailout' of the savings and loan industry. Further, government policies mandate minimum wage levels, enforce workplace safety standards, regulate corporate mergers, provide farm price supports, and funnel income in the form of social security, public assistance, student loans and veterans' benefits to a majority of people.

Capitalism comes in many forms. We have already seen the shift from Fordism to post-Fordism, described above. There are, then, contrasting cultures of capitalism: Japan and the United States, for instance work very differently. Generally, modern capitalism has moved though three phases. The first was a *liberal capitalism*, which dominated Britain and the United States in the early and middle nineteenth century and involved a free market, a 'facilitative' state and a legal framework which helps to maintain capitalism. Second was an *organised capitalism*, which involved an administered market and a more 'directive state'. There was, for example, in the UK between 1946 and 1979 much more 'state' intervention as governments often shaped economic policies. More recently a *disorganised/post-Fordist capitalism* has emerged, which involves an increase in the service sector, more global and dispersed operations and a decline of nation-states (Lasch and Urry, 1987).

Socialism

Socialism is *an economic system in which natural resources and the means of producing goods and services are collectively owned.* In its ideal form, a socialist economy opposes each of the three characteristics of capitalism just described.

Beijing 1997. Cyclists pass sign which features a painting of Hong Kong's skyline. It notes the commemoration day of the Chinese Communist Party, July 1, the same day as Hong Kong reverted to China after 150 years of British rule.

Source: Popperfoto

1. *Collective ownership of property*. An economy is socialist to the extent that it limits the right to private property, especially property used in producing goods and services. Laws prohibiting private ownership of property are designed to make housing and other goods available to all, not just to those with the most money. Karl Marx asserted that private ownership of productive property spawns social classes as it generates an economic elite. Socialism, then, seeks to lessen economic inequality while forging a classless society.

2. *Pursuit of collective goals*. The individualistic pursuit of profit also stands at odds with the collective orientation of socialism. Socialist values and norms condemn what capitalists celebrate as the entrepreneurial spirit. For this reason, private trading is branded as illegal 'black market' activity.

3. *Government control of the economy*. Socialism rejects the idea that a free-market economy regulates itself. Instead of a laissez-faire approach, socialist governments oversee a *centrally controlled* or *command economy*. Socialism also rejects the idea that consumers guide capitalist production. From this point of view, consumers lack the information necessary to evaluate products and are manipulated by advertising to buy what is profitable for factory owners rather than what they, as consumers, genuinely need. Commercial advertising thus plays little role in socialist economies.

The People's Republic of China and a number of nations in Asia, Africa and Latin America – some two dozen in all – model their economies on socialism, placing almost all wealth-generating property under state control (McColm et al., 1991). The extent of world socialism has declined in recent years, however, as societies in Eastern Europe and the former Soviet Union have forged new economic systems increasing the sway of market forces.

Socialism and communism

Some people equate the terms *socialism* and *communism*. More precisely, as the ideal spirit of socialism, **communism** is *a hypothetical economic and political system in which all members of a society are socially equal*. Karl Marx viewed socialism as a transitory stage on the path toward the ideal of a communist society that had abolished all class divisions. In many socialist societies today, the dominant political party describes itself as communist, but nowhere has the communist goal been achieved.

Why? For one thing, social stratification involves differences of power as well as wealth. Socialist societies have generally succeeded in reducing disparities in wealth only through expanding government bureaucracies and subjecting the population to extensive regulation. In the process, government has not 'withered away' as Karl Marx imagined. On the contrary, during this century socialist political elites have gained enormous power and privilege. Marx would probably have agreed that such a society is a *utopia* (from Greek words meaning 'not a place'). Yet Marx considered communism a worthy goal and might well have disparaged reputedly 'Marxist' societies such as North Korea, the former Soviet Union, the People's Republic of China and Cuba for falling far short of his ideal.

Democratic socialism and state capitalism

A limited measure of socialism, however, does not stifle democracy. In fact, some of the nations of Western Europe – including Sweden and Italy – have merged socialist economic policies with a democratic political system. Analysts call this 'third way' **democratic socialism**, *an economic and political system that combines significant government control of the economy with free elections*.

Under democratic socialism, the government owns some of the largest industries and services, such as transportation, the mass media and health care. In Sweden and Italy, about 12 per cent of economic production is state controlled or 'nationalised'. That leaves most industry in private hands, but subject to extensive government regulation. High taxation (aimed especially at the rich) funds various social welfare programmes, transferring wealth to less-advantaged members of society.

Yet another blend of capitalism and socialism is **state capitalism**, *an economic and political system in which companies are privately owned though they cooperate closely with the government*. Systems of state capitalism are common in the rapidly developing Asian countries along the Pacific Rim. Japan, South Korea and Singapore, for example, are all capitalist nations, but their governments work closely with large companies, supplying financial assistance or controlling imports of foreign products to help businesses function as competitively as possible in world markets.

Countries in East Asia and Western Europe illustrate that there are many ways in which governments and companies can work cooperatively (Gerlach, 1992).

The European success story

Swedish sociologist Goran Therborn, commenting on European economies, notes that 'by mid century the annually available economic resources of Europeans were about double of what they had been in 1913. This meant an annual growth rate of about 1.8%' (Therborn, 1995: 133). The Nordic countries have been hugely successful. Finland increased its national product 40 times between 1870 and 1990, Norway and Sweden some 30 times and Denmark 25 times. Many individual countries have not been as successful, but when the story is told for Europe as a whole, it becomes the most successful economic region on earth as Figure 15.3 on the GDP for selected countries shows.

Relative advantages of capitalism and socialism

In practice, how do economic systems differ? Assessing economic models is difficult because all countries mix capitalism and socialism to varying degrees. Moreover, each nation has distinctive cultural attitudes towards work, different natural resources, unequal levels of technological development and disparate patterns of trade. Some also carry more of the burdens of war than others (Gregory and Stuart, 1985).

Despite these complicating factors, some crude comparisons are revealing. The following sections contrast two categories of countries – those with predominantly capitalist economies and those with mostly socialist economies. The supporting data reflect economic patterns prior to recent changes in the former Soviet Union and Eastern Europe.

Economic productivity

The most important dimension of economic performance is productivity. A commonly used measure of economic output is gross domestic product (GDP), the total value of all goods and services produced annually by a nation's economy. 'Per capita' (or per person) GDP allows us to compare societies of different population size.

Historically, as Table 15.1 shows, important elements of GDP, such as the proportion of the international export market a country controls, have varied dramatically among capitalist countries. As a group, however, capitalist countries have generated more goods and services than socialist countries. Averaging the economic output of industrialised nations at the end of the last decade yields a per capita GDP of about US $13,500. The comparable figure for the former Soviet Union and the nations of Eastern Europe was about US $5,000. This means that capitalist countries outproduced socialist nations by a ratio of 2.7 to 1 (United Nations Development Programme, 1990).

Economic equality

How resources are distributed within a society stands as a second crucial issue. A comparative study completed in the mid-1970s calculated income ratios by comparing the earnings of the richest 5 per cent of the population and the poorest 5 per cent (Wiles, 1977). This research found that societies with predominantly capitalist economies had an income ratio of about 10 to 1; the corresponding figure for socialist countries was 5 to 1. This comparison of economic performance reveals that *capitalist economies produce a higher overall standard of living but also generate greater income disparity*. Or, put otherwise, *socialist economies create less income disparity but offer a lower overall standard of living*.

Civil liberties

A society's economic and political systems are closely linked. Capitalism depends on the freedom of producers and consumers to interact without extensive interference from the state. Thus economic capitalism fosters broad civil liberties and political freedom. For their part, socialist governments strive to maximise economic equality. This goal requires considerable state intervention in the economy, which limits the personal liberty of citizens in ways that the state deems beneficial to the public as a whole. Humanity has yet to devise a social system that ensures political liberty *and* economic equality. In tandem with the drive to improve living standards, many socialist societies are now striving to forge a new balance between these two other worthy objectives as well.

● Work in the postindustrial economy

In the spring of 1992, the UK Labour Force Survey found the active labour force population in Europe to be at 165 million people – nearly 60 per cent of the total European population of 367 million. Some

150 million people were in work at that time, with a working week of around 40 hours per week. Unemployment was very high – at around 10 per cent – just short of 17 million; its greatest impact was on women and the young. Contrary to a popular stereotype, the number of hours worked per week has been going up in recent years: in the UK from 44.5 hours per week for a man in 1985 to 45.8 hours in 1996 (*Social Trends*, 1997: 79).

Age also affects labour force participation. Typically, both women and men join the workforce in their teens and early twenties. During their child bearing years, however, women's participation lags behind that of men. After about the age of 45, the working profiles of the two sexes again become similar, with a marked withdrawal from the labour force as people approach age 65. After that point in life, only a small proportion of each sex continues to perform steady income-producing work.

The decline of agricultural work

When this century began, about 40 per cent of the labour force engaged in farming. By the time it ends, this proportion will have fallen to a mere 2 per cent, and many agricultural workers will work part time. France, Germany, Spain, Ireland and the UK have the largest agricultural areas in Europe. Total income from agriculture in the EU fell by 34 per cent between 1973–5 and 1990–2; an average drop of 2.4 per cent each year, with the steepest falls in Denmark, the UK and Germany (Eurostat, 1995: 255).

Even though today's agriculture involves fewer people, it is often more productive. A century ago, a typical farmer grew food for five people; today, one farmer feeds 75. This dramatic rise in productivity also reflects new types of crops, pesticides that increase yields, more efficient machinery and other advances in farming technology. Whilst, in southern Europe, holdings remain small (4 to 7 hectares in Greece, Portugal and Italy), in the north, the holdings are much larger (in the UK, the average is 68 hectares).

This process signals the eclipse of 'family farms', which are declining in number and produce only a small part of our agricultural yield, in favour of large *corporate agribusinesses*. But, more productive or not, this transformation has wrought painful adjustments for farming communities across the country, as a way of life is lost.

From factory work to service work

Industrialisation swelled the ranks of factory workers during the nineteenth century. But by 1911 more than 45 per cent of the United Kingdom workforce had service jobs (with 40 per cent in industry and only 14.7 per cent in agriculture) (Coleman and Salt, 1992: 375). By 1971, agriculture had declined to around 4 per cent, whilst service had increased to around 54 per cent. But this growth in the service industries has not been as pronounced in the UK as in some other industrialised countries. By 1994, 90 per cent of new jobs in the United States were in the service sector.

The growth of service occupations is one reason for the widespread description of Europe as a middle class society. As explained in Chapter 10 ('Social Class in Europe'), however, much service work – including sales positions, secretarial work and jobs in fast-food restaurants – yields little of the income and prestige of professional white-collar occupations, and often provides fewer rewards than factory work. In short, more and more jobs in this postindustrial era provide only a modest standard of living. According to Therborn, 'Sweden is the only country in the world that has gone from being an industrial society to a "knowledge and information society", having more "professional, technical and related workers" than production and related workers, including labourers' (1995: 76). Another notable occupation trend is the increase in the numbers of people working at home. In 1995, 29 per cent of employed men and 24 per cent of employed women in the UK worked some time at home. These were the highest rates in Europe (*Social Trends*, 1997). Britons also are more likely than other Europeans to work on weekends (Social Trends, 1997).

The dual labour market

The change from factory work to service jobs represents a shifting balance between two categories of work (Edwards, 1979). The **primary labour market** includes *occupations that provide extensive benefits to workers*. This favoured segment of the labour market contains the traditional white-collar professions and high management positions. These are jobs that people think of as *careers*. Work in the primary labour market provides high income and job security and is also personally challenging and intrinsically satisfying. Such occupations require a broad education rather than specialised training and offer solid opportunity for advancement.

But few of these advantages apply to work in the **secondary labour market**, *jobs providing minimal benefits to workers*. This segment of the labour force is employed in the low-skilled, blue-collar type of work found in routine assembly-line operations, and in low-level service-sector jobs including clerical positions. The secondary labour market offers workers much lower income, demands a longer working week and affords less job security and opportunity to advance. Not surprisingly, then, workers in the secondary labour market are most likely to experience alienation and dissatisfaction with their jobs. These problems most commonly beset women and other minorities, who are overly represented in this segment of the labour force (Kohn and Schooler, 1982). In Spring 1996, only 8 per cent of male employees worked part time, whilst some 45 per cent of women did (*Social Trends*, 1997: 71).

Most new jobs in our postindustrial economy fall within the secondary labour market, and they involve the same kind of unchallenging tasks, low wages and

FOCUS ON EUROPE

Women and work

Although women worked in the nineteenth century, by the end of the twentieth century, something between 40 per cent and 80 per cent of women had entered the labour market in the industrial world. In Scandinavian countries the figure hovers around 80 per cent; in the USA, it is about two-thirds; in the UK, it is around 47 per cent; and in Greece it is around 32 per cent. A recent report noted that women's proportions of the labour force in the EU rose from 39.3 per cent in 1987 to 41 per cent in 1992 (*Men and Women in the EU*, 1995) (see Figures 15.4 and 15.5). The traditional view that working for income is a 'man's role' no longer holds true.

In the EU, women are still concentrated in typically 'feminine' occupations. 'Feminine' qualities come to the fore and are seen as 'natural'. Thus women are much more likely to be found in supportive and caring roles: administrative support work (secretaries, typists) and service work (waitressing, food-service work, nursing,

Figure 15.4 ● Levels of economic activity rate of people aged 20–59, 1992

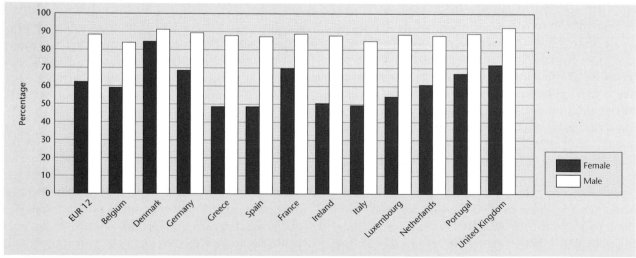

Source: *Women and Men in Europe: A Statistical Portrait*, Office for Official Publications of the European Community, Eurostat (1995), p. 123

poor working conditions characteristic of jobs in factories a century ago (Gruenberg, 1980). Moreover, as the box explains, job insecurity is on the rise as the economy shuttles an unprecedented share of workers from one temporary position to another.

The rise of part time and flexible work

Over the past decade, part time work has become more common – especially for women. One consequence of this is the undermining of job security. A decade ago, workers confidently assumed that hard work and playing by the rules all but guaranteed that their jobs would be there until they were ready to retire. No longer. As one analyst puts it:

The rise of the knowledge economy means a change, in less than twenty years, from an overbuilt system of large, slow-moving economic units to an array of small, widely dispersed economic centres, some as small as an individual boss. In the new economy, geography dissolves, the highways are electronic. Even Wall Street no longer has a reason to be on

child care). These jobs lie at the low end of the pay scale, offer limited opportunities for advancement and are subject to supervision – most often by men.

The key problem facing women's equal opportunities centres on the problems of balancing work and a private life. A woman's family situation shapes her work situation in ways it rarely does for men. Child bearing and child rearing, especially in countries with little child care provision, can weaken women's career structures.

Whilst most people in the EU are employed in the service sector, it is 76% for women and 52% for men; women were more likely to work part time (21% of women as opposed to 4% of men) . . . . Slightly more women (11.9%) than men (9.8%) are employed on temporary contracts . . . . There are flagrant pay differentials between men and women; women are more likely to get low pay and minimum wages. (Eurostat, 1995: 109, 121, 137) ●

Figure 15.5 ● Economic sectors with the highest and lowest feminisation rates, 1992

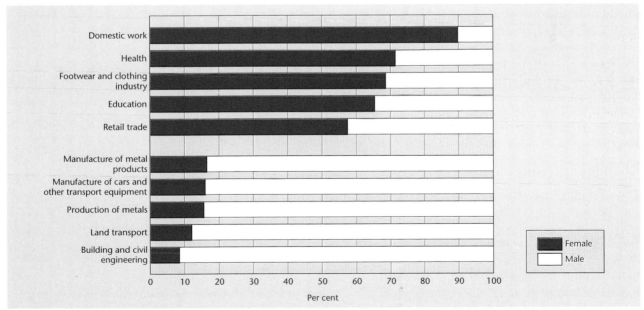

Source: *Women and Men in Europe: A Statistical Portrait*, Eurostat (1995)

Wall Street. Companies become concepts . . . and jobs are almost as susceptible as electrons to vanishing into thin air. (Morrow, 1993: 41).

In the short run, at least, the dislocation for workers is tremendous. Companies scrambling to 'remain competitive' in the global economy are 'downsizing' and decentralising to gain 'flexibility'. These trends mean not only cutting the number of people on the payroll – managers as well as secretaries – but also replacing long-term employees with temporary workers. By hiring 'temps', companies no longer have to worry about providing insurance, paid vacations or pensions. And, if next month workers are no longer needed, they can be released without further cost.

In the UK, between 1986 and 1996 (Table 15.2), the number of women in part time work increased by 18 per cent – to 5.3 million. Among men, the number doubled – but the total was only 1.2 million. Many who have these jobs say they do not want full time work (8 in 10 women; but only 4 in 10 men) (*Social Trends*, 1997: 76). In the EU as a whole, some 10 per cent of all employment is part time; and in some countries the figures soar: it is nearly 35 per cent of all employees in The Netherlands, and 22.5 per cent of Danes.

Recent trends are undoing workplace bonds with remarkable speed and at all levels of the labour force. Like workers at the dawn of the industrial era centuries ago, many of today's secretaries, engineers, bank staff and even corporate executives are finding their job security vanishing before their eyes. For the foreseeable future, most analysts agree, there is probably no going back to the traditional notion of lifetime employment with one company (Castro, 1993; Morrow, 1993).

Changes in trades unions

The changing economy has been accompanied by a declining role for **trades unions**, *organisations of workers seeking to improve wages and working conditions through various strategies, including negotiations and strikes*. Membership in trades unions increased rapidly in Europe through the earlier part of this century, peaking at 13 million people in the UK in 1979 (around 55 per cent). But by

Table 15.1 ● Britain's top ten leading companies, 1997

	Stockmarket value in 1997 pounds sterling, millions
BP	39424
Glaxo, Wellcome	39396
BT	28116
Lloyds TSB	27669
SmithKline Beecham	25268
Marks & Spencer	13977
NatWest Bank	11860
Grand Met	10562
GEC	10289
BTR	10241

Source: *Financial Times*

Table 15.2 ● Population of working age,[a] by gender and employment status, spring 1996

United Kingdom			Millions
	Males	**Females**	**All**
Economically active			
In employment			
Full-time employees	10.8	5.9	16.7
Part-time employees	0.8	4.5	5.3
All employees	11.6	10.4	22.0
Full-time self-employed	2.2	0.4	2.6
Part-time self-employed	0.2	0.4	0.5
All self-employed	2.4	0.7	3.1
Others in employment[b]	0.2	0.2	0.4
All in employment	14.2	11.3	25.4
ILO unemployed	1.5	0.8	2.3
All economically active	15.7	12.0	27.8
Economically inactive	2.9	4.9	7.8
Population of working age	18.6	17.0	35.5

[a]Males aged 16 to 64, females aged 16 to 59.
[b]Those on government employment and training programmes and unpaid family workers.
Source: Labour Force Survey, Office for National Statistics 1997

the mid-1990s it had dropped to 9 million (around 35 per cent) and further decline seems likely (McIlroy, 1995: 22–3). Indeed, during the 1980s, the British government under Margaret Thatcher was firmly committed to weakening the power of trades unions. Blaming unions for strikes and industrial unrest, the Thatcher government introduced such legislation as the 1980 Employment Act, making secret ballots on industrial action compulsory, and the Trade Union Act 1984, prohibiting 'secondary picketing' by restricting union members to picketing only at their own place of work. The Thatcher government also reduced consultation with union officials. Given also the increases in unemployment during this period, the unions' strengths were considerably undermined. Hyman sees all this as a process of 'coercive pacification' in which employers and government suppress and weaken union activities (Hyman, 1989).

But the decline of unions is not an isolated British phenomenon. In the United States, in absolute numbers, union membership peaked during the 1970s at almost 25 million people. Since then, it has steadily declined to about 16 per cent of non-farm workers, or about 18 million men and women. While a similar trend has emerged throughout Europe, in a few countries, particularly Denmark, trades union membership has actually increased. Roughly 80 per cent of workers in the Scandinavian countries belong to unions; and employer–union cooperation is high. In Europe as a whole about 40 per cent belong to unions, while in Canada and Japan the proportion is about one-third (Western, 1993, 1995).

The relative decline of unions stems from a number of trends already noted. First, industrial countries have lost tens of thousands of jobs in the highly unionised factories as industrial jobs are 'exported' overseas. Many plant managers have succeeded in forcing concessions from workers, including, in some cases, the dissolution of trades unions. Moreover, most of the new service-sector jobs being created today are not unionised, and hardly any temporary workers belong to a trade union.

As some analysts see it, however, falling job security may well make union membership a higher priority for workers in the years to come. But to expand their membership, unions will also have to adapt to the new global economy. Instead of seeing foreign workers as a threat to their interests, in short, union leadership will

have to forge new international alliances (Mabry, 1992; Church, 1994).

Professions

All kinds of work today are described as professional – we hear of professional tennis players, even professional insect exterminators. As distinct from an *amateur* (from Latin meaning 'lover', one who acts simply out of love for the activity itself), a professional pursues some task for a living. More precisely, though, a **profession** is *a prestigious, white-collar occupation that requires extensive formal education*. The term suggests a 'profession' – a public declaration of faith or willingness to abide by certain principles. Traditional professions include the ministry, medicine, law and academia (Goode, 1960). Today, workers describe their occupations as professions to the extent that they demonstrate the following four characteristics (Ritzer and Walczak, 1990).

1. *Theoretical knowledge.* Most jobs involve technical skills, but professions demand a theoretical understanding of a field, obtained through extensive schooling and regular interaction with one's peers. Anyone can master first-aid skills, for example, but doctors bring to their work a theoretical understanding of human health and illness.

2. *Self-regulated training and practice.* While in most workplaces people are under direct supervision, most professionals are self-employed. Professionals participate in associations that set standards for professional practice, typically including a formal code of ethics.

3. *Authority over clients.* Many jobs – sales work, for example – require people to respond directly to the wishes of customers. Professionals, by contrast, expect their clients to follow their direction and advice. Professionals claim this authority because they possess knowledge that lay people lack.

4. *Orientation to community rather than to self-interest.* The traditional 'professing' of faith or duty was a professional's declaration of intention to serve not self-interest but the needs of clients and the broader community. Most business executives readily admit to working in pursuit of profit, but professionals such as priests or university lecturers rarely admit to financial motives and prefer to think of their

work as contributing to the well-being of others. Some professional associations, including the British Medical Association, even forbid their members from advertising their services. This aura of altruism also makes many professionals reluctant to discuss the fees that contribute to their high incomes.

Alongside the traditional professions, a number of other occupations stand as *new professions*. These occupations, which include architecture, counselling, social work and accountancy, share most of the characteristics just presented. Many new service occupations in the postindustrial economy have also sought to *professionalise* their work. This claim to professional standing often begins with a new name for the work, one implying that practitioners have acquired special, theoretical knowledge. (These new names have the added benefit of distancing practitioners from their previously less-distinguished reputation.) Government bureaucrats, for example, become 'public policy analysts', and dog-catchers are reborn as 'animal-control specialists'.

Interested parties may also form a professional association that will formally attest to their specialised skills. This organisation then begins to license those who perform the work and develops a code of ethics that emphasises the occupation's contribution to the community. In its effort to win public acceptance, a professional association may also establish schools or other training facilities and perhaps start a professional journal (Abbott, 1988).

Not every category of workers tries to claim full professional status. Some *paraprofessionals*, including medical technicians, possess specialised skills but lack the extensive theoretical education required of full professionals.

Self-employment

Self-employment – earning a living without working for a large organisation – was once commonplace in Europe. Families owned and operated farms, and self-employed urban workers owned shops and other small businesses or sold their skills on the open market. With the onset of the Industrial Revolution, however, the economy became more centralised so that self-employment diminished. But more recently this has been changing. The number of self-employed people

in the UK increased throughout the 1980s to peak at 3.6 million in 1990. In spring 1996 there were 3.3 million – three-quarters of whom were men.

Most self-employed workers work in agriculture, fishing and construction, and are more likely to perform blue-collar than white-collar work. Society has always painted an appealing picture of working independently: no time clocks to punch, no one looking over your shoulder. For minorities who have long been excluded from particular kinds of work, self-employment has been an effective strategy for broadening economic opportunity (Evans, 1989). Further, self-employment holds the potential – though it is rarely realised – of earning a great deal of money. But for all its advantages, self-employment is vulnerable to fluctuations in the economy, one reason that only one-fifth of small businesses survive for more than ten years. Another common problem is that the self-employed generally lack pension and health-care benefits provided for employees by large organisations.

Unemployment

Every industrial society has some unemployment. Much of it is temporary. Few young people entering the labour force find a job right away; some workers temporarily leave the labour force while seeking a new job, to have children or because of a strike; others suffer from long-term illnesses; still others may lack skills to work.

But the economy itself also generates unemployment, often called structural unemployment. Jobs disappear as occupations become obsolete, as businesses close in the face of foreign competition and as recessions force layoffs and bankruptcies. Since 1980, for example, the 'downsizing' of US businesses has eliminated some 5 million jobs – a quarter of the total – in that country's 500 largest corporations.

Unemployment rates vary over time as they do from country to country. In Japan, for example, 2 per cent unemployment is common while 6 per cent of the US labour force lacked employment in 1994. In Europe, the unemployment rate rarely dips below 5 per cent of the labour force (Map 15.3) and no one speaks of an 'unemployment problem' until the rate exceeds 7 or 8 per cent. From the late 1940s to the 1970s in the UK, it was generally assumed that unemployment

Map 15.3 ● Unemployment rates in Europe, April 1993*

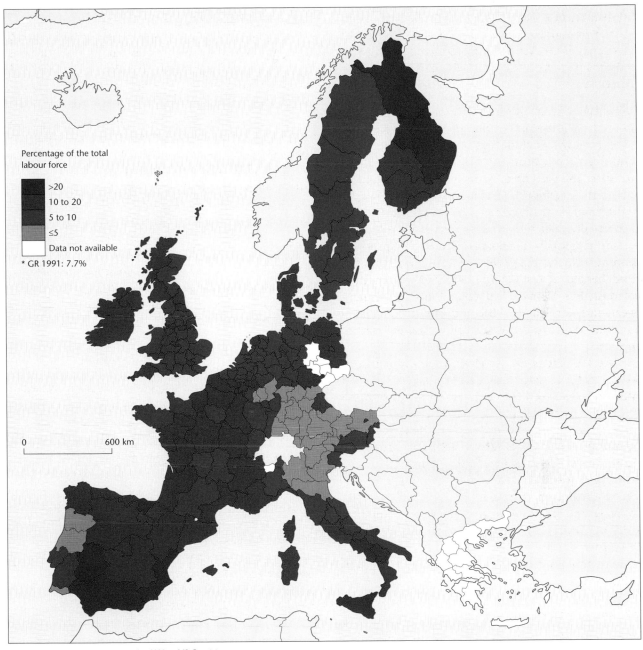

Source: *Women and Men in the European Union*, 1995, p. 163, Eurostats

should never rise above one million. But since that time there have been quite dramatic swings: 3 million by 1985, down again to 1.5 million by the early 1990s, and up again to 2.5 million people (8.5 per cent of the workforce) in 1994. This unemployment rate reflected large regional differences (Map 15.4), with the lowest rate in East Anglia (around 6.5 per cent) and the highest for the north of England (around 11 per cent) and Greater London (13 per cent). In 1997, unemployment was a little under 2 million.

Map 15.4 ● Male unemployment in the UK (%), 1991

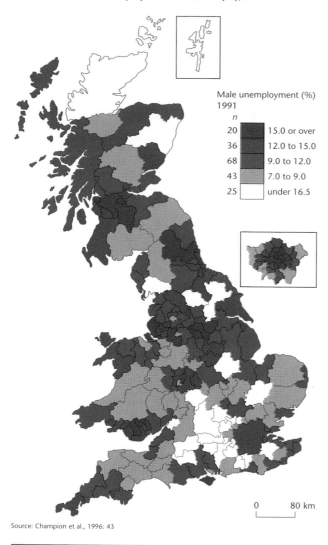

Male unemployment (%) 1991	
n	
20	15.0 or over
36	12.0 to 15.0
68	9.0 to 12.0
43	7.0 to 9.0
25	under 16.5

0   80 km

Source: Champion et al., 1996: 43

Unemployment in Europe

Since 1991, unemployment has been rising in all European Union countries (with the exception, periodically, of the UK); and in 1997, there were more than 18 million people unemployed and looking for work (*The Economist*, 5 April 1997: 21) – over 11 per cent of the labour force. The lowest rate is in Luxembourg (at around 2.5 per cent), the highest rates are in Spain (over 21 per cent), Ireland (over 18 per cent) and Finland (over 17 per cent).

Adrian Sinfield (1981) suggests five major groups who are more likely to become unemployed. These are:

- those who experience redundancies due to economic change;
- unskilled youth trying to make the transition from school to work;
- older workers who face enforced retirement;
- unemployed women; and
- the long-term unemployed.

In Europe, more than 40 per cent of the unemployed have been out of work for a year or more (compared with 11 per cent in the USA). The rate is higher for women than for men. And it particularly affects the young: in Spain, half of those under 24 are out of work; only in Germany, Austria and Denmark (with youth apprenticeships) is there reasonable employment of the young.

Experiencing unemployment

Unemployment can wreak havoc on lives and families. Many studies have suggested there is an initial shock, followed for a short while by denial and optimism (in which there may be a sense of being on holiday for a little while). But this is soon followed by distress and anxiety. If the unemployment continues for a long time, it may lead to resignation and adjustment. It has also been linked to 'ill health, premature death, attempted and actual suicide, marriage breakdown, child battering, racial conflicts and football hooliganism'. A subculture of despair can emerge, sometimes linked to the development of an underclass (see Chapter 10). For women who see work as an escape from the home, unemployment can be especially harsh (Jahoda, Larzersfeld and Zeisel, 1933; Fagin and Little, 1984) Generally, unemployment affects those with least resources most.

Problems of measuring unemployment

Measuring unemployment is no easy task. Although there are official figures, they can conceal the difficulties in recording practices. In low-income countries, for example, it is almost impossible to count the numbers out of work.

Government unemployment statistics, based on monthly national surveys, generally understate unemployment for three reasons. First, to be counted among the unemployed, a person must be actively seeking work; 'discouraged workers', those who have given up looking for a job, are omitted from the statistics.

Second, many people unable to find jobs for which they are qualified settle, at least for a while, for 'lesser' employment: A secretary works as a 'temp' several days a week or a former university lecturer drives a taxi while seeking a new teaching position. Such people are counted among the employed, though they might better be described as *under*employed.

Third, changes in policies towards the unemployed or in the procedures for measuring can conceal and distort the 'true picture'. In the UK, for instance, between 1982 and 1996 there were at least 14 changes that tended towards lowering the figures. For example, since 1982, only those eligible for benefits are included in the unemployment figures; and since 1988, most people in the UK under 18 became ineligible for benefits (income support) – resulting in 90,000 being taken off the register. Dan Finn suggests a lot of the youth training schemes have been designed to conceal unemployment by taking young people out of the unemployment statistics (Finn, 1987).

On the other hand, statistics also overlook the fact that many people officially out of work receive income 'under the table' from odd jobs or even from illegal activity. But, even considering this off-the-books income, the actual level of unemployment is probably several percentage points above the official figure.

The underground economy

Running parallel with the economic activity monitored and regulated by governments is the **underground economy**, *economic activity involving income unreported to the government as required by law*. On a small scale, most people participate in the underground economy on a regular basis. One family makes extra money by holding a car boot sale; another allows its teenage children to babysit for the neighbours without reporting the income received. Taken in total, such activities amount to millions of pounds in lost taxes annually. Much of the underground economy (or black economy) is attributable to criminal activity such as the sale of illegal drugs and weapons, trafficking of stolen goods, bribery, extortion, illegal gambling and money-laundering; and some countries, particularly parts of the Russian Federation, face larger problems with illicit activity than others.

Technology and work

The central technology of the emerging postindustrial economy is the computer and related devices for processing information. As we noted earlier, the Information Revolution is changing the character of the workplace and even of work itself. Shoshana Zuboff (1982) points to four additional ways in which computers are altering the character of work.

1. *Deskilling labour*. Just as industrial machinery 'deskilled' the master crafts workers of an earlier era, so computers now threaten to make the skills of managers obsolete. More and more business decisions are based not on executive decision-making but on computer modelling, in which a machine determines whether to buy or sell a product or to approve or reject a loan.

2. *Making work more abstract*. Industrial workers typically have a 'hands on' relationship with their product. Postindustrial workers manipulate words or other symbols in pursuit of more 'user-friendly' software or some other abstract definition of business success.

3. *Limiting workplace interaction*. The Information Revolution forces employees to perform most of their work at computer terminals; this system isolates workers from one another.

4. *Enhancing employers' control of workers*. Computers allow supervisors to monitor each worker's output precisely and continuously, whether employees are working at computer terminals or on an assembly line (Rule and Brantley, 1992). Making a broader point, Zuboff contends that technology is not socially neutral; rather, it *shapes* the way we work and alters the balance of power between employers and employees.

Understandably, then, while workers may hail some dimensions of the Information Revolution, they are likely to oppose others.

● Corporations

At the core of today's capitalist economy lies the **corporation**, *an organisation with a legal existence, including rights and liabilities, apart from those of its members*. By incorporating, an organisation becomes an entity unto itself, able to enter into contracts and own property.

The practice of legal incorporation accelerated with the rise of large businesses a century ago because it offered company owners two advantages. First, incorporation shields them from the legal liabilities of their businesses, protecting personal wealth from lawsuits arising from business debts or harm to consumers. Second, profits earned by corporations receive favourable treatment under the tax laws of Europe. The largest corporations are owned not by single families but by millions of stockholders, including other corporations. This dispersion of corporate ownership has spread wealth to some extent, making more people small-scale capitalists. Moreover, day-to-day operation of a corporation falls to white-collar executives, who may or may not be major stockholders themselves. Typically, however, a great deal of corporate stock is owned by a small number of the corporation's top executives and directors (Dahrendorf, 1959; Useem, 1980).

Economic concentration

While many corporations are small, with assets worth less than £75,000, the largest corporations dominate the global economy. In 1995, for example, the largest US corporation was car maker General Motors (GM), with more than £97 billion in revenue and £126 billion in total assets (*Fortune*, 1995). GM's sales during a single year roughly equalled the tax revenue of the smaller European countries. GM also employed more people (700,000) than did the government agencies in all the Western states in the United States.

Conglomerates and corporate linkages

Economic concentration has spawned **conglomerates**, *giant corporations composed of many smaller corporations*. Conglomerates emerge as corporations enter new markets, spinning off new companies or carrying out takeovers of existing companies. Forging a conglomerate is also a strategy to diversify a company, so that new products can provide a hedge against declining profits in the original market. Faced with declining sales of tobacco products, for example, R. J. Reynolds merged with Nabisco foods, forming a conglomerate called RJR-Nabisco. Coca-Cola's soft drink market is still growing, but this company now produces fruit drinks, coffee and bottled water, as well as movies and television programmes. Besides conglomerates, corporations are also linked through mutual ownership, since these giant organisations own each other's stock. In today's global economy, many companies have invested heavily in other corporations commonly regarded as their competitors. Indeed, in the summer of 1997, the European Union strove to block the merger of McDonnell-Douglas and Boeing, two US plane manufacturers, to protect the European aircraft conglomerate Airbus. In the end, the EU did not stop

the merger, but did negotiate that the new company would relinquish some of the exclusive contracts it had negotiated with US-based airline companies.

One more type of linkage among corporations is the *interlocking directorate*, a social network of people serving simultaneously on the boards of directors of many corporations. These connections give corporations access to valuable information about each other's products and marketing strategies. Laws forbid linkages of this kind among corporations that compete directly with one another. Yet beneficial linkages persist among non-competing corporations with common interests – for example, a corporation building tractors may share directors with one that manufactures tyres. Indirect linkages also occur when, for example, a member of General Motors' board of directors and a director of Ford both sit on the board of Exxon/Esso (Herman, 1981; Scott and Griff, 1985; Weidenbaum, 1995).

Corporate linkages do not necessarily run counter to the public interest, but they certainly concentrate power and they may encourage illegal activity. Price fixing, for example, is legal in much of the world (the Organisation of Petroleum Exporting Countries, OPEC, meets regularly to try to set oil prices), but not in Europe. By their nature, however, corporate linkages invite price fixing, especially when only a few corporations control an entire market.

Corporations and competition

The capitalist model assumes that businesses operate independently in a competitive market. But while smaller businesses and self-employed people do represent a competitive sector of the European economies, the corporate core is largely non-competitive. Large corporations are not truly competitive because, first, their extensive linkages mean that they do not operate independently. Second, a small number of corporations dominate many large markets.

With the exception of some public utility providers (such as water), no large company can establish an actual **monopoly**, *domination of a market by a single producer*. The law does permit lesser economic concentration called **oligopoly**, *domination of a market by a few producers*. Oligopoly results from the vast investment needed to enter a new market such as the car industry. Certainly, the successful entry of foreign-owned corporations into the European car markets

Chinese policeman directs traffic near McDonald's restaurant in central Beijing.

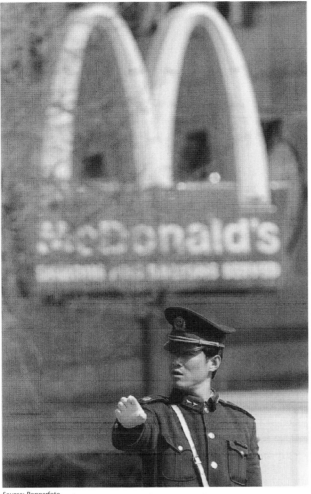

Source: Popperfoto

shows that new companies can successfully challenge the biggest corporations. But all large businesses strive to limit competition simply because it places profits at risk.

Although capitalism favours minimal government intervention in the economy, corporate power is now so great – and competition among corporations sometimes so limited – that government regulation may be the only way to protect the public interest. Yet, governments are also the corporate world's single biggest customer, and national governments frequently intervene to bolster struggling corporations. In short, corporations and governments typically work together to make the entire economy more stable and profitable (Madsen, 1980).

Corporations and the global economy

Corporations have grown in size and power so fast that they are now responsible for most of the world's economic output. In the process, the largest corporations – centred in Europe, Japan and the United States – have spilled across national borders and now view the entire world as one vast marketplace. As noted in Chapter 11 ('Global Stratification'), multinationals are large corporations that produce and market products in many different nations.

Corporations become multinational in order to make more money, since most of the planet's resources and three-quarters of the world's people are found in less-developed countries. Worldwide operations, then, offer access to plentiful materials and vast markets. In addition, labour costs are far lower in poor countries of the world. A manufacturing worker in Taiwan labours all week to earn what a German worker earns in a single day.

The impact of multinationals on poor societies is controversial, as Chapter 11 ('Global Stratification') explains in detail. On one side of the argument, modernisation theorists argue that multinationals unleash the great productivity of the capitalist economic system, which will boost economic development (Rostow, 1978; Madsen, 1980; Berger, 1986; Firebaugh and Beck, 1994). Cadbury-Schweppes alone, for example, far out-produces any one of the least-productive nations in the world. Corporations offer poor societies tax revenues, capital investment, new jobs and advanced technology – taken together, what modernisation theorists call a certain recipe for economic growth.

On the other side of the argument, dependency theorists who favour a socialist economy claim that multinationals only intensify global inequality (Vaughan, 1978; Wallerstein, 1979; Delacroix and Ragin, 1981; Bergesen, 1983; Walton and Ragin, 1990). Multinational investment, as they see it, may create a few jobs in poor countries but it also stifles the development of local industries, which are a better source of employment. Further, critics charge, multinationals generally push developing countries to produce expensive consumer goods for export to rich nations rather than food and other necessities that would bolster the standard of living in local communities. From this standpoint, multinationals establish a system of neocolonialism, making poor societies poorer and increasingly reliant on rich, capitalist societies.

The expansion of Western multinational corporations has altered patterns of consumption throughout the world, creating a homogeneous 'corporate culture' that is – for better or worse – undermining countless traditional ways of life.

Source: Gamma-Liaison, Inc. – Mayer

While modernisation theory hails the virtues of an unregulated market as the key to a future of progress and affluence for all the world's people, advocates of dependency theory call for the replacement of market systems by government regulation of economic affairs. The box on pages 418 and 419 takes a closer look at the issue of market versus governmental economies.

● Consumption

Until very recently the dominant approach to the economy by sociologists has been around the production of goods, with a focus on either businesses or workers and work. So far this has been the main focus of this chapter. But sociologists have increasingly come to recognise the importance of not just what we produce, but what – and how – we consume. Throughout most of history, the shop has been the 'open air market'. In Hong Kong or in Thailand's busy street markets today, there is a sense of historical continuity, of the bustle of the market. But with the arrival of the department store, and the rise of advertising in the nineteenth century, new worlds of consumption were slowly created.

Many suggest that Western societies are cultivating 'consumer societies'. Indeed, shopping has become one of the most popular leisure activities in Britain (see *Social Trends*, 1997). Think of your own life and how purchases – from buying clothes, CDs, tickets to sporting events and so forth – may play a part in it. Consider the following:

● *The growth of shopping malls* with megastores like Virgin Records, hypermarkets like Tesco, chain stores like Argos, retail parks and the endless proliferation of DIY stores across the country. Each Tesco store in Britain had a minimum area of 10,670 square metres in the 1990s (compared with 3,048 in the 1970s).

● *The growth of all kinds of commodities*. We now seem to need items that we did not need 50 years ago: sports clothes geared to every sport; new bathroom commodities like shower gels, foot creams and electric toothbrushes; new electronic gadgets ranging from computer toys and video games to mobile phones and multimedia computers; new forms of entertainment like multiplex cinemas and leisure complexes; new modes of eating out, from fast food McDonald's to upmarket dining; holidays that take us to Disneyland, on world cruises and to 'resort hotels'; and the rise in individual car ownership.

● *The spread of credit cards*. In the UK, at least a third of all consumption is based on credit; 25 million credit cards in the UK by 1998, but 'billions' in the United States (see Ritzer, 1995).

● *Teleshopping and netshopping*. After buying a digital television set-top box decoder, or a modem for your computer, an array of armchair services become available – from shopping and banking to travel and public services. Hundreds of channels with interactive shopping services come on stream through the television and the Internet, and all are purchasable through credit cards. British Interactive Broadcasting (BIB) is due to appear in 1998 and could change the face of British shopping. You lose the outing and the social functions of shopping, but you gain in convenience (*Guardian*, 8 May 1997: 3).

The rise of so much consumption has given sociologists much to discuss. In the first place, some argue that the 'consumerist' culture is having a deleterious effect on the quality of life. Socialist critic Jeremy Seabrook sees consumerism accelerating since 1945, and destroying traditional cultures and solidarities. The 'loadsa-money' culture promotes self-gratification, and with the market dominating , it leads to a general flattening of life – destroying differences and communities. It is the 'Coca-Colaisation of the world – Levi jeans are worn everywhere, all children consume McDonald's, and the trip to Tesco becomes the major communal activity. All this is seen to lead to the weakening of shared and moral values and the rise of a crass materialism.

Others, by contrast, argue that the new consumerism has been a major advance for most. It has become the means for a higher standard of living, as well as a chance not to deaden culture, but to enhance it. Goods and brands may spread through the world, but they are used differently and become different things. With the packaging of CDs in vast megastores, for instance, global music has developed – and the sheer range of musics available now has dramatically increased. The same is true of food, with supermarkets now making available ingredients and recipes unheard of 20 years ago. Far from flattening culture, consumerism has enriched it – giving us a greater choice and a better control of our lives. There has been a growing mass participation in creative activities, from DIY to music to cooking to reading to painting to all kinds of 'hobbies'.

Inequalities and consumption

Consumption is not available to all and thus becomes a major marker of inequalities. The sociologist Veblen recognised this some time ago when he identified conspicuous consumption – through which members of the elite engage in enhancing their status through commodities from dress and houses to cars and all the material symbols of wealth.

Consumption patterns lead to three ways of excluding people. The first is through money: many people simply do not have enough money to purchase all the latest foods or holidays on offer, and suffer economic exclusion as a result. Others may be excluded spatially; they live without a car or good public transport and hence are not able to make the trips to the shopping malls and places of consumption. Often indeed , if left to the devices of small local shops, they will find they pay more and have less choice. They become second class citizens. Finally, some people will be excluded because they lack the knowledge and skills to consume. Being a skilful consumer these days will mean you need knowledge of the metric system, computing or international food.

Not being part of the consumer world is therefore a form of social exclusion. Nowhere is this clearer than in the worlds of many elderly people: the new megastores are often inaccessible; the elderly are less likely to drive and their state of health may make time and travel hard; and even the design of stores, with high shelves, big trolleys and masses of people, makes the stores very inhospitable. Many of the new foodstuffs and gadgets may appear curiously threatening to them.

● Looking ahead: the economy of the twenty-first century

Social institutions are organisational strategies by which societies operate to meet the needs of their members. But societies themselves change over time, so the various institutions always seem somewhat at odds with their missions.

One important transformation highlighted in this chapter revolves around the Information Revolution. New information technology has defined a new era – the postindustrial economy. The share of the labour force engaged in manufacturing has been tumbling. For workers who depend on their industrial skills to earn a living, this major economic shift has brought rising unemployment and declining wages. As we look to the coming century, our society must face up to the fact that millions of men and women lack the language and computer skills needed to participate in the postindustrial economy. Can we afford to consign these workers to the margins of society? How should the government, schools and families prepare young people to perform the kind of work their society makes available to them?

A second transformation that will define the next century is the emergence of a global economy. Two centuries ago, the ups and downs of a local economy were guided by events or trends that took place within a single town. A century later, local communities throughout the country had become economically interconnected so that prosperity in one place depended on producing goods demanded by people elsewhere. As we approach the next century, economic links are intensifying at the global level. It now makes far less sense to speak of a national economy; what people, say, in a British farm town produce and consume may be affected more by what transpires in the wheat-growing region of Russia or changes in the European Union's Common Agricultural Policy than by events in their own country. In short, European workers are not only generating new products and services, but we do so in response to factors and forces that are distant and unseen.

Finally, change is causing analysts around the world to rethink conventional economic models. The emerging global economic system revealed socialist economies to be far less productive than their capitalist counterparts, one central cause of the recent collapse of socialist regimes in Eastern Europe and the former Soviet Union. At its peak, socialism organised the productive lives of about a quarter of humanity; now, the People's Republic of China and Cuba are among the few nations with government-based economies.

Capitalism, too, has seen marked changes and now operates with a significant degree of government regulation. The most significant change in the capitalist system is the emergence of multinational corporations. The global reach of today's giant businesses means that European corporations have expanded into more parts of the world, just as foreign-based corporations are increasing their investment in Europe.

What will be the long-term effects of all these changes? Two conclusions seem inescapable. First, the economic future of Europe and other nations will be played out in a global arena. The emergence of a postindustrial economy is, after all, inseparable from the increasing industrial production of other nations, especially in Asia's rapidly developing Pacific Rim. Second, everyone confronts the ever-pressing issue of global inequality. Whether the world economy ultimately reduces or deepens the disparity between rich and poor societies will be a key factor that steers the future towards peace or belligerence.

SUMMARY

1. The economy is the major social institution by which a society produces, distributes and consumes goods and services.

2. In technologically simple societies, the economy is subsumed within the family. In agrarian societies, most economic activity takes place outside the home. Industrialisation sparks significant economic expansion built around new energy sources, large factories, mass production and worker specialisation.

3. The postindustrial economy is characterised by a productive shift from tangible goods to services. Just as the technology of the Industrial Revolution propelled the industrial economy of the past, the Information Revolution is now advancing the postindustrial economy.

4. The primary sector of the economy generates raw materials; the secondary sector manufactures various goods; the tertiary sector focuses on providing services. In preindustrial societies, the primary sector predominates; the secondary sector is of greatest importance in industrial societies; the tertiary sector prevails in postindustrial societies.

5. Social scientists describe the economies of today's industrial and postindustrial societies in terms of two models. Capitalism is based on private ownership of productive property and the pursuit of personal profit in a competitive marketplace. Socialism is based on collective ownership of productive property and the pursuit of collective well-being through government control of the economy.

6. Although most European economies are predominantly capitalist, the European community and national governments are broadly involved in economic life. Governments play an even greater role in the 'democratic socialist' economies of some Western European nations and the 'state capitalism' of Japan. The Russian Federation has gradually introduced some market elements into its formerly centralised economy; the nations of Eastern Europe are making similar changes.

7. Capitalism is very productive, yielding a high overall standard of living with extensive civil liberties. Socialism is less productive and restricts civil liberties, but does generate greater economic equality than is found under capitalism.

8. The emergence of a global economy means that nations no longer produce and consume products and services within national boundaries. Moreover, the 600 largest corporations, operating internationally, now account for most of the earth's economic output.

9. In Europe, agricultural work has declined over the course of this century to just 2 per cent of the labour force. The share of blue-collar jobs has also diminished, now accounting for a quarter of the labour force. The share of white-collar service occupations, however, has been rising rapidly.

10. A profession is a special category of white-collar work based on theoretical knowledge, occupational autonomy, authority over clients and a claim to serving the community.

11. Work in the primary labour market provides far more rewards than work in the secondary labour market. Most new jobs in Europe are service positions in the secondary labour market, and about one-third of today's workers hold jobs classified as temporary, with no promise of job security.

12. Today, over 3 million British workers are self-employed. Although many professionals fall into this category, most self-employed workers have blue-collar occupations.

13. Unemployment has many causes, including the operation of the economy itself. The European unemployment rate is generally at least 5 per cent.

14. The underground economy, which includes both criminal and legal activity, generates income that goes unreported to tax agencies.

15. Corporations form the core of most European economies. Many large corporations operate as multinationals, producing and distributing products in most nations of the world, though the distribution of wealth resulting from this activity is often unequal.

16. Patterns of consumption play an important role in changes in the economy. Europeans are increasingly buying goods and services in large, centralised establishments, a pattern that has sapped the strength of small, local-based industries. Centralised shopping itself, however, faces drastic reduction as more people turn to television and Internet shopping services.

KEY CONCEPTS

capitalism an economic system in which natural resources and the means of producing goods and services are privately owned

communism a hypothetical economic and political system in which all members of a society are socially equal

conglomerates giant corporations composed of many smaller corporations

corporation an organisation with a legal existence, including rights and liabilities, apart from those of its members

democratic socialism an economic and political system that combines significant government control of the economy with free elections

economy the social institution that organises the production, distribution and consumption of goods and services

Fordism an economic system based on mass assembly line production, mass consumption and standardised commodities

global economy economic activity spanning many nations of the world with little regard for national borders

monopoly domination of a market by a single producer

oligopoly domination of a market by a few producers

post-Fordism an economic system emerging mainly since the 1970s and based on flexibility (rather than standardisation), specialisation and tailor-made goods

postindustrial economy a productive system based on service work and high technology

primary labour market occupations that provide extensive benefits to workers

primary sector the part of the economy that generates raw materials directly from the natural environment

profession a prestigious, white-collar occupation that requires extensive formal education

secondary labour market jobs that provide minimal benefits to workers

secondary sector the part of the economy that transforms raw materials into manufactured goods

socialism an economic system in which natural resources and the means of producing goods and services are collectively owned

state capitalism an economic and political system in which companies are privately owned but cooperate closely with the government

tertiary sector the part of the economy that generates services rather than goods

Thatcherism a system of political beliefs based on free markets and economic individualism

trades unions organisations of workers collectively seeking to improve wages and working conditions through various strategies, including negotiations and strikes

underground economy economic activity generating income that is kept hidden from government agencies

CRITICAL-THINKING QUESTIONS ....

1. How does the economy operate differently among societies at different stages of technological development?

2. Identify several ways in which the Industrial Revolution reshaped the economies of Europe. How is the Information Revolution transforming these economies once again?

3. What key characteristics distinguish capitalism, socialism and democratic socialism? Compare these systems in terms of productivity, economic inequality and support for civil liberties.

4. In light of the emerging global economy, some analysts suggest that measurements such as gross domestic product (GDP) are losing their utility. Do you agree?

5. Discuss the evidence for more flexible work patterns? Why have these emerged? What might be their advantages and disadvantages?

6. Why has unemployment been increasing in Europe? What solutions would you suggest to remedy this?

7. Make a critical analysis of your last 'shopping expedition'. Drawing from ideas in this chapter, discuss what you bought, the processes by which those items were produced, the people and agencies that benefited from your purchases, and why you felt motivated to purchase those goods and services.

GOING FURTHER ....

Introductory reading

Keith Grint, *The Sociology of Work: An Introduction* (Cambridge: Polity, 1991).
  Introduces the debates and evidence around theories of work.

Classical sources

Thorstein Veblen, *The Theory of the Leisure Class* (New York: New American Library, 1953; orig. 1899).
  One of the earliest US sociologists explains how patterns of consumption confer social status on

people in an increasingly affluent and upwardly mobile society.

Daniel Bell, *The Coming of Post-Industrial Society: A Venture in Social Forecasting* (New York: Harper Colophon, 1976).

Bell was among the first sociologists to recognise and analyse the emerging postindustrial society.

More advanced reading

David Harvey, *The Condition of Postmodernity* (Oxford: Blackwell, 1989).

Krishan Kumar, *From Post-Industrial to Post-Modern Society* (Oxford: Blackwell, 1995).

These two books provide detailed accounts of post-Fordism and review a number of explanations of the major changes in capitalist organisation.

Robert Bocock, *Consumption* (London: Routledge, 1993).

Mike Featherston, *Consumer Culture and Postmodernism* (London: Sage, 1991).

Daniel Miller (ed.), *Acknowledging Consumption* (London: Routledge, 1995).

These three books contain valuable reviews of writings on consumption.

D. Gallie, C. Marsh and C. Vogler, *Social Change and the Experience of Unemployment* (Oxford: Oxford University Press, 1993).

Looks at changes in British labour markets, and how British people have experienced unemployment.

Charles Hampden Turner and Fons Trompenaars, *The Seven Cultures of Capitalism* (London: Piatkus, 1993).

Based on a survey of 15,000 senior managers, the book explores the variety of forms of capitalism in Sweden, The Netherlands, Japan, Britain, France, the USA and Germany, showing how cultural habits shape business.

Suzan Lewis, Dafna N. Izraeli and Helen Hootsmans, *Dual-Earner Families: International Perspectives* (Newbury Park, CA: Sage, 1992).

This discussion highlights changing economic and family patterns in Hungary, Sweden, Singapore, Japan, India and elsewhere.

John McIlroy, *Trade Unions in Britain Today* (Manchester: Manchester University Press, 2nd edn, 1995).

A detailed, standard guide to the shifting fortunes of British trades unionism.

Bette Woody, *Black Women in the Workplace: Impacts of Structural Change in the Economy* (Westport, CT: Greenwood Press, 1992).

Economic changes have different effects on various segments of the labour force. This analysis highlights the consequences of the emerging postindustrial economy for women of colour in the USA.

James A. Yunker, *Socialism Revised and Modernized: The Case for Pragmatic Market Socialism* (New York: Praeger, 1992).

This author envisions how a fusion of capitalist and socialist models – involving public ownership of larger, profit-seeking corporations – would capitalise on the advantages of both economic systems.

Other sources

Eurostat: Statistical Offices of the European Communities.
http://europa.eu.int/en/comm/eurostat/ServEN/home.html

Gateway to official statistics of the EU, available in English, German, and French.

The World Bank Group Home Page
http://www.worldbank.org

Searches new publications, topics in development, countries and regions, and means of doing business with the World Bank.

chapter sixteen

Source: Popperfoto

Power, the State and Social Movements

Headlines

5 April 1997
The Grand National at Aintree on Merseyside is postponed because the Irish Republican Army (IRA) threaten to bomb it; 60,000 evacuated

Manchester, June 1988. Rescue services search the debris following the bomb blast which ripped through Manchester city centre. It was suspected to be the work of the IRA.

Source: Pepperdata

21 April 1997
London is gridlocked after multiple bomb threats bring the capital to chaos

16 June 1997
The IRA guns down John Graham, 34, and David Johnston, 30, both members of the Royal Ulster Constabulary in Lurgan, County Armagh

6 July 1997
The Drumcree Orange march in Portadown is attended by some 1,000 bowler-hatted members of the Protestant, unionist Orange Order. Catholic nationalists object, and three days of violence erupt. Petrol bombs, burnt out cars, gutted buildings, at least 130 injuries

15 July 1997
Catholic Bernadette Martin, 18, is shot dead in the home of her Protestant boyfriend – by a loyalist gunman

I n 1920, some 120 years after Britain and Ireland had been united, the Government of Ireland Act partitioned Ireland into two parts, each with its own parliament. In 1921, the 26 southern counties (mainly Catholic) became an independent Irish nation. The six northern counties (mainly Protestant) remained part of the UK. Economic, religious and nationalistic splits have left Northern Ireland with 'troubles' ever since. Especially since the late 1960s, conflicts, bombings and acts of terrorism have rarely been far away. The fight for a united Ireland is carried on by the Sinn Fein ('We Ourselves') party and a 'terrorist/political' organisation, the Irish Republican Army. By the end of 1994, the conflict had seen the deaths of over 3,000 people.

But the Northern Ireland conflict is only one amongst many. Throughout the world, many similarly charged events have transpired. This chapter investigates the dynamics of power within societies and among nations. **Politics** is *the social institution that distributes power, sets a society's agenda, and makes decisions*. Politics, in short, is about power.

● Power and authority

Max Weber (1978; orig. 1921) declared **power** to be *the ability to achieve desired ends despite resistance from others*. History reveals that force – physical might or psychological coercion – is the basic expression of power. But no society exists for long if power derives only from force, because people will break rules they do not respect at the first opportunity. Social organisation, therefore, depends on generating some consensus about proper goals (cultural values) and the suitable means of attaining them (cultural norms). As we have seen earlier, sociologists use concepts like ideology and hegemony to deal with this non-coercive power.

Northern Ireland, June 1996. Police block Orange order march from going down the Drumcree Road, preventing them from marching through the Catholic area of Portadown.

Source: Popperfoto

The key to social stability is exercising power within some framework of legitimacy. This insight led Weber to focus on the concept of **authority**, *power that people perceive as legitimate rather than coercive*. When parents, teachers or police perform their work in a normative way, their power generally wins respect as authority. The source of authority, Weber continued, differs according to a society's economy.

Traditional authority

Preindustrial societies, Weber explained, rely on **traditional authority**, *power legitimised through respect for long-established cultural patterns*. Traditional authority is power woven into a society's collective memory, so that it is not only legitimate but almost sacred. The might of Chinese emperors in antiquity was legitimised by tradition, as was the rule of nobles in medieval Europe. In both cases, hereditary family rule within a traditional, agrarian way of life imbued leaders with almost godlike authority.

Traditional authority declines as societies industrialise. Hannah Arendt (1963) explains that traditional authority is compelling only so long as everyone shares the same heritage and world view; this form of authority, then, is undermined by the specialisation demanded by industrial production, by modern, scientific thinking and also by the cultural diversity that accompanies immigration. Thus, no prime minister or president today, for example, would claim to rule by the grace of God. Even so, many monarchies have occupied a privileged position in European cultures and enter the political arena with some measure of traditional authority.

If traditional authority plays a smaller part in national politics, it persists in many dimensions of everyday life. Patriarchy, the traditional domination of women by men, is still widespread, although increasingly challenged. Traditional authority is also found in the power parents exert over their young children: traditional authority here is based on a person's status as parent rather than whatever wisdom the particular individual may have acquired. To children who ask why they should obey a parental order, parents have long retorted, 'Because I said so!' To debate the merits of such a command would defeat authority by placing parent and child on an equal footing. Nevertheless, with the growth of a children's rights movement, even this form of traditional authority is under question.

Everywhere in the modern world, it seems, traditional authority is being challenged.

Rational-legal authority

Weber defined **rational-legal authority** (sometimes called bureaucratic authority) as *power legitimised by legally enacted rules and regulations*. Rational-legal authority, then, is legitimised by **government**, *formal organisations that direct the political life of a society*.

As Chapter 7 ('Groups and Organisations') explains, Weber viewed bureaucracy as the organisational backbone of rational, industrial societies. Moreover, according to Weber, just as rationality promotes bureaucracy, so it erodes traditional customs and practices. In their search for justice, in other words, modern people are less likely to venerate the past and more apt to look to formal rules, especially law.

Rationally enacted rules not only guide government in Europe; they also underlie much of our everyday life. The authority of classroom teachers and lecturers, for example, rests on the offices they hold in bureaucratic schools and universities. The police, too, are officers within the bureaucracy of local government. Compared to traditional authority, then, rational-legal authority flows not from family background but from organisational position. Thus, while a traditional monarch rules for life, a modern prime minister or president accepts and relinquishes power according to law, with authority remaining in the office.

Charismatic authority

Max Weber identified charisma as one additional way in which power is transformed into authority. Charisma, a concept detailed in Chapter 18 ('Religion'), designates exceptional personal qualities that people take to be a sign of divine inspiration. In political terms, then, **charismatic authority** is *power legitimised through extraordinary personal abilities that inspire devotion and obedience*. Unlike tradition and rational law, then, charisma has less to do with social organisation and is more a trait of individual personality.

Members of societies throughout history have regarded some of their number as especially forceful, creative and magnetic. Charisma enhances the stature of an established leader, just as it strengthens the appeal of an outside challenger. By turning an audience into followers, charismatics often make their own rules, as if drawing on a higher power. The extraordinary ability of charismatics to challenge the status quo is deeply ingrained in global history: Vladimir Lenin guided the overthrow of feudal monarchy in Russia in 1917, Mahatma Gandhi inspired the struggle to free India from British colonialism after the Second World War and Martin Luther King, Jr, galvanised the civil rights movement in the United States.

Charisma may arise from personality, but it also reflects a society's expectations about what kind of people emerge as leaders. Patriarchy encourages us to choose men as our national officials, while steering charismatic women towards the arts, the family and other social contexts traditionally defined as feminine. Yet, in recent years, charismatic women, including Indira Gandhi of India, Benazir Bhutto of Pakistan, Golda Meir of Israel and Margaret Thatcher of the United Kingdom, have gained international political prominence.

Because charismatic authority emanates from a single individual, any charismatic regime faces a crisis of survival upon the death of its leader. Thus, Weber reasoned, the persistence of a charismatic movement depends on a process he called the **routinisation of charisma**, *the transformation of charismatic authority into some combination of traditional and bureaucratic authority*. Christianity, for example, began as a cult driven by the personal charisma of Jesus of Nazareth. After the death of Jesus, followers institutionalised his teachings in a church eventually centred in Rome and built on tradition and bureaucracy. Well routinised, the Roman Catholic church has flourished for 2,000 years.

● Politics in global perspective

Political systems display marked variety throughout history as well as around the world today. Looking back in time, technologically simple hunting and gathering societies operated like one large family, with few specialised roles. In general, leadership fell to a male with unusual strength, hunting skill or personal charisma. But leaders of these egalitarian societies exercised little actual power, since they lacked the resources to reward supporters or punish challengers. In the earliest societies, then, leaders were barely discernible from everyone else, and government did not exist as a distinct sphere of life (Lenski, Nolan and Lenski, 1995).

Agrarian societies, both larger and more complex, benefit from specialised activity and generate a material surplus. These societies become hierarchical, with a small elite gaining control of most wealth and power, and politics moving outside the family realm to become a social institution in its own right. Leaders who manage to pass along their power over several generations may acquire traditional authority, perhaps even claiming divine right to govern. Such leaders also may benefit from Weber's rational-legal authority as they are served by a bureaucratic political administration and system of law.

As politics expands in this way, societal power eventually takes the form of a national government or political state. But the political state could develop only according to available technology. Just a few centuries ago, armies moved slowly and communication over even short distances was uncertain. Thus governments could confidently control only very small areas. For this reason, early political empires – such as Mesopotamia in the Middle East about 5,000 years ago – actually took the form of many small city-states (Stavrianos, 1983).

More complex technology has helped the modern world develop the larger-scale system of nation-states. Currently, the world has around 190–200 independent nation-states, each of which operates a political system that is at least somewhat distinctive. Generally speaking, however, the world's political systems fall into four categories: monarchy, democracy, authoritarianism and totalitarianism.

Monarchy

Monarchy (with Latin and Greek roots meaning 'one ruler') is *a type of political system in which a single family rules from generation to generation*. Monarchy is typical of agrarian societies; the Bible, for example, tells of great kings such as David and Solomon. Today's British monarchy traces its lineage back roughly 1,000 years. In Weber's terms, then, monarchy is legitimised by tradition.

During the medieval era, absolute monarchy, in which hereditary rulers claimed a virtual monopoly of power based on divine right, flourished from England to China and in parts of the Americas. Monarchs in some nations – including Saudi Arabia – still exercise virtually absolute control over their people.

During this more egalitarian century, however, monarchs have gradually passed from the scene in favour of elected officials. Europe's remaining monarchs – in the UK, Spain, Norway, Sweden, Belgium, Denmark and the Netherlands – now preside over constitutional monarchies. They serve as symbolic heads of state, while actual governing is the responsibility of elected politicians, led by a prime minister, according to political principles embodied in a constitution. In these nations, then, the monarch may formally reign, but elected officials actually rule.

Democracy

The historical trend in the modern world has favoured **democracy**, *a political system in which power is exercised by the people as a whole*. Members of democratic societies rarely participate directly in decision-making; numbers alone make this an impossibility. Instead, a system of representative democracy places authority in the hands of elected leaders, who are accountable to the people. This needs to be contrasted with a system of participatory democracy where people represent themselves and take their own decisions. Such a system may often work amongst small groups: it is harder to organise at state and national levels!

High-income, industrial societies tend to embrace democratic political systems. Economic development and democratic government go together because both depend on a literate populace. Moreover, the traditional legitimisation of power in a monarchy gives way in democratic political systems to rational-legal authority. A rational election process places leaders in offices regulated by law. Thus democracy and rational-legal authority are linked just as monarchy and traditional authority are.

But democratic political systems are much more than just leaders and followers; they are built on extensive bureaucracy. Considerable formal organisation is necessary to carry out the expanding range of government activities undertaken by democratic societies. As it grows, government gradually takes on a life of its own, revealing an inherent antagonism between democracy and bureaucracy. The federal government of the United States, for example, employs more than 3 million people (excluding the armed forces), making it one of the largest bureaucracies in the world. Another 15 million people work in some 80,000 local governments. The great majority of these bureaucrats were never elected and are unknown to the public they purport to serve. To elect them would seem impractical given their numbers and the need for specialised training. But, ironically, while the public focuses attention on a small number of elected leaders, most everyday decision-making is carried out by career bureaucrats who are not directly accountable to the people (Scaff, 1981; Edwards, 1985; Etzioni-Halevy, 1985).

Democracy and freedom: contrasting approaches

Despite their distinctive histories and cultural diversity, virtually all industrialised nations in the world claim to be democratic and politically free. This curious fact might make us wonder what societies mean by being politically 'free'.

The political life of the West is largely shaped by the free-market economic principles of capitalism. Supporters argue that the operation of a market system affords individuals the personal freedom to pursue whatever they perceive as their self-interest. Thus, the argument continues, the capitalist approach to political freedom translates into personal liberty – freedom to vote for one's preferred leader or otherwise act with minimal interference from government.

Yet, as the last chapter explained, capitalist societies are marked by a striking inequality of wealth. Such economic disparity, critics counter, gives some people far more choices and opportunities than others. Thus, capitalism looks undemocratic insofar as such a system attends to the needs of only the well-to-do.

Supporters of a socialist economic system, by contrast, point out that socialist politics strives to meet every citizen's basic needs for housing, schooling, a job and medical care. Thus, the socialist approach to political freedom emphasises freedom from basic want. For example, there is little of the hunger and homelessness we associate with the capitalism of the United States in more socialist nations such as Norway and Sweden.

But critics of socialism counter that such systems are more likely to be unresponsive to people's needs and aspirations as well as heavy-handed in their suppression of any political opposition. Within the last decade, for example, people living under socialist governments in Eastern Europe overthrew that system in favour of a free market that would, presumably, reduce political repression (and, hopefully, raise living standards: something that is now in doubt).

Figure 16.1 ● The extent of global freedom, 1985 and 1995

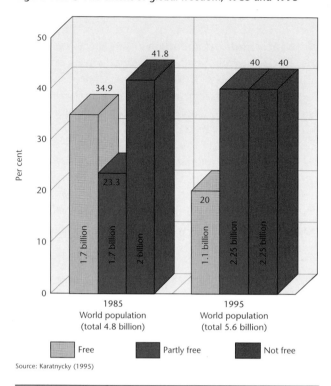

Source: Karatnycky (1995)

in places that were not free (Karatnycky, 1995). Figure 16.1 provides details.

Authoritarianism

As a matter of policy, some nations give their people little voice in politics. **Authoritarianism** refers to *a political system that denies popular participation in government*. An authoritarian government is not only indifferent to people's needs, it lacks the legal means to remove leaders from office and provides people with little or no way even to express their opinions. Polish sociologist Wlodzimierz Wesolowski (1990: 435) sums up authoritarianism this way: 'The authoritarian philosophy argues for the supremacy of the state [over other] organised social activity.'

The absolute monarchies in Saudi Arabia and Kuwait are highly authoritarian. Other examples of authoritarian regimes are military juntas, found today in Congo and Ethiopia, where political dissatisfaction has been widespread. But heavy-handed government does not always breed popular opposition, as we can see in the box – a look at the 'soft authoritarianism' that now thrives in the small Asian nation of Singapore.

Totalitarianism

The most restrictive political form is **totalitarianism**, *a political system that extensively regulates people's lives*. Totalitarian governments emerged only during this century, with the development of the technological means for rigid regulation of a populace. The Vietnamese government closely monitors the activities of its citizens and visitors. Similarly, the government of North Korea utilises surveillance equipment and sophisticated computers to store vast amounts of information on its citizenry and thereby manipulate an entire population.

Although some totalitarian governments claim to represent the will of the people, most seek to bend people to the will of the government. As the term itself implies, such governments represent total concentrations of power and prohibit organised opposition of any kind. Denying the populace the right to assemble for political purposes and controlling access to information, these governments thrive in an environment of fear and social atomisation.

Socialisation in totalitarian societies is intensely political, seeking not just outward compliance but

These contrasting views of freedom raise an important question: are economic equality and political liberty compatible? To foster economic equality, socialism tends to infringe on individual initiative. Capitalism, on the other hand, provides broad political liberties, which, in practice, mean little to the poor.

The discussions that follow in this chapter spotlight the varying positions of the world's countries with regard to how much economic inequality they tolerate and the extent of political freedoms they grant to their citizens. Map 16.1 provides one organisation's assessment of political freedom in the world today.

By the beginning of the 1990s, according to Freedom House, a New York-based organisation that tracks global political trends, more people in the world were 'free' than 'not free' for the first time in history. Since then, however, the tide has turned against democracy. In 1995, just 20 per cent of the world's people lived in nations that were free; 40 per cent resided in partly free countries, and 40 per cent lived

'Soft authoritarianism' or planned prosperity? A report from Singapore

Singapore, a tiny nation on the tip of the Malay Peninsula with a population of just over 3 million, seems to many to be an Asian paradise. Surrounded by poor societies that grapple with rapidly growing populations, squalid, sprawling cities and surging crime rates, the affluence, cleanliness and safety of Singapore make the European visitor think more of a theme park than a country.

In fact, since its independence from Malaysia in 1965, Singapore has startled the world with its economic development; today, the economy is expanding rapidly and per capita income now rivals that of the United States. But, unlike Europe or the United States, Singapore has scarcely any social problems such as crime, slums, unemployment or children living in poverty. In fact, people in Singapore do not even contend with traffic jams, graffiti on underground trains or litter in the streets.

The key to Singapore's orderly environment is the ever-present hand of government, which actively promotes traditional morality and regulates just about everything. The state owns and manages most of the country's housing and has a stake in many businesses. It provides tax incentives for family planning and completing additional years of schooling. To keep traffic under control, the government slaps hefty surcharges on cars, pushing the price of a basic saloon car up around £25,000.

Singapore made international headlines in 1994 after the government accused Michael Fay (from the United States) of vandalism and sentenced him to a caning – a penalty illegal in most Western countries. Singapore's laws also permit police to detain a person suspected of a crime without charge or trial and to mandate death by hanging for drug dealing. The government has outlawed some religious groups (including Jehovah's Witnesses) and bans pornography outright. Even smoking in public brings a heavy fine. To ensure that city streets are kept clean, the state forbids eating on the subway, imposes stiff fines for littering and has even outlawed the sale of chewing gum.

In economic terms, Singapore defies familiar categories. Government control of scores of businesses, including television stations, telephone services,

'Soft authoritarianism' or planned prosperity? A report from Singapore

Source: Picture Cube, Inc. – David Ball

airlines and taxis seems socialist. Yet, unlike socialist enterprises, these businesses are operated efficiently and very profitably. Moreover, Singapore's capitalist culture celebrates economic growth (although the government cautions its people about the evils of excessive materialism) and this nation is home to hundreds of multinational corporations.

Singapore's political climate is as unusual as its economy. Members of this society feel the hand of government far more than their counterparts in Europe. Just as important, a single political organisation – the People's Action party – has ruled Singapore without opposition since the nation's independence 30 years ago.

Clearly, Singapore is not a politically democratic country. But most people in this prospering nation seem content – even enthusiastic – about their lives. What Singapore's political system offers is a simple bargain: government demands unflinching loyalty from the populace; in return, it provides a high degree of security and prosperity. Critics charge that this system amounts to a 'soft authoritarianism' that stifles dissent and gives government unwarranted control over people's lives. Most of the people of Singapore, however, know the struggles of living elsewhere and, for now at least, consider the trade-off a good one. ●

Source: adapted from Branegan, 1993.

WINDOW ON THE WORLD

Map 16.1 ● Political freedom in global perspective

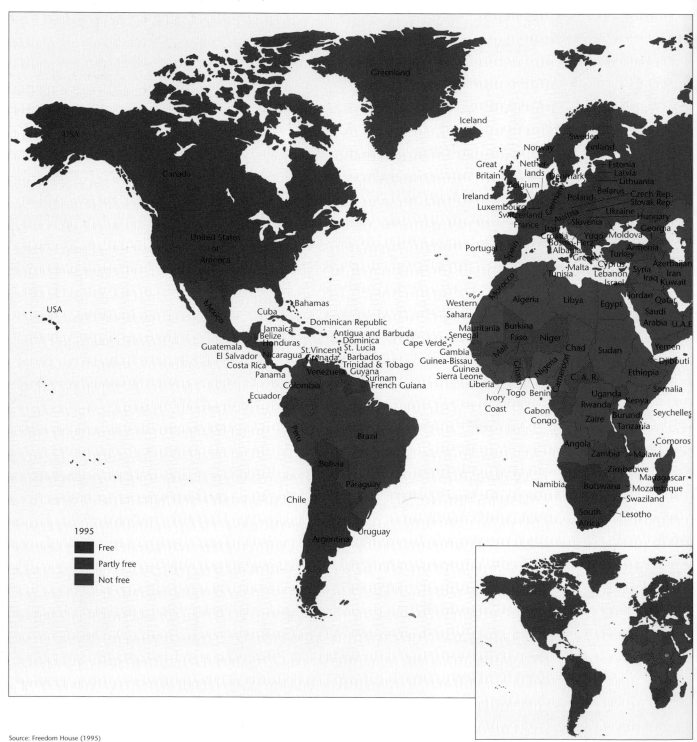

1995

- Free
- Partly free
- Not free

Source: Freedom House (1995)

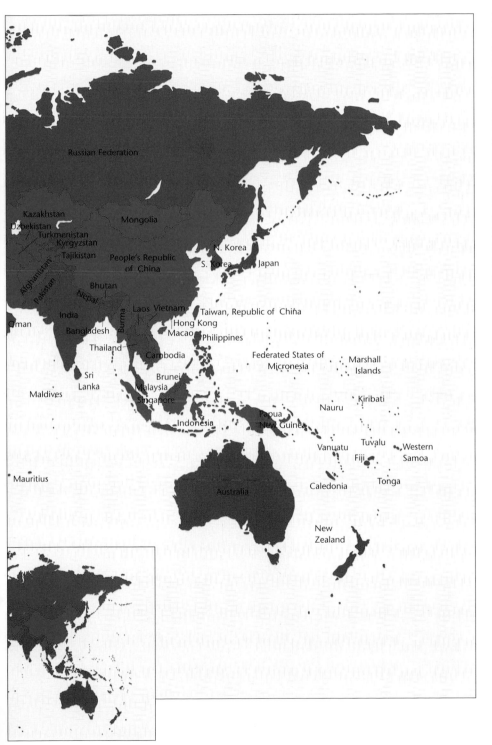

In 1995, 76 of the world's nations, containing 20 per cent of all people, were politically 'free' – that is, they offered their citizens extensive political rights and civil liberties. Another 61 countries that included 40 per cent of the world's people were 'partly free', with more limited rights and liberties. The remaining 54 nations, home to 40 per cent of humanity, fall into the category of 'not free'. In these countries, government sharply restricts individual initiative. Between 1980 and 1991 democracy made significant gains, largely centred in Latin America as well as Eastern Europe. Since 1991, however, the world has witnessed an erosion of political freedom on all continents.

inward commitment to the system. In North Korea, pictures of leaders and political messages over loudspeakers are familiar elements of public life that remind citizens that they owe total allegiance to the state. Government-controlled schools and mass media present only official versions of events.

Government indoctrination is especially stringent whenever political opposition surfaces in a totalitarian society. In the aftermath of the 1989 prodemocracy movement in the People's Republic of China, for example, officials demanded that citizens report all 'unpatriotic' people – even members of their own families. Further, Chinese leaders subjected all students at Beijing universities to political 'refresher' courses. Totalitarian governments span the political spectrum from the far right (including Nazi Germany) to the far left (North Korea).

● Nation-states and a global political system

Chapter 15 ('The Economy, Consumption and Work') pointed to the emergence of a global economy, meaning that increasing numbers of products and services routinely cross national boundaries. In part, the global economy reflects the expanding operations of multinational corporations; it also stems from the Information Revolution that has drawn together the various regions of the world.

Has there been a parallel development of a global political system? On one level, the answer is no. For the past 300 years or so, the dominant mode of governing has been through the nation-state (what is sometimes called the Westphalian Order, after the Peace of Westphalia (1648) which came to define the importance of nation-states). And it is still the case that we think primarily in terms of these **nation-states** – like Norway, Canada or Thailand. Each has its own political apparatus over a specific territory with its own citizens backed up by military force and a nationalistic, sovereign creed. Although most of the world's economic activity now involves more than one nation, the planet remains divided into nation-states, just as it has been for centuries. The United Nations (founded in 1945) might seem like a step towards global government, but it has played a limited role in global politics up to this point.

On another level, however, politics has clearly become a global process. In some ways, there is a long history of 'international governance': Ancient Greece or Renaissance Italy are two examples. Likewise, the

steady growth of political interconnectedness over large regions – notably the European Union comprising some 15 states, and ASEAN (the Association of South East Asian Nations: Indonesia, the Philippines, Malaysia, Singapore, Brunei, Thailand and Vietnam) (Naisbitt, 1997: 143) – signposts a continuing regional interconnectedness. But multinational corporations now represent a political order of a quite different kind. They have enormous power to shape social life throughout the world. From this point of view, politics is dissolving into business as corporations grow larger than governments. As one multinational leader asserted, 'We are not without cunning. We shall not make Britain's mistake. Too wise to govern the world, we shall simply own it' (quoted in Vaughan, 1978: 20).

Then, too, the Information Revolution has pulled even national politics on to the world stage. Hours before the Chinese government sent troops to Tiananmen Square to crush the 1989 prodemocracy movement, officials 'unplugged' the satellite transmitting systems of news agencies in an effort to keep the world from watching as events unfolded that day. Despite their efforts, news of the massacre was flashed around the world minutes after it began via the fax

Figure 16.2 ● **The size of government: tax revenues as share of Gross Domestic Product, 1992**

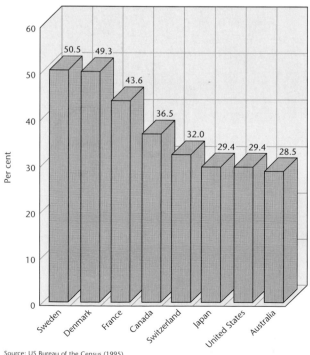

Source: US Bureau of the Census (1995)

machines in universities and private homes. In short, just as individual nations can no longer control their own economies, so no national government can fully manage the political events that occur within its borders (Baylis and Smith, 1997).

● Politics in the UK and the rest of Europe

Although this has not always been the case, all the countries of Western and East Central Europe may currently be seen as liberal democracies with a plurality of political parties and an electoral process. Spain, Germany, Greece and Italy have all at times been run by authoritarian governments. Portugal and Spain were right wing dictatorships till the mid-1970s. The situation in Eastern Europe is somewhat more complex. The Soviet Union dominated this bloc and most countries were communist until 1989. Since then, and often with much difficulty, they have been in the process of becoming democracies, too.

In most countries there is usually both a national system of government and a local one. This at times can cause major tensions, when different parties hold the balance of power in one but not the other. But in general, the political parties of Europe have been stable. Table 16.1 shows the main political parties in the European Union.

In the UK, the threefold split of liberal, labour and conservative (with minor challenges such as the breakaway labour Social Democratic Party in 1980) has been in place for much of the twentieth century. Yet a seeming growing consensus was challenged by the emergence of a New Right during the 1980s.

The European Union

Most European countries are standing at the threshold of major change. They have their own (usually long-standing) political system as a nation-state. The nation-states of Europe are the independent nations – with their own territories, military forces, sense of national identity, and their own forms of citizenship and government like Parliament in the UK and the Bundestag and Bundesrat in Germany.

But increasingly important is the fact that many of the nation-states have become member states of the European Union (Norway and Switzerland are major exceptions), sending their elected representatives to the Parliament at Strasbourg. As the map of Europe in Chapter 3 shows, there are a number of countries within Europe who are not yet members, but who are lining up to join. As Table 16.3 shows, there is a wide variation in participation and involvement in the EU across member countries.

The EU has developed a whole panoply of European institutions. Amongst these are:

● The Commission: with at least one member for each country; it proposes new laws, and implements them.

● The Council: each country has one seat; this is the main decision-making body.

● The Parliament: in 1995, there were 639 MEPs; they are allocated proportionally to population (the UK had 87 MEPs). See Figure 16.3. Turnout figures are given in Tables 16.2 and 16.3.

● The Court of Justice: monitors the EU laws and watches member states' compliance.

● European Court of Human Rights, established in 1959.

● Theoretical analysis of power in society

Sociologists and political scientists have long debated how power is distributed. Power is among the most difficult topics of scientific research because decision-making is complex and often occurs behind closed doors. It might be brutally visible in authoritarian societies, but in 'democratic' ones it is much harder to locate. Moreover, as Plato recognised more than 2,000 years ago, theories about power are difficult to separate from the beliefs and interests of social thinkers themselves. From this mix of facts and values, two competing models of power have traditionally been discussed.

The pluralist model

Formally, the **pluralist model** is *an analysis of politics that views power as dispersed among many competing interest groups*. This approach is closely tied to structural-functional theory. Pluralists claim, first, that politics is an arena of negotiation. With limited resources, no organisation can expect to realise all its goals. Organisations, therefore, operate as veto groups, achieving some success but mostly keeping opponents from reaching all their goals. The political process, then, relies heavily on negotiating alliances and compromises that bridge differences among numerous interest groups and, in the process, produce policies that generate broad-based support. In short, pluralists

Table 16.1 ● Political parties in the European Union

	Communist	Independent Socialist	Social Democrats	Liberal-Radicals	Centre	Christian Christian-Dem	Liberal Conservative	Conservative ('National')	Right Wing	Ethnic/Regional	'New Parties'
Austria	KPÖ		SPÖ			ÖVP			FRÖ		Green Alt. VGO
Belgium			BSP/PSB			CVP/PSC	VLD(PVV)/ PRL/FDF		Vlaams Blok	VB/Volksunie	Ecology/Alt Agalev
Denmark		Socialist (SF)	Social Democrats	Radical Venstre (RV)	Centre (CD)	Christian (KrF)	Venstre	Conservative (KF)	Progress		
Finland			Social (SSDP) Democrats		Centre (KESK)	Christian (SKL)		Conservative	Rural (SMP)	Swedish (SFP)	Greens
France	PCF		PS	Left-Rads (MRG)			UDF	RPR	FN		Green/Ecol MdC
Germany		PDS	SPD			CDU	FDP	CSU	Republikaner DVU		Greens Bundnis '90
Greece	KKE	Synaspismos	Pasok				POLA	New Democracy			
Ireland		Democratic Left/Workers Party	Labour	Fine Gael			Prog.Dems	Fianna Fail		Sinn Fein	Green Alliance
Italy	PDS(ex PCI)	La Rete	PSI	PRI PSDI		PPI (formerly DC)	PLI	Forza Italia	A.N. (formerly MSI/DN)	South Tyrol/ SVP Lega Nord	Radical Greens
Luxembourg	Communist		LSAP/PSOL			Christian Social CSV/PCS					Greens
Netherlands			PvdA	Dem.'66 Radical		CDA	VVD				
Portugal	Communist		Socialist (PS)			CDS	PSD				
Spain	(PCP)	IU (United Lef)	PSE (PSOE)		Soc-Dem Centre			Popular Party (PP)	FN	PNV/HB CIU	Union 55 + Green Left
Sweden	Communist		Soc. Dem. (SAP)		Centre		Liberal	Conservative			Greens/Ecol
UK			Labour SDLP (N Ireland)	Lib-Dems.				Conservative		SNP UUP DUP N.Sinn Fein Plaid Cymru	Green Party

Sources: 1. Keesings Record of World Events. 2. Gordon Smith, Politics in Western Europe (Aldershot: Dartmouth, 1990) 3. Party manifestos.

Table 16.2 ● Voter turnout in general elections for selected Western democracies

Country	Turnout (% eligible voters)
Sweden	86.6
UK	77.7
Germany	76.3
France	69.9
Italy	67
US	55.5

Based on Hancock et al, *Politics in Eastern Europe*, 1993: elections were between 1990–2.

Table 16.3 ● Participation in EU elections (per cent)

	1979	1984	1989	1994
Belgium	91.4	92.1	93.0	90.7
Luxembourg	88.9	88.8	87.0	86.6
Italy	86.0	83.4	81.5	74.8
Greece	–	78.4	77.7	71.2
Germany	65.7	56.8	61.5	60.1
Spain	–	–	54.8	59.6
France	61.2	57.4	50.4	53.7
Denmark	47.8	54.0	46.0	52.5
Irish Republic	63.6	47.6	68.5	44.0
United Kingdom	32.8	32.5	36.0	36.1
Portugal	–	–	51.2	35.6
Netherlands	58.2	50.9	47.2	35.6
EU average	62.5	60.1	58.5	56.8

Source: United Nations Economic Commission for Europe

believe that power is widely dispersed throughout society and that the political system takes account of all constituencies.

A second pluralist assertion holds that power has many sources – including wealth, political office, social prestige, personal charisma and organisational clout. Only in exceptional cases do all these sources of power fall into the same hands. Here, again, the conclusion is that power is widely diffused (Dahl, 1961, 1982).

Figure 16.3 ● Percentage of MPs* who are women: EU comparison, 1995
*Lower chamber in bicameral parliaments.

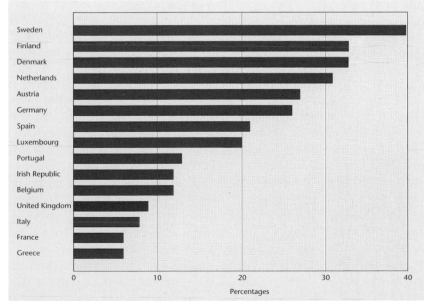

Source: United Nations Economic Commission for Europe

Research results

Supporting the pluralist model, Nelson Polsby (1959) found that in New Haven, Connecticut, key decisions on various issues – including urban renewal, the nomination of political candidates and the operation of the schools – were made by different groups. Polsby also noted that few of the upper-class families listed in New Haven's Social Register were also economic leaders. Thus, Polsby concluded, no one segment of society rules all the others.

Robert Dahl (1961) investigated New Haven's history and found that, over time, power had become increasingly dispersed. Dahl echoed Polsby's judgements, concluding that 'no one, and certainly no group of more than a few individuals, is entirely lacking in [power]' (1961: 228).

The pluralist model implies that 'democracies' are indeed reasonably democratic! They grant at least some power to everyone. Pluralists assert that not even the most influential people always get their way, and even the most disadvantaged are able to band together to ensure that some of their political interests are addressed.

The power elite model

The **power elite model** is *an analysis of politics that views power as concentrated among the rich.* This second approach is closely allied with the social-conflict paradigm. The term 'power elite' is a lasting contribution of C. Wright Mills (1956), who argued that the upper class holds the bulk of society's wealth, prestige and power. The power elite constitutes the 'super-rich' or, in Marxist terms, the capitalists who own and control the lion's share of the economy. These families, broadly linked through business dealings as well as marriage, are able to turn the national agenda towards their own interests.

Mills, writing about the power elite in the United States, claimed that historically that country has been dominated by three major sectors – the economy, the government and the military. Elites circulate from one sector to another, consolidating their power as they go. Alexander Haig, for example, has held top positions in private business, served as White House chief of staff under Richard Nixon, was secretary of state under Ronald Reagan, made a bid for the White House in 1988 as a presidential candidate, and is a retired army general. Haig is far from the exception: a majority of national political leaders enter public life from powerful and highly paid positions – 10 of 13 members of the Clinton cabinet are reputed to be millionaires – and most return to the corporate world later on.

Power elite theorists challenge claims that the United States is a political democracy; the concentration of wealth and power, they maintain, is simply too great for the average person's voice to be heard. Rejecting pluralist assertions that various centres of power serve as checks and balances on one another, the power elite model contends that those at the top encounter no real opposition.

Research results

Over more than fifty years, social scientists have conducted research that helps us evaluate these opposing views of government. Supporting the power elite position, Robert Lynd and Helen Lynd (1937) studied Muncie, Indiana (which they called 'Middletown', to indicate that it was a typical city). They documented the fortune amassed by a single family – the Balls – from their business manufacturing glass canning jars and showed how the Ball family dominated many dimensions of the city's life. If anyone doubted the Balls' prominence, the Lynds explained, there was no need to look further than the local bank, a university, a hospital and a department store, which all bear the family name. In Muncie, according to the Lynds, the power elite more or less boiled down to a single family.

Floyd Hunter's (1963) study of Atlanta, Georgia, provided further support for the power elite model. Atlanta, concluded Hunter, had no one dominant family; but there were no more than about 40 people who held all the top positions in the city's businesses and controlled the city's politics.

Critical evaluation

While these two models of power, summarised in Table 16.4, paint quite different pictures of US politics, some evidence validates each interpretation. Yet reviewing all the research on this issue, we find greater support for the power elite model. Even Robert Dahl (1982) – one of the strongest adherents of the concept of pluralism – concedes that the marked concentration of wealth and the barriers to equal opportunity faced by minorities constitute basic flaws in the US quest for a truly pluralist democracy.

Does this mean that the pluralist model is entirely wrong? No, but they do suggest that the US political system is not as democratic as some people think it is. The universal right to vote is a pluralist achievement, as is the right to form associations to pursue political ends. Even so, major political candidates usually support only those positions acceptable to the most powerful segments of society (Bachrach and Baratz, 1970).

● Marxist theories of the state

For Marxists, political equality is 'one of the great myths of our time' (Miliband, 1993). Basically, the state always works in the interests of the dominant, ruling, economic class: it favours and supports 'capital'. Although there may be many different groupings – elected parliaments, judiciaries, local government, pressure groups – which create a semblance of balance, checks and equality, in practice they simply serve as masks for what is really happening. There have been many prominent sociologists who have adopted variants of this position. Three will be introduced here.

The Italian Marxist Antonio Gramsci (1891–1937) was a leader in the Italian Communist Party.

Table 16.4 ● The pluralist and power elite models: a comparison (example of USA)

	Pluralist model	Power elite model
How is power distributed in the United States?	Dispersed	Concentrated
How many centres of power are there?	Many, each with a limited scope	Few, interconnected, with broad control over society
How do centres of power relate to one another?	They represent different political interests and thus provide checks on one another	They represent the same political interests and face little opposition
What is the relationship between power and the system of social stratification?	Some people have more power than others, but even minorities can organise to gain power. Wealth, social prestige and political office rarely overlap	Most people have little power, and the upper class dominates society. Wealth, social prestige and political office commonly overlap
What is the importance of voting?	Voting provides the public as a whole with a political voice	Voting involves choosing between alternatives acceptable to elites
What, then, is the most accurate description of the US political system?	A pluralist democracy	An oligarchy – rule by the wealthy few

Imprisoned from 1926 till his death by Mussolini's fascist government, his theory appears in his Prison Notebooks. For Gramsci : 'the state = political society + civil society'. The ruling class must gain the consent of the working class. No government can rule by force alone for long. He called this process **hegemony**, *the means by which a ruling/dominant group wins over a subordinated group through ideas*. To make hegemony work, dominated groups have to be taken into consideration, their interests noted and concessions given to them. Because dominated groups are always partially aware of their subordinated position, these concessions become vital to the smooth working of the state.

The English sociologist Ralph Miliband provides a lot of detail about the social background of cabinet ministers, senior police, top judges and the like, showing how they act in the interests of capital. Either these people occupy elite positions in the bourgeoisie or through education and culture they have come to identify with this group. Much work of the media disguises the real nature of the power, providing a process of legitimation.

The Greek sociologist Nicos Poulantzas adopts a wider (and much more abstract) approach. Individual politicians are not of interest to him. Instead, he looks at the state as part of a society, independent of people. It, so to speak, rolls on all on its own. The ruling class does not directly govern, but its interests are served through the autonomous functioning of a state which rises above sectional interests and maintains a myth of public interests and national unity. For Poulantzas, the state works through a repressive apparatus – army, police, etc. – using coercive power, and an ideological apparatus – church, schools, media and family – which 'manipulates' values and beliefs.

Poulantzas's theory is very abstract, and indeed he has been criticised for being too general and for seeing to little role (or indeed no role!) for people to play in shaping their own lives. More than this: he does not provide any evidence for his theories, and some have argued that the theory is impossible to prove or disprove.

Who rules Britain?

Which of these models – pluralist, power elite or ruling class – best fits Britain? Commentators on the political right often favour an elite view: that those who own wealth and land and come from better educated backgrounds should indeed have the majority say in the way the country is run. Commentators on the poitical left usually provide an analysis which sees a powerful ruling class furthering its own interests at the expense of the majority. 'A ruling class exists when there is both political domination and political rule by a capitalist class' (Scott, 1991: 124). Liberal commentators often favour pluralism – with power seen to be dispersed through society and with competing pressure groups.

John Scott has studied the power structures in the UK, asking who rules Britain? He suggests that 'there is in Britain today a ruling class' (1991: 4). Whilst there is an economically dominant class at the top of class structure, there is also a series of overlapping status circles at the top. Here there are strong alignments between educational backgrounds: 'private schooling remained the most important route to political success' (1991: 134). He suggests that Britain is run by an 'inner circle' of finance capitalists who represent a 'city' point of view. They fuse banking and industry, and play a key role in articulating capitalist industries within the power elite (Scott, 1991: 150–1; and see Chapter 10).

● The rise of social movements

Recent commentators on power structures have noticed the rise and proliferation of social movements, which are far more common today than in the past. Industrial societies foster diversity in the form of subcultures and countercultures, allowing social movements to develop around a wide range of public issues. In recent decades, for example, gays and lesbians have organised to combat discrimination. Like any social movement that challenges convention, this one has sparked a countermovement as traditionalists try to block greater social acceptance. In contemporary societies, almost every significant public issue gives rise to both a social movement favouring change and an opposing countermovement to resist change and reinforce the status quo (Lo, 1982).

Types of social movements

Sociologists have classified social movements according to several criteria (Aberle, 1966; Cameron, 1966; Blumer, 1969). One variable asks who is changed, since some movements target selected people while others try to change everyone. A second variable looks at how much change; some movements attempt to foster only superficial changes in how we live, while others pursue a radical transformation of society. Combining these variables, we can identify four types of social movements, shown in Figure 16.4.

Alternative social movements are the least threatening to the established social order, seeking limited change only in some narrow segment of the population. Planned Parenthood, one example of an alternative social movement, encourages individuals of childbearing age to take the consequences of sexual activity more seriously by practising birth control.

Redemptive social movements also have a selective focus, but they attempt to induce radical change in those they engage. Examples include fundamentalist Christian organisations that seek to win new members through conversion. The resulting transformation is sometimes so great that converts describe their experience as being 'born again'.

Reformative social movements aim for only limited social change but target everyone. The multiculturalism movement, described in Chapter 4 ('Culture'), is an educational and political initiative that advocates working towards social parity for all racial and ethnic categories of people. Reformative social movements generally work inside the existing political system. They can be progressive (promoting a new social pattern) or reactionary (countermovements trying to

Figure 16.4 ● Four types of social movements

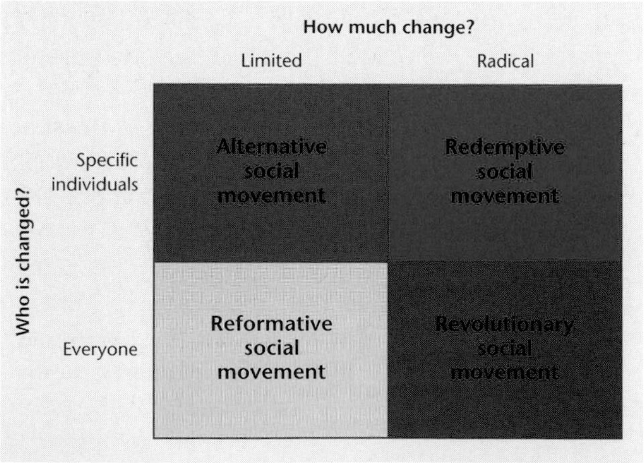

Source: Based on Aberle (1966)

preserve the status quo or to reinstate past social mores). Just as multiculturalists are pushing for greater racial equality, for example, so do various white supremacist organisations persist in their efforts to maintain the historical dominance of one racial category.

Revolutionary social movements have the most severe and far-reaching consequences of all, striving for basic transformation of a society. Sometimes pursuing specific goals, sometimes spinning utopian dreams, followers of these social movements reject established social institutions as inherently flawed while favouring radically new alternatives. Many environmental movements seek to radically change how we use and distribute resources in order to protect the planet. We will now look at five theories that are commonly used to explain the rise of social movements, summarised in Table 16.5. As we shall see, none of these theories is sufficient to stand on its own.

Deprivation theory

Relative deprivation theory holds that social movements arise among people who feel deprived. People who feel they lack sufficient income, satisfactory working conditions, important political rights or basic social dignity may engage in organised collective behaviour to bring about a more just state of affairs (Morrison, 1978; Rose, 1982).

As Chapter 7 ('Groups and Organisations') explained, deprivation is a relative concept. Regardless of how much money and power someone accumulates, people feel either well off or deprived compared to some category of others – a reference group. Relative deprivation, then, is a perceived disadvantage arising from some specific comparison (Stouffer et al., 1949; Merton, 1968).

More than a century ago Alexis de Tocqueville (1955; orig. 1856) studied the French Revolution. Why, he asked, did rebellion occur in progressive France rather than in more traditional Germany, where peasants were, by any objective measure, worse off? Tocqueville's answer was that, as bad as their condition was, German peasants had known nothing but feudal servitude and thus had no basis for feeling deprived. French peasants, by contrast, had seen various improvements in their lives that whetted their

Table 16.5 ● Theories of social movements: a summary

Deprivation theory	People forge a movement as a result of experiencing relative deprivation. The social movement is a means of seeking change that brings participants greater benefits. Social movements are especially likely when rising expectations are frustrated.
Mass-society theory	People who lack established social ties are mobilised into social movements. Periods of social breakdown are likely to spawn social movements. The social movement gives members a sense of belonging and social participation.
Structural-strain theory	People come together because of their shared concern about the inability of society to operate as they believe it should. The growth of a social movement reflects many factors, including a belief in its legitimacy and some precipitating event that provokes action.
Resource-mobilisation theory	People may join for all the reasons noted above and also because of social ties to existing members. The success or failure of a social movement depends largely on the resources available to it. Also important is the extent of opposition to its goals within the larger society.
New social movements theory	People who become part of social movements are motivated by 'quality of life' issues, not necessarily economic concerns. Mobilisation is national or international in scope. New social movements arise in response to the expansion of the mass media and the growing power of the state in modern industrial societies to affect people's lives for good or ill.

appetites for more. Thus the French – not the Germans – felt a keen sense of relative deprivation. Tocqueville pinpointed one of the notable ironies of human history: increasing prosperity, far from satisfying the population, is likely to promote a spirit of unrest (1955: 175; orig. 1856).

Deprivation theory has some problems, however. Most people experience some discontent at various times, yet social movements emerge among certain categories of people and not others. Deprivation theory also has a tendency towards circular reasoning: we assume that deprivation causes social movements, but often the only evidence of deprivation is the social movement itself (Jenkins and Perrow, 1977). A third limitation of this approach is that, while it focuses on the setting in which a social movement develops, it tells us little about movements themselves (McAdam, McCarthy and Zald, 1988). Fourth, some researchers have claimed that relative deprivation has not turned out to be a very good predictor of social movements (Muller, 1979).

Mass-society theory

William Kornhauser's mass-society theory (1959) argues that social movements arise in mass societies by providing socially isolated people with a sense of purpose and belonging (Melucci, 1989). People who have a strong sense of social integration, by contrast, are unlikely to join the ranks of a movement for change. Kornhauser regards activists as psychologically vulnerable individuals who eagerly join groups only to have leaders manipulate them, thereby subverting democratic principles. Thus extremist social movements on both ends of the political spectrum typically gain their most ardent support from people who have few other social affiliations.

The strength of Kornhauser's theory lies in its explanation of both the characteristics of the people who join social movements and the nature of the societies in which they form. Even so, it is extremely difficult to specify what constitutes a 'mass society'. Moreover, this theory minimises the importance of social justice. Put otherwise, Kornhauser suggests that flawed people, rather than a flawed society, underlie the emergence of social movements. Research support for this theory is mixed.

Structural-strain theory

One of the most influential approaches to understanding social movements is structural-strain theory, developed by Neil Smelser (1962). This analysis identifies six factors that foster social movements:

1. *Structural conduciveness*. Social movements arise when significant problems beset a society.

2. *Structural strain*. Relative deprivation and other kinds of strain stem from the inability of a society to meet the expectations of its people.

3. *Growth and spread of an explanation*. Any coherent social movement must formulate a clear statement of a problem, its causes and likely solutions. To the extent that these are well articulated, people are likely to express their dissatisfaction in an organised, goal-orientated way. If not, frustration may eventually explode in the form of unorganised and unproductive rioting.

4. *Precipitating factors*. Discontent frequently festers for a long time, only to be galvanised into collective action by a specific event.

5. *Mobilisation for action*. Widespread concern about a public issue sets the stage for collective action in the form of rallies, leafleting, building alliances with sympathetic organisations and similar activities.

6. *Lack of social control*. The responses of established authorities, such as political officials, police and the military, largely determine the outcome of any social movement. Firm repression by the state can weaken or even destroy a social movement, as demonstrated by the crushing of prodemocracy forces in the People's Republic of China. By contrast, Gorbachev adopted a policy of non-intervention in Eastern Europe, thereby increasing the possibility for change there.

The more prevalent these conditions are, Smelser suggests, the greater the likelihood that a social movement will emerge.

This theory recognises the complexity of social movements and points up how various factors encourage or inhibit their development, and also offers insights into which situations spark unorganised mobs or riots and which create highly organised social movements. Nevertheless, Smelser's theory incorporates some of the same circularity of argument found in Kornhauser's analysis. A social movement is caused by strain, he maintains, but frequently the only evidence of this underlying strain appears to be the emerging social movement itself. Finally, this theory overlooks the important role of resources such as the mass media or international alliances in the success or failure of a social movement (Oberschall, 1973; Jenkins and Perrow, 1977; McCarthy and Zald, 1977; Olzak and West, 1991).

Resource-mobilisation theory

An alternative approach, resource-mobilisation theory, notes that social movements are unlikely to succeed – or even get off the ground – without substantial resources, including money, human labour, office facilities, communications equipment, access to the mass media and a positive public image. In short, any social movement rises or falls on its capacity to attract resources, mobilise people and forge crucial alliances. The collapse of socialism in Eastern Europe was largely the work of dissatisfied people in those countries. But assistance from outside, including fax machines, copiers, telecommunications equipment, money and moral support provided by other nations, was instrumental in efforts first by the Poles and then by people in other nations to topple their leaders.

As this example demonstrates, supplying resources makes outsiders as important as insiders to the outcome of a social movement. Socially disadvantaged people generally lack the money, contacts, leadership skills and organisational know-how that a successful movement requires, and it is here that sympathetic outsiders often fill the resource gap.

To its credit, resource-mobilisation theory recognises that resources as well as discontent are critical to the success of a social movement. This theory also emphasises the interplay between social movements and other groups and organisations that are capable of providing or withholding valuable resources. Continuing research in this area suggests that a movement's position in the power structure also affects the strategies it can employ; violence, for example, is a resource that can be used by people seeking entrée into a political system (Grant and Wallace, 1991).

Critics of this approach maintain that even relatively powerless segments of a population can still promote successful social movements if they manage to organise effectively and have strongly committed members. A second problem with this theory is that it overstates the extent to which powerful people are willing to challenge the status quo. Overall, the success or failure of a social movement turns on the political struggle between challengers and supporters of intentional change. A strong and united establishment, perhaps aided by a countermovement, decreases the chances that any social movement will effect meaningful change. If, however, the established powers are divided, the movement's chances of success multiply.

New social movements theory

A final, more recent theoretical approach addresses the changing character of social movements. New social movements theory investigates the distinctive features of recent social movements in postindustrial societies of North America and Western Europe (Melucci, 1980; McAdam, McCarthy and Zald, 1988; Kriesi, 1989; Pakulski, 1993).

Today's most notable social movements are concerned with global ecology, the social standing of women and gay people, reducing the risks of war and animal rights, among others. One feature of these movements is their national and international scope. The power of the state continues to expand in postindustrial societies. Not surprisingly, then, the critical response to state policies has also assumed national proportions. As global political connections multiply, moreover, social movements respond by becoming international in scope.

Second, while traditional social movements, such as labour organisations, are concerned primarily with economic issues, new social movements tend to focus on cultural change and the improvement of our social and physical surroundings. The international environmental movement, for example, opposes practices that aggravate global warming and other worldwide threats to the environment.

Third, whereas most social movements of the past were guided by economic interests and elicited strong support from working-class people, new social movements often have non-economic agendas and usually draw disproportionate support from the middle and upper-middle classes.

Because new social movements theory is a recent development, sociologists are still assessing its usefulness. One clear strength of this analysis is its recognition that social movements are increasing in scale in response to the growing power of the state and the development of a global economic and political system. This theory also spotlights the power of the mass media to unite people around the world in pursuit of political goals.

Critics argue that this approach exaggerates differences between past and present social movements. The women's movement, for example, focuses on many of the same issues, including workplace conditions and pay, that consumed the energies of labour organisations for decades.

Stages in social movements

Researchers have identified four phases in the life of the typical social movement (shown in Figure 16.5): emergence, coalescence, bureaucratisation and decline (Blumer, 1969; Mauss, 1975; Tilly, 1978). In Stage 1, emergence, social movements build on the perception that all is not well. Some, such as the gay and lesbian rights and women's movements, are born of widespread dissatisfaction. Others emerge only as a small vanguard group increases public awareness of some issue.

By the second stage, coalescence, the movement must define itself and develop a strategy for 'going public'. Leaders must determine policies, decide on tactics, build morale and recruit new members. At this stage, the movement may engage in collective action like rallies or demonstrations to attract media attention in hopes of capturing public notice. Additionally, the movement may form alliances with other organisations to gain necessary resources.

To become an established political force, a social movement must bureaucratise, that is develop formal structures (Stage 3). As procedures become formal, the movement depends less on the charisma and talents of a few leaders and relies more on a capable staff. Social movements which avoid this stage, like campaigns organised to prod legislation against 'dangerous dogs' and handgun ownership in Britain, have short lives, fading when leaders lose energy or even die. Bureaucratisation can also weaken a movement by blunting the radical and innovative edge. On the other hand, the well-established Greenpeace, despite its changing leadership, offers a steady voice on behalf of environmentalists.

Social movements are inherently dynamic, so a decline (Stage 4) need not signal a demise (Wright, 1987). Eventually, however, most social movements do wither. This may occur when members achieve their primary goals, because of organisational factors, such as poor leadership or exhaustion of resources, or because hostile public or governmental reaction (sometimes literally) beats activists into submission. 'Selling out' is another possible outcome, when organisational leaders may use their positions to enrich themselves.

Figure 16.5 ● Stages in the life of social movements

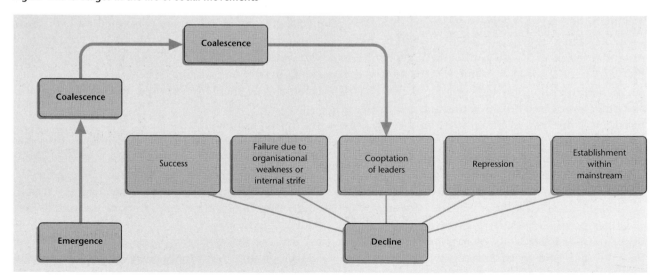

Social movements and social change

Social movements exist to encourage – or to resist – social change. Sometimes we overlook the success of past social movements and take for granted the changes that other people struggled so hard to win. Early workers' movements, for example, battled for decades to end child labour in factories, to limit working hours, to make the workplace safer and to establish the right to bargain collectively with employers. Legislation protecting the environment is also the product of successful social movements throughout this century. The women's movement has yet to attain full social equality for the sexes, but it has significantly extended the legal rights and economic opportunities of women. In fact, younger people can be surprised to learn that, earlier in this century, few women worked for income and none were permitted to vote.

Past social movements have shaped society in ways that people now take for granted. Just as movements produce change, so change itself sparks social movements. New social movements have been shaped by widespread dissatisfaction with the existing political system and debates. They bring new issues (especially issues linked to the environment, gender, peace, race, world development) and a broader conception of participatory politics, and often dissolve the clear distinction between public and private (Chapter 21, The Mass Media). As leading German sociologist Klauss Offe says 'the conflicts and contradictions of advanced industrial society can no longer be resolved by the state or by increasing bureaucracy' (Offe, 1985). New social movements are seen as the answer.

This broad view leads to one overarching conclusion: we can draw a direct link between social movements and change. In one direction, social transformations such as the Industrial Revolution and the rise of capitalism sparked the emergence of various social movements. Going the other way, the efforts of workers, women, racial and ethnic minorities and gay people have sent ripples of change throughout industrial societies. Thus social change is both the cause and the consequence of social movements.

Social movements have become a growing feature of globalised postindustrial life. The scope of social movements is likely to grow, for two reasons. First, the technology of the Information Revolution has drawn the world closer together than ever before. Today anyone with a satellite dish, personal computer or fax machine can stay abreast of political events, often as they happen. Second, as a consequence of new technology as well as the emerging global economy, social movements are now uniting people throughout the entire world. With the realisation that many problems are global in scope has come the understanding that they can be effectively addressed only on an international scale.

● Power beyond the rules

Politics is always a matter of disagreement about goals and the means to achieve them. Yet a political system tries to resolve controversy within a system of rules. The most heated debates in the European Community today surround efforts to synchronise these rules across the many, disparate countries. But political activity sometimes exceeds – or tries to do away with – established practices.

Revolution

Political revolution is *the overthrow of one political system in order to establish another*. In contrast to reform, which involves change within a system and rarely escalates into violence, revolution implies change of the system itself, sometimes sparking violent action. While the revolutions throughout Eastern Europe beginning in 1989 peacefully overthrew communist regimes in numerous countries, fighting in Romania ended thousands of lives.

No type of political system is immune to revolution; nor does revolution invariably produce any one kind of government. Colonial rule by the British monarchy in the United States was overthrown by the revolutionary war. The French revolutionaries in 1789 also overthrew a monarch, only to set the stage for the return of monarchy in the person of Napoleon. In 1917, the Russian Revolution replaced monarchy with a socialist government built on the ideas of Karl Marx (overturned, again, in 1992).

Despite their striking variety, revolutions share a number of traits, according to political analysts (Tocqueville, 1955, orig. 1856; also Davies, 1962; Brinton, 1965; Skocpol, 1979; Lewis, 1984; Tilly, 1986):

1. *Rising expectations.* Although common sense would dictate that revolution is more likely when people are grossly deprived, history shows that revolution generally occurs when people's lives are improving. Rising expectations, rather than bitter resignation, fuel revolutionary fervour.

2. *Unresponsive government.* Revolutionary zeal gains strength to the extent that a government is unwilling or unable to reform, especially when demands for change are made by large numbers of people or powerful segments of society.

3. *Radical leadership by intellectuals.* The English philosopher Thomas Hobbes (1588–1679) observed that political rebellion is often centred in universities. During the 1960s, throughout Europe and the United States, students were at the forefront of much of the political unrest that marked that tumultuous decade. Students also played a key role in China's recent prodemocracy movement, as they did in the toppling of socialist governments in Eastern Europe.

4. *Establishing a new legitimacy.* The overthrow of a political system rarely comes easily, but it is more difficult still to ensure a revolution's long-term success. Some revolutionary drives are unified merely by hatred of the past regime and fall victim to internal division once new leaders are installed. Revolutionary movements must also guard against counterrevolutionary drives spearheaded by past leaders; frequently, revolutionaries ruthlessly dispose of these former leaders.

Scientific analysis cannot pronounce the effects of revolution as good or bad. The full consequences of such an upheaval depend on one's values and, in any case, take many years to shake out. For example, in the wake of recent revolution, the future of the former Yugoslavia remains unsettled.

Terrorism

The activities of the IRA in the UK, Bader Meinhoff in Germany and the US bombing of the Oklahoma City federal building bring home the significance of **terrorism**, *violence or the threat of violence employed by an individual or a group as a political strategy.* Like revolution, terrorism is a political act beyond the rules of established political systems. Paul Johnson (1981) offers four insights about terrorism.

First, explains Johnson, terrorists try to cast violence as a legitimate political tactic, even though virtually every society condemns such acts. Terrorists also bypass (or are excluded from) established channels of political negotiation. Terror is thus a weak organisation's strategy to harm a stronger foe. For example, the people who held Western hostages in the Middle East until 1991 may have been morally wrong to do so, but they succeeded in directing the world's attention to that region of the globe.

Second, Johnson continues, terrorism is a tactic employed not only by groups but also by governments against their own people. **State terrorism** refers to *the use of violence, generally without support of law, against individuals or groups by a government or its agents.* While contrary to democratic political principles, state terrorism figures prominently in authoritarian and totalitarian societies, which survive by inciting fear and intimidation. From the left-wing regimes in North Korea and the former Soviet Union to the extreme right-wing regimes in Nazi Germany and Zaire, states have routinely employed terror against their own citizens. More recently, Saddam Hussein has ruled Iraq in the same manner.

Third, although democratic societies reject terrorism in principle, democracies are especially vulnerable to terrorists because they afford extensive civil liberties to their people and have minimal police networks. This susceptibility helps to explain the tendency of democratic governments to suspend civil liberties if officials perceive themselves to be under attack. Hostage taking and outright killing provoke widespread anger, but devising an effective response to such acts poses several thorny problems. Because most terrorist groups are shadowy organisations with no formal connection to any established state, targeting reprisals may be impossible. Yet the failure to respond can encourage other terrorist groups. Then, too, a forcible military reaction to terrorism may broaden the scope of violence, increasing the risk of confrontation with other governments.

Fourth, and finally, terrorism is always a matter of definitions. Governments claim the right to maintain order, even by force, and may brand opponents who use violence as 'terrorists'. Similarly, political differences may explain why one person's 'terrorist' is another's 'freedom fighter'.

Violence beyond the rules: a report from the former Yugoslavia

War is violent, but it also has rules. Many of the current norms of warfare emerged from the ashes of the Second World War, when German and Japanese military officials were brought to trial for war crimes. Subsequently, the United Nations has added to the broad principles of fair play in war that have become known as the 'Geneva Conventions' (the first of which dates back to 1864).

One of the most important principles of the rules of war is that, whatever violence soldiers inflict upon each other, they cannot imprison, torture, rape or murder civilians; nor can they deliberately destroy civilian property or wantonly bomb or shell cities to foster widespread terror. Even so, a growing body of evidence reveals that all these crimes have occurred as part of the protracted and bloody civil war in the former Yugoslavia. Serbs, Croats and Muslims have all committed war crimes – tens of thousands of deaths, rapes and serious injuries plus an incalculable

loss of property. Late in 1993, therefore, a United Nations tribunal convened in the Netherlands to assess

---

Civil wars, such as the conflict in the former Yugoslavia, are among the most tragic forms of bloodshed because a large proportion of causalities are not soldiers but civilians who find themselves in harm's way. Dozens of people died on this street in Sarajevo as mortar rounds fired from the mountains surrounding the city rained down on men, women and children who were going about their daily lives.

Source: Black Star – Peter Northall

the evidence and consider possible responses.

After the Second World War, the Allies successfully prosecuted (and, in several cases, executed) German officers for their crimes against humanity based on evidence culled from extensive Nazi records. This time around, however, the task of punishing offenders is proving to be far more difficult. For one thing, there appear to be no written records of the Balkan conflict; for another, United Nations officials fear that arrests may upset the delicate diplomatic efforts at bringing peace to the region.

Even so, since beginning their investigations in 1993, the United Nations has indicted more than 50 military officers on all sides of the conflict for war crimes. But many observers suspect that – despite a staggering toll in civilian deaths – very few will ever be convicted. ●

Sources: adapted from Nelan, 1993, and various news reports.

● War and peace

Perhaps the most critical political issue is **war**, *armed conflict among the people of various societies, directed by their governments*. War is as old as humanity, of course, but the awesome destructiveness of today's nuclear arsenals lends new urgency to understanding international confrontations. Thus, most scholarly investigation of war has the aim of promoting **peace**, *a state of international relations devoid of violence*. Peace implies the absence of war, although not necessarily the lack of all political conflict.

Many people think of war as extraordinary, yet it is peace that is actually rare, existing world-wide only for brief periods during this century. The scale of devastation across Europe during the World Wars of this century has been enormous; but there are at present over 30 wars being waged across the earth with millions of casualties.

The causes of war

The frequency of war in human affairs might imply that there is something natural about armed confrontation. Members of every culture embrace certain symbols and principles – such as patriotism and freedom – to the point that they are willing to fight to defend (or extend) them. But while many animals are naturally aggressive, research provides no basis for concluding that human beings inevitably wage war under any particular circumstances. Indeed, governments around the world have to use considerable coercion to enlist the support of their people for wars (Lorenz, 1966; Montagu, 1976).

Like all forms of social behaviour, warfare is a product of society that varies in purpose and intensity from culture to culture. The Semai of Malaysia, among the most peace-loving of the world's people, rarely resort to violence. By contrast, the Yanomamö, described in Chapter 4 ('Culture'), are quick to wage war with others.

If society holds the key to war or peace, under what circumstances do humans engage in warfare? Quincy Wright (1987) identifies five factors that promote war:

1. *Perceived threats*. Societies mobilise in response to a perceived threat to their people, territory or culture. The United States defined Iraq's invasion of Kuwait in 1990 as an immediate threat to national security and subsequently evicted Iraq using military force; by contrast, governments did not define the ethnic turmoil in the former Yugoslavia in these terms and the US military presence there has been more limited.

2. *Social problems*. Internal problems that generate widespread frustration may prompt a society's leaders to become aggressive towards others. In this way, societies 'construct' enemies as a form of scapegoating. Sluggish economic development in the People's Republic of China, for example, periodically touched off that nation's hostility towards Vietnam, Tibet and Russia.

3. *Political objectives*. Leaders sometimes settle on war as a desirable political strategy. Poor nations, such as Vietnam, have fought wars to end foreign domination. For powerful countries like the United States, a periodic 'show of force' (such as the recent deployment of troops in Somalia and Haiti) may enhance global political stature.

4. *Moral objectives*. Rarely do nations claim to fight merely to increase their wealth and power. Leaders infuse military campaigns with moral urgency, rallying people around religious values or secular visions of 'freedom'. Although few doubted that the 1991 Persian Gulf War was largely about oil, Western strategists portrayed the mission as a drive to halt a Hitler-like Saddam Hussein.

5. *The absence of alternatives*. A fifth factor promoting war is the absence of alternatives. Article 1 of the United Nations Charter defines that organisation's task as 'maintaining international peace'. Despite some notable successes, however, its ability to resolve tensions among self-interested societies has been limited.

In short, war is rooted in social dynamics – on a national and international level. Moreover, even combat has its own system of rules, the violation of which can lead to charges of war crimes. The box on page 464 takes a closer look.

The costs and causes of militarism

The costs of armed conflicts extend far beyond battle-field casualties. Together, the world's nations spend some £3.5 trillion annually for military purposes. Such expenditures, of course, divert resources from the desperate struggle for survival by millions of poor people throughout the world. Moreover, a large proportion of the world's top scientists concentrate on military research; this resource, too, is siphoned away from other work that might benefit humanity.

In recent years, defence has been the largest single expenditure of most governments. In the United States, for example, it accounts for 18 per cent of all federal spending, or £170 billion in 1995. This huge expenditure amounts to about £750 for every man, woman and child in the country.

The United States became a superpower as it emerged victorious from the Second World War with newly developed nuclear weapons. The atomic bomb

Although the two nuclear superpowers – the United States and the Russian Federation – have reduced their arsenals in recent years, global security is threatened by nuclear proliferation. Early in the next century, perhaps 50 nations – many engaged in regional conflicts – will have nuclear weapons.

Source: Baldeu/Sygma

broken out in Bosnia, Chechnya and Rwanda, and tensions still run high in a host of other countries, including Northern Ireland, Iraq and a divided Korea. Even wars of limited scope have the potential to escalate, involving other countries. And the danger of regional conflicts is growing as more and more nations gain access to nuclear weapons.

Nuclear weapons

Despite the easing of superpower tensions, the world still contains almost 25,000 nuclear warheads perched on missiles or ready to be carried by aircraft. This arsenal represents destructive power that one can barely imagine: five tons of TNT for every person on the planet. Should even a small fraction of this stockpile be detonated in war, life as we know it would cease on much of the earth. Albert Einstein, whose genius contributed to the development of nuclear weapons, reflected: 'The unleashed power of the atom has changed everything save our modes of thinking, and we thus drift toward unparalleled catastrophe'. In short, nuclear weapons have rendered unrestrained war unthinkable in a world not yet capable of peace.

At present, although the UK, France and the People's Republic of China have a substantial nuclear capability, the vast majority of nuclear weapons are held by the United States and Russia, which have agreed to reduce their stockpiles of nuclear warheads to about a quarter of their present size by 2003. But even as this rivalry winds down, the danger of catastrophic war is increasing along with **nuclear proliferation**, *the acquisition of nuclear-weapons technology by more and more nations*. Most experts agree that Israel, India, Pakistan, North Korea and South Africa already possess some nuclear weapons, and other nations (including Argentina, Brazil, Iraq and Libya) are in the process of developing them. By the year 2000, as many as 50 nations could have the ability to fight a nuclear war, a fact that underscores the dangers inherent in any regional conflict (Spector, 1988).

was first used in war by US forces to crush Japan in 1945. But the Soviet Union countered by exploding a nuclear bomb of its own in 1949, unleashing the 'cold war', by which leaders of each superpower became convinced that their counterparts were committed to military superiority. Ironically, for the next 40 years, both sides pursued a policy of escalating military expenditures that neither nation wanted nor could afford.

With the collapse of the Soviet Union in 1991, much of the cold war dissipated. Yet US military expenditures remain high. Some analysts have argued that, all along, the US economy has relied on militarism to generate corporate profits (Marullo, 1987). This approach, closely allied to power elite theory, maintains that the United States is dominated by a **military-industrial complex**, *the close association among the federal government, the military and defence industries*. The roots of militarism, then, lie not just in external threats to US security; they also grow from within the institutional structures of US society.

Another reason for persistent militarism in the post-cold war world is regional conflict. Since the collapse of the Soviet Union, for example, localised wars have

GLOBAL SOCIOLOGY

Beyond left and right: the politics of difference

Industrialisation, the emergence of modern nation-states and revolutionary movements on behalf of democracy have brought people to join together under the labels 'left' or 'right' for the past 200 years. (The terms originated in the French revolutionary assembly of the 1790s where the left were radicals and the right were moderates.) And for most of the twentieth century, the political divides have been very sharply drawn on these lines: capitalism versus communism, right versus left, the East versus the West. The demise of the cold war between the United States and what Reagan called the 'evil empire' of the USSR (Russia), was spectacularly symbolised at the end of 1980s by the fall of the Berlin Wall. At the time there was much jubilation. But the problem now – at the turn of the century – is where is all this heading? For many of the old communist countries a kind of chaos has been reached. For much of the old West, a kind of directionlessness has happened. If the old divides are crumbling, what is politics about in the twenty-first century?

One response was to see the end of these conflicts as the end of history. The fall of the Berlin Wall symbolised the final victory of capitalist democracy: this was the way of the world from now on. Francis Fukuyama sees 'the end of history' as nothing less than the worldwide triumph of modernity, capitalism and liberal democracy. The ideological battles are now over, and there are no alternatives. Fukuyama sees the 'universalisation of Western democracy as the final form of human government' (1989): Monarchism, fascism and communism have been rendered indefensible for all but a few

Source: Popperfoto

Information warfare

As earlier chapters have explained, the Information Revolution is changing almost every dimension of social life. In the next century, how will computers reshape warfare?

Currently, military strategists envision future conflict played out not with rumbling tanks and screaming aircraft but with electronic 'smart bombs' that would greatly reduce an enemy country's ability to transmit information. In such 'virtual wars', soldiers seated at workstation monitors would dispatch computer viruses to shut down an aggressor's communication lines, causing telephones to fall silent, air traffic control and railway switching systems to fail, computer systems to feed phoney orders to field officers, and televisions to broadcast 'morphed' news bulletins, prompting people to turn against their leaders.

Like the venom of a poisonous snake, the weapons of 'information warfare' can quickly paralyse an adversary, perhaps triggering a conventional military engagement. Another, more hopeful, possibility is that

extreme groups. Even the old left has died: Britain's New Labour, for instance, now champions policies that sound suspiciously like the old Conservative party. Similar moves are happening around the world.

But not all agree with Fukuyama. Many new 'politics' are being suggested. For instance, in Chapter 20 ('Environment') we will document the degradation of our environment; and here many argue for the world-wide development of a green politics.

Others, such as the English social theorist Anthony Giddens, are arguing for a 'democratic life politics' – a global politics which rethinks how we are to live and how we are to revitalise democracy through dialogue in a world which is changing globally at an accelerating rate. Arguing that both 'socialism and conservatism have disintegrated' (Giddens, 1994: 9), he champions a 'dialogic democracy' where importance is given to dialogues and the many different voices arguing for different ways to live. He seeks a radical rethinking of democracy – in opposition to fundamentalism of all kinds.

Others see these 'fundamentalisms' as the very basis of conflicts in the future. Benjamin Barber argues that the world is no longer divided between left and right. Instead the divide has shifted globally to one between consumerist capitalism (symbolised by a global McDonald's, or McWorld) and religious and tribal fundamentalisms (symbolised by the Islamic jihad). The former is rapidly dissolving nation-states and political boundaries, leading to the triumph of individualism and the marketplace all over the world. At the same time, the latter is forcing ethnic, religious and tribal conflicts into politics everywhere. This tension may be seen as one which goes to the heart of global modernity, and its manifestations in 'tribal warfare' are becoming increasingly apparent.

This is an important debate for the next century. Some argue that the old left and right positions of the twentieth century need a clear reasserting: they are still relevant. Others argue we have reached 'the end of history' and we are now, more or less, stuck with capitalist liberal democracies which in the twenty-

first century will rule the world. Still others see distinct dangers emerging in the continuing clashes between ethnic and religious fundamentalism and the free-for-all marketplace of consumer capitalism. And still others are looking to the creation of new political forms with social movements at the forefront, and new issues – green politics, lifestyles politics, differences – at the forefront.

● **Continue the debate:**

1. Have we really reached 'the end of history' and the triumph of liberal capitalism?

2. If fundamentalism is on the increase, will not this result in more and more bloody wars and conflicts?

3. Is not a politics based on lifestyle just an indulgence of the over-rich West?

4. How central do you think social movements around 'green politics' will become in the twenty-first century? ●

Sources: Francis Fukuyama, *The End of History*, 1989; Anthony Giddens, *Beyond Left and Right*, 1994; Benjamin Barber, *Jihad vs McWorld*, 1995.

new information technology might not just precede conventional fighting but prevent it entirely. Yet so-called 'infowar' also poses new dangers, since, presumably, a few highly skilled operators with sophisticated electronic equipment could also wreak havoc on communications in Europe and the rest of the world.

The pursuit of peace

How can the world reduce the dangers of war? Here are brief sketches of several recent approaches to promoting peace.

1. *Deterrence.* The logic of the arms race linked security to a 'balance of terror' between the superpowers. Based on the principle of mutually assured destruction (MAD) – meaning that either side launching a first-strike nuclear attack against the other would sustain massive retaliation – the strategy of deterrence has accompanied peace for almost 50 years. But it has three flaws. First, it has fuelled an exorbitantly expensive arms race. Second, missiles are now capable of delivering their warheads more quickly than when this strategy was first devised,

Patrick J. Garrity and Steven A. Maaranen (eds.), *Nuclear Weapons in the Changing World: Perspectives from Europe, Asia, and North America* (New York: Plenum, 1992).

This collection of essays by experts examines nuclear-weapons issues from the points of view of nations in various regions of the world.

Cynthia Enloe, *Bananas, Beaches, and Bases: Making Feminist Sense of International Politics* (Berkeley: University of California Press, 1990).

This feminist analysis of the world political scene maintains that gender is at the centre of global power structures.

Hanspeter Kriesi, Ruud Koopmans, Jan Willem Dyvendak and Marco G.Giuni, *New Social Movements in Western Europe* (London: UCL Press, 1995).

Many social movements have swept across Western Europe in recent decades; this book assesses what has changed and what has not.

Gao Yuan, *Born Red: A Chronicle of the Cultural Revolution* (Stanford, California: Stanford University Press, 1987).

This personal account of one teenager's experiences during the Cultural Revolution in China between 1966 and 1969 explores the causes and consequences of a mass movement that spun out of control.

chapter seventeen

Source: Popperfoto

Families

The Japanese are in the midst of a national debate on 'family values'. The problem is not divorce (relatively rare in Japan) or unmarried women having children (which is extremely rare). The Japanese are simply not having children – not enough, at least, to replace adults of childbearing age. Since 1950, in fact, the average number of children born to a Japanese woman during her lifetime has tumbled from almost five to just over one.

This precipitous decline is no indication that the Japanese have lost their love for children. Quite the contrary. Virtually all young Japanese couples claim to want children, and even screaming babies on a bus or train elicit smiles and sympathy from fellow travellers. The reason for the declining birth rate is that Japanese women display unprecedented reluctance to marry. Back in 1970, only 20 per cent of Japanese women reaching the age of 30 had yet to wed; today, that share has doubled to 40 per cent.

Why the second thoughts about marriage? For one thing, Japanese culture defines motherhood as a full-time responsibility, which precludes a career. Just as important, the typical Japanese husband works long hours – half are away from home at least 12 hours a day. When he is at home, moreover, the typical Japanese man performs almost no housework and spends little time with his children.

To young women in Japan, therefore, marriage commonly amounts to a daily round of housework, doting on youngsters and shuttling older children to special 'cram' schools where they prepare for all-important college entrance examinations. Faced with such prospects, more women are opting to stay single, live with parents, work and enjoy plenty of free time and spending money (The *Economist*, 1994).

The state of the family is a 'hot topic' all around the world, not just in Japan. In China, for instance, a population policy of one child per family was introduced in the 1970s – with enormous consequences.

In the UK fewer than one in four households now conform to the traditional image of a married or cohabiting couple with children. Indeed the often presumed model of the traditional nuclear family is now more likely to be found amongst households in Bangladeshi and Pakistani communities. In the United States the situation has developed further: one sociologist has suggested that by 1986 'only 7% of households conformed to the "modern" pattern of breadwinning father, homemaking mother and one to four children under the age of eighteen' (Stacey, 1992). And in many countries – especially the Nordic countries and the Netherlands – there are laws and debates emerging around same sex registered partnerships.

The opening box highlights a number of these changes in the UK. All taken together, a basic truth emerges: families in the UK, the rest of Europe and in other industrial societies are changing dramatically.

This chapter highlights important recent changes in family life and offers some insights to explain these trends. Yet, as we shall also point out, changing family patterns are nothing new to this country. Over a century ago, for example, concern over the decline of the

FOCUS ON EUROPE

What's going on in the family in the UK?

Marriage
In 1996, the number of marriages in the UK was at a 70 year low. There were 201,000 first marriages in 1994, half that of 1970. People are also marrying at older ages: the average age in the EU in 1993 was 28.5 for men and 26.1 for women. (The lowest marriage rate is Sweden, see box on pages 476 and 477: A report from Sweden.)

Cohabitation
This has risen significantly. The proportion of all non-married women aged 18 to 40 cohabiting has doubled since 1981 to 25 per cent. But cohabitation is often amongst the divorced and often ends through remarriage.

Divorces
The peak period for divorce was the 1970s, and it is now more stable (at around 160,000 a year). Between 1971 and 1994, the divorce rate more than

doubled, so that by 1994, the United Kingdom had the highest divorce rate in the European Union (but it was still not as high as that of some countries like the United States). It is expected that 40 per cent of recent UK marriages will end in divorce.

Roughly a quarter of children can now expect to find their original parents divorced by the time they are 16.

Home alone
More people are living alone. More than a quarter of all households are now one person households; this is double what it was in 1961. And household size fell from 3.09 in 1961 to 2.46 in 1990. In the UK, a curious new group of 'single men' is appearing.

Births outside of marriage
In the UK, about a third of all live births occur outside marriage; and in nearly

all European countries rate has doubled in the last 30 years. It is highest in Sweden and lowest in Greece (see map 17.2). Most of these births occur in stable relationships outside marriage (80 per cent are registered by both parents).

Lone parents
Almost one in five families with dependent children are lone parent families. Denmark and Sweden have the highest numbers in Europe. Most (52 per cent) are through divorce or separation; single mothers are around a third of this number and 42 per cent of them had incomes below £100 per week.

Women remaining childless
Whilst most women do have children, the number who do not has been growing (20 per cent of those born in 1954) and women are having children later in the lifecycle.

family swept the nation as the Industrial Revolution propelled people from farms to factories. Today, of course, many of the same concerns surround the rising share of women whose careers draw them away from home. In short, changes in other social institutions, especially the economy, are shaping ways of living together, including marriage and family life.

● The family: basic concepts

The **family** is *a social institution that unites individuals into cooperative groups that oversee the bearing and raising of children*. These social units are, in turn, built on kinship, *a social bond, based on blood, marriage or adoption, that joins individuals into families*. Although all societies contain families, just who is included under the umbrella of kinship has varied through history, and varies today from one culture to another.

During the twentieth century, most members of society have regarded a **family unit** as *a social group of two or more people, related by blood, marriage or adoption, who usually live together*. Initially, individuals are born into a family composed of parents and siblings, which is sometimes called the *family of orientation* because this group is central to socialisation. In adulthood, people forge a *family of procreation* in order to have or adopt children of their own.

Adoption
The numbers in adoption have sharply fallen. Six thousand in England and Wales in 1994, compared with 21,000 in 1971.

Diversity
There are now many different kinds of households. Fewer than one in four households now conform to the traditional image of a married or cohabiting couple with children. In the United States, one sociologist, Judith Stacey (1996), suggested that by 1986 only 7 per cent of households conformed to the modern patterns of breadwinning father, homemaking mother and one to four children under the age of eighteen. In the UK, the presumed model of the traditional nuclear family is now more likely to be found amongst households in Bangladeshi and Pakistani communities. There are debates about 'families of choice' especially where there are same sex registered partnerships (Denmark, Sweden, Norway, Finland).

Children
In 1901, 34.6 per cent of the population in the UK were under 16; in 1981 it was 22.3 per cent. The average number of children in a family was 1.8 (including adopted and step-children).

Working mothers
In 1931, 10 per cent of married women were economically active. By 1951 this had risen to 30 per cent and by 1987 it stood at 60 per cent. Most of this was in part-time employment and involved a 'second shift', making the women's week around 77 hours!

The generational gap
There is a large difference in attitude towards 'family' between those born before 1930 and those born since 1950. For example, 61–64 per cent of the former group would advise marriage without living together first; only 17 per cent of the younger group would now advise this.

Sexuality
The pill remains the most popular form of contraception – a quarter of all women aged 16 to 49 use it. In 1971, 21 per cent of births were conceived out of marriage; today it is around one in three and growing – especially in younger groups. In 1961 there were 54,000 births outside marriage; by 1991, the figure was 236,000. There has been a dramatic decline in the age of first intercourse: the median for young men and women (born between 1966 and 1975) was 17 years. Gay and lesbian sexualities have flourished.

Life expectancy
The twentieth century has seen 25 years added to human life expectancy, shifting the shape of the lifecycle. ●

Sources: Social Focus on Families, 1997; *Social Trends* 1997.

Throughout the world, families form around **marriage** *a legally sanctioned relationship, involving economic cooperation as well as normative sexual activity and childbearing, that people expect to be enduring.* Embedded in our language is evidence of a cultural belief that marriage alone is the appropriate context for procreation: traditionally, people have attached the label of *illegitimacy* to children born out of wedlock; moreover, *matrimony*, in Latin, means 'the condition of motherhood'. This link between childbearing and marriage has weakened, however, as the proportion of children born to single women has increased (noted earlier to be nearing one in four).

Many now object to defining as 'families' only married couples and children because that implies that everyone should embrace a single standard. As more and more people forge the non-traditional family ties, which we will discuss later, many are now thinking of

kinship in terms of *families of affinity* or **families of choice** (Weston, 1991), *people with or without legal or blood ties who feel they belong together and wish to define themselves as a family.* What does or does not constitute a family, then, is a moral and political matter that lies at the heart of the contemporary 'family values' debate, raised in the box on pages 496 and 497.

Global variety

Typically, members of preindustrial societies take a broad view of family ties, recognising the **extended family** as *a family unit including parents and children, but also other kin.* Extended families are also called *consanguine families*, meaning that they include everyone with 'shared blood'. Industrialisation, which sparks both geographic and social mobility (see Chapter 15, 'The Economy, Consumption and Work'),

FOCUS ON EUROPE

A less central family? A report from Sweden

Sweden is burdened with few of the social problems that are often identified with modern capitalism: in urban Sweden, there is little of the violent crime, drug abuse and grinding poverty that has blighted many other places. This Scandinavian nation seems to fulfil the promise of the modern welfare state, with an extensive and professional government bureaucracy that sees to virtually all human needs.

But Sweden also has very different kinds of families. Because people look to the government – not to spouses – for economic assistance, Swedes are less likely to marry than members of any other industrialised society. For

the same reason, Sweden also has a high share of adults living alone (more than 20 per cent). Moreover, a large proportion of couples live

In Sweden, unmarried women bear half of all children, twice the rate of births by single women in the United States.

Source: The Stock Market – Bo Zaunders

together outside of marriage (25 per cent) and half of all Swedish children (compared to about one in three in Europe) are born to unmarried parents.

Average household size in Sweden is also the smallest in the world (2.2 persons). Finally, Swedish couples (whether married or not) are more likely to break up than partners in any other country. US sociologist David Popenoe sums up by claiming that the family 'has probably become weaker in Sweden than anywhere else – certainly among advanced Western nations. Individual family members are the most autonomous and least bound by the group . . .' (1991: 69).

gives rise to the **nuclear family**, *a family unit composed of one or two parents and their children.* Because it is based on marriage, the nuclear family is also known as the *conjugal family.* Although many members of society live in extended families, nuclear families and families of choice, the nuclear family has become the predominant idealised image of the modern family. Di Gittins calls this 'familism': 'an ideology [which] claims there is only one type of family [that] can never be matched in reality . . .' (Gittins, 1985: 167).

Marriage patterns

Cultural norms, as well as laws, identify people as desirable or unsuitable marriage partners. Some marital norms promote **endogamy**, *marriage between people of the same social category.* Endogamy limits marriage prospects to others of the same age, race, religion or social class. By contrast, **exogamy** mandates *marriage between people of different social categories.* In rural India, for example, young people are expected to marry someone of the same caste (endogamy), but from a different village (exogamy).

Throughout the world, societies pressure people to marry someone of the same social background but of the other sex. The logic of endogamy is simple: people of similar social position pass along their standing to offspring, thereby maintaining traditional social patterns. Exogamy, by contrast, helps to forge useful alliances and promotes cultural diffusion.

In industrial societies today, laws prescribe **monogamy** (from Greek meaning 'one union'), *a form of marriage joining two partners.* The high level of divorce and remarriage, however, suggests that *serial monogamy* is a more accurate description of UK marital practice. Map 17.1 shows that while monogamy is the

Popenoe contends that a growing culture of individualism and self-fulfilment, coupled with the declining influence of religion, began to 'erode' Swedish families back in the 1960s. The movement of women into the labour force also plays a part. Sweden has the lowest proportion of women who are homemakers (10 per cent versus about 25 per cent in Europe) and the highest percentage of women in the labour force (77 per cent versus 59 per cent in Europe).

But, most important, according to Popenoe, is the expansion of the Swedish welfare state, one of the most far-reaching schemes of its kind. The Swedish government offers citizens a lifetime of services – and high taxes. Swedes can count on the government to give them jobs, sustain their income, deliver and educate their children, provide comprehensive health care

and, when the time comes, pay for their funeral.

Many Swedes supported this welfare programme, Popenoe explains, thinking it would strengthen families. But with the benefit of hindsight, he concludes, we see that proliferating government programmes actually have been replacing families. Take the case of child care. The Swedish government operates public child-care centres open to all. As officials see it, this system puts care in the hands of professionals, and makes this service equally accessible regardless of parents' income. At the same time, however, the government offers no subsidy for parents who want to care for children in their own home. In effect, then, government has taken over much of the traditional family function of child rearing.

If this system has solved so many social problems, why should anyone

care about the erosion of traditional family life? For two reasons, says Popenoe. First, government can do only at great cost what families used to do for themselves. Recently, Swedes voted to cut back on their burgeoning welfare system because of skyrocketing costs.

Second, can government employees in large child-care centres provide children with the level of love and emotional security they would receive from two parents living as a family? Unlikely, claims Popenoe, noting that small, intimate groups can accomplish some human tasks much better than formal organizations can.

David Popenoe uses the case of Sweden as part of his claim for a return to traditional families. We return to this issue in the concluding box. ●

Sources: Popenoe, 1991, 1994; also Herrstrom, 1990.

Map 17.1 ● Marital form in global perspective

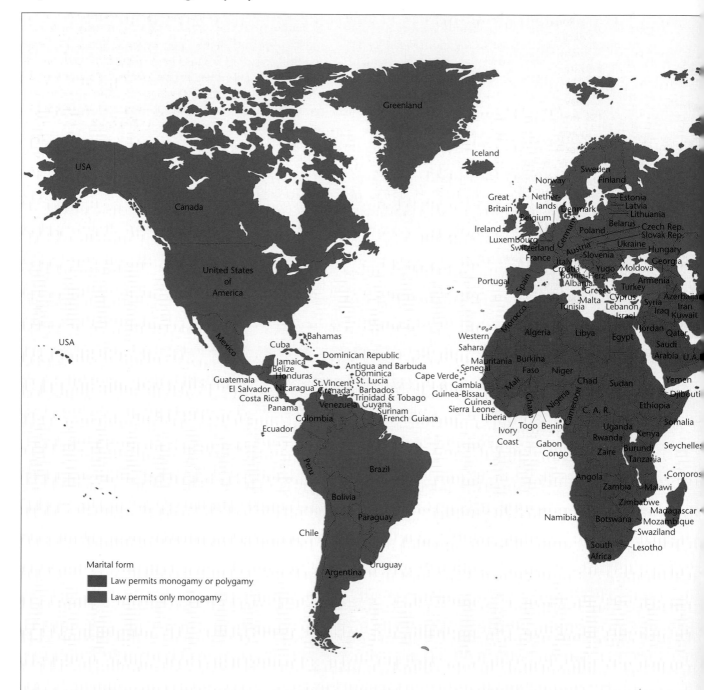

Marital form

■ Law permits monogamy or polygamy

■ Law permits only monogamy

Source: *Peters Atlas of the World (1990)*

Monogamy is the legally prescribed form of marriage in all industrial societies and throughout the Western hemisphere. In most African nations, as well as in southern Asia, however, polygamy is permitted by law. In many cases, this practice reflects the historic influence of Islam, a religion that allows a man to have no more than four wives. Even so, most marriages in these traditional societies are monogamous, primarily for financial reasons.

rule throughout the Americas and in Europe, many preindustrial societies – especially in Africa and southern Asia – prescribe **polygamy** (from Greek meaning 'many unions'), *a type of marriage uniting three or more people*. Polygamy takes two forms. By far the more common is **polygyny** (from Greek meaning 'many women'), *a type of marriage uniting one male and two or more females*. Islamic societies in Africa and southern Asia, for example, permit men up to four wives. In these societies, however, most families are monogamous all the same because few men have the wealth needed to support several wives and even more children.

Polyandry (from Greek meaning 'many men' or 'many husbands') is *a type of marriage joining one female with two or more males*. This pattern appears only rarely. One example can be seen in Tibet where agriculture is difficult. There, polyandry discourages the division of land into parcels too small to support a family and divides the work of farming among many men. Polyandry has also been linked to female infanticide – the aborting of female foetuses or killing of female infants – because a decline in the female population forces men to share women.

Historically, most world societies have permitted more than one marital pattern; even so, most actual marriages have been monogamous (Murdock, 1965). This cultural preference for monogamy reflects two key facts of life: the heavy financial burden of supporting multiple spouses and children and the rough numerical parity of the sexes, which limit the possibility of polygamy.

Residential patterns

Just as societies regulate mate selection, so they designate where a married couple resides. In preindustrial societies, most newlyweds live with one set of parents, thereby gaining economic assistance and security in the process. Most societies observe a norm of **patrilocality** (from meaning Greek 'place of the father'), *a residential pattern by which a married couple lives with or near the husband's family*. But some societies (such as the North American Iroquois) endorse **matrilocality** (Greek meaning 'place of the mother'), *a residential pattern by which couples live with or near the wife's family*. Societies that engage in frequent, local warfare tend towards patrilocality since families want their sons close to home to offer protection. Societies that

engage in distant warfare present a mixed picture, favouring patrilocality or matrilocality depending on whether sons or daughters have greater economic value (Ember and Ember, 1971, 1991).

Industrial societies show yet another pattern. When finances permit, at least, they favour **neolocality** (Greek meaning 'new place'), *a residential pattern by which a married couple lives apart from the parents of both spouses*.

Patterns of descent

Descent refers to *the system by which members of a society trace kinship over generations*. Most preindustrial societies trace kinship through only one side of the family – the father or the mother. The more prevalent pattern is **patrilineal descent**, *a system tracing kinship through men*. In a patrilineal system, children are related to others only through their fathers and fathers typically pass property on to their sons. Patrilineal descent generally characterises pastoral and agrarian societies, in which men produce the most valued resources. Less common is **matrilineal descent**, *a system tracing kinship through women*. Matrilineal descent, through which mothers pass property to their daughters, is found more frequently in horticultural societies where women are the primary food producers.

Industrial societies with greater gender equality recognise **bilateral descent** ('two-sided descent'), *a system tracing kinship through both men and women*. In this pattern, children recognise as relatives people on both the 'father's side' and the 'mother's side' of the family.

Patterns of authority

The predominance of polygyny, patrilocality and patrilineal descent in the world reflects the universal presence of patriarchy. Without denying that wives and mothers exercise considerable power in every society, as Chapter 13 ('Gender and Sexuality') explains, no truly matriarchal society has ever existed.

In industrial societies like Europe, more egalitarian family patterns are evolving, especially as increasing numbers of women enter the labour force. However, even here, men are typically heads of households. Parents in Europe also still prefer boys to girls and typically give children their father's last name.

● Families and social change

Di Gittins has argued that 'There is no such thing as *the* family – only families' (1993: 8) When we look at the debate amongst historians and sociologists over just how the family has changed over time, one thing is clear. The notion of an 'ideal' nuclear family of two parents and two children has, historically, been rare. Throughout history, there have been all kinds of combinations – shaped by age cycles, class, region, ethnicity and the like – which have made families very varied and complex. And at any one historical period, we would not expect families to be all the same. Jean-Louis Flandrin (1979) has shown how, for example, a whole array of family types existed at the same time in different parts of France. And British historian Peter Laslett (1972) studied parish records of English country villages from 1564 to 1821 and found that extended families were rare because of late marriage and shorter lives. But there were also large households – where the richer would take in the poorer as labourers and domestic servants.

Lawrence Stone in a classic study has charted three phases of the family in Western Europe between 1500 and 1800: the first was 'Open Lineage' and involved a lack of close relations and lack of privacy, but extensive kin. The second was 'Restricted Patriarchy' (1530–1640) where there were increased loyalties to state and church and less so to kin and community. The final stage – of 'Closed Domesticated' families – highlights privacy, bonds between children and parents and 'affective individualism'. It was 'an open ended, low keyed, unemotional, authoritarian institution' (Stone, 1977).

The English sociologists Michael Young and Peter Wilmott in a classic modern study have traced changing family form in modern Britain. In the 1950s they studied the very strong traditional family ties in 'traditional' Bethnal Green in East London and traced how they weakened as the families moved out to to new housing estates like Greenleigh in outer London. The three generation (grandparents, parents and child) and larger family gets replaced with a smaller nuclear pattern where the relationship between husband and wife becomes more intense. In a later study, they suggested that these newer families were becoming more 'symmetrical'. That is, the relationships were becoming increasingly equal with husband and wife spending more and more time together. These kinds of changes have become a common theme in much of the writing on the family. It is expected to find shifts from an extended and often patriarchal form of family to a more nuclear and symmetrical form. But it must be remembered that this is only one pattern – a largely traditional working-class one. Families vary and change with class and environment (see Young, 1977).

Three generations of women playing together

Source: Popperfoto

● Stages of family life

The family is dynamic, with marked changes across the life course. An ideal type model might suggest that family life begins with courtship, followed by settling into the realities of married life. Next comes the task of raising children, leading to the later years of marriage after children have left home to form families of their own ('the empty next' as it is called). But such a model does little justice to the dynamics of change. Thus, for example, cohabitation may lead to a family with children yet then, after divorce, become a lone parent family and then, on remarriage, a step-family.

A married couple with a child may divorce and the child is then adopted into the mother's newly formed lesbian partnership, whilst the husband becomes a single household. Figure 17.1 suggests something of the range of family types across the lifecycle.

● Theoretical analysis of the family

As in earlier chapters, several theoretical approaches offer a range of insights about the family.

Functions of the family: functionalist analysis

The functionalist paradigm contends that the family performs several vital tasks. From this point of view, the family operates as 'the backbone of society'.

1. *Socialisation.* As explained in Chapter 5 ('Socialisation'), the family is the first and most influential setting for socialisation. Ideally, parents teach children to be well-integrated and contributing members of society (Parsons and Bales, 1955). Of course, family socialisation continues throughout the life cycle. Adults change within marriage, and, as any parent knows, mothers and fathers learn as much from raising their children as their children learn from them.

2. *Regulation of sexual activity.* Every culture regulates sexual activity in the interest of maintaining kinship organisation and property rights. One universal regulation is the **incest taboo**, *a cultural norm forbidding sexual relations or marriage between certain kin.* Precisely which kin fall within the incest taboo varies from one culture to another. The matrilineal Navajo, for example, forbid marrying any relative of one's mother. Our bilateral society applies the incest taboo to both sides of the family but limits it to close relatives, including parents, grandparents, siblings, aunts and uncles. But even brother–sister marriages found approval among the Ancient Egyptian, Incan and Hawaiian nobility (Murdock, 1965). Reproduction between close relatives can adversely affect the mental and physical health of offspring. But this biological fact does not explain why, among all species of life, only human beings observe an incest taboo. The key reasons to control incest, then, are social. Why? First, the incest taboo minimises sexual competition within families by restricting legitimate sexuality to spouses. Second, it

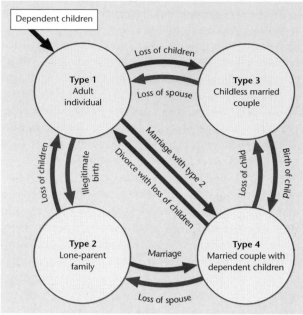

Figure 17.1 ● **Family types across the life course**

Source: Family Policy Studies Centre, October 1995

forces people to marry outside their immediate families, forging broader alliances. Third, since kinship defines people's rights and obligations towards each other, forbidding reproduction among close relatives protects kinship from collapsing into chaos.

3. *Social placement.* Families are not *biologically* necessary for people to reproduce, but they do provide for the *social* placement of children. Social identity based on race, ethnicity, religion and social class is ascribed at birth through the family. This fact explains the long-standing preference for so-called legitimate birth. Especially when parents are of similar social position, families clarify inheritance rights and allow for the stable transmission of social standing from parents to children.

4. *Material and emotional security.* People have long viewed the family as a 'haven in a heartless world', looking to kin for physical protection, emotional support and financial assistance. To a greater or lesser extent, most families do provide all these things, although not without periodic conflict.

Critical evaluation

Functionalism identifies a number of the family's major functions. From this point of view, it is easy to see that society as we know it could not exist without families. But this approach overlooks the great diversity in ways people can live together in the modern world. Children are being socialised outside of the traditional family; most people now have sexual relations outside of the family; and there is a lot of evidence of abuse and violence within the family that makes it seem a very dysfunctional place.

Moreover, functionalism pays little attention to how other social institutions (say, government) could meet at least some of the same human needs. Finally, it minimises the problems of family life. Established family forms reinforce patriarchy and incorporate a surprising amount of violence, with the dysfunctional effect of undermining individual self-confidence, health and well-being, especially of women and children.

Inequality and the family: conflict theory

Like the functional approach, the conflict paradigm sees the family as central to the operation of society. But rather than concentrating on ways that kinship benefits society, conflict theorists investigate how the family perpetuates social inequality. The role of families in the social reproduction of inequality takes several forms.

1. *Property and inheritance*. As noted in Chapter 13 ('Gender and Sexuality'), Friedrich Engels (1902; orig. 1884) traced the origin of the family to the need to identify heirs so that men (especially in the higher classes) could transmit property to their sons. Families thus support the concentration of wealth and reproduce the class structure in each succeeding generation (Mare, 1991).

2. *Patriarchy*. Engels also emphasised how the family promotes patriarchy. The only way men can know who their heirs are is to control the sexuality of women. Thus, Engels continued, families transform women into the sexual and economic property of men. A century ago in Europe, most wives' earnings belonged to their husbands. Although this practice is no longer lawful, men still exert power over women. Despite moving rapidly into the paid workforce, women continue to be paid less, work in more marginal occupations and still have to bear major responsibility for child rearing and housework (Fuchs, 1986; Hochschild, 1989; Presser, 1993; Keith and Schafer, 1994; Benokraitis and Feagin,

1995). As we shall see from the work of Delphy and Leonard later, patriarchal families offer considerable benefits to men. They also deprive men of the chance to share in the personal satisfaction and growth derived from close interaction with children.

3. *Race and ethnicity*. Racial and ethnic categories will persist over generations only to the degree that people marry others like themselves. Thus endogamous marriage also shores up the racial and ethnic hierarchy.

A radical feminist approach to the family

Many of the arguments above have been significantly developed by many feminists who see the family as the central location of women's oppression. They argue that men generally benefit greatly from families whilst women often do not. Until recently, men have nearly always been head of the household and made the key decisions about the family allocating rewards (often payment in kind, like holidays): even when women work, they often have little decision-making autonomy.

Christine Delphy and Diana Leonard in their book *Familiar Exploitation* (1992) argue that the family is an economic system, where men benefit from the work of women (and in many countries the work of children too). This is not just the work in the labour market (which they do increasing amounts of), but also the work they do at home. Family members work for the head of the household. As they say it is 'the work women do, the uses to which our bodies can be put, which constitutes the reason for our oppression'.

Many studies suggest that women still do more housework than men still spend more time looking after the children (especially in the more mundane and humdrum ways) and are much more likely to have to look after the sick and the elderly (Finch, 1989; Hochschild, 1989). They are also much more likely to have to give moral support to men (who often make little contribution to their wife's work).

These feminist arguments are strong claims and a careful evaluation of the evidence is needed to make sense of this. For instance, in modern families, there are now many single parent households where women are alone; further, women increasingly are choosing to not marry, to get divorced once married and to not have children. Twenty per cent of women remain childless, by choice.

Critical evaluation

Conflict theory reveals another side of family life: its role in maintaining social inequality. During his era, Engels condemned the family as part and parcel of capitalism. Yet non-capitalist societies have families (and family problems) all the same. Kinship and social inequality are deeply intertwined, as Engels argued, but the family appears to carry out various societal functions that are not easily accomplished by other means. And the arguments produced by radical feminists usually fail to take into account the growing trends towards equality in decision-making between men and women.

Micro-level analysis

Both functional and conflict analyses take a broad view of the family as a structural system with wide-ranging consequences for our lives. Micro-level approaches, by contrast, explore how individuals shape and experience family life.

Symbolic-interaction analysis

Seen from the inside, family life amounts to individuals engaging one another in a changing collage of meanings. People construct family life, building a reality that differs from case to case and from day to day.

In ideal terms, however, family living offers an opportunity for intimacy, a word with Latin roots meaning 'sharing fears'. That is, as a result of sharing a wide range of activities over a long period of time, members of families forge emotional bonds. Of course, the fact that parents act as authority figures often inhibits their communication with younger children. But, as young people reach adulthood, kinship ties typically 'open up' as family members recognise that they share concern for one another's welfare (Macionis, 1978).

Social-exchange analysis

Social-exchange analysis, another micro-level approach, depicts courtship and marriage as forms of negotiation (Blau, 1964). In the case of courtship, dating allows each person the chance to assess the likely advantages and disadvantages of taking the other as a spouse, always keeping in mind the value of what one has to offer in return. In essence, exchange analysts contend, individuals seek to make the best 'deal' they can in selecting a partner. Physical attractiveness is one critical dimension of social exchange. In patriarchal societies around the world, beauty has long been a commodity offered by women on the marriage market. The high value assigned to beauty explains women's traditional concern with physical appearance and their sensitivity about revealing their age. For their part, men have traditionally been assessed according to the financial resources they command. Recently, however, because increasing numbers of women are joining the labour force, they are less dependent on men to support them and their children. Thus, the terms of exchange have been converging for men and women.

Critical evaluation

Micro-level analysis offers a useful counterpoint to functionalist and conflict visions of the family as an institutional system. Adopting an interactional or exchange viewpoint, we gain a better sense of the individual's experience of family life and appreciate how people creatively shape this reality for themselves.

Using this approach, however, we run the risk of missing the bigger picture, namely, that family life is similar for people affected by any common set of economic and cultural forces. UK families vary in some predictable ways according to social class and ethnicity, and, as the next section explains, they typically evolve through stages linked to the life course.

● UK families: class, ethnicity and gender

Dimensions of inequality – social class, ethnicity and race and gender – are powerful forces that shape marriage and family life. While this section addresses each factor separately, they overlap.

Social class

Families can vary enormously across social class (see Chapter 10). Not only does class shape a family's financial security and range of opportunities, it can also affect the family size and shape. For instance, in the UK families are still likely to be larger amongst the working class, who also have higher rates of divorce.

In an influential North American study, Lillian Rubin (1976) found that working-class wives deemed a good husband to be one who refrained from violence and excessive drinking and held a steady job. Rubin's middle-class informants, by contrast, never mentioned such things; these women simply *assumed* a husband would provide a safe and secure home. Their ideal husband was a man with whom they could communicate easily and share feelings and experiences.

Such differences reflect the fact that people with higher social standing have more schooling, and most have jobs that emphasise verbal skills. In addition, middle-class couples share a wider range of activities, while working-class life is more sharply divided along gender lines. Conventionally masculine ideas of self-control, Rubin explains, can stifle emotional expressiveness on the part of working-class men, prompting women to turn to each other as confidantes.

Clearly, what women (and men) conclude that they can hope for in marriage – and what they end up with – is linked to their social class. Much the same holds true for children in families; boys and girls lucky enough to be born into more affluent families enjoy better mental and physical health, develop higher self-confidence, and go on to greater achievement than poor children do (Komarovsky, 1967; Bott, 1971; Rubin, 1976; Fitzpatrick, 1988; McLeod and Shanahan, 1993).

Ethnic minorities and family diversity

As Chapter 12 ('Race, Ethnicity and Migration') indicates, ethnicity and race are powerful social forces. The effects of both surface in family life. We must beware of stereotyping: just as there is enormous diversity behind the label 'white families', so there is great variety amongst ethnic families. But some differences do seem striking. Ethnic family forms in the UK have been subject to change over the past 40 years: in the early days of mass migration (1950–70), there was often a severe dislocation of family life, as patterns found in the former homes were disrupted. But subsequently new forms of stability emerged.

Asian families

The Asian population across the world generally has a very strong family system (Fukuyama, 1994). The first contact by Asians with UK culture after migration therefore often came as a culture shock. In the main Asian culture has continued to assert the importance of family life.

The village model of India was for a while transferred to the UK, with a complex network of kin and responsibilities. In some ways this is the classic 'extended family' model. On arrival initially in the UK, these traditional family structures were disrupted: there were smaller houses, there was less support and women became more isolated from other women. (Chain migration eventually restored this as families became reunited.) English families were often seen as 'morally bankrupt' (Elliot, 1997: 52).

In Asian families there are usually more people per household than in white families: three-quarters of Pakistani and Bangladeshi households have an average of five members and three-fifths of Indian households contain four or more people, compared with a quarter of white households (Skellington, 1996: 62; 49).

An ideal type would suggest a value that places family before individual self-interest, and one that is patrilineal, patrilocal and with a strong gender hierarchy. Marriage is a contract between two families not two individuals.

It is important to recognise again major differences between Asian communities (see Chapter 12). These can be compounded by gender. For instance, whilst East African and Indian women often work, taking them out of the house, Bangladeshi and Pakistani women's lives – more restricted by Islamic rules which do not permit women to be in close proximity to non-family men – lead to a much stronger home-based commitment, including 'homework'. Likewise, Muslims can marry close kin but this is not permitted for Sikhs and Hindus. Purdah is strong in Islam and restricts Islamic women more.

Sallie Westwood and Parminder Bhachu (1988) nevertheless see these traditions as evoking changes. Again, families do not remain static, but respond to current changes. Some become more nuclear and a diversity of Asian families starts to appear.

Afro-Caribbean families

These account for less than 1 per cent of all families in the UK (Skellington, 1996: 50). Thirty-seven per cent were headed by a female (compared with 9 per cent of white families). Marriage is often weaker, women headed households are more common, and the husband/father role is likely to be less strong. In a curious fashion, there is a resemblance to the United States situation where Afro-American families are also like this. Jocelyn Barrow explains this form of family by linking it to Caribbean society. Originally, whilst marriage is much valued in Caribbean societies, other patterns of sexual union were possible. There were common law family households with unmarried cohabitation, as well as women headed households.

In the main, extended kin units have not reappeared amongst Afro-Caribbean families in the UK. One study suggested that less than 1 per cent of childern are cared for by grandmothers as 'the grandmother family' disappears. The families often tend to be matrifocal, even though Afro-Caribbean women are more likely to be working and have less support than in the Caribbean. Men often become marginal to family life.

Lone parent families are highest amongst West Indian families (43 per cent in 1991 Census), but lowest for Asian: the figures were 6 per cent for Indian and Pakistani, 5 per cent for Bangladeshi and 11 per cent for white families (Skellington, 1996: 50, 60).

Gender

Among all races, Jessie Bernard (1982) asserts, every marriage is actually *two* different relationships: a woman's marriage and a man's marriage. Although the extent of patriarchy has diminished with time, even today few marriages are composed of two equal partners. Studies in the UK suggest that although there have been some moves towards equality, and that families do come in many forms, it remains the case that men still make most of the major decisions, and that wives generally are economically dependent upon husbands whilst still being more likely to be taking responsibility for child care and the housework within the family. (Devine, 1992; Pahl, 1989)

What is curious, in light of continuing patriarchy, is the persistent notion that marriage is more beneficial to women than to men (Bernard, 1982). The positive stereotype of the carefree bachelor contrasts sharply with the negative image of the lonely spinster. This idea is rooted in women's historic exclusion from the labour force, which made a woman's financial security dependent on marrying well.

But today, Bernard claims, compared to single women, married women have poorer mental health, evince more passive attitudes towards life and report less personal happiness. Married men, by contrast, live longer than single men, have better mental health and report being happier. These differences in marriage suggest why, after divorce, men are more eager than women to secure a new partner.

Bernard concludes that there is no better guarantor of long life, health and happiness for a man than a woman well socialised to perform the 'duties of a wife' by devoting her life to caring for him and providing the security of a well-ordered home. She is quick to add that marriage *could* be healthy for women if society would only end the practice of husbands' dominating wives and expecting them to perform all the housework.

● Transitions and problems in family life

Care in the family

One of the key tasks of families is 'caring': caring for partners, caring for children and caring for parents. This is a three or four generational span of care. And there is an important distinction here to be made between *caring about* – which is about love, feelings and emotions; and *caring for* – which is an active form of work: a 'labour of love' which involves looking after someone (Ungerson, 1983). They may, of course, be deeply interwoven; but they need not be. Overwhelmingly, this latter care process falls upon the women in the family, although it is usually invisible. Although there are signs that some men are playing a small role in it, feminist research has generally shown that the caring process is closely linked in modern societies to what it means to be a woman. Recall in Chapter 13 ('Gender and Sexuality') how Nancy Chodorow suggested that the social process of becoming a woman was closely linked to the social process of becoming a mother. It is the extension of this 'social mothering' that makes women more prone to look after the array of people within the family – and also outside it.

There has been quite a lot of research on 'care'. It suggests these commitments are rarely straightforward and always negotiated – often over long periods of time and implicitly. Sometimes there is an unwillingness to engage in care. Often the array of family members that will be carers is narrowly defined: usually from spouse, to daughter, to daughter-in-law and son. There is a hierarchy of care: sons and daughters define their care duties primarily to their own children and partners, only secondarily to their parents. Older people usually do not want to give up their independence – and so are looked after 'at a distance' ('intimacy at a distance'). Nevertheless, research strongly suggests that there is a great deal of care taking place amongst families today. But when governments cut back on public care, this can hit many families very hard, as they are already engaged in a great deal of unpaid care (Elliot, 1996: 122–40; Finch, 1989; Finch and Finch, 1993; Graham, 1991).

Family violence

The ideal family may serve as a haven from the dangers of the outside world; the reality is that many families are exceedingly dangerous places. From the Biblical story of Cain's killing of his brother Abel to the recent O. J. Simpson case, we see that the disturbing reality of many homes has been **family violence**, *emotional, physical or sexual abuse of one family member by another.* Sociologist Richard J. Gelles points to a chilling fact:

The family is the most violent group in society with the exception of the police and the military. You are more likely to get killed, injured or physically attacked in your home by someone you are related to than in any other social context. (quoted in Roesch, 1984: 75)

Violence against women

During the 1970s a seemingly new 'family problem' was discovered: men's violence against women. The women's movement responded by actively establishing women's refuges throughout the country and through a critical analysis of men's violence towards women (that often connected it to the rape and power debate discussed in Chapter 13 ('Gender and Sexuality')).

Erin Pizzey set up the first Women's Refuge in Chiswick in 1972 (Pizzey, 1974), and today almost every town in the UK has some such scheme (though usually, to avoid male harassers, they are kept fairly anonymous). A study by Jane Mooney (1994) in North London found that about half of all women surveyed had experienced threats of violence or actual violence – though many of these women had not told anybody.

The problem is even greater in the United States. As elsewhere, family brutality usually goes unreported to police, but the Bureau of Justice Statistics (1994) estimate that at least 600,000 women are victims of domestic violence each year. Women's activists say the figure may be as high as 8 million (Sasetti, 1993). Researchers note that men initiate most family violence and that women suffer most of the injuries (Straus and Gelles, 1986; Schwartz, 1987; Shupe, Stacey and Hazlewood, 1987).

US government statistics show that almost 30 per cent of women who are murdered – as opposed to 3 per cent of men – are killed by partners or ex-partners. In the USA the death toll from family violence is 1,500 women each year. Overall, women are more likely to be injured by a family member than to be mugged or raped by a stranger or hurt in a car accident.

Not long ago, US law declared wives the property of their husbands, so that no man could be charged with raping his wife. By 1995, however, 40 states had passed marital rape laws; in some cases, however, such a charge can be made only under specific circumstances, such as after a legal separation (Russell, 1982; O'Reilly, 1983; Margolick, 1984; Goetting, 1989). In the UK, changes in the law are only just beginning to take place.

People who hear about a case of abuse often shake their heads and wonder, 'Why didn't she just leave?' The answer is that most physically and emotionally abused women – especially those with children and without much money – have few options. Most wives are also committed to their marriages and believe (however unrealistically) that they can help abusive husbands to change. Some, unable to understand their husbands' violence, blame themselves. Others, raised in violent families, have learned to view assault as part of everyday family life.

In the past, the law regarded domestic violence as a private, family matter. Now, even without separation or divorce, a woman can obtain court protection from an abusive spouse. Today, half the states in the US have added 'stalking laws' that prohibit an ex-partner from following or otherwise threatening a woman. Finally, communities across Europe have established shelters that provide counselling as well as temporary housing for women and children driven from their homes by domestic violence.

The analysis has shifted from being based on individuals, to one based on the power relations – patriarchy – between men and women (see Chapter 13, 'Gender and Sexuality').

Violence against children

Family violence also victimises children. In the United States upwards of 3 million children – roughly 4 per cent of all youngsters – suffer abuse each year, including several thousand who die as a result. Child abuse entails more than physical injury because abusive adults misuse power and trust to undermine a child's emotional well-being. Child abuse is most common among the youngest and most vulnerable children (Straus and Gelles, 1986; Van Biema, 1994).

In the UK several noticeable cases have galvanised action and thinking. In 1973, the seven year old Maria Colwell was beaten to death by her stepfather after social workers had allowed her to return to her family from foster care. It led both to a moral panic (see Chapter 21, 'Mass Media') and the development of a public awareness of abuse. Later, in 1985, the death of Jasmine Beckford also served to highlight the continuing problem. As a consequence of such cases, social work intervention increased, and registers of children at risk were created. In the early 1990s, it was estimated that about four children in every 1,000 in the UK were on child protection registers (David, 1993: 4).

Many abused children suffer in silence, believing during their formative years that they are to blame for their own victimisation. The initial abuse, compounded by years of guilt, can leave lasting emotional scars that prevent people abused as children from forming healthy relationships as adults.

About 90 per cent of child abusers are men, but they conform to no simple stereotype. As one man who entered a therapy group reported, 'I kept waiting for all the guys with raincoats and greasy hair to show up. But everyone looked like regular middle-class people' (quoted in Lubenow, 1984). Most abusers, however, share one trait: having been abused themselves as children. Researchers have discovered that violent behaviour in close relationships is learned; in families, then, violence begets violence (Gwartney-Gibbs, Stockard and Bohmer, 1987).

● Towards the postmodern family?

At the turn of the twentieth century, families and relationships seem to be undergoing very significant changes. True, many of the older patterns persist – but there are certainly some new ones in the making. We have seen in Chapter 13 ('Gender and Sexuality') the emergence of a new flexible, highly individualistic, sexually 'plastic', 'pure relationship' where partners are mutually interdependent (Cancian, 1987; Beck and Beck-Gernsheim, 1990; Giddens, 1991). The suggestion is that for some (and it *may* be a blueprint for the future), relationships are emerging where men and women are more interdpendent and equal; where their child rearing is altogether part of a more egalitarian and democratic system; where sexuality and love become more 'plastic', diffuse, open. This is a relationship of choice, closely allied to individualism.

The changes we outline have been taken by many to herald a new form of family relationship. American family sociologist Judith Stacey has argued that we may be discovering the postmodern family. She writes

The postmodern family condition is not a new model of family life equivalent to that of the modern family; it is not the next stage in an orderly progression of stages in family history; rather the postmodern family condition signals the moment in history when our belief in a logical progression of stages has broken down. . . . The postmodern family condition incorporates both experimental and nostalgic dimensions as it lurches forward and backward into an uncertain future. (Stacey, *In the Name of the Family*, 1996: 8)

In what follows, we shall look in more detail at some of the changes.

Household size

Increasingly, sociologists focus on 'households', looking at their shape and size. In the UK, the average household size has almost halved since the start of the century – to 2.4 people per household. With this has come a decline in the traditional household of two parents and dependent children – 38 per cent of all households in 1961, but down to 24 per cent

Figure 17.2 ● Households by family type in the UK, 1993

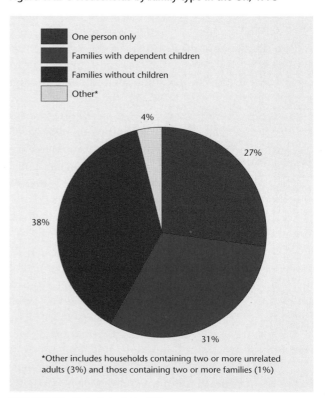

*Other includes households containing two or more unrelated adults (3%) and those containing two or more families (1%)

Source: Family Policy Studies Centre, October 1995

in 1995–6. There were more households with couples and no children than households with children. One in four households had a single person living alone. Figure 17.2 shows households by family type for the UK.

Marriage and divorce

One of the most striking features of modern societies has been the decline in first marriage and the rapid growth of divorce. There were 40 per cent fewer first marriages in the UK in 1994 than there were in 1971: a steep drop. By contrast, the number of divorces has more than doubled in the same period: a steep rise. There is also a general drift towards marrying at older ages.

These are trends found throughout Europe and other industrialising societies. Most countries in the European Union have seen a decline in marriage rates, with Sweden having the lowest. Taking Europe as a whole, the divorce rate quadrupled between 1960 and 1992, through as Figure 17.3 shows, there are significant differences across all countries. Divorce is highest in the UK and the Nordic countries, and lowest in the Mediterranean regions. US society has the highest divorce rate in the world: almost twice as high as Canada, four times as high as Japan, and ten times as high as Italy (US Bureau of the Census, 1995).

Nevertheless, since the mid 1980s, these rapid rises have stabilised. Although the trend of ending

Marriage is still an extremely popular institution and many celebrate it in the traditional way

Source: Popperfoto

Figure 17.3 ● **Marriage and divorce rates: EU comparison, 1994**

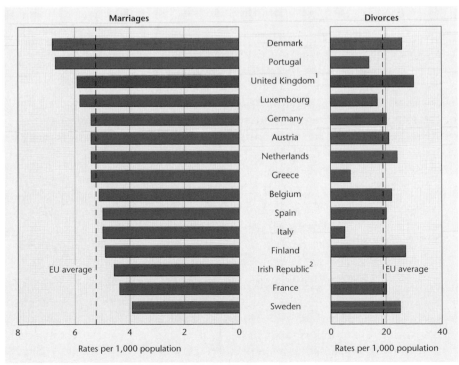

1. Marriages data are for 1993 2. Divorce is not permitted

Source: *Social Trends*, 27, 1992, p. 46, Social and Regional Statistics Office for National Statistics, Eurostat (1995)

marriage may have slowed for the moment, it does nevertheless seem a stable Western pattern.

The high UK divorce rate can be traced to a number of factors. The most common reason for women to be granted divorce in the UK is the 'unreasonable behaviour' of the man; for men, it is the adultery of the wife (*Social Trends*, 1997: 48). More broadly, we can see divorce rising because:

1. *Divorce is legally easier to accomplish.* For example, in the UK before 1857, divorces were almost impossible: they were only for wealthy men and required a private Act of Parliament. Legislation over the following century made divorce increasingly easy. But it was the Divorce Reform Act of 1969 (law from 1971) which shifted the grounds of divorce to the 'irretrievable breakdown of marriage' doctrine. Couples could now divorce after two years' separation (five years' if the partner objected). From this point onwards, divorces escalated. So there is little doubt that, formally, the changes in the law have made divorce possible. The key peaks of divorces in the UK in the 1970s were almost certainly due to the release of a backlog of long-dead marriages. But since the Matrimonial and Family Proceedings Act 1984, couples no longer have to be married for three years, which gave another impetus for increase.

2. *Demographic changes.* We commonly exaggerate the stability of marriage in the past, when the early death of a spouse ended as many marriages after a few years as divorce does now. When people lived less long, marriages were of shorter duration. These days, without divorce most people's marriages could last some 50 years or more – given current life expectancy and marriage rates.

3. *Individualisation is increasing.* Bech et al. (1995) see the rise of a modern society where both men and women expect choice, control over their lives and equality. We have become more individualistic, seemingly more concerned with personal happiness and success than with the well-being of families and children.

4. *Romantic love often subsides.* Modern cultures emphasise romantic love as a basis for marriage, rendering relationships vulnerable to collapse as sexual passion subsides. There is now widespread support for the notion that one may end a marriage in favour of a new relationship simply to renew excitement and romance.

5. *Women are now less dependent on men and have changed expectations.* Their increasing participation in the labour force has reduced wives' financial dependence on husbands. In addition, women have largely come to expect more from life than being the 'home maker' alone. They are more likely to demand equality from husbands, who may not have recognised the changing role of women. Changing expectations from women, then, may make it easier for them to walk away from unhappy marriages.

6. *Many of today's marriages are stressful.* With both partners working outside the home in most cases, jobs consume time and energy. In the past, wives looked after children, but now (and given the difficulty of securing good, affordable child care) raising children can be more difficult. Tensions may be increasing between men and women, as women come to demand and expect more. While children do stabilise some marriages, divorce is most common during the early years of marriage when many couples have young children.

7. *Divorce is more socially acceptable.* Divorce no longer carries the powerful, negative stigma it did a century ago. Couples considering divorce typically do not receive the discouragement from family and friends they once did.

Who divorces?

There is considerable discussion of the factors that put marriages at risk. They are varied but include:

● *age*: at greatest risk of divorce are young spouses, especially those who marry after a brief courtship and have few financial resources.

● *class*: those in the highest social class are least likely to divorce and those in the lowest social class are most at risk.

● *gender*: women who have successful careers are more prone to divorce, partly due to the strains that arise in two-career marriages but, more important, because financially independent women are less inclined to remain in an unhappy marriage.

● *prior marriage*: men and women who divorce once are more likely to divorce again, presumably because problems follow them from one marriage to another.

Finally, couples who have known their partners for short periods of time before marriage, those who marry in response to an unexpected pregnancy and people who are not religious divorce more readily than other couples (Booth and White, 1980; Burgoyne et al., 1987; Coleman and Salt, 1992; Yoder and Nichols, 1980; Glenn and Shelton, 1985).

Divorce as process

Divorce is a form of role exit, as described in Chapter 6 ('Social Interaction in Everyday Life'). Paul Bohannan (1970) and others point to six distinct adjustments divorcing people make:

1. *Emotional divorce.* Distancing oneself from the former spouse usually begins before the formal break occurs. A deteriorating marriage can be fraught with disappointment, indifference or outright hostility.

2. *Legal divorce.* Since marriage is a legal contract, divorce involves a legal change of status. Often financial settlements are central to a divorce agreement.

3. *Psychic reorganisation.* Many divorced people suffer not just from loneliness but from a sense that the ending of their marriage represents a personal failure.

4. *Community reorganisation.* Ending a marriage requires both partners to reorganise friendships and adjust relations with parents and other family members who are accustomed to seeing each one as part of a couple.

5. *Economic reorganisation.* Recent no-fault divorce laws have reduced the amount of alimony and child support paid by men to their former wives. Further, divorce courts often require ex-spouses to sell homes and divide marital assets equally. While divorce raises the living standards of many men (who no longer support wives and children), it can mean financial calamity to women whose earnings are lower than those of their husbands and who may be responsible for supporting children as well (Weitzman, 1985).

6. *Parental reorganisation.* More than half of all divorcing couples must resolve the issue of child custody. Society's conventional practice is still to award custody of children to mothers, based on the notion that women are better parents than men. A recent trend, however, is towards joint custody, whereby children divide their time between the new homes of their two parents. Joint custody is difficult if divorced parents live far apart or do not get along, but it has the advantage of keeping children in regular contact with both parents (Roman and Haddad, 1978; Cherlin and Furstenberg, 1983).

Because mothers usually gain custody of children but fathers typically earn more income, the well-being of children often depends on fathers making court-ordered child-support payments.

Financial support

In 1991 the UK's Conservative government of the day set up the Child Support Agency (CSA) which aimed to make absent parents (mainly fathers) contribute to their children's upbringing. An agency was set up to administer it and collect money from absent fathers – focusing especially in the first instance on low income fathers who were easier to locate (through social security offices). It led to considerable controversy and the campaign against CSA (APART, Absent Parents Asking for Reasonable Treatment). Partly, this was because it did not take into account the obligations a parent may have to a second family. But in addition, it was retrospective, overturning earlier court agreements. Further, if the parent with the child was already on income support, everything collected was recouped by the Benefits Agency.

Conventional wisdom holds that divorce is hardest on children. Divorce tears many young people from familiar surroundings, entangles them in bitter family feuds and frequently distances them from a parent they love. But the greatest tragedy of divorce is that, in their own minds, children often blame themselves for their parents' breakup. For this reason, concludes family counsellor Judith Wallerstein, divorce is a disaster for children that can change the trajectory of their entire lives. Perhaps, as others contend, children might better endure a parental divorce than remain in a family torn by tension or violence. But parents need to be mindful that, in a decision to divorce or not, much more than their own well-being is at stake (Goetting, 1981; Wallerstein and Blakeslee, 1989).

Remarriage

Despite the rising divorce rate, marriage – and remarriage – remain as popular as ever. In the UK over a third of all marriages each year are second marriages. Most people remarry within three to five years. Men, who derive greater benefits from wedlock, are more likely to remarry than women are.

Remarriage often creates *blended families*, composed of children and some combination of biological parents and step-parents. Members of blended families thus have to define precisely who is part of the child's nuclear family (Furstenberg, 1984). Blended families also require children to reorientate themselves; an only child, for example, may suddenly find she has two older brothers. And, as already noted, the risk of divorce is high for partners in such families. But blended families also offer both young and old the opportunity to relax rigid family roles.

Lone parent families

Lone parents headed some 23 per cent of all families with dependent children in the UK in 1994 (roughly one in ten of all households with children) – three times the proportion in 1971 (Figure 17.4). Lone parent families – over 90 per cent of which are headed by a single mother – may result from divorce, separation, death or the choice of an unmarried woman to have a child. Until the mid-1980s, most of the increase was due to divorce. But since then, the proportion of divorced mothers has remained stable, whilst that of single never-married mothers has doubled (Family Policies Study Centre, 1995: 2). There are at least five types of lone parent family (Haskey, 1994):

Single lone mothers	35 per cent
Divorced lone mothers	31 per cent
Separated lone mothers	21 per cent
Widowed mothers	4 per cent
Lone fathers	9 per cent

Map 17.2 shows that across Europe the percentage of births outside marriage has been significantly rising. The rate is highest in the Scandinavian countries and lowest in Greece. In the UK it is around 32 per cent, compared with 8 per cent in 1971.

Entering the labour force has bolstered women's financial capacity to be single mothers. But lone parenthood – especially when the parent is a woman – greatly increases the risks of poverty, as it can limit the

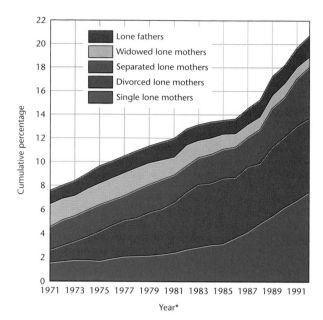

Figure 17.4 ● **Lone parent families by marital status in the UK, 1971–92**

*Three-year moving averages used (apart from 1971 and 1992)

Source: Family Policy Studies Centre, October 1995

woman's ability to work and to further her education. Many women in Europe now become pregnant as unmarried teenagers, and many decide to raise their children on their own. These young women with children – especially if they have the additional disadvantage of being minorities – form the core of the rising problem of child poverty in Europe.

Much contemporary research points to the conclusion that growing up in a lone parent family usually disadvantages children. Some studies indicate that a father and a mother each make a distinctive contribution to a child's social development, so it is unrealistic to expect one parent alone to do as good a job as two working together. But the most serious problem among families with one parent – especially if that parent is a woman – is poverty. On average, children growing up in a lone parent family start out with disadvantages and end up with lesser educational achievement and lower incomes, and face a greater chance of forming lone parent families themselves (Mueller and Cooper, 1984; McLanahan, 1985; Weisner and Eiduson, 1986; Wallerstein and Blakeslee, 1989; Astone and McLanahan, 1991; Li and Wojtkiewicz, 1992; Biblarz and Raftery, 1993; Popenoe, 1993; Shapiro and Schrof, 1995; Webster, Orbuch and House, 1995).

Map 17.2 ● Percentage of live births outside marriage, 1994

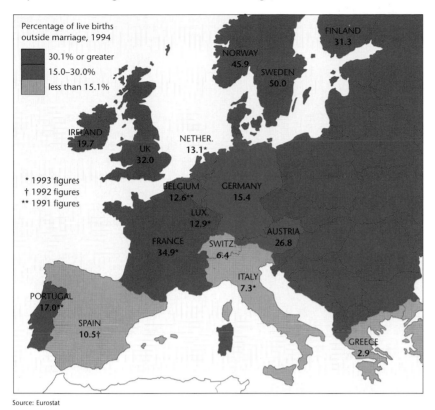

Source: Eurostat

Despite the growth of lone parent families, in 1996 four-fifths of children in the UK still lived in a family with two parents (*Social Trends*, 1997: 44).

Cohabitation

Cohabitation is *the sharing of a household by an unmarried couple*. A generation ago, widespread use of terms like 'living in sin' and 'premarital sex' indicated disapproval both of cohabitation and sex outside of marriage. But all this has changed. Attitudes surveys find a generational difference – with older people often disapproving of cohabitation, but younger people overwhelmingly in favour of it (*Social Trends*, 1997: 45–6). Since 1981, the proportion of all non-married women aged 18 to 49 who were cohabiting doubled – to a quarter of all couplings. Divorced women and younger women in their twenties were the most likely to cohabit. Cohabitation rarely lasts more than two years, and frequently leads to marriage.

Cohabitation is common in Europe as a whole. It is most pronounced in Sweden and other Scandinavian societies as a long-term form of family life, with or without children. By contrast, this family form is much rarer in more traditional (and Roman Catholic) nations such as Italy. While cohabitation is gaining in popularity in Europe – almost half of people between 25 and 44 years of age have cohabited at some point – such partnerships are still usually of short duration, with perhaps 40 per cent of couples marrying after several years, and the remainder splitting up (Blumstein and Schwartz, 1983; Macklin, 1983; Popenoe, 1988, 1991, 1992; Bumpass and Sweet, 1995).

Step-parenting

In 1991 there were around half a million step-families and around 1 million children (step-children and natural children) living in such families. There were three times as many step-fathers as step-mothers, as children are more likely to stay with their natural mothers (*Social Trends*, 1997: 44).

Gay and lesbian couples

In 1989, Denmark became the first country to formally recognise homosexual marriages, thereby extending social legitimacy to gay and lesbian couples as well as conferring legal advantages for inheritance, taxation and joint property ownership. All Nordic cultures and Sweden (1995) have followed suit. But none of these nations allows homosexual couples to adopt children. In the United States, while gay people cannot legally marry (but can adopt children), some cities (including San Francisco and New York) allow 'registered partnerships' that confer some of the legal benefits of marriage.

Most UK gay couples in households including children raise the offspring of previous, heterosexual unions; some couples have adopted children. But many gay parents are quiet about their sexuality, not wishing to draw unwelcome attention to their children. In several widely publicised cases in recent years, courts have removed children from homosexual couples, claiming to represent the best interests of the children.

Gay registered partnerships

On 28 June 1990, two men left the Town Hall in Copenhagen. Whilst there, they became the world's first gay 'registered partnership'. They were the first couple to take advantage of the new law which came into force on 1 October 1989. The ceremony used the same building, officials and similar working to those of civil marriages. A registered partnership gives two people of the same sex, the equivalent rights to heterosexual marriages except for the rights of adoption or a church marriage. One must be a Danish citizen. At the end of 1991, there were some 789 partnerships (191 of women). The numbers have subsequently declined.

Axel and Eigil Axgil, 67 and 72 years, the first homosexual couple to be legally married under a national law.

Source: Popperfoto

Versions of registered partnerhips are to be found in all the Nordic cultures: Denmark, 1989, Norway, 1993, Sweden, 1995, Iceland and Finland, 1996. Norway introduced a registered Partnership Act in 1993, with some 290 couples being registered by January 1995 (200 men couples, 90 women couples). In Sweden a law was passed in 1994.

There is an irony in all this. As gays and lesbians establish the legal basis for 'marriage' around the world, more and more heterosexuals are running away from it as marriage becomes less popular and divorce increases. ●

Source: Bech, 1992.

It has been estimated that there are as many as 1 million gay and lesbian couples in the United States who are now raising one or more children. While this pattern challenges many traditional notions about families in Europe, it also indicates that many gay and lesbian couples perceive the same rewards in child rearing that 'straight' couples do (Bell, Weinberg and Kiefer-Hammersmith, 1981; Gross, 1991; Pressley and Andrews, 1992; Henry, 1993).

Singlehood

Living alone is becoming more common in Europe. By 1995–6, a quarter of all households in the UK housed just one person living alone (about half of these were pensioners) and one in ten people lived alone.

Elderly widows have always represented a large share of single people. But a new group of men under the age of 65 have become the second biggest group to live alone: there were two and half times the number of men living alone in 1996 than in 1971. And it is

projected that this group will continue to rise. In the United States though the story is somewhat different. Here it is younger women who are staying single. In 1960, 28 per cent of US women aged 20 to 24 were single; by 1994 the proportion had soared to two-thirds. Underlying this trend is women's greater participation in the labour force: women who are economically secure view a husband as a matter of choice rather than a financial necessity.

● New reproductive technology and the family

In 1991, Arlette Schweitzer, a forty-two-year-old librarian living in Aberdeen, South Dakota, became the first woman on record to bear her own grandchildren. Because her daughter was unable to carry a baby to term, Schweitzer agreed to have her daughter's fertilised embryos surgically implanted in her own womb. Nine months later, her efforts yielded healthy twins – a boy and girl (Kolata, 1991).

FOCUS ON EUROPE

Family time

In 1961 women were only a quarter of the work force, now they are at least half. Domestic work has fallen substantially; for example, in 1961 it was 117 minutes per day in food preparation; by the mid 1990s it was 65 minutes. Working women have also reduced domestic work (from an average of 110 minutes a day in 1961 to 90 in the mid-1990s). (Men have increased domestic work from 15 minutes per day in 1961 to 45 minutes in 1995.)

But what is really important is that housework has been displaced for other things, for example, shopping, travel and the children. Child-care time has doubled. As Gershuny says: 'Full time-employed women with children in 1995 appear to devote more time to childcare than even non-employed did in 1961' (1997: 57).

Two factors may account especially for this. First, there is growing alarm about abuse and traffic danger, so parents are not letting their children roam too far. Second, there are all sorts of new services – sports, educational, lesiure – which require parents to take children there. Families are also going out more. ●

Source: Jonathan Gershuny, 'Time for the Family', *Prospect*, January 1997.

Such a case illustrates how *new reproductive technology* has created new choices for families and sparked new controversies for society as a whole. The benefits of this rapidly developing technology are exciting; but its use raises daunting ethical questions about the creation and manipulation of life itself.

In vitro fertilisation (IVF)

In 1978, in Britain, Louise Brown became the world's first 'test-tube' baby; since then, tens of thousands of people have been conceived in this way. Early in the next century, 2 or 3 per cent of the children in industrial societies may be conceived through new birth technologies.

Technically speaking, test-tube babies are the product of *in vitro fertilisation*, a procedure whereby the male sperm and the female ovum are united 'in glass'

Nirmala Devi and her lawyer Navjit Brar leave Chandigarh court on 9 June after she sought permission from a judge to 'rent her womb'. Devi offered her womb to a childless couple for 50,000 rupees (£1000) to bear a child, after conferring with her bed-ridden and paralysed husband. Police in the northern city of Chandigarh are threatening to prosecute Devi under the Suppression of Immoral Traffic Act. Devi approached the court to declare her 'renting of womb' as legal and said she had no other source of income and cannot bear the medical expenses of 700 rupees (£15) each month for her ailing husband.

Source: Popperfoto

Family values: have changes in the family gone too far?

Are 'traditional families' vital to our way of life? Or are they a barrier to progress? To begin, people typically use the term 'traditional family' to mean a married couple who, at some point in their lives, raise children. But the term is more than simply descriptive – it is also a moral and political statement. That is, support for the traditional family implies that people place a high value on getting and staying married, that parents should place more importance on raising children than on pursuing their own careers, and that society should accord special respect to two-parent families rather than various 'alternative lifestyles'.

On one side of the debate, Patricia Morgan, from a conservative view, and Norman Dennis and George Erdos from an ethical socialist view, argue that there has been a serious erosion of the traditional family since 1960. And this is not hard to see from the figures in the box on pages 474 and 475. There are fewer marriages, fewer children, more divorce, more singlehood, more single parents. Indeed, the number of children born out of wedlock has grown 'from one in ten in the late 1970s to over three in ten in the early 1990s (Morgan, 1995: 4). And, because of both divorce and increasing numbers of children born out of wedlock, the share of youngsters living with a single parent at some time before age 18 has quadrupled since 1960 to half of all children. Combining the last two

facts, just one in four of today's children will grow up with two parents and go on to maintain a stable marriage of their own.

In the light of such data, serious consequences follow. These include: the rise of delinquency, the growth of incivility, the huge welfare burden. The family is not just changing, it is heading towards total collapse. And it does not look good for the future of society.

Patricia Morgan suggests that the traditional family of man–wife–children is being replaced by the mother–child state. She deplores the rise of lone parent families, especially children born out of wedlock, and is very concerned about the growth of 'welfare dependency' for many of these poor lone parent families. Norman Dennis, with similar arguments, is most concerned with the ways in which a new family without fatherhood has been created. It is this lack of a father to be an adequate role model for children which has created many problems. In sum, and drawing from research, he suggests 'on average the life-long socially certified monogamous family of the pre-1960s pattern was better for children than any one of a variety of alternatives' (Dennis, 1993: 34).

The same debate is found in the United States. Here David Popenoe describes this breakdown as a fundamental shift from a 'culture of marriage' to a 'culture of divorce'. Traditional vows of marital commitment – 'till death us do part' – now

amount to little more than 'as long as I am happy'.

The negative consequences of the cultural trend towards weaker families, Popenoe continues, are obvious everywhere: as we pay less and less attention to children, the crime rate goes up along with a host of other problematic behaviours, including smoking, drinking and premarital sex.

As Popenoe sees it, then, we must work hard and quickly to reverse current trends. Government cannot be the solution (and may even be part of the problem): since 1960 as US government spending on social programmes has soared fivefold, the traditional family has grown weaker and weaker. The alternative, Popenoe reasons, is a cultural turnaround by which people will question and ultimately reject the recently popular 'me-first' view of our lives in favour of greater commitment to a spouse and children. (We have seen such a turnaround in the case of cigarette smoking.) Popenoe concludes we should save the traditional family, and that means we need to affirm publicly the value of marital permanence as well as endorse the two-parent family as best for the well-being of children.

On the other side of the debate, many sociologists argue that the recent changes in the family have mainly been for the good. They are really simply reflections of changes in the wider social world. As people's desire for choice, individuality, freedom, etc. has grown, so has their desire for more control over their personal life. The traditional families desired by the traditionalists are described in too romantic and nostalgic terms. Families of the past often meant that wives were stuck with violent husbands and large families of children lived in abject poverty. Equality was minimal, as was choice.

Instead of returning to a mythical past, a goal now is to achieve democracy in the personal sphere. Equality and choice become key features of modern families. In any event, it is no longer possible to have only one ideal family form – even if we should want it. The world has grown too complex. As Beck and Beck-Gernsheim argue in the *Normal Chaos of Love*, society has become individualised and with that 'It is no longer possible to pronounce in some binding way what family, marriage, parenthood, sexuality or love mean, what they should be or could be; rather they vary in substance, exceptions, norms and morality from individual to individual and from relationships to relationships' (1995: 5). The traditionalists are looking back to a world that has now gone, and cannot be returned to. They do not paint a rosy picture. They recognise that we are in a transition period – one in which there is likely to be 'a long and bitter battle – a war between men and women'.

Most of our current institutions were designed at a time when there was a sharp division between women in the home and men at work. Now this is changing: work situations, laws, town planning, school curricula all have to be changed.

For Judith Stacey, the traditional family is more problem than solution. Striking to the heart of the matter, Stacey writes (1990: 269):

The family is not here to stay. Nor should we wish it were. On the contrary, I believe that all democratic people, whatever their kinship preferences, should work to hasten its demise.

The main reason for rejecting the traditional family, Stacey explains, is that it perpetuates and enhances various kinds of social inequality. Families play a key role in maintaining the class hierarchy, transferring wealth as well as 'cultural capital' from one generation to another. Moreover, feminists charge that the traditional family is built on patriarchy, which subjects women to their husband's authority as well as saddling them with most of the responsibility for housework and child care. And from a gay-rights perspective, she adds, a society that values traditional families inevitably denies homosexual men and women equal dignity and participation in social life.

Stacey thus applauds the breakdown of the family as a measure of social progress. Indeed, she views the family not as a basic social institution but as a political construction that serves to elevate one category of people – affluent white males – at the expense of women, homosexuals and poor people who lack the resources to maintain middle-class respectability.

Moreover, Stacey continues, the concept of 'traditional family' is increasingly irrelevant to a diverse society in which people reject singular models of correct behaviour and in which both men and women must work for income. What society needs, Stacey concludes, is not a return to some golden age of the family but political and economic changes (including income parity for women, universal health care, programmes to reduce unemployment and expanded sex education in the schools) that will provide tangible support for children as well as ensure that people in diverse family forms receive the respect and dignity everyone deserves.

● **Continue the debate:**

1. To strengthen families, Popenoe urges parents to put children ahead of their own careers by limiting their joint working week to 60 hours. Do you agree? Why or why not?

2. Judith Stacey urges greater choice and equality in relationships and this means more diverse families. Do you agree?

3. What policies or programmes would you support to enhance the well-being of children?

4. Can you mount a 'defence of single parents', looking at evidence for their 'successes' and 'failures'. ●

Sources: Stacey, 1990, 1993; Abbot and Wallace, 1992; Dennis and Erdos, 1993; Popenoe, 1993; Council on Families in America, 1995; Morgan, 1995.

rather than in a woman's body. In this complex medical procedure, doctors use drugs to stimulate the woman's ovaries to produce more than one egg during a reproductive cycle. Then they surgically harvest eggs from her ovaries and combine them with sperm in a laboratory dish. The successful fusion of eggs and sperm produces embryos, which surgeons then either implant in the womb of a woman who is to bear the child or freeze for use at a later time.

The immediate benefit of *in vitro* fertilisation is to help couples who cannot conceive normally to have children. Looking further ahead, new birth technologies may eventually reduce the incidence of birth defects. By genetically screening sperm and eggs, medical specialists expect to increase the odds for the birth of a healthy baby (Vines, 1986; Ostling, 1987; Thompson, 1994).

Ethical issues

These are only a few of the new developments which have prompted much debate. Sperm banks, ovary and egg donation, embryo research, cloning, surrogacy and 'artificial wombs' are all issues of the future. Recognising this, in 1982, a government committee – The Warnock Committee – was set up in the UK to consider the ethical implications of such new reproductive issues, advocating in its final report very close regulation of such activities through a new body, the Human Fertilisation and Embryology Authority (HFEA) with the power, for example, to license IVF clinics. Unlike the system in the United States, the Warnock Committee (1984) was firmly against the commercialisation of such practices – where wombs can be sold (or rented!).

As doctors, politicians and lawyers decide when to employ or withhold these NRTs, they move into a new position to define what constitutes a family. In most cases, doctors and hospitals for instance have restricted in vitro fertilisation to women under forty years of age who have male partners. Single women, older women and lesbian couples are only slowly gaining access to this technology.

But all types of new reproductive technology – from laboratory fertilisation to *surrogate motherhood*, in which one woman bears a child for another – force us to confront the inadequacy of conventional kinship terms (is Arlette Schweitzer the mother of the twins she bore? Grandmother? Both?). Then, too, we need to consider

that, when it comes to manipulating life, what is technically possible may not always be morally desirable.

Whilst many women and some feminists have welcomed these developments as a way for women to gain more control over their bodies, others are more sceptical. Diane Richardson has summarised the key objections. She writes:

the new reproductive technologies are being used to uphold traditional notions of motherhood and femininity, have serious eugenic implications, have a low success rate and are expensive, pose health risks to women and, most importantly, they can be seen as extending control over women's reproductive capacities (Richardson, 1994: 87).

Clearly the introduction of such NRTs raises many challenging questions for the future.

● Looking ahead: families in the twenty-first century

In recent decades, transformation in family life throughout much of the world has generated controversy, with advocates of 'traditional family values' locked in debate with supporters of new family forms and greater personal choice. Whatever position one takes on the merits of current family trends, change is certain to continue into the coming century. Based on current evidence, we can make five predictions about the future of family life.

First, divorce rates are likely to remain high, even in the face of evidence that divorce can harm children. There may be some erosion of support for easy dissolution of marriage, yet several generations of high divorce rates have seriously weakened the idea that marriage is a lifetime commitment. Looking back through history, marital relationships are about as durable today as they were a century ago, when many marriages were cut short by death (Kain, 1990). But more couples now *choose* to end marriages that fail to live up to their expectations. Therefore, although the divorce rate has stabilised recently, it is unlikely that marriage will regain the durability characteristic of the 1950s. One major reason is that increasing numbers of women are able to support themselves, and traditional marriages appeal to fewer of them. Men, as well, are seeking more satisfying relationships. Perhaps we should view the recent trend towards higher divorce rates less as a threat to families than as a sign of change in family form. After all, most divorces still lead to remarriage, casting doubt on the notion that marriage itself is becoming obsolete. It is possible, too, that this trend may spread throughout parts of the non-Western world.

Second, family life in the twenty-first century will be highly variable. It may become increasingly 'postmodern'. We have noted an increasing number of cohabiting couples, lone parent families, gay and lesbian families and blended families. Most families may still be based on marriage and most married couples still have children. But, taken together, the variety of family forms observed today represents a new conception of family life as a matter of choice.

Third, men are likely to play changing roles in child rearing. For much of the nineteenth century and early twentieth century, men played limited roles in the raising of children. In the 1950s, a decade many people nostalgically recall as the 'golden age' of families, men began to withdraw from active parenting (Snell, 1990; Stacey, 1990). Since then, the share of children growing up in homes without their fathers has passed 25 per cent and is continuing to rise. A countertrend is

emerging as some fathers – older, on average, and more established in their careers – eagerly jump into parenting. There has also been the rise of the new man highly involved in child rearing. But, on balance, the high UK divorce rate and a surge in single motherhood point to more children growing up with weaker ties to fathers than ever before.

Fourth, economic changes will continue to reform marriage and the family. In many families, both household partners must work to ensure the family's financial security. As Arlie Hochschild (1988) points out, the economy is responsible for most of the change in society, but people *feel* these changes in the family. Marriage today is often the interaction of weary men and women: adults try their best to attend to children, yet often this can become minimal parenting. There are signs, however, that parents are giving increasing attention to their children in the UK (Gershuny, 1997).

Fifth, and finally, the importance of new reproductive technologies will increase. While ethical concerns will surely slow these developments, new methods of reproduction will continue to alter the traditional meanings of parenthood.

SUMMARY ....

1. All societies are built on kinship, although family forms vary considerably across cultures and over time.

2. In industrial societies such as Europe, marriage is monogamous. Many preindustrial societies, however, permit polygamy, of which there are two types: polygyny and polyandry.

3. In global perspective, patrilocality is most common, while industrial societies favour neolocality and a few societies have matrilocal residence. Industrial societies embrace bilateral descent; preindustrial societies tend to be either patrilineal or matrilineal.

4. Families in the past were varied, and indeed varied in the same historical period. There is no such thing as one family form.

5. Functionalist analysis identifies major family functions: socialising the young, regulating sexual activity, transmitting social placement and providing material and emotional support.

6. Conflict theories explore how the family perpetuates social inequality by strengthening divisions based on class, ethnicity, race and gender.

7. Micro-level analysis highlights the variable nature of family life both over time and as experienced by individual family members.

8. Families differ according to class position, race and ethnicity.

9. Gender affects family dynamics since husbands play a dominant role in the vast majority of families. Research suggests that marriage provides more benefits to men than to women.

10. Today's divorce rate is much higher than a century ago; four in ten current marriages will end in divorce. Most people who divorce – especially men – remarry, often forming blended families that include children from previous marriages.

11. Family violence, victimising both women and children, is far more common than official records

indicate. Adults who abuse family members most often suffered abuse themselves as children.

12. Society's family life is becoming more varied. Lone parent families, cohabitation, gay and lesbian couples and singlehood have proliferated in recent years. While the law does not recognise homosexual marriages, many gay men and lesbians form long-lasting relationships and, increasingly, are becoming parents.

13. Although ethically controversial, new reproductive technology is altering conventional notions of parenthood.

KEY CONCEPTS

bilateral descent a system tracing kinship through both men and women

cohabitation the sharing of a household by an unmarried couple

descent the system by which members of a society trace kinship over generations

endogamy marriage between people of the same social category

exogamy marriage between people of different social categories

extended family (consanguine family) a family unit including parents and children, but also other kin

family a social institution, found in all societies, that unites individuals into cooperative groups that oversee the bearing and raising of children

family of choice people with or without legal or blood ties who feel they belong together and wish to define themselves as a family

family unit a social group of two or more people, related by blood, marriage or adoption, who usually live together

family violence emotional, physical or sexual abuse of one family member by another

homogamy marriage between people with the same social characteristics

incest taboo a cultural norm forbidding sexual relations or marriage between certain kin

kinship a social bond, based on blood, marriage or adoption, that joins individuals into families

marriage a legally sanctioned relationship, involving economic cooperation as well as normative sexual activity and childbearing, that people expect to be enduring

matrilineal descent a system tracing kinship through women

matrilocality a residential pattern in which a married couple lives with or near the wife's family

monogamy a form of marriage joining two partners

neolocality a residential pattern in which a married couple lives apart from the parents of both spouses

NRT's new reproductive technologies

nuclear family (conjugal family) a family unit composed of one or two parents and their children

patrilineal descent a system tracing kinship through men

patrilocality a residential pattern in which a married couple lives with or near the husband's family

polyandry a form of marriage joining one female with two or more males

polygamy a form of marriage uniting three or more people

polygyny a form of marriage joining one male with two or more females

CRITICAL-THINKING QUESTIONS

1. How has the emerging postindustrial economy affected family life? What other factors are changing the family?

2. Why do some analysts describe the family as the 'backbone of society'? How do families perpetuate social inequality?

3. Do you think that lone parent households do as good a job as two-parent households in raising children? Why or why not?

4. On balance, are families in Europe becoming 'postmodern'? What evidence supports your contention?

GOING FURTHER ....

Introductory reading

Faith Robertson Elliot, *Gender, Family and Society* (London: Macmillian, 1996).

> Looks at a series of current debates around the family including ethnicity, masculinity, ageing, family violence and moralities.

Di Gittins, *The Family in Question* (London: Macmillan, 2nd edn, 1993).

> A useful series of questions are posed about the family.

Classic sources

Michael Young and Peter Willmott, *Family and Kinship in East London* (Middlesex, Penguin 1957).

> One of the best studies of the working-class family, this chronicle reveals the effect of class on family life.

More advanced reading

Ulrich Beck and Elisabeth Beck-Gernsheim, *The Normal Chaos of Love* (Cambridge: Polity Press, 1995). (translated by Mark Ritter and Jane Wiebel; and originally published in German as *Das ganz normale Chaos der Liebe*, 1990. Frankfurt)

> A highly readable account of changes in family and realtionships at century's end by leading German sociologists.

Anthony Giddens, *The Transformation of Intimacy* (Cambridge: Polity Press, 1992).

> A world renowned sociologist writes in a more accessible way and examines the major changes between men and women.

William J. Goode, *World Changes in Divorce Patterns* (New Haven, CT: Yale University Press, 1993).

> This global survey explains how divorce is affected by economic patterns such as industrialisation; it also explores variation in divorce by class.

Mark Mathabane, *African Women: Three Generations* (New York: HarperCollins, 1994).

> This personal look at three women – a grandmother, a mother and a sister – by a South African details the struggles common to women under a system of racial oppression.

On the family values debates, see:

Pamela Abbott and Claire Wallace, *The Family and the New Right* (London: Pluto Press 1992).

Judith Stacey, *In the Name of the Family: Rethinking Family Values in the Postmodern Age* (Boston: Beacon Press, 1996).

Norman Dennis and George Erdos, *Families without Fatherhood* (London: IEA Health and Welfare Unit, 1993).

Patricia Morgan, *Farewell to the Family* (London, IEA, 1995).

> The first two provide a critique of tradtional families; the last two a defence.

Nancy E. Dowd, *In Defense of Single-Parent Families* (New York: New York University Press, 1997).

> Reviews the case made against lone parents and argues against it.

Kath Weston *Families We Choose: Lesbians, Gays, Kinship* (New York: Columbia University Press, 1991).

> The first major study of the newly emerging gay and lesbian familes.

Other sources

For current information on UK families, contact :
The Family Policy Studies Centre, 231 Baker Street, London, NW1 6XE (0171 486 8179)

chapter eighteen

Source: Popperfoto

Religion

Salman Rushdie published his novel *The Satanic Verses* in Britain in 1989. The novel, addressing migration and exile, is set in contemporary London. One character in the book, the Prophet Mahound, appears as a figure of debauchery, foul language and obscenity. Sensing that this was a thinly disguised, blasphemous attack on Mohammed and the Islamic faith, British Muslims soon expressed their anger and requested a publisher's apology for misrepresenting the Islamic faith. Matters rapidly escalated: the book was ritually burned in Bolton and Bradford; the media accused the Muslims of intolerance; voices were raised against Rushdie in India and Pakistan. On Valentine's day 1989, the Iranian leader Ayatollah Khomeini issued his *fatwa* – or official call for execution – against Rushdie. Although initially a British affair, *The Satanic Verses* scandal escalated into an international one – symbolising battles between religious institutions and secular cultures, and accompanied a resurgence of anti-Islamic feeling in the West. Fearing for his life, Rushdie has been in hiding ever since. (Appignanesi and Maitland, 1989; Parek, 1989).

It is often argued that religion is in decline in the modern world – in the face of rising rationality and science. And it is true that in many European countries, church going and even Christian beliefs are becoming less common. But sociologists are clear that globally religion has remained a powerful force. As the Rushdie case well illustrates.

The timeless human fascination with other-worldly truth lies at the heart of religion. This chapter explains what religion is, explores the changing face of religious belief throughout history and around the world and examines the place of religion in today's modern, scientific and globalising cultures.

● Religion: basic concepts

Durkheim, whose ideas are discussed in detail in Chapter 3 ('Society'), claimed that the focus of religion is 'things that surpass the limits of our knowledge' (1965: 62; orig. 1915). As human beings, Durkheim explained, we organise our surroundings by defining most objects, events or experiences as **profane** (from Latin meaning 'outside the temple'), *that which is an ordinary element of everyday life*. But we set some things apart, Durkheim continued, by designating them as

Salmon Rushdie: the centre of a controversial debate between Islam and the west.

Source: Popperfoto

Religion is founded on the idea of the sacred, that which is set apart as extraordinary and which demands our submission. Bowing, kneeling or prostrating oneself – each a common element of religious devotion – symbolises this submissiveness.

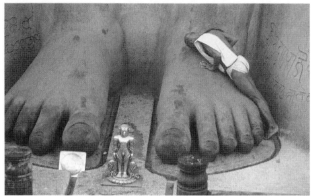

Source: Magnum Photos, Inc – R. Rai

sacred, *that which is defined as extraordinary, inspiring a sense of awe, reverence, and even fear.* Distinguishing the sacred from the profane is the essence of all religious belief. **Religion**, then, is *a social institution involving beliefs and practices based upon a conception of the sacred.*

Around the world, matters of faith vary greatly, with no one thing sacred to everyone. Although people regard most books as profane, Jews view the Torah (the first five books of the Hebrew Bible or Old Testament) as sacred, in the same way that Christians revere the entire Bible and Muslims exalt the Qur'an (Koran).

However, a community of believers draws religious lines, Durkheim (1965: 62) claimed. People understand profane things in terms of their everyday usefulness: we sit down at a computer or turn the key of a car to accomplish various tasks. What is sacred, however, we set apart from everyday life and regard with reverence. To make clear the boundary between the sacred and the profane, Muslims remove their shoes before entering a mosque to avoid defiling a sacred place of worship with soles that have touched the profane ground outside.

The sacred is the focus of **ritual**, which is *formal, ceremonial behaviour*. Holy communion is the central ritual of Christianity; the wafer and wine consumed during communion symbolise the body and blood of Jesus Christ, and are never treated as food.

Religiosity

Religiosity designates *the importance of religion in a person's life*. Years ago, Charles Glock (1959, 1962) distinguished five distinct dimensions of religiosity. *Experiential* religiosity refers to the strength of a person's emotional ties to a religion. *Ritualistic* religiosity refers to frequency of ritual activity such as prayer and church attendance. *Ideological* religiosity concerns an individual's degree of belief in religious doctrine. *Consequential* religiosity has to do with how strongly religious beliefs figure in a person's daily behaviour. Finally, *intellectual* religiosity refers to a person's knowledge of the history and doctrines of a particular religion. Anyone is likely to be more religious on some dimensions than on others; this inconsistency compounds the difficulty of measuring the concept of religiosity.

Religion and sociology

Because religion deals with ideas that transcend everyday experience, neither common sense nor any scientific discipline can verify or disprove religious doctrine. Religion is a matter of **faith**, *belief anchored in conviction rather than scientific evidence*. For instance, the New Testament of the Bible defines faith as 'the assurance of things hoped for, the conviction of things not seen' (Hebrews 11:1) and exhorts Christians to 'walk by faith, not by sight' (2 Corinthians 5:7).

Throughout most of human history, human beings living in small societies attributed birth, death and even what happened in between to the operation of supernatural forces. Over the course of the last several hundred years, however, science has emerged as an alternative way of understanding the natural world, and scientific sociology offers various explanations of how and why societies operate the way they do.

Some people with strong faith may be disturbed by the thought of sociologists turning a scientific eye to what they hold as sacred. Since religions vary a great deal around the world, with no one thing sacred to everyone on earth, this raises in an acute form *the problem of relativity* and leads to the question: just how can billions of people across the world organise their lives with such profoundly different belief systems, each of which claims its own god or gods? Sociologists recognise that religion is central to virtually every culture on earth, and they seek to understand how religious beliefs and practices guide human societies. But they offer no comment on the meaning and purpose of human existence, nor do they pass judgement on any religion as right or wrong. Rather, sociology delves into the consequences of religious activity for larger social life.

● Theoretical analysis of religion

Although, as individuals, sociologists may hold any number of religious beliefs – or none at all – they all agree that religion has major importance for the operation of society. Each theoretical paradigm suggests ways in which religion affects social life.

The functions of religion

Emile Durkheim (1965; orig. 1915) maintained that we confront the power of society every day. Society, he argued, has an existence and power all of its own beyond the life of any individual. Thus, society itself is 'godlike', surviving the ultimate deaths of its members whose lives it shapes. Durkheim contended that, in religious life, people celebrate the awesome power of their own society. This insight explains the practice, in every society, of transforming certain everyday objects into sacred symbols of collective life. Members of technologically simple societies, Durkheim explained, do this with the **totem**, *an object in the natural world collectively defined as sacred*. The totem – perhaps an animal or an elaborate work of art – becomes the centrepiece of ritual, symbolising the power of society to transform individuals into a powerful collectivity.

Durkheim pointed out three major functions of religion for the operation of society:

1. *Social cohesion*. Religion unites people through shared symbols, values and norms. Religious doctrine and ritual establish rules of 'fair play' that make organised social life possible. Religion also speaks eloquently about the vital human dimension of *love*. Thus, religious life underscores both our moral and emotional ties to others (Wright and D'Antonio, 1980).

2. *Social control*. Every society uses religious imagery and rhetoric to promote conformity. Societies infuse many cultural norms – especially mores relating to marriage and reproduction – with religious justification. Looking beyond behavioural norms, religion confers legitimacy on the political

system. In medieval Europe, in fact, monarchs claimed to rule by divine right. Few of today's political leaders invoke religion so explicitly, but many publicly ask for God's blessing, implying to audiences that their efforts are right and just.

3. *Providing meaning and purpose.* Religious beliefs offer the comforting sense that the vulnerable human condition serves some greater purpose. Strengthened by such convictions, people are less likely to collapse in despair when confronted by life's calamities. For this reason, major life-course transitions – including birth, marriage and death – are usually marked by religious observances that enhance our spiritual awareness.

Critical evaluation

Durkheim's structural-functional analysis contends that religion represents the collective life of society. The major weakness of this approach, however, is its tendency to downplay religion's dysfunctions – especially the capacity of strongly held beliefs to generate social conflict. During the early Middle Ages, for example, religious faith was the driving force behind the Crusades, in which European Christians sought to wrest from Muslim control lands that both religions considered to be sacred. Conflict among Muslims, Jews and Christians continues as a source of political instability in the Middle East today. Social divisions in Northern Ireland are also partly a matter of religious conflict between Protestants and Catholics; Dutch Calvinism historically supported apartheid in South Africa; and religious differences continue to fuel divisions in Algeria, Bosnia, India, Sri Lanka and elsewhere. In short, nations have long marched to war under the banner of their god: differences in faith have provoked more violence in the world than have differences of social class. Indeed, the history of the world may well be written as a history of religious war and conflict.

Constructing the sacred: the action paradigm

Max Weber's theory is usually considered a prime example of an action theory, and it is discussed below and elsewhere in this book. But there are many others. 'Society', asserts the Catholic sociologist Peter Berger (1967: 3) 'is a human product and nothing but a human product, that yet continuously acts back upon its producer'. From an action perspective, religion (like all of society) is socially constructed (although perhaps with divine inspiration!). It is one of the chief mechanisms through which meanings are constructed and people make sense of their lives. It is also one of the areas of life most shot through with symbolism and ritual. Thus, through various rituals, from saying grace before daily meals to annual religious observances such as Easter or Passover, individuals develop the distinction between the sacred and profane. Further, Berger explains, by placing everyday events within a 'cosmic frame of reference' people confer on their own fallible, transitory creations 'the semblance of ultimate security and permanence' (1967: 35–36).

Marriage is a good example. If we look on marriage merely as a contract between two people, we assume that we can end it whenever we want to. But if partners define their relationship as holy matrimony, this bond makes a far stronger claim on them. This fact, no doubt, explains why the divorce rate is lower among people who are more religious.

Especially when humans confront uncertainty and life-threatening situations – such as illness, war and natural disaster – we bring sacred symbols to the fore. By seeking out sacred meaning in any situation, in other words, we can lift ourselves above life's setbacks and even face the prospect of death with strength and courage. Interactionists have researched the ways in which many of the newer religions like the Moonies and Scientology give people meaning in the face of a modern world which can be deeply stressful (Lofland, 1977; Barker, 1984).

Critical evaluation

The action approach views religion as a social construction, placing everyday life under a 'sacred canopy' of meaning (Berger, 1967). Of course, Berger adds, the sacred's ability to legitimise and stabilise society depends on its constructed character going unrecognised. After all, we could derive little strength from sacred beliefs if we saw them to be mere devices for coping with tragedy. Then, too, this micro-level view pays scant attention to religion's link with social inequality, to which we now turn.

Inequality and religion: conflict analysis

The social-conflict paradigm highlights religion's support for social hierarchy. Religion, claimed Karl Marx, serves ruling elites by legitimising the status quo and diverting people's attention from the social inequities of society. Most religions create or reinforce systems of stratification. The caste system, as we have seen in Chapter 9, is a key feature of Hinduism and stratifies into layers of priests, rulers, merchants and servants – with a large 'outcast' group that does not fit (the untouchables). The structure of the Christian church, likewise, has often created considerable wealth for its religious leaders. The British monarch is crowned by the head of the Church of England, and The Vatican has status as an independent country in many international organisations, illustrating the close alliance between religious and political elites.

Gender and ethnicity also figure in religion's tie to social inequality. Virtually all the world's major religions have reflected and encouraged male dominance of social life, as the box explains. Many religions predominate in a specific geographical region or society. Islam commands the devotion of most (but not all) people within the Arab societies of the Middle East, Hinduism is closely fused with the culture of India, as is Confucianism with the Chinese way of life. During Marx's lifetime, powerful Christian nations of Western Europe justified colonial exploitation of Africa, the Americas and Asia by claiming that they were merely 'converting heathens'.

In practical terms, working for political change may mean opposing the church and, by implication, God. Religion also encourages people to look hopefully to a 'better world to come', minimising the social problems of this world. In one of his best-known statements, Marx offered a stinging criticism of religion as 'the sigh of the oppressed creature, the sentiment of a heartless world, and the soul of soulless conditions. It is the opium of the people.' (1964: 27; orig. 1848).

Critical evaluation
Social-conflict analysis reveals the power of religion to legitimise social inequality. Yet critics of religion's conservative face, Marx included, minimise ways in which religion has promoted change as well as equality. Nineteenth-century religious groups in the United Kingdom, for example, were at the forefront of the movement to abolish slavery. In the US, religious organisations and their leaders (including the Reverend Martin Luther King, Jr) were at the core of the civil rights movement and today serve as one of the main lobbies

for the needs of poor immigrants from Latin America. There has been a long-standing 'radical' Catholic movement in supporting revolutionary change in Latin America and elsewhere (discussed below).

● Types of religious organisation

Sociologists have devised broad schemes to categorise the hundreds of different religious organisations in the world: churches, sects, cults, ecclesia and denominations are the most common concepts used. The most widely used model takes the form of a continuum, with *churches* at one pole and *sects* at the other. We can describe any actual religious organisation, then, in relation to these two ideal types by locating it on the church–sect continuum.

Church

Drawing on the ideas of his teacher Max Weber, Ernst Troeltsch (1931) defined a **church** as *a type of religious organisation well integrated into the larger society*. Churchlike organisations usually persist for centuries and claim as adherents generations of the same family. Churches have well-established rules and regulations and expect their leaders to undergo approved training before being formally ordained.

While concerned with the sacred, a church accepts the ways of the profane world, which gives it broad appeal. Church doctrine conceives of God in highly intellectualised terms (say, as a force for good), and favours abstract moral standards ('Do unto others as you would have them do unto you') over specific mandates for day-to-day living. By teaching morality in safely abstract terms, a church can avoid social controversy. For example, many churches that, in principle, celebrate the unity of all peoples, have, in practice, all-white memberships. Such duality minimises conflict between a church and the surrounding political landscape (Troeltsch, 1931).

A church generally takes one of two forms. Islam in Morocco represents an **ecclesia**, *a church formally allied with the state*. Ecclesias have been common in history; for centuries Roman Catholicism animated the Roman Empire; Confucianism was the state religion in China until early in this century; the Anglican church remains the official Church of England, as Islam is the official religion of Pakistan and Iran. State churches typically define everyone in the society as a member; tolerance of religious difference, therefore, is severely limited. A **denomination**, by contrast, is *a church, independent of the state, that accepts religious pluralism.* Denominations are sects that have become incorporated into mainstream society. Thus Christian denominations include Baptists, Methodists and Lutherans, among others.

Sect

At the other end of our continuum is the **sect**, *a type of religious organisation that stands apart from the larger society.* Sect members hold rigidly to their own reli-

gious convictions while discounting what others around them claim to be true. In extreme cases, members of a sect may withdraw from society completely in order to practice their religion without interference from outsiders. When cultures view religious tolerance as a virtue, members of sects are sometimes accused of being dogmatic in their insistence that they alone follow the true religion (Stark and Bainbridge, 1979).

In organisational terms, sects are less formal than churches. Thus, sect members often engage in highly spontaneous and emotional practices as they worship, while members of churches tend to be passively attentive to their leader. Sects also reject the intellectualised religion of churches, stressing instead the personal experience of divine power. A further distinction

DIFFERENT VOICES

Religion and patriarchy: do gods favour men?

All world religions are patriarchal. They have male gods at the centre of their cosmologies; favour men to be their officials on earth; and frequently devise ways of excluding women both from church and society. Many more recent sects and cults that are emerging seem to keep this patriarchal order.

While many Christians revere Mary, the mother of Jesus, the New Testament also contrasts men made in 'the image and glory of God' with women, made for 'the glory of man', professing:

'For man was not made from woman, but woman from man. Neither was man created for woman, but woman for man' (1 Corinthians 11: 7–9). Another passage proclaims: 'Wives, be subject to your husbands, as to the Lord. For the husband is the head of

the wife as Christ is the head of the church' (Ephesians 5: 22–24), while the writings of Timothy declare 'I permit no woman to teach or to have authority over men; she is to keep silent. For Adam was formed first, then Eve; and Adam was not deceived, but the woman was deceived and became a transgressor. Yet woman will be saved through bearing children, if she continues in faith and love and holiness, with modesty' (1 Timothy 2: 11–15). Likewise, the Qur'an, the sacred text of Islam, contends

Bristol, England, March 1994. Rev. Susan Shipp, newly ordained woman priest.

Source: Popperfoto

between church and sect turns on patterns of leadership. The more churchlike an organisation, the more likely that its leaders are formally trained and ordained. Because more sectlike organisations celebrate the personal presence of God, members expect their leaders to exude divine inspiration in the form of **charisma** (from Greek meaning 'divine favour'), *extraordinary personal qualities that can turn an audience into followers*, infusing them with the emotional experience that sects so value.

Sects generally form as breakaway groups from established churches or other religious organisations (Stark and Bainbridge, 1979). Their psychic intensity and informal structure render them less stable than churches, and many sects blossom only to wither and disappear a short time later. The sects that do endure typically become more like churches, losing fervour as they become more bureaucratic and established.

To sustain their membership, many sects rely on active recruitment, or *proselytising*, of new members. Sects place great value on the experience of *conversion*, a personal transformation or religious rebirth. Members of Jehovah's Witnesses, for example, eagerly share their faith with others in hopes of attracting new members. Finally, churches and sects differ in their social composition. Because they are more closely tied to the secular world, well-established churches tend to include people of high social standing. Sects, by contrast, attract more disadvantaged people. A sect's openness to new members and promise of salvation and personal fulfilment

that 'men are in charge of women' (quoted in Kaufman, 1976: 163). Male Orthodox Jews include the following words in daily prayer:

Blessed art thou, O Lord our God, King of the Universe, that I was not born a gentile.

Blessed art thou, O Lord our God, King of the Universe, that I was not born a slave.

Blessed art thou, O Lord our God, King of the Universe, that I was not born a woman.

Historically, the major world religions have barred women from serving as priests. Islamic groups, Orthodox Jews and the Roman Catholic church continue to exclude women from the religious hierarchy. But a growing number of Protestant denominations – including the Church of England and Methodists – have overturned historical policies and now ordain women. In 1992, the Church of England voted to allow priesthood to be open to women, despite much opposition. Reform Judaism has long elevated women to the role of rabbi (and is the largest denomination to ordain gay and lesbian people). In 1985, the first woman became a rabbi in the Conservative denomination of Judaism.

Challenges to the patriarchal structure of organised religion – from the ordination of women to the introduction of gender-neutral language in hymnals and prayers – has sparked heated controversy, delighting progressives while outraging traditionalists. Propelling these developments is a lively feminism within many religious communities today. Feminist Christians contend that the rigid patriarchal traditions in many churches stand in stark contrast to the Biblical image of Jesus Christ as 'nonaggressive, non-competitive, meek and humble of heart, a nurturer of the weak and a friend of the outcast' – traits patriarchy associates with the feminine' (Sandra Schneiders, quoted in Woodward, 1989: 61).

Feminists argue that unless traditional notions of gender are removed from our understanding of God, women will never have equality with men in the church. Theologian Mary Daly puts the matter bluntly: 'If God is male, then male is God'. Mary Daly is, perhaps, the most outspoken, feminist critic (and was herself originally a Catholic). She sees Christianity as a patriarchal myth. For her, the Christian story served to eliminate earlier 'Goddess' religions and women: 'there is no female presence involved in this Monogender Male Automotherhood', she claims. She then goes on to argue that Christianity is rooted in male 'sado-rituals', with its 'torture cross symbolism', and that it embodies women hating. This leads her to mount a full-scale critique of male religions (Daly, 1973; 1978). ●

may be especially appealing to people who perceive themselves as social outsiders. However, as we shall explain presently, many established churches in the world have lost membership in recent decades. In the process, a number of sects, often global, now find themselves with more affluent members.

Cult

Finally, a **cult** is *a religious organisation that is substantially outside a society's cultural traditions*. Whereas a sect emerges from within a traditional religious organisation, a cult represents something else entirely. Cults typically form around a highly charismatic leader who offers a compelling message of a new way of life. Because some cult principles or practices may seem unconventional, the popular view of cults pictures them as deviant or even evil. Negative publicity given to a few cults has raised suspicion about any unfamiliar religious group. As a result of such aberrant behaviour, some scholars assert that to call a religious community a 'cult' amounts to declaring it unworthy (Richardson, 1990).

Many long-standing religions – Christianity, Islam and Judaism included – began as cults. Of course, not all or even most cults flourish for very long. Cults are more at odds with the larger society than sects; and many demand that members not only accept their doctrine but embrace a radically new lifestyle. As a result, people sometimes accuse cults of brainwashing new members, although research suggests that most people who join cults experience no psychological harm (Barker, 1981; Kilbourne, 1983). The rise in new cults is discussed further below.

● Comparative religions

Religion is found in virtually all societies, and the diversity of religious expression is almost as wide-ranging as culture itself. All religions have models of life by which people can organise their activities. Usually these include a cosmogony, a tale about how the world/universe was created; a theodicy, a tale about how evil and suffering is to be found in the world; and a broad vision of the ethical life – how people should behave. In addition they are likely to have many rituals: meditations and mantras, worship, regulations on hygiene, diet and sex; and festivals. Every Hindu

devotee must engage in ritual washings; whilst for Jews there are rites of passage like bar mitzvah for boys and bat mitzvah for girls (Kurtz, 1996: 25).

Religion in preindustrial societies

Religion predates written history. Archaeological evidence indicates that our human ancestors routinely engaged in religious rituals some forty thousand years ago. Early hunters and gatherers, and some modern non-Western peoples embrace **animism** (from Latin meaning 'the breath of life'), *the belief that elements of the natural world are conscious life forms that affect humanity*. Animistic people view forests, oceans, mountains, even the wind as spiritual forces. Hunters and gatherers conduct their religious life entirely within the family. Members of such societies may look to a *shaman* or religious leader, but there are no full-time, specialised religious leaders. Belief in a single divine power responsible for creating the world marked the rise of pastoral and horticultural societies. The Christian view of God as a 'shepherd', may be linked to earlier religions, all of whose original followers were pastoral peoples.

As societies develop more productive capacity, religious life expands beyond the family and priests take their place among other specialised workers. In agrarian societies, the institution of religion gains prominence, as evidenced by the centrality of the church in medieval Europe. Even the physical design of the city casts this dominance in stone, with the cathedral rising above all other structures.

● World religions

Many of the thousands of different religions are highly localised with few followers. *World religions*, by contrast, span large areas and have millions of adherents. We shall briefly describe six world religions, which together claim as adherents some 4 billion people – almost three-quarters of humanity.

Christianity

Christianity is the most widespread religion, with 1.9 billion followers, who constitute roughly one-third of humanity. Most Christians live in Europe or the Americas; more than 85 per cent of the people in the United States and Canada identify with Christianity.

Moreover, as shown on Map 18.1, people who are at least nominally Christian represent a significant share of the population in many other world regions, with the notable exceptions of northern Africa and Asia. This diffusion stems from the European colonisation of much of the world during the last 500 years. The dominance of Christianity in the West can be seen in the practice of numbering years on the calendar beginning with the birth of Christ.

Christianity originated as a cult, incorporating elements of its much older predecessor Judaism. Like many cults, Christianity was propelled by the personal charisma of a leader, Jesus of Nazareth, who preached a message of personal salvation. Jesus did not directly challenge the political powers of his day, calling on his followers to 'Render therefore to Caesar things that are Caesar's' (Matthew 22: 21). But his message was revolutionary, nonetheless, promising that faith and love would lead to triumph over sin and death.

Christianity is one example of **monotheism**, *belief in a single divine power*. This new religion broke with the Roman Empire's traditional **polytheism**, *belief in many gods*. Yet Christianity has a unique vision of the Supreme Being as a sacred Trinity: God the Creator; Jesus Christ, Son of God and Redeemer, and the Holy Spirit, a Christian's personal experience of God's presence. The claim that Jesus was divine rests on accounts of his final days on earth. Tried and sentenced to death in Jerusalem on charges that he was a threat to established political leaders, Jesus endured a cruel execution by crucifixion, which transformed the cross into a sacred Christian symbol. According to Christian belief, Jesus was resurrected – that is, he rose from the dead – showing that he was the Son of God.

The apostles of Jesus spread Christianity widely throughout the Mediterranean region. Although the Roman Empire initially persecuted Christians, by the fourth century Christianity had become an ecclesia – the official religion of what was known as the Holy Roman Empire. What had begun as a cult four centuries before was by then an established church.

Christianity took various forms, including the Roman Catholic church and the Orthodox church, centred in Constantinople (now Istanbul, Turkey). Further division occurred towards the end of the Middle Ages, when the Protestant Reformation in Europe sparked the formation of hundreds of denom-inations. Dozens of these denominations now command sizeable followings in Britain (see Figure 18.1).

Islam

Islam has some 1.1 billion followers (19 per cent of humanity), called Muslims. Like all religions, it is not uniform but made of many schisms – Sunnis, for example, are the more mystical branch of the Muslims. A majority of people in the Middle East are Muslims, which explains our tendency to associate Islam with Arabs in that region of the world. But most Muslims are *not* Arabs. Map 18.2 shows that a majority of people across northern Africa and western Asia are also Muslims. Moreover, significant concentrations of Muslims are found in Pakistan, India, Bangladesh, Indonesia and the southern republics of the former Soviet Union.

Islam is the second largest faith in Europe, with estimates of 6 million (3 per cent of most west European populations). If Eastern Europe were added in, the numbers would be significantly greater. Estimates place the number of British Muslims at 1,200,000 – most concentrated in the Midlands, London, Bradford, Strathclyde, Yorkshire and Lancashire. British Muslims are predominantly Sunni, with only around 25,000 Shias (Storry and Childs, 1997).

Followers of Islam reverently remove their shoes – which touch the profane ground – before entering this sacred mosque in the Southeast Asian nation of Brunei.

Source: Woodfin Camp & Associates – Hans Hoefer

Islam is the word of God as revealed to the prophet Mohammed, who was born in the city of Mecca (now in Saudi Arabia) around the year 570 CE. To Muslims, Mohammed, like Jesus, is a prophet, but not a divine being (as Christians define Jesus). The Qur'an (Koran), sacred to Muslims, is the word of God (in Arabic, 'Allah') as transmitted through Mohammed, God's messenger. In Arabic, the word 'Islam' means both 'submission' and 'peace', and the Qur'an urges submission to Allah as the path to inner peace. Muslims express this personal devotion in a daily ritual of five prayers.

Islam spread rapidly after the death of Mohammed, although divisions arose. All Muslims, however, accept the Five Pillars of Islam: (1) recognising Allah as the one, true God, and Mohammed as God's messenger; (2) ritual prayer; (3) giving alms to the poor; (4) fasting during the month of Ramadan; and (5) making a pilgrimage at least once in a lifetime to the Sacred House of Allah in Mecca (Weeks, 1988). Like Christianity, Islam holds people accountable to God for their deeds on earth. Those who live obediently will be rewarded in heaven, while evil-doers will suffer unending punishment.

Muslims are also obligated to defend their faith. Sometimes this tenet has justified holy wars against non-believers (in roughly the same way that medieval Christians joined the Crusades to recapture the Holy Land from the Muslims). Recently, in Algeria, Egypt, Iran and elsewhere, some Muslims have sought to rid their society of Western influences they regard as morally corrupting (Martin, 1982; Arjomand, 1988).

Map 18.1 ● Christianity in global perspective

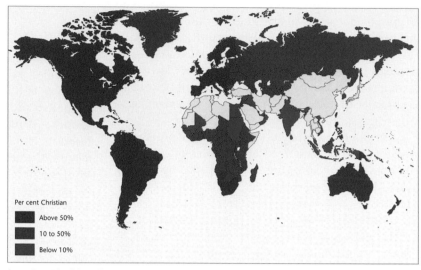

Per cent Christian

Above 50%

10 to 50%

Below 10%

Source: *Peters Atlas of the World* (1990)

Map 18.2 ● Islam in global perspective

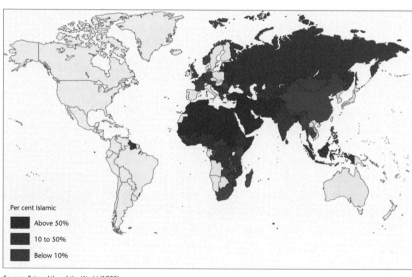

Per cent Islamic

Above 50%

10 to 50%

Below 10%

Source: *Peters Atlas of the World* (1990)

Many Westerners view Muslim women as among the most socially oppressed people on earth. Muslim women do lack many of the personal freedoms enjoyed by Muslim men, yet most accept the mandates of their religion. Moreover, patriarchy was well established in the Middle East before the birth of Mohammed. Some defenders of Islam's treatment of

Map 18.3 ● Hinduism in global perspective

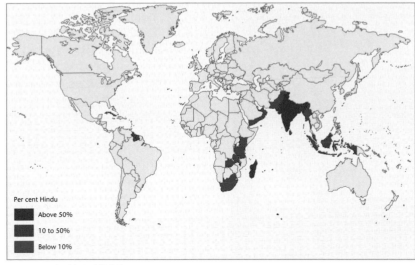

Source: *Peters Atlas of the World* (1990)

Map 18.4 ● Buddhism in global perspective

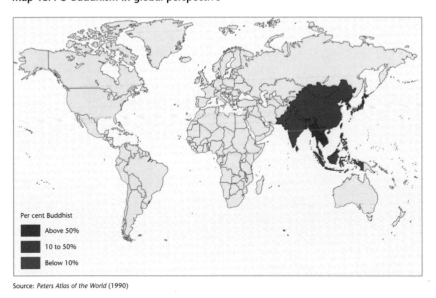

Source: *Peters Atlas of the World* (1990)

Judaism

Speaking purely in numerical terms, Judaism, with only 14 million adherents world-wide, is less prominent as a world religion. Only in Israel do Jews represent a national majority. But Judaism has significance in many countries. The United States has the largest concentration of Jews (6 million people); and the largest European communities are found in France (500,000–600,000) and Britain (300,000) (Davie, 1992: 225).

Jews look to the past as a source of guidance in the present and for the future. And Judaism has deep historical roots that extend back some 4,000 years before the birth of Christ to the ancient cultures of Mesopotamia. At this time, Jews were animistic; but this belief was to change after Jacob – grandson of Abraham, the earliest great ancestor – led his people to Egypt. Under Egyptian rule, Jews endured centuries of slavery. In the thirteenth century BCE, a turning point came as Moses, the adopted son of an Egyptian princess, was called by God to lead the Jews from bondage. This exodus (this word's Latin and Greek roots mean 'a marching out') from Egypt is commemorated by Jews today in the annual ritual of Passover. As a result of the Jews' liberation from bondage, Judaism became monotheistic, recognising a single, all-powerful God.

A distinctive concept of Judaism is the *covenant*, a special relationship with God by which Jews became a 'chosen people'. The covenant also implies a duty to observe God's law, especially the Ten Commandments as revealed to Moses on Mount Sinai. Jews regard the Bible (or, in Christian terms, the Old Testament) as both a record of their history and a statement of the obligations of

women argue that Islam actually improved the social position of women by demanding that husbands deal justly with their wives. Further, although Islam permits a man to have up to four wives, it admonishes men to have only one wife if having more than one would encourage him to treat women unjustly (Qur'an, 'The Women', v. 3).

Two Jewish boys read the Talmud, the Jewish sacred book.

Source: Popperfoto

Jewish life. Of special importance are the first five books of the Bible (Genesis, Exodus, Leviticus, Numbers and Deuteronomy), designated as the *Torah* (a word roughly meaning 'teaching' and 'law'). In contrast to Christianity's central concern with personal salvation, Judaism emphasises moral behaviour in this world.

Judaism is composed of three main denominations. Orthodox Jews strictly hold to traditional beliefs and practices, maintaining historical forms of dress, segregating men and women at religious services and consuming only kosher foods. Such traditional practices set off Orthodox Jews as the most sectlike. Hasidism is the most messianic and fosters a strong spiritual devotion to Judaism. In the mid-nineteenth century, many Jews sought greater accommodation to the larger society, leading to the formation of more churchlike Reform Judaism. More recently, a third segment – Conservative Judaism – has established a middle ground between the other two denominations.

All Jews, however, share a keen awareness of their cultural history, which has included battling against considerable prejudice and discrimination. A collective memory of centuries of slavery in Egypt, conquest by Rome and persecution in Europe have shaped Jewish identity. A militant Catholic church instigated a strong separation of Christian and Jew during the Crusades. Interestingly, the urban ghetto (derived from the Italian word *borghetto*, meaning settlement outside the city walls) was first home to Jews in Italy, and this form of residential segregation soon spread to other parts of Europe (Sowell, 1996: Chapter 6). Substantial numbers of Jews have lived in Eastern Europe since medieval times (with Poland often being the 'capital').

Around 120,000 Jews came to England as refugees from the pogroms of Russia between 1875 and 1914. Many settled in East London (Castles and Miller, 1993: 55). As larger numbers entered the country during the final decades of the nineteenth century, anti-Semitism increased. During World War II, anti-Semitism reached a vicious peak when Jews experienced the most horrific persecution in modern times as the Nazi regime in Germany systematically annihilated approximately 6 million Jews. The history of Judaism is a grim reminder of a tragic dimension of the human record – the extent to which religious minorities have been the target of hatred and even slaughter (Bedell, Sandon and Wellborn, 1975; Holm, 1977; Schmidt, 1980; Seltzer, 1980; Wilson, 1982; Eisen, 1983).

Hinduism

Hinduism is the oldest of all the world religions, originating in the Indus River Valley approximately forty-five hundred years ago. Hindus number some 775 million (14 per cent of humanity). Map 18.3 shows that Hinduism remains an Eastern religion, the predominant creed of India today with a significant presence in a few societies of southern Africa as well as Indonesia.

Hinduism differs from most other religions because it did not spring from the life of any single person. Hinduism also has no sacred writings comparable to the Bible or the Qur'an. Nor does Hinduism even envision God as a specific entity. For this reason, Hinduism – like other Eastern religions – is sometimes thought of as an 'ethical religion'. Hindu beliefs and practices vary widely, but all Hindus recognise a moral force in the universe that imposes on everyone responsibilities known as *dharma*. One traditional example of dharma is the need to act in concert with the traditional caste system, described in Chapter 9 ('Social Stratification').

A second Hindu principle, *karma*, refers to the belief in the spiritual progress of the human soul. To a Hindu, all actions have spiritual consequences and proper living contributes to moral development. Karma works through *reincarnation*, a cycle of new birth following death, so that individuals are reborn into a spiritual state corresponding to the moral quality of their previous life. Unlike Christianity and Islam, Hinduism proclaims no ultimate judgement at the hands of a supreme god, although in the cycle of rebirth, each person reaps exactly what that individual has sown. The sublime state of *nirvana* represents spiritual perfection: when a soul reaches this rarefied plateau, it exits the cycle of rebirth.

Looking at Hinduism, we see also that not all religions can be neatly labelled monotheistic or polytheistic. Hinduism may be described as monotheistic because it envisions the universe as a single moral system; yet Hindus perceive this moral order in every element of nature. Rituals, which are central to a Hindu's life, are performed in a variety of ways. Most Hindus practice private devotions, including, for example, ritual cleansing following contact with a person of lower caste. Many also participate in public rituals, such as the *Kumbh Mela*, during which pilgrims flock to the sacred Ganges River in India to bathe in its purifying waters. This ritual, which occurs every twelve years, attracts 15 to 20 million people, making it the largest gathering of people on earth (Pitt, 1955; Sen, 1961; Embree, 1972; Kaufman, 1976; Schmidt, 1980).

Buddhism

Some twenty-five hundred years ago, the rich culture of India also gave rise to Buddhism. Today more than 330 million people (6 per cent of humanity) embrace Buddhism, and almost all are Asians. As shown in Map 18.4, adherents to Buddhism represent more than half the population of Myanmar (Burma), Thailand, Cambodia and Japan; Buddhism is also widespread in India and the People's Republic of China. Of the world religions considered so far, Buddhism most resembles Hinduism in doctrine, but, like Christianity, its inspiration springs from the life of one individual.

Siddhartha Gautama was born to a high-caste family in Nepal about 563 BCE. As a young man, he was preoccupied with spiritual matters. At the age of twenty-nine, he underwent a radical personal transformation, setting off for years of travel and meditation. His path ended when he achieved what Buddhists describe as *bodhi*, or enlightenment. Understanding the essence of life, Gautama became a Buddha. During the third century BCE, the ruler of India joined the ranks of Buddhists, subsequently sending missionaries throughout Asia and elevating Buddhism to the status of a world religion.

Energised by the Buddha's personal charisma, followers spread his teachings – the *dhamma* – across India. The Buddhist ethics are found in the five Precepts: Do not kill; Do not steal; Do not lie; Do not be unchaste; Do not drink intoxicants. Central to Buddhist belief is the notion that human existence involves suffering. The pleasures of the world are real, of course, but Buddhists see such experiences as transitory. This doctrine is rooted in the Buddha's own travels throughout a society rife with poverty. But the Buddha rejected wealth as a solution to suffering; on the contrary, he warned that materialism inhibits spiritual development. Buddhism's answer to world problems is for individuals to pursue personal, spiritual transformation.

Buddhism closely parallels Hinduism in recognising no god of judgement; rather, it finds spiritual consequences in each daily action. Another similarity lies in its belief in reincarnation. Here, again, only full enlightenment ends the cycle of death and rebirth, thereby finally liberating a person from the suffering of the world (Schumann, 1974; Thomas, 1975).

Confucianism

From about 200 BCE until the beginning of this century, Confucianism was an ecclesia – the official religion of China. Following the 1949 Revolution, religion was suppressed by the communist government of the new People's Republic of China. Although officials provide little in the way of data to establish precise numbers, hundreds of millions of Chinese are still influenced by Confucianism. While almost all adherents to Confucianism live in China, Chinese immigration has introduced this religion to other societies in Southeast Asia.

When Western people perform religious rituals they typically do so collectively and formally as members of specific congregations. Eastern people, by contrast, visit shrines individually and informally, without joining a specific congregation. For this reason, Asian temples such as this one in Hong Kong, shown below, receive a steady flow of people – families praying, individuals engaged in business and foreign tourists just watching – that seems somehow inappropriate to the Western visitor.

Source: Sygma – Hans Kemp

Confucius or, properly, K'ung-Fu-tzu, lived between 551 and 479 BCE. Confucius shared with Buddha a deep concern for the problems and suffering of the world. The Buddha's response was a sectlike spiritual withdrawal from the world; Confucius, by contrast, instructed his followers to engage the world according to a strict code of moral conduct. Thus it was that Confucianism became fused with the traditional culture of China. Here we see a second example of what might be called a 'national religion'. As Hinduism has remained largely synonymous with Indian culture, Confucianism is enshrined in the Chinese way of life.

A central concept of Confucianism is *jen*, meaning humanness. In practice, this means that we must always subordinate our self-interest to moral principle. In the family, the individual must display loyalty and consideration for others. Likewise, families must remain mindful of their duties towards the larger community. In this way, layer upon layer of moral obligation integrates society as a whole. Most of all,

Confucianism stands out as lacking a clear sense of the sacred. We could view Confucianism, recalling Durkheim's analysis, as the celebration of society itself as sacred. Alternatively, we might argue that Confucianism is less a religion than a model of disciplined living. Certainly the historical dominance of Confucianism helps to explain why Chinese culture has long taken a sceptical attitude towards the supernatural. If we conclude that Confucianism is best thought of as a disciplined way of life, we must also recognise that it shares with religion a body of beliefs and practices that have as their goal goodness, concern for others and the promotion of social harmony (Kaufman, 1976; Schmidt, 1980; McGuire, 1987).

Religion: East and West

This overview of world religions points up two general differences between the belief systems that predominate in Eastern and Western societies. First, Western religions (Christianity, Judaism and Islam) are typically deity-based, with a clear focus on God. Eastern religions (Hinduism, Buddhism, Confucianism) tend to be more like ethical codes that make a less clear-cut distinction between the sacred and secular. Second, the operational unit of Western religious organisations is the congregation. That is, people attend a specific place of worship with others, most of whom are members. Eastern religious organisations, by contrast, are more broadly tied into culture itself. For this reason, for example, a visitor finds a Thai or Hong Kong temple awash with people – tourists and worshippers alike – who come and go on their own schedule, paying little attention to those around them.

These two distinctions do not overshadow the common element of all religions: having a conception of a higher moral force or purpose that transcends the concerns of everyday life. In all these religious beliefs, people of the world find guidance and a sense of purpose for their lives.

● Religion in Europe

Christianity is one of the foundations of European societies. For much of the past two millennia, Christianity has defined life in Europe – dignifying all major actions, from birth and baptism through marriage to death and burial. It has held out the hope of 'salvation'. In Pre-Reformation feudal society, the church was unitary – supported by royalty and the entire population. Hamiliton says:

The medieval world was Christian in the sense that everybody shared a common understanding of the world in which they lived based on Christian premises. Only the very learned had full and detailed knowledge of the whole world picture, but everybody understood some part of it. (Hamilton, 1986: 87)

Yet, whilst all the countries of Europe make some claim to be Christian and to have Christian values, there are significant religious divides both within and across countries. A potted history would have to include:

● The early combats with Judaism in the struggle to establish a dominant religion.

● The fourth Century split of the European Christian Church into Roman Catholicism in the West and Greek Orthodoxy in the East. While Roman Catholicism spread to the Americas, the Eastern Orthodox lost ground in central Europe and Asia to Islam during the eleventh century.

● The long struggles between empires and the papacy. Pope Innocent III (1198–1216) finally established a papal state in central Italy, the Holy Roman Empire.

● The conflicts within the church itself: the heretical struggles and executions of witches, etc. along with a rather dissolute clergy with an eye on wealth.

● The continuing conflicts with other religions, with high periodic violence (the Spanish Inquisition, the Crusades and the Nazi Holocaust).

● The Reformation: started in Germany with Martin Luther (1483–1546), reformists renounced allegiances to Rome in 1520. By 1570, Protestants had established a presence in many places – especially Scandinavia, Britain and 'Baltic Europe', moving later into the Netherlands, France, Spain and even Italy. Calvinism (formed by John Calvin 1509–64) emerged in France, the Netherlands and Scotland.

● Migration and missionary missions to colonies in the Americas and Africa.

● The rise of science, with its claims for rationality, as a serious challenge to Christianity during the Enlightenment and the Industrial Revolution.

Today, in Europe, divides and schisms continue. Yugoslavia, torn by divisions between Christians as well as between Christianity and Islam, dramatically revealed the sharper edge of the continuing conflicts. There are also deep seated conflicts between Protestants and Catholics (as in Northern Ireland) and between religion and humanism (as in the Netherlands). The Christian Democratic Parties in many European governments partly base their platforms on Christian principles. In the UK, the Queen is head of both Church and State and the two are interconnected. In Germany, the government collects church taxes (Kirchensteuer) on behalf of churches and uses it for social services. Abortion issues continue to preoccupy those countries with a strong Catholic base.

The most obvious divide lies between the more religious, Catholic countries of Southern Europe (Italy, Spain, Greece and Portugal) and the less religious Protestant north. But there are divergences: France and Ireland are predominantly Catholic. Belgium, the Netherlands, Britain and the Nordic countries are generally less religious. Islam now constitutes the second largest faith in Europe, claiming 6 million faithful – 3 per cent of most European populations (Clarke, 1988).

Religion in the UK

In contrast with the United States, where 90 per cent of adults voice a religious preference (NORC, 1994: 114), Britain is becoming a relatively non-religious country. Only 21 per cent of the British population say they have no doubts about the existence of God, whereas 26 per cent either do not believe in God or do not know if God exists (*Social Trends*, 1997: 13.23). Trinitarian churches have seen a fall in membership from 9.1 million adults in 1970 to 6.4 million in 1995 (*Social Trends*, 1997: 13.23).

In Britain, the Churches of England and Wales are formally tied to both Parliament and the monarchy, though the Church of England has shed its image as the 'Tory Party at prayer'. Indeed, during the long period of Conservative government from 1979 to 1997, the Church of England regularly provided reports which implicitly criticised the policies of the government, particularly *Faith in the City* (ACUPA, 1985) which highlighted the plight of the poor who had not benefitted from free market Thatcherism.

Membership in established, 'mainstream' churches has dwindled. Figure 18.1 demonstrates that support for the Anglican, Roman Catholic, Presbyterian and Baptist churches has declined significantly in recent

A Hindu praying.

Source: Popperfoto

Leader Ahmmedia Muslims in Britain in front of the oldest mosque, Earlsfield.

Source: Popperfoto

years. Nominally, there are around 27 million Anglicans (nearly two-thirds claimed to associate with the Church of England), but only 2 million have officially registered. There are some 5 million Catholics, who are much more likely to attend church (Liverpool is Britain's only mainly Catholic city). Nevertheless, the churches remain heavily involved in the cultural life of the UK, through such activities as play groups, jumble sales, youth clubs, care for the elderly and community centres. Christianity may now be more of a cultural force than a spiritual one.

As the established churches lose members, however, other religious organisations are showing surprising strength. As Figure 18.1 suggests, the UK now has substantial populations of Muslims, Sikhs, Hindus and Jews, which, in contrast to the Christian faiths, have generally grown significantly in recent years. Immigration initially underpinned the numbers of Muslims, Sikhs and Hindus, but now many of the 1,200,000 Muslims, who have established large communities to be found in London, the Midlands, West Yorkshire and Strathclyde, were born in the UK. Britain has the second largest Jewish community in Europe.

● Religion and social change

Religion is not just the conservative force portrayed by Karl Marx. Historically, as Max Weber (1958; orig. 1904) pointed out, religion often has promoted dramatic social change. It was in the wake of Calvinism, Weber noted, that Western Europe industrialised.

Figure 18.1 ● Church membership in the UK (millions)

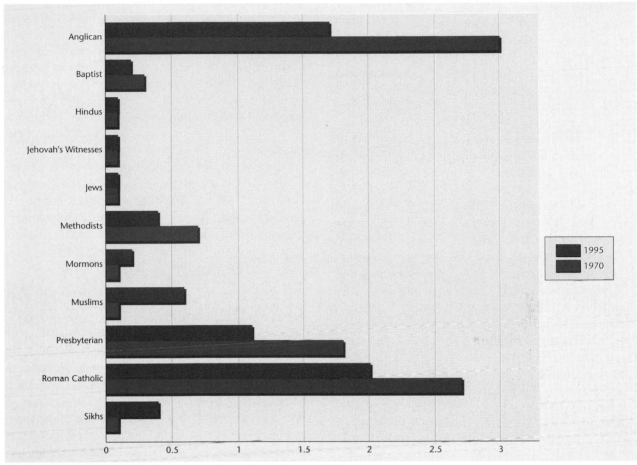

Source: *Social Trends*, 27, 1997, p. 224, Social and Regional Statistics Office for National Statistics, Eurostat (1995)

As Chapter 3 ('Society') explained, John Calvin (1509–1564), a leader in the Protestant Reformation, advanced the doctrine of predestination. Calvin held that an all-powerful and all-knowing God predestines some people for salvation while condemning most to eternal damnation. With each individual's fate sealed before birth and known to God alone, the only certainty is what hangs in the balance: eternal peace and glory or hellfire and brimstone. Driven by anxiety over their fates, Calvinists understandably sought signs of God's favour in *this* world and gradually settled on prosperity as a key symbol of divine favour. This conviction, coupled with their rigid devotion to duty, led Calvinists to become absorbed in the pursuit of success. But riches were never to fuel self-indulgent spending; nor were Calvinists moved to share their wealth with the poor, whose plight they saw as a mark of God's rejection.

As agents of God's work on earth, Calvinists believed that their lifelong 'calling' was best fulfilled by reinvesting profits and reaping ever-greater wealth in the process. All the while, they practised personal thrift and eagerly embraced technological advances that would enhance their efforts. Driven towards worldly success by religious motives, then, they laid the groundwork for the rise of industrial capitalism. In time, the religious fervour that motivated early Calvinists was transformed into a profane Protestant 'work ethic', prompting Weber to describe industrial capitalism as a 'disenchanted' religion. But his analysis leaves little doubt as to the power of religious thinking to alter the basic shape of society.

Liberation theology

Christianity has a long-standing concern for the suffering of poor and oppressed people. Historically, the Christian response to poverty has been to strengthen the believer's faith in a better life to come. In recent decades, however, some church leaders and theologians have embraced liberation theology, a fusion of Christian principle with (often Marxist) political activism.

This social movement started in the late 1960s in Latin America's Roman Catholic church. In addition to the church's efforts to free humanity from sin, Christian activists are helping people in low-income countries to liberate themselves from abysmal poverty. The message of liberation theology is simple: social oppression runs counter to Christian morality, and it is preventable. Therefore, as a matter of faith and social justice, Christians must promote greater social equality.

A growing number of Catholic people have allied themselves with the poor in the liberation theology movement. The costs of opposing the status quo, however, have been high. Church members – including Oscar Arnulfo Romero, the archbishop of San Salvador (the capital of El Salvador) – have been killed in the violence that engulfs much of that region.

Liberation theology has also polarised the Catholic community. Pope John Paul II condemns this movement for tainting traditional church doctrine with left-wing politics. Despite the Pontiff's objections, however, the liberation theology movement has attracted people receptive to the belief that Christian faith should strive to improve the condition of the world's poor (Boff, 1984; Neuhouser, 1989).

● Changing religions in the global village

The Industrial Revolution ushered in a growing emphasis on science. Increasingly, people looked to physicians and other practitioners of science for the comfort and certainty they had earlier sought from religious leaders. The growth of rationalism and science put the established church increasingly under threat. Even so, religious thought persists. Whatever the benefits of science to our material lives, then, religion has a unique capacity to address the spiritual dimension of human existence. Because they both offer powerful but distinct ways of viewing the universe, science and religion sometimes fall into an uneasy relationship. Yet, both science and religion play a central role in modern cultures, with each kind of truth focusing on different facets of human experience.

Religion can be seen as a force that largely opposes modernity. In 1863, Pope Pius IX said it was a heresy for anyone to believe that the 'Roman Pontiff can and ought to reconcile himself to, and agree with, progress, liberalism, and modern civilisation' (in Bettenson, 1974: 273). Indeed, the modern world has been roundly condemned by most religions.

Yet although the twentieth century was once predicted to be the age when 'the death of God' would be proclaimed, this has not been so. Indeed, religion is alive and well all over the world, and is undergoing a number of quite significant changes. In this section, we will detect some of these.

The secularisation myth

The first trend often discussed among sociologists is **secularisation**, *the historical decline in the importance of the supernatural and the sacred*. For society as a whole, secularisation points to the waning influence of religion in everyday life. And as religious organisations become more secular, they direct attention less to other worldly issues (such as life after death) and more to worldly affairs (such as sheltering the homeless, feeding the hungry and raising funds). In addition, secularisation means that functions once performed mostly by the church (such as charity) are now primarily the responsibility of businesses and government. More, it means that people are less likely to view the world in spiritual terms and more likely to see it in terms of material goods and consumption – a trend detected in Chapter 15 ('The Economy, Consumption and Work').

Secularisation, with Latin roots meaning 'the present age', is commonly associated with modern, technologically advanced societies (Cox, 1971; O'Dea and Aviad, 1983). Conventional wisdom holds that secularisation is one result of the increasing importance of science in understanding human affairs. Indeed, for many science takes over from religion. In broader terms, people perceive birth, illness and death less as the work of a divine power than as natural stages in the life course. Such events are now more likely to occur in the presence of physicians (scientific specialists) than religious leaders (whose knowledge is based on faith). With the rise of science, religion's sphere of influence has diminished. Theologian Harvey Cox elaborates:

The world looks less and less to religious rules and rituals for its morality or its meanings. For some, religion provides a hobby, for others a mark of national or ethnic identification, for still others an aesthetic delight. For fewer and fewer does it provide an inclusive and commanding system of personal and cosmic values and explanations. (1971: 3)

If Cox is correct, should we expect that religion will disappear completely some day? Does Modernity lend itself to a decline in religion? The consensus among sociologists is 'no' (Hammond, 1985; McGuire, 1987). And for two reasons:

1. If the world is looked at globally, then religion is still an overwhelming and dominant force, as the global maps indicate. While religion holds less sway in some regions (Scandinavian countries, for example) and some groups (Berger identifies an international subculture of humanists among academics), religious fervour is clearly rising in others (such as Iran, Algeria) (Cox, 1990). Peter Berger says: 'the world today, with some exceptions, is as furiously religious as it ever was, and in some places more so than ever' (1997: 32).

2. At the same time as it destroys traditional religious forms, modernity creates an ongoing requirement for something beyond itself (Davie, 1991: 234), generating three forms of religious revival: (i) fundamentalisms; (ii) the rise of new religious movements; and (iii) new forms of religion, including civil religion.

Religious fundamentalisms

The most extreme version of this change is the growth of **fundamentalism**, *a conservative religious doctrine that opposes intellectualism and worldly accommodation in favour of restoring traditional, otherworldly spirituality.* It believes in a timeless and absolute value given to sacred writings in all times and places. It is applied to a wide variety of groups: from the 'Moral Majority' in the USA, to Orthodox Jews in Israel and the Islamic government in Iran. In response to what they see as the growing influence of science and the erosion of the conventional family, religious fundamentalists defend their version of traditional values. From this point of

view, the liberal churches are simply too tolerant of religious pluralism and too open to change. Caplan (1987) and Hunter (1983, 1985, 1987) contend that a number of features distinguish religious fundamentalists of various stripes. They:

1. *Interpret 'infallible' sacred texts literally.* Fundamentalists, who see sacred texts as infallible blueprints for life, insist on literal interpretations of the sacred texts as a means of countering what they see as excessive intellectualism among more liberal and revisionist organisations.

2. *Reject religious pluralism.* Fundamentalists maintain that tolerance and relativism water down personal faith, and harshly judge most modern faiths as illegitimate.

3. *Find a personal experience of God's presence.* Fundamentalists seek to propagate spiritual revival. They define all areas of life as sacred. For example, fundamentalist Christians seek to be 'born again' to establish a personal relationship with Jesus that will shape a person's everyday life.

4. *Oppose secularisation and modernity.* Fundamentalists believe that accommodation to the changing world undermines religious conviction. *Secular humanism*, a general term referring to societies' tendency to look to scientific experts rather than God for guidance about how to live, leads to profane moral corruption.

5. *Promote conservative beliefs including patriarchal ones.* Fundamentalists argue that God intends humans to live in heterosexual societies dominated by men. They blame feminist and gay rights movements for contributing to moral decline. In particular, fundamentalists condemn abortion and decry lesbian and gay relations (Viguerie, 1981; Hunter, 1983; Speer, 1984; Ostling, 1985; Ellison and Sherkat, 1993; Green, 1993).

6. *Emerge in response to social inequality or a perceived social crisis.* Fundamentalists attract members by offering solutions to desperate, worried or dejected people.

Taken together, these traits have given fundamentalism a backward and self-righteous reputation. At the same time, this brief sketch also helps us to understand why adherents find such religions an appealing alternative to the more intellectual, tolerant and worldly 'mainstream' denominations.

Fundamentalist religions in the UK and across Europe have recently gained strength, but we must use the term with care. While conservative branches of many religions have turned fundamentalist, the term is often used pejoratively to dismiss religious movements which question the status quo. In parti-cular, as Chapter 12 noted, there has been the dev-elopment of 'Islamophobia', whereby the label 'fundamentalist' is often used in the West to dismiss the claims of a range of Islamic movements. Even in cases where Islam has evolved into an extreme form, fundamentalist extrem-ism often emerges in response to the capitalist version of modernity that has favoured the West while leaving extreme poverty elsewhere (Esposito, 1992: 14). As we have seen in Chapter 12, it is likely that issues of funda-mentalism will become more and more central in the coming twenty-first century.

The emergence of new religious movements (NRMs)

Whilst membership in established, 'mainstream' churches may have plummeted, affiliation with other religious organisations (including Seventh-Day Adventists and Christian sects) has risen just as dramat-ically. Indeed, secularisation itself may be self-limiting. As churchlike organisations become more worldly, some people within a religious 'marketplace' may sim-ply abandon them in favour of more sectlike religious communities that better address their spiritual con-cerns and whose members seem to exhibit greater religious commit-ment (Stark and Bainbridge, 1981; Roof and McKinney, 1987; Jacquet and Jones, 1991; Warner, 1993; Iannaccone, 1994). Thus, in the face of secularisation and the seeming decline in religion, many new NRMs have appeared. Indeed, one of the most striking developments of recent years has been the prolifera-tion of New Religious Movements. It is estimated that there may now be as many as 20,000 new religious groupings in Europe alone.

One way of thinking about these movements is to see their affinities with the traditional mainstream religions described above. Thus, some are linked to Hinduism (Hari Krishnas and the disciples of Bhagwan Rajneesh); oth-ers to Buddhism (various Zen groups); and others to Christianity (the Children of God). Some NRMs are eclectic (The Unification Church), while others have links with the Human Potential Movement (which advocate therapies to liberate human potential, such as transcendental meditation). Roy Wallis has pro-posed a typology of these growing groups. He suggests three main kinds of NRM's : world affirming, world rejecting and world accommodating.

The World Affirming groups are usually individualis-tic, life-positive and aim to release 'human potentials'. Research suggests that these are more common amongst middle-age, middle-class groups – often disil-lusioned and disenchanted with material values and in search of new positive meanings. These groups gener-ally lack a church, ritual worship or strong ethical sys-tems. They are often more akin to 'therapy groups' than traditional religions.

A major example of this is The *Church of Scientology*, founded by L. Ron Hubbard. Hubbard developed the philosophy of dianetics, which stresses the impor-tance of 'unblocking the mind' and leading it to becoming 'clear'. Hubbard believed in a rebirthing. His church spread throughout the world (with a base in California!) and it generated courses (usually

August 1996, Bulgarian Hare Krishna parade through the streets of Sofia.

Source: Popperfoto

expensive) and books galore (see Wall, 1976). A second example is Transcendental Meditation or TM. Brought to the West by the Hindu Mahareshi Mahesh Yogi in the early 1950s, it focuses upon building a personal mantra which is then dwelt upon for periods each day. Again, the focus is upon a good world – not an evil one – and a way of 'finding oneself' through positive thinking. Much of this mode of thinking has helped generate a major new linked movement: that of 'New Age'.

'New Age', a hybrid mix and match of religions, therapies and astrologies, has become increasingly important since the 1970s. Bruce (1996: 197) suggests these are largely 'audience' or 'client cults'. The former has led to a major market of 'self help therapy' books with mass distribution; the latter has led to the proliferation of new 'therapists' (from astrological to colour therapists) establishing new relationships between a consumer and a seller. Amongst the practices involved are Tarot readings, crystals, reflexology, channelling, I ching. Currently, many bookshops devote more to these sorts of books than to books on Christianity. The fascination with television programmes like 'The X Files' may also be seen as part of this. It brings a new science, a new ecology, a new psychology and a new spirituality.

The Word Rejecting groups are like the sects described above. In some ways they are quite like conventional religions in that they may require prayer and the study of key religious texts, and they have strong ethical codes. They are always highly critical of the outside (material evil) world and they demand change of their members through strong communal activities. They are exclusive, share possessions and seek to submerge identities to the greater whole. They are often millenarian – expecting God's intervention to change the world and inspiring activism to make this come about ('millenarian' is derived from the millennium, the 1,000 year reign of Christ). Researchers have suggested that it may well be people who live on the margins who are most attracted to these groups.

Perhaps the most widely cited example is the Unification Church (popularly the Moonies), founded in Korea by the Reverend Sun Myung Moon in 1954. It appeared in California in the early 1960s where it was studied by the sociologist John Lofland in his book *Doomsday Cult* (2nd edn, 1997). Later Eileen Barker studied it in England. The Unification Church

rejects the mundane secular world as evil and has strict moral rules: monogamous heterosexual sex, no smoking, no drinking etc. Another example is the Hare Krishna (Children of God, or ISKON – the International Society for Krishna Consciousness). The members are distinguished by their shaved heads, pigtails and flowing gowns; Hare Krishnas repeat a mantra 16 times a day.

These sects are the movements that have come under most public scrutiny in recent years, largely because of the fear of indoctrination and the problems of severe control and even mass suicide. There is a growing list of extreme examples – the mass suicide by Jim Jones's People Temple in Jonestown, Guyana (Hall, 1987); the Aum Supreme Truth (run by Shoko Ashara) which detonated poisonous gas canisters on a Tokyo underground in 1995, leaving 12 dead and 5,000 sick. The more recent suicidal death of the 39 members of the Heaven's Gate in California when they sighted the comet Hale-Bopp is another example. Heaven's Gate programmers posted a message on their web site saying: 'We are happily prepared to leave this world' (Christopher Reed, 'Gentle Preacher of Death' *Guardian*, 29 March, 1997: 2). While these new religious forms mirror the means and powers that other religions have continued to employ, they are seen by the press and public as deviant, and hence attract more attention.

World accommodating religions are more orthodox. They maintain some connections with mainstream religion, but give a high premium to the inner religious life. In England, the Neo-Pentecostals are a good example. The Holy Spirit 'speaks' through them, giving the gift of 'speaking in tongues'. Such religions are usually dismayed at both the state of the world and the state of organised mainstream religions. They seek to establish both older certainties and faith, whilst giving them a new vitality.

The arrival of new religious forms

One dimension of secularisation is the rise of what Robert Bellah (1975) has called **civil religion**. This is *a quasi-religious loyalty binding individuals in a basically secular society*. In other words, even if some traditional dimensions of religiosity are weakening, new religious qualities may be found in such things as patriotism, membership in associations, good citizenship and even sports meetings which can retain religious qualities. He conducted research in the United States, where, he argues, religious qualities appear in a range of rituals, from rising to sing the US national anthem at sporting events, to Presidential inauguration ceremonies, to sitting down to watch televised public parades several times a year. In England, ceremonies linked to the Royal Family (Coronations, Royal Weddings, etc.), as well as village fetes, town parades and similar gatherings – all may serve these same functions.

Most recently, the enormous outpouring of grief around the death of the People's Princess, Diana, could be taken as further evidence of civil religion. Immediately after her death in Paris on 31 August 1997, hundreds of thousands of people publicly showed their grief through sending flowers, attending the funeral, and signing 'commemoration books'. These people came from all walks of life and religions, but created a strong sense of group belonging and national – even international – grief.

The electronic church

In contrast to the small village congregations of years past, some religious organisations – especially fundamentalists – have become electronic churches dominated by 'prime-time preachers' (Hadden and Swain, 1981). Electronic religion has been especially strong in the United States and has propelled charismatic preachers like Oral Roberts, Pat Robertson, Robert

CONTROVERSY AND DEBATE

Does science threaten religion?

We live in a modern, rational scientific world. Almost everything we do – from driving a car to visiting a hospital for treatment, to travel and shopping, to using a computer – depends upon a rational, scientific use of our minds. These things do not work because of gods, but because of human activity and control over the environment. Sometimes, this 'rationality' gets carried away. As we have seen, McDonalds has spread throughout the world making food production a highly rational, predictable and efficient system. It is a model for many other things in the McDonaldisation of the world! So how does all this square with the more spiritual world, where rationality is less significant?

At the dawning of the modern age, the Italian physicist and astronomer Galileo (1564–1642) helped initiate the scientific revolution with a series of startling discoveries. Dropping objects from the Leaning Tower of Pisa, he discerned some of the laws of gravity. He also fashioned a telescope and surveyed the heavens, confirming a new proposition that the earth orbited the sun, rather than the other way around. But his lively scientific imagination got him into trouble: Galileo was denounced by the Roman Catholic church, which had preached for centuries that the earth stood motionless at the centre of the universe. Galileo only made matters worse by declaring that religious leaders and Biblical doctrine had no place in the building wave of science. Before long, he found his work banned and himself condemned to house arrest.

From its beginnings, science has maintained an uneasy relationship with religion. Indeed, as the course of Galileo's life makes clear, the claims of one sometimes infringe on the other's truth. Through this century, too, science and religion have battled over the issue of creation. In the wake of Charles Darwin's *On the Origin of Species* (1979 edn), scientists concluded that humanity evolved from lower forms of life over the course of a billion years. Yet the theory of evolution flies in the face of the Biblical account of creation found in Genesis, which states that 'God created the heavens and the earth', introducing life on the third day and, on the fifth and sixth days, creating animal life, including human beings, who were fashioned in God's own image.

Schuller and others to greater prominence than all but a few clergy have ever enjoyed in the past. About 5 per cent of the US television audience (around 10 million people) regularly tune into religious television, while perhaps 20 per cent (around 40 million) watch some religious programming every week (Martin, 1981; Gallup, 1982; NORC, 1994).

During the 1980s, regular solicitation of contributions brought a financial windfall to some religious organisations. Seen on thirty-two hundred stations in half the countries in the world, for example, Jimmy Swaggart received as much as $180 million annually in donations. But some media-based ministries were corrupted by the power of money. In 1989, Jim Bakker (who began his television career in 1965 hosting a children's puppet show with his wife Tammy Faye) was jailed following a conviction for defrauding contributors. Such cases, although few in number, attracted enormous international attention and undermined public support as people began to wonder whether television preachers were more interested in raising moral standards or private cash.

● Looking ahead: religion in the twenty-first century

As we have seen, two contradictory processes are happening at the end of the twentieth century. On the one hand, the process of 'secularisation', a growing disenchantment with the spiritual and the supernat-

---

Today, there is emerging a middle ground, which accepts that biblical accounts may be inspired by God and represent important philosophical truth without being literally correct in a scientific sense. That is, science and religion represent two different levels of understanding that respond to different kinds of questions. Both Galileo and Darwin devoted their lives to investigating how the natural world operates. Yet only religion can address why humans and the natural world exist in the first place.

The more scientists discover about the origins of the universe, the more overwhelming the entire process appears. Indeed, as one scientist recently pointed out, the mathematical odds that some cosmic 'Big Bang' 12 billion years ago created the universe and led to the formation of life on earth as we know it today are utterly infinitesimal – surely much smaller than the chance of one person winning a state lottery for twenty weeks in a row. Doesn't such a scientific fact point to the operation of an intelligent and purposeful power in our creation? Can't one be both a religious believer as well as a scientific investigator?

There is another reason to appreciate both scientific and religious thinking: The rapid advances of science continue to present society with vexing ethical dilemmas. Latter-day Galileos have unleashed the power of atomic energy, cloning and genetic engineering, yet we still struggle to find ethical uses for these powers. In 1992, a Vatican commission created by Pope John Paul II conceded that the church's silencing of Galileo had been in error. Today, most scientific and religious leaders agree that, while science and religion represent distinctive truths, their teachings may be complementary. And many believe – in the rush to scientific discovery – that our scientific world has never been more in need of the moral guidance afforded by religion.

● Continue the debate:

1. On what grounds do some scientists completely reject religious accounts of human creation? Why do some religious people completely reject scientific accounts?

2. Do you think the sociological study of religion challenges anyone's faith? Why or why not?

3. Do you think that the rate of scientific change has outstripped our ability to make moral judgements about the use of our new abilities? How might we best insert ethics into scientific research? ●

Sources: Based on Gould (1981) and Hutchinson (1994).

ural and a turn to rationality and science, has gained increasing support. Secularisation has spread across much of Europe and other Western cultures, with the partial exception of the United States, but remains relatively weak in the rest of the world, where traditional religions hold stronger sway. On the other hand, the growth of religious fundamentalism, the continuing adherence of millions to the 'mainstream' religions, alongside the development of many new religious forms, ensure that religion will remain a central element of modern societies.

The pace of social change is accelerating. As the world becomes more complex, rapid change often seems to outstrip our capacity to make sense of it all. Whilst technological advances undermine religiosity in some people, for others, religious guidance and religious communities offer the key for coping with change. Science alone is simply unable to address the most central human needs and questions. Moreover, new technology confronts us with vexing moral dilemmas – when and whether to use genetically modified organs in animals or aborted human foetal tissue in transplants, how to ethically regulate cloning, among many others. The final box explores the tensions between the spiritual world of religion and the secular sphere of science and technology which will continue to resonate throughout our lives. Against this backdrop of uncertainty, it is little wonder that many people continue to rely on their faith for assurance and hope. No doubt they will continue to do so for some time to come (Cox, 1977; Barker, 1981).

SUMMARY

1. Religion is a major social institution based on distinguishing the sacred from the profane. Religion is a matter of faith, not scientific evidence, which people express through various rituals.

2. Sociology analyses the social consequences and correlates of religion, but no scientific research can make claims about the ultimate truth or falsity of any religious belief.

3. Emile Durkheim argued that individuals experience the power of their society through religion. His structural-functional analysis suggests that religion promotes social cohesion and conformity by conferring meaning and purpose on life.

4. Using the symbolic-interaction paradigm, Peter Berger explains that religious beliefs are socially constructed as a means of responding to life's uncertainties and disruptions.

5. Using the social-conflict paradigm, Karl Marx charged that religion promotes social inequality. Historically, however, religious ideals have both supported hierarchy and motivated people to seek greater equality.

6. Max Weber's analysis of Calvinism's contribution to the rise of industrial capitalism demonstrates religion's power to promote social change.

7. Churches, which are religious organisations well integrated into their society, fall into two categories – ecclesias and denominations.

8. Sects, the result of religious division, are marked by suspicion of the larger society as well as charismatic leadership.

9. Cults are religious organisations that embrace new and unconventional beliefs and practices.

10. Many hunter-gatherer societies are and have been generally animistic, with religious life just one facet of family life; in more complex societies, religion emerges as a distinct social institution.

11. Followers of six world religions – Christianity, Islam, Judaism, Hinduism, Buddhism and Confucianism – represent three-quarters of all humanity.

12. Secularisation refers to the diminishing importance of the supernatural and the sacred. In Europe, while some indicators of religiosity (like membership in 'mainstream' churches) have declined, others (such as membership in sects) are on the rise. Such complexity suggests that secularisation will not bring on the demise of religion.

13. Civil religion is a quasi-religious belief by which people profess loyalty to their society, often in the form of patriotism.

14. Fundamentalists oppose secularisation, religious pluralism and the breakdown of heterosexual patriarchy, which they see as the only moral structure of human society. Fundamentalists advocate literal interpretation of sacred texts and pursue the personal experience of God's presence. Many such movements arise in response to a crisis or extreme social inequality.

15. New Religious Movements (NRMs) may be world affirming, world rejecting or world accommodating.

16. Some of the continuing appeal of religion lies in the inability of science to address timeless questions about the ultimate meaning of human existence or to provide clear answers to the moral dilemmas raised by new technologies.

KEY CONCEPTS

animism the belief that elements of the natural world are conscious life forms that affect humanity

charisma extraordinary personal qualities that can turn an audience into followers

church a type of religious organisation well integrated into the larger society

civil religion a quasi-religious loyalty binding individuals in a basically secular society

cult a religious organisation that is substantially outside a society's cultural traditions

denomination a church, independent of the state, that accepts religious pluralism

ecclesia a church that is formally allied with the state

faith belief anchored in conviction rather than scientific evidence

fundamentalism a conservative religious doctrine that opposes worldly accommodation in favour of restoring a traditional, otherworldly spirituality

liberation theology a fusion of Christian principles with political activism, often Marxist in character

monotheism belief in a single divine power

NRMs new religious movements

polytheism belief in many gods

profane that which is defined as an ordinary element of everyday life

religion a social institution involving beliefs and practices based upon a conception of the sacred

religiosity the importance of religion in a person's life

ritual formal, ceremonial behaviour

sacred that which is divine, inspiring a sense of awe, reverence and even fear

sect a type of religious organisation that stands apart from the larger society

secularisation the historical decline in the importance of the supernatural and the sacred

totem an object in the natural world collectively defined as sacred

CRITICAL-THINKING QUESTIONS

1. Explain the basic distinction between the sacred and the profane that underlies all religious belief.

2. Explain Karl Marx's contention that religion tends to support the status quo. Develop a counterargument that religion can serve as a major force for social change. Do you think religious-based social change generally has positive, negative or neutral implications?

3. Distinguish between churches, sects and cults. Is one type of religious organisation inherently better than another? Why or why not?

4. What evidence points to a decline in religion in Europe? In what ways does religion seem to be getting stronger?

5. Is there any reason to think that people in the twenty-first century will be any less religious than people today?

6. Why do you think some religious groups believe catastrophe will strike at the dawn of the new millennium?

GOING FURTHER ·

Introductory reading

Steven Bruce, *Religion in the Modern World: from Cathedrals to Cults* (Oxford: Oxford University Press, 1996).

> A readable review of the changing fortunes of religion in the modern world, especially the emergence of new cults and the 'new age movement'.

Lester Kurtz, *Gods in the Global Village: the World's Religions in Sociological Perspective* (London: Pine Forge Press, 1995).

> Detailed account of all the world's major religions and an analysis of how they are changing under the impact of globalisation and multiculturalsim.

Classic sources

Max Weber, *The Protestant Ethic and the Spirit of Capitalism* (New York: Charles Scribner's Sons, 1958; orig. 1904–5).

> This is the classic account of the power of religion to effect sweeping social change.

More advanced reading

Eileen Barker, *The Making of a Moonie* (Oxford: Blackwell, 1984).

> Examines life in the Unification church.

Eileen Barker, *New Religious Movements: A Practical Introduction* (London: HMSO, Fourth impression with amendments, 1995).

> A full account of NRMs which looks at their common characteristics, new converts and problems. An appendix lists some 30 examples of NRMs.

Richard W. Bulliet, *Islam: The View from the Edge* (New York: Columbia University Press, 1994).

> Although the heart of Islam lies in the Middle East, Muslims live in Europe and around the world. This book examines how Islam differs in its central and peripheral settings.

G. Davie, *Religion in Britain Since 1945: Believing without Belonging* (Oxford: Blackwell, 1994).

> Traces post war patterns of religion in the UK.

Helen Rose Ebaugh, *Women in the Vanishing Cloister: Organizational Decline in Catholic Religious Orders in the United States* (New Brunswick, NJ: Rutgers University Press, 1993).

> This account, written by a nun-turned-sociologist, explores the drop in the number of women in Catholic religious orders since the 1960s.

Christian Smith, *The Emergence of Liberation Theology: Radical Religion and Social Movement Theory* (Chicago: University of Chicago Press, 1991).

> This account of liberation theology among politically active Catholics during the 1960s assesses the movement's successes and failures.

Michael York, *The Emerging Network: A Sociology of the New Age & Neo-Pagan Movements* (London: Rowman and Littlefield, 1995).

> Empirical research on both the New Age and Neo-Pagan movements like Wicca, located in a New Religious Movement framework.

Roy Wallis, *The Road to Total Freedom: A Sociological Analysis of Scientology* (London: Heinemann, 1976).

> A critical and detailed analysis of the Church of Scientology.

Other sources

CULT INFORMATION CENTRE, an educational charity that provides information and can offer support to people in difficulties through cults. BCM Cults, London WC1N 3XX (Phone 0181 651 3322 Fax 0181 657 0204)

INFORM (Information Network Focus on Religious Movements) provides international information on Religious Movements. Houghton Street, London, WC2A 2AE; Phone: 0171 955 7654 Fax: 0171 955 7679; E-mail: inform@lse.ac.uk

INTERFAITH NETWORK, gives information on virtually every major religion from Afro-Caribbean Churches to the Vishhwa Hindu Parishad. 5-7 Tavistock Place, London WC1; Phone 0171 388 0008

The journal *Social Compass* (published by Sage) is an international journal of sociological studies of religion.

chapter nineteen

Source: Popperfoto

Education

Thirteen-year-old Naoko Matsuo has just returned from school to her home in suburban Yokohama, Japan. Instead of dropping off her books and beginning an afternoon of fun, she settles in to do her homework. Several hours later, Naoko's mother reminds her that it is time to leave for the *juku* or 'cram school' that she attends for three hours three evenings a week. Mother and daughter travel four stops on the subway to downtown Yokohama and climb to the second floor of an office building where Naoko joins dozens of other girls and boys for intensive training in Japanese, English, maths and science.

Tuition at the *juku* consumes several hundred pounds of the Matsuo family's monthly income. But they recognise the realities of the Japanese educational system and consider this investment a necessity. The extra hours in the classroom will soon pay off when Naoko takes a national examination to determine her school placement. Three years later, she will face another hurdle with the high school placement exam; this test, once again, will determine the quality of her education. Then will come the final challenge: earning admission to an exclusive national university, a prize won by the one-third of Japanese students who perform best on this examination. Stumbling in the race that is Naoko's next five years will mean learning to settle for less. Like most other Japanese families, the Matsuos are convinced that one cannot work too hard or begin too early to prepare for university admission (Simons, 1989).

W hy do the Japanese pay such attention to schooling? In this modern, industrial society, admission to an elite university all but ensures a high-paying, prestigious career. This chapter spotlights **education**, *the social institution guiding the transmission of knowledge, job skills, cultural norms and values*. In industrial societies, as we shall see, much education is a matter of **schooling**, *formal instruction under the direction of specially trained teachers*.

● Introducing education: a quick global tour

Most people in the Western world spend much of their first 20 years in school. Until recently, formal schooling in all societies was a privilege restricted to a small elite, and so it remains in most poor societies today.

In hunter-gatherer and small agrarian societies, people's survival depended on learning as much as they could about the plants, animals and landscape in their environment. Elders devoted much time to passing on both cultural beliefs and knowledge of the natural world to the younger generations. As agrarian societies grew in size and complexity, people needed to learn only specialised knowledge for their field of work, rather than general knowledge. The majority of people in such systems spent most of their time performing physical labour which required little training, while a minority with the greatest wealth and power enjoyed the spare time to study literature, art, history and science. Indeed, the English word 'school' comes from the Greek word for 'leisure'.

Traditionally, the Japanese have placed a strong emphasis on fitting in with the group. This cultural value is evident in the widespread wearing of school uniforms.

Source: Stock Boston – Charles Gupton

We find marked diversity in schooling throughout the world today. In some developing regions, like much of central Asia and central America, religious organisations play a major role in providing education to children. In other regions, particularly East Asia, Europe, the United States, Canada, Australia and New Zealand, the state formally coordinates and regulates the majority of schools. In most high income societies a growing number of young people are awarded first degrees: this is much less common in low income societies (see Figure 19.1).

All low-income countries have one trait in common: limited access to formal schooling. In the poorest nations, only half of all primary-aged children are in school; throughout the world, just half of all children attend secondary school (Najafizadeh and Mennerick, 1992). As a consequence, illiteracy disadvantages a third of Latin Americans, almost half of Asians and two-thirds of Africans. Observers like Ivan Illich argue that the answer to widespread illiteracy, displayed in Map 19.1, is not to transpose Western style schools into the rest of the world. Instead of formal degrees on paper, they suggest, people in developing areas need the practical knowledge and skills to provide for their basic life needs in a changing natural environment and to build small businesses that can generate wealth in ways sensitive to local cultural norms. In high-income societies, schooling for everyone serves as the means of training people to participate in democratic political life and apply the economic knowledge and technological skills increasingly important in the modern world. At the same time, however, schooling also can serve as a major mechanism for reproducing the social inequalities.

Schooling in the United States

The United States promoted mass education before most European countries. By 1850 about half the young people between the ages of five and 19 were enrolled in school. Today, four out of five have a secondary education, and more than one in five have a university degree. Both the national and state governments have striven to promote social mobility by funding state schools to offer *equal opportunity*, that is, the opportunity for all bright and motivated students to succeed in spite of the educational and economic background of their parents. The US educational system has also stressed the value of *practical* learning,

Figure 19.1 ● University degrees in global perspective

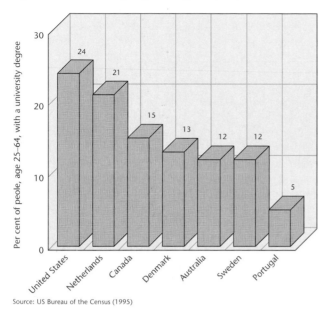

Source: US Bureau of the Census (1995)

that is, knowledge that has a direct bearing on people's work and interests.

Nevertheless, education has also played a role in maintaining social divisions. The top universities and secondary schools formally excluded women and people from most ethnic minorities until early this century. Indeed, the US formally segregated black and white students until 1954, when the US Supreme Court ruled that segregation had resulted in minorities receiving an inferior education. While schools generally have improved across the United States, young people in poor inner cities attend schools with increasingly larger class sizes, limited books and technological resources and decaying buildings. While many of the best teachers move to the more prosperous suburban schools, inner city schools face growing problems from drug use and violence among students.

Schooling in India

The wealthy in India enjoy high quality early schooling and many pursue university degrees. The majority of people in India cannot afford such privilege. Most people do now receive some primary education, typically in crowded schoolrooms where one teacher attends to upwards of 60 children. Children in the poorest families often begin full time work at an early age to help supplement the family income. Fewer than half of Indians pursue secondary education. Pronounced patriarchy also shapes Indian education; 45 per cent of boys but only 30 per cent of girls attend secondary school. While just over a third of the Indian population is illiterate, two-thirds of women lack basic literary skills. A large majority of the children working in Indian factories are girls (United Nations, 1995).

Schooling in Japan

Before industrialisation brought mandatory education to this country in 1872, only a privileged few enrolled in school. Today, Japan's educational system produces some of the highest achievers in maths and sciences (Brinton, 1988; Simons, 1989). Early grades concentrate on transmitting Japanese traditions, especially obligation to family. By their early teens, students encounter Japan's system of rigorous and competitive examinations. The Japanese government invests heavily in the education of students who perform well in these exams, while students performing poorly are pushed out of the system. Understandably, then, around half of Japanese students attend 'cram schools' to supplement their standard education and prepare for the exams. Japanese women, most of whom are not in the labour force, often devote themselves to their children's success in school.

Schooling in Europe

While all countries in the European Union agree that schooling is highly important, each takes a different approach to education, as Figure 19.2 displays. Luxembourg requires children to attend pre-school. In the Netherlands, primary school begins at four. While the UK introduced compulsory education in 1870, Italy and Greece did not follow suit until the 1950s, and Spain waited until the 1960s. Portugal introduced six years of compulsory elementary schooling in 1968, and did not fully implement this requirement until 1986 (Chisholm, 1992: 123). EU countries also require different minimum periods of study. Portugal, Spain and Italy require only eight years of schooling; Ireland, Greece, Luxemburg and Denmark require nine years; France, the Netherlands, and Germany 10 years, the United Kingdom 11 years, and Belgium 12 years (Chisholm, 1992: 133).

Many European countries have a multi-track secondary education system which channels some

WINDOW ON THE WORLD

Map 19.1 ● Illiteracy in global perspective

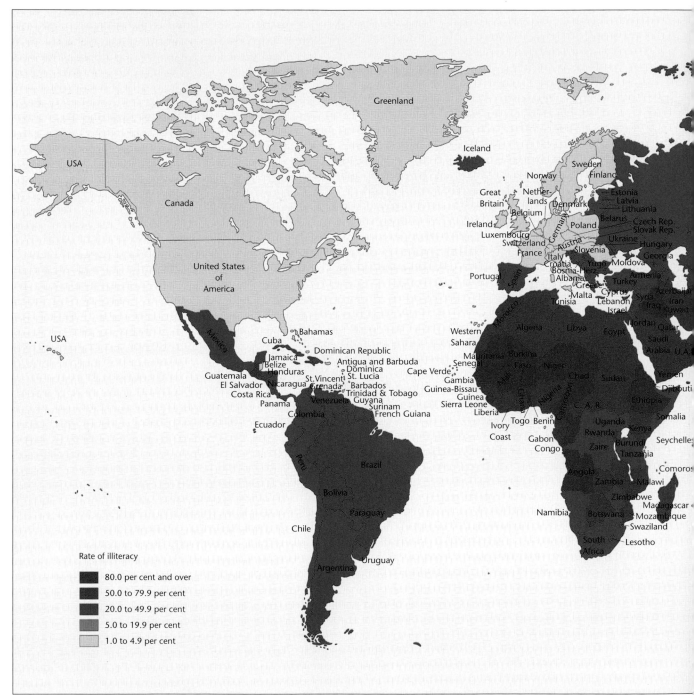

Rate of illiteracy

- 80.0 per cent and over
- 50.0 to 79.9 per cent
- 20.0 to 49.9 per cent
- 5.0 to 19.9 per cent
- 1.0 to 4.9 per cent

Source: *Peters Atlas of the World* (1990) and World Bank (1995)

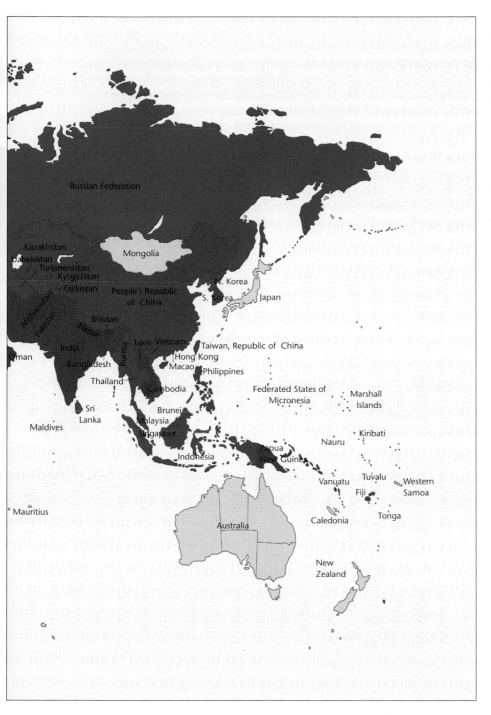

Reading and writing skills are widespread in every industrial society, with illiteracy rates generally below 5 per cent. Throughout Latin America, however, illiteracy is more commonplace – one consequence of limited economic development. In about a dozen nations of the world – many of them in Africa – illiteracy is the rule rather than the exception. In such societies, people rely on what sociologists call 'the oral tradition' of face-to-face communication rather than communicating by the written word.

Figure 19.2 ● Stages of schooling for children aged 2–18

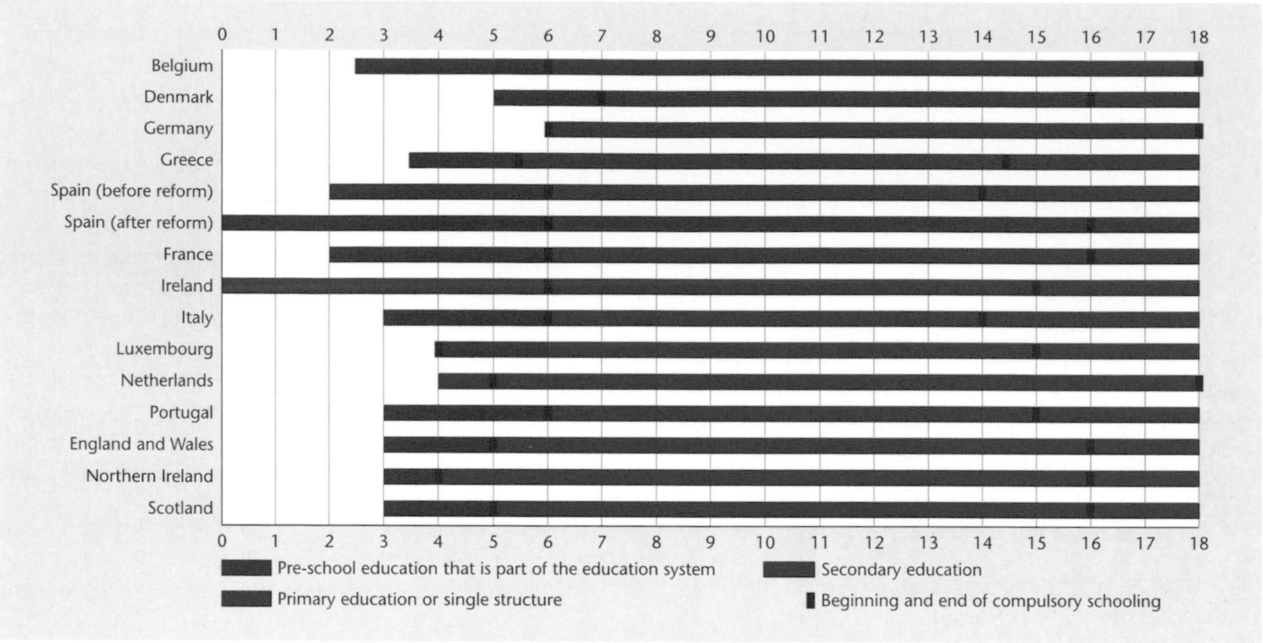

Source: *Women and Men in Europe: A Statistical Portrait*, Office for Official Publications of the European Community Luxembourg, Eurostats (1995)

students towards university and others towards various levels of vocational training. In Germany, for example, students undertake general secondary education for two years from age 12, then split into the university (*Gymnasium*), basic vocational (*Hauptschule*) and higher vocational (*Realschule*) groups. Some countries encourage greater educational specialisation from the secondary level onwards than others. Secondary students in Italy and Germany have more subjects to study at the post-16 level than students in the UK. As with the previous examples, European educational structures also help maintain the social power structures, as we shall now see by looking more closely at the UK.

Schooling in the UK

During the Middle Ages, schooling was a privilege of the British nobility, who studied classical subjects since they had little need for the practical skills related to earning a living. As the Industrial Revolution created a need for an educated labour force, a rising share of the population entered the classroom. In 1891, the Education Act made elementary education free to all citizens. Three major Acts have shaped British education during the twentieth century. These are:

● The Balfour Act in 1902, which established Local Education Authorities (LEAs), and gave these bodies powers over secondary and higher education;

● The Butler Act of 1944, which established a Ministry of Education and set up the tripartite system of three different kinds of schools – grammar, technical and secondary modern – to cater to the supposed differing intellectual abilities of students. The Act made education from 5 to 15 free for all people, improved equality of opportunity in education, and offered support services to students from poor families, including free milk, dental check-ups and health care.

● The Baker Act of 1988, which established the National Curriculum and reduced powers of LEAs.

Traditional social distinctions persist in British education. Many wealthy families send their children to *public schools*. Such elite schools not only teach academic subjects, they also convey to children from wealthy families the distinctive patterns of speech, mannerisms and social graces of the British upper class. These schools are far too expensive for most students. Until the 1970s another major divide in British education was between the grammar school and secondary schools, with the former being both more middle class and more successful. The Labour party in power at this time largely abolished grammar schools and introduced a 'comprehensive' system – ostensibly providing equality of education for all. In practice, some grammar schools remained and comprehensive schools became stratified into 'good' and 'bad'. Further, many prominent members of the Labour government in 1997 send their own children to grant-maintained schools rather than comprehensives, recognising the continuing difference in the standards of education at each level. Moreover, graduates from Oxford and Cambridge, or 'Oxbridge', often enter the core of the British power elite. More than two-thirds of the top members of the civil service and successive British governments have 'Oxbridge' degrees (Sampson, 1982; Gamble, Ludlam and Baker, 1993).

● Ways of studying schools

The previous brief comparisons illustrate that education is shaped by other institutions and social forces. Education transmits cultural values and can also contribute to social stratification. We will now look at the major sociological approaches to studying what happens in schools.

The microsociology of schools

One approach to studying education focuses on what goes on inside the classroom. Researchers, applying the theory of symbolic interactionism (Chapters 1 and 6) and the method of participant observation (Chapter 2), have documented the *perspectives* of teachers and students, the *processes* through which classes are constructed and negotiated, the different student roles and *cultures* which emerge within classes, and the impact of *stratifications* (gender, class and race) on these interactions.

An 'invisible pedagogy' (Bernstein, 1977), or hidden ranking system, in school culture can impact the academic performance – and long-term life chances of students. While teachers may strive to be impartial, they are culturally conditioned to assess their students' ability by ranking them on scales of other characteristics, such as appearance, personality, enthusiasm and conformity, which bear little relation to actual ability (Hargreaves, 1975). In Western societies, teachers often

favour boys over girls (Stanworth, 1983) and white boys over Afro-Caribbean boys, by giving them much more attention and opportunities to speak (Green, 1985). Asian girls are often stereotyped as 'passive' (Brah and Minhas, 1988). Labelling pupils in certain ways (as 'dumb' or 'delinquent') can bring about **self-fulfilling prophecies** whereby children defined as low achievers at school actually became low achievers. It is a matter of expectations.

The social background of the students also plays a role in how they experience education. Paul Willis looked at a small group of working class boys and studied their transition from school to work. He found that they generated an anti-school culture heavily focused upon their masculinity. They had little time for the middle class school values and for posh qualifications – seeing them as boring, effeminate and a waste of time. They castigated other boys who followed the rules as 'ear'oles' and saw them as cissies. Similar studies found such boys associating good grades with femininity and, to keep face in the eyes of their mates, boys may hand in work that is poor and disorganised. For these 'lads', 'having a laff' was especially important, and it is a value they then take to their workplace. For instance, in class there may be 'a continuous scraping of chairs, a bad tempered "tut-tutting" at the simplest request, and a continuous fidgeting which explores every permutation of sitting or lying on a chair'. They then carry this 'anti-authority', 'anti-achievement' culture to their place of work.

Critical evaluation
Symbolic interactionism highlights how relations between teachers and students, and between students themselves, both affect and are affected by the schooling process. This approach, however, tends to under-emphasise the relations between the activities within schools and the functioning of society as a whole, as we shall see by looking at the next approach.

The functions of schooling

A second approach, functionalism, directs attention to ways in which formal education enhances the operation and stability of society. Central to the socialisation process, schooling serves as a cultural lifeline linking the generations. In primary and secondary schools, government classes explicitly teach students how to participate in democracies. The operation of the classroom itself can also impart cultural values, such as respect for authority or a sense of fair play.

Educational systems create as well as transmit culture. Schools stimulate intellectual inquiry and critical thinking, sparking the development of new ideas. Inquiry in the humanities, the social sciences and the natural sciences is changing attitudes and behaviour throughout the world. Medical research, carried on at major universities, has increased life expectancy, just as research by sociologists and psychologists helps us to take advantage of this longevity.

Schooling works to forge a mass of people into a unified whole. This function is especially important in nations with pronounced social diversity, where various cultures are indifferent or even hostile to one another. In the past, the Soviet Union and Yugoslavia relied on schools to tie their disparate peoples together, without ultimately succeeding, and similar cultural strains mark the United Kingdom as well.

Societies in the Americas, Africa and Asia, encompassing hundreds of ethnic categories, all strive to foster social integration. Schools meet this challenge, first, by establishing a common language that allows for broad communication and forges a national identity. Of course, some ethnic minorities resist state-sponsored schooling for precisely this reason. In the former Soviet Union, for example, Lithuanians, Ukrainians and Azerbaijanis long chafed at having to learn Russian, which they saw as a threat to their own traditions and emblematic of their domination by outsiders. Similarly, the Welsh require students to learn in both English and Welsh to help preserve their cultural distinctiveness within the UK.

Formal education helps young people assume culturally approved statuses and perform roles that contribute to the ongoing life of society. To accomplish this, schooling operates to identify and develop people's various aptitudes and abilities. Ideally, schools evaluate students' performance in terms of achievement alone while downplaying their social background. In principle, teachers encourage the 'best and the brightest' to pursue the most challenging and advanced studies, while guiding students of more ordinary abilities into educational programmes well suited to their talents. Thus, in theory, schooling enhances **meritocracy**, *allocating positions according to merit based on universalist standards of achievement*, though in practice this goal has proved difficult to achieve.

Besides these manifest functions of formal education, a number of latent functions are less widely recognised. One is child care. As the number of one-parent families and two-career couples rises, schools have become vital to relieving parents of some child-care responsibilities. Among teenagers, too, schooling consumes much time and considerable energy, in many cases promoting conformity at a stage of life when the likelihood of unlawful behaviour is high. Because many students attend colleges and universities well into their twenties, education usefully engages thousands of young people for whom few jobs may be available.

Schools also set the stage for us to establish relationships and networks. In the social circles of the secondary school, college and university, many people meet their future spouses. In addition, affiliation with a particular school forms the basis of social ties that provide not only friendship but also valuable career opportunities later on in life.

Critical evaluation
Structural-functional analysis of formal education identifies both manifest and latent contributions of this social institution to an industrial way of life. Yet functionalism skims over one core truth: the quality of schooling is far greater for some than for others. Indeed, critics of European educational systems maintain that schooling actually operates to reproduce the class structure in each generation. In the next section, conflict analysis spotlights these issues.

Conflict analysis and social inequality

Conflict analysis is the third major approach to studying education. Far from seeing education as a tool for meritocracy, conflict theorists view schooling as a means for the reproduction of society's inequalities. Schooling can act as a means of social control, reinforcing acceptance of the status quo. In various, sometimes subtle, ways schools operate to reproduce the status hierarchy. Thus a number of sociologists have suggested that the origins of the UK system in the nineteenth century lay in class issues and control. The public schools came very early for the elite; then in the nineteenth century came the rather limited Sunday schools to provide a basic education for the working classes – often moral education. There was a continuous fear of an insurgent working class rising up once it had too much education.

Samuel Bowles and Herbert Gintis (1976) point out that the clamour for public education in the late nineteenth century arose precisely when capitalists were seeking a literate, docile and disciplined work force. In many countries with immigrants, but notably the USA, mandatory education laws ensured that schools would teach immigrants the dominant national language as well as cultural values supportive of capitalism. Compliance, punctuality and discipline were – and still are – part of what conflict theorists call the **hidden curriculum**, *subtle presentation of political or cultural ideas in the classroom*. It teaches young people 'to know their place and sit still in it' and 'reproduces inequality by justifying privilege and attributing poverty to personal failure' (Bowles and Gintis, 1976: 114).

Class differences

Conflict theorists argue that schools routinely tailor education according to students' social background, thereby perpetuating social inequality. Indeed, out of all major Western cultures, it has been argued that 'only the Netherlands and Sweden show persistent trends of equalising access to education in the course of the twentieth century' (Therborn, 1995: 257). By contrast, education in countries like the UK has reflected stratification in quality of provision both for individuals and for people of different social classes (MacKinnon, 1996: 173).

Figure 19.3 shows the differential performance of children at school from different classes. There is no doubt that children from working class homes consistently underachieve at every level of the educational system when compared to middle class and upper class children. Why should this be?

Some, like Charles Murray, have contended that genetic intellectual potential determines performance in school. Indeed, the tripartite system in Britain gave prominence to the results of IQ tests given to children at age 11 in helping divide students into their supposedly appropriate schools. The implication of this explanation, however, is that lower class people generally have lower genetic intellectual abilities – thus lower class people could be said to deserve their status because they lack the intellectual ability to compete with people from higher classes.

Many others reject this explanation, however, pointing out that governments have tended not to invest as heavily in the schools attended by the poorest people, that the less well off also tend to experience greater health problems, which in turn affect their performance at school. Moreover, poorer families cannot afford to send their children to nursery pre-school training and later to cram schools, to hire private tutors, or to purchase items like books or personal computers, which give children from more affluent backgrounds an advantage. Additionally, as the Willis study discovered, poorer children often grow up in environments where people see little hope of upward social mobility and rebel against the system rather than try to conform with it. In such an environment, adults often discourage rather than encourage success at school. To make matters worse, Basil Bernstein writes, people in different communities within a country often develop distinct dialects and colloquial vocabularies. While groups across the class divides do this, the dialects and words associated with richer and middle class communities gain status, while those associated with lower class communities get judged as 'uneducated'. In consequence, poor

Figure 19.3 ● Percentage of persons with higher or no educational qualifications, by social class, Great Britain, 1991–92

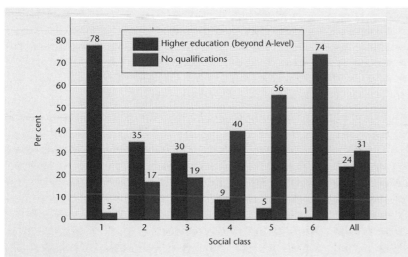

Source: General Household Survey, 1992

children are more likely to be more regularly criticised in school for 'weak' language skills and thus to develop lower educational confidence. These many factors, which have no relation to biological potential, have contributed to the educational class divide in countries like the UK (see Halsey et al., 1961; Douglas, 1964).

Ethnic differences

Not every country has adopted the extreme policy of racial segregation in classrooms once practised in the United States and South Africa, but racial differences in educational achievement appear in many countries – and these differences often coincide with social status differences between ethnic groups. Studies in the UK, like the reports of the Rampton Committee (1979) and the Swann Committee (1982), for example, found that in general West Indian children perform less well than Asian children, and in both cases boys do less well than girls. Asian girls may often do better than white boys; but black boys regularly come out at the bottom of the heap. This pattern continues through higher education. Part of this may be accounted for through links to class – Afro-Caribbean children are more likely to have parents in manual work.

Part of the explanation may also lie in what Smith and Tomlinson (1989) term 'the school effect'. While these authors argue that 'what school a child goes to makes far more difference than which ethnic group he or she belongs to' (1989: 281), they also note that people from ethnic minorities are more likely to be clustered into particular areas, and that their children's educational fate rests in the hands of the schools near where they live. For groups more likely to be poor, or immigrants clustered in poor sections of central cities to cut costs as they adjust to a new culture, this can be bad news.

Since schools tend to reinforce the dominant culture in a society, students from minority communities often face a confusing problem when trying to reconcile differences between their own culture and that of the larger society in which they live. This is particularly problematic in the case of people who came to live in a modern society originally by means not of their own choosing, like the Basques in Spain or the Welsh in the UK. People from former colonies likewise may not feel inclined to sever their roots with their homeland entirely. Gradually, many societies like Britain have moved from believing that children should be (a) fully assimilated into the dominant society, (b) to attempting to integrate cultures, (c) to promoting anti-racism and finally (d) to promoting multiculturalism in the 1990s.

Gender differences

Many of the world's societies have considered schooling more important for boys than for girls. Although the education gender gap has narrowed in Western countries in recent decades, many women still study traditionally feminine subjects such as literature, while men pursue mathematics and engineering. By stressing the experiences of people in traditionally masculine professions, like the military, while ignoring the lives of other, largely female work forces, like domestic workers, schools reinforce male dominance in society.

During the 1970s, sociologists discovered how girls were usually disadvantaged at school. Rosemary Deem demonstrated that education for girls in the past largely centred upon how it would prepare them for the family. Dale Spender found curricula riddled with 'sexism' and Sue Sharpe observed that schools steered girls towards 'feminine' subjects. Michelle Stanworth looked at a mixed group of students, finding that teachers gave more attention to boys than girls. As a result of such experiences, girls learned to lack faith in their abilities (Deem, 1980; Spender, 1982; Sharpe, 1995; Stanworth, 1983).

More recently, however, boys seem to be doing less well and girls doing better. Partly this is a consequence of a shift in educational policies. The National Curriculum in the UK, for example, insists that all boys have to take a language and all girls have to take a science subject; and most schools and universities now have equal opportunities policies. Girls in the 1990s have also become less family-focused, attaching more importance to education and work (Sharpe, 1995). At the same time, the continuing development of what is commonly called a 'lad culture' and a culture of underachievement has grown amongst boys (Willis, 1977; Ghail, 1995).

Although girls' education may have improved, women are still seriously disadvantaged. Only 8 per cent of British professors are women. Though at some newer universities, like South Bank, the proportion is as high as 30 per cent, in others it is as low as 3 per cent. Women also earn less than their male counterparts in the education professions (*Times Higher Education Supplement*, 6 June 1997: 19).

Structuring homosexuality out of education

What is it like to growing up gay in Europe? Many young people between 14 and 21, who generally seem to know they are gay quite early in life, find their experiences and feelings more or less completely overlooked whilst they are at school. Sociologists have suggested four ways in which schools make the situation of young gays and lesbians more difficult.

The first is through the hidden curriculum, which not only reproduces conventional gender roles in the classroom, but also reinforces heterosexuality. There have been attempts by some schools to introduce gay texts, but these attempts have caused much controversy. Indeed, UK law now explicitly prohibits 'the promotion of homosexuality' in schools.

A second mechanism concerns the absence of lesbian and gay role models in schools. Authorities have objected to teachers being 'known about' or openly discussing the issue of being gay. Yet it is precisely the quality of 'being out' that is required in schools if gay teenagers are to have the heterosexual assumption at least punctured and, more practically, if they are to have access to adults who may help them discuss their gay feelings.

A third mechanism, the social operation of youth peer groups 'structures out' homosexuality. Adolescent culture after the age of ten places much importance on going out with the opposite sex – a key way of validating one's normality.

And there is a fourth and final mechanism that comes into force if all else fails. This entails a direct homophobic response, through the harassment of gay youth by both teachers and other children. In a London survey, for example, about half of the respondents had been beaten up, teased, verbally abused or ostracised whilst at school. One boy, Peter, noted:

The biggest shock came when I went to a secondary school and discovered words like 'queer', 'poof', etc., and realised that I was one of these vile, disgusting perverts and as far as I knew the only one. (Burbidge and Walters, 1981).

As with each of the other mechanisms for making homosexuality invisible, this sort of direct homophobic response occurs in every setting a young person encounters. From mockery and abuse to physical violence, from being rejected by parents to losing one's job, from psychiatric treatment to imprisonment – all these remain distinct possibilities for those who dare to breach the heterosexual assumption.

● **Continue the debate:**

1. Briefly consider your own school experience. Did homosexuality get mentioned at all? If it was mentioned, was this a negative mention or a positive one?

2. Did you know any gays or lesbians when you were at school? If so, how did you respond to them? ●

Source: Herdt, 1989.

Sexuality, gender and the school

Gender segregation, whilst not total, is a common feature of children's and young people's lives. Playgrounds, classrooms, clubs and street life are all conspicuous for their spatial divisions into boys' worlds and girls' worlds. Here, in these segregated worlds, further divisions in gender identity are fashioned, particularly around sexuality. Especially among boys, calling each other queer, sissie or using other homophobic insults is a regular practice to isolate marginal children (Thorne and Luria, 1985). Such events make life particularly difficult for boys and girls who discover that they are gay.

Julian Wood (1984) found that not only is there a general highly charged, sexual atmosphere in schools – a point that few commentators seem to have noticed before – but that there is also a massive amount of sexism among the boys. Boys tended to deride women as collections of vital body parts or members of limited, sexually defined categories, and such an atmosphere not only generated negative perceptions of women, but also denied space to explore identity for boys who did not sexually identify with women. The box highlights how 'homosexuality' appears – or rather does not appear – in this context.

Critical evaluation
Conflict analysis points up the connection between formal education and social inequality and shows how schooling transforms privilege into personal worthiness, and social disadvantage into personal deficiency. Critics claim that conflict analysis minimises the extent to which schooling has met the intellectual and personal needs of students, propelling the upward social mobility of many young people in the process. Further, especially in recent years, 'politically correct' educational curricula, closely tied to conflict theory, are challenging the status quo on many fronts.

● Ability or merit: streaming and teaching

Despite continuing controversy over standardised tests, most schools use them as the basis for **streaming**, *the assignment of students to different types of educational programmes*. Streaming, or tracking, is a common practice in many industrial societies, including the UK, the USA, France and Japan. The educational justification for tracking is to give students the kind of schooling appropriate to their individual aptitude. For a variety of reasons, including innate ability and level of motivation, some students are capable of more challenging work than others are. Young people also differ in their interests, with some drawn to, say, the study of languages, while others seek training in art or science. Given this diversity of talent and focus, no single programme for all students would serve any of them well.

But critics see streaming as a thinly veiled strategy to perpetuate privilege. The basis of this argument is research indicating that social background has as much to do with streaming as personal aptitude does. Students from affluent families generally do well on standardised, 'scientific' tests and so are placed in university-bound streams, while schools assign those from modest backgrounds (including a disproportionate share of the poor) to programmes that curb their aspirations and teach technical trades. Streaming, therefore, effectively segregates students both academically and socially.

Most schools reserve their best teachers for students in favoured streams. Thus high-stream boys and girls find that their teachers put more effort into classes, show more respect towards students and expect more from them. By contrast, teachers of low-stream students concentrate on memorisation, classroom drill and other unstimulating techniques. Such classrooms also emphasise regimentation, punctuality and respect for authority figures.

In light of these criticisms, schools are now cautious about making streaming assignments and allow greater mobility between streams. Some have even moved away from the practice entirely. While some streaming seems necessary to match instruction with abilities, rigid streaming has a powerful impact on students' learning and self-concept. Young people who spend years in higher streams tend to see themselves as bright and able, whereas those in lower streams develop lower ambition and self-esteem (Rosenbaum, 1980; Oakes, 1982, 1985; Hallinan and Williams, 1989; Kilgore, 1991; Gamoran, 1992).

Just as students are treated differently within schools, schools themselves differ in fundamental ways. One key distinction separates state and public schools in the UK. State schools often have larger class sizes, insufficient libraries and fewer science labs. But money alone does not magically bolster academic quality. Even more important are the cooperative efforts and enthusiasm of teachers, parents and students themselves. In other words, even if school funding were exactly the same everywhere, the students whose families value and encourage education would still learn more than others (Jencks, 1972). In short, we should not expect schools alone to overcome the effects of marked social inequality.

Yet, schools certainly reflect privilege and disadvantage. As educational critic Jonathan Kozol (1992) concludes, 'savage inequalities' in our school system alert young children to the reality that our society has already defined them as winners or losers. And, Kozol continues, all too often the children go on to fulfil this labelling.

Finally, a key theme of conflict analysis deserves to be highlighted: *schooling transforms social privilege into personal merit*. Attending university, in effect, is a rite of passage for people from well-to-do families. People are more likely to interpret university degrees as 'badges of ability' rather than as symbols of family

Schooling raises acutely the issue of personal confidence for many children and young people.

  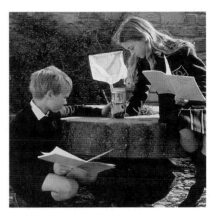

Source: Popperfoto

affluence (Sennett and Cobb, 1973). At the same time, people tend to transform social disadvantage into personal deficiency when they criticise school leavers.

● The bureaucratic school

A century ago, formal education in Europe took place in small, personal settings in countless local communities. Today, the one-room schoolhouse has been replaced by huge educational factories. A study of high schools in the United States (where the situation on this issue at least is broadly similar) led Theodore Sizer to identify five ways in which large, bureaucratic schools undermine education (1984: 207–9).

1. *Rigid uniformity*. Bureaucratic schools are typically insensitive to the cultural character of local communities. Outside 'specialists' (such as state education officials) operate schools with little understanding of the needs of particular students.

2. *Numerical ratings*. School officials define success in terms of numerical attendance records, dropout rates and achievement test scores. In doing so, they overlook dimensions of schooling difficult to quantify, such as the creativity of students and the energy and enthusiasm of teachers.

3. *Rigid expectations*. Officials expect 15-year-olds to be in the tenth grade, and eleventh-graders to score at a certain level on a standardised verbal achievement test. Rarely are exceptionally bright and motivated

students permitted to graduate early. Likewise, the system pushes along students who have learned little so they can graduate with their class.

4. *Specialisation*. High school students learn Spanish from one person, receive guidance from another and are coached in sports by still others. Although specialised teachers may have an in-depth grasp of their subjects, no school employee comes to know and appreciate the 'complete' student. Students experience this division of labour as a continual shuffling among 50-minute periods throughout the school day.

5. *Little individual responsibility*. Highly bureaucratic schools do not empower students to learn on their own. Similarly, teachers have little latitude in what and how they teach their classes; they dare not accelerate learning for fear of disrupting 'the system'.

Of course, some formal organisation in schools is inevitable, given the immense size of the task. The number of students in London comprehensive schools alone now exceeds the student population of the entire country a century ago. But, Sizer maintains, countries should 'humanise' schools to make them more responsive to those they claim to serve. He recommends eliminating rigid class schedules, reducing class size and training teachers more broadly to help them become more involved in the lives of their students. Overall, as James Coleman (1993) recently suggested, schools may need to be less 'administratively driven' and more 'output-driven'.

The politics of curriculum

The 1988 Education Act in England and Wales established for the first time a 'national curriculum'. Established by a committee of central government, it laid out what should be taught to children between 5 and 16 in state-sponsored (but not independent) schools. All pupils must study religion, English, maths, science, history, geography, design and technology, music, art, physical education and a modern language. Student are assessed at four key stages (between 5 and 7; between 7 and 11; between 11 and 14; and between 14 and 16). Schools have to train pupils to reach target scores on these assessments. Much of the national curriculum was seen to be controversial at the time, and creating new precedents.

But it was not at all new. A national curriculum has been standard practice for a long time in much of Europe. In some countries – Portugal, Greece, France – there is a centralised system of regulation. In other countries, variations occur across regions or even schools. In Germany, for instance, the curriculum is controlled by each of 16 separate provinces; while in Belgium and the Netherlands the curriculum reflects compromises between antagonistic religious and language groups. In Denmark, there are national guidelines but schools can make their own decisions. In any event, versions of national curricula are very common throughout Europe. England and Wales came in later.

But when it came, it came with a vengeance. The UK system introduced tighter centralised control of both what is taught and how it is taught. There are strict guidelines for assessment, and a rigorous new set of procedures for monitoring the skills of teachers was introduced. Unlike most other European countries, the curriculum was not built out of a consensus: it was imposed. For a government supposed to be committed to free markets and choice, the UK government of the day took an unusually centralist approach, rejecting the advice of official curriculum committees, and having their own say on what should or should not go in the curriculum.

Martin McLean, an English educationalist, has distinguished two approaches to the curricula across Europe. One, centralist, looks to a European-wide core curriculum; the other, centrifugalist, looks to the diversity of cultures across the European continent and seeks to incorporate these wide ranging elements in the curriculum. (This is similar to the debates around multiculturalism introduced in Chapter 4.)

Centralists are strongly identified with Maastricht, the need for a 'harmonisation' of curricula across Europe, and a federal, unified Europe. It is largely supported in Germany and largely opposed in Denmark, France and southern Europe. Centrifugalists look for a more diverse curricula. Pierre Bourdieu and François Gros have outlined six key principles:

● the need for constant revisions to meet the needs of changing societies

● teaching to focus on strengths rather than weaknesses

● coherence through interdisciplinary team teaching

● absolute standards to be tempered by questions about skills and knowledge and the best way to transmit them

● greater diversity of teaching methods

● excellence may be universal in science yet relative in historical and cultural areas

The trouble is that the UK curriculum fits neither of these positions. It has been structured as an 'increasingly authoritarian and monolithic national curriculum'. Its focus is on neither the unity of Europe nor its diversity. Whilst the idea of a national curriculum may be common now across Europe, in the UK, its suitability remains controversial. ●

Source: adapted from McLean, 1993.

● Current issues in education

Most Western cultures now place a high premium upon their educational systems. Education debates figure prominently at election times. Perhaps because we expect our schools to do so much – equalise opportunity, instil discipline, stimulate individual imagination, provide a labour force – they have remained at the centre of controversy for a number of years.

Introducing market forces

Following the recommendations of the previous year's Black Report, the British government enacted a series of sweeping and controversial changes in the Education Act 1988. These included:

● The introduction of the National Curriculum, with achievement targets for students at the ages of 7, 11, 14 and 16.

● The right for schools to 'opt out' of the Local Education Authority system if a majority of parents voting in a secret ballot wanted to do so. Any school with over 300 students could vote to 'opt out' of the LEA and become 'grant maintained' – in effect, becoming a business funded from central government. In 1994, 592 of 3,773 secondary schools and 334 of 18,828 primary schools exercised this option (though the Labour government in 1997 began reintegrating grant-maintained schools with the LEAs).

● Devolution of the financial management of schools from LEAs to boards of governors.

● The introduction of City Technology Colleges (15 in 1994).

The main thrust of the 1988 changes was to introduce market forces (supply, demand, competition and choice) into all levels of the education system. By more heavily assessing schools and publishing the results of assessments in 'league tables', the government of the time believed it would instil competition between schools and enable parents and students to make informed choices about where to study. While the Labour government reversed some aspects of the 1988 policy in 1997, it largely continued the process of marketisation in higher education, introducing student loans and fees in the name of making students more keen consumers (and saving public money), and also promoting the repackaging of knowledge into short, non-cumulative 'modules' – often with mass marketed text-books, like this one.

Yet whilst there is a concern with free markets at one level, at another level there has been increasing central state intervention in matters linked to the syllabus and assessment. A 1992 Education (Schools) Act introduced new centralised arrangements for school inspection (the Office for Standards in Education (OFSTED)). Textbooks geared to mass education and new standard curricula may mean much less flexibility. The box also shows how central government has played a role in the construction of national curricula.

The 'excellence and quality' debate

In many nations, concern has arisen about the standard of education. Some people in many industrialised nations fear that schools have done an increasingly poor job of motivating and training students, allowing the general intellectual and performance standards to slip. Others, however, argue that the increasing focus on market forces in some countries is itself undermining standards.

A Nation at Risk, a comprehensive report on the quality of schools in the United States prepared by the National Commission on Excellence in Education in 1983, opened with an alarming claim:

If an unfriendly foreign power had attempted to impose on America the mediocre educational performance that exists today, we might well have viewed it as an act of war. As it stands, we have allowed this to happen to ourselves. (1983: 5)

The report noted that 'nearly 40 per cent of seventeen-year-olds cannot draw inferences from written material; only one-fifth can write a persuasive essay; and only one-third can solve mathematical problems requiring several steps' (1983: 9). Furthermore, scores on national aptitude tests measuring preparation for university study had declined since the early 1960s. *A Nation at Risk* also noted an increase in **functional illiteracy**, *reading and writing skills insufficient for everyday living*. Roughly one in eight children in the United States completes secondary school without learning to read or write very well. For young African Americans,

Functional illiteracy in the United States

While the United States opened educational opportunities to all citizens long before most other industrialised countries, some 25 million adults read and write at no more than a fourth-grade level and another 25 million have only eighth-grade language skills. This means that one in four adults in the United States is functionally illiterate, and the proportion is higher among the elderly and minorities.

Functional illiteracy is a complex social problem. It is caused partly by an educational system that passes children from one grade to the next whether or not they master the academic skills spelled out in the grade curriculum. Another contributing factor is community indifference to local schools that prevents parents and teachers from working together to improve chil-

dren's learning. Still another cause is found in the home: millions of children grow up with illiterate parents who offer little encouragement to learn language skills.

Estimates place the societal cost of functional illiteracy at more than $100

Paco learned to read last year.
So did Dad.

Literacy
Volunteers
of America, Inc.

Source: Literacy Volunteers of America

billion a year. This total includes decreased productivity (by workers who perform their jobs improperly) and increased accidents (by people unable to understand written instructions). It also reflects the expense of supporting those unable to read and write well enough to find work who, unable to earn a living, end up either on welfare or in prison.

The problem of illiteracy in the United States is most serious among Latinos. In part this is due to a dropout rate among 14- to 24-year-olds of almost 30 per cent, which is three times the rate among whites or African Americans. The broader issue is that schools fail to teach many Spanish-speaking people to read and write any language very well. ●

Sources: based on Kozol, 1980, 1985a, 1985b.

the report continued, the proportion is more than one in three. Moreover, US students spend less time in the classroom (178 school days per year) than their counterparts in virtually every other industrial society: the British require 192 days in school, the Japanese 210 days, the Koreans 222 days and the Chinese 251 (Walters, 1994).

UK politicians of many colours have expressed alarm that 40 per cent of 11-year-olds and 30 per cent of 14-year-olds were not meeting national numeracy and literacy standards – well below international averages (see Figure 19.4). The Labour government which swept to power in the UK in 1997 claimed in its first White Paper, *Excellence in Schools*, that its main priorities were

Figure 19.4 ● National scores in mathematics: secondary pupils
The secondary pupil study was aimed at pupils aged 13 and surveyed two consecutive year groups (in England, years 8 and 9). The chart shows the results for the older year group who, in England, had an average age of 14.0, somewhat below the average age of pupils in most of the countries in the chart. The international average is of all countries taking part in TIMSS (*Third International Mathematics and Science Study* from *Education in Schools*, HMSO, 1997: 84).

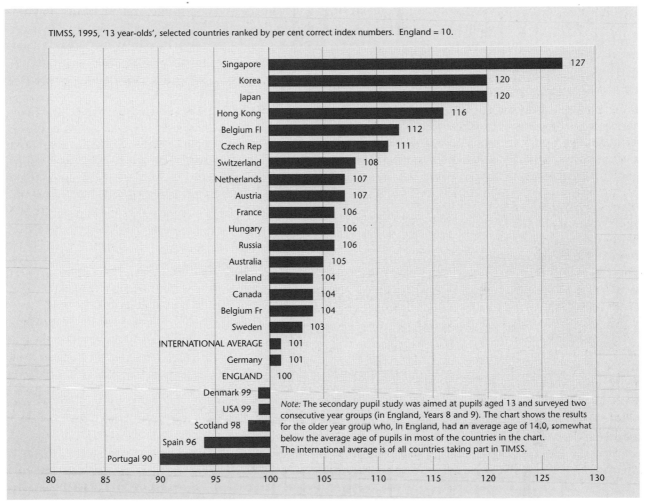

TIMSS, 1995, '13 year-olds', selected countries ranked by per cent correct index numbers. England = 10.

Note: The secondary pupil study was aimed at pupils aged 13 and surveyed two consecutive year groups (in England, Years 8 and 9). The chart shows the results for the older year group who, In England, had an average age of 14.0, somewhat below the average age of pupils in most of the countries in the chart. The international average is of all countries taking part in TIMSS.

Source: Department for Education and Employment, *Excellence in Schools*.

'education, education and education'. Following on from the preceding government, Labour has striven to expand monitoring of schools, through an improved Office for Standards in Education. Ministers have proposed testing children from the moment they start school, requiring primary schools to provide an hour a day on literacy and numeracy; weeding out the ranks of so-called incompetent teachers, and setting performance targets for each school – with those that fail to meet targets facing closure.

Some critics of both the former Conservative and the Labour government have suggested that the language of concern over decline has scapegoated teachers and LEAs for all the wider problems with education. Without a workforce able to feel confidence in itself, they claim, teachers can hardly encourage confidence among children. Some academics at the university level reject Labour's marketisation push as undermining the authority of 'pure knowledge' (Barnett, 1997).

From school to work: changing trends

The worlds of youth have been changing in the past two decades, and quite dramatically. The old model of school followed by work has, effectively, broken down. Young people at 16 now face the choice of staying at school, joining a youth training scheme or eventually joining the ranks of unemployed youth who have little or no benefits. Generally, young people who once expected to be independent now have to live at home – with university sometimes serving as an escape route from home! While some politicians believe these changes will make young people more responsible, critics charge that the changed policies promote an enforced dependency on school and parents (Furlong and Cartmeal, 1997; McDonald, 1997).

The ideology of parentocracy

Education in England and Wales (Scotland and Northern Ireland operate separate education systems) has gone through three phases: a concern for imparting basic information to the working classes; followed by a shift to a meritocratic ideology; followed by a new phase labelled **parentocracy**; *a system where a child's education is increasingly dependent upon the wealth and wishes of parents, rather than the ability and efforts of pupils* (Brown, 1990).

In part, the emphasis on parental choice in primary schools has fuelled this shift. One study of parents exercising choice over their children's schooling found that class plays a major influence. For working class parents, school had to be fitted into the demands of work and

PROFILE

Pierre Bourdieu: reproducing class

Pierre Bourdieu (1930–), a French sociologist, has made important contributions to the study of education, culture and class. Bourdieu has observed underlying patterns of class domination in education, art and 'culture' generally. He suggests that the primary roles of education are **social reproduction**, *the maintenance of power and privilege between social classes from one generation to the next*, and **cultural reproduction**, *the process by which a society transmits dominant knowledge from one generation to another.*

In his book *Distinction* (using large scale questionnaires on consumer activities), Bourdieu (1984) captures the profound sense of social difference and distance we often feel when faced with different cultures – some of which may even offend our own sensitivies. He is

concerned with our tastes for particular music (whether Blur or Mozart), foods (burgers or tofu), art and so forth, and with the ways items may move in and out of our scale of tastes. These can all be seen as ways of maintaining social distance, and reproducing class relations.

Each family teaches its children a certain cultural capital and a certain ethos. Starting in the pre-school years, children have different access to cultural capital. For instance, children taken by parents around the world have experiences of many different cultures with their different languages, manners, foods, arts and etiquettes. They build up experiences of travel, diversity and languages which other children may never know. Cultural capital, then, is much more than formal education – it is found often in person-

alities who 'know things' – about art or food or films or history – who have a stock of cultural knowledge.

Cultural reproduction, Bourdieu notes, does not involve the reproduction of the culture of all segments of society; only that of the dominant classes. People in each class transmit a distinctive 'habitus' (classifications, perceptions, ways of talking, moving and generally carrying oneself) down the generations, but schools pick up only on the habitus of the most powerful classes. He argues that the educational system has systematic biases against working-class knowledge and skills. ●

Source: For an introductory guide to Bourdieu, see Richard Jenkins, *Pierre Bourdieu*, London, Routledge, 1992.

other family matters, while middle class parents tended to reorganise their household arrangements to accommodate school. With the ideology of parentocracy, schools may be seen once again to disadvantage the less flexible working classes.

Another aspect of parentocracy is the rise of 'parent power' in the running of schools. Parents are invited to make their voices heard at school governors' meetings, and in the UK, vote on such matters as whether schools should 'opt out' of the LEA system. One study found that 'middle class white males still dominate the powerful positions in secondary schools governorship', although women have increasing influence at the primary school level (Deem, 1995, 1997: 28). Worryingly, though, the same study found that 'governors may turn out to have quite different characteristics from those of the pupils who attend the school they govern and to have much less interest in social justice than might be thought appropriate for those overseeing a public education service' (Deem, 1997: 31).

Credentialism

Randall Collins (1979) has coined the term *credential society*, for societies where people view diplomas and degrees as evidence of ability to perform specialised occupational roles. As modern societies have become more technologically complex, culturally diverse and socially mobile, a CV or résumé often says more about 'who you are' than family background does.

Credentialism, then, is *evaluating a person on the basis of educational degrees*. Functional analysis views credentialism is simply the way our modern society goes about ensuring that important jobs are filled by well-trained people. But Collins points out that credentials often bear little relation to the responsibilities of a specific job. In reality, then, advanced degrees serve as a shorthand way to sort out the people with the manners and attitudes sought by many employers. In short, credentialism operates much like family background as a gate-keeping strategy that restricts prestigious occupations to a small segment of the population. Finally, this emphasis on credentials can encourage *overeducation*, by which many workers have more schooling than they need to perform their jobs. As a result, although we see more and more people with advanced degrees, there are fewer jobs calling for highly educated workers, while the proportion of low-skill service jobs is expanding.

● Looking ahead: schooling in the twenty-first century

Many of the problems of schools have their roots in the larger society. As we approach the next century, we cannot expect schools to stay the same. One key trend now reshaping schools involves technology. Just as the Industrial Revolution had a major impact on schooling in the nineteenth century, computers and the Information Revolution are transforming formal education today. Most European schools have computers for instructional use. The promise of new information technology goes beyond helping students learn basic skills to improving the overall quality of learning. Interacting with computers prompts students to be more active learners and has the added benefit of allowing them to progress at their own pace. For students with disabilities who cannot write with a pencil, computers permit easier self-expression. The introduction of computers into schools appears to significantly increase learning speed and retention of information (Fantini, 1986). Nevertheless, computers alone cannot sort out the continued class, ethnicity and gender inequalities found in many schools. Many of the problems in education today will require dedicated effort for some years to come before a solution may be found.

SUMMARY ....

1. Education is the major social institution for transmitting knowledge and skills, as well as teaching cultural norms and values.
2. Symbolic interactionists have observed that relations between teachers and students play a role in maintaining social structures outside schools.
3. Structural-functional analysis highlights major functions of schooling, including socialisation, cultural innovation, social integration and placing people in the social hierarchy. Among the latent functions of schooling: providing child care and forging social networks.

4. Conflict analysis points out how differences in class, race, gender and sexuality promote unequal opportunities for schooling. Formal education also serves as a means of generating conformity to produce compliant adult workers.

5. When children get labelled as achievers or as failures at school, they learn to become the type of person which the label suggests they are.

6. Streaming, in theory, groups students of similar needs to maximise the appropriateness of teaching materials and the pace of learning. Critics maintain that schools stream students according to their social background, thereby providing privileged youngsters with a richer and more challenging education.

7. In some respects, the bureaucracy growing in schools facilitates the expansion of testing and assessment now common in many school systems, but bureaucracy also makes schools more rigid and less responsive to students needs.

8. The UK government has introduced market forces into the education system. Some believe that the market will improve services and choice, but others suggest that market forces are increasing inequalities and undermining the traditional principles of education.

9. Declining academic standards are reflected in today's lower average scores on achievement tests and the functional illiteracy of a significant proportion of secondary school graduates.

10. Many education systems encourage people to get credentials which are not necessarily related to the available jobs.

KEY CONCEPTS

credentialism evaluating a person on the basis of educational degrees

cultural reproduction the process by which a society transmits dominant knowledge from one generation to another

education the social institution guiding the transmission of knowledge, job skills, cultural norms and values

functional illiteracy reading and writing skills insufficient for everyday living

hidden curriculum subtle presentations of political or cultural ideas in the classroom

mainstreaming integrating special students into the overall educational programme

meritocracy allocating positions according to merit based on universalist standards of achievement

parentocracy a system where a child's education is increasingly dependent upon the wealth and wishes of parents, rather than the ability and efforts of pupils

schooling formal instruction under the direction of specially trained teachers

self-fulfilling prophecy children defined as low achievers at school learn to become low achievers

social reproduction the maintenance of power and privilege between social classes from one generation to the next

streaming the assignment of students to different types of educational programmes

CRITICAL-THINKING QUESTIONS

1. Why did widespread schooling develop in Europe only after the Industrial Revolution?

2. Referring to various countries, including the UK, describe ways in which schooling is shaped by economic, political or cultural factors.

3. From a functionalist perspective, why is schooling important to the operation of society? From a conflict point of view, how does formal education operate to reproduce social inequality?

4. How valuable do you find classroom interaction studies? Do one of your own, looking around your campus and class. Do the themes outlined in the text still apply?

5. Discuss the role of 'choice' in education. Does everyone have an equal choice? How might 'choice' be socially patterned? Do you agree that there is a growing ideology of parentocracy?

6. How would you explain the paradox that, whilst girls have been disadvantaged by sexism in schools, in recent years their performance has dramatically improved and often exceeds the performance of boys.

GOING FURTHER ....

Introductory reading

A. H. Halsey, Hugh Lauder, Phillip Brown and Amy Stuart Wells, *Education: Culture, Economy and Society* (Oxford: Oxford University Press, 1997).

Although not really introductory, this is a very valuable collection of up to date readings which mark out the field of the contemporary sociology of education.

Classic sources

Paul Willis, *Learning to Labour* (Farnborough: Saxon House, 1977).

This is the classic UK ethnography : a study of a small group of working class boys moving from school to work. Its fame may however be curiously misplaced: it studies only 12 boys and overlays the observation with a rather dense theoretical Marxism.

More advanced reading

Andy Green, *Education and State Formation: The Rise of Education Systems in England, France and the USA*, rev. edn (London: MacMillan, 1992).

A work of comparative sociology that details the rise of three major educational systems linked to the modern state.

HMSO, *Excellence in Schools*, Department of Education and Employment Cm 3681, July 1997.

As the Labour Government's first white paper when it swept into office in 1997 in the UK, this is an important statement of key issues in educational policy at the end of the century. It details a number of major goals to be achieved by the year 2002.

Mairtin Macan Ghaill, *The Making of Men: Masculinities, Sexualities and Schooling* (Buckingham: Open University Press, 1994).

Vivid study of gender, class and ethnicity in a secondary school.

Catherine Marshall, ed., *The New Politics of Race and Gender* (Falmer Press, 1993).

Essays in this collection examine the increasing importance of race and gender in shaping the curriculum, testing and staffing of schools in the United States, Australia and Israel.

Robert McDonald, *Youth, the Underclass and Social Exclusion* (London: Routledge, 1997).
Andy Furlong and Fred Cartmeal, *Young People and Social Change: Individualism and Risk in the Age of High Modernity* (Buckingham: Open University, 1997).

Two reviews of youth unemployment and education.

Sue Sharpe, *Just like a Girl: How Girls Learn to Become Women* (Middlesex: Penguin, 2nd edn, 1995).

The second edition in 1995 updates the original 1976 study and finds that girls have changed.

Nelly P. Stromquist (ed.), *Women and Education in Latin America: Knowledge, Power, and Change* (Boulder, Colorado: Lynne Rienner, 1992).

This book is a collection of thirteen essays that focus on the educational opportunities for women in this important world region.

Other sources

Donald Mackinnon, June Statham and Margaret Hales, *Education in the UK: Facts and Figures* (Buckingham: Open University, 1996).

One of a number of valuable overviews of the whole educational scene in the UK. It looks at its history, the main reports, legislation, the organisation and working of the system, and reviews matters linked to curriculum, preparation for employment and youth training. Not sociological as such, but helpful with facts, figures and information.

chapter twenty

Source: Popperfoto

Health and Medicine

At the start of the 1980s, 'AIDS' had not been invented. Throughout the previous decade, and maybe earlier, people had been contracting a peculiar *unnamed* disease and sometimes dying from it. The phenomenon of AIDS itself, however, had yet to be perceived. There were no people identified as suffering from it, and the 'AIDS spectrum' – of AIDS and HIV Seropositivity, of the 'worried well' and the fear of AIDS – had not been invented. There were no hospital beds for people with AIDS and no doctors and nurses dedicated to their care. No funds had been directed towards it, no research had been conducted upon it, no blood tests had been organised for it, no government had pronounced around it, no self-help groups had been established to deal with it, no media had talked about it, no moral crusader had campaigned against it, no household had been leafleted about it, no billboard had advertised it and no gay community had been disrupted by it. There were no articles, no journals, no legal handbooks, no nursing guides, no books, no films, no novels, no television programmes, no soap operas, no phone-ins, no videos, no posters, no red ribbons, no pamphlets, no conferences, no concerts, no sick jokes and no obituaries about AIDS. There were no experts on every conceivable aspects of AIDS – no oncologists or urologists, no haematologists or immunologists, no microbiologists or epidemiologists, no venereologists or sociologists, no psychiatrists or psychologists, no health educators or health counsellors, no condom specialists or fund-raisers. AIDS had not entered the discourses of sex and of drugs, of gayness and of prostitution, of race and religion, of haemophilia and blood transfusion, of third world and world health, of therapy and trade unionism, of science and literature, of law and ethics and of power and control.

Yet now, AIDS has become all of these things and more. First identified in 1981 and officially named in July 1982, AIDS signposts a syndrome in which the body's immune system is unable to function properly. But it is, however, much more than this, being also a set of powerful – often painful – *social meanings* that emerge through a host of social arenas and that are generated in many social practices. AIDS – the biological disease – must therefore be distinguished from 'AIDS' – the social institution (Plummer, 1988).

We tend to think of illness and disease as matters for doctors and biologists. But what this chapter will show is that disease is also very much a matter for sociologists. What happens to our bodies is very much a product of the kind of society we live in. And more: looking after our bodies has necessitated a major set of social institutions. In this chapter, we will start an exploration of all this.

● What is health?

Millions of people around the planet face major health problems, and some are in a position to cope more successfully than others. The World Health Organization (1946: 3) defines **health** as *a state of complete physical, mental and social well-being*. This definition underscores the major theme of this chapter: *health is as much a social as a biological issue.*

Health and society

The health of any population is shaped by traits of the surrounding society. Key aspects of health include the following:

1. *People judge their health relative to others.* Standards of health vary from society to society. Earlier this century, the contagious skin disease, yaws, was so common in sub-Saharan Africa that people there considered it normal (Dubos, 1980; orig. 1965). In truth, then, health is sometimes a matter of having the same diseases as one's neighbours (Crisp, 1989).

2. *People often equate 'health' with morality.* Many people look askance on those who contract a sexually transmitted disease. Indeed, some countries require potential immigrants to take HIV and syphilis tests before they are given visas. In short, ideas about good health constitute a type of social control that encourages conformity to cultural norms.

3. *Cultural standards of health change over time.* Early in this century, some prominent doctors condemned women for enrolling in universities, claiming that higher education placed an unhealthy strain on the female brain. Other specialists denounced

masturbation as a threat to health. Today, the medical community soundly rejects such notions. Conversely, few people 50 years ago recognised the dangers of cigarette smoking, a practice that is now widely regarded as a threat to health.

4. *Health and living standards are interrelated.* Poor societies routinely contend with malnutrition and poor sanitation, which promote high levels of infectious disease. Industrial development, taking little account of people's health, likewise has often lowered living standards.

5. *Health relates to social inequality.* Every society distributes resources unequally. The physical, mental and social health of the wealthy is far better than that of poor people. This pattern starts at birth, with infant mortality highest among the poor. Affluent people enjoy a greater chance of recovering from major illnesses and accidents than poor people.

● Health: a global survey

Because health is an important dimension of social life, we find pronounced change in human well-being over time. Historians of disease have identified three phases in human health. In a pre-agricultural phase, people lived short but healthy lives with few infectious diseases (McKeown, 1976). The Agricultural Revolution improved food security; but the accompanying increases in social inequality allowed elites to enjoy better health, while peasants and slaves often laboured for long hours and lived in crowded, insanitary shelters. In the cities of medieval Europe, human waste

Medieval medical practice was heavily influenced by astrology, so that physicians and lay people alike attributed disease to astral influence; this is the root of our word 'influenza'. In this woodcut by Swiss artist Jost Amman (1580), as midwives attend a childbirth, astrologers cast a horoscope for the new-born.

Source: The Granger Collection

and other refuse fuelled infectious diseases, including plagues that periodically wiped out entire towns (Mumford, 1961).

By the industrial era, people have learned to control many infectious diseases, but suffer from a range of diseases linked to environment, pollution and stress (such as cancers, strokes and heart disease). Contemporary ailments are more often helped by a change in lifestyle rather than by medications. Hence, as we shall see, medical work is increasingly preventive rather than curative (McKeown, 1976).

Health in low-income countries

Striking differences in health distinguish societies of the world today. The World Health Organization reports that 1 billion people around the world – one in five – suffer from serious illness due to poverty. Poor sanitation and malnutrition kill people of all ages,

especially children. Indeed, 10 per cent of the world's children die before the age of one (George, 1977; Harrison, 1984). Health is compromised not just by having too little to eat, but also by consuming only one kind of food, as the box on page 558 explains. A look back at Map 14.1 shows that average life expectancy in some of the world's poorest nations is as low as 40.

In impoverished countries, sanitary drinking water may be as scarce as the chance for a balanced diet. Contaminated water breeds many of the infectious diseases that imperil both adults and children. The leading causes of death in Europe a century ago, including influenza, pneumonia and tuberculosis, remain widespread killers in poor societies. As Map 20.1 shows, poor societies are further plagued by a shortage of doctors and other medical personnel.

Illness and poverty form a vicious cycle in much of the world – poverty breeds disease, which, in turn, undermines people's ability to earn income. Moreover, when medical technology does curb infectious disease, the populations of poor nations soar. Without resources to ensure the well-being of the people they have now, poor societies can ill afford surging population growth. Thus, efforts to lower death rates in poor countries will ultimately succeed only if they simultaneously reduce birth rates as well.

The Global Strategy of Health for All by the Year 2000, adopted by the WHO in 1982, argues that 'all the people in all the countries should have at least such a level of health that they are capable of working productively and participating actively in the social life of the community in which they live'. The WHO aims at ensuring all peoples have adequate access to safe water, sanitary facilities, immunisation against major infections and availability of local health care. Recent statistics strongly suggest these aims will not be met by the year 2000 (WHO, 1996; World Bank, 1997).

Health in high-income countries

Industrialisation dramatically changed patterns of human health in Europe, although, at first, not for the better. By 1800, as the Industrial Revolution was taking hold, factories were choking the cities with people drawn from the countryside in search of economic opportunity. Unprecedented population concentration spawned serious problems of sanitation and overcrowded housing. Moreover, factories continuously

Map 20.1 ● The availability of doctors in global perspective

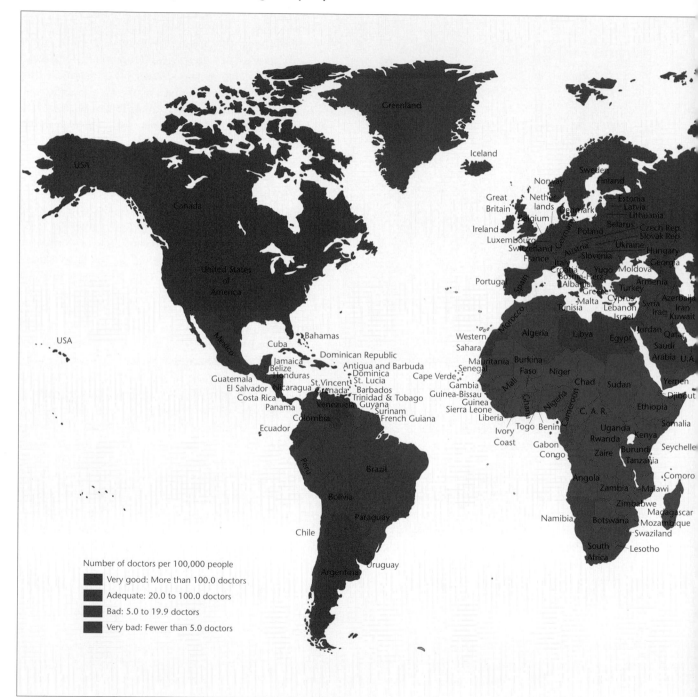

Number of doctors per 100,000 people

Very good: More than 100.0 doctors

Adequate: 20.0 to 100.0 doctors

Bad: 5.0 to 19.9 doctors

Very bad: Fewer than 5.0 doctors

Source: *Peters Atlas of the World* (1990)

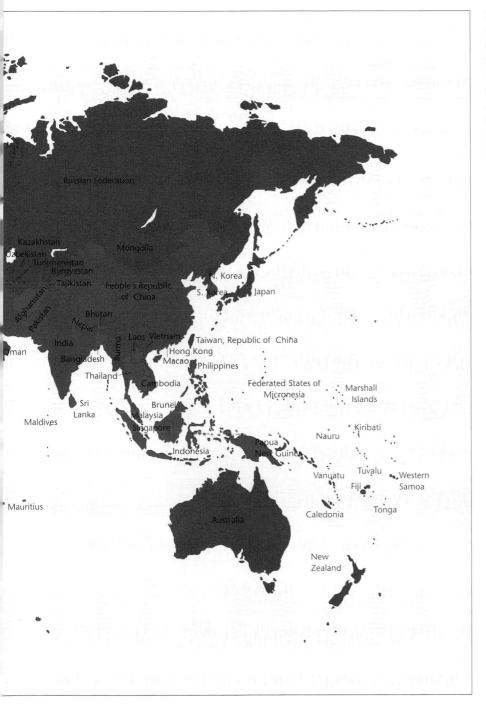

Medical doctors, widely available to people in rich nations, are perilously scarce in poor societies. While traditional forms of healing do improve health, antibiotics and vaccines – vital for controlling infectious diseases – are often in short supply in poor societies. In these countries, therefore, death rates are high, especially among infants.

Moreover, 'science' is not always neutral. Experiments have often been performed on the poor and ill-informed without their knowledge. Indeed, in 1997, US President Bill Clinton apologised to black men who were the subjects of studies of the cause of syphilis in the 1930s in the United States.

● Social causes of illness: inequalities in health

Most people in Europe are healthy by world standards. Some categories of people, however, enjoy far better health and well-being than others. Here we will look at some of the social patterns of health in Europe – which

is another way of saying that we will be looking at social inequalities. Once again, as we have seen throughout this book, one of the major mechanisms of social organisation is inequality. And just as we have seen that inequalities shape disease and health in low-income societies, so too they shape them in high-income societies.

Social epidemiology: the distribution of health

Social epidemiology is *the study of how health and disease are distributed throughout a society's population.* Just as early social epidemiologists examined the origin

---

Norbert Elias: the civilising of bodies and societies

The German–English sociologist, Norbert Elias (1897–1990) made important contributions both to the study of sociology and social change. A refugee from Hitler's Germany, his studies of *The Civilizing Process* (Germany in 1939!) suggests how from the Middle Ages onwards in most of Europe, people came to exert greater self control over their behaviour and their bodies. Through a series of studies of ways of eating, sleeping, dressing, spitting, having sex, defecating, dying and eliminating, he charts the changing ways of life.

Medieval life was unpredictable, highly emotional, often chaotic, frequently indulgent and there were few codes around bodily functions. Court society slowly started to change all this, by bringing about etiquette for body management, locations for defecation, and sleeping. Restraint appeared in

codes such as those managing table manners. The state developed side by side with a 'civilised' system of self-control. The civilised society has self-discipline, self-control, higher shame and embarrassment, etc.

Chris Shilling (1993) summarises three key processes involved in civilis-

Source: Popperfoto

ing: socialisation, rationalisation and individualisation. People are taught to hide natural functions – like defecating and urinating; rationalisation makes us less emotional; individualisation suggests we come to see ourselves and our bodies as distinctively separate.

All of this is part of Elias's wider approach to sociology, developed in his *What is Sociology?* (1970), and known as 'figurational sociology'. Interactions between individuals and societies are his area of study 'the network of inter-dependencies among human beings is what binds them together' (1978: 261).

Elias's work has been influential on a range of scholars who study everyday life processes. Stephen Mennell for instance has studied food. ●

Source: Norbert Elias, *The Civilizing Process* (originally published 1939).

and spread of epidemic diseases, researchers today find links between health and physical and social environments. Such analysis rests on comparing the health of different categories of people.

Social class

Lesley Doyal has argued that: 'Class differences in morbidity and mortality . . . provide strong evidence to support the argument that social and economic factors remain extremely important in determining the ways in which people live and die' (Doyal, 1979: 65). In 1993, for example, chronic sickness rates were over 10 per cent higher for the elderly unskilled worker than the professional worker (*Social Trends*, 1994: 86). And as Table 20.1 shows, infant mortality – the death rate among new-borns – is significantly higher among the children of unskilled workers than it is amongst children born to privilege. Note, though, that for all groups there have been significant improvements in the past two decades on this dimension.

The most important study to look at health inequalities in the UK was the Black Report (1980: *The Report of the Working Party on Inequalities in Health*; (updated in 1992 as *The Health Divide*). Townsend and Davidson (1982) argued that (1) inequalities in health are found at birth (as above), in childhood, in adolescence and throughout adult life; (2) some of these inequalities were amongst the worst in Europe; and (3)

inequalities have also been growing. One of its most famous findings was that the child of an unskilled manual worker will die around seven years earlier than a counterpart born to professional parents.

Linked closely to this is inequality in health care. Some research suggests that working class patients are treated somewhat differently. They may, for example, be given less time and be less well known to their doctors. More than this, there may be an 'inverse care law' – those whose need is less may get more resources, whilst those in greatest need get less – and the poorest may not get such good treatment from within the NHS (Cartwright and O'Brian, 1976; Hart, 1985; Tudor-Hart, 1971).

All in all, the link between class and inequality seems evident. But the question that is then posed concerns why. The Black Report looked at four main arguments which might explain social class differences around health. The four arguments have framed much of the debate in recent years. The competing arguments are:

● *Statistical artefacts*. This suggests there are real problems of measurement and the statistics themselves may not be reliable indicators.

● *Natural-Health selection explanations*. This suggests that health status itself may influence positioning in the class structure. The healthy drift upwards, the sick drift downwards. (Note that this has a social Darwinism ring to it.)

● *Materialist explanations*. This suggests that material deprivations – poverty, low incomes, bad housing conditions, pollution at work – shape the experiences of health.

● *Cultural explanations*. This suggests that certain class ways of life – more smoking in working class groups, poorer diets, less exercise – shape the health experiences.

The Black Report concluded that the last two explanations were the most satisfactory.

Ethnicity

Diseases can affect ethnic groups significantly differently. Thus, the infant mortality rate has been constantly higher for infants born in the New Commonwealth and Pakistan than for those born in the UK. There are also some diseases which disproportionately affect certain groups: sickle-cell anaemia

Table 20.1 ● Infant mortality[a]: by social class[b]

United Kingdom	Rates per 1,000 live births[c]		
	1981	1991	1994
Professional	7.8	5.0	4.5
Managerial and technical	8.2	5.3	4.5
Skilled non-manual	9.0	6.3	5.1
Skilled manual	10.5	6.3	5.5
Semi-skilled	12.7	7.1	6.4
Unskilled	15.7	8.2	6.8
Other	15.7	12.4	8.8
All social classes	10.4	6.4	5.4

[a] Deaths within one year of birth.
[b] Based on occupation of father.
[c] Inside marriage

Sources: Office for National Statistics; General Register Office (Scotland); General Register Office (Northern Ireland)

CRITICAL-THINKING QUESTIONS ....

1. Explain why health is as much a social as a biological issue.
2. In global context, which are the 'diseases of poverty' that kill people in poor countries? Which are 'diseases of affluence', the leading killers in rich nations?
3. Sexually transmitted diseases represent an exception to the historical decline in infectious illness. What social forces are reflected in the rise in STDs since 1960?
4. Do you think the United States should or should not follow the lead of other industrial countries by enacting a government programme of health care for everyone? Why?
5. Examine the reasons for 'inequalities of health'?.
6. How have 'bodies' changed in the twentieth century?

GOING FURTHER ....

Introductory reading

Sarah Nettleton, *The Sociology of Health and Illness* (Cambridge: Polity Press, 1995).

An introductory textbook guide to the whole field (it does not however discuss mental health).

Brian Turner, *Medical Power and Social Knowledge* (London: Sage, 1st edn, 1987; 2nd edn, 1996).

Fast becoming a classical textbook, but it is very theoretical.

Classic sources

Elisabeth Kübler-Ross, *On Death and Dying* (New York: Macmillan, 1969).

This study of the orderly process of dying illustrates how social research can assist terminally ill patients.

Michel Foucault, *The Birth of the Clinic: An Archaeology of Medical Perception* (New York: Vintage Books, 1975).

This history of medicine emphasises not scientific developments but the cultural forces that gradually changed how people thought about illness and health care.

Peter Townsend and Nick Davidson (eds), *Inequalities in Health: the Black Report* (Middlesex: Penguin, 1982). Margaret Whitehead, *The Health Divide: Inequalities in Health in the 1980s*. London: Health Education Authority, 1987.

The first is a highly influential study on inequalities, and the latter updates it.

British Medical Association BMA *Complementary Medicine: New Approaches to Good Practice* (London: BMA, 1993).

More advanced reading

Clyde B. McCoy and James A. Inciardi, *Sex, Drugs, and the Continuing Spread of AIDS* (Los Angeles: Roxbury, 1995).

The 'second wave' of the AIDS epidemic is placing poor people at risk, according to this book.

Susan Sherwin, *No Longer Patient: Feminist Ethics and Health Care* (Philadelphia: Temple University Press, 1992).

This author argues that ethical issues in medicine should be resolved in a feminist context.

Two books that consider women and health are:

Lesley Doyal, *What Makes Women Sick* (London, Macmillan, 1995).
P. Foster, *Women and the Health Care Industry* (Buckingham: Open University Press, 1995).

Kaja Finkler, *Women in Pain: Gender and Morbidity in Mexico* (Philadelphia: University of Pennsylvania Press, 1994).

Women in low-income countries face especially serious threats to health.

Richard Parker and Herbert Daniel *Sexuality, Politics and AIDS in Brazil: In Another World?* (Bristol, PA: Taylor & Francis, 1993).

Based on personal accounts of people with AIDS, the authors contend that the social dynamics linked to this deadly disease are not the same in Brazil as in Europe.

chapter twenty-one

Source: Popperfoto

The Mass Media

Let's start this chapter with an exercise. For the next few days, keep a detailed record of 'you and your media'. Keep a detailed log of just when you engage with the mass media, for how long and what was on. It may surprise you.

For instance, one of your authors gets up and amongst the first things he does most days will be to turn on the radio in the bathroom for music; turn on the TV whilst dressing for comments and news; and read the newspaper whilst getting breakfast. Once at work, on goes the CD player for background music; on goes the computer for the e-mail. Then the day has started. Nothing here is surprising; most people in the industrial world get up and start the day to various media. And as the day goes on, so the media continue to impinge on our lives.

The twentieth century has become the media century. Many of us live our lives increasingly in and through the media. To take television as a prime example: watching television is the most common home-based leisure activity for men and women in the UK. Virtually everyone watches it. Ninety-seven per cent of households in the UK own one television; 53 per cent own two or more (nearly 80 per cent of households have a video recorder; 7 per cent own two or more). Each individual watches it, on average, between 30 and 38 hours per day. Over one in five people have a satellite dish. In the United States the figures are even higher. Ninety-eight per cent own one television, 70 per cent own two or more, and these sets are on for an average of more than seven hours per day. And a 1996 survey of young people in 41 nations found they watched an average of six hours television per day (Allen, 1992: 1; Abercrombie, 1996: 2; Herman and McChesney, 1997: 4; Social Trends, 1997).

But television is only one media form. Half the UK population aged over 15 read a national daily newspaper and the same number hold library tickets. Some 140 million CDs were sold in 1995 (and 71 million singles): making roughly two CDs and one single per head of the population. Three-quarters of the population go to the cinema – and the figures are highest amongst the young: over 95 per cent.

Ownership and watching does not tell the full story. What is important about the mass media are the way in which they have come to play a prominent role in many aspects of our everyday lives. All the institutions discussed in this book have been changed by them: political elections, for example, are geared up to television; religion has got its televangelical networks; business and finance depend upon the new technologies for rapid information. And where would public events – like sport or parliament or news – be if they were not relayed in our homes on television?

Even the family has changed dramatically because of television. Many homes give pride of place to the TV set in their living room, draping it with family photos – symbolic of its importance in homes. Television becomes a part of everyday life, marking out family time and routines. It is the intimate machine – giving impressions of talking to you through its chat programmes, its advice programmes, its close-up interviews with all kinds of people. The media become friend and family. Indeed, much of what is shown on the screen actually depicts friends and families – the most popular programmes are the 'soap operas' which are always about this. But then we take to university or work all the details of the soap lives we have seen on TV and start to discuss them with friends. TV characters invade our lives as new friends (Abercrombie, 1996: 17–19 and Chapter 7).

We are media saturated. Indeed, one commentator has tellingly remarked that 'in one hour's television viewing, one of us is likely to experience more images than a member of a non-industrial society would in a life time. The quantitative difference is so great as to become categorical; we do not just experience more images, but we live with a completely different relationship between the image and other orders of experience' (Fiske, 1991: 58).

The Spanish sociologist, Manuel Castells, has argued that 'new information technologies are transforming the way we produce, consume, manage, live and die' (Castells, 1989: 15). In this chapter, we will look at how our modern mass media system developed and examine some of the theories that have tried to explain how it works. We will show how media research needs to look at what media messages contain, how media messages are made and how they are understood by the audiences. Finally, we will glimpse their coming importance in the twenty-first century, as the media becomes increasingly globalised.

● The media and social change

The history of societies can partially be written as the history of media communications. We have seen in Chapter 3 ('Society') how social life changed between hunting and gathering societies and industrial society and how technology is one guiding feature of social change. Technology can do nothing in itself: it takes people to act on the media to bring about change. But without the media themselves, no change would be possible. What we can see is direct one to one face to face communication developing into the **mass media**, *any social or technological device used for the selection, transmission, reception of some content like information.*

One aspect of that technology is the means of communication. As the means of communication change so do social lives. The major developments in human culture and consciousness are linked to changes in our modes of communication – the evolution from words and primitive speech through writing to typeface and now modern electronic worlds (Ong, 1982).

Our focus here is not upon the content of the media but on their form. In a famous phrase, US media guru Marshall McLuhan proclaimed that 'The Medium is the Message' (McLuhan, 1967). What he means by this is that independently of what is being said, it is the kind of 'medium which shapes and controls the scale of human association and action'. McLuhan sees the history of media as falling into three major periods. The first is an oral culture, where the ear is the important sense. Listening to the words is a harmonious, circular way of thought. The second is the writing and printing culture, where 'the ear' is exchanged for the 'eye'. It brings more linear thought. The third is the electronic culture. And here the media bring radical shifts again.

Consider Table 21.1 which outlines the evolution of the main forms of communication in society. We can return to our image of the world's history being scaled to be represented as a 24 hour clock starting at midnight and continuing till the next midnight, intro-duced in Chapter 3. Here, speech is invented around 9.30 in the evening. Writing is not invented till about eight minutes before midnight. Electronic devices appear some 11 seconds, and digital electronics 2 seconds, before the clock strikes midnight (Neuman, 1991: 7). Table 21.2 gives some landmarks in media history.

Oral cultures

For most of our history, then, societies have been entirely dependent upon face to face grunts! Language and speech only start to appear with more sophisti-cated societies, about 100,000 years ago. These are oral cultures, and culture here depends a great deal upon the ability to remember and to tell stories that get passed on from generation to generation. Without such stories, cultures and knowledge would die out. Certainly, these are 'slow societies' where not a great deal can be retained. For continuity, memory must have been vital. And stories played a crucial role.

Table 21.1 ● Stages in the development of human communication

1	The Age of Signs:	No speech or writing, only sounds and bodily gestures. Maybe 70 million years ago?
2	The Age of Speech:	Oral cultures, preliterate start to appear at most 100,000 years ago. cro Magna, Homo sapiens. Linguists can identify around 50 prehistoric vocabularies.
3	The Age of Writing:	Writing starts to appear around 5,000 years ago. Sumerians, Egyptian civilisation and in parts of Turkey, Iraq, Iran. Initially pictographs, hieroglyphics, clay tablets, later papyrus – a light and portable medium. Alphabets slowly replace images and songs and this promotes linear, rational and abstract thought. Problems of censorship start to appear. Chirography – or manuscripts – become main form in the Middle Ages.
4	The Age of Print:	Circa 1445/1456 the first printing press appears in the West; Gutenberg publishes the Bible (appeared in China nearly 800 years earlier). Greatly amplifies the reaches and impact of alphabet. Media censorship by church. Typography dominates. The whole process of printing speeds up with the Industrial Revolution.
5	The Age of Electronics:	Electrical and electronic media, from late 19th century. Emergence of photography.
6	The Future?	Digital, high tech, computers: The Information Age . . .

Writing cultures

Significant changes start to happen when the spoken word gets written down. This depends upon first, a written language system – an alphabet or code of some kind – and second, upon a means for writing and an object to write upon. Oral cultures depend upon memory. Poetry and stories become very important here in trying to pass on from generation to generation a sense of continuing culture. But writing makes it much easier to pass on this history.

And such a form will depend upon an alphabet. In China, some time around 3,000 years ago, an alphabet develops with some 50,000 characters! And with this emerges an elite who can master it: the mandarins. Phonetic alphabets – based on sounds – are more recent and mark a major advance in ease of use.

In some ancient civilisations, writing was carved on stone which was not at all easily transportable. Stone drawings are hard to change or revise – this medium therefore makes for relatively unchanging and stable societies. In Egypt, the dominance of stone as a medium gave a monopoly to those who owned it. But once papyrus was introduced, it played a major role in communication becoming more flexible.

The next major change comes when the churches start to develop significant manuscript writings. The medieval church had a monopoly over religious and all other information – controlled in manuscripts by a special class of priests. Again, these are far from available to most people.

Print cultures

And so we reach a time, just a few hundred years ago, when the method of print is invented. This is truly a revolution. Now the control of the elite church's scribes can be bypassed, because for the first time in history there arises the possibility that large numbers of people can become literate (an ability to read and write). This brings with it:

an ability to store and transmit culture much more readily;

the potential to include those people previously excluded from knowledge;

a potentially different way of thinking in which the person 'engages' with a text rather than another person;

● the potential for mass culture, mass society and mass education;

● the development of new minds in which literate modes of thought become part of our everyday consciousness;

● A new sense of 'authorship' and control over the text.

Despite the slow spreading of print, it is only really in the nineteenth century – with the birth of mass newspapers – that whole societies start to become literate. And at the same time, a mass education system is required to equip people for the new social order (see Chapter 19). Again, it was also a means of excluding people. There were constant fears of how this new literacy was 'dangerous'.

Electronic cultures

With the new electronic media, our experiences are no longer limited by where we are or who we are. Media, and especially television, weaken the strong sense we used to have of being in a place. Limited confines like the family home, the office or the prison are now invaded by the television, which starts to shift the boundaries of how we experience the world.

In an important recent study, Joshua Meyrowitz (1986) looks at how the pattern of information flow changes with television. With television we 'eavesdrop' on a host of different worlds. We can gain access to worlds that in the past were not accessible. Thus, for example, children's worlds and adult's worlds, men's worlds and women's worlds could in the past be kept separate. There were things that adults could talk about when children had gone to bed; things that men could talk about when women were not there. But television cuts out these separate spaces. We now inhabit 'no sense of place'. Our sense of place has changed.

Television weakens the traditional distinction between physical place and social situations. Public spheres now enter the living room; public and private get blurred. Television has changed our way of experiencing the world because it has changed what we know about everything – television parades before us an array of differences: men can learn about women, children about adult worlds, heterosexuals about gays, whites about blacks, the poor about the rich, the mass about the elite (Meyrowitz, 1986).

Table 21.2 ● Some modern landmarks in media history

1456	The Gutenberg Press: first book (The Bible) in the Western world (but evidence suggests China did this some 800 years earlier!)
17th century	Press starts to develop
1620–1	Corantos (news sheets) in Holland reporting (with King's authority) on wars
1665	Oxford – court news (later *London Gazette*)
1690	First American newspaper reporting on colonies . . .
1785	*The Times* was first published. Many of today's newspapers started in mid 19th century *News of the World* in 1843, *Daily Telegraph* in 1855 (Stamp duties abolished in 1855). *The Mail* was the first million selling mass circulation – edited by Lord Northcliffe.
1838	Morse code invented
1839	First photographs
1876	Alexander Graham Bell and the telephone
1877	Edison and the first replayable recording
1891	The kinetography and peep scopes. Late 1890s and 1900s short films like *How Bridget served the salad undressed* and in 1903 *The Great Train Robbery*
1910	Nickelodeon – some 10,000 family oriented exhibition halls exist in the USA
1915	*Birth of a Nation*: first 'major' film
1926	50 million people a week go to the movies in the US
1922	Radio arrives in Britain in 1922 with the British Broadcasting Company (The US started in 1921 with KDKA Pittsburgh)
1936	Television arrived in UK in 1936 at Alexandra Palace, for a small audience; but with the onset of World War II was not fully developed until the 1950s. ITV came in 1955; BBC2 in 1962; Channel 4 in 1982.
1950	The Univac (Universal Automatic Computer): the first mass produced computer
1960s	Emergence of Internet through the US Defense Department
1967	First local BBC
1981	MTV first televised (starts in US on 1 August 1981). Developed like a radio station, always on the air, appealing to the same market niche
1992	The Internet takes off.
1995	'Privatised Cyberspace': The Internet becomes commercial when the US government pulls out

● Media theories

The earliest theory of the mass media at the turn of the century – often called the magic bullet theory or the 'hypodermic' model of media effects – is the simplest propaganda model of the media. It assumes that people are passive and the media message has a direct impact upon them. It suggests that:

● Media messages are presented to members of a mass society, who receive them more or less uniformly.

● These messages are stimuli which influence the individual strongly.

● The stimuli lead individuals to respond in a similar, uniform fashion.

● The effects of mass communication are *powerful, uniform and direct* (our italics, adapted from Lowery and DeFleur, 1988: 23–4).

Although this theory can still be found in everyday debates (especially amongst those who see the media as dangerous), such an account has long been rejected by sociologists. We will now look at some of the theories that have been developed to replace this 'hypodermic syringe' model.

FOCUS ON EUROPE

History of television in Norway

Every country and culture now has its own media worthy of study. The history of various media provides clues as to a culture's social, economic and political history.

Norway came later to television than many other cultures, but the shape of its history is very similar to others. It falls into three waves:

1960–70: after an experimental period which started in 1954, 1960 saw the official opening of TV, a formal opening by the King, the Prime Minister and the Director-General. It was a continuation of the NRK (the Norwegian Broadcasting Corporation) which had been consolidated in 1933 through public radio; and it emerged through a close collaboration between the Norwegian Parliament and the NRK. It was also linked to industrial interests: the Norwegian radio industry was keen to produce television sets. Programming was limited – children's programmes at 6.00, a break; news at 8.00 and then programmes till 10.00 pm. In the early 1960s, education was seen as a major goal of what was effectively public tele-

vision. Although some 50–60 per cent of programming had to be home grown, there was quite an influx of UK and US programmes – bringing these cultures to the forefront of Norwegian life. There was also a classic debate between liberal values and conservative values. The period is summarised neatly: 'In 1960 a television set was regarded as a symbol of luxury and high social status. Ten years later it was a regular piece of furniture – a necessity for everybody' (Bastiansen and Syversten, 1996: 132).

1970–89: this was 'The Era of High Monopoly'. By the 1970s, television was the central medium in Norway. The one channel was a focus for the whole nation, especially over political debates. Programmes could attract 60 per cent of the nation's population. Throughout this period, the structure of programming was more or less the same. Children's shows at 6.00; three news programmes a day; mainly evening broadcasting. The monopoly was accused of bias – largely by conservatives who felt it was monopolised by the left. (It was not a total monopoly, as since the 1960s, access to

Swedish television had been possible.) Local and satellite broadcasting started in 1981 but on a limited scale and, as in so many countries, consumption was low initially. But significant changes can be heralded from 1989.

1989–now: by the end of 1990, almost 40 per cent could watch satellite television. The media age had arrived. There was a break up of the old public monopoly and the arrival of a new commercial era with a proliferation of channels. A second commercial channel opened in 1992.

What is interesting about this short television history is the pattern. Norway came later to television than many countries, but its three wave history is broadly comparable. What we see is a shift from a dominant 'public' medium of pervasive, but limited, scope to a proliferation of new channels and a commercialisation of the medium. Whilst each European country has its own history, this is the broad pattern. ●

Source: Bastiansen and Syversten, 1996: 127–55.

● Functionalist theories of the media

Functionalist theories of the media look at the ways in which the media serves to integrate society in different ways, and examine the role of media effects in doing this. Seeing media as working as part of the social system, media can provide information, education,

entertainment and diversion. Five functions have been particularly noted:

1. *The surveillance function.* The media provide a continuous flow of data about the world we live in. They can warn us of dangers (from hurricanes to wars to dangerous criminals) and be instrumental

in providing information on traffic jams, the stock market as well as all kinds of information linked to personal welfare. (They can also be dysfunctional – stirring up undue anxiety, for example.)

2. *The status conferral function.* Here, the media give status to people, public issues, organisations and social movements. Enhanced status comes to all who feature in the media – they become more known about, for good or bad. Not only do major events like political elections or famous criminal trials come to attention, many minor issues can be accorded status. Thus, a child with a life threatening illness, an old person on her hundredth birthday or environmental activists protesting a local pollution problem can all be accorded 'status'.

3. *The 'enforced application of social norms' function.* This highlights the public announcement of social norms, and publicity serves to close the gap between 'private attitudes and public morality'. Most noticeable here is the way in which the media can serve to dramatise deviance of all kinds. By bringing to our attention 'youth crime', 'rape', 'child sex offenders', 'drugs' or 'serial killers', the community's awareness is heightened and moral boundaries are drawn (see Chapter 8). The box describes how this often works as a moral panic.

4. *The transmission of culture function.* The media have become prime modern agents of socialisation (see Chapter 5). From young children's programmes like 'Teletubbies' to teenage chat shows, the media serve a key role in passing on elements of a society's culture and heritage.

5. *The narcotising function.* This is more of dysfunction than a function, and refers to the way in which a flood of information can lead to superficiality (Lazarsfeld and Merton, 1948 in Marris and Thornham, 1996: 16–18; Wright, 1967; McQuail, 1994).

Critical evaluation

Functionalist theories were popular during the middle part of this century, but have been much in decline since. The above listing suggests why. In many ways, all functionalist theories do is provide a descriptive listing of how an institution works in the current society. The functions listed here may be important, but it is not always clear that they add much depth of understanding.

● Conflict theories of the media

Much European work on the mass media has adopted a conflict (and often Marxist) approach to the media. Within this paradigm, the media are seen to be owned by dominant classes who use them as a mechanism to serve their own interests. The media thus come to play a major role in the transmission of ideologies. Broadly, conflict theories highlight two important matters. The first concerns the economic base of the media – in particular the ways in which they follow a profit motive, and the ways in which big business conglomerates come to shape them. The second concerns the ideological structuring of the media: in particular the ways in which certain conflicting interests – often of class, ethnicity, gender – are 'screened out' of the messages.

The political economy of the media: this stresses how the major means of communication in society come to be owned by private economic interests. Increasingly, it can be shown that these interests form giant interlocking directorates and are in the hands of powerful tycoons, like Rupert Murdoch and Silvio Berlusconi. (Berlusconi – who owns Finevest, with a virtual monopoly of Italian commercial television – was elected prime minister after much campaigning on his own television.) It has been true for some time that a country's media have been in the hands of a few powerful economic groups. Table 21.3 shows the approximate concentration in the UK in the mid-1990s. But even in the early 1970s, the top five media firms in the UK accounted for 71 per cent of daily newspaper circulation, 78 per cent of admissions to cinemas, 76 per cent of record sales and 74 per cent of homes with commercial television. But what has been happening since that time has been an increasing concentration of ownership globally. Thus Murdoch's transnational company has holdings in the United States, Latin America, Europe (especially the UK and Germany), Australia and Asia. This is discussed further below.

These powerful economic interests work to consistently exclude 'those voices lacking economic power or resources'. All kinds of minorities – from ethnic groups to disabled groups, from 'women' to 'gays' – may not be represented in media coverage. But more, much of the media will find that 'the voices which survive will largely belong to those least likely to criticise the prevailing distribution of power and wealth' (Murdock and Golding, 1977: 39).

DIFFERENT VOICES

Constructing moral panics

During the 1960s, Stanley Cohen investigated an emerging youth phenomenon: that of the Mods and Rockers (see Chapter 4). These young people appeared on the beaches and around the town of several south coast holiday resorts in England (including Clacton) over the Easter holiday of 1964. Although Cohen discovered that the amount of serious violence and vandalism was relatively little, he found that the media 'blew it up out of all proportions'. The media – and other 'moral crusaders' – saw the Mods and Rockers as terrorising the town and being 'hell bent on destruction'.

Cohen saw this as a 'moral panic' and defined it in the following way:

Societies appear to be subject, every now and then, to periods of moral panic. A condition, episode, person or group of persons emerges to become defined as a threat to societal values and interests; its nature is presented in a stylised and stereotypical fashion by the mass media; the moral barricades are manned (sic) by editors, bishops, politicians and other right thinking people; socially accredited experts pronounce their diag-

noses and solutions; ways of coping are evolved . . . (Cohen, 1972: 28)

Like Durkheim (in Chapter 8), Cohen argued that when societies entered times of anxiety and crisis, 'folk devils' were created through moral panics to reassert dominant values. For moral panics to exist, these responses have to be out of all proportion to the actual threat or danger. The media played a central role in stirring up concern, and often amplifying the problem. From a small initial issue, major hysteria could be created which often served the interest of specific groups worried about specific social issues – like teenage crime getting out of control.

Since Cohen's influential study, a great many 'folk devils and moral panics' have been identified. The media have mounted major concerns over drugs, mugging, baby battering, granny battering, child abuse of all forms, dole scroungers and welfare cheats, AIDS, video nasties, rapists and serial killers, paedophiles, Satanism and ritual abuse, religious cults, militant

trade unionism, 'blacks', pornography. In some cases the problems behind such issues have been found to be quite major; but in other cases, the hysteria is out of all proportion to the actual problem. Philip Jenkins has shown, for example, that serial killers in the UK are very rare indeed – and have remained at roughly the same low rate for the last 100 years (Jenkins, 1992).

To understand the workings of a moral panic, it is important to look at the way in which the media – newspapers and TV in particular – come to identify a 'problem' and present it in a particular way, and how this may 'fit' into a particular set of social anxieties or worries. Many moral panics for example depict dangerous threats to the traditional moral values of family life. When AIDS first appeared in the early 1980s, the media often handled it in a sensational way – depicting it as a dangerous threat to traditional sexuality. Look out for moral panics, and try to present your own analysis of one. ●

Sources: Cohen, 1972; Jenkins, 1992.

The culture industry and ideology: German critical theorists Adorno and Horkheimer saw the development of a 'culture industry' which 'transfers the profit motive naked on to cultural forms'. The multi-billion Hollywood empire sells its wares – from *Jurassic Park* to *Exterminator* – for huge profits. True 'culture' dissolves in the face of this commercial marketplace. And even 'great culture' will be dug up and recycled for new profits. Thus during the 1990s the work of the eighteenth-century novelist Jane Austen has been repack-

aged into films, television mini dramas and reworked books. Often this leads to her work becoming 'just like everything else': flattened for profit. And every aspect of the media is saturated with this. There are extremes – as in the hype and promotion of leading rock stars like the Spice Girls, or in a Madonna or Michael Jackson 'world concert'. Everywhere, media products 'are commodities through and through' and 'human beings are once more debased'. 'The colour film demolishes the genial old tavern to a greater extent

Table 21.3 ● Ownership of press media in the UK		
	Approximate share of market	
News International	35%	*Sun, Times, Sunday Times, News of the World*
Mirror Group	23–27%	*Mirror, Sunday Mirror, People*
United Newspapers	14% (9% for Sundays)	*Daily Express, Daily Star, Sunday Express*
Associated newspapers	15%	*Daily Mail, Mail on Sunday*

Note: These figures are approximate and meant only to indicate a broad level of concentration of the media in a few large firms

than bombs ever could: the film exterminates its imago.' It is 'mass deception', 'anti-enlightenment', and leads to subservience to blind authority (Adorno, 1991: 85–92).

Ideological state apparatuses: the French Marxist philosopher Louis Althusser (1918–90) saw a number of institutions (the media, but also education, religion, the family) as being independent of the state but functioning to reproduce the dominant ideologies through what he called the **ideological state apparatuses** (or ISAs as some have called them more popularly). These are *social institutions which reproduce the dominant ideology, independent of the state.* (In contrast, repressive apparatuses such as police and army employ more direct power.) Ideologies construct imaginary relations for people to live in, which help obscure the actual things that are going on (Althusser, 1971).

Critical evaluation
Conflict theories are persuasive in alerting us to media capital and bias. There is a growing world concentration of the mass media in the hands of a few major corporations and the research evidence suggests pervasive biases (especially over what is not allowed to be said in the media). But conflict theories may suffer from exaggeration. People are sometimes seen as being too much like passive victims and capital is seen as moving too coherently in favour of one outcome. In fact, media practices are complex and varied.

Symbolic interactionism

Hebert Blumer, the founder of symbolic interactionist analysis, was one of the first sociologists to conduct audience research on cinema going. As part of a widespread concern about the impact of films on young people, a series of investigations were set up in the late 1920s and early 1930s (popularly known as the Payne Studies, they were initiated by a pro-film censorship group, the Motion Picture Research Council). Blumer was involved with one of these that looked at young people. Straightforwardly, he asked some 1,500 young people to write 'motion-picture autobiographies', backed up with more selective interviews, group discussions and observations. He argued that to know what Impact media had on young people's lives, it is best to simply ask them. And following on from this, much of his ensuing book *Movies and Conduct* is given over to young people's first-hand accounts of the films they have seen – how they provide the basis of imitation, play, day dreams, emotional development and 'schemes of life'. He let the people speak for themselves. One entry – dealing with stereotypes – reads:

Female, 19, white college senior: – One thing these pictures did was to establish a permanent fear of Chinamen in my mind. To this day I do not see a Chinese person but what I think of him as being mixed up in some evil affair. I always pass them as quickly as possible if I meet them in the street, and refuse to go into a Chinese restaurant or laundry. (Blumer, 1933: 145)

Quite rightly, others more recently have been critical of his straightforward naiveté of approach. Denzin, for example, has recently been very critical of Blumer, suggesting that whilst progressive in method it was shrouded with Blumer's assumptions ('pro-middle class and anti-film', Denzin 1992: 107). It was also open to being used to crusade against film content and viewed texts unproblematically (Clough, 1992). True, Blumer's initial studies in the 1930s now look somewhat simple: but he was the first to take seriously audience responses.

Norman Denzin has focused on the importance of 'the movies' for understanding social life in the twentieth century. He considers the film and going to the cinema to be the key mode of narrative this century. Talking of the 'cinematic society', he suggests that watching films has shifted much of this century's experience by encouraging a more visual, looking society – a society which he sees as increasingly voyeuristic. Denzin's method is to look at films – ranging from *Blue Velvet* to *Rear Window* – to see how they display the cultural logic of society (Denzin, 1992, 1995).

Critical evaluation
Blumer was the founder of symbolic interactionism and Denzin is the leading proponent today. Whereas Blumer focused rather naively on what audiences said about films, Denzin ignores audiences altogether and engages in his own form of film theory.

Post-modern media theory

Over the past decade, a group of newer social theorists have come to highlight the centrality of the media in our lives. In particular, they have suggested that we now live our lives increasingly through the products of the mass media, which have come to have an autonomous existence of their own. We are media consumers. And the media messages – from Madonna's video to the soap opera *Brookside's* murder trials – become a new form of reality. We are awhirl and awash in signs.

Baudrillard (1929–) sees modern societies as concerned with the consumption of signs. Whilst in his earlier work he explored media 'codes', in his later work 'simulation' becomes the core of social life. Broadly, whatever is really happening in the world no longer matters, because people are coming to live so much in a media-mediated world, that reality gets bypassed. All we are left with are exploding (imploding) signs and **simulacra**, *worlds of media generated signs and images*. Just what these signs refer to in the world is no longer clearly distinguished.

One of Baudrillard's most famous (and disturbing) remarks concerned the Gulf War (16 January to 28 February 1991). He argued that it was a hyperreal representation on our television screens: the real battlefields were now replaced by media saturation. We can watch the bombings, hear the planning, see the war and all its atrocities from the comfort of our living room. The war is a simulation: we are not there, nor will we ever be there. All we will know is the hyperreality that media messages convey to us (Baudislland, 1991).

Once the media tried to provide copies of reality; but now they are their own reality. This is the post-modern world we live in. The masses for Baudrillard are mass media consumers. Everything is now reproduced – be it on video, TV, CDs or film. It comes to us already as a pre-experienced hyperreality.

Critical evaluation
This is a fashionable view that certainly places a great deal of importance on media images. But in that lies the critique. For Baudrillard is accused of excess. For him, it is often as if the Gulf War did not really happen, or indeed that any reality outside of the media really happens. This is a serious problem, not least since large numbers of the world's population are not caught up in the media – still millions have no access to the media. And of those that do, many can clearly distinguish between signs and realities.

Figure 21.1 ● A model of media analysis: Three questions

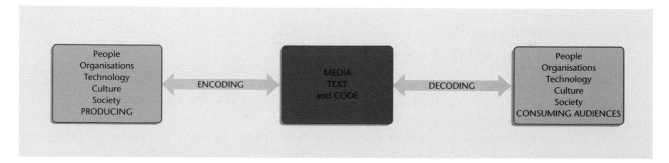

● The three questions of media analysis

Laswell once said that the goal of media research is to answer the question: who says what, in which channel, to whom with what effect? Following this, and putting it simply, we can say that media analysis directs our attention to three broad areas: codes, encoding and decoding (see Figure 21.1).

The first highlights the codes in **media texts**, *all media products such as television programmes, films, rock CDs, books, newspapers, web site pages etc.* **Codes** are *rule governed systems of signs.* The focus here is on the contents of the media and what organises them. It involves looking at specific contents like chat shows (on television and radio) film (for example, comedies or musicals) and 'stars' like Madonna or Oasis. Media texts are analysed for the messages they are trying to get across and their various biases.

A second area concerns the ways in which these media texts are produced. This involves looking at the technologies that emerge to present texts, along with the people who make programmes and their wider social locations. We are concerned here especially with **encoding**, *putting a message of any kind into a language* – spoken or written, verbal or pictorial. It involves looking at such matters as how journalists produce the news, how specific technologies like the Sony Walkman get manufactured for music production, or the organisation of finance in the ownership of media.

A third question looks at **decoding**, *the process by which we hear or read and understand a message.* Here the focus is on the audience. This involves looking at such matters as how families watch television, studying soap opera fans, or looking at the way gender may shape how films are viewed (Hall, 1980). All three act as a feedback loop.

In what follows, we will look at some examples of dealing with these questions.

Television news as an example

News is a central media product in modern societies. Not only was the news press the first major means of mass communication in the nineteenth century, today most TV channels adopt specific mechanisms for the delivery of news. Many radio stations in the UK punctuate their programmes with hourly or half-hourly news bulletins. And since the 1980s there have been continuous 'wall-to-wall' news channels like CNN which circulate around the world. Functionalist analysis may suggest that news serves an important information function in modern societies. Conflict theories may suggest that news presentation serves ideological functions and serves to mystify what is really going on through bias. Action theories would suggest the need to look at the ways in which people make the media and audiences come to 'read them'.

Codes: news may be seen as a coded text. It can be examined for the kinds of values and messages it gets across. We all know what televisions news is: many of us will watch it every day. But 'textual sociologists' attempt to see it as system of codes and values and, if the news does not fit these values, it will not work. Golding and Elliot in a classic study suggest that news values include:

● Featuring of personalities: stories need a human angle – people and personalities who have a story to tell. Abstractions and theories are not favoured, but interesting personal stories are.

● Elites: the featuring of big or well-known names is better than featuring 'nobodies'.

● Narrative structures that contains key elements of human drama: 'joy, sorrow, shock, fear, these are the stuff of news'.

● Good visuals and aesthetics: since television is a visual medium, news stories without good images becomes less newsworthy than ones with good images. Sometimes news stories may be included simply because there are good images!

● Entertainment values which attract large audiences: they must provide materials which are 'captivating, humorous, titillating, amusing or generally diverting'.

● Importance: the news item must have significance for large numbers of people in the audience.

● Proximity: news stories must be recent and relatively local. Foreign news must have local significance. The news in Norway cannot be the same as the news in Brazil.

● Brevity: nothing can last too long and everything must be packed with information. News is part of what has been called the 'three minute blip culture'.

● Negativity: 'bad news is good news'. It registers potential threats to social order.

● Recency: a premium is put on being first with the news. Once a competitor has the story, it becomes less significant. (Adapted from Golding and Elliott, 1979: 114–23)

Encoding: the encoding question asks about the ways in which a 'news story' is actually produced. Sociologists have done much work on this, and they have highlighted various layers of production.

A first layer looks at the actual *demands of the news programme* itself. Here there is an immediate daily time cycle, a planning structure which creates a routine agenda of predictable stories that provide the background of each day's production requirement' (Schlesinger, 1978: 79). Far from being 'news', much of it is planned and routine. Slots need filling: an opening story, a limited number of stories required to fill a fifteen minute space, good visuals, all following a regular schedule: it must be produced three times a day at the correct time. (If there is no news, something has to be found; and if there is too much news, some of it has to be edited out.) A second layer looks at the *day to day practices of news journalists*. Here a specific culture of work helps journalists look out for certain kinds of news and not others. It is 'purposive behaviour' (Molotch and Lester, 1974). A third layer sees the news as being structured by the *organisational demands of a bureaucracy*. We have seen in Chapter 7 how modern organisations tend to be highly ruled-governed agencies: news is produced through such rules. Most noticeable are the rules of news production that are tightly linked to a 'stop watch culture' (Schlesinger, 1978: 83). A fourth layer sees the news in the wider context of the *workings of the corporations*. Here such matters as its financial structure become important. News that is too offensive or disturbing may lose advertising revenue. Finally, the news may be linked up to wider concerns such as the *community needs and the dominant ideologies*. The Glasgow Media Group (1982) found that wider influences were at work, such that 'impartial news' often reflected a particular mind set of middle class values.

Decoding: the decoding issue turns to how actual audiences may interpret and watch the news. Here, the task is to get close to actual audiences to see the ways they make sense of the programmes they watch. Often this has a strongly gendered pattern; it may also be shaped by such things as class, age, ethnicity, sexuality. How we 'read' the media is known as audience ethnography (see below).

In one celebrated study, the UK media sociologist David Morley examined the audiences of *Nationwide* (a popular UK 1970s news programme). He works from the premise that the programme can be 'read' or viewed in a number of different ways. The text is **polysemic**, *open to many interpretations*. He was interested in showing the programme to a range of different groups (university arts students, trade unionists, apprentices, etc.) and getting their feed back. From this, Morley aimed to generate a typology of the 'decodings' made and to analyse their variety.

Broadly, what he found were three main positions in which the 'decoder' stood in relation to the text. For some, the meaning was taken fully within the framework which the message itself suggested (he calls this 'the dominant code'). For others, the meaning was broadly encoded this way, but through relating it to some specific concrete context which reflected the reader's own position the meaning was modified ('the negotiated code'). For still others, they recognised what was trying to be said, but rejected it and imposed a meaning that worked in an opposite way (an 'oppositional reading') (Morley, 1992: 89).

What is important about this approach is the way in which it never sees viewers as passive dummies just soaking up the news. Instead, the news is approached actively and audiences have to work to give it meanings.

● Looking at media content

A number of theories have been developed to help us analyse and 'read' the texts and images of the media. We will just look at two: genre theory and semiology. Others that could be looked at include narrative theory and code analysis.

Genre theory (from Latin 'genus' meaning type) helps us make sense of the seemingly chaotic flux of media programmes by identifying recognisable categories (Table 21.4). Each may then have its own set of rules and codes through which it is turned into a recognisable form.

As an example consider the soap opera – a very popular topic for media analysis. Whether one is a fan of *Eastenders, Home and Away, Emmerdale, Coronation Street* or countless others, certain broad features make them identifiable as a type of programme. Of course, the specific contents, characters and plots will vary. But as a type, soap operas are all likely to have:

Table 21.4 ● Television programmes and genre		
TV programmes can be identified by types		
Genre	**UK**	**Global**
News, current affairs	BBC News; ITN; *Panorama*	CNN
Documentaries	*Life on Earth*	*National Geographic*
Soap operas	*Archers* (Radio 4); *Eastenders*	*Home and Away* (Australian); *Dallas* (US)

- A never-ending story: story lines must always carry over to the next episode – there can be no closure as in a one hour drama.

- Regular cliff-hangers: each episode must come to some sort of climax. Every hour or half hour, the programme needs to have a crisis which will make the viewer wish to watch the next episode. The programme has to be a 'tease'.

- Core characters: the viewers become very familiar with the characters – they come to know a lot about them through watching many episodes. There are a lot of 'regulars' in soaps.

- Interweaving story lines: there is never just one or two plots, but a number. There are always several narrative strands proceeding at the same time.

- The unfolding text: narrative progression has to be fairly slow. Often a story line unfolds over weeks.

- A woman's genre: finally, women are more likely to feature in soaps – and women are more likely to watch them (see Allen, 1985, 1995; Geraghty, 1991)!

Semiology and the study of signs: As we have seen in Chapter 4, semiology is the study of signs. Semiology studies all signs: 'images, gestures, musical sounds, objects and the complex associations of all these, which form the content of ritual, convention or public entertainment' (Barthes, 1967: 9). Signs have no intrinsic or fixed meanings. Instead, their meaning is arbitrary and derived from the way they relate to other words and signs. Language has two components: *langue* (language) and *parole* (speech). The former is the rules and structures of language; the latter is its practice in actual speech and writing. Studying langue would enable the analyst to get at the underlying structures of language. Applied to the media, we become concerned with analysing the content of media as a system of signs, tracing out their relationships to each other – and possibly to an underlying pattern.

● Media audiences and media effects

One major concern in contemporary approaches to the mass media has been the audience and the impact of media upon them. Modern audiences differ from those of the past. Once – in theatres and stadiums – audiences were linked to a specific public setting, planned, organised and collectively shared. These days audiences have become much more fragmented and individualised. It is the difference between watching a film in a cinema and watching a video at home. One is public and shared; the other private and personalised.

The main concern of researchers has been to look at the ways in which media impacts audiences. One classic study which looked at the impact of television on children's lives gives a typically cautious conclusion:

For *some* children under *some* conditions *some* television is harmful. For *other* children under the *same* conditions, or for the *same* children under *other* conditions, it may be beneficial. For *most* children under *most* conditions, most television is neither harmful nor potentially beneficial! (Schramm, 1961)

Although there has been a long tradition of examining so-called media effects – what the media do to people – it is only fairly recently that researchers have switched the question from what the media do to people to what people do to the media. The classical 'effects literature' has tended to see audiences as fairly passive recipients of media messages. As we have seen above, the most extreme version of this is the hypodermic syringe model – where people are seen to be passively injected with media messages. Whilst no media analyst holds such a view today, it remains popular amongst public and media moralists. For instance, in the aftermath of the murder of a young child, Jamie Bulger, in the UK in 1993 by two young boys, the video of *Child's Play 2* (in which a similar kind of murder was to be seen) was evoked as a cause of the murder. Whilst it is possible to say the film may have

DIFFERENT VOICES

Race, gender and the mass media

Since it first captured the public imagination in the 1950s, television has placed the dominant segment of our population – white heterosexual males – at centre stage. Ethnic minorities were all but absent from television until the early 1970s; only in the last decade have programmes featured women in prominent roles; and only in the past few years have gay characters started to appear more regularly in programming.

Even when both sexes appear on camera, men generally play the brilliant detectives, fearless explorers and skilled surgeons. Women, by contrast, continue to be cast as the less capable characters, often prized primarily for their sexual attractiveness.

Change has come most slowly to advertising, which sells products by conforming to widely established cultural norms. Advertising thus presents the two sexes, more often than not, in stereotypical ways. Historically, ads have shown women in the home, happily using cleaning products, serving foods, modelling clothing and trying out new appliances. Men, on the other hand, predominate in ads for cars, travel, banking services, industrial companies and alcoholic beverages. The authoritative 'voiceover' – the faceless voice that promotes products on television and radio – is almost always male (Busby, 1975; Courtney and Whipple, 1983).

In a classic study of magazine and newspaper ads, Erving Goffman (1979) found other, more subtle biases. Men, he concluded, are photographed to appear taller than women, implying male superiority. Women were more frequently presented lying down (on sofas and beds) or, like children, seated on the floor. The expressions and gestures of men exude competence and authority, whereas women are more likely to appear in childlike poses. While men focus on the products being advertised, women direct their interest to men, conveying their supportive and submissive role.

Advertising also actively perpetuates Naomi Wolf's 'beauty myth', described in Chapter 13. The equation runs something like this: by embracing traditional notions of femininity and masculinity, we raise our prospects for personal and professional success. Thus, advertising commands masculine men to drive the 'right' car and feminine women to use beauty aids that will help them look younger and more attractive to men. ●

played a part – along with many other factors – it cannot be said to have simply caused it.

More recent approaches to the media audience tend to conduct ethnographic research on specific audiences. Thus, the researcher may enter a 'fan group' and see how they watch their favourite star. Or the researcher may observe and interview women as to how they watch soap operas and what they indeed like about them. In one celebrated study, David Morley entered families and observed the ways in which they watched the media.

Looking at 18 south London working-class families, Morley observed how they used television. One of his key themes is the way such viewing is structured by gender. Amongst his findings – which have to be seen as very provisional because of the scale of his study – he suggests:

- Adult men have most control over the programme choice, and the video is more likely to be controlled by 'dad'.

- Women are usually engaged in other domestic activities, and watch it more sporadically (except in 'solo' watching by day time). Husbands seem to watch more than wives.

- Men are more systematic and focused: they watch it more attentively.

- Men prefer sport and news, whilst women prefer drama and fiction features.

- Women are more likely to express guilt over their viewing habits; they also use it as a conversation piece more (Morley, 1986: Chapter 3).

The fragmentation of the mass audience

Although many critics have argued that this is the age of 'mass society', others have argued that what we are seeing is a breakdown of the population into hundreds of very different audiences. To take an example: the world of music used to be divisible into a few broad groupings. There was 'classical music', 'popular music', maybe 'jazz' and a few others. Now, as any browser at a mega record store will find, audiences for music have splintered in many directions: new age, ethnic, rock, classic rock, show tunes, country and western, punk, reggae, folk. But these break down categories further. Show tunes has its Sondheim *aficionados* who would not go near an Andrew Lloyd Weber score. And there are those who seek out the most obscure musicals that only ran for one night. And so on. What has happened is the emergence of many media markets – niche markets. At the same time, some 90 per cent of all albums sold in Europe are for rock or light music, 5–10 per cent are classical (Therborn, 1995: 224).

This may be depicted, as in Figure 21.2, as a move from media having elite audiences, through those having mass audiences to those having more specialised audiences. When a new medium appears it is usually adopted by an educational elite, before spreading out to a wider mass audience. After a while this splinters into a host of specialist groupings. What this means is that much media expansion takes place through increasingly specialised audiences.

● The globalisation of the media

Throughout the twentieth century, media have proliferated and become extended across the world. Indeed, they are one of the central mechanisms through which the processes of globalisation have taken place. Most countries are now connected to film, video, television satellites and cables. And the prognosis is that this will continue to grow in the twenty-first century.

The World Bank says that: 'The global economy is undergoing an Information Revolution that will be as significant in effect as the Industrial Revolution of the nineteenth century' (1997: 287). Indeed, worth some £1,000 billion in 1994, the World Bank reckons that it is growing faster than the global economy. Figure 21.4 charts some of the countries participating in the information economy.

In 1994 there were some 850 million television sets in more than 160 countries watched by 2.5 billion people per day. Since most of North America (with 110 million sets) and Europe (with over 140 million) are nearly saturated, the dominant growth areas are Africa, Asia and Central America (Barker, 1997: 4). Ien Ang's study of *Dallas* – a soap about a rich Texan oil family that was hugely popular in the mid-1980s – found it was being shown in 90 countries across the world (Ang, 1985).

We can distinguish three key aspects of this globalisation process.

The globalisation of means

The *means* for such proliferation have grown via new technologies. Many countries initially only had their own local systems, but with the growth of cable and satellite during the 1980s, this has changed (Table 21.5). Cable may not be very significant in the UK, but in the

Figure 21.2 ● Model of media specialisation

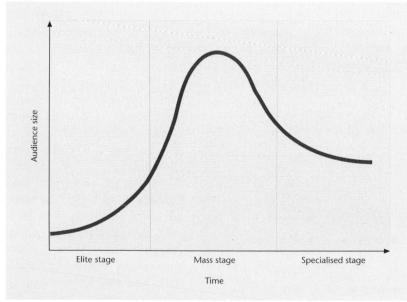

Source: W. Russell Neuman (1991)

Figure 21.3 ● **The size and fragmentation of audiences**

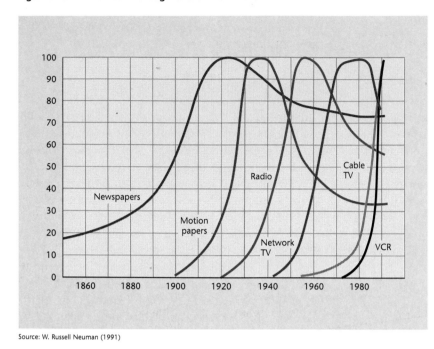

Source: W. Russell Neuman (1991)

The globalisation of content

The *content* of programmes has also become increasingly global. There are 'global totemic festivals' (Barker, 1997: 14) like Live Aid, World Cups, Olympics and the funeral of 'Diana', where it seems as if everyone in the world may be experiencing the same media events. This is also true of much live global coverage of many news events: wars, space probes, acts of terrorism, major new governments and disasters can all be screened around the world simultaneously.

Whilst all countries have their own specialist networks which usually provide their own local programming, much is also bought in. In Europe, it has been estimated that around two-thirds of TV programmes are 'home grown' European. The UK, the Netherlands and Belgium watch some 70 per cent European TV; in Denmark the figure is nearer 75 per cent; in Greece and Germany it is nearer 80 per cent. Nevertheless American films dominate West European markets. Likewise, the music market is strongly American although this is also an area where the British excel (Therborn, 1995: 223–4). It is not surprising that when people are questioned where they would like to live if they had to live abroad, most prefer the United States, Canada or Australia (Therborn, 1995: 224). And as Therborn (1995: 225) says, 'Europe is not a meaningful concept of current youth culture' (most of their popular music does not come from there).

Netherlands some 90 per cent of households are connected. Satellites increase the number of TV signals. ISDN networks (higher bandwidths) allow almost everyone to broadcast their own messages. During the 1990s, there has been a massive shift to 'digital transmission' of all kinds of data, and this – combined with satellite – has meant the rapid expansion of the super information highway: three cores of the global 'super information highway' are in North America, Europe and East Asia.

Barker has observed that there is a tendency for some genres of television to be recycled everywhere in approximately the same forms throughout the world. Thus, news and soap operas seem to travel very well. There *are* dif-

Table 21.5 ● **European cable and satellite reception equipment 1994 (percentage of equipped households)**

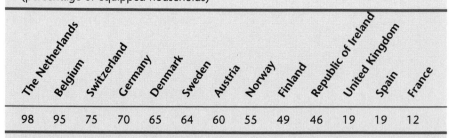

The Netherlands	Belgium	Switzerland	Germany	Denmark	Sweden	Austria	Norway	Finland	Republic of Ireland	United Kingdom	Spain	France
98	95	75	70	65	64	60	55	49	46	19	19	12

Source: Modified from *Cable and Satellite Europe*, September 1995. (Barker, 1997)

Jurgen Habermas: the changing public sphere

The German sociologist Jurgen Habermas (1929–) is considered one of the world's foremost contemporary social theorists.

Habermas has been concerned with the 'life world' (the immediate environment of the 'social actor') with knowledge and communication, and how it changes in the modern world.

Habermas is concerned with what he calls the changes in the public and private spheres of modern societies. The public sphere is 'a domain of our social life in which such a thing as public opinion can be formed . . . and is open in principle to all citizens' (Habermas, 1989). The public sphere is an arena where public debate flourishes, and ideas and opinions can grow. Habermas traces its history, suggesting that it was in seventeenth- and eigh-

teenth-century Europe that it developed a clear form. Between the realm of the state (see Chapter 16) and the private sphere of the family, there emerged a new public sphere which allowed people to exercise judgement and to critically engage in public debate. This may have been in the salons and coffee houses of the big European cities.

But nowadays, he worries, such debates have been narrowed by the collapse of this sphere into the mass media. It was originally the newspapers and the mass tabloids that first significantly brought about this change. They developed a much more commercial and consumer based culture which was linked much more to the privatised worlds of money and commerce rather than a public forum of debate.

He worries about the future of democracy as the media expand and proposes a theory of communicative action. He sees three forms of knowledge at work in society. First is instrumental knowledge which is technical and scientific. Much of this has worked against human progress and impoverished human lives. Second is hermeneutic knowledge, where the focus is on understanding. But Habermas looks for a third form of knowledge which could be 'emancipatory'. Believing in progress and modernity, he believes societies can only move forward if people can peel away all the irrationalities partially bestowed on them by media messages and arrive at a 'pure speech' situation in which they can understand clearly each other's ideas. At present this is made impossible because of technology. ●

ferences across cultures (there are still some 150 cultures to which the Australian soap *Neighbours* has not been exported! (Crofts, 1995: 102)). But overall Barker suggests a certain kind of international style may be developing. This includes:

● High production values: glossy and expensive
● Pleasing visual backgrounds: the landscapes of Australia, the beaches of California
● More action than in traditional soaps
● Hollywood style narrative mode
● Elements of melodrama over realism (Barker, 1997: 95)

Likewise, Barker finds news narration similar. What is news is fairly consistent from country to country, although there are some variations.

The globalisation of ownership and the decline of public television

Traditionally in Europe, radio and television have received *public finance* (via licences and taxes) to provide a *universal service for citizens* by producing programmes which have some form of public *accountability,* some r*egulation of content* and some *protection from competition.* The British Broadcasting Corporation is one classic instance of this. It accounts for about half of the viewing time but that proportion is now in decline. The BBC World Service – with a long history – is being overtaken by groups like CNN and MTV. And the story is the same throughout Europe. The Netherlands had 100 per cent public television in 1975; but by 1990 it had reduced to 58 per cent. In

France, it was 100 per cent in 1975, reduced to 33 per cent by 1990 (Barker, 1997: 32) (Figure 21.4).

Deregulated television is private and less accountable than public television. Its programmes are more 'market led'. There has been a real shift from a public service idea to a commercialised one with advertising at its core. But it goes further than this: the media is now often owned transnationally.

The five leading media firms in the world are Time-Warner (with sales approaching £17 billion in 1997), Disney (£16 billion), Bertelsmann (£10 billion, and the only Europe based firm), Viacom (£8 billion) and News Corporation (£7 billion). Typically, these firms have media holdings in a wider range of enterprises:

News Corporation, owned by Rupert Murdoch, has holdings in the following: Twentieth Century Fox (film, television and video and Fox News); 132 newspapers (in Australia, the UK, the United States); 25 magazines; book publishing; Asian Star Television; BSkyB Television satellite. Also large stakes in Germany's Vox channel; Sky Latin America; Japan Sky Broadcasting; Australian Foxtel Cable; Spanish El Canal Fox; India Sky Broadcasting; Channel V (an Asian music video channel); Hong Kong Phoenix satellite.

Rupert Murdoch: leading media tycoon

Source: Popperfoto

Time-Warner (the biggest, with an international labour force of around 340,000) has holdings in: 24 magazines (including *Time*), the second largest book publishing business in the world, Warner Bros. films, Warner music group, cinemas, comics, Home Box Office (the largest cable channel in the world), Six Flags theme parks, Warner Bros. retail stores, several global cable channels including CNN, TBS, TNY, Turner Classic movies, The Cartoon Network and CNN-SI all sports news channel, and on, and on (Herman and McChesney, 1997: Chapter 3).

Global media are transmitted internationally, received internationally, produced internationally; and they lead to massive international trading. Very often these transnational companies putting together the 'media texts' also connect with the equipment manufacturers, combining software and hardware, to make an overall 'synergy'. Barker cites the case of the film *The Last Action Hero*: 'This Schwarzenegger "blockbuster" was made by Columbia Pictures, owned by Sony Corporation. The soundtrack came from CBS, also owned by Sony, and it was screened in cinemas with digital sound systems made by Sony. In addition, Sony produced virtual reality and video games based on the film.' And, no doubt, these would be played on Sony screens (Barker, 1997: 25).

The rise of the Internet

Despite the significance of all the media forms discussed in this chapter – from film to television – there is one recent development that is generally considered to bring about the most profound changes of all. This is the emergence of the Internet. One study suggests that 25 per cent of US households will be connected by the end of 1997 (Herman and McChesney, 1997: 118). It is likely that this soon will be under the regulation of the media giants, as telecommunication firms merge and join forces with them. But it is also the case that at present it is the form of media which encourages globalisation in a highly individual and participatory manner.

The future of the media

Sociology has come increasingly to recognise that throughout the twentieth century, the mass media have come to play a growing importance in the lives of societies. This is not just true of the industrial West, but of nearly all cultures. Global 'mediasation' has become a major process as we enter the twenty-first

Figure 21.4 ● Global use of media: some examples

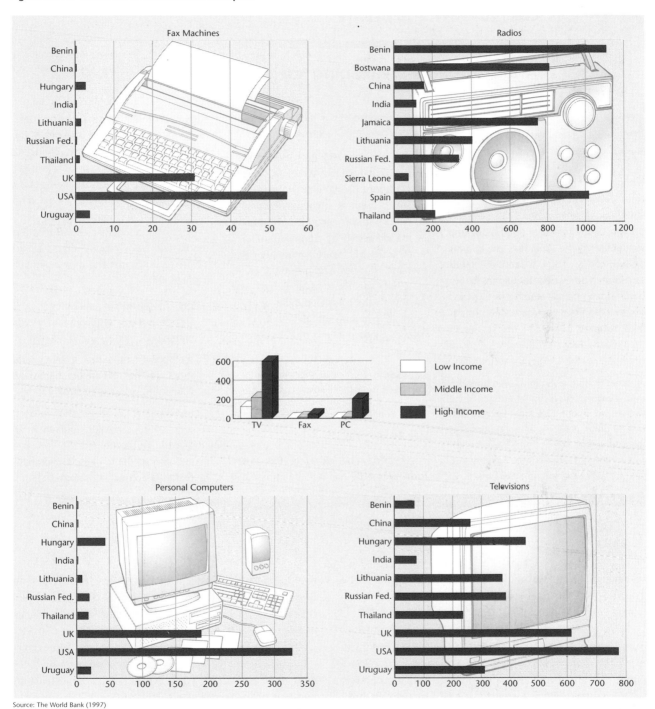

Source: The World Bank (1997)

CONTROVERSY AND DEBATE

Are the media weakening society?

Ever since its inception, the mass media have always been attacked as dangerous. It has at the centre of controversy. In the very earliest days, when books and novels started to be published, there were worries that these could be corrupting. As the earliest popular literature slowly became available to the 'masses', so it was denounced. In 1806, a Samuel P. Jarvis said that 'The evil consequences attendant upon novel reading are much greater than has generally been imagined' (Starker, 1989: 61). Much later, in the 1930s, radio programmes caused great alarm and Lyman Bryson wrote:

All great human inventions, even printing, even language itself, have proved to be two-edged swords. They can do as much evil as good. Radio is as great – and as dangerous – as any . . . and it can broadcast injury and discord and ugliness into the farthest reaches of inhabited space. To be lightminded about the radio is to jig along a precipice . . . Starker, 1989: 115

These days every new media form comes under attack. When Dungeons and Dragons (D&D) was first marketed in 1973 (with 8 million copies sold by 1985), it was accused of 'dabbling in the demonic' by *Christianity Today.* And attempts were made to link teenage suicides and murders to it. In 1992, the issue became 'rap and race' with the song Cop Killer by Ice-T prompting a boycott of Warner Bros. records by parents anxious about lyrics such as:

I'm 'bout to bust some shots off,
I'm 'bout to dust some cops off/

and a chant:

Die, Die, Die, Pig, Die.

This may be extreme. But every form of media has had its critics: the early tabloids and newspapers, Hollywood movies from the start of the twentieth century till now, children's comics, the 'plug in drug' of television, 'video nasties', pop music, computers. Over and over again, the media have been posed as a threat and a danger.

Media critics have claimed that the media can have serious effects on its audience. Amongst the many dangers it poses are:

● the fostering of passivity – the 'couch potato' syndrome of inertly watching;

● the growth of crime, violence and moral decline – the media shapes low values and provides bad role models;

● trivialisation: we are, in the words of one critic, 'amusing ourselves to death'. Authentic sports, religion and politics get trivialised. Even education becomes 'infotainment';

century. The full implications of this have yet to be grasped, but we need to consider at least three questions.

First, it seems likely that more and more of our lives – and those of our children – will come to be lived away from the real world and inside a media created one. Once the full implications of home multi-media start to be realised, will we spend less and less time in public space confronting real events and more and more time in a virtual space? Is the simulacrum arriving?

Second, the media world seems set to become increasingly a commercialised global one dominated by huge transnational corporations. To the extent that this happens, will this mean not only an increasing homogenisation of different cultures, but also a real threat to democracy as more and more of what we see in the world is regulated by high finance?

But third, the top Internet countries are overwhelmingly in the West: 90 per cent of users in 1995 were in North America and Western Europe. At least 80 per cent of the world's countries still lack communications technologies. And overwhelmingly, the typical user of the net is a North American male looking for entertainment. Although globalisation may be taking place, is this a process that will have serious consequences for the wider inequalities in society?

- the promotion of materialism and commercial values: most media comes with advertising to the forefront and this leads to a 'promotional culture'. Even the weather or the news gets identified with sponsorship;
- brainwashing, manipulation and mass conformity;
- the 'simulation' of the world, giving us pseudo-images and false realities. At its most extreme we come to inhabit an unreal media world, cut off from the more authentic experiences.

In short, mass media lead to a degenerating mass culture. As Bernard Rosenberg says: 'At its worst, mass culture threatens not merely to cretinise our taste but to brutalise our sense, while paving the way to totalitarianism' (in Starker, 1989: 13).

In contrast, media defenders reject these criticisms and argue that the media can:

- increase participation and creativity: viewers can be active and critical and use the media – they respond by writing letters, engaging in debates and the like;
- enhance the information a society has and help keep us aware of what is going on;
- increase public debate;
- extend access to all kinds of information and entertainment that previously were restricted to an elite class;
- provide diversity;
- reduce crime and enhance morality through making people more aware of issues.

In short, mass media can enhance a diverse, active and participatory culture.

Some modern media analysts such as Joli Jensen see the worry over the media as part of a continuing concern over modernity. The 'dangerous media', they suggest, are repeatedly compared with some mythical golden age in the past and taken to symbolise all the dangers of the modern world – rapid change, differences, a loss of clear authority, etc. They are constantly under attack because they are potent symbols of rapid change and a modern world hurtling into an unknown future. But media are in fact human made, are here to stay and we can shape them in the direction that we wish. They cannot in themselves be blamed for anything.

- **Continue the debate:**

1. Do you think that watching soap operas – the most popular form of television – can play any useful social role?
2. Do you think 'sport' has been degraded through being turned into a mass media event?
3. Look around you and see what form the attack on the media is currently taking. Dissect this latest example.
4. Weigh up the pros and cons of the new global communications systems. ●

Source: Joli Jensen, 1990.

KEY CONCEPTS ....

code rule governed system of signs

culture industry industry motivated by profit which produces all manner of cultural artefacts

cyber widely used prefix for anything connected to computers

cybernetics control systems using computers

decoding the process by which we hear or read and understand a message

encoding putting a message of any kind into a language

genre a species or type of media programme

ideological state apparatuses social institutions which reproduce the dominant ideology, independent of the state

mass medium any social or technological device used for the selection, transmission, reception of some information content

media texts all media products such as television programmes, films, rock CDs, books, newspapers, web site pages, etc.

oral culture culture with no written language,

dependent upon speech

polysemic open to many interpretations

simulacrum a world of media generated signs and images

CRITICAL-THINKING QUESTIONS ....

1. How does an 'oral culture' differ from a 'print culture'?

2. What are the three key areas of media study that need to be addressed? Select any one media item – such as a TV programme or a film – and examine the kinds of questions you would ask about it.

3. Compare the functionalist, conflict and interactionist theories of the media. What are the strengths and weaknesses of each?

4. Who owns the media? Using a reference book such as *Who Owns Whom?* examine the ownership of the

media and assess the concentration in a few powerful hands.

5. Examine one news programme on television. Consider the kinds of narratives that appear within it and discuss their appeal.

6. What is meant by 'audience ethnography'? Locate any one study which does this and review its findings. Then conduct one of your own on your favourite programme.

7. How far do you think mass media has now become globalised? Discuss the implications of this.

GOING FURTHER ....

Introductory reading

Media studies is a vast area of inquiry in itself and it clearly has strong links to cultural studies (introduced in Chapter 4). General introductions include:

Fred Inglis, *Media Theory: An Introduction* (Oxford: Blackwell, 1990).
    A short introduction to the whole field written in a readable and accessible fashion.

Denis McQuail, *Mass Communication Theory: An Introduction* (London: Sage, 3rd edn, 1993).
    A classic, comprehensive text book.

Paul Marris and Sue Thornham (eds.), *Media Studies: A Reader* (Edinburgh: Edinburgh University Press, 1996).
    A recent reader which covers the field broadly: there are now a great many of these! The first part looks at classical approaches, along with issues of production, text, ideology, feminism and reception. It ends with case studies of particular media forms such as soap operas, news and advertising.

Classic sources

Shearon A. Lowery and Melvin de Fleur (eds.), *Milestones in Mass Communication Research* (London: Longman, 1984, 1988).
    A text that discusses much of the earliest media work in the USA, focusing on 13 'milestones'. They are empirical, quantitative studies.

Peter Golding and Philip Elliot, *Making the News* (London: Longman, 1979).
    A now classic study which looks at the ways in which news is created.

Stan Cohen and Jock Young (eds.), *The Manufacture of News,* 2nd edn (London: Constable, 1981).
    A collection of articles on media and its construction, presentation and images. It includes an appendix on 'do it yourself' media sociology.

More advanced reading

Chris Barker, *Global Television: An Introduction* (Oxford: Blackwell, 1997).

Edward S. Herman and Robert W. McChesney, *The Global Media: The New Missonaries of Global Capitalism* (London: Cassell, 1997).

Two comprehensive reviews of the field and, in 1997, right up to date. The trouble is that this field changes so rapidly: by the time you read this it may already be out of date! The shape of things to come.

Dale Spender, *Nattering on the Net* (Melbourne, vii: Spinitex Press, 1996).

An important feminist contribution to the 'cyber' literature. Whilst she sees that women are excluded from this largely male space, she also sees its potential for women.

Nick Stevenson, *Understanding Media Cultures* (London: Sage, 1997).

A useful – though quite advanced – review of the major theories of the media, including Marxism, Baudrillard, Habermas and McLuhan – all briefly introduced in the chapter.

Shaun Moores, *Interpreting Audiences: the Ethnography of Media Consumption* (London: Sage, 1993).

Reviews the research on audiences whilst raising a series of critical problems with them.

R. Allen, *Channels of Discourse, Reassembled* (London: Routledge, 2nd edn, 1992).

The classic set of readings on all the major aspects of television. Required for 'telestudents'.

Joshua Meyrowitz, *No Sense of Place: The Impact of Electronic Media on Social Behaviour* (Oxford: Oxford University Press, 1986).

A classic study which draws upon Goffman and McLuhan to show the way in which television is changing the way we experience the world.

John Thompson, *The Media and Modernity: A Social Theory of Media* (Cambridge: Polity Press, 1995).

Examines the rise of media in modern societies.

Norman Denzin, *Images of the Postmodern: Social Theory and Contemporary Cinema* (London: Sage, 1991).

Introduces the idea of the postmodern, discusses the importance of cinema in the twentieth century, and analyses a number of films to show their relevance to modern thinking.

Other sources

A useful guide to the media in Europe is *The Media in Western Europe: The Euromedia Handbook* edited by Bernt Stubbe Ostergaard and the Euromedia Research Group (London: Sage, 2nd edn, 1997).

Based at London's South Bank, The Museum of the Moving Image (MOMI) provides an excellent documentary of the rise of the image society, especially television and film.

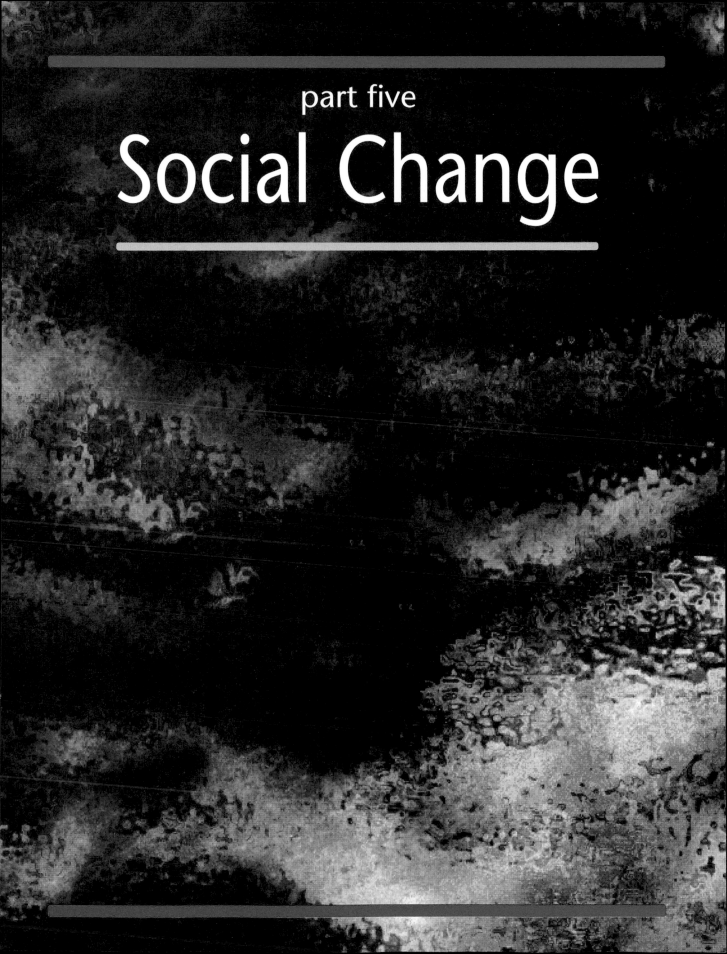

part five

Social Change

chapter twenty-two

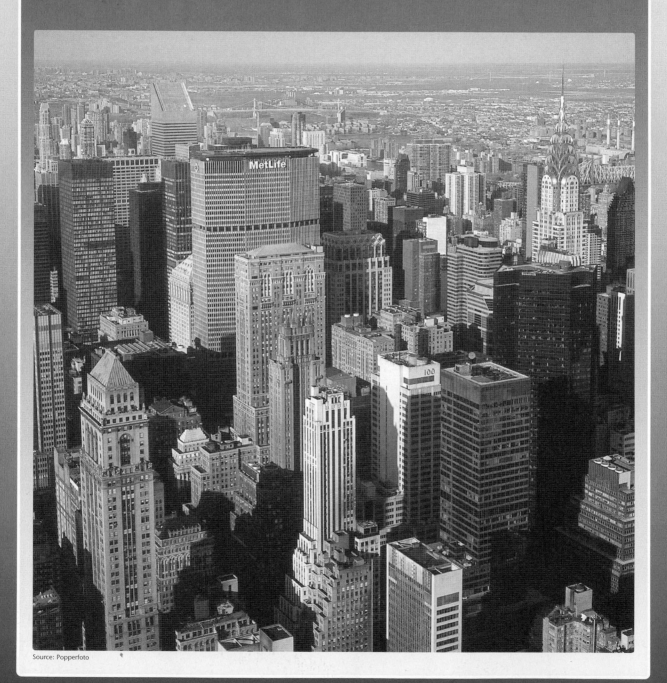

Source: Popperfoto

Population and Urbanisation

In 1519 a band of Spanish conquistadors led by Hernando Cortés reached Tenochtitlán, the capital of the Aztec empire. They were stunned by the beautiful, lake-encircled city, teeming with some 300,000 people – more than lived in any European city at that time. Gazing down broad streets, exploring magnificent stone temples, and examining the golden treasures of the royal palace, Cortés and his soldiers wondered if they were dreaming.

Cortés soon set his mind to looting the city's many priceless treasures. At first, he was repelled by the superior military forces of Montezuma and the Aztecs. But Cortés spent the next two years raising a vast army and finally returned to utterly destroy Tenochtitlán. On the rubble of this ancient urban centre, he constructed a new city in the European fashion – 'Ciudad Imperial de México', Mexico City.

Today Mexico City is once more fighting for its life. Its soaring population will reach 28 million by the end of this decade – 100 times the number that astonished Cortés. A triple burden of rising population, urban sprawl and desperate poverty weighs on Mexico as it does on much of today's world. This chapter examines both population growth and urbanisation – two powerful forces that have worked hand in hand to shape and reshape our planet for thousands of years. A steadily increasing population will be one of the most serious challenges facing the world in the coming century, and this compelling drama will be played out in cities of unprecedented size.

● Demography: the study of population

From the point at which the human species emerged about 250,000 BCE until several centuries ago, the population of the entire earth was only some 500 million – less than the number of Europeans today. Life for our ancestors was anything but certain; people were vulnerable to countless diseases, frequent injury and periodic natural disasters. Powerless in the face of such calamity, one might well be amazed that our species has managed to survive for 10,000 generations.

About 250 years ago, however, world population began to push upward. We now add around 90 million people to the planet each year, an increase that had made the global total 5.8 billion in mid-1996. There are twice as many people as there were in 1970; and the next 35 years will add another 2.5 billion – 90 per cent in the developing, low income regions. Thus in 2025, the population of the world is predicted to be 8.3 billion. Ironically, perhaps, human beings have been so successful in reproducing our species that the future well-being of humanity is again in doubt. Population density in the European Union is shown in Map 22.1.

The causes and consequences of this human drama form the core of **demography**, *the study of human population*. Demography (from Greek meaning 'description of people'), a close cousin of sociology, analyses the size and composition of a population as well as how people move from place to place. Although much demographic research is a numbers game, the discipline also poses crucial questions about the effects of population growth and its control. The following sections explain basic demographic concepts.

Fertility

The study of human population begins with how many people are born. **Fertility** is *the incidence of childbearing in a country's population*. During their childbearing years, from the onset of menstruation (typically in the early teens) to menopause (usually in the late forties), women are capable of bearing more than 20 children. But *fecundity*, or maximum possible childbearing, is sharply reduced in practice by cultural norms, finances and personal choice.

Demographers measure fertility using the **total period fertility rate (TPFR)**, *the average number of children each woman would have in her lifetime if the average number of children born to all women of childbearing age in any given year remained constant during that woman's childbearing years*. This measure tells us the average number of children women have had in the past, and allows us to project how many they may be likely to have in the future. In 1964, the TPFR for women in Britain was 2.95 children. By 1995, British women generally chose to have smaller families, and the TPFR dropped to 1.71 children (*Social Trends*, 1997: 32).

This measure has gained favour among demographers because the calculation is not affected if the proportion of women in different age groups changes. This flexibility is important, as was noted in Chapter 14 ('Ageing and the Elderly'), because the proportion of elderly women (as well as men) is increasing in industrialised societies. As will be discussed later in this chapter, the proportion of young people is increasing in many less developed countries. The TPFR thus allows for valuable comparisons between countries in the modern world.

The accuracy of the projections can weaken, however, if women change the average age at which they start having children. In Europe, women are generally waiting longer to have their first baby. While many women became pregnant in their teens prior to the Second World War, the average age of first birth had risen to the late twenties in many European countries by the 1990s. At the turn of the century, European women now have more educational and career opportunities than they enjoyed in earlier decades, as well as having access to more reliable family planning methods. Many women are choosing to seize these opportunities before they start a family. Even so, some demographers predict that women who have children, on average, are unlikely to wait much longer than they are now to have their first baby, and TPFRs may increase very slightly in the coming years (*Social Trends*, 1997: 32).

Mortality

Population size is also affected by **mortality**, *the incidence of death in a country's population*. In addition to the TPFR, demographers use a **crude death rate**, *the number of deaths in a given year for every thousand people in a population*. In 1995 there were 642,000 deaths in the UK population of 58.6 million, yielding a crude death rate of 10.9. The crude death rate in industrialised countries has fallen sharply over the last century. In the UK in 1900, over 17 of every thousand people died each year (*Social Trends*, 1997: 33). As Figure 22.1

Figure 22.1 ● Crude death rates, infant mortality rates and life expectancy, 1995

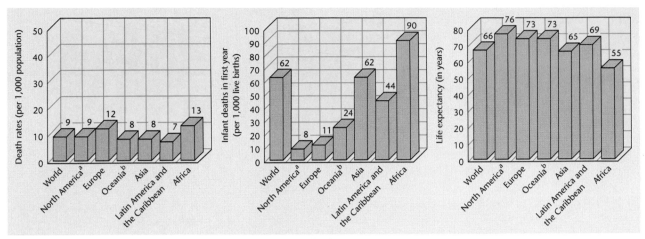

ªUnited States and Canada   ᵇAustralia, New Zealand and South Pacific Islands

Source: Population Reference Bureau (1995)

shows, higher crude death rates are still common in non-industrialised countries today. Mortality data also permits the calculation of **life expectancy**, *the average to which people in a given society are likely to live*. Males born in Britain in 1997 can expect to live 74 years, while females can look to nearly 80 years.

A fourth widely used demographic measure is the **infant mortality rate**, *the number of deaths among infants under one year of age for each thousand live births in a given year*. Again, as Figure 21.1 displays, infant mortality is generally higher in less developed countries than in the industrialised world – largely due to the higher standard of Western hospital facilities. In the UK, infant mortality has declined dramatically over the last 30 years, as Figure 22.2 shows. This figure also indicates that baby girls have a slightly higher

Figure 22.2 ● Infant mortality in Europe

	1961	1971	1981	1991	1995	2001*
Males	26.3	20.2	12.7	8.3	6.9	4.7
Females	18.2	15.5	9.5	6.3	5.4	4.0

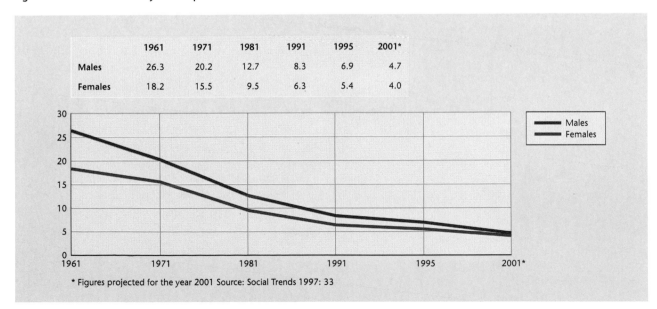

* Figures projected for the year 2001 Source: Social Trends 1997: 33

chance of survival than baby boys, though this gap is narrowing. Infant mortality can also vary between ethnic groups. In the United States, white and Asian babies are more likely to survive past infancy than African American babies, for example.

Migration

Population size is also affected by **migration**, *the movement of people into and out of a particular territory*. Migration is sometimes involuntary, such as the forcible transportation of 10 million Africans to the

Map 22.1 ● **Population density in the European Union, 1992**

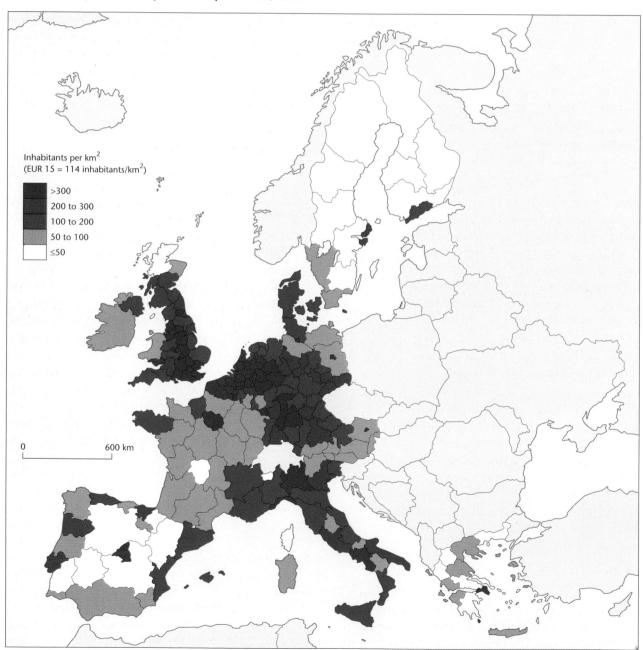

Inhabitants per km^2
(EUR 15 = 114 inhabitants/km^2)

- >300
- 200 to 300
- 100 to 200
- 50 to 100
- ≤50

0   600 km

Source: Europe in Figures, Eurostat (1995, p. 99)

Western Hemisphere as slaves (Sowell, 1981). Voluntary migration, however, is usually the result of complex 'push–pull' factors. Dissatisfaction with life in poor countries may 'push' people to move, just as the higher living standards of rich nations may exert a powerful 'pull'. England experienced no net change due to migration in 1995; by contrast, some 1.25 million immigrants enter the United States each year.

People's movement into a territory, commonly termed *immigration*, is measured as an *in-migration rate*, calculated as the number of people entering an area for every thousand people in the population. Movement out of a territory, or *emigration*, is measured in terms of the *out-migration rate*, the number leaving for every thousand people. Both types of migration usually occur simultaneously; their difference is called the **net migration rate**. All nations also experience internal migration, that is, movement within their borders from one region to another.

Migration has become an issue of particular social concern in many parts of Europe. As was discussed in Chapter 12 ('Race, Ethnicity and Migration'), some white Europeans fear the immigration of non-white peoples with different cultures and languages from other parts of the globe and seek to restrict numbers of immigrants from outside Europe as a response. Indeed, the rising number of racist attacks against immigrant communities in many European countries reflects the more extreme end of this spectrum. Many small rural communities also worry over the out-migration of young people and, in some cases, the in-migration of the elderly. Without new generations to carry on their traditions, some rural communities may disappear. Additionally, the member governments of the European Union periodically worry about so-called 'benefit tourists', people who move from one country offering less public support to the poor to another country with more generous benefits. For this reason, many politicians would like to standardise some benefits to spread the cost of supporting the less well off more evenly.

Population growth

Fertility, mortality and migration all affect a society's population. Map 22.2 shows that population growth in industrialised nations is well below the world average of 1.5 per cent. The earth's low-growth continents include Europe (shrinking by 0.1 per cent annually),

North America (0.7 per cent growth) and Oceania (1.2 per cent growth). Asia, with 1.7 per cent growth, stands near the global average; while Latin America (1.9 per cent growth) and Africa (2.8 per cent growth) comprise the high-growth regions of the world. *Natural increase* (more births than deaths) accounts for the majority of population expansion in the high-growth regions.

A handy rule of thumb is that dividing a society's population growth rate into the number 70 yields the *doubling time* in years. Thus, annual growth of 2.8 per cent means that the African population will double in twenty-five years. The population is growing most rapidly in countries with the fewest resources to cope with more people (Population Reference Bureau, 1995).

Population composition

Demographers also study the composition of a society's population at a given point in time. One simple variable is the **sex ratio**, *the number of males for every hundred females in a given population*. Sex ratios are usually below 100 because women typically outlive men. In India, however, the sex ratio is 108. More males than females survive in India, as well as in parts of East Asia, much of the Middle East and North Africa, because parents value sons more than daughters. Thus parents are more likely to abort a female foetus or, after birth, to provide less care to females than to males.

A more complex measure is the **age–sex pyramid**, *a graphic representation of the age and sex of a population*. Figure 22.3 presents the age–sex pyramid for the United Kingdom. The rough pyramid shape of these figures results from higher mortality as people age. Looking at the UK pyramid, the bulge corresponding to ages 20 to 49 reflects high birth rates from the mid-1940s to the late 1960s, resulting in the *baby boom*. The contraction just below this band represents the *baby bust* that followed as the birth rate dipped from 1957 to a low 1.71 children per woman in 1995 (*Social Trends* 1997: 32).

Age–sex pyramids not only reflect a society's history, they foretell its future. The age–sex pyramid for Mexico, like that of other lower-income nations, is wide at the bottom (reflecting higher birth rates) and narrows quickly by what we would call middle age (due to higher mortality). Mexico, in short, is a much

WINDOW ON THE WORLD

Map 22.2 ● Population growth in global perspective

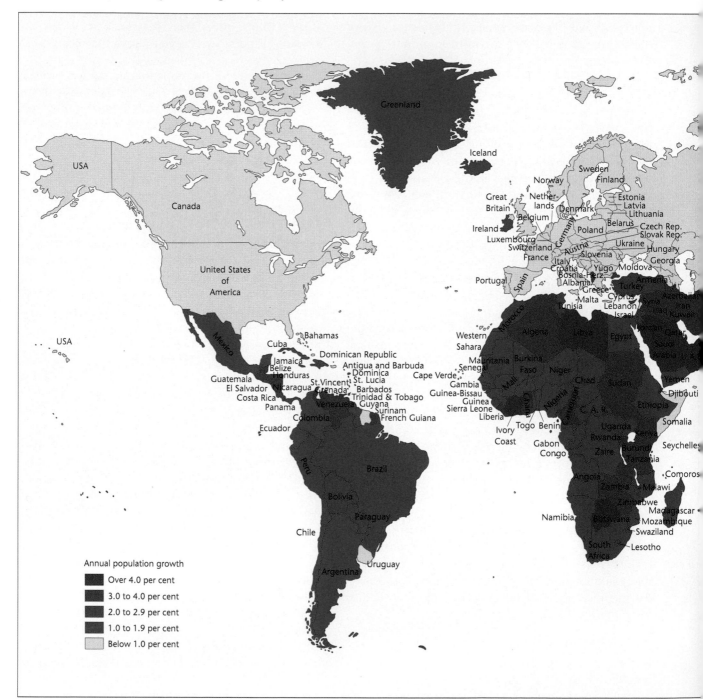

Annual population growth

- Over 4.0 per cent
- 3.0 to 4.0 per cent
- 2.0 to 2.9 per cent
- 1.0 to 1.9 per cent
- Below 1.0 per cent

Source: *Peters Atlas of the World* (1990), with statistics updated by the author.

The richest countries of the world – including the United States, Canada, and the nations of Europe – have growth rates below 1 per cent. The nations of Latin America and Asia typically have growth rates approaching 2 per cent, which double a population in 35 years. The continent of Africa has an overall growth rate of 2.8 per cent, which cuts the doubling time to less than 24 years. In global perspective, we see that a society's standard of living is closely related to its rate of population growth: Population is rising fastest in the world regions that can least afford to support more people.

Figure 22.3 ● Age–sex population pyramid: UK

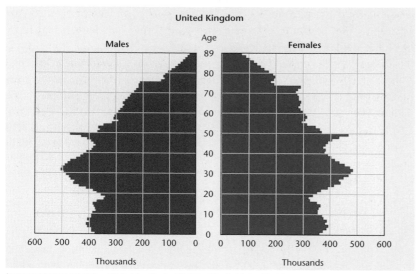

Source: *Social Trends*, 27, 1992, p. 29, Social and Regional Statistics Office for National Statistics, Eurostat (1995)

younger society with a median age of 20. With a larger share of females still in their childbearing years, we can understand why Mexico (Figure 22.4) has a relatively high TPFR, and why its annual rate of population growth (2.2 per cent) is rising almost four times higher than the 0.6 per cent growth rate in its northern neighbour, the United States.

Figure 22.4 ● Age–sex population pyramid: Mexico

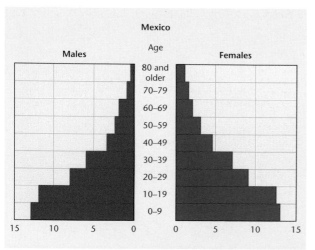

Source: US Bureau of the Census and Mexican Census data

● History and theory of population growth

Throughout most of human history, societies favoured large families since human labour was the key to productivity. Additionally, until the development of rubber condoms 150 years ago, controlling birth was uncertain at best. But if birth rates were high, so were death rates, as populations were periodically ravaged by infectious diseases. Thus world population at the dawn of civilisation, about 8000 BCE, hovered well below 100 million.

Figure 22.5 marks a demographic shift which began in about 1800, as the earth's population reached the 1 billion mark. Humans reached the next billion by 1930, barely a century later! The global population reached 3 billion by 1962 – after just 32 years and 4 billion by 1974, a scant twelve years later. The rate of world population increase has recently slowed, but in mid-1996, the

Figure 22.5 ● The increase in world population, 1700–2100

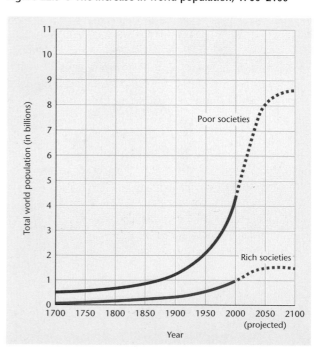

world population was estimated at 5.8 billion. In no previous century did the world's population even double. In the twentieth century, it has increased *fourfold*.

Currently, global population is increasing by 86 million people each year, with more than 90 per cent of this growth in poor societies. At this rate, the earth's people will number 6 billion early in the next century, probably reaching 8.3 billion by 2025 and passing 10 billion a century from now. Without a change in global consumption and living patterns, this increase will have dramatic social and environmental consequences. For this reason, a number of scholars have reflected on the potential impacts of population growth. This chapter now assesses some of the more influential perspectives.

Malthusian theory

The sudden population growth two centuries ago sparked the development of demography. Thomas Robert Malthus (1766–1834), an English clergyman and economist, noted that the number of people in the world had begun to increase geometrically (that is, doubling each time, 2, 4, 8, 16, 32, etc.). Even though people were improving farming technology and techniques, Malthus feared that the limited range of farmland could only sustain an *arithmetic increase* (as in the series 2, 3, 4, 5, 6) in the production of food (1926; orig. 1798). He concluded that the world might head towards a period of catastrophic starvation.

Malthus noted that people could slow the tide of population increase through *preventive checks*, like family planning, sexual abstinence and delayed marriages; however, people objected to birth control on religious grounds, and his common sense told Malthus that people would not abstain from sex or marry very much later. He also predicted that such *positive checks* as famine, disease and war would slow – but not prevent – the progression towards the final catastrophe, a vision that earned him the nickname of 'the dismal parson'.

Critical evaluation
Fortunately for us, Malthus's predictions were flawed. By 1850, the birth rate in Europe began to drop, partly because children were becoming more of an economic liability than an asset and partly because people began to use condoms. Second, Malthus underestimated human ingenuity. Irrigation, fertilisers and pesticides have increased farm production far more than he imagined. Some critics also noted that poor regions suffer deaths from war and famine disproportionately and objected to viewing suffering as a 'law of nature' rather than the product of inequality.

Still, we should not entirely dismiss Malthus's distressing prediction. First, habitable land, clean water and fresh air are certainly finite. Greater industrial productivity has taken a toll on the natural environment. Additionally, as medical advances have lowered death rates, the world population has risen even faster. This planet cannot sustain an indefinite increase in the number of people.

Demographic transition theory

Malthus's rather crude analysis has been superseded by **demographic transition theory**, *a thesis linking demographic changes to a society's level of technological development*. Why did world population soar after 1800? Why is population increase much higher in poor countries than in rich nations? Demographic transition theory answers these questions by analysing birth and death rates at four stages of a society's technological development. As shown in Figure 22.6, societies yet to industrialise, those at Stage 1, have high birth rates because of the economic value of children, the absence of effective family planning and the high risk that children will not survive to adulthood. Death rates, too, are high, due to periodic outbreaks of plague

Figure 22.6 ● Demographic transition theory

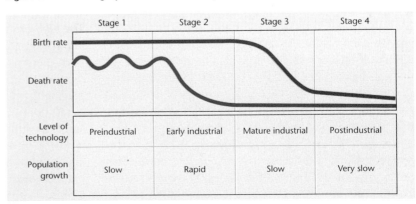

or other infectious disease, low living standards and a lack of medical technology. But deaths almost offset births, so population increase is modest.

Stage 2, the onset of industrialisation, brings a demographic transition as population surges upward. Technology expands food supplies and science combats disease. Death rates fall sharply but birth rates remain high, resulting in rapid population growth. It was in an era like this that Malthus formulated his ideas, and that goes a long way towards explaining his pessimism. Most of the world's least economically developed societies today are still in this high-growth stage.

In Stage 3, a mature industrial economy, birth rates drop, finally coming into line with death rates and, once again, curbing population growth. Fertility falls, because most children born do survive to adulthood, and rising living standards make raising children expensive. Affluence, in other words, transforms offspring from economic assets into economic liabilities. Smaller families, also favoured by women working outside the home, are made possible by the widespread availability of family planning. As birth rates follow death rates downward, population growth slows further.

The most recent stage corresponds to a post-industrial economy. The birth rate in such societies continues to fall, in part because dual-income couples gradually become the norm and partly because the costs of raising children continue to rise. This trend, coupled with steady death rates, means that, at best, population grows only very slowly. Recent years have witnessed a natural *decrease* in Europe's population.

Critical evaluation

Demographic transition theory suggests that technology holds the key to demographic shifts. Instead of the runaway population increase Malthus feared, this analysis foresees technology reining in population growth. Demographic transition theory dovetails with modernisation theory, one approach to global development examined in Chapter 11 ('Global Stratification').

Modernisation theorists are optimistic that industrialisation will also solve the population problems that now are placing strains on poor countries. But critics, notably dependency theorists, counter that current economic arrangements only ensure continued poverty in much of the world. Unless there is a significant redistribution of global resources, they maintain,

our planet will become increasingly divided into industrialised 'haves', enjoying low population growth, and non industrialised 'have-nots', struggling in vain to feed soaring populations.

Global population today

A brief survey of population trends around the world today reveals a growing gap between events in richer and poorer nations. Understanding these trends is the first step to understanding the nature of the population problem.

The low-growth North

When the Industrial Revolution began, growth in Western European and North American populations peaked at 3 per cent annually, doubling the population in little more than one generation. But, since then, growth rates have eased downward throughout the Northern hemisphere. The natural increase from births over deaths in Europe dropped from 7.7 per thousand in 1960 to 1.00 per thousand in 1990. As Europe entered Stage 4, the birth rate neared the replacement level of 2.1 children per woman, a point demographers designate as **zero population growth**, *the level of reproduction migration and death that maintains population at a steady state*. Demographers argue that most of Europe will be in steep population decline by the end of the first decade of the twenty-first century (Figure 22.7).

But at present Europe's population is actually increasing, due to a second key factor, in-migration. In 1993, the migratory balance in the EU worked out at 2.8 per 1,000 (Germany and Luxembourg had large increases, while Ireland lost almost 2 people per 1,000, though Irish outflow has begun to reverse in 1997). In 1992, there were some 16 million 'foreigners' living in Europe – 4.3 per cent of the total population.

The high-growth South

Population growth is a serious and increasing problem in the poor societies of the Southern hemisphere. Only a few nations lack industrial technology altogether, placing them at demographic transition theory's Stage 1. Most of Latin America, Africa and Asia has moved to Stage 2, still primarily agricultural but with some industry. In these nations, advanced medical technology (much supplied by rich societies) has sharply reduced death rates, but birth rates remain high. A look back at Figure 22.4 shows that poor societies now

Figure 22.7 ● Population of the EU as a percentage of world population

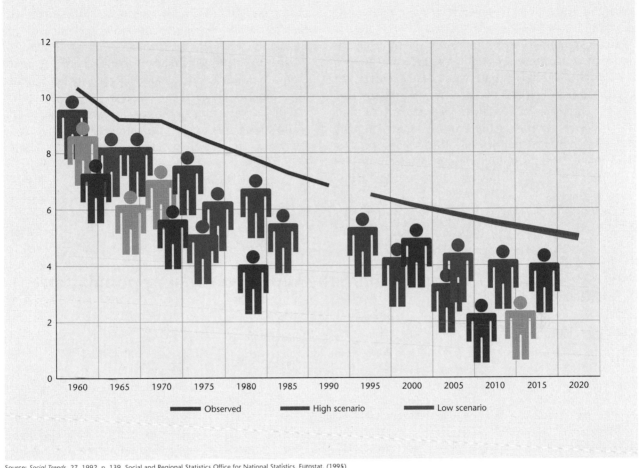

Source: *Social Trends*, 27, 1992, p. 139, Social and Regional Statistics Office for National Statistics, Eurostat, (1995)

account for two-thirds of the earth's people, a proportion that continues to rise.

In poor countries, urban families average four to five children; in rural areas, the number is often six to eight (The World Bank, 1991). No one doubts that world population simply cannot keep increasing at anything like its current rate. At a 1994 global population conference in Cairo, delegates from 180 nations agreed not only on the need for vigorous action to contain population growth, but also pointed out the crucial link between population control and the status of women. The box offers a closer look.

In the last decade, the world has made significant progress in lowering fertility. At the same time, however, mortality rates are falling. Although few would

oppose medical programmes that save lives, especially mostly of children, this trend exerts upward pressure on population. In fact, population growth in most low-income regions of the world is due *primarily* to declining death rates. After about 1920, when Europe and North America began to export advances in scientific medicine, nutrition and sanitation around the world, mortality tumbled. Since then, inoculations against infectious diseases and the use of antibiotics and insecticides have pushed down death rates with stunning effectiveness. For example, in Sri Lanka, malaria caused half of all deaths in the 1930s; a decade later, insecticides used to kill malaria-carrying mosquitoes cut the malaria death toll in half. Although we hail such an achievement, this technological advance sent Sri Lanka's population soaring. Similarly, India's infant mortality rate slid from 130 in 1975 to 74 in 1995, a decline that has helped boost that nation's population to 950 million.

Improvement in access to family planning in the developing world is clearly necessary, but how it should be introduced and who should direct the change in population is an open question. Many people in less developed countries view family planning initiatives coming from the West as racist – arguing that people in rich nations have little real regard for the welfare of the world's poor and instead only wish to curb the potential for immigration from the South to the North and the propensity for violence in overcrowded regions from which the North extracts natural resources. Policies of previous governments in India and China that have forced people to limit family size have proved highly unpopular among many groups in each country. Some people in both richer and poorer countries suggest that the best way to control population growth is to distribute the world's resources and wealth more fairly between all countries, and to expand educational and career opportunities for women everywhere.

CONTROVERSY AND DEBATE

Empowering women, the key to controlling population growth

Sohad Ahmad lives in a village 50 miles south of Cairo, Egypt's capital city. Her husband is a farmer and her family is poor. At first glance, one might conclude that this woman's situation fits a stereotype all too typical in low-income countries: desperate poverty pushing families to have more and more children to work the fields and earn more income. But this is not the case.

Sohad Ahmad has had only two children, and she and her husband will have no more. Egypt's rising population has already created such a demand for land that her family could not afford more even if they could farm it. More importantly, Sohad Ahmad does not want her life defined only by childbearing. Thus she has made a personal decision to have no more children.

Women like Sohad Ahmad who are taking control of their fertility and seeking greater opportunities are more and more common across Egypt. Indeed, this country has made great progress in reducing its annual population growth from 3.0 per cent just ten years ago to 2.3 per cent today. This is why the International Conference on Population and Development selected Cairo for its historic 1994 meeting.

The 1994 Cairo conference was not the first of its kind. But it stands out in several respects. First, it had an unprecedented base of participation, with representatives from 180 nations. In addition, delegates from more than 1,200 non-governmental organisations also attended the meeting. Second, the Cairo conference reached virtual consensus on a new path towards effective control of global population: elevating the standing of women.

In the past, population control programmes have been limited to making birth control technology available to women. This is a crucial objective, since only half the world's married women make use of effective birth control. But it has become clear that more than technology is needed to curb population increase. The larger picture shows that, even with available birth control, population continues to grow in societies that define women's primary responsibility as raising children.

Dr Nafis Sadik, an Egyptian woman who heads United Nations efforts at population control, sums up the new approach to lowering birth rates: give women more choices and they will have fewer children. In other words, women with access to schooling and jobs, who can decide when and if they wish to marry and who bear children as a matter of choice will limit their fertility. The door to schooling must be open to older women too, Dr Sadik adds, since they often exercise great influence in local communities. The lesson of the Cairo conference, and building evidence from countries around the world, is that controlling population and raising the social standing of women are inseparable objectives. ●

Sources: Linden, 1994; Ashford, 1995.

● Urbanisation: the growth of cities

For most of human history, the sights and sounds of great cities such as Hong Kong, Paris or Los Angeles were completely unknown. The world's people lived in small, nomadic groups, moving as they depleted vegetation or searched for migratory game. Humans survived for tens of thousands of years without permanent settlements. Cities first emerged in the Middle East, then arose on all the continents, but held only a tiny fraction of the earth's people until very recently.

Today, the population of the world's largest five cities exceeds the total planetary population when cities first developed. By 1950, nearly 80 cities had populations in excess of 1 million; by 1994, that number exceeded 280 (Figure 22.8, see page 623). The United Nations has predicted that within the next ten years, half of the world's population – half of the projected 6.6 billion people – will live in cities (*Social Trends*, 1997: 37). These figures testify to the steady march of **urbanisation**, *the concentration of humanity into cities*. Urbanisation both redistributes the popula-

Dr Nafiz Sadik is in charge of United Nations efforts to monitor and control the growth of world population. In her view, success in controlling population growth depends directly on our ability to expand the opportunities for education and paid employment for women – especially in poor countries.

Source: SABA Press Photos, Inc. – Nijlah Feanny

tion within a society and transforms many patterns of social life. We will trace these changes in terms of three urban revolutions: the emergence of cities beginning 12,000 years ago, the development of industrial cities after 1750 and the explosive growth of cities in low-income countries today.

The evolution of cities

Cities are a relatively new development in human history. Only about 12,000 years ago did our ancestors found the earliest permanent settlements, setting the stage for the *first urban revolution*. As glaciers drew back at the end of the last ice age, people congregated in warm regions with fertile soil. At the same time, humans discovered how to domesticate animals and cultivate crops. Whereas hunting and gathering demanded continual movement, raising food required people to remain in one place (Lenski, Nolan and Lenski, 1995). Domesticating animals and plants also yielded a material surplus, which freed some people from concentrating on food production and allowed them to build shelters, make tools, weave clothing and take part in religious rituals. Thus the founding of cities, made possible by favourable ecology and changing technology, was truly revolutionary, enhancing productive specialisation and raising living standards as never before.

The first cities

Historians identify Jericho as the first city. This settlement lies to the north of the Dead Sea in disputed land currently occupied by Israel. About 8000 BCE, Jericho contained about 600 people. By 4000 BCE, numerous cities were flourishing in the Fertile Crescent between the Tigris and Euphrates rivers in present-day Iraq, and urban settlement had begun along the Nile River in Egypt.

Some cities, with populations reaching 50,000, became centres of urban empires. Priest-kings wielded absolute power over lesser nobles, administrators, artisans, soldiers and farmers. Slaves, captured in frequent military campaigns, laboured to build monumental structures like the pyramids of Egypt (Kenyon, 1957; Hamblin, 1973; Stavrianos, 1983; Lenski, Nolan and Lenski, 1995).

In at least three other areas of the world, cities developed independently. Several large, complex settlements bordered the Indus River in present-day

Pakistan starting about 2500 BCE. Scholars date Chinese cities from 2000 BCE. And in Latin America, urban centres arose around 1500 BCE (Lamberg-Karlovsky, 1973; Change, 1977; Coe and Diehl, 1980).

Preindustrial European cities

Urbanisation in Europe began about 1800 BCE on the Mediterranean island of Crete. Cities soon spread throughout Greece, resulting in more than 100 city-states, of which Athens is the most famous. During its Golden Age, lasting barely a century after 500 BCE, Athenians made major contributions to the Western way of life in philosophy, the arts and politics. Yet Athenian society, numbering some 300,000, rested on the labour of slaves, who comprised a third of the population. Their democratic principles notwithstanding, Athenian men also denied the rights of citizenship to women and foreigners (Mumford, 1961; Gouldner, 1965; Stavrianos, 1983).

As Greek civilisation faded, the city of Rome grew to almost 1 million inhabitants and became the centre of a vast empire. By the first century CE, the militaristic Romans had subdued much of northern Africa, Europe and the Middle East. In the process, Rome spread its language, arts and technology. Four centuries later, the Roman Empire fell into disarray, a victim of its gargantuan size, internal corruption and militaristic appetite. Yet, between them, the Greeks and Romans founded cities across Europe from the Atlantic Ocean all the way to Asia, including Vienna, Paris, London and Constantinople.

The fall of the Roman Empire initiated an era of urban decline in Europe lasting 600 years. Cities became smaller as people drew back within defensive walls and competing warlords battled for territory. About the eleventh century, the 'Dark Ages' came to an end as a semblance of peace allowed trade to bring life to cities once again.

Expanding trade prompted medieval cities to tear down their walls. Amsterdam grew considerably from the fourteenth century, as it became more prominent in trade. Beneath towering cathedrals, the narrow and winding streets of London, Brussels and Florence soon teemed with merchants, artisans, priests, pedlars, nobles and servants. Typically, occupational groups such as bakers, keymakers and carpenters clustered together in distinct sections or 'quarters'. Ethnic groups also inhabited their own neighbourhoods, often because people kept them out of other districts. The term ghetto (from the Italian word *borghetto*, meaning 'outside the city walls') first described the segregation of Jews in medieval Venice.

The growth of industrial European cities

Throughout the Middle Ages, steadily increasing commerce enriched a new urban middle class or *bourgeoisie* (from the French, meaning 'of the town'). By the fifteenth century, the power of the bourgeoisie rivalled that of the hereditary nobility. In the 1400s Paris became the largest European city with a population of over a quarter of a million people.

By 1750 industrialisation was well under way, triggering a *second urban revolution*, first in Europe and then in North America. Factories unleashed productive power as never before, causing cities to grow to unprecedented size. London, the largest European city in 1700, with 550,000 people, swelled to 6.5 million by 1900 (A. Weber, 1963; orig. 1899; Chandler and Fox, 1974). Most of this increase was due to migration from rural areas by people seeking a better standard of living.

Cities not only grew but changed shape as well. The industrial-capitalist city replaced older irregular streets with broad, straight boulevards, which accommodated the increasing flow of commercial traffic. Steam and electric trams, too, criss-crossed the expanding cities. Lewis Mumford (1961) adds that developers divided cities into regular-sized lots, making land a commodity to be bought and sold. Finally, the cathedrals that had guided the life of medieval cities were soon dwarfed by towering, brightly lit and frantic central business districts made up of banks, retail stores and office buildings. Built for business, cities became increasingly crowded and impersonal. Crime rates rose. Especially at the outset, a small number of industrialists lived in grand style, while for most adults and children, factory work proved exhausting and provided bare subsistence.

In 1810, 20 per cent of the British population lived in cities and towns. By 1910 the figure was nearer 80 per cent (Kumar, 1978). Taking Europe as a whole, Therborn (1995: 184) notes that the proportion of European peoples living in cities escalated from a tenth in 1800, to a third by 1900, to two-thirds by 1989. Although European cities have often continued to grow significantly, they have usually had major geographical and political restrictions placed on their development. Consequently, European cities have not tended to reach the proportions of some cities in the newly industrialising world.

The shape of modern urban life

The twentieth century has seen living spaces changing in a number of directions, from the growth of central cities to expansion beyond suburbs. The pace of urban change has accelerated with time.

The great metropolis: 1860–1950

Following the First World War, waves of people deserted the countryside for cities in hopes of obtaining better jobs. This growth marked the era of the **metropolis** (from Greek words meaning 'mother city'), *a large city that socially and economically dominates an urban area*. Metropolises soon became the manufacturing, commercial and residential centres. The concentration of industrial technology not only generated expansion of the population but also changed the physical shape of cities. From the three- or four-storey towns in the United States in 1850, steel girders and mechanical lifts raised structures over ten storey high in 1880. In 1930, New York's Empire State Building became an urban wonder, a true 'skyscraper' stretching 102 storeys into the clouds.

Decentralisation: commuter towns and the suburbs

The industrial metropolis reached its peak during reconstruction after the Second World War. Since then, something of a turnaround, termed urban decentralisation, has occurred as people have deserted the city centres for outlying suburbs. Many large cities stopped growing, and some lost considerable population, after 1950. During the 1970s the population of Paris and London dropped by around 20 per cent. Instead of clustering in densely packed central cities, urban populations expanded outward.

Just as central cities flourished a century ago, we have recently witnessed the expansion of both new towns and **suburbs**, *urban areas beyond the political boundaries of a city*. They began to grow late in the nineteenth century as railways and buses enabled people to work in city centres yet leave behind the centralised congestion when they went home to quieter dormitory communities. The suburban trend caught on more quickly in the United States than in Europe.

Cheaper cars and declining land prices, and the need to move from seriously overcrowded cities like London, gradually also led to the development of new towns, like Stevenage in Hertfordshire or Basildon in Essex. Here home ownership catered to more prosperous working class people and council housing estates catered for the less well off.

Following the consumers, business, too, began moving to the new towns. And large, often impersonal, shopping centres started to replace the city centre stores of the metropolitan era. Manufacturing companies also decentralised into industrial parks far from the high property taxes, congested streets and crime growth identified with inner cities. The development of the motorway system, with its ring roads encircling central cities, made moving out to the new towns or the suburbs almost irresistible for residents and business people alike.

Suburbanisation also came at the cost of conformity. In the United States one of the most famous suburban sprawls was Levittown, the brainchild of the American developer Abraham Levitt. It was derided by critics as a field of look-a-like boxes – a label which aptly suits many of the council estates in Britain as well. Additionally, as businesses have centralised into large chain stores, suburban shopping districts increasingly resemble each other. The main variation often is only the order in which the major department stores and so forth are arranged. But these suburbs also developed a more worrying form of conformity, as communities like Levittown excluded black, Asian and Hispanic residents (Gans, 1982). Indeed, racial prejudice against increasing numbers of immigrants and ethnic minorities fuelled the growth of suburbs, prompting many whites to flee to homogeneous, high-prestige enclaves.

Moreover, this rapid growth in suburbs and new towns soon threw older cities into a financial problems. Population decline meant falling tax revenues. The overall result has often been inner-city decay. To many middle-class white people, the deteriorating inner cities became synonymous with slum housing, crime, drugs, unemployment, the poor and minorities. This perception fuelled wave after wave of 'white flight' and urban decline. Suburbs may have their share of poor housing, congestion and crime, but they still appeal to many people because they remain largely white, unlike the inner cities whose populations encompass a greater share of ethnic minorities.

Gentrification

The location of ghettos and centres of urban prosperity, however, do change over time. This change largely results from the process of gentrification, whereby areas in decline are transformed into areas of prosperity. Business and politicians periodically co-operate, with businesses providing the money and labour to restore or rebuild facilities and politicians providing tax and legal incentives to improve the profitability of these 'urban recycling' schemes. The London Docklands, eight and a half square miles of East London, was recently transformed from run-down docks and poverty-stricken dwellings to a prosperous business community dotted with luxury flats and trendy boutiques. Gentrification is a process of moving wealth back into the metropolis, but this process carries a heavy price. Urban ghettos are the homes of many poor people, and cheap housing and low wage jobs do not fit comfortably into high profit renewal programmes. Often, the poor residents of gentrified areas get pushed aside and are left to relocate themselves in other poor and overcrowded areas (Brownhill, 1990). Like suburbanisation, gentrification in Europe and the United States is a process which more often has worked to the benefit of white people at the expense of ethnic minorities.

Megacities and megalopolis: the rise of size

In 1950, only London (with 8 million residents) and New York (with 12.3 million residents) were megacities – defined as a city with a population exceeding 8 million (World Resources Unit, 1996). But by 1990 there were 21 megacities, with 16 in the developing world. Some such cities, like Shanghai and Seoul, are compact; others, like Bangkok and Manila, sprawl over a considerable area. The continuing decentralisation of cities has also produced vast urban areas that encompass numerous municipalities. In the early 1960s, the French geographer Jean Gottmann (1961) coined the term **megalopolis** to designate *a vast urban region containing a number of cities and their surrounding suburbs*. Although a megalopolis is composed of hundreds of separate cities and suburbs, from an airline at night, one observes what appears to be a single continuous city.

The world city

In 1986, John Friedman developed the idea of world cities – large, urban regions, highly interconnected, through which finance, economic decision-making and culture flows. These cities cannot be understood outside of the major world-wide network of finance. They are cities with much economic power, commanding global investments and the concentration and accumulation of capital. In Europe, only London and Paris can be seen as world cities (see Table 22.1 and Figure 22.8), though other cities, including Frankfurt, Brussels and Amsterdam are also important. London, along with Tokyo and New York, emerged as one of three leading centres of world finance. Whilst

Table 22.1 ● The world's ten largest urban areas, 1980 and 2000

1980	
Urban area	Population (in millions)
New York, USA	16.5
Tokyo–Yokohama, Japan	14.4
Mexico City, Mexico	14.0
Los Angeles–Long Beach, USA	10.6
Shanghai, China	10.0
Buenos Aires, Argentina	9.7
Paris, France	8.5
Moscow, USSR	8.0
Beijing, China	8.0
Chicago, USA	7.7

2000 (projected)	
Urban area	Population (in millions)
Tokyo–Yokohama, Japan	30.0
Mexico City, Mexico	27.9
São Paulo, Brazil	25.4
Seoul, South Korea	22.0
Bombay, India	15.4
New York, USA	14.7
Osaka–Kobe–Kyoto, Japan	14.3
Tehran, Iran	14.3
Rio de Janeiro, Brazil	14.2
Calcutta, India	14.1

Sources: United Nations (1995) and US Bureau of the Census (1995)

Figure 22.8 ● Hierarchy of world cities

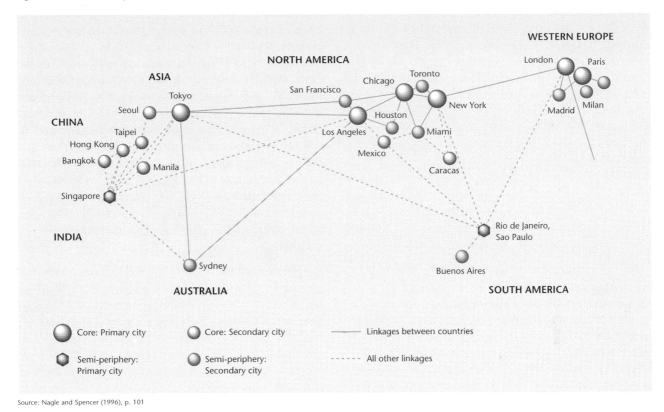

Source: Nagle and Spencer (1996), p. 101

these cities are the homes of stateless corporations and international systems of finance, often housed in spectacular sky scraping buildings, they also have a growing number of poor people – often immigrants – who work for low wages.

Urban tensions

With so many processes in the rise of cities, from the expansion of work with very low wages, low job security and few benefits, to suburbanisation and gentrification, working against the poorest residents, it is small wonder that tensions between city elites and poor people result. Sometimes these tensions arise on a small scale, such as with acts of vandalism and petty crime. Occasionally, they may erupt into riots. A series of riots broke out in the UK in the last decade, in

Major city

Source: Popperfoto

Bristol in 1980, in Brixton, Southall, Toxteth and Moss Side in 1981; and again in Brixton and Toxteth, as well as in Broadwater Farm (Tottenham) and Handsworth (Birmingham), in 1985. While these riots mainly reflected Afro-Caribbean grievances, they provided a forum for youths and older poor people from many ethnic groups to vent their frustrations. Like the more internationally famous riots in Los Angeles following the acquittal of white police officers who had beaten the black motorist Rodney King unconscious, these riots generally broke out in response to an act of violence perpetrated against a poor person. Such riots do nothing to solve the long-term problems of the poor and have served to reinforce the stereotypes held by the residents of gentrified city areas and suburbs that the poor constitute a problem which has to be controlled.

● Urbanisation as a way of life

Commentators have increasingly realised that contemporary cities have given rise to distinctive social experience. The Parisian poet Charles Baudelaire (1821–67) described the *flaneur*, *a social type who wanders cities, enjoying the sights and the crowd*. Subsequently a number of sociologists, Toennies, Durkheim, Simmel, Park and Wirth amongst them, started to analyse the city as a distinctly modern form which brought a pervasive newness, a concern with the transitory and obsessive individualism, along with a new excitement and sophistication.

Ferdinand Toennies: *Gemeinschaft* and *Gesellschaft*

A century ago, the German sociologist Ferdinand Toennies (1855–1937) set out to chronicle the social characteristics of the new industrial metropolis. He contrasted rural and urban life through two concepts that have become a lasting part of sociology's terminology.

Toennies (1963; orig. 1887) used the German word *Gemeinschaft* (meaning roughly 'community') to refer to *a type of social organisation by which people are bound closely together by kinship and tradition*. Rural villagers, Toennies explained, are joined by kinship, neighbourhood and friendship. *Gemeinschaft*, then, describes any social setting in which people form what amounts to a single primary group.

By and large, argued Toennies, *Gemeinschaft* is not found in the modern city. On the contrary, urbanisation fosters **Gesellschaft** (a German word meaning roughly 'association'), *a type of social organisation by which people have weak social ties and considerable self-interest*. In the *Gesellschaft* scheme, people are motivated by their own needs and desires rather than a drive to enhance the well-being of everyone. City dwellers, Toennies suggested, have little sense of community or common identity and look to others mostly as a means of advancing their individual goals. Thus Toennies saw in urbanisation the erosion of primary social relations in favour of the temporary, impersonal ties typical of business.

Emile Durkheim: mechanical and organic solidarity

Durkheim, whose ideas are detailed in Chapter 3 ('Society'), agreed with much of Toennies's thinking about cities. Yet Durkheim's analysis highlighted patterns of social solidarity, what binds people together. He conceptualised traditional, rural life as *mechanical solidarity*, social bonds based on shared moral sentiments. With its emphasis on conformity to tradition, this concept bears a striking similarity to Toennies's *Gemeinschaft*.

But if urbanisation erodes mechanical solidarity, Durkheim explained, it also generates a new type of bonding, which he termed *organic solidarity*, social bonds based on specialisation and interdependence. This concept, which parallels Toennies's *Gesellschaft*, reveals a key difference between the two thinkers.

While each thought the expansion of industry and cities would undermine traditional social patterns, Durkheim took a more optimistic view of this historical transformation. Where societies had been built on *likeness*, Durkheim now observed social organisation based on *difference*. Finally, as noted in Chapter 4, Durkheim did not miss the fact that urban society typically offers more individual choice, moral tolerance and personal privacy than people find in rural villages. In short, Durkheim concluded, something may be lost in the process of urbanisation, but much is gained.

Georg Simmel: the blasé urbanite

We previously encountered the ideas of German sociologist Georg Simmel (1858–1918) when we looked at how size affects the social dynamics of small groups

(Chapter 7, 'Groups and Organisations'). Simmel (1964; orig. 1905) also turned his characteristic micro-level focus to the city, probing how urban life shapes people's attitudes and behaviour. From the point of view of the individual, Simmel explained, the city is a crush of people, objects and events. Because the urbanite is easily overwhelmed with stimulation, he continued, a *blasé attitude* emerges as a coping strategy. That is, city people learn to respond selectively by tuning out much of what goes on around them. City dwellers are not without sensitivity and compassion for others, although they sometimes seem 'cold and heartless'. But urban detachment, as Simmel saw it, is better understood as a technique for social survival by which people stand aloof from most others so they can devote their time and energy to those who really matter.

The Chicago School: Robert Park and Louis Wirth

Sociologists in the United States eagerly joined their European colleagues in exploring the rapidly growing cities. The first major sociology programme in the United States took root a century ago at the University of Chicago. Chicago, then a new metropolis exploding with population and cultural diversity, became the research focus for generations of sociologists, and the work of these men and women yielded a rich understanding of many dimensions of urban life. Although inspired by European theorists like Toennies, Durkheim and Simmel, their unique contribution to urban sociology was in making the city itself a laboratory for actual research.

Perhaps the greatest urban sociologist of all was Robert Park, who for decades provided the leadership that established sociology in the United States. Park is introduced in the box. A second major figure in the Chicago School of urban sociology was Louis Wirth (1897–1952). Wirth's (1938) best-known contribution is a brief essay in which he systematically blended the ideas of Toennies, Durkheim, Simmel and Park into a comprehensive theory of urban life.

Wirth began by defining the city as a setting with a large, dense and diverse population. These traits, he argued, combine to form an impersonal, superficial and transitory way of life. Sharing the teeming streets, urbanites surely come into contact with many more people than rural residents do. But, if city people pay any mind to others, they usually know them only in terms of *what they do*: as bus driver, florist or shop assistant, for instance.

Urban relationships are not only specialised and impersonal, Wirth explained, they are also founded on self-interest. For example, shoppers view grocers as the source of goods, while grocers see shoppers as a source of income. Urban people may pleasantly exchange greetings, but friendship is not the reason for their interaction. Finally, limited social involvement coupled with great social diversity also make city dwellers more tolerant than rural villagers. Rural communities often jealously enforce their narrow traditions, but the heterogeneous population of a city rarely shares any single code of moral conduct (T. C. Wilson, 1985, 1995).

Critical evaluation

On balance, early European and US urban sociological research offers a mixed view of urban living. Toennies and Wirth, especially, worried that the personal ties and traditional morality of rural life are lost in the anonymous rush of the city. On the other hand, Durkheim and Park emphasised urbanism's positive face, including greater personal autonomy and a wider range of life choices.

What of Wirth's specific claims about urbanism as a way of life? Decades of research have provided support for only some of his conclusions. Wirth correctly maintained that urban settings do sustain a weaker sense of community than do rural areas. But one can easily forget that conflict is found in the countryside as well as the city. Furthermore, while urbanites treat most people impersonally, they typically welcome such privacy and, of course, they do maintain close personal relationships with a select few (Keller, 1968; Cox, 1971; Macionis, 1978; Wellman, 1979; Lee et al., 1984). Where the analysis of Wirth and others falls short, too, is in painting urbanism in broad strokes that overlook the effects of class, race and gender. Herbert Gans (1968) explains that there are many types of urbanites, rich and poor, Asian, black and white, women and men – all leading distinctive lives. In fact, cities often intensify these social differences. That is, we see the extent of social diversity most clearly in cities where different categories of people reside in the largest numbers (Spates and Macionis, 1987).

chapter twenty-three

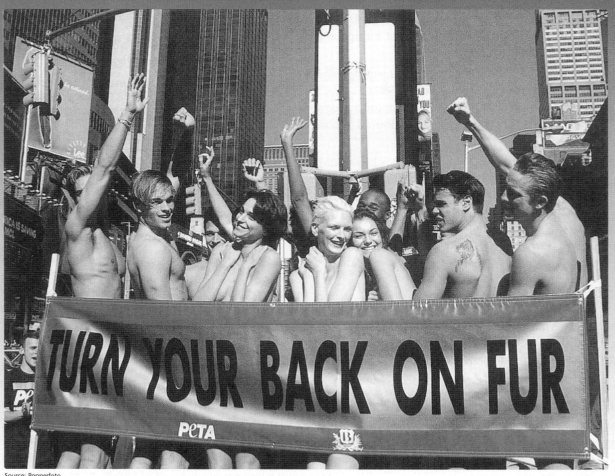

Source: Popperfoto

Environment and the Risk Society

The tiny island of Nauru (pronounced NAH-roo) is the world's smallest and most isolated country. Just eight square miles of windswept sand and coral reef, Nauru lies in the South Pacific, roughly 1,700 miles north-east of Australia and hundreds of miles from its nearest neighbour.

Another notable fact is that Nauru's 7,500 people are among the richest on earth. Do they own petrol wells? No, their wealth comes from bird droppings. Over hundreds of thousands of years, the excrement from sea birds roosting here has

Source: Woodfin Camp & Associates – Michael Friedel

fossilised into a rich phosphate fertiliser. In 1907, German colonists began mining the phosphate, an industry the Australians continued after they took control of the island in 1917. In 1968, Nauru became independent, so that the mining revenues went to the local people, who control a trust fund valued at almost £64 million.

But all is not well on Nauru. Ninety per cent of the island has now been strip-mined. This gives the island yet another distinction – as the most environmentally ravaged place on earth. Its once lush vegetation is all but gone, and in its place lies an eerie moonscape of bare rock canyons. The people, whose easy income from phosphate led them to abandon farming decades ago, now import their food – mostly high-fat tinned meats enjoyed with crisps and beer. As a result, most Nauruans are overweight, suffering from diabetes and high blood pressure. Today, few live past the age of 60. Most now realise that their island is no longer habitable. The Nauruans may have money in the bank, but they have lost their way of life and now face the grim reality of abandoning their ancestral home (Shenon, 1995).

Nauru may seem too far removed from our lives to have much meaning. But the tragic events that turned this one-time island paradise into an ugly and desolate wasteland are instructive for people everywhere. There have been many similar disasters that have gained wider public attention: the slag heap slide at Aberfan in Wales which buried a school in 1966; the industrial accident in Bhopal, India, which killed 3,000 and injured hundreds of thousands; the spate of oil tanker groundings which have decimated sea life off the shores of Alaska, Britain and Ireland in the 1990s; the nuclear explosion at Chernobyl; and even the scare over 'mad cow disease' and its links to CJD. In the modern world, environmental disasters have become common.

These 'symbolic' disasters can conceal a much more pervasive damage. For instance, the Torrey Canyon oil slick deposited some 117,000 tons of oil in 1967 and killed between 40,000 and 100,000 birds. Significant as this was, it fades when compared to the total annual oil spillage of around 3.6 million tons! As one analyst concluded, humanity's remaking of the earth during the last two centuries may well exceed changes to our planet from all causes over the last billion years (Milbrath, 1989).

These disasters often arise from the human pursuit of improvements in mining, agriculture, housing, industry and transportation. Many of these changes have benefited some people. A high proportion of people in rich nations now enjoy a level of material comfort that our ancestors scarcely could have imagined. However, as the Nauruans learned, such achievements carry both costs and risks. As this chapter explains, the way of life that has evolved in rich societies places such great strain on the earth's natural environment that it threatens the future of the entire planet.

● Ecology: the study of the natural environment

This chapter draws on **ecology**, *the study of the interaction of living organisms and the natural environment.* Researchers from many disciplines have contributed to this field, but this chapter will focus on those aspects of ecology that have a direct connection to the human social interactions.

The concept of the **natural environment** refers to *the earth's surface and atmosphere, including various living organisms as well as the air, water, soil and other resources necessary to sustain life.* Like every other living species, humans are dependent on the natural environment for everything from basic food, clothing and shelter to the materials and advanced sources of energy needed to construct and operate our vehicles and all kinds of electronic devices. Yet humans stand apart from other species in our capacity for culture; we alone take deliberate action to remake the world according to our own interests and desires. Thus our species is unique in its capacity to transform the world, for better and worse.

The role of sociology

One might wonder what many of the topics found in this chapter – including solid waste, pollution, acid rain, global warming and loss of biodiversity – are doing in a sociology text. Yet, as Leo Marx (1994) points out, all of these problems arise from human activities, not the 'natural world' operating on its own. Thus, such ecological issues are also *social* issues.

Though most social scientists may not have the technical training to assess the scientific evidence accumulating about climate change, sociologists can make three vital contributions to ecological debates. First, and perhaps most important, sociologists can demonstrate how human social patterns have caused mounting stress on the natural environment. That is, sociologists can spotlight how environmental problems are linked to particular cultural values, as well as specific political and economic arrangements (Cylke, 1993, 1995; Redclift and Benton, 1994).

Second, sociologists can monitor the public pulse on many environmental issues, reporting people's thoughts and fears (whether grounded or not) about these controversies. Moreover, sociologists analyse why certain categories of people fall on one side of political debates over an environmental issue or another (Roberts, 1993). Third, sociologists can explore what 'the environment' means to people of varying social backgrounds.

The global dimension

Any comprehensive study of the natural environment must also be global in scope. Regardless of humanity's political divisions into nation-states, the planet constitutes a single **ecosystem**, defined as *the system composed of the interaction of all living organisms and their natural environment*. The Greek meaning of eco is 'house', which reminds us of the simple fact that our planet is our home.

Even a brief look at the operation of the global ecosystem confirms that all living things and their natural environment are *interrelated*. Changes to any part of the natural environment ripple through the entire ecosystem, so that what happens in one part of the world inevitably has consequences in another.

Advocates of the Gaia hypothesis have suggested that planet earth itself should be seen as a living organism, inside which humans and other species each have a vital part to play.

Consider the effects of our use of chlorofluorocarbons (CFCs) as a propellant in aerosol spray cans and as a gas in refrigerators, freezers and air conditioners. CFCs may have improved our lives in various ways; but as they were released into the atmosphere, they reacted with sunlight to form chlorine atoms, which, in turn, depleted ozone. The ozone layer in the atmosphere serves to limit the amount of harmful ultraviolet radiation reaching the earth from the sun. Thus, recent evidence of a 'hole' in the ozone layer (in the atmosphere over Antarctica) may produce a rise in human skin cancers and countless other effects to plants and animals (Clarke, 1984a). While an international agreement has been reached to phase out the use of CFCs, many unscrupulous people continue to prefer to maximise their short-term convenience by continuing to use CFCs. By 1997, the black market global trade in CFCs rivalled the trade in narcotics (Clover, 1996). Moreover, in spite of global efforts to cut other emissions, some soft drink companies seek to market a new self-cooling can, which will chill warm drinks in two minutes when opened – and release nearly as much pollution as the cars we drive today (Clover, 1997).

Given the complexity of the global ecosystem, many threats to the environment go unrecognised. Few Australians who purchased fertiliser for their gardens gave any thought to how they were contributing to the destruction of the island of Nauru, described in the chapter opening. Similarly, as the box explains, the popular, although seemingly innocent, act of eating fast-food has significant environmental effects in other parts of the world.

The historical dimension

How did humanity gain the power to threaten the natural environment? The most basic part of the answer lies in our capacity for culture, that is, to cultivate the earth. As humans have devised more powerful forms of *technology*, humans have gained the ability to make and remake the world as we choose.

Members of societies with simple technology – the hunters and gatherers described in Chapter 3

GLOBAL SOCIOLOGY

The global ecosystem: the environmental consequences of everyday choices

People living in high-income countries, such as most of those in Europe, have the greatest power to affect the earth's ecosystem for the simple reason that they consume so much of the planet's resources. Thus, small, everyday decisions about how to live can add up to large consequences for the planet as a whole.

Consider the commonplace practice of enjoying a burger. McDonald's and dozens of other fast-food chains serve billions of burgers each year to eager customers across the world. This appetite for beef creates a large market for cattle throughout the world. The UK briefly experimented with cheap feeding strategies to reduce the price of beef – only to gain problems with BSE, or 'mad cow disease', as a result. Yet even with the outbreak of the BSE scare in 1995, the European Community as a whole did not apply equally stringent regulations for the slaughter of cattle across member states until July 1997!

Other countries, particularly in Latin America, have responded to the demand for beef by expanding cattle ranching. As consumption of burgers has grown, ranchers in Brazil, Costa Rica and other countries are devoting more and more land to cattle grazing. Latin American cattle graze on grass. This diet produces the lean meat demanded by the fast-food corporations, but it also requires that a great deal of land be dedicated to grazing.

Where is the land to come from? Ranchers in Latin America are solving their land problem by clearing forests at the rate of thousands of square miles each year. These tropical forests, as we shall explain presently, are vital to maintaining the earth's atmosphere. Therefore, forest destruction threatens the well-being of everyone – even the people back in Europe who enjoy burgers without giving a thought to the environment.

Enhancing global consciousness is thus a vital dimension of increasing environmental awareness. Ecologically speaking, our choices and actions ripple throughout the world, even though most of us never realise it. People in Europe are simply looking for a quick burger. Fast-food companies are making a profit by serving meals that people want. Ranchers are trying to earn a living by raising beef cattle. No one intends to harm the planet but, taken together, these actions can have serious consequences for everyone. All people on this planet inhabit a single ecosystem. In a world of countless environmental connections, we need to think critically about the effects of choices we make every day – like what's for lunch! ●

Source: Based on Myers (1984a).

('Society') – have scarcely any ability to affect the environment, whether they want to or not. Indeed, members of such societies are so directly dependent on nature, that their lives are guided by the migration of game and the rhythm of the seasons. They remain especially vulnerable to natural events, such as fires, floods, droughts and storms.

Societies at intermediate stages of technological development have a somewhat greater capacity to shape the environment. But the environmental impact of horticulture (small-scale farming), pastoralism (the herding of animals) and even agriculture (the use of animal-drawn ploughs), is limited by the reliance on muscle power for production of food and other goods.

Dramatic change in humans' relationship with the natural environment takes place with the development of industrial technology. Industry replaces muscle power with combustion engines that burn fossil fuels, including coal and oil. Such machinery affects the environment in two ways – by consuming natural resources and by releasing pollutants into the atmosphere. Humans armed with industrial technology become able to bend nature to their will far more than ever before, tunnelling through mountains, damming rivers, irrigating deserts and drilling for oil on the ocean floor.

Map 23.1 shows energy use around the world. The general pattern is clear. High-income, industrial societies place the greatest demands on the planet's ecosystem. Whilst low-income societies use only 14 per cent of the total world energy, high-income societies use 57 per cent (World Bank, 1997: 93). The United States, home to 5 per cent of the world's population, consumes roughly a third of the world's energy – more than any other country. The typical US adult consumes 100 times more energy annually than the average member of the world's poorest societies. Taking a broader perspective, the members of all high-income societies represent 20 per cent of humanity, but utilise 80 per cent of all energy (Connett, 1991; Miller, 1992).

But the environmental impact of industrial technology is not limited to energy consumption. Just as important, industrial societies produce 100 times more goods than agrarian societies do. While these products raise the material standard of living, they greatly escalate the problem of solid waste (because people ultimately throw away most of what they produce) and pollution (because industrial production generates smoke and other toxic substances).

People have been eager to acquire many of the material benefits of industrial technology. But a century after the dawn of industrial development people began to gauge the long-term consequences of this new technology on the natural environment. Indeed, one defining trait of post-industrial societies is a growing concern for environmental quality.

From today's vantage point, we draw an ironic and sobering conclusion: as we have reached our greatest technological power, we have placed the natural environment – including ourselves and all other living things – at greatest risk (Voight, cited in Bohrmann and Kellert, 1991: ix–x). The evidence is mounting that, in our pursuit of material affluence, humanity is running up an **environmental deficit**, *a situation in which our relationship to the environment, while yielding short-term benefits, will have profound, negative long-term consequences* (Bohrmann, 1990).

The concept of environmental deficit implies three important ideas. First, it reinforces the key assertion that the state of the environment is a *social issue*, reflecting choices people make about how they live. Second, this concept suggests that environmental damage – to the air, land or water – is often *unintended*. By focusing on the short-term benefits of, say, cutting down forests or using easily disposable packaging, we

Chernobyl, Ukraine, April 1996. Aerial view of the exploded block of the Chernobyl nuclear power plant which spread its radioactive clouds across Europe.

Source: Popperfoto

fail to see (or choose to ignore) their long-term environmental effects. Third, in some but not all respects, the environmental deficit is *reversible*. Inasmuch as societies have created environmental problems, in other words, societies can undo most of them.

Population increase

Paralleling the development of more powerful technology is a second underlying cause of environmental problems. At the dawn of human civilisation, the entire world's population barely reached 100 million people, roughly double the size of Britain today! Furthermore, population growth was very slow, with gradual increases periodically offset by plagues and other catastrophes.

Map 23.1 ● Energy consumption in global perspective

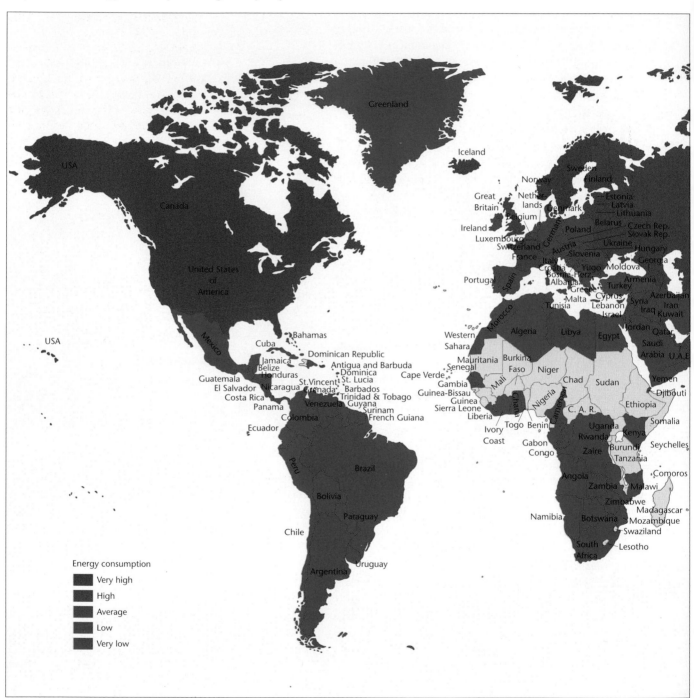

Energy consumption

- Very high
- High
- Average
- Low
- Very low

Source: *Peters Atlas of the World* (1990)

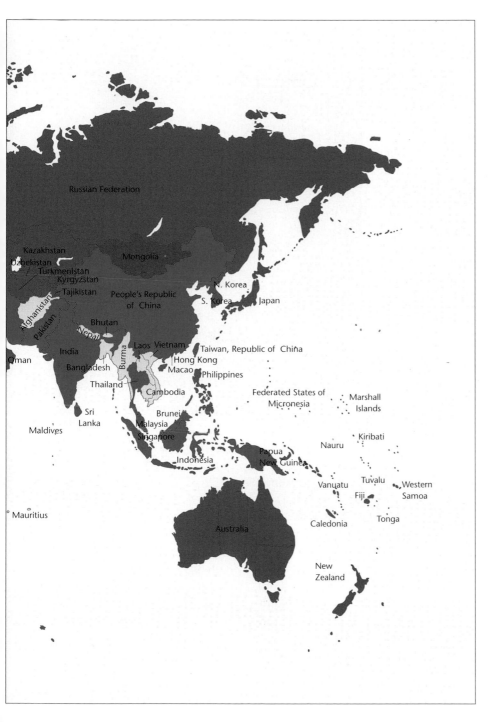

The members of industrial societies consume far more energy than others on the planet. The highest consumption in the world is in the USA. One person uses the same amount of energy in a year as 100 people in the Central African Republic. This means that the most economically productive societies are also those that place the greatest burden on the natural environment.

With the advent of the Industrial Revolution, rising living standards and improving medical technology, death rates have plummeted, resulting in a sharp rise in population. By 1800, global population had soared to the unprecedented level of 1 billion. But that was just the beginning. In the decades that followed, global population growth accelerated, reaching the 2 billion point by 1930, 3 billion in 1962, 4 billion in 1974 and 5 billion by 1987. In 1996, the world's population stood at roughly 5.8 billion, with 90 million people added to the world's total annually. To put it another way: the population is growing by 250,000 every day.

The danger of population growth is that it can quickly overwhelm available resources. Consider this old illustration about how runaway growth can wreak havoc on the natural environment (Milbrath, 1989: 10):

A pond has a single water lily growing on it. The lily doubles in size each day. In thirty days, it covers the entire pond. On which day did the lily cover half the pond?

The answer that comes readily to mind – the fifteenth day – is wrong because the lily was not increasing in size by the same amount every day. The correct answer is that the lily covered half the pond on the twenty-ninth day. The lesson of the riddle is that, at an increasing rate of growth, the small lily increases from covering an eighth of the surface to covering the entire pond in just three days.

To apply the same logic to the earth, most experts now conclude that between 8 and 10 billion people will inhabit the planet by the end of the next century. As Chapters 11 ('Global Stratification') and 22 ('Population and Urbanisation') explain, the most rapid population growth now is occurring in the poorest regions of the world. A glance back at Map 22.2 reveals that the nations of Africa, taken together, are adding to their population at an annual rate approaching 3 per cent. If sustained, this high growth rate will almost double that continent's population over the course of the next generation.

Rapid population growth goes hand in hand with poverty. For one thing, a surging population quickly neutralises any increase in a society's living standards. If a nation's population doubles, doubling its productivity amounts to no gain at all. And poverty itself strains the environment. Preoccupied with survival, people living on the edge of existence are driven to consume whatever resources are at hand – with little

Beijing – early morning rush hour. Beijing is seeking to limit the number of vehicles in the city centre to ease conjestion.

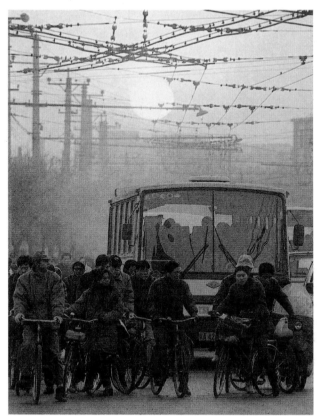

Source: Popperfoto

hope of change in the long-term for themselves, they can give little thought to the long-term environmental consequences of their actions.

The risk society

These long-term consequences of both population and technology have led sociologists to talk of 'the risk society'. The German sociologist Ulrick Beck (1992) has been to the fore in suggesting that the new technologies are generating risks which are of a quite different order from those found throughout earlier human history. Beck argues that the risks associated with new technologies generate new dangers to lives and the planet itself which may take many, many thousands of years to reverse. They are taking us to the edge of catastrophe: to 'threats to all forms of life on this planet'; to 'the exponential growth of risks and the impossibility of escaping them'.

Cultural patterns: growth and limits

If the world as a whole were suddenly blessed with the material prosperity that people in much of the Western world take for granted, humanity would soon overwhelm the global environment. This conclusion suggests that our planet suffers not just from the problem of economic *under*development in some regions but also from economic *over*development in others. Consider how we construct our cultural notion of 'the good life'. This is crucial because our cultural outlook, in addition to technology and population growth, is a third factor underlying the environmental deficit.

The logic of growth

One of the driving assumptions of modern Western societies is that of progress and material, economic advance. Moreover, we rely on *science*, looking to experts to apply technology to make our lives better. Taken together, such cultural values form the foundation for *the logic of growth*.

This logic of growth looks like an optimistic view of the world, suggesting, first, that people have improved their lives by devising more productive technology and, second, that we shall continue to do so into the future. The logic of growth thus amounts to the assertions that 'people are clever', 'having things is good (having more is better)', and 'life will improve'. A powerful force throughout the history of the Western, capitalist and industrial societies, the logic of growth has driven individuals to sail the seas, clear the land, build towns and roads and pursue material affluence.

But even optimistic people realise that 'progress' generates unanticipated problems, environmental and otherwise. The logic of growth responds by arguing that people (especially scientists and other technology experts) are inventive and will find a way out of any problems that growth places in our path. If, say, present resources should prove inadequate for our future needs, we will come up with new alternative resources that will do the job just as well.

To illustrate, most people in Europe would probably agree that cars have greatly improved our lives by providing us with a swift and comfortable means of travel. The counterargument, however, highlights some of the hazards car culture raises. Cars have also made us dependent on petrol, and Europe has previously suffered when conflicts in the Middle East have slowed the sale of oil resources. Even if the logic of growth rightly suggests that scientists will develop cars needing an alternate fuel source by the time the planet's oil reserves run dry, today's millions of cars will make mountains of rubbish in the future.

This is one of many reasons why most environmental scientists criticise the logic of growth. Lester Milbrath (1989) argues that natural resources such as oil, clean air, fresh water and the earth's topsoil – all *finite* – simply cannot be replaced by technologically engineered alternatives. He warns that we can and will exhaust them if we continue to pursue growth at any cost.

And what of our faith in human ingenuity and especially the ability of science to resolve problems of scarcity? While conceding that humans are clever at solving problems, Milbrath adds that human resourcefulness, too, has its limits. Do we dare to assume that we will be able to solve every crisis that confronts us, especially those wreaking serious damage on the life-giving environment? Moreover, the more powerful and complex the technology (nuclear reactors, say, compared to petrol engines), the greater the dangers posed by miscalculation and the more significant the unintended consequences are likely to be. Thus, Milbrath concludes that as we call on the earth to support increasing numbers of people with finite resources, we will almost certainly cause serious injury to the environment and, ultimately, to ourselves.

The limits to growth

If we cannot 'invent' our way out of the problems created by the 'logic of growth', perhaps we have to come up with an alternative way of thinking about the world. Environmentalists, therefore, propose the counterargument that growth must have limits. The *limits to growth thesis*, stated simply, is that humanity must implement policies to control the growth of population, to cut back on production and to use fewer resources in order to avoid environmental collapse.

The Limits to Growth, a controversial book published in 1972 that had a large hand in launching the environmental movement, uses a computer model to calculate the planet's available resources, rates of population growth, amount of land available for cultivation, levels of industrial and food production, and amount of pollutants released into the atmosphere. The authors contend that the model reflects changes that have occurred since 1900, then projects forward

A well known scene throughout the world. As population grows and environmental degradation increases, it becomes harder and harder to find an empty beach. Here a lifeguard sits over a beach at Gijon, Spain.

Source: Popperfoto

to the end of the next century. Long-range predictions using such a complex model are always speculative and some critics think they are simply wrong (Simon, 1981). But many find the general conclusions of the study, shown in Figure 23.1, convincing.

Following the limits to growth logic, humanity is quickly consuming the earth's finite resources. Supplies of oil, natural gas and other sources of energy will fall sharply, a little faster or slower depending on policies in rich nations and the speed at which other nations industrialise. While food production per person should continue to rise into the next century, the authors calculate, millions will go hungry because existing food supplies are so unequally distributed throughout the world. By mid-century, the model predicts a hunger crisis serious enough that rising mortality rates will first stabilise population and then send it plunging downward. Depletion of resources will eventually cripple industrial output as well. Only then will pollution rates fall.

The lesson of this study is grim: current patterns of life are not sustainable for even another century. This leaves us with the fundamental choice of making deliberate changes in how we live or allowing calamity to force changes upon us.

● Environmental issues

We have reviewed how technological development, population growth and cultural orientations have placed increasing demands on the natural environment. What, then, is the state of the natural environment today? Public opinion surveys reveal serious concern about the natural environment. In general, people in low-income societies who contend with the greatest problems of over-population and poverty are most unhappy with their surroundings. Figure 23.2 compares environmental attitudes in selected industrialising and industrial countries (Dunlap,

Figure 23.1 ● The limits to growth: projections

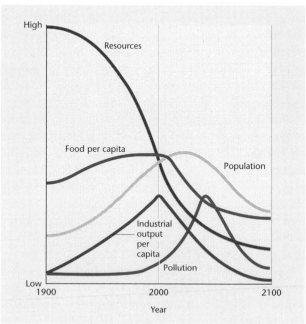

Source: Based on Meadows et al. (1972)

A dramatically changing environment

The weather
The hottest ten years in recorded history have happened since 1980. Within the next 40 year period, ocean temperatures could rise by 7°C (enough to melt polar ice caps!)

The earth
The world is losing seven million hectares of fertile land a year due to soil degradation, and about 10 million hectares of forest land a year (about the size of South Korea!). Whilst there is less land, more food is needed (see 'People' above).

Forests and biodiversity
Between 70 and 95 per cent of the Earth's species live in the world's disappearing tropical forest. We are losing 50 species a day. By 2020, 10 million species are likely to become extinct.

The water
By 2025, as many as 3 billion people could be living with chronic water scarcity. Freshwater ecosystems are in decline everywhere. Some 25 million people die every year from pollution in contaminated drinking water.

Air
Fossil fuel burning releases about 6 billion tons of carbon into the air each year, adding about 3 billion tons annually to the 170 billion tons that have settled since the Industrial Revolution. The rate of growth in carbon emissions is around 2 per cent per year.

People
World population grows by about 90 million people a year.

Cars
In 1993, of the world's 607 million cars, a third were in the US, and another third were to be found in six other industrialised countries. ●

Sources: *New Internationalist*: Numbers: 269, 278, 287, 289
Lester R. Brown et al., *State of the World*, A Worldwatch Institute Report, London: Earthscan Publications, 1996

Figure 23.2 ● Rating the local environment: a global survey
Survey question: 'When we say environment, we mean your surroundings – both the natural environment, namely, the air, water, land, plants and animals – as well as buildings, streets and the like. Overall, how would you rate the quality of the environment in your local community: very good, fairly good, fairly bad or very bad?'

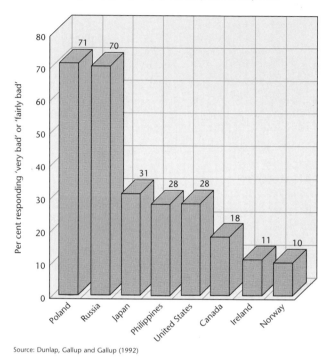

Source: Dunlap, Gallup and Gallup (1992)

Gallup and Gallup, 1992). In sum, we certainly *perceive* threats to the natural environment. But does our perception accurately mirror reality? In the following survey, we shall briefly examine several key environmental issues. The box shows some of the major issues.

Solid waste: 'disposable societies'

As an interesting exercise, carry a rubbish bag over the course of a single day and collect all the materials you throw away. Most people would be surprised to find out how much waste they generate! Rubbish is a feature of all modern societies, but the most extreme case is the United States – the classic 'disposable society'. In the United States, an average person tosses out close to five pounds of paper, metal, plastic and other disposable materials daily (about 50 tons over a lifetime). For that country as a whole, this amounts to about 1 billion pounds of solid waste produced *each and every day*.

The United States is not the only culprit. In the European Union, legislation designed to facilitate the *safe* transport of goods around the common market and to protect consumer health has led to an escalating use of packaging. Everything from baked goods to hammers to bicycle helmets increasingly is sold with excessive packaging – a trend which many manufacturers and retailers have welcomed, as packaging can make a product more attractive to the customer (or harder to shoplift).

Consider, too, that manufacturers market soft drinks, beer and fruit juices in aluminium cans, glass jars or plastic containers, which not only consume finite resources but also generate mountains of solid waste. Then there are countless items intentionally designed to be disposable. A walk through any local supermarket reveals shelves filled with pens, razors, flashlights, batteries and even cameras, intended to be used once and dropped in the nearest bin. Other products – from light bulbs to washing machines – are designed to have a limited useful life, and then become unwanted junk. As Paul H. Connett (1991) points out, even the words we use to describe what we throw away – *waste, litter, rubbish, refuse, garbage* – reveal how little we value what we cannot immediately use and how quickly we push it out of sight and out of mind. Living in a 'disposable society', the average person in the United States consumes 50 times more steel, 170 times more newspaper, 250 times more petrol and 300 times more plastic each year than the typical individual in India (Miller, 1992). Comparable high levels of consumption in Europe mean that Western societies not only use a disproportionate share of the planet's natural resources, but also generate most of the world's refuse (Figure 23.3).

Solid waste that is not burned or recycled never 'goes away'; rather, it ends up in landfills. The practice of using landfills, originally intended to improve sanitation, is now associated with several threats to the natural environment. First, the sheer volume of discarded material is literally filling up landfills. Especially in large cities like London, there is simply little room left for disposing of rubbish. Second, material placed in landfills contributes to water pollution. Although laws now regulate what can be placed in a landfill, there are dump sites across Europe containing hazardous materials that are polluting water both above and below the ground. Third, what goes into

European environmental policy

Environmental issues are truly global. Many of the problems – like the releasing of CFC's into the atmosphere – have global effects and require global action. Some problems link to the exploitation of **global commons** – *the resources shared by the international community*, like deep sea beds and the atmosphere. Sometimes small local problems – such as poisonous gases leaking from landfills and water pollution – are multiplied so many times in many local contexts that they become major world hazards. The environment is a global concern requiring global policies.

The UN Conference on the Human Environment in 1972 at Stockholm was the first major international conference on the environment. It led to a Declaration and an Action Plan with 109 recommendations in six broad areas (including human settlements, natural resource management, pollution, educational and social aspects of the environment, development, and international organisations). It led to a programme to manage the 'global commons', and established a UN environment programme. Subsequent world conferences include the Earth Summit held at Rio in 1992 and the Earth Summit 2 in New York in 1997.

Uniquely amongst international organisations, the European Union has 'the power to agree environmental policies binding on its members' (McCormick, 1991: 128). Since 1957, some 300 pieces of environmental legislation have been passed. Four periods of European policy have been identified:

1957–72 The original Treaty of Rome did not raise environmental issues and there was minimal involvement

1973–85 In the wake of *Limits to Growth* report (see discussion in text), the First Environmental Action Programme gave the EU power to act whenever 'real effectiveness' on environmental issues seemed possible. Water quality, air quality and hazardous waste policies (120 directives, 27 decisions and 14 regulations) were implemented.

1986–92 A formal legal framework emerged.

1993–97 In the wake of Maastricht, integration curiously becomes weaker as the Union expands to include new members and as members defend their national self interest. Nonetheless, the EU continues to promote sustainable environmental policies through such measures as the regulation of fish stocks and funding of sustainable development research.

Interestingly, the World Watch Institute has recently remarked that: 'The European Union, consisting of some 15 countries and containing 360 million people, provides a model for the rest of the world of an environmentally sustainable food/population balance . . . one seventh of humanity is already there' (Brown, 1997: 12–13). ●

Sources: based on Brown, 1997; Hildebrand, 1992.

landfills all too often stays there – sometimes for centuries. Tens of millions of tyres, nappies and other items that we bury in landfills each year do not readily decompose, leaving an unwelcome legacy for future generations.

Preserving clean water

The oceans, lakes and streams supply the lifeblood of the global ecosystem. Throughout human history, people have relied on water for drinking, bathing, cooling, cooking, recreation and a host of other activities. Yet, the oceans have long served as a vast dumping ground for all kinds of waste – including nuclear submarines and human excrement. No-one can calculate the precise amount of waste that has been poured into the world's oceans, but the total certainly exceeds millions of tons. The problems caused by disposing of solid waste in this way are crystal clear: polluted water kills fish or makes them dangerous to eat, and also spoils a source of great beauty and pleasure.

Through the process which scientists call the *hydrological cycle*, the earth naturally recycles water and

Figure 23.3 ● **Composition of household waste**

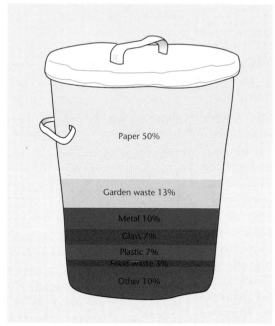

Paper 50%

Garden waste 13%

Metal 10%

Glass 7%

Plastic 7%

Food waste 3%

Other 10%

Source: Based on Franklin Associates (1986) and Corley et al. (1993)

refreshes the land. The process begins as heat from the sun causes the earth's water, 97 per cent of which is in the oceans, to evaporate and form clouds. Next, water returns to earth as rain, which drains into streams and rivers and rushes towards the sea. The hydrological cycle not only renews the supply of water but cleans it as well. Because water evaporates at lower temperatures than most pollutants, the water vapour that rises from the seas is relatively pure and free of contaminants, which are left behind. Although the hydrological cycle generates clean water in the form of rain, it does not destroy pollutants that steadily build up in the oceans – and clean rain can collect pollutants in the air as it falls back to earth. Two key concerns, then, dominate discussions of water and the natural environment. The first is supply; the second is pollution.

Water supply

Talk about a 'drought' along with discussions of the amount of rainfall each month has become a common concern in European societies, where the weather is

relatively kind. But concern over an ample supply of water is hardly new. For thousands of years, since the time of the ancient civilisations of China, Egypt and Rome, water rights have figured prominently in codes of law. Throughout Europe, aqueducts of brick, built by the ancient Romans, stand as testimony to the historical importance of readily available water.

Today, as Map 23.2 shows, some regions of the world, especially the tropics, enjoy a plentiful supply of water, although most of the annual rainfall occurs over a relatively brief season. High demand for water, coupled with more modest reserves, makes water supply a matter of concern in much of Europe and North America as well as most of Asia; in these areas people look to rivers – rather than rainfall – for their water. Especially in the Middle East and parts of Africa, water supply has already reached a critical level. Egypt, for instance, is located in an arid region of the world, where people have long depended on the River Nile for most of their water. But, as the Egyptian population increases, shortages are becoming commonplace. Egyptians today must make do with a sixth as much water per person from the Nile as they did in 1900 and experts project that the supply will shrink by half again over the next 20 years (Myers, 1984c; Postel, 1993).

Within 30 years, according to current predictions, 1 billion people throughout the Middle East and parts of Africa will lack sufficient water. The world has recently witnessed the tragedy of hunger in the African nations of Ethiopia and Somalia. While we recognise the impact of food shortages there, an even more serious problem for these societies is the lack of adequate water for irrigation and drinking.

Surging population and complex technology – especially in manufacturing and power-generating facilities – have greatly increased our appetite for water. The global demand for water (estimated at about 5 billion cubic feet per year) has tripled since 1950 and is expanding faster than the world's population (Postel, 1993). As a result, even in areas that receive significant rainfall, people are using groundwater faster than it can be naturally replenished. Take the Tamil Nadu region of southern India, for example. There, the rapidly growing population is drawing so much groundwater that the local water table has fallen 100 feet over the last several decades.

In light of such developments, we must face the reality that water is a valuable, finite resource. Greater conservation of water by individuals (who consume, on average, 10 million gallons over a lifetime) is part of the answer. However, households around the world account for no more than 10 per cent of water use. We need to curb water consumption by industry, which currently uses 25 per cent of the global total.

Irrigation channels two-thirds of humanity's water use on to croplands. New irrigation technology may well reduce this demand in the future. But, here again, we see that population increase, as well as economic growth, is placing increasing strains on the eco-system (Myers, 1984a; Goldfarb, 1991; Falkenmark and Widstrand, 1992; Postel, 1993).

Water pollution

In large cities – from Mexico City to Cairo to Shanghai – many people have little choice but to drink contaminated water. The poor people of the world suffer most as a result of unsafe water. As Chapter 20 ('Health and Medicine') noted, infectious diseases like typhoid, cholera and dysentery, all caused by micro-organisms that contaminate water, run rampant in poor nations. Throughout the low-income regions of the world, then, the source of much illness and death can be traced to microbes thriving in polluted water (Clarke, 1984b; Falkenmark and Widstrand, 1992).

Thus, besides ensuring ample *supplies* of water, we must recognise that no society has done an exemplary job of protecting the *quality* of its water. In most areas of the world, tap water is not safe for drinking.

Most people living in Europe take for granted that tap water is free from harmful contaminants, and water quality in Europe is generally good by global standards. However, even here the problem of water pollution is growing steadily. The Rhine drainage basin (connecting the Netherlands, Germany, France and Switzerland) contains about 20 per cent of the EU's population, along with its industry. Large quantities of toxic waste – chemicals, heavy metals and sewage – have been found to be entering the river. Although actions have since been taken to reduce the quantities of waste, the possibility of contaminated water remains (Drake, 1994: 218–20). Likewise, the pollution all round the Mediterranean is well known. And in the UK, pollution incidents in rivers have doubled in recent years (Pickering and Owen, 1994).

Clearing the air

Most people in Europe are more aware of air pollution than they are of contaminated water, in part because air serves as our constant and immediate environment. Then, too, many urbanites are familiar with the mix of smoke and fog (the origin of the word 'smog') that hangs over cities.

One of the unanticipated consequences of the development of industrial technology – especially the factory and the motor vehicle – has been a deterioration of air quality. The thick, black smoke belched from factory chimneys, often 24 hours a day, alarmed residents of early industrial cities a century ago. By the end of World War II, air pollution was commonplace in most industrial cities. In London, factory discharge, car emissions and smoke from coal fires used to heat households combined to create what was probably the worst urban air quality of the century. In the course of just five days in 1952, an especially thick haze – the infamous 'pea-souper' – hung over London, killing 4,000 people (Clarke, 1984).

Recently, improvements have been made in combating air pollution brought on by industry. Laws now mandate the use of low-pollution heating fuels in most cities; the coal fires that choked London a half-century ago, for example, are now forbidden (the Clean Air Act of 1956 helped to end much of this pollution – though in December 1991, a severe smog did reappear). In addition, scientists have effectively devised new technologies to reduce the noxious output of factory chimneys and, even more important, to lessen the pollution caused by the growing number of cars and lorries. The switch to unleaded petrol, coupled with changes in engine design and exhaust systems, has reduced the car's detrimental environmental impact. Still, with cars accounting for around 80 per cent of all travel in Europe (and 96 per cent in the United States!), the challenge of cleaning the air remains daunting (*Social Trends*, 1997: 202). See Table 23.1.

If the rich societies of the world can breathe a bit more easily than they once did, poor societies contend with an increasing problem of air pollution. For one thing, people in low-income countries still rely on wood, coal, peat or other 'dirty' fuels for cooking fires

Map 23.2 ● Water consumption in global perspective

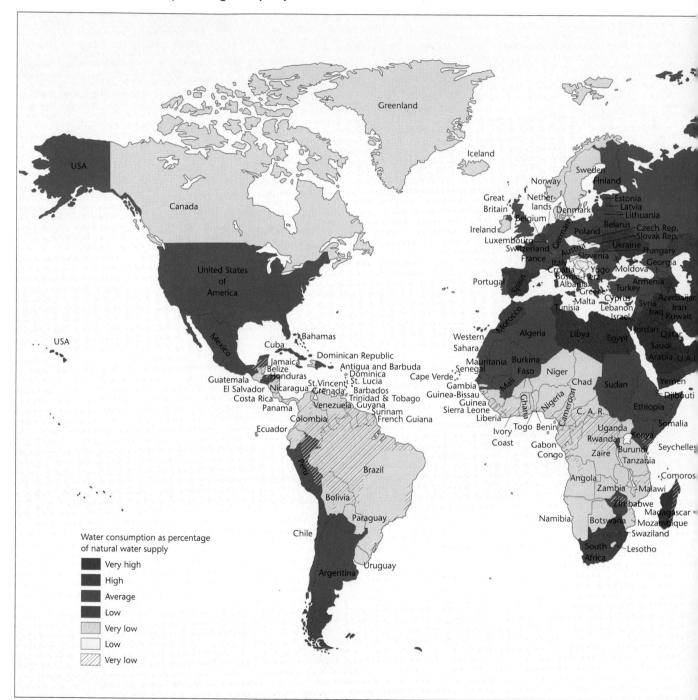

Water consumption as percentage of natural water supply

- Very high
- High
- Average
- Low
- Very low
- Low
- Very low

Source: United Nations Development Programme (1995)

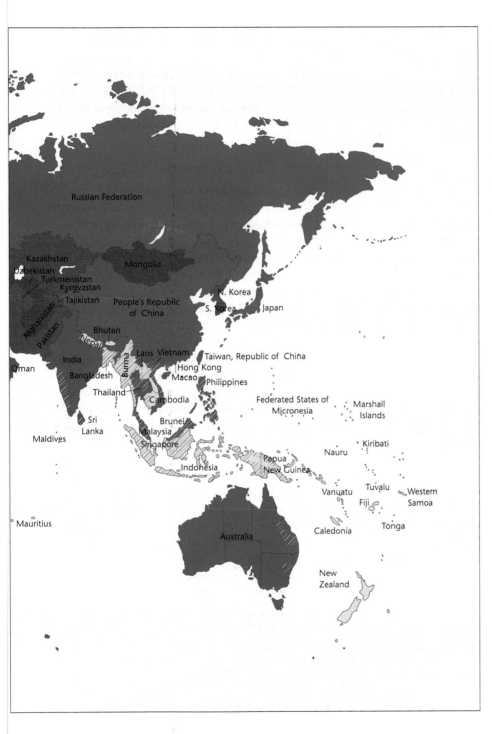

This map shows each country's water consumption as a percentage of its internal renewable water resources. Nations near the equator consume only a tiny share of their available resources; indeed, as the map shows, much of this region is covered with rain forest. Northern Africa and the Middle East are a different story, however, with dense populations drawing on very limited water resources. As a result, in Libya, Egypt, Saudi Arabia and other countries, people (especially the poor) do not have as much water as they would like or, often, as they need.

Taking sides with the environmental movement: how radical should it be?

It isn't much, really, in dispute – only the land we live on, the water we drink, the air we breathe, the food we eat, and the energy that supports us (Aaron Wildavsky).

Whilst many people believe that science and technology will improve their lives; environmentalists aren't so sure. For them, the world is hurtling towards an ecological disaster. All the evidence described in this chapter must lead one to conclude that our environment is under severe risk, and planet earth could face its own destruction in the not too distant future.

The earliest manifestations of the Environmental Movement (EM) in Britain appeared as early as the sixteenth century with people's concerns for the countryside. The movement developed more focus in the nineteenth century through the emergence of groups like the National Trust (1895) and the Royal Society for the Protection of Birds (created in 1889). It takes its distinctively modern form from the late 1950s onwards, and, by 1980, around 5 per cent of the population in the UK belonged to one of several thousands environmental groups. By 1989, a MORI poll revealed that 18 million people regarded themselves as envi-

ronmentally conscious shoppers; and some 17 to 35 per cent of people rated the environment as the most important political issue (Garner, 1996: 62–3). At the forefront of these newer groups were Friends of the Earth and Greenpeace. Greenpeace emerged in the late 1960s and, by 1989, had attracted an estimated 3.5 million members. Friends of the Earth was founded in 1969 in the USA, and by the early 1980s had branches in some 29 countries (Garner, 1996: 66)

How might this growth be explained? Martell (1994) and Garner (1996) suggest three possible sources. One is a cultural shift in values – what they call a post materialist view. Second, it has been suggested that a new largely middle-class lobby from the non-productive service sector – doctors, teachers, social workers – insulated from the dominant values of the society has emerged which follows different goals (Cotgrove et al. 1982). Finally, the sheer scale of environmental worries has inspired some to join the movement.

Whatever the explanation, there is no doubt that an important Environmental Movement is a major feature of the late twentieth-century world.

The movement itself has changed over time. Whilst the 'first wave' of environmentalism was little more than a conservation movement that focused on protecting the natural environment, during the 1960s a 'second wave' of environmentalism took root in Europe and became decidedly more radical and critical. In 1962, in the USA, Rachel Carson's book *Silent Spring* explored the dangers of spreading pesticides across the land. Agricultural 'business as usual', Carson warned, was courting disaster. Before long, environmental concerns had become part of the activist culture that marked the decade with people chaining themselves to trees to halt logging and blocking ships armed with nuclear weapons.

By 1970, with the celebration of the first 'Earth Day', the environmental movement had come of age. Its adherents addressed a wide range of issues – including those covered in this chapter – and, increasingly, they directly challenged many of the practices and priorities that had long marked out the western way of life. But in the early 1980s, conservative administrations often adopted a strong pro-business agenda and soon governments and the

tested tens of thousands of plants for their medical properties, and they have developed hundreds of new medicines each year based on this research.

Third, with the loss of any species of life – whether

it is one variety of ant, the spotted owl, the magnificent Bengal tiger or the famed Chinese panda – the beauty and complexity of our natural environment is diminished. And there are clear warning signs. Three-

environmental movement were locking horns over population control, land development and other matters.

Today, the Environment Movement falls into three main groupings. One groups comprises mainstream lobbyists who usually work in formal organisations and are often professional and well funded. A second group encompasses popular movements where people lobby for specific issues and work to change things in their own lives, be it picketing the transportation of live stock and concern over 'animal rights' in the UK, marching on railway carriages transporting nuclear waste in Germany, or landless peasants marching on Brasilia to address land rights issues. The third, more radical wing of environmentalism, draws on Marxism and feminism and takes drastic action to instil a sense of urgency among governments.

Many environmentalists think there is nothing at all radical about their movements. From their point of view, we must learn to live in concert with the environment because, politics aside, humanity cannot survive otherwise. In the end, what

these environmentalists are saying is that, in light of the risks we face, making basic changes is common sense. On the surface, at least, the public has come to accept environmentalism. And everywhere one looks, governments are acting to reduce the dangers : under the buzz phrase of sustainable development.

But other environmentalists do not think the problem and solution is so simple. These 'ecological radicals' argue that basic changes are necessary in our way of life if we are to head off disaster down the road. In particular, they believe, we can no longer place economic growth at the heart of culture because this core value is causing an increasing environmental deficit. The

materialist and consumerist vision of the good life can no longer be sustained because it leads to the degradation of the environment. Perhaps society has come to accept the idea that environmentalism is good in principle. But it is far from clear that most people are willing to make the hard choices to achieve a sustainable way of life.

● **Continue the debate:**

1. Do you think limiting economic growth is necessary in order to secure our environmental future? Would you be willing to accept a lower standard of living to protect the natural environment?

2. What action have you ever taken (signing a petition, participating in a demonstration, modifying your consumption patterns) in support of the environment?

3. Where do you think the major European political parties stand on environmental issues? ●

Sources: Based on Dunlap and Mertig, 1992; survey data from Dunlap, Gallup and Gallup, 1992, NORC, 1994, and Benton, 1997

New York, 1996. Models from the Boss Modelling Agency posed naked in Times Square to promote the agency's announcement that it is 'fur free'.

Source: Popperfoto

quarters of the world's 9,000 species of birds are currently declining in number. Finally, keep in mind that, unlike pollution and other environmental problems, the extinction of species is irreversible and final. As a

matter of ethics, then, should those who live today make decisions that will impoverish the world for those who live tomorrow (Myers, 1984b, 1991; Wilson, 1991; Brown, 1993)?

Members of small, simple societies, such as the Tan't Batu, who thrive in the Philippines, live in harmony with nature; such people do not have the technological means to greatly affect the natural world. Although we in complex societies like to think of ourselves as superior to such people, the truth is that there is much we can – and must – learn from them.

Source: Sygma - Eric Pasquier

● Society and the environment: theoretical analysis

We have now introduced a number of key concepts and outlined prominent issues facing the natural environment. Sociological theory can help tie this material together to see how environmental concerns reflect the operation of society.

Functional analysis

The structural-functional paradigm offers three significant insights about the natural environment. First, as earlier chapters have made clear, this approach highlights the fundamental importance of *values* and *beliefs* to the operation of a social system. Thus, in simple terms, the state of the environment depends largely on our attitude towards the natural world, for values guide human actions.

Members of industrial societies generally see nature as a set of resources to serve our needs. This perspective (examined earlier as the 'logic of growth') justifies imposing our human will on the planet. With this orientation, our forebears cleared forests for farmland, dammed rivers for irrigation and water power, covered vast areas with asphalt and concrete and erected buildings to make cities. Moreover, Western cultures historically have embraced both materialism and acquisitiveness. That is, we have looked to *things* (sometimes more than, say, kinship or spirituality) as a source of comfort, happiness and fulfilment. At the same time, we tend to think that if owning *some* things is good, having *more* things is better. Our tendency towards 'conspicuous consumption' leads us to purchase and display things as a way to indicate our social position to others. Such values, not surprisingly, set the stage for the kinds of environmental stress this chapter has described.

Second, functional theory points up the interconnectedness of various dimensions of social life. Our ideas about efficient and private travel, for example, have much to do with the dizzying rate at which industrial societies have produced and consumed motor vehicles. Building and operating hundreds of millions of lorries and cars, in turn, has depleted natural resources (like oil) and the quality of the overall environment (especially the air).

Third, functional analysis suggests that, given the many ways in which the operation of society interacts with the natural environment, environmental problems demand far-reaching and multifaceted solutions. We cannot hope to curb the rate at which humanity is consuming the earth's resources, for example, as long as 250,000 people are added to the global population each day. Controlling population growth, in turn, depends on expanding the range of occupational and educational opportunities open to women, so they can opt for alternatives to having more children.

However difficult the task may be, functionalism provides grounds for optimism that societies can constructively respond to threats to the environment. Consider, once again, the case of air pollution. Air quality plunged with the onset of the Industrial Revolution. But gradually societies in Europe and North America recognised and responded to this problem, enacting new laws and employing new technology to improve air quality. Similarly, just as companies once fouled the natural environment in the process of making money, now new companies are profiting by cleaning up our physical surroundings. In short, because we need a liveable natural environment, determined efforts will undoubtedly be brought to bear on whatever environmental problems may arise.

Cultural ecology

Closely allied with functional theory is **cultural ecology**, *a theoretical paradigm that explores the relationship of human culture and the physical environment.* This paradigm broadens our analysis by exploring not just how culture affects the environment but also how the environment (say, climate or the availability of natural resources) shapes human culture.

First-time travellers to India might well wonder why this nation, that contends with widespread hunger and malnutrition, prohibits the killing of cows. According to Hindu cultural beliefs, cows are sacred animals. To many European and North Americans who enjoy so much beef, this way of thinking is puzzling. Investigating rural India's ecology, Marvin Harris (1975) concluded that the Hindu veneration of the cow makes sense because cattle's importance extends well beyond their value as a food source. Harris points out that cows cost little to raise, since they consume grasses of no interest to humans.

And cows produce two valuable resources: oxen (their neutered offspring) and manure. Unable to afford expensive farm machinery, Indian farmers rely on oxen to power their ploughs. For Indians, killing cows would be as silly as farmers in Europe destroying

factories that build tractors. Furthermore, each year Indians process millions of tons of cow manure into building material and burn 'cowpats' as fuel (India has little oil, coal or wood). Culture, in short, is shaped by the ecology: killing cows for food would deprive Indians of homes and a major source of heat.

Critical evaluation
Functional analysis, including the cultural ecology approach, shows that the condition of the natural environment cannot be analysed apart from the operation of society itself. To its credit, this paradigm reveals the extent to which the environment is a sociological concern. But critics have pointed out various weaknesses in this paradigm. With regard to cultural ecology, we can see how the natural environment shapes the culture of people with limited technology, but this connection is less obvious in societies with industrial technology.

More broadly, structural-functionalism overlooks issues of social inequality. As we shall note presently, the burdens of environmental pollution are shouldered disproportionately by people with less social power – the poor and minorities. Furthermore, many environmentalists are sceptical of structural-functionalism's optimism about society's capacity to restore the natural world. On the one hand, many people have vested interests in the status quo, even if that threatens the well-being of the general public. Moreover, many of the environmental problems we face – especially rapid population growth – are simply too far out of control at present to justify the optimism voiced by functionalists.

Conflict analysis

Conflict theory highlights the very issues that structural-functionalism tends to overlook: power and inequality. Far from being inevitable, conflict theorists maintain that problems of the natural environment result from social arrangements favoured by elites. It is critical of powerful groups for directly or indirectly aggravating environmental problems as they pursue their self-interest. Moreover, conflict theory highlights the serious environmental consequences of the global disparity of wealth and power.

First, there is the issue of elites. As conflict theorists see it, in the hierarchical organisation of societies, a small proportion of our population – what Chapter 16

('Power, the State and Social Movements') called the 'power elite' – sets the national and global agenda by controlling the world's economy, law and view of the natural environment. Early capitalists shepherded Europe into the industrial age, hungrily tapping the earth's resources and frantically turning out manufactured goods in pursuit of profits. By and large, it was they who reaped the benefits of the new industrial wealth, while workers toiled in dangerous factories and lived in nearby localities blighted with smoke, racked with noise and shaken by the vibrations of the big machines.

Just as important, many societies have just ignored the most blatant instances of environmental destruction, even when elite perpetrators run foul of the law. Corporate pollution, as Chapter 8 ('Deviance') explains, falls under the category of white-collar crime. Such offences typically escape prosecution; when action is taken, it is usually in the form of fines levied on a company rather than criminal penalties imposed on individuals. Thus, corporate executives who order the burning or burying of toxic waste have been subject to penalties no greater (and sometimes less) than ordinary citizens who throw rubbish from car windows.

Conflict theorists, who embrace a Marxist view of society, argue that capitalism itself poses a threat to the environment. The logic of capitalism is the pursuit of profit, and that pursuit demands continuous economic growth. What is profitable to capitalists does not necessarily advance the public welfare, nor is it likely to be good for the natural environment. As noted earlier in this chapter, capitalist industries have long ensured ongoing profits by designing products to have a limited useful life (the concept of 'planned obsolescence'). Such policies may improve the 'bottom line' in the short term, but they raise the long-term risk of depleting natural resources as well as generating overwhelming amounts of solid waste.

A second issue raised by conflict theory is inequality. As shown earlier in Map 22.1, a small share of the earth's population currently consumes most of its energy. Generally, members of rich societies use most of the earth's resources and, in the process, produce the most pollution. By exploiting both the earth and the poor of the less developed countries, these countries have poisoned the air and water in the process. From this point of view, rich nations are actually *over*developed and consume too much. No one should expect that the majority of the earth's people, who live in poor

societies, will be able to match the living standard in these countries; nor, given the current environmental crisis, would that be desirable. Instead, conflict theorists call for a more equitable distribution of resources among all people of the world as both a matter of social justice and as a strategy to preserve the natural environment (Schnaiberg and Gould, 1994; Szasz, 1994).

Environmental racism

An important aspect of this inequality is the worrying growth of **environmental racism**, *the pattern by which environmental hazards are perceived to be greatest in proximity to poor people and especially minorities*. Historically, factories that spew pollutants have been built in and near districts inhabited by the poor and people of colour, who often work there. As a result of their low incomes, many could afford housing only in undesirable localities, sometimes in the very shadow of the plants and mills. Although workers in many manufacturing industries have organised in opposition to environmental hazards, they have done so with limited success, largely because the people facing the most serious environmental threats have the least social power to begin with.

Critical evaluation

The conflict paradigm complements other analyses by raising the important questions of who sets a society's agenda and who benefits (and suffers) most from decisions that affect us all. Environmental problems, from this point of view, are consequences of a society's class structure and, globally, the world's hierarchy of nations. Like functionalism, this approach is subject to criticism. While it may be true that elites have always dominated industrial society, they have not been able to stem a steady tide towards legal protection of the natural environment. These protections, in turn, have yielded significant improvements in our air and water quality.

And what of the charge that capitalism is particularly hostile to the natural world? There is little doubt that capitalism's logic of growth does place stress on the environment. At the same time, however, capitalist societies in North America and Europe have made notable strides towards environmental protection. By contrast, the environmental record of socialist societies is far from exemplary. A look back to Figure 23.3 shows that citizens of Poland and Russia – two nations ruled for half a century by socialist governments – are highly critical of environmental quality in their local communities (Dunlap, Gallup and Gallup, 1992; Olsen, Lodwick and Dunlap, 1992). This record reflects policies that, for decades, pursued industrialisation in utter neglect of environmental concerns, without challenge and with tragic consequences in terms of human health.

Finally, there is little doubt that high-income countries currently place the greatest demands on the natural environment. However, this pattern is already beginning to shift as global population swells in poor countries. And environmental problems are also likely to grow worse to the extent that poor societies develop economically, using more resources and producing more waste and pollutants in the process. In the long run, all nations of the world share a vital interest in protecting the natural environment. This concern leads us to the final topic of this chapter, the concept of a sustainable environment.

● Looking ahead: towards a sustainable society and world

India's great leader Mahatma Gandhi once declared that societies must provide 'enough for people's needs, but not for their greed'. From an environmental point of view, this means that the earth will be able to sustain future generations only if humanity refrains from rapidly and thoughtlessly consuming finite resources such as oil, hardwoods and water. Nor can we persist in polluting the air, water and ground at anything like the current levels. The loss of global forests – through cutting of trees and the destructive effects of acid rain – threatens to undermine the global climate. And we risk the future of the planet by adding people to the world at the rate of 90 million each year.

Today, on every part of the earth inhabited by humanity, the environmental deficit is growing. In effect, our present way of life is borrowing against the well-being of our children and their children. And, taking a global perspective, we see that members of rich societies, who currently consume so much of the earth's resources, are mortgaging the future security of the majority of people who live in the poor countries of the world.

In principle, we could solve the entire range of environmental problems described in this chapter by living in a more *ecocentric* manner, one that makes environmental consequences central to our actions. This is the path to a culture that is sustainable, one

that does not increase the environmental deficit. An **ecologically sustainable culture**, then, refers to *a way of life that meets the needs of the present generation without threatening the environmental legacy of future generations*. (The concept of 'sustainable development' was popularised through the 1987 UN Commission Report on the Environment – the Brundtland Commission.)

Sustainable living calls for three basic strategies. The first is the *conservation of finite resources*. We must balance the desire to satisfy our present wants with our responsibility to preserve what will be needed by future generations. Conservation means using resources more efficiently, seeking alternative resources and, in some cases, learning to live with less.

Technology, no doubt, will provide the key to household devices (from light bulbs to boilers) that are far more energy efficient than those available at present. Moreover, we should expand development of alternative energy sources, including harnessing the power of the sun, wind and tides. But while relying on help from new technology, a sustainable way of life will require rethinking the pro-consumption attitudes formed during decades of 'cheap electricity' and 'cheap petrol'.

The second basic strategy is *reducing waste*. Whenever possible, simply using less is the most effective way to reduce waste. In addition, societies around the world need to expand recycling programmes. Success will depend both on dual incentives of educational efforts to enlist widespread support for these initiatives and on legislation requiring the recycling of certain materials. Looking down the road, as recycling programmes become commercially profitable, they will be adopted more readily by market-based economies around the world.

The third key element in any plan for a sustainable ecosystem is *bringing world population growth under control*. As we have explained, the 1996 global population of 5.75 billion was already straining the natural environment. Clearly, the higher world population climbs, the more difficult environmental problems will become. Global population is now increasing by about 1.5 per cent each year, a rate that will double the world's people in fewer than 50 years. Few analysts think that the earth can support a population of 10 billion or more; most argue that we must hold the line at about 7 billion. Controlling population growth will require urgent steps in poor regions of the world where growth rates are highest.

GLOBAL SOCIOLOGY

Turning the tide: a report from Egypt

Cairo, like many large cities, has become a mess of pollution. No sooner had we left the bus then smoke and stench, the likes of which we had never before encountered, swirled around us. Eyes squinting, handkerchiefs pressed against noses and mouths, we moved slowly uphill along a path ascending mountains of trash and garbage that extended for miles. We had reached the Cairo dump, where the refuse generated by 15 million people in one of the world's largest cities ends up. We walked hunched over and with great care, guided by only a scattering of light from small fires smouldering around us. Up ahead, through clouds of smoke, we saw blazing piles of trash encircled by people seeking warmth and enjoying companionship.

Human beings actually inhabit this inhuman place, creating a surreal scene, like the aftermath of the next global war. As we approached, the fires cast an eerie light on their faces. We stopped some distance from them, separated by a vast chasm of culture and circumstances. But smiles eased the tension and soon we were sharing the comfort of their fires. At that moment, the melodious call to prayer sounded across the city.

The people of the Cairo dump, called the Zebaleen, belong to a religious minority – Coptic Christians – in a predominantly Muslim society.

Barred by religious discrimination from many jobs, the Zebaleen use donkey carts and small trucks to pick up the city's refuse and haul it here. For decades, the routine has reached a climax at dawn when hundreds of Zebaleen gather at the dump, swarming over the new piles in search of anything of value.

Upon our visit in 1988, we observed men, women and children picking through Cairo's refuse, filling baskets with anything of value: bits of metal, strips of ribbon, even scraps of discarded food. Every now and then, someone gleefully displayed a 'precious' find that would bring the equivalent of a few dollars in the city. Watching in silence, we became keenly aware of our sturdy shoes and warm clothing and self-conscious that our watches and cameras represented more money than most of the Zebaleen earn in a year.

Today, the Cairo Zebaleen still work the city's streets collecting trash.

But much has changed, as they now represent one of the world's environmental success stories. The Zebaleen now have a legal contract to perform this work and, most important, they have established a large recycling centre near the dump. There, dozens of workers operate large machines that shred discarded cloth into stuffing to fill furniture, car seats and pillows. Others separate plastic and metal into large bins for cleaning and sale. In short, the Zebaleen are big business people. Using start-up loans from the World Bank, not only have the Zebaleen constructed an efficient recycling centre, they also have built for themselves a modern apartment complex, with electricity and running water.

The Zebaleen are still poor by European standards. But they now own the land on which they live and work, and they are prospering. Certainly, they no longer inhabit the bottom rung of Egyptian society. And many international environmental organisations hope their example will inspire others elsewhere. When the 1992 environmental summit meeting convened in Rio de Janeiro, officials presented the Cairo Zebaleen with the United Nations award for environmental protection. ●

The Zebaleen people of Cairo have amazed the world with their determination and ingenuity, turning one of the planet's foulest dumps into an efficient recycling centre and providing new apartment units for themselves in the process.

Source: Sygma – Thomas Hartwell

Source: based on Macionis's visits to Egypt, 1988 and 1994.

But even sweeping environmental strategies – put in place with the best intentions – will fail without some fundamental changes in the ways in which we think about ourselves and our world. By taking an *egocentric* view that sets up our own immediate interests as the standards for how to live, we have obscured several key connections that become clear as we shift to a more *ecocentric* outlook. First of all, we need to realise that, environmentally speaking, *the present is tied to the future*. Simply put, today's actions shape tomorrow's world. Thus, we must learn to evaluate our short-term choices in terms of their long-range consequences for the natural environment.

Second, rather than viewing humans as 'different' from or 'better' than other forms of life and assuming that we have the right to dominate the planet, we must acknowledge that *all forms of life are interdependent*. Ignoring this truth not only harms other life forms; it will eventually undermine our own well-being. From the realisation that all life figures in the ecological balance must follow specific programmes that will protect the earth's biodiversity.

Third, and finally, achieving a sustainable ecosystem will require *global cooperation*. The planet's rich and poor nations are currently separated by a vast chasm of divergent interests, cultures and living standards. On the one hand, most countries in the northern half of the world are overdeveloped, using more resources than the earth can sustain over time. On the other hand, most nations in the southern half of the world are underdeveloped, unable to meet the basic needs of many of their people. A sustainable ecosystem depends on bold and unprecedented programmes of international cooperation. And, while the cost of change will certainly be high, it pales before the eventual cost of not responding to the growing environmental deficit (Humphrey and Buttel, 1982; Burke, 1984; Kellert and Bohrmann, 1991; Brown, 1993). Along with the transformations just noted, we will reach the goal of a sustainable society only by critically re-evaluating the logic of growth that has dominated our way of life for several centuries.

In closing, we might well consider that the great dinosaurs dominated this planet for some 160 million years and then perished forever. Humanity is far younger, having existed for a mere quarter of a million years. Compared to the rather dim-witted dinosaurs, our species has the gift of great intelligence. But how wisely will we use this ability? What are the chances that our species will continue to flourish on the earth 160 million years – or even a few thousand years – from now? As Tom Burke (1984) points out, it would be foolish to assume that our present civilisation is about to collapse. But it would be equally foolish to ignore the warning signs. One certainty is that the state of tomorrow's world will depend on choices we make today.

SUMMARY

1. Because the most important factor affecting the state of the natural environment is the way in which human beings organise social life, ecology – the study of how living organisms interact with their environment – is one important focus of sociology.

2. Societies increase the environmental deficit by focusing on short-term benefits and ignoring the long-term consequences brought on by their way of life.

3. Studying the natural environment demands a global perspective. All parts of the ecosystem – including the air, soil and water – are interconnected. Similarly, actions in one part of the globe have an impact on the natural environment elsewhere.

4. Humanity's enormous influence on the natural environment springs from our capacity for culture. Our manipulation of the environment has expanded over time with the development of both complex technology and capitalism.

5. Through population growth, too, humanity affects the natural environment. The world population has soared upward over the course of the last two centuries and now threatens to overwhelm available natural resources.

6. Modern societies are 'risk societies'. New Technologies are generating 'risks' of a quite new order.

7. The 'logic of growth' argument defends economic development and asserts that people can solve environmental problems as they arise. Countering this view, the 'limits to growth' thesis states that societies have little choice but to curb development to head off eventual environmental collapse.

8. European and other Western countries have transformed into 'disposable societies', generating billions of pounds of solid waste each day. Even though recycling efforts have increased, the majority of waste continues to be dumped in landfills.

9. Water consumption is rapidly increasing throughout the world. Much of the world – notably Africa and the Middle East – is currently approaching a water-supply crisis.

10. The hydrological cycle purifies rainwater, but water pollution from dumping and chemical contamination still poses a serious threat to water quality in Europe. This problem is even more acute in the world's low-income countries.

11. Air quality became steadily worse in Europe and North America after the Industrial Revolution. About 1950, however, a turnaround took place and these societies have made significant progress in curbing air pollution. In low-income countries, particularly in cities, air quality remains at unhealthy levels due to burning of 'dirty' fuels and little regulation of pollution.

12. Acid rain, the product of pollutants entering the atmosphere, often contaminates land and water thousands of miles away.

13. Rainforests play a vital role in removing carbon dioxide from the atmosphere. Under pressure from commercial interests, the world's rainforests are now half their original size and are shrinking by about 1 per cent annually.

14. Global warming refers to predictions that the average temperature of the earth will rise because of increasing levels of carbon dioxide in the atmosphere. Both carbon emissions from factories and cars and the shrinking rainforests, which consume carbon dioxide, aggravate this problem.

15. The elimination of rainforests is also reducing the planet's biodiversity, since these tropical regions are home to about half of all living species. Biodiversity, a source of natural beauty, is also critical to agricultural and medical research.

16. Functional theory points out that cultural values have much to do with a society's orientation to the natural environment. Cultural ecology, one application of this approach, explains that a society's climate and natural resources influence culture.

17. Conflict analysis highlights the importance of inequality in understanding environmental issues. This perspective blames environmental decay on the self-interest of elites, and notes the pattern of environmental racism whereby the poor, especially minorities, disproportionately suffer from proximity to environmental hazards. It also places responsibility for the declining state of the world's natural environment primarily on rich societies, which consume the most resources.

18. A sustainable environment is one that does not threaten the well-being of future generations. Achieving this goal will require conservation of finite resources, reducing waste and pollution, and controlling the size of the world's population.

KEY CONCEPTS

acid rain precipitation that is made acidic by air pollution so that it destroys plant and animal life

cultural ecology a theoretical paradigm that explores the relationship of human culture and the physical environment

ecologically sustainable culture a way of life that meets the needs of the present generation without threatening the environmental legacy of future generations

ecology the study of the interaction of living organisms and the natural environment

ecosystem the system composed of the interaction of all living organisms and their natural environment

environmental deficit the situation in which our relationship to the environment, while yielding short-term benefits, will have profound, negative long-term consequences

environmental racism the pattern by which environmental hazards are greatest in proximity to poor people, especially minorities

global commons resources shared by all members of the international community, such as ocean-beds and the atmosphere

greenhouse effect a rise in the earth's average temperature due to increasing concentration of carbon dioxide in the atmosphere

natural environment the earth's surface and atmosphere, including various living organisms as well as the air, water, soil and other resources necessary to sustain life

rainforests regions of dense forestation, most of which circle the globe close to the equator

risk society society where risks are of a different magnitude because of technology and globalisation

CRITICAL-THINKING QUESTIONS ....

1. At one level, chemical spills are technical glitches that we sometimes dismiss as mere 'accidents'. But what social patterns and cultural values combine to make such occurrences regular events in our lives?

2. What special role can sociology play in understanding the natural environment?

3. What is meant by 'sustainable development' and what evidence supports the contention that humanity is running up an 'environmental deficit'?

Is there any evidence suggesting that some environmental problems are subsiding?

4. In what specific ways would your own life change if we were to establish an environmentally sustainable society?

5. Discuss the ways in which 'the environment' has become a global issue in the late twentieth century.

6. Examine the idea of 'the risk society'. Do you agree that risk is qualitatively different for modern societies than earlier ones?

GOING FURTHER ....

Introductory reading

Robert Garner, *Environmental Politics* (London: Prentice Hall, 1996).

Provides a succinct summary of the main issues, splits and groupings around 'environmentalism'.

A. J. McMichael, *Planetary Overload: Global Environment Change and the Health of the Human Species* (Cambridge: Cambridge University Press, 1993).

Focuses upon how the major ecological disruptions are posing a threat to the health and very existence of the human species. Provides detailed accounts of all the major threats.

Classic sources

Ulrich Beck, *Risk Society* (London: Sage, 1992).

The now classic and key statement of the emergence of a risk society, though it is far from being an 'easy read'.

Rachel Carson, *Silent Spring* (Boston: Houghton Mifflin, 1962).

This book about the dangers of chemical pollution helped launch the environmental movement in the United States and elsewhere.

Donella H. Meadows et al., *The Limits to Growth: A Report for the Club of Rome's Project on the Predicament of Mankind* (New York: Universe Books, 1972).

This study draws on computer modelling to predict future ecological trends. Its conclusions support the 'limits to growth' thesis.

More advanced reading

Ted Benton (ed.), *The Greening of Marxism* (New York: Guildford Press, 1996).

A collection of essays which show the close affinities between a revised Marxism and world concerns for the environment.

Lester R. Brown, et al., *State of the World: A Worldwatch Institute Report on Progress Toward a Sustainable Society* (New York: W. W. Norton, 1997).

 Published annually, this collection of essays focuses on a range of environmental dangers in global perspective.

Charles L. Harper, *Environment and Society: Social Perspectives on Environmental Issues and Problems* (Englewood Cliffs, NJ: Prentice Hall, 1995).

 This new text applies various sociological approaches, including major theoretical paradigms, to the study of the environment.

Other sources

Activist resources in the UK include such groupings as:

Friends of the Earth, 26–28 Underwood Street, London N1 7JQ, 0171 490 1555, web page http://www.foe.co.uk

Greenpeace, Canonbury Villas, London N1 2PN, 0171 865 8100 (membership line 0800 269 065); web page http://www.greenpeace.org.uk

The Red-Green Study Group (particularly its pamphlet *What on Earth is to be Done* 1995) at 2 Hamilton Road, Manchester M13 OPB

A compendium of ideas is to be found in:

Howard Rheingold *The Millenium Whole Earth Catalogue* San Francisco: Harper 1994/6

chapter twenty-four

Source: Popperfoto

Social Change: Traditional, Modern and Postmodern Societies

The firelight flickers in the gathering darkness as Chief Kanhonk sits, as he has done at the end of the day for many years, ready to begin an evening of animated talk and storytelling (Simons, 1995). This is the hour when the Kaiapo, a small society in Brazil's lush Amazon region, celebrate their heritage. Because the Kaiapo are a traditional people with no written language, the elders rely on evenings by the fire to teach their culture and instruct the grandchildren. In the past, evenings like this have been filled with tales of brave Kaiapo warriors fighting off Portuguese traders in pursuit of slaves and gold. But as the minutes pass, only a few villagers assemble for the evening ritual.

'It is the Big Ghost,' one man grumbles, explaining the poor turnout. The 'Big Ghost' has indeed descended upon them; its bluish glow spilling from windows of homes throughout the village. The Kaiapo children – and many adults as well – are watching television. The consequences of installing a satellite dish in the village several years ago have turned out to be greater than anyone imagined. In the end, what their enemies failed to do to the Kaiapo with guns, they may well do to themselves with prime-time programming.

The Kaiapo are among the 230,000 native peoples who inhabit the country we call Brazil. They stand out because of their striking body paint and ornate ceremonial dress. Recently, they have become rich as profits from gold mining and harvesting mahogany trees have flowed into the settlement. Now they must decide if their new-found fortune is a blessing or a curse.

To some, affluence means the opportunity to learn about the outside world through travel and television. Others, like Chief Kanhonk, are not so sure. Sitting by the fire, he thinks aloud, 'I have been saying that people must buy useful things like knives and fishing hooks. Television does not fill the stomach. It only shows our children and grandchildren white people's things.' Bebtopup, the oldest priest, nods in agreement: 'The night is the time the old people teach the young people. Television has stolen the night' (Simons, 1995: 471).

The transformation of the Kaiapo raises profound questions about the causes of change and whether change – even in pursuit of a higher material standard of living – is always for the better. Moreover, the drama of the Kaiapo is being played out around the globe as more and more traditional cultures are being lured away from their heritage by the materialism and affluence of rich societies. This chapter examines social change as a process with both positive and negative consequences. Of particular interest to people in the Western world is what sociologists call *modernity*, changes brought about by the Industrial Revolution, and *postmodernity*, more recent transformations sparked by the Information Revolution and the post-industrial economy, which are affecting both Europe and the rest of the world.

● What is social change?

Earlier chapters have examined human societies in terms of both stability and change. Relatively *static*

social patterns include status and roles, social stratification and various social institutions. The *dynamic* forces that have recast humanity's consciousness, behaviour and needs range from innovations in technology to the growth of bureaucracy and the expansion of cities. These are all dimensions of **social change**, *the transformation of culture and social institutions over time*. The process of social change has four key characteristics:

1. Social change happens everywhere, although the rate of change varies from place to place. 'Nothing is constant except death and taxes', goes the old saying. Yet social patterns related to death have changed dramatically as life expectancy in the Western world has nearly doubled over the last two centuries. Taxes, meanwhile, unknown through most of human history, emerged only with complex social organisation several thousand years ago. In short, one is hard-pressed to identify anything that is not subject to the twists and turns of change.

Still, some societies change faster than others. As Chapter 3 ('Society') explained, hunting and gathering societies tend to change quite slowly. Members of technologically complex societies, on the other hand, can sense significant change even within a single lifetime. Moreover, even in a given society, some cultural elements change more quickly than others. William Ogburn's (1964) theory of *cultural lag* (see Chapter 4) recognises that material culture (that is, things) usually changes faster than non-material culture (ideas and attitudes). For example, medical techniques that prolong life have developed more rapidly than have ethical standards for deciding when and how to use them.

2. Social change is sometimes intentional but often unplanned. Industrial societies actively promote many kinds of change. For example, scientists seek more efficient forms of energy and advertisers try to convince consumers that life is incomplete without some new gadget. Yet even the experts rarely envisage all the consequences of the changes they promote.

   Early car manufacturers certainly understood that cars would allow people to travel in a single day distances that had required weeks or months to traverse a century before. But no one foresaw how profoundly the mobility provided by cars would reshape European societies, scattering family members, threatening the environment and reshaping cities and suburbs. In addition, automotive pioneers could hardly have predicted the 50,000 deaths each year in car accidents in the Western world alone.

3. Social change often generates controversy. As the history of the car demonstrates, most social change yields both positive and negative consequences. Capitalists welcomed the Industrial Revolution because advancing technology increased productivity and swelled profits. Many workers, however, fearing that machines would make their skills obsolete, strongly resisted 'progress'. In the Western world, changing patterns of interaction between black people and white people, between women and men and between gays and heterosexuals give rise to misunderstandings, tensions and, sometimes, outright hostility.

4. Some changes matter more than others. Some social changes have only passing significance, whereas other transformations resonate for generations. At one extreme, clothing fads among the young burst on the scene and dissipate quickly. At the other, we are still adjusting to powerful technological advances such as television half a century after its introduction. Looking ahead, who can predict with any certainty how computers will transform the entire world during the next century? Will the Information Revolution turn out to be as pivotal as the Industrial Revolution? Like the car and television, computers will have both beneficial and deleterious effects, providing new kinds of jobs while eliminating old ones, joining people together in ever-expanding electronic networks while threatening personal privacy.

● Causes of social change

Social change has many causes. And in a world linked by sophisticated communication and transportation technology, change in one place often begets change elsewhere.

Culture and change

Culture is a dynamic system that continually gains new elements and loses others. Chapter 4 ('Culture') identified three important sources of cultural change. First, *invention* produces new objects, ideas and social patterns. Through rocket propulsion research, which began in the 1940s, we have engineered high-tech vehicles for space flight. Today we take such technology for granted; during the next century a significant number of people may well travel in space.

Second, *discovery* occurs when people first take note of certain elements of the world or learn to see them in a new way. Medical advances, for example, offer a growing understanding of the human body. Beyond the direct effects for human health, medical discoveries have also stretched life expectancy, setting in motion 'the greying of the Western World' (see Chapter 14, 'Ageing and the Elderly').

Third, *diffusion* creates change as trade, migration and mass communication spread cultural elements throughout the world. Ralph Linton (1937) recognised that many familiar elements of a culture have come to us from other lands. For example, cloth was developed in Asia whilst coins were devised in Turkey. Generally, material things diffuse more readily than non-material cultural traits. The Kaiapo, described at the beginning of this chapter, have been quick to adopt television but reluctant to embrace the materialism and individualism that sometimes seize those who spend hours watching Western commercial programming.

Through much migration, the Western world has steadily changed in response to cultural diffusion. In recent decades, people from Africa, Asia and other parts of the world have been introducing new cultural patterns, clearly evident in the sights, smells and sounds of cities across European countries. Conversely, the global power of the Western world ensures that much of Western culture – from the taste of beefburgers to the sounds of Pavarotti – is being diffused to other societies.

Conflict and change

Tension and conflict within a society also produce change. Marx heralded class conflict as the engine that drives societies from one historical era to another (see Chapter 3, 'Society', and Chapter 9, 'Social Stratification'). In industrial-capitalist societies, he maintained, struggle between capitalists and workers propels society towards a socialist system of production. In the century since Marx's death, this model has proven simplistic. Yet, he correctly foresaw that social conflict arising from inequality (involving race, gender and sexuality as well as social class) would force changes in every society, including our own.

Ideas and change

Max Weber, too, contributed to our understanding of social change. While Weber acknowledged the importance of conflict based on material production, he traced the roots of social change to the world of ideas. He illustrated his argument by showing how people who display charisma (described in Chapter 16, 'Power, the State and Social Movements', and Chapter 18, 'Religion') can convey a message that sometimes changes the world.

Weber also highlighted the importance of ideas by revealing how the world view of early Protestants prompted them to embrace industrial capitalism (see Chapter 3, 'Society'). By showing that industrial capitalism developed primarily in areas of Western Europe where the Protestant work ethic was strong, Weber (1958; orig. 1904–5) concluded that the disciplined rationality of Calvinist Protestants was instrumental in this change.

Ideas also fuel social movements. Chapter 16 looked at social movements and showed how they may emerge from the determination to modify society in some manner (say, to clean up the environment) or from a sense that existing social arrangements are unjust. The international gay rights movement draws strength from the contention that lesbians and gay men should enjoy rights and opportunities equal to those of the heterosexual majority. Opposition to the gay rights movement, moreover, reveals the power of ideas to inhibit as well as to advance social change.

The natural environment and change

As Chapter 23 ('Environment and the Risk Society') detailed, human societies are closely connected to their natural environment. For this reason, change in one tends to produce change in the other. By and large, 'modern' culture has cast nature as a force to be tamed and reshaped to human purposes. From the onset of industrialisation and the rise of capitalism, people have systematically cut down forests to create fields for farming and to make materials for building; they have established towns and cities, extended roads in every direction and dammed rivers as a source of water and energy. Such human construction not only reflects a cultural determination to control the natural environment; it also points up the centrality of the idea of 'growth' in our way of life.

But the consequences of this thinking have placed increasing stress on the natural environment. Western societies confront problems from growing mountains of solid waste, as well as air and water pollution, all the while consuming the lion's share of global resources. A growing awareness that such patterns are not sustainable in the long term is forcing us to confront the need to change our way of life in some basic respects.

Demographic change

Population growth places escalating demands on the natural environment, and also alters cultural patterns. In cities of the Netherlands, a high-density nation, homes are small and narrow with extremely steep staircases to make efficient use of space. In Tokyo, Japan, commuters routinely endure crowding on subways that would challenge the patience of a lifelong Londoner or Parisian. The fast-paced and anonymous way of life that is typical of populous cities barely resembles that found in the rural villages and small towns common to our past.

Profound change also results from the shifting composition of a population. As Chapter 14 ('Ageing and the Elderly') explained, many societies are growing older. Soon nearly one in five people in Western countries will be 65 or older. Medical research and health care services already focus extensively on the elderly, and common stereotypes about old people will be undermined as more men and women enter this stage of life. Ways of life may change in countless additional directions as homes and household products are redesigned to meet the needs of growing ranks of older people.

Migration within and among societies is another demographic factor that promotes change. Between 1870 and 1930, millions of rural peoples in Western societies, along with millions of immigrants from poorer countries, swelled the industrial cities. As a result, farm communities declined, metropolises burgeoned and the Western world became for the first time a predominantly urban society. Similar changes are taking place today as people moving between European Union member states interact with new immigrants from Africa and Asia.

● Modernity

A central concept in the study of social change is **modernity**, *social patterns linked to industrialisation*. In everyday usage, modernity (its Latin root means 'lately') designates the present in relation to the past. Sociologists include within this catchall concept the many social patterns set in motion by the Industrial Revolution beginning in Western Europe in the mid-eighteenth century. **Modernisation**, then, is *the process of social change initiated by industrialisation*. The time line inside the front cover of the text highlights important events that mark the emergence of modernity.

Key dimensions of modernisation

Peter Berger (1977) notes four major characteristics of modernisation:

1. *The decline of small, traditional communities.* Modernity involves 'the progressive weakening, if not destruction, of the concrete and relatively cohesive communities in which human beings have found solidarity and meaning throughout most of history' (Berger, 1977: 72). For thousands of years, in the camps of hunters and gatherers and in the rural villages of Europe, people lived in small-scale settlements with family and neighbours. Such traditional worlds – based on sentiments and beliefs passed from generation to generation – afford each person a well-defined place. These primary groups limit people's range of experience while conferring a strong sense of identity, belonging and purpose.

   Small, isolated communities still exist in the Western world, of course, but they are now home to only a small percentage of people. Even for rural people, rapid transportation and efficient communication, including television, have brought individuals in touch with the pulse of the larger society and even the entire world.

2. *The expansion of personal choice.* To people in traditional, preindustrial societies, life is shaped by forces beyond human control – gods, spirits or, simply, fate. Steeped in tradition, members of these societies grant one another a narrow range of personal choices. As the power of tradition erodes, however, people come to see their lives as an unending series of options, a process Berger calls *individualisation*. Many people respond to the alternatives in modern societies by changing their 'lifestyles' over time.

3. *Increasing diversity in beliefs.* In preindustrial societies, strong family ties and powerful religious beliefs enforce conformity while discouraging diversity and change. Modernisation promotes a more rational, scientific world view, in which tradition loses its force and morality becomes a matter of individual attitude. The growth of cities, the expansion of impersonal organisations and social interaction among people from various backgrounds combine to foster a diversity of beliefs and behaviour.

4. *Future orientation and growing awareness of time.* People in modern societies think more about the future, while preindustrial people focus more on the past. Modern people are not only forward looking but optimistic that discoveries and new inventions

will enhance their lives. In addition, modern people organise daily routines according to precise units of time. With the introduction of clocks in the late Middle Ages, sunlight and seasons faded in importance as measures of time's forward march in favour of hours and minutes. Preoccupied with personal gain, modern people calculate time to the moment and generally believe that 'Time is money!' Berger points out that one key indicator of a society's degree of modernisation is the proportion of people wearing wristwatches.

Finally, recall that modernisation touched off the development of sociology itself. As Chapter 1 ('The Sociological Perspective') explained, the discipline

originated in the wake of the Industrial Revolution in Western Europe, precisely where social change was proceeding most rapidly. Early sociologists tried to analyse and explain modernisation and its consequences – both good and bad – for human beings.

Ferdinand Toennies: the loss of community

The German sociologist Ferdinand Toennies, whose brief biography appears in the box, produced the theory of *Gemeinschaft* and *Gesellschaft* (see Chapter 21, 'Population and Urbanisation'). Like Peter Berger, whose work he influenced, Toennies (1963; orig. 1887) viewed modernisation as the progressive loss of *Gemeinschaft*, or human community. As Toennies saw

PROFILE
. . . .

Ferdinand Toennies: is there virtue in modern society?

Can traditional virtues such as selflessness and honour survive in the rapidly changing modern world? Pioneering sociologist Ferdinand Toennies (1855–1936) spent his life pursuing the answer to this important question. In the process, along with his colleagues, Max Weber and Georg Simmel, Toennies helped to establish sociology as an academic discipline in Germany.

Born to a wealthy family in the German countryside, Toennies was raised in comfortable surroundings and received an extensive education. He also learned a great deal from observing the world about him – he was especially fascinated by how the Industrial Revolution was transforming Germany and other European countries. Toennies's work displays a deep distrust of the notion of 'progress', which he

feared amounted to the steady loss of traditional morality. His influential book *Gemeinschaft und Gesellschaft* (1887) is therefore both a chronicle of modernisation and an indictment of an increasingly impersonal world.

Toennies's thesis is that traditional societies, built on kinship and

Ferdinande Toennies

Source: Bildarchiv Preussischer Kulturbesitz – Gelehrte Dtld

neighbourhood, nourish collective sentiments, virtue and honour. Modernisation washes across traditional society like an acid, eroding human community and unleashing rampant individualism. Toennies stopped short of claiming that modern society was 'worse' than societies of the past and he made a point of praising the spread of rational, scientific thinking. Nevertheless, the growing individualism and selfishness characteristic of modern societies troubled him. Knowing that there could be no return to the past, he looked to the future, hoping that new forms of social organisation would develop that would combine modern rationality with traditional collective responsibility. ●

Source: based on Cahnman and Heberle, 1971.

it, the Industrial Revolution undermined the strong social fabric of family and tradition by fostering individualism and a businesslike emphasis on facts and efficiency. European and North American societies gradually became rootless and impersonal as people came to associate mostly on the basis of self-interest – the condition Toennies dubbed *Gesellschaft*.

Early in this century, at least some areas of the Western world approximated Toennies's concept of *Gemeinschaft*. Families that had lived for generations in rural towns and villages were tightly integrated into a hard-working, slow-moving way of life. Before telephones (invented in 1876) and television (introduced in 1939, widespread after 1950), families and communities entertained themselves, communicating with distant members by letters. Before private cars became commonplace after the Second World War, many people viewed their home town as their entire world.

Inevitable tensions and conflicts – sometimes based on race, ethnicity and religion – characterised past communities. According to Toennies, however, the traditional ties of *Gemeinschaft* bound people of a community together, 'essentially united in spite of all separating factors' (1963: 65; orig. 1887).

Modernity turns societies inside out so that, as Toennies put it, people are 'essentially separated in spite of uniting factors' (1963: 65; orig. 1887). This is the world of *Gesellschaft* where, especially in large cities, most people live among strangers and ignore those they pass on the street. Trust is hard to come by in a mobile and anonymous society in which, according to researchers, people tend to put their personal needs ahead of group loyalty and a majority of adults claim that 'you can't be too careful' in dealing with people (Russell, 1993). In the United States, 15 million people attend weekly support groups to establish temporary emotional ties and find someone who is willing simply to *listen* (Leerhsen, 1990).

Critical evaluation

Toennies's theory of *Gemeinschaft* and *Gesellschaft* stands as the most widely cited model for describing modernisation. The theory's strength lies in its synthesis of various dimensions of change – growing population, the rise of cities, increasing impersonality in social interaction. One problem with Toennies's theory, however, is that modern life is not completely devoid of *Gemeinschaft*. Even in a world of strangers, friendships are often strong and lasting. Traditions are especially pronounced in many ethnic communities where residents maintain close community ties. Another criticism is that Toennies's approach says little about which factors (industrialisation, urbanisation, weakening of families) are cause and which are effect. Some analysts have also argued that Toennies overlooked the negative sides of traditional community organisations.

Emile Durkheim: the division of labour

Durkheim, whose work has appeared throughout this book, shared Toennies's interest in the profound social changes wrought by the Industrial Revolution. For Durkheim, modernisation is marked by an increasing *division of labour*, or specialised economic activity (1964b; orig. 1893). Whereas every member of a traditional society engages in a wide range of activities, people in modern societies perform highly specialised roles.

Durkheim contended that *mechanical solidarity*, social bonds arising from shared moral sentiments, held preindustrial societies together. Members had a sense that everyone was basically alike and belonged together. Mechanical solidarity – similar to Toennies' *Gemeinschaft* – depends on a minimal division of labour, so that everyone's life follows much the same path.

With modernisation, the division of labour becomes increasingly pronounced. Mutual dependency among people with specialised occupations, or *organic solidarity*, thus holds modern societies together. Difference, rather than likeness, integrates modern societies. All of us depend on others to meet most of our needs. Organic solidarity corresponds to Toennies's concept of *Gesellschaft*.

Despite obvious similarities, Durkheim and Toennies interpreted modernity somewhat differently. To Toennies, modern *Gesellschaft* amounts to the loss of social solidarity – the inevitable result of the gradual erosion of 'natural' and 'organic' bonds of the rural past, leaving only the 'artificial' and 'mechanical' ties of the present. Durkheim disagreed and even reversed Toennies's language to bring home the point. He labelled modern society 'organic', suggesting that today's world is no less natural than before, and he described traditional societies as 'mechanical' because they are so regimented. Thus Durkheim viewed modernisation not so much as a loss of community as a change in the basis of community – from bonds of likeness (kinship and community) to economic interdependence (the division of labour). Durkheim's perspective on modernity is both more complex and more positive than that of Toennies.

Critical evaluation

Durkheim's work stands alongside that of Toennies as a highly influential analysis of modernity. Of the two, Durkheim is clearly more optimistic; though he feared that modern societies might become so internally diverse that they would collapse into *anomie*, a condition in which norms and values are so weak and inconsistent that society provides little moral guidance to individuals. In the midst of weak moral claims from society, modern people tend to be egocentric, placing their own needs above those of others.

Evidence supports Durkheim's contention that anomie plagues modern societies. Suicide rates – which Durkheim considered a good index of anomie – have, in fact, risen throughout this century. Increasingly, people feel less commitment to a standard of 'right and wrong' and instead apply more flexible (or disconnected) moral ideals to different situations. On the other hand, shared norms and values are still strong enough to give individuals some sense of meaning and purpose. Additionally, whatever the hazards of anomie and atomisation, most people seem to value the privacy and personal autonomy that modern society affords.

Max Weber: rationalisation

For Max Weber, whose work is also detailed in Chapter 3 ('Society'), modernity amounts to the progressive replacement of a traditional world-view with a rational way of thinking. In preindustrial societies, tradition acts as a constant brake on change. To traditional people, Weber explains, 'truth' is roughly synonymous with 'what has always been' (1978: 36; orig. 1921). In modern societies, by contrast, people see truth as a more personal matter of deliberate calculation. Because efficiency is valued more than reverence for the past, individuals adopt whichever social patterns will allow them to achieve their goals.

Echoing the claims of Toennies and Durkheim that industrialisation weakens traditions, Weber declared that people in modern societies feel 'disenchanted'. Once unquestioned truths have become subject to matter-of-fact calculations. In embracing rational, scientific thought, modern societies turn away from the gods. Throughout his life, Weber explored various modern 'types' – the capitalist, the scientist, the bureaucrat – all of whom share the rational and detached world-view Weber believed was coming to dominate humanity.

Critical evaluation

Compared with Toennies, and especially Durkheim, Weber profoundly criticised modern societies. He recognised that science could produce technological and organisational wonders, yet he worried that it was carrying us away from more basic questions about the meaning and purpose of human existence. Weber feared that rationalisation, especially in bureaucracies, would erode the human spirit with endless rules and regulations. However, some of Weber's critics think that the alienation he attributed to bureaucracy is actually a product of social inequality. The contention leads us to the ideas of Karl Marx.

Karl Marx: capitalism

Instead of examining social order, Marx focused on social conflict. For Marx, modern society was synonymous with capitalism. He saw the Industrial Revolution primarily as a *capitalist revolution*. As Chapter 3 ('Society') explained, Marx contended that the bourgeoisie in medieval Europe emerged as a force to wrest control of society from the feudal nobility. The bourgeoisie were finally successful when the Industrial Revolution placed a powerful new productive system under their control.

Marx agreed that modernity weakened small-scale communities (as described by Toennies), sharpened the division of labour (as noted by Durkheim), and fostered a rational world-view (as argued by Weber). Nevertheless, he considered these factors simply as conditions necessary for capitalism to flourish. Capitalism, according to Marx, draws populations from farms and small towns into an ever-expanding market system centred in the cities. Specialisation underlies efficient factories and rationality is exemplified by the capitalists' relentless quest for profits.

Even so, Marx's vision of modernity incorporates a considerable measure of optimism. Unlike Weber, who viewed modern society as an 'iron cage' of bureaucracy, Marx believed that social conflict within capitalist social systems would sow the seeds of revolutionary social change, ultimately producing an egalitarian socialism. Such a society, as he envisioned it, would harness the wonders of industrial technology to enrich people's lives and also rid the world of social classes, the prime source of social conflict and dehumanisation. While Marx's evaluation of modern capitalist society was highly negative, then, he imagined a bright future of greater human freedom, blossoming human creativity and renewed human community.

Critical evaluation
Marx's theory of modernisation weaves together many threads in a fabric dominated by capitalism. Yet Marx underestimated the dominance of bureaucracy in modern societies. And in a twist never predicted by Marx, the bloated government apparatus in socialist societies actually stifled the human spirit. The recent upheavals in Eastern Europe and the former Soviet Union reveal the depth of popular opposition to rigid state-controlled bureaucracies.

● Theoretical analysis of modernity

The rise of modernity is a complex process involving many dimensions of change, described in previous chapters and summarised in Table 24.1. How is one to make sense of so many changes going on all at once? Sociologists have devised two overarching explanations of modern society, one derived from the functional paradigm and one based on the conflict approach.

Functional theory: modernity as mass society

One broad approach – drawing on the ideas of Ferdinand Toennies, Emile Durkheim and Max Weber – understands modernisation as the emergence of *mass society* (Dahrendorf, 1959; Kornhauser, 1959; Nisbet, 1966, 1969; Baltzell, 1968; Stein, 1972; Berger, Berger and Kellner, 1974; Pearson, 1993). A **mass society** is *a society in which industry and expanding bureaucracy have eroded traditional social ties*. A mass society is marked by weak kinship, impersonal communities and socially atomised individuals. As isolated units in mass societies, people typically experience feelings of moral uncertainty and personal powerlessness.

The mass scale of modern life
Mass-society theory points, first, to the rapidly increasing scale of modern life. Before the Industrial Revolution, Europe and North America constituted an intricate mosaic of countless rural villages and small towns. In these small communities, which inspired Toennies's concept of *Gemeinschaft*, people lived out their lives surrounded by kin and guided by a shared heritage. Gossip was an informal, yet highly effective, means of ensuring rigid conformity to community standards. Limited community size combined with strong moral values to stifle social diversity – the mechanical solidarity described by Durkheim.

For example, in England before 1690, both law and local custom demanded that all people regularly participate in the Christian ritual of Holy Communion (Laslett, 1984). Because social differences were repressed, subcultures and countercultures rarely flourished and change proceeded slowly. Individuals' social positions were more or less set at birth, with little social mobility.

A surge in population, the growth of cities and specialised economic activity driven by the Industrial Revolution gradually changed all this. People came to know one another by their functions (as a 'doctor' or a 'clerk') rather than by their kinship group or home town. The majority of people looked on others simply as strangers. The mass media – newspapers, radio, television and computer networks – replaced the face-to-face communication of the village, furthering the process of social atomisation. Large organisations steadily assumed more and more responsibility for daily needs that had once been fulfilled by family, friends and neighbours; universal public education enlarged the scope of learning; police, solicitors and formal courts supervised a wide-ranging criminal justice system. Even charity became the work of faceless bureaucrats working for various social welfare agencies.

Geographical mobility, mass communications and exposure to diverse ways of life erode traditional values. Less certain about what is worth believing, people become more tolerant of social diversity, trumpeting individual rights and freedom of choice. Subcultures and countercultures multiply. Making categorical distinctions among people – that is, treating people differently based on their race, sex or religion – has come to be defined as backward and unjust. In the process, minorities who have long lived at the margins of society have gained greater power and broader participation in public life. Yet, mass-society theorists fear, transforming people of various backgrounds into a generic mass may end up dehumanising everyone.

Table 24.1 ● Traditional and modern societies: the big picture

Elements of society	Traditional societies	Modern societies
Cultural patterns		
Values	Homogeneous; sacred character; few subcultures and countercultures	Heterogeneous; secular character; many subcultures and countercultures
Norms	High moral significance; little tolerance of diversity	Variable moral significance; high tolerance of diversity
Time orientation	Present linked to past	Present linked to future
Technology	Preindustrial; human and animal energy	Industrial; advanced energy sources
Social structure		
Status and role	Few statuses, most ascribed; few specialised roles	Many statuses, some ascribed and some achieved; many specialised roles
Relationships	Typically primary; little anonymity and privacy	Typically secondary; considerable anonymity and privacy
Communication	Face to face	Face-to-face communication supplemented by mass media
Social control	Informal gossip	Formal police and legal system
Social stratification	Rigid patterns of social inequality; little mobility	Fluid patterns of social inequality; considerable mobility
Gender patterns	Pronounced patriarchy; women's lives centred on the home	Declining patriarchy; increasing number of women in the paid labour force
Economy	Based on agriculture; some manufacturing in the home; little white-collar work	Based on industrial mass production; factories become centres of production; increasing white-collar work
State	Small-scale government; little state intervention in society	Large-scale government; considerable state intervention in society
Family	Extended family as the primary means of socialisation and economic production	Nuclear family retains some socialisation functions but is more a unit of consumption than of production
Religion	Religion guides world view; little religious pluralism	Religion weakens with the rise of science; extensive religious pluralism
Education	Formal schooling limited to elites	Basic schooling becomes universal, with growing proportion receiving advanced education
Health	High birth and death rates; brief life expectancy because of low standard of living and simple medical technology	Low birth and death rates; longer life expectancy because of higher standard of living and sophisticated medical technology
Settlement patterns	Small scale; population typically small and widely dispersed in rural villages and small towns	Large scale; population typically large and concentrated in cities
Social change	Slow; change evident over many generations	Rapid; change evident within a single generation

The ever-expanding state

In the small-scale, preindustrial societies of Europe, government amounted to little more than a local noble. A royal family formally reigned over an entire nation but, without efficient transportation or communication, the power of even absolute monarchs fell far short of that wielded by today's political leaders.

As technological innovation allowed government to expand, the centralised state grew in size and importance. Government has entered more and more areas of social life – regulating wages and working conditions, establishing standards for products of all sorts, schooling the population and providing financial assistance to the ill and the unemployed. Taxes covering such programmes consume several months of most people's annual earnings.

In a mass society, power resides in large bureaucracies, leaving people in local communities little control over their lives. For example, state officials mandate a standardised educational programme for local schools, local products must earn government certification, and every citizen must maintain extensive records for purposes of taxation. While such regulations may protect people and enhance uniformity of treatment, they force us to deal more and more with nameless officials in distant and often unresponsive bureaucracies, and they undermine the autonomy of families and local communities.

Critical evaluation

The theory of mass society concedes that the transformation of small-scale communities has positive aspects, but it sees in historical change the loss of an irreplaceable heritage. Modern societies increase individual rights and tolerance of social differences, and raise standards of living. Nevertheless, they seem prone to what Weber feared most – excessive bureaucracy – as well as Toennies's feared self-centredness and Durkheim's predicted anomie. The size, complexity and tolerance of diversity in modern societies all but doom traditional values and family patterns, leaving individuals isolated, anxious and materialistic. As we noted in Chapter 16 ('Power, the State and Social Movements'), voter apathy has become a serious problem in the Western world. But is it surprising that people in vast, impersonal societies tend to conclude that no one person can make a difference?

Critics of mass-society theory contend that it romanticises the past. They remind us that many people in small towns were actually eager to set out for the excitement and higher standard of living found in cities. Critics also point out that this approach pays little attention to problems of social inequality. Mass-society analysis, critics conclude, attracts social and economic conservatives who defend conventional morality and often seem indifferent to the historical plight of women and other minorities.

Conflict theory: modernity as class society

A second interpretation of modernity derives largely from the ideas of Karl Marx. From this point of view, modernity takes the form of a **class society**, *a capitalist society with pronounced social stratification*. This theory holds that inequality underlies widespread feelings of powerlessness. While acknowledging that modern societies have expanded to a mass scale, this approach views the heart of modernisation as an expanding capitalist economy with its inevitable inequality (Miliband, 1969; Habermas, 1970; Blumberg, 1981; Harrington, 1984).

Capitalism

Class-society theory follows Marx in claiming that the growing scale of social life has resulted from the insatiable appetite of capitalism. Because a capitalist economy pursues ever-increasing profits, both production and consumption steadily rise. According to Marx, capitalism rests on 'naked self-interest' (1972: 337; orig. 1848). This self-centredness erodes the social ties that once cemented small-scale communities. Capitalism also fosters impersonality and anonymity by transforming people into commodities, both as a source of labour and a market for capitalist production. The net result is that capitalism reduces human beings to cogs in the machinery of material production.

Capitalism also embraces science, not just as the key to greater productivity but also as an ideology that justifies the status quo. In modern societies, people view their own well-being as a *technical* puzzle to be solved by engineers and other experts rather than through the pursuit of *social* justice (Habermas, 1970). A capitalist culture, for example, seeks to improve health through scientific medicine rather than by eliminating poverty, which undermines many people's health in the first place.

Businesses also raise the banner of scientific logic when they claim that efficiency is achieved only through continual growth. As Chapter 15 ('The Economy, Consumption and Work') explains, capitalist corporations have reached enormous size and control almost unimaginable wealth. They have done so by 'going global', operating as multinationals throughout the world. From the class-society point of view, then, the expanding scale of life is less a function of *Gesellschaft* than the inevitable, destructive consequence of capitalism.

Persistent inequality

Modernity has gradually worn away some of the rigid categorical distinctions that divided nobles and commoners in preindustrial societies. Even so, class-society theory maintains that wealthy business elites wield considerable power. In many countries today, the richest 5 per cent of the population controls over half of the national wealth.

While mass-society theorists believe that government has an expanding role in combating social problems, Marx was sceptical that the state could accomplish more than minor reforms. As he saw it, the state mostly defends the wealth and privileges of capitalists. Other class-society theorists add that working peoples and minorities have clawed out expanded political rights and a higher standard of living only by organising against hostile capitalists and government officials.

Critical evaluation

Table 24.2 summarises the interpretations of modernity offered by mass-society theory and class-society theory. While the former focuses on the increasing life spans

and the growth of government, the latter stresses the expansion of capitalism and the persistence of inequality. Class-society theory also dismisses Durkheim's argument that people in modern societies suffer from anomie, claiming, instead, that they grapple with alienation and powerlessness. People adopting this interpretation of modernity call for the extensive regulation (or the abolition) of the capitalist marketplace.

To critics of class-society theory, this analysis overlooks the many ways in which modern societies have grown more egalitarian. While discrimination based on race, ethnicity, gender and sexuality persists, such discrimination is increasingly perceived as deviant, rather than acceptable, behaviour. Further, most people in the Western world favour unequal rewards, at least insofar as they reflect differences in personal talent and effort. Moreover, many of the social problems found in the Western world – from unemployment, industrial pollution and unresponsive government – have also been commonplace in socialist nations such as North Korea.

Modernity and the individual

Both mass-society theory and class-society theory focus on broad patterns of change that have taken place since the Industrial Revolution. From each macro-level approach we can also draw micro-level insights into how modernity shapes individual lives.

Micro-action/mass society: problems of identity

Modernity liberated individuals from small, tightly knit communities of the past. Most people in modern societies possess unprecedented privacy and freedom to express their individuality. Mass-society theory suggests, however, that extensive social diversity, atomisation and rapid social change make it difficult for many people to establish any coherent identity at all (Wheelis, 1958; Riesman, 1970; Berger, Berger and Kellner, 1974).

Chapter 5 ('Socialisation') explained that people forge distinctive personalities based on their social experience. The small, homogeneous and slowly changing societies of the past provided a firm (if narrow) foundation for building meaningful identity. The Amish communities that flourish in parts of the United

Table 24.2 ● Two interpretations of modernity: a summary

	Key process of modernisation	Key effects of modernisation
Mass-society theory	Industrialisation; growth of bureaucracy	Increasing scale of life; rise of the state and other formal organisations
Class-society theory	Rise of capitalism	Expansion of the capitalist economy persistence of social inequality

States teach young people 'correct' ways to think and behave. Not everyone born into an Amish community can tolerate these demands for conformity, but most members establish a well integrated and satisfying personal identity (see Hostetler, 1980; Kraybill and Olshan, 1994).

Mass societies, with their characteristic diversity and rapid change, offer only shifting sands on which to build a personal identity. Left to make our own life decisions, many of us – especially those with greater affluence – confront a bewildering array of options. Autonomy has little value without standards for making choices and, in a tolerant mass society, people may find one path no more compelling than the next. Not surprisingly, many people shuttle from one identity to another, changing their lifestyle, relationships and even religion in search of an elusive 'true self'. Beset by the widespread 'relativism' of modern societies, people without a moral compass have lost the security and certainty once provided by tradition.

To David Riesman (1970; orig. 1950), modernisation brings on changes in **social character**, *personality patterns common to members of a particular society.* Preindustrial societies promote what Riesman calls **tradition-directedness**, *rigid conformity to time-honoured ways of living.* Members of traditional societies model their lives on what has gone before so that what is 'good' is equivalent to 'what has always been'.

Tradition-directedness, then, carries to the level of individual experience Toennies's *Gemeinschaft* and Durkheim's mechanical solidarity. Culturally conservative, tradition-directed people think and act alike because everyone draws on the same solid cultural foundation. Amish people exemplify tradition-direction; in Amish culture, tradition ties everyone to ancestors and descendants in an unbroken chain of righteous living.

Many members of diverse and rapidly changing societies define a tradition-directed personality as deviant because it seems so rigid. Modern people, by and large, prize personal flexibility, the capacity to adapt and sensitivity to others. Riesman describes this type of social character as **other-directedness**, *a receptiveness to the latest trends and fashions, often expressed in the practice of imitating others.* Because their socialisation occurs within societies that are constantly in flux, other-directed people develop fluid identities marked by superficiality, inconsistency and change. They try

on different 'selves', almost like so many pieces of new clothing, seek out 'role models' and engage in varied 'performances' as they move from setting to setting (Goffman, 1959). In a traditional society, such 'shiftiness' marks a person as untrustworthy, but in a changing, modern society, the chameleon-like ability to fit in virtually anywhere stands as a valued personal trait.

In societies that value the up-to-date rather than the traditional, people anxiously solicit the approval of others, looking to members of their own generation rather than to elders as significant role models. 'Peer pressure' can sometimes be irresistible to people with no enduring standards to guide them. Our society urges individuals to be true to themselves. But when social surroundings change so rapidly, how can people determine to which self they should be true? This problem lies at the root of the identity crisis so widespread in industrial societies today. 'Who am I?' is a nagging question that many of us struggle to answer. In truth, this problem is not so much psychological as sociological, reflecting the inherent instability of modern mass society.

Class society: problems of powerlessness

Class-society theory paints a different picture of modernity's effects on individuals. This approach maintains that persistent social inequality undermines modern society's promise of individual freedom. For some, modernity delivers great privilege, but, for many, everyday life means coping with economic uncertainty and a gnawing sense of powerlessness (Newman, 1993).

For ethnic minorities, the problem of relative disadvantage looms even larger. Similarly, although women enjoy expanded opportunities and gay men and lesbians increasing acceptance as normal people, these groups continue to confront traditional barriers of sexism and homophobia. In short, this approach rejects the mass-society theory claim that people suffer from too much freedom. Instead, class-society theory holds, our society still denies a majority of people full participation in social life.

As we saw in Chapter 11 ('Global Stratification'), the expanding scope of world capitalism has placed more of the earth's population under the influence of multinational corporations. As a result, about two-thirds of the world's income is concentrated in high-income countries, where only 15 per cent of its people live. Is it any wonder, class-society theorists ask, that people in poor nations also seek greater power to shape their own lives?

Such problems led Herbert Marcuse (1964) to challenge Max Weber's contention that modern society is rational. Marcuse condemned modern society as irrational because, he maintained, it fails to meet the needs of so many people. While modern capitalist societies produce unparalleled wealth, poverty remains the daily plight of more than a billion people. Moreover, Marcuse argues, technological advances typically reduce people's control over their own lives. The advent of high technology has conferred great power on a core of specialists – not the majority of people – who now control events and dominate the public agenda, whether the issue is energy production or health care. Countering the common view that technology *solves* the world's problems, Marcuse contended that science actually *causes* them. In sum, class-society theory asserts that people suffer because modern societies have concentrated both wealth and power in the hands of a privileged few.

Modernity and progress

In modern societies, most people expect – and applaud – social change. We link modernity to the idea of *progress* (from Latin, meaning 'moving forward'), a state of continual improvement. By contrast, we denigrate stability as stagnation. This chapter began by describing the Kaiapo of Brazil, for whom affluence has broadened opportunities but weakened traditional heritage. In examining the Kaiapo, we see that social change, with all its beneficial and detrimental consequences, is too complex simply to be equated with progress.

Whether or not we see a given change as progress depends on our underlying values. A rising standard of living among the Kaiapo – or among the European populations – has helped make lives longer and more comfortable. But affluence has also fuelled materialism at the expense of spiritual life, rendering any simplistic notions of 'progress' suspect. In global context, as Figure 24.1 shows, people in Western countries have considerable confidence in the ability of science to improve their lives. Yet, recent surveys show that many adults also feel that science 'makes our way of life change too fast' (NORC, 1994: 321).

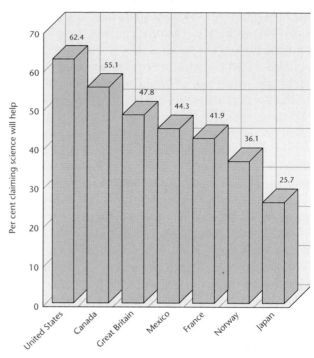

Figure 24.1 ● **Support for science: a global survey**

Survey question: 'In the long run, do you think the scientific advances we are making will help or harm humankind?'

Per cent claiming science will help:
- United States: 62.4
- Canada: 55.1
- Great Britain: 47.8
- Mexico: 44.3
- France: 41.9
- Norway: 36.1
- Japan: 25.7

Source: World Values Survey (1994)

Social change, then, is inherently complex and controversial. We in the Western world are proud of our pursuit of basic human rights. Yet, as Chapter 4 ('Culture') explained, we now have something of a 'culture of rights' that emphasises what others owe us but overlooks our obligations to one another.

In principle, almost everyone in our society supports the idea that individuals should have considerable autonomy in shaping their own lives. Thus, many people will applaud the demise of traditional conceptions of honour, viewing this trend as a sign of progress. Yet, as people exercise their freedom of choice, they inevitably challenge social patterns cherished by those who maintain a more traditional way of life. For example, people may choose to live with someone without marrying, or may feel more comfortable in an intimate same sex partnership. To those who endorse individual choice, such changes symbolise progress; to those who value traditional family patterns, however, these developments signal societal decline.

New technology, too, sparks controversy. More rapid transportation and more efficient communication may improve our lives in some respects. However, complex technology has also eroded traditional attachments to home towns and even to families. Industrial technology has also unleashed an unprecedented threat to the natural environment. In short, we know that change is accelerating over time, but views may differ sharply as to whether any particular change amounts to progress.

Modernity: global variation

While it is often useful to contrast traditional and modern social patterns, actual societies often fuse the old and the new in unexpected ways. In the People's Republic of China, ancient Confucian principles coexist with contemporary socialist thinking. Similarly, in Mexico and much of Latin America, people engage in centuries-old Christian rituals even as they struggle valiantly to pursue economic development. The description of Brazil's Kaiapo that opened this chapter points up the tensions that typically surround the mixing of traditional and modern social patterns. The broader point is that such combinations are far from unusual – indeed, they are found throughout the world.

● Postmodernity

If modernity was the product of the Industrial Revolution, has the Information Revolution propelled us into the postmodern era? A number of scholars answer affirmatively, and use the term **postmodernity** to refer to *social patterns characteristic of postindustrial societies.*

Looking more closely, however, we find disagreement about precisely what constitutes postmodernism. This term – long used in literary, philosophical and even architectural circles – has edged into sociology on a wave of social criticism that has been building since the surge of left-leaning politics in the 1960s. Although there are many variants of postmodern thinking, all share the following

five themes (Bernstein, 1992; Borgmann, 1992; Crook, 1992; Hall and Neitz, 1993):

1. In important respects, modernity has failed. The promise of modernity was a life free from want. As many postmodernist critics see it, however, the twentieth century was unsuccessful in eradicating social problems like poverty or even ensuring financial security for many people.

2. The bright light of 'progress' is fading. Modern people typically look to the future expecting that their lives will improve in significant ways. Members (even leaders) of a postmodern society, however, have less confidence about what the future holds. Furthermore, the buoyant optimism that swept society into the modern era more than a century ago has given way to stark pessimism on the part of most adults that life is getting worse.

3. Science no longer holds the answers. The defining trait of the modern era was a scientific outlook and a confident belief that technology would make life better. But postmodern critics contend that science has created more problems (such as degrading the environment) than it has solved. More generally, postmodernist thinkers discredit the

The Pompidou cultural centre in Paris: a postmodern building?

The communitarian debate

Shortly after midnight on a crisp March night in 1964, Kitty Genovese pulled into the car park of a New York tower block, locked the doors of her vehicle and headed towards the entrance to her building. Moments from safety, she was accosted by a man wielding a knife. As she screamed, he stabbed her repeatedly. Windows opened above, as curious neighbours searched for the cause of the commotion. But the attack continued – for more than 30 minutes – until Genovese lay dead in the doorway. Subsequent investigation failed to identify the assailant but did confirm a stunning fact: not one of dozens of neighbours who witnessed the attack on Kitty Genovese went to the trouble to come to her aid or even to call the police.

Like the scores of homeless people begging for money on many city streets, the Genovese tragedy forces us to confront the question of what we owe others. Members of modern societies prize their individual rights and personal privacy, sometimes withdrawing from public responsibility to the point that society itself seems to collapse. When a cry for help is met by the silence of indifference, have we pushed our modern conception of personal autonomy too far? In a cultural climate of expanding individual rights, can we sustain a sense of human community?

These questions point up the tension between traditional and modern social systems, which is evident in the writings of all the sociologists discussed in this chapter. Toennies, Durkheim and others concluded that, in a fundamental respect, traditional community and modern individualism are incompatible. That is, society can unite its members in a moral community only to the extent that it limits their range of personal choices about how to live. In short, while we value both community and autonomy, we cannot have it both ways.

In recent years, sociologist Amitai Etzioni (1993) has tried to strike a middle ground. The 'communitarian movement', formed in the United States, rests on the simple premise that 'strong rights presume strong responsibilities' or, put otherwise, that an individual's pursuit of self-interest must be balanced by a commitment to the larger community. Etzioni's critique of modernity focuses on the proliferation of individual rights. As he sees it, while people expect the system to provide for them, they are reluctant to support that system. For example, the public is

---

foundation of science – the assertion that objective reality and truth exists at all. *Reality* is socially rather than naturally constructed, they claim; moreover, 'deconstructing' science shows that this system of ideas has been widely used for political purposes, especially by powerful segments of society.

4. Cultural debates are intensifying. As we have already explained, modernity came wrapped in the bright promise of enhanced individuality and expanding tolerance. Critics claim, however, that the emerging postmodern society falls short of that promise. Queer theorists assert that heterosexism continues to shape society today. Multiculturalism seeks to empower minorities long pushed to the margins of social life and left to languish there.

5. Social institutions are changing. Industrialisation brought sweeping transformation to social institutions; the rise of a postindustrial society is remaking society once again. For example, just as the Industrial Revolution placed *material things* at the centre of productive life, now the Information Revolution has elevated the importance of *ideas*. Similarly, the postmodern family no longer conforms to any singular formula; on the contrary, individuals are devising varied ways of relating to one another.

Critical evaluation
Postmodern critics contend that the Western world has failed in important ways to meet human needs. Yet few would argue that modernity has failed

quick to accept government services, but increasingly reluctant to pay taxes.

Specifically, the communitarians advance four proposals designed to balance individual rights with public responsibilities. First, societies should halt the expanding 'culture of rights' by which people have placed their own interests ahead of social responsibility. Second, communitarians argue that all rights involve responsibilities – we cannot simply take from society without giving something back. Third, there are certain responsibilities that no one is free to ignore, such as protecting the natural environment. Fourth, defending some community interests may require limiting individual rights, such as installing security cameras in high streets to photograph human interactions to help identify criminals.

The communitarian movement appeals to many people who, along with Etzioni, seek to balance personal freedom with social responsibility. But critics have attacked this initiative. Some argue that the vague notion of 'social reintegration' falls flat when it comes to addressing problems ranging from voter apathy to street crime. Instead, these critics contend, we need expanded government efforts to enhance equality in modern societies by curbing the political influence of the rich, as well as actively combating racism, sexism and homophobia.

Conservative critics fault Etzioni's proposals as little more than a rerun of the failed leftist ideals of previous decades. Conservatives question whether a free society should engage in the kind of social engineering that Etzioni advocates (such as institutionalising programmes in schools to foster tolerance and requiring young people to perform a year of national service).

While some believe that Etzioni has identified a moderate, sensible answer to vexing problems, it may well be that people in the diverse European nations will never readily agree about what they owe themselves – and each other.

● **Continue the debate:**

1. Have you ever failed to come to the aid of someone in need or danger? Why?

2. The UK Prime Minister Tony Blair has pushed to reform the British benefit system by requiring young people and single parents to take up training or jobs identified by government agencies – or face losing state support. Do you think this policy fairly addresses the needs of the poor as well as of society at large? Provide some examples to illustrate your view.

3. Do you agree or disagree that your society needs to balance individual rights with more responsibility? Why? ●

completely; after all, we have seen marked increases in the length and quality of life over the course of this century. Moreover, even if we were to accept postmodernist criticism that science and traditional notions about progress are bankrupt, what are the alternatives? Then, too, many voices offer strikingly different understandings of recent social trends.

● **Looking ahead: modernisation and the global future**

Back in Chapter 1, we imagined the entire world reduced to a village of 1,000 people, where 175 residents live in luxury, while 200 struggle to survive. The tragic plight of the world's poor shows that some desperately needed change has not occurred at all. Chapter 11 ('Global Stratification') detailed two competing views of why 1 billion people the world over are poor. *Modernisation theory* claims that in the past the entire world was poor and that technological change, especially the Industrial Revolution, enhanced human productivity and raised living standards. From this point of view, the solution to global poverty is to promote technological development in poor nations.

For reasons suggested earlier, however, global modernisation may be difficult. Recall that David Riesman portrayed preindustrial people as *tradition-directed* and likely to resist change. In response to this cultural brake on development, modernisation theorists call for the world's rich societies to offer assistance to poor countries to encourage productive innovation. Industrial nations can speed development by

SOCIOLOGICAL SPOTLIGHT

Putting it all together: sensing a postmodern future

At the turn of the millennium, many sociologists have suggested a rupture is happening within the modern world, and a new social order is starting to appear on a global scale. Postmodernism, late-modernism and post-industrial are all terms used to signify the emergence of this new social order. Jean-Francois Lyotard has defined postmodernism 'as an incredulity towards metanarratives'. By this he means that we can no longer believe in one all encompassing story or truth. We can now see there are many paths, routes, possibilities, truths. Indeed, for another leading French sociologist, Jean Baudrillard, the argument is that the postmodern is: 'the characteristic of a universe where there are no more definitions possible. . . . It has all been done. . . . So all that are left are pieces. All that remains to be done is play with the pieces – that is postmodern'.

These controversial theories and ideas have been used throughout this book, and it should be clear that not all sociologists agree with their use. In this chapter, we have suggested five key themes associated with postmodernism. But almost every chapter in this book suggests that something is indeed happening at the end of the twentieth century which must be seen as significant change. Thus Chapter 1 ends by suggesting that new ways of approaching society through multiple voices is starting to happen: the old orthodoxies of functionalism, conflict and actions are being challenged. Chapter 2 suggests that new methods are in the making in sociological research. Chapter 3 captures the idea of a new kind of 'post-industrial' society in the making and Chapter 4 highlights multiculturalism and post-colonialism. Then in Chapter 7, we see a new kind of postmodern organisation, whilst in Chapter 8, all manner of new kinds of surveillance techniques in crime control appear. In Chapter 15 we see a new kind of economy and pattern of work emerging – which we call 'post-Fordist'. And so it goes on: new forms of 'post-modern family', new patterns of gender and sexual relations, new modes of consumption, new social movements and even new religions. We have also seen debates around class which suggest it may be becoming less important (Chapter 10) whilst ethnicity (Chapter 12), gender (Chapter 13) and age (Chapter 14) become more important. We have seen the rise of the new computer society – cybersociety – saturated with information and communication (Chapter 21). And the chapter on the environment (Chapter 23) hurtles us towards a new kind of 'risk society'. Even in this final chapter, we have highlighted new forms of self and identity.

Along with all this has been another closely linked theme: globalisation. Here we start to see a major shift in the way the world exists in time and in space. More and more countries live in a space between countries: there are global religions, global media, global inequalities, global cities, global finance centres and even global power structures appearing. We are moving out of the era of the 'Nation-state' and into a new period where countries are profoundly interconnected.

To conclude your reading of this text, you may now like to review it in its entirety and try to draw up a catalogue of the major kinds of changes indicated in each chapter. When it is all put together, it will not be hard to see why there is so much talk of a new kind of society appearing. ●

exporting technology to poor regions, welcoming students from abroad, and providing foreign aid to stimulate economic growth.

The review of modernisation theory in Chapter 11 points to some limited success for these policies in Latin America, Taiwan, South Korea, Singapore and Hong Kong. But jump-starting development in the poorest countries of the world poses the greatest challenges. And even where dramatic change has occurred, modernisation entails a trade-off. Traditional people, such as Brazil's Kaiapo, may gain wealth through economic development, but only at the cost of losing their cultural identity and values as they are drawn into the 'global village' of McCulture, based on Western materialism, pop music, trendy clothes and fast food.

One Brazilian anthropologist expressed hope about the future of the Kaiapo: 'At least they quickly understood the consequences of watching television . . . Now [they] can make a choice' (Simons, 1995: 471). But not everyone thinks that modernisation is really an option. According to a second approach to global stratification, *dependency theory*, today's poor societies have little ability to modernise, even if they wanted to. From this point of view, the major barrier to economic development is not traditionalism but the global domination of rich, capitalist societies. Initially, as Chapter 11 explains, this system took the form of colonialism, whereby European societies seized much of Latin America, Africa and Asia. Trading relationships soon enriched England, Spain, Portugal, France and other colonial powers and their colonies simultaneously became dependent and poor. Almost all societies subjected to this form of domination are now politically independent, but colonial-style ties continue in the form of neo-colonialism, with multinational corporations operating throughout the world.

In effect, dependency theory asserts, rich nations achieved their modernisation at the expense of poor ones, which provided valuable natural resources and human labour. Even today, the world's poorest countries remain locked in a disadvantageous economic relationship with rich nations, dependent on wealthy countries to buy their raw materials and in return sell them whatever manufactured products they can afford. Overall, dependency theorists conclude, continuing ties with rich societies will only perpetuate current patterns of global inequality.

Whichever approach one finds more convincing, we can no longer isolate the study of the Western world from the rest of the world. At the beginning of the twentieth century, a majority of people in today's high-income countries lived in relatively small settlements with limited awareness of the larger world. Now, at the threshold of the twenty-first century, people everywhere participate in a far larger human drama. The world seems smaller and the lives of all people are increasingly linked. We now discuss the relationships among countries in the same way that people a century ago talked about the expanding ties among cities and towns.

The century now coming to a close has witnessed unprecedented human achievement. Yet solutions to many problems of human existence – including finding meaning in life, resolving conflicts among societies and eradicating poverty – have eluded us. To this list of pressing matters new concerns have been added in recent years, such as controlling population growth and establishing a sustainable natural environment. As we approach the twenty-first century, we must be prepared to tackle such problems with imagination, compassion and determination. The challenge is great, but our wide-ranging understanding of human society gives us reason to look to the task ahead with optimism.

SUMMARY

1. Every society changes continuously, intentionally or not, and at varying speeds. Social change often generates controversy.

2. Social change results from invention, discovery and diffusion as well as social conflict.

3. Modernity refers to the social consequences of industrialisation, which, according to Peter Berger, include the erosion of traditional communities, expanding personal choice, increasingly diverse beliefs and a keen awareness of time, especially the future.

4. Ferdinand Toennies described modernisation as the transition from *Gemeinschaft* to *Gesellschaft*, which signifies the progressive loss of community amid growing individualism.

5. To Emile Durkheim, modernisation occurred as a function of a society's expanding division of labour. Mechanical solidarity, based on shared activities and beliefs, gradually gives way to organic solidarity, in which specialisation makes people interdependent.

6. According to Max Weber, modernity replaces traditional beliefs with a rational world view. He feared the dehumanising effects of rational organisation.

7. Karl Marx saw modernity as the triumph of capitalism over feudalism. Viewing capitalist societies as fraught with social conflict, Marx advocated

revolutionary change to achieve a more egalitarian, socialist society.

8. According to mass-society theory, modernity increases the scale of life, enlarging the role of government and other formal organisations in carrying out tasks that previously were performed by family members and neighbours. Cultural diversity and rapid social change make it difficult for people in modern societies to develop stable identities and to find certainty and meaning in their personal lives.

9. Class-society theory states that capitalism is central to Western modernisation. This approach charges that, by concentrating wealth, capitalism generates widespread feelings of powerlessness.

10. Social change is too complex and controversial simply to be equated with social progress.

11. Postmodernity refers to cultural traits of post-industrial societies. Postmodern criticism of society centres on the failure of modernity, and specifically science, to fulfil its promise of prosperity and well-being.

12. In a global context, modernisation theory links global poverty to the power of tradition. Therefore, some modernisation theorists advocate intentional intervention by rich societies to stimulate the development of poor nations.

13. Dependency theory explains global poverty as the product of the world economic system. The operation of multinational corporations ensures that poor societies will remain economically dependent on rich ones.

KEY CONCEPTS

class society a capitalist society with pronounced social stratification

mass society a society in which industry and expanding bureaucracy have eroded traditional social ties

modernity social patterns linked to industrialisation

modernisation the process of social change initiated by industrialisation

other-directedness a receptiveness to the latest trends and fashions, often expressed in the practice of imitating others

postmodernity social patterns characteristic of post-industrial societies

social change the transformation of culture and social institutions over time

social character personality patterns common to members of a particular society

tradition-directedness rigid conformity to time-honoured ways of living

CRITICAL-THINKING QUESTIONS

1. Do you think Toennies, Durkheim, Weber and Marx accurately predicted the character of modern society? How do their visions of society differ?

2. What traits render your country a 'mass society'? Do you consider yourself and most of your friends to be 'other-directed'?

3. What is the difference between *anomie* (a trait of mass society) and *alienation* (a characteristic of class society)? Among which sections of the population would you expect each to be pronounced?

4. What developments lead some analysts to claim that European countries have become postmodern societies?

5. Do you think there are any postmodern societies in the world today? Which ones are they?

GOING FURTHER ....

Introductory reading

Richard Appignanesi and Chris Garratt, *Postmodernism for Beginners* (Cambridge: Icon Books, 1995).

> This book is fun but at the same time looks at the world of the 'postmodern' in some 'depth'. A good opening introduction for 'would-be postmodernists'!

Amitai Etzioni, *The Spirit of Community: Rights, Responsibilities, and the Communitarian Agenda* (New York: Crown Publishers, 1993).

> In what might be called the 'handbook of the communitarian movement', Etzioni suggests ways to fuse individual rights with collective responsibility.

Derek Sayer, *Capitalism and Modernity: An Excursus on Marx and Weber* (London: Routledge, 1991).

> Examines the limits of modernity and prospects for postmodernity by reviewing the ideas of two seminal sociologists.

Classic sources

Frederick Jameson, *Postmodernism or the Logic of Late Capitalism* (London: Verso, 1992).

J. F. Lyotard, *The Postmodern Condition* (Manchester: Manchester University Press, 1992).

> These are two major statements of postmodernism: widely citied but not readily accessible.

More advanced reading

Peter Berger, Brigitte Berger and Hansfried Kellner, *The Homeless Mind: Modernisation and Consciousness* (New York: Vintage Books, 1974).

> Discusses what modernity means.

Steven Connor, *Postmodernist Culture* (Oxford: Blackwell, 2nd edn, 1997).

> A clear, intelligible guide that examines 'culture' with lots of examples.

Glossary

absolute poverty a deprivation of resources that is life threatening

achieved status a social position that someone assumes voluntarily and that reflects personal ability and effort

acid rain precipitation that is made acidic by air pollution and destroys plant and animal life

actors assemble social meanings

activity theory the proposition that a high level of activity enhances personal satisfaction in old age

Afrocentrism the dominance of African cultural patterns

ageism prejudice and discrimination against the elderly

age–sex pyramid a graphic representation of the age and sex of a population

age stratification the unequal distribution of wealth, power, and privileges among people at different stages in the life course

agriculture the technology of large-scale farming using plows harnessed to animals or more powerful sources of energy

alienation the experience of isolation resulting from powerlessness

animism the belief that elements of the natural world are conscious life forms that affect humanity

anomie Durkheim's designation of a condition in which society provides little moral guidance to individuals

anticipatory socialisation social learning directed toward gaining a desired position

ascribed status a social position that someone receives at birth or assumes involuntarily later in life

assimilation the process by which minorities gradually adopt patterns of the dominant culture

authoritarianism a political system that denies popular participation in government

authority power that people perceive as legitimate rather than coercive

beliefs specific statements that people hold to be true

bilateral descent a system tracing kinship through both men and women

blue-collar occupations lower-prestige work involving mostly manual labour

body projects the process of becoming and transforming a biological entity through social action

bureaucracy an organisational model rationally designed to perform complex tasks efficiently

bureaucratic inertia the tendency of bureaucratic organisations to perpetuate themselves

bureaucratic ritualism a preoccupation with rules and regulations to the point of thwarting an organisation's goals

capitalism an economic system in which natural resources and the means of producing goods and services are privately owned

capitalists people who own factories and other productive enterprises

caste system a system of social stratification based on ascription

cause and effect a relationship in which change in one variable (the independent variable) causes change in another (the dependent variable)

charisma extraordinary personal qualities that can turn an audience into followers

charismatic authority power legitimised through extraordinary personal abilities that inspire devotion and obedience

church a type of religious organisation well integrated into the larger society

civil religion a quasi-religious loyalty binding individuals in a basically secular society

class conflict wealth and power in society

class consciousness Marx's term for the recognition by workers of their unity as a social class in opposition to capitalists and to capitalism itself

class society a capitalist society with pronounced social stratification

class system a system of social stratification based on individual achievement

code rule governed system of signs

cohabitation the sharing of a household by an unmarried couple

cohort a category of people with a common characteristic, usually their age

collective behaviour activity involving a large number of people, often spontaneous, and typically in violation of established norms

collectivity a large number of people whose minimal interaction occurs in the absence of well-defined and conventional norms

colonialism the process by which some nations enrich themselves through political and economic control of other countries

communism a hypothetical economic and political system in which all members of a society are socially equal

concept a mental construct that represents some part of the world, inevitably in a simplified form

concrete operational stage Piaget's term for the level of human development at which individuals first perceive causal connections in their surroundings

conflict paradigm a framework for building theory that envisions society as an arena of inequality that generates conflict and change

conglomerates giant corporations composed of many smaller corporations

control holding constant all relevant variables except one in order to observe its effect

corporation an organisation with a legal existence, including rights and liabilities, apart from those of its members

correlation a relationship by which two (or more) variables change together

counterculture cultural patterns that strongly oppose those widely accepted within a society

credentialism evaluating a person on the basis of educational degrees

crime the violation of norms a society formally enacts into criminal law

crimes against the person (violent crimes) crimes that direct violence or the threat of violence against others

crimes against property (property crimes) crimes that involve theft of property belonging to others

criminal justice system a societal reaction to alleged violations of the law utilising police, courts, and prison officials

criminal recidivism subsequent offences committed by people previously convicted of crimes

crowd a temporary gathering of people who share a common focus of attention and whose members influence one another

crude birth rate the number of live births in a given year for every thousand people in a population

crude death rate the number of deaths in a given year for every thousand people in a population

cult a religious organisation that is substantially outside a society's cultural traditions

cultural conflict political opposition, often accompanied by social hostility, rooted in different cultural values

cultural ecology a theoretical paradigm that explores the relationship of human culture and the physical environment

cultural integration the close relationship among various elements of a cultural system

cultural lag the fact that cultural elements change at different rates, which may disrupt a cultural system

cultural relativism the practice of judging a culture by its own standards

cultural reproduction the process by which a society transmits dominant knowledge from one generation to another

cultural transmission the process by which one generation passes culture to the next

cultural universals traits that are part of every known culture

culture the beliefs, values, behaviour, and material objects that constitute a people's way of life

culture shock personal disorientation that comes from encountering an unfamiliar way of life

cyber widely used prefix for anything connected to computers

cybernetics control systems using computers

Davis–Moore thesis the assertion that social stratification is a universal pattern because it has beneficial consequences for the operation of a society

decoding the process by which we hear or read and understand a message

deductive logical thought reasoning that transforms general ideas into specific hypotheses suitable for scientific testing

democracy a type of political system in which power is exercised by the people as a whole

democratic socialism an economic and political system that combines significant government control of the economy with free elections

demographic transition theory a thesis linking population patterns to a society's level of technological development

demography the study of human population

denomination a church, independent of the state, that accepts religious pluralism

dependency ratio the numbers of dependent children and retired persons relative to productive age groups

dependency theory a model of economic and social development that explains global inequality in terms of the historical exploitation of poor societies by rich ones

dependent variable a variable that is changed by another (independent) variable

descent the system by which members of a society trace kinship over generations

deterrence the attempt to discourage criminality through punishment

deviance the recognised violation of cultural norms

direct-fee system a medical-care system in which patients pay directly for the services of physicians and hospitals

discrimination any action that involves treating various categories of people unequally

disengagement theory the proposition that society enhances its orderly operation by disengaging people from positions of responsibility as they reach old age

division of labour specialised economic activity

documents of life research documents produced in the natural world by the subjects themselves, like letters and diaries

dramaturgical analysis Erving Goffman's term for the investigation of social interaction in terms of theatrical performance

dyad a social group with two members

dysfunction (*See* social dysfunction)

eating disorder an intense involvement in dieting or other forms of weight control in order to become very thin

ecclesia a church that is formally allied with the state

ecologically sustainable culture a way of life that meets the needs of the present generation without threatening the environmental legacy of future generations

ecology the study of the interaction of living organisms and the natural environment

economy the social institution that organises the production, distribution, and consumption of goods and services

ecosystem the system composed of the interaction of all living organisms and their natural environment

education the social institution guiding the transmission of knowledge, job skills, cultural norms and values

ego Freud's designation of a person's conscious efforts to balance innate, pleasure-seeking drives and the demands of society

empirical evidence information we can verify with our senses

encoding putting a message of any kind into a language

endogamy marriage between people of the same social category

environmental deficit the situation in which our relationship to the environment, while yielding short-term benefits, will have profound, long-term consequences

environmental racism the pattern by which environmental hazards are greatest in proximity to poor people-and especially minorities

epistemology branch of philosophy that investigates the nature of knowledge and truth

ethnic antagonism hostilities between different ethnic groups

ethnic cleansing see genocide

ethnicity a shared cultural heritage

ethnocentrism the practice of judging another culture by the standards of one's own culture

ethnomethodology Harold Garfinkel's term for the study of the way people make sense of their everyday lives

Eurocentrism the dominance of European (especially English) cultural patterns

euthanasia (mercy killing) assisting in the death of a person suffering from an incurable disease

exogamy marriage between people of different social categories

experiment a research method for investigating cause and effect under highly controlled conditions

expressive leadership group leadership that emphasises collective well-being

extended family (consanguine family) a family unit including parents and children, but also other kin

fad an unconventional social pattern that people embrace briefly but enthusiastically

faith belief anchored in conviction rather than scientific evidence

false consciousness Marx's term for explanations of social problems grounded in the shortcomings of individuals rather than the flaws of society

family a social institution, found in all societies, that unites individuals into cooperative groups that oversee the bearing and raising of children

family of choice people with or without legal or blood ties who feel they belong together and wish to define themselves as a family

family unit a social group of two or more people, related by blood, marriage, or adoption, who usually live together

family violence emotional, physical, or sexual abuse of one family member by another

fashion a social pattern favoured for a time by a large number of people

feminism the advocacy of social equality for the sexes, in opposition to patriarchy and sexism

feminisation of poverty the trend by which women represent an increasing proportion of the poor

fertility the incidence of childbearing in a country's population

flaneur a social type who wanders cities, enjoying the sights and the crowd

folkways a society's customs for routine, casual interaction

Fordism an economic system based on mass assembly line production, mass consumption and standardised commodities

formal operational stage Piaget's term for the level of human development at which individuals think abstractly and critically

formal organisation a large secondary group organised to achieve its goals efficiently

functional illiteracy reading and writing skills insufficient for everyday living

functional paradigm a framework for building theory that envisions society as a complex system whose parts work together to promote solidarity and stability

fundamentalism a conservative religious doctrine that opposes intellectualism and worldly accommodation in favour of restoring a traditional, otherworldly spirituality

Gemeinschaft Toennies's term for a type of social organisation by which people have weak social ties and considerable self-interest

gender the significance members of a society attach to being female or male

gender identity traits that females and males, guided by their culture, incorporate into their personalities

gender roles (sex roles) attitudes and activities that a society links to each sex

gender stratification a society's unequal distribution of wealth, power, and privilege between the two sexes

generalised other George Herbert Mead's label for widespread cultural norms and values that we use as references in evaluating ourselves

genocide the systematic annihilation of one category of people by another

genre a species or type of media programme

gerontocracy a form of social organisation in which the elderly have the most wealth, power, and prestige

gerontology the study of aging and the elderly

Gesellschaft Toennies's term for a type of social organisation by which people have weak social ties and considerable self-interest

global commons resources shared by all members of the international community, such as ocean beds and the atmosphere

global economy economic activity spanning many nations of the world with little regard for national borders

global perspective the study of the larger world and our society's place in it

globalisation the increasing interconnectedness of societies

gossip rumour about the personal affairs of others

government formal organisations that direct the political life of a society

greenhouse effect a rise in the earth's average temperature (global warming) due to increasing concentration of carbon dioxide in the atmosphere

gross domestic product (GDP) all the goods and services on record as produced by a country's economy in a given year

gross national product (GNP) all a country's goods and services, as for GDP, with the addition of foreign earnings

groupthink the tendency of group members to conform by adopting a narrow view of some issue

hate crime a criminal act against a person or a person's property by an offender motivated by racial or other bias

Hawthorne effect a change in a subject's behaviour caused simply by the awareness of being studied

health a state of complete physical, mental, and social well-being

health care any activity intended to improve health

health maintenance organisation (HMO) an organisation that provides comprehensive medical care to subscribers for a fixed fee

hegemony the means by which a ruling/dominant group wins over a subordinate group through ideas

hermaphrodite a human being with some combination of female and male internal and external genitalia

hidden curriculum subtle presentations of political or cultural ideas in the classroom

high culture cultural patterns that distinguish a society's elite

high-income countries industrial nations in which most people enjoy material abundance

holistic medicine an approach to health care that emphasises prevention of illness and takes account of a person's entire physical and social environment

homogamy marriage between people with the same social characteristics

horticulture technology based on using hand tools to cultivate plants

humanism stance that takes the human subjects seriously and is concerned with their meanings

humanising bureaucracy fostering a more democratic organisational atmosphere that recognises and encourages the contributions of everyone

hunting and gathering simple technology for hunting animals and gathering vegetation

hypothesis an unverified statement of a relationship between variables

id Freud's designation of the human being's basic drives

ideal culture (as opposed to real culture) social patterns mandated by cultural values and norms

ideal type Weber's term for an abstract statement of the essential characteristics of any social phenomenon

ideal types an abstract statement of the essential, though often exaggerated, characteristic of any social phenomenon

ideology cultural beliefs that serve to justify social stratification

incest taboo a cultural norm forbidding sexual relations or marriage between certain kin

income occupational wages or salaries and earnings from investments

ideological state apparatuses social institutions which reproduce the dominant ideology, independent of the state

independent variable a variable that causes change in another (dependent) variable

inductive logical thought reasoning that transforms specific observations into general theory

industrialism technology that powers sophisticated machinery with advanced sources of energy

infant mortality rate the number of deaths among infants under one year of age for each thousand live births in a given year

ingroup a social group commanding a member's esteem and loyalty

institutional prejudice or discrimination bias in attitudes or action inherent in the operation of society's institutions

instrumental leadership group leadership that emphasises the completion of tasks

intergenerational social mobility upward or downward social mobility of children in relation to their parents

interview a series of questions a researcher administers personally to respondents

intragenerational social mobility a change in social position occurring during a person's lifetime

juvenile delinquency the violation of legal standards by the young

kinship a social bond, based on blood, marriage, or adoption, that joins individuals into families

labelling theory the assertion that deviance and conformity result, not so much from what people do, as from how others respond to those actions

labour unions organisations of workers seeking to improve wages and working conditions through various strategies, including negotiations and strikes

language a system of symbols that allows members of a society to communicate with one another

latent functions consequences of any social pattern that are unrecognised and unintended

liberation theology a fusion of Christian principles with political activism, often Marxist in character

life expectancy the average life span of a society's population

looking-glass self Cooley's term for the image people have of themselves based on how they believe others perceive them

low-income countries nations with little industrialisation in which severe poverty is the rule

macro-level orientation a focus on broad social structures that characterise society as a whole

mainstreaming integrating special students into the overall educational program

manifest functions the recognised and intended consequences of any social pattern

marketisation an economic system based on the principles of the market, including supply, demand, choice and competition

marriage a legally sanctioned relationship, involving economic cooperation as well as normative sexual activity and childbearing, that people expect to be relatively enduring

mass behaviour collective behaviour among people dispersed over a wide geographical area

mass hysteria a form of dispersed collective behaviour by which people respond to a real or imagined event with irrational, frantic, and often self-destructive behaviour

mass media impersonal communications directed toward a vast audience

mass medium any social or technological device used for the selection, transmission, reception of some information content

mass society a society in which industry and expanding bureaucracy have eroded traditional social ties

master status a status that has exceptional importance for social identity, often shaping a person's entire life

material culture the tangible things created by members of a society

matriarchy a form of social organisation in which females dominate males

matrilineal descent a system tracing kinship through women

matrilocality a residential pattern in which a married couple lives with or near the wife's family

mean the arithmetic average of a series of numbers

measurement the process of determining the value of a variable in a specific case

mechanical solidarity Durkheim's designation of social bonds, based on shared morality, that unite members of preindustrial societies

media texts all media products, such as television

median the value that occurs midway in a series of numbers arranged in order of magnitude or, simply, the middle case

medicalisation of deviance the transformation of moral and legal issues into medical matters

medicine a social institution concerned with combating disease and improving health

megalopolis a vast urban region containing a number of cities and their surrounding suburbs

meritocracy a system of social stratification based on personal merit

metropolis a large city that socially and economically dominates an urban area

micro-level orientation a focus on patterns of social interaction in specific situations

middle-class slide a trend towards declining living standards and economic security at the centre of industrial societies

middle-income countries nations characterised by limited industrialisation and moderate personal income

migration the movement of people into and out of a specified territory

military–industrial complex the close association among the federal government, the military, and defence industries

minority a category of people, distinguished by physical or cultural traits, who are socially disadvantaged

miscegenation biological reproduction by partners of different racial categories

mob a highly emotional crowd that pursues some violent or destructive goal

mode the value that occurs most often in a series of numbers

modernity social patterns linked to industrialisation

modernisation the process of social change initiated by industrialisation

modernisation theory a model of economic and social development that explains global inequality in terms of differing levels of technological development among societies

monarchy a type of political system in which a single family rules from generation to generation

monogamy a form of marriage joining two partners

monopoly domination of a market by a single producer

monotheism belief in a single divine power

mores a society's standards of proper moral conduct

mortality the incidence of death in a country's population

multiculturalism an educational program recognising past and present cultural diversity in U.S. society and promoting the equality of all cultural traditions

multinational corporation a large corporation that operates in many different countries

nation-state a political apparatus over a specific territory with its own citizens backed up by military force and a nationalistic, sovereign creed

natural environment the earth's surface and atmosphere, including various living organisms as well as the air, water, soil, and other resources necessary to sustain life

neocolonialism a new form of global power relationships that involves not direct political control but economic exploitation by multinational corporations

neolocality a residential pattern in which a married couple lives apart from the parents of both spouses

net migration rate the number of people who enter a territory (in-migration) minus the number of people who leave (out-migration) in a given year

network a web of social ties that links people who identify and interact little with one another

new racism racism based upon cultural, rather than biological, values

newly industrialising countries (NICs) lower-income countries that are fast becoming higher income countries

nonmaterial culture the intangible world of ideas created by members of a society

nonverbal communication communication using body movements, gestures, and facial expressions rather than speech

norms rules and expectations by which a society guides the behaviour of its members

nuclear family (conjugal family) a family unit composed of one or two parents and their children

nuclear proliferation the acquisition of nuclear weapons technology by more and more nations

objectivity a state of personal neutrality in conducting research

occupational prestige the value that people in a society associate with various occupations

oligarchy the rule of the many by the few

oligopoly domination of a market by a few producers

operationalising a variable specifying exactly what one intends to measure in assigning a value to a variable

oral culture culture with no written language, dependent upon speech

organic solidarity Durkheim's designation of social bonds, based on specialisation, that unite members of industrial societies

organisational environment a range of factors external to an organisation that affects its operation

other-directedness a receptiveness to the latest trends and fashions, often expressed in the practice of imitating others

outgroup a social group toward which one feels competition or opposition

panic a form of localised collective behaviour by which people react to a perceived threat or other stimulus with irrational, frantic, and often self-destructive behaviour

paradigm (*See* theoretical paradigm)

parentocracy a system where a child's education is increasingly dependent upon the wealth and wishes of parents, rather than the ability and efforts of pupils

participant observation a research method in which researchers systematically observe people while joining in their routine activities

pastoralism technology based on the domestication of animals

patriarchy a form of social organisation in which males dominate females

patrilineal descent a system tracing kinship through men

patrilocality a residential pattern in which a married couple lives with or near the husband's family

peace a state of international relations devoid of violence

peer group a social group whose members have interests, social position, and age in common

personality a person's fairly consistent patterns of thinking, feeling, and acting

personal space the surrounding area to which an individual makes some claim to privacy

plea bargaining a legal negotiation in which the state reduces the charge against a defendant in exchange for a guilty plea

pluralism a state in which racial and ethnic minorities are distinct but have social parity

pluralist model an analysis of politics that views power as dispersed among many competing interest groups

political action committee (PAC) an organisation formed by a special-interest group, independent of political parties, to pursue political aims by raising and spending money

political revolution the overthrow of one political system in order to establish another

politics the social institution that distributes power, sets a society's agenda, and makes decisions

polyandry a form of marriage joining one female with two or more males

polygamy a form of marriage uniting three or more people

polygyny a form of marriage joining one male with two or more females

polysemic open to many interpretations

polytheism belief in many gods

popular culture cultural patterns that are widespread among a society's population

population the people who are the focus of research

positivism a means to understand the world based on science

postcolonialism recognises how many cultures have been made through oppressor subject relationships and seeks to unpack these, showing how cultures are made

post-Fordism an economic system emerging mainly since the 1970s and based on flexibility (rather than standardisation), specialisation and tailor-made goods

postindustrial economy a productive system based on service work and high technology

postindustrialism technology that supports an information-based economy

postmodernity social patterns characteristic of postindustrial societies

power the ability to achieve desired ends despite resistance from others

power-elite model an analysis of politics that views power as concentrated among the rich

prejudice a rigid and irrational generalisation about an entire category of people

preoperational stage Piaget's term for the level of human development at which individuals first use language and other symbols

presentation of self an individual's effort to create specific impressions in the minds of others

primary group a small social group in which relationships are both personal and enduring

primary labour market occupations that provide extensive benefits to workers

primary sector the part of the economy that generates raw materials directly from the natural environment

primary sex characteristics the genitals, used to reproduce the human species

profane that which is defined as an ordinary element of everyday life

profession a prestigious, white-collar occupation that requires extensive formal education

programmes films, rock CDs, books, newspapers, web site pages, etc.

proletariat people who provide labour necessary to operate factories and other productive enterprises

propaganda information presented with the intention of shaping public opinion

qualitative research investigation by which a researcher gathers impressionistic, not numerical, data

quantitative research investigation by which a researcher collects numerical data

questionnaire a series of written questions a researcher supplies to subjects requesting their responses

race a category composed of people who share biologically transmitted traits that members of a society deem socially significant

racialisation process of ranking people on the basis of their presumed race

racism the belief that one racial category is innately superior or inferior to another

rain forests regions of dense forestation, most of which circle the globe close to the equator

rationality deliberate, matter-of-fact calculation of the most efficient means to accomplish a particular goal

rationalisation of society Weber's term for the historical change from tradition to rationality as the dominant mode of human thought

rational-legal authority (bureaucratic authority) power legitimised by legally enacted rules and regulations

real culture (as opposed to ideal culture) actual social patterns that only approximate cultural expectations

realism scientific method that theorises a 'problematic' in order to see what is really going on

reference group a social group that serves as a point of reference in making evaluations or decisions

rehabilitation a program for reforming the offender to preclude subsequent offences

relative deprivation a perceived disadvantage arising from a specific comparison

relative poverty the deprivation of some people in relation to those who have more

reliability the quality of consistent measurement

religion a social institution involving beliefs and practices based upon a conception of the sacred

religiosity the importance of religion in a person's life

replication repetition of research by others

research method a systematic plan for conducting research

resocialisation radically altering an inmate's personality through deliberate manipulation of the environment

retribution moral vengeance by which society inflicts suffering on an offender comparable to that caused by the offence

retrospective labelling the interpretation of someone's past consistent with present deviance

riot a social eruption that is highly emotional, violent, and undirected

risk society society where risks are of a different magnitude because of technology and globalisation

ritual formal, ceremonial behaviour

role behaviour expected of someone who holds a particular status

role conflict incompatibility among the roles corresponding to two or more statuses

role set a number of roles attached to a single status

role strain incompatibility among roles corresponding to a single status

routinisation of charisma the transformation of charismatic authority into some combination of traditional and bureaucratic authority

rumour unsubstantiated information people spread informally, often by word of mouth

sacred that which is defined as extraordinary, inspiring a sense of awe, reverence, and even fear

sample a part of a population researchers select to represent the whole

Sapir–Whorf hypothesis the hypothesis that people perceive the world through the cultural lens of language

scapegoat a person or category of people, typically with little power, whom people unfairly blame for their own troubles

schooling formal instruction under the direction of specially trained teachers

science a logical system that bases knowledge on direct, systematic observation

secondary analysis a research method in which a researcher utilises data collected by others

secondary group a large and impersonal social group devoted to some specific interest or activity

secondary labour market jobs that provide minimal benefits to workers

secondary sector the part of the economy that transforms raw materials into manufactured goods

secondary sex characteristics bodily development, apart from the genitals, that distinguishes biologically mature females and males

sect a type of religious organisation that stands apart from the larger society

secularisation the historical decline in the importance of the supernatural and the sacred

segregation the physical and social separation of categories of people

self George Herbert Mead's term for a dimension of personality composed of an individual's self-awareness and self-image

self-fulfilling prophecy children defined as low achievers at school learn to become low achievers

sensorimotor stage Piaget's designation for the level of human development at which individuals experience the world only through sensory contact

sex the biological distinction between females and males

sexism the belief that one sex is innately superior to the other

sex ratio the number of males for every hundred females in a given population

sexual harassment comments, gestures, or physical contact of a sexual nature that are deliberate, repeated, and unwelcome

sexual orientation an individual's preference in terms of sexual partners: same sex, other sex, either sex, neither sex

sexuality aspects of the body and desire that are linked to the erotic

sick role patterns of behaviour defined as appropriate for those who are ill

simulacrum a world of media generated signs and images

slavery a form of stratification in which people are owned by others as property

social change the transformation of culture and social institutions over time

social character personality patterns common to members of a particular society

social conflict struggle between segments of society over valued resources

social-conflict paradigm a framework for building theory that envisions society as an arena of inequality that generates conflict and change

social construction of reality the process by which people creatively shape reality through social interaction

social control various means by which members of a society encourage conformity to norms

social dysfunction the undesirable consequences of any social pattern for the operation of society

social epidemiology the study of how health and disease are distributed throughout a society's population

social function the consequences of any social pattern for the operation of society

social group two or more people who identify and interact with one another

social institution a major sphere of social life, or societal subsystem, organised to meet a basic human need

social interaction the process by which people act and react in relation to others

social mobility change in people's position in a social hierarchy

social movement organised activity that encourages or discourages social change

social reproduction the maintenance of power and privilege between social classes from one generation to the next

social stratification a system by which society ranks categories of people in a hierarchy

social structure relatively stable patterns of social behaviour

socialisation the lifelong social experience by which individuals develop their human potential and learn patterns of their culture

socialised medicine a health-care system in which the government owns and operates most medical facilities and employs most physicians

socialism an economic system in which natural resources and the means of producing goods and services are collectively owned

societal protection a means by which society renders an offender incapable of further offences temporarily through incarceration or permanently by execution

society people who interact in a defined territory and share culture

sociobiology a theoretical paradigm that explores ways in which our biology affects how humans create culture

sociocultural evolution the Lenski's term for the process of change that results from a society's gaining new information, particularly technology

socioeconomic status (SES) a composite ranking based on various dimensions of social inequality

sociology the systematic study of human society

special-interest group a political alliance of people interested in some economic or social issue

spurious correlation an apparent, although false, relationship between two (or more) variables caused by some other variable

state see nation state

state capitalism an economic and political system in which companies are privately owned but cooperate closely with the government

state terrorism the use of violence, generally without support of law, against individuals or groups by a government or its agents

status a recognised social position that an individual occupies

status consistency the degree of consistency of a person's social standing across various dimensions of social inequality

status set all the statuses a person holds at a given time

stereotype an exaggerated description applied to every person in some category

stigma a powerfully negative social label that radically changes a person's self-concept and social identity

streaming the assignment to students to different types of educational programmes

structural-functional paradigm a framework for building theory that envisions society as a complex system whose parts work together to promote solidarity and stability

structural social mobility a shift in the social position of large numbers of people due more to changes in society itself than to individual efforts

subculture cultural patterns that set apart some segment of a society's population

suburbs urban areas beyond the political boundaries of a city

superego Freud's designation of the operation of culture within the individual in the form of internalised values and norms

survey a research method in which subjects respond to a series of items in a questionnaire or an interview

symbol anything that carries a particular meaning recognised by people who share culture

symbolic-interaction a theoretical framework that envisions society as the product of the everyday interactions of people doing things together

technology knowledge that a society applies to the task of living in a physical environment

terrorism violence or the threat of violence employed by an individual or group as a political strategy

tertiary sector the part of the economy that generates services rather than goods

Thatcherism a system of political beliefs based on free markets and economic individualism

theoretical paradigm a basic image of society that guides sociological thinking and research

theory a statement of how and why specific facts are related

Thomas theorem W. I. Thomas's assertion that situations we define as real become real in their consequences

total institution a setting in which people are isolated from the rest of society and manipulated by an administrative staff

total period fertility rate the average number of children each women would have in her lifetime if the average number of children born to all women of childbearing age in any given year remained constant during that woman's childbearing years

totalitarianism a political system told collectively defined as sacred

tracking the assignment of students to different types of educational programs

trade unions organisations of workers collectively seeking to improve wages and working conditions through various strategies, including negotiations and strikes

tradition sentiments and beliefs passed from generation to generation

traditional authority power legitimised through respect for long-established cultural patterns

tradition-directedness rigid conformity to time-honoured ways of living

transsexuals people who feel they are one sex though biologically they are the other

triad a social group with three members

underclass a group 'under the class structure' which is economically, politically and socially marginalised and excluded

underground economy economic activity generating income that one does not report to the government as required by law

urban ecology the study of the link between the physical and social dimensions of cities

urbanisation the concentration of humanity into cities

validity the quality of measuring precisely what one intends to measure

values culturally defined standards by which people assess desirability, goodness, and beauty, and which serve as broad guidelines for social living

variable a concept whose value changes from case to case

victimless crimes violations of law in which there are no readily apparent victims

war armed conflict among the people of various societies, directed by their governments

wealth the total value of money and other assets, minus outstanding debts

white-collar crime crimes committed by persons of high social position in the course of their occupations

white-collar occupations higher-prestige work involving mostly mental activity

zero population growth the level of reproduction that maintains population at a steady state

References

Abercrombie, Nicholas. *Television and Society*. Cambridge: Polity, 1996.

Aberle, David F. *The Peyote Religion Among the Navaho*. Chicago: Aldine, 1966.

Abbott, Andrew. *The System of Professions: An Essay on the Division of Expert Labor*. Chicago: University of Chicago Press, 1988.

Abbott, Pamela and George Giacinto Giarchi. 'Health, Healthcare and Health Inequalities'. In Tony Spybey, ed., *Britain in Europe*. London: Routledge, 1997, Chapter 18.

Abbott, Pamela and Claire Wallace. *The Family and the New Right*. London: Pluto Press, 1992.

——. *An Introduction to Sociology*. London: Routledge, 1996; 2nd edn. 1997.

ACUPA (Archbishop's Commission on Urban Priority Areas). *Faith in the City*. London: Church of England, 1985.

Adler, Jerry. 'When Harry Called Sally . . . '. *Newsweek* (1 October 1990): 74.

Adorno, Theodore. *The Culture Industry*. London: Routledge, 1991.

Adorno, Theodore and Max Horkheimer. *Dialectic of Enlightment*. New York: Seabury Press, 1972

Adorno, Theodore, et al. *The Authoritarian Personality*. New York: Harper & Brothers, 1950.

Agger, B. *Cultural Studies as Critical Theory*. London: Falmer, 1992.

Akers, Ronald L., Marvin D. Krohn, Lonn Lanza-Kaduce and Marcia Radosevich. 'Social Learning and Deviant Behavior'. *American Sociological Review*. Vol. 44, No. 4 (August 1979): 636–55.

Alam, Sultana. 'Women and Poverty in Bangladesh'. *Women's Studies International Forum*. Vol. 8, No. 4 (1985): 361–71.

Alba, Richard D. *Italian Americans: Into the Twilight of Ethnicity*. Englewood Cliffs, NJ: Prentice Hall, 1985.

——. *Ethnic Identity: The Transformation of White America*. Chicago: University of Chicago Press, 1990.

Allan, Emilie Andersen and Darrell J. Steffensmeier. 'Youth, Underemployment and Property Crime: Differential Effects of Job Availability and Job Quality on Juvenile and Young Adult Arrest Rates'. *American Sociological Review*. Vol. 54, No. 1 (February 1989): 107–23.

Allen, R. *To be Continued . . . . Soap Operas Around the World*. London: Routledge, 1995.

Allen, Shiela and Carol Walkowitz. *Homeworking: Myths and Realities*. London: Macmillan, 1987.

Allport, Gordon. *The Use of Personal Documents in Psychological Science*. New York: Social Science Research Council, 1942.

Allsop, Kenneth. *The Bootleggers*. London: Hutchinson and Company, 1961.

Altheide, David L. and Robert P. Snow. *Media Worlds in the Postjournalism Era*. New York: Aldine de Gruyter, 1991.

Altman, Dennis. *Aids and the New Puritanism*. London: Pluto Press, 1986.

Altman, Drew, et al. 'Health Care for the Homeless'. *Society*. Vol. 26, No. 4 (May–June 1989): 4–5.

Althusser, Louis. *Lenin and Philosophy and Other Essays*. New Left Books, 1971.

Ambert, Alba N. and Marie D. Alvares, eds. *Puerto Rican Children on the Mainland: Interdisciplinary Perspectives*. New York: Garland, 1992.

Anderson, John Ward and Molly Moore. 'World's Poorest Women Suffer in Common'. *Columbus Dispatch* (11 April 1993): 4G.

Ang, Ian. *Watching Dallas: Soap Opera and the Melodramatic Imagination*. London: Methuen, 1985.

Angelo, Bonnie. 'Assigning the Blame for a Young Man's Suicide'. *Time*. Vol. 138, No. 2 (18 November 1991): 12–14.

Anthias, Floya and Nira Yuval Davis. *Racialised Boundaries*. London: Routledge, 1993.

Appignanesi, L. and S. Maitland. *The Rushdie File*. London: Fourth Estate, 1989.

Appignanesi, Richard and Chris Garratt. *Postmodernism for Beginners*. Cambridge: Icon Books, 1995.

Arber, Sara and Jay Ginn, eds. *Connecting Gender and Ageing: A Sociological Approach*. Buckingham: Open University Press, 1995.

Archer, Dane and Rosemary Gartner. *Violence and Crime in Cross-National Perspective*. New Haven, CT: Yale University Press, 1987.

Arendt, Hannah. *The Origins of Totalitarianism*. Cleveland, OH: Meridian Books, 1958.

——. *Between Past and Future: Six Exercises in Political Thought*. Cleveland, OH: Meridian Books, 1963.

Aries, Philippe. *Centuries of Childhood: A Social History of Family Life*. New York: Vintage Books, 1965.

——. *Western Attitudes Toward Death: From the Middle Ages to the Present*. Patricia M. Ranum, trans. Baltimore: Johns Hopkins University Press, 1974.

Arjomand, Said Amir. *The Turban for the Crown: The Islamic Revolution in Iran*. New York: Oxford University Press, 1988.

Asante, Molefi Kete. *The Afrocentric Idea*. Philadelphia: Temple University Press, 1987.

——. *Afrocentricity*. Trenton, NJ: Africa World Press, 1988.

Asch, Solomon. *Social Psychology*. Englewood Cliffs, NJ: Prentice Hall, 1952.

Ashford, Lori S. 'New Perspectives on Population: Lessons from Cairo'. *Population Bulletin*. Vol. 50, No. 1 (March 1995).

Ashworth, Andrew and Edmund Daises. 'Race and Criminal Justice'. Institute for Study and Treatment of Delinquency, Fact Sheet No. 1, 1997.

Astone, Nan Marie and Sara S. McLanahan. 'Family Structure, Parental Practices and High School Completion'. *American Sociological Review*. Vol. 56, No. 3 (June 1991): 309–20.

Atchley, Robert C. 'Retirement as a Social Institution'. *Annual Review of Sociology*. Vol. 8. Palo Alto, CA: Annual Reviews, 1982: 263–87.

——. *Aging: Continuity and Change*. Belmont, CA: Wadsworth, 1983; 2nd edn, 1987.

Aviad, Janet O'Dea, *Return to Judaism: Religious Renewal in Israel*. Chicago. London: University of Chicago Press, 1983.

Axtell, Roger E. *Gestures: The DOs and TABOOs of Body Language Around the World*. New York: Wiley, 1991.

Ayensu, Edward S. 'A Worldwide Role for the Healing Powers of Plants'. *Smithsonian*. Vol. 12, No. 8 (November 1981): 87–97.

Back, Les. *New Ethnicities and Urban Cultures: Racisms and Multiculture in Young Lives*. London: UCL Press, 1996.

Bachrach, Peter and Morton S. Baratz. *Power and Poverty*. New York: Oxford University Press, 1970.

Backman, Carl B. and Murray C. Adams. 'Self-Perceived Physical Attractiveness, Self-Esteem, Race, and Gender'. *Sociological Focus.* Vol. 24, No. 4 (October 1991): 283–90.

Bahl, Vinay. 'Caste and Class in India'. Paper presented to the Southern Sociological Society, Atlanta, April 1991.

Bailey. Joe, ed. *Social Europe.* London: Longman, 1992.

Bailey, William C. 'Murder, Capital Punishment and Television: Execution Publicity and Homicide Rates'. *American Sociological Review.* Vol. 55, No. 5 (October 1990): 628–33.

Bailey, William C. and Ruth D. Peterson. 'Murder and Capital Punishment: A Monthly Time-Series Analysis of Execution Publicity'. *American Sociological Review.* Vol. 54, No. 5 (October 1989): 722–43.

Baldovino, Angelo. *The Pleasure of Honesty.* 1962, pp. 57–58, 157–58.

Bales, Robert F. 'The Equilibrium Problem in Small Groups'. In Talcott Parsons, et al., eds., *Working Papers in the Theory of Action.* New York: Free Press, 1953: 111–15.

Bales, Robert F. and Philip E. Slater. 'Role Differentiation in Small Decision-Making Groups'. In Talcott Parsons and Robert F. Bales, eds., *Family, Socialization and Interaction Process.* New York: Free Press, 1955: 259–306.

Baltes, Paul B. and K. Warner Schaie. 'The Myth of the Twilight Years'. *Psychology Today.* Vol. 7, No. 10 (March 1974): 35–39.

Baltzell, E. Digby. *The Protestant Establishment: Aristocracy and Caste in America.* New York: Vintage Books, 1964.

——. 'Introduction to the 1967 Edition'. In W. E. B. Du Bois, *The Philadelphia Negro: A Social Study.* New York: Schocken, 1967; orig. 1899.

Baltzell, E. Digby, ed. *The Search for Community in Modern America.* New York: Harper & Row, 1968.

Banks, James A. *Multiethnic Education: Theory and Practice.* Boston: Allyn and Bacon, 1981.

Banks, Olive. *Faces of Feminism.* Oxford: Martin Robertson, 1981.

Barash, David. *The Whispering Within.* New York: Penguin Books, 1981.

Barber, Benjamin. *Jihad vs McWorld.* New York: Ballatine Books, 1995.

Barbour, Phillippe, ed. *The European Union Handbook.* London: Fitzroy Dearborn, 1996.

Barker, Chris. *Global Television: An Introduction.* Oxford: Blackwell, 1997.

Barker, Eileen. 'Who'd Be a Moonie? A Comparative Study of Those Who Join the Unification Church in Britain'. In Bryan Wilson, ed., *The Social Impact of New Religious Movements.* New York: The Rose of Sharon Press, 1981: 59–96.

——. *The Making of a Moonie.* Oxford: Basil Blackwell, 1984.

——. *New Religious Movements: A Practical Introduction.* 4th edn. London: HMSO, 1995.

Barker, Martin. *The New Racism.* London: Junction Books, 1981.

Barnett, Bernice McNair. *Sisters in Struggle: Invisible Black Women in the Civil Rights Movement.* London: Routledge, 1997.

Barnett, Hilaire A. *Sourcebook on Feminist Jurisprudence.* London: Cavendish, 1997.

Barrett, Michele. *Women's Oppression Today.* London: Verso, 1980.

Barry, Kathleen. 'Feminist Theory: The Meaning of Women's Liberation'. In Barbara Haber, ed., *The Women's Annual 1982–1983.* Boston: G. K. Hall, 1983: 35–78.

Barthes, Roland. *Elements of Semiology*, Annette Lavers and Colin Smith, trans. London: Cape, 1967.

Bastiansen, Henrik and Trine Syversten. 'Towards a Norwegian Television History'. In Bondenberg and Francesco Bono, eds., *Television in Scandinavia.* Luton: John Libby, 1996.

Bateson, Gregory and Margaret Mead. *Balinese Character.* New York: New York Academy of Science, 1942.

Baudrillard, Jean. 'The Reality Gulf'. *The Guardian* (11 January 1991): 25.

Bauer, P. T. *Equality, the Third World and Economic Delusion.* Cambridge, MA: Harvard University Press, 1981.

Bauman, Zygmunt. *Modernity and the Holocaust.* Cambridge: Polity Press, 1989.

Baylis, John and Steve Smith, eds. *The Globalization of World Politics.* Oxford: Oxford University Press, 1997.

Bech, Henning. 'Report from a Rotten State: Marriage and Homosexuality in Denmark'. In Ken Plummer, ed., *Modern Homosexualities: Fragments of Lesbian and Gay Experience.* London: Routledge, 1992, pp. 134–47.

Beck, Ulrich. *Risk Society.* London: Sage, 1992.

Beck, Ulrich and Elisabeth Beck-Gernsheim. *The Normal Chaos of Love.* Cambridge: Polity Press, 1995.

Becker, Howard S. *Outside: Studies in the Sociology of Deviance.* New York: Free Press, 1966.

——. *Doing Things Together.* Chicago: Aldine, 1986.

Bedell, George C., Leo Sandon, Jr. and Charles T. Wellborn. *Religion in America.* New York: Macmillan, 1975.

Beeghley, Leonard. *The Structure of Social Stratification in the United States.* Needham Heights, MA: Allyn & Bacon, 1989.

Bekker, Simon. *Ethnicity in Focus: The South African Case.* Durban: Indicator South Africa, 1993.

Bell, Alan P., Martin S. Weinberg and Sue Kiefer-Hammersmith. *Sexual Preference: Its Development in Men and Women.* Bloomington: Indiana University Press, 1981.

Bell, Daniel. *The Coming of Post-Industrial Society: A Venture in Social Forecasting.* New York: Harper Colophon, 1976.

Bell, Judith. *Doing your Research Project: A Guide for First-Time Researchers in Education and Social Science.* 2nd edn. Buckingham: Open University Press, 1993.

Bellah, Robert N. *The Broken Covenant.* New York: Seabury Press, 1975.

Bellah, Robert N., Richard Madsen, William M. Sullivan, Ann Swidler and Steven M. Tipton. *Habits of the Heart: Individualism and Commitment in American Life.* New York: Harper & Row, 1985.

Belsky, Jay, Richard M. Lerner and Graham B. Spanier. *The Child in the Family.* Reading, MA: Addison-Wesley, 1984.

Benedict, Ruth. 'Continuities and Discontinuities in Cultural Conditioning'. *Psychiatry.* Vol. 1 (May 1938): 161–67.

Benet, Sula. 'Why They Live to Be 100, or Even Older, in Abkhasia'. *New York Times Magazine* (26 December 1971): 3, 28–29, 31–34.

Benjamin, Bernard and Chris Wallis. 'The Mortality of Widowers'. *The Lancet.* Vol. 2 (August 1963): 454–56.

Benjamin, Lois. *The Black Elite: Facing the Color Line in the Twilight of the Twentieth Century.* Chicago: Nelson-Hall, 1991.

Benjamin, Walter. *The Work of Art in the Age of Mechanical Reproduction.* London: Cape, 1970.

Benokraitis, Nijole and Joe Feagin. *Modern Sexism: Blatant, Subtle and Overt Discrimination.* 2nd edn. Englewood Cliffs, NJ: Prentice Hall, 1995.

Benton, Douglas A. *Applied Human Relations; An Organizational and Skill Development Approach.* 6th edn. Englewood Cliffs, NJ: PrenticeHall, 1997

Benton, Ted, ed. *The Greening of Marxism.* New York: Guildford Press, 1996.

Berger, Alan L. *Children of Job: American Second-generation Witnesses to the Holocaust.* New York: State University of New York Press, 1997.

Berger, Peter L. *Invitation to Sociology.* New York: Anchor Books, 1963.

——. *The Sacred Canopy: Elements of a Sociological Theory of Religion.* Garden City, NY: Doubleday, 1967.

——. 'Against the Current'. *Prospect (UK).* Issue 17 (March 1977a), 32–6.

——. *Facing Up to Modernity: Excursions in Society, Politics and Religion.* New York: Basic Books, 1977b.

——. *The Capitalist Revolution: Fifty Propositions About Prosperity, Equality and Liberty.* New York: Basic Books, 1986.

Berger, Peter, Brigitte Berger and Hansfried Kellner. *The Homeless Mind: Modernization and Consciousness.* New York: Vintage Books, 1974.

Berger, Peter and Hansfried Kellner. *Sociology Reinterpreted: An Essay on Method and Vocation.* Garden City, NY: Anchor Books, 1981.

Berger, Peter and Thomas Luckman. *The Social Construction of Reality: A Treatise in the Sociology of Knowledge*. Garden City, NY: Anchor Books, 1967

Bergesen, Albert, ed. *Crises in the World-System*. Beverly Hills, CA: Sage, 1983.

Bernard, Jessie. *The Female World*. New York: Free Press, 1981.

——. *The Future of Marriage*. New Haven, CT: Yale University Press, 1982; orig. 1973.

Bernstein, Richard J. *The New Constellation: The Ethical-Political Horizons of Modernity/Postmodernity*. Cambridge, MA: MIT Press, 1992.

Berrill, Kevin T. 'Anti-Gay Violence and Victimization in the United States: An Overview'. In Gregory M. Herek and Kevin T. Berrill, *Hate Crimes: Confronting Violence Against Lesbians and Gay Men*. Newbury Park, CA: Sage, 1992: 19–45.

Berry, Brian L. and Philip H. Rees. 'The Factorial Ecology of Calcutta'. *American Journal of Sociology*. Vol. 74, No. 5 (March 1969): 445–91.

Best, Raphaela. *We've All Got Scars: What Boys and Girls Learn in Elementary School*. Bloomington: Indiana University Press, 1983.

Beauvoir, Simone de. *The Woman Destroyed*, Patrick O'Brian, trans. London: Fontana/Collins, 1971.

——. *The Second Sex*. Harmondsworth: Penguin, 1972 (originally published in English 1952).

Beynon, Huw, Ray Hudson and David Sadler. *A Tale of Two Industries: The Contraction of Coal and Steel in the North East of England*. Buckingham: Open University Press, 1991.

Bhavnani, Kum Kum. 'Talking Racism and the Reality Of Women's Studies'. In D. Richardson and V. Robinson, eds., *Introducing Womens Studies*. London: Macmillan, 1993.

Biblarz, Timothy J. and Adrian E. Raftery. 'The Effects of Family Disruption on Social Mobility'. *American Sociological Review*. Vol. 58, No. 1 (February 1993): 97–109.

Blakemore, Ken and Margaret Boneham. *Age, Race and Ethnicity: A Comparative Approach*. Buckingham: Open University Press, 1993.

Blau, Peter M. *Exchange and Power in Social Life*. New York: Wiley, 1964.

——. *Inequality and Heterogeneity: A Primitive Theory of Social Structure*. New York: Free Press, 1977.

Blau, Peter M., Terry C. Blum and Joseph Schwartz. 'Heterogeneity and Intermarriage'. *American Sociological Review*. Vol. 47, No. 1 (February 1982): 45–62.

Blau, Peter M. and Otis Dudley Duncan. *The American Occupational Structure*. New York: Wiley, 1967.

Blumer, Herbert G. 'Collective Behavior'. In Alfred McClung Lee, ed., *Principles of Sociology*. 3rd edn. New York: Barnes & Noble Books, 1969: 65–121.

Blumstein, Philip and Pepper Schwartz. *American Couples*. New York: William Morrow, 1983.

Bocock, Robert. *Consumption*. London: Routledge, 1993.

Bodenheimer, Thomas S. 'Health Care in the United States: Who Pays?' In Vicente Navarro, ed., *Health and Medical Care in the US: A Critical Analysis*. Farmingdale, NY: Baywood Publishing Co., 1977: 61–68.

Boff, Leonard and Clodovis. *Salvation and Liberation: In Search of a Balance Between Faith and Politics*. Maryknoll, NY: Orbis Books, 1984.

Bogardus, Emory S. 'Comparing Racial Distance inEthopia, South Africa, and the United States'. *Sociology and Social Research*. Vol. 52, No. 2 (January, 1968): 149–56.

Bohm, Robert M. 'American Death Penalty Opinion, 1936–1986: A Critical Examination of the Gallup Polls'. In Robert M. Bohm, ed., *The Death Penalty in America: Current Research*. Cincinnati: Anderson Publishing Co., 1991: 113–45.

Bohrmann, Herbert F. and Stephen R. Kellert, eds., *Ecology, Economics and Ethics: The Broken Circle*. New Haven, CT: Yale University Press, 1991: 205–10.

Booth, Alan and Lynn White. 'Thinking About Divorce'. *Journal of Marriage and the Family*. Vol. 42, No. 3 (August 1980): 605–16.

Bondenberg and Francesco Bono, eds. *Television in Scandinavia*. Luton: John Libbey, 1996: 127–55.

Bonner, Jane. Research presented in 'The Two Brains', Public Broadcasting System telecast, 1984.

Borgmann, Albert. *Crossing the Postmodern Divide*. Chicago: University of Chicago Press, 1992.

Bormann, F. Herbert and Stephen R. Kellert. 'The Global Environmental Deficit'. In F. Herbert Bormann and Stephen R. Kellert, eds., *Ecology, Economics and Ethics: The Broken Circle*. New Haven, CT: Yale University Press, 1991: ix–xviii.

Bornhoff, Nicholas. *Pink Samurai: An Erotic Exploration of Japanese Society*. London: Grafton Books, 1992.

Boswell, Terry E. and William J. Dixon. 'Marx's Theory of Rebellion: A Cross-National Analysis of Class Exploitation, Economic Development and Violent Revolt'. *American Sociological Review*. Vol. 58, No. 5 (October 1993): 681–702.

Bott, Elizabeth. *Family and Social Network*. New York: Free Press, 1971; orig. 1957.

Bottoms, Anthony F. 'Some Neglected Features of Modern Penal Systems'. In D. Garland and P. Young, eds., *The Power to Punish*. London: Heinemann, 1988.

Boulding, Elise. *The Underside of History*. Boulder, CO: Westview Press, 1976.

Bourdieu, Pierre. *Distinction*. London: Routledge, 1984.

Bowles, Samuel and Herbert Gintis. *Schooling in Capitalist America: Educational Reform and the Contradictions of Economic Life*. New York: Basic Books, 1976.

Boyle, Kevin. *Freedom of Religion and Belief: A World Report*. London: Routledge, 1997.

Branegan, Jay. 'Is Singapore a Model for the West?' *Time*. Vol. 141, No. 3 (18 January 1993): 36–37.

Bratlinger, Patrick. *Crusoe's Footprints: Cultural Studies in Britain and America*. New York: Routledge, 1990.

Breen, Leonard Z. 'The Aging Individual'. In Clark Tibbitts, ed., *Handbook of Social Gerontology*. Chicago: University of Chicago Press, 1960: 145–62.

Breen, Richard and David B. Rottman. *Class Stratification: A Comparative Perspective*. Hemel Hempstead: Harvester Wheatsheaf, 1994.

Brightman, Joan. 'Why Hillary Chooses Rodham Clinton'. *American Demographics*. Vol. 16, No. 3 (March 1994): 9–11.

Brinton, Crane. *The Anatomy of Revolution*. New York: Vintage Books, 1965.

Brinton, Mary C. 'The Social-Institutional Bases of Gender Stratification: Japan as an Illustrative Case'. *American Journal of Sociology*. Vol. 94, No. 2 (September 1988): 300–34.

British Medical Association. *Complementary Medicine: New Approaches to Good Practice*. London: BMA, 1993.

Brown, Lester R., et al., eds. *State of the World 1993: A Worldwatch Institute Report on Progress Toward a Sustainable Society*. New York: W. W. Norton, 1993 and 1997.

Brown, Lester R. 'Reassessing the Earth's Population'. *Society*. Vol. 32, No. 4 (May–June 1995): 7–10.

Brown, Mary Ellen, ed. *Television and Women's Culture: The Politics of the Popular*. Newbury Park, CA: Sage, 1990.

Brownhill, Sue. *Housing London: Issues of Finance and Supply: The Final Report of the Greater London Study*. York: Joseph Rowntree Foundation, 1990.

Bruce, Steven. 'The Twilight of the Gods', *Sociology Review* (November 1992).

——. *Religion in the Modern World: From Cathedrals to Cults*. Oxford: Oxford University Press, 1996.

Bruno, Mary. 'Abusing the Elderly'. *Newsweek* (23 September 1985): 75–76.

Bryman, Alan. *Disney and His Worlds*. London: Routledge, 1995.

Bryson. 'Of Mice and Millions'. *Observer Magazine* (28 March 1993): 16–23.

Bulliet, L. Richard W. *Islam: The View from the Edge.* New York: Columbia University Press, 1993.

Bulmer, Martin and Anthony M. Rees, eds. *Citizenship Today: The Contemporary Relevance of T.H. Marshall.* London: UCL Press, 1996.

Bumpass, Larry and James A. Sweet. 1992–1994 National Survey of Families and Households. Reported in 'Report from PPA'. *Population Today.* Vol. 23, No. 6 (June 1995): 3.

Burbridge, Mikey and J. Walters, eds. *Breaking the Silence: Gay Teenagers Speak for Themselves.* London: Joint Council of Gay Teenagers, 1981.

Burgess, Robert. *In the Field London.* London: Allen & Unwin, 1984.

Burgoyne, Jacqueline, Roger Ormrod and Martin Richards. *Divorce matters.* Harmondsworth: Penguin, 1987.

Burke, Tom. 'The Future'. In Sir Edmund Hillary, ed., *Ecology 2000: The Changing Face of the Earth.* New York: Beaufort Books, 1984: 227–41.

Bury, M.R. 'Social Constructionism and the Development of Medical Sociology'. *Sociology of Health and Illness.* Vol. 8 (1986): 137–68.

——. 'The Sociology of Chronic Illness'. *Sociology of Health and Illness.* Vol. 13, No. 4 (1991): 451–68.

Busby, Linda J. 'Sex Role Research on the Mass Media'. *Journal of Communications.* Vol. 25 (Autumn 1975): 107–13.

Busfield, Joan. *Women, Men and Madness.* London: Macmillan, 1997.

Butler, Robert N. *Why Survive? Being Old in America.* New York: Harper & Row, 1975.

Butterworth, Douglas and John K. Chance. *Latin American Urbanization.* Cambridge: Cambridge University Press, 1981.

Bytheway, Bill. *Ageism.* Buckingham: Open University Press, 1995.

Cahnman, Werner J. and Rudolf Heberle. 'Introduction'. In *Ferdinand Toennies on Sociology: Pure, Applied, and Empirical.* Chicago: University of Chicago Press, 1971: vii–xxii.

Callahan, Daniel. *Setting Limits: Medical Goals in an Aging Society.* New York: Simon & Schuster, 1987.

Calley, Malcolm J. C. *God's people: West Indian Pentecostal Sects in England.* London: Oxford University Press, 1965.

Calmore, John O. 'National Housing Policies and Black America: Trends, Issues and Implications'. In *The State of Black America 1986.* New York: National Urban League, 1986: 115–49.

Cameron, William Bruce. *Modern Social Movements: A Sociological Outline.* New York: Random House, 1966.

Cancian, Francesca M. *Love in America: Gender and Self-development.* Cambridge: Cambridge University Press,1987.

Caplan, Lionel. 'Popular Conceptions of Fundamentalism'. In L. Caplan, ed., *Studies in Religious Fundamentalism.* Albany: State University of New York, 1987: 1–24.

Caplan, Patricia. *Class and Gender in India: Women and Their Organisation in a South Indian City.* New York: Tavistock, 1985.

Caplow, Theodore, Howard M. Bahr, John Modell and Bruce A. Chadwick. *Recent Social Trends in the United States, 1960–1990.* Montreal: McGill-Queen's University Press, 1991.

Carley, Kathleen. 'A Theory of Group Stability'. *American Sociological Review.* Vol. 56, No. 3 (June 1991): 331–54.

Carlson, Norman A. 'Corrections in the United States Today: A Balance Has Been Struck'. *The American Criminal Law Review.* Vol. 13, No. 4 (Spring 1976): 615–47.

Carmichael, Stokely and Charles V. Hamilton. *Black Power: The Politics of Liberation in America.* New York: Vintage Books, 1967.

Carson, Rachel. *Silent Spring.* Boston: Houghton Mifflin, 1962.

Cartright, Ann and M. O'Brian. 'Social Class: Variations in Health Care'. In M. Stacey, *The Sociology of the NHS, Sociological Review Monograph,* No. 22, Keele, 1976.

Castells, Manuel. *The Informational City.* Oxford: Blackwell, 1989.

Castles, Stephen, H. Booth and T. Wallace. *Here for Good: Western Europe's New Ethnic Minorities.* London: Pluto, 1984.

Castles, Stephen and Mark J. Miller. *The Age of Migration: International Population Movements in the Modern World.* London: Macmillan, 1993.

Castro, Janice. 'Disposable Workers'. *Time.* Vol. 131, No. 14 (29 March 1993): 43–47.

Chagnon, Napoleon A. *Yaïnomamŏ: The Fierce People.* 5th edn. New York: Holt, Rinehart & Winston, 1997.

Champion, A.G. *Social and Economic Atlas of the UK.* Oxford: Oxford University Press, 1996

Chandler, Tertius and Gerald Fox. *3000 Years of Urban History.* New York: Academic Press, 1974.

Change, Kwang-Chih. *The Archaeology of Ancient China.* New Haven, CT: Yale University Press, 1977.

Cherlin, Andrew and Frank F. Furstenberg, Jr. 'The American Family in the Year 2000'. *The Futurist.* Vol. 17, No. 3 (June 1983): 7–14.

Chisholm, Patricia. 'To Celebrate Our Love Publicly'. *Maclean's* (28 June 1993): 29.

Chodorow, Nancy. *The Reproduction of Mothering.* Berkeley: University of California Press, 1978.

Chown, Sheila M. 'Morale, Careers and Personal Potentials'. In James E. Birren and K. Warner Schaie, eds., *Handbook of the Psychology of Aging.* New York: Van Nostrand Reinhold, 1977: 672–91.

Church, George J. 'Unons Arise – With New Tricks'. *Time.* Vol. 143, No. 24 (13 June 1994): 56–58

Clark, Curtis B. 'Geriatric Abuse: Out of the Closet'. In *The Tragedy of Elder Abuse: The Problem and the Response.* Hearings before the Select Committee on Aging, House of Representatives (1 July 1986):49–50.

Clark, Margaret S., ed. *Prosocial Behavior.* Newbury Park, CA: Sage, 1991.

Clark, Thomas A. *Blacks in Suburbs.* New Brunswick, NJ: Rutgers University Center for Urban Policy Research, 1979.

Clarke, P. 'Islam in Contemporary Europe'. In S. Sutherland, et al., eds., *The World's Religions.* London: Routledge, 1988.

Clarke, Robin. 'Atmospheric Pollution'. In Sir Edmund Hillary, ed., *Ecology 2000: The Changing Face of the Earth.* New York: Beaufort Books, 1984: 130–48.

Clegg, Stuart R. *Modern Organisation: Organisation Studies in the Postmodern World.* London: Sage, 1990.

Clinard, Marshall and Daniel Abbott. *Crime in Developing Countries.* New York: Wiley, 1973.

Clough, Patricia Ticineto. *The Ends of Ethnography: From Realism to Social Criticism.* Newbury Park, CA: Sage Publications, 1992.

Cloward, Richard A. and Lloyd E. Ohlin. *Delinquency and Opportunity: A Theory of Delinquent Gangs.* New York: Free Press, 1966.

Cochrane, Alan and John Clarke. *Comparing Welfare States: Britain in International Context.* London: Sage, 1993.

Coe, Michael D. and Richard A. Diehl. *In the Land of the Olmec.* Austin: University of Texas Press, 1980.

Cohen, Albert K. *Delinquent Boys: The Culture of the Gang.* New York: Free Press, 1971; orig. 1955.

Cohen, Joel E. *How Many People Can the Earth Support.* New York: W. W. Norton, 1995.

Cohen, Lloyd R. 'Sexual Harassment and the Law'. *Society.* Vol. 28, No. 4 (May–June 1991): 8–13.

Cohen, P. 'Subculture Conflict and Working Class Community'. In S. Hall, et al., *Culture, Media, Logica.* London: Hutchinson, 1980; orig. 1972.

Cohen, Stanley. *Visions of Social Control.* Cambridge: Polity Press, 1985.

Cohen, Stanley and Laurie Taylor. *Escape Attempts: The Theory and Practice of Resistance to Everyday Life.* 2nd edn. London: Routledge, 1995.

Cohen, Stanley and Jock Young, eds. *The Manufacture of News.* 2nd edn. London: Constable, 1981.

Cohn, Richard M. 'Economic Development and Status Change of the Aged', *American Journal of Sociology.* Vol. 87, No. 2 (March 1982):1150–61.

Coleman, Clive and Jenny Moynihan. *Understanding Crime Data.* Buckingham: Open University Press, 1996.

Coleman, David, ed. *Europe's Population in the 1990s.* Oxford: Oxford University Press, 1992

Coleman, David and John Salt. *The British Population: Patterns, Trends and Processes*. Oxford: Oxford University Press, 1992

Coleman, James S. 'Rational Organization'. *Rationality and Society*. Vol. 2 (1990): 94–105.

——. 'The Design of Organizations and the Right to Act'. *Sociological Forum*. Vol. 8, No. 4 (December 1993): 527–46.

Coleman, Richard P. and Lee Rainwater. *Social Standing in America*. New York: Basic Books, 1978.

Collins, Patricia Hill. *Black Feminist Thought*. London: Routlege, 1991.

Collins, Randall. 'A Conflict Theory of Sexual Stratification'. *Social Problems*. Vol. 19, No. 1 (Summer 1971): 3–21.

——. *The Credential Society: An Historical Sociology of Education and Stratification*. New York: Academic Press, 1979.

Colloway, N. O. and Paula L. Dollevoet. 'Selected Tabular Material on Aging'. In Caleb Finch and Leonard Hayflick, eds., *Handbook of the Biology of Aging*. New York: Van Nostrand Reinhold, 1977: 666–708.

Comte, Auguste. *Auguste Comte and Positivism: The Essential Writings*. Gertrud Lenzer, ed., New York: Harper Torchbooks, 1975.

Connell, R.W. *Masculinities*. Cambridge: Polity Press, 1995.

Connett, Paul H. 'The Disposable Society'. In F. Herbert Bormann and Stephen R. Kellert, eds., *Ecology, Economics and Ethics: The Broken Circle*. New Haven, CT: Yale University Press, 1991: 99–122.

Connor, Steven. *Postmodern Culture*. 2nd edn. Oxford: Blackwell, 1997.

Conrad, Peter and Joseph Schneider. *Deviance and Medicalization: From Badness to Sickness*. London: Routledge (originally Free Association), 1990.

Contreras, Joseph. 'A New Day Dawns'. *Newsweek* (30 March 1992): 40–41.

Cooley, Charles Horton. *Human Nature and the Social Order*. New York: Schocken Books, 1964; orig. 1902.

Coran, Tony. *Between the Sheets*. London: Cassell, 1997.

Corbin, J. and Anslem Stauss. 'Managing Chronic Illness at Home', *Qualitative Sociology*, Vol. 8, No. 3 (1985): 224–47.

Corley, Robert N., O. Lee Reed, Peter J. Shedd and Jere W. Morehead. *The Legal and Regulatory Environment of Business*. 9th edn. New York: McGraw-Hill, 1993.

Coser, Lewis A. *Masters of Sociological Thought: Ideas in Historical and Social Context*. 2nd edn. New York: Harcourt Brace Jovanovich, 1977.

Cotgrove, Stephen. *Catastrophe or Cornucopia: The Environment, Politics and the Future*. Chichester: Wiley, 1982.

Cottrell, John and The Editors Of *Time-Life*. *The Great Cities: Mexico City*. Amsterdam: Time-Life, 1979.

Council on Families in America. *Marriage in America: A Report to the Nation*. New York: Institute for American Values, 1995.

Counts, G. S. 'The Social Status of Occupations: A Problem in Vocational Guidance'. *School Review*. Vol. 33 (January 1925): 16–27.

Courtney, Alice E. and Thomas W. Whipple. *Sex Stereotyping in Advertising*. Lexington, MA: D.C. Heath, 1983.

Coveney, Lal, et al. *The Sexuality Papers*. London: Hutchinson, 1984.

Cowan, Carolyn Pope. *When Partners Become Parents*. New York: Basic Books, 1992.

Cowgill, Donald and Lowell Holmes. *Aging and Modernization*. New York: Appleton-Century-Crofts, 1972.

Cowley, Geoffrey. 'The Prescription That Kills'. *Newsweek* (17 July 1995): 54.

Cox, Harvey. *The Secular City*. Rev. edn. New York: Macmillan, 1971; orig. 1965.

——. *Turning East: The Promise and Peril of the New Orientalism*. New York: Simon and Schuster, 1977.

——. 'Church and Believers: Always Strangers?' In Thomas Robbins and Dick Anthony, *In Gods We Trust: New Patterns of Religious. Pluralism in America*. 2nd edn. New Brunswick, NJ: Transaction, 1990: 449–62.

Coxon, Anthony P. M. *Between the Sheets: The Sexual Diaries of Gay Men*. London: Cassell, 1997.

Craib, Ian. 'Masculinity and Male Domination'. *Sociological Review*, Vol. 35, No. 4 (November 1987): 721–43.

——. *Classical Social Theory*. Oxford: Oxford University Press, 1997.

——. *Modern Social Theory*. 2nd edn. Hemel Hempstead: Harvester Wheatsheaf, 1992.

Craig, Grace. *Human Development*. 7th edn. Englewood Cliffs, NJ: Prentice Hall, 1995.

Crofts, S. 'Global Neighbours'. In R. Allen, *To be Continued . . . . Soap Operas Around the World*. London: Routledge, 1995.

Crompton, Rosemary. *Class and Stratification*. Cambridge: Polity, 1993.

Crook, Stephan, Jan Pakulski and Malcolm Waters. *Postmodernity: Change in Advanced Society*. Newbury Park, CA: Sage, 1992.

Crossette, Barbara. 'Female Genital Mutilation by Immigrants is Becoming Cause for Concern in the US'. *New York Times International* (10 December 1995): 11.

Crystal, David. *English as a Global Language*. Cambridge: Cambridge University Press, 1997

Cuff, E. C. and G. C. F. Payne, eds. *Perspectives in Sociology*. London: Allen and Unwin, 1979.

Cuff, E. C., Wes Sharrock and D. Francis. *Perspectives in Sociology*. 3rd edn. London: Allen and Unwin, 1990.

Cumming, Elaine and William E. Henry. *Growing Old: The Process of Disengagement*. New York: Basic Books, 1961.

Curtis, James and Lorne Tepperman, eds. *Haves and Have Nots: An International Reader on Social Inequality*. Englewood Cliffs, NJ: Prentice Hall, 1994.

Curtiss, Susan. *Genie: A Psycholinguistic Study of a Modern-Day 'Wild Child'*. New York: Academic Press, 1977.

Cutler, David M. and Lawrence F. Katz. 'Rising Inequality? Changes in the Distribution of Income and Consumption in the 1980s'. Working Paper No. 3964. Cambridge, MA: National Bureau of Economic Research, 1992.

Cutright, Phillip. 'Occupational Inheritance: A Cross-National Analysis'. *American Journal of Sociology*. Vol. 73, No. 4 (January 1968): 400–16.

Cylke, F. Kurt, Jr. *The Environment*. New York: HarperCollins, 1993.

Dahl, Robert A. *Who Governs?* New Haven, CT: Yale University Press, 1961.

——. *Dilemmas of Pluralist Democracy: Autonomy vs. Control*. New Haven, CT: Yale University Press, 1982.

Dahrendorf, Ralf. *Class and Class Conflict in Industrial Society*. Stanford, CA: Stanford University Press, 1959.

Daly, Martin and Margo Wilson. *Homicide*. New York: Aldine, 1988.

Daly, Mary. *Beyond God the Father*. Boston: Beacon Press, 1973.

——. *GYn/Ecology: The Metaethics of Radical Feminism*. Boston: Beacon, 1978.

Daniel, W. W. *Racial Discrimination in England* (based on the PEP Report). Harmondsworth: Penguin, 1968.

Dannefer, Dale. 'Adult Development and Social Theory: A Reappraisal'. *American Sociological Review*. Vol. 49, No. 1 (February 1984): 100–16.

Darnton, Nina and Yuriko Hoshia. 'Whose Life Is It, Anyway?' *Newsweek*. Vol. 113, No. 4 (13 January 1989): 61.

Darwin, Charles. *The Illustrated Origin of the Species*, abridged by Richard Leakey. London: Faber and Faber, 1979.

Davidson, Julia O'Connell and Derek Layder. *Methods, Sex and Madness*. London: Routledge, 1994.

Davie, Grace. 'God and Caesar: Religion in a Rapidly Changing Europe'. In J. Bailey, ed., *Social Europe* (1992), pp. 216–38

——. *Religion in Britain since 1945: Believing without Belonging*. Oxford: Blackwell, 1994.

Davies, Christie. *Ethnic Humor Around the World: A Comparative Analysis*. Bloomington: Indiana University Press, 1990.

Davies, James C. 'Toward a Theory of Revolution'. *American Sociological Review*. Vol. 27, No. 1 (February 1962): 5–19.

Davies, Malcolm, Hazel Croall and Jane Tyrer. *Criminal Justice: An Introduction to the Criminal Justice System in England and Wales.* London: Longmans, 1995.

Davies, Mark and Denise B. Kandel. 'Parental and Peer Influences on Adolescents' Educational Plans: Some Further Evidence'. *American Journal of Sociology.* Vol. 87, No. 2 (September 1981): 363–87.

Davis, Kingsley. 'Extreme Social Isolation of a Child'. *American Journal of Sociology.* Vol. 45, No. 4 (January 1940): 554–65.

——. 'Final Note on a Case of Extreme Isolation'. *American Journal of Sociology.* Vol. 52, No. 5 (March 1947): 432–37.

Davis, Kingsley and Wilbert Moore. 'Some Principles of Stratification'. *American Sociological Review.* Vol. 10, No. 2 (April 1945): 242–49.

De Cecco, John. 'Homophobia: An Overview'. *Journal of Homosexuality.* Vol. 10, No. 11 (1987).

De Mente, Boye. *Japanese Etiquette and Ethics in Business.* 5th edn. Lincolnwood, IL: NTC Business Books, 1987.

Dedrick, Dennis K. and Richard E. Yinger. 'MAD, SDI and the Nuclear Arms Race'. Manuscript in development. Georgetown, Ky.: Georgetown College, 1990.

Deegan, Mary Jo. *Jane Addams and the Men of the Chicago School.* New Jersey: Transaction, 1988.

Deem, Rosemary, ed. *Schooling for Women's Work.* London: Routledge and Kegan Paul, 1980.

——. 'Governing schools in the 1990s'. *Sociology Review.* Vol. 6, No. 3 (1997): 28–31.

Deem, Rosemary, K. J. Brehony and S. Heath. *Active Citizenship and the Governing of Schools.* Buckingham: Open University Press, 1995.

Delacroix, Jacques and Charles C. Ragin. 'Structural Blockage: A Crossnational Study of Economic Dependency, State Efficacy and Underdevelopment'. *American Journal of Sociology.* Vol. 86, No. 6 (May 1981): 1311–47.

Delphy, Christine and Diana Leonard. *Familiar Exploitation: A New Analysis of Marriage in Contemporary Western Societies.* Cambridge: Polity Press, 1992.

Dennis, Norman and George Erdos. *Families without Fatherhood.* London: IEA Health and Welfare Unit, 1993.

Dennis, Norman, Fernando Henriques and Clifford Slaughter. *Coal is Our Life: an Analysis of a Yorkshire Mining Community.* London: Eyre & Spottiswoode, 1956.

Denzin, Norman K. *Images of Postmodern Society.* London: Sage, 1991.

——. *Symbolic Interactionism and Cultural Studies: The Politics of Interpretation.* Oxford: Basil Blackwell, 1992.

——. *The Cinematic Society.* London: Sage, 1995.

Denzin, Norman K. and Yvonna S. Lincoln, ed. *Handbook of Qualitative Research.* London: Sage, 1994.

Der Spiegel. 'Third World Metropolises Are Becoming Monsters; Rural Poverty Drives Millions to the Slums'. In *World Press Review* (October 1989).

Devine, Fiona. *Affluent Workers Revisited.* Edinburgh: Edinburgh University Press, 1996.

——. *Class in Britain and America.* Edinburgh: Edinburgh University Press, 1996.

DGAA Homelife. *100 at 100: An Interview Study with 100 Centenarians.* London: 1 Dery St. W8 5HY.

Dickens, Charles. *Oliver Twist.* 1886: 36; orig. 1837–39.

Dobson, Richard B. 'Mobility and Stratification in the Soviet Union'. *Annual Review of Sociology.* Vol. 3. Palo Alto, CA: Annual Reviews, 1977: 297–329.

Dollard, John, et al. *Frustration and Aggression.* New Haven, CT: Yale University Press, 1939.

Domhoff, G. William. *Who Rules America Now? A View of the '80s.* Englewood Cliffs, NJ: Prentice Hall, 1983.

Donovan, Virginia K. and Ronnie Littenberg. 'Psychology of Women: Feminist Therapy'. In Barbara Haber, ed., *The Women's Annual 1981: The Year in Review.* Boston: G. K. Hall, 1982: 211–35.

Douglass, Richard L. 'Domestic Neglect and Abuse of the Elderly: Implications for Research and Service'. *Family Relations.* Vol. 32 (July 1983): 395–402.

Dowd, Nancy E. *In Defense of Single-Parent Families.* New York: New York University Press, 1997.

Downes, David and Paul Rock. *Understanding Deviance.* 2nd edn. Oxford: Clarendon Press, 1988.

Downs, Anthony. *New Visions for Metropolitan America.* Washington, DC: Brookings Institute, 1994.

Doyal, Lesley. *The Political Economy of Health.* London: Pluto, 1979.

——. *What Makes a Women Sick.* London: Macmillan, 1995.

Drake, Graham. *Issues in the New Europe.* London: Hodder & Stoughton, 1994.

Du Bois, W. E. B. *Dusk of Dawn.* New York: Harcourt, Brace & World, 1940.

——. *The Philadelphia Negro: A Social Study.* New York: Schocken Books, 1967; orig. 1899.

——. *The Souls of Black Folk.* New York: Penguin Books, 1982; orig. 1903.

Dubos, René. *Man Adapting.* New Haven, CT: Yale University Press, 1980; orig. 1965.

Duhl, Leonard J. 'The Social Context of Health'. In Arthur C. Hastings, et al., eds., *Health for the Whole Person: The Complete Guide to Holistic Medicine.* Boulder, CO: Westview Press, 1980: 39–48.

Duhring, Simon, ed. *The Cultural Studies Reader.* London: Routledge, 1993.

Dunlap, Riley E., George H. Gallup, Jr. and Alec M. Gallup. *The Health of the Planet Survey.* Princeton, NJ: The George H. Gallup International Institute, 1992.

Dunlap, Riley E. and Angela G. Mertig. 'The Evolution of the US Environmental Movement from 1970 to 1990: An Overview'. In Riley E. Dunlap and Angela G. Mertig, eds., *American Environmentalism: The US Environmental Movement, 1970–1990.* New York: Taylor & Francis, 1992: 1–10.

Dunn, Ashley. 'Ancient Chinese Craft Shifts Building Designs in the US'. *The New York Times* (22 September 1994): IA, B4.

Durkheim, Emile. *The Division of Labor in Society.* New York: Free Press, 1964a; orig. 1895.

——. *The Rules of Sociological Method.* New York: Free Press, 1964b; orig. 1893.

——. *The Elementary Forms of Religious Life.* New York: Free Press, 1965; orig. 1915.

——. *Suicide.* New York: Free Press, 1966; orig. 1897.

——. *Selected Writings.* Anthony Giddens, ed., Cambridge: Cambridge University Press, 1972.

——. *Sociology and Philosophy.* New York: Free Press, 1974; orig. 1924.

Durning, Alan Thein. 'Supporting Indigenous Peoples'. In Lester R. Brown, et al., eds., *State of the World 1993: A Worldwatch Institute Report on Progress Toward a Sustainable Society.* New York: W. W. Norton, 1993: 80–100.

Dworkin, Andrea. *Pornography: Men Possessing Women.* New York: Pedigree, 1981.

——. *Intercourse.* New York: Free Press, 1987.

Ebaugh, Helen Rose Fuchs. *Becoming an EX: The Process of Role Exit.* Chicago: University of Chicago Press, 1988.

——. *Women in the Vanishing Cloister: Organisational Decline in Catholic Religious Orders in the United States.* New Brunswick, NJ: Rutgers University Press, 1993.

Economist, The. 'Cockfighting: 'Til Death Us Do Part'. Vol. 333, No. 7851 (19 February 1994): 30.

——. 'Japan's Missing Children'. Vol. 333, No. 7889 (12 November 1994): 46.

Eder, Klaus. *The New Politics of Class.* London: Sage, 1993.

Edgell, Steven. *Class.* London: Routledge, 1993.

Edwards, David V. *The American Political Experience.* 3rd edn. Englewood Cliffs, NJ: Prentice Hall, 1985.

Edwards, Richard. *Contested Terrain: The Transformation of the Workplace in the Twentieth Century.* New York: Basic Books, 1979.

Edye, David and Valerio Lintner, eds. *Contemporary Europe*. Hemel Hempstead: Prentice Hall, 1996.

Ehrenreich, John. 'Introduction'. In John Ehrenreich, ed., *The Cultural Crisis of Modern Medicine*. New York: Monthly Review Press, 1978: 1–35.

Ehrlich, Paul R. *The Population Bomb*. New York: Ballatine Books, 1968.

Eichler, Margrit. *Nonsexist Research Methods: A Practical Guide*. Winchester, MA: Unwin Hyman, 1988.

Eisen, Arnold M. *The Chosen People in America: A Study of Jewish Religious Ideology*. Bloomington: Indiana University Press, 1983.

Eisenstein, Zillah R., ed., *Capitalist Patriarchy and the Case for Socialist Feminism*. New York: Monthly Review Press, 1979.

Ekman, Paul. 'Biological and Cultural Contributions to Body and Facial Movements in the Expression of Emotions'. In A. Rorty, ed., *Explaining Emotions*. Berkeley: University of California Press, 1980a: 73–101.

——. *Face of Man: Universal Expression in a New Guinea Village*. New York: Garland Press, 1980b.

——. *Telling Lies: Clues to Deceit in the Marketplace, Politics, and Marriage*. New York: W. W. Norton, 1985.

Ekman, Paul, Wallace V. Friesen and John Bear. 'The International Language of Gestures'. *Psychology Today* (May 1984): 64–69.

Eldridge, John. *C. Wright Mills*. London: Tavistock/Routledge, 1983.

Elias, Norbert. *The Civilizing Process*, Edmund Jephcott, trans. Oxford: Blackwell, 1978a.

——. *What is Sociology?*, Stephen Mennell and Grace Morrissey, trans. London: Hutchinson, 1978b.

Elkind, David. *The Hurried Child: Growing Up Too Fast Too Soon*. Reading, MA: Addison-Wesley, 1981.

Elliot, Faith Robertson. *Gender, Family and Society*. London: Macmillan, 1976, 1996.

Ellison, Christopher G. and Darren E. Sherkat. 'Conservative Protestantism and Support for Corporal Punishment'. *American Sociological Review*. Vol. 58, No. 1 (February 1993): 131–44.

Elmer-DeWitt, Philip. 'First Nation in Cyberspace'. *Time*. Vol. 142, No. 24 (6 December 1993): 62–64.

——. 'The Genetic Revolution'. *Time*. Vol. 143, No. 3 (17 January 1994): 46–53.

Ember, Melvin and Carol R. Ember. 'The Conditions Favoring Matrilocal versus Patrilocal Residence'. *American Anthropologist*. Vol. 73, No. 3 (June 1971): 571–94.

——. *Anthropology*. 6th edn. Englewood Cliffs, NJ: Prentice Hall, 1991.

Emerson, Joan P. 'Behavior in Private Places: Sustaining Definitions of Reality in Gynecological Examinations'. In H. P. Dreitzel, ed., *Recent Sociology*. Vol. 2. New York: Collier, 1970: 74–97.

Endicott, Karen. 'Fathering in an Egalitarian Society'. In Barry S. Hewlett, ed., *Father–Child Relations: Cultural and Bio-Social Contexts*. New York: Aldine, 1992: 281–96.

Engels, Friedrich. *The Origin of the Family*. Chicago: Charles H. Kerr & Company, 1902; orig. 1884.

Enloe, Cynthia. *Bananas, Beaches, and Bases: Making Feminist Sense of International Politics*. Berkeley: University of California Press, 1990.

Enzansberger, Hans Magnus. *The Consciousness Industry*. New York: Seabury Press, 1974.

Erikson, Erik H. *Childhood and Society*. New York: W. W. Norton, 1963; orig. 1950.

——. *Identity and the Life Cycle*. New York: W. W. Norton, 1980.

Erikson, Kai T. *Wayward Puritans: A Study in the Sociology of Deviance*. New York: Wiley, 1966.

Erikson, Robert and John H. Goldthorpe. *The Constant Flux: A Study of Class Mobility in Industrial Societies*. Oxford: Clarendon Press, 1992.

Esping-Anderson, C. *The Three Worlds of Welfare Capitalism*. Cambridge: Polity Press, 1990.

Esposito, John L. *The Islamic Threat: Myth or Reality*. New York: Oxford University Press, 1992.

Etzioni, Amitai. *A Comparative Analysis of Complex Organization: On Power, Involvement and Their Correlates*. Rev. and enlarged edn. New York: Free Press, 1975.

——. 'How to Make Marriage Matter'. *Time*. Vol. 142, No. 10 (6 September 1993): 76.

——. *The Spirit of Community: Rights, Responsibilities, and the Communitarian Agenda*. New York: Crown Publishers, 1993.

Etzioni-Halevy, Eva. *Bureaucracy and Democracy: A Political Dilemma*. Rev. edn. Boston: Routledge & Kegan Paul, 1985.

Eurostat. *Europe in Figures*. 4th edn. Luxembourg: Office for Official Publication of the European Community, 1995.

——. *Women and Men in Europe: A Statistical Portrait*. Luxembourg: Office for Official Publication of the European Community, 1995.

Evans, M. D. R. 'Immigrant Entrepreneurship: Effects of Ethnic Market Size and Isolated Labor Pool'. *American Sociological Review*. Vol. 54, No. 6 (December 1989): 950–62.

Evans-Pritchard, John. *Living and Working in Europe*. London: Pitman Publishing, 1997.

Edye, Dave and Valerio Lintner. *Contemporary Europe : Economics, Politics and Society*. London : Prentice Hall, 1996.

Fagin, Leonard and Martin Little. *The Forsaken Families: The Effects of Unemployment on Family Life*. Harmondsworth: Penguin, 1984.

Falk, Gerhard. Personal communication to J. J. Macionis, 1987.

Falkenmark, Malin and Carl Widstrand. 'Population and Water Resources: A Delicate Balance'. *Population Bulletin*. Vol. 47, No. 3 (November 1992). Washington, DC: Population Reference Bureau.

Family Policy Studies Centre. *Families in Britain*. London, 1995.

Fanon, Frantz. *The Wretched of the Earth*. New York: Grove Press, 1963.

Fantini, Mario D. *Regaining Excellence in Education*. Columbus, Ohio: Merrill, 1986.

Farley, Reynolds and William H. Frey. 'Changes in the Segregation of Whites From Blacks During the 1980s: Small Steps Toward a More Integrated Society'. *American Sociological Review*. Vol. 59, No. 1 (February 1994): 23–45.

Farrell, Michael P. and Stanley D. Rosenberg. *Men at Midlife*. Boston: Auburn House, 1981.

Fausto-Sterling, Anne . *Myths of Gender: Biological Theories about Men and Women*. New York: Basic Books, 1985.

Feagin, Joe. *The Urban Real Estate Game*. Englewood Cliffs, NJ: Prentice Hall, 1983.

——. 'The Continuing Significance of Race: Antiblack Discrimination in Public Places'. *American Sociological Review*. Vol. 56, No. 1 (February 1991): 101–16.

Featherman, David L. and Robert M. Hauser. *Opportunity and Change*. New York: Academic Press, 1978.

Featherstone, Mike. *Consumer Culture and Postmodernism*. London: Sage, 1991.

Featherstone, Mike, ed. *Global Culture: Nationalism, Globalization and Modernity*. London: Sage, 1990.

Fennell, Graham, Chris Phillipson and Helen Evers. *The Sociology of Old Age*. Buckingham: Open University Press, 1988.

Fennell, Mary C. 'The Effects of Environmental Characteristics on the Structure of Hospital Clusters'. *Administrative Science Quarterly*. Vol. 29, No. 3 (September 1980): 489–510.

Ferguson, Tom. 'Medical Self-Care: Self Responsibility for Health'. In Arthur C. Hastings et al., eds., *Health for the Whole Person: The Complete Guide to Holistic Medicine*. Boulder, CO: Westview Press, 1980: 87–109.

Finch, Janet. *Family Obligations and Social Change*. Cambridge: Polity Press, 1989.

Finch, Janet and Jennifer Mason. *Negotiating Family Responsibilities*. London: Routledge, 1993.

Fine, Michele and Adrian Ash. *Women with Disabilities*. Philadelphia: Temple University Press, 1990.

Finkelstein, Neal W. and Ron Haskins. 'Kindergarten Children Prefer Same-Color Peers'. *Child Development*. Vol. 54, No. 2 (April 1983): 52–8.

Finkler, Kaja. *Women in Pain: Gender and Morbidity in Mexico*. Philadelphia: University of Pennsylvania Press, 1994.

Finn, Dan. *Training without Jobs: New Deals and Broken Promises: From Raising the School Leaving Age to the Youth Training Scheme*. London: Macmillan, 1987.

Firebaugh, Glenn. 'Growth Effects of Foreign and Domestic Investment'. *American Journal of Sociology*. Vol. 98, No. 1 (July 1992): 105–30.

Firebaugh, Glenn and Frank D. Beck. 'Does Economic Growth Benefit the Masses? Growth, Dependence and Welfare in the Third World'. *American Sociological Review*. Vol. 59, No. 5 (October 1994): 631–53.

Fischer, Claude S. *The Urban Experience*. 2nd edn. San Diego: Harcourt Brace Jovanovich, 1984.

Fischer, Claude S., et al. *Networks and Places: Social Relations in the Urban Setting*. New York: Free Press, 1977.

Fisher, Elizabeth. *Woman's Creation: Sexual Evolution and the Shaping of Society*. Garden City, NY: Anchor/Doubleday, 1979.

Fisher, Roger and William Ury. 'Getting to YES'. In William M. Evan and Stephen Hilgartner, eds., *The Arms Race and Nuclear War*. Englewood Cliffs, NJ: Prentice Hall, 1988: 261–68.

Fiske, Alan Paige. 'The Cultural Relativity of Selfish Individualism: Anthropological Evidence that Humans Are Inherently Sociable'. In Margaret S. Clark, ed., *Prosocial Behavior*. Newbury Park, CA: Sage, 1991: 176–214.

Fiske, John. *Television Culture*. London: Methuen, 1987.

——. 'Postmodernism and Culture'. In James Curran and Michael Gurevitch, eds., *Mass Media and Society*. London: Metheun, 1991.

Fitzpatrick, Mary Anne. *Between Husbands and Wives: Communication in Marriage*. Newbury Park, CA: Sage, 1988.

Flaherty, Michael G. 'A Formal Approach to the Study of Amusement in Social Interaction'. *Studies in Symbolic Interaction*. Vol. 5. New York: JAI Press, 1984: 71–82.

——. 'Two Conceptions of the Social Situation: Some Implications of Humor'. *The Sociological Quarterly*. Vol. 31, No. 1 (Spring 1990).

Flandrin, Jean Louis. *Families in Former Times: Kinship, Household and Sexuality*. Richard Southern, trans. Cambridge: Cambridge University Press, 1979.

Flynn, Patricia. 'The Disciplinary Emergence of Bioethics and Bioethics Committees: Moral Ordering and its Legitimation'. *Sociological Focus*. Vol. 24, No. 2 (May 1991): 145–56.

Fornas, Johan, Ulf Lindeberg and Oue Sernhede. *In Garageland: Rock, Youth and Modernity*. London: Routledge, 1995.

Foster, P. *Women and the Health Care Industry*. Buckingham: Open University Press, 1995.

Foucault, Michel. *Discipline and Punish: the Birth of the Prison*, translated from the French by Alan Sheridan. Harmondsworth: Penguin, 1979.

——. *The Birth of the Clinic: An Archaeology of Medical Perception*. New York: Vintage Books, 1975.

Frank André Gunder. *On Capitalist Underdevelopment*. Bombay: Oxford University Press, 1975.

——. *Crisis: In the World Economy*. New York: Jameson & Meier, 1980.

——. *Reflections on the World Economic Crisis*. New York: Monthly Review Press, 1981.

Franklin Associates. *Characterization of Municipal Solid Waste in the United States, 1960–2000*. Prairie Village, KS: Franklin Associates, 1986.

Frayman, Harold. *Breadline Britain 1990s: the Findings of the Television Series*. London: LWT, 1991

Frazier, E. Franklin. *Black Bourgeoisie: The Rise of a New Middle Class*. New York: Free Press, 1965.

——. *The Negro Church in America*. New York: Schocken, 1963.

Fredrickson, George M. *White Supremacy: A Comparative Study in American and South African History*. New York: Oxford University Press, 1981.

Free, Marvin D. 'Religious Affiliation, Religiosity and Impulsive and Intentional Deviance'. *Sociological Focus*. Vol. 25, No. 1 (February 1992): 77–91.

Freedom House. *Freedom in the World*. New York: Freedom House, 1995.

French, Marilyn. *Beyond Power: On Women, Men, and Morals*. New York: Summit Books, 1985.

Friedan, Betty. *The Fountain of Age*. New York: Simon and Schuster, 1993.

Friedman, Milton and Rose Friedman. *Free to Choose: A Personal Statement*. London: Secker and Warburg, 1980.

Friedrich, Otto. 'A Proud Capital's Distress'. *Time*. Vol. 124, No. 6 (6 August 1984): 26–30, 33–35.

——. 'United No More'. *Time*. Vol. 129, No. 18 (4 May 1987): 28–37.

Frisby, David. *George Simmel*. London: Tavistock, 1984.

Frisby, David and Derek Sayer. *Society*. London: Routledge, 1986.

Fuchs, Victor R. 'Sex Differences in Economic Well-Being'. *Science*. Vol. 232 (25 April 1986): 459–64.

Fukuyama, Francis. *The End of History*, Irving Kristol, Washington, 1989 (Offprint from: *The National Interest*, Summer 1989 issue).

Funken, Klaus and Penny Cooper, eds. *Old and New Poverty: The Challenge for Reform*. London: Rivers Oram Press, 1995.

Furlong, Andy and Fred Cartmeal. *Young People and Social Change: Individualism and Risk in the Age of High Modernity*. Buckingham: Open University Press, 1997.

Furstenberg, Frank F., Jr. 'The New Extended Family: The Experience of Parents and Children After Remarriage'. Paper presented to the Changing Family Conference XIII: The Blended Family. University of Iowa, 1984.

Furstenberg, Frank F., Jr. and Andrew Cherlin. *Divided Families: What Happens to Children When Parents Part*. Cambridge, MA: Harvard University Press, 1991.

Gagnon, J. and W. Simon. *Sexual Conduct*. Chicago: Aldine, 1973.

Gagliani, Giorgio. 'How Many Working Classes?' *American Journal of Sociology*. Vol. 87, No. 2 (September 1981): 259–85.

Gallie, D., C. Marsh and C. Vogler. *Social Change and the Experience of Unemployment*. Oxford: Oxford University Press, 1993.

Gallup, George, Jr. *Religion in America*. Princeton, NJ: Princeton Religion Research Center, 1982.

Galster, George. 'Black Suburbanization: Has It Changed the Relative Location of Races?' *Urban Affairs Quarterly*. Vol. 26, No. 4 (June 1991): 621–28.

Gamoran, Adam. 'The Variable Effects of High-School Tracking'. *American Sociological Review*. Vol. 57, No. 6 (December 1992): 812–28.

Gans, Herbert J. *People and Plans: Essays on Urban Problems and Solutions*. New York: Basic Books, 1968.

——. *Popular Culture and High Culture*. New York: Basic Books, 1974.

——. *The Urban Villagers: Group and Class in the Life of Italian-Americans*. New York: Free Press, 1982; orig. 1962.

Garfinkel, Harold. 'Conditions of Successful Degradation Ceremonies'. *American Journal of Sociology*. Vol. 61, No. 2 (March 1956): 420–24.

——. *Studies in Ethnomethodology*. Cambridge: Polity Press, 1967.

Garland, David. *Punishment and Modern Society*. Oxford: Clarendon, 1990.

Garner, Robert. *Environmental Politics*. London: Prentice Hall, 1996.

Garrity, Patrick J. and Steven A. Maaranen, eds., *Nuclear Weapons in the Changing World: Perspectives from Europe, Asia, and North America*. New York: Plenum Press, 1992.

Gay, Peter. *The Enlightment: An Interpretation*. London: Weidenfeld & Nicolson, 1969.

Geertz, Clifford. *The Interpretation of Cultures*. New York: Basic Books, 1973; London: Hutchinson, 1995.

Geertz, Hildred and Clifford Geertz. *Kinship in Bali*. Chicago: University of Chicago Press, 1975.

Gelder, Ken and Sarah Thornton, eds. *The Subcultures Reader*. London: Routledge, 1997.

Gelman, David. 'Who's Taking Care of Our Parents?' *Newsweek* (6 May 1985): 61–64, 67–68.

George, Susan. *How the Other Half Dies: The Real Reasons for World Hunger*. Totowa, NJ: Rowman & Allanheld, 1977.

Geraghty, Christine. *Women and Soap Operas*. Cambridge: Polity Press, 1991.

Gergen, Kenneth J. *The Saturated Self: Dilemmas of Identity in Contemporary Life*. New York: Basic Books, 1991.

Gerlach, Michael L. *The Social Organization of Japanese Business*. Berkeley: University of California Press, 1992.

Gershuny, Jonathan. 'Time for the Family'. *Prospect* (January 1997).

Gerstel, Naomi. 'Divorce and Stigma'. *Social Problems*. Vol. 43, No. 2 (April 1987): 172–86.

Gerth, H. H. and C. Wright Mills, eds. *From Max Weber: Essays in Sociology*. New York: Oxford University Press, 1946; London: Routledge and Kegan Paul, 1948.

Gerzina, G. *Black England*. London: Routledge, 1995.

Geschwender, James A. *Racial Stratification in America*. Dubuque, IA: Wm. C. Brown, 1978.

Ghaill, Martin M. *The Making of Men: Masculinities, Sexualities and Schooling*. Buckingham: Open University Press, 1994

Gibbons, Don C. and Marvin D. Krohn. *Delinquent Behavior*. 4th edn. Englewood Cliffs, NJ: Prentice Hall, 1986.

Gibbs, Nancy. 'How Much Should We Teach Our Children About Sex?' *Time*. Vol. 141, No. 21 (24 May 1993): 60–66.

Giddens, Anthony. Sociology: *A Brief but Critical Introduction*. New York: Harcourt Brace Jovanovich, 1982.

——. *Self Identity and Late Modernity*. Cambridge: Polity Press, 1991.

——.*The Transformation of Intimacy*. Cambridge: Polity Press, 1992.

——.*Beyond Left and Right : The Future of Radical Politics*. Cambridge: Polity Press, 1994.

Giele, Janet Z. 'Gender and Sex Roles'. In Neil J. Smelser, ed., *Handbook of Sociology*. Newbury Park, CA: Sage, 1988: 291–323.

Gilligan, Carol. *In a Different Voice: Psychological Theory and Women's Development*. Cambridge, MA: Harvard University Press, 1982.

——. *Making Connections: The Relational Worlds of Adolescent Girls at Emma Willard School*. Cambridge, MA: Harvard University Press, 1990.

Gilroy, Paul. *The Black Atlantic: Modernity and Double Consciousness*. London: Verso, 1993.

Giovannini, Maureen. 'Female Anthropologist and Male Informant: Gender Conflict in a Sicilian Town'. In John J. Macionis and Nijole V. Benokraitis, eds., *Seeing Ourselves: Classic, Contemporary and Cross-Cultural Readings in Sociology*. 2nd edn. Englewood Cliffs, NJ: Prentice Hall, 1992: 27–32.

Gittins, Diana. *The Family in Question: Changing Households and Familiar Ideologies*. Basingstoke: Macmillan, 1st edn. 1985; 2nd edn. 1993.

Glaab, Charles N. *The American City: A Documentary History*. Homewood, IL: Dorsey Press, 1963.

Glaser, Barney and Anselm Stauss. *Awareness of Dying*. London: Weidenfeld and Nicolson, 1967.

Glasgow Media Group. *Really Bad News*. London: Writers and Readers, 1982.

Glasner, Angela. 'Gender and Europe: Cultural and Structural Impediments to Change'. In Joe Banks, ed., *Social Europe*. London: Longman, 1992.

Glass, Ruth. *Newcomers*. London: Allen & Unwin, 1960.

Glazer, Nathan and Daniel P. Moynihan. *Beyond the Melting Pot*. 2nd edn. Cambridge, MA: MIT Press, 1970.

Glendenning, F. 'What is Elder Abuse and Neglect?'. In P. Decalmer and F. Gendenning, eds., *The Mistreatment of Elderly People*. London: Sage, 1993.

Glendinning, Caroline and Jane Millar, eds. *Women and Poverty in Britain*. Brighton: Wheatsheaf, 1987.

Glendon, Mary Ann. *Rights Talk: The Impoverishment of Political Discourse*. New York: The Free Press, 1991.

Glenn, Norval D. and Beth Ann Shelton. 'Regional Differences in Divorce in the United States'. *Journal of Marriage and the Family*. Vol. 47, No. 3 (August 1985): 641–52.

Glock, Charles Y. 'The Religious Revival in America'. In Jane Zahn, ed., *Religion and the Face of America*. Berkeley: University of California Press, 1959: 25–42.

——. 'On the Study of Religious Commitment'. *Religious Education*. Vol. 62, No. 4 (1962): 98–110.

Gluck, Peter R. and Richard J. Meister. *Cities in Transition*. New York: New Viewpoints, 1979.

Glueck, Sheldon and Eleanor Glueck. *Unraveling Juvenile Delinquency*. New York: Commonwealth Fund, 1950.

Goetting, Ann. 'Divorce Outcome Research'. *Journal of Family Issues*. Vol. 2, No. 3 (September 1981): 350–78.

——. Personal communication to J. J. Macionis, 1989.

Goffman, Erving. *The Presentation of Self in Everyday Life*. Garden City, NY: Anchor Books, 1959.

——. *Asylums: Essays on the Social Situation of Mental Patients and Other Inmates*. Garden City, NY: Anchor Books, 1961.

——. *Stigma: Notes on the Management of Spoiled Identity*. Englewood Cliffs, NJ: Prentice Hall, 1963.

——. *Interactional Ritual: Essays on Face to Face Behavior*. Garden City, NY: Anchor Books, 1967.

——. *Gender Advertisements*. New York: Harper Colophon, 1979.

Goldberg, Steven. *The Inevitability of Patriarchy*. New York: William Morrow, 1974.

Goldfarb, William. 'Groundwater: The Buried Life'. In F. Herbert Bormann and Stephen R. Kellert, eds., *Ecology, Economics and Ethics: The Broken Circle*. New Haven, CT: Yale University Press, 1991: 123–35.

Golding, Peter and Philip Elliot. *Making the News*. London: Longmans, 1979.

Goldsby, Richard A. *Race and Races*. 2nd edn. New York: Macmillan, 1977.

Goldsmith, H. H. 'Genetic Influences on Personality from Infancy'. *Child Development*. Vol. 54, No. 2 (April 1983): 331–35.

Goldthorpe, John H. (in collaboration with Catriona Llewellyn and Clive Payne). *Social Mobility and Class Structure In Modern Britain*. Oxford: Clarendon Press, 1980.

——. 'On the Service Class, Its Formation and Future'. In A. Giddens and G. Mackenzie, eds., *Social Class and the Division of Labour*. Cambridge: Cambridge University Press, 1982.

——. *Family Life in Western Societies: a Historical Sociology of Family Relationships in Britain and North America*. Cambridge: Cambridge University Press, 1987.

Goode, William J. *World Changes in Divorce Patterns*. New Haven, CT: Yale University Press, 1993.

Goodman, Alissa, Paul Johnson and Steven Webb. *Inequality in the UK*. Oxford: Oxford University Press, 1997.

Gordon, James S. 'The Paradigm of Holistic Medicine'. In Arthur C. Hastings, et al., eds., *Health for the Whole Person: The Complete Guide to Holistic Medicine*. Boulder, CO: Westview Press, 1980: 3–27.

Goring, Charles Buckman. *The English Convict: A Statistical Study*. Montclair, NJ: Patterson Smith, 1972; orig. 1913.

Gorman, Christine. 'Mexico City's Menacing Air'. *Time*. Vol. 137, No. 13 (1 April 1991): 61.

Gorssberg, Lawrence, Cary Nelson and Treichler, Paula. *Cultural Studies*. London: Routledge, 1992.

Gortz, André. 'Immigrant Labour'. *New Left Review* (1961): 28–30.

——. *Farewell to the Working Class: An Essay on Post-industrial Socialism*. London: Pluto Press, 1982 (original French edition 1980).

Gottdiener, M. 'Field Research and the Video Tape'. *Sociological Inquiry*. Vol. 49, No. 4 (1980): 59–66.

Gottfredson, Michael R. and Travis Hirschi. 'National Crime Control Policies'. *Society*. Vol. 32, No. 2 (January–February 1995): 30–36.

Gottmann, Jean. *Megalopolis*. New York: Twentieth Century Fund, 1961.

Gould, Stephen J. 'Evolution as Fact and Theory'. *Discover* (May 1981): 35–37.

Gouldner, Alvin. *Enter Plato*. New York: Free Press, 1965.

——. 'The Sociologist as Partisan: Sociology and the Welfare State'. In Larry T. Reynolds and Janice M. Reynolds, eds., *The Sociology of Sociology*. New York: Avon Books, 1970a: 218–55.

——. *The Coming Crisis of Western Sociology*. New York: Avon Books, 1970b.

Graham, Hilary. 'The Concept of Caring in Feminist Research: The Case of Domestic Service'. *Sociology*. Vol. 25 (1991): 61–78.

——. *Hardship and Health in Women's Lives*. Hemel Hempstead: Harvester Wheatsheaf, 1993.

Gramsci, A. *Selections for the Prison Notebooks*. London: New Left Books, 1971.

Granovetter, Mark. 'The Strength of Weak Ties'. *American Journal of Sociology*. Vol. 78, No. 6 (May 1973): 1360–80.

Grant, Don Sherman, II and Michael Wallace. 'Why Do Strikes Turn Violent?' *American Journal of Sociology*. Vol. 96, No. 5 (March 1991): 1117–50.

Grant, Karen R. 'The Inverse Care Law in the Context of Universal Free Health Insurance in Canada: Toward Meeting Health Needs Through Public Policy'. *Sociological Focus*. Vol. 17, No. 2 (April 1984): 137–55.

Gray, Chris Hables, ed. *The Cyborg Handbook*. London: Routledge, 1995.

Gray, Paul. 'Whose America?' *Time*. Vol. 137, No. 27 (8 July 1991): 12–17.

Green, Andy. *Education and State Formation: The Rise of Education Systems in England, France and the USA*. Rev. edn. London: Macmillan, 1992.

Green, John C. 'Pat Robertson and the Latest Crusade: Resources and the 1988 Presidential Campaign'. *Social Sciences Quarterly*. Vol. 74, No. 1 (March 1993): 156–68.

Greenhouse, Linda. 'Justices Uphold Stiffer Sentences for Hate Crimes'. *New York Times* (12 June 1993): 1, 8.

Gregory, Paul R. and Robert C. Stuart. *Comparative Economic Systems*. 2nd edn. Boston: Houghton Mifflin, 1985.

Griffin, Christine. *Typical Girls*. London: Routledge, 1985.

Grint, Keith. *The Sociology of Work: An Introduction*. Cambridge: Polity Press, 1991.

Gross, Jane. 'New Challenge of Youth: Growing Up in a Gay Home'. *New York Times* (11 February 1991): A1, B7.

Gruenberg, Barry. 'The Happy Worker: An Analysis of Educational and Occupational Differences in Determinants of Job Satisfaction'. *American Journal of Sociology*. Vol. 86, No. 2 (September 1980): 247–71.

Gwartney-Gibbs, Patricia A., Jean Stockard and Susanne Bohmer. 'Learning Courtship Agression: The Influence of Parents, Peers and Personal Experiences'. *Family Relations*. Vol. 36, No. 3 (July 1987): 276–82.

Habermas, Jurgen. *Towards a Rational Society: Student Protest, Science, and Politics*. Jeremy J. Shapiro, trans. Boston: Beacon Press, 1970.

Hacker, Helen Mayer. 'Women as a Minority Group'. *Social Forces*. Vol. 30 (October 1951): 60–69.

——. 'Women as a Minority Group: 20 Years Later'. In Florence Denmark, ed., *Who Discriminates Against Women?* Beverly Hills, CA: Sage, 1974: 124–34.

Hackman, J. R. 'The Design of Work Teams'. In J. Lorch, ed., *Handbook of Organizational Behavior*. Englewood Cliffs, NJ: Prentice Hall, 1988: 315–42.

Hadden, Jeffrey K. and Charles E. Swain. *Prime Time Preachers: The Rising Power of Televangelism*. Reading, MA: Addison-Wesley, 1981.

Hafner, Katie. 'Making Sense of the Internet'. *Newsweek* (24 October 1994): 46–48.

Haig, Robin Andrew. *The Anatomy of Humor: Biopsychosocial and Therapeutic Perspectives*. Springfield, IL: Charles C. Thomas, 1988.

Hakken, David and Barbara Andrews. *Computing Myths, Class Realities: An Ethnography of Technology and Working People in Sheffield, England*. Boulder, CO: Westview Press, 1993.

Hall, John H. *Gone from the Promised Land: Jonestown in American Cultural History*. New Brunswick, NJ: Transaction, 1987

Hall, John R. and Mary Jo Neitz. *Culture: Sociological Perspectives*. Englewood Cliffs, NJ: Prentice Hall, 1993.

Hall, Stuart. 'Encoding and Decoding'. In *Culture, Media, Language*. London: Hutchinson, 1980.

——. 'The Question of Cultural Identity'. In S. Hall, D. Held and T. McGrew, eds., *Modernity and Its Futures*. Cambridge: Polity Press, 1992.

Hall, Stuart and Martin Jacques. *New Times*. London: Laurence and Wisehart, 1989.

Hallinan, Maureen T. and Richard A. Williams. 'Interracial Friendship Choices in Secondary Schools'. *American Sociological Review*. Vol. 54, No. 1 (February 1989): 67–78.

Halsey, A.H. *Change in British Society*. Oxford: Oxford University Press, 1986.

Halsey, A.H., Jean Floud and C. Arnold Anderson, eds. *Education, Economy, and Society: A Reader in the Sociology of Education*. New York, London: Free Press, Collier-Macmillan, 1961.

Halsey, A.H., Hugh Lauder, Phillip Brown and Amy Stuart Wells. *Education: Culture, Economy and Society*. Oxford: Oxford University Press, 1997.

Hamblin, Dora Jane. *The First Cities*. New York: Time-Life Books, 1973.

Hamel, Ruth. 'Raging Against Aging'. *American Demographics*. Vol. 12, No. 3 (March 1990): 42–45.

Hamrick, Michael H., David J. Anspaugh and Gene Ezell. *Health*. Columbus, OH: Merrill, 1986.

Hamilton, George. *Religion in the Medieval West*. London: Edward Arnold, 1986.

Hammersley, Martin and Paul Atkinson. *Ethnography: Principles in Practice*. 2nd edn. London: Routledge, 1995.

Hancock, M. Donald. *Politics in Western Europe: An Introduction to the Politics of the United Kingdom, France, Germany, Italy, Sweden, and the European Community*. Basingstoke: Macmillan, 1993.

Hannerz, Ulf. 'Cosmopolitans and Locals in World Culture'. In Mike Featherstone, ed., *Global Culture: Nationalism, Globalisation, and Modernity*. London: Sage, 1990.

Hare, Paul A., Edgar F. Borgatta and Robert F. Bales. *Small Groups: Studies in Social Interaction*. Rev. edn. New York: Alfred A. Knopf, 1965.

Hareven, Tamara K. 'The Life Course and Aging in Historical Perspective'. In Tamara K. Hareven and Kathleen J. Adams, eds., *Aging and Life Course Transitions: An Interdisciplinary Perspective*. New York: Guilford Press, 1982: 1–26.

Hargreaves, David H. *Interpersonal Relations and Education*. London, Boston: Routledge and Kegan Paul, 1975.

Harlan, William H. 'Social Status of the Aged in Three Indian Villages'. In Bernice L. Neugarten, ed., *Middle Age and Aging: A Reader in Social Psychology*. Chicago: University of Chicago Press, 1968: 469–75.

Harlow, Harry F. and Margaret Kuenne Harlow. 'Social Deprivation in Monkeys'. *Scientific American*. Vol. 207 (November 1962): 137–46.

Harper, Charles L. *Environment and Society: Social Perspectives on Environmental Issues and Problems*. Englewood Cliffs, NJ: Prentice Hall, 1995.

Haraway, Donna. *Simians, Cyborgs and Women: The Reinvention of Nature*. London: Free Association, 1991.

——. *Primate Visions : Gender, Race and Nature in the World of Modern Science*. London: Verso, 1992.

——. '"Cyborgs and Symbiants": Living Together in the New World Order'. In C. G. Hay, ed. *The Cyburg Handbook*. London: Routledge, 1995: xi–1.

Harris, Chauncey D. and Edward L. Ullman. 'The Nature of Cities'. *The Annals*. Vol. 242 (November 1945): 7–17.

Harris, Jack Dash. Lecture on Cockfighting in the Phillipines. *Semester at Sea* (October 1994).

Harris, Marvin. *Cultural Anthropology*. 2nd edn. New York: Harper & Row, 1987.

Harrison, Paul. *Inside the Third World: The Anatomy of Poverty*. 2nd edn. New York: Penguin Books, 1984; 3rd edn. 1993.

Hart, Nicky. *The Sociology of Health and Medicine*. Ormskirk, Lancashire: Causeway Press, 1985.

Hartmann, Betsy and James Boyce. *Needless Hunger: Voices From a Bangladesh Village*. San Francisco: Institute for Food and Development Policy, 1982.

Harvey, David. *The Condition of Postmodernity*. Oxford: Blackwell, 1989.

——. 'Between Time and Space: Reflections on the Geographical Imagination'. *Annals, Association of American Geographers*. Vol. 80 (1990): 418–34.

Haskey, J. 'Estimated Numbers of One-parent Families and Their Prevalence in Great Britain in 1991'. *Population Trends*. London: HMSO, 1992.

Havighurst, Robert J., Bernice L. Neugarten and Sheldon S. Tobin. 'Disengagement and Patterns of Aging'. In Bernice L. Neugarten, ed., *Middle Age and Aging: A Reader in Social Psychology*. Chicago: University of Chicago Press, 1968: 161–72.

Hawkes, Gail. *A Sociology of Sex and Sexuality*. Buckingham: Open University Press, 1996.

Haxekamp, Jan Laurens and Keith Popple, eds. *Racism in Europe: A Challenge for Youth Policy and Youth Work*. London: UCL Press, 1997.

Hay, Chris Gable, ed. *The Cyborg Handbook*. London: Routledge, 1995.

Hay, D. *Europe: The Emergence of an Idea*. 2nd edn. Edinburgh: Edinburgh University Press,1968.

Hayles, N. Katherine. 'The Life Cycle of Cyborgs'. In C. G. Hay, ed., *The Cyburg Handbook*. London: Routledge, 1995: 321–38.

Health Insurance Association Of America. *Source Book of Health Insurance Data*. Washington, DC: The Association, 1991.

Heath, Julia A. and W. David Bourne. 'Husbands and Housework: Parity or Parody?' *Social Science Quarterly*. Vol. 76, No. 1 (March 1995): 195–202.

Heilbroner, Robert L. *The Making of Economic Society*. 7th edn. Englewood Cliffs, NJ: Prentice Hall, 1985.

Helgesen, Sally. *The Female Advantage: Women's Ways of Leadership*. New York: Doubleday, 1990.

Helmuth, John W. 'World Hunger Amidst Plenty'. *USA Today*. Vol. 117, No. 2526 (March 1989): 48–50.

Henley, Nancy, Mykol Hamilton and Barrie Thorne. 'Womanspeak and Manspeak: Sex Differences in Communication, Verbal and Nonverbal'. In John J. Macionis and Nijole V. Benokraitis, eds., *Seeing Ourselves: Classic, Contemporary and Cross-Cultural Readings in Sociology*, 2nd edn. Englewood Cliffs, NJ: Prentice Hall, 1992: 10–15.

Henry, William A., III. 'Gay Parents: Under Fire and On the Rise'. *Time*. Vol. 142, No. 12 (20 September 1993): 66–71.

Herek, Gregory M. and Kevin T. Berrill. *Hate Crimes: Confronting Violence against Lesbians and Gay Men*. Newbury Park, CA: Sage, 1992.

Herdt, Gilbert. *Guardians of the Flutes: Idioms of Masculinity*. London: McGraw-Hill, 1981.

Herdt, Gilbert, ed., *Gay and Lesbian Youth*. London: Haworth Press, 1989.

Herman, Edward S. and Robert W. McChesney. *The Global Media: The New Missionaries of Global Capitalism*. London: Cassell, 1997.

Herman, Edward S. *Corporate Control, Corporate Power: A Twentieth Century Fund Study*. New York: Cambridge University Press, 1981.

Herrnstein, Richard J. *IQ and the Meritocracy*. Boston: Little, Brown, 1973.

Herrnstein, Richard J. and Charles Murray. *The Bell Curve: Intelligence and Class Structure in American Life*. New York: Free Press, 1994.

Herrstrom, Staffan. 'Sweden: Pro-Choice on Child Care'. *New Perspectives Quarterly*. Vol. 7, No. 1 (Winter 1990): 27–28.

Hersch, Joni and Shelly White-Means. 'Employer-Sponsored Health and Pension Benefits and the Gender/Race Wage Gap'. *Social Science Quarterly*. Vol. 74, No. 4 (December 1993): 850–66.

Hewitt, John P. *Self and Society*. 5th edn. London: Allyn and Bacon, 1991.

Hewlett, Barry S. 'Husband-Wife Reciprocity and the Father-Infant Relationship Among Aka Pygmies'. In Barry S. Hewlett, ed., *Father–Child Relations: Cultural and Bio-Social Contexts*. New York: Aldine, 1992: 153–76.

Hewlett, Sylvia Ann. 'The Feminization of the Work Force'. *New Perspectives Quarterly*. Vol. 7, No. 1 (Winter 1990): 13–15.

Hill, Michael. *Understanding Social Policy*. 5th edn. Oxford: Blackwell, 1997.

Hiroshi, Mannari. *The Japanese Business Leaders*. Tokyo: University of Tokyo Press, 1974.

Hirschi, Travis. *Causes of Delinquency*. Berkeley: University of California Press, 1969.

HMSO. 'Excellence in Schools'. Department of Education and Employment, CM 3681, July 1997.

Hobsbawm, Eric. *The Age of Revolution*. Weidenfeld and Nicolson, 1962.

——. *The Age of Capital*. Weidenfeld and Nicolson, 1975.

——. *The Age of Empire*. Weidenfeld and Nicolson, 1987.

——. *Age of Extremes: The Short Twentieth Century, 1914–1991*. London: Michael Joseph, 1994.

Hochschild, Arlie. *The Second Shift: Working Parents and the Revolution at Home*. London: Judy Piatkus Ltd, 1989.

Hodge, Robert W., Donald J. Treiman and Peter H. Rossi. 'A Comparative Study of Occupational Prestige'. In Reinhard Bendix and Seymour Martin Lipset, eds., *Class, Status and Power: Social Stratification in Comparative Perspective*. 2nd edn. New York: Free Press, 1966: 309–21.

Hoggart, R. *The Uses of Literacy*. Harmondsworth: Penguin, 1958.

Hohenberg, Paul and Lynne Hollen Lees. *The Making of Urban Europe 1000–1950*. Cambridge, MA: Harvard University Press, 1985.

Holm, Jean. *The Study of Religions*. New York: Seabury Press, 1977.

Holmes, C. *Anti-Semitism in British Society*. London: Arnold, 1979.

Holmes, Malcolm D., Harmon M. Hosch, Howard C. Daudistel, Dolores Perez and Joseph B. Graves. 'Judges, Ethnicity and Minority Sentencing: Evidence Among Hispanics'. *Social Science Quarterly*. Vol. 74, No. 3 (September 1993): 496–506.

Holmstrom, David. 'Abuse of Elderly, Even by Adult Children, Gets More Attention and Official Concern'. *Christian Science Monitor* (28 July 1994): 1.

Homans, George C. *The Human Group*. New Brunswick, NJ: Transaction, 1992; orig. 1950.

Hostetler, John A. *Amish Society*. 3rd edn. Baltimore: Johns Hopkins University Press, 1980.

Hout, Mike, Clem Brooks and Jeff Manza. 'The Persistence of Classes in Post-Industrial Societies'. *International Sociology*. Vol. 8, No. 3 (September 1993): 259–77.

Howlett, Debbie. 'Cruzan's Struggle Left Imprint: 10,000 Others in Similar State'. *USA Today* (27 December 1990): 3A.

Hoyt, Homer. *The Structure and Growth of Residential Neighborhoods in American Cities*. Washington, DC: Federal Housing Administration, 1939.

Huls, Glenna. Personal communication to J. J. Macionis, 1987.

Humphrey, Craig R. and Frederick R. Buttel. *Environment, Energy and Society*. Belmont, CA: Wadsworth, 1982.

Humphrey, Derek. *Final Exit: The Practicalities of Self-Deliverance and Assisted Suicide for the Dying*. Eugene, Ore.: The Hemlock Society, 1991.

Hunter, Floyd. *Community Power Structure*. Garden City, NY: Doubleday, 1963; orig. 1953.

Hunter, James Davison. *American Evangelicalism: Conservative Religion and the Quandary of Modernity*. New Brunswick, NJ: Rutgers University Press, 1983.

——. 'Conservative Protestantism'. In Philip E. Hammond, ed., *The Sacred in a Secular Age*. Berkeley: University of California Press, 1985: 50–66.

——. *Evangelicalism: The Coming Generation*. Chicago: University of Chicago Press, 1987.

Hutchinson, James E. 'Science and Religion'. *The Herald* (Dade County, Florida) (25 December 1994): 1M, 6M.

Hutter, Bridget and Gillian Williams. *Controlling Women*. London: Croom-Helm, 1981.

Hutton, Ronald. *The Stations of the Sun: A History of the Ritual Year in Britain*. Oxford: Oxford University Press, 1996.

Hutton, Will. *The State We're In*. London: Cape, 1995.

Hwang, Sean-Shong, Steven H. Murdock, Banoo Parpia and Rita R. Hamm. 'The Effects of Race and Socioeconomic Status on Residential Segregation in Texas, 1970–1980'. *Social Forces*. Vol. 63, No. 3 (March 1985): 732–47.

Hyman, Richard. *Strikes*. Basingstoke: Macmillan, 1989.

——. *The Political Economy of Industrial Relations: Theory and Practice in a Cold Climate*. Basingstoke: Macmillan, 1989.

Ide, Thomas, R. and Arthur J. Cordell. 'Automating Work'. *Society*. Vol. 31, No. 6 (September–October 1994): 65–71.

Illich, Ivan. *Medical Nemesis: The Expropriation of Health*. New York: Pantheon Books, 1976.

Inglis, Fred. *Media Theory: An Introduction*. Oxford: Blackwell, 1990.

Iannaccone, Laurence R. 'Why Strict Churches Are Strong'. *American Journal of Sociology*. Vol. 99, No. 5 (March 1994): 1180–1211.

Ignatieff, Michael. *A Just Measure of Pain: The Penitentiary in the Industrial Revolution*. 1750–1850. London: Macmillan, 1978.

ISTD 'Race and Criminal Justice'. Factsheet, 1997.

Jackman, Mary J. *The Velvet Glove: Paternalism and Conflict in Gender, Class. and Race Relations*. Berkeley and Los Angeles: University of California Press, 1994.

Jacob, John E. 'An Overview of Black America in 1985'. In James D. Williams, ed., *The State of Black America 1986*. New York: National Urban League, 1986: i–xi.

Jacobs, James B. 'Should Hate Be a Crime?' *The Public Interest*. No. 113 (Fall 1993): 3–14.

Jacobs, Jane. *The Economy of Cities*. New York: Vintage Books, 1970.

Jacobson, Jodi L. 'Closing the Gender Gap in Development'. In Lester R. Brown, et al., eds., *State of the World 1993: A Worldwatch Institute Report on Progress Toward a Sustainable Society*. New York: Norton, 1993: 61–79.

Jacoby, Russell and Naomi Glauberman, eds. *The Bell Curve Debate*. New York: Random House, 1995.

Jacquet, Constant H. and Alice M. Jones. *Yearbook of American and Canadian Churches 1991*. Nashville, Tenn.: Abingdon Press, 1991.

Jahoda, M., P. Lazersfeld and H. Zeizel. *Marienthal: Sociology of an Unemployed Community*. 1933; 2nd edn. London: Tavistock, 1972.

Jagarowsky, Paul A. and Mary Jo Bane. *Neighborhood Poverty: Basic Questions*. Discussion paper series H-90–3. John F. Kennedy School of Government. Cambridge, MA: Harvard University Press, 1990.

Jagger, Alison. 'Political Philosophies of Women's Liberation'. In Laurel Richardson and Verta Taylor, eds., *Feminist Frontiers: Rethinking Sex, Gender, and Society*. Reading, MA: Addison-Wesley, 1983.

James, Adrian L., Keith Bottomley, Alison Liebling and Emma Clare. *Privatising Prisons: Rhetoric and Reality*. London: Sage, 1997.

Jameson, Frederick. *Postmodernism or the Logic of Late Capitalism*. London: Verso, 1992.

Jamieson, Anne, Sarah Harper and Christian Victor, eds. *Critical Approaches to Ageing and Later Life*. Buckingham: Open University Press, 1995.

Jeffreys, Sheila. *The Sexuality Debate*. New York, London: Routledge & Kegan Paul, 1987.

Jencks, Christopher. 'Genes and Crime'. *The New York Review* (12 February 1987): 33–41.

Jencks, Christopher, et al. *Inequality: A Reassessment of the Effect of Family and Schooling in America*. New York: Basic Books, 1972.

Jenkins, Holman, Jr. 'The 'Poverty' Lobby's Inflated Numbers'. *Wall Street Journal* (14 December 1992): A10.

Jenkins, J. Craig and Charles Perrow. 'Insurgency of the Powerless: Farm Worker Movements (1946–1972)'. *American Sociological Review*. Vol. 42, No. 2 (April 1977): 249–68.

Jenkins, Phillip. *Intimate Enemies. Moral Panics in Contemporary Great Britain*. New York: Aldine de Gruyte, 1992.

Jensen, Joli. *Redeeming Modernity: Contradictions in Media Criticism*. Newbury Park, CA, London: Sage, 1990.

Johnson, Cathryn. 'Gender, Legitimate Authority and Leader-Subordinate Conversations'. *American Sociological Review*. Vol. 59, No. 1 (February 1994): 122–35.

Johnson, Paul. 'The Seven Deadly Sins of Terrorism'. In Benjamin Netanyahu, ed., *International Terrorism*. New Brunswick, NJ: Transaction Books, 1981: 12–22.

Johnson, Paul, ed. *20th Century Britain: Economic, Social and Cultural Change*. London: Longman, 1994.

Johnston, R. J. 'Residential Area Characteristics'. In D. T. Herbert and R. J. Johnston, eds., *Social Areas in Cities*. *Vol. 1: Spatial Processes and Form*. New York: Wiley, 1976: 193–235.

Joll, James. *Europe: A Historian's View*. Leeds: Leeds University Press, 1969.

Jones, Huw. *Population Geography*. 2nd edn. London: Paul Chapman, 1990.

Joseph Rowntree Foundation. Income and Wealth Inquiry Group. *Inquiry into Income and Wealth*. York: Joseph Rowntree Foundation, 1995.

Kadushin, Charles. 'Friendship Among the French Financial Elite'. *American Sociological Review*. Vol. 60, No. 2 (April 1995): 202–21.

Kain, Edward L. *The Myth of Family Decline: Understanding Families in a World of Rapid Social Change*. Lexington, MA: Lexington Books, 1990.

Kalish, Richard A. 'The New Ageism and the Failure Models: A Polemic'. *The Gerontologist*. Vol. 19, No. 4 (August 1979): 398–402.

Kaminer, Wendy. 'Volunteers: Who Knows What's in It for Them'. *Ms.* (December 1984): 93–94, 96, 126–28.

Kanter, Rosabeth Moss. *Men and Women of the Corporation*. New York: Basic Books, 1977.

——. *The Change Masters: Innovation and Entrepreneurship in the American Corporation*. New York: Simon and Schuster, 1983.

——. *When Giants Learn to Dance: Mastering the Challenges of Strategy, Management and Careers in the 1990s*. New York: Simon and Schuster, 1989.

Kanter, Rosabeth Moss and Barry A. Stein. 'The Gender Pioneers: Women in an Industrial Sales Force'. In R. M. Kanter and B. A. Stein, eds., *Life in Organizations*. New York: Basic Books, 1979: 134–60.

——. *A Tale of 'O': On Being Different in an Organization*. New York: Harper & Row, 1980.

Kaplan, E. Ann. *Rocking Around the Clock: Music, Television, Postmodernism and Consumer Culture*. London: Routledge, 1987.

Kaplan, Eric B., et al. 'The Usefulness of Preoperative Laboratory Screening'. *Journal of the American Medical Association*. Vol. 253, No. 24 (28 June 1985): 3576–81.

Karatnycky, Adrian. 'Democracies on the Rise, Democracies at Risk'. *Freedom Review*. Vol. 26, No. 1 (January–February 1995): 5–10.

Katz, Jonathan. *Gay American History*. New York: Thomas and Cromwell, 1976.

Kaufman, Walter. *Religions in Four Dimensions: Existential, Aesthetic, Historical and Comparative*. New York: Reader's Digest Press, 1976.

Kaufman, Robert L. and Seymour Spilerman. 'The Age Structures of Occupations and Jobs'. *American Journal of Sociology*. Vol. 87, No. 4 (January 1982): 827–51.

Keith, Jennie, et al. *The Ageing Experience: Diversity and Commonality across Cultures*. London: Sage, 1994.

Keith, Pat M. and Robert B. Schafer. 'They Hate to Cook: Patterns of Distress in an Ordinary Role'. *Sociological Focus*. Vol. 27, No. 4 (October 1994): 289–301.

Keller, Helen. *The Story of My Life*. New York: Doubleday, 1903.

Keller, Suzanne. *The Urban Neighborhood*. New York: Random House, 1968.

Kellert, Stephen R. and F. Herbert Bormann. 'Closing the Circle: Weaving Strands Among Ecology, Economics and Ethics'. In Herbert F. Bohrmann and Stephen R. Kellert, eds., *Ecology, Economics and Ethics: The Broken Circle*. New Haven, CT: Yale University Press, 1991: 205–10.

Kelly, Elinor. *Racism in Schools: New Research Evidence*. Stoke-on-Trent: Trentham Books, 1988.

Kelly, Liz. *Surviving Sexual Violence*. Cambridge: Polity, 1998.

Kelner, Douglas. *Television and the Crisis of Democracy*. Boulder, CO: Westview Press, 1990.

Kenyon, Kathleen. *Digging Up Jericho*. London: Ernest Benn, 1957.

Kidron, Michael and Ronald Segal. *The New State of the World Atlas*. New York: Simon and Schuster, 1991.

Kilbourne, Brock K. 'The Conway and Siegelman Claims Against Religious Cults: An Assessment of Their Data'. *Journal for the Scientific Study of Religion*. Vol. 22, No. 4 (December 1983): 380–85.

Kilgore, Sally B. 'The Organizational Context of Tracking in Schools'. *American Sociological Review*. Vol. 56, No. 2 (April 1991): 189–203.

King, Anthony, et al. *Britain at the Polls, 1997*. Chatham, NJ: Chatham House, 1997.

King, Martin Luther, Jr. 'The Montgomery Bus Boycott'. In Walt Anderson, ed., *The Age of Protest*. Pacific Palisades, CA: Goodyear, 1969: 81–91.

Kinkead, Gwen. *Chinatown: A Portrait of a Closed Society*. New York: HarperCollins, 1992.

Kinsey, Alfred. *The Sexual Behaviour of the Human Male*. Philadelphia, PA: Saunders, 1948.

——. *The Sexual Behaviour of the Human Female*. Philadelphia, PA: Saunders, 1953.

Kiser, Edgar and Joachim Schneider. 'Bureaucracy and Efficiency: An Analysis of Taxation in Early Modern Prussia'. *American Sociological Review*. Vol. 59, No. 2 (April 1994): 187–204.

Kishor, Sunita. '"May God Give Sons to All": Gender and Child Mortality in India'. *American Sociological Review*. Vol. 58, No. 2 (April 1993): 247–65.

Kitson, Gay C. and Helen J. Raschke. 'Divorce Research: What We Know, What We Need to Know'. *Journal of Divorce*. Vol. 4, No. 3 (Spring 1981): 1–37.

Kittrie, Nicholas N. *The Right To Be Different: Deviance and Enforced Therapy*. Baltimore: Johns Hopkins University Press, 1971.

Kleinman, Arthur. *The Illness Narratives*. New York: Basic Books, 1988.

Kohlberg, Lawrence. *The Psychology of Moral Development: The Nature and Validity of Moral Stages*. New York: Harper & Row, 1981.

Kohlberg, Lawrence and Carol Gilligan. 'The Adolescent as Philosopher: The Discovery of Self in a Postconventional World'. *Daedalus*. Vol. 100 (Fall 1971): 1051–86.

Kohn, Melvin L. and Carmi Schooler. 'Job Conditions and Personality: A Longitudinal Assessment of Their Reciprocal Effects'. *American Journal of Sociology*. Vol. 87, No. 6 (May 1982): 1257–83.

Kolata, Gina. 'When Grandmother Is the Mother, Until Birth'. *New York Times* (5 August 1991): 1, 11.

Komarovsky, Mirra. *Blue Collar Marriage*. New York: Vintage Books, 1967.

——. 'Cultural Contradictions and Sex Roles: The Masculine Case'. *American Journal of Sociology*. Vol. 78, No. 4 (January 1973): 873–84.

——. *Dilemmas of Masculinity: A Study of College Youth*. New York: W. W. Norton, 1976.

Kornhauser, William. *The Politics of Mass Society*. New York: Free Press, 1959.

Kozol, Jonathan. *Prisoners of Silence: Breaking the Bonds of Adult Illiteracy in the United States*. New York: Continuum, 1980.

——. 'A Nation's Wealth'. *Publisher's Weekly* (24 May 1985a): 28–30.

——. *Illiterate America*. Garden City, NY: Doubleday, 1985b.

——. *Savage Inequalities: Children in America's Schools*. New York: Harper Perennial, 1992.

Kramarae, Cheris. *Women and Men Speaking*. Rowley, MA: Newbury House, 1981.

Kraybill, Donald B. *The Riddle of Amish Culture*. Baltimore: Johns Hopkins University Press, 1989.

——. 'The Amish Encounter With Modernity'. In Donald B. Kraybill and Marc A. Olshan, eds., *The Amish Struggle with Modernity*. Hanover, NH: University Press of New England, 1994: 21–33.

Kraybill, Donald B. and Marc A. Olshan, eds. *The Amish Struggle with Modernity*. Hanover, NH: University Press of New England, 1994.

Kriesi, Hanspeter. 'New Social Movements and the New Class in the Netherlands'. *American Journal of Sociology*. Vol. 94, No. 5 (March 1989): 1078–116.

Kriesi, Hanspeter, Ruud Koopmans, Jan Willem Dyvendak and Marco G. Giuni. *New Social Movements in Western Europe*. London: UCL Press, 1995.

Kübler-Ross, Elisabeth. *On Death and Dying*. New York: MacMillan, 1969.

Kuhn, Thomas. *The Structure of Scientific Revolutions*. 2nd edn. Chicago: University of Chicago Press, 1970

Kumar, Krishan. *Prophecy and Progress: The Sociology of Industrial and Post-Industrial Society*. Harmondsworth: Penguin, 1978.

——. *From Post-Industrial to Post-Modern Society: New Theories of the Contemporary World*. Oxford: Blackwell, 1995.

Kurtz, Lester. *Gods in the Global Village: The World's Religions in Sociological Perspective*. London: Pine Forge Press, 1995.

Kuznets, Simon. *Modern Economic Growth: Rate, Structure and Spread*. New Haven, CT: Yale University Press, 1966.

Kvale, Steiner. *Interviews: An Introduction to Qualitative Research Interviewing*. London: Sage, 1996.

Ladd, John. 'The Definition of Death and the Right to Die'. In John Ladd, ed., *Ethical Issues Relating to Life and Death*. New York: Oxford University Press, 1979: 118–45.

Lamberg-Karlovsky, C. C. and Martha Lamberg-Karlovsky. 'An Early City in Iran'. *Cities: Their Origin, Growth and Human Impact*. San Francisco: Freeman, 1973: 28–37.

Landers, Rene M. 'Gender, Race, and the State Courts'. *Radcliffe Quarterly*. Vol. 76, No. 4 (December 1990): 6–9.

Lane, David. 'Social Stratification and Class'. In Erik P. Hoffman and Robbin F. Laird, eds., *The Soviet Polity in the Modern Era*. New York: Aldine, 1984: 563–605.

Lappé, Frances Moore and Joseph Collins. *World Hunger: Twelve Myths*. New York: Grove Press/Food First Books, 1986.

Lappé, Frances Moore, Joseph Collins and David Kinley. *Aid as Obstacle: Twenty Questions about Our Foreign Policy and the Hungry*. San Francisco: Institute for Food and Development Policy, 1981.

Larmer, Brook. 'Dead End Kids'. *Newsweek* (25 May 1992): 38–40.

Lash, Scott and John Urry. *The End of Organized Capitalism*. Cambridge: Polity, 1987.

Laslett, Peter, ed. *Household and Family in Past Time: Comparative Studies in the Size and Structure of the Domestic Group over the Last Three Centuries in England, France, Serbia, Japan and Colonial North America, with further materials from Western Europe*. Cambridge: Cambridge University Press, 1972.

——. *The World We Have Lost: England Before the Industrial Age*. 3rd edn. New York: Charles Scribner's Sons, 1984.

——. *Fresh Map of Life: Emergence of the Third Age*. Basingstoke: Macmillan, 1st edn. 1989; 2nd rev. edn. 1995.

Laumann, Edward O., John H. Gagnon, Robert T. Michael and Stuart Michaels. *The Social Organization of Sexuality: Sexual Practices in the United States*. Chicago: University of Chicago Press, 1994.

Lazarsfeld, Paul F. and Robert K. Merton. 'Mass Communication, Popular Taste and Organized Social Action'. In Paul Marris and Sue Thornham, eds., *Media Studies*. Edinburgh: Edinburgh University Press, 1996.

Lazreg, Marnia. *The Eloquence of Silence: Algerian Women in Question*. New York: Routledge, 1994.

Le Grand, Julien. *The Strategy of Equality*, 1982.

Leacock, Eleanor. 'Women's Status in Egalitarian Societies: Implications for Social Evolution'. *Current Anthropology*. Vol. 19, No. 2 (June 1978): 247–75.

Leavitt, Judith Walzer. 'Women and Health in America: An Overview'. In Judith Walzer Leavitt, ed., *Women and Health in America*. Madison: University of Wisconsin Press, 1984: 3–7.

Lee, Barrett A., R. S. Oropesa, Barbara J. Metch and Avery M. Guest. 'Testing the Decline of Community Thesis: Neighborhood Organization in Seattle, 1929 and 1979'. *American Journal of Sociology*. Vol. 89, No. 5 (March 1984): 1161–88.

Lee, David and H. Newby. *The Problem of Sociology*. London: Hutchinson, 1983.

Lee, David and Bryan Turner, eds. *Conflict about Class: Debating Inequality in Late Industrialism*. London: Longman, 1996.

Lees, Sue. *Sugar and Spice*. Harmondsworth: Penguin, 1993.

Lehne, Gregory. 'Homphobia among Men'. In D. David and R. Brannon, eds., *The Forty-Nine Per Cent Majority: The Male Sex Role*. London: Addison Wesley, 1976

Lemert, Edwin M. *Social Pathology*. New York: McGraw-Hill, 1951.

——. *Human Deviance, Social Problems and Social Control*. 2nd edn. Englewood Cliffs, NJ: Prentice Hall, 1972.

Lemert, Edwin M., ed. *Social Theory: The Multicultural and Classic Readings*. Oxford: Westview, 1993.

Lengermann, Patricia Madoo and Ruth A. Wallace. *Gender in America: Social Control and Social Change*. Englewood Cliffs, NJ: Prentice Hall, 1985.

Lennon, Mary Clare and Sarah Rosenfeld. 'Relative Fairness and the Doctrine of Housework: The Importance of Options'. *American Journal of Sociology*. Vol. 100, No. 2 (September 1994): 506–31.

Lenski, Gerhard. *Power and Privilege: A Theory of Social Stratification*. New York: McGraw-Hill, 1966.

Lenski, Gerhard, Patrick Nolan and Jean Lenski. *Human Societies: An Introduction to Macrosociology*. 7th edn. New York: McGraw-Hill, 1995.

Leonard, Eileen B. *Women, Crime and Society: A Critique of Theoretical Criminology*. New York: Longman, 1982.

Leerhsen, Charles. 'Unite and Conquer'. *Newsweek* (5 February 1990): 50–55.

Lester, David. *The Death Penalty: Issues and Answers*. Springfield, IL: Charles C. Thomas, 1987.

Lever, Janet. 'Sex Differences in the Complexity of Children's Play and Games'. *American Sociological Review*. Vol. 43, No. 4 (August 1978): 471–83.

Levinson, Daniel J., with Charlotte N. Darrow, Edward B. Klein, Maria H. Levinson and Braxton McKee. *The Seasons of a Man's Life*. New York: Alfred A. Knopf, 1978.

Levitas, Ruth and Will Guy, eds. *Interpreting Official Statistics*. London: Routledge, 1996.

Levy, Frank. *Dollars and Dreams: The Changing American Income Distribution*. New York: Russell Sage Foundation, 1987.

Lewis, Flora. 'The Roots of Revolution'. *New York Times Magazine* (11 November 1984): 70–71, 74, 77–78, 82, 84, 86.

Lewis, Jane. 'Gender and the Development of Welfare Regimes'. *European Journal of Social Policy*. Vol. 2, No. 2 (1992): 159–74.

Lewis, Oscar. *Five Families*. New York: Basic Books, 1959.

——. *The Children of Sanchez*. New York: Random House, 1961.

Lewis, Susan, Dafna N. Isreali and Helen Hootsmans. *Dual-Earner Families: International Perspectives*. Newbury Park, CA: Sage, 1992.

Li, Jiang Hong and Roger A. Wojtkiewicz. 'A New Look at the Effects of Family Structure on Status Attainment'. *Social Science Quarterly*. Vol. 73, No. 3 (September 1992): 581–95.

Lin, Nan and Wen Xie. 'Occupational Prestige in Urban China'. *American Journal of Sociology*. Vol. 93, No. 4 (January 1988): 793–832.

Linden, Eugene. 'Can Animals Think?' *Time*. Vol. 141, No. 12 (22 March 1993): 54–61.

——. 'More Power to Women, Fewer Mouths to Feed'. *Time*. Vol. 144, No. 13 (26 September 1994): 64–65.

Linton, Ralph. 'One Hundred Percent American'. *The American Mercury*. Vol. 40, No. 160 (April 1937): 427–29.

——. *The Study of Man*. New York: D. Appleton-Century, 1937.

Lipset, Seymour Martin and Reinhard Bendix. *Social Mobility in Industrial Society*. Berkeley: University of California Press, 1967.

Liska, Allen E. *Perspectives on Deviance*. 3rd edn. Englewood Cliffs, NJ: Prentice Hall, 1991.

Liska, Allen E., and Mark Tausig. 'Theoretical Interpretations of Social Class and Racial Differentials in Legal Decision Making for Juveniles'. *Sociological Quarterly*. Vol. 20, No. 2 (Spring 1979): 197–207.

Liska, Allen E and Barbara D. Warner. 'Functions of Crime: A Paradoxical Process'. *American Journal of Sociology*. Vol. 96, No. 6 (May 1991): 1441–63.

Lo, Clarence Y. H. 'Countermovements and Conservative Movements in the Contemporary US'. *Annual Review of Sociology*. Vol. 8. Palo Alto, CA: Annual Reviews, 1982: 107–34.

Lockwood, David. *Solidarity and Schism: The Problem of Disorder in Durkheimian and Marxist Sociology*. Oxford: Clarendon Press, 1992.

Lockwood, David, John Goldthorpe, Frank Beckhoffer and Jennifer Platt. *The Affluent Worker*. Cambridge: Cambridge University Press, 1967.

Lofland, J. *Doomsday Cult*. 2nd edn. New York: Irvington

Logan, John R. and Mark Schneider. 'Racial Segregation and Racial Change in American Suburbs, 1970–1980'. *American Journal of Sociology*. Vol. 89, No. 4 (January 1984): 874–88.

Longino, Jr., Charles F. 'Myths of An Aging America'. *American Demographics*. Vol. 16, No. 8 (August 1994): 36–42.

Lopez, Barry. *Arctic Dreams: Imagination and Desire in a Northern Landscape*. London: Picador, 1986.

Lorber, Judith. *Paradoxes of Gender*. New Haven, CT: Yale University Press, 1994.

Lord, Walter. *A Night to Remember*. Rev. edn. New York: Holt, Rinehart & Winston, 1976.

Lorenz, Konrad. *On Aggression*. New York: Harcourt, Brace & World, 1966.

Lovenduski, J. 'Feminism and West European Politics: An Overview'. In D.W. Unwin and W.E. Pateson, *Politics in Western Europe Today*. London: Longman, 1990.

Lowery, A. and Melvin de Fleur, eds. *Milestones in Mass Communication Research*. London: Longman, 1984, 1988.

Loy, Pamela Hewitt and Lea P. Stewart. 'The Extent and Effects of Sexual Harassment of Working Women'. *Sociological Focus*, Vol. 17, No. 1 (January 1984): 31–43.

Lubenow, Gerald C. 'A Troubling Family Affair'. *Newsweek* (14 May 1984): 34.

Lull, James. *Media, Communication, Culture: A Global Approach*. Cambridge: Polity Press, 1995.

Lund, Dale A. 'Conclusions about Bereavement in Later Life and Implications for Interventions and Future Research'. In Dale A. Lund, ed., *Older Bereaved Spouses: Research With Practical Applications*. London: Taylor-Francis-Hemisphere, 1989: 217–31.

Lund, Dale A., Michael S. Caserta and Margaret F. Dimond. 'Gender Differences Through Two Years of Bereavement Among the Elderly'. *The Gerontologist*. Vol. 26, No. 3 (1986): 314–20.

Lutra, Mohan. *Britain's Black Population*. London: Arena, 1997.

Lutz, Catherine A. *Unnatural Emotions: Everyday Sentiments on a Micronesia Atoll and Their Challenge to Western Theory*. Chicago: University of Chicago Press, 1988.

Lutz, Catherine A. and Jane L. Collins. *Reading National Geographic*. Chicago: University of Chicago Press, 1993.

Lutz, Catherine A. and Geoffrey M. White. 'The Anthropology of Emotions'. In Bernard J. Siegel, Alan R. Beals and Stephen A. Tyler, eds., *Annual Review of Anthropology*. Palo Alto, CA: Annual Reviews, Vol. 15 (1986): 405–36.

Lynd, Robert S. *Knowledge For What? The Place of Social Science in American Culture*. Princeton, NJ: Princeton University Press, 1967.

Lynd, Robert S. and Helen Merrell Lynd. *Middletown in Transition*. New York: Harcourt, Brace & World, 1937.

Lynott, Patricia Passuth and Barbara J. Logue. 'The "Hurried Child": The Myth of Lost Childhood on Contemporary American Society'. *Sociological Forum*. Vol. 8, No. 3 (September 1993): 471–91.

Lyotard, J.F. *The Postmodern Condition*. Manchester: Manchester University Press, 1992.

Ma, Li-Chen. Personal communication to J. J. Macionis, 1987.

McAdam, Doug, John D. McCarthy and Mayer N. Zald. 'Social Movements'. In Neil J. Smelser, ed., *Handbook of Sociology*. Newbury Park, CA: Sage, 1988: 695–737.

McCarthy, John D. and Mayer N. Zald. 'Resource Mobilization and Social Movements: A Partial Theory'. *American Journal of Sociology*. Vol. 82, No. 6 (May 1977): 1212–41.

McColm, R. Bruce, James Finn, Douglas W. Payne, Joseph E. Ryan, Leonard R. Sussman and George Zarycky. *Freedom in the World: Political Rights & Civil Liberties, 1990–1991*. New York: Freedom House, 1991.

McCormick, John. *British Politics and the Environment*. London: Earthscan, 1991.

McCoy, Clyde B. and James A. Inciardi. *Sex, Drugs and the Continuing Spread of AIDS*. Los Angeles: Roxbury, 1995.

McDonald, Robert. *Youth, the Underclass and Social Exclusion*. London: Routledge, 1997.

Macionis, John J. 'Intimacy: Structure and Process in Interpersonal Relationships'. *Alternative Lifestyles*. Vol. 1, No. 1 (February 1978): 113–30.

——. 'The Search for Community in Modern Society: An Interpretation'. *Qualitative Sociology*. Vol. 1, No. 2 (September 1978): 130–43.

McIllroy, John. *Trade Unions in Britains Today*. 2nd edn. Manchester: Manchester University Press, 1995.

Mack, Joanna and Stewart Lansley. *Poor Britain*. London: Allen & Unwin, 1985.

MacKay, Donald G. 'Prescriptive Grammar and the Pronoun Problem'. In Barrie Thorne, Cherls Kramarae and Nancy Henley, eds., *Language, Gender and Society*. Rowley, MA: Newbury House, 1983: 38–53.

McKeown, T. *The Role of Medicine: Dream, Mirage and Nemesis*. London: Nuffield Provincial Hospital Trust, 1976.

MacKinnon, Catharine A. *Feminism Unmodified: Discourses on Life and Law*. Cambridge, MA: Harvard University Press, 1987.

Mackinnon, Donald, June Statham and Margaret Hales. *Education in the UK: Facts and Figures*. Buckingham: Open University Press, 1996.

Macklin, Eleanor D. 'Nonmarital Heterosexual Cohabitation: An Overview'. In Eleanor D. Macklin and Roger H. Rubin, eds., *Contemporary Families and Alternative Lifestyles: Handbook on Research and Theory*. Beverly Hills, CA: Sage, 1983: 49–74.

McLanahan, Sara. 'Family Structure and the Reproduction of Poverty'. *American Journal of Sociology*. Vol. 90, No. 4 (January 1985): 873–901.

McLean, Gill L. *Facing Death: Conversations with Cancer Patients*. Edinburgh: Churchill Livingstone, 1993.

McLeod, Jane D. and Michael J. Shanahan. 'Poverty, Parenting and Children's Mental Health'. *American Sociological Review*. Vol. 58, No. 3 (June 1993): 351–66.

McLuhan, Marshall. *The Medium is the Message*. Harmondsworth: Penguin, 1963.

McMichael, A.J. *Planetary Overload: Global Environment Change and the Health of the Human Species*. Cambridge: Cambridge University Press, 1993.

McQuail, Denis. *Mass Communication Theory: An Introduction*. 3rd edn. London: Sage, 1993.

McRae, Susan. *Cross-Class Families: A Study of Wives' Occupational Superiority*. New York: Oxford University Press, 1986.

McRobbie, Angela. *Feminism and Youth Culture*. London: Macmillan, 1991.

Mabry, Marcus. 'New Hope for Old Unions?' *Newsweek* (24 February 1992): 39.

Mack, Joanna and S. Lansley. *Poor Britain*. 2nd edn. London: Routledge, 1993.

Maddox, Setma. 'Organizational Culture and Leadership Style: Factors Affecting Self-Managed Work Team Performance'. Paper presented at the annual meeting of the Southwest Social Science Association, Dallas, February, 1995.

Madood, Tariq, et al. *Ethnic Minorities in Britain*. 4th edn. London: Policy Studies Institute, 1997.

Madsen, Axel. *Private Power: Multinational Corporations for the Survival of Our Planet*. New York: William Morrow, 1980.

Maguire, Mike, R. Morgan and R. Reiner, et al. *The Oxford Handbook of Criminology*. 2nd edn. Oxford: Clarendon Press, 1988.

Majka, Linda C. 'Sexual Harassment in the Church'. *Society*. Vol. 28. No. 4 (May–June 1991): 14–21.

Malcolm, Noel. *Bosnia: A Short History*. Rev. edn. London: Macmillan, 1996.

Manning, Philip. *Erving Goffman and Modern Sociology*. Cambridge: Polity, 1992.

Marcuse, Herbert. *One-Dimensional Man*. Boston: Beacon Press, 1964.

Mare, Robert D. 'Five Decades of Educational Assortative Mating'. *American Sociological Review*. Vol. 56, No. 1 (February 1991): 15–32.

Margolick, David. 'Rape in Marriage Is No Longer Within the Law'. *New York Times* (13 December 1984): 6E.

Markoff, John. 'Remember Big Brother? Now He's a Company Man'. *New York Times* (31 March 1991): 7.

Markson, Elizabeth W. 'Moral Dilemmas'. *Society*. Vol. 29, No. 5 (July–August 1992): 4–6.

Marris, Paul and Sue Thornham, eds. *Media Studies*. Edinburgh: Edinburgh University Press, 1996.

Marris, Robin. *How to Save the Underclass*. Basingstoke: Macmillan, 1996.

Marsden, Peter. 'Core Discussion Networks of Americans'. *American Sociological Review*. Vol. 52, No. 1 (February 1987): 122–31.

Marshall, Catherine, ed. *The New Politics of Race and Gender*. Washington, DC; London: Falmer Press, 1993.

Martell, Luke. *Ecology and Society: An Introduction*. Cambridge: Polity, 1994.

Martin, John M. and Anne T. Romano. *Multinational Crime: Terrorism, Espionage, Drug and Arms Trafficking*. Newbury Park, CA: Sage, 1992.

Martin, Richard C. *Islam: A Cultural Perspective*. Englewood Cliffs, NJ: Prentice Hall, 1982.

Martin, William. 'The Birth of a Media Myth'. *The Atlantic*. Vol. 247, No. 6 (June 1981): 7, 10, 11, 16.

Marullo, Sam. 'The Functions and Dysfunctions of Preparations for Fighting Nuclear War'. *Sociological Focus*. Vol. 20, No. 2 (April 1987): 135–53.

Marx, Karl. 'Excerpt from "A Contribution to the Critique of Political Economy"'. In Karl Marx and Friedrich Engels, *Marx and Engels: Basic Writings on Politics and Philosophy*. Lewis S. Feurer, ed., Garden City, NY: Anchor Books, 1959: 42–46, 1977; orig. 1859.

——. *Karl Marx: Selected Writings in Sociology and Social Philosophy*. T. B. Bottomore, trans. New York: McGraw-Hill, 1964.

——. *Capital*. Friedrich Engels, ed., New York: International Publishers, 1967; orig. 1867.

——. 'Theses on Feuer'. In Robert C. Tucker, ed., *The Marx–Engels Reader*. New York: W. W. Norton, 1972: 107–9; orig. 1845.

Marx, Karl and Friedrich Engels. 'Manifesto of the Communist Party'. In Robert C. Tucker, ed., *The Marx–Engels Reader*. New York: Norton, 1972: 331–62; orig. 1848.

——. *The Marx–Engels Reader*. Robert C. Tucker, ed., New York: W. W. Norton, 1977.

Marx, Leo. 'The Environment and the 'Two Cultures' Divide'. In James Rodger Fleming and Henry A. Gemery, eds., *Science, Technology and the Environment: Multidisciplinary Perspectives*. Akron, OH: University of Akron Press, 1994: 3–21.

Massey, Douglas S. and Nancy A. Denton. 'Hypersegregation in US Metropolitan Areas: Black and Hispanic Segregation Along Five Dimensions'. *Demography*. Vol. 26, No. 3 (August 1989): 373–91.

Mathabane, Mark. *African Women: Three Generations*. New York: HarperCollins, 1994.

Matthews, Roger. 'Criminal Statistics'. *Criminal Justice Matters*, No. 27 (1977): 14–15.

Matthiessen, Peter. *Indian Country*. New York: Viking Press, 1984.

Mauro, Tony. 'Cruzan's Struggle Left Imprint: Private Case Triggered Public Debate'. *USA Today* (27 December 1990): 3A.

Mauss, Armand L. *Social Problems of Social Movements*. Philadelphia: Lippincott, 1975.

Mead, George Herbert. *Mind, Self and Society from the Standpoint of a Social Behaviourist*. Charles W. Morris, ed., Chicago: University of Chicago Press, 1962; orig. 1934.

Mead, Margaret. *Coming of Age in Samoa*. New York: Dell, 1961; orig. 1928.

——. *Sex and Temperament in Three Primitive Societies*. New York: William Morrow, 1963; orig. 1935.

Meadows, Donella H., Dennis L. Meadows, Jorgan Randers and William W. Behrens, III. *The Limits to Growth: A Report on the Club of Rome's Project on the Predicament of Mankind*. New York: Universe, 1972.

Meltzer, Bernard N. 'Mead's Social Psychology'. In Jerome G. Manis and Bernard N. Meltzer, eds., *Symbolic Interaction: A Reader in Social Psychology*. 3rd edn. Needham Heights, MA: Allyn & Bacon, 1978.

Melucci, Alberto. 'The New Social Movements: A Theoretical Approach'. *Social Science Information*. Vol. 19, No. 2 (May 1980): 199–226.

——. *Nomads of the Present: Social Movements and Individual Needs in Contemporary Society*. Philadelphia, PA: Temple University Press, 1989.

Mennell, Stephen. *All Manners of Food: Eating and Taste in England and France from the Middle Ages to the Present*. Oxford: Basil Blackwell, 1985.

Merton, Robert K. 'Social Structure and Anomie'. *American Sociological Review*. Vol. 3, No. 6 (October 1938): 672–82.

——. *Social Theory and Social Structure*. New York: Free Press, 1968.

——. 'Discrimination and the American Creed'. In *Sociological Ambivalence and Other Essays*. New York: Free Press, 1976: 189–216.

Meyrowitz, Joshua. *No Sense of Place: The Impact of Electronic Media on Social Behavior*. New York and Oxford: Oxford University Press, 1986.

'Migrants and Refugees'. Briefing paper in the series 'Understanding Global Issues', Richard Buckely, ed. (The Runnings, Cheltenham GL51 9PQ, UK), 1966.

Michels, Robert. *Political Parties*. Glencoe, IL: Free Press, 1949; orig. 1911.

Milbrath, Lester W. *Envisioning A Sustainable Society: Learning Our Way Out*. Albany: State University of New York Press, 1989.

Milgram, Stanley. 'Behavioral Study of Obedience'. *Journal of Abnormal and Social Psychology*. Vol. 67, No. 4 (1963): 371–78.

——. 'Group Pressure and Action Against a Person'. *Journal of Abnormal and Social Psychology*. Vol. 69, No. 2 (August 1964): 137–43.

——. 'Some Conditions of Obedience and Disobedience to Authority'. *Human Relations*. Vol. 18 (February 1965): 57–76.

Miliband, Ralph. *The State in Capitalist Society*. London: Weidenfield and Nicolson, 1969.

Miliband, Ralph and Leo Panitch. *Socialist register, 1993: Real Problems, False Solutions*. London: Merlin Press, 1993.

Mill, John Stuart and Harriet Taylor Mill. *The Subjection of Women*. 1869.

Miller, Arthur G. *The Obedience Experiments: A Case of Controversy in Social Science*. New York: Praeger, 1986.

Miller, Daniel, ed. *Acknowledging Consumption*. London: Routledge, 1995.

Miller, G. Tyler, Jr. *Living in the Environment: An Introduction to Environmental Science*. Belmont, CA: Wadsworth, 1992.

Miller, Walter B. 'Lower Class Culture as a Generating Milieu of Gang Delinquency'. In Marvin E. Wolfgang, Leonard Savitz and Norman Johnston, eds., *The Sociology of Crime and Delinquency*. 2nd edn. New York: Wiley, 1970: 351–63; orig. 1958.

Millet, Kate. *Sexual Politics*. Garden City, NY: Doubleday, 1970.

Milliband, Ralph. *The State of Capitalist Society*. London: Weidenfeld & Nicolson, 1969.

Mills, C. Wright. *The Power Elite*. New York: Oxford University Press, 1956.

——. *The Sociological Imagination*. New York: Oxford University Press, 1959, 1967 and 1970.

——. *Power, Politics, and People: The Collected Essays of C. Wright Mills*. London and New York: Oxford University Press, 1967.

Mink, Barbara. 'How Modernization Affects Women'. *Cornell Alumni News*. Vol. III, No. 3 (April 1989): 10–11.

Mirowsky, John. 'The Psycho-Economics of Feeling Underpaid: Distributive Justice and the Earnings of Husbands and Wives'. *American Journal of Sociology*. Vol. 92, No. 6 (May 1987): 1404–34.

Mirza, Heidi Safia, ed. *British Black Feminism*. London: Routledge, 1997.

Modood, Tariq. 'Political Blackness and British Asians', *Sociology*. Vol. 28, No. 4 (1994): 859–76.

Moen, Phyllis. *Women's Two Roles: A Contemporary Dilemma*. New York, London: Auburn House, 1992.

Molotch, Harvey. 'The City as a Growth Machine'. *American Journal of Sociology*. Vol. 82, No. 2 (September 1976): 309–33.

Molotch, Harvey and Marilyn Lester. 'News as Purposive Behaviour'. *American Sociological Review*. Vol. 39 (1974): 101–12.

Montagu, Ashley. *The Nature of Human Aggression*. New York: Oxford University Press, 1976.

Mooney, Jane. *The Hidden Figure: Domestic Violence in North London*. Middlesex: Middlesex University, 1994.

Moore, Gwen. 'Structural Determinants of Men's and Women's Personal Networks'. *American Sociological Review*. Vol. 55, No. 5 (October 1991): 726–35.

——. 'Gender and Informal Networks in State Government'. *Social Science Quarterly*. Vol. 73, No. 1 (March 1992): 46–61.

Moore, Wilbert E. 'Modernization as Rationalization: Processes and Restraints'. In Manning Nash, ed., *Essays on Economic Development and Cultural Change in Honor of Bert F. Hoselitz*. Chicago: University of Chicago Press, 1977: 29–42.

——. *World Modernization: The Limits of Convergence*. New York: Elsevier, 1979.

Moores, Shaun. *Interpreting Audiences: The Ethnography of Media Consumption*. London: Sage, 1993.

Morgan, Rod and Tim Newburn. *The Future of Policing*. Oxford: Clarendon Press, 1997.

Morgan, Patricia. *Farewell to the Family*. London: IEA, 1995.

Morin, S. and E. Garfinkle. 'Male Homophobia'. *Journal of Social Issues*. Vol. 34, No. 1: 29–47.

Morley, David. *Family Television: Cultural Power and Domestic Leisure*. London: Comedia, 1986.

——. *Television: Audiences and Cultural Studies*. London: Routledge, 1992.

Morris, Lydia. *Dangerous Classes: The Underclass and Social Citizenship*. London: Routledge, 1994.

Morrison, Denton E. 'Some Notes Toward Theory on Relative Deprivation, Social Movements, and Social Change'. In Louis E. Genevie, ed., *Collective Behavior and Social Movements*. Itasca, IL: Peacock, 1978: 202–9.

Morrow, Lance. 'The Temping of America'. *Time*. Vol. 131, No. 14 (29 March 1993): 40–41.

Morton, Jackson. 'Census on the Internet'. *American Demographics*. Vol. 17, No. 3 (March 1995): 52–53.

Mosley, W. Henry and Peter Cowley. 'The Challenge of World Health'. *Population Bulletin*. Vol. 46, No. 4 (December 1991). Washington, DC: Population Reference Bureau.

Mueller, Daniel P. and Philip W. Cooper. 'Children of Single Parent Families: How Do They Fare as Young Adults?' Presentation to the American Sociological Association, San Antonio, Texas, 1984.

Muller, Edward N. *Aggressive Political Participation*. Princeton, NJ: Princeton University Press, 1979.

Mumford, Lewis. *The City in History: Its Origins, Its Transformations and Its Prospects*. New York: Harcourt, Brace & World, 1961.

Murdoch, Graham and P. Golding. 'Capitalism, Communication and Class Relations'. In James Curran, et al. *Mass Communication and Society*. London: Edward Arnold, 1977.

Murdock, George Peter. 'The Common Denominator of Cultures'. In Ralph Linton, ed., *The Science of Man in World Crisis*. New York: Columbia University Press, 1945: 123–42.

——. *Social Structure*. New York: Free Press, 1965; orig. 1949.

Murray, Charles. *Losing Ground: American Social Policy 1950–1980*. New York: Basic Books, 1984.

Myers, Norman. 'Humanity's Growth'. In Sir Edmund Hillary, ed., *Ecology 2000: The Changing Face of the Earth*. New York: Beaufort Books, 1984a: 16–35.

——. 'The Mega-Extinction of Animals and Plants'. In Sir Edmund Hillary, ed., *Ecology 2000: The Changing Face of the Earth*. New York: Beaufort Books, 1984b: 82–107.

——. 'Disappearing Cultures'. In Sir Edmund Hillary, ed., *Ecology 2000: The Changing Face of the Earth*. New York: Beaufort Books, 1984c: 162–69.

——. 'Biological Diversity and Global Security'. In F. Herbert Bormann and Stephen R. Kellert, eds., *Ecology, Economics and Ethics: The Broken Circle*. New Haven, CT: Yale University Press, 1991: 11–25.

Myers, Sheila and Harold G. Grasmick. 'The Social Rights and Responsibilities of Pregnant Women: An Application of Parsons' Sick Role Model'. Paper presented to Southwestern Sociological Association, Little Rock, Arkansas, March 1989.

Myrdal, Gunnar, et al. *An American Dilemma The Negro Problem and Modern Democracy*. New York: Harper & Brothers, 1944.

Nagle, Garrett and Kris Spencer. *A Geography of the European Union*. Oxford: Oxford University Press, 1996.

Naisbitt, John. *Megatrends Asia*. London: Nicholas Brealey, 1997.

Nakx, K. 'The "Eclipse" of Folk Medicine in Western Society'. *Sociology of Health and Illness*. Vol. 13, No. 1 (1991): 203.

Nash, J. Madeleine. 'To Know Your Own Fate'. *Time*. Vol. 145, No. 14 (3 April 1995): 62.

National Commission on Excellence in Education. *A Nation at Risk*. Washington, DC: US Government Printing Office, 1983.

Navarro, Vicente. 'The Industrialization of Fetishism or the Fetishism of Industrialization: A Critique of Ivan Illich'. In Vicente Navarro, ed., *Health and Medical Care in the US: A Critical Analysis*. Farmingdale, NY: Baywood Publishing Co., 1977: 38–58.

——. *Crisis, Health and Medicine*. London: Tavistock Institute, 1986.

Nelan, Bruce W. 'Crimes Without Punishment'. *Time*. Vol. 141, No. 2 (11 January 1993): 21.

Nettleton, Sarah. *Power, Pain and Denistry*. Buckingham: Open University, 1992.

——. *The Sociology of Health and Illness*. Cambridge: Polity, 1995.

Neugarten, Bernice L. 'Grow Old with Me. The Best Is Yet to Be'. *Psychology Today*. Vol. 5 (December 1971): 45–48, 79, 81.

——. 'Personality and Aging'. In James E. Birren and K. Warner Schale, eds., *Handbook of the Psychology of Aging*. New York: Van Nostrand Reinhold, 1977: 626–49.

Neuhouser, Kevin. 'The Radicalization of the Brazilian Catholic Church in Comparative Perspective'. *American Sociological Review*. Vol. 54, No. 2 (April 1989): 233–44.

Neuman, W. Russell. *The Future of the Mass Audience*. Cambridge: Cambridge University Press, 1991.

Newman, Katherine S. *Declining Fortunes: The Withering of the American Dream*. New York: Basic Books, 1993.

Newman, William M. *American Pluralism: A Study of Minority Groups and Social Theory*. New York: Harper & Row, 1973.

Nielsen, Joyce McCarl, ed. *Feminist Research Methods: Exemplary Readings in the Social Sciences*. Boulder, CO: Westview Press, 1990.

Nisbet, Robert A. *The Sociological Tradition*. New York: Basic Books, 1966.

——. *The Quest for Community*. New York: Oxford University Press, 1969.

——. 'Sociology as an Art Form'. In *Tradition and Revolt: Historical and Sociological Essays*. New York: Vintage Books, 1970. (Published as *Sociology as an Art Form*. London: Heinemann, 1976.)

Norbeck, Edward. 'Class Structure'. In *Kodansha Encyclopedia of Japan*. Tokyo: Kodansha, 1983: 322–25.

NORC. *General Social Surveys, 1972–1991: Cumulative Codebook*. University of Chicago: National Opinion Research Center,1991

NORC. *General Social Surveys, 1972–1994: Cumulative Codebook*. University of Chicago: National Opinion Research Center, 1994.

Oakes, Jeannie. 'Classroom Social Relationships: Exploring the Bowles and Gintis Hypothesis'. *Sociology of Education*. Vol. 55, No. 4 (October 1982): 197–212.

——. *Keeping Track: How High Schools Structure Inequality*. New Haven, CT: Yale University Press, 1985.

Oberschall, Anthony. *Social Conflict and Social Movements*. Englewood Cliffs, NJ: Prentice Hall, 1973.

Offir, Carole Wade. *Human Sexuality*. New York: Harcourt Brace Jovanovich, 1982.

Ogburn, William F. *On Culture and Social Change*. Chicago: University of Chicago Press, 1964.

Okin, Susan Moller. *Justice, Gender and the Family*. New York: Basic Books, 1989.

Olsen, Marvin E., Dora G. Lodwick and Riley E. Dunlap. *Viewing the World Ecologically*. Boulder, CO: Westview Press, 1992.

Olzak, Susan. 'Labor Unrest, Immigration and Ethnic Conflict in Urban America, 1880–1914'. *American Journal of Sociology*. Vol. 94, No. 6 (May 1989): 1303–33.

Olzak, Susan and Elizabeth West. 'Ethnic Conflict and the Rise and Fall of Ethnic Newspapers'. *American Sociological Review*. Vol. 56, No. 4 (August 1991): 458–74.

Ong, A. *Orality and Literacy*. London: Sage, 1982.

Oppenheim, C. *Poverty: The Facts*. 2nd edn. London: Child Poverty Action Group, 1993.

OPCS. *1991 census Preliminary Report for England and Wales*. London: HMSO, 1991.

O'Reilly, Jane. 'Wife Beating: The Silent Crime'. *Time*. Vol. 122, No. 10 (5 September 1983): 23–24, 26.

Orlansky, Michael D. and William L. Heward. *Voices: Interviews With Handicapped People*. Columbus, OH: Merrill, 1981: 85, 92, 133–34, 172.

Orshansky, Mollie. 'How Poverty is Measured'. *Monthly Labor Review*. Vol. 92, No. 2 (February 1969): 37–41.

Ostling, Richard N. 'Jerry Falwell's Crusade'. *Time*. Vol. 126, No. 9 (2 September 1985): 48–52, 55, 57.

——. 'Technology and the Womb'. *Time*. Vol. 129, No. 12 (23 March 1987): 58–59.

Ouchi, William. *Theory Z: How American Business Can Meet the Japanese Challenge*. Reading, MA: Addison-Wesley, 1981.

——. 'Personality and the Aging Process'. *The Gerontologist*. Vol. 12, No. 1 (Spring 1972): 9–15.

——. 'Personality and Aging'. In James E. Birren and K. Warner Schaie, eds., *Handbook of the Psychology of Aging*. New York: Van Nostrand Reinhold, 1977: 626–49.

Pahl, Jan, *Money and Marriage*. Basingstoke: Macmillan Education, 1989.

Pakulski, Jan. 'Mass Social Movements and Social Class'. *International Sociology*. Vol. 8, No. 2 (June 1993): 131–58.

Palmore, Erdman. 'Predictors of Successful Aging'. *The Gerontologist*. Vol. 19, No. 5 (October 1979a): 427–31.

——. 'Advantages of Aging'. *The Gerontologist*. Vol. 19, No. 2 (April 1979b): 220–23.

——. 'What Can the USA Learn from Japan About Aging?' In Steven H. Zarit, ed., *Readings in Aging and Death: Contemporary Perspectives*. New York: Harper & Row, 1982: 166–69.

Parekh, Bhiku. 'The Rushdie Affair and the British Press'. *Social Studies Review* (November, 1989): 44.

Park, Robert E. *Race and Culture*. Glencoe, IL: Free Press, 1950.

——. 'The City: Suggestions for the Investigation of Human Behavior in the Human Environment'. In Robert E. Park and Ernest W. Burgess, *The City*. Chicago: University of Chicago Press, 1967; orig. 1925: 1–46.

Parker, Richard and Herbert Daniel. *Sexuality, Politics and AIDS in Brazil: In Another World?* Bristol, PA: Taylor & Francis, 1993.

Parkin, Frank. *Class Inequality and Political Order: Social Stratification in Capitalist and Communist Societies*. London: MacGibbon & Kee, 1971.

Parkinson, C. Northcote. *Parkinson's Law and Other Studies in Administration*. New York: Ballantine Books, 1957.

Parrillo, Vincent N. *Diversity in America*. Thousand Oaks, CA: Pine Forge, 1996.

Parsons, Talcott. 'Age and Sex in the Social Structure of the United States'. *American Sociological Review*. Vol. 7, No. 4 (August 1942): 604–16.

——. *The Social System*. New York: Free Press, 1964; orig. 1951.

——. *Essays in Sociological Theory*. New York: Free Press, 1954, 1964.

——. *Societies: Evolutionary and Comparative Perspectives*. Englewood Cliffs, NJ: Prentice Hall, 1966.

Parsons, Talcott and Robert F. Bales, eds. *Family, Socialization and Interaction Process*. New York: Free Press, 1955.

Patterson, Shiela. *Dark Strangers*. Harmondsworth: Penguin, 1963.

Pear, Robert, with Erik Eckholm. 'When Healers are Entrepreneurs: A Debate Over Costs and Ethics'. *New York Times* (2 June 1991): 1, 17.

Pennings, Johannes M. 'Organizational Birth Frequencies: An Empirical Investigation'. *Administrative Science Quarterly*. Vol. 27, No. 1 (March 1982): 120–44.

Pessen, Edward. *Riches, Class and Power: America Before the Civil War*. New Brunswick, NJ: Transaction Books, 1990.

Peter, Laurence J. and Raymond Hull. *The Peter Principle: Why Things Always Go Wrong*. New York: William Morrow, 1969.

Peters Atlas of the World. New York: Harper & Row, 1990.

Peters, Thomas J. and Robert H. Waterman, Jr. *In Search of Excellence: Lessons From America's Best-Run Companies*. New York: Warner Books, 1982.

Phillips, Adam. *On Flirtation*. Cambridge, MA: Harvard University Press, 1994.

Phillipson, Chris. *Capitalism and the Construction of Old Age*. London: Macmillan, 1982.

Phizacklea, Annie. *One Way Ticket: Migration and Female Labour*. London: Edward Arnold, 1993.

Pickering, K. T. and Lewis A. Owen. *An Introduction to Global Environmental Issues*. London: Routledge, 1994.

Pietroni, P. *Reader's Digest Guide to Alternative Medicine*. London: Readers Digest Association, 1991.

Pillemer, Karl. 'Maltreatment of the Elderly at Home and in Institutions: Extent, Risk Factors, and Policy Recommendations'. In US Congress. House, Select Committee on Aging and Senate, Special Committee on Aging. *Legislative Agenda for an Aging Society: 1988 and Beyond*. Washington, DC: US Government Printing Office, 1988.

Pines, Maya. 'The Civilization of Genie'. *Psychology Today*. Vol. 15 (September 1981): 28–34.

Pitt, Malcolm. *Introducing Hinduism*. New York: Friendship Press, 1955.

Piven, Frances Fox and Richard A. Cloward. *Regulating the Poor: the Functions of Public Welfare*. London: Tavistock Publications, 1972.

Pizzey, Erin. *Scream Quietly or the Neighbours Will Hear*. Harmondsworth: Penguin: 1974.

Plomin, Robert and Terryl T. Foch. 'A Twin Study of Objectively Assessed Personality in Childhood'. *Journal of Personality and Social Psychology*. Vol. 39, No. 4 (October 1980): 680–88.

Plummer, Kenneth. *Documents of Life: An Introduction to the Problems and Literature of a Humanistic Method*. London: Allen & Unwin, 1983

——. 'Organising AIDS'. In Peter Aggleton and Hilary Homans, *Social Aspects of AIDS*. London: Falmer Press, 1988.

——. 'Speaking its Name: Inventing Gay and Lesbian Studies'. In Ken Plummer, ed., *Modern Homosexualities*. London: Routledge, 1992.

Polsby, Nelson W. 'Three Problems in the Analysis of Community Power'. *American Sociological Review*. Vol. 24, No. 6 (December 1959): 796–803.

Popenoe, David. *Disturbing the Nest: Family Change and Decline in Modern Societies*. New York: Aldine, 1988.

——. 'Family Decline in the Swedish Welfare State'. *The Public Interest*. No. 102 (Winter 1991): 65–77.

——. 'The Controversial Truth: Two-Parent Families are Better'. *New York Times* (26 December 1992): 21.

——. 'American Family Decline, 1960–1990: A Review and Appraisal'. *Journal of Marriage and the Family*. Vol. 55, No. 3 (August 1993): 527–55.

——. 'Scandinavian Welfare'. *Society*. Vol. 31, No. 6 (September–October, 1994): 78–81.

Population Reference Bureau. *1995 World Population Data Sheet*. Washington, DC: Population Reference Bureau, Inc., 1995.

——. 'Past and Future Population Doubling Times, Selected Countries'. *Population Today*. Vol. 23, No. 2 (February 1995): 6.

Population Today. 'Majority of Children in Poverty Live with Parents Who Work'. Vol. 23, No 4 (April 1995): 6.

Population Trends. London: The Stationery Office, 1997.

Postel, Sandra. 'Facing Water Scarcity'. In Lester R. Brown, et al., eds., *State of the World 1993: A Worldwatch Institute Report on Progress Toward a Sustainable Society*. New York: W. W. Norton, 1993: 22–41.

Powell, Chris and George E. C. Paton, eds. *Humour in Society: Resistance and Control*. New York: St. Martin's Press, 1988.

Presser, Harriet B. 'The Housework Gender Gap'. *Population Today*. Vol. 21, No. 7/8 (July–August 1993): 5.

Pressley, Sue Anne and Nancy Andrews. 'For Gay Couples, the Nursery Becomes the New Frontier'. *Washington Post* (20 December 1992): A1, A22–23.

Price, Simon. *Human Capital, Hysteresis and Unemployment among Workers with Finite Lives*. London: ESRC Research Council on Micro-Social Change, 1991.

Primeggia, Salvatore and Joseph A. Varacalli. 'Southern Italian Comedy: Old to New World'. In Joseph V. Scelsa, Salvatore J. LaGumina and Lydio Tomasi, eds., *Italian Americans in Transition*. New York: The American Italian Historical Association, 1990: 241–52.

Pryce, Ken. *Endless Pressure*. 2nd edn. Harmondsworth: Penguin, 1986; orig. 1979.

Quinney, Richard. *Class, State and Crime: On the Theory and Practice of Criminal Justice*. New York: David McKay, 1977.

Rademacher, Eric W. 'The Effect of Question Wording on College Students'. *The Pittsburgh Undergraduate Review*. Vol. 8, No. 1 (Spring 1992): 45–81.

Rademaekers William and Rhea Schoenthal. 'Iceman'. *Time*, Vol. 140, No. 17 (26 October 1992): 62–66.

Randall, Vicki. *Women and Politics: An International Perspective*. 2nd edn. London: Macmillan, 1987.

Rathje, William and Cullan Murphy. *Rubbish: The Archeology of Garbage*. New York: HarperCollins, 1991.

Reckless, Walter C. and Simon Dinitz. 'Pioneering With Self-Concept as a Vulnerability Factor in Delinquency'. *Journal of Criminal Law, Criminology, and Police Science*. Vol. 58, No. 4 (December 1967): 515–23.

Redclift, Michael and Ted Benton, eds. *Social Theory and the Global Environment*. London: Routledge, 1994.

Reich, Robert B. 'As the World Turns'. *The New Republic* (1 May 1989): 23, 26–28.

——. *The Work of Nations: Preparing Ourselves for 21st-Century Capitalism*. New York: Alfred A. Knopf, 1991.

Reinharz, Shulamit. *Feminist Methods in Social Research*. New York: Oxford University Press, 1992.

Remoff, Heather Trexler. *Sexual Choice: A Woman's Decision*. New York: Dutton/Lewis, 1984.

Renard, W. *A Future for the NHS? Health Care in the 1990s*. London: Longman, 1994.

Rex, John and Robert Moore. *Race, Community and Conflict*. London: Oxford University Press, 1967.

Richards, Janet. *The Sceptical Feminist: A Philosophical Enquiry*. Harmondsworth: Penguin, 1982.

Richardson, Diane. *Women, Motherhood and Children*. London: Macmillan, 1993.

——. *Women, Motherhood and Childrearing*. London: macmillan, 1994.

Richardson, James T. 'Definitions of Cult: From Sociological-Technical to Popular Negative'. Paper presented to the American Psychological Association, Boston, August 1990.

Riesman, David. *The Lonely Crowd: A Study of the Changing American Character*. New Haven, CT: Yale University Press, 1970; orig. 1950.

Ridgeway, Cecilia L. *The Dynamics of Small Groups*. New York: St. Martin's Press, 1983.

Reid, Ivan. *Social Class Differences in Britain*. 3rd edn. London: Fontana, 1989.

Rieff, Philip. 'Introduction'. In Charles Horton Cooley, *Social Organization*. New York: Schocken Books, 1962.

Riis, Joseph. *How the Other Half Lives*. New York: Dover Books, 1971.

Riley, Matilda White, Anne Foner and Joan Waring. 'Sociology of Age'. In Neil J. Smelser, ed., *Handbook of Sociology*. Newbury Park, CA: Sage, 1988: 243–90.

Ritzer, George. *Sociological Theory*. New York: Alfred A. Knopf, 1983: 63–66; 3rd edn. New York, McGraw-Hill, 1992.

——. *The McDonaldization of Society: An Investigation Into the Changing Character of Contemporary Social Life*. Thousand Oaks, CA: Pine Forge Press, 1993.

Ritzer, George and David Walczak. *Working: Conflict and Change*. 4th edn. Englewood Cliffs, NJ: Prentice Hall, 1990.

Roberts, J. Deotis. *Roots of a Black Future: Family and Church*. Philadelphia: Westminster Press, 1980.

Roberts, J. Timmons. 'Psychosocial Effects of Workplace Hazardous Exposures: Theoretical Synthesis and Preliminary Findings'. *Social Problems*. Vol. 40, No. 1 (February 1993): 74–89.

Robinson, Vera M. 'Humor and Health'. In Paul E. McGhee and Jeffrey H. Goldstein, eds., *Handbook of Humor Research, Vol. II: Applied Studies*. New York: Springer-Verlag, 1983: 109–28.

Robinson, Joyce and Glenna Spitze. 'Whistle While You Work? The Effect of Household Task Performance on Women's and Men's Well-Being'. *Social Science Quarterly*. Vol. 73, No. 4 (December 1992): 844–61.

Rockett, Ian R. H. 'Population and Health: An Introduction to Epidemiology'. *Population Bulletin*. Vol. 49, No. 3 (November 1994). Washington, DC: Population Reference Bureau.

Roesch, Roberta. 'Violent Families'. *Parents*. Vol. 59, No. 9 (September 1984): 74–76, 150–52.

Roethlisberger, F. J. and William J. Dickson. *Management and the Worker*. Cambridge, MA: Harvard University Press, 1939.

Rokove, Milton L. *Don't Make No Waves, Don't Back No Losers*. Bloomington: Indiana University Press, 1975.

Roman, Mel and William Haddad. *The Disposable Parent: The Case for Joint Custody*. New York: Holt, Rinehart & Winston, 1978.

Róna-Tas, Ákos. 'The First Shall Be Last? Entrepreneurship and Communist Cadres in the Transition From Socialism'. *American Journal of Sociology*. Vol. 100, No. 1 (July 1994): 40–69.

Roof, Wade Clark. *A Generation of Seekers: The Spiritual Journeys of the Baby Boom Generation*. New York: HarperCollins, 1992.

Roof, Wade Clark, and William McKinney. *American Mainline Religion: Its Changing Shape and Future*. New Brunswick, N.J.: Rutgers University Press, 1987.

Rose, Jerry D. *Outbreaks*. New York: Free Press, 1982.

Rosen, Ellen Israel. *Bitter Choices: Blue-Collar Women In and Out of Work*. Chicago: University of Chicago Press, 1987.

Rosenbaum, Alan S., ed. *The Philosophy of Human Rights: International Perspectives*. London: Aldwych Press, 1980.

Rosenthal, Elizabeth. 'Canada's National Health Plan Gives Care to All, With Limits'. *New York Times* (30 April 1991): A1, A16.

Rosenthal, Jack. 'The Rapid Growth of Suburban Employment'. In Lois H. Masotti and Jeffrey K. Hadden, eds., *Suburbia in Transition*. New York: New York Times Books, 1974: 95–100.

Rossi, Alice S. 'Gender and Parenthood'. In Alice S. Rossi, ed., *Gender and the Life Course*. New York: Aldine, 1985: 161–91.

Rostow, Walt W. *The Stages of Economic Growth: A Non-Communist Manifesto*. Cambridge: Cambridge University Press, 1960.

——. *The World Economy: History and Prospect*. Austin: University of Texas Press, 1978.

Rowbottom, Sheila. *A Century of Women: The History of Women in Britian and the United States*. London: Viking, 1997.

Rowe, David C. 'Biometrical Genetic Models of Self-Reported Delinquent Behavior: A Twin Study'. *Behavior Genetics*. Vol. 13, No. 5 (1983): 473–89.

Rowe, David C. and D. Wayne Osgood. 'Heredity and Sociological Theories of Delinquency: A Reconsideration'. *American Sociological Review*. Vol. 49, No. 4 (August 1984): 526–40.

Rubenstein, Eli A. 'The Not So Golden Years'. *Newsweek* (7 October 1991): 13.

Rubin, Beth A. 'Class Struggle American Style: Unions, Strikes and Wages'. *American Sociological Review*. Vol. 51, No. 5 (October 1986): 618–31.

Rubin, Lillian Breslow. *Worlds of Pain: Life in the Working-Class Family*. New York: Basic Books, 1976.

Ruggiero, Vincento, Mick Ryan and Joe Sim, eds. *Western European Penal Systems: A Critical Anatomy*. London: Sage, 1995.

Runciman, W. G. 'How Many Classes are There in Society?'. *Sociology*. Vol. 24: 377–96.

Runnymede Trust. *Multi-ethnic Britain – Facts and Trends*. London: Runnymede Trust, 1994.

Rushdie, Salman. *Midnight's Children*. London: Picador, 1982.

Russell, Cheryl. 'The Master Trend'. *American Demographics*. Vol. 15, No. 10 (October 1993): 28–37.

Russell, Diana E. H. *Rape in Marriage*. New York: Macmillan, 1982.

Ryan, William. *Blaming the Victim*. Rev. edn. New York: Vintage Books, 1976.

Rymer, Russ. *Genie*. New York: HarperPerennial, 1994.

Sagan, Carl. *The Dragons of Eden*. New York: Ballantine, 1977.

Saks, M. *Alternative Medicine*. Oxford: Clarendon Press, 1992.

Sale, Kirkpatrick. *The Conquest of Paradise: Christopher Columbus and the Columbian Legacy*. New York: Alfred A. Knopf, 1990.

Saltman, Juliet. 'Maintaining Racially Diverse Neighborhoods'. *Urban Affairs Quarterly*. Vol. 26, No. 3 (March 1991): 416–41.

Sampson, Anthony. *The Changing Anatomy of Britain*. London: Hodder and Stoughton, 1982.

Sampson, Robert J. 'Urban Black Violence: The Effects of Male Joblessness and Family Disruption'. *American Journal of Sociology*. Vol. 93, No. 2 (September 1987): 348–82.

Sampson, Robert J. and John H. Laub. 'Crime and Deviance Over the Life Course: The Salience of Adult Social Bonds'. *American Sociological Review*. Vol. 55, No. 5 (October 1990): 609–27.

Santoli, Al. 'Fighting Child Prostitution'. *Freedom Review*. Vol. 25, No. 5 (September-October 1994): 5–8.

Sapir, Edward. 'The Status of Linguistics as a Science'. *Language*. Vol. 5 (1929): 207–14.

——. *Selected Writings of Edward Sapir in Language, Culture and Personality*. David G. Mandelbaum, ed. Berkeley: University of California Press, 1949.

Sargent, Lyman Tower, ed. *Extremism in America: A Reader*. New York: New York University Press, 1995.

Sassen, Saskia. *The Global City: New York, London, Tokyo*. Princeton: Princeton University Press, 1991.

Sato, Ikuyo. *Kamikaze Biker: Parody and Anomie in Affluent Japan*. Chicago: University of Chicago Press, 1991.

Saunders, Peter. *Social Class and Stratification*. London: Routledge. 1990.

Savage, Mike. *Walter Benjamin and Urban Meaning*. Keele: University of Keele, 1993.

Savage, Mike, J. Burlow, P. Dickens and T. Fielding. *Property Bureaucracy and Culture: Middle Class Formation in Contemporary Britain*. London: Routledge, 1992.

Savage, Mike and Alam Warde. *Urban Sociology, Capitalism and Modernity*. London: Macmillan, 1993.

Sayers, Janet. *Biological Politics*. London: Tavistock, 1982.

Scaff, Lawrence A. 'Max Weber and Robert Michels'. *American Journal of Sociology*. Vol. 86, No. 6 (May 1981): 1269–86.

Scarman, Leslie George. T*he Brixton Disorders, 10–12 April 1981: Report of an Inquiry: Presented to Parliament by the Secretary of State for the Home Department, November 1981*. London: HMSO, 1981.

Schaie, I. Warner. 'Intelligence and Problem Solving'. In James E. Birren and R. Bruce Sloane, eds., *Handbook of Mental Health and Aging*. Englewood Cliffs, NJ: Prentice Hall, 1980: 262–84.

Scheff, Thomas J. *Mental Illness and Social Processes*. New York: Harper & Row, 1967.

——. *Being Mentally Ill: A Sociological Theory*. 2nd edn. New York: Aldine, 1984.

Schellenberg, James A. *Masters of Social Psychology*. New York: Oxford University Press, 1978: 38–62.

Scheper-Hughes, Nancy. *Death Without Weeping: The Violence of Everyday Life in Brazil*. Berkeley: University of California Press, 1992

Schilling, Chris. *The Body and Social Theory*. London: Sage, 1993.

Schlesinger, Philip. *Putting 'Reality' Together: BBC News*. London: Constable, 1978.

Schmidt, Roger. *Exploring Religion*. Belmont, CA: Wadsworth, 1980.

Schnaiberg, Allan and Kenneth Alan Gould. *Environment and Society: the Enduring Conflict*. New York: St. Martin's Press, 1994.

Schodt, Frederick. *Manga! Manga! The World of Japanese Comics*. London: Kodansha Europe, 1986.

Scholte, Jan Aart. 'The Globalisation of World Politics'. In John Bayles and Steve Smith, eds., *The Globalisation of World Politics*. Oxford: Oxford University Press, 1997.

Schooler, Carmi, Joanne Miller, Karen A. Miller, and Carol N. Richtand. 'Work for the Household: Its Nature and Consequences for Husbands and Wives'. *American Journal of Sociology*. Vol. 90, No. 1 (July 1984): 97–124.

Schramm, Wilbur. *TV in the Lives of our Children*. California: Stanford University Press, 1961.

Schulte, Joachim. *Experience and Expression: Wittgenstein's Philosophy of Psychology*. Oxford: Clarendon Press, 1995.

Schumann, Hans Wolfgang. *Buddhism: An Outline of Its Teachings and Schools*. Wheaton, IL: The Theosophical Publishing House/Quest Books, 1974.

Schwartz, Martin D. 'Gender and Injury in Spousal Assault'. *Sociological Focus*. Vol. 20, No. 1 (January 1987): 61–75.

Scott, John. *Who Rules Britain*. Cambridge: Polity, 1991.

——. *Poverty and Wealth*. London: Longman, 1994.

——. *Stratification and Power: Structures of Class, Status and Command*. Cambridge: Polity Press, 1996.

Scott, John, and Catherine Griff. *Directors of Industry: The British Corporate Network, 1904–1976*. New York: Blackwell, 1985.

Scott, W. Richard. *Organizations: Rational, Natural and Open Systems*. Englewood Cliffs, NJ: Prentice Hall, 1981.

Seabrook, Jeremy. *In the Cities of the South*. London: Verso, 1996.

Segal, Lynne. *Is the Future Female?: Troubled Thoughts on Contemporary Feminism*. London: Virago, 1994.

——. *Straight Sex: The Politics of Pleasure*. London: Virago, 1994; 2nd edn. 1997.

Seidman, Steven, ed. *Queer Theory/Sociology*. Oxford: Blackwell, 1996.

Sekulic, Dusko, Garth Massey and Randy Hodson. 'Who Were the Yugoslavs? Failed Sources of Common Identity in the Former Yugoslavia'. *American Sociological Review*. Vol. 59, No. 1 (February 1994): 83–97.

Sellin, Thorsten. *The Penalty of Death*. Beverly Hills, CA: Sage, 1980.

Seltzer, Robert M. *Jewish People, Jewish Thought: The Jewish Experience in History*. New York: Macmillan, 1980.

Sen, K. M. *Hinduism*. Baltimore: Penguin Books, 1961.

Sennett, Richard and Jonathan Cobb. *The Hidden Injuries of Class*. New York: Vintage Books, 1973.

Shapiro, Joseph P. and Joannie M. Schrof. 'Honor Thy Children'. *US News and World Report*. Vol. 118, No. 8 (27 February 1995): 39–49.

Sharpe, Sue. *Just Like a Girl: How Girls Learn to Become Women*. 2nd edn. Harmondsworth: Penguin, 1994.

Shawcross, William. *Sideshow: Kissinger, Nixon and the Destruction of Cambodia*. New York: Pocket Books, 1979.

Sheehan, Tom. 'Senior Esteem as a Factor in Socioeconomic Complexity'. *The Gerontologist*. Vol. 16, No. 5 (October 1976): 433–40.

Sheehy, Gail. *Passages: Predictable Crises of Adult Life*. New York: Dutton, 1976.

Sheldon, William H., Emil M. Hartl, and Eugene McDermott. *Varieties of Delinquent Youth*. New York: Harper, 1949.

Sheley, James F., Joshua Zhang, Charles J. Brody and James D. Wright. 'Gang Organization, Gang Criminal Activity and Individual Gang Members' Criminal Behavior'. *Social Science Quarterly*. Vol. 76, No. 1 (March 1995): 53–68.

Shenon, Philip. 'A Pacific Island Nation is Stripped of Everything'. *New York Times* (10 December 1995): 3.

Sherman, Lawrence W. and Douglas A. Smith. 'Crime, Punishment and Stake in Conformity: Legal and Informal Control of Domestic Violence'. *American Sociological Review*. Vol. 57, No. 5 (October 1992): 680–90.

Sherwin, Susan. *No Longer Patient: Feminist Ethics and Health Care*. Philadelphia, PA: Temple University Press, 1992.

Shevky, Eshref and Wendell Bell. *Social Area Analysis*. Stanford, CA: Stanford University Press, 1955.

Shilling, Chris. *Schooling for Work in Capitalist Britain*. London: Falmer, 1989.

Shils, Edward and Henry Finch, eds. *Max Weber and the Methodology of the Social Sciences*. New York: Free Press, 1949.

Shipler, David K. *Russia: Broken Idols, Solemn Dreams*. New York: Penguin Books, 1984.

Shipley, Joseph T. *Dictionary of Word Origins*. Totowa, NJ: Roman & Allanheld, 1985.

Shupe, Anson, William A. Stacey and Lonnie R. Hazlewood. *Violent Men, Violent Couples: The Dynamics of Domestic Violence*. Lexington, MA: Lexington Books, 1987.

Sidel, Ruth and Victor W. Sidel. *A Healthy State: An International Perspective on the Crisis in United States Medical Care*. Rev. edn. New York: Pantheon Books, 1982a.

——. *The Health Care of China*. Boston: Beacon Press, 1982b.

Sills, David L. 'The Succession of Goals'. In Amitai Etzioni, ed., *A Sociological Reader on Complex Organizations*. 2nd edn. New York: Holt, Rinehart & Winston, 1969: 175–87.

Silverberg, Robert. 'The Greenhouse Effect: Apocalypse Now or Chicken Little?' *Omni* (July 1991): 50–54.

Simmel, Georg. *The Sociology of Georg Simmel*. Kurt Wolff, ed. New York: Free Press, 1950: 118–69; orig. 1902.

——. 'The Metropolis and Mental Life'. In Kurt Wolff, ed., *The Sociology of Georg Simmel*. New York: Free Press, 1964: 409–24; orig. 1905.

Simon, Julian. *The Ultimate Resource*. Princeton, NJ: Princeton University Press, 1981.

Simons, Carol. 'Japan's Kyoiku Mamas'. In John J. Macionis and Nijole V. Benokraitis, eds., *Seeing Ourselves: Classic, Contemporary and Cross-Cultural Readings in Sociology*. Englewood Cliffs, NJ: Prentice Hall, 1989: 281–86.

Simons, Marlise. 'The Price of Modernization: The Case of Brazil's Kaiapo Indians'. In John J. Macionis and Nijole V. Benokraitis, eds., *Seeing Ourselves: Classic, Contemporary, and Cross-Cultural Readings in Sociology*. 3rd edn. Englewood Cliffs, NJ: Prentice Hall, 1995: 470–76.

Simpson, George Eaton and J. Milton Yinger. *Racial and Cultural Minorities: An Analysis of Prejudice and Discrimination*. 4th edn. New York: Harper & Row, 1972.

Sinfield, Adrian. *What Unemployment Means*. Oxford: Martin Robertson, 1981.

Sivard, Ruth Leger. *World Military and Social Expenditures, 1987–88*. 12th edn. Washington, DC: World Priorities, 1988.

Sizer, Theodore R. *Horace's Compromise: The Dilemma of the American High School*. Boston: Houghton Mifflin, 1984.

Skellington, R. *'Race' in Britain Today*. 2nd edn. London: Sage, 1996

Skocpol, Theda. *States and Social Revolutions: A Comparative Analysis of France, Russia and China*. Cambridge: Cambridge University Press, 1979.

Skolnick, Arlene. *The Psychology of Human Development*. New York: Harcourt Brace Jovanovich, 1986.

Slater, Philip E. 'Contrasting Correlates of Group Size'. *Sociometry*. Vol. 21, No. 2 (June 1958): 129–39.

——. *The Pursuit of Loneliness*. Boston: Beacon Press, 1976.

Smart, Carol. *Women, Crime and Criminology: a Feminist Critique*. London: Routledge and Kegan Paul, 1977.

——. *The Ties that Bind*. London: Routledge, 1984.

Smelser, Neil J. *Theory of Collective Behavior*. New York: Free Press, 1962.

Smith, Christian. *The Emergence of Liberation Theology: Radical Religion and Social Movement Theory*. Chicago: Chicago University Press, 1991.

Smith, David J. and Sally Tomlinson. *The School Effect: A Study of Multi-racial Comprehensives*. London: Policy Studies Institute, 1989.

Smith, Douglas A. 'Police Response to Interpersonal Violence: Defining the Parameters of Legal Control'. *Social Forces*. Vol. 65, No. 3 (March 1987): 767–82.

Smith, Douglas A. and Patrick R. Gartin. 'Specifying Specific Deterrence: The Influence of Arrest on Future Criminal Activity'. *American Sociological Review*. Vol. 54, No. 1 (February 1989): 94–105.

Smith, Douglas A. and Christy A. Visher. 'Street-Level Justice: Situational Determinants of Police Arrest Decisions'. *Social Problems*. Vol. 29, No. 2 (December 1981): 167–77.

Smith, Gordon. *Politics in Western Europe*. Aldershot: Dartmouth, 1990.

Smith, Robert B. 'Health Care Reform Now'. *Society*. Vol. 30, No. 3 (March–April 1993): 56–65.

Smith, Tom W. Research results reported in 'Anti-Semitism Decreases But Persists'. *Society*. Vol. 33, No. 3 (March/April 1996): 2.

Smith-Lovin, Lynn and Charles Brody. 'Interruptions in Group Discussions: The Effects of Gender and Group Composition'. *American Journal of Sociology*. Vol. 54, No. 3 (June 1989): 424–35.

Smolowe, Jill. 'When Violence Hits Home'. *Time*. Vol. 144, No. 1 (4 July 1994): 18–25.

Snell, Marilyn Berlin. 'The Purge of Nurture'. *New Perspectives Quarterly*. Vol. 7, No. 1 (Winter 1990): 1–2.

Social Trends. 27. London: The Stationery Office, 1997.

Sorokin, Pitrim and C. Berger. *Time Budgets of Human Behaviour*. Cambridge, MA: Harvard University Press, 1938.

South, Scott J. and Steven F. Messner. 'Structural Determinants of Intergroup Association: Interracial Marriage and Crime'. *American Journal of Sociology*. Vol. 91, No. 6 (May 1986): 1409–30.

Sowell, Thomas. *Ethnic America*. New York: Basic Books, 1981.

——. *Race and Culture*. New York: Basic Books, 1994.

——. 'Ethnicity and IQ'. In Steven Fraser, ed., *The Bell Curve Wars: Race, Intelligence and the Future of America*. New York: Basic Books, 1995: 70–79.

——. *Migrations and Cultures: A World View*. New York: Basic Books, 1996.

Soysal, Yasemin. *Limits of Citizenship: Migrants and Postnational Membership in Europe*. Chicago: University of Chicago Press, 1994.

Spates, James L. 'Counterculture and Dominant Culture Values: A Cross-National Analysis of the Underground Press and Dominant Culture Magazines'. *American Sociological Review*. Vol. 41, No. 5 (October 1976): 868–83.

——. 'The Sociology of Values'. In Ralph Turner, ed., *Annual Review of Sociology*. Vol. 9. Palo Alto, CA: Annual Reviews, 1983: 27–49.

Spates, James L. and John J. Macionis. *The Sociology of Cities*. 2nd edn. Belmont, CA: Wadsworth, 1987.

Spates, James L. and H. Wesley Perkins. 'American and English Student Values'. *Comparative Social Research*. Vol. 5. Greenwich, CT: JAI Press, 1982: 245–68.

Spector, Leonard S. 'Nuclear Proliferation Today'. In William M. Evan and Stephen Hilgartner, eds., *The Arms Race and Nuclear War*. Englewood Cliffs, NJ: Prentice Hall, 1988: 25–29.

Speer, James A. 'The New Christian Right and Its Parent Company: A Study in Political Contrasts'. In David G. Bromley and Anson Shupe, eds., *New Christian Politics*. Macon, GA: Mercer University Press, 1984: 19–40.

Spender, Dale. *Man Made Language*. London: Routledge & Kegan Paul, 1980.

——. *Women of Ideas and What Men Have Done to Them: From Aphra Behn to Adrienne Rich*. London: Routledge & Kegan Paul, 1982.

Spitzer, Steven. 'Toward a Marxian Theory of Deviance'. In Delos H. Kelly, ed., *Criminal Behavior: Readings in Criminology*. New York: St. Martin's Press, 1980: 175–91.

Spybey, Tony, ed. *Britain in Europe: An Introduction to Sociology*. London: Routledge, 1997.

Stacey, Judith. *Patriarchy and Socialist Revolution in China*. Berkeley: University of California Press, 1983.

——. *Brave New Families: Stories of Domestic Upheaval in Late Twentieth-Century America*. New York: Basic Books, 1990.

——. 'Good Riddance to "The Family": A Response to David Popenoe'. *Journal of Marriage and the Family*. Vol. 55, No. 3 (August 1993): 545–47.

——. *In the Name of the Family: Rethinking Family Values in the Postmodern Age*. Boston: Beacon Press, 1996: 8.

Stack, Carol B. *All Our Kin: Strategies for Survival in a Black Community*. New York: Harper & Row, 1975.

Stahura, John M. 'Suburban Development, Black Suburbanization and the Black Civil Rights Movement Since World War II'. *American Sociological Review*. Vol. 51, No. 1 (February 1986): 131–44.

Stanley, Liz, ed. *Feminist Praxis: Research, Theory and Epistemology in Feminist Sociology*. London: Routledge & Kegan Paul, 1990.

Stanley, Liz and Sue Wise. *Breaking Out: Feminist Consciousness and Feminist Research*. London: Routledge & Kegan Paul, 1983.

Stanworth, M. D. *Gender and Schooling: A Study of Sexual Divisions in the Classroom*. London: Hutchinson in association with the Explorations in Feminism Collective, 1983.

Stark, Rodney. *Sociology*. Belmont, CA: Wadsworth, 1985.

Stark, Rodney and William Sims Bainbridge. 'Of Churches, Sects and Cults: Preliminary Concepts for a Theory of Religious Movements'. *Journal for the Scientific Study of Religion*. Vol. 18, No. 2 (June 1979): 117–31.

——. 'Secularization and Cult Formation in the Jazz Age'. *Journal for the Scientific Study of Religion*. Vol. 20, No. 4 (December 1981): 360–73.

Starker, Steven. *Evil Influences: Crusades Against the Mass Media*. New Brunswick: Transaction Publishers, 1989.

Stavrianos, L. S. *A Global History: The Human Heritage*. 3rd edn. Englewood Cliffs, NJ: Prentice Hall, 1983.

Steele, Shelby. *The Content of Our Character: A New Vision of Race in America*. New York: St. Martin's Press, 1990.

Stein, Dorothy. *People Who Count: Population and Politics, Women and Children*. London: Earthscan, 1995.

Stein, Maurice R. *The Eclipse of Community: An Interpretation of American Studies*. Princeton, NJ: Princeton University Press, 1972.

Stephens, John D. *The Transition From Capitalism to Socialism*. Urbana: University of Illinois Press, 1986.

Stern, Steve J. *The Secret History of Gender; Women, Men, and Power in Late Colonial Mexico*. Chapel Hill: University of North Carolina Press, 1997.

Sternlieb, George and James W. Hughes. 'The Uncertain Future of the Central City'. *Urban Affairs Quarterly*. Vol. 18, No. 4 (June 1983): 455–72.

Stone, Lawrence. *The Family, Sex and Marriage in England 1500–1800*. New York: Harper & Row, 1977.

Storey, John. *Cultural Studies and the Study of Popular Culture*. Edinburgh: Edinburgh University Press, 1996.

Storry, Mike and Peter Childs, eds. *British Cultural Identities*. London: Routledge, 1997.

Storti, Craig. *The Art of Crossing Cultues*. Yarmouth, MN: Intercultural Press, 1990.

Stouffer, Samuel A., et al. *The American Soldier: Adjustment During Army Life*. Princeton, NJ: Princeton University Press, 1949.

Strang, John and Gerry Stimson. *AIDS and Drug Misuse: The Challenge for Policy and Practice in the 1990s*. London: Routledge, 1990

Straus, Murray A. and Richard J. Gelles. 'Societal Change and Change in Family Violence From 1975 to 1985 as Revealed by Two National Surveys'. *Journal of Marriage and the Family*. Vol. 48, No. 4 (August 1986): 465–79.

Streib, Gordon F. 'Are the Aged a Minority Group?' In Bernice L. Neugarten, ed., *Middle Age and Aging: A Reader in Social Psychology*. Chicago: University of Chicago Press, 1968: 35–46.

Stromquist, Nelly P., ed. *Women and Education in Latin America: Knowledge, Power and Change*. Boulder, CO: Lynne Rienner, 1992.

Strong, Philip. *The Ceremonial Order of the Clinic*. London: Routledge, 1979.

Sudnow, David N. *Passing On: The Social Organization of Dying*. Englewood Cliffs, NJ: Prentice Hall, 1967.

Sumner, William Graham. *Folkways*. New York: Dover, 1959; orig. 1906.

Sutherland, Edwin H. 'White Collar Criminality'. *American Sociological Review*. Vol. 5, No. 1 (February 1940): 1–12.

Szasz, Thomas S. *The Manufacturer of Madness: A Comparative Study of the Inquisition and the Mental Health Movement*. New York: Dell, 1961.

——. *The Myth of Mental Illness: Foundations of a Theory of Personal Conduct*. New York: Harper & Row, 1970; orig. 1961.

——. 'Mental Illness Is Still a Myth'. *Society*. Vol. 31, No. 4 (May–June 1994): 34–39.

——. 'Idleness and Lawlessness in the Therapeutic State'. *Society*. Vol. 32, No. 4 (May/June 1995): 30–35.

Taeuber, Karl and Alma Taeuber. *Negroes in Cities*. Chicago: Aldine, 1965.

Tajfel, Henri. 'Social Psychology of Intergroup Relations'. *Annual Review of Psychology*. Palo Alto, CA: Annual Reviews, 1982: 1–39.

Tannen, Deborah. *You Just Don't Understand Me: Women and Men in Conversation*. New York: Wm. Morrow, 1990.

——. *Talking from 9 to 5: How Women's and Men's Conversational Styles Affect Who Gets Heard, Who Gets Credit and What Gets Done at Work*. New York: Wm. Morrow, 1994.

Tekce, Belgin, Linda Oldham and Frederick Shorter. *A Place to Live: Families and Health Care in a Cairo Neighborhood*. Cairo: American University in Cairo, 1994.

Terkel, Studs. *Working*. New York: Pantheon Books, 1974: 1–2, 57–59, 65, 66, 69, 221–22.

Terry, Don. 'In Crackdown on Bias, A New Tool'. *New York Times* (12 June 1993): 8.

Theen, Rolf H. W. 'Party and Bureaucracy'. In Erik P. Hoffmann and Robbin F. Laird, eds., *The Soviet Polity in the Modern Era*. New York: Aldine, 1984: 131–65.

Therborn, Goran. *European Modernity and Beyond: The Trajectory of European Societies 1945–2000*. London: Sage, 1995.

Thernstrom, Melanie. *The Dead Girl*. London: Kyle Cathie, 1990.

Thomas, Piri. *Down These Mean Streets*. New York: Signet, 1967.

Thomas, W. I. 'The Relation of Research to the Social Process'. In Morris Janowitz, ed., *W. I. Thomas on Social Organization and Social Personality*. Chicago: University of Chicago Press, 1966: 289–305; orig. 1931.

Thomas, W. I. and Florian Znaniecki. *The Polish Peasant in Europe and America* (original 1918). New York: Dover Publications, 1958.

Thompson, E.P. *The Making of the English Working Class*. Harmondsworth: Penguin, 1968.

Thompson, Kenneth, ed. *Readings from Emile Durkheim*. London: Routledge, 1985.

Thompson, Larry. 'The Breast Cancer Gene: A Woman's Dilemma'. *Time*. Vol. 143, No. 3 (17 January 1994): 52.

Thompson, Paul, Catherine Ibsen and Michele Auerldstern. *I don't feel old: the experience of later life*. Oxford: Oxford University Press, 1990.

Thorne, Burrie and Z. Luria. 'Sexuality and Gender in Children's Daily Worlds'. *Social Problems*. Vol. 33, No. 3: 176–90.

Thornton, Arland. 'Changing Attitudes Toward Separation and Divorce: Causes and Consequences'. *American Journal of Sociology*. Vol. 90, No. 4 (January 1985): 856–72.

Thornton, Sarah. *Club Cultures*. Cambridge: Polity Press, 1995.

Thurnbull, Colin. *The Human Cycle*. London: Cape, 1984.

Thurow, Lester C. 'A Surge in Inequality'. *Scientific American*. Vol. 256, No. 5 (May 1987): 30–37.

Tilly, Charles. *From Mobilization to Revolution*. Reading, MA: Addison-Wesley, 1978.

——. 'Does Modernization Breed Revolution?' In Jack A. Goldstone, ed., *Revolutions: Theoretical, Comparative, and Historical Studies*. New York: Harcourt Brace Jovanovich, 1986: 47–57.

Tobin, Gary. 'Suburbanization and the Development of Motor Transportation: Transportation Technology and the Suburbanization Process'. In Barry Schwartz, ed., *The Changing Face of the Suburbs*. Chicago: University of Chicago Press, 1976.

Tocqueville, Alexis de. *The Old Regime and the French Revolution*. Stuart Gilbert, trans. Garden City, NY: Anchor/Doubleday Books, 1955; orig. 1856.

——. *Democracy in America*. Garden City, New York: Doubleday–Anchor Books, 1968; orig. 1834, 1840.

Toennies, Ferdinand. *Community and Society (Gemeinschaft und Gesellschaft)*. New York: Harper & Row, 1963; orig. 1887.

Tolson, A. *The Limits of Masculinity*. London: Tavistock, 1977.

Tolson, Jay. 'The Trouble With Elites'. *The Wilson Quarterly*. Vol. 19, No. 1 (Winter 1995): 6–8.

Tong, Rosemarie. *Feminist Thought: A Comprehensive Introduction*. London: Unwin Hyman, 1989.

Towers, Heather. 'From AIDS to Alzheimer's: Policy and Politics in Setting New Health Agendas'. In Joe Bailey, *Social Europe*. London: Longman, 1992: 190–215.

Townsend, Peter. *The Family Life of Old People*. Harmondsworth: Penguin, 1957.

——. *Poverty & Labour in London: Interim Report of a Centenary Survey*. London: Low Pay Unit, in conjunction with the Poverty Research (London) Trust, 1987.

——. *Poverty in the UK*. Harmondsworth: Penguin, 1979.

Townsend, Peter and Nick Davidson, eds. *Inequalities in Health: The Black Report*. Harmondsworth: Penguin, 1982.

Treas, Judith. 'Socialist Organization and Economic Development in China: Latent Consequences for the Aged'. *The Gerontologist*. Vol. 19, No. 1 (February 1979): 34–43.

——. 'Older Americans in the 1990s and Beyond'. *Population Bulletin*. Vol. 50, No. 2 (May 1995). Washington, DC: Population Reference Bureau.

Trebilcot Joyce, ed. *Mothering: Essays in Feminist Theory*. Totowa, NJ: Rowman & Allanheld, 1984.

Treiman, Donald J. 'Industrialization and Social Stratification'. In Edward O. Laumann, ed., *Social Stratification: Research and Theory for the 1970s*. Indianapolis, Ind.: Bobbs-Merrill, 1970.

Trenchard, I. and H. Warren. *Something to Tell You: The Experiences and Needs of Young Lesbians and Gay Men in London*. London: Gay Teenage Group, 1984.

Troeltsch, Ernst. *The Social Teaching of the Christian Churches*. New York: Macmillan, 1931.

Tucker, R.C., ed. *The Marx–Engles Reader*. 2nd edn. New York: W. W. Norton, 1978.

Tudge, Colin. *The Day before Yesterday: Five Million Years of Human History*. London: Cape, 1995.

Tudor-Hart, J. 'The Inverse Care Law'. *The Lancet* (27 February 1971): 405–12.

Tumin, Melvin M. 'Some Principles of Stratification: A Critical Analysis'. *American Sociological Review*. Vol. 18, No. 4 (August 1953): 387–94.

——. *Social Stratification: The Forms and Functions of Inequality*. 2nd edn. Englewood Cliffs, NJ: Prentice Hall, 1985.

Tunstall, Jeremy. *Old and Alone : A Sociological Study of Old People*. London: Routledge & Kegan Paul, 1966.

Turkel, Sherry. *Life on the Screen: Identity in the Age of the Internet*. London: Weidenfeld & Nicolson, 1996.

Turner, Brian. *The Body and Society*. Oxford: Blackwell, 1984.

——. *Medical Power and Social Knowledge*. London: Routledge, 1st edn. 1987; 2nd edn. 1996.

Turner, Bryan F. 'Outline of a Theory of Citizenship'. *Sociology*. Vol. 24, No. 2 (1990): 189–217.

Turner, Charles Hampden and Fons Trompenaars. *The Seven Cultures of Capitalism*. London: Piatkus, 1993.

Turner, G. *British Cultural Studies*. London: Unwin Hyman/Routledge, 1990.

Turner, Ian, Paul Walker and Jack Young. *The New Criminology*. London: Routledge, 1977.

Turner, Johnathan. *Herbert Spencer*. London: Sage, 1985.

Tyree, Andrea, Moshe Semyonov and Robert W. Hodge. 'Gaps and Glissandos: Inequality, Economic Development and Social Mobility in 24 Countries'. *American Sociological Review*. Vol. 44, No. 3 (June 1979): 410–24.

Uchitelle, Louis. 'But Just Who is That Fairy Godmother?' *New York Times* (29 September 1991): Section 4, p. 1.

Ungerson, Clare. *Policy is Personal: Sex, Gender and Informal Care*. London: Tavistock, 1987.

United Nations Development Programme. *Human Development Report 1993*. New York: Oxford University Press, 1993.

——. *Human Development Report 1994*. New York: Oxford University Press, 1994.

——. *Human Development Report 1995*. New York: Oxford University Press, 1995.

——. *Human Development Report 1996*. New York: Oxford University Press, 1996.

Unnever, James D., Charles E. Frazier and John C. Henretta. 'Race Differences in Criminal Sentencing'. *The Sociological Quarterly*. Vol. 21, No. 2 (Spring 1980): 197–205.

US Bureau Of The Census. Prepublication data on income and wealth provided by the Census Bureau, 1994, 1995,1996.

US Bureau Of Justice Statistics. *Sourcebook of Criminal Justice Statistics 1990*. Timothy J. Flanagan and Kathleen Maguire, eds. Washington, DC: US Government Printing Office, 1991.

US Equal Employment Opportunity Commission. Response to personal query, 1996.

US House of Representatives, 1992.

Useem, Michael, and Jerome Karabel. 'Pathways to Corporate Management'. *American Sociological Review*. Vol. 51, No. 2 (April 1986): 184–200.

Van Biema, David. 'Parents Who Kill'. *Time*. Vol. 144, No. 20 (14 November 1994): 50–51.

Van den Haag, Ernest and John P. Conrad. *The Death Penalty: A Debate*. New York: Plenum Press, 1983.

Vance, Carole S., ed. *Pleasure and Danger*. London: Routledge, 1984.

Varawa, Joana McIntyre. *Changes in Latitude: An Uncommon Anthropology*. New York: Harper & Row, 1990.

Vaughan, Mary Kay. 'Multinational Corporations: The World as a Company Town'. In Ahamed Idris-Soven et al., eds., *The World as a Company Town: Multinational Corporations and Social Change*. The Hague: Mouton Publishers, 1978: 15–35.

Vayda, Eugene and Raisa B. Deber. 'The Canadian Health Care System: An Overview'. *Social Science and Medicine*. Vol. 18, No. 3 (1984): 191–97.

Veblen, Thorstein. *The Theory of the Leisure Class*. New York: The New American Library, 1953; orig. 1899.

Veum, Jonathan R. 'Accounting for Income Mobility Changes in the United States'. *Social Science Quarterly*. Vol. 73, No. 4 (December 1992): 773–85.

Viguerie, Richard A. *The New Right: We're Ready to Lead*. Falls Church, Va.: The Viguerie Company, 1981.

Vincent, John A. *Inequality and Old Age*. London: UCL Press, 1996.

Vines, Gail. 'Whose Baby Is It Anyway?' *New Scientist*. No. 1515 (3 July 1986): 26–27.

Vogel, Ezra F. *The Four Little Dragons: The Spread of Industrialization in East Asia*. Cambridge, MA: Harvard University Press, 1991.

Vogel, Lise. *Marxism and the Oppression of Women: Toward a Unitary Theory*. New Brunswick, NJ: Rutgers University Press, 1983.

Vold, George B. and Thomas J. Bernard. *Theoretical Criminology*. 3rd edn. New York: Oxford University Press, 1986.

Von Hirsh, Andrew. *Past or Future Crimes: Deservedness and Dangerousness in the Sentencing of Criminals*. New Brunswick, NJ: Rutgers University Press, 1986.

Vonnegut, Kurt, Jr. 'Harrison Bergeron'. In *Welcome to the Monkey House*. New York: Delacorte Press/Seymour Lawrence, 1968: 7–13; orig. 1961.

Wadsworth, M.E.J. *The Imprint of Time: Childhood History, and Adult Life*. Oxford: Clarendon Press, 1991.

Walby, Sylvia. *Theorizing Patriarchy*. Cambridge: Polity Press, 1990.

Walker, Alan and Tony Maltby. *Ageing Europe*. Buckingham: Open University Press, 1997.

Wall, Thomas F. *Medical Ethics: Basic Moral Issues*. Washington, DC: University Press of America, 1980.

Wallerstein, Immanuel. *The Modern World-System: Capitalist Agriculture and the Origins of the European World-Economy in the Sixteenth Century*. New York: Academic Press, 1974.

——. *The Capitalist World-Economy*. New York: Cambridge University Press, 1979.

——. 'Crises: The World Economy, the Movements and the Ideologies'. In Albert Bergesen, ed., *Crises in the World-System*. Beverly Hills, CA: Sage, 1983: 21–36.

——. *The Politics of the World Economy: The States, the Movements and the Civilizations*. Cambridge: Cambridge University Press, 1984.

Wallis, Roy. *The Road to Total Freedom: A Sociological Analysis of Scientology*. London: Hienemann, 1976.

Walsh, John P. *Supermarkets Transformed: Understanding Organisational and Technological Innovations*. New Brunswick, NJ: Rutgers University Press, 1993.

Walters, Laurel Shaper. 'World Educators Compare Notes'. *The Christian Science Monitor: Global Report* (7 September 1994): 8.

Walton, John and Charles Ragin. 'Global and National Sources of Political Protest: Third World Responses to the Debt Crisis'. *American Sociological Review*. Vol. 55, No. 6 (December 1990): 876–90.

Warner, R. Stephen. 'Work in Progress Toward a New Paradigm for the Sociological Study of Religion in the United States'. *American Journal of Sociology*. Vol. 98, No. 5 (March 1993): 1044–93.

Warner, W. Lloyd and J. O. Low. *The Social System of the Modern Factory*. Yankee City Series, Vol. 4. New Haven, CT: Yale University Press, 1947.

Warner, W. Lloyd and Paul S. Lunt. *The Social Life of a Modern Community*. New Haven, CT: Yale University Press, 1941.

Warnock Committee. *Report of the Committee of Inquiry into Human Fertilisation and Embryology*. CM9314. London: HMSO, 1984.

Watson, John B. *Behaviorism*. Rev. edn. New York: Norton, 1930.

Waxman, Chaim I. *The Stigma of Poverty: A Critique of Poverty Theories and Policies*. 2nd edn. New York: Pergamon Press, 1983.

Weber, Adna Ferrin. *The Growth of Cities*. New York: Columbia University Press, 1963; orig. 1899.

Weber, Max. *Max Weber on the Methodology of the Social Sciences*. E.A. Shils and H.A. Finch, trans., eds. Glencoe, IL: Free Press, 1949.

——. *The Protestant Ethic and the Spirit of Capitalism*. New York: Charles Scribner's Sons, 1958; orig. 1904–5.

——. *Economy and Society*. G. Roth and C. Wittich, eds. Berkeley: University of California Press, 1978; orig. 1921.

Webster, Pamela S., Terri Orbuch and James S. House. 'Effects of Childhood Family Background on Adult Marital Quality and Perceived Stability'. *American Journal of Sociology*. Vol. 101, No. 2 (September 1995): 404–32.

Weeks, J. *Coming Out: Homosexual Politics in Britain from the Nineteenth Century to the Present*. London: Quartet, 1977.

Weeks, Jeffrey. *Sexuality*. London: Routledge, 1986.

Weeks, John R. *Population*. 6th edn. Belmont, CA: Wadsworth, 1996.

Weidenbaum, Murray. 'The Evolving Corporate Board'. *Society*. Vol. 32, No. 3 (March/April 1995): 9–20.

Weinberg, George. *Society and the Healthy Homosexual*. New York: Doubleday, 1973.

Weisner, Thomas S. and Bernice T. Eiduson. 'The Children of the '60s as Parents'. *Psychology Today* (January 1986): 60–66.

Weitzman, Lenore J. *The Divorce Revolution: The Unexpected Social and Economic Consequences for Women and Children in America*. New York: Free Press, 1985.

Weitzman, Lenore J., Deborah Eifler, Elizabeth Hodaka and Catherine Ross. 'Sex-Role Socialization in Picture Books for Preschool Children'. *American Journal of Sociology*. Vol. 77, No. 6 (May 1972): 1125–50.

Welfare (United States Department of Health, Education and Welfare Library). *Words on Ageing: A Bibliography of Selected Annotated References* (UK Edition). London: Greenwood Press, 1981.

Wellings, Kaye, et al. *Sexual Behaviour in Britain : The National Survey of Sexual Attitudes and Lifestyles*. Harmondsworth: Penguin, 1994.

Wellman, Barry. 'The Community Question: Intimate Networks of East Yorkers'. *American Journal of Sociology*. Vol. 84, No. 5 (March 1979): 1201–31.

Wenke, Robert J. *Patterns of Prehistory*. New York: Oxford University Press, 1980.

Wesolowski, Wlodzimierz. 'Transition From Authoritarianism to Democracy'. *Social Research*. Vol. 57, No. 2 (Summer 1990): 435–61.

Western, Bruce. 'Postwar Unionization in Eighteen Advanced Capitalist Countries'. *American Sociological Review*. Vol. 58, No. 2 (April 1993): 266–82.

——. 'A Comparative Study of Working-Class Disorganization: Union Decline in Eighteen Advanced Capitalist Countries'. *American Sociological Review*. Vol. 60, No. 2 (April 1995): 179–201.

Weston, Kath. *Families We Choose: Lesbians, Gays, Kinship*. New York: Columbia University Press, 1991.

Westwood, Sallie and Parminder Bhachu, eds. *Enterprising Women: Ethnicity, Economy, and Gender Relations*. London: Routledge, 1988.

Wheelis, Allen. *The Quest for Identity*. New York: Norton, 1958.

White, Merry. *The Material Child: Coming of Age in Japan and America*. New York: Free Press, 1993.

White, Ralph and Ronald Lippitt. 'Leader Behavior and Member Reaction in Three "Social Climates".' In Dorwin Cartwright and Alvin Zander, eds., *Group Dynamics*. Evanston, IL: Row, Peterson, 1953: 586–611.

Whitehead, Margaret. *The Health Divide: Inequalities in Health in the 1980's*. London: Health Education Authority, 1987

Whittaker, James K. *Caring for Troubled Children: Residential Treatment in a Community*. New York: Aldine de Gruyter, 1997.

Whyte, William Foote. *Street Corner Society*. 3rd edn. Chicago: University of Chicago Press, 1981; orig. 1943.

Whyte, William H., Jr. *The Organization Man*. Garden City, NY: Anchor Books, 1957.

Wiarda, Howard J. 'Ethnocentrism and Third World Development'. *Society*. Vol. 24, No. 6 (September–October 1987): 55–64.

Wiatrowski, Michael A., David B. Griswold and Mary K. Roberts. 'Social Control Theory and Delinquency'. *American Sociological Review*. Vol. 46, No. 5 (October 1981): 525–41.

Williams, Raymond. *Culture*. London: Fontana, 1981.

——. *Culture and Society: Coleridge to Orwell*. London: Hogarth Press, 1987.

Williams, Robin M., Jr. *American Society: A Sociological Interpretation*. 3rd edn. New York: Alfred A. Knopf, 1970.

Williamson, Jeffrey G. and Peter H. Lindert. *American Inequality: A Macroeconomic History*. New York: Academic Press, 1980.

Willis, Paul. *Learning to Labour*. Farnborough: Saxon House, 1977.

Wilson, Bryan. *Religion in Sociological Perspective*. New York: Oxford University Press, 1982.

Wilson, Edward O. *Sociobiology: The New Synthesis*. Cambridge, MA: Belknap Press of the Harvard University Press, 1975.

——. *On Human Nature*. New York: Bantam Books, 1978.

Wilson, Logan. *American Academics Then and Now*. New York: Oxford University Press, 1979

Wilson, James Q. *Bureaucracy: What Government Agencies Do and Why They Do It*. New York: Basic Books, 1991

Wilson, James Q. and Richard J. Herrnstein. *Crime and Human Nature*. New York: Simon and Schuster, 1985.

Wilson, Thomas C. 'Urbanism and Tolerance: A Test of Some Hypotheses Drawn From Wirth and Stouffer'. *American Sociological Review*. Vol. 50, No. 1 (February 1985): 117–23.

——. 'Urbanism and Unconventionality: The Case of Sexual Behavior'. *Social Science Quarterly*. Vol. 76, No. 2 (June 1995): 346–63.

Wilson, William Julius. *The Declining Significance of Race*. Chicago: University of Chicago Press, 1978.

Winkler, Karen J. 'Scholar Whose Ideas of Female Psychology Stir Debate Modifies Theories, Extends Studies to Young Girls'. *Chronicle of Higher Education*. Vol. 36, No. 36 (23 May 1990): A6–A8.

Winn, Marie. *Children Without Childhood*. New York: Pantheon Books, 1983.

Wintle, Michael, ed. *Culture and Identity in Europe*. London: Avebury, 1996.

Wirth, Louis. 'Urbanism As a Way of Life'. *American Journal of Sociology*. Vol. 44, No. 1 (July 1938): 1–24.

Witte, Rob. *Racist Violence and the State: A Comparative Analysis of Britain, France and the Netherlands*. Harlow: Longman Group, 1996.

Wolfe, David B. 'Targeting the Mature Mind'. *American Demographics*. Vol. 16, No. 3 (March 1994): 32–36.

Wolfgang, Marvin E., Robert M. Figlio and Thorsten Sellin. *Delinquency in a Birth Cohort*. Chicago: University of Chicago Press, 1972.

Wollstonecraft, Mary. *A Vindication of the Rights of Woman*. 1792 (new ed. Everyman's Library, 1992).

Wood, John. 'Groping towards Sexism: Boys' Sex Talk'. In A. McRobbie and M. Nava, eds., *Gender and Generation*. London: Macmillan, 1984.

Woodward, Kenneth L. 'Feminism and the Churches'. *Newsweek*. Vol. 13, No. 7 (13 February 1989): 58–61.

Woody, Bette. *Black Women in the Workplace: Impacts of Structural Change in the Economy*. Westport. CT: Greenwood Press, 1992.

Wooley, Orland W., Susan C. Wooley and Sue R. Dyrenforth. 'Obesity and Women – II: A Neglected Feminist Topic'. *Women's Studies International Quarterly*. Vol. 2 (1979): 81–92.

World Bank. *World Tables 1991*. Baltimore, London: Johns Hopkins University

———.*World Development Report 1993*. New York: Oxford University Press, 1993

———.*World Development Report 1995*: *Workers in an Integrating World*. New York: Oxford University Press, 1995.

———. *World Development Report 1997*. *Workers in an Integrating World*. New York: Oxford University Press, 1997.

———. *Averting the Old Age Crisis: Policies to Protect the Old and Promote Growth*. Oxford: Oxford University Press, 1997.

World Health Organization. *Constitution of the World Health Organization*. New York: World Health Organization Interim Commission, 1946.

World Values Survey, 1990–1993. Ann Arbor, MI: Inter-university Consortium for Political and Social Research, 1994.

Worsley, Peter. 'Models of the System'. In Mike Featherstone, ed., *Global Cluture: Nationalism, Globalization, and Modernity*. Newbury Park, CA: Sage, 1990.

Wren, Christopher S. 'In Soweto-by-the-Sea, Misery Lives On as Apartheid Fades'. *New York Times* (9 June 1991): 1, 7.

Wright, Charles R. *Mass Communications*. New York: Random House, 1967.

Wright, Erik Olin. *Classes*. London: Verso, 1985.

Wright, Erik Olin, Andrew Levine and Elliott Sober. *Reconstructing Marxism: Essays on Explanation and the Theory of History*. London: Verso, 1992.

Wright, Erik Olin and Bill Martin. 'The Transformation of the American Class Structure, 1960–1980'. *American Journal of Sociology*. Vol. 93, No. 1 (July 1987): 1–29.

Wright, Quincy. 'Causes of War in the Atomic Age'. In William M. Evan and Stephen Hilgartner, eds., *The Arms Race and Nuclear War*. Englewood Cliffs, NJ: Prentice Hall, 1987: 7–10.

Wright, Richard A. *In Defense of Prisons*. Westport, CT: Greenwood Press, 1994.

Wright, Stuart A. and William V. D'Antonio. 'The Substructure of Religion: A Further Study'. *Journal for the Scientific Study of Religion*. Vol. 19, No. 3 (September 1980): 292–98.

Yates, Ronald E. 'Growing Old in Japan; They Ask Gods for a Way Out'. *Philadelphia Inquirer* (14 August 1986): 3A.

Yeatts, Dale E. 'Self-Managed Work Teams: Innovation in Progress'. *Business and Economic Quarterly* (Fall–Winter 1991): 2–6.

———. 'Creating the High Performance Self-Managed Work Team: A Review of Theoretical Perspectives'. Paper presented at the annual meeting of the Social Science Association, Dallas, February 1995.

Yoder, Jan D. and Robert C. Nichols. 'A Life Perspective: Comparison of Married and Divorced Persons'. *Journal of Marriage and the Family*. Vol. 42, No. 2 (May 1980): 413–19.

York, Michael. *The Emerging Network: A Sociology of the New Age and Neo-Pagan Movements*. London: Rowman and Littlefield, 1995.

Yoshizumi, Kyoko. 'Marriage and Family: Past and Present'. In Kumiko Fojimura–Famslow and Atsuko Kameda, eds., *Japanese Women: New Feminist Perspectives of the Past, Present and Future*. New York: The Feminist Press at the City University of New York, 1995.

Young, Gerald. *Adult Development, Therapy, and Culture: A Postmodern Synthesis*. New York, London: Plenum Press, 1997.

Young, Michael and Peter Willmott. *Family and Kinship in East London*. Basingstoke: Penguin, 1957.

Young, Michael and Peter Willmott. *The Symmetrical Family*. London: Routledge and Kegan-Paul, 1973.

Yuan, Gao. *Born Red: A Chronicle of the Cultural Revolution*. Stanford, CA: Stanford University Press, 1987.

Yunker, James A. *Socialism Revised and Modernized: The Case for Pragmatic Market Socialism*. New York: Praeger, 1992.

Zangwill, Israel. *The Melting Pot*. New York: MacMillan, 1921; orig. 1909. (Also London: William Heinemann, 1919 and Ayer Company Publishers (USA), 1994.)

Zaslavsky, Victor. *The Neo-Stalinist State: Class, Ethnicity and Consensus in Soviet Society*. Armonk, NY: M. E. Sharpe, 1982.

Zeitlin, Irving M. *The Social Condition of Humanity*. New York: Oxford University Press, 1981.

Zellner, William W. *Counter Cultures: A Sociological Analysis*. New York: St Martin's Press, 1994.

Zola, Irving. 'Medicine as an Institution of Social Control'. *Sociological Review* (1972): 487–504.

Zuboff, Shoshana. 'New Worlds of Computer-Mediated Work'. *Harvard Business Review*. Vol. 60, No. 5 (September–October 1982): 142–52.

Name Index

Subject Index

sex (continued)
  discrimination 277
  premarital and extra-marital 370
  ratio 611
  see also sexual/sexuality
sexism 241, 359, 399, 681, 685
  see also gender and sexuality
sexual/sexuality 475
  activity, regulation of 484
  autonomy 367
  behaviour 52
  differences 352
  education 541–2
  harassment 371–3, 378
  and languages 227
  modernization and women 310
  orientation 108, 219
  plastic 377
  repression 134
  slavery 305
  social change 680
  social stratification 241
  Sweden 205
  violence 219, 367
    see also date rape; rape
  see also gender and sexuality; heterosexuality
shamans 70, 510
shelters 489
shopping malls 432
Sicily 54
Sierra Leone 105
Singapore 8, 209, 279, 295, 686
  economy 419
  global inequality 309, 311, 314, 316
  politics 444, 445
  technology 85
single parents *see* lone parents
singlehood 495, 497
skills, interpersonal 192
slavery 242–3, 248, 312, 366
smiling 166
smoking 554, 562
social
  background 37, 144, 156, 161, 186
  boundaries 186
  care 403
  change 210, 377, 669–89
    Communitarian debate 684–5
    conflict 672, 679–80
    culture 671–2
    definition 670–1
    demographic causes 672–3
    ever-expanding state 679
    functional theory 677
    ideas 672
    and mass media 582–5
    modern societies 678
    modernisation and global future 685–7
    modernity 673–7, 680–3
    natural environment 672
    postmodernity 683–6
    and religion 518–19
    scale of modern life 677–8
    traditional societies 678
  character 681
  civility 167
  cohesion 505
  conditions 224

conflict 78, 89, 676–7
construction *see* social interaction
construction of illness 569–70
control 220, 505–6
crises 12, 17, 521
democatic welfare 286, 287
differentiation 241
distance 331
diversity 140, 186
division 89
domination and racism 329
dysfunctions 20
experience 132, 138, 139
functions 19
groups *see* groups and organisations
habit 113
hierarchy 186, 506
identity 147, 156
inclusiveness 196
inequality 71, 240, 255, 477, 521, 560–6, 572
  see also class, poverty and welfare
inferiority 334
institutions 77, 86
integration 6, 18, 20
interaction 138, 155–75, 184
  embarrassment and tact 167
  emotions in global perspective 164
  gender and personal performances 165–6
  humour 168–73
  idealisation 166–7
  non-verbal communication 162–4
  performances 162
  social construction of reality 159–62
  social structure 156–9
  technology 172
isolation 131–2, 393
learning theories 354
life 184, 185, 658
marginality 12
mobility 240–1, 244, 247, 269, 275, 276
  assimilation 336
  class, poverty and welfare 266
  education 532
  upward 275, 280
movements 454–5, 672
  see also power, the state and social movements
norms 587
order 18
organisation 23, 39, 86, 370–1
parity 186
patterns 12, 20, 22, 38
placement 484
policy 403
position 140
power 209
prestige 20, 254
privilege 215
processes 185
psychology 137
relations 185
reproduction 548
rights 286

security 252
self 137–9
significance *see* ethnicity/race and migration
skills 134
solidarity 20, 66
standing 21, 248
stratification 239–62, 306
  bell curve debate 256–7
  caste system 242–4
  class 244–5, 250–5
  definition 240–1
  facts and values 260
  functions 248–50
  horticultural, pastoral and agrarian societies 255
  hunter gatherer societies 255
  ideology 247–8, 249
  income disparity 258–9
  industrial societies 255–6
  Japan 245
  Russian Federation 245–7
  slavery system 242–3
  technology 248, 256–9
structure 19, 193
  see also social interaction
survey approach 370
unity 210
welfare agencies 217
worth 251
  see also socialisation
Social Protection in Europe Directive 285
social-conflict analysis/paradigm 218, 250, 254, 451, 506, 507
social-exchange analysis 24, 486
socialisation 129–52, 444–5, 484
  adult 358
  agents 139–41
  anticipatory 141
  cognitive development 134–5
  freedom within society 148
  gender, and girls' self-esteem 136–7
  health and medicine 560
  human development: nature and nurture 130–1
  and life course 141–7
    adolescence 144
    adulthood 144–5
    childhood 141–4
    dying 146–7
    old age 145–6
    overview 147
  moral development 135–6
  personality, elements of 132–4
  resocialisation: total institutions 147–9
  social isolation 131–2
  social self 137–9
socialism 81, 120, 257, 294, 316, 373, 375, 418–20, 434
  advantages 420
  collapse 457, 460
  democratic 419–20
  economy 415
  health and medicine 566
  politics 443, 444, 466
  power 459
society 65–94
  changing patterns 66–76
    agrarian 71–3

Europe 68–9
  horticultural and pastoral 70–1
  hunting and gathering 67, 70
  industrial 73–4
  postindustrial 74–5
  sociocultural evolution 74–5
  technology 67, 72, 76
cohesion 89–90
and conflict (Karl Marx) 76–81
  capitalism and alienation 80–1
  capitalism and class conflict 79–80
  in history 78–9
  production 76–8
  revolution 81
evolutionary cycle 89
and function (Emile Durkheim) 87–9
future prospects 90
how societies change 89
interconnectedness 8–9
progress 90
protection 229–31
rationalisation (Max Weber) 81–7
  alienation 87
  bureaucracy 86
  Calvinism and industrial capitalism 83
  social organisation 86
  technology in global perspective 84–5
  and tradition 81–3
social stratification 250
sociobiology 121–2
sociocultural evolution 67, 74–5, 255
socioeconomic status 40
sociological investigation 33–62
  basics 34–5
  epistemology 35–6
  ethics 34–5, 54–5
  feminist research 53–4
  humanism 36, 39
  methods 42–53
    African-American elite, study of 45–7
    asking questions: survey research 43
    emerging research tools 51–3
    participant observation: field work 48–9
    population and sample 43–4
    questionnaires and interviews 44–5
    secondary and historical analysis 50
    table-reading 47
    testing a hypothesis: the experiment 42–3
  planning 58–9
  politics and ethics 34–5, 52
  positivism 36–8
  realist sociology 36
  statistics and deception 56–7
  technology and research 34, 39–42, 55